Poetry Criticism

Guide to Gale Literary Criticism Series

For criticism on	Consult these Gale series
Authors now living or who died after December 31, 1999	*CONTEMPORARY LITERARY CRITICISM (CLC)*
Authors who died between 1900 and 1999	*TWENTIETH-CENTURY LITERARY CRITICISM (TCLC)*
Authors who died between 1800 and 1899	*NINETEENTH-CENTURY LITERATURE CRITICISM (NCLC)*
Authors who died between 1400 and 1799	*LITERATURE CRITICISM FROM 1400 TO 1800 (LC)* *SHAKESPEAREAN CRITICISM (SC)*
Authors who died before 1400	*CLASSICAL AND MEDIEVAL LITERATURE CRITICISM (CMLC)*
Authors of books for children and young adults	*CHILDREN'S LITERATURE REVIEW (CLR)*
Dramatists	*DRAMA CRITICISM (DC)*
Poets	*POETRY CRITICISM (PC)*
Short story writers	*SHORT STORY CRITICISM (SSC)*
Literary topics and movements	*HARLEM RENAISSANCE: A GALE CRITICAL COMPANION (HR)* *THE BEAT GENERATION: A GALE CRITICAL COMPANION (BG)*
Asian American writers of the last two hundred years	*ASIAN AMERICAN LITERATURE (AAL)*
Black writers of the past two hundred years	*BLACK LITERATURE CRITICISM (BLC)* *BLACK LITERATURE CRITICISM SUPPLEMENT (BLCS)*
Hispanic writers of the late nineteenth and twentieth centuries	*HISPANIC LITERATURE CRITICISM (HLC)* *HISPANIC LITERATURE CRITICISM SUPPLEMENT (HLCS)*
Native North American writers and orators of the eighteenth, nineteenth, and twentieth centuries	*NATIVE NORTH AMERICAN LITERATURE (NNAL)*
Major authors from the Renaissance to the present	*WORLD LITERATURE CRITICISM, 1500 TO THE PRESENT (WLC)* *WORLD LITERATURE CRITICISM SUPPLEMENT (WLCS)*

ISSN 1052-4851

Poetry Criticism

Excerpts from Criticism of the Works of the Most Significant and Widely Studied Poets of World Literature

Volume 55

Timothy J. Sisler
Project Editor

GALE®

THOMSON
✦
GALE

Detroit • New York • San Diego • San Francisco • Cleveland • New Haven, Conn. • Waterville, Maine • London • Munich

THOMSON

GALE

Poetry Criticism, Vol. 55

Project Editor
Timothy J. Sisler

Editorial
Jenny Cromie, Kathy D. Darrow, Lemma
Shomali, Carol Ullmann

Indexing Services
Laurie Andriot

Rights Acquisition and Management
Denise Buckley, Ann Taylor, Jackie Key

Imaging and Multimedia
Dean Dauphinais, Leitha Etheridge-Sims,
Lezlie Light, Dan Newell

Composition and Electronic Capture
Kathy Sauer

Manufacturing
Lori Kessler

LIBRARY OF CONGRESS CATALOG CARD NUMBER 91-118494

ISBN 0-7876-7453-2
ISSN 1052-4851

Printed in the United States of America
10 9 8 7 6 5 4 3 2 1

Contents

Preface vii

Acknowledgments ix

Literary Criticism Series Advisory Board xi

Preface

*P*oetry Criticism (PC) presents significant criticism of the world's greatest poets and provides supplementary biographical and bibliographical material to guide the interested reader to a greater understanding of the genre and its creators. Although major poets and literary movements are covered in such Gale Literary Criticism series as *Contemporary Literary Criticism (CLC)*, *Twentieth-Century Literary Criticism (TCLC)*, *Nineteenth-Century Literature Criticism (NCLC)*, *Literature Criticism from 1400 to 1800 (LC)*, and *Classical and Medieval Literature Criticism (CMLC)*, *PC* offers more focused attention on poetry than is possible in the broader, survey-oriented entries on writers in these Gale series. Students, teachers, librarians, and researchers will find that the generous excerpts and supplementary material provided by *PC* supply them with the vital information needed to write a term paper on poetic technique, to examine a poet's most prominent themes, or to lead a poetry discussion group.

Scope of the Series

PC is designed to serve as an introduction to major poets of all eras and nationalities. Since these authors have inspired a great deal of relevant critical material, *PC* is necessarily selective, and the editors have chosen the most important published criticism to aid readers and students in their research. Each author entry presents a historical survey of the critical response to that author's work. The length of an entry is intended to reflect the amount of critical attention the author has received from critics writing in English and from foreign critics in translation. Every attempt has been made to identify and include the most significant essays on each author's work. In order to provide these important critical pieces, the editors sometimes reprint essays that have appeared elsewhere in Gale's Literary Criticism Series. Such duplication, however, never exceeds twenty percent of a *PC* volume.

Organization of the Book

Each *PC* entry consists of the following elements:

- The **Author Heading** cites the name under which the author most commonly wrote, followed by birth and death dates. Also located here are any name variations under which an author wrote, including transliterated forms for authors whose native languages use nonroman alphabets. If the author wrote consistently under a pseudonym, the pseudonym will be listed in the author heading and the author's actual name given in parenthesis on the first line of the biographical and critical introduction. Uncertain birth or death dates are indicated by question marks. Single-work entries are preceded by the title of the work and its date of publication.

- The **Introduction** contains background information that introduces the reader to the author and the critical debates surrounding his or her work.

- A **Portrait of the Author** is included when available.

- The list of **Principal Works** is ordered chronologically by date of first publication and lists the most important works by the author. The first section comprises poetry collections and book-length poems. The second section gives information on other major works by the author. For foreign authors, the editors have provided original foreign-language publication information and have selected what are considered the best and most complete English-language editions of their works.

- Reprinted **Criticism** is arranged chronologically in each entry to provide a useful perspective on changes in critical evaluation over time. All individual titles of poems and poetry collections by the author featured in the entry are printed in boldface type. The critic's name and the date of composition or publication of the critical work are given at the beginning of each piece of criticism. Unsigned criticism is preceded by the title of the source in which it appeared. Footnotes are reprinted at the end of each essay or excerpt. In the case of excerpted criticism, only those footnotes that pertain to the excerpted texts are included.

- Critical essays are prefaced by brief **Annotations** explicating each piece.

- A complete **Bibliographical Citation** of the original essay or book precedes each piece of criticism.

- An annotated bibliography of **Further Reading** appears at the end of each entry and suggests resources for additional study. In some cases, significant essays for which the editors could not obtain reprint rights are included here. Boxed material following the further reading list provides references to other biographical and critical sources on the author in series published by Gale.

Cumulative Indexes

A **Cumulative Author Index** lists all of the authors that appear in a wide variety of reference sources published by the Gale Group, including *PC*. A complete list of these sources is found facing the first page of the Author Index. The index also includes birth and death dates and cross references between pseudonyms and actual names.

A **Cumulative Nationality Index** lists all authors featured in *PC* by nationality, followed by the number of the *PC* volume in which their entry appears.

A **Cumulative Title Index** lists in alphabetical order all individual poems, book-length poems, and collection titles contained in the *PC* series. Titles of poetry collections and separately published poems are printed in italics, while titles of individual poems are printed in roman type with quotation marks. Each title is followed by the author's last name and corresponding volume and page numbers where commentary on the work is located. English-language translations of original foreign-language titles are cross-referenced to the foreign titles so that all references to discussion of a work are combined in one listing.

Citing *Poetry Criticism*

When writing papers, students who quote directly from any volume in the Literary Criticism Series may use the following general format to footnote reprinted criticism. The first example pertains to material drawn from periodicals, the second to material reprinted from books.

Sylvia Kasey Marks, "A Brief Glance at George Eliot's *The Spanish Gypsy*," *Victorian Poetry* 20, no. 2 (Summer 1983), 184-90; reprinted in *Poetry Criticism*, vol. 20, ed. Ellen McGeagh (Detroit: The Gale Group), 128-31.

Linden Peach, "Man, Nature and Wordsworth: American Versions," *British Influence on the Birth of American Literature*, (Macmillan Press Ltd., 1982), 29-57; reprinted in *Poetry Criticism*, vol. 20, ed. Ellen McGeagh (Detroit: The Gale Group), 37-40.

Suggestions are Welcome

Readers who wish to suggest new features, topics, or authors to appear in future volumes, or who have other suggestions or comments are cordially invited to call, write, or fax the Project Editor:

Project Editor, Literary Criticism Series
The Gale Group
27500 Drake Road
Farmington Hills, MI 48331-3535
1-800-347-4253 (GALE)
Fax: 248-699-8054

Acknowledgments

The editors wish to thank the copyright holders of the criticism included in this volume and the permissions managers of many book and magazine publishing companies for assisting us in securing reproduction rights. We are also grateful to the staffs of the Detroit Public Library, the Library of Congress, the University of Detroit Mercy Library, Wayne State University Purdy/Kresge Library Complex, and the University of Michigan Libraries for making their resources available to us. Following is a list of the copyright holders who have granted us permission to reproduce material in this volume of *PC*. Every effort has been made to trace copyright, but if omissions have been made, please let us know.

COPYRIGHTED MATERIAL IN *PC*, VOLUME 55, WAS REPRODUCED FROM THE FOLLOWING PERIODICALS:

African American Review, v. 31, autumn, 1997 for "Two Writers Sharing: Sterling A. Brown, Robert Frost, and 'In Divés' Dive'" by John Edgar Tidwell. Copyright © 1997 by John Edgar Tidwell. Reproduced by permission of the author.; v. 31, autumn, 1997 for "Authenticity and Elevation: Sterling Brown's Theory of the Blues" by Lorenzo Thomas. Copyright © 1997 by Lorenzo Thomas. Reproduced by permission of the author.—*The American Poetry Review,* v. 28, March-April, 1999 for "Reverberations of a Work Song" by Edward Hirsch; v. 29, July-August, 2000 for "A Future for Modernism: Barbara Guest's Recent Poetry" by Robert Kaufman; v. 31, September-October 2002 for "Three Essays" by Barbara Guest. Copyright © 1999, 2000, 2002 by World Poetry, Inc. All reproduced by permission of the respective authors.—*Black American Literature Forum,* v. 16, spring, 1982 for "The Distant Closeness of Dancing Doubles: Sterling Brown and William Carlos Williams" by Vera M. Kutzinski; v. 23, spring, 1989 for "The New Negro Poet and the Nachal Man: Sterling Brown's Folk Odyssey" by John S. Wright. Copyright © 1982, 1989 by Indiana State University. Both reproduced by permission of the publisher and the respective authors.—*The Black Scholar,* v. 12, March-April, 1981. Copyright © 1981 by *The Black Scholar.* Reproduced by permission.—*Chicago Review,* v. 47, fall, 2001. Copyright © 2001 by *Chicago Review.* Reprinted by permission.—*CLA Journal,* v. 32, June, 1989; v. 34, March, 1993; v. 38, December, 1994. Copyright © 1989, 1993, 1994 by the College Language Association. All reproduced by permission.—*Contemporary Literature,* v. 38, summer, 1997. Copyright © 1997 by the Board of Regents of the University of Wisconsin System. Reprinted by permission.—*English Language Notes,* v. 37, March, 2000. Copyright © 2000 by Regents of the University of Colorado. Reproduced by permission.—*English Studies,* v. 81, February, 2000. Copyright © 2000 by Swets & Zeitlinger. Reproduced by permission.—*The Journal of Pre-Raphaelite and Aesthetic Studies,* v. 1, fall, 1987. Copyright © 1987 by *The Journal of Pre-Raphaelite and Aesthetic Studies.* Reproduced by permission.—*The Journal of Pre-Raphaelite Studies,* v. 2, November, 1981. Copyright © 1981 by *The Journal of Pre-Raphaelite Studies.* Reproduced by permission.—*MELUS,* v. 21, spring, 1996. Copyright © 1996, MELUS: The Society for the Study of Multi-Ethnic Literature of the United States. Reproduced by permission.—*The New Republic,* v. 187, December 20, 1982. Copyright © 1982 by The New Republic, Inc. Reproduced by permission of *The New Republic.*—*Philological Quarterly,* v. 39, April, 1960. Reproduced by permission.—*The Russian Review,* v. 57, April, 1998. Copyright © 1998 by *The Russian Review.* All rights reserved. Reproduced by permission of Blackwell Publishers.—*Slavic and East European Journal,* v. 43, summer, 1999. Copyright © 1999 by the American Association of Teachers of Slavic and East European Languages. Reproduced by permission.—*Slavic Review,* v. 49, fall, 1990. Copyright © 1990 by the American Association for the Advancement of Slavic Studies, Inc. Reproduced by permission.—*Southern Cultures,* v. 5, summer, 1999. Copyright © 1999 by the Center for the Study of the American South. Reproduced by permission.—*Studies in Philology,* v. 84, spring, 1987. Copyright © 1987 by The University of North Carolina Press. Reproduced by permission.—*Victorian Poetry,* v. 7, autumn, 1969 for "'Rapunzel' Unravelled."; v. 15, fall, 1977 for "The Embodiment of Dreams: William Morris's 'Blue Closet' Group" by Margaret A. Lourie; v. 15, winter, 1977 for "Love is Enough: A Crisis in William Morris's Poetic Development" by Frederick Kirchhoff; v. 29, summer, 1991 for "'A Strange Diagonal': Ideology and Enclosure in the Framing Sections of 'The Princess' and the 'Earthly Paradise'" by Isolde Karen Herbert; v. 30, summer, 1992 for "Morris' Medieval Queen: A Paradox Resolved" by Virginia S. Hale and Catherine Barnes Stevenson; v. 35, spring, 1997 for "The 'Pomona' Lyric and Female Power" by Norman Talbot; v. 38, fall, 2000 for "Medieval Drama and Courtly Romance in William Morris' 'Sir Galahad, A Christmas Mystery,'" by Catherine Stevenson and Virginia Hale. Copyright © 1969, 1977, 1991, 1992, 1997, 2000 by West Virginia University. All reproduced by permission of the respective authors.—*Women's Studies: An Interdisciplinary Journal,* v. 30, 2001. Copyright © 2001 by OPA (Overseas Publishers Association). All rights reserved. Reprinted by permission.

Gale Literature Product Advisory Board

The members of the Gale Group Literature Product Advisory Board—reference librarians from public and academic library systems—represent a cross-section of our customer base and offer a variety of informed perspectives on both the presentation and content of our literature products. Advisory board members assess and define such quality issues as the relevance, currency, and usefulness of the author coverage, critical content, and literary topics included in our series; evaluate the layout, presentation, and general quality of our printed volumes; provide feedback on the criteria used for selecting authors and topics covered in our series; provide suggestions for potential enhancements to our series; identify any gaps in our coverage of authors or literary topics, recommending authors or topics for inclusion; analyze the appropriateness of our content and presentation for various user audiences, such as high school students, undergraduates, graduate students, librarians, and educators; and offer feedback on any proposed changes/enhancements to our series. We wish to thank the following advisors for their advice throughout the year.

Requiem

Anna Akhmatova

Russian poem of the twentieth century.

The following entry provides criticism of Akhmatova's *Requiem* from 1972 through 1999. For discussion of her life and career, see *PC,* Volume 2.

INTRODUCTION

Rekviem (1963), translated into English as *Requiem,* is the one of the best known works of the Russian poet Anna Akhmatova. The composition consists of a series of numerous short poems that reflect the anguish of the Russian people during years of persecution and purges under the rule of Joseph Stalin. Although it was composed in large part prior to 1940, Akhmatova considered *Requiem* too dangerous to be written down, much less published, at the time, so until the mid-1960s it remained unpublished, and existed only as individual verses memorized by the poet and a handful of her most trusted confidants.

BIOGRAPHICAL INFORMATION

Akhmatova (also transliterated as Axmatova) was born Anna Andreevna Gorenko in Odessa, a coastal town along the Black Sea in the Ukraine, on June 23, 1888. She was raised in Tsarskoye Selo, near St. Petersburg. Her affinity for writing poetry began during childhood. In 1910, she married the poet Nikolai Gumilyov, with whom she was a founding member of the Acmeist group of poets who rejected the mysticism and stylistic obscurity of Symbolism and attempted to restore clarity to poetic language. She gave birth to a son in 1912 and was divorced from Gumilyov following an unhappy marriage in 1918. Gumilyov was executed by the Soviet regime for treason in 1921. An unofficial ban by the Communist party on the publication of Akhmatova's works was imposed starting in 1925; this was due in some measure to her previous association with Gumilyov, but it was also a consequence of her popularity as a poet in pre-Revolutionary years and her choice of themes such as death, poverty, and the fear of war. Her son, too, suffered at the hands of the Stalinist regime through repeated arrests for no discernible "crime" other than being the son of literary parents whose works were

regarded with suspicion by the political leaders of the day. During the 1920s, 1930s, and 1940s, Akhmatova continued to write and translate verse, but much of the work attributed to these decades, including *Requiem,* remained unpublished until the late 1950s and mid-1960s, well after the death of Stalin. She died on March 5, 1966.

PLOT AND MAJOR CHARACTERS

Requiem is a cycle of fifteen short poems introduced with a paragraph of prose that, taken as a whole, constitutes an epic of grief and remembrance. Although the work possesses no conventionally defined plot, the ten internal numbered poems form a chronological revelation that documents the suffering of the Russian people during the years of Stalinist terror. Through the eyes of the women—who stood outside prisons for days, hoping for word about their loved ones, hoping to deliver a hat or a pair of salvaged gloves or shoes, hoping for one last glimpse before the inevitable sentence of death or exile for a beloved son or husband—Akhmatova plumbs the depths of unimaginable suffering, and charts the journey of mourning and memorial. The poem opens with a declaration of the pain of one woman, an individual circumstance but recognizable to all who lived through the era. With each successive poem, the central figure experiences a new stage of suffering: mute grief, growing disbelief, rationalization, raw mourning, steely resolve. Sometimes writing in the first person, sometimes in the third person, Akhmatova becomes the voice of the people as she universalizes her personal pain over the repeated imprisonment of her son and the loss of friends and literary peers to execution and exile.

Throughout much of the cycle the suffering Russian woman, one yet universal, is the central figure. At the climax of the cycle of grief, however, three figures of Christian religious significance appear: Mary Magdalene, Mary the Mother of Christ, and John, the beloved disciple. Critics hold various opinions about why Akhmatova incorporated these personages who are closely associated with Catholic religious beliefs, and about whom significant people in the poet's life each figure represents. Within the work as a whole, however, these religious figures, placed outside the context of their New Testament roles, reinforce the poet's subtext of the inevitability of suffering. Akhmatova allows the central figure to transcend her personal circumstances in an almost mystical, supernatural way—not to mitigate her pain or allow her a measure of peace, but to dignify and honor the ability of this woman, and all women, to confront their deepest grief and fear and survive. In *Requiem,* writes Amanda Haight, Akhmatova "has taken suffering to its limit and so there is nothing to fear."

MAJOR THEMES

Requiem has been called an elegy, a poem of memorial and mourning, for the people of Russia. Critic Sam Driver wrote in 1990 that the work was conceived by the poet as "a combination of the epic and the lyric." Constructed as a lament for the people of Russia, its scale is simultaneously enormous and intimate: although it chronicles a nearly unfathomable episode of terror and persecution in a specific historic time period, it is characterized by short, almost episodic pieces of verse. Not incidentally, even this characteristic of structure is integral to the work's thematic core: the short elements that comprise the work as a whole are of such length that they could be committed to memory in a short period of time and carried, in secret, in the hearts of those for whom it had meaning. This is how the work

was preserved for several decades by the poet and her closest confidants; the danger of being caught with such words on paper was considered too great by Akhmatova. The composition of the poem in this manner is representative of the ways in which the Russian people communicated with each other and offered one another support and assistance during the years of the Stalinist regime: in secret, in veiled language, and without a trail of evidence that could be used in further persecution.

Although the work is recognizable as an epic lament for a particular people in response to specific circumstances of history, Akhmatova couches references to actual times and places in such a way that the work transcends its era and becomes a universal and timeless voice for the victims of persecution anywhere and any time. Images evoked by the poet's words—for example, women waiting wearily outside prisons for word from loved ones, their faces ravaged by raw grief and fear—may be visualized as belonging to a particular episode of Russian history. Yet they also possess a timelessness that allows them to serve as icons of the universality of human cruelty and human pain. Throughout this work, Akhmatova explores the role of the poet as the voice of truth, and the role of poetry, the language of both suffering and redemption, as a weapon of resistance and solidarity. Thematically, the poem also honors love and remembrance as forces that transcend evil and empower the powerless.

CRITICAL RECEPTION

Akhmatova's *Requiem* is considered to be one of the most significant works of her long career. Until it appeared in print for the first time in the 1960s, Akhmatova's considerable reputation as a poet had been based primarily on the love poems she composed during her youth, and on her role as a founding member of the Acmeist school. She had fallen from favor in her own country, and been virtually forgotten by readers and critics elsewhere. Following the death of Stalin in 1953, Akhmatova gradually felt more secure and safe as a poet in her homeland, and her work was tolerated, though not celebrated, by the Soviet leadership. Her literary voice was renewed, and her works once again came to the attention of scholars and critics. In the years prior to her death works such as *Requiem* and *Poema bez geroya* (1960; *Poem without a Hero*) saw publication, and a new body of work emerged for critical scrutiny. National and international critics had lauded Akhmatova's early works for their blend of graceful language and complex classical Russian forms of poetry. As the full breadth of her achievement became visible and was published first in Russian and then in translation throughout the world, she was recognized as not only one of the few poets of her generation to survive to old age in her country, but as one of the most accomplished Russian poets of the twentieth century. Sam Driver notes that in *Requiem,* in particular, Akhmatova managed to "generalize her own shattering experience into an epic cry for her people." The work is accepted as one of the masterpieces of her career, and it continues to receive critical attention, not simply as an example of laudable art emerging from the fire of persecution, but as a carefully crafted masterwork composed by a master poet.

PRINCIPAL WORKS

Poetry

Vecher [*Evening*] 1912
Chetki [*Rosary*] 1914
Belaya staya [*White Flock*] 1917
U samogo morya 1921
Podorozhnik 1921
Anno Domini MCMXXI 1921
Iz shesti knig [*From Six Books*] 1940
Izbrannye stikhi 1943
Stickhotvoreniia, 1909-1957 1958
Poema bez geroya; Triptych [*Poem without a Hero*] 1960
Stikhi, 1909-1960 1961
Stikhotvoreniia, 1909-1960 1961
Rekviem [*Requiem*] 1963
Poeziya 1964
Beg Vremeni 1965
Sochineniya. 3 vols. 1965
Stikhotvoreniia i poemy 1976
Sochineniia v dvukh tomakh. 2 vols. 1986
Severnye elegii: stikhotvoreniia, poetry, o poetakh 1989

Principal English Translations

Forty-Seven Love Songs 1927
Collected Poems: 1912-1963 1963
Selected Poems 1969
Poems of Akhmatova 1973
Poem without a Hero 1973
Tale without a Hero and Twenty-two Poems by Anna Axmatova 1973
Requiem and Poem without a Hero 1976
White Flock 1978
Way of All the Earth 1979
Poems 1988
The Complete Poems of Anna Akhmatova [translated by Judith Hemschemeyer] 2 vols. 1990

CRITICISM

Sam N. Driver (essay date 1972)

SOURCE: Driver, Sam N. "Later Works." In *Anna Akhmatova,* pp. 125-55. New York: Twayne Publishers, 1972.

[*In the following excerpt, Driver offers a thematic overview of Akhmatova's* Requiem.]

Unlike the **Poem Without a Hero, Requiem** is not a private poem. It is not so much a new experiment in Akhmatova's poetry as a culmination of a style perfected over the decades preceding; Akhmatova organizes her characteristic devices and techniques into an amazingly powerful statement which requires no elaboration or "explanation."

Neither is the **Requiem** a private poem in the sense that the subject, unlike that of the **"Petersburg Tale,"** is immediately accessible to anyone with a knowledge of Russia's recent history—and all too well-known to those who lived in Russia during the late 1930's. The poem is, if not private, deeply personal: but Akhmatova is able to generalize her own shattering experience into an epic cry for her people. It was a time when "The stars of death stood above us, / And guiltless Russia huddled trembling / Under bloody boots / And under the tires of the Black Moriahs."

For the introduction to **Requiem,** Akhmatova wrote: "In the terrible years of the Ezhovshchina[1], I spent seventeen months in the prison lines in Leningrad." Time has dulled the mind to the enormity of what happened in Russia in the late 1930's, but Akhmatova's contemporaries can recall the horror bound up in her simple statement.

After the murder of the Leningrad Party Secretary Sergey Kirov in 1934, there started a chain reaction of political arrests, interrogations and executions which climaxed in the Great Purge of 1935-38. The show trials and the liquidation of the "enemies of the people" began. The population of the prison camps grew from six million in 1937 to ten million by 1940-42.[2] Even ordinary and innocent people were denounced in the general hysteria. In the cities, the prisons filled the minds of everyone; scarcely a family was not in some way affected. Long lines of mothers, wives and sisters formed beneath the prison walls. It is here that Akhmatova stood, waiting for news of her imprisoned son, Lev; it is here that she raised her cry for Russia's suffering, and it is here she would have her monument raised:

And if someone in this land
Thinks to raise a monument to me,

I agree to this honor
But with a condition—place it not

Near the sea, where I was born,
My last tie with the sea is broken,

Nor near that sacred stump in the garden at Tsarskoe,
Where an inconsolable shade searches for me,

But here where I stood for three hundred hours,
And where they did not draw back the bolts for me.

Because, even in blessed death I'm afraid
I'll forget the rumble of the Black Moriahs,

Forget how the hateful door clanged shut,
And how an old woman howled like a wounded beast.

As part of the introduction, Akhmatova gives a brief reminiscence from the days spent in the prison lines:

Once somebody somehow "recognized" me. Then a woman behind me, lips blue from the cold, who had never before heard my name, wakened from the stupor common to us all and asked close to my ear (we all spoke in whispers there): "And you can describe this?" And I said, "I can." Then something like a smile slipped over what had once been her face.

It is to these women that Akhmatova dedicates her poem, and with their voices that she speaks:

I would like to name them all by name,
But the list has been taken away and there's nowhere
  to find out.

For them I wove a wide cover
Out of the poor words I overheard from them.

I remember them always and everywhere,
And I shall not forget them even in some new sorrow.

And if they shut my tortured mouth
Which shouts with the voices of a hundred million,

Let the women remember me likewise
On the eve of my memorial day.

These lines come from the **"Second Epilogue"**; the structural divisions in the poem are quite complex. There is the prose **"In Place of an Introduction,"** a dedication, a poetic **"Introduction,"** and then a series of ten lyrical poems, not directly related to one another, and employing a variety of styles and moods, but each representing a step in a progression which replaces the usual poetic narrative. The two epilogues follow, returning from the lyric to the epic stance of the **"Dedication"** and **"Introduction."**

The **"Dedication"** begins: *Pered etim gorem gnutsya gory, / Ne techyot velikaya reka /* (Before such grief mountains bend, / The great river does not flow).

Akhmatova's genius at orchestration makes the opening line a wonderfully powerful one.[3] The **"Dedication"** continues to state the theme of the poem, and the **"Introduction"** repeats it: "It was when only the dead / Smiled, glad to be at peace. / And Leningrad, like a useless appendage, / Flapped beside its prisons."

From the general and epic tone of the prefatory pieces, the first poem of the cycle shifts to the specific and individual, a short lyric with the distinctive marks of Akhmatova's style:

They led you away at dawn;
I walked behind you as in a funeral,
The children wept in the darkened chamber,
The candle at the shrine overflowed.
On your lips, an icon-like coldness.
Deathly sweat on your brow . . . not to be forgotten.
And I like the wives of the Streltsy[4]
Will howl under the Kremlin's towers!

The suggestion of a funeral is not an unusual one in Akhmatova's early poetry (compare from *1916* the lines: *ya plakal'shchits stayu vedu za soboy*—I lead behind me a flock of mourners).

Also, the rich lexicon borrowed from an older Russia is, as we have seen, a characteristic feature of Akhmatova's earlier work: the almost obsolete *gornitsa* (chamber), the Orthodox associations of the word *bozhnitsa* (shrine, perhaps icon stand or icon corner), and the comparison using the word "icon" itself.

The breathless hesitancy of the lyrical moment which marks so many of the early lyrics is here. At the full realization of the emotion, there is a breaking point; the melted wax on the votive candle trembles and spills over. The wire snaps; control is gone: *"Budu ya kak streletskie zhonki / Pod kremlyovskimi bashnyami vyt'!"/* (And I like the wives of the Streltsy / Will howl under the Kremlin's towers!)

This is an astonishingly forceful evocation of another tragic time in Russian history: the wives wailing near the walls of the Kremlin, their husbands executed before their eyes. Into this powerful image, Akhmatova introduces a note of pathos in the unexpected diminutive of "wives" *(zhonki)*. In the tension created, she has produced two of her most striking lines. The wail of the Streltsy women is echoed again in the **"Epilogue"**—in the howl of the old woman as the prison door slams shut on her loved one. There arises a whole series of associations with the brave and loyal Russian women who followed their men into prison and exile—from Nataliya Dolgorukaya to Maria Volkonskaya and beyond.

After a complete emotional break in Akhmatova's poems, we have come to expect a quick return to calm. In the early lyrics, it is often the calm of resignation, or that brought on by force of will. In the later poetry, there is the suggestion of an unnatural calm, a calm that is not quite sane. It is as though the mind, to protect itself, loses touch with reality and its unbearable grief. The tendency in some early poems for the *persona* to stand aside and apparently observe herself as a separate person is even more marked in the later poetry. Here, the separation can become complete.

The second lyric has meaning in this sense: a calm with a suggestion of madness after intense grief, and the dissociation of the poet from herself.

> Quietly flows the quiet Don,
> Into the house comes the yellow moon.
>
> Comes in with his hat cocked jauntily,
> The yellow moon sees a shadow.
>
> This woman is sick,
> This woman is alone
>
> Husband in the grave, son in prison,
> Pray for me a little.

The shift from the emotional break in the first lyric is abrupt; quiet is introduced in one line. The evocation of the Don also suggests a kind of epic calm, and is part of the epic motif of Russia's mighty rivers: the unnamed "great river" and the misty Neva of the **"Dedication,"** the quiet Don here, the swirling Yenisei, and at the very end, once more the Neva.

Calm is reestablished, but it is only apparent: the odd impression of the moonlight suggests the mind disordered by grief, and there is a confusion between first and third persons. In the following lyric, the confusion is resolved: the *persona* divorced entirely from the suffering self. "No, that is not I, that is someone else who is suffering. / I couldn't suffer like that, and as to what happened— / Let it be covered over with black cloths, / And let the lamps be carried out . . . / Night."

The gesture of covering here is not simply suggestive of covering the dead; there is a subtle use here of a mainly Orthodox association which is not infrequent in Akhmatova's verse. It carries the idea of comfort and protection. In the **"Epilogue,"** Akhmatova wrote of the women standing in the prison lines: "For them I wove a wide cover / Out of the poor words I heard from them."

The word used for cover is *pokrov*, and the Orthodox association is with the veil of the Virgin, its comfort and protection.[5]

With the finality of the single word "night" of the last line, the poem draws to a complete stop. The next part takes up a theme which is to be central to *The Poem Without a Hero*: time past in the present. The young noblewoman and fashionable poetess of Petersburg in 1913 reappears momentarily standing "three hundredth or so" in the line under the grim walls of the Kresty prison. There are now three *personae* present, the same and yet not the same: the grief-stricken mother, the person speaking here who cannot bear to suffer so, and the "gay little sinner of Tsarskoye Selo."

> You should be shown, you who loved to make fun of
>   things,
> You who were the favorite of all your friends,
> The gay little sinner of Tsarskoe Selo,
> What will happen in your life—
> As three hundredth or so in line
> You will stand under the Kresty walls,
> And with your hot tear
> Burn through the New Year's ice.
> And not a sound—and how many
> Innocent lives are ending there . . .

The next two poems are lyrical treatments of the poet's apprehension of her terror and despair. They are followed by the central poem of *Requiem,* wonderfully simple and deeply moving in its simplicity.

"The Sentence"

> And the stone word fell
> Upon my still living breast.
> Never mind, I was ready after all,
> I'll manage somehow or other.
>
> I have lots to do today:
> I have to kill my memory utterly,
> I've got to turn my soul to stone,
> I've got to learn to live again—
>
> And if not . . . The hot rustle of summer
> Is like a holiday outside my window.
> For a long time I've had a presentiment of this
> Bright day and empty house.

For the central poem in her long work, Akhmatova chooses restraint where one might expect a complete breakdown or histrionics. After all, the fifth poem in the cycle begins "For seventeen months I've been crying out, / I am calling you home. / I have thrown myself at the feet of the hangman; / You are my son and the terror of my life."

In **"The Sentence,"** however, there is extreme understatement, a simple, workaday vocabulary and tone. It is not simply epic calm in the face of tragedy, or a kind of resignation and acceptance. The intensity of the moment is increased many times by the pathetic effort of the will to overcome a grief that borders on madness.

In the context of all Akhmatova's poetry up to this point, the poet's very own familiar devices and symbols, already perfected in less tragic days, lend an extraordinary pathos. The conversational tone, the stone imagery, the suggestion of clairvoyance, the peculiar use of bright/radiant, the pervasive symbol of the empty or abandoned house—all these things were once, after all, the stock-in-trade of the "gay little sinner of Tsarskoe Selo." Their reappearance here subtly compounds the emotional charge of this "restrained" lyric.

An apostrophe to death follows: "You will come anyway—so why not now?" The *persona* will greet death in any form he chooses—even in "the little game which he himself invented, and with which everyone is familiar to the point of nausea": "That I may see the top of a blue cap⁶ / And the superintendent pale from fear. / It's all the same to me. The Yenisei swirls / And the polar star shines . . ."

The next poem and the last lyric in the series takes up directly the theme of madness, again with the suggestion of another person suffering:

> Madness has already covered
> Half my soul with its wing,
> And gives to drink of a fiery wine
> And beckons into a dark valley.
>
> And I understood that
> I must lose the battle to it,
> Listening to my own raving
> As though it were someone else's.
>   . . . . .

The last part of the poem proper is entitled **"Crucifixion."** In the brief space of two quatrains, Akhmatova is able to generalize the intensely lyrical emotion of the preceding cycle of nine poems. To do this, she relies once again on the universality of the mother suffering for the son sentenced and persecuted. From the mother and son, the poem moves to the Mother and the Son:

> A mighty choir of angels praised the hour,
> And the skies melted in fire.
> To the Father He said: "Why hast thou forsaken me!"
> And to the Mother: "Oh, do not weep for me . . ."
>
> The Magdalene struck her breast and sobbed,
> The beloved disciple turned to stone,
> But there, where the Mother stood silent
> No one dared even to glance.

The poem ends with this brief and extremely effective generalization of human experience, and in the **"Epilogues,"** the epic stance of the introductory poems is again assumed. In the second **"Epilogue,"** the theme receives its final statement. The pounding, compelling amphibracs give the impression that no force can stay the completion of that statement. And when it is completed, the poet returns again to the motif of the great rivers of Russia, here as in the first part, to the Neva and its association with Pushkin, *The Bronze Horseman,* with Peter the Great and Russian history:

> *I tikho idut po Neve korabli.*
> And the ships go quietly along the Neva.

Notes

1. The "Ezhov time"; from N. I. Ezhov, head of the N.K.V.D. (Secret Police) from 1936-38, who led the Terror.

2. Georg von Rauch, *History of Soviet Russia.* New York: Praeger (1967), p. 242.

3. The close juxtaposition of gutturals suggests a throat constricted by grief. Akhmatova consciously used juxtapositions of glottal stops for emotional signification; elsewhere she notes the use of juxtaposed "k"s to suggest extreme agitation. The vowel sounds are carefully ordered in a progression from front to back. The line descends in intonation as in physical articulation. The following line, as characteristic of Akhmatova's earlier orchestrations, reverses the procedure.

4. The Streltsy were a standing infantry which sided with the Tsarevna Sophia against Peter the Great in an attempt to preserve their power and privileges. After their second rebellion in 1698, Peter executed over seven hundred of the Streltsy, and many of them were killed before the walls of the Kremlin.

5. The Feast of the Protection of the Mother of God, which is little known in the West, is an important Orthodox festival, commemorating her appearance in Constantinople in the Tenth Century. Kneeling in tears in the center of a church, she extended her veil over all the people, who felt the grace of her protection. See Leonid Ouspensky and Vladimir Lossky, *The Meaning of Icons.* Boston: Book and Art Shop (1952), pp. 153-54.

6. The blue cap (*golubaya shapka*) is meant to suggest the N.K.V.D.; the superintendent (*upravdom*) is a kind of concierge and also a minor functionary who manages the building.

Sonia I. Ketchian (essay date 1986)

SOURCE: Ketchian, Sonia I. "An Inspiration for Anna Akhmatova's *Requiem*: Hovannes Tumanian." In *Studies in Russian Literature In Honor of Vsevolod Setchkarev,* edited by Julian W. Connolly and Sonia I. Ketchian, pp. 175-188. Columbus, Ohio: Slavica Publishers, 1986.

[*In the following essay, Ketchian proposes that one source of inspiration for Akhmatova's* Requiem *was a Tumanian.*]

Numerous literary, cultural, and historical sources have enriched Akhmatova's masterpiece **Requiem** (1935-1961). Some have been studied, but many more await their turn.[1] The present objective is to illuminate a source of inspiration for ***Requiem,*** the poem "Requiem" ("Hogehangist") by Hovannes Tumanian (1869-1923).[2] While there is no written reference to familiarity with Tumanian's poem and its translator Naum Grebnev, the likelihood of Akhmatova being familiar with the poem is great, particularly in interlinear translation.[3] For, on the one hand, attested acquaintance of Akhmatova with Armenian poetry dates to the mid-thirties, when she commenced her own ***Requiem.*** At that time she published her translation of the Symbolist poet Daniel Varuzhan's (1884-1915) poem "First Sin" in the journal *Zvezda* (1936) and was translating two poems of the fiery Eghishe Charents (1897-1937), according to her prose piece "What I Am Working on":

> I have devoted much time to translations. Recently in *Zvezda* appeared my translation of a long poem by the Armenian poet Daniel Varuzhan—"First Sin." Now I have completed the translation of two poems by the contemporary Armenian poet Charents.[4]

On the other hand, Akhmatova's poem **"Imitation from the Armenian,"** broadly dated "the 1930's," most certainly designates an Armenian source through its title alone, which specifies the poem's genre and general source. This poem of Akhmatova derives from a quatrain from the philosophical cycle *Quatrains* by Tumanian, as demonstrated in my article "The Genre of Imitation and Anna Akhmatova."[5] The allegoric theme of Tumanian's quatrain is the Turkish genocide of the Armenian nation in 1915. There are three translations of the quatrain into Russian, that of M. Pavlova, K. Lipskerov, and N. Grebnev.[6] A literal translation from the Armenian reads:

> In my dream a ewe
> Came up to me with a question:
> "May God protect your son,
> How was the taste of my child?"
>
> (1917)

In her **"Imitation"** Akhmatova retains the forced servility of the wronged one, who can seek no justice from the perpetrator:

"Imitation from the Armenian"

> I shall come into your dream
> As a black ewe, approach the throne
> On withered and infirm
> Legs, bleating: 'Padishah,
> Have you dined well? You who hold
> The world like a bead, beloved
> Of Allah, was my little son
> To your taste, was he fat enough?'
>
> (the 1930's)

Given these premises connecting Akhmatova with Tumanian in a certain theme, I will investigate similarities in the two Requiems with attention directed first to general parallels and then to the individual pieces which comprise Akhmatova's poem. A literal translation of Tumanian's poem (1915) and its Armenian title reads:

"Requiem"

> And I arose that, in accordance with our ancestral laws,
> I might read the last repose for the hapless victims of my nation,
> Who in the country and city, and on the hills and plains, from sea to sea
> Are expired, dead, sprawled and scattered in myriads
> . . .
>
> And I took fire from the red flames of the Armenian conflagration,
> And I relighted one by one in the bosom of the serene and cold heaven
> The great votive candles of the Armenian land,
> The Massis and the Ara, the Sipan and the Sermantz, the Nemruth, the Tandurek,
> As well as the lamp of the Holy Arakadz, which, like the distant sun,
> Is unattainable, interminable, refulgent, and bright above my head.
> I stood, grave, alone, and solid, like Mount Massis,
> I called out to those tragic souls, scattered forever,
> As far as Mesopotamia, Assyria, the Armenian Sea,
> As far as Hellespont, as far as the stormy shores of Pontus.
> "Repose, my orphans . . . in vain is sorrow, in vain and useless. . . .
> Man—the man-eating beast—will remain so for yet a long time" . . .
>
> To my right the Euphrates, to my left the Tigris passed by,
> Reading psalms in formidable voices and going through deep-deep valleys.
> And the clouds arising from the Tsirac, the enormous censer,
> Set out from the Flowering Hills, from the Armenian Range;
> Fragrant, aromatic, they moved toward faraway places,
> To sprinkle gems, to make flowers fragrant, to incense perfume
> As far as Mesopotamia, as far as Assyria, as far as the Armenian Sea,
> As far as Hellespont, as far as the stormy shores of Pontus . . .
> "Repose, my orphans . . . in vain is sorrow, in vain and useless. . . .
> Man—the man-eating beast—will remain so for yet a long time". . . .[7]

The similarities in the two poems are not at all obvious, as they were in the poem titled **"Imitation from . . ."** Still, if Akhmatova once achieved striking emphasis in equating the Genocide of the Armenians with Stalinist Terror (for which now in ***Requiem*** she employs the narrower definition of Ezhovist Terror to protect herself), she could easily have resorted to the same theme a second time, if more obliquely, in conjunction with various other allusions from Russian and world culture and literature.

Both of Tumanian's poems were created in the same period, 1915-1917, and treat the theme of "man—the man-eating beast." Both works of Akhmatova involve a mother, a son, and a seen, or unseen (in *Requiem*), villain (*palach*—executioner). The villain of *Requiem,* Stalin, is intimated in the poem and understood by those conversant with the times. In the case of both poets the main perpetrator of the crimes comes from a different ethnic origin—a Georgian persecuting Russians and other peoples in Akhmatova's work, Turks persecuting Armenians in Tumanian's work. There is, then, the distinct possibility that the title for Akhmatova's work was inspired by Tumanian's Armenian equivalent, without discounting the influence of musical requiems. Importantly, Tumanian's title refers mainly to a ceremony for the dead and only incidentally calls out to the orphans of the atrocities, whereas many of Akhmatova's victims are still living.[8] Yet she fears a terrible death for them. Akhmatova develops funereal images for her living son, Lev Gumilev: "I followed you as at a wake." In this way she underscores the fate of those who perished and those who are to follow.

In composition, the poems are dissimilar: Tumanian has twenty-six long, ponderous lines of fourteen and fifteen syllables. The verse is syllabic—customary for Armenian prosody. By contrast, Akhmatova's long poem consists of sixteen pieces. One is in prose—**"In Lieu of a Foreword"** (1957). Among the verse pieces there are one epigraph, two introductions—**"Dedication"** and **"Introduction,"** a two-part **"Epilog"** and ten core poems, all featuring various metrical and compositional form.

The Requiems of both poets commemorate the tragic fate of a nation and of millions of its victims. Their striking similarity lies in the fact that neither poet eulogizes a singular or single fate. As Sam Driver has aptly observed in his book *Anna Akhmatova,* in this deeply personal poem, "Akhmatova is able to generalize her own shattering experience into an epic cry for her people."[9]

Further, there is correspondence of ambience in both poets. Tumanian and even Akhmatova, despite her poetic persona being three hundredth in line, stand isolated in the face of personal and national tragedy. Both are observers, but secondhand observers, or outside participants in the calamity. For Tumanian, the persona stands alone with the aftermath of the slaughter beneath him in the distance; he was spared this fate, because he is an Eastern Armenian, less subject to these particular horrors, insofar as the massacres engulfed chiefly the greater, Western part of the Armenian nation. His speaker moves magically in thought over distance to places beyond the borders of historical Armenia. Akhmatova, too, moves great distances in imagination over land. Similarly, although residing in the same political entity as the prisoners, Akhmatova is physically removed from them, i.e. from those suffering firsthand in prison and in concentration camps. She is, however, surrounded by sufferers like herself, the families of the incarcerated—secondhand, as it were, sufferers, while Tumanian mourns the victims alone and is removed from all other people. Both speakers, then, are grieving for others, not for themselves.

Both personas are strong and brave. Tumanian's speaker is almost detached from his sorrow. As for Akhmatova, Sam Driver points out her method of "extreme understatement" in the piece "Sentence." Still, Akhmatova's speaker breaks down emotionally following the sentencing of her son; hers is an attempt to seek oblivion in madness and death. Tumanian's speaker, on the other hand, is beyond the stage of sentencing. In fact, the victims he mourns were slaughtered without trial. Nonetheless, Akhmatova's speaker is sufficiently stoic to create, in the words of Pushkin, her "monument unwrought by human hands" to personal and national tragedy.[10] In light of these facts, it is difficult to agree with the Soviet composer Dmitrii Shostakovich's statement that in *Requiem* "protest is lacking, the note of Christian humility is too strong" or with Alexander Solzhenitsyn who chided the poet, "This was a tragedy of the people, but you have only the tragedy of a mother and son."[11] On the contrary, Akhmatova merely avoids histrionics. Her main protest is firmly embodied in her monumental poem, as noted by M. Yovanovich (171).

Neither poet attempts to describe the atrocities committed. For Akhmatova, such reticence is in keeping with her unique circumspect style. Indeed, it is well known that she rarely describes in the true sequential sense, notwithstanding the presence in *Requiem*'s prefatory prose piece, **"In Lieu of a Foreword,"** of the query by the emaciated woman in the line:

"And can you describe this?"

"And I said, 'I can.'"

Conversely, Tumanian's customary style is not devoid of sequential description; still, he presents here images without detailing, or naming the crimes. His attitude is: the less said, the better one is able to cope with the atrocities and to assume the difficult task of living.

Above all, both poets try to kill memory. Akhmatova is specific: "I must kill my memory totally." Tumanian eradicates memory by meticulously avoiding mention of the perpetrators of the heinous crimes: to name the brutes would be to immortalize them. Instead, in the words of the contemporary poet Vahagn Davtian, the universal criteria denominating Tumanian's poem break down the general concepts of power and subjugation, and

> . . . the weak and the strong acquire relative values. You begin to feel and realize, quite unexpectedly, the purity and strength of the slaughtered, dead people, whose literary patriarch is sufficiently strong to suffer his immense sorrow in dignity and has the power to say, "Repose, my orphans . . . vain are the emotions . . . vain and inept . . ."[12]

In Akhmatova the distancing of the self in her mind— that is intellectually—from the grief exhibited physically and emotionally, is akin to the stoicism in Tumanian. Compare the piece, "No, it is not I," which clarifies the image in the **"Dedication"**—"Yet goes . . . swaying . . . Alone."—as well as that in the piece "Gently flows the quiet Don"—"Of a woman lying ill." Understandably, making personal experience intellectually strange through defamiliarization results in a form of muting or killing of memory.[13] The quietness of the religious rites discharged by Tumanian's persona, the matter-of-fact manner of their performance is the result of numbness. Correspondingly, his attitude deadens the pain sufficiently to give rise to philosophical and social contemplation, which will raise the persona above disruptive depression. Thus for both poets a kind of numbness exists as a result of horror. It can, in the words of Sam Driver, "take the form of madness (losing one's right mind, seeing oneself as someone else) or apparent calm in monumental self-abnegation, mechanically following rituals (another kind of madness)."[14]

In surveying vast expanses of the land, both speakers, in addition to the epic range, provide specific geographic names. Clearly, through toponymy (Tsushima, the epic rivers of the Soviet Union—the Yenisei, the Neva, and the Don, the steppes of Central Asia, the Black Sea shore where she was born) Akhmatova demonstrates the magnitude of the tragedy's grip on her country. Following this she moves out into the realm of Russian history through her comparison with the seventeenth century wailing wives of the executed *strelets* soldiers and of religion—to Jerusalem and to Christ. Tumanian intimates the devastated barrenness of an area, whose formerly thriving roots go back to Biblical times and places. He appears to be negating the painful present and the current sole masters of the area by using classical and purely Armenian toponymy in some cases ("Pontus" for "Black Sea"; the Armenian "Massis" for "Ararat"). The two speakers also present mountains in a figurative sense. Akhmatova alliterates the *dr* and *gr* sounds in **"Dedication"** to evoke Marina Tsvetaeva's *Poem About a Mountain* in introducing her mountain imagery: "Pered etim gorem gnutsia gory" (The mountains buckle before this grief).[15] Akhmatova even replicates the stressed front vowels and the repeated *o*.

While Yovanovich, like others before her, has noticed the play in Akhmatova on the root *gor,* she does not connect it with the interplay of *gore—gor'kii* (grief— bitter), so pivotal to Akhmatova's poetics.[16] Nor does she draw parallels with Tsvetaeva.

After naming mountains, Tumanian speaks of them symbolically, as religious votive candles:

> And I relighted one by one . . .
> The great votive candles of the Armenian land,
> The Massis and the Ara, the Sipan and the Sermantz,
>   the Nemruth, the Tandurek, . . .

Through simile Tumanian equates stoicism with mighty Mount Massis: "I stood, grave, alone and solid, like Mount Massis." Both speakers mention rivers. Akhmatova shows that tears are more multitudinous and swift than a certain river: "The great river does not flow." Instead, "tears gush." The river in question is not the Don, it is probably the Volga, or one of the great Siberian rivers or none at all. Later the speaker will refer to the Don: "Tikho l'etsya tikhii Don" (The quiet Don quietly pours), using the verb "pours" in lieu of the more usual "flows" to bring movement closer to an image of tears. Sam Driver comments on the river:

> The evocation of the Don also suggests a kind of epic calm, and is part of the epic motif of Russia's mighty rivers: the unnamed "great river" and the misty Neva of the **"Dedication,"** the quiet Don here, the swirling Yenisei, and at the very end, once more the Neva.
>
> (129)

The tautology of the word *tikhii* (quiet) in the line is probably an ironic reference to Mikhail Sholokhov's *Tikhii Don* (*Quiet Flows the Don*) and evokes images of tears of despair.[17] The image of the Siberian river in the piece **"To Death"** adds scope to the poem's geographic space and, conceivably, incorporates indignant supportive emotion. Similarly, Tumanian's mind and voice reach out to Mesopotamia with its two famous rivers and to other bodies of water:

> I called out to those tragic souls, scattered forever,
> As far as Mesopotamia, Assyria, the Armenian Sea,
> As far as Hellespont, as far as the stormy shores of
>   Pontus.

He then names two rivers that participate openly in the rites:

> To my right the Euphrates, to my left the Tigris passed
>   by,
> Reading psalms in formidable voices . . .

Tumanian, then, is clear about the rivers' participation in the lament, whereas Akhmatova intimates it.

The perpetrated evil represents such immense proportions in **Requiem** that the normal benevolent mind cannot grasp it; in the piece "The light years are flying"

Akhmatova's speaker says, "What has happened, I can't take in." There is the same bewilderment in Tumanian, although he is less vocal and accepts philosophically, as it were, the atrocities due to their recurring nature. Although convinced of the evil's inevitability, he, like Akhmatova, transcends spiritually, and even physically, the tragedy at hand. Further, Tumanian's image of "man—the man-eating beast" is reflected in Akhmatova's piece "For seventeen months I have called you" in the lines:

> . . . I can't say who's
> Man, who's beast any more. . . .

Both utterances evoke the devouring image in the quatrain of Tumanian used by Akhmatova in her "Imitation from the Armenian."

In Akhmatova's piece **"The Sentence"** the stony word of the sentencing—"There fell the word of stone"—induces the persona's desire for numbing her heart or "turning her soul into stone" in order to relearn how to continue living. Tumanian's heart is likewise numbed through the horrors, yet he masks the numbness under valor.

In the piece **"To Death"** Akhmatova calls for death so that she may not witness the living sacrifices. The thought of death never even crosses Tumanian's mind, since he must live on to remember and to record the atrocities through art. Where Akhmatova alludes to the culprit—the NKVD, the Secret Police, whose uniform sports a blue-topped hat—through "the top of the light-blue cap," Tumanian maintains a chilling silence on the topic of the executioners, unlike in his quatrain with its startling revelation at the end. Only a hint is provided in the ominous "man—the man-eating beast" that the deaths were not caused by any natural disaster, such as an earthquake.

Since requiems are religious rites, it is to be expected that both personas appear to find solace in religion. Akhmatova's imagery includes the Crucifixion of Christ, Magdalene, the Virgin Mary, "the cold of an icon," "your high cross," "the ringing of censers," "Rising as though for early mass," "in the image-case candlelight guttered." The name of the prison, Kresty (Crosses), resounds with irony, evoking both the image of graveyard crosses and the Russian idiom "nesti svoi krest" (to bear one's cross). Mountains as lighted candles figure in Tumanian in performing the mechanical aspect of the ancient rites for the dead; the rivers intone psalms. In Akhmatova the Biblical imagery gains prominence in the piece **"Crucifixion,"** when insanity seems to overcome her narrator, conceivably, as the only salvation, and certainly as a fitting comparison between the loss of an only son by the Virgin Mary and by the persona. Insanity, however, eludes the speaker,

as if the popular denouement of literary tragedies were too simplistic a solution in "real life." Importantly, both mothers grow stony in their grief, and one of the memories the speaker must leave behind is the terrible eyes of her son which embody "petrified suffering."

As already mentioned, the bipartite **"Epilog"** to Akhmatova's *Requiem* represents a hymn whose tribute surmounts the personal sorrow. In its first part the narrator becomes specific:

> And I pray not only for myself,
> But also for all those who stood there.

Her focus rests on those suffering outside the prisons and the camps:

> And if they shut my tormented mouth,
> Through which a hundred million of my people
> cry, . . .

The second piece of **"Epilog"** finds the persona disassociating herself from the perpetrators of the terrors through her protest that a future monument to her may be erected only at the site of the Kresty Prison to memorialize her tears and anguish:

> And if ever in this country they should want
> To build me a monument
>
> I consent to that honor,
> But only on condition that they
>
> Erect it not on the sea-shore where I was born: . . .
>
> But here, where I stood for three hundred hours
> And where they never, never opened the doors for me.
>
> Lest in blessed death I should forget
> The grinding scream of the Black Marias,
>
> The hideous clanging gate, the old
> Woman wailing like a wounded beast.

Curiously, the speaker uses the phrase "in this country," which may sound neutral in English, since it is used by Americans to speak of their own country; however, in Russian only a foreigner would use the expression within Russia itself. A Russian would say "v nashei strane," or "u nas (v Rossii)" (in our country). Her use distances the country.

Most important, in the **"Epilog"** Akhmatova overtly transcends the particular, or personal, in favor of the general. In this narrative poem she has crafted a lasting monument to the victims of the years of the Terror on both sides of the bars, while depicting only the families outside the prisons. The prisoners remain a blur, as if they were already in Hades, or their suffering were too terrible for poetry. The silence with which Akhmatova shrouds the prisoners is akin to that of Tumanian for the dead victims. Tumanian proffers a spiritual monument, as it were, by transforming the mountain peaks into religious votive candles, where Akhmatova, in turn, rejects any future monument to herself as a poet, with one possible stipulation for acceptance—that it be erected on the very site of her greatest torment and where so many suffered with her. Accordingly, she transforms even a personal literary monument into a general one with political overtones.

Tumanian's rhythm and sounds are beautifully solemn. Their resigned majestic notes evoke a musical requiem for his dead victims. Akhmatova's victims, on the other hand, are mostly living at present, which is one reason she does not imitate a single-motif piece of music. Nor does she evoke Tumanian's rhythm. If Akhmatova had tried to imitate the fourteen and fifteen syllabic line in Russian, the result would have sounded like a throwback to the eighteenth century and to Vasilii Trediakovskii's verse in particular. Its impact would have been negligible. Instead, she chose variation, as if she were searching in all directions and trying to release the prisoners in a thousand ways. In her imagination, at least, she was. The ten core poems are preceded by an epigraph and three introductory pieces, as if a work on imprisonment were difficult to commence. Once begun, however, the surge subsides slowly, as evidenced by the ponderous bipartite **"Epilog."** Lacking consecutive narration, these poems of diverse rhythm shift their focus to various aspects of the leitmotif of prison and suffering. Each poem has a different rhythmic approach, as if anguish had sent the mother's head reeling, with her mind fixated on her loss.

Akhmatova's **Requiem** is not totally isolated from the body of her *oeuvre*. Its continuation is observed by Jeanne van der Eng-Liedmeier in her seminal article "Reception as a Theme in Achmatova's Later Poetry," where Akhmatova's heroic attempt will be paralleled in her later war poems in which she emerges as a poet crying out on behalf of her countrymen, her "people." Eng-Liedmeier states that the poem **Requiem,** which describes the reign of terror:

> . . . contains at the same time an accusation of those responsible and preserves the memory of what happened for future generations. "Do not forget," "remember always," is indeed the central motif in *Requiem*.[18]

The same statements are true of Tumanian.

Both poets display guarded optimism at best for the future, expressed by nature imagery. Tumanian turns to the clouds that:

> Set out from the Flowering Hills, from the Armenian
>   Range; . . .
> To sprinkle gems, to make flowers fragrant, to incense
>   perfume.

The tears bringing rain that will renew nature and life in the form of growth and development are far away from the present locus. Akhmatova's perorating lines likewise feature the image of tears in the guise of snow melting on the persona's future statue. She seems to be dispatching the prison pigeon far away with a message to distant friends. The image of the ships sailing down the Neva River evokes trips to foreign shores. There is a hint here at the dispersal of her family and people. Her two brothers, Andrei and Victor Gorenko, were living abroad. Similarly, the remnants of Tumanian's people had dispersed throughout the world.

Thus, although Akhmatova never translated Tumanian's poetry, she appears to have been sufficiently familiar with it to incorporate aspects of it into her own verse in an attempt to render more memorable and forceful her own art. Her own leitmotif acquired a greater universality through her homage to another master and the tragedy of another people.

Notes

1. For influences from various literatures see Milovoe Yovanovich "K razboru 'chuzhikh golosov' v *Rekvieme* Akhmatovoi," *Russian Literature,* 15, No. 1 (1984), 10.

2. For the text of Akhmatova's *Requiem* see A. Akhmatova, *Sochineniya,* 2 ed., ed. G. P. Struve *et al.* (Munich: Inter-Language Literary Associates, 1967-68, vols. I-II; Paris: YMCA, 1983, vol. III), I, 359-70. All translations of texts into English are mine, other than the translations of Akhmatova's "Imitation from the Armenian" and *Requiem,* which are translated by D. M. Thomas. See his A. Akhmatova, *Way of All Earth* (London: Secher and Warburg, 1979), 22; A. Akhmatova, *Requiem and Poem without a Hero* (London: Paul Elek, 1976), 23-32. In some instances, where exact wording was needed for *Requiem,* I have used my own literal translation.

3. This is the only Russian version known to me. It was published three years after Akhmatova's death in 1966, long after it would have been useful to her. Grebnev alters the poem noticeably, beginning with his title "Oplakivanie" ("Mourning"). Compositionally, he reduces it to fourteen rhyming couplets, where the Armenian has four stanzas of uneven length (4+6+6+10). For Grebnev's translation see Ovannes Tumanyan, *Izbrannye proizvedeniya v trekh tomakh* (Yerevan: Ayastan, 1969), I, 100-101. Grebnev has translated a fair amount of Tumanian, including an entire booklet of the *Quatrains*: Ovannes Tumanyan, *Chetverostishiya* (Yerevan: Ayastan, 1968). For the Armenian text of Tumanian's "Requiem" see H. Tumanian, *Banasteghtsutiunner* (Constantinople: K. Keshishian, 1922), 37-38.

4. A. Akhmatova, *Sochineniya,* III, 126. Interestingly, Charents has a long poem with the title partly in Latin, similar to Akhmatova's, *Requiem Aeternam Komitasu. Otryvki,* dedicated to the great Armenian composer Komitas, who lost his mind when witnessing the Turkish genocide of the Armenians in 1915. See Egishe Charents, *Stikhotvoreniya i poemy.* Biblioteka poeta. Bol'shaya seriya. (Leningrad: Sov. pisatel', 1973), 471-82.

5. S. Ketchian, "The Genre of *Podražanie* and Anna Achmatova," *Russian Literature,* 15, No. 1 (1984).

6. The two Russian translations, other than Grebnev's, are found in Ovannes Tumanyan, *Izbrannye proizvedeniya* (M.: Gos. izd. khud. lit., 1946), 89 (the translation of M. Pavlova) and in Ovannes Tumanyan, *Izbrannye sochineniya* (Yerevan: Arm. gos. izd., 1956), 101 (the translation of K. Lipskerov). Mention of Akhmatova's friendship with Lipskerov is found in Lidiya Chukovskaya, *Zapiski ob Anne Akhmatovoi* (Paris: YMCA, 1976-), II, 533, 29.

7. I am indebted to poet Diana Der Hovanessian and Dr. Marzbed Margossian for locating the Armenian version of the poem for me after I had found the English excerpts in *Kroonk* (1982). An English poetic translation, "Rest in Peace," is available in Hovannes Toumanian, *Selected Works* (Moscow: Progress, 1969), 25.

8. Apart from *Requiem . . .* by Charents mentioned in note 4, similarly titled poems can be found in other literatures. My thanks to Prof. Helen Vendler of Harvard University who has found a "Requiem" by the Scottish poet Robert Louis Stevenson. It is like a final instruction from the deceased on the site of his burial and on the contents of his epitaph. The time for the poem's action is projected into the future. See *The Poems of Robert Louis Stevenson* (New York: Thomas Y. Crowell, 1900), 293. Aleksandr Blok has translated a "Rekviem" ("Requiem") by the Latvian poet Vilis Plūdons (1874-1940). Written in 1912, it was translated in 1915. Like Stevenson's, it is a final instruction, the statement of a young man who has died for love in this case. Begging forgiveness of his mother, he brings his instructions to the act of burial. A. Blok, *Sobranie sochinenii v vos'mi tomakh* (Moscow: Gos. izd. khud. lit., 1960-62), III, 399-402. By contrast, Tumanian's poem is a requiem for the dead by a third party, where the present glosses over the past and bravely tries to project into the future. Akhmatova's poem is a requiem that probably intended to include past (dead) victims but concentrates on those living under hellish conditions on both sides of the bars. Since many will perish, her poem projects from the present into the not very distant future.

9. Sam Driver, *Anna Akhmatova* (New York: Twayne, 1972), 139.

10. Quoted from Pushkin's poem "Monument" ("Ya pamyatnik sebe vozdvig nerukotvornyi"). A. S. Pushkin, *Polnoe sobranie sochinenii* (Moscow: AN SSSR, 1962-68), III, 373.

11. S. Volkov, "'Rekviem' Anny Akhmatovoi i Dzhona Tavenera," *Novoe russkoe slovo,* April 4, 1984, 10. For a truly personal focus on the suffering of the speaker and her son see Akhmatova's five-piece cycle "Cherepki" ("Shards"), written in the late 1940's and early 1950's in A. Akhmatova, *Sochineniya,* III, 73-74.

12. Vahagn Davtian, "The 'Requiem' of Hovannes Toumanian," *Kroonk,* No. 4 (1982), 19.

13. This impactful image has served as a title for the last volume, . . . *Kill Memory . . .* (N. Y.: New Directions, 1983), in the political trilogy by William Herrick.

14. Quoted from Sam Driver's letter of comments.

15. Compare Tsvetaeva's opening lines:

> Vzdrognut'—i gory s plech,
> I dusha—gore!
> Dai mne o gore spet':
> O moei gore.
> (To shudder—and a load off one's shoulders,
> And one's soul to grief!
> Let me sing of grief:
> About my mountain.)

16. On the interplay of grief—bitter see S. Ketchian, *The Poetry of Anna Akhmatova: A Conquest of Time and Space,* Slavistische Beiträge, vol. 196 (Munich: Otto Sagner, 1986), 39-55. Intonations of Nikolai Nekrasov are evident in the sound play as well (the repetition of the "u" sounds, as in his poem "Zheleznaya doroga" ("The Railroad").

17. For a different explanation see Yovanovich, 170.

18. Jeanne van der Eng-Liedmeier, "Reception as a Theme in Achmatova's Later Poetry," *Russian Literature,* 15, No. 1 (1984), 110.

Susan Amert (essay date fall 1990)

SOURCE: Amert, Susan. "Akhmatova's 'Song of the Motherland': Rereading the Opening Texts of *Rekviem.*" *Slavic Review* 49, no. 3 (fall 1990): 374-89.

[*In the following essay, Amert offers a close reading of the first two texts of Akhmatova's* Requiem.]

Pokoinyi Alig'eri sozdal by desiatyi krug ada.

Anna Akhmatova

Hostias et preces tibi,
Domine, laudis offerimus:
tu suscipe pro animabus illis,
quarum hodie memoriam facimus:
fac eas, Domine, de morte
transire ad vitam.

the requiem mass

Anna Akhmatova's **Rekviem** is a deceptively simple piece. Compared to the opacity and self-conscious literariness of **Poema bez geroia, Rekviem** seems transparent, much like Akhmatova's early lyrics, and appears to demand little in the way of commentary or elucidation.[1] Its very form and scope, however, as well as the dates of its composition (1935-1961), identify it as a product of the "later Akhmatova"—the Akhmatova who resumed writing in the mid-1930s after a decade of relative poetic inactivity, the Akhmatova who created **Poema bez geroia. Rekviem** fully adheres to the poetics of the later work,[2] most strikingly in the salient role of intertextual references—allusions to Russian literature and the western European literary tradition—in the generation of meaning, a role that has only recently begun to be acknowledged.[3] The workings of intertextuality in **Rekviem** are a primary focus of this article, which offers a close reading of the first two texts of the *poema*[4]—**"Vmesto predisloviia,"** the short prose preface written in 1957, and the **"Posviashchenie,"** twenty-five lines of verse composed in March 1940. Although they have as yet received little critical attention,[5] these texts are of pivotal importance in **Rekviem**: Together, they image the poet and her addressees, defining their relations through references to Dante and Pushkin, among others. By incorporating these allusions into **Rekviem,** Akhmatova places herself in the tradition of Dante and Pushkin, claiming their moral authority as her own. The opening text, **"Vmesto predisloviia,"** tells the story of the genesis of **Rekviem,** concomitantly elucidating its very nature and purpose. The **"Posviashchenie,"** which constitutes a brilliant recasting of the genre of the "mass song," serves as the overture of **Rekviem,** prefiguring the tragic progression of the ten numbered texts and the restorative impulse of the **"Epilog."**

The laconic **"Vmesto predisloviia"** sets the stage. Its power in large part stems from the author's use of understatement; a strong tension exists between the text's matter-of-fact narrative tone, recalling reportage, and its subject matter. Understatement and restraint are, of course, distinctive features of Akhmatova's poetry, and, despite its markedly unpoetic tone, **"Vmesto predisloviia"** is in fact couched in terms of Akhmatova's poetic idiom; it employs a number of devices central to the early poetry, and likewise recasts certain prominent images and motifs. Here is the whole text:

В страшные годы ежовщины я провела семнадцать месяцев в тюремных очередях в Ленинграде. Как-то раз кто-то «опознал» меня. Тогда стоящая за мной женщина с голубыми губами, которая, конечно, никогда не слыхала моего имени, очнулась от свойственного нам всем оцепенения и спросила меня на ухо (там все говорили шепотом):

—А это вы можете описать?

И я сказала:

—Могу.

Тогда что-то вроде улыбки скользнуло по тому, что некогда было ее лицом.[6]

This first-person narrative begins by identifying the historical context, seventeen months during the "terrible years of the Ezhovshchina."[7] Declaring her presence in Leningrad's prison lines during that period, the author goes on to relate a specific incident that occurred. An estranged act of recognition initiates the episode: "Kak-to raz kto-to 'opoznal' menia." The neutral verb *uznal* is replaced here by the specialized *opoznal,* which literally means "identified," as in the judicial expression "opoznat' prestupnika," suggesting the narrator's complicity in the crime of being closely related to an "enemy of the nation" inside the prison—a crime often sufficient during those years to result in incarceration. The verb also figures in the forensic expression "opoznat' trup," and connotations of lifelessness predominate in **"Vmesto predisloviia."** The woman behind the speaker is distinguished by her "golubye guby" (replacing the customary alliteration "golubye glaza"), an emblem of lifelessness.[8] In the phrase "svoistvennoe nam vsem otsepenenie," this deathlike condition is defined as the common bond uniting all those present, for *otsepenenie* conjures up paralysis, insensibility, and even rigor mortis.

The theme of lifelessness finds its ultimate development in the telling evocation of a gesture in the final sentence: "Togda chto-to vrode ulybki skol'znulo po tomu, chto nekogda bylo ee litsom." The foregrounding of this gesture recalls the importance of gestures in Akhmatova's early poetry, their crucial role in conveying emotion.[9] Movements of the mouth and lips are particularly prominent in the early lyrics. Smiles, for instance, serve to express a whole range of emotions—from happiness and pleasure, to mere civility, to contempt, to intense pain and anguish. As Boris Eikhenbaum observed, movements of the lips are not just described but are accentuated in the sound orchestration of the poetry.[10] This reflects the special valuation of the lips in the early lyrics: Besides conveying emotion, they figure as bearers of eros (for example, "I ulybaesh'sia, o ne odnu pchelu / Rumianaia ulybka soblaznila" [1:207]; compare the prominent motif of the "potselui"); moreover, they are both integral to speech and instrumental in the creative process (compare their prominence in "V to vremia ia gostila na zemle").[11] In **"Vmesto predis-loviia,"** lips are first mentioned in passing in the phrase "zhenshchina s golubymi gubami." The early lyrics paint lips in shades of red and pink, connoting vitality and sensuality (compare "Rumianaia ulybka" [1:207]; "Eti vishnevye videt' usta" [1:178]; "Moi rot trevozhno zaalel" [1:81]), or else in pale hues, to express tension or anxiety. The unprecedented appearance of the epithet *golubye* in **"Vmesto predisloviia"** measures the change from the world of the early poetry to the lifeless world of **Rekviem.** The modifier suggests numbness from a lack of air or from the cold, precluding sensation and hindering movement. Devoid of eros, these lips are impaired in their ability to convey emotion, and speech itself is threatened.

The final sentence of **"Vmesto predisloviia"** portrays a movement made by these selfsame lips: "I togda chto-to vrode ulybki skol'znulo po tomu, chto nekogda bylo ee litsom." Estrangement operates on a number of levels here to undermine the meaningfulness of this gesture. The indefinite locution "chto-to vrode ulybki" leaves in question the actual identity of the gesture by telling what it resembles but not naming it directly. The locus of this quasi-smile is described in similarly indefinite terms; it is named by what it was formerly (*nekogda*) but is no longer—the woman's face. There is a play here on the idiom "net na nei litsa," a figurative expression used to describe momentary yet drastic changes in a person's face effected by an intense emotional or physical shock. Literally the phrase means "there is no face on her," and it is precisely this grotesque notion which is conveyed in **"Vmesto predisloviia"** through the use of the past tense: The state of "facelessness" dominates the present and shows no signs of passing.[12] The notion of facelessness has ominous implications, for the face has long been valued as the incarnation of spirituality, as in Cicero's aphorism "imago animi vul-tus est." The Russian Orthodox church teaches that the face embodies the highest spiritual qualities and values, reflecting the divine in human beings;[13] accordingly, facelessness would betoken the loss of the spirit or soul and would represent yet another sign of lifelessness. By metonymy, the word *litso* also means individual or person (compare the latter's grammatical usage); from this perspective, loss of the *litso* would symbolize a loss of individuality, of personal identity. All those standing in line are indeed shown to be depersonalized, from the blue-lipped woman to the narrator herself, for the verb "opoznat'" in the text's second sentence "identifies" the narrator's former personal identity, which no longer applies in the present context.[14] All this reveals the absolute devastation of the lyric realm, the domain of the *lichnoe*—the personal and the individual. Yet, there is a faint hope in the fleeting glimpse of something resembling a smile on that "no-longer-face;" a hint, however disfigured, of a solace that is possible if their shared suffering is not ceded to oblivion—faceless

and nameless horror—but described and thus remembered as a testimonial to endurance and love.

What elicits the quasi-smile is a dialogue,[15] a dialogue that tells the story of the genesis of **Rekviem.** By narrating the origins of **Rekviem, "Vmesto predisloviia"** explains the very nature and purpose of the *poema.*[16] As has been already noted, the faculty of speech is imperiled in this setting, and the dialogue reflects this peril in two ways: First, for fear of reprisal, it is conducted in whispers ("tam vse govorili shepotom"), and, second, it is maximally abbreviated, consisting of just six words. Brief as it is and softly as it is uttered, the dialogue does nevertheless occur, marking a break with the prevailing state of lifelessness. Symbolically, the dialogue represents the relationship between the author and her people, for its participants are the poet and a random, anonymous woman of the people. One crucial fact about the nameless woman's relation to the poet is supplied: "[ona], konechno, nikogda ne slykhala moego imeni."[17] This statement clearly reflects the poet's peripheral place in society during the 1930s: Her work had been barred from publication since the mid-1920s, her readership for the most part no longer existed, and her life as a poet was generally believed to be over, another level of meaning inherent in the verb *opoznat'.*

An ironic reversal of the Stalinist *sotsial'nyi zakaz,* the woman's question—"A eto vy mozhete opisat'?"—challenges the poet to render in words the nightmarish reality of the Ezhovshchina. The challenge is a daunting one. Those standing in line resemble the dead, and the task of describing the scene recalls Dante's task in the *Inferno,* with one crucial difference: Dante visited the Underworld as a living man, but in **"Vmesto predisloviia"** the poet inhabits the deathly realm and shares the lifeless state of the others. Despite her condition, however, the poet self-confidently declares her ability to carry out the task: "'Mogu.'" This bold assertion of her verbal powers contrasts forcefully with the enervation and lifelessness that dominate the scene, foreshadowing the poet's ultimate triumph over these conditions through the writing of **Rekviem.**

Dante's importance as a model for Akhmatova in **Rekviem** finds confirmation in her lyric entitled **"Muza"**; its final lines record an exchange between the poet and her Muse: "Ei govoriu: 'Ty l' Dantu diktovala / Stranitsy Ada?' Otvechaet: 'Ia'" (1:230). The resemblance of this exchange to that recorded in **"Vmesto predisloviia"** is striking: Both consist of a brief question and a one-word affirmative response. Akhmatova is underscoring here that her Muse and the Muse of Dante's *Inferno* are identical, establishing a parallel, as Milivoe Iovanovich has noted, between the object of Dante's description and what Akhmatova is to depict.[18] While **Rekviem**'s indebtedness to the *Inferno* merits separate treatment, two key connections between them are germane to the present discussion. First, the condition of the women as portrayed in **"Vmesto predisloviia"** and elsewhere in the *poema* recalls Dante's experiences in the frozen ninth circle of hell. Their *otsepenenie,* for example, echoes the evocation in Canto 33 of Dante's numbness: "sì come d'un callo, / per la freddura ciascun sentimento / cessato avesse del mio viso stallo."[19] In Canto 34, Dante describes his terror upon seeing Satan: "Io non mori' e non rimasi vivo; / pensa oggimai per te, / s'hai fior d'ingegno, / qual io divenni, d'uno e d'altro privo."[20] Dante's fear deprives him of life yet does not kill him, a state paralleled by the women's lifelessness in **"Vmesto predisloviia."** The **"Posviashchenie"** goes on to describe the women as "mertvykh bezdykhannei" (1:362), a phrase that separates the women from both the living and the dead, implying that their condition is worse than that of the dead.[21] The **"Posviashchenie"** also qualifies the poet's two years in Leningrad's prison lines as *osatanelye,* from the root *satana,* implying that the city was under Satan's dominion during that period; the epithet could be translated as "hellish," for it bears connotations of madness, evil, and frenzy. These similarities to Dante's *Inferno* point back to the title of Akhmatova's *poema* and illuminate her intention in writing it: to bring *requiem aeternam* to the victims of the Ezhovshchina. The second crucial link between *Rekviem* and the *Inferno* involves another key aim of the poet. As Dante reveals in Canto 29, his mission is to preserve a memory of the dead "nel primo mundo," among the living.[22] As revealed in the **"Epilog,"** Akhmatova's aim in *Rekviem* is similar—to preserve for posterity the memory of those who suffered in the Ezhovshchina.

The poet's declaration of her ability "to describe this" immediately raises questions as to the form such a description could take. With what kind of voice could Akhmatova, a lyric poet par excellence, convey the devastation of the lyric domain? What kind of poetry could adequately express the depersonalized, lifeless state of those evoked in **"Vmesto predisloviia"**? These questions are addressed in the **"Posviashchenie,"** given below in full (1:362):

> Перед этим горем гнутся горы,
> Не течет великая река,
> Но крепки тюремные затворы,
> А за ними «каторжные норы»
> И смертельная тоска.   5
> Для кого-то веет ветер свежий,
> Для кого-то нежится закат—
> Мы не знаем, мы повсюду те же,
> Слышим лишь ключей постылый скрежет
> Да шаги тяжелые солдат.   10
> Подымались как к обедне ранней,

> По столице одичалой шли,
> Там встречались, мертвых бездыханней,
> Солнце ниже и Нева туманней,
> А надежда все поет вдали.   15
> Приговор . . . И сразу слезы хлынут,
> Ото всех уже отделена,
> Словно с болью жизнь из сердца вынут,
> Словно грубо навзничь опрокинут,
> Но идет . . . Шатается . . . Одна . . .   20
> Где теперь невольные подруги
> Двух моих осатанелых лет?
> Что им чудится в сибирской вьюге,
> Что мерещится им в лунном круге?
> Им я шлю прощальный свой привет.   25

The **"Posviashchenie"** begins impersonally, with a powerful double image of the misfortune that has struck—"eto gore"—as reflected in the natural world: The mountains' bending down [l. 1] vividly depicts catastrophe (in the sense of an unexpected, violent change in the earth's surface); the great river's ceasing to flow [l. 2] suggests that life itself has been brought to a standstill, harking back to the theme of *otsepenenie* in **"Vmesto predisloviia."**[23] This use of natural imagery recalls the rendering of disaster in the Russian epic tradition, specifically in *Slovo o polku Igoreve* and the *Zadonshchina,* which sing of national misfortune through the anthropomorphized image of trees bowing down to the earth in sorrow. Akhmatova's choice of mountains, which is obviously motivated by the phonological similarity between *góre* and *góry,* accentuates the immense scale of the misfortune.[24]

The catastrophe proper is revealed in the evocation of the prison realm [ll. 3-5]. The quotation "'katorzhnye nory'" (l. 4)—puts the scene into perspective. The source is Pushkin's 1827 lyric "Vo glubine sibirskikh rud," an epistle to the Decembrists sentenced to hard labor in Siberia, exhorting them to endure in the first stanza and predicting relief in the final three quatrains:

> Несчастью верная сестра,
> Надежда в мрачном подземелье
> Разбудит бодрость и веселье,
> Придет желанная пора:

> Любовь и дружество до вас
> Дойдут сквозь мрачные затворы,
> Как в ваши каторжные норы
> Доходит мой свободный глас.

> Оковы тяжкие падут,
> Темницы рухнут—и свобода
> Вас примет радостно у входа,
> И братья меч вам отдадут.[25]

Far from simply reiterating Pushkin's words, Akhmatova foregrounds the fact of quotation by supplying his collocation with quotation marks. In addition, she preserves Pushkin's rhyme "zatvory"/"nory," establishing "Vo glubine sibirskikh rud . . ." as one of the primary subtexts of the **"Posviashchenie."**

While both texts conjure up scenes of captivity, the striking differences between them effectively contrast Stalin's rule with that of Nicholas I a century before. Pushkin's text is dominated by the antithesis between the inner realm of captivity—bounded by the "mrachnye zatvory"—and the outer domain of freedom and traces freedom's incursion into the prison in the form of the poet's "svobodnyi glas." It concludes by envisaging freedom's complete triumph in the prison's destruction and the liberation of those incarcerated. The **"Posviashchenie"** borrows Pushkin's *zatvory* to demarcate its prison realm, but while "Vo glubine" underscores the bolts' penetrability, Akhmatova emphasizes their strength ("No *krepki* tiuremnye zatvory").[26] By naming what is situated behind those bolts with Pushkin's phrase "katorzhnye nory," she alludes to the *katorga* in prison camps awaiting those within the Leningrad prison. While the prison's gloom in "Vo glubine" is alleviated by the presence of hope, which inspires courage and good cheer, the prison realm in the **"Posviashchenie"** is dominated by "smertel'naia toska" (l. 5), suggesting that what the prisoners face is death, not liberation, as Pushkin predicts for his addressees.[27]

The grim import of line 5—"I smertel'naia toska"—is accentuated in the way it violates the metrical scheme of the **"Posviashchenie"**: the line is truncated, containing only four feet.[28] This violation, the only one of its kind in the **"Posviashchenie,"** is motivated in another way as well, for Akhmatova is recalling a line from the following quatrain of Pushkin's 1826 "Zimniaia doroga":

> Что-то слышится родное
> В долгих песнях ямщика:
> То разгулье удалое,
> То сердечная тоска.[29]

Akhmatova's echoing of the last line in "I smertel'naia toska" once again contrasts Pushkin's age with her own; Pushkin's "dull" winter road has been transformed a century later into the road to prison, the road to Siberia. Under Stalin, not only is Russian life devoid of "razgul'e" and full of misery, it is lived in extremis, as underscored in the replacement of the epithet *serdechnaia* by *smertel'naia*. This change eloquently testifies to the devastation of the lyric domain.[30]

Another key difference between the **"Posviashchenie"** and "Vo glubine sibirskikh rud" involves the portrayal of the world outside the prison: while "Vo glubine" represents it as the realm of freedom, in the **"Posviashchenie"** life outside the prison mirrors that within. In the first stanza, the deep sorrow of the outer world (ll.

1-2) reflects the "smertel'naia toska" within the prison. This mirroring becomes more explicit in the second stanza, where the adverb *povsiudu* (l. 8) in the phrase "my povsiudu te zhe" blurs the distinction between those outside and inside. That all share the captive state is also suggested in what is heard: "Slyshim lish' kliuchei postylyi skrezhet / Da shagi tiazhelye soldat." The mirroring of the prison in the outside world is likewise supported by the image of Leningrad evoked in the **"Posviashchenie."** The third stanza's "Po stolitse odichaloi shli" (l. 12), as Sharon Leiter has observed, harks back to the beginning of Akhmatova's 1923 lyric **"Sograzhdanam,"** which like the **"Posviashchenie"** is spoken in the first-person plural:

> И мы забыли навсегда,
> Заключены в столице дикой,
> Озера, степи, города
> И зори родины далекой.

$$(1:213)^{31}$$

The city is pictured here as a place of confinement; later in the same text it is pointedly associated with the absence of freedom. In **Rekviem,** the prison-like nature of the former capital is explicitly expressed in the grotesque portrayal of the city in the **"Vstuplenie"** (1:362-363):

> И ненужным привеском болтался
> Возле тюрем своих Ленинград.
> И когда, обезумев от муки,
> Шли уже осужденных полки. . . .

Here, in what constitutes a brilliant image of the prison lines, the city proper has been reduced to a useless appendage to its prisons; dominated by those prisons and the masses of condemned innocents, the scene reeks of butchery, through the use of the word *privesok*.[32]

One other important difference between Pushkin's epistle and Akhmatova's **"Posviashchenie"** concerns the status of the poet. "Vo glubine" emphasizes the poet's freedom when it pictures his "free voice" reaching the prisoners and inspiring them with courage. In the **"Posviashchenie,"** by contrast, the "free voice" of the poet is conspicuous by its absence. The poet is just one of the many languishing in captivity, a point made directly in the text's final stanza, when the women who stood in line together are in retrospect called "nevol'nye podrugi," companions through circumstances beyond their control, those circumstances themselves—*nevolia*—named by the epithet *nevol'nye*. The first-person plural *my,* which dominates lines 8-10, belongs to these women, and the poet is just one of their number.[33]

Pushkin is not the only Russian poet to whom Akhmatova alludes. Toward the beginning of the text there is an enigmatic reference to some person or persons evidently untouched by suffering: "Dlia kogo-to veet veter svezhii, / Dlia kogo-to nezhitsia zakat" (ll. 6-7). Set apart by their markedly unpoetic anaphora, flat diction, and banal imagery,[34] these lines conjure up a state of well-being that clashes with the prevailing misery and grief.[35] The solution to this riddle lies in a most unlikely subtext. "Dlia kogo-to veet veter svezhii" pointedly recalls "Nad stranoi vesennii veter veet, / S kazhdym dnem vse radostnee zhit'"—lines penned by Vasilii Lebedev-Kumach. The text in question is his "Pesnia o rodine" (1935),[36] a paean to Soviet life under Stalin. It epitomizes the aggressively nationalistic, radiantly optimistic spirit of Stalinism in the later 1930s, when it enjoyed the status of a "sort of unofficial national anthem."[37] An exemplar of the propagandistic genre of the "mass song," "Pesnia o rodine" is mainly spoken in the first-person plural and purports to represent the voice of the people. Employing the same meter—trochaic pentameter—as Lebedev-Kumach, Akhmatova weaves into her **"Posviashchenie"** allusions to his Stalinist hymn only to subvert its claim to speak for the people: By replacing Lebedev-Kumach's *my* with the indefinite pronoun *kto-to* in ll. 6-7, she indicates that his song speaks only for some unspecified individuals and not for the people as a whole. When the first-person plural sounds forth emphatically in l. 8 of the **"Posviashchenie"** ("My ne znaem, my povsiudu te zhe"), immediately following the allusion to "Pesnia o rodine," it represents the authentic voice of the Russian people, singing the truth about the motherland under Stalin's rule.[38]

Akhmatova's intention for *Rekviem* to be, at least in part, a recasting of the "mass song" is confirmed in the second part of the **"Epilog,"** when the theme of the mass song resurfaces in the following lines: "I esli zazhmut moi izmuchennyi rot, / Kotorym krichit stomil'onnyi narod" (1:369). Akhmatova is referring here to a different poet of the masses, Vladimir Maiakovskii, and specifically to the fourth line of his blatantly propagandistic *massovaia poema 150,000,000* (1919-1920): "150 000 000 govoriat gubami moimi."[39] In Akhmatova's treatment, the mass song becomes a vehicle for protest, not for propaganda. The dirgelike **"Posviashchenie"** bitterly parodies Lebedev Kumach's joyful mass song, giving the lie to it, contradicting point by point the picture of Russian life it draws. "Pesnia o rodine" extols, for instance, the plenitude of Russian life in a trite metaphor: "Vsiudu zhizn' i vol'no i shiroko, / Tochno Volga polnaia, techet."[40] The **"Posviashchenie"** clearly harks back to and negates that metaphor in the line "Ne techet velikaia reka" (l. 2). Lebedev-Kumach time and again praises the freedom enjoyed in his homeland, most saliently in the last two lines of the song's famous refrain:

Широка страна моя родная,
Много в ней лесов, полей и рек.

Я другой такой страны не знаю,
Где так вольно дышит человек![41]

Akhmatova, by contrast, as has already been amply demonstrated, portrays the Russian people in a state of captivity. For the women of the **"Posviashchenie,"** the question of breathing freely does not even arise, for they are described as "mertvykh bezdykhannei."[42] Two other lines from "Pesnia o rodine" are pertinent to the representation of the women in the **"Posviashchenie,"** namely, the final stanza's concluding lines: "Kak nevestu, rodinu my liubim, / Berezhem, kak laskovuiu mat'."[43] This hackneyed comparison of the motherland to bride and mother points toward the symbolic dimension of the women's representation in the **"Posviashchenie"**: In their captivity and suffering, they stand for the nation as a whole, and their plight represents a travesty of the lofty pledge of love and protection sounded in "Pesnia o rodine."

Nowhere is this more evident than in the critical fourth stanza, the climax of the **"Posviashchenie."** Until this point in the text, in keeping with the mass song model, the women have been portrayed en masse, emphasizing their lack of individuality—a theme first sounded in **"Vmesto predisloviia"** and expressed in the **"Posviashchenie"** both explicitly ("my povsiudu te zhe") and indirectly (through the use of impersonal verbal forms in the third stanza's account of the women's common actions: "Podymalis' . . . / . . . shli, / Tam vstrechalis'" [ll. 11-13]). In the fourth stanza, however, the focus unexpectedly shifts from the mass of women to just one of their number:

Приговор . . . И сразу слезы хлынут,
Ото всех уже отделена,
Словно с болью жизнь из сердца вынут,
Словно грубо навзничь опрокинут,
Но идет . . . Шатается . . . Одна . . .

Individuality is restored here to one woman through a brutal *prigovor* isolating her from the others. The *prigovor* clearly refers to the sentencing of her loved one within the prison, yet it is portrayed solely through its violent effect on the woman herself,[44] an effect that is likened both to a painful deathblow (l. 18) and to her being thrown on her back (l. 19), an oblique yet unmistakeable reference to rape. On the symbolic level of Lebedev-Kumach's "bride" and "affectionate mother," Akhmatova is evoking here the murder and rape of the motherland.

The **"Posviashchenie"** hinges on the fourth stanza's shift in focus from the many to the individual: The text traces an arc from a national catastrophe of epic proportions, as sketched in the first stanza, to the personal catastrophe of one woman, as evoked in the fourth stanza. This arc is inscribed in the text through a number of parallels between the two stanzas. Phonetically, the beginning of the first line—"*Pered* etim *gor*em"—is echoed in the first word of the fourth stanza, "*Prigovor.*" The dominant theme of the first stanza—the *gore* that has struck—is clearly evidenced in the woman's reaction to the sentence, the flood of tears she sheds; in addition, likening the sentence's effect to a deathblow quite pointedly recalls the idiom *ubita gorem.* Finally, the bowing down of the mountains (l. 1) is mirrored in the image of the woman's being cast down (l. 19). Through this series of correspondences, the national catastrophe is embodied in the fate of one woman.[45] The movement traced in the **"Posviashchenie"** from captivity to a sentencing cast as a figurative execution foreshadows the progression from arrest to execution in *Rekviem*'s central sequence of ten poems.[46]

The fifth and final stanza leaves behind the mass song model, for in it there emerges a new, truly lyric voice that speaks in the first-person singular of the present tense:

> Где теперь невольные подруги
>
> Двух моих осатанелых лет?
>
> Что им чудится в сибирской вьюге,
>
> Что мерещится им в лунном круге?
>
> Им я шлю прощальный свой привет. 25

These lines reverse the theme of the suppression of the poet's voice, introduced through the multiple allusions to "Vo glubine sibirskikh rud," for what sounds forth is the voice of the poet, speaking in a present tense that for the first time in the **"Posviashchenie"** refers to the time of the text's writing (emphasized in l. 21's "teper'"), not to the time of the narrated events. Having recollected the Ezhovshchina in a voice speaking for her people, the poet now speaks for herself, turning her attention to the present circumstances of the women who stood in the prison lines with her.

As anticipated by the fourth stanza's portrayal of one woman's separation from the group, the poet has been separated from the other women. She speaks of them through a network of references to a different poem by Pushkin, one that brings out the profoundly lyric tenor of the concluding lines of the **"Posviashchenie."** The text in question is the 1826 "Niane," written shortly after the end of Pushkin's exile in Mikhailovskoe:

> Подруга дней моих суровых,
> Голубка дряхлая моя!
> Одна в глуши лесов сосновых
> Давно, давно ты ждешь меня.
> Ты под окном своей светлицы
> Горюешь, будто на часах,
> И медлят поминутно спицы
> В твоих наморщенных руках.
> Глядишь в забытые вороты
> На черный отдаленный путь:
> Тоска, предчувствия, заботы
> Теснят твою всечасно грудь.
> То чудится тебе . . .[47]

These lines invoke Arina Rodionovna, the poet's faithful companion in exile, about whom he wrote from Mikhailovskoe in 1824, "vecherom slushaiu skazki moei niani, originala niani Tat'iany; . . . ona edinstvennaia moia podruga—i s neiu tol'ko mne ne skuchno."[48] Akhmatova is recalling Pushkin's address to Arina Rodionovna—"Podruga dnei moikh surovykh"—when she calls the women who stood with her outside the prison "podrugi / Dvukh moikh osatanelykh let." She actually spent seventeen months in the lines, as the first sentence of **"Vmesto predisloviia"** and the beginning of the fifth numbered text of *Rekviem* ("Semnadtsat' mesiatsev krichu, / Zovu tebia domoi" [1:364]) indicate;[49] two years was the term of Pushkin's days in exile at Mikhailovskoe.

Akhmatova is drawing a parallel between Pushkin's exile and her own plight during the Ezhovshchina, while highlighting the radical differences between their experiences through the two telling epithets in lines 21-22. First, her characterization of those years as *osatanelye* contrasts with Pushkin's assessment of his days of exile as *surovye.* Second, while Pushkin spent his exile in the company of his doting nurse, Akhmatova's companions were bound to her not by love but by force of circumstance ("nevol'nye podrugi," l. 21).[50] The stance of the poet, however, is identical in "Niane" and the **"Posviashchenie"**: Just as Pushkin looks back on the difficult period of his exile and evokes his faithful nanny alone at Mikhailovskoe, so Akhmatova looks back on the Ezhovshchina and recalls those who stood in the prison lines with her. Pushkin describes Arina Rodionovna and her activities in detail, but Akhmatova is uncertain of the fate of her former companions, and she builds this uncertainty into the text by posing three questions about them. While the first question echoes Pushkin's address to Arina Rodionovna, the second and third are inspired by the phrase on which his text breaks off—"To chuditsia tebe"; they both articulate the question implicit in the truncation of "Niane" by asking what "appears" to the women (Pushkin's verb *chudit'sia* and the synonymous *mereshchit'sia* are used). The query "Chto im chuditsia v sibirskoi v'iuge" indicates that at least some of them are in Siberia, whether in prison camp or in exile.[51]

The repetition of the pronoun *im* in each of the last three lines of the **"Posviashchenie"** sounds the theme of dedication, harking back to the title of the text. Literary dedications are typically addressed to acquaintances or close personal friends of the author as a sign of respect or affection. Pushkin, for example, dedicated *Kavkazskii plennik* to his good friend N. N. Raevskii, *Poltava* to an unnamed but beloved woman, and *Evgenii Onegin* to his friend and publisher P. A. Pletnev. The **"Posviashchenie"** of *Rekviem,* by contrast, is addressed to a large group of nameless women; yet it similarly expresses the author's feelings toward them, suggesting that they provided the impetus for the writing of the *poema*.[52] The story of the work's genesis given in **"Vmesto predisloviia"** confirms this,[53] as does the "Niane" subtext in the **"Posviashchenie."** "Niane" provides at least a partial answer to the questions posed by Akhmatova about the women's fate. Pushkin writes to Arina Rodionovna, "Davno, davno ty zhdesh' menia." On one level, this indicates that the women from the prison lines are alone, still separated from their loved ones. On another level, however, it implies that they are waiting for the poet, for Akhmatova, to describe their shared experience.[54] Still troubled ("Toska, predchuvstviia, zaboty / Tesniat tvoiu vsechasno grud'"), they await the peace that **Rekviem** will bring.

Through the allusions to Pushkin's "Niane," Akhmatova likens the women to Arina Rodionovna, suggesting their importance as a source not only of comfort but of inspiration as well. Pushkin drew many memorable verse portraits of Arina Rodionovna, but what distinguishes "Niane" among them is its heightened lyricism: The poet's strong affection for her is reflected in the text's tender forms of address, as well as in the sharp detail with which her image is evoked. When Akhmatova couches her questions about the women in Pushkin's words, she demonstrates her profound concern and solicitude for them, elevating them to the status of intimate friends. In so doing, she restores to them their dignity as human beings, symbolically redressing the wrongs they suffered during the Ezhovshchina.

This restorative impulse is the mainspring of **Rekviem.** Prefigured in **"Vmesto predisloviia,"** it resurfaces at the end of the *poema* to dominate the **"Epilog,"** where it is manifested in the poet's stance as intercessor for her "nevol'nye podrugi," in her memorialization of their shared suffering, as well as in the ritual of remembrance that she creates to ensure the preservation of their memory. Evident everywhere in the **"Epilog,"** the healing impulse is emblematized in the image of the text as a *pokrov* for the poet's former companions: "Dlia nikh sotkala ia shirokii pokrov / Iz bednykh, u nikh zhe podslushannykh slov" (1:369). The *pokrov,* woven from the *bednye slova* of these ordinary women,[55] is a burial shroud that preserves and sanctifies; it is the shroud that the Virgin Mary spreads "nad skorbiami velikimi,"[56] providing comfort and protection; it is, finally, a shroud woven of words, bringing deliverance from oblivion and silence.

Notes

This article is part of a broader study of the framing texts of *Rekviem,* to be published as the second chapter of my forthcoming book *In a Shattered Mirror: The Poetics of Akhmatova's Later Work* (Stanford University Press).

1. Compare Sam Driver's description of *Rekviem* as "an amazingly powerful statement which requires no elaboration or 'explanation'" (*Anna Akhmatova* [New York: Twayne, 1972], 125).

Unlike *Poema bez geroia, Rekviem* has received relatively little critical attention. The most comprehensive study of it to date is Efim Etkind's "Die Unsterblichkeit des Gedächtnisses: Anna Achmatovas Poem 'Requiem'," *Die Welt der Slaven* 29,2 (1984): 360-394. Kees Verheul discusses *Rekviem* in his "Public Themes in the Poetry of Anna Achmatova," *Russian Literature* 1 (1971): 73-112, especially 79-82, 89-90, 93, 98-100, 105-112. Among others who have written on it are Sam Driver, *Anna Akhmatova,* 125-132; Sharon Leiter, *Akhmatova's Petersburg* (Philadelphia: University of Pennsylvania Press, 1983), 90-97, and Amanda Haight, *Anna Akhmatova: A Poetic Pilgrimage* (New York: Oxford University Press, 1976), 99-108. Two specialized studies of *Rekviem* also deserve mention: Milivoe Iovanovich treats the problem of intertextual references in his valuable "K razboru 'chuzhikh golosov' v *Rekvieme* Akhmatovoi," *Russian Literature* 15 (1984): 169-182, while T. Voogd-Stojanova provides an extensive syntacticometrical analysis in "Tsezura i slovorazdely v poeme A. Akhmatovoi *Rekviem,*" in *Dutch Contributions to the Seventh International Congress of Slavists,* ed. André Van Holk (The Hague: Mouton, 1973), 317-333.

For decades unpublished in the Soviet Union, *Rekviem* was long off-limits to Soviet specialists and could be referred to only in passing or obliquely. Its recent publication in *Oktiabr',* No. 3 (1987), and *Neva,* no. 6 (1987), however, may pave the way for the appearance of serious critical studies of it in the Soviet Union.

2. Compare Milivoe Iovanovich's dating of the beginning of Akhmatova's later period: "pozdniaia Akhmatova nachinaetsia imenno s *Rekviema*" ("K razboru 'chuzhikh golosov'," 171).

Here is Akhmatova's own characterization of her later poetry: "I tak pozdniaia A[khmatova] vykhodit iz zhanra 'liubovnogo dnevnika' . . . i perekhodit na razdum'ia o roli i sud'be poeta, o remesle, na legko nabrosannye shirokie polotna. Poiavliaetsia ostroe oshchushchenie istorii" (quoted in V. M. Zhirmunskii, *Tvorchestvo Anny Akhmatovoi* [Leningrad, 1976], 26). *Rekviem* reflects the new thematic concerns—in particular, the preoccupation with history and with the poet's role in society—and the turn to larger forms, which in Akhmatova's view typify the later poetry. For a fuller discussion of the poetics of her later work, see the first chapter of my "Axmatova's Later Lyrics: The Poetics of Mediation" (Ph.D. diss., Yale University, 1983), 1-39.

Verheul sees *Rekviem* as transitional between Akhmatova's early and later styles ("Public Themes," 112). While the ten numbered texts of the *poema* do manifest certain features of the early style, as Verheul notes, together they trace a distinct narrative progression from arrest to execution, which sharply distinguishes them from the early work.

3. Milivoe Iovanovich's "K razboru 'chuzhikh golosov'" is the only article specifically devoted to the problem of intertextuality in *Rekviem*. Particularly useful are Iovanovich's remarks on Akhmatova's incorporation of reminiscences—mainly for parodic ends—from Nekrasov's "Russkie zhenshchiny," Lermontov's "Kazach'ia kolybel'naia pesnia," and Blok's *Na pole Kuliko-vom* (170-171). Kees Verheul explores some of the biblical and liturgical subtexts in *Rekviem* ("Public Themes," 111-112), and Sharon Leiter discusses some examples of a different kind of intertextual references in *Rekviem*—Akhmatova's incorporation of self-reminiscences—allusions to her own poetry (*Akhmatova's Petersburg*, 90-97).

4. Akhmatova herself classified *Rekviem* as a *poema*. The list of titles she intended to publish in the collection *Beg vremeni* concludes with a section called "Poemy," to consist of *Putem vseia zemli*, *Rekviem*, and *Poema bez geroia*. See *Pamiati Anny Akhmatovoi* (Paris: YMCA, 1974), 29-30.

For a discussion of *Rekviem*'s status as a *poema*, see Etkind, "Die Unsterblichkeit des Gedächtnisses," 362-365. Compare Verheul's remarks on the same issue ("Public Themes," 107-108).

5. "Vmesto predisloviia" has been widely quoted but has received virtually no commentary. Neither Verheul nor Etkind mentions it in the articles cited above. Among those who quote it without commentary are Sharon Leiter (*Akhmatova's Petersburg*, 91-92) and Amanda Height (*Anna Akhmatova*, 99). Sam Driver quotes it and does comment on it, but only by describing the historical context (*Anna Akhmatova*, 125-127).

The most detailed comments on the "Posviashchenie" have been provided by Etkind, "Die Unsterblichkeit des Gedächtnisses," 387-388. Compare Verheul, "Public Themes," 80-81.

6. Anna Akhmatova, *Sochineniia*, ed. G. P. Struve and B. A. Filippov, 2nd ed. ([Munich]: Interlanguage Literary Associates, 1967) 1:361. Henceforth, references to this edition, as well as to volumes 2 (1968) and 3 (ed. G. P. Struve, N. A. Struve, and B. A. Filippov [Paris: YMCA, 1983]), will be given in parentheses in the body of the text.

7. The epithet *strashnye*, the sole affective epithet in the text, does not belie the narrative's prosaic tone, since "strashnye gody Ezhovshchiny" is, generally speaking, a fixed expression.

8. Lidiia Chukovskaia has asserted that the image of the "woman with blue lips" originated in her novel *Sof'ia Petrovna*, which she read to Akhmatova in February 1940. See Chukovskaia, *Zapiski ob Anne Akhmatovoi* (Paris: YMCA, 1980) 2:305.

Milivoe Iovanovich provides an unwitting proof of the strength of the customary formula when he quotes from "Vmesto predisloviia" and twice erroneously replaces Akhmatova's "gubami" with "glazami" ("K razboru 'chuzhikh golosov'," 177n7).

9. In Boris Eikhenbaum's formulation, "emotsiia peredaetsia opisaniem zhesta ili dvizheniia, t.e., imenno tak, kak eto delaetsia v novellakh i romanakh." Boris Eikhenbaum, *Anna Akhmatova: Opyt analiza* (Petrograd, 1923; Paris: Izdatel'stvo Lev, 1980), 127. Eikhenbaum is pointing to what Osip Mandel'shtam had described in his 1922 "Pis'mo o russkoi poezii" as Akhmatova's indebtedness to the nineteenth century Russian psychological novel. See Osip Mandel'shtam, *Sobranie sochinenii v trekh tomakh* (New York: Inter-Language Literary Associates, 1969), 3:34.

10. Eikhenbaum writes, "Poeticheskaia rech' Akhmatovoi kak by sosredotochena na perednem artikuliatsionnom plane i okrashena mimicheskim dvizheniem gub ('molitva gub moikh nadmennykh,' 'dvizhenie chut' vidnoe gub')" (*Anna Akhmatova*, 87).

11. The persona describes the name given her at baptism, Anna, as "Sladchaishee dlia gub liudskikh" and remarks on the strangeness of the lips of the "inostranka," a Muse figure who visits her (1:191).

12. The first volume of Chukovskaia's *Zapiski ob Anne Akhmatovoi* devotes a number of passages to the faces of the women standing in line. In the entry dated 22 February 1939, Akhmatova is quoted as saying, "Ia ne mogu videt' etikh glaz. Vy zametili? Oni kak by otdel'no sushchestvuiut, otdel'no ot lits." See *Zapiski*, 1:18.

13. "The face of a human being represents the highest spiritual gifts: the forehead represents heavenly love; the eyes—understanding, intelligent contemplation; the ears—understanding and obedience; the nose—the grasping of the good; the cheeks—the grasping of spiritual truths; the mouth—thought and teaching; the lips—spiritual praise. . . ." See Vladimir Dal', *Tolkovyi slovar' zhivago velikorusskago iazyka*, 2nd ed., 4 vols. (St. Petersburg and Moscow: Vol'fe, 1881), 2:258.

14. This imagery resurfaces in the collective portrait of the faces of those who stood outside the prison

given in the first part of the "Epilog," which begins "Uznala ia, kak opadaiut litsa" (1:368) and proceeds to trace, in a technique reminiscent of time-lapse photography, the impact of the Terror on the fragile human visage.

15. Akhmatova's early lyrics abound in reported speech, another mark of their indebtedness to the novelistic tradition. V. V. Vinogradov devotes a chapter of his study of the early Akhmatova to this feature of her work; see "Grimasy dialoga" in his *O poezii Anny Akhmatovoi (Stilisticheskie nabroski)* (Leningrad, 1925), reprinted with a commentary by R. D. Timenchik and A. P. Chudakov in V. V. Vinogradov, *Poetika russkoi literatury* (Moscow: Nauka, 1976), 451-459. Timenchik and Chudakov's comments on "Grimasy dialoga" are directly relevant to *Rekviem*: "'adresaty' i 'personazhi' ee poezii privnosiat s soboi v tekst fragmenty i obraztsy razlichnykh stilisticheskikh sistem, 'sbornye tsitaty' iz literaturnykh i bytovykh 'stilei rechi.' Eto vvedevnie razlichnykh vidov 'chuzhogo slova' sluzhit glavnym sredstvom 'polifonizatsii' ee liriki, pridavaia ei v tselom dialogicheskii kharakter" (506). In "Vmesto predisloviia" and the "Posviashchenie," two different types of "chuzhoe slovo" are foregrounded through the use of direct quotation, signaling their prominent role in *Rekviem*—discourse from everyday life and literary discourse.

16. To indicate the origins of a phenomenon is to explain it. Compare Iu. M. Lotman on the category of beginnings: "Nachalo . . . ne tol'ko svidetel'stvo sushchestvovaniia, no i zamena (sic) bolee pozdnei kategorii prichinnosti. Ob''iasnit' iavlenie—znachit ukazat' na ego proiskhozhdenie" (*Struktura khudozhestvennogo teksta* [Moscow, 1970; Providence, R.I.: Brown University Press, 1971], 260).

17. In her entry for 10 November 1938, Chukovskaia records Akhmatova's account of an episode antithetical to this one: "'Zhenshchina v ocheredi, stoiavshaia pozadi menia, zaplakala, uslykhav moiu familiiu'" (*Zapiski,* 1:16). In "Vmesto predisloviia," Akhmatova chooses to portray the contrary—the nonrecognition of her name—as typical of the 1930s.

18. "K razboru 'chuzhikh golosov'," 176-177, n. 6. Iovanovich does not discuss the role of references to the *Inferno* itself in *Rekviem*.

While "Muza" bears the date 1924, it was in the later 1930s that Dantean themes and motifs became prominent in Akhmatova's work; compare the obviously related line—"I prosto prodiktovannye strochki" (1:251)—from the 1936 poem "Tvorchestvo"; her "Dante" ("On i posle smerti

ne vernulsia" [1:236]) dates from the same year. For an excellent introduction to the role of Dante in Akhmatova's life and works, see M. B. Meilakh and V. N. Toporov, "Akhmatova i Dante," *International Journal of Slavic Linguistics and Poetics* 15 (1972): 29-75. The authors do not comment directly on *Rekviem*.

19. In Singleton's translation, "as in a callus, all feeling, because of the cold, had departed from my face." Dante Alighieri, *Inferno,* trans. and with a commentary by Charles S. Singleton, 2nd ed. (Princeton, N.J.: Princeton University Press, 1977), 354-355, ll. 100-102.

20. In Singleton's translation, "I did not die and I did not remain alive: now think for yourself, if you have any wit, what I became, deprived alike of death and life!" (ibid., 362-363, ll. 25-27).

21. According to the beginning of *Rekviem*'s "Vstuplenie," true death brings peace: "Eto bylo, kogda ulybalsia / Tol'ko mertvyi, spokoistviiu rad" (1:363). Compare the suppressed tenth and eleventh stanzas from the "Reshka" segment of *Poema bez geroia,* which deal with the Ezhovshchina and share much of *Rekviem*'s imagery. In stanza 11, the condition of the poet and her female contemporaries is defined in a sentence that plays on the notion of the "potustoronnii mir": "'Po tu storonu ada—my!'" (3:116).

22. Dante, *Inferno,* 310-311, ll. 103-105.

23. Sam Driver has described well the first line's brilliant sound orchestration: "The close juxtaposition of gutturals suggests a throat constricted by grief. . . . The vowel sounds are carefully ordered in a progression from front to back. The line descends in intonation as in physical articulation" (*Anna Akhmatova,* 155-156, n 18).

24. Tsvetaeva exploits almost the same resemblance in her *Poema gory* (*góre / gorá*); compare the phrase in English poetry "mountains mourn." Akhmatova's *gnutsia gory* appears to hark back to and realize the apocalyptic prediction of the "glas vopiiushchego v pustyne" in Isaiah 40:3-4 that "vsiakaia gora i kholm da poniziatsia."

25. Aleksandr Pushkin, *Sobranie sochinenii v desiati tomakh* (Moscow, 1974-1978) 2:97. This edition will henceforth be referred to as *SS.*

26. Milivoe Iovanovich notes a somewhat similar line in a Russian translation of Euripides' *Iphigenia in Aulis,* where Clytemnestra says, "O, tam zapory krepki" ("K razboru 'chuzhikh golosov'," 173). The lack of a series of textual correspondences between the "Posviashchenie" and Euripides' tragedy in translation suggests that the parallel is coincidental.

27. The motif of hope is not entirely absent from the "Posviashchenie"; l. 15 locates it not within the prison, as in Pushkin's text, but in the distance: "A nadezhda vse poet vdali." What is portrayed in ll. 16-20 dashes even this distant hope.

   One of Akhmatova's remarks to Chukovskaia, recorded in the entry of 18 May 1939, helps elucidate this line's significance in the *poema*: "Vy znaete, chto takoe pytka nadezhdy? Posle otchaianiia nastupaet pokoi, a ot nadezhdy skhodiat s uma" (*Zapiski* 1:24). Compare the deployment of imagery relating to madness throughout *Rekviem.*

28. In her metrical analysis of the "Posviashchenie," T. Voogd-Stojanova notes this violation but comments only that the line is perceived as "contrastive in form" in relation to the rest ("Tsezura i slovorazdely," 318).

29. Pushkin, *SS* 2:92.

30. Voogd-Stojanova suggests that the "Posviashchenie" represents a variation on what Kiril Taranovsky has identified as the trochaic pentameter theme initiated in Lermontov's "Vykhozhu odin ia na dorogu," where the "dinamicheskii motiv puti protivopostavliaetsia staticheskomu motivu zhizni, odinochestvu i razdum'iam o zhizni i smerti" ("Tsezura i slovorazdely," 319). In Akhmatova's transformation of this theme, the road leads only to imprisonment and death.

31. Sharon Leiter, *Akhmatova's Petersburg,* 92-93, 73-74. See also 61-64 for a discussion of the first occurrence of this imagery in a 1915 poem about the beginning of World War I, "Tot avgust, kak zheltoe plamia" (1:194-195).

   "Sograzhdanam" appears under the title "Petrograd, 1919" with a number of substantial changes in Anna Akhmatova, *Stikhotvoreniia i poemy* (Leningrad, 1976), 149. See that volume, 471, and 1:398-399, for its publication history.

32. Compare Akhmatova's description of the city to Lidiia Chukovskaia in 1939; confessing that she is fed up with the city, she explains, "Dal', doma—obrazy zastyvshego stradaniia" (*Zapiski* 1:21). The final phrase recalls the prominent motif of "okameneloe stradanie" in *Rekviem.*

33. The theme of the suppression of the poet's voice, introduced obliquely into the "Posviashchenie" through the allusions to Pushkin's "Vo glubine," looms large in *Rekviem,* emerging explicitly in the second part of the "Epilog": "I esli zazhmut moi izmuchennyi rot" (1:369).

34. Compare with l. 6 the young Akhmatova's "Zharko veet veter dushnyi" (1:58).

35. This conflict is vividly embodied in the sound orchestration of the text: first, the mellifluous paronomasia of l. 6—"*veet veter svezhii*"—contrasts with the first line's abrasive "*gorem gnutsia gory*"; similarly, the pleasing near rhyme "svezhii" / "nezhitsia" in ll. 6-7 finds a jarring third in l. 9's "skrezhet," which itself recalls the apocalyptic gospel phrase "tam budet plach i skrezhet zubov," envisaging the suffering of those in hell.

36. My thanks go to Alexander Lehrman for calling this subtext to my attention in the fall of 1986. See V. Lebedev-Kumach, "Pesnia o rodine," in *Kniga pesen* (Moscow, 1938), 9-10. The lines occur in the third verse, which has since Stalin's death been regularly excised from printings of the song for praising the "Vsenarodnyi Stalinskii Zakon." Compare, for instance, Lebedev-Kumach, *Pesni i stikhotvoreniia* (Moscow, 1960), 27-29.

   Akhmatova's use of Lebedev-Kumach's hacksong as a subtext in the "Posviashchenie" forces one to recall the lines from her "Tainy remesla" cycle: "Kogda b vy znali, iz kakogo sora / Rastut stikhi, ne vedaia styda" (1:251).

37. See Gleb Struve, *Russian Literature under Lenin and Stalin* (Norman: University of Oklahoma Press, 1971), 312. Featured in the popular film *Tsirk,* the song was played repeatedly on the radio and was "printed in *Pravda, Izvestiia, Komsomol'skaia pravda,* and in a number of newspapers, journals, and collections" (Lebedev-Kumach, *Kniga pesen,* 193).

38. In the rest of *Rekviem,* the first-person plural occurs only once, in passing, making its role in the "Posviashchenie" highly marked. It comes toward the end of the "Vstuplenie" in the line "Zvezdy smerti stoiali nad nami" (1:363). "Eto bylo, kogda ulybalsia" became the "Vstuplenie" of *Rekviem* only in 1962, when the first typewritten copy of the *poema* was prepared. See Chukovskaia, *Zapiski* 2:473-474.

39. Vladimir Maiakovskii, *Sobranie sochinenii v dvenadtsati tomakh,* 12 vols. (Moscow: Pravda 1978) 1:317. On the *poema*'s failure as a work of propaganda, see Edward J. Brown, *Mayakovsky: A Poet in the Revolution* (Princeton, N.J.: Princeton University Press, 1973), 204-206.

   Akhmatova's allusion to Maiakovskii calls to mind Kornei Chukovskii's 1921 comparison of the two writers (Korney Chukovsky, "Akhmatova and Mayakovsky," trans. John Pearson, in *Major Soviet Writers: Essays in Criticism,* ed. E. J. Brown [London: Oxford University Press, 1973] 33-53). Maiakovskii figures as "the poet of the colossal" for whom "words like 'thousand,' 'million,' and 'billion' are commonplace" (44), a fact that, in Chukovskii's view, reflected the cataclysmic times (45). Akhmatova, on the contrary, is the poet of "the microscopic detail" (40), in whose verse "not a single 'million' is to be found" (46). The appearance of the epithet "stomil'onnyi" in Akhmatova's poetry in 1940 is unprecedented, but not the theme to which it is attached—the fate of the Russian nation. As Chukovskii wrote in 1921, "When the war broke out Akhmatova . . . saw only Russia" (46); the same could be said of her response to the revolution. By contrast, Chukovskii calls Maiakovskii an internationalist ("Work is our homeland!") with "no feeling" "for the motherland" (47). Maiakovskii's point of departure in *150,000,000* is identical to Akhmatova's in *Rekviem*—the destruction of Russia: "Propala Rosseichka! / Zagubili bedniuiu!" (Maiakovskii, *Sobranie,* 1:318). Rather than mourning this fact, as Akhmatova does in *Rekviem,* Maiakovskii immediately calls for the creation of a "new Russia," a universal one ("Novuiu naidem Rossiiu. / Vsekhsvetnuiu!" [Maiakovskii, *Sobranie,* 1:318]), which gives rise in turn to the *poema*'s plot—an allegorical treatment of class struggle.

40. Lebedev-Kumach, *Kniga pesen,* 9.

41. Ibid., 9-10.

42. Akhmatova seems to echo "Pesnia o rodine" in other parts of *Rekviem* as well. To give but one example, the line "Starikam—vezde u nas pochet" is contradicted in the second part of the "Epilog": "I vyla starukha, kak ranenyi zver'" (1:370).

43. Ibid., 10.

44. This is yet another instance of the outside world mirroring life within the prison. In his brief discussion of the "Posviashchenie," Efim Etkind speaks of the woman as "die Verurteilte," without noting that she is "sentenced" only figuratively. See "Die Unsterblichkeit des Gedächtnisses," 387-388.

45. This design vividly illustrates Akhmatova's fusion in the "Posviashchenie" of lyric and epic elements, of the personal and the national. That the two are conjoined in *Rekviem* is a commonplace in the critical literature, although the actual workings of this conjunction have received little attention. Kees Verheul has written that in *Rekviem* the "lyrical-autobiographical and the national . . . coincide" ("Public Themes," 108). According to Efim Etkind, "'Requiem' ist ein *episches* Poem, das aus einzelnen *lyrischen* Gedichten aufgebaut ist. Jedes dieser Gedichte ist dem Aufbau nach lyrisch, hat aber eine Tendenz zur Epik" ("Die Unsterblichkeit des Gedächtnisses," 392). See also

Lidiia Chukovskaia's discussion of the tension in *Rekviem* between the personal and the national (*Zapiski* 2:473-474), and Joseph Brodsky's comments on the same in Akhmatova's poetry as a whole in "The Keening Muse," published in his collection *Less than One: Selected Essays* (New York: Farrar, Straus, Giroux, 1986), 34-52, especially 42-44.

46. The close link between the dedicatory poem and that central sequence is signaled at the beginning of the fourth stanza of the "Posviashchenie," for its first word—"Prigovor"—recurs as the title of the sequence's seventh poem. *Rekviem* in fact offers two versions of the same event, one as described in the third person and the other as told from the point of view of a single victim. This is another salient example of the blending of epic and lyric elements in *Rekviem.*

47. Pushkin, *SS* 2:85. In the first volume of her memoirs of Akhmatova, Lidiia Chukovskaia unwittingly hints at the importance of allusions to Pushkin in *Rekviem* by enciphering references to it as "*Rekviem* Pushkina." For instance, she encodes a reference to the "Posviashchenie" as follows: "Potom ona prochitala mne novonaidennye pushkinskie stroki—iz ego *Rekviema.* 'Lunnyi krug.'" See the entry for 3 March 1940, *Zapiski* 1:76.

48. Pushkin, *SS* 9:120. The source of these remarks is a letter to D. M. Shvarts dated 9 December 1824. In his commentary to *Evgenii Onegin,* Nabokov argues that Pushkin intentionally encouraged the confusion of Arina Rodionovna "with the generalized nurse [he] gives the Larin girls" and claims that Pushkin generally "romanticized her in his verse." See *Eugene Onegin,* trans. with a commentary by Vladimir Nabokov, rev. ed., 4 vols. (Princeton, N.J.: Princeton University Press, 1975) 2:452.

In an essay called "Iavleniia muzy," V. F. Khodasevich offers some concrete textual evidence linking Tat'iana's nanny to Arina Rodionovna. Khodasevich traces the connection between Arina Rodionovna and the poet's many-faced Muse, asserting that the Muse appeared to Pushkin in the guise of his nanny. It appears in Khodasevich's *O Pushkine* (Berlin: Petropolis, 1937), 8-38; see especially 37-38 and 14-20.

49. Lev Gumilev was arrested on 10 March 1937 and was imprisoned in Leningrad until 17 or 18 August 1939 (Haight, *Anna Akhmatova,* 97). Compare Lidiia Chukovskaia's description, in the entry for 28 August 1939, of Akhmatova's visit to the prison to see her son on the eve of his transfer to a prison camp in the north (*Zapiski* 1:38-40).

50. Friendship was for Akhmatova an expression of spiritual freedom; compare her definition of *druzhba* as "Dushi vysokaia svoboda" (1:229) in "Nadpis' na knige," written in May 1940, just two months after the "Posviashchenie," and dedicated to Mikhail Lozinskii.

51. The same notion is conveyed in the second part of the "Epilog," when the speaker recalls one woman "chto rodimoi ne topchet zemli" (1:369). The question posed in l. 23 recalls yet another text from the period of Pushkin's exile in which Arina Rodionovna figures—"Zimnii vecher" (1825), which conjures up a snowstorm weathered by the persona and his "dobraia podruzhka" at Mikhailovskoe.

52. I am indebted here to Stephanie Sandler's discussion of the dedication of *Kavkazskii plennik* in chapter 4 of her *Distant Pleasures: Alexander Pushkin and the Writing of Exile* (Stanford, Calif.: Stanford University Press, 1989), 155-161. Sandler writes, "To say to someone 'I write these lines for you' is to say that a prior relationship exists to make the addressee an especially knowledgeable or valuable reader; it is also to say that he or she has in some way made it possible for the lines to be written in the first place" (160).

53. So does the following couplet from the second part of the "Epilog": "Dlia nikh sotkala ia shirokii pokrov / Iz bednykh, u nikh zhe podslushannykh slov" (1:369). Not only did those she addresses impel the poet to write *Rekviem,* they unwittingly provided her with the material from which it was composed.

54. I am grateful to Catherine Ciepiela for calling to my attention this parallel between "Niane" and the "Posviashchenie."

55. Akhmatova is underscoring here once more that *Rekviem* is a genuine *massovaia poema,* representing the true voice of the Russian people. The words of these women, quoted directly in "Vmesto predisloviia" and at the beginning of the second part of the "Epilog," are called "poor" in contrast to the bombast of which official mass songs are made, as demonstrated, for instance, in the following lines from Lebedev-Kumach's "Pesnia o rodine": "Etikh slov velichie i slavu / Nikakie gody ne sotrut: /—Chelovek vsegda imeet pravo / Na uchen'e, otdykh i na trud!" (Lebedev-Kumach, *Kniga pesen,* 10).

56. The reference is to Akhmatova's "Iiul' 1914": "Bogoroditsa belyi rasstelet / Nad skorbiami velikimi plat" (1:134).

Sam Driver (essay date 1990)

SOURCE: Driver, Sam. "Anna Akhmatova." In *European Writers: The Twentieth Century,* vol. 10, edited by George Stade, pp. 1521-42. New York: Charles Scribner's Sons, 1990.

[*In the following excerpt, Driver provides a brief overview of Akhmatova's* Requiem.]

Now that Akhmatova has been for so long fixed among the premier poets of Russia, it is difficult to recall that in the middle to late 1950's she was very nearly forgotten in the West and that in the Soviet Union she was considered to be an obscure figure, certainly not one who was very "relevant." Older readers typically remembered "the left-hand glove drawn onto the right" and often a good deal more, but most were surprised that Akhmatova was still among the living. As individual poems found their way into print both in the Soviet Union and abroad, it became clear that Akhmatova not only had retained both a high level of creativity and a consistency of style throughout the decades of enforced silence but had also undergone a remarkable development in her worldview. Her themes and images once carefully restricted to the worlds familiar to her from personal experience, now open out to encompass the whole world, and draw deeply on the European cultural tradition as well as the Russian.

This is partially illustrated by the rather spare total of representative poems from the 1920's and 1930's. At critical times during those years Akhmatova had to burn her archive, and much was lost simply in the vicissitudes of those years. Around 1939-1940, however, there was an extraordinary burst of creative activity. Along with a large number of poems in the usual short format, Akhmatova wrote the better part of two long narrative poems. She brought to completion *Requiem* and composed the **"Petersburg Tale,"** which served as the narrative line for the lengthy and complex *Poem Without a Hero.* If the latter was a markedly new departure for Akhmatova, *Requiem* was a natural development from her earlier work, a kind of culmination.

It is clear from Akhmatova's comments on Blok's *Vozmezdie (Retribution,* 1939) that she thought narrative poems could be successful only if they did not repeat forms already used (like Pushkin's, for example). Akhmatova worked out an original form for *Requiem,* a combination of the epic and the lyric. In one sense, it is an epic lament for Russia caught in the Terror, but it is made up of short lyrical poems and incidental pieces (introductions, dedication, epilogues). The means of expression in the lyric poems is essentially the one worked out in the six books up to 1922. Her techniques and versification, her idiosyncratic symbolic system, her diction and tone are all immediately recognizable here. The central poem of the work is an excellent example. It is entitled **"Prigovor" ("The Sentence")**, and while its simplicity and understatement suggest an epic calm in the face of tragedy, the intensity of the moment is increased many times by the pathetic effort of the will to overcome a grief that borders on madness:

> And the stone word fell
> On my still living breast.
> Never mind, I was ready after all,
> I'll manage somehow or other.
>
> I have lots to do today:
> I have to kill my memory completely,
> I've got to turn my soul to stone,
> I've got to learn to live again—
>
> And if not . . . The hot rustle of summer
> Is like a holiday outside my window.
> For a long time, I've had a presentiment of this
> Bright day and empty house.
>
> Summer 1939

The quiet conversational tone, the simple, workaday words contrast with the high seriousness of the content. The transformation of abstracts into concretes, the special meaning given the interior through the image of the window, and finally the image of the abandoned house all have—just because they fall within the context of Akhmatova's poetry—an immeasurably greater impact than they would in isolation.

According to the short prose introduction, **Requiem** had its genesis in Akhmatova's experience of the long lines of women outside the Leningrad prisons, where they waited for news of their loved ones imprisoned there. It was a time when "only the dead smiled, glad to be at peace, and Leningrad flapped like a useless appendage around its prisons."

The body of the work itself opens with a lyric poem about someone beloved who was swept up in the Terror, someone who might stand for Lev, for Mandelshtam, for Akhmatova's third husband Nikolai Punin, or for all those arrested in the night and taken away in those frightful years. Note once again how the images and devices already characteristic of Akhmatova in the first period transmit the import of the poem. There are rich lexical borrowings from an earlier Russian culture with its Orthodox foundations. (The word for chamber, *gornitsa,* is almost obsolete; *bozhnitsa,* here translated literally as "shrine," could be an icon corner or icon stand; an icon itself figures in one image.) Further, there is the familiar image of an interior setting and the symbolic doorway. And again, the Russia of history, of medieval Muscovy, is evoked—this time through the reference to the Kremlin walls—in **"Uvodili tebia na rassvete" ("They Led You Away at Dawn")**:

> They led you away at dawn;
> I went after, as if following your coffin.
> Children wept in the darkened chamber
> The candle at the shrine spilled over.
> The cold of an icon on your lips,
> A deathly sweat on your brow . . . Can't be forgotten!
> And I, like the wives of the Streltsy
> Shall howl under the Kremlin's towers.
>
> (*Sochineniia* 1. 355)

The Streltsy were a standing infantry at the time of Peter the Great who sided against him in a palace plot. Many were beheaded on the square in front of the Kremlin, others hanged before its wall—in full sight of their wives and families. In this context, then, Peter figures as cruel despot (and in the eyes of the Orthodox common folk of his time, the Antichrist). The relationship is clear enough between the "poor little wives of the Streltsy"—the tender diminutive is used—and the women of **Requiem** standing in lines at the prison walls.

The breathless hesitancy that marks so many of the early lyrics is also here. There is a rapid build-up to a breaking point; the melted wax on the votive candle spills over. Control is gone, and the lyric persona "howls like the wives of the Streltsy."

But it is restraint of emotion, rather than release, that we have come to expect in Akhmatova's poetry, or at least a return to a kind of resignation after the breaking point. In **Requiem** this indeed follows; in the next lyric, the contrast is complete. There is a certain calm, but it is a calm that is not quite sane, for the persona of the poem is divorced from her suffering self. A jingly meter jars with the content, and madness hovers:

> Quietly flows the quiet Don,
> Into the house comes the yellow moon,
>
> Comes in with his hat cocked jauntily,
> The yellow moon sees a shadow.
>
> This woman is sick,
> This woman is alone,
>
> Husband in the grave, son in prison,
> Pray for me a little.

In the following brief lyric, **"Net, eto ne ia" ("No, That Is Not I,"** 1940), the separation becomes complete, and before the halting rhythms quite resolve themselves, the poem comes to a full stop: ". . . what happened, let black cloths cover over / And let the lamps be carried out . . . Night."

There follows a jumble of impressions: a memory of happier days, before the revolution in Tsarskoe Selo, contrasted with the lines of disheartened women outside the prisons in the bitter winter cold; the utter horrors of the time, and of men of the time; the poet's grief for her son and for her people.

And only dusty flowers,
And the clinking of the censer chain, and footprints
Going nowhere.

This leads to the central poem, **"The Sentence."** The extraordinary effect of this poem and those preceding it depends in large part on recognition of the style of the early Akhmatova, and on the irony engendered as a result of the discrepancy between her younger self and the present person—between "the gay little sinner of Tsarskoe Selo," as she is called here, and the shabby, gray-faced woman standing in the prison lines, just another among a nation of suffering women.

From **"The Sentence,"** the *Requiem* moves on again through changes of atmosphere and diction until it reaches the end in two final, moving quatrains. Here, Akhmatova generalizes the properly lyrical cry of the passages just preceding into the universality of the Mother suffering for the Son.

> The Magdalene struck her breast and sobbed,
> The beloved disciple turned to stone,
> But there, where the Mother stood silent,
> No one even dared to look.

> (*Stikhotvoreniia i poemy,* p. 192)

The two epilogues that follow take up the themes, progressing once again from lyric to epic in stance. Here, the poet becomes not only witness and chronicler, but ultimately judge.

The epilogues close with a reference to the great rivers of Russia, echoing the first lines of the dedication: "Before such grief, mountains bend, / The great river cannot flow. . . ." There are reprises in the body of the poem—the quietly flowing Don, the swirling Yenisei—resolving at the end in the river of Petersburg/Leningrad: "And ships go quietly along the Neva."

Michael Basker (essay date 1990)

SOURCE: Basker, Michael. "Dislocation and Relocation in Akhmatova's *Rekviem*." In *The Speech of Unknown Eyes: Akhmatova's Readers on Her Poetry,* edited by Wendy Rosslyn, pp. 5-25. Cotgrave, Nottingham, England: Astra Press, 1990.

[*In the following essay, Basker examines aspects of Akhmatova's* Requiem *that project qualities of disorientation and dislocation.*]

The American critic Sam Driver has described **Rekviem** as 'an amazingly powerful statement which requires no elaboration or "explanation"'.[1] A 'public' work, woven, we are told, from the 'poor words' of the ordinary victims of the events described,[2] **Rekviem** indeed seems readily accessible and intensely moving. In lines such as:

Я жду тебя—мне очень трудно

it achieves a pathos-laden directness, and an absolute simplicity at the very limits of poetic art, which make the critical elucidation vital to an appreciation of so much of Akhmatova's later poetry appear lamely redundant. This, as much as previous political constraints, perhaps accounts for a relative critical neglect of this major work.

Naturally enough, those who have written in most detail on *Rekviem* have concentrated primarily on 'ideational' aspects and, to a lesser extent, on narrative progression and structural unity. The main themes of the cycle have been identified as memory, the poetic word, and their triumph over persecution and death, Akhmatova's main endeavour being 'to eternally preserve the memory of what occurred; and to distill from that experience its innermost spiritual significance'.[3] Haight has written lucidly on the cycle as the 'map of a journey leading through hell into the light', 'an organic unity documenting a precise progression through all the stages of suffering';[4] while Etkind, in the fullest study to date, has paid particular attention to architectonic symmetry and to a series of bipartite structural oppositions.[5] It has also been made increasingly clear, by revealing asides in the articles of distinguished Soviet-based critics, by Etkind, and in an article by Milivoe Jovanović,[6] that beneath its apparent simplicity *Rekviem,* too, reveals an extensive тайнопись, a more complex, hidden structure, based in considerable part on intertextual allusion. The smooth unelaborated reading in other words proves insufficient. Under the broad heading of dislocation and relocation this paper looks briefly at various aspects of *Rekviem* to suggest that in some respects the cycle is in fact challengingly disorienting.

I

Something of its disorienting, dislocative quality might be illustrated at the outset by Akhmatova's choice of epigraph:

> Нет, и не под чуждым небосводом,
> И не под защитой чуждых крыл,—
> Р была тогда с моим народом,
> Там, где мой народ, к несчастью, был.

This is, most obviously, an impassioned statement of location (тогда—там), in which the resounding negative of the first two lines emphasised by syntactic parallelism and repetition of key lexemes (нет—не—не; чуждым—чуждых), is forcefully juxtaposed to the no-less-insistently repetitive, unequivocally positive identification of self with time, place and people in lines 3-4. The epigraph takes up a theme familiar from earlier poems by Akhmatova, of the moral opposition between emigration and Russia, and reads in context as 'a triumphant vindication of a conviction Akhmatova had first formulated in 1917, that it was right and necessary for her to stay in Russia and die with her country if need be'.[7] Yet beneath their powerful rhetorical sweep the precise meaning of Akhmatova's lines is perhaps not entirely clear: in particular, the metaphor of the 'shelter of alien wings' might seem obscure. The imagery of wings is ubiquitous in the poetry of Akhmatova, and recurs with connotations of madness in a striking instance of etymological root-play (крыло—закрыло) in poem **"#9"** of the cycle.[8] A different gloss might be provided here, however, by the opening verses of the 90th (91st) Psalm:

> Живущий под кровом Всевышняго под сению Всемогущаго покоится. Говори Господу: "прибежище мое и защита моя Бог мой, на Котораго я уповаю!:" . . . Перьями Своими осенит тебя, и под крыльями Его будешь безопасен . . .

If the words of the Psalm suggest that the 'defending wings' might be those of God, then the чуждые крылья of Akhmatova's epigraph would allude to a foreign faith.[9] At the head of **Rekviem,** the implications are profoundly disjunctive: for if an alien faith, as well as an alien land, might seem to beckon, this is presumably because in the people's misfortune the Russian faith has failed to provide that defence from 'terror by night and the arrow that flieth by day' promised by the 90th Psalm (appropriately enough, one of those included in the Orthodox funeral service).[10] The poet, though united with her people, may have been abandoned by her God: and her overtly religious poem-cycle thus opens with a covert note of religious disquiet. This will be sustained through such dislocated religious symbolism as the черные Марусьи of poem **"#1"**, Kresty as name of a Communist prison (**"#4"**), or the огромная звезда (with its obvious allusion to the stars on the Kremlin towers) which presages not the Nativity but the imminent death of mother or son (**"#5"**), to culminate, as we shall see, in poem #10, **"Raspiatie."**

Though the epigraph, dated 1961, adumbrates a theme familiar from such poems as "Mne golos byl. On zval uteshno" and "Ne s temi ia, kto brosil zemliu", its meaning is perhaps also modified in the light of the notorious Party resolution of 1946. Despite a disorienting anachronism in relation to the main subject matter of **Rekviem,** it is difficult not to detect in Akhmatova's prominently positioned later lines a defiant rejoinder to Zhdanov's denunciation of her poetry as 'utterly remote from the people', even, perhaps, an implicit reply to his rhetorical question: 'What is there in common between this poetry, the interests of our people and the State?'[11] in **Rekviem** the interests of poet and people are one, and though the epigraph draws an overt distinction between народ and emigration, Russia and abroad, the shadow of Zhdanov brings into consideration an underlying third force. The fundamental disjuncture, it is intimated, is an eternal one, between the interests of poet and people on the one hand, and those of the State on the other, between безвинная Русь (**"Vstuplenie"**) and the 'alien' force of her палачи (**"#6"**). The powerful locative statement of Akhmatova's epigraph is thus predicated upon an apprehension of profound dislocation. The sense of disjuncture, disunity and fragmentation that it introduces is the central experience of the cycle.

From the very start of **Rekviem** the natural order is disrupted. The mountains are bowed with grief, the 'great river' does not flow, and the 'capital' (which, unnervingly, is no longer the capital) has 'grown wild' (**"Posviashchenie"**). The experience of the prison queues has blotted out all ordinary perception, so that a very literal dis-location has taken place:

> И ненужным привеском болтался
> Воале тюрем своих Ленинград
>
> (**"Vstuplenie"**)

Subsequent locations shift, abruptly and disconcertingly, from Leningrad to Moscow and back again, from the Neva to the Don to the Enisei, but in a sense this is immaterial: Мы не знаем, мы повсюду те же (**"Posviashchenie"**). All places coalesce undifferentiatedly into one, the only significant topography a 'blind red wall' which might itself be either Kremlin or prison (**"Epilog (1)"**). Essentially, it seems, the place which the poet shared with her people (Я была тогда с моимнародом) was a non-place.

Further disorientation is expressed through a series of unnatural inversions and conceptual incongruities. The condemned walk in regiments like soldiers. Песни разлукн mark their disappearance, but they are sung by locomotive whistles, not the loved ones we might expect in a military context (**"Vstuplenie"**). The son whose return is longed for passionately for seventeen months is equated with horror: ты сын и ужас мой (**"#5"**), his eyes are страшные (**"#9"**). Amongst other elements of religious inversion, leaving each day for the prison queues is like leaving for early-morning service (**"Posviashchenie"**). Much else, from the oxymoron мертвых бездыханней in the opening poem, betrays a confusion of life and death. Living is dependent upon killing memory and stifling the soul (**"#7"**), and death, in whatever odious guise, is простая и чудная (**"#8"**). Only the dead smile, pleased to have found peace; and if this defies logic, then another emphatically locative statement—Это было, когда улыбался / Только мертвый . . . at the start of **"Vstuplenie"**—is also divested of its overt meaning to suggest that time too (300 hours or 17 months), is out of joint: a dislocated non-time or a time suspended. All is subject to the irreality of a sickeningly 'familiar' сказка, utterly disruptive of familiar life (**"#8"**).

At worst the poet and the people with whom she identifies are divorced each from the other in the depths of their suffering (**"Posviashchenie"**), while the numbing dislocation of normal perception obliterates, seemingly irrevocably, moral as well as physical distinctions:

> Все перепуталось навек,
> И мне не разобрать
> Теперь, кто зверь, кто человек . . .
>
>   (**"#5"**)

Victims as well as executioners are dispossessed of their human attributes: poet and people cease to be people. **Rekviem** is framed by the 'semblance of a smile that flits across something that was once a face' (**"Vmesto predisloviia"**) and the closing memory of an old woman who 'howled . . . like a wounded animal' (**"Epilogue (2)"**). In between we see the harrowing and protracted process of dislocation of personality: of loss of identity (**"#3"**); self-dissociation (**"#3", "#4", "#9"**); surrender of moral integrity: Кидалась в ноги палачу (**"#5"**); attempted moral suicide through extinction of memory and feeling (**"#7"**); longing for physical death (**"#8"**) and incipient descent into the oblivion of madness (**"#9"**). The emergence from such experience of the poetic self with whom the poem begins and ends is, indeed, a spiritual and moral triumph, а подвиг to which no purely literary commentary can do justice. As we shall see, however, it involves not a restoration of the dislocated self and world, but their denatured relocation.

II

Motifs of dislocation are amply mirrored in the style and structure of **Rekviem**. Indeed, the cycle abounds in what Roman Timenchik defines as devices of автометаописание:

> the presence within a poetic text of an ideational motivation for the reduction of sense precisely to a given number of syllables and—more broadly—any emphasis within a poetic text of the ideational link between different levels.[12]

There is, in other words, an exceptional degree of correlation between form and content, and the reader is in consequence subjected to a variety of dislocative devices.

Some of the simplest of such devices are syntactic. To cite just two examples, the declaration of a final indifference at the end of poem **"#8"** (Мне все равно теперь . . .) is mirrored by the disorienting syntactic indifference of the last lines, in which subject and object cannot ultimately be distinguished:

> И синий блеск возлюбленных очей
> Последний ужас застилает.

And in **"Posviashchenie"** suspension of pronominal reference, temporal shifts and fragmentation of syntax combine to convey the violent separation of the individual both from the mass and from her own sense of reality. After a passage of first person plural past tense narrative the reader is disoriented by the shift from a naturally assumed first person (отделена) to third (идет):

> Приговор . . . И сразу слезы хлынут,
> Ото всех уже отделена,
> Словно с болью жизнь иа сердца вынут,
> Словно грубо навзничь опрокинут,
> Но идет . . . Шатается . . . Одна . . .

Confusion is increased by the switch to third person impersonal verbs, and from past through future perfective to present, until by the fifth line the syntax is clearly disrupted (шатается), and the words expressive of dislocation themselves become graphically isolated.

Metrical irregularity, too, may be an autometapoetic expression of dislocation. So, in **"Prigovor"** (**"#7"**), the unexpected truncation of a regular five-foot trochaic metre to four feet:

> Справлюсь с этим как-нибудь

might be construed as a significant subversion of stated meaning: the failure, as it were, to cope with metre is silent testimony to an underlying inability to cope with the sentence that has been passed. More striking is the suspension of entire lines—as in poem **"#4"**, where the twelfth line, the anticipated completion of the third rhyming quatrain, is withheld. The poem breaks off at the end of line 11, with the suggestion of a thought too awful to articulate, while the descent into distressed silence is also the formal realisation of the deathly hush described in the preceding line:

> Там тюремный тополь качается,
> И ни звука—а сколько там
> Неповинных жизней кончается . . .

Such fragmentation is more complete in poem **"#3"** ("Net, eto ne ia, eto kto-to drugoi stradaet"), where the regular structure of metre and rhyme is abandoned to represent the disintegration of self. The poem moves from prosaic colloquialism and complete rhythmic irregularity towards 'poetic' metaphor and an emergent amphibrachic metre, but the fourth line tails off with suspension points, and all development is halted by the single disruptive monosyllable of the fifth: Ночь. The poem breaks off into another premature silence, the formal counterpart of unutterable darkness.

In broad outline, at least, it might also be argued that the entire structure of **Rekviem** is mimetic of the thematics of dislocation. It is made up of a series of short poems (some ostensibly fragmented), of differing length and metre and, where given, of widely differing date,[13] preceded by an anachronistic epigraph which is itself a fragment from a longer poem,[14] and a brief passage of prose which, however conventional its designation in Russian, is denied the full-fledged status of a foreword (**"Vmesto predisloviia"**). Although Haight and others demonstrate a general narrative progression (more obvious, in fact, over the second half of the cycle), *Rekviem* shifts abruptly from poem to poem in mood and tone as well as metre and setting, and lacks both a conventional plot (contrast, for example, Blok's polymetric *Dvenadtsat'*) and consistent personal referents: autobiographically, as we know, poem **"#1"** was written on the arrest of Punin;[15] others refer to L. N. Gumilev. Within the text, however, there is a more striking discontinuity, reinforced by shifts of grammatical person and point of view, between, say, the woman who will wail like the wives of the Strel'tsy at the Kremlin wall (**"#1"**) and the woman associated with the muted madness of the quiet Don (**"#2"**); or between these women, and the царскосельская веселая грешница and her dispossessed heir (**"#4"**), and Mary (**"#10"**); or between the woman who descends into madness (**"#9"**) and the poetic voice of the epilogue poems. The opening of poem **"#3,"** "Net, eto ne ia, eto kto-to drugoi stradaet", points, in other words, to a fundamental contradiction, realised not just within the self of individual poems, but between the (dislocated) selves of the different fragments. Dislocation of experience and personality is presented as a cycle of disparate, discontinuous fragments, without a consistently recognisable, conventional persona.

Other elements of style and structure, which cannot be deemed mimetic or autometapoetic, further contribute to the overall sense of dislocation. In some poems there is discordance between the thematic expectation created by choice of metre, and actual content.[16] Clash of semantic registers is another effective device, as in the jarring intrusion of modernity into a description 'which at first seems to be presented in a purely traditional allegorical form':[17]

И безвинная корчилась Русь
Под кровавыми сапогами
И под шинами черных марусь.

Broadly analogous is the chilling substitution of губы for the strongly anticipated глаза in Женщины с голубыми губами (**"Vmesto predisloviia"**), or the incursion of 'Soviet reality' (the 'blue hat' which we realise must belong to the NKVD, and the управдом, pale from fright) into the seemingly timeless, folk-tale-based evocation of death's monstrous guises in **"K smerti"** (**"#8"**). Despite elements of structural symmetry between the disparate component parts of *Rekviem* (in particular with regard to the outer framework of **"Posviashchenie," "Vstuplenie"** and the epilogues),[18] there is also a pervasive undercurrent of contradiction between one segment of text and another, clearly disrup-

tive of any symmetrical patterning. Thus, синий блеск возлюбленных очей (**"#8"**) conflicts with сына страшные глаза (**"#9"**); все говорили шепотом (**"Vmesto predisloviia"**) with Буду . . . выть (**"#1"**); Не течет великая река (**"Posviashchenie"**) with Тихо льется тихий Дон (**"#2"**); or the grand pathetic fallacy of the opening with the depiction of nature's ordinary dispassionate round, painfully out of step with emotional trauma (**"#6"**). The strong implication that the present era is without precedent is at variance with historical reference which suggests a continuity of suffering (the wives of the Strel'tsy, the Bronze Horseman); and emphatic statements of location (там, тогда, это было, когда) contrast with shifting scenes and a sense of irreality. Beneath, as we have seen, lies the disjuncture of the *He* . Plainly such contradictions, hitherto largely neglected by critics, vary in both significance and degree of eventual resolution. At one extreme, the contrary impulses to remember and forget (Не забыть! [**"#1"**]; Надо память до конца убить [**"#7"**]) are resolved in the second epilogue (О них вспоминаю всегда и везде). At the other, the assertion that the cycle is composed of the simple words of other women, иа бедных, у них же подслушанных слов, is so at odds with the profusion of literary allusion that Akhmatova's much-quoted assertion can only be considered deliberately misleading. In all, however, such inconsistency evidently further contributes to the disturbing sense of dislocation with which *Rekviem* confronts the reader.

III

Literary allusion is itself also frequently used to dislocative effect, creating and simultaneously subverting a context of expectation for what is described. Milivoe Jovanović, in an article on *Rekviem* dealing primarily with Akhmatova's use of quotations from Euripides and Shakespeare, has made brief reference to certain parodic or polemical reworkings of Russian literary tradition: of Nekrasov's "Russkie zhenshchiny", Lermontov's "Kazach'ia kolybel'naia pesnia", and, perhaps most significantly, Blok's "Na pole Kulikovom".[19] In fact, *Rekviem* is replete with other such dissociative echoes of Russian literature, Blok, together with Mandel'shtam and, above all, Pushkin, providing their most frequent source.[20]

Jovanović is persuasive in detecting in Не течет великая река at the start of Akhmatova's **"Posviashchenie"** an inversion (or what R. Timenchik has defined as a 'shadow quotation')[21] of Река раскинулась. Течет, грустит лениво from the opening of "Na pole Kulikovom", and thus the first in a series of implicit refutations of the historiosophical vision of Blok's cycle. However, the most obvious literary allusion of Akhmatova's opening poem (uniquely in *Rekviem* accorded the emphasis of quotation marks) is to the каторжные норы of Pushkin's "Vo glubine sibirskikh rud". Yet the confident optimism of Pushkin's epistle to the incarcerated Decembrists:

> . . . Любовь и дружество до вса
> Дойдут сквозь мрачные затворы,
> Как в ваши каторжные норы
> Доходит мой свободный глас.
>
> Оковы тяжкие падут,
> Темницы рухнут—и свобода
> Вас примет радостно у входа . . .[22]

stands in jarring contrast to Akhmatova's poem, throwing into emphatic relief the utter bleakness of the modern period, in which all else distintegrates but prison bolts remain firm and prison walls impenetrable (Но крепки тюремные затворы, / А за ними «каторжные норы»), 'love and friendship' have been replaced by смертельная тоска, and the 'free voice' by howls and silence. To similar effect, in the description of the одичалая столица in which the women met ritually together (как к обедне ранней) while hope still sang in the background (все поэт) **"Posviashche-nie"** perhaps also contains an understandably more muted evocation of Mandel'shtam's "V Peterburge my soidemsia snova", where the 'capital' (already, as in Akhmatova, a misnomer) is hunched like a 'wild' cat (дикой кошкой) but the 'blessed women' with their singing eyes (Все поют блаженных жен родные очи) at least live on together as an enduring source of inspiration during present darkness, the guardians of a cult and token of spiritual survival and reunion.[23] In **"Posviash-chenie"** in *Rekviem,* by contrast, the community of women seems irrevocably broken asunder, and a final oxymoron underlines that no future meeting can be envisaged (Где теперь невольные подруги . . . Им я шлю прощальный свой привет). Not only Pushkin's optimism, but also Mandel'shtam's sombre prognostication has proved an inadequate measure of the blackness of the 'Soviet night' by which he had himself been engulfed. For as Akhmatova later remarked to Lidiia Chukovskaia:

> What we lived through then . . . has not been recorded by any literature. Shakespeare's dramas—all those flamboyant villains, passions, duels—are trivia, child's play, by comparison with the lives of each one of us. I dare not speak of what those who were sentenced to execution or camp underwent. It cannot be named in words. But each one even of our fortunate (благополучный) lives was a Shakespearean tragedy a thousand times over.[24]

The disjunctive allusion, evoking unprecedented horror by its distance from the familiar pattern of a more ordered past, thus assumes special importance.

The voices of Mandel'shtam and Pushkin might again be heard in Akhmatova's already quoted lines:

> Все перепуталось навек
> И мне не разобрать
> Теперь, кто зверь, кто человек . . .
>
> ("#5").

The finality of Akhmatova's *ек* contrasts with the now appropriate equivocation of another of Mandel'shtam's political poems of the *Tristia* period, "Dekabrist":

> Все перепуталось, и некому сказать,
> Что, постепенно холодея,
> Все перепуталось и сладко повторять . . .[25]

while the attendant confusion between man and animal might recall Pushkin's Evgenii, beaten by coachmen because он не разбирал дороги / Уж никогда:

> . . . И так он свой несчастный век
> Влачил, ни зверь, ни человек . . .[26]

In *Mednyi vsadnik,* Evgenii is a lone victim who loses his human respect. In *Rekviem,* the calamity extends to all around.

Similar use of allusion might also provide a clue towards deciphering in poem **"#2"**:

> Тихо льется тихий Дон
> Желтый месяц входит в дом.
> Входит в шапке небекрень.
> Видит желтый месяц тень.
> Эта женщина больна,
> Эта женщина одна,
> Муж в могиле, сын в тюрме,
> Помолитесь обо мне.

The poem is based on a number of startling incongruities, culminating in the agonised immediacy of the final line, where impersonal presentation is suddenly disrupted both by the supplication of an imperative address, and by the disorienting double shift from third person to first of the final мне, which displaces both 'this woman' as the subject of depiction, and 'husband and son' as the strongly anticipated object of the imperative verb. The poem is also troublingly enigmatic in its relation to other poems of *Rekviem,* not least, as Lidiia Chukovskaia's bewildered question 'Почему Дон? indicates,[27] in its seemingly unparalleled remoteness from the known facts of Akhmatova's biography. By a characteristic twist, however, it is possible that beneath the painful urgency of its first-person conclusion this seemingly least autobiographical poem conceals an exceptional intrusion of autobiographical reality. Approaching it as the deliberate puzzle which Chukovskaia's remarks suggest, one might detect encoded anagrammatically in the words муж в могиле the name of Akhmatova's dead husband Gumilev;[28] and if he is indeed intended, then the phrase муж в могиле contains a further jarring contrariety. Gumilev had no grave, and the missing grave was an enormity on which Akhmatova wrote elsewhere with encoded eloquence.[29] The possibility of verbal play might also lead one to re-examine the poem's opening lines, to recognise if not the name of Lev/Leva, then that stifled sighing of his name ('даже не звук—тень звука, стона или зова') which Chukovskaia heard in 1940,[30] or, perhaps, to regard *До* as abstract sound, evoking one of those 'infrequent and remote strokes of the funeral bell' which Akhmatova described as the only fitting accompaniment, besides silence, to her **Rekviem**.[31] The opening of another poem by Pushkin might, however, provide a more straightforward explanation for Akhmatova's 'quietly flowing quiet Don':

> Блеща средь полей широких
> Вон он льется! . . . Здравствуй, Дон!

Pushkin's poem (which includes the epithet тихий Дон) coincides with Akhmatova's in metre as well as in its first main verb, and the point of the correspondence becomes clear from its continuation:

> От сынов твоих далеких
> Я привез тебе поклон.[32]

Pushkin brings advance greetings from those soon to return victorious from the Russo-Turkish war.[33] Akhmatova, too, is concerned with 'distant sons', but as victims not victors, and from them no news issues forth: in place of Pushkin's ebullient *окло* the only messenger is the intruding, seemingly malevolent moon. Once again, the preoccupations of a more ordinary age form a dislocative background, chilling not least in the implication that the words of the первый поэт have become comfortlessly redundant. In Akhmatova, this alone is perhaps tantamount to divorce from self.[34]

To similar contrastive effect, Akhmatova instills new content into old forms in **"K Smerti" ("#8")**. The pattern of her familiar invocation of death (Ты все равно придешь, зачем же не теперь? / Я жду тебя . . . Прими для этого какой угодно вид . . . Мне все равно теперь) seems to be modelled, amongst other possible sources,[35] upon Pushkin's invocation of the deceased Leila in his "Zaklinanie" (. . . Я тень зову, я жду Лейлу: . . . Явись возлюбленная тень . . . Приди, как дальная звезда, / Как легкий звук иль дуновенье, / Иль как ужасное виденье, / Мне все равно: сюда! сюда! . . .).[36] But where Pushkin, in wistful sorrow, addresses a dead lover,[37] Akhmatova's desperate appeal, from one forcefully deprived of her loved ones, is the sombre conjuration of a violent death.

Given the extensive Pushkinian background, one might also read Akhmatova's ninth poem, on encroaching madness, in the context of Pushkin's famous treatment in "Ne dai mne Bog soiti s uma"[38]—with the difference

that in Akhmatova God, as we have seen, does not forestall madness, while the брань смотрителей ночных, / Да визг, да звон оков, with abjuration of which Pushkin's poem closes, has become ubiquitous reality. The short dramatically disrupted third poem might seem by contrast an intensification of Pushkin, at least in terms of Akhmatova's own observations on the *Malen'kie tragedii,* where 'everything has already happened (случилось) somewhere outside the given work' and where, 'in essence . . . the tragedy begins when the curtain falls':[39]

> Нет, это не я, это кто-то другой страдает.
> Я бы так не могла, а то, что случилось,
> Пусть черные сукна покроют,
> И пусть унесут фонари . . .
> 　　　　Ночь.

In this case, however, the main disjunctive voice is perhaps that of Blok. Etkind has described the poem as 'Shakespearean', and Jovanović discerns here echoes of both Shakespeare and Euripides;[40] but it seems equally possible to detect behind at least the closing words of Akhmatova's short piece an inverted echo of Blok's almost equally short, no less formally self-conscious poem from "Pliaski smerti", "Noch', ulitsa, fonar', apteka".[41] The implication is clear. The purely abstract horror of a metaphorical living death has been replaced by the concrete reality of physical annihilation, the apparently hopeless, meaningless eternal round of the beginning of the century (Исхода нет. / Умрешь—начнешь опять сначала . . .) broken by the onset of that unrelieved darkness which Akhmatova, in the lines added after Mandel'shtam's death to her poem on his Voronezh exile, called 'the night which knows no dawn'.[42] The horror of the Ezhov terror surpasses anything of which Blok—or his comtemporary, the царскосельская веселая грешница, castigated in the following poem, primarily, it would seem, for the insouciant immorality characteristic of her age—were able to conceive.[43]

IV

It now remains to consider how far the darkness is indeed unrelieved, or to what extent the last numbered poem of the cycle, **"Raspiatie",** and the two epilogues, present a resolution of dislocation.

There can be little doubt that **"Raspiatie"**, with its image of a Mary who 'understands that the Crucifixion is the greatest moment in history',[44] concludes the numbered poems on a cathartic note of high solemnity and awe-inspiring spiritual triumph. By ordinary criteria it is, nevertheless, a poem of considerable dislocation. It consists of two stanzas written at different times,[45] in different metres (five-foot iambic and five-foot trochaic), and with opposing sequences of masculine and feminine rhymes. The triumphant opening, Хор ангелов великий час воссиавил, constitutes an abrupt shift from the encroaching madness of poem **"#9"**. Yet it might also seem a shocking, almost irreverent disruption of the sombre tone of all that has preceded (the funeral bell, not the angelic host, is indeed the appropriate accompaniment to **Rekviem**), all the more discordant in that the великий час which the angels praise is that of the Crucifixion, not, as might be expected, the Resurrection. The words of Christ which follow also seem harsh and divisive. Father is set off against Mother; and although the possibility of an autobiographical reading, with further reference to the dead Gumilev, would cast the son's reproach (Почто Меня оставил!) in a different light, its obvious sense is that, as elsewhere in **Rekviem,** Mother and Son are abandoned by God to a cruel world. The words to the Mother (О, не рыдай Мене) suggest, moreover, that they are scarcely united in their suffering. In the Orthodox Eastern ritual these are words of tender comfort, connected with the promise of resurrection (Восстасну бо и прославлюся . . .);[46] in the context of the sustained and powerful 'mother's lament' of **Rekviem,** the injunction not to lament seems curiously heartless. And though the Passion might seem a more fitting analogue for the Ezhov terror than any of the secular texts discussed above, it is difficult to see how the promise of resurrection on the third day, traditionally implicit in Christ's words to Mary, might be appropriate to the modern reality. As title, epigraph and opening line imply, the emphasis of this poem is entirely upon death.

The second stanza is accordingly also one of disassociation. In further contrast to traditional expectation, Mary is emphatically separated from Mary Magdalene and from the 'beloved disciple' with whom, in the Gospels, the dying Christ sought to reconcile her.[47] As Amanda Haight has indicated, these three figures may readily be identified with different stages of suffering:[48] Mary Magdalene (билась и рыдала) with the initial 'howl' of poem **"#1"**; the disciple turning to stone perhaps not just, as Haight suggests, with the stone imagery of poem **"#7,"** but with the entire process of spiritual and emotional atrophy depicted in poems [**"#2"**, **"#3"**, **"#4"**, **"#5"**, **"#6"**, **"#7"**, **"#8"**, **"#9"**,]; and the silent, inscrutable Mary presumably with transcendence of these stages of self-dislocation—not, however, to the restoration of human aspect but to a state which appears impersonal or supra-personal. To the extent that the three disunited figures may be seen as projections of the self, Mary evidently symbolises no harmonious, healing reintegration; while the final locative statement establishes that her place is a kind of no-man's land, inaccessible to normal human emotion (А туда, где молча мать стояла / Так никто взглянуть и не посмел.) From the context of the entire poem it must be concluded that Mary has come to terms with suffering and terror not through mystic transcendence or divine intervention, but by complete divorce of self from all that is most dear in the normal world, a fiercely cruel purging of all ordinary emotional response.

This conclusion is borne out by each of the two epilogues. The figure of Mary is clearly implicit behind the 'I' of the first: Узнала я, как опадают лица. The pun лица—листья of the opening line reintroduces the tree imagery, sustained though улыбка вянет and в сухоньком смешке (cf сухие листья), which is one of the leitmotifs of the cycle and, following **"Raspiatie"**, perhaps evokes the traditional identification of tree and cross:[49] unlike those who dare not look upon Mary, the transfigured self is now able to look upon those disfigured each by their own individual Passion. In contrast to the desperate appeal for prayer in poem **"#2"**, she has crossed beyond the dislocation of self-engrossed suffering to pray on behalf of all who were with her. In this she approaches the traditional role of the Mother of God as Intercessor.

This role is further developed in the immensely powerful lines of **"Epilog (2)"**, culminating in the theme of the bronze памятник. And although this final poem, with its temporal distancing from events, marks an obvious movement towards the resumption of calm normality, elements of dislocation remain intense. Instead of looking upon and praying for the suffering and sundered народ, the poet now merges completely with them as the instrument of their expression, the измученный рот / Которым кричит стомильонный народ. The image of the disembodied mouth is one of grotesque dislocation, and suggests an impersonal voice that arises out of agonised obliteration of individual traits. Consistent with this, the siting of the monument represents an explicit rupture from the past self and its dearest associations: the last ties with the person born by the sea have been severed, and the безутешная тень in the town of Pushkin and Gumilev is abandoned to its inconsolable search. The cruel severity of this very literal self-renunciation even precludes final repose, in a startlingly paradoxical expression of fear, not of the terror but of forgetting its emblems 'even in blessed death'. The proximity to the austere, trans-personal figure of Mary is as clear as the contrast to the norm of Pushkin's 'personal' monument, erected from the entirety of his work on a basis of чувства добрые and любезность народу.[50] The identity of poet and Mary is reinforced by an implicit association of the poetic 'veil' (Покров) woven from the people's words and the Protecting Veil with which the Mother of God is entreated—in the *Troparion* of the Feast in its honour (Покров)—to cover the people and deliver them from evil.[51] The Russian connotations of Покров—a celebration of Mary's special importance as Intercessor for the Russian people[52]—deepen the association already implicit in the preceding poem. In addition, it is the chief function of Akhmatova's monument, too, to 'deliver the people from evil', perpetuating memory to eschew repetition.

The site of this hypothetical monument could scarcely be more emphatically defined; but its location is that dislocated non-place (by the blind wall, outside the unopened door) which is the main setting of the cycle, and might now be identified as well with the no-man's land of Mary. It is also unmistakably dislocative in relation to the city's most famous bronze statue, the Bronze Horseman. In public terms what it therefore betokens is not restoration of an earlier order but *relocation* of a tradition horribly distorted and dislocated, a shift from the values of the Petrine (and Pushkinian) city perhaps commensurate with the calamity that has intervened. Previous normality cannot be restored; and thus, though harmony with nature is re-established and the great river flows once more, the pathetic fallacy is also resumed to close in the form of snow that will melt each year as tears from the immovable lids of the bronze statue. Even the ships on the Neva—in contrast to the animated vigour of the Introduction to Pushkin's *Mednyi vsadnik*[53]—will pass in fitting silence. Similarly, what the monument signifies in private terms is not restoration of the dislocated self, but a relocation of the stricken centre of personality. The ferociously concentrated trans-personal strength which monument and Mary both represent brings them to occupy the symbolic no-man's land, for their strength is built on inconsolable loss and pitilessly searing detachment from the broken and now redundant ordinary self. Majestic impersonality is perhaps all that can be retrieved from the dislocative trauma of the terror.

It might therefore be argued in conclusion that *Rekviem,* lacking a conventionally unified persona, finally advances an unconventional model of personality. And by a further disorienting paradox this impersonal personality is presented in very personal terms; for behind the images of Mary and monument stands the real author whom the monument represents, and who speaks in the epilogue with quite exceptional autobiographical directness. We are thus prompted to regard this personality not as a literary convention but as non-literary reality—and consequently, perhaps, to regard the discontinuous personae of the numbered cycle as fragmented projections of the same real self. To the end, literary convention—but to a lesser extent, it may be hoped, conventional literary commentary—remains inadequate to the experience *Rekviem* records.

Notes

1. S. N. Driver, *Anna Akhmatova* (New York, 1972), p. 125.

2. "Epilog (2)". *Rekviem* is quoted according to *Neva*, 6 (1987), 74-9. References to individual sections are given as, for example, #2 in the text. The *Neva* version is close to that published by G. P. Struve and B. A. Filippov (*S*, I, 361-70) with variants generally as indicated by L. Chukovskaia (*Zapiski*, I-II, 1976-80, *passim*) and Akhmatova's own recordings. It has been preferred to the version in *Oktiabr'*, no. 3 (1987), 130-5.

3. S. Leiter, *Akhmatova's Petersburg* (Philadelphia, 1983), p. 92.

4. A. Haight, *Anna Akhmatova: A Poetic Pilgrimage* (Oxford, 1976), pp. 108, 100.

5. E. Etkind, 'Die Unsterblichkeit des Gedächtnisses: Anna Achmatovas Poem "*Requiem*", *Die Welt der Slaven,* 29 (1984) 360-94.

6. M. Iovanovich, 'K razboru "chuzhikh golosov" v *Rekvieme* Akhmatovoi', *Russian Literature,* 15 (1984), 169-82.

7. Haight, *Akhmatova,* p. 100.

8. K. Verheul, 'Public Themes in the Poetry of Anna Akhmatova', in J. van der Eng-Liedmeier & K. Verheul, *Tale Without a Hero and Twenty-Two Poems by Anna Axmatova* (The Hague, 1973), pp. 32-3.

9. It might be recalled that N. S. Gumilev had also used an image of the wings of an alien faith to conclude a 1912 poem on the seductive power of Catholicism: Скорей! Одно последнее усилье! / Но вдруг слабеешь, выходя на двор,— / Готические башни, словно крылья, / Католицизм в лазури распростер (*Sobranie sochinenii* [Washington, 1962], vol. 1, p. 237).

10. *Pravoslavnyi tolkovyi molitvoslov* (St Petersburg, 1907), p. 27.

11. KPSS, 'O zhurnalakh *Zvezda* i *Leningrad*: iz postanovleniia TsVKP (B) ot 14-ogo avgusta 1946g.', *Zvezda,* nos. 7-8 (1946), 4, 6.

12. R. D. Timenchik, 'Avtometaopisanie u Akhmatovoi", *Russian Literature,* 10-11 (1975), 213.

13. Fuller information on dates of composition and the in part fortuitous final shape of *Rekviem* is to be found in *Zapiski*, I, 65, 73, 110; *Zapiski*, II, 414-15, 453, 473-4; and Etkind, 'Unsterblichkeit des Gedächtnisses', pp. 381-4.

14. "Net, ne zria my vmeste bedovali" (*S*, III, 94-5).

15. *S*, II, 181. It is typical of the uncertainty of referents that, as Akhmatova notes here, Mandel'shtam mistakenly took this poem to refer to his own arrest. Yet a clear echo of "Za gremuchuiu doblest' griadushchikh vekov" at the end of poem #8 (see Etkind, 'Unsterblichkeit des Gedächtnisses', p. 378) evidently does superimpose the image of the dead Mandel'shtam on that of the son whom the lines overtly concern.

16. See Etkind, 'Unsterblichkeit des Gedächtnisses', pp. 367, 369-70, 373.

17. Verheul, 'Public Themes', p. 32.

18. Cf Etkind's particularly elaborate but by no means uncontroversial analysis of symmetrical structure, summarised in his 'Unsterblichkeit des Gedächtnisses', pp. 362-3.

19. Iovanovich, 'K razboru', pp. 170-1.

20. Not considered here, for reasons of space, is the question of similar echoes of Akhmatova's own earlier poetry. Etkind, 'Unsterblichkeit des Gedächtnisses', provides some valuable observations on the subject.

21. R. Timenchik, 'Printsipy tsitirovaniia u Akhmatovoi v sopostavlenii s Blokom', in *Tezisy I Vsesoiuznoi (III) konferentsii "Tvorchestvo A. A. Bloka i russkaia kul'tura XX veka"* (Tartu, 1975), p. 124.

22. A. S. Pushkin, *Sobranie sochinenii, 10 vols. (Moscow, 1974-78), vol.2*, p. 97.

23. *O. E. Mandel'shtam, Sobranie sochinenii,* 2nd. edn. (n.p., 1967), vol. 1, pp. 85-6.

24. *Zapiski,* II, 137.

25. Mandel'shtam, *Sobranii sochinenii,* vol. 1, p. 66.

26. Pushkin, *Sobranie sochinenii,* vol. 3, p. 265.

27. *Zapiski,* I, 73 fn. 34.

28. For another possible example of anagram in *Rekviem,* see Iovanovich, 'K razboru', p. 179 fn.22.

29. "Pushkin i nevskoe vzmor'e", *S,* III, 251-61. On Akhmatova's attitude to Gumilev's absent grave, see also *Zapiski,* II, 432.

30. *Zapiski,* I, 143. See also in this context R. D. Timenchik's suggestion of an etymological link between $_u x_u \check{u}$ and the surname Gumilev, cited in M. B. Meilakh, 'Ob imenakh Akhmatovoi: I, Anna', *Russian Literature,* 10-11 (1975), 55 fn. 57.

31. *S,* III, 159.

32. "Don", *Sobranie sochinenii,* vol.2, p. 186. Pushkin used the same epithet in *Kavkazskii plennik* (*Sobranie sochinenii,* vol. 3, p. 89); other possible sources for Akhmatova's line are suggested in Iovanovich, 'K razboru', pp. 177-8 fns. 12, 15.

33. Pushkin, *Sobranie sochinenii,* vol.2, p. 580.

34. Cf. R. D. Timenchik's comment: 'For Akhmatova reading Pushkin inevitably became a form of analytical self-cognition' ('Anna Akhmatova i Pushkinskii Dom', in *Pushkinskii Dom: Stat'i. Dokumenty. Bibliografiia* [Leningrad, 1982], p. 112).

35. Etkind, 'Unsterblichkeit des Gedächtnisses', pp. 376-7, refers to Chénier; Iovanovich, 'K razboru', pp. 175-6, 181 fns. 42-3; to Euripides' *Andromache* and Shakespeare's *Macbeth* and *Hamlet.*

36. Pushkin, *Sobranie sochinenii,* vol.2, p. 245.

37. Akhmatova herself (*S,* III, 317) noted the derivation of "Zaklinanie" from the ending of Byron's *The Giaour.* The name Leila is from Byron. The identity of Pushkin's addressee remains uncertain (see *Stikhotvoreniia Pushkina 1820-1830-x godov* [Leningrad, 1974], p. 115).

38. Pushkin, *Sobranie sochineii,* vol.2, pp. 313-14.

39. *S,* III, 182.

40. Etkind, 'Unsterblichkeit des Gedächtnisses', p. 363; Iovanovich, 'K razboru', pp. 174-5, 181 fn. 41.

41. A. A. Blok, *Sobranie sochinenii* (Moscow-Leningrad, 1960), vol. 3, p. 337. Cf. Akhmatova's more overt reworking of this poem in: "On prav—opiat' fonar', apteka".

42. "Voronezh". On the date of these lines, see *Zapiski,* II, 233.

43. Akhmatova, again linked Blok with her own past self in polemic with the immorality of the 1910s in *Poéma bez geroia.* See, e.g., S. Driver, "Axmatova's *Poéma bez geroia* and Blok's *Vozmezdie'*, in *Aleksandr Blok Centennial Conference,* ed. by W. Vickery & B. Sagatov (Columbus, OH, 1984), p. 95 and *passim.*

44. Haight, *Akhmatova,* p. 100.

45. Dated '1940-1943' in published versions other than *Neva,* 6 (1987).

46. *Pravoslavnyi tolkovyi molitvoslov,* p. 155.

47. John xix, 26-7.

48. Haight, *Akhmatova,* p. 105.

49. Cf Akhmatova's own poem of 1946 "V kazhdom dreve raspiatyi Gospod".

50. "Ia pamiatnik sebe vozdvig nerukotvornyi", *Sobranie sochinenii,* vol.2, p. 385. Contrast the impersonality of Akhmatova's Воздвигнуть задумают памятник мне.

51. *Pravoslavnyi tolkovyi molitvoslov,* p. 212. Driver, *Akhmatova,* p. 130, and J. van der Eng-Liedmeier, 'Reception as a Theme in Achmatova's Later Poetry', *Russian Literature,* 15 (1984), 110, each refer to the religious connotations of покров in connection with 'its comfort and protection'.

52. *Pravoslavnyi tolkovyi molitvoslov,* p. 212.

53. Cf Все флаги в гости будут к нам, / И за-
    пируем на иростране; . . . корабли / Толпой
    со всех концов земли / К богатым пристаням
    стремятся (Pushkin, *Sobranie sochinenii,* vol. 3,
    p. 255).

Roberta Reeder (essay date 1994)

SOURCE: Reeder, Roberta. "The Great Terror: 1930-
1939." In *Anna Akhmatova: Poet and Prophet,* pp. 211-
22. New York: St. Martin's Press, 1994.

*[In the following excerpt, Reeder provides a biographi-
cal and thematic overview of Anna Akhmatova's career
during the composition of her* Requiem.*]*

Indeed, Akhmatova had begun to write brilliant poems
again. Her "mute" period was over, as the impressions
of the many years of quiet suffering finally rose to the
surface. Philosophical themes, such as humanity's place
in the universe and the role of suffering in the life of
those who believe in a benevolent God, now began to
play a more dominant role in her work. "In 1936 I began
to write again, but my handwriting changed, my voice
sounded different, and my life passed under the reins of
a Pegasus which somehow reminds one of the apocalyptic White Horse or Black Horse of poems that were yet
to be born—a return to my first style is impossible.
Whether it is better or worse one cannot judge."[1]

When her creative powers returned, Akhmatova wrote
the cycle of poems about the Great Terror that have
since made her world-famous—*Requiem* (1935-40).
Anatoly Naiman, Akhmatova's literary secretary at the
end of her life, points out how very personal this work
is:

> The hero of this poetry is the people. Not a larger or
> smaller plurality of individuals called "the people" for
> political, nationalist, or other ideological reasons, but
> the whole people, every single one of whom participates
> in what is happening on one side or the other. . . .
> What differentiates it from, and thus contrasts it to,
> even ideal Soviet poetry is the fact that it is personal,
> just as profoundly personal. . . . The personal attitude
> is not a rejection of anything; it is an affirmation which
> is manifest in every word of *Requiem.* This is what
> makes *Requiem* poetry—not Soviet poetry, but simply
> poetry: it could be personal only if it dealt with
> individuals, their loves, their moods, and their selves in
> accordance with the officially sanctioned formula of
> "joys and sorrows."[2]

Another critic maintains that the cycle places the suffering heroine in the context of important literary works
on the suffering of mothers and wives, such as Nekrasov's portrayal of the wives of Decembrists who followed their husbands into exile at the beginning of the
nineteenth century, poems Akhmatova heard as a child.
Earlier examples are the heroines of Euripides—Andromache, Hecuba, the Trojan women. All of them share a
similar range of emotions: hope, the threat of death,
madness, indifference, and a readiness to accept death.[3]

The portrayal of intense suffering does not mean that
the poet has lost her faith. Inherent in the works of
great Russian writers like Dostoyevsky and Berdyaev is
the Orthodox belief that suffering is an important aspect
of life, by which one's faith is tested. One has three
choices: to overcome one's doubt and accept the idea
that suffering is part of a divine plan, whose meaning is
known to a benevolent God; to become immoral, give
up one's faith, and turn to demonic forces; or to become
totally amoral, in the belief that the individual is the
sole arbiter of his or her own destiny. Never in any of
Akhmatova's writings or conversations with trusted
friends did she admit to doubt or lack of faith in the
mysterious and often incomprehensible ways of a
Divine Creator. She would not agree with Albert Camus's philosophy of the absurd. In his *Myth of Sisy-
phus,* Camus finds no way out of his metaphysical
dilemma—either we are not free and almighty God is
responsible for evil; or we are free and responsible, but
God is not omniscient, all-powerful. Camus prefers to
accept a world without God, an essentially amoral
universe where good and evil coexist without aim or
meaning. But there is another answer—that it is possible to believe in a God who created a universe
containing both good and evil, and the individual has
the freedom to choose between the two. Only in such a
universe, rather than one in which one's fate is
predestined, can people be judged as moral human beings who will ultimately be rewarded for their actions.

The poet Joseph Brodsky saw the text of *Requiem* itself
as a confirmation of Akhmatova's faith, saying:

> The degree of compassion with which the various
> voices of *Requiem* are rendered can be explained only
> by the author's Orthodox faith; the degree of under-
> standing and forgiveness which account for this work's
> piercing, almost unbearable lyricism, only by the
> uniqueness of her heart, herself, and this self's sense of
> time. No creed would help to understand, much less
> forgive, let alone survive this double widowhood at the
> hands of the regime, this fate of her son, these forty
> years of being silenced and ostracized.[4]

Akhmatova did not foresee the Terror, but by 1930 she
certainly knew what probably lay ahead, considering all
that had already occurred to her and to millions of others under the Soviet regime. Yet she chose to stay and
suffer with her people. This is made clear in the
epigraph to *Requiem,* which was added in 1961, from
the poem **"No, we didn't suffer together in vain"**
(1961), not published in the Soviet Union until after her
death:

No, not under the vault of alien skies,
And not under the shelter of alien wings—
I was with my people then,
There, where my people, unfortunately, were.

(II, p. 95)[5]

The epigraph does not ground the poem in any particular historical context, hence the theme becomes universal. In typical Akhmatova fashion, much is said in few words. Through the metaphor of a sheltering wing, the first two lines convey the idea that no matter where the foreign land may be, it promises comfort, refuge. One word, "unfortunately," in the last line, is enough to let the reader imagine that in the poet's own land the situation is grimmer; but this situation is unspecific and therefore universal—it could be war, natural catastrophe, or (as is implicit in the cycle) political oppression.

"Instead of a Preface," a short prose piece, introduces the cycle:

> In the terrible years of the Yezhov terror, I spent seventeen months in the prison lines of Leningrad. Once, someone "recognized" me. Then a woman with bluish lips standing behind me, who, of course, had never heard me called by name before, woke up from the stupor to which everyone had succumbed and whispered in my ear (everyone spoke in whispers there): "Can you describe this?" And I answered: "Yes, I can." Then something that looked like a smile passed over what had once been her face.

(I, p. 95)

Now Akhmatova fulfills her destiny as the voice of her people, taking on the persona of the village Wailer and the Madonna—the religious prototype for all mothers who must watch helplessly while their children suffer, somehow fulfilling an incomprehensible destiny. The mother can only provide comfort and prayer so that the pain and agony may be somehow alleviated.

The **"Dedication"** was written in March 1940, introducing the theme of "mortal woe" that permeates the cycle:

Mountains bow down to this grief,
Mighty rivers cease to flow,
But the prison gates hold firm,
And behind them are the "prisoners' burrows"
And mortal woe.
For someone a fresh breeze blows,
For someone the sunset luxuriates—
We wouldn't know, we are those who everywhere
Hear only the rasp of the hateful key
And the soldiers' heavy tread.
We rose as if for an early service,
Trudged through the savaged capital
And met there, more lifeless than the dead;
The sun is lower and the Neva mistier,
But hope keeps singing from afar.
The verdict . . . And her tears gush forth,
Already she is cut off from the rest,
As if they painfully wrenched life from her heart,

As if they brutally knocked her flat,
But she goes on . . . Staggering . . . Alone . . .
Where now are my chance friends
Of those two diabolical years?
What do they imagine is in Siberia's storms,
What appears to them dimly in the circle of the moon?
I am sending my farewell greeting to them.

(II, p. 97)

As Michael Basker has shown, the opening reveals that the natural order has been disrupted, part of a general pattern in the entire poetic cycle reflecting a disruption of the universe caused by the Terror.[6] The early lines evoking nature mourning in sympathy recall Akhmatova's earlier poem **"July 1914,"** part of a two-poem cycle, about another catastrophe, World War I:

"July 1914"

1

It smells of burning. For four weeks
The dry peat bog has been burning.
The birds have not even sung today,
And the aspen has stopped quaking. . . .

(I, p. 427)

Both reach back to the famous medieval Russian epic the *Igor Tale*. On the day of battle black clouds come in from the sea, streaks of blue lightning quiver within them, the birds in the oak trees lie in wait for misfortune, eagles screech and foxes yelp.[7]

Through literary allusion Akhmatova adds implicit interpretations to the text. The phrase "prisoners' burrows" refers to Pushkin's poem "Message to Siberia," where the poet encourages his exiled friends who participated in the Decembrist rebellion to have hope, "his free music pours round their prisoners' burrows," giving them faith. But Akhmatova's lines are bitterly ironic, for here "the prison gates hold firm," and hope is distant, "singing from afar."

Akhmatova progresses from seeing herself at first as one with the other women through most of the poem, to feeling cut off from them while still physically among them, to becoming totally detached, separate: "But she goes on . . . Staggering . . . Alone." The last lines bring us to the present (1940), as the poet asks where those friends are who came together not out of choice but by chance, because they shared one thing in common—they had come to communicate with loved ones in prison through the package they shoved through the little prison window.

The Prologue makes no direct allusion to the poet herself, but to all women:

"Prologue"

That was when the ones who smiled
Were the dead, glad to be at rest.
And like a useless appendage, Leningrad

Swung from its prisons.
And when, senseless from torment,
Regiments of convicts marched,
And the short songs of farewell
Were sung by locomotive whistles.
The stars of death stood above us
And innocent Rus writhed
Under bloody boots
And under the tires of the Black Marusyas.

(II, p. 99)

The first line leads us to believe a happy event is being described, but we soon learn that the only ones smiling are the dead. Implicit is the idea that those alive in this situation are going through an unbearable hell, while peace and rest come only to those already beyond. Although rare in Akhmatova's poetry, when simile is used it is a powerful device. Leningrad as a useless appendage becomes a city no longer fulfilling a useful function in life: it has become a city of the dead. Short songs of farewell become a simple, everyday symbol of the thousands leaving Leningrad for exile, for the trip the passengers are taking leads them to Siberia and the camps. Basker perceptively interprets the "stars of death" as the red stars above the Kremlin.

Instead of "Russia," Akhmatova purposely uses the term "Rus"—the medieval name for the territory which included parts of present-day Russia, Ukraine, and Belorussia. It was composed of wealthy city-states equaling Florence and Venice in power and beauty. In this way the poem is transformed from a description of one particular city during the Terror to a symbol of the entire land in historical and mythical time. This ancient land is now writhing under the boots and tires of the modern Soviet police state, conveyed by the metonymic image of the police vans called *chyrnaya Marusya* or the Black Marusya, taking prisoners away. This was not the big, black van known as *chyrnyi voron* ("black raven") which every Russian would recognize, similar to the American Black Maria, but a regular delivery truck carrying bread, milk, and other ordinary products.[8] The name "Marusya" is the village version of Maria, and lacks the more elevated overtones of Maria the Madonna, although the allusion to the Madonna is clear—the Black Marusya is a religious inversion. The Madonna is holy, with the ability to intercede between man and God, to bring comfort and solace to humanity; but the Black Marusya strikes terror and fear in the hearts of men and carries out the dark work of the forces of evil.

In **"Poem #1"** (1935), the poet compares herself to a peasant woman performing the ancient Russian ritual of *vynos*—the carrying out of the dead from the house to the vehicle that will take the body to the cemetery. Instead of a dead body, however, this time it is a live prisoner, someone beloved, perhaps on the biographical level Punin or Mandelstam.[9]

They led you away at dawn,
I followed you, like a mourner,
In the dark front room the children were crying,
By the icon shelf the candle was dying.
On your lips was the icon's chill.
The deathly sweat on your brow . . . Unforgettable!
I will be like the wives of the *Streltsy*,
Howling under the Kremlin towers.

(II, p. 99)

The *vynos* is one of several episodes in the funeral rite, which is accompanied by laments, usually sung by a professional wailer from the village, the *prichitalnitsa*. The laments are improvised recitatives, incorporating traditional stock phrases adapted by the lamenter to the person who has died and the woman who is grieving.

The clue that the speaker is from the peasant milieu is provided by the reference to the *gornitsa,* a special room where rich peasants received guests. The religious associations are conveyed through motifs such as icons, the sacred images painted on wood to which the Orthodox pray, and the *bozhnitsa* or icon shelf, placed in a special corner of the house where meals are held and rituals like match-making take place.

In the end the poet compares herself to the wives of the *Streltsy,* or Archers, the elite military corps employed by Sophia, Peter the Great's half sister. They supported Sophia in her fight for the throne in 1798 because they believed Peter was godless, the Anti-Christ who would destroy Russia. Their wives lamented for them under the Kremlin towers, and the event was immortalized in Vasily Surikov's famous nineteenth-century painting, *The Morning of the Execution of the Streltsy.*

In **"Poem #2"** a playful moon is contrasted with the lone figure of the suffering woman:

Quietly flows the quiet Don,
Yellow moon slips into a home.

He slips in with cap askew,
He sees a shadow, yellow moon.

This woman is ill,
This woman is alone,

Husband in the grave, son in prison,
say a prayer for me.

(II, p. 101)

The poem sounds like a nursery rhyme or lullaby—a Cossack lullaby because of the reference to the Don, where Cossacks lived. The phrase "quiet Don" connotes folklore since it is used in numerous historical songs.[10] For example, there is a famous soldiers' song in which the land has been ploughed with horses' hooves, sown with Cossack heads, and blossomed with orphans. It ends:

> What are the waves of the glorious quiet Don filled
>   with?
> The waves of the quiet Don are filled with fathers'
>   and mothers' tears.[11]

Cossack sons were constantly exposed to danger, which meant the women were subject to loss, to the pain of a "Husband in the grave, a son in prison." A "Husband in the grave" may refer to Gumilyov. The deceptively simple structure of the poem accounts for the shock that occurs when we learn only in the last line that the woman ill and alone is the poet herself. Suddenly the objective narrative is transformed into vividly personal perceptions.

"Poem #3" (1940) again shows how Akhmatova's use of structure influences the meaning and impact of a poem:

> No, it is not I, it is somebody else who is suffering.
> I would not have been able to bear what happened,
> Let them shroud it in black,
> And let them carry off the lanterns . . .
> Night.

> (II, p. 101)

Basker has explained that the regular structure of meter and rhyme in Russian is abandoned to represent the disintegration of the self. He adds that "The fourth line tails off with suspension points, and all development is halted by the single disruptive monosyllable of the fifth: *Noch* [Night]. The poem breaks off into another premature silence, the formal counterpart of unutterable darkness."[12]

The next poem, **"#4"** (no date), articulates the theme underlying *Poem Without a Hero,* that the "gay little sinner" and her whole generation would pay for their indifference to the sufferings of their land and their people:

> You should have been shown, you mocker,
> Minion of all your friends,
> Gay little sinner of Tsarskoye Selo,
> What would happen in your life—
> How three-hundredth in line, with a parcel,
> You would stand by the Kresty prison,
> Your tempestuous tears
> Burning through the New Year's ice.
> Over there the prison poplar bends,
> And there's no sound—and over there how many
> Innocent lives are ending now . . .

> (II, p. 101)

The poet herself pays by standing three-hundredth in line with her parcel by the Kresty [Crosses] prison. The name as well as the cross-shape of the prison evokes the Christian symbolism of the Cross, standing for atonement and redemption.

The poems ["**#5**," "**#6**," "**#7**," "**#8**," "**#9**"] (1939-40) trace the poet's state of mind, moving from a wish for death to being overcome by madness, which she welcomes because she hopes it will help her achieve oblivion, total forgetfulness. In **"#8," "To Death"** (1939), the speaker no longer wishes to reconcile herself to the situation and only begs for death to bring her comfort. It is a theme that has a long tradition in Russian literature. In Mussorgsky's song cycle *Songs and Dances of Death,* death brings peace to a soldier on the battlefield, to a sick child whose mother is grieving; and in Nekrasov's poem "Grandfather Frost," the cold brings comforting death to a poor peasant woman who has just buried her husband.

"To Death"

> You will come in any case—so why not now?
> I am waiting for you—I can't stand much more.
> I've put out the light and opened the door
> For you, so simple and miraculous.
> So come in any form you please,
> Burst in as a gas shell
> Or, like a gangster, steal in with a length of pipe,
> Or poison me with typhus fumes.
> Or be that fairy tale you've dreamed up—
> So sickeningly familiar to everyone—
> In which I glimpse the top of a pale blue cap
> And the house attendant white with fear.
> Now it doesn't matter anymore. The Yenisey swirls,
> The North Star shines.
> And the final horror dims
> The blue luster of beloved eyes.

> (II, p. 107)

The fairy tale that death may bring is not a harmless piece of fantasy, but what has by now become an "old story"—the search, arrest, exile, and perhaps death. The secret police wore light blue caps, and a house attendant had to be present at an arrest. The reference to the Yenisey River is not a stereotyped cliché of time being compared to a rolling river, but is directly associated with the Great Terror—the Yenisey is the site of many prison camps in Siberia, including Norilsk, where her son was exiled. As Etkind points out, this recalls a Mandelstam poem from the same period, "Beyond the thundering voice of future centuries" (1931):

> Lead me way into the night, where the Yenisey flows
> And the pine reaches to the stars
> Because I am not a wolf by blood
> And only someone my equal will be the death of me.[13]

The real subject of Akhmatova's poem is probably Mandelstam, especially since in 1939 she received the news that he had died.[14]

The cycle reaches its culmination in **"#10," "Crucifixion,"** consisting of two poems. The first was written in 1940:

"Crucifixion"

1

> "Do not weep for Me, Mother,
> I am in the grave."

A choir of angels sang the praises of that momentous
   hour,
And the heavens dissolved in fire.
To his Father He said: "Why hast Thou forsaken me!"
And to his Mother: "Oh, do not weep for Me . . ."

(II, p. 109)

The epigraph is in Church Slavonic, the sacred language
of the Orthodox Slavs. It is based on lines from the
ninth chant of the Holy Week service, which are "Do
not weep for Me, Mother, as you gaze upon the tomb."[15]
On the Cross, first expressing his human aspect, Christ
addresses God the Father, asking why he has been
abandoned and forced to experience the suffering of an
ordinary man: "Eloi, Eloi, lama sabachthani" (My God,
my God, why hast thou forsaken me? [Mark 15:34]).
But to his Mother he says, "Oh, do not weep for Me,"
because he knows he is divine and will be resurrected.
Christ must feel human pain, or his sacrifice is meaningless, but he suffers as part of a divine destiny in order
to bring salvation to humanity—therefore his mother
should not weep. In the Annunciation, Mary received
the message that her son would have a unique destiny
when she was told he would reign over the house of Jacob forever, "and of his kingdom there shall be no end"
(Luke 1:33).

Amanda Haight suggests that the cycle's second poem
(1943) illustrates different kinds of suffering:
Magdalene, the suffering of rebellion, John, the silent
suffering of one trying to kill memory and feeling; but
the Mother's suffering is so great no one can bear to
look at her.[16]

2

Mary Magdalene beat her breast and sobbed,
The beloved disciple turned to stone,
But where the silent Mother stood, there
No one glanced and no one would have dared.

(II, p. 111)

Akhmatova is faithful to the original description of the
apostle in John 19:26-27, where no specific person is
named: "When Jesus therefore saw his mother, and the
disciple standing by, whom he loved, he saith unto his
mother, 'Woman, behold thy son!' Then saith he to the
disciple, 'Behold thy mother!' And from that hour that
disciple took her unto his own home." Over the
centuries in depictions of the Crucifixion the disciple
has been portrayed as John. Akhmatova's version differs dramatically from the original. Here the disciple,
rather than acting as a comforter, himself becomes helpless, and the mother remains alone and unprotected.

In "Epilogue I" the poet reconfirms that hers is the
voice of all those who have experienced what she has.
The cycle ends with "Epilogue II," whose theme is
"remembrance," which would become a major motif in

Akhmatova's later works. Memory becomes a moral
imperative, for the indifference of her own generation
to the sufferings of the people, the years of Terror, is a
sin.

In the Orthodox ritual, Remembrance Day marks the
anniversary of the death of a member of the Orthodox
Church, and a service is held in his honor.[17] If the poet
is to be remembered by her country, she asks that it not
be near the sea, the scene of her childhood (Akhmatova
was born by the Black Sea and spent many of her childhood summers there), nor near the pine stump in the
tsar's garden. Presumably this refers to Tsarskoye Selo,
where Akhmatova grew up and spent her early married
years. Further, an allusion to a tree stump also appears
in her poem "Willow," written in 1940, the same year
as this poem, contrasting the tranquillity enveloping her
in the peaceful environment of Tsarskoye, of which the
silver willow is a symbol, and her later years, when the
tree is nothing but a stump—like the dead willow, the
tranquillity of Tsarskoye Selo has disappeared. Instead
of these happy allusions, though, the poet wishes her
monument to be where she stood for three hundred
hours—in front of the prison.

In the fifth stanza, she says she will weave a *pokrov*
(mantle) to protect the women who waited in line with
her:

I have woven a wide mantle for them
From their meager, overheard words.

I will remember them always and everywhere,
I will never forget them no matter what comes.

And if they gag my exhausted mouth
Through which a hundred million scream,

Then may the people remember me
On the eve of my remembrance day.

(II, p. 113)

The word *pokrov* evokes a network of associations in
Russian culture. It is connected with the holiday of
Intercession celebrated on October 1, the feast day commemorating Andrew, a "holy fool," gifted by madness
and prophecy, who had a vision of the Madonna in a
Byzantine church in Constantinople. The holiday is the
subject of many icons and the name of numerous Russian churches. The Madonna took off her mantle and
laid it over the congregation as a sign of her intercession between humanity and heaven, a gesture symbolizing her role as protector of the people. In the context
of *Requiem,* the word *pokrov* associates the poet with
the Madonna—Akhmatova becomes an intercessor and
voice of her people, although her mantle will be "woven
of words."

In the last stanza there is another covert biblical reference, this time an ironic allusion to the dove. Since the

time of Noah, the dove has been associated with peace and renewal of life; but in this poem we hear a "*prison dove*" cooing in the distance, caught like the prisoners in the nightmarish world of the Terror, while boats quietly sail on the Neva River, symbolic of people in the outside world who remain totally indifferent to the suffering of those inside Russia and inside the prison walls.

Akhmatova was afraid to write **Requiem** down. Lydia Chukovskaya, an author and daughter of the eminent critic Korney Chukovsky, was one of the few people to whom the poet recited the work when it was first composed, and who committed it to memory. Akhmatova would visit her and read her the poems in a whisper, but when Chukovskaya came to see her in her own apartment, Akhmatova would stop suddenly in the midst of a conversation and glance up at the ceiling and walls, where she assumed there were hidden microphones. Then she would say something quite ordinary like, "Would you like a cup of tea?", while scribbling swiftly on a piece of paper and handing it over. "Autumn is so early this year," Akhmatova would say, and after Chukovskaya had memorized the lines, Akhmatova would light a match and burn the paper in an ashtray.[18]

Chukovskaya first came to visit Akhmatova because her own husband, the brilliant physicist Matthew Bronstein, had been exiled, and Chukovskaya had heard about Akhmatova's letter to Stalin which resulted in the release of Punin and her son. She thought Akhmatova could give her good advice. However, times were different, and Akhmatova could no longer even help her own son.[19]

Chukovskaya kept a diary of her conversations with Akhmatova from 1939 to 1942, when they quarreled. In 1952, they became friends again and Chukovskaya continued her diary until Akhmatova's death in 1966. In her preface to the diaries, Chukovskaya mentions what an important role Akhmatova played in her own life:

> I felt drawn to write about her because she herself, her words and deeds, her head, shoulders and movements, her hands, possessed a perfection usually found in this world only in great works of art. The fate of Akhmatova—something more than her own particular personality—carved before my very eyes a statue of grief, orphanhood, pride and courage out of this famous and abandoned, strong and helpless woman. I had known Akhmatova's earlier poems by heart since childhood, but the new ones, together with the movements of her hands burning the paper above the ashtray, together with the aquiline profile standing out like a blue shadow on the white wall of the deportation prison, entered my life as naturally as long ago the bridge, St. Isaac's Cathedral, the Summer Garden or the Embankment had done.[20]

By this time Akhmatova perceived her relationship with Punin as disintegrating rapidly. In a poem written in 1936, she likens herself to a domesticated animal in his house:

> I hid my heart from you
> As if I had hurled it into the Neva.
> Wingless and domesticated,
> I live here in your home.
> Only . . . at night I hear creaking.
> What's there—in the strange gloom?
> The Sheremetev lindens . . .
> The roll call of the spirits of the house . . .
> Approaching cautiously,
> Like gurgling water,
> Misfortune's black whisper
> Nestles warmly to my ear—
> And murmurs, as if this were
> Its business for the night:
> "You wanted comfort,
> Do you know where it is—your comfort?"
>
> (II, p. 83)

According to Chukovskaya, Akhmatova finally left Punin on September 19, 1938. She said they had lived together for sixteen years.

Notes

1. Akhmatova, "Pages from a Diary," MHC [*My Half Century: Selected Prose,* ed. Ronald Meyer. Ann Arbor: Ardis, 1992], p. 13.

2. Nayman-Rosslyn [*Remembering Anna Akhmatova.* London: P. Halban, 1991], p. 127.

3. Milivoe Jovanovich, "K razboru . . . ," p. 171.

4. Joseph Brodsky, "The Keening Muse," in Brodsky, *Less Than One: Selected Essays* (New York: Farrar, Straus & Giroux, 1986), p. 51.

5. Amanda Haight, Akhmatova's first biographer, suggests that these lines harken back to the poems written right after the Revolution, such as "To the Many":

   > I—am your voice, the warmth of your breath,
   > I—am the reflection of your face,
   > The futile trembling of futile wings,
   > I am with you to the end, in any case.
   >
   > (I, p. 619)

   H-N [Amanda Haight. *Anna Akhmatova: A Poetic Pilgrimmage.* Oxford: Oxford University Press, 1990], p. 100.

6. Michael Basker, "Dislocation and Relocation in Akhmatova's *Rekviem,*" SUE [*The Speech of Unknown Eyes: Akhmatova's Readers on Her Poetry,* ed. Wendy Rosslyn. 2 vols. Nottingham: Astra Press, 1990], I, p. 9.

7. See "The Lay of Igor's Campaign," *The Heritage of Russian Verse,* p. 4.

8. In America the black prison van is known as "the Black Maria." A poem by Langston Hughes incorporates this image in his poem "Must be the Black Maria," in which the poet says he hopes "it ain't coming for me." See Langston Hughes, *Selected Poems of Langston Hughes* (New York: Vintage Books 1974,), p. 118.

9. In Akhmatova, "Mandelstam," MHC, p. 101, Akhmatova says she quoted lines from this poem when she was visiting Mandelstam, and he thanked her for them. However, she makes it clear she originally wrote it for Punin: "That poem is from *Requiem* and refers to the arrest of Nikolai Punin in 1935."

10. See Efim Etkind, "Die Unsterbichkeit des Gedachtnisses: Anna Achmatova's poem 'Requiem,'" *Die Welt der Slaven,* 29 (1984), p. 363.

11. Roberta Reeder, *Russian Folk Lyrics,* [Bloomington: Indiana University Press, 1993] p. 155.

12. Basker, "Dislocation," p. 11.

13. Trans. Roberta Reeder.

14. See Etkind, "Ob Fontanki," p. 373.

15. Zoya Tomashevskaya, "Introduction" to Anna Akhmatova, "Requiem," *Oktyabr,* no. 3 (1987), p. 130.

16. H-N, p. 105.

17. The Requiem service, called *pannykhida,* is held immediately after death, when the reading of the Psalter begins by the dead person's coffin. The body is later taken to a church burial, and a funeral service is held. A manual of the Orthodox Church's Divine Service describes the remembrance days— days set apart by the Church for the commemoration of all deceased Christians, apart from private commemoration of the deceased at the wish of friends and relatives. The services for these general days are called "Universal Requiems" and the days are called "ancestral days." One of the most important is on Monday or Tuesday of St. Thomas week, the week after Easter, when families go to the cemetery and feast at the side of the ancestral graves. D. Sokolof, *A Manual of the Orthodox Church's Divine Services* (Jordanville, N.Y.: Holy Trinity Monastery, 1975), p. 157.

18. Lydia Chukovskaya, ZAA [*Zapiski ob Anne Akhmatovoi.* Vol. I (1938-1941). Paris: YMCA Press, 1976. Vol. II (1952-1962). Paris: YMCA Press, 1980.], I, p. 8.

19. Ibid.

20. Ibid., p. 10. Chukovskaya recorded this conversation November 10, 1938.

David N. Wells (essay date 1996)

SOURCE: Wells, David N. "Stalinism and War: Works of the 1930s and 1940s." In *Anna Akhmatova: Her Poetry,* pp. 64-95. Oxford, England: Berg, 1996.

[*In the following excerpt, Wells discusses structure, theme, and inspirational sources of Akhmatova's* Requiem.]

Akhmatova's most sustained piece of overtly oppositional writing in the 1930s is the cycle *Requiem* (I, 359-70).[1] Although the epigraph and prose introduction to the cycle were both added later, the cycle as such was put together in 1940.[2] The poems which make it up appear to have been inspired by several different episodes in Akhmatova's biography. Although the most immediate impetus is clearly Akhmatova's experience, following her son's arrest in 1938, in the queues of women waiting outside prisons attempting to receive news of their imprisoned menfolk, there are also additional sources. The first of the ten numbered poems, **'Uvodili tebya na rassvete'** (**'They took you away at dawn'**, I, 363) is dated 1935, and according to Akhmatova's memoir of Mandelstam, refers to the arrest that year of Nikolai Punin (II, 181). Mandelstam, it appears, took this poem to refer to his own arrest. But the exact biographical referents are perhaps not important. Akhmatova, by combining them in her cycle has produced what is, in its own way, a comprehensive social history of the Terror, what Haight has called 'an organic unit documenting a precise progression through all the stages of suffering'.[3]

Although **Requiem** has no plot in any conventional sense, the ten numbered poems which form its centre do represent a process of emotional change. They do this through a lyrical examination of a series of emotional states presented in a chronological sequence which is rendered coherent by the two unnumbered introductory poems entitled **'Posvyashchenie'** (**'Dedication'**) and **'Vstuplenie'** (**'Introduction'**). **'Dedication'** in particular not only makes it clear that the poems which follow are written in the name of a large and anonymous group of women, but also specifies the time frame of the cycle:

> Gde teper' nevol'nye podrugi
> Dvukh moikh osatanelykh let?

> Where now are the chance friends
> Of those two demoniacal years?

'Introduction', on the other hand, focuses rather on place:

> I nenuzhnym priveskom boltalsya
> Vozle tyurem svoikh Leningrad.

> And Leningrad dangled around its prisons
> Like a useless appendage.

By later referring more broadly to the sufferings of 'Rus'', it affirms that the description of Leningrad is meant to stand also for the entire country.

The central section of the poem begins with an arrest, laconically described in the first line of poem **No. 1**: 'They took you away at dawn.' The scene is likened to a funeral, but a note of defiance is implied by the heroine's comparison of herself to the wives of the Strel'tsy in the last two lines:

> Budu ya, kak streletskie zhenki,
> Pod kremlevskimi bashnyami vyt'.

> Like the wives of the Strel'tsy
> I shall howl under the Kremlin towers.

In the poems which follow, however, this defiance gives way to passivity and to a gradual breakdown of personality. In the second poem the speaker sees herself partly as someone else:

> Eta zhenshchina bol'na,
> Eta zhenshchina odna,
> Muzh v mogile, syn v tyur'me,
> Pomolites' obo mne.

> This woman is ill,
> This woman is alone,
> Son in prison, husband in the grave,
> Pray for me.

And in the third poem the gap between mental processes that predate the arrest and the current reality is rendered explicit. The speaker is unable to believe that it is indeed her own actions that she is watching:

> Net, eto ne ya, eto kto-to drugoi stradaet.
> Ya by tak ne mogla

> No, it is not I, it is somebody else who is suffering
> I should not have been able to bear it.

The fourth poem marks a particular stage in the history of individual prisoners—their mothers and wives queuing outside the Kresty prison in Leningrad in order to hand over parcels, and shows the speaker, more resignedly now, contrasting her present fate with her life in earlier years. The fifth, explicitly situated seventeen months after the arrest, shows increasing disorientation:

> Vse pereputalos' navek,
> I mne ne razobrat'
> Teper', kto zver', kto chelovek

> Everything has been muddled for ever,
> And now I cannot work out
> Who is a beast and who is a human being.

This is also reflected in the sixth poem. The seventh, entitled **'Prigovor'** (**'Sentence'**), initiates a further new stage. Notification that her son has been sentenced—presumably to death—throws the speaker back into despair:

> I upalo kamennoe slovo
> Na moyu eshche zhivuyu grud'.

> And the word fell like a stone
> On my still living breast.

She is led into another round of denial and suppression of her emotions:

> U menya segodnya mnogo dela:
> Nado pamyat' do kontsa ubit',
> Nado, chtob dusha okamenela,
> Nado snova nauchit'sya zhit'

> Today I have many things to do:
> I must kill my memory off completely,
> My heart must turn to stone,
> I must relearn how to live.

The next two poems deal with different and more extreme manifestations of despair: in the first ('**No. 8**') the speaker invites death to come to her to release her from her torments; in the second ('**No. 9**') it is insanity which is seen as the only possible form of consolation even though it will remove all memories of the past, the welcome as well as the terrible.

Up to this point the numbered poems of the narrative sequence had been written almost entirely in the first person. (The exceptions are **'No. 2'**, which is written partly in the third person, and **'No. 4'**, which is written as a second-person address by the speaker to herself.) The tenth and final poem of the inner narrative, which represents the carrying out of the sentence passed in the seventh poem, that is the execution of the heroine's son, switches to the third person, discursively reflecting her inability to speak after this latest shock. In order to describe this culmination of the narrative, Akhmatova has recourse to Biblical history and finds a model in the crucifixion of Jesus, and particularly in the responses of female figures—Mary Magdalene and Mary the Mother of Jesus—to the crucifixion:

> Magdalina bilas' i rydala,
> Uchenik lyubimyi kamenel,
> A tuda, gde molcha Mat' stoyala,
> Tak nikto vzglyanut' i ne posmel.

> Mary Magdelene beat her breast and sobbed,
> The beloved disciple turned to stone,
> But no one even dared to look
> At where the Mother stood in silence.

Haight has suggested that the three figures here represent three different stages of suffering: Mary Magdalene the defiance of poem **'No. 1'**, John the beloved disciple the paralysis of, for example, **'No. 7'**, and Mary the Mother a deep understanding arrived at by passing through all stages.[4] The silence of Mary the Mother at the moment of the crucifixion, however, may represent not so much wisdom as a state of catatonia induced in her, as in the first-person heroine of the narrative, by the finality of her son's death.

However, invoking the crucifixion is not merely a method for projecting the sufferings of women in Russia in the late 1930s on to a universal plane. In theological terms the crucifixion implies the resurrection, and the memorialising function of the *Requiem* cycle foreshadowed in 'Dedication' (and affirmed in the introductory prose passage added in 1957) is rendered explicit in the two poems which form its **'Epilogue'**. Having passed through the Terror documented in the ten poems of the narrative, the speaker finds she has survived and is able to record the experience of her sisters:

> I ya molyus' ne o sebe odnoi,
> A obo vsekh, kto tam stoyal so mnoyu,
> I v lyutyi kholod, i v iyul'skii znoi,
> Pod krasnoyu oslepsheyu stenoyu.

> And I pray not for myself alone,
> But for all those who stood there with me
> In the bitter cold and in the heat of July
> Under that blind red wall.

The final poem contains an affirmation of the power of words to recall the female, indirect victims of Stalinism and also an assertion that the act of recalling has its own therapeutic and protective effect:

> Dlya nikh sotkala ya shirokii pokrov
> Iz bednykh, u nikh zhe podslushannykh slov.

> For them I have woven a broad shroud
> From poor words, overheard from them.

Having established the power of such a monument, Akhmatova then, secure in the knowledge of its durability, turns to the question of a sculptural monument to herself as the author of *Requiem*. In considering where such a monument should be placed, Akhmatova rejects locations that have associations with her life and poetry before *Requiem*—the Black Sea coast and the park at Tsarskoe Selo—and insists that it should be outside the prison walls in Leningrad, so that even in death she should not forget the events of the 1930s. This choice too marks a partial rejection of the poetry of Akhmatova's youth now that her pen has found its vocation as public chronicler of the Terror.

The superficial clarity and simplicity of the *Requiem* cycle belie a considerable underlying complexity of imagery, allusion and compositional technique. As Michael Basker has argued, the disorientation of the heroine is mirrored stylistically in the cycle in many ways.[5] Most obviously, there is no unequivocal link between the various poems that make up *Requiem*: they vary greatly in length, metrical format and rhyme scheme; they do not maintain unity of place—some are clearly set in Leningrad, while others are on the river Don (**'No. 2'**) or in Biblical Palestine (**'No. 10'**); they do not contain a consistent narrative viewpoint, chang-ing abruptly, for example, between the first and third person (**'Dedication'**, **'No. 2'**). Much of the imagery is similarly dislocated, even verging on the surreal, as in the opening lines of **'Dedication'**:

> Pered etim gorem gnutsya gory,
> Ne techet velikaya reka.

> Mountains bend down before this grief,
> The great river does not flow.

or the description of prisoners in **'Introduction'**:

> Shli uzhe osuzhdennykh polki,
> I korotkuyu pesnyu razluki
> Parovoznye peli gudki.

> Regiments of the already condemned were marching
> And the whistles of steam engines
> Sang brief songs of farewell.

This is much more nearly the Leningrad of Nikolai Zabolotskii than of Akhmatova's early poems. Expressions from different semantic registers are placed in juxtaposition. Thus 'Rus'' ('Russia') is made to rhyme with 'chernykh marus'' ('black marias'); in **'No. 8'** (**'To Death'**) terms of Soviet *realia*—'verkh shapki goluboi' ('the top of a pale blue cap', alluding to the NKVD uniform), and 'upravdom' ('house manager')—appear in the middle of an otherwise broadly abstract invocation of death. The religious metaphors which abound in the cycle serve to highlight the enormity of events by their incongruity: 'Kresty' ('Crosses') is the name of a prison (**'No. 4'**); the scene of arrest is compared to a funeral (**'No. 1'**). Even the title of the work, *Requiem,* with its associations above all with Catholic Christianity and the civilisation of western Europe, sits uneasily with the Orthodox tradition evoked in the poems themselves by references, for example, to icons (**'No. 1'**), to the 'pominal'nye dni' ('remembrance days') of the Orthodox funeral ritual (**'Epilogue'**) and to the language of the Church Slavonic Bible: 'Ottsu skazal: "Pochto Menya ostavil!" / A Materi: "O, ne rydai Mene . . ."' ('To the Father he said, "Why hast thou forsaken me", but to his Mother, "Oh, do not weep for me . . .", **'No. 10'**). The numerous allusions to Old Russia further serve to set the work in an Orthodox historical context rather than in a more broadly European one.

At the same time, as with the early books discussed in chapter three, the architectonics of the cycle are calculated with deliberate rhetorical precision. Various schemes have been devised to show a symmetry of themes and images around a central poem operating as a pivot.[6] While these are apt to overstate their case, at the very least it can be said that the ten 'narrative' poems are situated within a symmetrical framework of two introductory and two concluding poems which emphasise the courage and persistence of Russian women outside the prisons of the 1930s and lay great weight on the power of poetry to record their sufferings and to transcend them. The 'narrative' sequence is organised around three points of transformation, beginning with an arrest (**'No. 1'**), ending with an execution (**'No. 10'**) and articulating itself around the seventh poem, in which the sentence is pronounced.

As might be expected from a knowledge of Akhmatova's early poems, the superficially limpid poetry of **Requiem** is rich in evocations of other literary works. Allusions have been detected to a very wide range of authors from Euripides, Dante and Shakespeare to Tyutchev, Nekrasov and Mayakovskii.[7] The most salient is highlighted by Akhmatova herself when she places quotation marks around a phrase from Pushkin which occurs in **'Dedication'**:

> No krepki tyuremnye zatvory,
> A za nimi 'katorzhnye nory'

> But the prison bolts are firm,
> And behind them lie the 'convicts' burrows'.

Pushkin's 1827 poem 'Vo glubine sibirskikh rud' ('In the depths of the Siberian mines'), from which the quoted phrase is taken, is addressed to the participants of the abortive Decembrist uprising.

Pushkin's poem was designed to encourage the convicted Decembrists and to reassure them that the ideals of freedom which they had attempted unsuccessfully to uphold were still alive in the outside world and would eventually prevail. The poem concludes:

> Lyubov' i druzhestvo do vas
> Doidut skvoz' mrachnye zatvory,
> Kak v vashi katorzhnye nory
> Dokhodit moi svobodnyi glas.
> Okovy tyazhkie padut,
> Temnitsy rukhnut—i svoboda
> Vas primet radostno u vkhoda,
> I brat'ya mech vam otdadut.[8]

> Love and friendship will reach you
> Past the sombre bolts,
> As my free voice reaches you
> In your convicts' burrows.
> Your heavy fetters will fall,
> Your dungeons will collapse,
> And freedom will greet you at the entrance,
> And your brothers will give you back your sword.

The position in **Requiem,** however, is quite different. The prisons of the GULag are seen as impenetrable ('But the prison bolts are firm'); there is no hope of Akhmatova's voice reaching them, and it is to the survivors that the cycle is addressed. The contrast with Pushkin's poem, as Basker notes, throws 'into emphatic relief the utter bleakness of the modern period'.[9]

Similar effects are achieved by other references to external texts throughout **Requiem.** The pathos of the description of the woman crushed by the totalitarian state in poem **'No. 2'** is increased by its overtly folkloric language, alluding to a pre-industrial world. The invocation of death in **'No. 8'** achieves a particular intensification of emotion from its similarities to Pushkin's appeal to a dead lover in his poem 'Zaklinanie' ('Incantation') and from parallels in a poem by Chénier, 'Vienne, vienne la mort!—Que la mort me délivre' ('Let death come!—Let death deliver me'), with its appeals to the notions of justice and truth.[10] As Amert has noted, there are also ironic allusions to works of officially promoted Soviet literature which project a contented world grotesquely at variance with the one described by Akhmatova. In **'Dedication',** for example, the lines 'Dlya kogo-to veet veter svezhii, / Dlya kogo-to nezhitsya zakat' ('For someone a fresh wind is blowing, For someone the sunset is luxurious') are a contemptuous echo of Vasilii Lebedev-Kumach's widely disseminated hymn to Stalinism, 'Pesnya o rodine' ('Song of the Motherland'), written in 1935, and in particular the lines:

> Nad stranoi vesennii veter veet,
> S kazhdym dnem vse radostnee zhit'.[11]

> A spring wind is blowing across the country,
> With every day life is more joyous.

Another function of literary allusion in **Requiem** is to indicate and memorialise poets known personally to Akhmatova who became victims of Soviet repression. There are, for example, several more or less direct allusions to the work of Mandelstam and Gumilev, who were by this stage completely unable to reach an audience directly.[12]

Notes

1. The work has also, with some reason, been called a narrative poem (*poema*). For a discussion of its genre see E. Etkind, 'Bessmertie pamyati. Poema Anna Akhmatovoi *Rekviem*', *Studia Slavica Finlandensia,* vol. 8, 1991, pp. 100-3.

2. One poem, 'Eto bylo, kogda ulybalsya', although written in 1940, was not included in the cycle until 1962, see Chukovskaya, *Zapiski,* vol. 1, p. 65.

3. Haight, *Anna Akhmatova*, p. 100.

4. Ibid., p. 105.

5. M. Basker, 'Dislocation and Relocation in Akhmatova's *Rekviem*', in Rosslyn, *The Speech of Unknown Eyes,* vol. 1, pp. 5-25.

6. Etkind, 'Bessmertie pamyati'; A. L. Crone, 'Antimetabole in *Rekviem*: The Structural Disposition of Themes and Motifs', in Rosslyn, *The Speech of Unknown Eyes,* vol. 1, pp. 27-41.

7. See M. Jovanović, 'K razboru "chuzhikh golosov" v *Rekvieme* Akhmatovoi', *Russian Literature,* vol. 15, 1984, pp. 169-81; Etkind, 'Bessmertie pamyati'; M. M. Kralin, 'Nekrasovskaya traditsiya u Anny Akhmatovoi', *Nekrasovskii sbornik,* no. 8, 1983, pp. 74-86.

8. Pushkin, *PSS,* vol. 3, p. 7.

9. Basker, in Rosslyn, *The Speech of Unknown Eyes,* p. 14.

10. Ibid., pp. 17-18; Pushkin, *PSS,* vol. 3, p. 193; Etkind, 'Bessmertie pamyati', pp. 114-15.

11. See S. Amert, *In a Shattered Mirror: The Later Poetry of Anna Akhmatova,* Stanford, Calif. 1992, pp. 42-3.

12. See Basker, in Rosslyn, *The Speech of Unknown Eyes.*

Select Bibliography

Akhmatova, A. A., *Vecher,* St Petersburg, 1912.

—, *Chetki,* St Petersburg, 1914.

—, *Belaya staya,* Petrograd, 1917.

—, *Podorozhnik,* Petrograd, 1921.

—, *U samogo morya,* Petrograd, 1921.

—, *Anno Domini MCMXXI,* Petrograd, 1921.

—, *Anno Domini,* 2nd edn, Petrograd, 1923.

—, *Iz shesti knig,* Leningrad, 1940.

—, *Izbrannoe,* Tashkent, 1943.

—, *Izbrannye stikhi,* Moscow, 1946 (edition not released to the public).

—, *Stikhotvoreniya 1909-1945,* Moscow, 1946 (edition not released to the public).

—, *Stikhotvoreniya,* Moscow, 1958.

—, *Stikhotvoreniya (1909-1960),* Moscow, 1961.

—, *Beg vremeni,* Moscow, 1965.

—, 'Avtobiograficheskaya proza', *Literaturnoe obozrenie,* no. 5, 1989, pp. 3-17.

—, 'Otryvok iz perevoda "Makbeta"', *Literaturnoe obozrenie,* no. 5, 1989, pp. 18-21.

Amert, S., 'Akhmatova's "Pushkin i nevskoe vzmor'e"', *Transactions of the Association of Russian-American Scholars in the U.S.A.,* vol. 23, 1990, pp. 193-211.

—, *In a Shattered Mirror: The Later Poetry of Anna Akhmatova,* Stanford, Calif., 1992.

Annenkov, Yu., *Dnevnik moikh vstrech: tsikl tragedii,* Leningrad, 2 vols, 1991.

Bazhenov, M. N., 'Anna Akhmatova—Osip Mandel'shtam: biobibliografiya', *Sovetskaya bibliografiya,* no. 2, 1991, pp. 86-100.

Berlin, I., *Personal Impressions,* London, 1980.

Bobyshev, D., 'Akhmatova i emigratsiya', *Zvezda,* no. 2, 1991, pp. 177-80.

Bowra, C. M., *Poetry and Politics, 1900-1960,* Cambridge, 1966.

Braun, E., *The Theatre of Meyerhold: Revolution on the Modern Stage,* London, 1979.

Brown, C., *Mandelstam,* Cambridge, 1973.

Childers, R. and A. L. Crone, 'The Mandel'štam Presence in the Dedications of Poèma bez geroja', *Russian Literature,* vol. 15, 1984, pp. 51-82.

Chukovskaya, L. K., *Zapiski ob Anne Akhmatovoi,* vol. 1, Paris, 1976; vol. 2, Paris, 1980.

Chukovskii, K., 'Chitaya Akhmatovu', *Moskva,* no. 5, 1964, pp. 200-3.

Chumakov, Yu. N., 'Ob avtorskikh primechaniyakh k "Evgeniyu Oneginu"', *Boldinskie chteniya,* Gor'kii, 1976, pp. 58-72.

Crone, A. L., 'Blok as Don Juan in Akhmatova's "Poema bez geroia"', *Russian Language Journal,* nos. 121-2, 1981, pp. 147-55.

Dedyulin, S., "Maloizvestnoe interv'yu Anny Akhmatovoi', *Voprosy literatury,* no. 7, 1978, pp. 313-14.

Dedyulin S. and G. Superfin (eds), *Akhmatovskii sbornik,* vol. 1, Paris, 1989.

Dodero Costa, M. L. (ed.), *Anna Achmatova (1889-1966): Atti del Convegno nel centenario della nascita, Torino, Villa Gualino, 12-13 dicembre 1989,* Allessandria, 1992.

Doherty, J., *The Acmeist Movement in Russian Poetry: Culture and the Word,* Oxford, 1995.

Driver, S., *'Axmatova's Poèma bez geroja* and Blok's *Vozmezdie',* in W. N. Vickery (ed.), *Aleksandr Blok Centenary Conference,* Columbus, Ohio, 1984, pp. 89-99.

Dzhandzhakova, E. V., 'Smuglyi otrok brodil po alleyam', *Russkaya rech',* no. 5, 1976, pp. 16-19.

Eikhenbaum, B., *Anna Akhmatova: opyt analiza,* Petrograd, 1922.

Ecker, N., 'Elemente der Volksdichtung in der Lyrik Anna Achmatovas', unpublished D.Phil. thesis, University of Vienna, 1973.

Erdmann-Pandžić, E. von, *'Poèma bez geroja'von Anna A. Achmatova: Varientenedition und Interpretation von Symbolstrukturen,* Cologne, 1987.

Etkind, E., 'Bessmertie pamyati. Poema Anny Akhmatovoi Rekviem', *Studia Slavica Finlandensia,* vol. 8, 1991, pp. 98-133.

Faryno, J., 'Kod Akhmatovoi', *Russian Literature,* vol. 7/8, 1974, pp. 83-102.

—, 'Akhmatova's *Poem Without a Hero* as a *Moneta* and as a Revelation, *Essays in Poetics,* vol. 16, no. 2, 1991, pp. 75-93.

Genin, L., 'Akhmatova i tsarskaya tsenzura', *Zvezda,* no. 4, 1967, pp. 203-4.

Gershtein, E. G., 'Memuary i fakty (ob osvobozhdenii L'va Gumileva)', *Russian Literary Triquarterly,* no. 13, 1975, pp. 645-57.

—, 'Posleslovie', in A. Akhmatova, *O Pushkine,* Leningrad, 1977, pp. 277-317.

—, *Novoe o Mandel'shtame,* Paris, 1986.

Ginzburg, L. Ya., *O starom i novom: stat'i i ocherki,* Leningrad, 1982.

Graf-Schneider, M., '"Musa" dans l'oeuvre d'Anna Akhmatova', *Slavica Helvetica,* vol. 16, 1981, pp. 187-203.

Haight, A., *Anna Akhmatova: A Poetic Pilgrimage,* New York, 1976.

Hartman, A., 'The Metrical Typology of Anna Akhmatova', in L. Leighton (ed.), *Studies in Honor of Xenia Gasiorowska,* Columbus, Ohio, 1982, pp. 112-23.

Ivanova, L. V., *Vospominaniya: kniga ob ottse,* Moscow, 1992.

Jovanović, M., 'K razboru "chuzhikh golosov" v *Rekvieme* Akhmatovoi', *Russian Literature,* vol. 15, 1984, pp. 169-81.

Kaji, S., 'O slavoslovii Anny Akhmatovoi', *Japanese Slavic and East European Studies,* vol. 12, 1991, pp. 45-60.

Karpiak, R., 'The Sequels to Pushkin's *Kamennyi gost*': Russian Don Juan Versions by Nikolai Gumilev and Vladimir Korvin-Piotrovskii', in S. D. Cioran, W. Smyrniw, G. Thomas (eds), *Studies in Honour of Louis Shein,* Hamilton, Ont., 1983, pp. 79-92.

Kats, B. and R. D. Timenchik, *Anna Akhmatova i muzyka: issledovatel'skie ocherki,* Leningrad, 1989.

Kelly, C., *A History of Russian Women's Writing, 1820-1992,* Oxford, 1994.

Ketchian, S. I., 'Akhmatova's Civic Poem "Stansy" and its Pushkinian Antecedent', *Slavic and East European Journal,* vol. 37, no. 2, 1993, pp. 194-210.

— (ed.), *Anna Akhmatova 1889-1989: Papers from the Akhmatova Centennial Conference, Bellagio Study and Conference Center, June 1989,* Oakland, Calif., 1993.

Kolmogorov, A. N. and A. V. Prokhorov, 'O dol'nike sovremennoi russkoi poezii', *Voprosy yazykoznaniya,* no. 6, 1963, pp. 84-95 and no. 1, 1964, pp. 75-94.

Kralin, M. M., 'Nekrasovskaya traditsiya u Anny Akhmatovoi', *Nekrasovskii sbornik,* no. 8, 1983, pp. 74-86.

— (ed.), *Ob Anne Akhmatovoi: stikhi, esse, vospominaniya,* Leningrad, 1990.

Kushner, A., *Apollon v snegu: zametki na polyakh,* Leningrad, 1991.

Landsman, I. M. and E. B. Naumov, 'Iz nablyudenii nad yazykom A. Akhmatovoi', *Voprosy russkogo i obshchego yazykoznaniya* (Sbornik nauchnykh trudov (Tashkentskii un-t), 580), 1979, pp. 75-82.

Leiter, S., *Akhmatova's Petersburg,* Cambridge, 1983.

Lisnyanskaya, I., *Muzyka 'Poemy bez geroya' Anny Akhmatovoi,* Moscow, 1991.

Loseff, L. and B. Scherr (eds), *A Sense of Place: Tsarskoe Selo and its Poets: Papers from the 1989 Dartmouth Conference Dedicated to the Centennial of Anna Akhmatova,* Columbus, Ohio, 1993.

Luknitskaya, V. K., *Nikolai Gumilev: zhizn' poeta po materialam domashnego arkhiva sem'i Luknitskikh,* Leningrad, 1990.

—, *Pered toboi—zemlya,* Leningrad, 1990.

—(ed.), 'Rannie pushkinskie shtudii Anny Akhmatovoi (po materialam arkhiva P. Luknitskogo)', *Voprosy literatury,* no. 1, 1978, pp. 185-228.

Luknitskii, P. N., *Acumiana: vstrechi s Annoi Akhmatovoi,* vol. 1, Paris, 1991.

Maksimov, D. E., 'Akhmatova o Bloke', *Zvezda,* no. 12, 1967, pp. 187-91.

Mandel'shtam, N. Ya., *Vospominaniya,* 3rd edn, Paris, 1982.

—, *Vtoraya kniga,* 4th edn, Paris, 1987.

—, *Kniga tret'ya,* Paris, 1987.

Meilakh, M. B. and V. N. Toporov, 'Akhmatova i Dante', *International Journal of Slavic Linguistics and Poetics,* vol. 15, 1972, pp. 29-75.

Metcalf, A. and J. Neville, '1940: Not So Much a Thaw—More a Change in the Air', in M. Pavlyshyn (ed.), *Glasnost' in Context: On the Recurrence of Liberalizations in East European Literatures and Cultures,* New York, 1990, pp. 117-26.

Nabokov, V. (ed.), *Eugene Onegin,* 4 vols, rev. edn, London, 1975.

Naiman, A., *Rasskazy o Anne Akhmatovoi,* Moscow, 1989.

—, 'Uroki poeta', *Literaturnaya gazeta,* 14 June 1989, p. 8.

Panchenko, A. M. and N. V. Gumileva (eds), 'Perepiska A. A. Akhmatovoi s L. N. Gumilevym', *Zvezda,* no. 4, 1994, pp. 170-88.

Pavlovskii, A. I., *Anna Akhmatova: zhizn' i tvorchestvo,* Moscow, 1991.

Reeder, R. (ed.), *The Complete Poems of Anna Akhmatova,* trans. Judith Hemschemeyer, 2 vols, Somerville, Mass., 1990, pp. 21-183.

—, *Anna Akhmatova: Poet and Prophet,* New York, 1994.

Reeve, F. D., *Aleksandr Blok: Between Image and Idea,* New York, 1962.

Roskina, N., *Chetyre glavy: iz literaturnykh vospominanii,* Paris, 1980.

Rosslyn, W. A., *The Prince, the Fool and the Nunnery: The Religious Theme in the Early Poetry of Anna Akhmatova,* Amersham, 1984.

—, 'Don Juan Feminised', in A. McMillin (ed.), *Symbolism and After: Essays on Russian Poetry in Honour of Georgette Donchin,* London, 1992, pp. 102-21.

— (ed.), *The Speech of Unknown Eyes: Akhmatova's Readers on her Poetry,* 2 vols, Nottingham, 1990.

Sandler, S., 'The Stone Guest: Akhmatova, Pushkin and Don Juan', *Stanford Slavic Studies,* vol. 4, no. 2, 1992, pp. 35-49.

Satin, M. R., 'Akhmatova's "Shipovnik Tsvetet": A study of Creative Method', unpublished Ph.D. thesis, University of Pennsylvania, 1977.

Saulenko, L. L., 'Pushkinskaya traditsiya v "Poeme bez geroya" Anny Akhmatovoi', *Voprosy russkoi literatury* (L'vov), vol. 36, no. 2, 1980, pp. 42-50.

—, 'Imya knigi (o traditsii v poetike A. Akhmatovoi)', *Voprosy russkoi literatury* (L'vov), vol. 40, no. 1, 1984, pp. 89-94.

Shilov, L., *Anna Akhmatova (100 let so dnya rozhdeniya),* Moscow, 1989.

Subbotin, A., 'Mayakovskii i Akhmatova', *Ural,* no. 6, 1983, pp. 177-84.

—, *Gorizonty poezii,* Sverdlovsk, 1984.

Sukhanova, M., 'Fuga temporum', *Russian Literature,* vol. 30, 1991, pp. 337-42.

Thompson, R. D. B., 'The Anapaestic Dol'nik in the Poetry of Axmatova and Gumilev', in D. Mickiewicz (ed.), *Toward a Definition of Acmeism (Russian Language Journal,* Supplementary Issue), East Lansing, Mich., 1975, pp. 42-58.

Timenchik, R. D., 'Akhmatova i Pushkin: razbor stikhotvoreniya "Smuglyi otrok brodil po alleyam"', *Pushkinskii sbornik,* Riga, 1968, pp. 124-31.

—, 'Akhmatova i Pushkin: zametki k teme', *Pushkinskii sbornik,* no. 2, Riga, 1974, pp. 35-48.

—, 'Rizhskii epizod v "Poeme bez geroya" Anny Akhmatovoi', *Daugava,* no. 80, 1984, pp. 113-21.

— (ed.), *Anna Akhmatova: Desyatye gody,* Moscow, 1989.

— (ed.), *Anna Akhmatova: Requiem,* Moscow, 1989.

Timenchik, R. D., V. N. Toporov and T. V. Tsiv'yan, 'Akhmatova i Kuzmin', *Russian Literature,* vol. 6, 1978, pp. 213-305.

Tlusty, I. A., 'Anna Akhmatova and the Composition of her *Poema bez geroya* 1940-1962', unpublished D.Phil. thesis, University of Oxford, 1984.

Toporov, V. N., *Akhmatova i Blok (k probleme postroeniya poeticheskogo dialoga: 'blokovskii' tekst Akhmatovoi),* Berkekey, 1981.

—, 'Ob istorizme Akhmatovoi', *Russian Literature,* vol. 28, 1990, pp. 277-418.

Toporov, V. N. and T. V. Tsiv'yan, 'O nervalianskom podtekste v russkom akmeizme (Akhmatova i Mandel'shtam)', *Russian Literature,* vol. 15, 1984, pp. 29-50.

Tsiv'yan, T. V., 'Zametki k deshirovke "Poemy bez geroya"', *Trudy po znakovym sistemam,* no. 5, 1971, pp. 255-77.

Verheul, K., *The Theme of Time in the Poetry of Anna Axmatova,* The Hague, 1971.

—, 'Public Themes in the Poetry of Anna Axmatova', in J. van der Eng-Liedmeier and K. Verheul (eds), *Tale Without a Hero and Twenty-Two Poems by Anna Axmatova,* The Hague, 1973, pp. 9-46.

Vilenkin, V. Ya., *V sto pervom zerkale,* 2nd edn, Moscow, 1990.

—, 'Obraz "teni" v poetike Anny Akhmatovoi', *Voprosy literatury,* no. 1, 1994, pp. 57-76.

Vinogradov, V., *O poezii Anny Akhmatovoi (stilisticheskie nabroski),* Leningrad, 1925.

Wells, D. N., 'Folk Ritual in Anna Akhmatova's *Poema bez geroya*', *Scottish Slavonic Review,* no. 7, 1986, pp. 69-88.

—, 'Akhmatova and Pushkin: The Genres of Elegy and Ballad', *Slavonic and East European Review,* vol. 71, no. 4, 1993, pp. 631-45.

—, *Akhmatova and Pushkin: The Pushkin Contexts of Akhmatova's Poetry,* Birmingham, 1994.

Zhirmunskii, V. M., *Voprosy teorii literatury,* Leningrad, 1928.

—, *Tvorchestvo Anny Akhmatovoi,* Leningrad, 1973.

Zykov, L., 'Nikolai Punin—adresat i geroi liriki Anny Akhmatovoi', *Zvezda,* no. 1, 1995, pp. 77-114.

Boris Katz (essay date April 1998)

SOURCE: Katz, Boris. "To What Extent is *Requiem* a Requiem? Unheard Female Voices in Anna Akhmatova's *Requiem.*" *The Russian Review* 57, no. 2 (April 1998): 253-63.

[*In the following essay, Katz traces musical, literary, and religious subtexts in Akhmatova's* Requiem.]

> Some cry up Haydn, some Mozart,
> Just as the whim bites. For my part,
> I do not care a farthing candle
> For either of them, nor for Handel.
> Cannot a man live free and easy,
> Without admiring Pergolesi?
>
> —Charles Lamb, "Free Thoughts on Several Eminent
> Composers" (1830).

It is obvious that not every poet would share Charles Lamb's attitude toward music in general, and toward "several eminent composers" in particular. Anna Akhmatova certainly would not. There is no need to cite a great deal of evidence; it is sufficient to recall one passage from the memoirs of Anatoly Naiman, a Russian poet who was close to Akhmatova in her later years. The passage presents a good picture of Akhmatova's diverse and selective preferences in the world of music:

> At the head of the truckle-bed was a low table with an electric record player: either I had hired it locally or someone had brought it from town. She listened to music frequently and for long periods; she listened to various kinds of music, but sometimes she would be especially interested in a particular piece or pieces for a certain time. In the summer of 1963 it was the Beethoven's sonatas, in the autumn—Vivaldi; in the summer of 1964—Shostakovich's *Eighth Quartet,* in the spring of 1963—Pergolesi's *Stabat Mater,* and in the summer and autumn—Monteverdi's *L'incoronazione di Poppea* and, especially often, Purcell's *Dido and Aeneas,* the British recording with Schwartzkopf. She liked listening to Beethoven's *Bagatelles,* much of Chopin (played by Sofronitskii), *The Four Seasons* and other Vivaldi's concertos, and also Bach, Mozart, Haydn, and Handel. As we know, Vivaldi's *Adagio* appears in **Midnight Verses**: "We shall meet again in music, in Vivaldi's bold *Adagio.*" One day she asked me to find some music on the radio for a change. I began moving the needle along the dial and observed aloud that it was all light music. Akhmatova replied, "Who needs that?" "Ah, here's some opera." "Operas aren't always bad." "When aren't they bad?" "When they're *Khovanshchina,* or *Kitezh Town.*"[1]

But since some require evidence to be convinced, one interesting bit of it belongs to Akhmatova herself and is expressed in her poetry—specifically, in the poem with the significant title **"A Poet"**:

> Подумаешь, тоже работа,—
> Беспечное это житье:
> Подслушать у музыки что-то
> И выдать шутя за свое.
>
> И чье-то веселое скерцо
> В какие-то строки вложив,
> Поклясться, что бедное сердце
> Так стонет средь блещущих нив.[2]

Here we have an authorial confession of a great importance, for one of the distinctive features of Akhmatova's poetry (especially that of the late period) is the abundance of so-called subtexts.[3] Akhmatova's poetry of the late period is literally woven from threads connecting a poem with numerous other texts, often of a very different nature. Such texts may be facts of biography, history, art, and so forth. Literary subtexts, of course, play the most essential part. "In the later period," Susan Amert noted, "the role of literary quotations and references takes on pivotal importance: the identification and interpretation of literary references becomes crucial to an understanding of Akhmatova's poetry, which speaks through such echoes and allusions."[4] That is why intertextual approaches to Akhmatova's poetry have been so widely adopted. Immersion into what Akhmatova herself called "the subtextual depth" seems to be one of the most adequate methods for analyzing her works.

In this regard, at least two points should be emphasized. The first is Akhmatova's well-known, frequent use of the device of concealment. The line from the *Poem without a Hero,* «У шкатулки ж тройное дно», could serve as a motto for studies on Akhmatova's way of referring to different subtexts. One of them may conceal another, the latter may conceal yet another, and so on. A different motto for the same kind of research could be borrowed from the early Akhmatova poem **"Pesnia poslednei vstrechi,"** «Я на правую руку надела / Перчатку с левой руки», for Akhmatova rarely uses any sources directly.[5] Usually, she intentionally fuses and transforms them into something new and—quite often—hardly commensurate to the original. That is why it is not easy to recognize Akhmatova's subtexts.

The second point to be emphasized is the most important for these considerations. "The box with a triple bottom" of Akhmatova's poetry conceals not only different literary sources but also musical ones. Akhmatova scholars often neglect these musical sources (especially if they are inclined to share Charles Lamb's attitude toward music). But the stanzas from **"A Poet"** cited above point to the existence of musical subtexts in Akhmatova's verse, at the same time that they underline their transformation and complex encoding. This being the case, Akhmatova's musical subtexts may be divided into two categories: "heard" and "unheard" melodies. My terms are taken from John Keats' lines from the *Ode on a Grecian Urn* (1820): "Heard melodies are sweet, / But those unheard are sweeter."[6] By "heard melodies" I mean those musical subtexts which are disclosed to the reader by the author herself; by "unheard melodies," those which the author either vaguely hints at or entirely conceals. Three examples will make my division clear. In the first **"Dedication"** from the *Poem without a Hero* we read:

> Не море ли?
> Нет, это только хвоя
>
> Могильная, и в накипанье пен
> Все ближе, ближе . . .
> *Marche funèbre* . . .
> Шопен . . .[7]

Undoubtedly, the piece by Chopin serves as an audible (as though heard by inner ear) musical accompaniment to these lines. Here we have, so to speak, the heard melody.

The poem **"The Call"** (**"Zov,"** from the cycle *Polnochnye stikhi*), meanwhile, places us in quite another situation: «В которую-то из сонат / Тебя я спрячу осторожно . . . »[8] To whose sonata did Akhmatova refer? The answer may be found in the previous variants of the poem, and in Akhmatova's drafts. In an early variant of **"The Call,"** the first line reads: «И в предпоследней из сонат». This version does not make the reference absolutely clear, but it tells us that the poem deals with a certain musical piece. The reader does not know which piece it is, but the author does. Fortunately, in Akhmatova's drafts one can find the discarded motto to this poem, "Arioso Dolente. Beethoven. Op. 110," so we now know that Akhmatova had in mind the lamenting melody from the finale of Beethoven's *Piano Sonata No. 31*, which is indeed the composer's penultimate sonata.

In this way, Akhmatova transformed the "heard melody" into an "unheard" one. Without touching upon all the reasons for this transformation, let us remember that "unheard melodies are sweeter."[9]

The third example presents the first lines from a poem written in 1914: «Вечерний звон у стен монастыря / Как некий благовест самой природы».[10] Here we have a telling example of a combination of both types of musical subtexts within one line, or, to put it another way, a combination of heard and unheard melodies. The heard one is the melody of the ringing church bells directly mentioned in the text.

At the same time, the first two words refer to the famous Russian romance which eventually became a folk song.

The initial words of the song (as well as its title) are the same: "Vechernii zvon." Incidentally, the text of the song is a translation of a poem by Thomas Moore (1779-1852) entitled *Those Evening Bells,* made by the Russian poet Ivan Kozlov, who wrote in the beginning of the nineteenth century. This translation had been set to music several times during the nineteenth century, although the most popular melody belongs to an unknown composer. This melody is well known in Russia and, beyond any doubt, it was known to Akhmatova. Thus her poem imperceptibly evokes two "melodies" at one and the same time: the "heard" sounding of the church bells and the "unheard melody" of the old Russian song.

Turning to the problem of musical subtexts in Akhmatova's *Requiem,* one might suppose that the very title of the poem points to the musical setting of the Latin text that is used in Roman Catholic liturgy. The first composer to come to mind as a potential reference is, of course, Mozart, for it is his *Requiem* that became one of the most famous examples of the genre. Considering Akhmatova's lifelong admiration for Mozart's music one could easily conclude that the identity of the main musical subtext for her *Requiem* is established. The problem cannot be solved so easily, however, because "the box has a triple bottom." First of all let us note that the only explicit statement by Akhmatova on musical subtexts in her *Requiem* is found among her notes on *Poem without a Hero*: "Next to it [this poem] . . . so motley and saturated with music, went [my] funereal *Requiem,* which can only be accompanied by Silence and occasional, distant strokes of funeral bells."[11] If these words refer in any way to musical compositions, it may be to those of one of the greatest Russian composers—Modest Mussorgsky, for the funeral bells sounding behind the stage are among the distinctive features of his best-known operas, *Boris Godunov* and *Khovanshchina.*

In the first, funeral bells resound in one of the opera's most impressive scenes, when the dying Tsar Boris exclaims, «Звон! Погребальный звон!» But the use of the funeral bells in *Khovanshchina* is perhaps even more striking, for here we have precisely the combination of Silence and the distant, sparse tolling of funeral bells. I have in mind the scene from Act 4, when the stroke of a bell breaks a terrifying silence and announces the beginning of the mass execution.

As many readers know, *Khovanshchina* deals with certain historical events at the end of the seventeenth century in Russia. The climax of Act 4 represents the tragic result of the Strel'tsy mutiny of 1698, which Peter I severely suppressed. Many rebels were executed on Red Square in Moscow just at the Kremlin walls. In his opera Mussorgsky presents (not without some deviations from history) the beginning of the execution, and—what is of special importance for our subject—he includes in this scene a choir of female voices. This choir is one of the most impressive musical episodes of the opera. The wives of the doomed victims are crying and wailing. According to Mussorgsky's realistic principles, this musical fragment is more akin to the real wailing of womenfolk than to traditional operatic female choirs.

Remembering that just before this choir the funeral bells ring out in the silence, it is not so difficult to discover the unheard music implied in the last lines of the first poem from Akhmatova's *Requiem*: «Буду я, как стрелецкие женки, / Под кремлевскими башнями выть».[12] And this "unheard melody" is quite definite: it is the abundantly chromatic music of the Choir of Strel'tsy Wives.

It seems that *Khovanshchina* (incidentally, one of Akhmatova's favorite operas) provided more than one melody as musical subtext for *Requiem.* The only heroine of the opera, Marfa, stands on the stage in silence listening to the funeral bells. Marfa is a strong, determined woman, extremely (almost fanatically) religious, yet also a passionate lover. She is absolutely fearless, scorns any danger, and in the end burns herself for the sake of the true faith. Moreover, she has the gift of prophesy and is able to predict the future.

This character had a historical prototype in seventeenth-century Russia. The resistance to the innovations being introduced by Peter the Great and his predecessors was supported to a great degree by the Old Believers. There was one woman among their leaders—the noblewoman Morozova, who was sentenced to exile, imprisonment, and eventually to death. In several poems Akhmatova explicitly identified herself with Morozova.[13] So it comes as no surprise that Akhmatova may well have identified herself with the character of Mussorgsky's opera—with the Morozova-type character Marfa.

One of the most striking episodes involving Marfa is the scene in Act 2 where she foretells the sad destiny that is awaiting the hero in spite of his current prosperity:

> Тебя ожидают опала и ссылка и заточенье в
> дальнем краю.
> Отнимется власть, и богатство и знатность навек
> от тебя.
> Ни слава в минувшем, ни доблесть, ни знанья,
> ничто не спасет . . .
> Узнаешь великую страду, печаль и лишенья . . .
> в той страде, горючих слезах познаешь всю
> правду земли . . .[14]

The echoes of this aria, *Gadanie Marfy,* may be heard at the beginning of the **"Epilogue"** in Akhmatova's *Requiem*:

> Узнала я, как опадают лица,
> Как из-под век выглядывает страх,
> Как клинописи жесткие страницы
> Страдание выводит на щеках.[15]

But Marfa's aria seems to be even closer to the *Requiem*'s **"Poem 4,"** which also deals with the prophesy, with the foretelling of a prosperous life turned disastrous:

> Показать бы тебе, насмешнице
> И любимице всех друзей,
> Царскосельской веселой грешнице,
> Что случится с жизнью твоей—
> Как трехсотая с передачею
> Под Крестами будешь стоять
> И своею слезою горячею
> Новогодний лед прожигать.[16]

Besides the obvious similarities («горючих слезах» and «слезою горячею») it is remarkable that Akhmatova uses «показать» (to show) instead of the seemingly more suitable «рассказать» (to tell). The point is, Mussorgsky's Marfa does not merely foretell the future in her aria, she shows it, because this future became visible to her in water. *Gadanie Marfy,* then, might well serve as the musical subtext to **"Poem 4,"** and if this is the case, the sad and gloomy melody sung by a low female voice constitutes its "unheard counterpoint."

This poem also offers one of the most telling examples of Akhmatova's subtextual technique, for in it we see how the different subtexts are combined and how they intersected in her verse. The phrases «царскосельской веселой грешнице» and «под Крестами будешь стоять» deserve special attention. "Kresty" is the name of the Petersburg prison where many victims of Stalin's terror, including the poet's son, were held. The word "kresty" means "the crosses," hence the expression «стоять под Крестами» means more than "to stand near a prison." It has the second meaning of "to stand by the cross." Here it is not difficult to recall the Gospel according to St. John (19:25): "Now there stood by the cross of Jesus his mother, and his mother's sister, Mary the wife of Cleophas, and Mary Magdalene." Mary Magdalene is traditionally identified with the woman characterized in the Gospel according to St. Luke (7:37) as "a woman in the city, who was a sinner."

It seems, then, that the female sinner of Tsarskoe selo who stands by the Crosses in Akhmatova's *Requiem,* and the female sinner of the city who stood by the cross of Jesus, have much in common. She who stood by Jesus was forgiven by Him, as is mentioned in the Latin text of the Requiem service (in *Recordare*): "Qui Mariam absolvisti [It was You to Mary pardon gave]."

Hence, in **"Poem 4"** from Akhmatova's *Requiem* cycle one may see at least two "hidden" faces belonging to one and the same heroine: she is Marfa from Mussorgsky's opera and she is Mary Magdalene from the New Testament and from the canonical text of the Roman Catholic Requiem. Having established this, it is easy to see why precisely these two very different characters became united: there are two sisters in the New Testament who knew Jesus—Mary and Martha (or Marfa in Russian). However, it seems that our heroine has one more "hidden" face, and perhaps this is the most important one.

Before uncovering this third face, let us note that Akhmatova's text does not contain very many references to the text of the Latin Requiem. In addition to the "sinner of the city" one could point to only one more detail: «Это было, когда улыбался / Только мертвый, спокойствию рад».[17] The words «мертвый» and «спокойствию» in these initial lines of **"Vstuplenie"** obviously echo the initial words of the Latin prayer: "Requiem aeternam dona eis, Domine! [Eternal rest grant to them [the dead], O Lord]!" This complicates matters, however. The Requiem Mass prays for peace for the dead. Akhmatova's **Requiem** asserts that the dead are happy because they already have been granted peace. They are even smiling, in contrast to those still among the living. Indeed, Akhmatova's poem begins as something like an Anti-Requiem, and it continues in the same direction, contradicting the traditional contents of the Requiem Mass.

Many readers noticed the contradiction between the real biographical events reflected in Akhmatova's poem, on the one hand, and its title on the other. Let us briefly recall these events. In 1935, Akhmatova's husband, Nikolai Punin, and Akhmatova's son by her first marriage, Lev Gumilev, were arrested. Akhmatova did her best to save them: she appealed to Stalin personally («Кидалась в ноги палачу»), as a result of which both Punin and Gumilev were soon released. These events inspired Akhmatova's writing some short poems which were eventually turned into the **Requiem** cycle. In 1938, Gumilev was re-arrested and imprisoned in Leningrad. He was sentenced to death, but in August 1939 his sentence was commuted and he was deported from Leningrad, first to a camp, and then into exile. Later he was released, again re-arrested, and finally freed in 1956. Punin was re-arrested in 1949 and died in prison camp in 1953. It is worth stressing that **Requiem** as a cycle of poems was completed in a first version in 1940, while both Gumilev and Punin were alive, though the former was still in prison.

The traditional Requiem, however, is a Mass for the Dead (*Missa pro defunctis*). The implication, therefore, seems to be that when Akhmatova was crafting her **Requiem** she bore in mind not only her own loved ones, but all the victims of Stalin's terror. Still, there are only two more lines (in **"Poem 4"**) actually dealing with the dead, or, strictly speaking, with those who are almost dead, or dying: «И ни звука—а сколько там / Неповинных жизней кончается . . . »[18] Are there too few lines about the dead for the genre, then? Is it not strange, in a cycle of poems entitled **Requiem,** to speak about living (albeit doomed) persons, rather than dead ones?

In view of the numerous discrepancies between Akhmatova's text and that of the Catholic Mass for the Dead (there also are no equivalents to, say, the *Dies Irae, Tuba mirum, Rex tremendae, Sanctus, Benedictus, Agnus Dei, Lux aeterna,* and to other important parts of the Requiem Mass), let us put the crucial question: Is Akhmatova's **Requiem** a requiem at all? Did the Requiem Mass serve as both a verbal and musical subtext for Akhmatova's poem?

It seems to me that the answer must be no. The title **Requiem,** in my opinion, illustrates Akhmatova's typical manner of hiding one source under the name of another one, for it was another Catholic prayer that served as verbal and musical subtext for Akhmatova's **Requiem.** We can easily disclose this subtext, for Akhmatova explicitly points to it in the second part of **"Poem 10," "Raspiatie" ("Crucifixion"):**

> Магдалина билась и рыдала,
> Ученик любимый каменел,
> А туда, где молча М с о л ,
> Так взглянуть никто и не посмел.[19]

The italicized words reproduce almost exactly the initial words of the famous medieval devotional poem about the Virgin Mary's vigil by Christ's Cross—*Stabat Mater* ("Stabat Mater dolorosa [A grief-striken Mother was standing]"). This text goes back to the thirteenth century and is still sung in the Roman Catholic rites at the Feast of the Seven Sorrows of the Virgin Mary. It was also set to music by many composers (Palestrina, Pergolesi, Haydn, Rossini, Verdi, and Dvorzak, among others) in numerous oratorios with the same title.

Indeed, it was not only Mary Magdalene, who stood by the Cross: Mary, the mother of Christ, stood there as well. Her suffering is the main subject of *Stabat Mater,* and it is a mother's suffering that is the main subject of Akhmatova's **Requiem.** Let us add to this, that the traditional Requiem does not include a description of the Crucifixion, while *Stabat Mater* does, and with many touching details.

Comparing Akhmatova's **Requiem** with *Stabat Mater,* several parallelisms of different kinds become apparent. Touching upon the lexical ones, let us note the key words common to both texts: "mother," "son," "to stand," "death," "tears," "suffering," and "to weep." The word "cross" may be found in Akhmatova's text not only as the name of the prison: the cross appears to be a symbolic instrument of execution of the son. Without quoting from **"Raspiatie"** again, let us note the last two lines from **"Poem 6,"** addressed directly to the son: «О твоем кресте высоком / И о смерти говорят».[20] Some of Akhmatova's metaphors may be understood as transformed metaphors from *Stabat Mater.* For example, the sword that pierced the Virgin Mary's grieving, anguished, and lamenting heart ("Cujus animam gementem / Contristatam et dolentem / Pertransivit gladius") seems to be turned into the "stone word" that fell upon the "still-living breast" in Akhmatova's **Requiem**: «И упало каменное слово / На мою еще живую грудь».[21]

The suffering of the afflicted Mother of an only Son ("O quam tristis et afflicta / Fuit illa benedicta / Mater Unigeneti") as well as the appeal for compassion to the loving mother grieving for her Son ("Quis non posset contristari / Piam matrem contemplari / Dolentem cum Filio?") appear to be condensed in Akhmatova's lines dealing with the ill and lonely woman:

> Эта женщина больна,
> Эта женщина одна,
> Муж в могиле, сын в тюрьме
> Помолитесь обо мне.[22]

The motif of "Mater Unigeneti" may well have been especially moving for Akhmatova. Certainly in some poems which are close to **Requiem,** but not included in the cycle, the motif of "an only Son" occurs rather often: «Разлучили с единственным сыном», (**"Vse ushli, i nikto ne vernulsia"**),[23] «Разлученной с единственным сыном», «Мне он—единственный сын» (**"Cherepki"**).[24]

One more example of Akhmatova's compressing several images of *Stabat Mater* in her own poems may be shown by comparing the words "Inflammatus at accensus" ("Inflamed and burning") and "Cruce hac inebriari" ("intoxicated by his Cross") with the words from **"Poem 9"**: «И поит огненным вином». The notion of "inflamation," "intoxication," and "burning" are condensed here in one line.

It is, of course, inappropriate to claim direct structural and metrical influence exerted by the medieval verses of *Stabat Mater,* with its three-line stanzas (trochaic tetrameter with the dactylic foot to conclude the third line) upon Akhmatova's cycle, with its diverse and changeable meters and stanzas. Nonetheless, it is noteworthy that three consecutive poems from **Requiem** (**"4,"** **"5,"** and **"6"**) provide us with examples of parallelisms. Thus the lines from **"Poem 4,"** «Там тюремный тополь качается» and «Неповинных жизней кончается», are the only two lines in the whole cycle to have a dactylic foot in their ends. **"Poem 5"** gives the only example of three-line structures united in one six-line stanza:

> И только пышные цветы,
> И звон кадильный, и следы
> Куда-то в никуда.
> И прямо мне в глаза глядит
> И скорой гибелью грозит
> Огромная звезда.[25]

Finally, **"Poem 6"** is the only one written in trochaic tetrameter. The sequence of two rhyming lines coincides almost exactly with a similar pattern in *Stabat Mater:*

> Ястребиным жарким оком,
> О твоем кресте высоком . . .

> Stabat Mater dolorosa
> Juxta crucem lacrymosa . . .

Perhaps all this is not pure coincidence. In any case, the juxtaposition of the concluding sections of Akhmatova's **Requiem** with *Stabat Mater* is certainly fruitful. The last stanza of *Stabat Mater* reads: "Quando corpus morietur, / Fac ut animae donetur / Paradisi gloria [When my body dies / Let my soul be granted the glory of Heaven]." The end of **Requiem** is also strongly marked by references to a time when the author of **Requiem** will be no more: «И если когда-нибудь в этой стране / Воздвигнуть задумают памятник мне . . . »[26]

Yet **Requiem**—in contrast to *Stabat Mater*—deals with the dream of glory on Earth, not heavenly glory. It is a dream of a posthumous monument which would represent not only the poet's magnificence but first of all the mother's suffering. This monument of the poet's dreams must be erected on the same place where the mother from Akhmatova's **Requiem** "was standing for three hundred hours" («Здесь, где стояла я триста часов»), namely, "by the Crosses"—(«под Крестами»). Thus Akhmatova once more identified herself with the Mother of God while at the same time stressing the special aspect of such an identification: a destiny of a mother who is doomed to see her only son being unjustly imprisoned, sentenced, tormented, and executed.

Thus, ultimately, it is not a requiem that Akhmatova wrote, in spite of the title **Requiem.** Rather, it is a very Russian, even very Soviet, and, of course, very Akhmatovian version of *Stabat Mater.*

In Akhmatova's opinion, Solzhenitsyn was wrong when in a conversation with the poet (as recorded by one of her friends), he said: "It was a national tragedy, but you made it only the tragedy of a mother and son." According to the same source, Akhmatova "repeated these words with her usual shrug of the shoulders, and a slight grimace."[27]

Indeed, another writer (an émigré who belonged to Akhmatova's generation) seems to have had a better understanding of **Requiem** when he called it a "lament, a female, motherly, lament, not only for herself but also for all those who are suffering, for all wives, mothers, brides, and in general for all those who are being crucified."[28] Nevertheless, Solzhenitsyn's judgment contains a grain of truth. Akhmatova's *Requiem*, although it presents, of course, the tragedy of the entire nation, does so through the prism of her personal tragedy, of a mother watching her tormented and dying son.

This fact explains why precisely *Stabat Mater*—the best exemplification of such a Mother-Son tragedy in European literature—may be considered the hidden subtext of Akhmatova's *Requiem*. Akhmatova's knowledge of Latin is beyond any doubt. Her acquaintance with medieval Catholic prayers might have its origin in her close contacts (in the mid-1910s and early twenties) with Arthur Lourie (1892-1966), the avant-garde composer who, after his conversion to Catholicism, wrote several liturgical compositions on the texts of medieval Latin prayers. One of them—*Salve Regina*—is mentioned (rather enigmatically) in Akhmatova's long poem **Putem vseia zemli,** written the same year in which Akhmatova completed her *Requiem*, 1940.[29]

Akhmatova may have had several reasons for hiding the subtext *Stabat Mater* in "the box with a triple bottom" (and the very deepest one at that). For one thing, we know that Akhmatova, for both political and personal reasons, would carefully conceal everything that could shed light on her relationship with Arthur Lourie. For another, *Stabat Mater* was too closely connected with Catholic liturgy and had no equivalents among the Orthodox prayers. Moreover, "requiem" was a term that (at least in Russian culture) had lost, to a certain degree, both its religious and Catholic flavor and turned into something neutral enough to be applied to secular memorial works of art. Finally, if I may say it again, "unheard melodies are sweeter."

With respect to the melodies which Akhmatova's *Requiem* may have secretly implied, this issue is fairly easy to resolve. One of the most famous musical settings of *Stabat Mater* is the oratorio composed by Giovanni Batista Pergolesi (probably in 1739). Anatoly Naiman, as we remember, mentions this oratorio among Akhmatova's favorite musical pieces. It seems to be particularly important that Pergolesi's *Stabat Mater* (in contrast to Mozart's *Requiem*, which usually is performed by a mixed choir with orchestra) is to be sung only by female voices—by two female singers (Soprano and Alto) accompanied by strings and harpsichord. This feminine-sounding image, so to speak, strengthens, in my opinion, the resemblance between Pergolesi's oratorio and Akhmatova's poem.

So, Lamb's ironic question, "Cannot a man live free and easy, / Without admiring Pergolesi?" may be answered: Perhaps men can, but women cannot. At least one of them could not.

Notes

1. Anatoly Naiman, *Remembering Anna Akhmatova*, trans. Wendy Rosslyn (New York, 1991), 147. Both operas mentioned by Akhmatova were written by Russian composers—*Khovanshchina* by Modest Mussorgsky, and *The Legend of the Invisible City of Kitezh and the Maiden Fevronia* by Nikolai Rimsky-Korsakov.

2. Anna Akhmatova, *Posle vsego* (Moscow, 1989), 145. Unless otherwise noted, all further citations of Akhmatova's texts are from this excellent edition, which combines Akhmatova's works with numerous valuable materials for Akhmatova studies and comprises five books published simultaneously by the Moscow Pedagogical Institute in 1989 (compilers and commentators R. Timenchik, K. Polivanov, and V. Morderer). Unfortunately, the edition lacks any general title and none of the books (*Desiatye gody, Poema bez geroia, Rekviem, Posle vsego,* and *Fotobiografiia*) has a number. Therefore, all further references mention the title of each book and the page number.

3. By "subtext" I mean, following Kirill Taranovskii and Omry Ronen, the source of a literary citation or allusion.

4. Susan Amert, *In a Shattered Mirror: The Later Poetry of Anna Akhmatova* (Stanford, 1992), 14.

5. *Desiatye gody,* 57.

6. These lines were used as the motto to the only (posthumous) collection of the poems by Vsevolod Kniazev (*Stikhi* [St. Petersburg, 1914]) who was to become the prototype for "dragunskii kornet" in Akhmatova's *Poem without a Hero*. For more details see Roman Timenchik, "Zametki o 'Poeme bez geroja,'" in Akhmatova, *Poema bez geroia,* 4-9.

7. *Poema bez geroia,* 33.

8. *Posle vsego,* 188.

9. For elucidation of links between Beethoven's Sonata, op. 110 and Akhmatova's poem *The Call* see B. Kats and R. Timenchik, *Anna Akhmatova i muzyka* (Leningrad, 1989), 148-52.

10. Anna Akhmatova, *Stikhotvoreniia i poemy* (Leningrad, 1977), 280.

11. *Poema bez geroia,* 62.

12. *Rekviem,* 304.

13. «Мне с Морозовою класть поклоны . . . » (*Posledniaia roza,* 1962), «О, если бы вдруг откинуться / В какой-то семнадцатый век . . . С боярынею Морозовой / Сладимый

медок попивать . . . Какой сумасшедший Суриков / Мой последний напишет путь?» (*Ia znaiu, s mesta ne sdvinut'sia* . . . , 1939 [?]). Judith Hemschemeyer comments on the last lines: "A picture of the Boyarynya Morozova by Vasily Surikov (1848-1916) depicts her on a sleigh, in chains, being taken into exile. According to Nadezhda Mandelstam in *Hope against Hope* . . . the last two lines of this poem originated in a remark made by Punin to Akhmatova in the Tretyakov Gallery: 'Now let's go and see how they'll take you to your execution.'" See *The Complete Poems of Anna Akhmatova,* trans. Judith Hemschemeyer, vol. 2 (Somerville, MA, 1990), 784. Perhaps it is worth adding that another famous picture by V. I. Surikov depicts the execution of Strel'tsy (*Utro Streletskoi kazni*).

14. M. Mussorgskii, *Khovanshchina: Narodnaia muzykal'naia drama* (Moscow, 1932), 140-42.

15. *Rekviem,* 311.

16. Ibid., 306.

17. Ibid., 304.

18. Ibid., 306.

19. Ibid., 310 (emphasis added).

20. Ibid., 307.

21. Ibid.

22. Ibid., 304.

23. Ibid., 293.

24. Ibid., 282.

25. Ibid., 306.

26. Ibid., 312.

27. Natalia Roskina, "Good-by Again," in *Anna Akhmatova and Her Circle,* comp. Konstantin Polivanov, trans. Patricia Beriozkina (Fayetteville, AR, 1994), 193.

28. Boris Zaitsev, "Dni," *Russkaia mysl'* (Paris), 7 January 1964, cited in Akhmatova, *Rekviem,* 299.

29. *Posle vsego,* 120. For more details about this reference to Lourie's *Salve Regina,* as well as about Lourie himself (he emigrated in 1922) and his influence upon Akhmatova's life and works, see Kats and Timenchik, *Anna Akhmatova i muzyka,* 147, 31-36, 170-72; and *Poema bez geroia,* 338-51.

Sharon M. Bailey (essay date summer 1999)

SOURCE: Bailey, Sharon M. "An Elegy for Russia: Anna Akhmatova's *Requiem.*" *Slavic and East European Journal* 43, no. 2 (summer 1999): 324-46.

[*In the following essay, Bailey defines Akhmatova's* Requiem *as an elegy of mourning, particularly giving voice to the grief of the women whose loved ones were imprisoned or executed during the years of Stalinist rule in the Soviet Union.*]

INTRODUCTION

In the final lines of Akhmatova's **Requiem** is the image of a bronze monument to the poet, standing motionless in front of the Leningrad Prison and crying with each spring thaw. Although this statue has not yet been erected, **Requiem** itself is nothing less than such a monument. Within the course of the cycle, Akhmatova reconstructs her experience of the Stalinist Terror. After the arrest of her son, the fabric of her life dissolves in grief, loneliness and despair. Reconciliation is, however, eventually found in the verbal commemoration of the grief. With **Requiem,** Akhmatova weaves a veil of words that articulates her pain of those years, acknowledges the crimes which were the cause, and perpetuates the memory of it in defense against the forgetfulness of time.

This complex cycle of fifteen poems and one prose paragraph was written during the height of the Stalinist Terror, in which as many as 40 million people were arrested, exiled or executed. The earliest poems were written in 1935, after her son Lev Gumilev and her third husband Nikolai Punin were arrested within two weeks of each other. Lev Gumilev was arrested probably for no other reason than that he was the son of Nikolai Gumilev (Akhmatova's first husband), who had sympathized with the White Army during the Civil War and was executed for that in 1921. Lev Gumilev was released shortly after his arrest, rearrested in 1937, held for 17 months, and sentenced to death. Gumilev's sentence was commuted to exile and hard labor, however, when those who had handed down his sentence were themselves purged (see Haight 92-100). The subject of **Requiem** is the experiences of the mother during the 17 months of waiting to hear from her son and the experience of hearing the sentence. The cycle consists of an epigraph, three introductions, and ten poems which are organized chronologically documenting the arrest and sentencing, periods of overwhelming grief, denial, incomprehension, and withdrawal. The cycle closes with a two-part **"Epilogue"** in which Akhmatova begins to react against the destructiveness of the Terror by consciously developing a verbal strategy of remembrance.

A requiem is a mass for the dead or a musical composition in honor of the dead. The funeral elegy, the literary equivalent of a requiem, is traditionally a poem written on the occasion of a death, serving the dual function of commemorating the deceased and of contemplating the nature of death in general.[1] At first glance, Akhmatova's **Requiem** would seem to have little in common with either a requiem or an elegy, for the son had not died, and in fact very little is said about the son personally. However, despite the lack of funeral or eulogistic elements, many of the most fundamental elegiac conventions can be found in the cycle. In particular, the elements which I will be discussing in this paper include the loss of the loved one, usually by death in a traditional elegy but represented by arrest in *Requiem,* the universal significance of that loss, the pathetic fallacy, which is intimately tied to the theme of the universality of death, the progression from grief to consolation, and the ultimate resolution of the work of mourning.

Critics of the elegy repeatedly point out that the conventions of the genre have their roots in the human psyche. Far from being artificial, writes Ellen Zetzel Lambert, "A literary convention is, like a convention of behavior, always something more than a series of allusions or inherited forms: it is a way of seeing things" (xi). Many of the images in Requiem spring from the author's experience of and need to express grief, and most can be understood as permutations of elegiac conventions. Yet even while much of *Requiem* can be understood within the paradigm of the traditional elegy, the unique circumstances of the Terror also add a moral aspect to the process of elegiac commemoration. Akhmatova's articulation of her son's and her own suffering is a monument to the suffering of an entire nation. As David Wells writes, *Requiem* emphasizes "the courage and persistence of Russian women outside the prisons of the 1930s and lay[s] great weight on the power of poetry to record their sufferings and to transcend them" (75). Akhmatova has written this cycle not only for herself, but for all of the women of Leningrad and for their sons and husbands.

I

The definition of the word elegy in the *Princeton Encyclopedia of Poetry and Poetics* is representative of that given by most critics and handbooks of literature. It states that "the elegy is a short poem, usually formal or ceremonious in tone and diction, occasioned by the death of a person" (322). The first obvious question is whether a poem written on the occasion of an arrest can be described as an elegy. One response to this objection would be to point out that, for a vast number of victims of the Terror, arrest resulted in death, whether immediately by execution or slowly in Siberia, so that it might be assumed that the one leads directly to the other. This correlation is in fact present within Akhmatova's cycle. In the **"Prologue,"** for example, we read,

Звезды смерти стояли над нами,
И безвинная корчилась Русь
Под кровавыми сапогами
И под шинами черных марусь.

The stars of death stood above us
And innocent Russia writhed

Under bloody boots
And under the tires of the Black Marias.[2]

Similarly, in the fifth poem, the final lines tell of a star which threatens impending death. Akhmatova also knew intimately how arrest could result in death; the final lines of **"VIII,"** "I sinii blesk vozliublennykh ochei / Poslednii uzhas zastilaet" ("And the final horror dims / The blue luster of beloved eyes"), have been read as a homage to Osip Mandelstam, whose death in a camp near Vladivostok Akhmatova heard rumored in 1939 (Etkind 378), and the first poem, **"Uvodili tebia na rassvete"** (**"They led you away at dawn"**), with its reference to execution in both the first and the last lines, might easily be read as an allusion to the arrest and execution of Nikolai Gumilev in 1921.[3] Even though Akhmatova was not present at N. Gumilev's arrest, and though his arrest predated the purges by a decade, this potential reading is reinforced by the second poem, **"Muzh v mogile, syn v tiur'me"** (**"Husband in the grave, son in prison"**), which leaves it yet ambiguous as to whether the first poem refers to husband or son. Michael Basker also points out that the first half of this line may have been intended as an anagram for Gumilev (16-17). Finally, in **"IV,"** the executions which took place in the cellars of the prison are alluded to through a missing line of verse:

Там тюремный тополь качается,
И ни звука—а сколько там
Неповинных жизней кончается . . .

Over there the prison poplar bends,
And there's no sound—and over there how many
Innocent lives are ending now . . .

Through most of the cycle the events are couched in aesthetic euphemism; reality is displaced by a literary reflection. The amount of time the mother stood in line, for example, is said to be 300 hours (**"Epilogue II"**), and her place in the line is 300th (**"IV"**; cf. Basker 9). In these lines, however, the aesthetic mask has fallen away, and poet and reader are faced with a reality that defies speech. Efim Etkind writes,

> Das autobiographische Element dieses "Ichs" steigert sich fast bis zur Deckung mit dem Leben und wird derart verstärkt, daß außerliterarische Realität ins Gedicht eindringt und den Text abbricht. . . . Der vierte Vers fehlt, das Versende "tam" bleibt ohne Reim im Raum stehen, die Stimme wird von Schluchzen unterbrochen: der letzte Vers sollte wohl von den Erschießungen in den Kellern des Lubjanka-Gefängnisses berichten.

> The autobiographical element of this "I" approaches a direct correlation to life and intensifies to the point that extra-literary reality breaks into the poem and silences the text. . . . The fourth verse is missing, the word "tam" remains standing in space without a rhyme, the voice is interrupted by sobbing: the final verse should

probably inform us of the executions in the cellars of the Lubjanka Prison.

(370; Translation mine)[4]

Although it is never stated explicitly that the son has been executed (on the contrary, we know that he has been exiled), his impending death is the occasion for which **Requiem** is written.

However, in spite of the fact that incarceration likely meant death for those arrested, the dead are for the most part absent from the cycle. For example, despite its allusions to a funeral procession and to execution, the first poem shows a still living person being led out of the house. Instead of playing the central role in the cycle, death is used as a foil or as a background against which the experiences of the poet and her son are projected. In contrast to the pain of living during those times, actual physical death is portrayed as desirable, as in the first lines of the **"Prologue"**: "Eto bylo, kogda ulybalsia / Tol'ko mertvyi spokoistviiu rad" ("That was when the ones who smiled / Were the dead, glad to be at rest"). Likewise, in **"To Death,"** death becomes an avenue of escape from the misery of living. With death presented more as a *leitmotiv* against which arrest is projected, we again return to the question of whether a poem written on the occasion of an arrest can be described as an elegy.

This question loses its relevance if we recognize the fact that mourning is necessitated not so much by death as by loss, and that it is the sudden absence of a loved one that is the cause of grief. Peter Sacks begins his discussion of the elegy with the statement, "An elegist's language emerges from, and reacts upon, an originating sense of loss" (1). He argues that there is a fundamental similarity between the mourning process and the oedipal resolution, in that both processes consist primarily of coming to terms with separation from or depravation of an object of affection (8-17). However, since historically many of the most famous elegies were written for people whom the elegist barely knew, if at all (e.g., Thomas Gray's *Elegy Written in a Country Churchyard*), the emphasis should be placed on the elegist's *sense of loss* of the object of affection, and not on that object itself (see Sacks 1, quoted above). It is in this sense that Eric Smith defines the elegy as a poem about "what is missing and also about what is more certainly known to have been formerly possessed" (2). Thus, while an elegy may be (and usually is) *occasioned* by death, it is more accurately defined as a poem *about* loss. Consequently, the grammatical subject of the elegy, so to speak, is the poet, who experiences the loss, and not the deceased, who functions in the poem only by his/her absence.

The suffering of the survivor is, even in traditional criticism, a recognized aspect of the elegy. The tragedy of death (or of arrest in the case of **Requiem**) is not so much the changes that have taken place for the victim, but rather the implications of that event for the lives of the survivors. Kinereth Meyer writes,

> Smith's formulation of the elegy [. . .] takes on its full significance only when we realize that for the elegist, "what is missing" refers not only to the subject of the poem, but also to the poet's projection of his own absence, and that "what is . . . known to have been formerly possessed" refers to his own life as well as to that of another.
>
> (25)

In **Requiem,** it is apparent perhaps to a greater degree than in the traditional elegy, that the subject is not so much the son as the mother. In fact, the framing poems make no mention of the son, and barely discuss the prisoners at all. The epigraph, which answers the question "Where did this happen?," answers without alluding to the arrests, and defines, for the remainder of the cycle, the subject as "I"—Akhmatova herself. Dan Latimer also emphasizes the survivor over the deceased in his definition of the elegy. The most essential theme, he writes, is the disruption of the survivor's sense of justice in the universe:

> The first [essential theme of any elegy] is the expression of disbelief that death would come to one so beautiful, so vital (Adonis), so gifted (Bion, Keats), so noble (Caesar, Lincoln), so earnest and dedicated (Eduard King). This question involves what Rilke calls "des Unrechts Anschein," the appearance of injustice.
>
> (25-26)

A slight reformulation of this idea would be that the events have disrupted the survivor's sense of a rational and predictable order in his or her own life. At the same time as Akhmatova is grieving the loss of her son in **Requiem,** she is also grieving, for example, the lack of continuity between her own happy youth in Tsarskoye Selo in poem **"IV"** or her childhood by the sea in **"Epilogue II"** and her present misery. The arrest of her son initiates a breakdown of the poet's perception of an understandable reality.

The loss in **Requiem,** however, is more than nostalgia for lost youth. At this point **Requiem** exhibits a complexity that goes beyond that of a traditional elegy. In the traditional elegy, much of the suffering of the survivor stems from a consciousness that he/she is not immune from the fate of the deceased. In **Requiem,** the suffering of the survivor is real and not just the result of an awareness of potentialities. The same political machinery which is responsible for the arrests and executions of the sons also sentences the wives and mothers to a different type of suffering. The uncertainty, helplessness and injustice that accompany arrest of a family member is a fate that makes life outside the prison no more desirable than arrest itself, and in this sense, *Requiem* is an elegy written on the occasion of the arrest of the son and the subsequent "living death" of the mother.[5] This living death is reflected in the depictions of the women, which show them lacking social qualities, such as speech and identity, and physical qualities, such as warmth and breath.

Analogous to the isolation imposed on the prisoners, the wives and mothers are shown to be essentially deprived of speech—a deprivation which prevents them from joining into a healthy community. On the one hand, this speechlessness is a consequence of the physical suffering. Even to produce her whispered question, one of only two examples of spoken communication in the cycle, the woman of **"Instead of a Preface"** had to rouse herself from a stupor into which everyone had fallen. On the other hand, there is a disconcerting absence of anyone to whom the women could speak. The arresting soldier is represented only by a blue-topped cap (**"To Death"**), the executioner by feet (**"V"**), and guard and warden by bolted doors (**"Epilogue II"**) or the rasping key (**"Dedication"**). Denied articulate, human speech, the women wail like the wives of the Streltsy (**"I"**), cry like the mother pleading for her son or Mary Magdalene (**"V"** and **"Crucifixion"**), howl like the woman against whom the door is slammed (**"Epilogue II"**), or fall silent like John and the Mother (**"Crucifixion"**). Speech is above all a social act, but the arrest of their sons and husbands have left the women isolated, not only from the one arrested, but even from each other. Even though the women stand in line together, they are unable to form a community. In this respect, their experience is much like the isolation imposed on the prisoners within the prison.

In addition to being deprived of perhaps the most fundamental of social functions, speech, the women are also depicted as lacking even more basic human qualities, such as warmth, breath, and identity. Nearly all of the physical descriptions of the women in the lines show them to be like corpses; in **"Epilogue I"** their cheeks are stiffened and etched as if petrified and their hair is turned gray, and in **"Instead of a Preface"** the woman is described as faceless with blue lips, the second image of which is also echoed in **"I,"** where the arrested son is described as having cold lips. These descriptions of the women emphasize the loss of individuality and a reduction to an almost animal-like state, for as Susan Amert writes, "Russian Orthodoxy teaches that the face embodies the highest spiritual qualities and values, imaging the divine in human beings; accordingly, facelessness would betoken the loss of the spirit or soul" (34). Just as the women are faceless, hence without souls, they are also nameless. The woman in **"Instead of a Foreword"** has "identified" (*opoznal*) the poet, but even this does not imply that Akhmatova's individual worth had been validated. Whereas to "recognize" a person is to separate that

person out from the crowd as someone with familiar characteristics and a history, to "identify," here with its implication of guilt, strips the person of individuality and worth and broadly classifies that person as criminal. Finally, in the **"Dedication"** the women are described as more breathless than dead, and when the sentence is announced, it is as if the life is wrenched from their hearts. Amert compares this limbo between death and meaningful human life to Dante's experience in the ninth circle of hell, where "fear deprives him of life yet does not kill him" (36). Even more than mourning the arrest and possible death of the son, *Requiem* is an elegy mourning the loss of life for the wives and mothers left behind.

The occasion of an elegy, we have established, is absence and loss. In *Requiem* the loss takes place on several levels. First, the mother has lost her son to arrest, and with justification she anticipates a final loss through death. Second, at the same time as the poet is experiencing the absence of her son, she is aware of the loss of her earlier belief in a just and secure natural order. But above all, the poet has lost a part of herself to a living death at the hands of the Terror.

II

At the foundation of the elegy is the rediscovered knowledge on the part of the poet and reader that they are also subject to the same fate, that all are mortal. The loss felt by one individual (the poet) only becomes a compelling theme, when it appeals to similar sentiments in another individual (the reader). The failure to tap into this universal emotion or to reawaken the reader's sense of mortal vulnerability is, warns Sacks, the failing of many contemporary elegies:

> How many elegies console more readers than the poet, the particular bereaved, and their immediate circle? This question suggests both a problem besetting the contemporary elegy and a criterion by which to judge its individual examples. Often, these poems are too narrowly based, too private in their expression of grief and too idiosyncratic in their use of anecdote, description, or recollection.
>
> (325-26)

Although Sacks chides the modern elegist in particular for a disregard for generic convention and literary tradition, his overriding concern is for the lack of thematic universality to which the elegy should appeal, through its roots in human psychology and expressed through its natural conventions. The arrest that occasioned the writing of *Requiem* does not seem to be one that would naturally tap into universal sentiment, for as time passes, an ever larger percentage of the readers of the cycle will not have experienced an atrocity of this kind. Yet we know that *Requiem* does hold appeal for readers. One reason for this appeal may be the tone of the framing poems, in which Akhmatova invites the reader to place him/herself into the setting of the cycle. In **"Instead of a Preface,"** Akhmatova uses a narrative tone to define the time and place: "V strashnye gody ezhovshchiny ia provela semnadtsat' mesiatsev v tiuremnykh ocherediakh v Leningrade" ("In the terrible years of the Yezhov terror, I spent seventeen months in the prison lines of Leningrad"), and in **"Epilogue I"** she again steps back, almost as if to gloss the ten poems with a brief but straight-forward summary: "Uznala ia, kak opadaiut litsa, / Kak iz-pod vek vygliadyvaet strakh" ("I learned how faces fall, / How terror darts from under eyelids"). The reader is drawn into the cycle without having the feeling of eavesdropping on the poet's private grief. In addition to inviting the reader to witness her grief, Akhmatova also makes clear that the grief she expresses is not hers alone. She accomplishes this by overlaying the specific subjects of *Requiem* (mother and son) with a collective subject, developed through grammatical ambiguity and cultural subtexts. Thus, she raises the private expression of grief to the level of a national and cultural outcry.

Just as the fear occasioned by one death, as addressed in a traditional elegy, is the realization that all people are mortal, in *Requiem* the significance of the Terror lay in the fact that what happened to the poet and her son could and did happen to countless others. This is reflected in the cycle on several levels. Most intimately, Akhmatova had not only to mourn the arrest of her son, but also that of her third husband Nikolai Punin and of her close friend Osip Mandelstam. Furthermore, references such as that in the **"Prologue"** to "regiments of convicts" or in the **"Dedication"** and **"IV"** to the long lines outside the prisons—women in the same predicament as Akhmatova—indicate how common and how much a part of life in Leningrad the arrests had become. Akhmatova uses references to Russian history, such as the reference to the wives of the Streltsy Guard in **"I,"** particularly in the cultural incarnations, to place the events on a more national scale. Boris Katz has argued that the reference to the Streltsy wives in **"I"** is more accurately a reference to V. I. Surikov's painting as well as to Modest Mussorgsky's opera *Khovanshchina,* both of which depict the execution of the Streltsy (256-57). In this manner, Akhmatova places the arrests within a Russian tradition of oppression and suffering and herself within a continuum of Russian cultural self-identity.

The magnitude of this atrocity can also be seen in poem **"IV,"** in which Akhmatova invokes details of her personal life, not only to show how much of her individual identity had been lost, but also to show the extent to which her fate has dovetailed with the fates of so many other women:

> Показать бы тебе, насмешнице
> И любимице всех друзей,

Царскосельской веселой грешнице,
Что случится с жизнью твой—
Как трехсотая, с передачею,
Под Крестами будишь стоять.

> You should have been shown, you mocker,
> Minion of all your friends,
> Gay little sinner of Tsarskoye Selo,
> What would happen in your life—
> How as the three-hundredth in line, with a parcel,
> You would stand by the Kresty prison.

Finally, the experiences of the women in the prison lines are described in terms of arrest and death, pointing to a common experience for those inside the prison and those waiting in the lines outside its walls.

The transferal of emphasis from the arrested sons to the mothers and the element of a shared experience is foreshadowed in the **"Dedication,"** which functions as an overture to the whole cycle. The first five lines of the **"Dedication"** describe those arrested and in the prisons, and the next five lines, quoted here, continue a description of despair and fear:

> Для кого-то веет ветер свежий,
> Для кого-то нежится закат—
> Мы не знаем, мы повсюду те же,
> Слышим лишь ключей постылый скрежет
> Да шаги тяжелые солдат.

> For someone a fresh breeze blows,
> For someone the sunset luxuriates—
> We wouldn't know, [we are everywhere the same],
> We hear only the rasp of the hateful key
> And the soldiers' heavy tread.

The ambiguous, collective "we" may be the prisoners of the previous stanza, but it might well refer also to the wives and mothers of the following stanza. Here Akhmatova uses an ambiguous grammatical construction to create a complex subject. In the second half of the **"Dedication"** she further develops this multi-leveled subject. The subject of the third and fourth stanzas could be either third person ("they" and "she," respectively) or else first person ("we" and "I"). We do not know whether the poet is describing her own experiences or that of the other women. The use of first person in the second stanza and the third person in the fifth may justify the translation of the subjects as "we" and "she" in the third and fourth stanzas respectively, as Judith Hemschemeyer, D. M. Thomas and others have done. However, the second and fifth stanzas are in the present tense while the third and fourth stanzas are in the past tense. Thus the "they" of the fifth stanza may be referring to the subjects remembered in the third and fourth stanzas, justifying the use of a third person subject in both of those stanzas. On the other hand, the facts that the poet's own son was also sentenced (**"The Sentence"**) and that in the fifth stanza the poet is separated from her "involuntary friends," a separation which could be seen as taking place in the fourth stanza, the subject of the fourth stanza could justifiably be first person. Anna Ljunggren points out that Akhmatova moves easily from "we" to "she" to "I": "All these variations on the protagonist are seen as though through various foreshortening" (111). Many critics have commented on this device, finding significance on many levels. Basker writes that this grammatical ambiguity is a reflection of the dislocation of the individual's sense of self and of temporal continuity: "In **'Posviashchenie'** suspension of pronominal reference, temporal shifts and fragmentation of syntax combine to convey the violent separation of the individual both from the mass and from her own sense of reality" (10). Anna L. Crone likewise comments on this multi-leveled subject and its function in the cycle when she writes, "In no work does Akhmatova merge with the nation and set herself apart from it so many times. Paradoxically, the shared common experience is the loneliness and isolation of grief" (28). The experiences described can not be understood as simply the poet's own or as those of another woman; the ambiguous syntax points to the paradoxical reality of blurred distinction between the free and the captive, between community and isolation, between self-recognition and self-estrangement.

At its simplest, an elegy can be defined as a poem occasioned by the death of an individual, but even at its simplest there is an allegorical essence to the genre. A poem about one death becomes a meditation on mutability and mortality. For Akhmatova, the arrest of her son becomes the starting point for a meditation on the pain and suffering caused by the arrests for those arrested, and even more importantly, for the families left behind, as she grammatically and figuratively proceeds to include all of these individuals under the rubric of son and mother. As Joseph Brodsky writes, "[It is] autobiographical indeed, yet the power of *Requiem* lies in the fact that Akhmatova's biography was all too common. This requiem mourns the mourners. . . . This is a tragedy where the chorus perishes before the hero" (51). Just as the traditional elegist foresees his own death in the death which he mourns, Akhmatova recognizes an essential correlation between the experiences of all Russians, whether locked inside the prisons or waiting outside its walls.

III

It has been shown that *Requiem* achieves universal significance by appealing to a broad audience and, more importantly, by emphasizing the magnitude of the atrocity—repeatedly focusing first on the victims as individuals and then on the victims as part of a countless mass. Sacks also stresses the importance of generic convention to the universal appeal of an effective elegy. He argues throughout his book that the conventions are not artificial literary devices, but are reflections of natural human impulses. Due to space limitations it is not possible to list all of the conventions and their examples in *Requiem*. I will therefore limit my discussion to the one convention which, in my opinion, is used most effectively in the cycle. The pathetic fallacy, according to Lambert, is one of the most universal conventions of the elegy and basic to grief itself:

> In funeral laments from all cultures and from all stages of civilization we see a desire on the part of the mourner (expressed either as wish or as fact) to involve the whole world in his own particular sorrows. Nature is made culpable, is made to suffer, is made to sympathize.
>
> (xxvi)

A predictable, perhaps even cliché, example of this can be found in the first lines of the **"Dedication"**: "Pered etim gorem gnutsia gory, / Ne techet velikaia reka" ("Mountains bow down to this grief, / Mighty rivers cease to flow"). In other instances, the moon visits the grieving woman of **"II,"** and the White Nights keep watch over the son and speak of his suffering. However, it is not only nature that participates in the grief, but also the man-made environment of Leningrad, and even Russia as a symbolic cultural and ethnic entity.

The pathetic fallacy springs from the rupture—caused by death—of the human's perception of his relationship to nature. For the conscious and self-contemplating human, the natural cycle of death and rebirth creates a dilemma; as Smith writes, "The one thing which appears to be exempt from rebirth is conscious being. Thus the conservation of Nature's store in endless cycles is not calculated to inspire confidence in the immortality, the eternal significance, of the individual" (5). The immortality humans wish for is not so much of the body as of the mind, and essential to that immortality is eternal communion with other humans. Smith points out, if the human soul were subject to rebirth within the natural order, eventual reunion of mourned and mourner would be impossible, the dream of eternal spiritual communion between individuals would be shattered, and the loss would be permanent. Human souls would become trapped in what Smith calls an "unearthly game of tag" (6). On the other hand, nature is the elemental force "which govern[s] man in all his social relations and all aspects of his conscious being" (5). In short, the death of an individual tears apart the mourner's perception of unity between nature, death and humanity—death comes out of season, spring branches wither and freeze, and the eternal cycle is broken. Thus the pathetic fallacy has its root in the human need to recreate an order in which man, rather than nature, is supreme. Sacks, who like Smith essentially subordinates all other elegiac conventions to the pastoral,[6] writes that the pathetic fallacy allows the elegist to create a fiction whereby the mutability of nature is not the cause of his suffering, but rather changes in nature appear to depend on him (20).

The loss grieved in a traditional elegy falls within the natural order, and consequently nature is appropriately implicated in grief. The loss in *Requiem* is a result of arrest and transpires at the hands of the poet's own government. Therefore, following the logic of Smith and Sacks, the most appropriate place to grieve would be the city. Just as nature and death are in essence intricately bound, but forcibly separated and made independent of each other within the context of the elegy, the city and the government are two aspects of civilization in general and of Russian identity in particular which are forcibly divorced from each other. In other words, the city, the government and the citizen depend on each other for their identity, but when the government turns on its citizens, the unity is broken and order falls apart. Basker describes a pervasive dislocation and disjuncture throughout the cycle, indicating the extent to which nothing is as it once was or as it should naturally be:

> Locations shift, abruptly and disconcertingly, from Leningrad to Moscow and back again, from the Neva to the Don to the Enisei, but in a sense this is immaterial: Мы не знаем, мы повсюду те же (**"Posviashchenie"**). All places coalesce undifferentiatedly into one, the only significant topography a "blind red wall" which might itself be either Kremlin or prison.
>
> (8)

The government is reduced to disjointed physical minutia: the boots of the soldiers (**"Dedication," "Prologue"**) or of the executioner (**"V"**), the blue-topped cap of the secret police (**"To Death"**), the Black Marias (**"Prologue," "Epilogue II"**), and the bolted prison door (**"Dedication," "Epilogue II"**; cf. Jeanne van der Eng-Liedmeier 324). Meanwhile, the city becomes savage (**"Dedication"**) and train whistles sing songs of farewell (**"Prologue"**). Leningrad in the **"Prologue"** is described as hanging uselessly from its prisons and filled with people being marched to the trains that will take them into exile. In **"V"** the city is reduced to tracks that lead from somewhere to nowhere, suggesting that all of Russia has been transformed into a prison.[7] The epigraph implies that Russia should and normally would protect its citizens:

> Нет, и не под чуждым небосводом,
> И не под защитой чуждых крыл,—
> Я была тогда с моим народом,
> Там, где мой народ, к несчастью, был.
>
> No, not under the vault of alien skies,
> And not under the shelter of alien wings—
> I was with my people then,
> There, where my people, unfortunately, were.

However, throughout the cycle, Leningrad and Russia are the homeland which has been made impotent by the terror and forced to share in the suffering.

Akhmatova not only implicates the Russian cityscape, but also the very idea of the Russian nation in the grief of the years of the Terror. Amert shows that in the **"Dedication"** there is a parody of an unofficial national hymn of the late 1930's (43-45). In "Song of the Motherland," Vasilii Lebedev-Kumach extols life in the Soviet Union under Stalin's rule. The line "Dlia kogo-to veet veter svezhii" ("For someone a fresh breeze blows") refers to Lebedev-Kumach's lines, "Nad stranoi vesennii veter veet, / S kazhdym dnem vse radostnee zhit'" ("Over the country a spring wind blows, / With every day living grows more joyful"; quoted in Amert 43), and in every following line, Akhmatova continues to parody and lay bare the lie of Lebedev-Kumach's patriotic optimism. In "Song of the Motherland," Lebedev-Kumach presumes to voice the sentiments of the entire Russian nation, but Akhmatova alienates his sentiment from its intended subject, ascribes it to "someone" (*kogo-to*), and proceeds to give voice to the reality of Russians' daily experiences. Ironically, in the fourth stanza, where the **"Dedication"** becomes most personal—the only stanza in the **"Dedication"** to have a singular subject—the allusion to Lebedev-Kumach's hymn implies a broad, allegorical intention. This stanza, about the mother who has heard the sentence of her son, plays off two other lines of "Song of the Motherland": "Kak nevestu, rodinu my liubim, / Berezhem, kak laskovuiu mat'" ("We love our motherland like a bride, / We cherish it like an affectionate mother"). Amert writes that in *Requiem,*

> [The] sentence is portrayed solely as mirrored in its violent effect on the woman herself, an effect that is likened both to a painful deathblow (line 18) and to her being thrown on her back (line 19), an oblique yet unmistakable reference to rape. On the symbolic level of Lebedev-Kumach's "bride" and "affectionate mother," Akhmatova is imaging here the murder and rape of the motherland.
>
> (44-45)

Juxtaposed with the "Song of the Motherland" and its allegorical treatment of mother and bride, the assault of a single woman in **"Dedication"** or in **"The Sentence"** is likewise lifted to the allegorical level of the rape of Mother Russia.

In this far-reaching elegy, not only nature, but also the cityscape and even the cultural self-identity of Russia are laid low before the suffering. Yet the shared suffering of the city and nation offers little comfort to the women, and indeed only throws into sharper relief the extent to which the women and their arrested sons and husbands have been betrayed and abandoned by the social structures which molded them. Smith writes that the fallacy fulfills the basic human need for a sense of kinship between man and nature to offset a feeling of the "essential loneliness of man in the face of forces which appear to make a mockery of all that he holds valuable" (7). It is then a gross irony that the values which are undermined—e.g., freedom, security, community and cultural identity in *Requiem*—originally spring from the same "forces" which have now violated the poet.

IV

The *Princeton Encyclopedia of Poetry and Poetics* definition, quoted at the beginning of this article, continues, "The elegy frequently includes a movement from expressed sorrow toward consolation" (322). While this may seem a very straight-forward statement, G. W. Pigman argues that the two elements—expressed grief and consolation—are, in fact, in opposition to each other. He writes, "The major purpose of consolation is to induce the bereaved to suppress grief" (2), and that "for the consoler, in prose or in verse, consolation is a defense against the breakdown of an ideal of rational self-sufficiency" (6). Pigman argues that, while any given elegy may both express grief and offer consolation, the balance between these two elements indicates the degree to which the elegist (and his or her contemporaries) are comfortable with the inherently irrational displays of sorrow (3-4). While such exercises are admittedly artificially schematic, it is possible to find markers of the poet's grief at various stages in the mourning process. However, consolation plays a minor role in the cycle as a whole. The ten central poems of *Requiem* fall exclusively into the realm of expressions of sorrow, while the framing poems, in particular the "Epilogue," offer a degree of consolation, albeit in a form that testifies to the flexibility of the genre in general.

Therese A. Rando outlines three broad grief reactions: 1) avoidance, 2) confrontation, and finally 3) reestablishment (28). In *Requiem* the poet progresses through these three stages twice, once after the arrest, portrayed in "I," and the second time after the sentencing in "VII."[8] The first stage is characterized by shock, disbelief and denial. The bereaved may be unable or unwilling to comprehend the loss, or she/he may carry out social obligations (making funeral arrangements, etc.) while emotionally denying the loss (29). In *Requiem* this can be seen in "III," in which the poet states, "Net, eto ne ia, eto kto-to drugoi stradaet. / Ia by tak ne mogla" ("No, it is no I, it is somebody else who is suffering. / I would not have been able to bear what has happened"), and again after hearing her son's sentence in "VII," "Nichego, ved'ia byla gotova, / Spravlius' s etim kak-nibud'" ("Never mind, I was ready. / I will manage somehow"). In the second stage, Rando writes, extremes of emotions are felt, including

anger, depression (its symptoms including withdrawal, apathy, feelings of helplessness, feelings of depersonalization, somatic problems, etc.), thoughts of suicide, obsessive rumination about the deceased, active searching for the deceased, identification with the deceased, spatial disorientation, and a feeling of going crazy (30-35). Nearly all of these symptoms can be found in poems ["II," "III," "IV," "V"] and "VIII"-"IX." In "II" we find the grieving woman distressed and unable to sleep. In "IV" the poet remembers her youth, full of friends and gatherings, but the present shows her in line at the prison and crying, oblivious to the festivities which should mark the New Year. In "V" the poet is confused and there are images of spatial bewilderment, as if she is unable to recognize the city in which she lives. In "VIII" the poet expresses anger at the death (by extension also at life, and in particular at the government) for its cruelly arbitrary approach to choosing whom and when to attack. And in "IX" the poet is perilously close to insanity, though not yet insane, for as Crone points out, the poet is able to list off what she claims insanity will not allow her to remember (38). J. Bowlby delineates another stage of disorganization and despair, which would mark the beginning of final reestablishment, when the bereaved resumes social contacts. In this stage, the bereaved loses hope of recovering the deceased, he/she begins to form more accurate memories of the deceased, the intense emotions subside, and the bereaved may become depressed (quoted in Rando 23; cf. Also Rando 26, Pigman 7-9). A mixture of memory, sorrow and reconciliation is especially noticeable in "VI," in which the confusion and anger expressed in "V" have given way to a relatively clear-minded reflection on the year that had passed while the son was in prison. And in "X" the sense of the mother having accepted her loss and her burden of sorrow is so strong that ironically there is no hint of the resurrection and the promise of eternal life that the Crucifixion usually signifies. Akhmatova only begins to show signs of having reached the final stage of reestablishment in "Epilogue II."

If it is indeed the case, as Pigman writes, that "consolation is a defense against the breakdown of an ideal of rational self-sufficiency" (6), one might infer that Akhmatova is not terribly concerned with imposing a rational explanation on the events which occasioned *Requiem*. The greater bulk of the cycle is devoted to her grief, leaving only the "Epilogue" to the task of finding some kind of consolation. This, John Harris suggests in "An Elegy for Myself: British Poetry and the Holocaust," is the appropriate response, possibly the only response, to a large-scale atrocity. The traditional elegist places the tragedy of an individual's death within a larger context that grants it reason, makes it understandable and leads to consolation.[9] Harris writes that there is no larger, rationalizing context to the Holocaust of Nazi Germany:

The first problem facing any attempt to write about the atrocities of those times is that of conceiving their scale, both in sheer numbers and in terms of the lack of humanity which caused them. . . . Secondly, in claiming that we can conceive the horror of the Holocaust we lay ourselves open to the accusation that by imposing a critical form and structure on it we are *ipso facto* justifying it; by attributing a rationale of any sort to it, we admit that the Holocaust could be seen as a rational act.

(213)

It is in fact for this reason that George Steiner speaks of the necessity not to write at certain points in history:

The temptation of silence [is] the belief that in the presence of certain realities art is trivial or impertinent. . . . The world of Auschwitz lies outside speech as it lies outside reason. To speak of the *unspeakable* is to risk the survivance of language as creator and bearer of humane, rational truth.

(123; emphasis in original)

The sense of injustice in a traditional elegy lay not in the fact that death strikes, but in that death struck this once, in an untimely manner, an individual whom we wish would have stayed with us longer. Death is cruel, it is arbitrary, it is indifferent to the accomplishments or promise of its victims, but for all this, it is not without rationale (Smith 8).[10] An atrocity such as the Holocaust or the Terror, on the other hand, defies comprehension. What words can describe a situation that has no meaning? However, this leads to the moral problem of acknowledging the events; if there are no words with which to speak of the atrocity, how will it be remembered? Thus Brodsky writes, "At certain periods of history it is only poetry that is capable of dealing with reality by condensing it into something graspable, something that otherwise could not be retained by the mind" (52). Theodor Adorno, who is famous for his proclamation that it is "barbaric to continue to write poetry after Auschwitz" (87), also admits that poetry is indispensable: "Suffering—what Hegel called the awareness of affliction—also demands the continued existence of the very art it forbids; hardly anywhere else does suffering still find its own voice, a consolation that does not immediately betray it" (88).[11] The successful poem portrays the events without rationalization, preserving the memory of those who suffered, while at the same time preserving the sense of overwhelming chaos. The elegy for such an atrocity must find consolation through memory that does not impose reason.

This complicated task is achieved even within the ten central poems of *Requiem.* In addition to expressing her grief with nearly textbook accuracy, Akhmatova conveys historical information about what happened, and more importantly its toll on the men who were arrested and the women who were left behind. Many of the images used to describe the poet's state of mind are images of arrest and death and serve the dual function of describing what happened to the son and what the mother felt as a result. For example, in **"To Death"** the poet wishes desperately to be in her son's place: to be arrested, dead or in Siberia, and in **"IX"** she recreates the experience of half-death, "Uzhe bezumnie krylom / Dushi zakrylo polovinu" ("Now madness half shadows / My soul with its wing"). Here, insanity is personified as one who comes to arrest her:

И не позволит ничего
Оно мне унести с собою
(Как ни упрашивай его
И как ни докучай мольбою)

And it does not allow me to take
Anything of mine with me
(No matter how I plead with it,
No matter how I supplicate)

The image of insanity again sets on equal terms death, which allows nothing to be carried away, and arrest, against which supplication is useless (see **"V"**: "Kidalas' v nogi palachu"; "I flung myself at the hangman's feet"). Also, in **"The Sentence",** the poet entertains two possible reactions to the news of her son's sentence:

Надо память до конца убить,
Надо, чтоб душа окаменела,
Надо снова научиться жить,—
А не то . . .

I must kill memory once and for all,
I must turn my soul to stone,
I must learn to live again—
[Otherwise] . . ."

The former wish—to turn her soul to stone—echoes her son's fate in **"IX,"** where suffering has turned his eyes to stone, the new life which the poet must learn echoes the new life of exile which the son is now learning, and the final "Otherwise" represents the possibility of escaping suffering through death—an option for mother and son alike (see Etkind 375). Even though the mother's experience was in actuality not the same as her son's, she constructs the events and her feelings in terms which strongly imply a shared experience.

The correlation between the son's actual experience and the mother's perception of her own has significance on several levels. In psychological terms, the mother's construction of her own experiences in terms reminiscent of arrest and imprisonment is yet another step in the mourning process. Sigmund Freud writes that one of the symptoms of mourning is "loss of capacity to adopt any new object of love, which would mean replacing of the one mourned, [and] turning from every active effort that is not connected with thoughts of the dead" ("Mourning" 153). In light of this, one might argue that the poet attempts to live her son's experiences, perhaps even to become him, in order to postpone the separation. In generic terms, the vicarious death of the poet is the avenue by which the poet explores the meaning of loss, the nature of the self, and the function of art. Meyer writes,

> The poet undergoes a self-imposed death and catharsis, achieving a reconstruction of the self through the construction of the poem. The mythology of modern death, one may say, represents not a radical shift away from the elegiac tradition, but rather a further intensification of its basic concerns: the "I" and the other, the contemplation of death and the celebration of life, the fragmentation of the self and its reconstruction through art.
>
> (24-25)

However, it is a final, moral aspect that sets *Requiem* apart from the traditional elegy and forces us to look for a new definition of consolation. The vicarious arrest and imprisonment of the mother conveys the memory of the suffering felt both by the arrested men within the prison and the women waiting outside. *Requiem* aspires not only to immortalize the son or even the mother's love for her son, but to acknowledge the reality of the Terror in such a way that will not allow history to forget. The poetic consolation, which Adorno writes does not immediately betray the suffering it portrays, is the memorialization of the events as they truly happened. Akhmatova's overarching goal in the ten central poems is to immortalize an entire nation victimized by the Terror.

The consolation which Adorno speaks of, which does not betray suffering by offering rationale, is not the same kind of consolation which Pigman discusses. The former consolation is the result of the knowledge that the suffering has been recognized as the atrocity it is, while the latter consolation is the result of a belief that grief is not necessary, for the deceased is not truly lost and the separation is only temporary. The former consolation involves admission of suffering, the latter suppression. *Requiem* as a whole can be said to offer consolation of the former type, but lacks the latter type completely. This does not, however, imply that *Requiem* is in some way an abortive elegy. Sacks, in his discussion of the psychological foundations of the elegy, speaks not so much of consolation as of resolution, i.e., of the successful result of the work of mourning, or what Rando calls "reestablishment." The work of mourning, as Freud calls it, consists of detaching one's affection (libido) from the lost object and reattaching it elsewhere ("Mourning" 154; cf. Rando 35-36). This is not the same as consolation, for Freud also writes,

> Although we know that after such a loss the acute state of mourning will subside, we also know we shall remain inconsolable and will never find a substitute.

> No matter what may fill the gap, even if it be filled completely, it nevertheless remains something else. And actually this is how it should be. It is the only way of perpetuating that love which we do not want to relinquish.
>
> (*Letters* 386)

According to Sacks, for the elegist, whose reality is intimately bound together with words, the object to which affection is reattached is language (xii, 1, 18-19).[12]

The grief expressed in the central ten poems is raw, internal, not inherently within the realm of language, and expressed without a strong sense of an implied reader. This is not the case in the framing poems. These poems, as already pointed out above, seem to address the reader directly. The **"Dedication,"** for example, prepares the reader with an outline of the sequence of events to be portrayed in the cycle: the arrest and imprisonment, the waiting in line, and the sentencing and isolation (Amert 45-46). The **"Prologue"** and **"Epilogue I"** summarize the Terror from the perspective of the arrested and the women left behind, respectively. These three poems demonstrate the successful resolution of the poet's work of mourning, insofar as they state with relative directness what the poet only intimates in the central poems. However, it is in **"Epilogue II"** and **"Instead of a Foreword"** that Akhmatova most clearly articulates her strategies to overcome the suffering of the Terror.

Whereas the ten central poems are by their very existence a memorial to the victims of the Terror, **"Epilogue II"** lays emphasis on the act of articulating memory as a defense against the continued suffering. In this poem, Akhmatova purposefully invokes language itself as a weapon. Throughout the cycle the poet, as well as all of the women, are shown bewildered, speechless and defeated. In **"Epilogue II"** Akhmatova overcomes this. Geographic locations distinguish themselves from each other and remain fixed to their proper historical significance. The women with whom Akhmatova stood in line begin to stand out from the mass as individuals, for as Amert writes,

> In contrast to the collective portrait evoked in the first part of the **"Epilogue,"** the poet conjures up brief yet individualized portraits of three of her addressees and then articulates her unrealizable wish to call all of the women by name, thereby commemorating them individually—the antithesis of their depersonalization during the Ezhov Terror.
>
> (52)

Akhmatova even restores to the women the power of speech. Aside from the whispered question in **"Instead of a Preface,"** the only moment of articulate speech is by the beautiful woman in the **"Epilogue"**: "Siuda prikhozhu, kak domoi!" ("Coming here's like coming home").

On a more fundamental level, however, **"Epilogue II"** makes clear that Akhmatova intends for the cycle to itself supply the words to name the atrocities which could only be met with silence at the time. Sacks writes that the poetic form of the elegy is a verbal "presence" which fills the "absence" caused by death (xi-xiii). The need to create a "presence" through language is only that much more acute when the elegy is for victims of an atrocity, since, as we have seen, Terror deprives the victims of the means of articulating their pain and, by isolating the women at the time and then finally scattering them, eliminates the potential audience. Akhmatova uses the image of weaving a cloth of words as a means of creating a tangible "presence" to displace the "absence" created by the Terror. Sacks writes that it is

> worth noting the significant frequency with which the elegy has employed crucial images of weaving, of creating a fabric in the place of a void. . . . To speak of weaving a consolation recalls the actual weaving of burial clothes and shroud and this emphasizes how mourning is an action, a process of work.
>
> (18-19)

Akhmatova uses exactly the image of weaving a cloth of words. Unable to name each woman and not knowing what has become of them, she nevertheless seeks to fill the void of their silence with a veil of their own words: "Dlia nikh sotkala ia shirokii pokrov / Iz bednykh, u nikh zhe podslushannykh slov" ("I have woven a wide mantle for them / From their meager, overheard words"). On the one hand, this cloth she weaves may be seen as a burial shroud, with which, perhaps, she offers a token rite to those who had been executed in secret and buried without a memorial service or grave marker. Perhaps also it is a shroud with which Akhmatova puts to rest her grief of the ten central poems. But more than just covering and concealing what has happened, this cloth also makes it visible. The women have been scattered without any record of their having been there. Akhmatova's veil of words solidifies them into a group, protects them from obscurity, and replaces their physical absence with a verbal presence.

The poet does not simply present the atrocity to the reader, but she incorporates it into herself. She succumbs together with the other victims to the Terror, knows first-hand their suffering, but then overcomes the silence, resurrects herself, and presents herself verbally, not only on behalf of the victims but also for her own sake. When in **"Instead of a Foreword"** Akhmatova answers the nameless woman's question "Can you describe this?", Akhmatova is accepting the call to be a prophet and taking upon herself the burden of not forgetting nor allowing history to forget. She accepts the call to perpetually relive the pain through her poetry and, above all, to speak it. Sam Driver writes, "It is this self-abnegation and acceptance of responsibility for

universal brotherhood that raises **'Poem without a Hero'** and **'Requiem'** to the level [Osip] Mandel'shtam foresaw—where the true poet stands on moral grounds, not only as a symbol of rectitude, but as judge" ("Theory and Practice" 349). It is she who weaves the veil of words to spread over the other women, giving them definition and protecting them from obscurity, just as the veil of the Virgin protects her people (see Amert 52-53; Driver, *Akhmatova* 155 n. 19). It is she who with the confidence of a prophet affirms with a simple "Mogu"/"I can" her ability to describe the unspeakable.

Notes

1. Elegy can be understood as two distinct types of poetry. The first classification, often also called the "elegiac mode," is defined primarily by form. This type of elegy can be written on any subject, but the content most often is dominated by themes of love and the passage of time, and is usually pervaded by a melancholic mood. This application of the term "elegy" is the most common one in Russian poetics. According to L. G. Frizman, for example, the elegy is above all characterized by the melancholic mood, sadness, lamentation, etc., but it is usually not related to death and mourning. This definition fits Akhmatova's *Northern Elegies*, but not *Requiem*. The second definition of elegy, the definition which I will be using, is "a poem about death and mourning." Meter and rhyme do not usually play a role in this generic classification; psychology, however, does. This type of elegy is also often called the "elegy of mourning," the "funeral elegy," or sometimes in discussions of twentieth-century elegies "poetry of mourning."

2. All translations of *Requiem* are by Judith Hemschemeyer. Where the translation has been modified to be more literal, brackets have been used. Quotes from the cycle are identified by either the title of the poem or its Roman numeral.

3. Amanda Haight writes that the first poem (I) was written on the occasion of the arrest of Punin, Akhmatova's third husband, and that Akhmatova's son was arrested shortly before Punin (92). Furthermore, the loss of Akhmatova's third husband and son may have triggered grief for her first husband, especially if she had not yet resolved her grief for that loss. Rando outlines various social factors which may inhibit normal grief work, two of which may apply to Akhmatova's situation at the time of N. Gumilev's death. First, Akhmatova and Gumilev were already divorced at the time of his death. Consequently, her loss would not necessarily be socially recognized as a loss, since it might be assumed that he was not a significant part of her life. Second, the fact that he

was executed for his service in the White Army might make his death a "socially unspeakable loss" (66). In these cases of "social negation of loss" and "socially unspeakable loss," Rando writes, "Although grief work is necessary, the social support for it is inadequate or non-existent," and in the latter case, "members of the social system . . . tend to shy away [from the bereaved] out of ignorance of what to say to help or moral repugnance" (66).

4. Michael Basker also discusses this missing line, with its "suggestion of a thought too awful to articulate," adding that "the descent into distressed silence is also the formal realization of the deathly hush described in the preceding metrical line" (11). Basker further points to two other examples of metrical truncation in the cycle. In "the Sentence," the last line of the first stanza is four rather than five metrical feet, formally undermining the verbal statement that the author will cope with what has happened. Finally, in III, the last monosyllabic line "Noch'" represents a break, as in IV, into a formally premature silence (11).

5. Boris Katz also notes the irony of a requiem written about living, "albeit doomed," persons. He concludes that the penultimate line of "Crucifixion," "A tuda, gde molcha Mat' stoiala" ("But there, where the silent Mother stood") alludes to the opening lines of the *Sabat Mater* (260). He writes, "Thus, ultimately, it is not a requiem that Akhmatova wrote, in spite of the title *Requiem*. Rather, it is a very Russian, even very Soviet, and, of course, very Akhmatovian version of *Sabat Mater*" (262).

6. To give two examples, Sacks describes how the procession of mourners, which functions to place a distance between the dead and the still living, can be traced to the yearly departure and return of the vegetation god (19-20), and he traces the convention of a repetition of words and phrases to the cycle of the seasons (23-24). Sacks summarizes the elegiac conventions on pages 18-37.

7. Sharon Leiter writes, "Living in a city which for thousands, in point of fact, became a 'transfer point' to Siberian imprisonment, Akhmatova, who was spared, experienced this freedom as both exile and imprisonment" (89). Leningrad had become a prison and intermediate station for all of its citizens, not just for those who had been arrested.

8. "Anticipatory grief" might be experienced, writes Rando, when a family member becomes terminally ill, when a family member is missing in action or a prisoner of war, or even when one is scheduled for amputation of a limb (37-39). One might argue that Akhmatova experiences anticipatory grief

after the arrest of her son, and the true loss is marked by the sentence—the difference between a death sentence and exile being negligible for the family, after all. Support for this can be found in IX, in which we learn that Akhmatova did have at least one opportunity to meet with her son in prison, giving her an opportunity to resolve unfinished business with him and to prepare an image of him to endure after the final loss (see Rando 37-38). Also, in "The Sentence," the reference to the empty house implies that Akhmatova had not yet really felt her son to be absent until that time. However, a detailed psychological analysis of Akhmatova's grief work based on a reading of *Requiem* would certainly have a large margin of error.

9. This larger context usually involves immortality of one of two kinds. Elegies such as John Milton's *Lycidas* or Percy Shelley's *Adonis* offer the consoling argument that the deceased is now in the immortal company of God (or the Muses). These two elegies remove the deceased from Earth to an eternal Hereafter, where the poet hopes to eventually join the deceased. Other elegies, such as Brodsky's "Verses on the Death of T. S. Eliot," argue that the works of the deceased will perpetuate his existence; although the body has died, the soul of the deceased has achieved immortality. In either case, the grief caused by loss and the fear of mortality is countered by the projection of an immutable realm in which the deceased continues to exist.

10. This is perhaps one reason why the elegy has traditionally been a proving-ground for young poets (see Pigman 43). The paradoxes of the human versus nature and of the feeling that death is unjust versus the knowledge that death is both inevitable and not necessarily bad make the writing of the elegy an excellent language exercise.

11. Adorno's justification for the prohibition of poetry is that poetry threatens to make the atrocity aesthetically pleasing. Even as he admits that effective poems have been written about the Holocaust and even as he recognizes the futility of calling for an end to poetry, he argues that the memory of the victims is compromised if a reader were to derive even a small amount of pleasure from reading about their suffering. This is a very different argument than Harris's, Steiner's or Brodsky's. Insofar as *Requiem* is a well-wrought and effective cycle, Akhmatova can hardly be defended against this charge. Furthermore, whether we would want to defend Akhmatova, and the manner in which it could be done, are questions of theory and beyond the scope of this paper.

12. Sacks defines the process of writing an elegy as one analogous to the psychological paradigm of Lacan, for whom language emerges as a result of the loss of a child's undifferentiated union with the mother (8-12).

Works Cited

Adorno, Theodor W. "Commitment." *Notes to Literature.* Vol. 2. Ed. Rolf Tiedemann. Trans. Shierry Weber Nicholsen. New York: Columbia UP, 1992. 76-94.

Akhmatova, Anna. *Anna Akhmatova: Polnoe sobranie stikhotvorenii. The Complete Poems of Anna Akhmatova.* Vol. 2. Trans. Judith Hemschemeyer. Ed. Roberta Reeder. Somerville: Zepher P, 1992.

Amert, Susan. *In a Shattered Mirror: The Later Poetry of Anna Akhmatova.* Stanford: Stanford UP, 1992.

Basker, Michael. "Dislocation and Relocation in Akhmatova's *Rekviem.*" *The Speech of Unknown Eyes: Akhmatova's Readers on Her Poetry.* Vol 1. Ed. Wendy Rosslyn. Nottingham: Astra P, 1990. 5-25.

Brodsky, Joseph. "The Keening Muse." *Less than One: Selected Essays.* New York: Farrar Straus Giroux, 1986. 34-52.

Brogan, T. V. F., Peter Sacks, and Stephen F. Fogle. "Elegy." *The New Princeton Encyclopedia of Poetry and Poetics.* Ed. Alex Preminger, T. V. F. Brogan, et al. New York: MJF Books, 1993. 322-25.

Crone, Anna L. "Antimetabole in *Rekviem*: The Structural Disposition in Themes and Motifs." *The Speech of Unknown Eyes: Akhmatova's Readers on Her Poetry.* Vol 1. Ed. Wendy Rosslyn. Nottingham: Astra P, 1990. 27-41.

Driver, Sam. *Anna Akhmatova.* New York: Twayne, 1972.

————. "Anna Akhmatova: Theory and Practice." *Canadian-American Slavic Studies* 22. 1-4 (1988): 343-51.

Eng-Liedmeier, Jeanne van der. "Aspects of the Prophetic Theme in Akhmatova's Poetry." *The Speech of Unknown Eyes: Akhmatova's Readers on Her Poetry.* Vol 2. Ed. Wendy Rosslyn. Nottingham: Astra P, 1990. 315-32.

Etkind, Efim. "Die Unsterblichkeit des Gedächtnisses: Anna Achmatovas Poem 'Requiem.'" *Die Welt der Slaven* 29. 2 (1984): 360-94.

Freud, Sigmund. *Letters of Sigmund Freud.* Trans. Tania Stern and James Stern. Ed. Ernst L. Freud. New York: Basic Books, 1960.

————. "Mourning and Melancholia." *Collected Papers.* Vol 4. Trans. Joan Riviere. London: Hogarth P, 1950. 152-70.

Frizman, L. G. "Dva veka russkoi elegii." *Russkaia elegiia xviii-nachala xx veka.* Sost. L. G. Frizman. Leningrad: Sovetskyi Pisatel', 1991. 5-48.

Haight, Amanda. *Anna Akhmatova: A Poetic Pilgrimage.* New York: Oxford, 1976.

Katz, Boris. "To What Extent is *Requiem* a Requiem? Unheard Female Voices in Anna Akhmatova's *Requiem.*" *Russian Review* 57. 2 (1998): 253-63.

Lambert, Ellen Zetzel. *Placing Sorrow: A Study of the Pastoral Elegy Convention from Theocritus to Milton.* Chapel Hill: U of North Carolina P, 1976.

Latimer, Dan. *The Elegiac Mode in Milton and Rilke: Reflections on Death.* Frankfurt a. M.: Peter Lang, 1977.

Leiter, Sharon. *Akhmatova's Petersburg.* Philadelphia: U of Pennsylvania P, 1983.

Ljunggren, Anna. "Anna Akhmatova's *Requiem*: A Retrospective of the Love Lyric and Epos." *Anna Akhmatova 1889-1989. Papers from the Akhmatova Centennial Conference* Ed. Sonia Ketchian. Oakland: Berkeley Slavic Specialities, 1993.

Meyer, Kinereth. "The Mythology of Modern Death." *Genre* 19. 1 (1986): 21-35.

Pigman, G. W. III. *Grief and English Renaissance Elegy.* Cambridge: Cambridge UP, 1985.

Rando, Therese A. *Grief, Dying, and Death: Clinical Interventions for Caregivers.* Champaign, IL: Research Press Company, 1984.

Sacks, Peter M. *The Engligh Elegy.* Baltimore: Johns Hopkins UP, 1985.

Smith, Eric. *By Mourning Tongues: Studies in English Elegy.* Ipswich, England: Boydell, 1977.

Steiner, George. *Language and Silence: Essays on Language, Literature and the Inhuman* New York: Atheneum, 1967.

Thomas, D. M. "Introduction." *Selected Poems of Anna Akhmatova.* Trans. and ed. D. M. Thomas. New York: Penguin, 1988.

Wells, David. *Anna Akhmatova: Her Poetry.* Oxford: Berg, 1996.

FURTHER READING

Criticism

Crone, Anna. "Antimetabolie in *Rekviem*: The Structural Disposition of Themes and Motifs." In *The Speech of Unknown Eyes: Akhmatova's Readers on Her Poetry,* edited by Wendy Rosslyn, pp. 27-41. Cotgrave, Nottingham, England: Astra Press, 1990.

Structural analysis of Akhmatova's *Requiem.*

Kemball, Robin. "Anna Akhmatova's 'Requiem, 1935-1940.'" *The Russian Review* 33, no. 3 (July 1974): 303-12.

    English translation of Akhmatova's *Requiem* that purports to retain the meter, line-length and rhyme-scheme of the original Russian.

Stone, Carole. "Elegy as Political Expression in Women's Poetry: Akhmatova, Levertov, Forché." *College Literature* 18, no. 1 (February 1991): 84-91.

    Comparison of elegies composed by women poets.

Terras, Victor. *Poetry of the Silver Age: The Various Voices of Russian Modernism.* Dresden, Germany: Dresden University Press, 1998, 353 p.

    Poets highlighted in the chapter about the Acmeism movement include Nikolai Gumilyov, Akhmatova's first husband, and Akhmatova.

Thomas, D. M. *Anna Akhmatova: Requiem* and *Poem without a Hero.* Athens, Ohio: Ohio University Press, 1976, 78 p.

    Translations of two of Akhmatova's master works, including a critical introduction by the translator.

Additional coverage of Akhmatova's life and career is contained in the following sources published by the Gale Group: *Contemporary Authors,* **Vols. 19-20;** *Contemporary Authors New Revision Series,* **Vol. 35;** *Contemporary Authors—Obituary,* **Vols. 25-28R;** *Contemporary Authors Permanent Series,* **Vol. 1;** *Contemporary Literary Criticism,* **Vols. 11, 25, 64, 126;** *DISCovering Authors 3.0; DISCovering Authors Modules: Poets; Encyclopedia of World Literature in the 20ᵗʰ Century,* **Ed. 3;** *European Writers,* **Vol. 10;** *Literature Resource Center; Major 20ᵗʰ-Century Writers,* **Eds. 1, 2;** *Poetry Criticism,* **Vol. 2; and** *Reference Guide to World Literature,* **Eds. 2, 3.**

Sterling Allen Brown
1901-1989

American poet, folklorist, editor, critic, and essayist.

The following entry provides information on Brown's life and works from 1934 through 1999.

INTRODUCTION

An important American poet and critic, Brown was one of the first writers to infuse his poetry with black folklore. In his first collection, *Southern Road* (1932), he wove elements of ballads, spirituals, work songs, and the blues into narrative poems generally written in a southern black dialect. Although Brown published little poetry after this collection, many critics believe that his work was significant in the development of black writing.

BIOGRAPHICAL INFORMATION

Brown was born in Washington, D.C., on May 1, 1901. His father, Sterling Nelson Brown, taught in the department of religion at Howard University and was pastor of Washington's historic Lincoln Temple Congregational Church. Among the minister's associates were black leaders Frederick Douglass and Booker T. Washington, senators B. K. Bruce and John R. Lynch, sociologist W. E. B. Du Bois, and cultural critic Alain Locke. Brown was inspired by his acquaintance with these men to study black history and the importance of black life in America. After he graduated from Williams College in 1922, Brown enrolled at Harvard University and received a master's degree in English in 1923. After graduation Brown taught in the rural South—despite his contemporaries' attempts to dissuade him. It was during this time he gathered the material for *Southern Road,* which was published in 1932. He accepted a teaching position at Howard University, where he would remain for forty years. Despite the success of *Southern Road,* his publisher rejected what would have been his second published volume of poetry, *No Hiding Place,* and declined to issue a second printing of *Southern Road.* These decisions had a devastating effect on Brown's reputation as a poet; because no new poems appeared, many of his admirers assumed that he had stopped writing. Brown subsequently turned his attention to teaching and to writing criticism, producing several major works on African-American studies. In 1971 Howard University granted Brown an honorary degree. A republication of *Southern Road* and a new volume of poetry, *The Last Ride of Wild Bill and Eleven Narrative Poems* (1975), followed. He died on January 13, 1989.

MAJOR WORKS

Southern Road is Brown's best-known and most highly acclaimed volume of poetry. Viewed as a breakthrough for black poetry, it incorporates the dialect, music, folklore, and rhythms of rural African Americans in the South. In the poems in the collection, Brown focuses on farmers, preachers, prisoners, prostitutes, and itinerant workers who are at home in their surroundings and preoccupied with the business of survival. The volume includes poems such as "Sam Smiley," in which a World War I veteran returns home to find his woman in prison for having killed the baby she conceived by a rich white man in Sam's absence. Sam is lynched for murdering the man. In poems "Memphis Blues" and "Ma Rainey," he celebrates the strength and stoicism of the African American people. Brown looked humorously at race relations in other poems, particularly in a series featuring the character Slim Greer. In the poem "Slim in Atlanta," the protagonist discovers that blacks are forbidden to laugh in public, and are lining up to laugh in the security of a telephone booth. Slim finds the situation so absurd that he jumps to the front of the line, seizes the telephone booth, and proceeds to laugh for four hours, much to the dismay of the three hundred blacks in line. Brown's later collection, *The Last Ride of Wild Bill,* focuses on tales of black heroism. In the title poem, Wild Bill defiantly battles a corrupt chief of police who is out to eliminate Bill's numbers business. Although Wild Bill eventually loses to the lawman, he is viewed as an enduring and courageous figure who refuses to be pushed around by the white man.

CRITICAL RECEPTION

Southern Road was a critical success, prompting James Weldon Johnson to change his mind about dialect poetry. Johnson, who had previously said that dialect verse could only depict humor and pathos, now saw a greater depth with Brown's poetry, which he praised in the introduction to *Southern Road.* Although critics often cite Brown as one of the most neglected poets of the twentieth century, they have also undertaken to correct that notion. In recent years several critical studies of Brown's poetry and career have appeared, and many critics note that he has now received the attention he lacked in his lifetime. Several commentators have praised his work as important to the development of African American poetry and perceive Brown to be a seminal figure in African American letters.

PRINCIPAL WORKS

Poetry

Southern Road 1932

The Last Ride of Wild Bill and Eleven Narrative Poems 1975

*The Collected Poems of Sterling A. Brown 1980

Other Major Works

Outline for the Study of the Poetry of American Negroes (criticism) 1931

The Negro in American Fiction (criticism) 1937

Negro Poetry and Drama (criticism) 1938

A Son's Return: Selected Essays of Sterling A. Brown (essays) 1996

*This work includes many of the poems in Brown's unpublished *No Hiding Place*.

CRITICISM

E. Clay (essay date June 1934)

SOURCE: Clay, E. "Sterling Brown: American Peoples' Poet." *International Literature* 8, no. 2 (June 1934): 117-22.

[*In the following essay, Clay assesses Brown's contribution to African American poetry.*]

Somewhere a long time ago, I ran across this apt couplet in an old poem, "The Singer:"

> Thus in his manhood, clean, superb and strong
> To him was born the priceless gift of song.

That fits Sterling Brown exactly: Brown is a singer, a rhapsodos, a singer of his people. The Greek rhapsodos was a reciter of the epic also. Epic poetry is usually great poetry and requires mighty subject matter. There is vast, unmined material for epic poetry in the Negro race and one hopes fervently that Sterling Brown will fulfill the fine echoed prophecy of Stephen Vincent Benet in his *John Brown's Body*:

> Oh, blackskinned epic, epic with the black spear
> I cannot sing you, having too white a heart
> And yet some day a poet will rise to sing you
> And sing you with such truth and mellowness. . . .

Yes, that is the kind of poet Brown is, a poet who, we hope, is conscious that his is at last the task of singing the Negro as he is and not as he has been written about or sung. And the fecundity with which he endows his explicit characterizations ensures his poetry a well placed niche in the American poetic scene.

Sterling Brown has never written for any special group, black or white. He has no pandering, truculent desire to appeal to the genteel diversion and tradition. That is his real value. He has created new values, or rather transvalued old dog-eared ones. In his indigenous, of-the-earth poetry, there is never any lachrymose piddling. The darts he sends find their destination almost anywhere:

> They cooped you in their kitchens,
> They penned you in their factories,
> They gave you the jobs they were too good for
> They tried to guarantee happiness to themselves
> By shunting dirt and misery to you.

There are others writing poetry similar to this, but as will be shown, Brown's poetry has somehow struck a newer note in Negro poetry. We have been waiting for this note a long time—a divergence of our racial stream performed by a poet who has his gaze riveted upon the social panorama—a poet whose social sensitivity enables him to draw in his poetry those psychologic, historic and sociologic ideologies so peculiar to American Negro life. He has tried to see his Negro life whole and this in itself is significant. He has sterilized Negro art forms and purged them of their decadent white-washed effusions. He has returned to the dialect form—for much the same reasons as Synge and McKay—and he uses it with a truly novel effect.

There had to arise some day a poet who would be conscious of the social maladjustments of the Negro scene, who could drink in the kaleidoscope of rich and varied living with thirsty attention. Toomer has enriched our poetic vaults with his unforgettable characterizations of Southern life as he saw it. But here we have a poet who has given us the cross-section, country and city, North, South, East and West. None are missing from his canvas, Big Boy, Jack Johnson, Sporting Beasley, Slim Greer, dicties, dudes, Bessie "gaunt of flesh and painted," Ma Rainy, Harlem street-walkers, John Henry, Jewish cabaret owners, convicts, Hardrock Gene, Mississippi and Father Missouri "children," Hambone, the whole gamut is on his page.

To be worthwhile today, an artist must have his roots in the social soil, he must have something new. And Brown's poetry startles us because we see in it a razing of washed-out nostrums into fresh components, a creation of new social values into the alembic of social reality. His poetry makes for discovery because it is socially significant, because his poetic gaze is fixed upon that part of humanity who feel, suffer and produce. He does not romanticize or idealize those he portrays. These people are real to him:

> These folks knew then the hints of fear
> For all their loafings on the levee
> Unperturbably spendthrifts of time.
>
> ("**Children of the Mississippi**"[1])

He does have faith in them and the humanity they typify. He is glad they can laugh and sing even if

> They bought off some of your leaders
> You stumbled as blind men will. . . .
> They coaxed you, unwontedly, soft voiced
> You followed a way
> Then laughed as usual
> They heard the laugh and wondered
> Uncomfortable
> Unadmitting a deeper terror
>
> ("**Strong Men**")

Do any escape this fear? Not many, for Brown writes of them all with amazing fidelity, of Long Gone who

> Aint never caught you wrong,
> But it jes aint nachal
> Fo' to stay here long

of Big Boy who

> Done shocked de co'n in Marylan'
> In Georgia done cut cane
> Done planted rice in South Caline

of Maumee Sal, Maumee Ruth, elders, deacons, of handsome Daniel who became a pimp, of Lulu and Jim who "found religion in a chubby baby boy," of Georgie Grimes who murdered his woman, of wise old men and women, of those who must abide by the uncontrollable Father Missouri and Ole Man Mississippi, of those who are victims of destructive tornadoes, and of those unfortunate children who do not know what is to be their lot in a capitalistic society:

> They have forgotten
> What had to be endured

He portrays with equal warmth the lot of the sharecroppers who

> Buy one rusty mule
> We stays in debt
> Until we're dead.

He knows well the problems of debt slavery, economic injustice, trials by prejudice, wage slavery, discrimination, segregation, slums, peonage, starvation and he scalpels them all with broad swathes.

Sterling Brown is a product of the Negro upper middle class. This bourgeois heritage has not deterred him in laying bare the surface superfluities of Negro "society." His environment has been the parsonage of educated parents, Williams College, Harvard and university teaching. He has been able to pierce through the vanities, shams and fictions of bourgeois existence. In "**Tin Roof Blues**" he writes of the

> Gang of dicties here, and de rest wants to git dat way
> Dudes and dicties, others strive to git dat way.
> Put pennies on de numbers from now unto de judgment day

There is always an agonized awareness of macabre decadence and revolt, of the ineffable vacuities of middle-class life and of the inevitableness of their social counter-parts. In this quotation from "**Sun Down**," the poet seems to be convinced that there is no earthly way in which the social directives or class ideologies can be avoided:

> Churches don't help me cause I aint got no Sunday clothes
> Preachers and deacons, dont look to git no help from those

and from "**Salutamus**" this:

> What was our crime that such a searing brand
> Not of our choosing keeps us hated so

Of course there is still noticeable the imprint of his class in his work. This is unavoidable and is not to be wondered at, for the emotional content cannot be entirely done away with nor can an artist immediately resolve the dialectical antitheses of his personal and social life.

There are two very important aspects of his poetry that must be considered—his attitudes toward race consciousness and his ruthless bludgeoning of the American created, fictionized stereotyped Negro. Certainly Brown is very well acquainted with the phenomena of racial pride, "ethnocentrism," oppression psychoses, discrimination and their concomitant incunabula. What one misses in his work, though, is the overemphasis on these American institutions seen in the work of other Negro poets. He has written often of Salisbury Md., of Tuscoloosa, Scottsboro and of other outrages. There is very much the same pent up fury and scorn that so colors the incendiary poetry of McKay and Hughes. And he does display in his poems an intuitive acuity of group consciousness, as in his **"Strong Men:"**

> Walk together, chillen
> Dontcha get weary
> The strong men keep-a-comin' on
> The strong men git stronger
>
>   . . . . .
>
> One thing they cannot prohibit
> The strong men . . . carrying on
> The strong men gittin stronger
> Strong men
> Stronger.

It seems to me, that in poetry of this stripe, there is a tendency toward an ideological identification with a racial group rather than mere race consciousness. He recognizes all too poignantly the presence of "oppression psychoses." But there is a different kind of defiance in this recognition:

> What reaches them
> Ill at ease, fearful?
> Today they shout prohibition at you
> "Thou shalt not this
> Thou shalt not that"
> "Reserved for whites only"
> You laugh

Again there is no fawning self-pity, as in so many poems of the older Negro poets, no pitying his race. Perhaps in the poems **"Children of the Mississippi,"** **"Father Missouri," "Sam Smiley," "Tornado Blues"** and others, this might seem so, but they seem to be rather a faithful depiction of a deterministic, long-suffering minority. If the charge be proven, then his pity is cool and detached rather than the sickening gush and tearfulness of other poets. There is dignity here, yes, nonchalance, with head thrown back as he writes of the victims of Father Missouri,

> Who takes what was loaned so very long ago
> And leaves puddles in the parlor, and useless lakes
> In his fine pasture land.
> Sees years of labor turned into nothing
> Curses and shouts in his hoarse old voice
> "Aint got no right to act dat way at all!
> No right at all!"

Like the other poets, he resents the efforts made to impugn the moral status of the race. He despises any kind of stereotype and in especial the sex and morality fixations. And he is never slow to portray with telling and vital truth the critical facts as to white and black morality as in **"Frankie and Johnny," "Slim Greer,"** **"Sam Smiley"** and **"Cabaret."**

Nor is there any personalization of the race as in Cullen's "Heritage" nor any pedestalizing as in McKay's poetry. There is, however, always the unspoken resentment toward the poetry that evokes gaudy plaudits and purple encomia as to the race's greatness. Maybe in **"Salutamus"** there is a touch of race pride but it is not over-weaning:

> And yet we know relief will come some day
> For these seared breasts; and lads as brave again
> Will plant and find a fairer crop than ours
> It must be due our hearts, our mind, our powers. . . .

All in all, **"Strong Men," "Salutamus"** and **"Strange Legacies"**—among others—point his attitude unmistakeably. In these he says that he believes in the potentialities of a handicapped minority, and if he must serve this tychistic attitude, fight for it, be loyal to it, he will do it in quite such a way as Claude McKay once did, standing up, going onward.

> It is a gloomy path that we must go
> We must plunge onward, onward gentlemen.

Brown has torn down another stale concept which had become a cancerous growth in Negro ideology. He has failed to idealize its "great men." Recognizing that this is the malignant weapon wielded by the Negro literati and the weekly Negro press to such a harmful extent, he has reversed the process and told the truth. He sees the ineradicable harm that does arise from this magnifying the great man as a symbolic prototype. He tells us that

> They bought your leaders
> You stumbled as blind men will.

but

> The strong men keep-a-comin' on.

Sterling Brown realizes that there is only irreparable injury in empty idealizing, giving the masses a chance to achieve vicarious existence by needlessly exalting the race. He would rather that his audience listen to the epic grandeur and Olympian humor of his John Henry, Stagolee Bill, Sporting Beasley and Slim Greer.

He is determined to demolish the stereotype Negro and in his poetry and critical work he has accomplished this. In his poetry, there is no special attention paid to the Contented Negro, no unequal emphasis on the Brute Negro, no ridiculing of the Comic Negro. No, he destroys such notions and attacks the cork face comedians, manumitted psychology (that Negroes are congenitally joyous), and all the Nordic accolades as to his gentleness and faithfulness. This from Mr. Samuel and Sam is convicting,

> Mister Samuel, he belong to the Rotary,
> Sam to de Sons of Rest

Both wear red hats lak monkey men
An' you caint say which is de best.

. . . . .

Mister Samuel die, and de folks all know
Sam die without no noise;
De world go by in de same ol' way,
And dey's both of 'em po' los' boys. . . .

He wants to create what has been the residue and mir-roring of his individual experiences. So often we at-tribute to an artist motives of which he is ignorant. But in Brown's case, it can be seen easily that his creation of the worker, lover, street walker, pimp, sharecropper, chain gang convict are not types. They are people whom he has known, people whose lives are known to him. This poetic attitude and social gaze are important. They make all of his objections to classification justifiable. And that is because he is against the attempts to place Negro character into neat bifurcations. Brown felt the need for this overturning of manufactured concepts. It is in this way that he can break through Southern cavalier, bourgeois standards. He replies to the Agrar-ians, Allen Tates and to all those who so pontifically rant "we know the Negro,"

"that shrapnel bursts and poison gas
Were inextricably color blind."

It might be objected that Brown occasionally falls victim to those very things against which he fulminates. Perhaps he too generalizes. Perhaps he is often the local colorist in his Chicago and New York poems. If this is so, there is something else. He sees in his performers action and release, disquietude, cynicism, and emotional deshabille.

His characters are his friends. And because he is such a humorist, his friends have been endowed with this fun making capacity. In almost every poem, there is rich humor, a philosophy of humor and laughter. He draws in bold gargantuan strokes characters remindful of Lau-trec and Hogarth and there is such irony mixed in this mould that his poetry lives gustatorily. The masterpieces he has created, **"Ma Rainey," "Slim Greer," "Big Boy," "Sporting Beasley"** deserve to be quoted in full, but space forbids. Mention should be made also of the perfect rhythms, blues and Spirituals idioms and craftsmanship in his work. As a craftsman, both in dialect and the purer English form, Sterling Brown has few equals among modern poets.

It is seldom that the Negro poet today brings to his work an understanding of the class struggle, of the social and economic forces which go to make up the pot-pouri conditions of Negro life. Sterling Brown's work definitely heads in this direction. His poetry shows that he is conversant with the social, psychological, biological and economic arguments. And most impor-tant, he roots his work in the social soil of life he knows.

This knowledge, derived from his varied experience has sharpened his poetic acumen, brought him nearer to his objective . . . and closer to our ranks.

Note

1. *Southern Road,* Sterling Brown, Harcourt, Brace & Co. New York, N. Y., USA.

Sterling Stuckey (essay date 1974)

SOURCE: Stuckey, Sterling. Introduction to *The Col-lected Poems of Sterling A. Brown,* selected by Michael S. Harper, pp. 3-15. New York: Harper & Row, 1980.

[*In the following essay, which was originally published in 1974, Stuckey considers the critical reaction to Brown's poetry.*]

Unlike the others, the poet had not introduced himself. He had simply said, **"Ma Rainey,"** and continued in a way that indicated an unusual affinity between author and poem, between voice and word. It seemed the most natural and impressive delivery I had ever heard:

I talked to a fellow, an' the fellow say,
"She jes' catch hold of us, some kindaway.
She sang Backwater Blues one day . . ."

"An' den de folks, dey natchally bowed dey heads an'
    cried,
Bowed dey heavy heads, shet dey moufs up tight an'
    cried,
An Ma lef' de stage, an' followed some de folks
    outside."

And then those lines which say so much, which enable one to *feel* so much, about the great Blues singer and her followers:

Dere wasn't much more de fellow say:
She jes' gits hold of us dataway.

It was a weekend in the summer of '62 at a resort near Detroit, just on the other side of the Canadian border. We were listening to a recording being amplified throughout the grounds of poets reading their works. Just standing at that early hour on a Sunday morning would have been, under most circumstances, an achieve-ment, but this time I was startled upright and determined to get to the record player to discover whose voice it was. The voice belonged to Sterling A. Brown. I wondered then and later how a Williams College Phi Beta Kappa, a Harvard man, a college professor, and eminent writer could have a voice with so much of earth and sky and sunlight and dark clouds about it; a voice unafraid, an instrument Blues-tinged.[1]

With W. E. B. Du Bois in Ghana, Brown was even then the Dean of American Negro scholars, a man noted especially for his brilliant defenses of Negro character in literature. But for decades he had operated almost exclusively on the Howard campus, and there was some reason to wonder whether the Negro literati at Howard and at other centers of learning had much conception of why he was important, apart from the fact that he was known to be a man of learning with a rather inexplicable interest in Blues, Jazz, and Negro Spirituals. Even then—especially then, for it was at the height of the Civil Rights Movement—one sensed in Sterling Brown's voice a connecting timbre, a feel for reciprocity between past and present. If listened to, if called upon, some of us thought he could speak to the spiritual state of his people. But civil rights leaders were not overly interested in matters of culture or heritage.[2] And members of the black bourgeoisie were scarcely in the mood to seek counsel from poets, especially from one who might speak of slavery and provide a glimpse of a future which, even in freedom, would not be easy. Besides, the sixties seemed to belong to younger, "angrier" writers.

Later in 1962 Sterling Brown lectured on folklore for Chicago's Amistad Society and made a big impression on hundreds of people on the South Side. After his lecture before a small group, he read poems until daybreak—from a sheaf of yellowed pages, some of them tattered at the edges—poems never before anthologized, poems not found in *Southern Road*—and they did not appear to be the least dated.

After his lecture and poetry reading (his first in Chicago), Brown returned several times—"my best audiences are in Chicago," he has said. Each time, whatever the age group or racial composition of the audience, his reading was singularly successful, which buoyed his spirits, for he had in fact wondered perhaps more than he ever let us know how the younger generation would relate to his poetry.[3] It was evident that despite his great gifts as a poet, he was troubled by a not inconsiderable lack of recognition. Those who knew and respected him assumed that he had fallen silent, had stopped writing poetry, shortly after the appearance of *Southern Road.* That assumption, together with sadly deficient criticism from some quarters, helped to fix his place in time—as a not very important poet of the past.[4]

A man who has gone his own way most of his life, Brown has not been noted for asking favors, for seeking the easy way out by playing games with critics or with other people of influence. Among his favorite lines are these from Robert Frost's "In Dives' Dive":

> It is late at night and still I am losing,
> But still I am steady and unaccusing.

However, Sterling Brown was once taken far more seriously than he is today—and by critics who had done their homework. That was roughly forty years ago, and those critics had offered high praise.

I

Alain Locke, perhaps the chief aesthetician of the New Negro Movement and clearly its most effective defender, acknowledged that numerous critics, on the appearance of *Southern Road,* had hailed Brown "as a significant new Negro poet." For Locke, that was not sufficient: "The discriminating few go further; they hail a new era in Negro poetry, for such is the deeper significance of this volume." Locke identified the principal objective of Negro poetry "as the poetic portrayal of Negro folklife," suggested that such portraits should be "true in both letter and spirit to the idiom of the folk's own way of feeling and thinking," and declared that with the publication of *Southern Road* it could be said "that here for the first time is that much-desired and long-awaited acme attained or brought within actual reach."[5] As the folk-poet of the new Negro, Brown was for Locke the most important of Negro poets. This folk-poet appellation was an appropriate one, for Brown had recognized and begun to mine the rich veins of Negro folklore and found there almost boundless artistic possibilities for exploring the human condition.

Not meaning to ascribe perfection and complete maturity to Brown's art, Locke described him as "a Negro poet with almost complete detachment, yet with a tone of persuasive sincerity, whose muse neither clowns nor shouts. . . ." In Locke's view Brown had been able to create with the naturalness and freshness integral to folk balladry, and he called attention to **"Maumee Ruth," "Sam Smiley," "Dark of the Moon," "Johnny Thomas," "Slim Greer,"** and **"Memphis Blues"** as convincing proof that a Negro poet could "achieve an authentic folk-touch."[6]

Locke was fond of **"Maumee Ruth,"** a poem in which Brown, as he did on a number of occasions, linked North and South, countryside and city; a poem which Locke considered as uniquely racial as **"Southern Road,"** the title poem with work-song rhythms:

> White man tells me—hunh—
> Damn yo' soul;
> White man tells me—hunh—
> Damn yo' soul;
> Got no need, bebby,
> To be tole.

In Locke's opinion a number of Negro poets had been too reluctant to show their own people in a truer light, though they had become increasingly bold and now were no longer "too gingerly and conciliatory to and about the white man. The Negro muse weaned itself of that in McKay, Fenton Johnson, Toomer, Countée Cullen and Langston Hughes. But in Sterling Brown it has learned to laugh at itself and to chide itself. . . ."[7] Locke considered Brown a finer student of folk-life, more thoughtful, more detached, more daring than the others. Here was a poet who had gone further still and had explored, "with deeply penetrating genius," fundamental and abiding qualities of Negro feeling and thought, establishing "a sort of common denominator between the old and the new Negro."[8]

Louis Untermeyer, in a review of *Southern Road,* warned against ranking other poets of the New Negro Movement with Brown. But for those who "insist that such strains have been played before by the darker-minded of Brown's race, I would reply that Brown achieves a detachment which Claude McKay, for all his ardor, or Countée Cullen, for all his fluency, never achieves."[9] Untermeyer, in his appreciation of Brown's detachment, pointed to one of Brown's characteristics which should be pondered by many of the new black poets. Brown's mastery of a first principle of his craft: the poet should not shout or scream but, through singular command of language, perspective, mood, and event, win his way toward triggering a desire to shout *in the reader.* Brown's detachment, according to Untermeyer, allows him "to expostulate without ranting, or even raising his voice. . . ." "Only the most purblind—or prejudiced—will refuse to admit," thought Untermeyer, the strength and power of *Southern Road.*[10]

While he found **"Odyssey of Big Boy"** and **"Frankie and Johnny"** not to his liking, Untermeyer considered *Southern Road* as a whole "not only suffused with the extreme color, the deep suffering and high laughter of workers in cabins and cottonfields, of gangs and gutters, but it vibrates with a less obvious glow—the glow which, however variously it may be defined, is immediately perceived and ultimately recognized as poetry."[11] "Brown," Untermeyer concluded, "has expressed sources and depths which a pioneer like Dunbar might have felt but could never voice. . . . Thus 'Southern Road' reveals old material and a new utterance. Another light has emerged from the dark, unexhausted mine."[12]

The reviewer for *The New Republic* praised Brown for genuine originality in handling folk materials, noted the absence of pretension in his work, and hailed his "forthright use of realistic Negro material" as a characteristic worthy of emulation by those following him.[13] The reviewer for *The Nation* shrewdly realized that Brown's poems on the folk Negro experience were not conventional dialect renderings of that reality but were written in the natural, vigorous speech of the contemporary Negro. *The Nation* critic had put his finger on an aspect of Brown's poetry that has been misunderstood by a number of critics.[14]

That Brown's treatment of the folk Negro was destitute of maudlin sentimentality and outlandish humor, hallmarks of most traditional dialect poetry, was

altogether clear to William Rose Benét. Commenting on *Southern Road* in the *Saturday Review of Literature,* Benét also called the reader's attention to Brown's qualities as a narrative poet: "The fact that Brown is so good a narrative poet has inclined me toward him," he wrote. Benét found a command of real pathos and grimness in Brown's treatment of **"Sam Smiley,"** the buckdancer and veteran of foreign wars who, on returning home, put to use, without, color discrimination, his martial skills; Sam Smiley, who in the end:

> Buckdanced on the midnight air.

Brown's ability to "strike out original simile," as in **"Tornado Blues"** (from **"New St. Louis Blues"**):

> Black wind come a-speedin' down de river from de
>   Kansas plains,
> Black wind come a-speedin' down de river from de
>   Kansas plains,
> Black wind come a-roarin' like a flock of giant
>   aeroplanes—

impressed the reviewer. Benét also considered "peerless" some of the verses in the three **"Slim Greer"** poems, a series in which he thought humorous Negro fables were related with "inimitable unction."[15]

In several Slim Greer stanzas, Brown shows the reader how the suggestive powers of language can call reality into play with uncommon force, revealing terrible potential for turbulence beneath mirth that is in the final analysis no more than surface deep. Slim Greer seeking to pass for white romancing the Southern white woman was faced with an especially deadly moment of racial truth when his love

> Crept into the parlor
> Soft as you please
> Where Slim was agitatin'
> The ivories.
>
> Heard Slim's music—
> An' then, hot damn!
> Shouted sharp—"Nigger!"
> An' Slim said, "Ma'am?"

And the reviewer found, in the last section of *Southern Road,* **"Thoughts of Death," "Against That Day,"** and the sonnet **"Rain"** to be "entirely uncolloquial . . . unusually well-fashioned." The overall estimate was glowing: Brown's work had "distinctly more originality and power than that of Countée Cullen, and more range than that of Langston Hughes." Of the younger Negro poets, he closed, "I consider Sterling A. Brown to be the most versatile and the least derivative."[16]

The *New York Times* printed a lengthy review of *Southern Road* which also drew attention to the E. Simms Campbell illustrations. The reviewer found race on every page, "but it is 'race' neither arrogant nor servile. There is pathos, infinite pathos; but everywhere there is dignity that respects itself." The reviewer, unafraid of Negro bitterness, called the reader's attention to **"Maumee Ruth,"** finding in it sentiments that have been expressed "from the earliest poetry of the Hebrews down to the present day." He also trenchantly observed that the gayety found in *Southern Road* is "on the whole gayety restrained."[17] One must differ with the assertion that race is on every page, but that objection is little more than quibbling since race is indeed prominent in *Southern Road.* The *New York Times* review could scarcely have offered a finer tribute, one worth quoting in full: "*Southern Road* is a book the importance of which is considerable. It not only indicates how far the Negro artist has progressed . . . but it proves that the Negro artist is abundantly capable of making an original and genuine contribution to American literature . . . there is everywhere art, such a firm touch of artistry as is only seldom found among poets of whatever descent."[18]

That James Weldon Johnson introduced *Southern Road* when it first appeared in 1932 suggests something of the powerful effect which Sterling Brown's poetry had upon him. Perhaps by then Johnson had realized that, while his earlier strictures about dialect poetry had been correct enough when applied to the verse of others, they were simply not applicable to the poetry of Sterling Brown. Citing Brown's use of ballads and folk epics, he suggests that when the raw material upon which the poet works is radically different from the excessive geniality and optimism, the sentimentality and artificiality found in poetry based on the minstrel tradition, one is on the threshold of a breakthrough in poetic experimentation and achievement. Brown, Johnson tells us, mastered the spirit of his materials to the point of absorption and, "adopting as his medium the common, racy, living speech of the Negro in certain phases of *real* life," re-expressed that spirit with artistry and greater power.

If my reading of Johnson is correct, then his statement that "Mr. Brown's work is not only fine, it is also unique" is all the more comprehensible. Unique as well, Johnson correctly notes, are many of Sterling Brown's poems, which "admit of no classification or brand, as, for example, the gorgeous **'Sporting Beasley.'**" In that poem, the **"Slim Greer"** cycle, and in others, Johnson added, "[Brown] gives free play to a delicious ironical humor that is genuinely Negro." Johnson ventured to classify **"Sporting Beasley,"** calling it "Sterling-Brownian." He concluded his remarks with the observation that while there are "excellent poems written in literary English and form" in *Southern Road* "it is in his poems whose sources are the folk life that [Brown] makes, beyond question, a distinctive contribution to American poetry."

And so it was a remarkable achievement for a young poet: not one of the major reviewers hailed Brown as a poet of promise, as a talented young man awaiting creative maturity; on the contrary, he was regarded as a poet of uncommon sophistication, of demonstrated brilliance whose work had placed him in the front rank of working poets here and elsewhere. And the critics had been correct in noting that the maturity of Sterling Brown's poetic vision, the success with which he focused and ranged it over the varied terrain of Southern Negro experience, venturing now and again into higher latitudes such as Chicago, was not a result of unpracticed, intuitive genius. To be sure, most of Brown's years before the completion of his manuscript were helpful in preparing him for *Southern Road.*

II

In ways both subtle and obvious Sterling Nelson Brown, distinguished minister and father of the poet, influenced his son's attitude toward life and literature. Born a slave in eastern Tennessee, the elder Brown, unlike many of similar origin, was not ashamed of his slave heritage, nor was he ashamed of rural Negro descendants of slaves. The sense of continuity with the past and the considerable attention devoted to the folk Negro in Brown's poetry probably owe as much to his having been the son of such a father as they do to the valuable experiences which the young poet had in the South following his graduation from Williams College and Harvard University.[19]

Fortunately Sterling A. Brown, exposed to the critical realist approach to literature of George Dutton of Williams and the realism that characterized some of the best of American poetry of the twenties, especially the work of Edwin Arlington Robinson, Robert Frost, and Carl Sandburg, was all the more prepared to take an uncondescending, that is to say genuinely respectful, attitude toward the folk whom he encountered in the South. And there he discovered a wealth of folk material waiting to be fashioned into art, and a number of quite ordinary people who, thanks to his artistry, would teach us unusual things about life. Brown realized the need to explore the life of the Southern Negro below the surface in order to reveal unseen aspects of his being, his strength and fortitude, his healing humor, and his way of confronting tragedy. As a young man he began meeting and talking to a variety of people, some of whom, such as Big Boy Davis, a traveling guitar player after whom the character in **"Southern Road,"** the title poem, is modeled, would win permanent places in our literature. The fact that Brown, with his sharp eye, fine ear, and excellent mind, spent so many of his early years in the South helps us understand the sensibility behind a volume which reads like the work of a gifted poet who has lived a lifetime.

Just as Brown's creation of folk characters presents individualized portraits revelatory of interior lives, his

uses of the great body of Negro music, of the Spirituals, Blues, Jazz, and Work Songs, extend rather than
reflect meanings. Sadly enough, there is reason to
believe that many students of Negro literature, as I have
implied, are unfamiliar with most of the poems in
Southern Road. Numerous major poems have never
been anthologized; and some, such as **"Cabaret,"** have
only recently been brought to our attention by critics.[20]
Yet a specialist on the "Harlem Renaissance," of which
Brown was not a part, *places him in that movement*
with a number of references, including one to **"Memphis Blues,"** while omitting mention of **"Cabaret,"**
perhaps the single most important New Negro Movement poem dealing with the exploitation of Negro
performing artists, especially members of orchestras
and chorus lines, during the twenties and since.[21]

Though **"Cabaret"** is by no means the only significant
Brown poem that numerous scholars don't seem to
know exists, it deserves attention because of its brilliant
multi-level interplay between appearance and reality:
between life as Negroes live it and life as projected
onto them by white audiences. **"Cabaret"** stands as a
starkly eloquent emblem of the frustrations, cleverly
masked, of Negro entertainers before the bizarre
expectations of white patrons of black arts of the twenties. The inexorably grim logic of the poem unfolds to
the accompaniment of Negro music in a Chicago Black
and Tan club in 1927. The poet employs symbolically
the Blues, Jazz, the corruptions of Tin Pan Alley, the
perversions of genuine Negro music, the dirty misuse
of Negro chorus girls and musicians—all set against the
rural tragedy of a desperate people in the terrible flood
of 1927.

Though I had the rare pleasure of hearing Brown recite
the following lyrical, gut-bucket stanzas—recite them
magnificently—to my knowledge **"Kentucky Blues"**
has never been anthologized:

> I'm Kentucky born,
> Kentucky bred,
> Gonna brag about Kentucky
> Till I'm dead.
>
> . . . . .
>
> Ain't got no woman,
> Nor no Man O' War,
> But dis nigger git
> What he's hankering for—
>
> De red licker's good,
> An' it ain't too high,
> Gonna brag about Kentucky
> Till I die. . . .

The narrator of **"Kentucky Blues"** would be completely
at home in **"Memphis Blues,"** whose last grim stanza
closes with a brilliantly conceived reference to another
art form, not unknown for qualities of stoicism, to the
mood of the poem:

> Memphis go
> By Flood or Flame;
> Nigger don't worry
> All de same—
> Memphis go
> Memphis come back,
> Ain' no skin
> Off de nigger's back.
> All dese cities
> Ashes, rust. . . .
> De win' sing sperrichals
> Through deir dus'.

As a student of the relationship between past and
present, of the effects of time and circumstance upon
human beings, Sterling Brown has demonstrated, as
well as any artist known to this writer, how music and
myth function in the lives of ordinary people. In but a
portion of a single stanza from **"Ma Rainey,"** perhaps
the Blues poem, Brown manages to capture in a few
lean lines the essence of the Blues singer as repository,
as explicator of the values of her people, as Priestess.

> O Ma Rainey,
> Sing yo' song;
> Now you's back
> Whah you belong,
> Git way inside us,
> Keep us strong. . . .

And in **"Strange Legacies,"** we encounter perhaps the
greatest of all Negro folk heroes:

> Brother,
> When, beneath the burning sun
> The sweat poured down and the breath came thick,
> And the loaded hammer swung like a ton
> And the heart grew sick;
> You had what we need now, John Henry.
> Help us get it.
>
> *So if we go down*
> *Have to go down*
> *We go like you, brother,*
> *'Nachal' men. . . .*

But in **"Children's Children"** the poet turns to discontinuities, to a poignant breakdown in racial memory:

> When they hear
> These songs, born of the travail of their sires,
> Diamonds of song, deep buried beneath the weight
> Of dark and heavy years;
> They laugh.
>
> . . . . .
>
> They have forgotten, they have never known,
> Long days beneath the torrid Dixie sun
>
> . . . . .
>
> With these songs, sole comfort.

As remarkable as many of the poems in this volume
are, they can, like arresting but isolated portions of a
vast canvas, be done full justice only when seen within

the framework of the overall artistic conception. This is so because Sterling Brown, despite the impressive range of characterization and technique revealed in this volume, builds from a unified, integrated conception of reality. The happy effect of such architecture is that individual poems, however much they dazzle when read apart from others, gain new and deeper meaning, and a new resonance, when the entire volume is read.

Given the experiences of his people in America, it is especially worth noting that Brown has been able to take attributes that appear greatly susceptible to stereotypical treatment—cheating, flight, laughing, dancing, singing—and, never losing control of them, in fact utilizing them repeatedly, to establish the irreducible dignity of a people. So powerful is his vision of their humanity, so persuasive his powers of poetic transmutation, that his utilization of the most distinctly Negroid accents serves to enlarge, rather than diminish, that humanity. In a word, Brown makes no concessions to white prejudice or to Negro pretense.

If Sterling Brown speaks of tragedy, he also holds out the ultimate hope of triumph, the possibility of which, paradoxically, is heightened, not lessened, by the tough-minded quality of his way of reckoning events and determining what is important in life. His disclosures of largely unappreciated qualities, though they range over myriad concerns, are on balance values, sacred and secular, hidden in the hearts of a people. **"Strong Men"** gives us a better sense of what the long haul has meant, of how a people has not merely survived but projected its sense of what is meaningful, than any other poem in Afro-American literature. The vision which informs this poem is essentially the same which courses through a volume offering no easy optimism and no quick victories but all the determination in the world. And so there is a promise of eventual relief. The poet's vision is, in the end, tragic—triumphant.

In spite of all, whatever his setbacks, whatever his triumphs, Sterling Brown has maintained through it all possession of his soul and kept the faith with his fellows, living and dead. He is an artist in the truest sense: the complete man, he has attempted to master the art of living. One is reminded, when thinking of him, of Lionel Trilling's reference to certain "men who live their visions . . . who *are* what they write."²²

As Sterling Brown reveals the world of *Southern Road,* he leads us ultimately, through the Negro, to a conception of the nature of man. There is a noticeable absence of the questionable poetic ideal of being "difficult," which too frequently has come to mean, in our time, impenetrability. Yet Brown's genius is such that as he sculpts simple, plain speech into poetry, as he unveils the value ensemble of a people, the reader will discover, almost in a flash, that he has entered a world as wondrously complex as life itself.

Notes

1. Sterling A. Brown was born in Washington, D.C., in 1901. He has taught at Virginia Seminary, at Lincoln University (Missouri), at Fisk, and, since 1929, at Howard University. From 1936 to 1939 he was Editor of Negro Affairs for the Federal Writers' Project. He was also a staff member of the Carnegie-Myrdal Study of the Negro. He has, in addition to having authored scores of scholarly articles, published *The Negro in American Fiction* (1938), *Negro Poetry and Drama* (1938), and, with Ulysses Lee and Arthur P. Davis, edited the noted anthology *The Negro Caravan* (1941). A collection of Brown's essays, *A Different Drummer,* is being readied for publication by Howard University Press.

2. A number of leading figures in SNCC were interested in cultural questions. Mike Thelwell, Charlie Cobb, Stokely Carmichael, Bill Mahoney, and Courtland Cox—all students of Brown at Howard—possessed more than a little knowledge of the folk heritage of Afro-America, which was not altogether unrelated to that consciousness within SNCC which led to the call for black power.

3. Actually, few people relate to younger people as well as Sterling Brown, who somehow, despite his age, does not seem "old." Hoyt Fuller, editor of *Black World,* has captured a number of Brown's qualities: "Settle him down, loosen his tie, provide him with some congenial and intelligent company, and turn him on. The stories flow. Out of his fascinating past, a life filled with both raw and genteel adventures in that mad, rich, vibrant world on the mellow sidelines of America, he serves up a living history of the past forty years. . . . Who are the others who can sit among a roomful of men and women young enough to be their children and meld in spirit and mood with no hint of pomp and no suggestion of paternalism? . . . His books are where the minds are which have been touched by his vivid stories, his subtle and unsettling legends, his images of yesterday designed to guard against undue folly today" [Hoyt W. Fuller, "The Raconteur," *Black World,* April 1967, 50]. Brown's poetry readings to the young were no less successful than his renderings of the extraordinary stories to which Fuller alluded.

4. As a consequence of such a judgment, editors of anthologies and professors of Negro literature apparently assumed that the only Brown poems worth reading were those which had appeared in previous anthologies. How else, after all, can one account for the same Sterling Brown poems in anthology after anthology? Perhaps a second printing of *Southern Road* would have militated against

such a trend. Frederic Ramsey, Jr., distinguished folklorist and jazz authority, was employed at Harcourt, Brace and Company at the time the decision was made not to order a second printing of *Southern Road.* Ramsey "Protested the book's going out of print, and can remember the answer that came back from the head of the sales department: 'It wouldn't pay us.' Possibly not" [Frederic Ramsey, Jr., editor, "Sixteen Poems of Sterling A. Brown read by Sterling A. Brown," *Folkway Records,* album no. FL9794, 1973].

Southern Road constitutes slightly less than one-third of Sterling Brown's poetry. A few years following the publication of *Southern Road,* Brown submitted his second manuscript to Harcourt, Brace and Company, to be entitled *No Hiding Place*; it was rejected. The rejection of that manuscript, said to be on a level with *Southern Road,* remains something of a mystery. There is reason to believe, however, that more than possible sales considerations figured into the decision. *No Hiding Place* and *36 Poems 36 Years Later* are expected to be published soon. The appearance of these volumes, together with this reprint of *Southern Road,* should move Brown back to the center of Negro poetry—indeed, toward the center of American poetry, a position which he occupied shortly after the publication of *Southern Road.*

5. Alain Locke, "Sterling Brown: The New Negro Folk-Poet," Nancy Cunard, *Negro Anthology* (Wishart Co., 1934), p. 111.

6. *Ibid.,* p. 112.

7. *Ibid.,* p. 114.

8. *Ibid.,* p. 115.

9. Louis Untermeyer, "New Light from an Old Mine," *Opportunity,* August 1932, p. 250.

10. *Ibid.*

11. *Ibid.*

12. *Ibid.,* p. 251.

13. *The New Republic,* July 27, 1932, p. 297.

14. *The Nation,* July 13, 1932, p. 43. It should be noted that Sterling Brown has no objections to his poetry's being called dialect, providing it is understood that he rejects, through his poetry, the constricted definition earlier given to dialect by James Weldon Johnson—that is, that dialect has but two stops: humor and pathos. Brown has shown the remarkable resources of the language, demonstrating that dialect has as many stops as there are human emotions. Brown, in fact, has

given us the first real look at the written language, in all its variety and richness, linked as it should be to the real-life people who created it. Thus, if the term *dialect* is to be used at all in describing much of the work of Brown, it should be understood that his is a wholly new conception.

15. William Rose Benét, "A New Negro Poet," *The Saturday Review of Literature,* May 14, 1932, p. 732.

16. *Ibid.*

17. "A Notable New Book of Negro Poetry," *The New York Times Book Review,* May 15, 1932.

18. *Ibid.,* p. 13.

19. See Sterling Nelson Brown, *My Own Life* (Hamilton, 1924).

20. Stephen Henderson's *Understanding the New Black Poetry* (Morrow, 1973) contains "Cabaret." Henderson's criticism of Brown in *Black World* was perhaps the first sensitive and scholarly treatment of Brown's poetry by a Negro since the generation of Locke and James Weldon Johnson. In providing a level of criticism worthy of the seriousness of Brown's art, Jean Wagner, in *Black Poetry* (University of Illinois Press, 1973), joins Henderson. For Henderson's essay on Brown's poetry, see "A Strong Man Called Sterling Brown," *Black World,* September 1970.

21. See Nathan Irvin Huggins, *Harlem Renaissance* (Oxford University Press, 1971), pp. 78, 221, 222, 225-227, 228. But Brown has challenged the very conception that a "Harlem Renaissance" took place: "The New Negro is not to me a group of writers centered in Harlem during the second half of the twenties. Most of the writers were not Harlemites; much of the best writing was not about Harlem, which was the show-window, the cashier's till, but no more Negro America than New York is America" [Sterling A. Brown, "The New Negro in Literature, 1925-1955," in *The New Negro Thirty Years Afterwards,* edited by Rayford Logan et al. (Washington: Howard University Press, 1955), p. 57].

22. See Lionel Trilling's introduction to George Orwell, *Homage to Catalonia* (New York: Harcourt, Brace and World, Inc., A Harvest Book, 1952), p. viii. Daisy Turnbull Brown, the wife of Sterling Brown, has helped him live this vision—in his poetry as in life. She is introduced in several poems in the last section of the volume, including "Thoughts of Death":

> *Death will come to you, I think,*
> *Like an old shrewd gardener*

Culling his rarest blossom . . .

and the magical "Mill Mountain"
  . . . We have learned tonight
  That there are havens from all desperate seas,
  And every ruthless war rounds into peace.
  It seems to me that Love can be that peace . . .

Clyde Taylor (essay date March-April 1981)

SOURCE: Taylor, Clyde. "The Human Image in Sterling Brown's Poetry." *The Black Scholar* 12, no. 2 (March-April 1981): 13-20.

[In the following essay, Taylor offers an appreciation of Brown's work, contending that the poet's significance "is that he planted foundations beneath modern black verse, and in so doing, provided the core of identity of imaginative Afro-American writing."]

  So if we go down
  Have to go down
  We go like you, brother,
  'Nachal' men. . . .

                                        —"**Strange Legacies**"

The failure to recognize the central place of Sterling Brown as one of its most necessary innovators is an embarrassment to Afro-American writing. The publication of his *Collected Poems*[1] offers one more chance to end this severe case of cultural absent-mindedness.

Brown's achievement, which he shares with his contemporary, Langston Hughes, is that he planted foundations beneath modern black verse, and in so doing, provided the core of identity for imaginative Afro-American writing. Not knowing this is like not knowing what Louis Armstrong and Duke Ellington added to instrumental black music.

Brown completed the indispensible task of naturalizing black verse within black vernacular. The earliest dialect efforts of Dunbar and his school had never shaken off the reductive mimicry of minstrelism. Brown and Hughes rescued the use of Black English in literature from the confines of a specialty gimmick in black writing (like a buck and wing in a coon show) and liberated its possibilities to the widest ranges of modern art. They found ways to make poetry in black people's own linguistic and artistic idioms: the blues, "ballits," proverbs, "lies," toasts, spirituals, oral histories and myths that are still the better half of black verbal creativity. They put the blackness into black writing, democratizing it by creating a comfortable, legitimate space where everyday black folks could be expressed. They did this along with other writers of the New Negro era, but none with Brown's depth and originality.

A particular kind of genius is needed to do what Brown and Hughes did, no matter how inevitable it looks now. Every group that has a modern literature had to wait for the right maker to come along and do the obvious—seize the instrument of literacy to capture the speech, myths and values of his/her people, instead of slavishly following the verbal and intellectual precedents of some older, imperial example, like Latin or Victorian English. For the inventor of a script for the poetry of his or her people, the difficulty is something like discovering your own speech in the flow of an alien medium. It's a job remotely related to the invention of the alphabet, also easily taken for granted by later users.

Brown, then, is a major example of the *national* poet described by Carolyn Rodgers.[2] The writer who polishes the language of the tribe is likely to be also one who opens his voice so his people can speak through it on his pages. The role is well recognized in Chaucer, Dante, Robert Burns, but is also illustrated by Nicolas Guillen, Hughes, Henry Dumas, Margaret Walker, E. A. Robinson, Edgar Lee Masters, the poets of Haitian indigenism, Yeats, Sembene and hundreds of others.

The movement of Brown's poetry within black writing is towards re-rootment, a return to the source. After he began a commanding acquaintance with western literature at Williams and Harvard, he went South to teach and to learn from his "own-folk," like DuBois before him. Thus armed, he pitched himself without possibility of retreat into the basic struggle of intellectuals of his breed, the defense of national culture against the official, pseudo-universal culture of the dominant elite.

What needs to be observed is the subtlety and honesty Brown brings to this version of the writer's craft. His resettlement falls outside the too rigid characterization Fanon draws of the "native intellecutal" who, after frustrated social climbing, suddenly discovers that he has a people. Brown escaped the fate of the poet described by Baraka, who "loves his people with an abstract love."

In his campaign of literary reconstruction, Brown had to steer a course between two extremes. One is the smothering force pressed against the possibilities of finished art in black speech. He rankles still at inanities like one white critic's assertion that in sixteen lines of Brer Turtle you have the whole range of Negro character. He is also challenged by James Weldon Johnson's ranking of Negro dialect poetry as capable of but two stops, pathos and humor. The other danger, often betrayed in *negritude* and the Harlem school of New Negro writing, is the leap into escapist mysticism and counter-elitism. In a rare self-characterization of his mission, he says "I didn't want to attack a stereotype by idealizing. I wanted to deepen it. I wanted to show that what you think this is has these other dimensions."[3]

The magic slides sidemouth out his downhome verse like a wink, stories in homespun pirouette on their points, wry sociologies mount syncopations, convicting details ripple insinuations in pools of rime, the aphoristic rewards of slavery stand tethered in under-statements. Sterling knows how folkspeech in the face of Standard picks up the quality of metaphor, opens ethnographic sorties into other cultural worlds. Part of his music is the play between meanings of the same words in different tongues, a play kept lively by exchanges between rhythms. And he can swing, like a streamline special.

> I got me a Blackcat's wishbone,
> Got some Blackcat's ankle dus'
> An' yuh crackers better watch out
> Ef I sees yo' carcass fus'.

He is the master of Afro-American humor, wild, vagrant laughter, the merry side of madness. His talent for deep song, where the word becomes thing, can remind you of Billie Holiday:

> The poor-white and nigger sinners
> Are low-down in the valley,
>   The rider is a devil
> And there's hell to pay;
>   The devil is a rider,
> God may be the owner,
> But he's rich and forgetful,
>   And far away.

It's poetry earned by one who holds as touchstone, this: "I don't know what my mother wants to stay here for. This old world ain't been no friend to her."

The best appraisal of the success of Brown's enterprise remains Alain Locke's essay "Sterling Brown: The New Negro Folk-Poet."[4] Locke acknowledges Brown's singular, elusive gift in capturing "the ancient common wisdom of the folk." It is worth the trouble, though, to modify some of the key terms Locke used in conveying the departures implied in Brown's art. Where Locke says "ancient," we might think and use *ancestral*. For *dialect,* better read *Black English*. Better, too, to see Brown as national poet than "folk-poet." For honorable as that title might be, the wear and prejudices of usage make calling Brown a folk-poet a bit like describing Duke Ellington as a jungle-music entertainer. For similar reasons, many black musicians, Ellington first among them, have rejected the term "jazz."[5]

The description of Brown as "folk-poet" is cramped, even at the coordinates of his leading strengths, character and language. The expression being national, concern for character flows naturally from it. Hence, Brown's work comprises a panoramic Afro-American gallery, although our memories are most swiftly seized by his "portraitures," as he calls them, of root people. A census of this gallery, however, includes peasants, farmers, yes, but also coal-truck drivers, blues singers, streetcar conductors, gangsters, levee workers, gamblers, prostitutes, domestics, pullman porters, railroad men, chain gang convicts, true, but also city slickers, chorus girls, politicians, college students, preachers, doctors, teachers, society belles, business men, professors, himself. Thinking of the spread of his characters, we should remember the adjoining galleries of Edgar Lee Masters and E. A. Robinson.

The reach of Brown's language is equally palpable. "Dialect poetry" is too narrow, a falsification. Less than half his collected poems are in dialect orthography. An attractive formulation for me once seemed to be a breakdown of the voices in his verse into three kinds: literary, as in the Vestiges section of *Southern Road*; Black English, as in the poem "Southern Road"; and a mix of the two—a sophisticated observer narrating a framework for folk documentaries, as in "Odyssey of Big Boy" and "Strong Men." This third category waits for special attention, because it holds some of Brown's most powerful pieces, "Strange Legacies," "Old Lem," "Saints," "Ma Rainey."

But this breakdown won't stand up. Long ago, Locke noted the full black-folk expressiveness of poems *not* in dialect, like "Maumee Ruth." The poems in deepest Black English reverberate so strongly that we hear their twang and cadence even in absence of phonetic orthography. (The greater breadth of "Black English" over "dialect" is also demonstrated.) Further, there are linkages and continuities in the voices used over a wide spread of sociology and geography—Louisiana, Georgia, Kentucky, Virginia, Boston, New York, D.C., and the roads between. His poetic forms are drawn from both oral and literary traditions, from the too fine "New St. Louis Blues" ("Whoever runs dis gamble sholy runs it well"), through ballads, high barroom boasts like "The Last Ride of Wild Bill," dramatic monologues (sometimes as versified oral histories), straight through to romantic lyrics, free verse and black verse introspections, to posied sonnets, like "Nous n'irons plus au bois. . . ."

Mostly, poetic form conforms to the social background of the speaker; and poetic devices notable in English poetic tradition, like incremental repetition, fabliau, dramatic monologue are used overlapping with parallels in Afro oral tradition. But there is always the possibility of tonal and sociological complexity. The blues singer in "Long Track Blues," the last poem in his collection, is Sterling himself; the "babe" is his wife, Miss Daisy, who died shortly before publication.

> Went down to the yards
> To see the signal lights come on;

Looked down the track
Where my lovin' babe done gone.

OTHER DIMENSIONS OF BROWN'S POETRY

It is easy to mistake the interest of scholars and artists in the lore of the folk for solidarity. Since the 60's, the use of Black English in Afro literature has become commonplace, and in recent novels almost standard. Some of the most crafty exploiters of the new literary idiom use it with little commitment to the people who supply its raw materials, individualists seeing in the new medium their main chance for fame and wealth. Brown's project of reducing the costly separation of oral and literate media in his society was pursued with motives grounded differently from those of many folk-based black writers of the 20s' black awakening and after.

His concentration on precise, reportorial detail plus his celebrated detachment can raise a false impression of Brown as a kind of candid camera realist, free of moralizing, sentiment or ideology. The publication at last of *No Hiding Place* after forty years (one of three complete volumes in this collection) should change that impression. As a whole, the book is urban, populist and militantly democratic and anti-racist. It is a tough-lipped book, laced with biting satires and a strain of 30's social radicalism. The folk are transformed here into an embattled people—the Depression perfecting their traditional afflictions—but fighting back, as in the much-loved **"Old Lem,"** possibly the most effective use of incremental repetition in the English language ("They don't come by one's, they don't come by two's . . .") and **"An Old Woman Remembers."** *No Hiding Place* also dramatizes the commonalities of black and white workers, divided and usually conquered by capitalistic racism. Was the new tone, after the more objective *Southern Road,* the reason Harcourt Brace turned the book down after announcing its forthcoming publication?

All along, Brown had been more closely allied to the intellectuals of the New Negro movement, to social scientists like Ralph Bunche, E. Franklin Frazier, Allison Davis and Rayford Logan, than he was to the literati of Harlem. The ideology of New Negro intellectuals shared more of the spirit of Europe's Enlightenment than its Renaissance. It saw more progress (a "key word") coming from the application of critical social thought to the problems of the "American Negro", here and now, than from utopian, morale-building fantasies like yearning for Africa. It was anticlerical, secular, down on all forms of social escapism. It concentrated on the issues and problems of black individuals and communities instead of celebrating black people's intuitive knowledge "how to live". It leaned toward environmentalism to explain weaknesses in Afro-American society, as opposed to the Harlemite account of Afro personality through primitivism and exoticism. Its efforts reached its scholarly peak in *An American Dilemma,* its practical triumph in the U.S. Supreme Court decision desegregating public schools.

So Brown's persistent deconstruction of "the Harlem Renaissance" has more to it than cursing a missed boat. It has to do with his resistance to intellectuals bandwagoning through shortcuts. By contrast, the New Negro movement offered a more commonsensical, representative, *national* frame of reference. The issue Brown raises with the concept of the Harlem "renaissance" still has some bite. What would Afro-America be if it allowed its brains and nerves to be represented by intellectuals of New York, or any other single city? What would Afro-American literature be—a literature, remember, whose first, most important body of work is its Southern-based oral traditions—if it allowed its character to be shaped by the speakeasy exoticism of the Harlem literary extravaganza?

The Harlem "renaissance" in Brown's thought and poetry is encapsulated in **"Cabaret,"** written before the craze faded, albeit after a visit to a nightclub in *Chicago,* 1927. The "renaissance" and its writers are imaged in those painted, theatrical chorus girls, mimicking for "Hebrew and Anglo-Saxon overlords" a parody of Southern creole beauties longing for home: "I've got my toes turned Dixie ways / Round that Delta let me laze", while

> (In Mississippi
> the black folk huddle, mute, uncom-
> prehending,
> Wondering how come the good lord
> Could treat them this way.)

It's not just people who are stereotyped; stereotyping is also stamped on places, historical eras, causes, large ideas. The "Harlem renaissance" is a stereotype that was believed by many of its victims, and still claims good brains. Brown's position on the "renaissance" was critical from the beginning, consistent with his life-long intellectual outlook and literary project: "I wanted to show that what you think this is has these other dimensions."

Responses to the new material in the collected poems should include surprise. We have comfortably accepted his persona as cracker-barrel humorist and raconteur, local-colorist and snap-shot chronicler, while Brown has also been a "long-breath singer", one of those few black artists whose work taken whole carries a broad structured, nearly programmatic vision of Afro-American reality, punctuated by a sharply defined order of values. It should be clear now that Brown's critical writing is part of his creative project—its debunking of fraudulent ideas, its anecdotal method, its reticence regarding sweeping constructs. *The Negro Caravan,* the first major anthology of black American writing which Brown edited along with Arthur P. Davis and Ulyssees Lee, reinforces a diverse and national perspective. While the "renaissance" was oceans wider than sixteen lines of Brer Turtle, it shrinks, along with other fads, in the *Caravan*'s generous oral and literate dimensions.

Brown's intellectual stance actually outflanks even New Negro ideology. To paraphrase a remark made of Henry James, his is a mental process too fine for all but the most compelling natural ideas to penetrate. Ideas are there, and we should search the poetry more shrewdly for them; but they hold a different weight in the scheme of things. He is more skeptical of bulky conclusions, even from the academy, than many of his social scientist colleagues of the New Negro movement. He has never, for instance, shared their seduction by the idea of progress, instead crediting the variances of history to a kind of seasonal flow, "the swing of the pendulum." From **"Memphis Blues"**:

> Memphis go
> Memphis come back,
>   Ain' no skin
> Off de nigger's back.

His concept of man and of the Negro is more natural and commodious than the theorems of *An American Dilemma* (some of which he used). Some idea of his worldview lies in the order of values surrounding the people in his poetry. Those hopelessly beguiled by pretensions, modish escapisms, whether of religion, politics or art become the butts of uproarious yarns— the foolish militant in **"Crispus Attucks McKoy,"** the Garveyite in **"The Temple."** Appreciating this vein of his work should help set apart his version of national poetry from the black nationalist poetry of the 60's and early 70's. And for all his devotion to root people, his realism fends off sentiment or *miserabilism* in witnessing their flaws and weaknesses. At the extreme, note his meditation on race traitors in **"Memo: For the Race Orators."** It is the house servant who blows the whistle:

> Show how he remains: a runner to the master,
> To the time-keeper, the warden, the straw boss, the
>   brass-hat,
> The top-hat, the big shot, the huge noise, the power,
> Show him running, hat in his hand,
> Yelping, his tail and his hindquarters drooping.

The folly and tragedy people bring upon themselves in Brown's poetic tales arise out of their drifting from ancestral stabilities, trying to assimilate into vanities— into movie images of bad dudes, and jail, into the glitter-lights of tin-roofed towns, and prostitution. The cities are markets of glitter and de-naturalization, the traffic of loss and assimilation. The last lines of **"Memphis Blues"** read:

> All dese cities
> Ashes, rust . . .
> De win' sing sperrichals
> Through deir dus'.

The folk values of his world, which are also his values, are kin to the "core black culture" revealed in *Dry-longso.* Brown's world shows a fuller appreciation for the hustling Slim Greers, the Sporting Beasleys, the Scrappys, putting on dog, than Gwaltney's crime-beseiged respondents can muster. The order of values here admires the vitality and heart of these high, wild spirits, but it does not heroize them. He does not say of *them,* "You had what we need now, John Henry / Help us get it." They are not asked, as is Ma Rainey, "Git way inside us, / Keep us strong. . . ."

Beneath the glare of false idols, the idea of humanity in Brown's world is a strength in moving on, in face of natural and social obstacles, in full knowledge and acceptance of the limitations of mortality, the ultimate source of laughter. To acknowledge death and, therefore, limits, means to accept contradictions and complexity; the Panzaic principle outlasting Quixotic idealisms. The balance of contradictory, vital forces, which never add up to absolute salvation, being what is meant by "nature". The refusal to assimilate to less than naturally grounded ideas, racism among them, being its notion of strength. It is the old, Adamic affirmation of the value of being above all else. It holds, as Goethe did, that life is more interesting than the interpretation of life. The possibilities of social advance in this view lie within the people conceived in this image, not within quickie political nostrums or their spokesmen. Leaders are mentioned in **"Strong Men,"** Brown's great poem of ethnic identity, only obliquely:

> They bought off some of your leaders
> You stumbled, as blind men will . . .

Any such paraphrase takes a risk. The suspicion of words outside their context of actuality, where they become abstractions or the reveries of bourgeois lyricists, accounts for the prevalence in Brown's work, of narrative, story, action and character, the carpet of experience in specific settings.

Still one more limitation accepted is the lack of novelty in this human image, a vision shared with multitudes, expressed by Homer, Chaucer, Burns, and so many others, we should not be thrown off its track by local colorations, confusing them with chauvinism. Brown's originality lies in his ability to realize this human image with the sonority, depth and accent it also finds in the blues, gaining over them on the printed page as much as is lost to voice and guitar. Old Man Buzzard spews his evil prophecies at Fred in his fields: your woman won't be true, your friends won't last, good luck and health will soon be gone and death will find you alone.

> 'Doan give a damn
> Ef de good things go,
> Game rooster yit,
> Still kin crow,
> Somp'n in my heart here
> Makes me so.
>
> . . . . .
>
> No need in frettin'
> Case good times go,
> Things as dey happen
> Jes' is so;
> Nothin' las' always
> Farz I know . . .'

The "other dimensions" Brown's poetry aims for beneath the stereotypes are those of whole life, without additives, preservatives or debilitating refinements. The basic contradiction he attacked is not DuBois' noted "twoness—an American, a Negro," though his work capitalizes the overlap of much Afro and WASP experience. He attacked, at greater depth, the supposed contradiction outlined by Frederick Douglass who said he thanked God for making him a man, while Martin Delaney thanked God for making him a black man. Beyond the stereotypes and the elitist, colonialist and racist dreck, Brown's poetry asks, where's the difference? "What it means to be a Negro in the modern world," he wrote in the 30's, "is a revelation much needed in poetry. But the Negro poet must write so that whosoever touches his book touches a man."[6]

A couple of years ago he said, "I am an integrationist, though that is an ugly word, because I know what segregation really was. And by integration, I don't mean assimilation. I believe what the word means—an integer is a whole number . . . I want to be accepted as a whole man." In his battles against racism and its first line of defense in the arts—inferiorized, distorted images of other people—it is this drive toward wholeness that makes his poetry national. "I love the blues, I love jazz, and I'm not going to give them up."[7]

Conclusion

It is time, now, to go beyond particularist appreciations of Sterling's art, to do more than rifle through his works for personal favorites. His commitment to wholeness and complexity urges us to envision his work as a whole. It's a fool's errand to look for some blueprint or grand plan there. But there are proportions: folk and bourgeoisie, South and North, country and town are given space in his work gauged to their importance in his perception of his times. And the subtitled sectioning of the poems is a key to some sense of design.

There are groupings among the poems, the most essential coming in pairs, as contrasting opposites, or complements, sometimes as two dialoguing voices within the same poem. The martyred hero is admired in **"Old Lem"** while the foolish martyr in **"Crispus Attucks McKoy"** is satirized in riming, footstomping guffaws. **"Children of Mississippi"** is available for stark contrast to **"Children's Children."** Every melancholy dirge has its uproarious, tall-tale twin. The call and response of distinctive fates and voices multiply finally into the ensemble improvisation of a community expressing itself. Though a production mounted in Washington, D.C. by actor-director Robert Hooks in the mid-70's made a beginning, the full realization is yet to be made that the work of Sterling Brown is, more than a gallery, a national theater.

Brown's collected poetry, then, stands as an effective integration of certain elements of Euro-American literacy with Afro-oral consciousness, placed in the deep center. In his poems, the already created consciousness of his race is forged into a modular replication of black culture. Seen whole, as a kind of narrative minus a dominating plot, the interaction of contrasting values, the lines of character-destiny, provide the motivations and dynamics of the society reverberated there, where the major themes—the twisting paths of human motivations, pride in work, the ruin of children, love, death and the sweetness of life in its shadow, wanderlust, the adhesiveness of men to women, the irredeemable evil of ritual murder, the wit of the trickster, the kinship of laughter and courage—are the scaffolds of its dialectics. This work, based on principled, studied observation, offers a synopsis of black consciousness in the decades after the Great War, yet with ringing implications for the present. When Afro-American social thinkers end their neglect of literature as an analytical probe, they will find in Brown's collected poetry an important document for their study.

As for the literary generation of the 60's, with the notable exception of Stephen Henderson and Sterling Stuckey, it has mostly failed to recognize the central precedent in Brown's literary project of goals it claims as its own. As Alain Locke observed a half century ago, "Gauging the main objective of Negro poetry as the poetic portrayal of Negro folk-life true in both letter and spirit to the idiom of the folk's own way of feeling and thinking, we may say that here for the first time is that much desired and long-awaited acme attained. . . ."

Notes

1. *The Collected Poems of Sterling A. Brown,* selected by Michael Harper (New York: Harper & Row, 1980).

2. "The Literature of Black," *Black World* (June 1970).

3. Hollie I. West, "The Teacher," *The Washington Post* (Nov. 16, 1969), F2.

4. Reprinted in Nathan Huggins, ed., *Voices from the Harlem Renaissance* (New York: Oxford University Press, 1976), pp. 251-257.

5. One problem with such redesignations is that they risk the wrath of Brown's own learned insistence. Armies of linguistic and semantic debate stand at the ready over these questions. Michael Harper, in his preface to the *Collected Poems,* avoids all ethnic reference; and Sterling Stuckey, in his introduction to *Southern Road,* avoids *black* in favor of *American Negro,* Brown's emphatic self-description. The hazard of the newer terms pays off in fuller appreciation for the scope and reference of Brown's work in contemporary discourse, providing we respect the battles Brown fought during the New Negro era regarding the ideas behind these terms.

6. "Contemporary Negro Poetry, 1914-1936," in Sylvestre C. Watkins, ed., *An Anthology of American Negro Literature* (New York: Random House, 1944), p. 261.

7. "A Son's Return: 'Oh, Didn't He Ramble,' in Michael S. Harper and Robert B. Stepto, eds., *Chant of Saints* (University of Illinois Press, 1979), p. 18.

Vera M. Kutzinski (essay date spring 1982)

SOURCE: Kutzinski, Vera M. "The Distant Closeness of Dancing Doubles: Sterling Brown and William Carlos Williams." *Black American Literature Forum* 16, no. 1 (spring 1982): 19-25.

[*In the following essay, Kutzinski compares* Southern Road *and William Carlos Williams's* Paterson *in order to derive insights into the definition of American poetry.*]

> I call to the mysterious one who yet
> Shall walk the wet sands by the edge of the stream
> And look most like me, being indeed my double,
> And prove of all imaginable things
> The most unlike, being my anti-self,
> And, standing by these characters, disclose
> All that I seek. . . .
>
> —W. B. Yeats, "Ego Dominus Tuus"

> I hold my breath,
> and try not to shake my tree house,
> so high away I only hear
> the melancholy slap of their hands,
> and see them move from side to side,
> dressing the cypress in their wet clothes,
> passing and coming so close to each other
> that I cannot tell them apart,
> cannot separate them when they part.
>
> —Jay Wright, "Baptism in the Lead Avenue Ditch"

"American poetry is a very easy subject to discuss for the simple reason that it does not exist."[1] Without being particularly attracted to the role of the *advocatus diaboli,* I find it nevertheless hard, if not impossible, to resist the discursive potential of what might strike us as an extravagantly patronizing, though not altogether unfamiliar, remark. To be more precise, I'm interested in re-examining here one of the questions which is most frequently prompted by this quotation from William Carlos Williams' *Paterson* of a quotation from Englishman George Barker: How can American poetry *not* exist? This response, colored by feelings of defensive indignation and a certain degree of innocence or naivete, is as obvious as it is problematic. The dilemma becomes clear once one attempts to define "American poetry" or "American literature."

What, precisely, is "American poetry"? How does its "Americanness" manifest itself and where does it come from? Is it poetry written by Americans about America? Is it poetry that is characterized by a particular practice of genre that could be called American? None of the answers inherent in the questions appear fully satisfactory, which may well lead to the analyst's increasing discomfort with the implicit assertion that instigated the search—namely, that "American poetry" *exists*—and strengthen the claim of George Barker that "American poetry," whatever it is, does, in fact, not exist. What's more, if one continues to pursue the path of Cartesian (or, shall I say, Derridian) skepticism, one will inevitably be driven toward the painful realization that this problematic non-existence or "absence" of "American poetry" is not only due to the elusiveness of its particular mode of existence but, perhaps more importantly, to the general indeterminacy of poetry's or literature's mode of being; that is, if we are prepared to contend that "existence" requires a certain kind of "visibility" or "presence." The shadow of Derridian deconstruction does indeed loom large to remind us, time and again, that any text (or body of texts), not just "American poetry," is, in effect, an extremely difficult subject to discuss *because* it does not, as it were, exist:

> . . . there is no present text in general, and there is not even a past text, a text which is past as having been present. The text is not conceivable in an originary or modified form of presence. The unconscious text is already a weave of pure traces, differences in which meaning and force are united—a text nowhere present, consisting of archives which are always already transcriptions. Originary prints. *Everything begins with reproduction.* (italics added) Always already: Repositories of a meaning which was never present, whose signified presence is always reconstituted by deferral, *nachträglich,* belatedly, *supplementarily;* for the *nachträglich* also means *supplementary.*[2]

"Everything begins with reproduction"—curiously enough, this statement does not strike us as being far removed from the notion implicit in George Barker's

remark that "American poetry" does not exist, for the simple reason that it is nothing but a reproduction or imitation of English poetry and, after all, has to use a borrowed language for lack of an idiom of its own. Put in other words, originality, or lack thereof, becomes the convenient criterion for determining the presence or non-presence of a "text" or an entire body of "texts." At the same time, this is exactly the point at which our comparison of the two quotations is bound to come to a rather abrupt halt: George Barker and others like him, expressing what was by no means an unusual sentiment earlier in this century, would hardly have stopped to question the so-called "originality" of their own national literatures.

The controversial issue of originality vs. reproduction finds a striking parallel in the relation between what might be termed Anglo-American and Afro-American literature. More often than not, Afro-American literature is viewed as a mere subcategory of American letters in much the same way, and for much the same reasons, that George Barker's Eliotic remark implies the derivative status of Anglo-American poetics in relation to the European literary tradition. It has to be admitted that the distinction between Anglo- and Afro-American is somewhat awkward; but, after all, it has to be kept in mind that what Joseph Riddel has called the "oxymoronic" existence of American literature[3] is, at least to some extent, an adequate reflection of this hyphenation, which defies any preconceived notions about America as a unified cultural entity. Unless one is willing to subscribe to Moynihan's convenient fable of the "melting pot," one is forced to acknowledge that American literature is a multitude, a varied song indeed, to paraphrase Whitman or, for that matter, W. E. B. Du Bois.[4]

How, then, can we possibly assert that "American literature" does exist? Are not the common features far out-matched by the differences? While it would be unreasonable to pretend to possess an all-inclusive solution to this problem, I would like to suggest a few points of departure for what could be called an answer-in-progress. Let me then begin to begin again, as Williams would have it, by quoting a passage from T. S. Eliot's "Tradition and the Individual Talent" which will help to clarify some of the assumptions underlying this essay:

> No poet, no artist of any art, has his complete meaning alone. His significance, his appreciation is the appreciation of his *relation* to the dead poets and artists. You cannot value him alone; you must set him, for contrast and comparison, among the dead. I mean this as a principle of aesthetic, not merely historical, criticism. The necessity that he shall conform, that he shall cohere, is not one-sided; what happens when a new work of art is created is something that happens *simultaneously* to all works of art which preceded it. The existing monuments form an ideal order among themselves, which is modified by the introduction of the new (the really new) work of art among them.[5]

Although I question Eliot's notion of an "ideal order" of literary of artistic "monuments," as well as the inevitably resulting definition of artistic "progress" as a "continual self-sacrifice, a continual extinction of personality,"[6] I find his remarks valuable because they stress the importance of the intertextual relation of the individual work of art and its pretextual tradition along with the aspect of simultaneity that characterizes the creative and the interpretive process. American literature, Joseph Riddel suggests, "begins with the contradiction inherent in the notion of original or creative 'literature,' of original secondariness."[7] One could argue that this is equally true of all literatures, and I'm quite prepared to agree. On the other hand, American literature in general and Afro-American literature in particular, due to its precarious hyphenated status, offer an excellent prism from which to view this paradox and the ways in which it gives rise to a variety of "stages" on which the already-familiar dances with its "new" and unfamiliar doubles. This *dance* as an expression of the Eliotic idea of simultaneity is the result of repeating or "reproducing" the past, of beginning (again), and can be regarded as the act of establishing a *visible* relationship between the old and the new, the familiar and the unfamiliar, that goes beyond mere derivation. As Wilson Harris points out, "There are two kinds of relationship to the past—one which *derives* from the past, and one which is profound *dialogue* with the past (one which asks impertinent questions of the past). The nature of *tradition is,* in some degree, *a ceaseless question* about the nature of exploitation, self-exploitation, as well as the exploitation of others, the exploitation of one culture by another."[8] Harris' allusion to a specific historical phenomenon, the relationship between Europe and its overseas colonies, by no means distracts from "literary" issues. Rather, colonialism offers an appropriate and illuminating metaphor that introduces an important geocultural dimension to our previous discussion.

I'm only too aware at this point that, by leaving what Edward Said describes as the "conservative safety of language without history,"[9] I might well be accused of breaking the rules, as it were, of the kind of criticism my initial reference to Derrida might have seemed to inaugurate. If this is the case, then so be it. At any rate, we have to be conscious of the fact that any definition of language—or of writing, to be more precise—as a particular form of communication almost automatically requires us to include the element of *intention* into our analysis. While it is true that no linguistic sign in any text—and I'm talking about the rhetorically *conscious* and not the "unconscious" text here—ever refers only to itself, I'm not entirely satisfied with placing an emphasis on its referring to that which *has always already been* there at the expense of that which *will always already have been* there—the reader. The initial *dialogue* thus turns out to be, in effect, a *tri-alogue,* or put in Derridian terms, "[a] signifier is from the very beginning the *possibility of its own repetition,* of its own image or resemblance."[10] Quite to the point, intention, as the will to be present and to communicate that which manifests itself in the form of a text, not only occupies a *place,* but creates for itself a *space* with distinct geo-cultural and historical dimensions. In Said's words, "a signifier occupying a *place,* signifying *in place is*—rather than *represents*—an act of will with ascertainable political and intellectual consequences and an act fulfilling a strategic desire to administer a vast and *detailed* field of material."[11]

These linguistic as well as geo-cultural spaces, called into being by the triangulation of the various doubles which cohabit the poem—text, pre-text, and con-text—will constitute the central focus of my following interpretive response to the poems of Sterling Brown and William Carlos Williams. American poetics, I hope to show by comparing Anglo-American with Afro-American poetry, derives its validity as an ordering concept not from any notions about a common origin, but from the particular ways in which its multi-cultural components and participants are visible, textual expressions of the continuous quest for forms and shapes that would actualize their own (inter)textual dynamics by drawing together past and future in this timeless category we have come to know as the present. While most of my examples in this quest for poetic, and for critical, authenticity will be taken from Brown's *Southern Road* and Williams' *Paterson,* it often seems inevitable to refer to other texts as well. Although one could argue that the poetic features of *Paterson* and *Southern Road* are far too different to provide a basis for any fruitful comparison, I wish to point to the shared concern for language as an "energy" or "force" that is capable of calling into existence its own spaces. Williams' claim that language's "highest dignity [is] its illumination in the environment to which it is native,"[12] which revoices his earlier notions about the "local" being the only manifestation of the universal, holds true for a poet like Sterling Brown as well. While terms such as "native environment" or "local" could easily be viewed as direct references to the "verbal" spaces of the poems themselves, both Williams and Brown are quite explicit about the geo-cultural dimensions of their poetic spaces.

The two titles, *Paterson* and *Southern Road,* already articulate such an intention. It might be worth noting here that what I am calling geo-cultural referentiality has nothing to do with "local color" or some sort of literary regionalism; nor does it depend on the actual existence of a place or a region called "Paterson" or "the South" respectively. Neither Williams nor Brown is interested in "realistic" portraits or representative "copies" of an external reality or world. The fact that Brown calls his poetry "portraitures," which Henry-Louis Gates, Jr., interprets as "close and vivid detail-

ings of a carefully delineated subject that suggested a sense of place,"[13] illustrates the concern for an imaginary reality that shapes and, in its turn, is shaped by the poem itself. It is, to paraphrase Williams, not a matter of representation, but of separate existence.[14] The tension between this so-called external reality and the imaginary symbolic space of the poems creates a contrapuntal movement that is appropriated by the figurative dynamics evoked by the choice of language in the two titles. The genealogical transitions inscribed in the combination of "Pater"-"son" identifies this figure as a "befitting emblem of adversity"[15] as well as transmuting it into what Robert B. Stepto has termed a "spatial expression of *communitas* and *genius loci.*"[16] The effect of the combination "Southern"-"Road" is quite similar to that of "Pater"-"son." The kinetic trope of the road suggests two kinds of seemingly opposed movements which are ultimately but two different versions of the same activity. Ascent and separation figure as much in this image of transition as do descent and immersion.[17] The characteristic referential ambiguity of "Southern *Road*" derives from the fact that it leads both *away* from the South (to a symbolic North), and thus becomes an emblem of adversity, as well as *back toward* the South, in which case it is transformed into an "image of kin," in Michael S. Harper's words.[18] Brown's Southern Road interconnects two symbolically charged landscapes, the South and the North, in much the same way that the genealogical line from Pater to son is both an expression of the simultaneous distance and closeness between father and son—in this case, between Europe and America. In this sense, the poems of both Williams and Brown become figures of their own referential doubleness or what Jay Wright has very appropriately termed "emblems of the ecstatic connection."[19] They are the visible manifestations of those peculiar dialogues with the past—in effect, trialogues between past, present, and future—that textualize themselves as "performances," in the Derridian sense, or, to be even more accurate, as *dances:*

> The law? The law gives us nothing
> but a corpse, wrapped in a dirty mantle.
> The law is based on murder and confinement,
> long delayed,
> but this, following the insensate music,
> is based on the dance:
>   an agony of self-realization
> bound into a whole
> by that which surrounds us
>   I cannot escape
> I cannot vomit it up
> Only the poem!
> Only the poem made, the verb calls it
>   into being.[20]

This "agony of self-realization" vis-à-vis the "law" of a dominant literary tradition and its "legal" confinements links the different, yet analogous, cases of Williams and Brown as American poets.[21] The following two stanzas, which provide the *frame* for one of Sterling Brown's best poems, **"Odyssey of Big Boy,"** offer an excellent example of how a poem is indeed drawn out of the structural and figurative isolation of its alleged self-referentiality and bound into a whole by that which surrounds it:

> Lemme be wid Casey Jones,
>   Lemme be wid Stagolee,
> Lemme be wid such like men
>   When Death takes hol' on me,
>   When Death takes hol' on me. . . .
>   . . . . .
> An' all dat Big Boy axes
>   When times comes fo' to go,
> Lemme be wid John Henry, steel drivin' man,
>   Lemme be wid old Jazzbo,
>   Lemme be wid ole Jazzbo. . . .[22]

The **"Odyssey of Big Boy"** realizes the full potential of *Southern Road*'s figurative and structural design. The structural topography created by Big Boy's journey ranges from the "Kentucky hills" to "li'l New York" and back to "Southwest Washington." This private ritual ground is framed, if you will, by a variety of "ghostly presences" that people the poetic space and thus transform it into a symbolic landscape which figures as a spatial expression of poetic storytelling as a communal rite of passage. Big Boy, himself a twin version of Du Bois' "weary traveller," invites these not-so-ghostly ghosts of the past to share the "food," which is the poem. J. Hillis Miller's intriguing discussion of the figurative and the etymological interdependence of host and parasite, of text and pre-text, might be profitably extended to this poem to illustrate the relationship between Big Boy and the "guests" conjured up by his voice: The poem as the visible resonance of his "call" provides the figurative food for its mythic guests—Casey Jones, Stagolee, John Henry, ole Jazzbo—, whose existence depends as much on their "host" as the poem-as-host needs these guests to achieve a particular kind of visibility or presence.[23]

The poem's will to communicate with its historical-mythical past as well as with its contextual future, the reader, is by no means limited to the figurative level of its Afro-American idiom, but finds its structural equivalent in the call-and-response relations which govern the individual stanzas as well as the frame. The poem is set in motion by the call of the first stanza, whose open form already anticipates the response of the final one. In fact, the anticipation is really a formal prefiguration: The response repeats or revoices the call in such a way that it inverts the lines of the initial stanza. Put differently, the response appears as the inverted *double* of the call, so that the beginning is, in a sense, indeed the end. More to the point, the conspicuous absence of a poetic closure leaves us with a circular movement which could be described as the macro-

rhythmic version of the micro-rhythms generated by each of the individual stanzas. Throughout the poem, the final line in each stanza either literally repeats the next-to-last line ("Won't work in no mo' mine, / Won't work in no mo' mine") or improvises upon it ("But won't do dat again, / Do dat no mo' again"). This rhetorical device is a direct reference to the blues and thus invites yet another ghostly presence which concretizes the figurative dialogue by carrying it over into the structural sphere of the poem. It might be worth noting here that such rhythmic properties can dominate a poem to such an extent that the figurative qualities of its language are almost literally smothered by the embrace. The best example for such a "strangulation" is the title poem, **"Southern Road,"** in which the underlying work-song structure is modified by the call-and-response pattern of the traditional blues stanza:

> Doubleshackled—hunh—
> Guard behin';
> Doubleshackled—hunh—
> Guard behin';
> Ball an' chain, bebby,
> On my min'.
> **(*CP* [*The Collected Poems of Sterling A. Brown*], p. 52)**

In **"Odyssey of Big Boy,"** however, the successful interaction of micro- and macro-rhythms render visible the poem's continuous quest for its own figurative and structural form. The double circular movement, generated by the call-and-response patterns of the dialogue between figuration and structure, gives birth to one of the most striking emblems of the ecstatic connection, the dance of doubles—

> For the beginning is assuredly
> the end—since we know nothing, pure
> and simple, beyond
> our own complexities.
> (*P* [*Paterson*], pp. 11-12)

Although this passage from the "Preface" of *Paterson* invites us to participate in a very similar circular movement, I'm far from suggesting that Williams' poetry is a product of the same call-and-response network that readily and consistently draws attention to itself as method and poetic intention in the texts of Sterling Brown. However, one can hardly ignore the fact that the rhetorical effects of the interplay between the already-familiar and its most unlike twin, "something else, something else the same" (*P,* p. 44) in *Paterson* are at least comparable to those in **Southern Road.** *Paterson* is set in motion by a citation, this most parasitical of all presences, which is immediately answered, if you will, by the subsequent stanza so that, in essence, we can legitimately regard the resulting relation between the two as a dialogue with the past:

> "Rigor of beauty is the quest. But how will you find beauty when it is locked in the mind past all remonstrance?"

To make a start,
out of particulars
and make them general, rolling
up the sum, by defective means
Sniffing the trees,
just another dog
among a lot of dogs. What
else is there? And to do?

                                              (*P,* p. 11)

As we can clearly see in this passage, "to make a start" means, in effect, to *repeat,* "to begin to begin again" and to find a *shape* that will offer evidence of at least some innovation—of *having begun.*[24] Therefore it is not at all surprising that the communicative motion incited by this repetition multiplies and continues to call attention to itself as a dynamic process throughout *Paterson* in particular and Williams' poetry in general. If the following citation does indeed revoice the above dialogue, and I think it does, then the way in which the evidence of having begun is presented to us is most striking in the context of the statements made in its opposing parts:

> How to begin to find a shape—to begin to begin again,
> turning the inside out: to find one phrase that will
> lie married beside another for delight   ?
> —seems beyond attainment.
>
> *American poetry is a very easy subject to discuss for*
> *the simple reason that it does not exist*

                                              (*P,* p. 167)

As in **"Odyssey of Big Boy,"** the two dance partners have exchanged places, and this structural inversion itself is sufficient proof that the dance has indeed begun! At the same time, the figure of the dance attests to the impossibility of Williams' quest for "one phrase that will / lie married beside another for delight" and opens the insight that "Dissonance / (if you are interested) / leads to discovery" (*P,* p. 207). Put in other words, the dance is not a structural figure that is characterized by harmony. On the contrary, it is moved by oppositions which are inextricably locked in a rather ambiguous embrace, because one is always inherent in the other. The emphatic detachment of the sign *will* from its syntagmatic context, *will/lie,* in conjunction with drawing together *married* and *beside,* already prefigures the larger contrapuntal rhythm of the poem as a whole and elucidates Williams' concept of poetic "marriage." "The dance! The verb detaches itself / seeking to become articulate" (*PB* [*Pictures from Brueghel and Other Poems*], p. 120). I wish to point out that my frequent references to "The Desert Music" are largely prompted by the poem's intimate structural and figurative ties to *Paterson.* In fact, "The Desert Music" seems to start exactly where *Paterson* "ends," which is clarified by the following juxtaposition:

> We know nothing and can know nothing
>   but

the dance, to dance to a measure
contrapuntally,
                    Satyrically, the tragic foot.

                                              (*P,* p. 278)

—the dance begins: to end about a form
propped motionless—on the bridge
between Juárez and El Paso—unrecognizable
in the semi-dark

                                              (*PB,* p. 108)

Since any attempt to do full justice to either of the two poems within the confines of this essay is doomed to fail from the very start, "The Descent" (*Paterson,* Book Two) will have to serve as a representative response to the perpetual search for formal realization of this emblem of simultaneous kinship and adversity which is the dance. Or, as Williams himself put it so much better, "How shall we get said what must be said? / Only the poem" (*PB,* p. 108).

> The descent beckons
>   as the ascent beckoned
>   Memory is a kind
> of accomplishment
>   a sort of renewal
>   even
> an initiation, since the spaces it opens are new
> places
>   inhabited by hordes
>   heretofore unrealized,
> of new kinds—
>   since their movements
>   are towards new objectives
> (even though formerly they were abandoned)

                                              (*P,* p. 96)

The poem as verbal space is the perfect realization of the dynamic potential of the two central nouns, descent and ascent, in precisely that order. Their order derives its significance from the fact that the memory of the third line is experienced, both figuratively and structurally, as the *measured* simultaneity of the two movements, which are logically separated by their attachment to sequential time-categories. While the poetic space outlined by the rhythmic interaction of this particular pair of etymological doubles seems largely self-referential and self-contained when divorced from the context of *Paterson,* it cannot be overlooked that the space it breaks open is indeed a new, "unsuspected" *place,* in the sense of a private ritual ground for the initiated individual, Paterson, the man-city, the poet. As in the parallel case of **"Odyssey of Big Boy,"** this personal ritual ground assumes the features of a *genius loci* once the ghostly guests, the "hordes heretofore unrealized," are invited to participate in this special rite of passage, which is to transform the space laid out by the poem into a spatial and temporal expression of *communitas.* Williams' idea of "marriage" as the contrapuntal dance without beginning or end is, in the final analysis, as much an image of kinship and immersion, with all that is implied here in terms of intimacy and adversity, as is Brown's *Southern Road,* to which we now return. Although my following example, **"Transfer,"** is taken from a later collection of Brown's poetry entitled *No Hiding Place,* it clearly revoices the rhetorical strategies inscribed in the **"Southern Road"** metaphor.

Like **"Odyssey of Big Boy"** and other poems such as **"Long Gone," "Transfer"** begins with a journey which is set in motion by the stubborn absence of articulation presented to us, quite ironically, as "tongue-tied" absent-mindedness:

> It must have been that the fellow was tongue-tied,
> Or absent-minded, or daft with the heat,
> But howsoeverbeit he didn't say sir,
> So they took and bounced him out on the street.
>
> > (*CP,* p. 180)

But the journey does not end out on the street, as it were; it leads us to a figurative inversion of the referential significance of "tongue-*tied*" as an act of resistance. By the end of the fourth stanza, the persona is indeed physically *tied up* on "the prison farm," and this image of actual confinement prefigures, by contrast, the flight to Atlanta which culminates in the textual revoicing of a Du Boisian "Sorrow Song," indeed a familiar "sermon." The initial images of spiritual and physical imprisonment and violence undergo a figurative transformation in the second part of the poem, which, significantly, is underscored by the narrative movement away from those manifestations of oppressive "justice" and toward those "images of kin" inaugurated by the distinct echoes of both W. E. B. Du Bois and Richard Wright in the fifth and sixth stanzas.[25]

> But one day a red sun beat on the red hills
> As he was in the pasture, haltering a mare,
> And something went snap in his trusty old head
> And he started a-riding away from there.
>
> When he got to Atlanta, the folks took him in,
> And fed him and clothed him, and hid him away;
> And let him out only when the cops disappear
> From the streets of Darktown at the dusk of day:
>
> > (*CP,* p. 180)

And it is at this point that the poem's narrative structure does indeed become a "transfer" to a new direction: The rebellious inarticulateness of the first stanza, which is narratively figured as an act of separation, gives rise, at the end of the poem, to a most powerful image of articulateness, the "one text" which all have heard; and the persona's retelling of this "text" is an act of liberation which asserts its own literacy in the process of assuming control over one's own "tale." In this sense, the (re)turn to Atlanta is an act of descent and immersion, suggesting a strong sense of place, tradition, and, ultimately, kinship:

> "I stayed in my place, and my place stayed wid me,
> Took what I was dished, said I liked it fine:
> Figgered they would see that I warn't no trouble,
> Figgered this must be the onliest line.
>
> "But this is the wrong line we been ridin',
> This route doan git us where we got to go.
> Got to git transferred to a new direction.
> We can stand so much, then doan stan no mo'."
>
> > (*CP,* p. 181)

The persona's transition or "transfer" from a "tongue-tied" fellow to a virtual storyteller, which is effectively signaled by Brown's conspicuous shift to the vernacular in the last two stanzas, is textualized as the gaining of a personal voice ("*I* stayed in my place . . ."), extends into an embrace of the collective "we" in the poem's final line. This articulation of a sense of community may be regarded as an emblem of kinship and love renewed vis-à-vis an oppressive cultural context, and this process is comparable, at least rhetorically, to the poetic message emanating from the following passage from Williams' "The Descent":

> With evening, love wakens
> > > though its shadows
> > > > which are alive by reason
> > of the sun shining—
> > > > grow sleepy now and drop away
> > > > > > from desire
> > Love without shadows stirs now
> > > > beginning to waken
> > > > > > > as night
> > advances.
>
> > (*P,* pp. 96-97)

Within the context of the poem, this passage provides the transition from the new "places" and their anonymous inhabitants to this hopeful new awakening "which is a reversal / of despair" and as such announces the culmination of the idea of love in the collective "we" of the adjacent lines. These final lines of the poem are a fascinating realization of this particular kind of reversal or inversion which reaffirms, on the micro-structural level of "The Descent" itself, the macro-rhythmic circle of *Paterson*'s more elaborate dance:

> > > For what we cannot accomplish, what
> > is denied to love,
> > > > what we have lost in the anticipation—
> > > > > a descent follows,
> > endless and indestructible
>
> > (*P,* p. 97)

When compared to the structural movement at the beginning of the poem, these lines present themselves as variations on the initial triangulation: descent—ascent—memory. Curiously enough, the order within the triangle has changed to such an extent that the former positions of its constituents are now inverted.

This reversal, which is announced by the introduction of the negative *cannot accomplish,* effectively draws attention to itself as the very accomplishment it denies. In fact, this accomplishment is the only one that is possible because it is neither denied to the renewed love, the "love without shadows," nor has it been lost in the ascending anticipation. To be more specific, what has indeed (or better, *in deed*) been accomplished is the visibility of the inherence of one part of the binary pair in the other, which takes a form of *a* descent (as opposed to *the* descent), and this descent is a *new* beginning in the sense that it repeats the *old* one. It is thus both a beginning and an end at the same time, a *perpetuum mobile* whose openendedness becomes even clearer once the poem is recontextualized within the body of *Paterson.* The following two lines should suffice to re-establish this context: "Listen!— / The pouring water!" Quite to the point, this is the same water that "encircles" *Paterson.* Interestingly enough, the rhetorical effect here is quite similar to the "pouring" voice at the end of Brown's **"Transfer"**; like in *Paterson,* we as readers are indeed listening, as it were, to the pouring language of the descent.

I would now like to close the circle of my own discussion by offering a few comments about yet another striking configuration of such a poetic "descent," Sterling Brown's **"Ma Rainey."**

I

When Ma Rainey
Comes to town,
Folks from anyplace
Miles aroun',
From Cape Girardeau,
Poplar Bluff,
Flocks in to hear
Ma do her stuff;
Comes flivverin' in,
Or ridin' mules,
Or packed in trains,
Picknickin' fools. . . .
That's what it's like,
Fo' miles on down,
To New Orleans delta
An' Mobile town,
When Ma hits
Anywheres aroun'.

III

O Ma Rainey,
Sing yo' song;
Now you's back
Whah you belong,
Git way inside us,
Keep us strong. . . .
O Ma Rainey,
Li'l an' low;
Sing us 'bout de hard luck
Roun' our do';

Sing us 'bout de lonesome road
We mus' go. . . .

                                        (*CP,* pp. 62-63)

In this juxtaposition of Parts I and III of the poem, the poetic transmutation of the symbolic landscape outlined by the variations on the journey motif, in the first part, into a geo-cultural ritual ground becomes even more lucid than in **"Odyssey of Big Boy"** or **"Transfer."** The way in which the "folks," the "picknickin' fools" from "anyplace," actually ascend from their initial obscurity and congregate in the process of gaining a collective voice, which is achieved in the act of repetition that connects the two parts, is already a remarkable anticipation of the descent that follows:

I talked to a fellow, an' the fellow say,
"She jes' catch hold of us, somekindaway.
She sang Backwater Blues one day:
  '*It rained fo' days an' de skies was dark as night,*
  Trouble taken place in de lowlands at night.

  '*Thundered an' lightened an' the storm begin to roll*
  Thousan's of people ain't got no place to go.

  '*Den I went an' stood upon some high ol' lonesome hill,*
  An' looked down on the place where I used to live.'

An' den de folks, dey natchally bowed dey heads an' cried,
Bowed dey heavy heads, shet dey moufs up tight an' cried,
An' Ma lef' de stage, an' followed some de folks outside."
Dere wasn't much more de fellow say:
She jes' gits hold of us dataway.

                                        (*CP,* p. 63)

Ma Rainey's song, unmistakably the ghost conjured up by the poem's call to invest this mythic blues singer with a visible shape and an audible voice, turns the carefree audience described in Part II into compassionate listeners and kinsmen, and thereby accomplishes an interesting figurative reversal. But the ascent to voice and the descent to song are not only textualized by the apparent simultaneity of the two actions, which receive additional support from the consistent use of the synchronizing *an'* and thus draw this particular version of Du Bois' Sorrow Songs into the present of the poem's performance. On the one hand, Ma Rainey steps up onto this *"high ol' lonesome hill,"* which figures as the singer's *stage,* only to descend to the audience's space and thus to concretize and symbolically complete the restoration of the communicative ties between past and present, between artist and reader/listener, which had been invoked by her song. In that sense, the poem becomes a powerful vision or revision of Afro-American cultural history and thus re-creates its own tradition, which is significantly bound to the sense of place as expressed by the interdependency of place and voice described above. On the other hand, this reinvocation of the collective assumption that, when the blues singer says "I," the audience hears "we" extends into the future by including the readers as well as the imaginary listeners. The resulting sets of relationships clearly assume the shape of what I have referred to as trialogue. Put in other words, the accomplishment of the poem, which is the movement from "somekindaway" to the more specific "dataway," lies in the act of rendering visible its own contrapuntal call-and-response pattern, not by eliminating the ascent/descent polarity, but by controlling its structural and figurative dynamics. Brown and Williams evidently agree that "everything we do must be a repetition of the past with a difference."[26]

It ought to be clear by now that Williams' emblem of love is no more confined to a self-referential space than is Brown's emblem of the ecstatic connection. Both poets share the insight that the end is nothing but a transfiguration of the beginning, in which always already inheres the possibility of its own repetition or double. Interestingly enough, the dance of such doubles is already inscribed in the etymological structure of *repetition* and its verbal dynamics. To *repeat*, as the compound of the prefix *re* ('back, again') and the root *petere,* is divided into two seemingly polar clusters of meanings: The first one is characterized by a notion of hostility—*petere* 'to assault'; *re-petere* 'to attach again, to renew, to recommence'—which is significantly absent from the other: (*re*)-*petere* 'to embrace (again)'. The way in which the interaction of the two different semantic fields re-voices the relation between host and parasite, which J. Hillis Miller has described as intimate kinship and enmity at the same time,[27] adds to an understanding of the third dimension of (*re*)*petere*: 'to seek (again), to travel to a place, to go in quest of, to claim or demand what is due.' In light of this etymology, the act of repeating can be defined as an ambiguous embrace which is always the beginning of a continuous quest that creates a poetic space for itself. The poem, in turn, becomes the visible resonance of this self-perpetuating search for a communicative form. In this sense, the poem is neither the host nor the parasite, but the dramatization and the articulation of the ambiguous, but not necessarily strangling, embrace in which the two doubles are locked. Hence the "being" born in the process of dancing has only one form of articulation: "the tight voice of becoming,"[28] which does indeed and in deed disclose all we seek and all we can know;

> But only the dance is sure!
> make it your own.
> Who can tell
> what is to come of it?

(*PB,* p. 33)

Notes

1. William Carlos Williams, *Paterson* (New York: New Directions, 1963), p. 167. All further references to this volume will appear in the text as *P.*

2. Jacques Derrida, *Writing and Difference,* trans. with an intro. and notes by Alan Bass (Chicago: Univ. of Chicago Press, 1978), p. 24.

3. "Decentering the Image: The 'Project' of 'American' Poetics?" in *Textual Strategies,* ed. Josué V. Harari (Ithaca, NY: Cornell Univ. Press, 1979), p. 322.

4. Whitman's original in *Leaves of Grass* reads, "I hear America singing, the varied carols I hear"; see also W. E. B. Du Bois, *The Souls of Black Folk* (1903; rpt. New York: New American Library, 1969), p. 209.

5. In *Selected Prose of T. S. Eliot,* ed. Frank Kermode (London: Faber and Faber, 1975), p. 38; italics added.

6. Ibid., p. 40.

7. Riddel, "Decentering the Image," p. 322.

8. "A Talk on the Subjective Imagination," *New Letters,* 40, No. 1 (1973), 45; italics in second sentence added.

9. *Beginnings: Intention and Method* (Baltimore, MD: The Johns Hopkins Press, 1975), p. xiii.

10. Jacques Derrida, *Of Grammatology,* trans. Gayatri Chakravorty Spivak (Baltimore, MD: The Johns Hopkins Press, 1974), p. 91; italics added.

11. "The Problem of Textuality: Two Exemplary Positions," *Critical Inquiry,* 4 (1978), 709.

12. *The Collected Later Poems of William Carlos Williams* (New York: New Direction, 1967), p. 5.

13. "Songs of a Racial Self," *The New York Times Book Review,* 11 Jan. 1981, p. 11.

14. *Spring and All,* in *Imaginations* (New York: New Directions, 1970), p. 117.

15. W. B. Yeats, "My House," in *The Variorum Edition of the Poems of W. B. Yeats* (New York: Macmillan, 1977), p. 420.

16. *From Behind the Veil: A Study of Afro-American Narrative* (Urbana: Univ. of Illinois Press, 1979), p. 67

17. The terms "ascent," "descent," and "immersion" are taken from Stepto's study.

18. *Images of Kin* (Urbana: Univ. of Illinois Press, 1970).

19. *Dimensions of History* (Santa Cruz, CA: Kayak, 1976), p. 34.

20. Williams, "The Desert Music," in *Pictures from Brueghel and Other Poems* (New York: New Directions, 1949), pp. 109-10. All further references to this volume will appear in the text as *PB*.

21. Unlike Williams, Brown did not have to free himself from *his* literary tradition to assert himself as an Afro-American poet. What he was suffering from was not the impact of the steel-chains of the tradition he sought to reclaim, but the denial of its very existence by those participants of the Harlem Renaissance who had discarded dialect poetry in favor of so-called standard English. Black oral and musical forms in general and dialect in particular were viewed as archaic remnants of the plantation tradition that perpetuated the stereotypical images poets such as Countee Cullen, Claude MacKay, and, above all, James Weldon Johnson were out to correct. In short, dialect poetry such as Paul Laurence Dunbar's "jingles in a broken tongue" were all too readily associated with the political conservatism of a Booker T. Washington and his disciples, which made them an embarrassment. As a result, Johnson announced in 1931 that the passing of traditional dialect as a medium for Negro poets was complete (it might be worth noting here that Johnson's "Jingles and Croons," published in 1917, was one of the worst examples of the use of black dialect!). Ironically, Johnson was the one to write the preface to Sterling Brown's *Southern Road* only one year later, in which he admitted, albeit reluctantly, that he had been mistaken about the "passing" of dialect poetry and that Brown's poems were indeed valuable contributions to American literature.

22. *The Collected Poems of Sterling A. Brown,* ed. Michael S. Harper (New York: Harper and Row, 1980), pp. 20-21. All further references to this edition will appear in the text as *CP*.

23. See J. Hillis Miller, "The Critic as Host," in *Deconstruction and Criticism* (New York: Continuum, 1979), pp. 217-53.

24. Said, *Beginnings,* p. xiii.

25. See Du Bois, *The Souls of Black Folk,* and Richard Wright, *Black Boy.*

26. Williams, *The Great American Novel,* in *Imaginations,* p. 210.

27. "The Critic as Host," pp. 224-25.

28. Jay Wright, *The Double Invention of Komo* (Austin: Univ. of Texas Press, 1980), p. 36.

John F. Callahan (essay date 20 December 1982)

SOURCE: Callahan, John F. "In the Afro-American Grain." *The New Republic* 187, no. 24 (December 20, 1982): 25-8.

[*In the following essay, Callahan asserts that Brown's emphasis on African American oral tradition and dialect is central to his poetic achievement.*]

On May 1, 1901—the same year W. E. B. DuBois wrote his prophetic line: "The problem of the twentieth century is the problem of the color line"—Sterling Brown was born in a house then near and now part of the Howard University campus. His father was Sterling Nelson Brown, minister of Lincoln Temple Congregational Church, professor of religion at Howard, and for a time member of the District of Columbia Board of Education. His parents met at Fisk, where his mother was valedictorian of her class and a relative had been one of the original Fisk Jubilee singers back in the Reconstruction.

Brown grew up in a time when the flavor of Washington, D.C. was becoming more and more bitterly Southern for Negroes, as Woodrow Wilson's New Freedom tightened the noose of segregation and Jim Crow. Along with contemporaries Allison Davis, Montague Cobb, William Hastie, and Charles Drew, Brown went to Dunbar High School and from there, on scholarship, to Williams, then one of the few New England colleges to admit a token one or two Negro students a year. At Williams, Brown remembers, his classmates

> had never seen a Negro, and I had hardly ever seen a white man their age. Until I came to Williams, I had never spoken to a white boy except the little son of the drugstore man where we used to go to get sundaes for my family, and he and I were friends until Negroes came around with me or whites came around with him. Then we didn't know each other.

At Williams, class of 1922, he learned from George Dutton.

> Dutton was teaching Joseph Conrad. He said Joseph Conrad was being lionized in England—H. G. Wells and Galsworthy and all the ladies and lords and the rest were making a fuss over Joseph Conrad, and Conrad was sitting over in the corner, quiet, not participating. Dutton said he was brooding and probably thinking about his native Poland and the plight of his people. He looked straight at me. I don't know what he meant, but I think he meant, and this is symbolic to me, I think he meant don't get fooled by any lionizing, don't get fooled by being here at Williams with a selective clientele. There is business out there that you have to take care of. Your people, too, are in a plight. I've never forgotten it.

After Williams, Brown took his Masters from Harvard in 1923 and studied under Bliss Perry and George Lyman Kittredge. "At Harvard," he remembers—again in "A Son's Return: 'Oh Didn't He Ramble,'" an autobiographical address given at Williams in 1973,

> I went into careful study of American poetry. I learned from Edwin Arlington Robinson's *Tilbury Town* where he took up the undistinguished, the failures, and showed the extraordinary in ordinary lives. I learned from Robert Frost. I learned from my own; the man I was brought up on was Dunbar. I learned from Claude McKay.

During Brown's year at Harvard, McKay's *Harlem Shadows* came out and also Jean Toomer's *Cane.* As a boy in D.C., Sterling Brown had imitated some of Toomer's moves on the basketball court. Now, Williams and Harvard behind him, he began, as Toomer had done a few years before, a geographical and spiritual journey that was to culminate in **Southern Road** nine years later and influence profoundly the rest of his poetry and criticism. "I went South," he says.

> I taught at Virginia Seminary, where I learned a great deal that I could not learn at Williams. I learned the strength of my people, I learned the fortitude. I learned the humor. I learned the tragedy. I learned from a wandering guitar player [the Big Boy Davis who is such an important voice and presence in Brown's great ballads] about John Henry, about Stagolee, about 'The Ballad of the Bollweevil.' I learned folktales. I learned folkstuff.

Brown learned folklore firsthand from the folk in rural Virginia, Missouri, and Tennessee, while he taught at Virginia Seminary, Lincoln, and Fisk. These Negro colleges were more important to the Negro folk than Brown knew when, only twenty-two or twenty-three himself, he rebuked a student for falling asleep in class. When he investigated, Brown discovered the young man both went to school and plowed and tilled his people's farm. Brown met the family and was introduced by the student's mother, Mrs. Bibby, to the complexity of folk idiom. Speaking of a ne'er-do-well neighboring farmer of whom others were saying he do this or that but *he mean good,* the old woman, after she had removed a corncob pipe from her mouth and spat precisely onto the hottest chunk in the fire, told the assembled company: "Well, he may mean good, but he *do so doggone po'.*" This and other sayings that Sterling Brown heard from the surviving folk in the 1920s and 1930s found their way into the aphorisms he, along with Arthur Davis and the late Ulysses Lee, included in the still unequaled gathering of American Negro writing and folkstuff, *The Negro Caravan* (1941).

Brown brought this rich folk speech to the literary forms of poetry. And while he wrote the poems for **Southern Road** (1932), Brown honed the principles of critical realism in a regular column for *Opportunity.* In "Our Literary Audience" (February 1930), he made close connections between literature and history, literature and society, and, above all, between writer and audience. For him the act of writing involved attention to talking and listening as well as reading, the ear as well as the eye. "We are not a reading folk," he observed and reaffirmed Whitman's belief: "Without great audiences we cannot have great poets." Brown's purpose was to develop kinships between literary forms of expression and an Afro-American audience.

> I have a deep concern with the development of a literature worthy of our past, and of our destiny; without which literature certainly, we can never come to much. I have a deep concern with the development of an audience worthy of such a literature.

And Brown's work enacts this profound relationship between literature and democracy. It is his achievement to have fulfilled the complex double purpose of writing poetry worthy of a great audience and of helping to shape that diverse, responsive, critical, and inclusive audience through his essays and criticism.

In his poetry, now gathered in **The Collected Poems of Sterling A. Brown,** Brown forged an alliance between two essential traditions: the American vernacular of critical realism—of Robinson, Frost, Sandburg—and the Afro-American vernacular derived from folk speech and folktales, from the spirituals and work songs and carried on in the ballads and the blues. Voice, he realized, was the core of his task. Like Dunbar before him, he knew that for oral tradition to survive, the spoken word must be heard on the page.

But what was the oral tradition?

In *Negro Poetry and Drama* (1938), Brown noted Dunbar's idealization of Negro rural life in the dialect poems and commented gently but with the bite of understatement that "No picture of Negro life that is only pastoral can be fully true." This was an old battle over the nature of reality going back to Frederick Douglas and beyond, even to the utterance of Phyllis Wheatley. At stake was nothing less than the meaning and direction of Afro-American idiom and personality. Already in his own folk poems Sterling Brown had answered James Weldon Johnson's characterization of Negro dialect as "an instrument with but two full stops, humor and pathos." In his preface to the *Book of American Negro Poetry* (1922), Johnson had claimed that "there are phases of Negro life in the United States which cannot be treated in the dialect either adequately or artistically." But Johnson was talking of dialect as a literary convention. Recalling Louis Untermeyer's remark that traditional dialect was "an affectation to please a white audience," Brown added that its practitioners were often "preachers and teachers, consciously literary," who "seldom saw the wit and beauty possible to folk speech, the folk-shrewdness, the humanity, the stoicism of those people."

About tradition Brown is committed, critical, and unerringly explicit:

> I love Negro folk speech and I think it is rich and wonderful. It is not *dis* and *dat* with a split verb. But it is "Been down so long that down don't worry me," or it is what spirituals had in one of the finest couplets in American literature:

> "I don't know what my mother wants to stay here for. This old world ain't been no friend to her."

To Sterling Brown, "Dialect, or the speech of the people, is capable of expressing whatever the people are." And such expression is the achievement of Brown's poetry. His best work touches greatness. As Alain Locke contended in what remains the finest piece on *Southern Road,* "The New Negro Folk Poet (1934),"

> Sterling Brown has listened long and carefully to the folk in their intimate hours, when they are talking to themselves not, so to speak, as in Dunbar, but actually as they do when the masks of protective mimicry fall.

Of course Brown's poetry comes also from gifts other than that of listening. He makes rhythm, cadence, and a carefully wrought vocabulary reverberate with the experience and feelings of folk characters. Because he understood that folk speech in poetry, like good dialogue in fiction, is something other than exact imitation of conversation, he was able to create a speech that functions powerfully both as written and as spoken word. This comes from his ear, his eye, his sense of line, of beat. It also flows from his sense of tradition and his will to put his gifts to work in literary forms capable of carrying on the great tradition of Afro-American oral culture—the sorrow songs, work songs, the ballads, the blues.

In the accessible way of good poetry, Brown's folk-spoken ballads and blues poems summon images and voices from that enduring and, in Faulkner's sense, prevailing Afro-American past so essentially bound up with the nation's culture and condition.

Listen. Hear Big Boy stake out a place in the pantheon of stoical folk heroes:

> An' all dat Big Boy axes
>   When time comes fo' to go,
> Lemme be wid John Henry, steel drivin'
>   man,
> Lemme be wid old Jazzbo,
>   Lemme be wid ole Jazzbo . . .

Overhear a lifer on the chain gang hold his own by holding it in, honing his fury to the low growl of a last irrevocable word, his hammer in his hand all the while:

> White man tells me—hunh—
> Damn yo' soul;
> White man tells me—hunh—

> Damn yo' soul;
> Got no need, bebby,
> To be tole.

Listen to the double changes, religious and historical, aspired to in the advice the poet gives old Sister Lou in an idiom tender, strong, and soulfully hers:

> Honey
> Don't be feared of them pearly gates,
> Don't go 'round to de back,
> No mo' dataway
> Not evah no mo'.

Catch the simple, subtle beat of an epic blues about the ebb and flow of cities and civilizations and pick up the bluesman's onomatopoeic insinuations of tradition in the sighting of the elemental, everlasting wind:

> Memphis go
> Memphis come back,
> Ain' no skin
> Off de nigger's back.
> All dese cities
> Ashes, rust . . .
> De win' sing sperrichals
> Through deir dus'.

Literary variations on the oral forms of ballad, work song, spiritual, and blues, these poems prepare the ear for the voices of *No Hiding Place,* Brown's second book of poetry, a volume turned down in the late 1930s and seen for the first time in its entirety only in the *Collected Poems.* In "Old Lem," an old Southern Negro spits out a story so strongly and stubbornly paced that each word seems a stone that might indeed break bones some day:

> I had a buddy
> Six foot of man
> Muscles up perfect
> Game to the heart
>   They don't come by ones
> Outworked and outfought
> Any man or two men
>   They don't come by twos
> he spoke out of turn
> At the commissary
> They gave him a day
> To git out the county.
> He didn't take it.
> He said 'Come and get me.'
> They came and got him.
>   And they came by tens.

Other poems are spoken in double voices. Folk speech counterpoints a plain-spoken American vernacular. And sometimes the narrator's American vernacular modulates into the Afro-American folk voice. Consider, for example, the opening and closing couplets from the last stanza of the blues-ballad, "Ma Rainey":

> I talked to a fellow, an' the fellow say,
> 'She jes' catch hold of us

some kind away.' . . .
Dere wasn't much more de fellow say:
She jes' gits hold of us dataway.

Notice the changes. The indefinite "somekindaway" yields to the definite "dataway" because between the two couplets the fellow has testified to Ma Rainey's effect on the people, on an occasion when he and the poet were witnesses to her performance. And there is something else. The poet's idiom becomes one with the fellow's folk speech. *The* becomes *de,* and the quotation marks fall away to signify that the poet's voice has become truly the voice of the folk. In such poetry Brown writes what Yeats called "the book of the people."

Unsurprisingly, in view of Brown's commitment to critical realism, the song Ma Rainey sings to "get way inside" the folk is "Backwater Blues," a blues Bessie Smith was moved to write when, riding the train, she witnessed the devastation of the 1927 flood. ("Bessie had a greater voice," according to Brown. "Bessie was the empress of the blues, but Ma taught her and Ma was really the authentic folk singer.") That authenticity enables Brown, like Ma Rainey, to move the people beyond pain and loss to a depth of wonder akin to love, and to a will to overcome. In **"Cabaret,"** Brown superimposes on the Southern landscape a Chicago nightclub scene. Underneath, like the discontinuous layers of allusion in *The Waste Land,* are other landscapes: the natural one of bottom land and backwater in Arkansas and Mississippi, the moral one of the folk as they "huddle, mute, uncomprehending," and beneath these the historical landscape of slavery. Of the 1927 flood Brown recalls: "I was in Missouri teaching then. And I saw the Missouri in flood. I saw the Mississippi, I saw Arkansas at that time. And then I go into the cabaret [the Black and Tan in Chicago] and hear the popular muddy water business and the contrast struck me." In **"Cabaret,"** an M.C. shows off falsely the Negro chorus girls, his voice receding before the unforgotten voice of a slave auctioneer. These Brown interrupts with two vernaculars, one satiric, the other brooding and biblical, but all of the above yield to the vicious sentimentality of the *Muddy Water* lyrics. In these cabaret landscapes the folk are wholly mute, voiceless. Here the musicians are exploited and worse off spiritually than the Southern Negroes who are casualties of the flood. Here there is no performance in the testamental, rejuvenating manner of the blues, only an entertainment degrading to both Negro personality and tradition.

In still other poems Brown assumes the voice of a chronicler who, as poet and storyteller too, weaves fact and fiction, anecdote and legend together into narrative portraits and commentaries. And the voice reflects Brown's fidelity to a vernacular shared by all Americans. The climax of **"Strange Legacies,"** for instance, is spoken by an "old nameless couple in Red River bottom." To utter their will to continue in the teeth of their lives' devastation by the forces of man and nature, they use a vernacular similar to that spoken by Frost's or Robinson's people:

> Guess we'll give it one mo' try.
> Guess we'll give it one mo' try.

For Brown the courage of actual and legendary heroes like Jack Johnson and John Henry flows from, and is nourished by, the folk. In addition, and here is where American vernacular and Brown's overall American audience come in, the old nameless couple's effort and idiom are in the best American tradition. It is a tradition whose democratic voice and responsibility were affirmed by Robert Frost in "In Dives' Dive," a poem repeatedly quoted and brilliantly commented on by Sterling Brown:

> As long as the Declaration guards,
> My right to be equal in number of cards,
> It is nothing to me who runs the Dive.
> Let's have a look at another five.

Declaring himself once more in the 1970s—his seventies as well—Sterling Brown uttered a confession of faith.

> I am an integrationist, though that is an ugly word, because I know what segregation really was. And by integration, I do not mean assimilation. I believe what the word means—an integer is a whole number. I want to be in the best American tradition. I want to be accepted as a whole man.

Nothing he has written better testifies to that wholeness of tradition and personality than **"Strong Men."** To make it, Brown cast Carl Sandburg's vernacular line into the Afro-American vernacular:

> *The strong men keep coming on.*
>
> —Sandburg

> The strong men keep a-comin' on
> The strong men git stronger . . .

Written in 1929, the poem and its superb refrains express a gathering of forces as Brown anticipates the people massing their voices and bodies as of course men, women, and children were to do in the South and in Brown's Washington, D.C. during the 1950s and 1960s. Like so much of Brown's best work, **"Strong Men"** recapitulates the past and points the way to the toughness of character and vision required for the struggle in coming days.

The same compassionate, continuing, compelling strength marks the more intimate poems. **"Long Track**

Blues" testifies to the grief of love in a particularly haunting way because its singer speaks of losses both calculable and incalculable, the twin losses of departure and death:

> Went down to the yards
> To see the signal lights come on'
> Looked down the track
> Where my lovin' babe done gone.
> Red light in my block
> Green light down the line
> Lawdy, let yo' green light
> Shine down on that babe o'mine.

From the whistle of distant trains, from the expanse of track, from the hurt, Brown's sure simplicity of rhythm and idiom makes affirming music.

What better homage to Sterling Brown than the wish of **"Long Track Blues"**? A book of essays in the works, his memoirs in progress, a poem or two forming in his head, "Sister Goose" and other tales waiting to be told again, at eighty-one Sterling Brown lives the refrain from **"Strong Men,"** that poem he believes "still tells the essential truth about the position of my people." Like the archetypal Afro-Americans in his poem, he remains out there, exposed, on the line: a strong man, gittin' stronger.

John S. Wright (essay date spring 1989)

SOURCE: Wright, John S. "The New Negro Poet and the Nachal Man: Sterling Brown's Folk Odyssey." *Black American Literature Forum* 23, no. 1 (spring 1989): 95-105.

[*In the following essay, Wright explores the impact of African American folklore on Brown's career and finds him uniquely qualified to provide an understanding of the work of Walter "Leadbelly" Boyd, the infamous African American Depression-era blues singer.*]

In 1936, the year Sterling Brown and John Lomax joined forces supervising the collection of oral slave narratives for the Federal Writers' Project (see Mangione 257-63), Lomax and his son Alan published the first extended study of an American folksinger. That singer, one Walter Boyd, alias Hudie Ledbetter, alias "Leadbelly," had been the self-proclaimed "King of the Twelve String Guitar Players of the World," as well as the number one man in the number one gang on the number one convict farm in Texas. He had fought his way into prison and had sung his way to freedom, to fleeting fame, and to what would be a pauper's death in Bellevue in 1949. A man of prodigious physical strength, emotional volatility, unpredictable violence, and indisputable creativity, unschooled if not unassum-

ing, he was shaped by record, film, and the printed page into the prototypic national image of the "folk Negro." For the recording industry, his songs were a golden hedge against hard times. For the generation of newly professional folklorists that the Lomaxes represented, he was a "find" that helped buttress the assault of the Depression era folklore radical democrats against the old aristocratic folklore scholarship. For the thinkers and artists of the black world-within-a-world from which he came, however, Leadbelly made concrete an old enigma alternately energizing and embarrassing— and one left largely unplumbed by the outspokenly "folk conscious" New Negro movement of the twenties. Lawbreaker, illiterate, brawler, boozer, womanizer, cottonpicker, and vagrant; singer of prison dirges, work songs, cowboy ballads, children's songs, spirituals, lullabies, and barrel-house blues, Leadbelly was a grinning, gold-toothed incongruity. Vernacular tradition's "nachal man" incarnate, he was in one rough frame the bruised and imbruted "man farthest down" for whom Booker T. Washington and the organizations of racial uplift had lowered their proverbial buckets, *and* he was the voice of that transcendent "Negro genius" which W. E. B. Du Bois and the Talented Tenth had exalted as creator of "the most beautiful expressions of human experience born this side of the seas" (265). In the preceding decade Jean Toomer, Claude McKay, Zora Neale Hurston, and Langston Hughes had all directed their imaginative energies to penetrating the layers of abstraction that created incongruity from the folklife Leadbelly nonetheless had to live. But perhaps nowhere had so clear a perspective emerged for seeing such a man whole as in the work of Sterling Brown.

In 1932 Brown had published *Southern Road*; and with a social realism honed to poetic precision, he had struck through the masks with which minstrelsy, local color, the plantation tradition, and Jazz Age primitivism had defaced the folk. Alain Locke, self-professed "literary midwife" of the New Negro movement, in reviewing *Southern Road* hailed Sterling Brown as "The New Negro Folk Poet" and described him as an artist who had revealed better than any of his contemporaries the "racial touch," independent of dialect, which enabled him to catch the deeper "idiom of feeling" (89). Locke had predicted some years earlier that "the soul of the Negro will be discovered in a characteristic way of thinking and in a homely philosophy rather than in a jingling and juggling of broken English" (89). The secret of Sterling Brown's poetic effects was that he had "listened long and carefully to the folk in their intimate hours," talking to themselves, their protective masks dropped. A "more reflective, a closer student of the folk-life, . . . a bolder and more detached observer" than his fellow poets, Sterling Brown had recaptured what was "more profoundly characteristic" than types of metaphors or mannerisms of speech—he had recaptured the philosophic attitudes, material and metaphysical, that lay beneath the surface of folksongs, fables, proverbs, and argot (90). And in giving the folk credit for thinking he had discovered the "poetic divining-rod" for rendering, with Aesopian clarity and Aesopian candor, that ancient common wisdom of the group which promised to bridge the then highly publicized gap between the Old Negro and the New.

Rejecting the Old Negro and the traditional poetry of folk caricature, James Weldon Johnson had advocated a symbolic rather than a phonetic literary mimesis, and had forecast the doom of dialect poetry. But Sterling Brown perceived that the problem of defining a poetic language for folk portraiture was a problem not so much of materials as of perspective. "Dialect, or the speech of the people," he maintained, "is capable of expressing whatever the people are. And the folk Negro is a great deal more than a buffoon or a plaintive minstrel. Poets more intent upon learning the ways of the folk, their speech, and their character, that is to say, better poets, could have smashed the mold. But first they would have to believe in what they were doing. And this was difficult in a period of conciliation and middle class striving for recognition and respectability" (qtd. in Redmond 227-28). Brown's less conventional strivings provided critical as well as poetic demonstrations of his own unshakable belief in "the validity, the power, and the beauty of folk culture." His was an aesthetic of reorientation, and its achievement rested no less surely on his poems than on the critical paths he cut through the jungle of theory and interpretation, censorship and commercialization, romanticism and mysticism, that engulfed the study of Afro-American folklore between the 1920s and the 1950s.

The twenties, besides hosting the New Negro movement, fostered another phenomenon not unconnected to the black cultural ferment of the time with its artistic focus on, in Locke's terms, "the revaluation of the Negro": After a war decade remarkable for the *accumulation* of major folklore collections in America, the twenties became a decade remarkable for the *publication* of folklore collections. Several decades earlier, in 1888, the American Folklore Society had been founded as a kind of rescue operation to record what were thought to be the "fast vanishing relics" of rural folk groups before their projected disappearance from an urbanizing, industrializing modern culture (Brunvand 9). Though the academic study of folklore would not be established in the United States until the 1940s, an interim throng of avid amateurs and bootlegging scholars trained in other fields—English literature, anthropology, sociology, musicology, history, and languages—began consolidating in the twenties a vast repository of folklore and folksong which by the forties had tapped extensively the traditions of such occupational, regional, ethnic, and racial groups as Western cowboys, Nova Scotian sailors, Midwestern

lumberjacks, Pennsylvania Germans, Southwest Mexican-Americans, Utah Mormons, and Ozark mountaineers (Brunvand 9, 19).

In this surge of folklore collecting, studies of Afro-American lore and song loomed large. Such collecting was not new, of course: The first serious collection, *Slave Songs of the United States,* had been made in 1867. Between the end of Reconstruction and the turn of the century, a series of literary figures, beginning with William Wells Brown (*My Southern Home,* 1880) and including Joel Chandler Harris, with his Uncle Remus collections, and Charles Chesnutt (*The Conjure Woman,* 1899), made literary capital from black folktales and anecdotes. White collectors like C. C. Jones, Jr., and Virginia Boyle transcribed folk myths and devil tales in the Sea Islands Gullah dialect. And during the 1880s and '90s a black folklore group met regularly at Hampton Institute in Virginia and published summaries of papers and the texts of oral lore in the *Southern Workman* (Dorson 110). Interest in the folk, though, had waned enough by the opening years of the new century to lead Booker T. Washington to complain, in his 1904 introduction to Samuel Coleridge-Taylor's *Twenty-Four Negro Melodies,* that the plantation songs were dying out with the generation that had given them birth (Lovell 494).

When the resurgence of Afro-American folklore collecting appeared early in the twenties, it was with the force of a revitalized national interest in native traditions behind it. John Lomax's publication of *Cowboy Songs and Other Frontier Ballads* in 1910 and Cecil Sharp's *English Folksongs from the Southern Appalachians* in 1917 had pioneered a turnabout in American folklore research by revealing living folksong traditions that were not vanishing but instead surviving and in fact being continually reborn. In 1915, amidst a flurry of regional collecting, music critic Henry Krehbiel had directed attention away from the ongoing "ballad wars" and toward the Afro-American folksongs he sought "to bring into the field of scientific observation" (v). Krehbiel had centered his study around the questions of "whether or not the songs were original creations of these native blacks, whether or not they were entitled to be called American, and whether or not they were worthy of consideration as foundation elements for a school of American composition" (vi). Krehbiel had answered all these in the affirmative; and his formulation then of the problems of origins, of methods of composition, and of provenience did much to set the terms of discourse for the new black folklore studies that flowed out into the public arena in the twenties and early thirties.

Those studies revealed a body of Afro-American oral tradition that was massive, vital, and portentous. The published collections included Thomas Talley's *Negro*

Folk Rhymes (secular songs and linguistic lore) and Ambrose Gonzales' *With Aesop Along the Black Border* (coastal fables in Gullah dialect) in 1922; Elsie Parson's *Folklore of the Sea Islands* in 1923; Dorothy Scarborough's *On the Trail of Negro Folk-Songs* in 1925; Howard Odum and Guy Johnson's *The Negro and His Songs* and *Negro Workaday Songs* in 1925 and 1926, respectively; James Weldon Johnson's *Book of American Negro Spirituals* and *Second Book . . .* in 1925 and 1926; Newbell Niles Puckett's *Folk Beliefs of the Southern Negro* in 1926; Newman White's *American Negro Folk Songs* in 1928; E. C. L. Adams' *Congaree Sketches* and *Nigger to Nigger* (coastal jokes and tales) in 1927 and 1928. Howard Odum's novelistic trilogy about travelin' man Left Wing Gordon—*Rainbow Round My Shoulder, Wings on My Feet,* and *Cold Blue Moon*—appeared in 1928, 1929, and 1930; Guy Johnson's *Folk Culture on St. Helena Island* in 1930; J. Mason Brewer's slave tale collection *Juneteenth* in 1932; Zora Neale Hurston's *Mules and Men* in 1935; and John and Alan Lomax's *Negro Folk Songs as Sung by Leadbelly* in 1936.

In the face of this expanding repository of traditional art and customs, the prevailing notion that no distinctive Afro-American culture existed, or that such culture as did exist was one of either fossilized African survivals or debased imitations of white models, began to give ground. And the folk ideology so central to the New Negro creed formulated by Alain Locke received a concrete foundation of folk myths, legends, symbols, and character types upon which many of the major black literary achievements of the next two decades would build. Prospects for employing the new folklore studies either for aesthetic purposes or in support of the socio-political "literature of racial vindication," however, were vitiated by a trio of conceptual problems and controversies that implicated the whole of folklore research and interpretation at the time.

First, American folklorists, who, as Richard Dorson has noted, were rarely trained in folklore and rarely Americanists, subscribed heavily to Eurocentric theories that (a) predicated the existence of folklore on the presence of a traditional peasantry that did not exist in America, (b) treated folklore genres hierarchically, with the Anglo-Saxon ballad first and foremost, and (c) approached American folk forms generally as corrupted, inherently inferior imitations of Old World originals (Dorson 4-7). Under the disabling influence of these theories, Fisk professor Thomas Talley, for example, in his pioneering study of Afro-American folk rhymes, labored tortuously to force his materials into an elaborate system of ballad classification based on his defensively mystical proposition that "all [Negro] Folk Rhymes are Nature Ballads" with call-and-response structures that somehow "hover ghostlike" over them (250, 285).

Second, nineteenth-century racist ethnology, though under attack in the anthropological work of Franz Boas and his students, remained a potent force in the new folklore research—reinforced by lingering Social Darwinism and the currents of popular nativism and racism. The mystique of racial "gifts," "temperaments," and "geniuses" helped contort the endless debate over the origins of folk forms waged between diffusionists, who believed in a single origin of folk themes with their subsequent spread, and polygeneticists, who argued for the repeated reinvention of similar materials because of similar psychological or historical conditions (Brunvand 11). Their romantic racialism made studies like Odum and Johnson's *The Negro and His Songs,* which presented the earliest extended analysis of the blues, read, as contemporary folklorists have acknowledged, "like a Music of the Darkies with a bit of enlightened sociological body English" (Jackson 7).

Third, the new folklore studies were hampered by the absence of any scientific or humanistic theory of American culture and national character capable of comprehending, as a cultural matrix for folklife, this country's modernity, its radical heterogeneity, and its peculiar blend of social fixedness and fluidity. Moreover, the folkloric enterprise was subject to pressures from popularization, commercialization, and the emerging mass media that were plagued with distortions and fabrications of folk culture that produced the "bankrupt treasuries" Stanley Edgar Hyman lambasted in the mid-forties and that led Richard Dorson eventually to coin the distinction between folklore and the rising tide of "fakelore" (Dorson 5-7).

Into this fray Sterling Brown brought a keen critical intelligence, his convictions about the cultural integrity and aesthetic significance of folklife, and his instincts as a creative writer. Afro-American folklorists were scarce to say the least, and in the quarter-century of folkloric fervor that spanned the Jazz Age, the Great Depression, and the Second World War, Sterling Brown's essays in *Opportunity* and *Phylon,* and his editorial and scholarly work with the Federal Writers' Project Negro Affairs division, filled the void with a wide-ranging folklore critique fully cognizant of the shifting grounds of folklore scholarship yet fixed unerringly on the perspectives of the folk themselves. Brown had spent the years after the publication of **Southern Road** absorbed in Afro-American literary history and the iconography of racial stereotypy—preoccupations fleshed out in his *The Negro in American Fiction* and *Negro Poetry and Drama.* With his appointment to the Federal Writers' Project in the spring of 1936, he turned toward the socio-historical study of the black folk and urban experience, immersing himself first in the gathering of ex-slave narratives which was then underway and which would be perhaps the Writers' Project's greatest contribution to the study of Afro-American life.

The collection of slave narratives had been begun in 1934 by the Federal Emergency Relief Administration, at the instigation of black historian Lawrence Reddick, who had voiced the growing historical consensus that the story of slavery and Reconstruction could not be complete "until we get the view as presented through the slave himself" (Mangione 257). The Writers' Project had inherited the undertaking; and in 1936, when John Lomax became the Project's first folklore editor, Sterling Brown began guiding the interviewing efforts that would lead finally to the publication of seventeen volumes of manuscripts containing over two thousand slave narratives (Mangione 263). Under Lomax's supervision, and after 1938 under the leadership of Benjamin Botkin, the Project proceeded to collect folk materials on a scale larger than ever previously attempted.

Under Botkin's influence especially, the Project countered the antiquarian orientation of academic folklorists with an emphasis on oral history and "living lore." Sterling Brown, who had contributed poems and critical reviews to Botkin's four-volume regional miscellany *Folk-Say* between 1929 and 1932, found Botkin's proletarian emphasis congenial to his own. "The folk movement must come from below upward rather than from above downward," Botkin contended; "otherwise it may be dismissed as a patronizing gesture, a nostalgic wish, an elegiac complaint, a sporadic and abortive review—on the part of paternalistic aristocrats going slumming, dilettantish provincials going native, defeated sectionalists going back to the soil, and anybody and everybody who cares to going collecting" (Mangione 270). Folk imagination more than folk knowledge became the Project's aim, and the outlook and skills of writers such as Sterling Brown became crucial to capturing it.

For Sterling Brown the aim also was, in his words, to "produce an accurate picture of the Negro in American social history," to reveal him as an integral part of American life and to do so in a way that mediated between the competing chauvinisms of both white and black historians (Mangione 259). The device of correlating folklore with social and ethnic history was the tactic Brown emphasized in his editorial role and in his efforts to have Afro-American materials included in the Project's state guidebooks then being compiled around the country. The publication of *The Negro in Virginia* in 1940 demonstrated the value of this approach. It was produced under the local supervision of black historian Roscoe Lewis, but Brown's role in this field project was considerable. Built upon years of carefully collected oral histories and interviews and on painstaking research that traced neglected materials back to the arrival in Virginia of the first Africans in 1619, *The Negro in Virginia* became a model of documentary research and narrative drama (Mangione 260-61).

In a talk before the Conference on the Character and State of Studies in Folklore in 1946, Brown looked back at his years with the Project: "I became interested in folklore," he recalled, "because of my desire to write poetry and prose fiction. I was first attracted by certain qualities I thought the speech of the people had, and I wanted to get for my own writing a flavor, a color, a pungency of speech. Then later I came to something more important—I wanted to get an understanding of people" ("Approach" 506). Respectful of the scientific approaches to folklore but untroubled by any definitional or procedural obstacles that might block his access to the "living-people-lore" of, for instance, so fascinating a tribe as urban jazzmen, Sterling Brown had developed a flexible, functionalist approach to folklore. It was an approach that, as Alan Lomax advocated in the same session, rejected views of the folk "as ignorant receptacles for traditions and ideas which they do not themselves understand, and which make very little sense until they are pieced together and explained in historical terms by the comparative scholar." Such an approach instead saw folklore as "equipment for living," saw the folklorist as performing not only an archaeological role but one of recording a vigorous human tradition, and it recognized that "the best interpretations of folklore may be obtained in the end from the folk themselves" (Lomax, "Functional Aspects" 507).

In the early forties, the conviction that the folk may be their own best interpreters became one of the trademarks of Sterling Brown's series of articles on black folk expression. His synoptic essay in *The Negro Caravan* in 1941, on the sources and genres of black oral literature, stands even today as the single best introduction to the subject because, in threading its way through all the scholarship and interpretative quandaries of the previous decades, it maintains its balance by never falling victim to the disorienting proposition that, as Newman White had myopically insisted, "the Negro never contemplated his low estate."

"Nigger, your breed ain't metaphysical," one of the voices in Robert Penn Warren's poeticized fable "Pondy Woods" had proclaimed, confronting New Negroes with the old stereotype of the crusading New South. "Cracker, *your* breed ain't exegetical," Sterling Brown responded dialectically, as he outlined a critique that treated black forms as distillations of communal *mind* and *ethos* (Brown interview). In his essays on the blues in particular, Brown treated the products of folk imagination as *self-conscious* wisdom—tragic, comic, ironic, shrewd, emotionally elastic and attitudinally complex, capable of supporting a variety of stances toward life, and resistant, as such, to ideological straitjacketing or implications of naïveté. Worldly and self-aware, the spirit of the blues, he submitted, is defined by the songs themselves, in lines which assert that "the blues ain't nothin' but a poor man's heart disease" or "the blues ain't nothin' but a good man way, way down" or, more obliquely, "Woke up this morning, blues walking round my bed / Went in to eat my breakfast, blues was all in my bread." The blues fused stoicism in a concrete, *metaphoric metaphysic*: It was a frank Chaucerian *attitude* toward sex and love that kept even the bawdiest authentic blues from being prurient and pornographic. It was "elemental *honesty*," "depth of *insight*," and *sophistication* about human relations that lay behind their appeal across caste lines. It was *imagination* making the love of life and the love of words memorably articulate which turned the best blues into potent lyric poetry.[1]

Brown's reading of the blues tradition did not go uncontested. In a lengthy, two-part essay on the spirit and meaning of black folk expression published in *Phylon* in the early fifties, he acknowledged that "the field of folklore in general is known to be a battle area, and the Negro front is one of the hottest sectors" (Autumn 1950: 319). But he needed no new battlepieces, no defensive ethnic chauvinism. Incorporating the insights of Stith Thompson's then definitive study of the folktale, he found, in the newly revealed patterns of interchange and diffusion characteristic of even Old World African folklore, support for his vision of the underlying unity of the world's and the nation's many cultural traditions. After all, he noted, in the cosmology of black folk traditions themselves, "tales about the origin of the races leave little room for chauvinism about a chosen people. The slaves knew at first hand that the black man had a hard road to travel, and they tell of the mistakes of creation with sardonic fatalism" (Autumn 1950: 325). Looking then at the prospects for the future of folklife, he knew that hard road was all too literal. Black folk culture was breaking up, he thought. In migrating to the city "the folk become a submerged proletariat. Leisurely yarn-spinning, slow paced aphoristic conversation become lost arts; jazzed-up gospel hymns provide a different sort of release from the old spirituals; the blues reflect the distortions of the new way of life. Folk arts are no longer by the folk for the folk; smart businessmen now put them up for sale. Gospel songs often become showpieces for radio-slummers, and the blues become the double talk of the dives." And yet, he interjected, "the vigor of the creative impulse has not been snapped, even in the slums," and the folk roots "show a stubborn vitality" (Winter 1953: 60-61).

Leadbelly was a few years dead then, his pauperized last seasons spent as a resident "living legend" in Greenwich Village coffeehouses. The "blues boom," the "rediscovery" of New Orleans jazz, and the folk revivals of the fifties were taking hold. *Southern Road*, though, was out of print and Sterling Brown's poetry largely unremarked since the thirties by the canonizers of American verse. In his various roles as teacher,

scholar, poet, husband, mentor, and self-confessed "Teller of Lies," Brown weathered those years, and the years after, sustained by the same lyric loves he found in the blues—the love of words, the love of life, and the love of all things musical, as he was wont to say, "from Beethoven to the boogie-woogie." And perhaps concluding with this one of Brown's own pointed incongruities makes sense if, blues-like, we "worry" it a bit. Beethoven, save for the tarbrushings that allege him to be quite literally a "soul brother," is a relatively unambiguous reference for defining one aesthetic pole and one kind of hero on the spectrum of "strange legacies" Sterling Brown's work embraces. The boogie-woogie, though, evokes almost as unruly an image as Leadbelly, for the phrase masks onomatopoetically a complex legacy of juxtaposed folk meanings: The boogie-woogie was simultaneously a fast-stepping, Kansas City Jazz-influenced piano blues in which the bass figure comes in double time; it was the knee-flexing jitterbug one danced in accompaniment; it was a racial epithet; it was a wartime moniker for enemy aircraft; it was an intransitive vernacular verb connoting the uninhibited pursuit of pleasure; it was a reference to the devil and all the troubles associated with him; and it was, less openly but no less significantly, a Southern euphemism for a case of secondary syphilis. There was a multilayered joke proffered, in other words, in Brown's wry conflation of Beethoven with the boogie-woogie, an irreverent populist riff that counterpointed democratically the classical with the vernacular, the academy with the Southern road, white icons with black reprobates; and that now, in remembrance, binds Brown the scholar/poet with the many-monikered chaingang songster as nachally as a professing Teller of Lies might be to the legend with the gold-toothed grin.

Note

1. Sterling Brown, "The Blues as Folk Poetry," *Folk-Say*, 4 vols., ed. Benjamin Botkin (Norman: U of Oklahoma P, 1930) 1: 324-39; "Blues, Ballads and Social Songs," *Seventy-five Years of Freedom* (Washington: Library of Congress, 18 December 1940) 17-25; "The Blues," *Phylon* 13 (Autumn 1952): 286-92.

Works Cited

Brown, Sterling. "The Approach of the Creative Artist," *Journal of American Folklore* 59 (Oct. 1946): 506-07.

———. "Folk Literature." *The Negro Caravan*. Ed. Sterling Brown, Arthur Davis, and Ulysses Lee. 1941. New York: Arno and The New York Times, 1970. 412-34.

———. Interview with Sterling Brown. With John Edgar Tidwell and John S. Wright. Washington, 13 July 1980.

————. "Negro Folk Expression." *Phylon* 11 (Autumn 1950): 318-27.

————. "Negro Folk Expression: Spirituals, Seculars, Ballads and Work Songs." *Phylon* 14 (Winter 1953): 45-61.

Brunvand, Jan Harold. *Folklore: A Study and Research Guide.* New York: St. Martin's, 1976.

Dorson, Richard. *American Folklore and the Historian.* Chicago: U of Chicago P, 1971.

Du Bois, W. E. B. *The Souls of Black Folk* (1903). *Three Negro Classics.* Ed. John Hope Franklin. New York: NAL, 1969. 207-389.

Jackson, Bruce. Foreword. *American Negro Folksongs.* By Newman White. 1928. Hatbora, PA: Folklore Associates, 1965.

Krehbiel, Henry. *Afro-American Folksongs: A Study in Racial and National Music.* New York: Schirmer, 1914.

Locke, Alain. "Sterling Brown: The New Negro Folk Poet." *Negro Anthology.* Ed. Nancy Cunard. 1934. New York: Ungar, 1970. 88-92.

Lomax, Alan. "The Functional Aspects of Folklore." *Journal of American Folklore* 59 (Oct. 1946): 507-10.

Lomax, John, and Alan Lomax. *Negro Folk Songs as Sung by Leadbelly.* New York: Macmillan, 1936.

Lovell, John. *Black Songs: The Forge and the Flame.* New York: Macmillan, 1972.

Mangione, Jerre. *The Dream and the Deal: The Federal Writers' Project, 1935-1943.* New York: Avon, 1972.

Redmond, Eugene. *Drumvoices: The Mission of Afro-American Poetry.* Garden City: Anchor, 1976.

Talley, Thomas. *Negro Folk Rhymes.* 1922. Port Washington: Kennikat, 1968.

Gary Smith (essay date June 1989)

SOURCE: Smith, Gary. "The Literary Ballads of Sterling A. Brown." *CLA Journal* 32, no. 4 (June 1989): pp. 393-409.

[*In the following essay, Smith discusses the "complexity of Brown's artistic vision" and views the poet's major achievement as the restoration and recreation of African American folk literature.*]

> Sterling Brown, more reflective, a closer student of folk-life, and above all a bolder and more detached observer, has gone deeper still, and has found certain basic, more sober and more persistent qualities of Negro thought and feeling; and so has reached a sort of common denominator between the old and the new

Negro. Underneath the particularities of one generation are hidden universalities which only deeply penetrating genius can fathom and bring to the surface. Too many of the articulate intellects of the Negro group—including sadly enough the younger poets—themselves children of opportunity, have been unaware of these deep resources of the past.

> —Alaine Locke[1]

Although one might now quibble with the limitations of Alaine Locke's perceptive review of Sterling Brown's poetry—especially in light of the 1980 publication of Brown's **Collected Poems**[2] and the numerous reconsiderations[3] that have placed Brown's poetry within the mainstream of both American and Afro-American literature—Locke nonetheless touches upon what is still Brown's major achievement as a poet: his restoration and recreation of black American folk literature. In retrospect, Brown's achievement clearly overshadows his contemporaries, Jean Toomer, Countee Cullen, Langston Hughes, and Claude McKay, all of whom, in their poetry, were important architects of the New Negro but who did considerably less than Brown to restore the ethnic identity of black Americans.[4] The vitality of Brown's poetry is the constant tension between the old and new, between what is ostensibly a traditional way of viewing black Americans and a radical reconstruction. While New Negro poetry generally portrayed black Americans as militantly determined to participate in America's democratic processes, Brown's poetry first assumes that black Americans are as inherently complex and diverse as white Americans; hence, the essential and perhaps more meaningful dialogue is not between new and newer representations of black Americans but rather between what is old and new.

This dialogue leads, in part, to Locke's second insight into Brown's poetry: its detached observation. Brown neither idealizes the past nor romanticizes the present. As the title of his first published work, **Southern Road,**[5] indicates, he creates a dynamic, almost seamless, relationship or quest between the past and present; the road that leads away from the South also leads back.[6] His characters, in such poems as **"The Ballad of Joe Meek"** and **"The Odyssey of Big Boy,"** are not in conflict with the past as much as they are with the inherent paradoxes of the human heart. Joe, for example, is both an old and new Negro. He is self-effacing and deferential to white authority; however, when provoked by what he considers a gross miscarriage of justice, he becomes militantly self-assertive. The odyssey of Big Boy is also a circuitous journey from self-discovery to self-recovery; he finds his presence in his past.[7] In his characterizations, Brown does not overlook the particular issues of poverty, racism, and social injustice, but these issues, however important, are interwoven with the universals that underscore his characters' lives. These universals include not only love and brotherhood but also their antitheses, hate and cruelty. Indeed, his best poetry engages the energetic hope and idealism of the New Negro as well as the resigned pessimism and realism of the old Negro.

The complexity of Brown's artistic vision is nowhere better illustrated than in his choice of poetic forms. While trained academically at Williams College and Harvard in traditional English and Anglo-American literature, he wrote the bulk of his poetry in ballads and blues poems.[8] His rejection of Modernism—what he termed the "puzzle poetry" of T. S. Eliot and Ezra Pound—was not, however, prompted by his search for an idealized folk past. The hallmarks of Modernist poetry, socio-psychological fragmentation and displacement of human values, are also important themes in Brown's poetry. However, these themes do not replace the need for social and aesthetic continuities within black American literature. For Eliot and, to a lesser degree, Pound, the past constitutes an idealized order, although the poet's relationship with this order is often antithetical.[9] For Brown, though, the past is not a static, idealized order; the poet is as responsible for the past as he is responsive to it. Indeed, his choice of ballads and blues, as poetic forms, is reflective of his need to invoke continuities between the past and present.

Stylistically, ballads and blues are more dynamic and open than closed poetic forms such as the Petrarchan sonnet. While the latter, traditionally written in syllogistic form, offers the poet discursive possibilities, ballads and blues are primarily performative. The blues singer/poet is more directly or intimately engaged with his audience, and his performances/poems often occur as spontaneous creative exchanges with his audience. Similarly, the traditional ballad is a communal art form that originates in rhythmic group action.[10] The balladist is thus an inextricable part of his folk community. Indeed, in poems such as **"Ma Rainey"** (*CP* [*Collected Poems*], pp. 62-63) and **"When de Saints Go Ma'ching Home"** (*CP,* pp. 26-30), Brown explores the relationship between the singer, song, and folk community. The famous blues singer, Ma Rainey, is both the poem's subject and its performer:

> O Ma Rainey,
> Sing yo' song;
> Now you's back
> Whah you belong,
> Git way inside us,
> Keep us strong. . . .

Similarly, Big Boy Davis, as a "saint," provides subject and style in his song, **"When de Saints Go Ma'ching Home"**:[11]

> He'd play, after the bawdy songs and blues,
> After the weary plaints
> Of "Trouble, Trouble deep down in muh soul,"

> Always one song in which he'd lose the role
> Of entertainer to the boys. He'd say,
> "My mother's favorite." And we knew
> that what was coming was his chant of saints,
> "When de saints go ma'chin' home. . . ."
> And that would end his concert for the day.

With ballads and blues, Brown was also able to personalize his otherwise tragically ironic and objectively detached artistic vision. This dynamic viewpoint permits him to focus objectively and ironically upon the individual plight of blacks within American society, yet underscore the paradoxical relationship of blacks to America's democratic ideals and harsh realities. The ballad, historically, has always been a vehicle by which the folk masses could realize a measure of poetic understanding in an unjust world.[12] And the blues, an art form that originates in the slave seculars and work songs, invokes the human injustice of slavery as well as the universal plight of the underclass. This poetic strategy juxtaposes personal, deep-seated longings for socioeconomic justice with public performances.

While Brown found certain continuities between the past and present within black American life and literature, he also found discontinuities. He is acutely aware of how, in spite of their dynamic interrelationship, the past differs from the present in style and substance. **"Children's Children"** (*CP,* p. 94) and **"Cabaret"** (*CP,* p. 101) are poems that portray black Americans who, while they have definite affinities with the past, are essentially at odds with it. "They have forgotten / What had to be endured," or they are simply apathetic to the past:

> I've been away a year today
> To wander and roam
> I don't care if it's muddy there

Therefore, Brown is interested in both the continuities and discontinuities that underscore his generation. His poems are paradoxical bridges and sometimes gaps between traditional rural and contemporary urban representations of black Americans. He is as mindful of what makes the new Negro old as he is of what makes the old Negro new. This poetry of paradox is nowhere better illustrated than in Brown's literary ballads. In them, Brown has freely adopted the traditional features of black folk ballads, while radically altering their themes and styles. In ballads such as **"Frankie and Johnny," "A Bad, Bad Man,"** and **"Break of Day,"** Brown portrays traditional folk characters restored and recreated within his dynamic perception of the continuities and discontinuities of black American literature.

"Frankie and Johnny"[13] is arguably one of the oldest and best known black folk ballads. Although its title often varies, its narrative usually tells the story of Frankie and her unfaithful lover, Johnny, whom she kills after finding him in bed with another woman. Structurally, the folk ballad leaps from one moment to another in the ill-fated romance. The first three stanzas quickly establish the basic plot: Frankie and Johnny are lovers who have sworn to be true to each other, but Johnny's infidelity leads to Frankie's murderous revenge:

> Frankie went down to the hotel
> Looked over the transom so high,
> There she saw her lovin' Johnnie
> Making love to Nelly Bly
> He was her man; he was doing her wrong.

> Frankie threw back her kimono,
> Pulled out her big forty-four;
> Rooty-toot-toot: three times she shot
> Right through that hotel door,
> She shot her man, who was doing her wrong.

The final three stanzas turn upon Johnny's confession of infidelity, "I was your man, but I done you wrong." The *noncupative testament* that follows includes the sheriff's sentence, "It's the 'lectric chair for you," and Frankie's remorseless testimony:

> Frankie says to the sheriff,
> "What are they going to do?"
> The sheriff he said to Frankie,
> "It's the 'lectric chair for you.
> He was your man, and he done you wrong."
> "Put me in that dungeon,
> Put me in that cell,
> Put me where the northeast wind
> Blows from the southeast corner of hell,
> I shot my man, 'cause he done me wrong."

As a black folk ballad, **"Frankie and Johnny"** is distinguishable from "Fuller and Warren" and "The Jealous Lover," American folk ballads of similar romantic crimes, by the fulsome details in which Frankie's actions are described and the precise nature of her punishment.[14] The incremental refrain clearly establishes that the narrator's and, presumably, the reader's sympathies are with Frankie's plight; yet, in spite of the mitigating circumstances, she, as well as Johnny, dies.

This rather simple tragic irony informs the larger complexities of Brown's **"Frankie and Johnny"** (*CP*, p. 44). Structurally, he shortens his version of the folk ballad by three stanzas and eliminates the incremental refrain and testament. The burden of the narrative is thus more forcefully rendered, and the reader plays a larger role in determining the motivation of Frankie and Johnny. In the case of Frankie, her innocence is based upon her demented psychology and equally demented "cracker" father:

> Frankie was a halfwit, Johnny was a nigger,
> Frankie liked to pain poor creatures as a little 'un,
> Kept a crazy love of torment when she got bigger,
> Johnny had to slave it and never had much fun.

> Frankie liked to pull wings off of living butterflies,
> Frankie liked to cut long angleworms in half,
> Frankie liked to whip curs and listen to their drawn
>   out cries,
> Frankie liked to shy stones at the brindle calf.

> Frankie took her pappy's lunch week-days to the
>   sawmill,
> Her pappy, red-faced cracker, with a cracker's thirst,
> Beat her skinny body and reviled the hateful imbecile,
> She screamed at every blow he struck, but tittered
>   when he curst.

In spite of their racial differences, Johnny is at least Frankie's equal as a victim. As a "nigger," he is as much a social outcast as she is though not as depressed. Their romance is thus a macabre parody of the folk ballad.[15] In this regard, the mismatched lovers are a reversal of our expectations for love and fidelity; their romance is not reflective of communal norms, but rather of its abnormalities.

In the next three stanzas of his version, Brown shifts his focus from Frankie to Johnny. His tone also changes from melodramatic to tragic:

> Frankie had to cut through Johnny's field of sugar
>   corn
> Used to wave at Johnny, who didn't '*pay no min*'—
> *Had had to work like fifty from the day that he was*
>   *born,*
> *And wan't no cracker hussy gonna put his work*
>   *behind*—.

> But everyday Frankie swung along the cornfield lane,
> And one day Johnny helped her partly through the
>   wood,
> Once he had dropped his plow lines, he dropped them
>   many times again—
> Though his mother didn't know it, else she'd have
>   whipped him good

> Frankie and Johnny were lovers; oh Lordy how they
>   did love!
> But one day Frankie's pappy by a big log laid him
>   low,
> To find out what his crazy Frankie had been speaking
>   of;
> He found that what his gal had muttered was exactly
>   so.

Brown transforms Johnny from social outcast to victim. Unlike Frankie, his relationship with nature and his mother is wholesome, and his dedication to hard work and self-discipline is admirable. Ironically, the moral edge Johnny has over Frankie and her father lies in his simple determination to work within an unjust socio-economic system. His tragic fate, then, seems doubly cruel. He is a victim not only of racism and socio-economic injustice, but also his own emotional vulnerability. His fidelity to hard work, of course, does not mitigate his fate but instead leads to his death. In Brown's version, then, the final stanza does not conclude the poem in the usual way as much as it circles back to the initial dilemma of injustice and victimization:

> Frankie, she was spindly limbed with corn silk on her
>   crazy head,
> Johnny was a nigger, who never had much fun—
> They swung up Johnny on a tree, and filled his swing-
>   ing hide with lead,
> And Frankie yowled hilariously when the thing was
>   done.

Here, Johnny becomes one of the "poor creatures" victimized by Frankie's dementia. In this, he is a part of the natural order in the poem—butterflies, angle-worms, curs and brindle calf—subject to Frankie's cruelty. The ballad is thus still an indictment of racism and, more importantly, the psychological disorders that racism often precipitates in human beings, but by reversing the traditional roles of Frankie and Johnny, Brown changes the narrative from simple melodrama to complex tragedy. Its complexity lies in the gross miscarriage of justice that leads to Johnny's lynching: the reader must decide whether he is a victim of his own vulnerability to racism or Frankie's wanton pathology.

Brown's ballad **"A Bad, Bad Man"** (*CP*, pp. 144-45), is based, in part, on the folk ballad "Bad Man Ballad."[16] As with his version of **"Frankie and Johnny,"** Brown made substantial changes in theme and style. In the original folk ballad, Lee Brown, a bad man, kills his "woman" for no apparent reason:

> Late las' night I was a-makin' my rounds,
> Met my woman an' I blowed her down,
> Went on home an' I went to bed,
> Put my hand cannon right under my head.

His escape from justice is cut short in Mexico, where another bad man, "Bad Texas Bill," takes him into custody:

> "Yes, oh, yes" says. "This is him.
> If you got a warrant, jes' read it to me."
> He says: "You look like a fellow that knows what's
>   bes'.
> Come 'long wid me—you're under arres'."
>
> When I was arrested, I was dressed in black;
> Dey put me on a train, an' dey brought me back.
> Dey boun' me down in de county jail;
> Couldn' get a human for to go my bail.

As a traditional black folk ballad, "Bad Man Ballad" emphasizes the vulnerability of the black criminal who is often victimized by the justice system.[17] Lee Brown's trial lasts only five minutes, and he is sentenced to "Ninety-nine years on de hard, hard groun'."

The testament that closes the ballad again highlights Lee Brown's ironic vulnerability and the price he has to pay for his crime:

> Here I is, bowed down in shame,
> I got a number instead of a name.
> Here for de res' of my nachul life,
> An' all I ever done is kill my wife. . . .

Lee Brown's simple, remorseless testimony reinforces his reputation as a "bad man." Ironically, he is more concerned about his loss of identity and freedom than his dead wife. Moreover, his testimony does not reveal why he murdered his wife. On one level, his motiveless malignancy substantiates the moral rigidity of the poem; good and evil are inherent, often inexplicable human qualities. On another level, though, the poem indicts America's judicial system. Lee Brown's misfortune, however justly deserved, is compounded by the mistreatment he receives during his trial.

By its title alone, Brown's **"A Bad, Bad Man"** is suggestive of the farcical nature of his ballad. He has transformed the tragedy of Lee Brown's misfortune into comic burlesque. The narrative remains basically the same, but the indictment is rendered in terms that belie its seriousness; **"A Bad, Bad Man"** is actually a parody of "Bad Man Ballad." This parody begins with an epic invocation:

> Forget about your Jesse James,
> And Billy the Kid;
> I'll tell you instead what
> A black boy did.

Here, Brown invokes the legendary outlaws from American folklore as company for his character. In so doing, he not only places John Bias, "a black boy," within the American folk tradition of outlaws and bad men, but he also debunks the prevalent myth that black bad men somehow exist apart from this tradition. That Jesse James and Billy the Kid are celebrated as heroes is yet another way of illustrating the double standards of American socio-history and justice.

The character sketch that follows the invocation, however, places John Bias in opposition to the outlaw tradition. He is a "squinchy runt, / Four foot two" and married to a "strapping broad. / Big-legged Sue." The grotesque humor that informs his character also informs the plot. The narrative begins with the misadventures of another "black boy," Sam Johnson:

> Another boy, Sam Johnson,
> Was getting lynched because
> His black mule had bust
> A white man's jaws.
>
> The crackers gathered in the woods
> Early that night.

Corn liquor in pop bottles
Got 'em right.

They tied Sam Johnson to a tree.
Threw liquor on the fire.
Like coal oil it made the flames
Shoot higher.

The tragic possibilities of this scene are undermined, however, by the appearance of John Bias, who rushes to Sam Johnson's rescue, "Waving a great big / Forty-four." The caliber of his gun is, of course, larger than John Bias' physical size, but, more to the point, his disruption of the lynching places him on the side of the good man. His character thus changes from a bad man to a serio-comic Robin Hood. Ironically, John Bias' legendary stature, as a bad man, then grows in reverse proportion to his physical size:

The crackers spoke, from then on,
Of the giant nigger,
Every day he grew a
Little bigger.

The testament, in part, provides a psychological motive for John Bias' actions that, in the folk ballad, is missing:

Johnnie was told the next day
What he had done for Sam,
Scratched his head and said, "Well
I be dam!

"Never had no notion
To save nobody's life,
I was only jes a-lookin'
For my wife."

Here, again, tragedy is transformed into comedy. John Bias is not simply a hero or antihero: he is a complex mixture of both. As his name changes—from the serious John Bias to the playful Johnnie—he is a would-be sinner as well as a reluctant saint. He thus straddles several important traditions in the black folk ballad.

Big Jess, in Brown's ballad **"Break of Day"** (*CP*, p. 146) is also a complex mixture of personality traits. His story is actually a conflation of several versions of the folk ballad "Casey Jones."[18] In the first, Joseph Mica, a railroad engineer, represents the heroic ideal of a faithful worker, whose dedication to his job transcends his own personal safety:

Joseph Mica was good engineer,
Told his fireman not to fear,
All he want is water'n coal,
Poke his head out, see drivers roll.

Early one mornin' look like rain,
'Round de curve come passenger train,
On powers lie ole Jim Jones,
Good ole engineer, but daid an' gone.

Another version generally repeats this simple narrative of the engineer's ill-fated train ride, but adds three stanzas that further develop the engineer's heroism in contrast to the fireman's cowardice:

Casey Jones, I know him well,
Tole de fireman to ring de bell;
Fireman jump an' say good-by,
Casey Jones, you're bound to die.

Went on down to de depot track,
Beggin' my honey to take me back,
She turn 'round some two or three times,
"Take you back when you learn to grind."

Womens in Kansas all dressed in red,
Got de news dat Casey was dead;
De womens in Jackson all dressed in black,
Said, in fact, he was a cracker-jack.

Here, the testament reinforces the difference between the engineer and the fireman. The engineer is mourned by women dressed symbolically in red and black for his reckless courage, whereas the fireman is suspected of impotent cowardice: "Take you back when you learn to grind."

Within the conventional moral code of the ballad, the fireman's censure is justly deserved. Outside this code, however, the fireman's misdeed presents the same problem of interpretation as John Bias' crime; in both instances, the key element of motive is missing. The poem never makes clear whether the fireman abandons the train because he is a coward or, perhaps, wiser than the engineer.

The final three stanzas of a third version of "Casey Jones" substantially alters the nature of the fireman's cowardice and the engineer's heroism:

Just as he got in a mile of the place,
He spied number Thirty-five right in his face.
Said to the fireman, "You'd better jump!
For these locomotives are bound to bump."

When Casey's family heard of his death,
Casey's daughter fell on her knees,
"Mamma! mamma! how can it be,
Papa got killed on the old I. C.?"

"Hush your mouth, don't draw a breath;
We'll draw a pension from Casey's death!"

Here, the engineer's command prompts the fireman's actions; he "jumps" the train under orders from the engineer. On the other hand, the testament does not affirm the engineer's tragic heroism. Although his daughter mourns his death, his wife quickly sees economic advantage in his misfortune: "We'll draw a pension from Casey's death!" The wife thus not only trivializes the engineer's heroism; she also raises doubts about his wisdom in remaining aboard the ill-fated train. Indeed, her greed undermines the engineer's reckless courage.

In his ballad **"Break of Day,"** Brown further alters the folk ballad by reversing the dramatic roles of the fireman and engineer. The fireman, Big Jess, is presented as the main character, whereas the engineer, Mister Murphy, is his foil. More importantly, Brown increases the racial tension in the poem by making Jess a black man whose heroic ideals of hard work, fair play, and devotion to his family are jeopardized by white racism. The plot, therefore, develops in a melodramatic fashion, but with the forces of good and evil clearly identified:

> Big Jess fired on the Alabama Central,
> Man in full, babe, man in full.
> Been throwing on coal for Mister Murphy
> From times way back, baby, times way back.
>
> Big Jess had a pleasing woman, name of Mamie,
> Sweet-hipted Mama, sweet-hipted Mame;
> Had a boy growing up for to be a fireman,
> Just like his pa, baby, like his pa.
>
> Out by the roundhouse Jess had his cabin,
> Longside the tracks, babe, long the tracks,
> Jess pulled the whistle when they high-balled past it
> "I'm on my way, baby, on my way."
>
> Crackers craved the job what Jess was holding,
> Times right tough, babe, times right tough,
> Warned Jess to quit his job for a white man,
> Jess he laughed, baby, he jes' laughed.

Structurally, the incremental refrain, absent from the folk ballad, underscores the realities of Jess' heroism: his fidelity to his job and family as well as his single-minded, rugged individualism. The refrain also slows the pace of the narrative. Rather than leap from one select moment to another in the story, the forward thrust of each stanza is slowed by the counterweight of the repetitive refrain. On another level, the refrain, with its insistent repetition of "baby," forces the tone of the melodramatic ballad toward a tragic-comic blues poem. In this, it invokes the themes of tragic fate and personal loss that characterize the traditional blues song.

Indeed, the next two stanzas further close the aesthetic distance between the poem's melodramatic plot and its tragic theme. Big Jess becomes more of a doomed figure whose ritualized actions do not create suspense within the narrative as much as they foretell his doom:

> He picked up his lunch-box, kissed his sweet woman,
> Sweet-hipted Mama, sweet-hipted Mame,
> His son walked with him to the white-washed palings,
> "Be seeing you soon, son, see you soon."
>
> Mister Murphy let Big Jess talk on the whistle
> "So long sugar baby, so long babe";

> Train due back in the early morning
> Breakfast time, baby, breakfast time.

The final two stanzas, therefore, do not close the poem as much as they conclude the simple rituals of Jess' work day:

> Mob stopped the train crossing Black Bear Mountain
> Shot rang out, babe, shot rang out.
> They left Big Jess on the Black Bear Mountain,
> Break of day, baby, break of day.
>
> Sweet Mame sits rocking, waiting for the whistle
> Long past due, babe, long past due.
> The grits are cold, and the coffee's boiled over,
> But Jess done gone, baby he done gone.

Here, Brown has omitted the testament that, in the folk ballad, usually resolves the conflict between good and evil. The mob prevails against Jess' rugged individualism, and the values that inform Jess' character are undermined by the mob's racism and vengeful terror. As the poem's title suggests, the circle of Jess' work day as well as the self-sustaining rituals within his family are now hollow: "Sweet Mame sits rocking, waiting for the whistle."

Brown's literary ballads reinforce his achievement and importance within the black American literary tradition. His ballads successfully bridge the gap between rural and urban representations of black Americans and underscore the essential continuities between these representations. In this, Brown's ballads underscore the persistent themes of black American literature: the need for freedom and socio-economic justice. His relationship with the ballad tradition, however, is not simply that of a restorer. As his complex literary ballads suggest, he has effectively recreated the folk ballad in terms that reflect the complexity of our modern age. In this, too, his ballads are radical reconstructions of the past that demythologize the present. His poetry of paradox recreates and restores the universals that belie the particularities of our generation.

Notes

1. Alaine Locke, "Sterling Brown: The New Negro Folk-Poet," in *Negro Anthology,* ed. Nancy Cunard (New York: Negro Universities Press, 1969), p. 115.

2. Sterling A. Brown, *Collected Poems* (New York: Harper, 1980). Subsequent references to this source will be cited parenthetically in the text as *CP.*

3. See Robert G. O'Meally, "Reconsideration: Sterling A. Brown," *The New Republic,* 11 February 1978, pp. 33-36; Stephen E. Henderson, "Sterling Brown: The Giant Unbowed," *The Black Collegian,* April/May 1981, pp. 138-40; Philip Le-

vine, "A Poet of Stunning Artistry," *Saturday Review,* October 1981, pp. 42, 47; and John F. Callahan, "Sterling Brown: In the Afro-American Grain," *The New Republic,* 20 December 1982, pp. 25-28.

4. It should be further noted that Brown, along with Zora N. Hurston, were unique among the writers of the Harlem Renaissance, since they conducted actual fieldwork in the South to substantiate their artistic visions. See Clyde Taylor, "The Human Image in Sterling Brown's Poetry," *The Black Scholar,* March/April 1981, p. 13.

5. Sterling Brown, *Southern Road* (New York: Harcourt, 1932).

6. See Vera M. Kutzinski, "The Distant Closeness of Dancing Doubles: Sterling Brown and William Carlos Williams," *Black American Literature Forum,* 16 (1982), 21.

7. See Kimberly W. Benston, "Sterling Brown's After-Song: 'When De Saints Go Ma'ching Home' and the Performances of Afro-American Voice," *Callaloo,* 5 (1982), 34.

8. See Sterling Brown, "A Son's Return: 'Oh, Didn't He Ramble'," *Chant of Saints,* ed. Michael S. Harper and Robert B. Stepto (Urbana: Univ. of Illinois Press, 1979), pp. 3-22.

9. T. S. Eliot, *The Sacred Wood: Essays on Poetry and Criticism* (London: Methuen, 1920), pp. 49-53.

10. See Robert Graves, *The English Ballad: A Short Critical Survey* (London: Ernest Benn Ltd., 1927), p. 8.

11. Benston, "Sterling Brown's After-Song," p. 39.

12. See Alan Bold, *The Ballad* (London: Methuen, 1979), p. 49.

13. "Frankie and Johnny," *The Negro Caravan,* ed. Sterling A. Brown, Arthur P. Davis, and Ulysses Lee (New York: Dryden, 1941), pp. 461-62. For other variants of this folk ballad, see *Folk Ballads of the English Speaking World,* ed. Albert B. Friedman (New York: Viking, 1956), pp. 211-17.

14. See G. Malcolm Laws, Jr., *Native American Balladry* (Philadelphia: The American Folklore Society, 1964), 86-87.

15. For two other interesting interpretations of this poem, see Charles H. Rowell, "Sterling A. Brown and the Afro-American Folk Tradition," *Studies in the Literary Imagination,* 7 (1974), 148-49, and Jean Wagner, *Black Poets of the United States* (Urbana: Univ. of Illinois Press, 1973), p. 489.

16. "Bad Man Ballad," *Negro Caravan,* pp. 455-56.

17. For a general study of the bad man in black folklore, see Lawrence W. Levine, *Black Culture and Black Consciousness* (Oxford: Oxford Univ. Press, 1977), pp. 404-20, and for a specific discussion of the bad man in Brown's poetry, see Robert G. O'Meally, "'Game to the Heart': Sterling Brown and the Bad Man," *Callaloo,* 5 (1982), 43-54.

18. For several variants of this folk ballad, see *Folk Ballads of the English Speaking World,* pp. 309-17.

Stephen E. Henderson (essay date 1991)

SOURCE: Henderson, Stephen E. "Sterling Brown: 1901-1989." In *African American Writers,* edited by Lea Baechler and A. Walton Litz, pp. 45-55. New York: Charles Scribner's Sons, 1991.

[*In the following essay, Henderson offers an overview of Brown's life and career.*]

Sterling Allen Brown, a pioneering and gifted poet, a seminal scholar, a brilliant critic, a master teacher, and mentor to hundreds, is generally acknowledged as the dean of African American literature. He was born in Washington, D.C., on 1 May 1901, the youngest of the six children (and the only son) of Rev. Sterling Nelson Brown, minister of Lincoln Temple Congregational Church and professor of religion at Howard University, and of Adelaide Allen Brown, who had been valedictorian of her class at Fisk University.

Brown received an excellent education both in the classroom and outside it. He heard learned discourse in his father's church and at home, where he was awakened to the love of poetry by his mother. He attended Lucretia Mott School and later distinguished himself at Dunbar High School, where Angelina Weld Grimke taught him English and Jessie Redmon Fauset taught him French, and where his classmates included Allison Davis, Montague Cobb, William Hastie, and Charles Drew. Brown received a scholarship to Williams College, from which he graduated in 1922 as a member of Phi Beta Kappa and with a scholarship to Harvard, where he received a master's degree in 1923. At Williams, inspired by George Dutton, he became deeply involved in the new realistic poetry of Edwin Arlington Robinson, Carl Sandburg, and Robert Frost. The example of the Irish writers Sean O'Casey and J. M. Synge led him to resolve to write about black life as it truly was, without resorting to stereotypes or gloss. Education in black culture came while he was teaching in Virginia. This resolve gradually became his life's mission.

After graduation from Harvard, spurred on by his father and the historian and educator Carter G. Woodson, Brown took a teaching post at Virginia Theological Seminary and College at Lynchburg, Virginia (1923-1926). Although he acquired a reputation for stringent grading, he was a popular teacher who was both admired and respected by his students. And from them Brown learned the great life lessons of racial strength and cultural resiliency. He admired his students' dedication, their faith, and their wonderful speech, which he studied and winnowed and incorporated into his poetry. His students also introduced him to the "songster" Calvin "Big Boy" Davis, from whom he acquired ballads, spirituals, and blues. Brown made Davis the subject of three of his earliest poems: **"When de Saints Go Ma'ching Home," "Odyssey of Big Boy,"** and **"Long Gone."** He also devoted two poems, **"Virginia Portrait"** and **"Sister Lou,"** to Mrs. Bibby, the mother of one of his students. To Brown she signified a kind of wisdom and, in effect, offered a lesson that he never forgot and that provided a resonant awareness throughout his poetry and his life. It was also in Lynchburg in December, 1927, that Brown married Daisy Turnbull. The couple later adopted a son.

Although Brown called himself an "amateur folklorist," since he was seeking artistic and philosophical (not scientific) truth, he is held in high esteem by folklorists, especially for the accuracy of his investigation of folk forms such as blues, ballads, and folktales. Indeed, the hallmark of Brown's poetry is its exploration of the bitter dimension of the blues, which he links with a view of humankind that he shares with Sandburg, Frost, Robinson, and Edgar Lee Masters. Their influence helped to catalyze Brown's work without diluting it, and he extended the literary range of the blues without losing their authenticity. When he employed other folk forms, such as the ballad, the "folk epic," the "lie," and the song-sermon, he did so with complete confidence, not only in his skill but also in his models, both the literary (Sandburg, Frost, James Weldon Johnson, and Robinson) and the folk (blues, ballads, and the people who created them).

Brown, a complex man of enormous energy and a masterful talent, gained the admiration and respect of professionals and authorities in the fields of sociology, history, education, and government. Among his earliest and closest friends were the sociologists Charles S. Johnson and E. Franklin Frazier, who inscribed a copy of *Black Bourgeoisie* "To my favorite literary sociologist." In the mid 1930s Brown was consultant to Gunnar Myrdal while the latter was preparing his encyclopedic study of black life, *An American Dilemma* (published in 1944). For this project Brown produced a monumental study of black theater and culture that has served generations of scholars as an introduction to the subject. Although this study was left unpublished, it remains indispensable to a knowledge of the subject.

Among Brown's oldest friends—those who called him "Dutch"—were men and women destined for historical distinction: Ralph Bunche, statesman; Rayford W. Logan, historian; Mercer Cook, linguist and mentor to the Negritude movement; and William Hastie, judge. However, not all of his friends were from the intellectual elite, for Brown always went where the people were, refusing to disown them (as many black intellectuals did). Instead, he stood up for them, and the dignity and wisdom that they embodied. In a moving statement on his relationship to Brown, anthropologist Alan Lomax said in 1975:

> I saw Sterling not in classrooms but standing up for the right of his people's culture in governmental and scholarly circles. I saw the inspiring work that he did on the WPA Writers' Project and in the American Council of Learned Societies; I appeared on platforms with him when he spoke with passion and with double-edged laughter about the things he knew and loved. One of America's greatest poets and one of America's authentically original and beautiful people.

Brown was a teacher for over fifty years (including forty years at Howard, 1929-1969), and teaching was his greatest source of pride. In an interview with Genevieve Ekaete in 1974, Brown stated, "My legacy is my students." Although he retired in 1969, by 1973 he was placing his battered briefcase on the desk and arranging a small library in front of a new class. His former students were as excited as the new ones. One of the latter, Michael Winston, then director of the Moorland-Spingarn Research Center and later Howard University's vice-president for academic affairs, mused, "This great man thought that I could *be* somebody." Among the many other students who became his life-long friends were Clyde Taylor, Eugenia Collier, Bernard Bell, the Dasein poets (among them Percy Johnston, Al Frazier, Ozzie Govan, Joseph White, Nate Richardson, and Leroy Stone), Eloise Spicer, Amiri Baraka, Sherley Anne Williams, Oscar Brown, Jr., and Ossie Davis.

As a writer, Brown produced important work both as a critic and scholar and as a poet. As a scholar he was instrumental in defining and critiquing the African American literary canon. His work in this area, self-assured and reliable, converges in *Negro Poetry and Drama* and *The Negro in American Fiction* (both 1937); *The Negro Caravan,* edited with Arthur P. Davis and Ulysses Lee (1941); and *Outline for the Study of the Poetry of American Negroes* (1931). In addition, he produced for the Myrdal project the previously mentioned study of blacks in the American culture, which, though incomplete, is invaluable. Darwin Turner, distinguished scholar of American and African American literature, sums up the scholarly achievement of Brown in these words:

I had completed research in Afro-American fiction and drama and had known of Brown's work. But, as I probed further, I discovered that all trails led, at some point, to Sterling Brown. His *Negro Caravan* was *the* anthology of Afro-American literature. His unpublished study of Afro-American theatre was *the* major work in the field. His study of images of Afro-Americans in American literature was a pioneer work. His essays on folk literature and folklore were preeminent. He was not always the best critic (I still have a fondness for Saunders Redding's *To Make a Poet Black*), but Brown was and is the literary historian who wrote the Bible for the study of Afro-American literature. Moreover, he seemed to enjoy and respect all Afro-American writers, the folk as well as the elite.

For the study of African American poetry, Brown's 1937 book is still valuable, still fresh. It is comprehensive and challenging, full of insights into the texts. Especially noteworthy is the inclusion of "Negro" poetry in the tradition of American poetry. This was a crucial position, shared by many, to which Brown clung throughout his career. There was no sufferance of double standards, no confusion of a "racial bunt with an Aryan home-run," as it sometimes seemed in the 1960s, but neither was there any sufferance of prejudice or any hesitation in pointing to the limitations of the cultural mainstream. Brown believed in one standard—excellence—and one of his chief discoveries was that excellence was found in cultural tributaries, if one understood the connections and history of the literature and the people who produced it.

Brown argued the uniqueness of the folk forms and demonstrated their power, especially when contrasted with the contemporary romantic poetry in standard English produced by black poets who patterned their work on traditional European forms and themes. His discussion of "Negro folk poetry" encompasses crucial issues of theme, structure, and propriety that still confront black writers and critics. Thus he took up the debate on the originality of spirituals and the opposition of African and Euro-American models to the form, concluding that there are elements of both in the songs. The ultimate creators, however, were the slaves, he stated, and even Southern white scholars admitted that "The words of the best White spirituals cannot compare as poetry with the words of the best Negro spirituals." To which Brown added: "It remains to be said that for the best Negro spirituals, camp-meeting models remain to be discovered."

Brown discussed the philosophy of the spirituals and refuted the notion that they were merely escapist in nature. They reflected real suffering and real longing for freedom, both earthly and spiritual. He singled out "He Never Said a Mumbling Word" and "Were You There," which tell of Jesus' suffering on the cross, and saw them as "among the most lyrical cries of all literature." From this we see Brown's emotional and philosophical

kinship not only with the "black and unknown bards" who created this moving expression but also with the scholars and poets who preceded him in their spiritual and aesthetic discovery: Thomas Wentworth Higginson, W. E. B. Du Bois, and James Weldon Johnson, whom Brown called "mentor." Understanding this kind of faith in the folk creators of the spiritual, we begin to observe the origin and evolution of Brown's aesthetic and philosophy.

The other side of the coin is the social realism expressed in secular rhymes, ballads, work songs, and blues. "At times they belong with the best of folk poetry," Brown said, "and the people who create them at their best cannot be dismissed as clowns." Indeed, these people (designated blues people by LeRoi Jones, one of Brown's protégés) would become the subjects of Brown's portraiture in **Southern Road** and other poems. Still, as James Weldom Johnson notes in his introduction to that volume, Brown does not make mere transcriptions of this vital speech but deepens its meanings.

Like Johnson before him, Brown takes up the hard question posed by the use of dialect, with its associated vilification of black people. He considers the compromises that Paul Laurence Dunbar had to make as he sought to straddle two differing poetry traditions. And with acerbic wit he considers the "contemporary" poetry scene (1914-1936). He dismisses those poets who ignore the real world for one of romantic escape. Their own personalities and struggles should have been recorded: "They refused to look into their own hearts and write." Interestingly, Brown's discussion of dialect and European models is still relevant, for the clash of opposing factions is still to be heard in the arena of the black aesthetic. Also implied in Brown's discussion is the still debated question of identification or identity— What is a "black" poem? Poets of the recent Black Arts movement contend that a criterion of the black poem is black authorship, whereas Brown has always acknowledged the skill and craftsmanship of such writers as Vachel Lindsay and Carl Sandburg, their usefulness as models, and their influence upon his own work. For Brown, the standard of measurement is realism, fidelity to the spirit and objective reality of his subjects. This honesty is consistent in Brown and is the cornerstone of all of his achievement.

In his discussions of blacks in the area of drama, Brown provides the reader with a fact-filled history of American drama and the roles played by blacks both as subjects and as writers. His informed and subtle judgments still provide a valuable introduction to the subject, and scholars and critics of blacks in the cinema also find Brown's pioneering studies relevant to their efforts. He discusses stereotypes; blackface minstrelsy; early black actors such as Ira Aldridge, who played

Othello to Edmund Kean's Iago; and The African Company, dating from 1821, which specialized in Shakespeare. The historical popularity of stage versions of Harriet Beecher Stowe's *Uncle Tom's Cabin* and other abolitionist propaganda, the emergence of the comic black stereotypes, and the evolution of blackface minstrelsy in the "Negro Show" contributed to the climate in which the latter emerged.

According to Brown, however, serious comprehensive treatment and the important relation of black life and character were left waiting for the advent of realism. Contributing to this development was the sympathetic, understanding treatment of folk life, as in the Irish theater, and "the careful study of the Negro's social experience." The ultimate appearance of the realism that Brown speaks of intersects his own work at Howard University, where he served as director of the Howard Players. The theater remained an integral part of Brown's artistic and educational interests. One sees this in his lectures and in his poetry readings—his diction is precise; his timing, perfect.

If Sterling Brown had created nothing else, the anthology *The Negro Caravan* (1941) would have accorded him a secure place in literary history. This book was not the first anthology of African American writing, but it was the most comprehensive and the best until then. It is still the best. As the editors point out, earlier anthologies were more narrowly literary, sometimes focusing on a single genre, such as poetry, or on a particular period, as did Benjamin Brawley's *Early Negro American Writers*. According to the preface of *Negro Caravan*:

> This anthology of the writings of American Negroes has three purposes: (1) to present a body of artistically valid writings by American Negro authors, (2) to present a truthful mosaic of Negro character and experience in America, and (3) to collect in one volume certain key literary works that have greatly influenced the thinking of American Negroes, and to a lesser degree, that of Americans as a whole.

To achieve their purposes, the editors covered the whole range of black writing—from Phillis Wheatley and Jupiter Hammon to Richard Wright. The selections are arranged in eight sections according to type, with selections arranged chronologically. Each author's work is preceded by a brief biographical and bibliographical note. Among the selections are speeches, pamphlets, letters, biography and autobiography, and essays classified into historical, social, cultural, and personal types. There is also a generous representation of folk literature, the direct influence of Brown, preceded by a brilliant essay on the literary and social importance of the texts. Finally, there is a useful chronology of historical and cultural events in America as a whole, and in black America. The book is a classic, and its influence has been fundamental.

Brown's first published poem was **"When de Saints Go Ma'ching Home"** (*Opportunity* 5:48 [July 1927]). Other poems appearing before the publication of his first volume include **"Challenge," "Odyssey of Big Boy," "Return," "Salutamus,"** and **"To a Certain Lady, in Her Garden"** (all in *Caroling Dusk,* edited by Countee Cullen [1927]). Additional poems are **"Thoughts of Death"** (*Opportunity* 6:242 [6 August 1928]); **"Riverbank Blues"** (*Opportunity* 7:148 [May 1929]); **"Effie"** (*Opportunity* 7:304 [October 1929]); **"Long Gone," "Memphis Blues," "Slim Greer," "Southern Road," "Strong Men"** (in *The Book of American Negro Poetry,* edited by James Weldon Johnson [1931]); **"Convict," "New St. Louis Blues," "Old King Cotton," "Pardners," "Revelations," "Slow Coon"** (later **"Slim Lands a Job?"**), and **"Tin Roof Blues"** (in *Folk-Say* edited by Benjamin A. Botkin [1931]).

Although the above listing tells us nothing about the order of composition, it does imply something about order of publication and the configuration that this group of poems makes: for example, the sonnet **"Salutamus"** and the poems **"Challenge"** and **"Return"** from the "Vestiges" section of **Southern Road,** as well as the contrasting poem **"Odyssey of Big Boy,"** which represents a turning away from the genteel and the lyrical to the folk model. We can see how the poet selects and melds these different styles in a process everywhere evident in **Southern Road.** One must marvel at the skill, the ear, the touch by which this mosaic of black life becomes a book, an organic entity that over the years has achieved legendary, at times archetypal, character.

Brown chooses the road, one of the central metaphors of the black experience—indeed, of the human experience—as the unifying motif of his book. Many critics have commented on the felicity of that choice, reflecting as it does powerful connections in the history and culture of the group. Among the forms that the road has taken are the creeks and the rivers, the railroad, the Underground Railroad, the gospel train, the way of survival, the slippery path to hell, the lonesome valley, the Big Road of Life. Immersed as he was in folklore, Brown could ring many changes on the "lonesome road," the junction "where the Southern cross the Yellow Dog," John Henry, the poor wayfaring traveler, and the restless spirit that drives the blues man with a hell hound on his trail. Joanne Gabbin emphasizes the road as "a path of knowledge and experience" epitomized in the words of an old spiritual:

> O de ole sheep dey knows de road,
> Young lambs gotta find de way.

This communication between the old and the young establishes a bond and a continuity between the generations that give "credence to the idea that the Black literary tradition is one continuous line of development issuing from the earliest folk thought and utterance." In several respects the organization of *Southern Road* implies the dynamics of the social and moral forces whose struggle the poems amplify and illumine.

Southern Road is divided into four parts, each preceded by an epigraph and a dedication, as follows:

> Part One: Road So Rocky. "Road May be Rocky / Won't Be Rocky Long . . ." (spiritual), for Anne Spencer
>
> Part Two: On Restless River. "O, de Mississippi River, so deep an' wide . . ." (blues), for Allison Davis
>
> Part Three: Tin Roof Blues. "I'm got de tin roof blues, / Got dese sidewalks on my mind." (**"Tin Roof Blues"**), for Poodle Williams
>
> Part Four: Vestiges. "When I was one-and-twenty: I heard a wise man say:" (A. E. Housman), for Rose Anne.

With his talent for architectonics Brown sets up a controlled field, a kind of grid, on which to situate our responses. Each of the "pylons" that link the book can also be recognized as chords, each chord consisting of four terms or tones, from the enumeration to the title to the quotation to the dedication. Each level builds to the final nomination, and each element affects us on a different level, though the levels overlap and converge. The last, the deepest level, is the personal, the level of friendship and love. With the passing of time that level becomes a de facto monument against the day when nothing remains of the specific identity but the "sounds of our names."

That movement of names through present time to future time, I submit, is a movement toward a final object that is expressed thus in the dedication of *Collected Poems*: "To Rose Anne [Brown's wife, Daisy], as ever." Characteristically, the epigraphs and dedications move from the literary to the folk to the vernacular, and this practice continues elsewhere in the *Collected Poems,* where the poet moves from his circle of recent friends in *No Hiding Place* to those of his youth, friends of Dunbar days who called him Dutch. They appear in dedications of *The Last Ride of Wild Bill.* The dedication reads: "To the Dunbar Independents (who prodded my tall tales) Axe/Bill/Forty-Five/Flap/Ike/Lancess/Sam/In memory of Charlie and Ralph." The last two names are those of the medical scientist Charles Drew and of the statesman Ralph Bunche.

The opening poem of *Southern Road,* **"Odyssey of Big Boy,"** is one of Brown's best and most popular. It also sets the tone for the collection. A delightful ballad, the poem is characterized by humor, stoicism and endurance, racial pride, and technical virtuosity. The hero of the poem, Calvin "Big Boy" Davis, is the "songster"

Brown met while at Virginia Seminary. His identification with Davis extends beyond personal friendship to an absorption of the qualities that the man, as the epitome of a culture and a tradition, embodied. And at the end of the poem Big Boy identifies not only with the legendary John Henry but also with the prototypical blues wanderer, "the po' boy a long ways from home," the Original Brother, "old Jazzbo." It is not accidental that the SNCC (Student Nonviolent Coordination Committee) Freedom Fighters in the deep South in the 1960s occasionally signed their names as "Junebug Jazzbo Jones"—they, in effect, led that life. In this poem a full life has been recorded. A life marked by good times and bad, but one that, with all of its dangers and hardships, was eagerly embraced. It is a quality occasionally heard in the blues: "I have had my fun, if I don't get well no mo'." But, like the singer in the blues, Big Boy is in the prime of a life that he, for all his good timing, has lived to the fullest.

> Done took my livin' as it came,
>   Done grabbed my joy, done risked my life;
> Train done caught me on de trestle,
>   Man done caught me wid his wife,
>   His doggone purty wife. . . .

Another poem inspired by "Big Boy" brings an intimate touch to the portrait of the itinerant musician. In **"Long Gone,"** the wanderlust seizes Big Boy's mind as he lies on his pallet listening to the lonely sounds of the trains. He remembers the woman at his side:

> When I oughta be quiet,
>   I is got a itch
> Fo' to hear de whistle blow
>   Fo' de crossin' or de switch,
>
> An' I knows de time's a nearin'
>   When I got to ride,
> Though it's homelike and happy
>   At yo' side.
>
> Ain't no call at all, sweet woman,
>   Fo' to carry on—
> Jes' my name and jes' my habit
>   To be Long Gone. . . .

There are hundreds of blues songs that sound these feelings of restlessness and nameless dissatisfaction, but Brown captures the mood in his ballad form before it is shaped by the bitter sensuality of the blues. As it stands, it retains a certain lyricism that one associates with youth and the passing of time.

Brown develops these feelings into a spacious composition that enables him to comment on the final leaving as adumbrated in a homely but powerful vision of the Last Judgment, as it were. Appropriately, **"When de Saints Go Ma'ching Home"** opens with the following dedication:

(To Big Boy Davis, Friend.
In Memories of Days Before He Was
Chased Out of Town for Vagrancy.)

There is an effective interplay of memory, mutability, and imagination that forces the seminarians, the professor, and, indeed, the readers to understand more fully the meaning of their association with Big Boy—he is a repository and a guardian of their past, their culture, and somehow they will not let that die. The poem begins ". . . his chant of saints, / 'When de saints go ma'chin home. . . .' / and that would end his concert for the day." Brown's handling of the narrative elements is excellent, especially the shifting perspectives. First there is the close-up of the tuning of the guitar:

> He would forget
> The quieted bunch, his dimming cigarette
> Stuck into a splintered edge of the guitar;
> Sorrow deep hidden in his voice, a far
> And soft light in his strange brown eyes;
> Alone with his masterchords, his
>   memories. . . .
> *Lawd I wanna be one in nummer*
> *When de saints go ma'chin' home.*

Seemingly transfixed, Davis was absorbed by the vision of a Beulah Land created by the mingling of faith, imagination, and music. In that vision, there follows a processing "Of saints—his friends—'a-climbin' fo' deir wings,'" created again out of faith and incorruptible song.

Section two of the poem presents the saints, including asthmatic Deacon Zachary, "A-puffin' an' a-wheezin' / up de golden stair." There is "ole Sis Joe / In huh big straw hat, / An' huh wrapper flappin' . . . in de heavenly win'. . . ." There's "Ole Elder Peter Johnson" puffing on his corncob pipe, and the "little brown-skinned chillen" dancing to the heavenly band. There is "Maumee Annie," with her washing done, and old Grandpa Eli, puzzling on a question to ask St. Peter.

In this poem, the procession melds several literary traditions—the classical, the romantic, and the folk minstrel (including the dialect poems of Paul Laurence Dunbar). In the classical, there is the roll call of heroes as in the *Iliad,* the procession of negative characters in *Lycidas*; in the romantic, the procession of mourners in *Adonais*; in the folk minstrel, the revelers in Dunbar's "The Party," and its descendants in black popular song, such as Little Richard's "Long Tall Sally," who is "built for speed," who has "everything Uncle Tom needs." After the concert is over, Big Boy would go where "we / Never could follow him—to Sophie probably, / Or to his dances in old Tinbridge flat." After one such concert Davis never came back. Before he disappeared, however, he had allowed Brown to take his picture and had taught him about John Henry, the ballads, the work songs, and the blues.

Just as he had developed friendships and had virtually soaked up black folk culture during his years at Virginia Seminary, Brown in his next two teaching jobs continued his self-education: at Lincoln University in Missouri (1926-1928) and at Fisk University (1928-1929). At both places he got to know the hotels, the barber shops, the shoeshine parlors, and other black businesses that were special gathering places for local wits and raconteurs. He visited rural communities and learned their ways first hand. At Jefferson City, Missouri, he spent long hours listening to tall tales told by a waiter named Slim who kept everyone in stitches and was the prototype for the character Slim Greer, one of Brown's best-known creations. At Fisk, Brown met "the best liar I ever ran across." This was Will Gilchrist, the master yarn spinner, the immortal "Gillie," who probably influenced Brown's performance style as much as anyone other than Calvin "Big Boy" Davis. To a degree, Gilchrist and Davis were co-creators with the poet, as Brown himself would readily concede. Later, Brown would playfully refer to himself as Slim and would, in turn, be called "Slim" by friends. In fact, the identification at times is so amazing that Edward A. Jones, a colleague from Atlanta, called Slim "Brown's poetic alter ego."

There are five Slim Greer poems: three in **"On Restless River"** and two, **"Slim Hears the Call"** and **"Slim in Hell,"** omitted from *The Collected Poems.* Briefly these poems exploit the racial, male, unself-conscious lore that never appears in Paul Laurence Dunbar or James Weldon Johnson. This is the dimension of the vernacular that Johnson calls "the common, racy, living speech of the Negro in certain phases of real life." In **"Slim Lands a Job?"** the hero goes to Big Pete's Cafe, looking for a job. Pete warns Slim that he has a "slow nigger" whom he's going to fire. Then:

> A noise rung out
>   In rush a man
> Wid a tray on his head
>   An' one on each han'
>
> Wid de silver in his mouf
>   An' de soup plates in his vest
> Pullin' a red wagon
>   Wid all de rest. . . .
>
> De man's said, "Dere's
>   Dat slow coon now
> Dat wuthless lazy waiter!"
>   An' Slim says, "How?"
>
> An' Slim threw his gears in
>   Put it in high,
> An' kissed his hand to Arkansaw,
>   Sweetheart . . . good-bye!

There are other stunning portraits throughout Brown's poems, a number of them in *Southern Road.* In **"Vir-**

ginia Portrait" a formal rendering of Mrs. Bibby, the wise mother of one of his students, is presented with monumental dignity and grace:

> Even when winter settles on her heart,
> She keeps a wonted, quiet nonchalance,
> A courtly dignity of speech and carriage,
> Unlooked for in these distant rural ways.

There is the tragic Johnny Thomas (in the poem bearing his name), taken by everyone for a "consarned fool." He gets hooked on gambling and a "fancy woman":

> De jack run low
> De gal run out
> Johnny didn't know
> What 'twas all about.

He then commits murder and is executed:

> Dropped him in de hole
> Threw de slack lime on,
> Oughta had mo' sense
> Dan to evah git born.

A similar fate dogs the convict in **"Southern Road."** Aside from the drama and the metaphoric extensions of the poem, especially noteworthy is the manner in which the poet takes a three-line blues stanza and transforms it into a work song. The lines are punctuated by the convict's breath, which also regulates the rhythm of his swing. This practice in the oral tradition—in black preaching—is still widely employed even by urban ministers. The virtuoso handling of rhetorical devices, especially those which are endemic to the black tradition, undergirds many aspects of literary performance, from folk rhymes to sermons to contemporary "rap" songs. A kind of revival of these practices has taken place since the early 1970s, not only in poetry but also in fiction. Brown (with **"Strong Men"** and **"Ma Rainey"** in *Southern Road,* **"The Last Ride of Wild Bill"** in the collection of that title, and **"Old Lem"** in *No Hiding Place*), Zora Neale Hurston, James Weldon Johnson, and Langston Hughes were forerunners in their use of this style.

Brown's rhetoric—the rhetoric of the black tradition—is greatly influenced by music in both obvious and subtle ways. A good deal of this word play still remains in the black community; even when it appears to be on the wane, it reappears somewhere else. The golden solemnity of Martin Luther King, Jr., and the fire darts of Malcolm X's wit are fused and subsumed in the torrential talent of Jesse Jackson. In similar manner the apocalyptic be-bop of Larry Neal and Amiri Baraka, the popular prophecy of Nikki Giovanni and Sonia Sanchez—all poets of the 1960s—have been reborn in "rap" music. Larry Neal, poet and theorist of the Black Arts movement, called for a poet who had the drive and skill of James Brown: "Did you ever hear a poet scream like that?" The poets arrived with the Last Poets (among them Felipe Luciano and Gylan Kain), whose kinetic chanting provided a generational link with the "rappers" of the 1980s and 1990s, and with other performer "poets." The point is that the pattern had already been established by Brown and Langston Hughes; and before them, James Weldon Johnson; and before him, Frances Ellen Watkins Harper, whose animated delivery style was geared to maximum audience impact.

It is virtually impossible to read Brown's poetry aloud and not realize his masterful skills. His effects are not accidental, and he doesn't have to scream. When he wants it to, the poem screams, as in **"The Ballad of Joe Meek."** In poem after poem he never falters and always delights. In a live reading by the poet, one would note his powerful and sonorous voice, capable of myriad shadings and inflections. In **"Sister Lou,"** for example, which fuses the poem's images with its rhythms and musicality, the voice of an old woman speaking softly to a dying friend becomes the overwhelming presence:

> Jesus will find yo' bed fo' you
> Won't no servant evah bother wid yo' room.
> Jesus will lead you
> To a room wid windows
> Openin' on cherry trees an' plum trees
> Bloomin' everlastin'
> An' dat will be yours
> Fo' keeps.
> Den take yo' time. . . .
> Honey, take yo' bressed time.

Fascination with music is not confined, of course, to Brown. It is a feature of African American writing in general, especially the poetry, and it would be strange indeed if the poets neglected so prominent a part of their heritage. In Brown's **"Ma Rainey"** the Mother of the Blues performs to an audience of poor working people. The laughing, cackling crowd quiets down when Ma comes on stage. In his famous description Brown suggests her role of healer, consoler, and priestess:

> O Ma Rainey,
> Sing yo' song;
> Now you's back
> Whah you belong,
> Get way inside us,
> Keep us strong. . . .
>
> O Ma Rainey,
> Lil' an' low;
> Sing us 'bout de hard luck
> Roun' our do';
> Sing us 'bout de lonesome road
> We mus' go. . . .

Ma's rendering of "Backwater Blues" brings comfort and solace to the weeping audience. The delineation of the spirit is precise, pure, and presented with economy. It answers all of the questions regarding the use of dialect that James Weldon Johnson raises.

Another example of Brown's incorporating music into his rhetoric is found in **"Strong Men."** Like powerful hammer blows, the accusatory rhythm is driven by the syntax. Rewritten, the framing lines read: "They dragged you . . . They chained you . . . They huddled you . . . They sold you. . . . They broke you. . . . They scourged you. . . . They branded you. . . ." This pattern is a kind of call and response, although the "call" is more an attack or command. But there's no doubting the response: "You sang. . . . You sang. . . . You sang. . . . You sang. . . . You sang."

Again comes the negative call to despair: "They cooped you. . . . They penned you. . . ." And you sang, and they were afraid. And what did you sing? Spirituals, work songs, ragtime and jazz.

> You sang:
> Me an' muh baby gonna shine, shine
> Me and muh baby gonna shine.

The Charleston set to poetry.

In **"Cabaret,"** a truly remarkable poem, Brown shows how the economic and political power of the "overlords" exploits and perverts African American creativity, as a complex stream of consciousness is juxtaposed to recollection of the disastrous floods of 1927, which the poet had addressed earlier in **"Ma Rainey"** and **"Children of the Mississippi."**

"Vestiges," Part Four of *Southern Road,* is quite different from the others and poses certain problems for the reader. Anticipating its difficulty, Brown smoothly works this section into the design of the book. First, according to Brown himself, the title "Vestiges" signifies an earlier group of writings in traditional Euro-American forms from which he had turned away. It also implies that those works and lines were not being renounced, but superseded by the new realism. So he is salvaging the best work of his youth with full knowledge that he would not pass that way again.

Mechanically, "Vestiges" is connected to the other three parts of *Southern Road* by the dedication to "Rose Anne" (his wife, Daisy) and by the poem **"To a Certain Lady, in Her Garden"** which bears a parenthetical dedication to Anne Spencer—to whom Part One was dedicated. Thematically, "Vestiges" addresses the perennial concerns of the young artist: romantic love, mutability, fame, and the passing of youth. Stylistically, the poems are written in sonnet form (**"Challenge"**), in iambic pentameter quatrains (**"To a Certain Lady"**), iambic tetrameter quatrains (**"Against That Day"**), in free verse (**"Thoughts of Death"**), and in a blank verse reminiscent of James Thomson and William Cooper (**"Mill Mountain"**). These connections are indicative of Brown's poetic range and the kinds of literary options available to him before he chose his realistic models.

Between the publication of *Southern Road* in 1932 and its republication in 1974, there is a strange and disturbing lapse. Certainly Brown was not silent, for in 1937 he had scheduled *No Hiding Place,* his second book of poems, for publication. The book was rejected for reasons that are unclear, and Brown became bitter. In the 1960s Brown's popularity soared, buoyed by the discovery of his work by a larger audience, some of whom were stirred by the Black Consciousness movement of the 1960s and 1970s. In 1975, Brown was persuaded to publish *The Last Ride of Wild Bill and Eleven Narrative Poems.* In the title poem the headlong, rhythmic rush of the poem is driven by a witty, audacious "skeletonic" verse in which Brown is fluent.

In 1980 *The Collected Poems of Sterling A. Brown* appeared. *No Hiding Place,* published as a section of *Collected Poems,* lacks the symmetry and range of *Southern Road* but is nonetheless a worthy effort. Its eight parts, when considered together, create a kind of personal odyssey (or travelogue): Part One: Harlem Stopover; Part Two: The Cotton South; Part Three: Down in Atlanta; Part Four: "Rocks Cried Out"; Part Five: Road to the Left; Part Six: Frilot Cove; Part Seven: Washington, D.C.; Part Eight: Remembrances. As in *Southern Road,* the last part is devoted to memories.

Although frequent reprinting had made a few of the poems fairly well known—**"Old Lem," "An Old Woman Remembers," "Remembering Nat Turner," "Puttin' on Dog,"** and **"Long Track Blues"**—most of them were hardly known and others, such as the Cajun poems of **"Frilot Cove,"** were total surprises to most readers. In a few cases one senses directions and leads that the poet briefly followed and then, apparently, dropped. There is a satirical critique of self-appointed race leaders in **"The Temple," "The New Congo,"** and **"Memo: For the Race Orators"** (on black traitors); there are perversions of history through excess racial zeal in **"The Temple,"** and through prejudice in **"Remembering Nat Turner."** In these poems Brown is rather close in tone to Melvin Tolson and Frank Marshall Davis. Class struggle and dignity and unity among the working classes are themes of the "Road to the Left" section. Class, not race, is the unifying factor. In **"Raise a Song,"** music functions as a mask and ironic bandage to physical and spiritual injuries of the poor and the homeless. **"Colloquy"** is a satire on the "solidarity" of black worker and white worker. The touchstone is the wisdom of the black folk tradition:

> But dere's hard times comin'—wuss'n hard tmes now.
> An' in de hard times dat I recollec'
> De whites stood together on top of our shoulders
> An' give it to us square in de neck.

In **"Street Car Gang"**—a litany of social and economic woes, the urban parallel to **"Old Lem"** in its description of the oppression of black manhood by the whites in power—a younger worker calls for revolutionary change of the entire system:

> By Gawd we do the work
> What come from it is ours.

Although not much is known about why *No Hiding Place* was not published earlier, some suggest that Brown was simply involved with too many projects during this period. A glance at his publications list is thus revealing. In addition, Brown taught a full course load of fifteen hours at Howard, served as director and adviser to the Federal Writers' Project and similar efforts, and was involved in academic politics. Brown himself felt that the sharp social threats and reactions to the militancy of the period made him politically suspect. There were also difficult professional and personal decisions to be made. For example, his acceptance of a position at Vassar College in 1945 received national attention and promised the kind of recognition he wanted. But the returning veterans of World War II needed him, too. And Howard University needed him, and his people needed him, so he remained there. Brown had touched many lives, and when he came out of retirement in 1973-1975, he helped to energize a new generation of scholars and artists at the Howard University Institute for the Arts and the Humanities. During this time he was becoming more widely known, for his lectures and poetry readings. A new generation had thus discovered him, and at long last some of the symbols of acceptance and appreciation were bestowed upon him. He received honorary doctorates from Howard University, Williams College, Boston University, Harvard, Vassar, and Brown, and other academic institutions. He also was elected to the Academy of American Poets and proclaimed poet laureate of the District of Columbia.

A personal subtext to Brown's poetry, especially as it is shaped by *Southern Road* and *No Hiding Place,* is his love for "Rose Anne" (actually Daisy, his wife of more than fifty years), and his abhorrence of pomposity and fakery. His courtship and youth speak in a variety of voices, one of which appears in **"Honey Mah Love"**:

> Dear child
> Someday there will be truce from quarreling.
> And someday all our silly fears will cease.
> Someday there will be ways that we shall learn
> To bilk old clandestine Time, and to return
> His cheats, with one on him. Oh we shall bring
> Someday to our ecstatic worshiping
> More than our fretting fervor; something nearer peace,
> Something near the surety we have been dreaming of.
> Happy at last. . . . Oh happy! Honey, mah love. . . .

Brown died in Washington, D.C. on 17 January 1989.

Angela E. Chamblee (essay date March 1993)

SOURCE: Chamblee, Angela E. "Slim's Heaven and Hell." *CLA Journal* 36, no. 3 (March 1993): 339-42.

[*In the following essay, Chamblee elucidates Brown's conception of Heaven and Hell in his poem "Slim in Hell."*]

There are many definitions of the word *heaven.* Heaven can be the repository of the ideals of all that is good in life. Heaven can be the stars in the sky. There can be heaven on earth, and the kingdom of heaven can be within.

Hell too can be on earth, and Hell can be in one's mind. In Sterling Brown's poem **"Slim in Hell,"** Heaven is not a solemn, ethereal place, nor is Hell exclusively an abode of torture and pain. Both Heaven and Hell are variations on everyday life. Ultimately, Slim's mind—his consciousness—determines his Heaven and Hell.

The Heaven of **"Slim in Hell"** does not seem to be a reverent, pious place. Slim calls St. Peter "Pete." St. Peter winks at Slim and calls him a "travelin' rascal," which is a somewhat disparaging term. The dictionary defines the word "rascal" to mean "a base, dishonest, unscrupulous person, or a mischievous person." If Slim is a rascal, then why is he in Heaven? The Heaven that Brown creates is not dull and staid. There is humor, and evidently some devilishness is allowed. In Brown's poem, Heaven seems to be a place where the earthy warmth, love, and humor of African-American life reign supreme.

In most cultures Heaven is a place of luxury, where there is an abundance of food. In ancient Egypt, for example, the followers of Osiris believed that

> the righteous dead would find their everlasting abode in the kingdom of that god [Osiris] and would enjoy in a fertile land, with running streams, a life very like that which the well-to-do Egyptian lived upon earth. . . . In the kingdom of Osiris the beatified dead ate bread-cakes made from one wonderful kind of grain, and drank beer made from another kind, and enjoyed conjugal intercourse and the company of their relations and friends.[1]

Brown's poem **"Sister Lou"** suggests a Heaven of rest and ease, where African-American people no longer have to work like slaves. People sit leisurely and talk to family and friends. In Brown's Heaven people eat greengrape jellies, golden biscuits, and spoonbread.

In **"When De Saints Go Ma'ching Home"** a musician, Big Boy, sings a spiritual to end his nightclub act. He dedicates the song to his mother, and as he sings, he and the audience become transformed. They both get caught up in a vision of Heaven, which is also a vision of human possibility on earth.[2] Heaven and the march towards Heaven become "understood as one and the same event."[3]

We really do not see much of Heaven in **"Slim in Hell,"** but the Heaven we do see is similar to the Heaven of such Spirituals as "Walk All Over God's Heaven" (also known as "I Got a Robe") and "Swing Low, Sweet Chariot." There is no mention of food. The focus is on clothes, and not only on adequate clothing, but on fine-looking, ostentatious clothes—clothes fit for a king. There is also a verse about getting wings with which to fly. What are wings but a sophisticated, rich man's mode of travel? "Swing Low, Sweet Chariot" also suggests a Heaven where people can meet and talk with friends. Moreover, a chariot could have been the opulent version of an automobile in the ancient world. One might note a jazz version of the spiritual that Dizzy Gillespie recorded: "Swing Low, Sweet Cadillac." Brown's use of the words "parked," as in "he parked his wings," highlights the connection between wings and cars. Heaven is the place for fashionable clothes and fast automobiles, the perfect domain for a rascal.

If a certain amount of devilishness can be allowed in Heaven, then, by contrast, a certain amount of heavenly bliss can be allowed in Hell. Hell has plenty of wine, women, and song, and it evidently is a very pleasurable place for some people to go. If it were exclusively a place of pain and terror, Peter would not have winked at Slim, and Slim would not be so happy to take a trip there.

The Devil at the entrance to Hell is very civil and polite—formal, with Slim. He calls Slim "Mr. Greer." Hence, the tone at the entrance to Hell is markedly different from Peter's easygoing tone at the entrance to Heaven. Considering the African-American cultural feelings about honorific titles, it is significant that the Devil would refer to Slim as "Mr. Greer." The Devil could have grinned and addressed Slim using a derogatory name, but he did not.

The Devil does not insult Slim, but neither is he jokingly friendly with him, as Peter is. The Devil is indifferent, neither an angel who would help Slim nor an ugly, evil creature who would destroy him. Formality is a form of indifference. The Devil is symbolic of Hell itself, because Hell is whatever Slim wants to make of it.

Although the Devil may not necessarily seem to be a monstrous-looking fiend, the dog that runs up to Slim certainly is. Nevertheless, oddly, the dog does not attack Slim. Why? Because Slim is not afraid of him. His mind does not allow for the reality of the dog's attacking him, so the bloodhound runs off to attack somebody else.

Slim is not afraid of the Devil, the dog, or the various devils he sees in Hell. It is the European-American sheriff who unsettles him. Slim is so terrified of such an authority figure that he has to run away. After Slim makes a hasty retreat back to Heaven, St. Peter tells him that he is "a leetle too dumb" to stay in Paradise. To stay in Heaven Slim needs to have attained a certain level of understanding of the nature of racial oppression.

Hell is encountered on earth, and it takes the form of police brutality. Slim has learned an important lesson. However, there is still more for him to learn. A higher level of understanding would reveal that Hell is not found on earth but in the mind. Just as dogs can sense fear in people, people can sense fear in each other. When Slim learns to view the monstrous sheriff as he views the monstrous dog, then he will be able to stay in Heaven.

Notes

1. E. A. Wallis Budge, *The Egyptian Heaven and Hell* (La Salle, Illinois: Open Court Publishing Co., 1989), p. 20. Reprinted from a clothbound edition of the same title, 1925.

2. Kimberly W. Benston, "Sterling Brown's After-Song: 'When de Saints go Ma'ching Home' and the Performances of Afro-American Voice," *Callaloo: An Afro-American and African Journal of Arts and Letters,* 5 (Feb.-May, 1982), 38.

3. Ibid., p. 36.

Mark A. Sanders (essay date December 1994)

SOURCE: Sanders, Mark A. "The Ballad, the Hero, and the Ride: A Reading of Sterling A. Brown's *The Last Ride of Wild Bill.*" *CLA Journal* 38, no. 2 (December 1994): 162-82.

[*In the following essay, Sanders perceives* The Last Ride of Wild Bill *as a collection of ballads that focus on the fundamental nature of heroism.*]

In 1975 one of the most aggressive proponents of the Black Arts Movement (BAM), Broadside Press, published *The Last Ride of Wild Bill and Eleven Narrative Poems,* Sterling A. Brown's final collection. As he points out in his preface, Dudley Randall had been requesting, for some time, permission from Brown to reissue much of his poetry; Randall was especially concerned that *Southern Road* was out of print and therefore largely unavailable to a new generation of highly politicized readers. But Brown's sight was on a new configuration of older works—most of them not found in *Southern Road*—and a new poem to introduce the collection.

Broadside, a press very much involved in the heated racial politics of the late sixties and early seventies, by definition sought out writers who directly engaged the various ideologies of Black Power and Black Arts. It serves as testament to Brown's longevity and insight that such a press would aggressively pursue a figure much less preoccupied with the immediate polemic than with the continuum of cultural aesthetics. But this is not inconsistent with the times, for throughout the Civil Rights Movement and the subsequent Black Power Movement, Brown was lionized for his strident defense of grassroots folk and for his acute understanding of African-American culture. As an immensely popular teacher at Howard University, he served as mentor to a number of future political leaders—Stokely Carmichael (Kwame Toure) being one of the most prominent—and worked as advisor to the Nonviolent Action Group (NAG). In fact, more radical students at Howard agitated to rename the institution "Sterling Brown University."[1] And as James G. Spady aptly illustrates, Brown's poetry and politics fostered a conceptual and cultural continuum from New Negro to Black Power activist. At a tribute to Brown, Spady commented on the political climate of the sixties and the reception of Brown's poetry:

> Remember this was doing [sic] the seething sixties when some considered anyone over thirty to be an uncle tom [sic]. As a matter of fact some of Howard University's finest professors had been burned in effigy. Why were Sterling Brown's poems so enthusiastically applauded? . . . They have simplicity, they are vivid, they are often humorous, sometimes sad, more often heroic but always capable of moving the listener. They have sense and sound. Most important they are timeless. That is the reason **"Old Lem"** could move both my grandparents and me. And everybody knows that Jim Fox ain't easily moved.[2]

In short, both the political activists of the Black Power Movement and the aestheticians of the Black Arts Movement fully embraced Brown as mentor and progenitor. In him they found a viable antecedent for their political and cultural agendas; and as such, Brown was celebrated as a Black Arts activist far ahead of his time.

Yet given the accolades and attention produced in the late sixties and early seventies, Brown's poetics stood apart from, if not in direct opposition to, the dominant aesthetics of the day. Although *Last Ride* occupies the same historical moment as BAM poets such as Nikki Giovanni and Don L. Lee, Brown continues a much older tradition focused on rural and Southern idioms. By presenting the dynamics of African-American culture as its own liberating agent, the poem, for Brown, does not become the polemic but an aesthetic means of celebrating essential strengths and potential. In a sense *Last Ride* is largely anachronistic; Black Arts aesthetics

notwithstanding, Brown rejects the encroaching dissonance of postmodern poetics and its emphasis on language's chronic instability. Instead Brown harkens back to the forms and traditions which shaped his first collection. Indeed, completing a continuum beginning with *Southern Road* and advanced in *No Hiding Place*, Brown's *Last Ride* reconceptualizes African-American culture in modal process. Like his previous collections, *Last Ride* explores the means by which the culture itself actualizes its own progression and propels itself toward its own visions. In this particular collection Brown cites heroism and the omnipresent heroic spirit as the catalytic agents animating African-American culture. Brown's cultural heroes—figures produced by the folk and embodying their essential strengths and aspirations—singularly confront the multiple forms of white authority and its stifling influences. Through defiance, and often martyrdom, these figures reveal a vital impulse toward autonomy and self-realization. Be they perpetually rebellious or only occasionally so, all reflect a cultural will which continues to inspire defiant acts commensurate with heroism.

With this in mind, our understanding of *Last Ride* as a book of and about ballads becomes vitally important. Brown takes the ballad, an essential medium of folk culture (a "communal art form"[3]), and reconstructs it in a search for essential cultural strengths. As a collection of ballads the process of narrating itself holds center stage; the tradition of exaggeration and tall tales fuels the collection and points to its metaphoric focus. Both the folk ballad and Brown's literary ballads take up the figure of the folk hero, but where the folk ballad validates the hero's mythic stature, *Last Ride* seeks to examine the fundamental nature of heroism: how and why it exists, and what broader meaning it imports. Brown presents an extended address of the cultural hero, invoking the conventions of lies and toasts, but goes beyond the mere appropriation of folk idioms in order to examine the essential motivations behind the hero's perpetual rebelliousness.

If heroism is predicated upon the physical act of rebellion, so too are the various iconographic forms which Brown's heroes take. The bad man, the renegade, and the humble worker trying to do right all combine to provide an array of personas destabilizing social conventions. By creating a diversified or multidimensional face for the heroic impulse, Brown eventually makes a strong case for its ubiquitousness. Moving beyond the stasis of a single cultural image, Brown attempts to portray the cultural dynamic, the specific catalyst which prompts the culture as a whole to confront imposed limitations. In short, *Last Ride,* moving through various avatars of the heroic spirit, asserts the ubiquitous yet often hidden heroic impulse anterior to the heroic act yet gesturing toward numerous possibilities. Thus Brown's ballads seek to locate power and potential implicit yet latent within the culture.

This gesture toward hidden potential fixes the hero in the broadest metaphoric spheres; here the hero is an ultimately transformational figure, one alluding to liberation through reformulation of self, community, and relations with white authority. The collection begins with an examination of the hero's power to transform confining surroundings, then embarks upon a linear progression in two modes, comic and tragic, toward ever expansive implications in transformation. Each specific face of the cultural hero reveals new possibilities, both individual and collective, culminating in Joe Meek's encompassing gesture toward the transcendent nature of heroism itself. Brown enriches the metaphoric development of heroism and its transformational potential with an intricate dialogue between comic and tragic modes. Beginning with the comic, Brown establishes the resonant folk voice. Invoking the tradition of the toast, tall tales, and hyperbole, Wild Bill, Slim Greer, and John Bias offer various forms of the exaggerated and the burlesque but gradually adopt undertones of tragic implications. Brown effectively blurs the distinctions between the two modes, achieving a final unity in Joe Meek, a product of the tall tale yet a tragic hero of epic proportions. Thus by reformulating the mode of their representation, Brown underscores the overt transformational qualities of his heroes. Yet on a more fundamental level, Brown critiques traditional balladry through his experimentation with new narrative forms. As we will see in **"The Last Ride of Wild Bill,"** the ballad form itself serves as yet another site for Brown's invocation of liberating and rejuvenating potential in heroic resistance.

Finally, Brown serves both formal and thematic unity through his central metaphor, "the ride." In practical terms the trope refers to the narrative itself, both the episodic progression toward resolution and the revelation of formal transformation which the narrative progression exposes. As central metaphor the trope invokes the liberating possibilities inherent in the heroic act. It is the superlative romantic gesture toward freedom and autonomy, and as such the ride signals the broadest symbolic movement from the palpability of the physical act itself to its expansive metaphoric implications.

Thus Brown introduces this collection of ballads and heroes with a signature poem which largely defines the tenor and import of the book. In **"The Last Ride of Wild Bill,"** Brown concerns himself primarily with transformation itself; in terms of form, theme, action and final metaphor, **"Last Ride"** points toward the

power and agency of change, the potential in reordering and redefining oppressive circumstances, and ultimately toward the fundamental value systems which create them.

Furthermore, **"Last Ride"** establishes the expansive implications of the central trope and, by extension, those of the entire collection by laying claim to epic stature. As the embodiment of collective cultural aspirations and as one willing to battle forces threatening the community, Wild Bill serves as epic hero in folk form. From Wild Bill's extended and detailed journey to his descent into the underworld, the poem takes on the trappings of high epic and thus a depth and breadth in metaphoric resonance.

But even with its epic scope, **"Last Ride"** announces itself as a ballad in the traditional sense: "verse narratives that tell dramatic stories in conventionalized ways."[4] Yet immediately evident are the reordered conventions. Brown replaces the standard quatrain structure and its regular meter with a new form which self-consciously calls attention to its own unconventionality. In fact Brown holds true to only the most basic tenets of balladry, often constructing for the reader a set of expectations, then systematically violating them, thereby instituting the concept of flux within the very matrix of the poem. Brown's lines range broadly in length. And though most lines consist of two or three stresses, the stresses themselves constantly move; so too, quasi-conventional lines seldom succeed each other for more than two or three lines, again breaking a regularity which is tenuous at best. For example, **"Challenge"** begins the poem with a six-line stanza proclaiming volatility and flux as major organizing principles for the poem:

> The new chief of police
> Banged his desk
> Called in the force, and swore
> That the number-running game was done
> And Wild Bill
> Would ride no more.

Here Brown demonstrates his range in length of line and the perpetual movement in stress within each line. That he consistently uses masculine endings and rhymes "swore" and "more" serve to create some sense of regularity. Throughout the poem these nearly sporadic reminders of regularity (hard stops, masculine endings, and occasional rhymes) strain to harness the potentially discursive energies of the poem, strain, in effect, to hold the poem back from free verse and thus from a full departure from folk oral and musical traditions. Yet all the while Brown utilizes short lines, enjambement, and irregular stresses in order to sustain a sense of rapid movement, almost a sense of tumbling.

As a result of this perpetual tension between regularity and irregularity, between conformity and freedom, the larger metaphoric implications of poetic form come into focus. Here Brown's self-conscious denial of formal expectations stresses the palpable and symbolic importance of transformation. By consistently breaking convention and refusing to meet standard expectations, Brown underscores Wild Bill's significance beyond the immediate poem. As motion and progression emerge from the very matrix of the poem, they contribute directly to the effect of the narrative and the symbolism of the ride. Perhaps this symbolism goes so far as to suggest Brown's own transformational powers in his revision of Western balladry in order to create new conceptual space for black agency.

As the narrative structure begins to give itself over to metaphor, it gives rise to the progression of the ride— the physical movement across the city and the symbolic agitation against confinement. In both senses the ride serves as a transformative act with Wild Bill looming as the symbolic figure embodying potential in transformation. As a folk form of the epic hero, the bad man, Wild Bill possesses special qualities in subverting and transforming the status quo. Stressing such abilities, Brown devotes a conspicuously large section of the poem to the reaction of the community rather than focusing strictly on the dramatic events of the chase. The wit and humor with which the various communities respond to the central conflict reveal the essential power behind Wild Bill and his ride:

> These were the people
> That the bug had bit,
> Betting now
> On a sure-fire hit:
> Kiwanians, and Rotarians
> Daughters, Sons, Cousins
> Of Confederate Veterans,
> The Kleagle of the Ku Klux Klan,
> The Knights of the Pantry
> And Dames of the Pan,
> The aristocrats, the landed gentry,
> The cracker, and the jigaboo
> Hoi-polloi
> All seemed to think well
> Of their boy,
> Were eager to lay
> Their bucks on Bill.

> On Druid Hill
> An old-stock cavalier tried to bet
> His yard-boy part of his back-pay due
> But Mose he believed in Wild Bill too.

Here, with much ironic humor, Brown allies groups which ordinarily would be diametrically opposed due to class and racial divisions. White/black, rich/poor, powerful/powerless, Wild Bill effectively dismantles these oppositions fundamental to the very meaning of the community. In subverting the status quo, he creates new conceptual ground where the rudimentary potential for redefinition lies.

Much of this potential rests on Wild Bill's symbolic meaning assigned by the newly united community. Even beyond the prospect of making money off his triumph, the community at large embraces Wild Bill as a repository of values far more significant than monetary gain. Thus being "their boy," he implicates an expansive iconographic field incorporating the American bad man, renegade, and hero. Defining himself on his own terms and thus occupying conceptual space outside of cultural conventions, Wild Bill invokes fundamental American myths celebrating the frontiersman, independence, and unbridled individuality; and it is precisely his ability to embody these mythic precepts which draws the admiration of the community. He sets conformity and self-reliance in practical and symbolic opposition by stating:

> "Ride my route
> Again today;
> Start at noon,
> End at three.
> Guess it will have
> To be you and me."

By responding to the demands of the authorities with an aggressive proclamation to defy them, he invokes an American romantic impulse toward individual freedom and independence. In this sense he does not so much threaten the community but upholds its fundamental beliefs. Here Wild Bill as outlaw is not simply a defensive metaphor,[5] temporarily thwarting the homogenizing effects of authority, but he looms as an aggressive representation of agency. More than checking the forces of authority, he agitates for space within the community for both freedom and independence.

Brown completes this notion of liberating transformation through an apotheosis redefining a highly symbolic space. Although Wild Bill lands in hell, the final site and evidence of his transformational abilities, his hell is a reconstructed one which reverses the assumed value of temporal and permanent life:

> The devils rushed at him
> In a swarm,
> And the cool
> Wild Bill
> Grew awful warm.
> It looked like he'd
> Broke up a meeting;
> But this was the Convocation's
> Greeting:
> They climbed all over
> His running board,
> "Wild Bill, Wild Bill!"
> Their shouting roared
> And rang through all the streets of Hell:

> "Give us the number,
> Wild Bill,
> Tell us
> What fell!"

Underestimating his own prowess, Wild Bill expects the Judeo-Christian notion of hell, one in which he will pay for a life of sin through eternal torment. But instead he finds a transformed hell which ultimately affirms the qualities for which he was killed. Here the final reversal relies on the juxtaposition of earth and hell. As the devils embrace Wild Bill as hero, earth and temporal reality become the site of perpetual persecution; conversely, Wild Bill's reconstructed hell then becomes the final site of resolution. In this apotheosis he expands as metaphor to represent a myriad of regenerative transformations. By subverting traditional and confining oppositions, by militating against oppressive authority, by living and dying according to self-defined principles, Wild Bill points toward a range of possibilities which lie beyond stasis and conventionality.

Thus by creating conceptual space for himself, he also points toward the possibilities suggested by the ensuing heroes and ballads. In short, **"The Last Ride of Wild Bill"** launches a collection of poems celebrating African-American heroism and its liberating potential. In response to this potential suggested through comedy, **"He Was a Man"** pursues potential in tragic representation. Returning to conventional balladry, Brown addresses the sobering brutality of folk life and the exorbitant costs of self-assertion. The poem, like **"Last Ride,"** works through ironic inconsistencies which conspire to defeat heroism; yet Brown meticulously constructs Will as the embodiment of social stability, one firmly grounded within the community and defined by stabilizing notions of work and family. As such he affirms the fundamental ties which supposedly hold cultures together. And in order to add pathos to Wild Bill's stature, the speaker declares that these attributes disqualify Will as hero:

> He wasn't nobody's great man,
>   He wasn't nobody's good,
> Was a po' boy tried to get from life
>   What happiness he could,
> He was a man, and they laid him down.

Brown pits Will's agency against that of the community; in these tragic circumstances Will's act of self-assertion in self-defense is met with a greater act of assertion. Killing a man in self-defense, he willfully accepts the truth of his actions: "Didn't catch him in no manhunt." But even more boldly the whites "Didn't hide themselves, didn't have no masks, / Didn't wear no Ku Klux hoods." And with a final ironic twist, at the site of social justice they destroy his claim to autonomy. Clearly Brown calls into question the concept of justice and ultimately deems the term void of meaning as the Sheriff and Coroner decline to pursue it. Thus irony becomes tragic as allegedly just officials turn murderous, killing one wholly in support of the community they vow to protect.

Brown's elliptical style also contributes to the cathartic force of the poem. As opposed to **"Last Ride,"** which provides an abundance of detail and celebrates the process of telling the tale, **"He Was a Man"** gains much of its force through omission. Simply the facts of the lynching speak for themselves, and only the one-line incremental refrain allows for much editorial comment. As this refrain connotes a fatigued and tragic inevitability, it also identifies the essential vitality of the hero, a vitality which exists beyond physical life, a vitality that, in fact, emerges through martyrdom. Because Will is a man, a black man no less, in the scheme of this poem the broader politics of the South demand his destruction; yet his destruction validates his agency. For both Will and Wild Bill, much of their heroism derives from their willingness to die for their convictions and from the culture's compulsion to curtail such rebellious assertions of self. Although the individual impulse toward self-assertion and the societal impulse to deny black self-hood collide to destroy the physical hero, they also conspire to create the symbol and thus the sustenance of the omnipresent spirit. Therefore the poem laments Will's loss but implicitly validates an immortality which will manifest itself in ensuing poems.

As this second poem inaugurates the theme of tragic representation, it looks forward to **"Sam Yancey"** and the further extension of the tragic mode. **"Sam Yancey,"** **"Crispus Attucks McKoy,"** and **"Break of Day"** all represent the hero as a liberating potential tragically cut short. In each poem the hero embodies essential strengths common to the culture yet threatening to white authority. And in each instance, in the classic mode of the hero, he asserts these strengths, strives to defend them, and ultimately dies as a result of his agency. Martyrdom serves as the supreme affirmation of heroism, where superlative sacrifice in defense of self and culture ostensibly points toward an irrepressible continuity in heroic spirit. Each time the physical avatar is struck down, another manifestation of the spirit appears, insuring sustained agitation for freedom and independence.

Having established this strident sense of agency in both comic and tragic modes, Brown presents the Slim Greer series, which examines both the strengths and limitations of the comic hero. Following **"Sam Yancey,"** Brown moves away from the high price of heroism to complete the Slim Greer series and its exploration of humor's potential. In 1932 Brown first presented Slim Greer in *Southern Road,* with only the first three poems: **"Slim Greer,"** **"Slim Lands a Job?"** and **"Slim in Atlanta."** With this configuration Greer clearly conforms to the standard definition of the trickster, consistently subverting white authority through wit and humor. His introductory poem, **"Slim Greer,"** outlines his persona and demonstrates both his ability to circumvent social restrictions and his ability to use them for his own gain. Beyond the immediate action of the drama though, Slim's ability as comic figure reveals his superlative gifts in absurdity and burlesque. His outlandishness and the circumstances in which he finds himself acquire dramatic force in their power to diffuse oppressive situations, transforming them into moments of celebration.

It is within this context that the first three Slim Greer poems add a humorous dimension to the master trope, "the road" in *Southern Road.* But by completing the series and placing all five poems in *Last Ride,* Brown implies critically different connotations. First, by moving away from high burlesque, the latter two poems incorporate more ominous implications for both Greer's character and his ability to affect his surroundings. Furthermore, in relation to the broader signifying field of *Last Ride,* the Slim Greer series exposes the limitations of comic representation and thereby alludes to its final subsumption in **"The Ballad of Joe Meek."**

Following **"Slim in Atlanta,"** **"Slim Hears 'The Call'"** continues the mode of burlesque but raises serious questions concerning Slim's use of his transformative powers. Simply the title's calling special attention to "the call" questions its ultimate meaning, finally resulting in an ironic call to make money rather than to serve God. Furthermore, **"Slim Hears 'the Call'"** deviates from standard presentation in that it is Greer's own narrative. Rather than a third-person narrative celebrating Greer's ability to outwit whites and to undermine potentially oppressive circumstances, Greer tells his own story of victimizing the powerless. The poem begins invoking the tradition of exaggeration and hyperbole, and much of its amusing quality stems from Greer's mastery of style and form. In the first two stanzas Greer recreates his adversity in order to illicit laughter, not pity. Rather than illustrating the severity of his condition, he better demonstrates his rhetorical skills and mastery of form, a mastery implicitly asserting control over much more than oratorical tropes:

> Down at the barbershop
>   Slim had the floor,
> "Ain't never been so
> Far down before.
>
>   "So ragged, I make a jaybird
>   About to moult,
>   Look like he got on gloves
>   An' a overcoat
>
> "Got to walk backwards
>   All de time
> Jes' a-puttin' on front
>   Wid a bare behime."

Indeed Greer's display of rhetorical expertise serves as a prelude to his mastery of a cultural form, "de bishopric"; thus his tale is one of apprenticeship in

preparation for his next money-making scheme. Greer retells, with humorous irony, the mercenary practices of a fraudulent clergyman that his friend misrepresents himself, steals from his congregation, and ultimately undermines the religious imperative of his position, for Greer constitutes the epitome of cunning and shrewdness. Greer's admiration ultimately is for the ability to control, manipulate, and make money with the least amount of effort:

> So here he was de head man
>   Of de whole heap—
> Wid dis solemn charge dat
>   He had to keep:
>
>   "A passel of Niggers
>   From near an' far
>   Bringin' in de sacred bucks
>   Regular."

And Greer ends his apprenticeship and his amusing tale with a resounding endorsement of this enterprise and with an embracing call for everyone so inclined to do as he does. On the one hand Greer successfully promotes the same persona celebrated in the previous three poems: he is witty, resourceful, and, above all, farcically entertaining. But as he shifts the focus of his talents away from the empowered to the dispossessed, he begins to work against the iconography previously assigned him. He no longer ridicules and dismantles figures and forces of oppression; he now reinforces them. Clearly Brown pokes fun at the disreputable figures in the African-American clergy; and clearly enough, too, is the attempt to add levity to the sobering reality of African-American exploitation in one of its most important institutions. But in terms of Greer's development, and in terms of his broader implications within the collection, **"Slim Hears 'the Call'"** constitutes a serious departure from the established metaphoric development.

Greer's willful exultation of his own ability to exploit begins to indicate the limitations of burlesque. At this point the mode of the tale subsumes the overt politics of the content; humor begins to serve its own ends— pure entertainment—and thus divorces itself from a broader political context.

This implication, that the very form which Greer represents necessarily embodies severe limitations in terms of historical vision, receives further treatment in the last poem of the series. **"Slim in Hell"** entertains a number of potentially sobering ironies while sustaining the tradition of the burlesque. The premise of the poem—Greer in an odd situation—automatically advances the comic mode of the series. But given the comic conventions, that Greer finds hell to be in truth the South strikes a poignantly accurate note. As St. Peter corroborates Greer's encroaching suspicions, comedy quickly becomes satire:

Then Pete say, "You must
　　Be crazy, I vow,
Where'n hell dja think Hell *was,*
　　Anyhow?

This acerbic indictment of the South and its racial politics works in and of itself to darken the implications of the poem. But that the poem ends not with the realization of such a harsh reality but with Greer's expulsion from heaven due to his limited vision shifts the focus from the injustice of the South to Greer's misunderstanding of its ramifications:

"Git on back to de yearth,
Cause I got de fear
You'se a leetle too dumb,
　　Fo' to stay up here . . ."

As a product of the South and as one having resisted many of its stifling forces, Greer fails to perceive the literally cosmic implications of racial oppression. In the broadest of religious schemes hell and Dixie hold the same literal meaning which its victims are expected to understand. That Greer fails calls into question his understanding of his own gifts and the implications of their application. Although he perceives and fights the oppression directed specifically at him, he does not read beyond his own circumstances; nor does he invoke an appreciation for a continuum of oppressive forces. Simply put, Greer exists in an historical vacuum, employing only ad hoc measures of resistance; therefore, due to an extremely truncated view of his own condition, Greer's talents remain restricted to his specific circumstances. That Brown ends the series with Greer's expulsion from heaven due to his misreading implicates the entirety of his progression and finally raises the issue of his limitations. As the trickster fails to see or act beyond his own self-interest—thus perpetually assuming a defensive rather that offensive political position—Brown begins to circumscribe the comic mode of the hero within a limited metaphoric and political sphere, limited at least relative to the final expansion of the tragic hero and his import.

Brown responds to the subtle but serious encroachment upon Slim Greer's levity with an unequivocal canonization of a figure fully aware of the political imperatives of his circumstances. **"Crispus Attucks McKoy"** explores the transcendent heroic spirit, a spirit completely dedicated to both individual and collective liberation. As in **"Last Ride,"** Brown creates a dramatically new ballad form in order to stress the monumental precedent which McKoy represents. Yet in contrast to the continual changes in **"Last Ride,"** the form of **"Crispus Attucks McKoy"** is ultimately uniform and immediately self-evident. Brown's regimented eight-line stanzas, complete with regular rhyme and meter, first create a strident sense of regularity and clarity. As the speaker asserts an uncompromising vision of hero-

ism, so, too, does the form affirm a sense of strength and assurance. Equally as important, but somewhat less obvious, Brown borders on formal rigidity in order to emphasize a consistent historical progression linking past, present, and future. Just as each stanza succeeds the previous one in a predictable fashion—almost marching toward the inevitable apotheosis in martyrdom—that "The soul of our hero / Goes marching on . . ." ultimately affirms the inevitable progression of the heroic spirit.

Following the profundity of martyrdom, Brown advances the exchange between comic and tragic, presenting John Bias in **"A Bad, Bad Man."** Setting **"A Bad, Bad Man"** against **"Break of Day,"** John Bias serves as the farcical antithesis to the self-determined tragic hero, while Big Jess epitomizes the tragic martyr. Here, where Big Jess completes the tragic lineage begun with Sam Yancey, Joe Meek picks up both strands of representation in order to provide the broadest array of transformational possibilities for both kinds of heroes.

As the first and last stanzas indicate, Brown frames Joe Meek's ballad within two illustrations suggesting a wealth of meanings residing just below surface appearances. **"The Ballad of Joe Meek,"** as Brown's final representation of the hero, affirms the ubiquitous nature of the heroic spirit and thus completes Wild Bill's transformational ride. Joe Meek becomes "Joe Hero," a compelling combination of ordinariness and extraordinariness, championing the cause of the downtrodden and illustrating the heroic potential lurking in the most unlikely individuals.

Stressing the intrinsic meaning hidden behind deceptive surfaces, Brown constructs the entire poem around the tension between the external and internal, between superficial illusion and permanent meaning: "You cain't never tell, / How far a frog will jump, / When you jes' see him planted / On his big broad jump." In a conversation with Clark White, Brown comments: "[T]he Joe Meek piece is an ideal peace and it's [sic] meaning is: don't believe the appearance of my people by the way they look. . . . [W]ith Joe Meek the dramatic turn was the injustice. . . . [W]e can take so much and then take no more."[6] Initially the form itself invokes and advances the absurdity developed in the Slim Greer series. The short lines and regular quatrains convey a light, homespun folk voice which seems to indicate yet another tall tale in the burlesque. Yet the form and its comic implications belie the intrinsically political ramifications of Joe Meek's narrative. In sharp contrast to its form, the poem's content follows the basic pattern of hero construction initiated in **"Last Ride."** The solitary figure, stridently committed to his own principles, dares to combat the established order bent on compromising those principles. Of course this battle ends in martyrdom; thus in terms of fundamental patterns, Joe Meek echoes Wild Bill's implications and completes a lineage including Will, Sam Yancey, Crispus McKoy, and Big Jess.

Thus we find that beneath the surface of the comic voice and form lie both the tragedy of potential destroyed and the promise of transformation. In this sense **"The Ballad of Joe Meek"** culminates the exploration of the heroic nature and finds its potential omnipresent. The title itself constructs Joe as the most unlikely candidate for martyrdom. Mild mannered and conciliatory to a fault, his fundamental disposition would usually allow the status quo to exist undisturbed and unchallenged. Yet given a catalyst for transformation, Meek becomes the epitome of the cultural hero. The catalyst here, heat, promotes aberrant behavior in beetles, pet bunnies, and babies, but exposes in Meek an essential and permanent nature. That "Joe didn't feel / So agreeable" is certainly a direct result of the heat, but after "The sun had gone down" and "The air it was cool," Joe continues his defiant behavior. In both cases, Joe's actions serve as manifestations of a latent heroic nature. In a typically mild manner he asks the officers whether they had done "just right," and asks at his death for "one kindness / Fo' I die." These gestures and his willingness to battle an entire police department transform his "meekness" into strength and conviction, and finally reveal his heroic essence.

Finally affirming his heroism Brown places Meek in direct reference to John Henry:

> "Won't be here much
>   To bother you so,
> Would you bring me a drink of water
>   Fo' I go?"

Just as John Henry asks for a "Cool drink of water 'fore I die," Joe Meek asks for the same practical and symbolic solace. In a mode similar to Big Boy Davis, of **"Odyssey of Big Boy"** fame, Joe Meek invokes the tradition which holds permanent meaning for both his life and death. Where Big Boy Davis invokes the rhetorical form of his idol John Henry, Joe Meek quotes him directly, attempting to achieve a similar affinity. Furthermore, Brown assigns Joe a greater degree of metaphoric weight by linking his martyrdom, and the vision of justice which his martyrdom represents, to that of John Henry, perhaps the broadest symbol of black cultural agency.

In addition, Brown lends even greater resonance to his encompassing notion of transformation through the conversion of the comic into the tragic. **"The Ballad of Joe Meek"** serves as an apt conclusion to a collection of ballads and heroes in that it combines the two dominant modes of portrayal in order to utilize the most expressive traits of each. As an exaggerated tall tale,

this ballad reinvokes the tradition of lies. But as we have already seen, Brown calls into question the broader scope of the comic hero's abilities. As Slim Greer makes explicit, neither he nor Wild Bill see or act beyond their own self-interest. Moving beyond the confines of self-concern, it is the tragic hero's task, particularly Joe Meek's, to exercise agency in a public sphere, to act on behalf of the surrounding community, and in doing so the tragic hero extends the nearly limitless potential of transformation to incorporate acts of liberation. Thus both in mode and metaphor Joe Meek successfully subsumes the comic hero and reconstructs him as a public agent for the greater community.

Returning to the framing notion of deceptive appearance, Joe Meek's tale ends alluding to the heroic possibilities lying dormant in unlikely places, thus ending a collection which celebrates the folk hero by ultimately democratizing the figure. Here, finally, Brown's notion of heroic transformation achieves its broadest scope. With Joe Meek as central metaphor for the collection Brown ultimately creates conceptual space for the reader. Joe the commoner validates the patently unromantic, yet he stresses that we all are heir to the legacy which John Henry and Wild Bill represent. As the collection ends, "The soul of our hero / Goes marching on. . . ." Unimpeded by the murders of specific figures, the idea and symbol of the hero remain immortal and continue to point toward future incarnations.

Indeed, by employing a number of cultural icons—the badman, the renegade, the humble worker trying to do right, etc.—and various ballad forms, the collection creates a diversified or multidimensional face for the heroic impulse, one perpetually agitating against social conventions and white authority. The ride, formally and metaphorically, invokes progression, movement from specific to general, from renegade (and therefore aberration) to commoner, symbolically embracing all. Through this movement beyond the stasis of a singular cultural image, Brown attempts to portray a dynamic which prompts the culture as a whole to confront imposed limitations. In short, Brown's ballads seek to locate power and potential implicit yet latent within the culture. And having done so, the collection has discovered and affirmed an essential means by which African-American culture attempts to realize its own liberation.

Notes

1. Joanne V. Gabbin, *Sterling Brown: Building the Black Aesthetic Tradition* (Westport: Greenwood, 1985) 59.

2. James G. Spady, "Ah! To Have Lived in the Days of the 'Senegambian,' Sterling Brown," *Sterling A. Brown: A UMUM Tribute,* ed. Black History Museum Committee (Philadelphia: Black History Museum Publishers, 1982) 35.

3. Gary Smith, "The Literary Ballads of Sterling Brown," *CLA Journal* 32 (June 1989): 396.

4. Malcolm Laws, Jr., *The British Literary Ballad: A Study in Poetic Imagination* (Carbondale: Southern Illinois UP, 1972) xi.

5. Bruce Jackson, in "Get Your Ass in the Water and Swim Like Me": *Narrative Poetry from Black Oral Tradition* (Cambridge: Harvard UP, 1974) 31, suggests that the prototypical badman serves as a "challenge to hegemony."

6. Clark White, "Sterling Brown, 'The Ole Sheep, They Know the Road . . . Young Lambs Gotta Find the Way': An Essay Dedicated to Ole 'Skeeta Brown," *Sterling A. Brown: A UMUM Tribute,* ed. Black History Museum Committee, (Philadelphia: Black History Museum Publishers, 1982) 114-15.

Michael Tomasek Manson (essay date spring 1996)

SOURCE: Manson, Michael Tomasek. "Sterling Brown and the 'Vestiges' of the Blues: The Role of Race in English Verse Structure." *MELUS* 21, no. 1 (spring 1996): 21-40.

[*In the following essay, Manson analyzes the verse structure of Brown's "Challenge" and explores the role of race in the poem.*]

Although poets continue to discuss the significance of particular poetic forms or verse schemes, literary critics less frequently examine the constitutive nature of such structures.[1] We usually comment on large structures like the sonnet or small ones like metrical variations only in order to drive home a point that originated elsewhere, in some other textual, biographical, historical, or cultural inquiry. Less often do we *begin* with versification as a way of understanding history or ideology, even though it is frequently the starting place for poets.

This trivialization of prosody in literary criticism has as much to do with the dominance of the field by linguists as with the desire of literary critics to move beyond the formalism of the New Criticism and embrace psychoanalysis, marxism, feminism, new historicism, and other extratextual literary theories. The "scientific" density of linguistic analyses of versification make prosody seem stuffy and pointless, while the New Criticism has made verse structure difficult to imagine as anything but a closed, coherent linguistic universe outside history.

The most successful attempt to break these habits has been Antony Easthope's 1983 study, *Poetry As Discourse*. Drawing on Ferdinand de Saussure, Louis Althusser, and Jacques Lacan, Easthope first approaches poetry as verse structure and then finds in that structure history, psychology, and materialism. In short, he finds *in* formalism what others have tried to find *beyond* it. Looking at the most common structure in English verse, Easthope describes iambic pentameter as "an epochal form, co-terminous with the capitalist mode of production and the hegemony of the bourgeoisie as the ruling class" (24) and explains not only how it differs from the hegemonic poetic discourse of the feudal era, but also how it developed from the Renaissance to the Augustan and Romantic periods to unravel during Modernism.

Easthope's work thus lays a foundation for a truly *literary* history by arguing that verse scheme—the very materiality of poetry—is a discourse, fully embedded in a dialectical history. With this important step made, we can now examine how the intersection of "poetic" discourse with other discourses, like race, produces poetry. Easthope tells the story of the emergence, consolidation, and disintegration of iambic pentameter as a hegemonic discourse, but of necessity he focuses on the poets who made that history—Shakespeare, Pope, Wordsworth, and Pound—not the poets who resisted that history even while they were constituted by it. I will examine **"Challenge,"** a sonnet from Sterling Brown's 1932 volume **Southern Road,** because it offers a particularly dramatic example of how Easthope's terms produce a partial reading of the poem that requires the insights of African American literary theory to produce a fuller and more satisfying account. The result will be a union of linguistic and literary theory that begins in an analysis of verse schemes. I hope to show that a better formalism will yield a better material and cultural analysis.

1

I SAID, IN DRUNKEN PRIDE OF YOUTH AND YOU,
THAT MISCHIEF-MAKING TIME WOULD NEVER DARE
PLAY HIS ILL-HUMORED TRICKS UPON US TWO,
STRANGE AND DEFIANT LOVERS THAT WE WERE.
I SAID THAT EVEN DEATH, HIGHWAYMAN DEATH,   5
COULD NEVER MASTER LOVERS SUCH AS WE,
THAT EVEN WHEN HIS CLUTCH HAD THROTTLED BREATH,
MY HYMNS WOULD FLOAT IN PRAISE, UNDAUNTEDLY.
I DID NOT THINK SUCH WORDS WERE BRAVADO.
OH, I THINK HONESTLY WE KNEW NO FEAR,   10
OF TIME OR DEATH. WE LOVED EACH OTHER SO.
AND THUS, WITH YOU BELIEVING ME, I MADE MY
PROPHECIES, REBELLIOUS, UNAFRAID. . . .
AND THAT WAS FOOLISH, WASN'T IT, MY DEAR?

"Challenge" exhibits many of the features Easthope discerns in William Shakespeare's sonnet 73 (97-109). Sonnet 73 serves Easthope as an example of the "founding moment" of bourgeois poetic discourse, and he contrasts its prosodic effects with those of the feudal ballad. He argues that the ballad (and other accentual schemes) form a "sociolect" by drawing "on a common and intersubjective discourse" (160). Its loose syntax, its use of parataxis, and its nonsense rhymes all celebrate the play of the signifier and ask the reader to think of it as "an act of pleasurable speaking." The result is "a poetic discourse that offers a *relative* position for the ego, a position produced in acknowledged relationship to a field of forces, social, subjective, linguistic" (93).

The bourgeois discourse created by iambic pentameter, however, "aims first of all to represent an individual speaking" (93). Instead of parataxis, we have a strong syntagmatic structure of subordinated sentences and clauses that lead inexorably to the final line, and, instead of the pleasure of nonsense rhymes, the rhymes are subordinate to the meaning. Whatever pleasure we derive from hearing Brown rhyme "we" with "undauntedly" is subordinated to the rhyme's thematic significance: it is the solidity of the union (of the "we") that makes the undaunted posture possible.

Finally, the very structure of iambic pentameter creates the effect of an idiosyncratic, speaking voice, the sound of a single person referring to a reality beyond himself and thus guaranteeing "the speaker's existence as a subject" (100). Accentualism—now used almost exclusively in nursery rhymes, jump rope chants, football cheers, and marching and protest chants—produces a community even when it speaks the word "I." For example, Brown's **"Odyssey of Big Boy"** begins with an individual's voice,

> Lemme be wid Casey Jones,
> Lemme be wid Stagolee,
> Lemme be wid such like men
> When Death takes hol' on me,
>   When Death takes hol' on me. . . .
>
>   (20)

But, although Big Boy was Brown's friend, we do not hear an individual's voice as much as we hear the voice of a tradition and a community. This "sociolect" is created by references to other, perhaps historical, characters who have achieved mythic status (Odysseus, Casey Jones, Stagolee), but more importantly, it is created by an accentual scheme that asks us to chant along with it and feel it as our own. Although she does not remark on accentualism's role in producing this effect, Hazel Carby captures it when she follows John Coltrane in noting that the "I" of the blues singer always suggests the "we" of the blues community (15). The subjectivity created by accentualism is relative rather than transcendent.

Iambic pentameter, however, creates a reality in which the subjective is contrasted with the objective. Big Boy's mythic community (which is chanted into exist-ence with our voices) gives way in **"Challenge"** to a contrast between the "I" of the speaker and the "you" of the lover. As John Stuart Mill suggested, we overhear the lyric. Instead of chanting iambic pentameter, we follow its logic as it engages the objective world. In accentual meter, there is usually only one way to perform a verse—the voice is a collective one, just as in a chant—but in iambic pentameter, the fifth stress evens out intonation along the line and allows readers to find their own, idiosyncratic representation of the speaker's lone voice (72-74).[2] For us as readers, pentameter gives the speaker of **"Challenge"** a concreteness that Big Boy does not possess; Big Boy is a character, almost as much a stock figure as Stagolee.[3] The primary aim of iambic pentameter, however, is "to make the subject 'see' itself as a transcendental ego, an *absolutely* free agent, centre and origin of action, unproduced, given once and for all" (28).[4]

Concluding his description of iambic pentameter, Easthope says,

> Clearly, in the aggressive early days of the struggle for bourgeois hegemony, especially around 1600, the pentameter had a novelty and glamour that was long gone in 1900. Now the pentameter is a dead form and its continued use (e.g. by Philip Larkin) is in the strict sense reactionary.
>
>   (76)

Logically, Easthope's comments here about Larkin and any post-1900 use of pentameter would extend to Brown's work, and indeed Brown's own comments and practice seem to justify Easthope's conclusions.

In his critical essays, Brown maintained a distinction between "subjective" and "objective" verse. Subjective verse expresses the poet's "deepest thoughts and feelings" (*Negro Poetry and Drama* 80), usually in "lyrics on the ageless and raceless themes of love and disappointed youth and death" (*Caravan* 280).[5] Objective verse, however, is "dramatic" (*Negro Poetry and Drama* 71), focused on the lives of others. Brown reinforces this distinction in the structure of **Southern Road** by placing all the portraits of African American life in the first three sections and all the personal lyrics of love and loss in the final section. Furthermore, he thematizes the distinction by organizing the four sections of **Southern Road** into a narrative sequence. The first two sections describe the life of rural Southern blacks, the third portrays the migration north into the cities, and the fourth delineates Brown's own inner life, that of an urban intellectual, a member of the talented tenth. This final section is entitled "Vestiges," raising an ambiguity about this road out of the South. Literally a footprint, a vestige can be a point of pride, the tracks in the road still present in the urban son's life; but in Darwinian terms, a vestige can also be a remnant from some previous stage of evolution. The dramatic shift from the vernacular verse schemes of the first three sections of **Southern Road** to the traditional European American ones of the last section could suggest either that we should search the poems in "Vestiges" for the footprints of Scotty and Maumee Ruth or that we applaud the evolution of these poems beyond the earlier ones.[6]

Using Easthope's theory alone, we might thus see **Southern Road** as doubly reactionary—first in its use of pentameter and second in its implication that progress for African Americans lies in writing sonnets on what Brown himself called "ageless and raceless themes." Easthope's theory can help us ground prosody in material history, but unaided it cannot theorize the role of race in English verse structure. It cannot help us understand the seeming contradiction between the implied narrative of **Southern Road** and its stature as one of the great works of African American poetry. For that, we need to examine the intersection of poetic discourse with other discourses.

2

In trying to describe what is specifically "African American" in African American literature, many theorists have argued that these writers have constructed a literary tradition out of such extra-literary structures as jazz, the blues, signifying, call-and-response, and speaking-in-tongues.[7] In *Blues, Ideology, and Afro-American Culture* (1984), Houston Baker, like Easthope, focuses on the material: troping Karl Marx's notion of wage slavery, Baker argues that African American life is shaped by the "economics of slavery," the continuing intersection of class and race in the United States. He prefers terms like "vernacular" over "dialect" and "expressive culture" over "literature," because he wants to preserve the literal meaning of "vernacular" ("of a slave") and because "expressive culture" includes the full range of African American creativity. Taking the blues as a metaphor for all of this creativity, Baker argues that African American expressivity creates "the blues" whenever it resists the "economics of slavery," producing a "racial sounding" that gathers class and mass into a "nation."

Baker's terminology can help us build on Easthope and complete our partial reading of Brown if we think of it as acting as a bridge between scheme and trope. As an "expressive structure," a "racial sounding" would include both scheme and trope; it would refer to a "structure" (a word pattern or scheme) that "expresses" (or tropes) some meaning. For example, we say the scheme for most blues is AAB (the first line is repeated), but, as Sherley Anne Williams notes, the scheme acts as a trope for community, the B line answering the A lines, as in call-and-response (77).

How then do we hear a racial sounding in **"Challenge,"** in a poem that seems utterly European American in

both scheme and trope, in a poem that seems to carry no racial markers at all? Baker points to a methodology when he ends *Blues, Ideology, and Afro-American Literature* with a call for scholars to situate themselves at a railroad "crossing sign in order to materialize vernacular faces" and to respond to those faces as energetically as blues artist Sonny Terry did to guitarist Brownie McGhee. When McGhee intones,

> "Let me hear you squall, boy, like you never squalled before!" The answer is a whooping, racing, moaning harmonica stretch that takes one's breath away, invoking forms, faces, and places whose significance was unknown prior to the song's formidable inscriptions.

> (203)

Baker's call here is one that Brown himself answered much earlier when he rejected dialect poetry and attended to the voices of rural Southern blacks. He studied the blues, visited juke joints, and got to know blues artists like Big Boy in order to write a poetry and a criticism that responded to those vernacular voices. If we follow Brown to the crossroads, we can hear four distinct racial soundings in a sonnet about the "ageless and raceless" theme of love.

3

As we have seen, for Easthope, modern poems in pentameter are "reactionary" because their reproduction of an individual speaking voice reinscribes the hegemonic individualism of the bourgeois social order. Pentameter is particularly insidious because it makes us feel we are in the presence of a person actually speaking at the same time that it requires that we *mouth* that person's speech. In other words, we both watch a transcendent subjectivity in action and are required to feel our own subjectivity as transcendent. While accentualism requires a communal intonation and an intersubjective interpretation, pentameter allows a person to give a line a number of intonations depending on his or her own interpretation.

We find a rather different kind of mouth at Baker's crossroads. When Terry makes his harmonica squall, he puts the instrument to a use unintended by its European inventors. Designed so that any blow or suck on the instrument creates a harmonious chord, the harmonica was transformed by blues artists who reshaped their mouths and throats in order to bend the reeds and make the instrument whoop and moan. By the time we reach **"Challenge,"** we have read almost fifty poems in a vernacular, accentual verse. We have heard Brown play a blues harmonica on the English language almost fifty times, creating sounds (and soundings) not available to standard English. If we take Easthope seriously when he describes the different subjectivities and "mouths" created by accentual and pentameter verse, reading any of the poems in "Vestiges" requires that we reshape our mouths just as harmonica players do in shifting from bluesy bends to harmonious chords. Prosodically, then, **"Challenge"** is not an isolated text but is accompanied by our awareness that Brown's mouth—and our own as we have reproduced Brown's in the collective chanting of accentual verse—has undergone a great transformation. In other words, by the time we reach **"Challenge,"** the previous accentual prosody has prepared us to hear in pentameter not the voice of a transcendent, bourgeois subjectivity but the specific voice of an African American.

The specificity of Brown's mouth is further highlighted—not deemphasized—by the poem's conventional treatment of love. To help explain this paradox, we can turn to legal scholar Patricia J. Williams, who has described how hegemonic discourse takes on a radically different meaning when uttered from African American mouths. Williams's specific target is those members of the Critical Legal Studies movement (CLS) who have argued that the fight for equal rights is "'positively harmful'" (151). She agrees with their poststructuralist analysis of rights as "unstable and indeterminate," but she also realizes that the alternative ("needs" talk) works only for privileged European Americans (148). While CLS desires a world without boundaries, African Americans remember that they have never had boundaries and have always been "free" for intrusion. They remember how they nurtured civil rights:

> . . . we gave them life where there was none before; we held onto them, put the hope of them into our wombs, mothered them and not the notion of them. And this was not the dry process of reification, from which life is drained and reality fades as the cement of conceptual determinism hardens round—but its opposite. This was the resurrection of life from ashes four hundred years old.
>
> (163)

This long labor of resurrection is why

> "Rights" feel new in the mouths of most black people. It is still deliciously empowering to say. It is the magic wand of visibility and invisibility, of inclusion and exclusion, of power and no power. The concept of rights, both positive and negative, is the marker of our citizenship, our relation to others.
>
> (164)

While European Americans have used rights as a tool of power, that same tool in African American mouths, Williams says, creates a "relation to others."

Once we attend to race, then, the use of pentameter—which for Easthope is "reactionary"—becomes in addition liberatory. If Williams is right, when Brown utters a transcendent self in "Challenge," he must be feeling something "new" and "deliciously empowering" in his mouth. He is "mouthing off" to those who would deny him his humanity. Indeed, to insist that he produce a more intersubjective, destabilized self would be to ask him to "free" himself for more intrusion.[8] Moreover, such a request ignores Brown's achievement in persuading his readers, black and white, to listen to a specifically African American mouth speak as a voice of power and authority. There is a racial sounding in the poem and in Brown's transcendent subjectivity after all.

4

Standing at the crossroads Baker describes, Sonny Terry is not alone. His "squalls" answer guitarist Brownie McGhee in the call-and-response pattern familiar to readers of African American literature and literary theory. The two blues artists create a racial sounding when they build a community or a "nation" out of their personal whoops and moans. By comparison, **"Challenge"** seems impoverished because it lacks a nation to which it either calls or responds. But the poem seems so only if we forget that the blues are not solely an expression of African American creativity, but also arise from an intersection with the country and folk music created by impoverished European Americans: African Americans met other people at the crossroads with guitar in hand. Once we examine the diction of **"Challenge,"** we can hear a racial sounding neither as the vernacular (Baker), nor as a tool for empowerment (Williams), but as a call for a "chorus," a nation of nations, the second of my four perspectives.

Although standard literary histories of twentieth century verse still focus on experimental modernism, Brown himself claimed that the New Poets were far more important to the development of African American verse than was the avant-garde. "The New Poetry Movement," he tells us,

> sponsored by critics like Amy Lowell, Harriet Monroe, and Louis Untermeyer, anthologized by Untermeyer and Braithwaite, and producing such important poets as Edwin Arlington Robinson, Robert Frost, Vachel Lindsay, Edgar Lee Masters, and Carl Sandburg, had a nationwide influence. The movement repudiated sentimentality, didacticism, optimism, romantic escape, and "poetic" diction. The lessons it taught were beneficial to Negro poets.
>
> (*Caravan* 280)

For Brown, the lessons of the New Poets involved both trope (sentimentality, and so on) and scheme ("poetic" diction). In saying so, he followed the lead of Louis Untermeyer. Untermeyer's 1919 anthology, *Modern American Poetry,* represented the New Poets' departure from the genteel tradition epitomized by Jessie Rittenhouse's 1913 collection, *The Little Book of Modern Verse.*[9] Rittenhouse included love sonnets whose diction was self-consciously "poetic":

My love for thee doth take me unaware,
  When most with lesser things my brain is wrought,
  As in some nimble interchange of thought
The silence enters, and the talkers stare.

(128)

The poeticisms in these lines by Richard Hovey range from archaisms ("thee") to syntactic inversions ("When most with lesser things my brain is wrought").[10] In his introduction, Untermeyer recommends discarding these schemes or word patterns. He notes that he has collected poets who no longer use contractions like "'twixt," padded phrases like "doth smile," or clichés like "heavenly blue." These changes have resulted in a "great gain in sincerity and intensity" (xlvi).

Untermeyer connects these changes in scheme to the development of the United States as a "nation." Unlike standard literary histories, then and now, Untermeyer's locates the beginning of a national literature not with the Puritans or the American Renaissance but in the West. The Civil War marks for him the end of a New England "aristocracy" governed by Emerson and Longfellow and the beginnings of a "political nationalism and industrial reconstruction" led by "new men" who "must have seemed like a regiment recruited from the ranks of vulgarity." These new men included Walt Whitman, Mark Twain, and dialect writers like Joel Chandler Harris, "men who had graduated from the farm, the frontier, the mine, the pilot-house, the printer's shop!" (xvii-xviii). This "spontaneous national expression," Untermeyer argues, was "averted" (xviii) by establishment poets and the moral lassitude of the Gilded Age, but then "the war with Spain, the industrial turmoil, the growth of social consciousness and new ideas of responsibility made America look for fresh valuations, more searching songs" (xxviii). The ultimate result was the 1913 "renascence," the New Poetry (xxx).

Through Untermeyer, Brown's work thus contributes to an American nationalism as well as to a black one. His poetry makes apparent what has always been true in the United States: that Slim Greer and Ma Rainey work alongside Miniver Cheevy, Chicago meat packers, and those who live in Spoon River or north of Boston. Although **"Challenge"** is not concerned with folk life, the syntactic clarity and simple diction of lines like "Oh, I think honestly we knew no fear, / Of Time or Death" communicates Brown's earnest desire to speak to an audience of his equals, to men and women of all races and classes who are struggling for the recognition of their humanity against institutional oppression. Untermeyer's list of radical causes—the protest against the United States's imperialist war with Spain (1898) and the struggle for the rights of workers at home—does not explicitly include the fight against Jim Crow and for an anti-lynching law, but, by speaking in the language of the New Poets, Brown invites that audience to add racism to their agenda. However flawed in its practice, this poetry was more concerned with the politics and possibilities of the Progressive era than with T. S. Eliot's fear that a common European culture had collapsed. For the New Poets, a truly common culture was just beginning to be born through a diversity of voices.

If we understand racial sounding to include the sound of a chorus of nations within the U.S. demanding a more democratic society, then a racial sounding issues through **"Challenge"**'s colloquial diction and syntax: the diction is not black vernacular, but it appreciatively alludes to work being done by other poets to bring forward other forgotten peoples. This appreciation reaches its finest moment when Brown allows the tone to elevate around the thoroughly conventional and "poetic" image of "Highwayman Death." The simple, New Poetical syntax opens up the conventional image to a new meaning, a special, ironic significance for all the impoverished nations that travel U.S. highways, nations from every continent who fear that Death may yet rob them before they find the economic and social peace they seek. A chorus can be made at any crossroads where people meet with a guitar and, with Blind Lemon Jefferson, wonder "would a matchbox hold my clothes."

5

In describing the discourse created by an African American use of Anglo-American verse schemes, we have imagined Brown's mouth around a harmonica, and we have imagined him playing at the crossroads with Frost and Sandburg, but we have not yet imagined him standing next to Brownie McGhee replying to McGhee's call to squall "like you never squalled before." We have not yet imagined **"Challenge"** as a "blues sonnet."

Earlier, we watched the shape of Brown's mouth change as he switched from playing a blues harmonica in the early sections of *Southern Road* to playing harmonious chords in "Vestiges," but we did not examine what it might mean to Brown personally for Brownie McGhee to ask him to "squall like you never squalled before." To expect Brown to squall the blues, however, would be to flatten the variety of African American life, reduce it to a singular "black experience," and to trivialize the blues, for such an expectation would miss the economic/racial component that Baker places at their center. Baker defines the blues as an "affirmation of human identity in the face of dehumanizing circumstance" and argues that they are a "product of the actual impoverishment of blacks in America" (*Blues* 190, 197). The blues, he claims, are "unthinkable in well-endowed circumstances" (197). The alienation of a Sonny Terry, then, his blues, is so keen because after he has lost his lover, he has nowhere else to turn for community in this racist and impoverished world. Everything else in his life denies his humanity.

What makes Brown's sonnet so unlike the blues is a confident air breathed by those born to privilege. And relatively speaking, Brown was privileged. Born to a middle-class family and living not in the Deep South but in the border city of Washington, D.C., Brown had the opportunity to attend not only college but also graduate school, and it was his relative class privilege that placed him where he could learn the sonnet tradition, the Latin title that graces the first sonnet in "Vestiges," and the poetic techniques that enabled him to render the blues with a craft exceeding even that of Langston Hughes. When he stands at the crossroads, his squall does not have the same urgency as Sonny Terry's, because Brown carries his clothes not in a matchbox but in a valise.

Many African American artists of the 1920s and '30s who were also born to such relative privilege argued that mastery of traditional Anglo-American schemes would prove to white Americans that blacks were intelligent and deserved equal rights and treatment. Brown takes a step further by placing his sonnets in the context of the blues poems that appear in earlier sections. By doing so, he emphasizes that the blues—in both scheme and trope—are different from the sonnet, that they both are social products.

As verse scheme, then, this traditional Anglo-American sonnet can be heard as making a rather different racial sounding. By resisting the blues and by refusing to act as if that sensibility were Brown's own, the poem testifies to the importance of class in the constitution of subjectivity. The craft that produced the first three quarters of **Southern Road** was the result of Brown's years of loving study of a people who shared his racial identity, but not his class privilege. To rural Southern blacks, **"Challenge"** thus humbly acknowledges class difference; and to white Americans, it stands as a reminder that if they are waiting for great, universal, "ageless and raceless" "Art" from African Americans, then they will have to help create new social and economic conditions. The fact that **"Challenge"** contains no hint of the black vernacular thus ironically serves to illustrate how much the U.S. must change before men like Long Gone and women like Sister Lou can attain the education and class status that European Americans require of "Poets" before they are allowed institutional recognition. In this way, the prosody of **"Challenge"** acts as a "blues sonnet" by refusing to create such a thing at all. Like the blues, **"Challenge"** calls for economic justice for African Americans, and it does so by making no attempt to *be* the blues. Yes, Brown needs love, but it is not the only thing left standing between him and his humanity. There are others more needy than Brown himself.

6

When African American culture met European American culture at the crossroads, it created not only the blues but also jazz, an improvisational form which, as James A. Snead explains, resists European notions of progress in favor of a cyclical world view. I want to argue now that **"Challenge"** is a "jazz sonnet" insofar as it resists pentameter's desire to legislate progress.

When Easthope explains how pentameter functions as an ideological discourse in promoting some meanings over others, he lists four items: abstraction, concealed production, necessity and freedom, and proper speaking. He suggests, for example, that the "universalizing, essentializing tendency" found in post-feudal culture is recreated in verse by pentameter's own abstract pattern. Pentameter is thus abstract insofar as it "represents a systemic totality, an explicit preconception legislating for every unit of stress and syllable" (66).

Easthope is thinking here of lines like that which ends the octave:

$$. \quad / \quad . \quad / \quad . \quad / \quad . \quad / \quad . \quad /$$
My hymns would float in praise, undauntedly.

Outside of verse, we would scan "undauntedly" with only one stress, but, as Easthope puts it, pentameter "legislates" stress by requiring the promotion of the final syllable, "-ly," so that the line might conform to the abstract pattern of five alternating stresses. The ideological effects of this promotion are not unexpected in light of feminist criticism and theory: by protecting the line from a weak or "feminine" ending, the promotion enables a masculine posture of transcendence over Time. Brown can stand undaunted in the face of Time's threats because pentameter has helped create a technology of the self based on such abstractions.

In order to hear **"Challenge"** as a jazz sonnet, we first need to add a fifth item to Easthope's list of pentameter's ideological preferences: progress. The prosodist Derek Attridge has explained why pentameter prefers a rising rhythm and thus chooses iambs over trochees.[11] Extending Easthope, we can interpret this phenomenon as part of the ideological structure of the transcendent self. One illusion central to capitalism is the appearance of an ever-expanding self, nation, and economy. The iambic pentameter line, with its predominantly rising rhythm, reproduces this ideology by promising and "legislating" accretion, an ever-building sense of arrival.

Easthope discusses the significance of the fundamentally stichic nature of pentameter and describes the importance of evening the stress over the course of the line, but we can add that some stresses are more important than others, that the rising rhythm of the pentameter line promises a final stress that will climax either in a satisfying (and masculine) end stop or an enjambment, a structure which, as another prosodist argues, creates transcendence through a masculine figure for sexual intercourse, the overflow of one line into another.[12] Since pentameter is stichic, it produces a repetitive need for such transcendent, masculine climaxes. The beginning of each line creates a new need to build to another climax. Like the self, a nation, or an economy, pentameter can never possess too much. Its constant rising builds and adds. It makes progress.

This progress is reproduced not only on the level of the line but also on the level of the sonnet scheme. In *The Birth of the Modern Mind: Self, Consciousness, and the Invention of the Sonnet,* Paul Oppenheimer explains that the sonnet was the first lyric scheme since the fall of Rome *not* to be for music, thus becoming the first lyric of self-consciousness, of a lone voice speaking (3). It is personal in that the speaker is presented as someone actually speaking, rather than as a character type (30-31). Oppenheimer's account of the sonnet scheme thus parallels Easthope's account of pentameter.

But Oppenheimer also emphasizes that the scheme is structured to accomplish progress. The sonnet was invented by Giacomo da Lentino, a lawyer for Frederick the Great, whose reign (1215-1250) is considered to be one of the birthplaces of the modern. Giacomo structured the sonnet specifically to create a logical solution to emotional problems, to the problems of the individual self (24). While the songs of the troubadours were built around repetition (or cycle), Giacomo's sonnets relied on a logical progression from the statement of a problem in the octave to its resolution in the sestet (177).

Throughout the octave, **"Challenge"** reproduces this abstract progress, thus reinforcing the hegemony of the sonnet and its insistence on the idea that, through verse, the poet can make his love transcend Time. Progress is measured by the number of Time's "ill-humored tricks" vanquished by the lover. Brown probably met this tradition in *Palgrave's Golden Treasury,* which was the most popular collection at the turn of the century, defining for more than one generation (in fact, since 1861) the meaning, function, and importance of the lyric. The fourth poem in the 1906 edition is Shakespeare's sonnet 65 which vividly describes Time's "rage," its "wreckful siege of battering days," against which beauty's "action is no stronger than a flower." The couplet ends the poem with the assertion that Time's "spoil of beauty" can only be "forbid" if "this miracle have might, / That in black ink my love shall still shine bright." Time's "progressive" decay is thus resisted by love and poetry, and their success is measured by the years vanquished.

Although **"Challenge"** begins by appealing to this sonnet tradition, the poem falters at the beginning of the sestet, when the opening line fails to achieve iambic pentameter:

> . / . / . / . ./ .
> I did not think such words *were bravado.*

In studying the linguistic rules which govern whether a line is *heard* as iambic pentameter, Derek Attridge has accounted for the ear's acceptance of what prosodists used to call "substitutions":

> . . . Time would never dare
> . . / / . / . ./ /
> *Play his ill-hu*mored tricks upon us two,
> / . ./ / . / . /
> *Strange and* defiant lovers that we were.

Prosodists have long recognized double iambs[13] and initial trochees as common and thus acceptable variations, but Attridge argues that such traditional terminology does not help us explain *why* some variations are acceptable and others are not. In generating the rules for English verse, he explains that these common lines are not "variations" but refigurations. In the double iamb above, for example, the consecutive unstressed syllables compensate for an "implied offbeat" between the two stressed syllables: we can just hear a slight pause between "ill" and "humored," and thus the line produces the characteristic alternation of stressed and unstressed syllables that iambic pentameter requires. In Easthope's terms, such devices in pentameter legislate a particular abstract rhythm.

Line 9, however, has no such devices; such a pattern at the end of a line appears nowhere else in iambic pentameter. While line 8 ("My hymns would float in praise, undauntedly") relies on promotion to create the fifth stressed syllable ("-ly"), no such candidate appears in line 9. Attridge would thus call the line "unmetrical." Creating only four stresses, the line is not heard as iambic pentameter; it has an unlegislated rhythm of its own.[14]

In jazz terms, line 9 is a "cut." James A. Snead explains that

> In jazz improvisation, the "cut" . . . is the unexpectedness with which the soloist will depart from the "head" or theme and from its normal harmonic sequence or the drummer from the tune's accepted and familiar primary beat.
>
> (69)

In **"Challenge,"** the "'head' or theme" is eternal love, a theme that is built by the "normal harmonic sequence" and the "accepted and familiar primary beat" of iambic pentameter. Line 9 is thus an "unexpected" "cut" away from pentameter and into a different discourse.

According to Snead, such cuts have a broad philosophical and cultural significance. In fact, he divides cultures into those which give prominence to the cut and those which emphasize progression. He favors the former because such cultures come to terms with the inevitable and fundamental repetitiveness of existence. Instead of a world of eternal novelty, these cultures describe a world marked by cycles: the recurrence of the seasons, of birth and death, of particular issues, ideas, events, and people. Some cultures choose to celebrate this repetitiveness by calling attention to it, and they come to terms with the changes that do occur from year to year by means of the cut, a figure which interrupts one cycle of repetition and introduces another. This new cycle is neither better nor worse; it is just different.

Snead calls cultures based on the cut "black," because current European culture created itself in opposition to a culture it called "black" (62). It had to invent the idea of a "black" culture, because only 500 years ago it too was based on cycles and repetitions. Instead of using the cut, however, current European culture, comes to terms with repetition and change by denying repetition and emphasizing change, in terms of either progress or regress. Every year must bring greater abundance and development of whatever type, whether it is an expanding economy, a New Year's resolution to be a better person (66), or, we might add, an accounting of how much more Time has been vanquished in the name of love.

Thus, when line 9 cuts away from iambic pentameter, it also cuts away from the notion of progress. The question for us is why, and the answer lies in the line itself. Instead of an iambic rhythm progressing toward a climax at the end of the line, we have instead a deflation around the word "bravado." When Brown confesses to "bravado," to an unwarranted confidence in the self's power to transcend adversities like Time, he admits that his boasts were empty. This revelation differs from the opening claim of the octave. He no longer argues that youth and passion dulled his powers of judgment or suggests he was ruined by a woman. Instead, he realizes that the problem was his own inability to judge language: he believed that his words accurately represented reality. He now faces the "challenge" of explaining what failed and of determining what that failure means to his own desire to progress and to transcend Time.

What troubles Brown most deeply is that the bravado worked, despite its non-transcendent and un-pentameter-like posturing. It did not work in the way he desired; he and his lover do not stand entirely clear and free of Time, but they still possess a kind of eternal love. She is still his "dear."[15] In fact, we might say that Brown has completed a cycle and has returned to the originating moment of his love. Instead of finding progress—a

love that is greater because more Time has challenged him and has been vanquished—Brown cuts away from the cycle and produces another vision of love, one less interested in transcendence, progress, or victory, one that accepts the contingency of love and time.

This poem, then—which appears so traditional, so unlike the blues poems for which Brown is best known—expresses a racial sounding in an unmetrical line that cuts away from the very notion of a transcendent love and self that the sonnet and pentameter schemes desire to encode and legislate. Brown's poem thus "challenges" the racist economy and hegemony that Baker claims produced the blues in the first place. The "vestiges" he records here are not the remaining fragments of a racial identity, but the still glimmering shards of an illusion, of a European dream of transcendence. In this "jazz sonnet," Brown cuts away to another—more "black"—vision of love. He squalls on the sonnet like no one has ever squalled before.

7

Although I have explored above Brown's use of traditional Anglo-American verse schemes, I am cautious about extending my conclusions beyond him to Countee Cullen, Claude McKay, or Anne Spencer, because I believe the embeddedness of poetic work in material history is specific to author, volume, and culture. Easthope's theory works as a broad guide, but his account of pentameter is modified by Brown's own understanding of versification, by his construction of **Southern Road,** and by his African American heritage. Any discursive theory of poetry must both develop race as a category of analysis and develop a method of inquiry sensitive to individual prosodic interventions.

Bringing together the work of linguists and the expressive concerns of African American theory can yield a profoundly material analysis of poetry by focusing on the several meanings of "material": desiring to produce a material object (a poem), Brown refashioned the materials at hand (the blues and the sonnet), which were themselves products of material history (the "economics of slavery" which produced the blues and the bourgeois hegemony which produced both the sonnet and iambic pentameter). The resulting poem captures Brown's historical moment, a moment in which he redefined the material possibilities within the United States first by partially accepting an Anglo-American subjectivity and then by complexly asserting his civil rights, addressing the New Poets as fellow travelers, acknowledging his class position within his race, and returning to a cyclical understanding of existence. A method that takes prosody as its starting place thus gives fullness to literary history by perceiving history embedded in every level of the literary. Without such an approach, we cannot do justice to Sterling Brown's poetic work, to the work he did in history.

Notes

1. I will use the traditional rhetorical distinction between "scheme" and "trope" rather than the more common and misleading distinction between "form" and "content." Recent literary criticism has been far more concerned with trope—such figures of meaning as metaphor, metonymy, or representations of race or gender—than with scheme—such surface patterns of words as anaphora, sonnet, iambic pentameter, or call-and-response. I find the scheme/trope distinction useful for its ambiguity: while the form/content distinction implies that verse conveniently contains particular meanings, scheme/trope suggests an ambiguous interrelation.

2. Easthope refers here to what Otto Jespersen calls the "principle of relative stress." For prosodists like Paul Fussell iambic pentameter is an abstract pattern which is not necessarily realized in every line. Fussell would find six stresses and an initial spondee in the first line and four stresses and a medial pyrrhic in the second (both lines are from Robert Frost's "The Vantage Point"):

    / / . / . / . / . /
    Far off the homes of men, and farther still,
    . / . / . . / . /
    The graves of men *on an* opposing hill,

Jespersen and his followers (including Easthope and Attridge), however, believe that iambic pentameter is realized in every line. They would argue that *relative* to "off" the word "far" is unstressed and that relative to "on" and "o-" the word "an" is stressed. Seen from this perspective, both lines have five stresses and are in regular iambic pentameter. Relative stress is what Easthope means when he says that pentameter "evens intonation out across the line." The effect of an individual speaking voice thus arises between the principle of relative stress and the way that different readers will actually stress ambiguities like "far" and "an."

3. Much of the power of *Southern Road* comes from its redefinition of character. Figures like Big Boy, Georgie Grimes, Sister Lou, and Maumee Ruth exist somewhere between type and three-dimensional character. The techniques, effects, and significance of Brown's experimentation with character need to be explored in depth and contrasted not only with Plantation Literature but also with Wordsworth's "literary ballads."

4. Easthope's work is sometimes described as deterministic, mistaking coincidence for causation and convention for structure—just because pentameter has *usually been used* to express a

transcendent subjectivity does not mean it *must*. Easthope, however, is discussing linguistic realities, not "content," "convention," or "intention." Ask a class of thirty to read Shakespeare aloud, and the result is cacophony, thirty voices never falling into rhythm; ask them to read a ballad, and they produce a single, full voice (see note 2, above). This will be true even if the pentameter piece praises community or the ballad individuality. The two schemes have particular linguistic features creating such effects. As a discourse theorist, Easthope is interested in why particular periods create different poetic discourses, elevating some linguistic features of the language over others. Here and elsewhere, I have tried to complicate his account (which is more complex than I have represented) by examining what results when poetic discourse (pentameter) intersects with other discourses, like race, in a particular body of poetry.

5. Brown's history of African American verse, *Negro Poetry and Drama* (1937), was published just five years after *Southern Road* and was later condensed in *The Negro Caravan* (1941). His evaluations of these writers are generous and yet contain an implicit outline of his poetic program. For a further description of the meaning of the lyric at the turn of the century, see Lentricchia.

6. Baker makes a similar point: "Sterling Brown—in a gesture that implies self-conscious evolutionism in craftsmanship (and, one suspects, a masterful black 'craftiness' as well)—entitles the last section of his vernacular *Southern Road* 'Vestiges.' He fills the section with standard poems such as '*Nous n'irons plus au bois*'" (*Modernism* 100). The section title could also refer to the poems as vestiges, footprints, of his own life, the life larger than the poems that carry the traces of that life.

7. For jazz, see Snead; for the blues, see Baker (*Blues*) and Sherley Anne Williams; for signifying, see Gates ("Blackness"); for call-and-response, see Bowen; and for speaking-in-tongues, see Mae Gwendolyn Henderson. For essays that discuss Brown's vernacular work in these terms, see Baker (*Modernism*), Benston, Gabbin, Gates ("Dis"), and Stephen Henderson.

8. Williams explains that although describing needs has failed as a political activity, it has succeeded in literature. But even there it "has been compartmentalized by the larger culture as something other than political expression." The result is that "white descriptions of 'the blues' tend to remove the daily hunger and hurt from need and abstract it into a mood" (151-52). I would argue that Brown describes needs in the first three sections of *Southern Road* and asserts rights in "Vestiges,"

thus resisting the impulse of European American readers to reduce the blues to a mood. See section five, which discusses "Challenge" as a "blues sonnet."

9. For a fuller discussion of Untermeyer and Rittenhouse, see Lentricchia.

10. At the time, Hovey was considered a challenge to the genteel tradition. One of the "vagabond" poets, he was more conventional than he seemed, as the above poem demonstrates. However, the fact that Rittenhouse chose this sonnet over Hovey's more challenging work indicates that her choices were again guided by the lyric ideal.

11. A rising rhythm is not, of course, the same thing as an iamb, but Attridge argues linguistically that iambic pentameter prefers a rising rhythm (113).

12. In *Celestial Pantomime: Poetic Structures of Transcendence* (1979), Lawler argues that enjambment structurally reenacts sexual intercourse (74). Despite the acuity of many of Lawler's insights into verse structure, he does not perceive these structures as gendered, nor the transcendence as a historical product.

13. The term "double iamb" is Robert Bridges's, and it refers to the common figure of a pyrrhic followed by a spondee (.. / /). Although recent metrical theory has rejected as misleading such terms as "iamb," "trochee," "substitution," and "variation," I use them here to avoid the introduction of unfamiliar terminology.

14. For Easthope's critique of attempts like Attridge's to generate rules for iambic pentameter and thus distinguish between metrical and unmetrical lines, see 58-59. A theoretical defense of Attridge on this point is outside the bounds of this essay, but we can note that unmetrical lines are extremely rare and that attempts to find five stresses in line 9, however abstract, are doomed.

For a tour de force demonstration of unmetricality, see Hollander, 23-24, in which he composes lines of ten syllables that have five stresses but do not *sound* like iambic pentameter. Hollander demonstrates this lack of sound by rhyming the last lines. We cannot *hear* the rhyme because the intervening lines are, by Attridge's definition, unmetrical.

15. In the only book-length study of Brown, Gabbin interprets the poem as one of lost love and "personal tragedy" (172), but I take the last line ironically. The only "loss" is a belief in a love that *never* wavers or changes shape. The lovers, I assume, have not parted: "my dear" is deictic, pointing to a lover present at the poem's occasion.

Works Cited

Attridge, Derek. *The Rhythms of English Poetry.* London: Longman, 1982.

Baker, Houston A., Jr. *Blues, Ideology, and Afro-American Literature: A Vernacular Theory.* Chicago: U of Chicago P, 1984.

———. *Modernism and the Harlem Renaissance.* Chicago: U of Chicago P, 1987.

Benston, Kimberly W. "Sterling Brown's After-Song: 'When de Saints go Ma'ching Home' and the Performances of Afro-American Voice." *Callaloo* 5. 1-2 (1982): 33-42.

Bowen, Barbara E. "Untroubled Voice: Call and Response in *Cane.*" Gates, *Black* 187-203.

Brown, Sterling A. *Negro Poetry and Drama* and *The Negro in American Fiction.* 1937. New York: Atheneum, 1969.

———. *Southern Road.* New York: Harcourt, 1932.

Brown, Sterling A., Arthur P. Davis, and Ulysses Lee, eds. *The Negro Caravan.* 1941. New York: Arno, 1969.

Carby, Hazel V. "'It Jus Be's Dat Way Sometime': The Sexual Politics of Women's Blues." *Radical America* 20. 4 (1986): 9-24.

Easthope, Antony. *Poetry as Discourse.* London: Methuen, 1983.

Fussell, Paul. *Poetic Meter and Poetic Form.* Rev. ed. New York: Random, 1979.

Gabbin, Joanne V. *Sterling A. Brown: Building the Black Aesthetic Tradition.* Westport, CT: Greenwood, 1985.

Gates, Henry Louis, Jr., ed. *Black Literature and Literary Theory.* New York: Methuen, 1984.

———. "The Blackness of Blackness: A Critique of the Sign and the Signifying Monkey." Gates, *Black* 285-321.

———. "Dis and Dat: Dialect and the Descent." *Afro-American Literature: The Reconstruction of Instruction.* Ed. Dexter Fisher and Robert B. Stepto. New York: MLA, 1979.

Henderson, Mae Gwendolyn. "Speaking in Tongues: Dialogics, Dialectics, and the Black Woman Writer's Literary Tradition." *Reading Black, Reading Feminist: A Critical Anthology.* Ed. Henry Louis Gates, Jr. New York: Penguin, 1990. 116-42.

Henderson, Stephen E. "The Heavy Blues of Sterling Brown: A Study of Craft and Tradition." *Black American Literature Forum* 14 (1980): 32-44.

Hollander, John. *Rhyme's Reason: A Guide to English Verse.* New Haven: Yale UP, 1981.

Hovey, Richard. "The Thought of Her." *The Little Book of Modern Verse.* Ed. Jessie B. Rittenhouse. Boston: Houghton, 1913. 128.

Lawler, Justus George. *Celestial Pantomime: Poetic Structures of Transcendence.* New Haven: Yale UP, 1979.

Lentricchia, Frank. "The Resentments of Robert Frost." *Out of Bounds: Male Writers and Gender(ed) Criticism.* Ed. Laura Claridge and Elizabeth Langland. Amherst: U of Massachusetts P, 1990. 268-89.

Oppenheimer, Paul. *The Birth of the Modern Mind: Self, Consciousness, and the Invention of the Sonnet.* New York: Oxford UP, 1989.

Shakespeare, William. Sonnet 65. *Palgrave's Golden Treasury.* Ed. F. T. Palgrave. 1861. London: Dent, 1906. 3-4.

Snead, James A. "Repetition as a Figure of Black Culture." Gates, *Black* 59-79.

Untermeyer, Louis. Introduction. *Modern American Poetry.* Ed. Louis Untermeyer. 1919. New York: Harcourt, 1921.

Williams, Patricia J. *The Alchemy of Race and Rights.* Cambridge: Harvard UP, 1991.

Williams, Sherley Anne. "The Blues Roots of Contemporary Afro-American Poetry." *Afro-American Literature: The Reconstruction of Instruction.* Ed. Dexter Fisher and Robert B. Stepto. New York: MLA, 1979. 72-87.

John Edgar Tidwell (essay date autumn 1997)

SOURCE: Tidwell, John Edgar. "Two Writers Sharing: Sterling A. Brown, Robert Frost, and 'In Divés' Dive.'" *African American Review* 31, no. 3 (autumn 1997): 399-408.

[*In the following essay, Tidwell considers the influence of Robert Frost's "In Divés' Dive" on Brown's verse.*]

It is late at night and still I am losing,
But still I am steady and unaccusing.

As long as the Declaration guards
My right to be equal in number of cards,

It is nothing to me who runs the Dive.
Let's have a look at another five.

                                (Robert Frost, "In Divés' Dive")

In the recent proliferation of conference papers, critical articles, and books discussing the pioneering innovation and enduring significance of Sterling A. Brown's poetry, literary critics and historians have enthusiastically shown a propensity toward tracing the resonance of "influence" in his work. The persistence of this practice can hardly be faulted because, starting in the early 1960s, Brown began explicating himself to younger generations whom he felt were unacquainted with his seminal efforts to define the distinctiveness of African American literature and culture. In numerous formal and informal interviews, poetry readings, and public lectures, Brown professed an indebtedness to precursing and contemporary writers, including English poets (Ernest Dowson, Rudyard Kipling, Thomas Hardy, A. E. Housman), African American poets (Paul Laurence Dunbar, Langston Hughes, James Weldon Johnson, and nameless vernacular artists), and the New American Poets (E. A. Robinson, Edgar Lee Masters, Carl Sandburg, Vachel Lindsay, and Robert Frost):

In between professing and practice, though, lies a fundamental problem, if we elect to follow Brown's "stage directions" for understanding his poetic apprenticeship. We are challenged by the paradox engendered in his revelation: How can we effectively describe the uniqueness of his poetry and, at the same time, locate it within a tradition of poetry making? Brown, as James Weldon Johnson discovered, always followed his supposed confessions about literary debt with denials about the extent to which anyone shaped and molded his work. Faced with the prospect that readers would interpret Johnson's use of "ultimate source," in his introduction to **Southern Road** (1932), to mean inartistic, salvish imitation, Brown stubbornly resisted Johnson's analysis with this rejoinder: "I think . . . you overstress the influence of the so-called folk epics. These have hardly been my *sources*. Folk experience *has* been" (Letter to Johnson). As a consequence of Brown's retreat, seekers after literary indebtedness find themselves entrapped in poetic miasmas, where the illusory substitutes for the real. I will argue that a relational strategy called "sharing" enables a more appropriate description of the category of influence informing Brown's uniqueness and his participation in a tradition of poetry-making.

My argument involves three basic concerns. I shall describe the concept of "influence" to reveal how its flexibility as a critical term enables a broader discussion of Brown's claim to poetic uniqueness than is generally found in previous studies of his work. Using arguably the most pointed example of Brown's acknowledged "indebtedness," that of Robert Frost and his poem "In Divés' Dive," I take up the question of how a feature of "influence" I call "sharing" provides both points of convergence and divergence between Frost's and Brown's vision of American poetic tradition. Finally, from my account of "sharing," I derive three general criteria I consider important to describing Brown's poetic distinctiveness and employ these criteria to advocate a relational strategy I believe most effectively applies to reading his work.

Recent study of "influence," as related especially to African American literature, has shown, among other things, that the way of reading literary interaction has generally centered on the imitation of white authors by African American writers. Essentially this relationship has been seen as a one-way street, with the motives of African American authors evolving out of a felt need to prove their "personal merit" and "racial merit" to whites. It's no small wonder, then, that, especially in the mid-eighteenth century, when "originality gained prominence and [when] influence [that is, homage to a venerated predecessor] grew suspect" (Mishkin 5), African American writers came to be viewed negatively as imitative and derivative. In his response cited above to James Weldon Johnson, Brown demonstrates a certain defensiveness about or sensitivity to such accusations.

In addition to showing us feelings of sensitivity, Brown's response to Johnson perfectly illustrates the usual way in which "influence" has been defined— poetic relationships having a generic or thematic connection, in which a younger writer adopts and subsequently modifies a precursing writer's subject matter, form, or style. Out of this pursuit, which theorist Tracy Mishkin develops more fully, came the critics' "interest in source-hunting" (5), which further crystalized "influence" as denoting a "father-son" relationship. Brown himself struggled against this familial metaphor in his denial to Johnson, but it is precisely the imposition of a precursor-imitator relational strategy that constrains many critics writing about Brown.

Joanne Gabbin, in the first book-length bio-critical study of Brown, has good intentions but is only partially correct when she argues that "the poets who most appealed to Brown during [his apprenticeship period] were those who used freedom as their banner: freedom to choose new materials; freedom from stilted, florid poetic diction; freedom to experiment with language, form, and subject matter in new, unconventional ways; and freedom from the kind of provincialism and Puritanism that Van Wyck Brooks said in *America's Coming of Age* has stymied the growth of literature and art in America" (31). This argument illustrates the tendency to see African American poets in terms of the "influence" exerted on them by white precursors, or even contemporaries. In her otherwise perceptive observation, Gabbin finds it unnecessary to interrogate the practitioners of florid language in an effort to determine where Brown agreed or disagreed with their practice. Nor does she explore the remnants of his apprenticeship work, found in the "Vestiges" section of his ***Southern Road*** (1932), to determine the origins of these poems in earlier poetic practice. Moreover, Gabbin's argument

neglects to probe the intraracial conversation that took place among whites, whose preeminence became the standard critics used in defining "the tradition."

As critics writing about Brown, we can find ourselves caught in the same dilemma that Brown had to face: how to demonstrate his participation in a tradition of poetry-making while simultaneously showing his uniqueness. For Brown, the dilemma had personal implications: Like his integration-minded fellow poets, he sought to prove that he belonged socially to the American mainstream while maintaining his racial integrity as an individual.[1]

I would argue that one way out of the dilemma of precursor and imitator, of provider and receiver, and of group member and individual is through the complementarity of "influence" and "intertextuality." These two approaches, as Mishkin persuasively writes, are complementary, "for they can identify each other's weaknesses . . . thereby enhancing the study of literary interaction" (8). In a fuller, more serviceable explanation, Clayton and Rothstein observe that

> Strictly, influence should refer to relations built on dyads of transmission from one unity (author, work, tradition) to another. More broadly, however, influence studies often stray into portraits of intellectual background, context. . . . The shape of intertextuality in turn depends on the shape of influence. One may see intertextuality either as the enlargement of a familiar idea or as an entirely new concept to replace the outmoded notion of influence. In the former case, intertextuality might be taken as a general term, working out from the broad definition of influence to encompass unconscious, socially prompted types of text formation (for example, by archetypes or popular culture); modes of conception (such as ideas "in the air"); styles (such as genres); and other prior constraints and opportunities for the writer. In the latter case, intertextuality might be used to oust and replace the kinds of issues that influence addresses, and in particular its central concern with the author and more or less conscious authorial intentions and skills.
>
> (3)

Although the terms "influence" and "intertextuality" are often distinguished by the question of agency, the issue of concurrent or overlapping features is of interest to the argument I wish to develop about Brown and Frost. To make the claim for two writers sharing is to argue the significance of intellectual background or aesthetic context. As "influence," the mode of literary interaction I call "sharing" is broadly concerned with questions of context, intellectual background, and tradition. However, "sharing," from a basis in "intertextuality," results not from the relationship between two writers but from literary interactions based on "the enlargement of a familiar idea." Clayton and Rothstein state this idea in a different way when they write: "An expanded sense of influence allows one to shift one's attention from the transmission of motifs between authors to the transmission of historically given material. This shift does not do away with author-centered criticism so much as broaden it to take into account the multifarious relations that can exist among authors" (6). Implicit in the notion of expanding ideas is not a doctrinaire set of assumptions, to which a group of writers would pay obeisance; instead, expansion places ideas in conversation with each other, permitting us to examine points of convergence and divergence.

I have chosen as a case in point the literary interaction of Brown and Frost, using their only personal meeting—an occasion so poignant that it almost appears the archetypal example of "literary influence." In this momentous June 1, 1960, meeting, which held deep symbolic significance for Brown, these two venerable veterans of the culture wars paused briefly to reflect on the convergence and divergence of their lives and careers. Their animated conversation focused on the relative importance of Frost's poem "In Divés' Dive." In my mind, the exchange distilled dialogically the most important moment the two poets shared aesthetically.

We can perhaps distrust the authority of the few extant accounts of this fortuitous meeting because they're anecdotal; however, Frost biographer and *Negro Caravan* publisher Stanley Burnshaw offers the most persuasive rendering of the moment. In his *Robert Frost: Himself,* Burnshaw remembers Brown's response to his question probing the nature of Brown's conversation with Frost: "Six great lines from *A Further Range.* Nobody mentions them. He says I'm the only one he knows who knows that poem" (138).

From this brief moment of reflection emerge two distinct and often overlapping views of poetry and literary history. For Brown, the "six great lines" revealed an essential commitment to a democratic vision of America, in which principle and practice coalesced in the body of governing documents that defined America. In his now familiar speech "A Son's Return. 'Oh, Didn't He Ramble,'" Brown tells us in an "autobiographical sounding off" how "In Divés' Dive" reveals "a strong statement of a man's belief *in America* and *in himself*" (22; emphasis added). To understand the significance of Brown's self-disclosure and to see how it accords with Frost's ideas, we must review some of Brown's cultural and political beliefs.

If we use Houston Baker's theory of "AMERICA," we can profitably explore Brown's self-described commitment to America. Baker argues that the defining signification of "AMERICA" is an inscribing and reinscribing discourse based in an "immanent idea of boundless, classless, raceless possibility in America" (65); in short, a committed belief in American demo-

cratic principles embraces egalitarianism and racial equality. That Brown was quite committed to these values is clear in his now familiar declaration, "I am an integrationist. . . . And by integration, I do not mean assimilation. I believe what the word means—an integer is a whole number" ("Son's Return" 18). In effect, Brown's quest to achieve full integration took him through the process of filling in the fractional status that existed vestigially for African Americans in the U.S. Constitution. Complete racial integration would be achieved, Brown believed, when the "three-fifths" clause placed in the Constitution for purposes of taxing Black slaves would be supplemented with the other two-fifths, thereby making a whole number and representing the achievement of complete humanity. Despite the survival of the "three-fifths compromise" in a body of de jure and de facto Jim Crow practices, Brown remained hopeful about the boundless possibility of America. The context provided by this socio-cultural pursuit frames Brown's exegesis of "In Divés' Dive."

The poem focuses ingeniously on gambling, specifically playing poker, a game Brown says neither he nor Frost indulged in ("Son's Return" 20). In the representation of poker as a game, Frost creates a virtual setting to suggest larger ideas about full, participatory democratic politics. Brown found kinship with the speaker of the poem, who finds himself, late at night, losing in the game. "But still," the speaker proclaims, "I am steady and unaccusing." Brown saw himself in this line: Even at seventy-three (his age when he gave this presentation at Williams College), he was not "laying blame on anybody. If I lose I am not singing blues about anybody else causing it" (21). The source supporting his belief in the game and his right to participate in it was the Declaration of Independence. Shrouded in its protections, Brown agreed with the poem's speaker: "I'm not a good poker player, but . . . I'm going to play my hand out with the cards that come. And that to me is a strong statement of a man's belief in America and in himself" (22).

While "In Divés' Dive" no doubt reaffirmed Brown's passion for courage, belief in democratic principles, and more, Frost probably recalled these same qualities in the context of the controversy that surrounded *A Further Range* (1936), the collection in which "Divés'" was originally published. Although Frost's poetry, like that of most writers in the 1930s, was consumed with issues of social significance, he nevertheless found himself at the vortex of controversy with *A Further Range* because his conservative politics were misread or undervalued. Indeed, an argument can be made that *A Further Range* came under unusual critical scrutiny precisely because Frost's audience was divided on the question of art and its relation to social significance.

Part of the acclaim and part of the contentiousness for *A Further Range* derives from Frost's announcement of what he considered new poetic paths. He dedicated the collection "to E. F. for what it may mean to her that beyond the White Mountains were the Green; beyond both were the Rockies, the Sierras, and, in thought, the Andes and the Himalayas—range beyond range even into the realm of government and religion." As aesthetic statement, the dedication to Frost's wife Elinor tells us much about his charting new poetic territories. According to biographer Lawrance Thompson, Frost hit upon the idea of using "as metaphor the fact that his experiences had caused him to look across all the ranges of mountains in the United States, and thus to endow his poetry with a further range of themes, even social and political" (440). It is in this context that Burnshaw's observations must be viewed: Frost had a consuming concern for gambling; that is, not playing cards, but taking chances. What ranged beyond the mountains, beyond the explicitness of actual place was an implicit realm—the imagination. With this collection, Frost's approach was not so much one of imagined flight as of imagined confrontation, and as a consequence of this new direction, Frost suffered the ignominy of being accused of writing his first seriously flawed or simply bad book.

Critic George Nitchie typifies a large number of commentators when he called *A Further Range* "Frost's first bad book." He adds that his assessment is

> not based on the dubious proposition that a poet is somehow obligated to deal with certain preeminently social issues from a certain set of premises. Rather . . . it is based on the propositions, that, as poet, Frost seldom exhibits any very vital or immediate sense of collective aims, of broadly social values, and that in *A Further Range* he implies that such aims and such values are somehow undesirable in themselves, are absurd or unnecessary, wasteful or destructive.
>
> (112)

In this view, "social significance" means very little if it refers to proselytizing, propagandizing, or inspiring collective action. Frost seldom missed an opportunity to tout the virtues of New England life, as he saw them: independence, self-sufficiency, individualism, and so forth. Yet precisely these terms drew tremendous heat from reviewers and critics of *A Further Range,* who seemed to be divided on the significance of these qualities and on Frost's treatment of them.

Among the many critics, biographers, and literary historians who have written on Frost, Richard Poirier, in *Robert Frost: The Work of Knowing,* has emerged as one of the most articulate and persuasive spokespersons. By positioning Frost's popularity with a literate general public and a college audience that rejected modernism and Europeanized New York intellectuals against the poet's critical detractors, Poirier adeptly shows the mixed constituency to which Frost's poetry played

(227). Frost was either soundly greeted or assailed, depending on the audience. Connected to this issue of audience is the problem of Frost's response. He felt that it was necessary to explicate himself, partly in response to the negative reviews of *A Further Range,* and also in an effort to gain acceptance from the very group that had lambasted him. To understand this issue is to accept the premise that Frost's politics and poetics became, as Poirier observed, "inseparable" (236-37). In an extended passage, Poirier discusses the implications of this claim:

> Frost takes his place in an American tradition which proposes that since you are most inconsequential when you are most "included" in any system or "stated plan" you are, paradoxically, most likely to find yourself, and to be saved, when you risk being excluded or peripheral. This is a tradition full of political implications. The placement of the self in relation to the apparent organizations of things is one of the major concerns of Frost's later poetry, but it is a political concern only while it also reveals his more general contempt for a tendency in modern liberalism to discredit the capacity of ordinary, struggling people to survive in freedom and hope without the assistance of the state or any other kind of planning and despite the arrogant solicitude of those who think that such people would be better off if "provided" for.
>
> (264)

I wish briefly to consider one implication of this marvelous observation. Frost, rooted in the New England-Yankee tradition of self-help, railed against the New Deal fashioned by President Franklin Delano Roosevelt. The consensus among reviewers and critics that *A Further Range* was Frost's most polemical collection to date focused squarely upon its aphoristic, didactic quality as masking a rather thinly veiled but scathing denunciation of authority. Frost's conservative politics were fairly well-known, and thus this collection revealed to critics a direct opposition to Franklin Delano Roosevelt, an attack which they characterized as ad hominem. It is true, as Burnshaw writes, that the New Deal represented for Frost an erosion of sorts. The dignity, the courage, the spirit of self-help that had made America *America* had suffered because of the Depression. To Frost, though, the New Deal not only bailed out many American people but threatened to create a class of "no-good dependents" by "infantilizing" them. The New England virtues of self-reliance, courage, and independence defined, for Frost, the quintessential American citizen, and the New Deal, according to this perspective, threatened to "take the starch out of self-reliant people" (Burnshaw interview).

Along with the question of denouncing authority, more than one critic wondered whether *A Further Range* represented a further elucidation of the human condition or a shriveling up of an enervated poetic talent capable only of a polemic masquerading as poetry. The basis for attacking this collection usually focused on its moralistic or didactic features, not Frost's poetic experimentation and ingenuity. It is precisely this kind of "telling" that many reviewers—some of whom were Leftists anyway—seized upon as evidence of a diminishing poetic talent whose political conservatism was out of step with current thought.

Brown, of course, agreed with Frost regarding the necessity of people to be free from systems or institutions that abridged individual freedoms. Like Frost, he appreciated the ruggedness of individual efforts and initiatives. The characterological qualities often found in Brown's portrait poems include stoicism, philosophical indifference, tonic shrewdness, and the like. However, Brown did not enjoy Frost's racial privilege, and, as a consequence, he parted company with Frost on the role of governmental systems. Brown's editorship for the Federal Writers' Project was made necessary by the proliferation of stereotyped representations of African Americans. The self—the *Black* self—in Brown's view declared itself against a world view of racial stereotyping. What rescued the dignity of Blacks from warped imaginations and projections of difference was sheer will or an indomitable spirit. And it is this will that forced Brown into an imagined reckoning with the self and with the self in society.

Finally, if "In Divés' Dive" can be used as evidence, Brown departed from Frost regarding the relative use of folk traditions in advancing his views about democracy. The principal reference in the title of Frost's poem represents an important demarcation between Brown and Frost. Frost, in 1960, apparently knew nothing of the well-known Negro spiritual containing the Divés reference. It is quite possible that he knew about Divés through the biblical parable (Luke 16: 19-31) and maybe Elizabeth Gaskill's novel *Mary Barton* (1848), whose theme "the rich don't get it" (45) foregrounds an idea that differs from Frost's. By turning to the formal differences in the several versions of the Divés story, we can infer more clearly the character of African American life as Brown represented it and begin to see how he enlarged an idea in ways Frost did not.

How Brown came to know the Divés-Lazarus story is not difficult to discern. The son of a renowned Congregationalist pastor and theologian, Brown admitted his thorough acquaintance with biblical readings. As a student of Harvard's legendary Shakespearian and folk song collector George Lyman Kittredge, Brown no doubt knew quite well the different folk songs versions, too. And as principal editor of *The Negro Caravan*, Brown wrote with unusual sensitivity and insight about the Negro spiritual based on the Divés-Lazarus story, "I Got a Home in That Rock."

Fundamentally, as biblical parable, the Rich Man-Lazarus story anticipates a theme that resonates throughout the various forms containing this story: "the

reversal of fortune" that takes place when both men die. In life, according to the Gospel of St. Luke, Divés (so-named because *dives* in Latin means "rich man"), bedecked in his finest clothing, hosts a lavish banquet but fails to see (or sees but ignores!) the starving, sore-infested Lazarus (whose name means 'God helps') who lies, at Divés's doorstep, begging crumbs from the bounteous table. At their death, Lazarus is borne away by angels to rest in the bosom of Abraham in heaven, while Rich Man Divés is ferried to hell, where his perpetually parched throat becomes his unending punishment and his anguish increases to the point of making him beg Abraham to send Lazarus with a cooling drop of water. Having been denied this wish, Divés pleads that Lazarus be sent to warn Divés's five brothers to repent of their selfish ways before they incur the fate he now experiences in hell. Abraham once again denies Divés's request because, "if they hear not Moses and the prophets, neither will they be persuaded, though one rose from the dead" (Luke 16: 31).

This sparse rendering hardly probes the complexities and interpretative debates about this parable: "If man chooses heaven on earth, will he sacrifice a real heaven after death?" "Was Divés intentionally cruel or did he mistakenly pass by Lazarus?" An analogy posed by one writer to demonstrate what he understands to be Divés's charitable nature reads: "Divés spoke about the colored races, but never saw the Negro who passed his gate. Divés discussed employment statistics, but never imagined himself a man out of work. *He did not see*" (*Interpreter's Bible* 291; emphasis added). Before one can be blamed for not taking an appropriate measure, one has to see the problem wholly and steadily. Although Brown never commented directly on this parable, it is possible to infer from his scholarship and poetry how "the reversal of fortunes" theme informs his vision of the folk.

As a folk song, "Divés and Lazarus" is only minimally related to the biblical parable, but Brown would hardly find this distinction or the problems posed by the song's encapsulating form compelling. In the ballad stanza, where the story is generally rendered in four iambic lines (the first and third being tetrameter and others trimeter, with the second and fourth lines rhyming), the song is characteristically condensed, dramatic, and impersonal. The narrator often begins with the climactic episode and tells the story's action tersely by means of action or dialogue. Most importantly, the narrator usually tells the story without self-reference or expressions of personal attitude or feelings. With little of the intrusiveness of the narrator, the situation is presented dramatically, often with a view that is unsentimental or ironic. Finally, because the narrative often has no connection between verses or scenes, there is no explanation of the events leading up to the climax of the narrative.

Consider these two verses from the *Traditional Ballads of Virginia*:

> There was a man in ancient times,
> Dressed in purple and fine linen;
> He ate, he drank, but scorned to pray,
> Spent all of his days in sinning
>
> Poor Lazarus lying at his gate,
> All helpless in his condition,
> He asked the crumbs fell to the floor
> That fell from his rich table.

> (Davis)

Brown would see the rather impersonal narrative voice as making almost no intrusion upon the text of the story and would understand that the listener is only brought into the narrative conflict through the song's lyrics. Brown's own artful use of the tall-tale tradition, which I've commented on elsewhere, effectively refutes the assumed formal qualities of the folk song.[2] Through his Slim Greer poems, for example, he establishes the necessity for a personal relationship through storytelling as a prerequisite for community.

But a significant feature of the Negro spiritual "I Got a Home in That Rock" is its capacity to represent, like most spirituals, a sense of community and an inspiration for changing the status quo. In *Black Song,* still the most comprehensive study of Negro spirituals, John Lovell poignantly observes that "the folk community of the spiritual believed in *poetry* as a maker and a reflector of change so powerful as to constitute magic" (196; emphasis added). The poetry and incipient political force of the lyrics identified by Lovell accord with Brown's scholarship on the spirituals.

In *The Negro Caravan* (1941), unarguably the most comprehensive literary anthology of its time, Brown wrote with assuredness and cogency about the "folk stuff," including the spirituals. In summarizing the major issues of this genre, using the precursing scholarship of Thomas Wentworth Higginson, James Weldon Johnson, W. E. B. Du Bois, Alain Locke, and Newman White, among many others, Brown wrote incisively about the folk origins of the spirituals (that is, whether they were composed by individuals or groups, derived from African or European music or combined, etc.) and especially its poetry. For Brown, the difference in metaphoric range functioned as an important difference between white and Negro spirituals:

> To hide yourself in the mountaintop
> To hide yourself from God.

> (white)

> Went down to the rocks to hide my face,
> The rocks cried out no hiding place.

> (Negro) (*Caravan* 417)

The similarity that exists between the two sets of lines lies in their "general idea, certainly not in the poetry" (*Caravan* 417). In these two very different sets of lyrics rests a fundamental belief that permeates Brown's folk-based metaphysic: that the "poetry" of Negro folk language revealed wit, wisdom, and a world view. Distilled in these two lines is an anthropomorphized vision of nature itself. The idea, once we leave the realm of the religious for the social, is that no place can provide refuge or escape from the encroachments or assaults made against African American humanity.

As Lovell stated this argument, the "magic" of the spirituals was not simply rescue but empowerment. It provided justice, "an irresistible force against strong earthly powers" (Lovell 340). Lovell finds no better instance of universal justice than that portrayed in "I Got a Home in That Rock":

> Poor old Lazarus, poor as I, Don't you
> see? Don't you see? (repeat)
> Poor old Lazarus, poor as I, When he
> died had a home on high.
> He had a home in-a-that Rock, Don't
> you see?
>
> Rich man, Dives, lives so well, Don't
> you see? Don't you see? (repeat)
> Rich man, Dives, lived so well, When
> he died he found home in hell,
> Had no home in that Rock, Don't you
> see?

> (qtd. in Lovell 340)[3]

Brown and Lovell agreed that, in Lovell's words, ". . . in the Afro-American spiritual, universal justice straightens all, clarifies all, judges all, at long last" (Lovell 340).

The Negro spiritual thus emerges as a music of political as well as religious significance. Brown understood that the "I" in "I Got a Home in That Rock" signifies not just the individual but also the community. In this way, the Rich Man-Lazarus parable represents more than a reversal of fortunes in the next world; it offers profound hope to sustain aggrieved singers/listeners in this world. "The spirituals," Brown argues, "were born of suffering" (*Caravan* 420). Rather than supporting a case for "You take dis worl', and give me Jesus," the spirituals derive their strength, their raison d'être as "tragic poetry." That is, the language of the spirituals is rooted in a nearly cathartic emotional response to hardship, trial, and tribulation. In effect, the Divés-Lazarus parable teaches the listeners/singers that understanding selfishness, self-interest, and irresponsibility has consequences *in this world* and in the world that follows; therefore, the individual is connected to the community by love, care, and concern, and the community, in turn, is responsible to its individual members. By maintaining this sense of community, whatever befalls the group can be properly withstood.

Principally, then, the points of convergence and divergence in Brown's and Frost's use of the Divés-Lazarus story focus on the two poets' respective associations of art and the social significance of art. Among the most focused critical comparisons of these two poets, Mark Jeffreys vacillates tellingly between Brown's indebtedness to and departure from Frost and other "New American Poets." Ultimately, though, Jeffreys is most serviceable and cogent when he comments that "Brown's acknowledgment of Frost is one of kindred spirit more than kindred technique" (214). Unlike Frost, who never had his identity of being an American questioned, Brown had to argue for recognition that he was "a part of," not relegated to being "apart from," America.

Even though Frost never had to argue for his identity as an American, he nevertheless attempted to define the meaning of being one. But being an American was important to Brown, too, as many of his poems suggest. In **"Old Lem,"** for example, Brown subtly suggests a protracted history of legal and social customs in contrasting, minute gestures: "Their fists stay closed / Their eyes look straight / Our hands stay open / Our eyes must fall" (*Collected Poems* 81). Or in the raucous **"Slim in Atlanta,"** in which Brown skillfully uses the techniques of the tall tale, the peripatetic Slim satirizes racial proscription and laughs the reader into understanding the ridiculousness of such practices: "Down in Atlanta, / De whitefolks got laws / For to keep all de niggers / From laughin' outdoors" (*Collected Poems* 81). Frost never had to write a poem like **"Sam Smiley,"** whose last two lines elevate the poem out of the more direct social protest against lynching and into a cultural moment resonating with impressive power of human emotion: "And big Sam Smiley, King Buckdancer, / Buckdanced on the midnight air" (*Collected Poems* 46).

"In Divés' Dive" served quite different aesthetic and political purposes for these two writers. The traditional claim for "influence," as Mark Jeffreys correctly observes (see, especially, 221), has no merit if one poem or poet is set forth in hegemonic relation with the other. However, the special form of sharing that takes place between both writers rescues Brown from his own dilemma of how to acknowledge his participation in modifying a given body of ideas without accepting the burden of being "influenced."

Notes

1. This difficulty with racial integration was only one of many dilemmas confronting Brown. See, for example, his steadfast disavowal of being included as a New Negro, only to contradict his own claims, as Robert Stepto has persuasively shown, by locating himself in the center of New Negro activity in New York during the 1920s.

2. See my essay "The Art of Tall Tale in the Slim Greer Poems."

3. It bears mentioning that either Brown misremembers or the editors mistranscribe these lines in "A Son's Return." The two published verses are interposed. More importantly, the published line "[Divés] had a home in that Rock" alters dramatically the meaning of the biblical parable, since he had *no* home in the kingdom.

Works Cited

Baker, Houston. *Blues, Ideology, and Afro-American Literature: A Vernacular Theory.* Chicago: U of Chicago P, 1984.

Brooks, Van Wyck. *America's Coming-of-Age.* New York: Huebsch, 1915.

Brown, Sterling A. *The Collected Poems of Sterling A. Brown.* Ed. Michael S. Harper. 1980. Evanston: Tri-Quarterly Books, 1989.

———. Letter to James Weldon Johnson. 17 Feb. 1932. Yale U Library.

———. Personal Interview. 2 December 1982.

———. "A Son's Return: 'Oh, Didn't He Ramble.'" 1974. Ed. Michael S. Harper and Robert Stepto. *Chant of Saints: A Gathering of Afro-American Literature, Art and Scholarship.* Champaign: U of Illinois P, 1979. 3-22.

———. "Steady and Unaccusing: An Interview With Sterling A. Brown." With John S. Wright and John Edgar Tidwell. 2 August 1980 and 2 May 1981.

———, Arthur P. Davis, and Ulysses Lee, eds. *The Negro Caravan.* New York: Dryden P, 1941.

Burnshaw, Stanley. *Robert Frost: Himself.* New York: Braziller, 1986.

———. Telephone Interview. 12 September 1990.

Clayton, Jay, and Eric Rothstein. "Figures in the Corpus: Theories of Influence and Intertextuality." *Influence and Intertextuality in Literary History.* Ed. Clayton and Rothstein. Madison: U of Wisconsin P, 1991. 3-36.

Davis, Arthur Kyle, Jr., ed. "Divés and Lazarus." *Traditional Ballads of Virginia.* Cambridge: Harvard UP, 1929. 175-76.

Frost, Robert. *A Further Range.* New York: Holt, 1936.

The Interpreter's Bible. Vol. 8. New York: Abingdon-Cokesbury P, 1952.

Gaskell, Elizabeth. *Mary Barton.* 1848. New York: Viking Penguin, 1970.

Gabbin, Joanne V. *Sterling A. Brown: Building the Black Aesthetic Tradition.* Westport: Greenwood, 1985.

Jeffreys, Mark. "Irony Without Condescension: Sterling A. Brown's Nod to Robert Frost." *Literary Influence and African American Writers.* Ed. Tracy Mishkin. New York: Garland, 1996. 211-29.

Lovell, John, Jr. *Black Song: The Forge and the Flame, The Story of How the Afro-American Spiritual Was Hammered Out.* New York: Macmillan, 1972.

Meyers, Jeffrey. *Robert Frost: A Biography.* Boston: Houghton, 1996.

Mishkin, Tracy. "Theorizing Literary Influence and African-American Writers." Ed. Mishkin. *Literary Influence and African-American Writers: Collected Essays.* New York: Garland, 1996. 3-20.

Nitchie, George W. *Human Values in the Poetry of Robert Frost.* Durham: Duke UP, 1960.

Poirier, Richard. *Robert Frost: The Work of Knowing.* Stanford: Stanford UP, 1977.

Stepto, Robert B. "Sterling A. Brown: Outsider in the Harlem Renaissance?" *The Harlem Renaissance: Revaluations.* Eds. Amritjit Singh, et al. New York: Garland, 1989. 73-81.

Thompson, Lawrance. *Robert Frost: The Years of Triumph, 1915-1938.* New York: Holt, 1970.

Tidwell, John Edgar. "The Art of Tall Tale in the Slim Greer Poems." *Cottonwood* 38-39 (1986): 170-76.

———. "Recasting Negro Life History: Sterling A. Brown and the Federal Writers' Project." *Langston Hughes Review* 13. 2 (1995): 77-82.

Wagner, Linda W., ed. *Robert Frost: The Critical Reception.* New York: Burt Franklin, 1977.

Lorenzo Thomas (essay date autumn 1997)

SOURCE: Thomas, Lorenzo. "Authenticity and Elevation: Sterling Brown's Theory of the Blues." *African American Review* 31, no. 3 (autumn 1997): 409-16.

[*In the following essay, Thomas discusses Brown's incorporation of the blues tradition in his poetry, maintaining that he was able to "identify the authentic poetic voice of black America."*]

Every poet must confront a serious problem: how to reconcile one's private preoccupations with the need to make poetry that is both accessible and useful to others. A failure in this area does not, of course, prevent the production of poems. Indeed, some poems—like many of T. S. Eliot's—may be records of this struggle, while others have the disturbingly eloquent beauty of Church testifying or 12-step program witness. One manner of reconciliation is an embrace of what may be called *tradition,* but even this is problematic.

The idea of tradition made Eliot uneasy; at best he saw it as a living artist's colloquy and competition with the dead (48-50). In his essay "Tradition and the Individual Talent" (1920), Eliot points out that acquiring the "consciousness of the past" is both necessary and perilous for a poet; and eventually, in his description of it, tradition begins to assume the proportions of a face that "sticks that way" (52-53).

As a poet somewhat younger than Eliot, Sterling A. Brown delighted in experimentation yet also valued his role as a contributor to a tradition. In the poems he composed in the 1920s, Brown "sought to combine the musical forms of the blues, work songs, ballads, and spirituals with poetic expression in such a way as to preserve the originality of the former and achieve the complexity of the latter" (Gabbin 42). Brown's relationship to tradition was, in other words, something like a mirror-image of Eliot's. Where Eliot cringed before a weighty past, Brown—focusing on the African American vernacular tradition—perceived an originality and creativity to be mastered and then practiced in an even more original manner. In fact, Brown's poetics document an attitude toward tradition that is not very different than the one held by the blues singers themselves.[1] It is worth noting, also, that Brown did not necessarily see his valorization of African American folk tradition as inconsistent with his practice of contemporary poetic experiment. Just as Hart Crane and others fled the stultifying worldview of their parents, Brown could warn against "an arising snobbishness; a delayed Victorianism" among educated African Americans ("Our Literary Audience" 42). And when he analyzed the blues, Brown discerned a poetic approach that paralleled the Imagists and other Modernists "in substituting the thing seen for the bookish dressing up and sentimentalizing" that characterized nineteenth-century literary verse ("The Blues as Folk Poetry" 378).

In addition to addressing the dilemma of privacy and access, of the proper value of tradition, Sterling Brown's work also shows how one writer negotiated the relationship of the creative arts—both "highbrow" and "folk"—to the political agenda of the African American struggle for self-determination as it developed in the period between the two world wars. In choosing to study the blues, Brown found himself engaged with a genre of poetry that offers its own clever solution to these problems. The blues, Brown discovered, "has a bitter honesty. This is the way the blues singers and their poets have found life to be. And their audiences agree" ("The Blues" 288). Indeed, it is this agreement between poet and audience that is the reality and the purpose of the blues.

Houston A. Baker, Jr., has rightly noted the unusual circumstance of the awesomely intellectual young Sterling Brown embracing a form devised by the unlettered (92-95), and perhaps an important clue is found in Brown's poem **"Ma Rainey."** Rainey's art and its powerful effect on her audience, her ability to "'jes catch hold of us, somekindaway'" (*Collected Poems* 63) through song, is precisely the ambition of every poet, and may explain one source of Brown's attraction to the blues. There are some other possibilities as well. Whether or not one sees Brown's poetry as part of the Modernist direction—or of the Regionalism that seemed to make a number of largely regional "splashes" during the 1930s—Brown's poems also clearly embody and represent two decidedly pre-Modern projects. One of these is the "corrective" gesture of African American scholarship, and the other is the desire of both poets and critics to create a "national literature" for black Americans.

In 1930, Brown declared "a deep concern with the development of a literature worthy of our past, and of our destiny; without which literature we can never come to much." He added, "I have deep concern with the development of an audience worthy of such literature" ("Our Literary Audience" 42). In a sense this aim balances Brown's Modernist tendencies and leads him toward the compilation of "antiquities" found in the folk tradition. As Charles H. Rowell has noted, Brown belonged to a group of writers who "realized that to express the souls of black folk, the artist has to divest himself of preconceived and false notions about black people, and create an art whose foundation is the ethos from which spring black life, history, culture, and traditions" (131). This effort is also consistent with the "Correctionist" mission first assumed by David Walker in his 1829 rebuttal of Thomas Jefferson's racial slurs in *Notes on the State of Virginia* (1785) and continued by Carter G. Woodson, J. A. Rogers, Lerone Bennett, Jr., Ivan van Sertima, and others.

Sterling Brown's contribution to this effort was to identify and analyze the stereotypes—derogatory in varying degrees but *never* "just clean fun"—that proliferate in literature and the media. This he did in both scholarly and popular arenas—as both critic and poet. The urgency of Brown's efforts derive from his understanding, as stated in *The Negro Caravan* (1941), that "white authors dealing with the American Negro have interpreted him in a way to justify his exploitation. Creative literature has often been a handmaiden to social policy" (3). As critic Brown exposed these vicious and persistent stereotypes; as a creative artist, he sought to counter them with a social realist portraiture based on forms indigenous to the African American community.

The need for this type of work should not be underestimated. Although minstrelsy began in the 1830s, it was—incredibly—still going strong a century later. In 1922, for example, George Gershwin and Buddy DeSylva wrote *Blue Monday Blues,* a one-act "jazz opera," for a Broadway musical production. As a run-up to Gershwin's classic *Porgy and Bess* (1935) this was more like a stumble. The review in the New York *World* called it "the most dismal, stupid and incredible blackface sketch that has probably ever been perpetrated. In it a dusky soprano finally killed her gambling man. She should have shot all her associates the moment they appeared and then turned the pistol on herself" (qtd. in Goldberg 122). As late as 1932, *George White's Scandals* filled seats on Broadway with songs such as "That's Why Darkies Were Born." Writing in *Opportunity,* Brown acknowledged the popular and degradingly inaccurate depictions of the Negro from Stephen Foster to Al Jolson as an "epidemic" which spread its contagion anywhere money was to be made: "Tin Pan Alley, most of whose dwellers had been no further south than Perth Amboy, frantically sought rhymes for the southern states, cheered over the startling rediscovery of Alabammy and Miami for their key word Mammy . . ." ("Weep" 87). It is against this tide of doggerel that Brown built a levee of authentic African American folksong.

As poet also, notes Stephen E. Henderson, Brown's subtle and insightful understanding of the folk forms "extends the literary range of the blues without losing their authenticity." In fact, Brown approaches the African American folk forms of spiritual, shout, work song, and blues exactly as he had used "the formal measures of the English poets" in his earliest attempts at writing poetry (Henderson 32). It is clear that, for Brown, these stanzas had achieved an equal dignity and utility as literary models.

Among the formal qualities of the blues, Brown's study also focused on language and dialect. Brown's important essay "The Blues as Folk Poetry" (1930) is not so theoretically elaborate or ambitious as the archetype of "Ebonics" offered in Zora Neale Hurston's "Characteristics of Negro Expression" (1934). While the dialect recorded in folklore is integral for Brown, it is *not* of mystical import:

> There is nothing "degraded" about dialect. Dialectical peculiarities are universal. There is something about Negro dialect, in the idiom, the turn of phrase, the music of the vowels and consonants that is worth treasuring.

> ("Our Literary Audience" 45)

In "The Blues as Folk Poetry," Brown finds that the images presented in this dialect form are "highly compressed, concrete, imaginative, original" (383). He cites beautifully conceived lines such as

> My gal's got teeth lak a lighthouse on de sea.
> Every time she smiles she throws a light on me.

But Brown was not primarily interested in collecting poetic, or the more numerous quaint, expressions. As he noted in 1946, his interest in folk materials "was first attracted by certain qualities that I thought the speech of the people had, and I wanted to get for my own writing a flavor, a color, a pungency of speech. Then later I came to something more important—I wanted to get an understanding of people, to acquire an accuracy in the portrayal of their lives" ("Approach" 506).

Brown's work also participates in the creation of an African American "national literature" by endorsing and contributing to a project carefully outlined by Alain Locke in the 1920s. This is not a Modernist program but a modernized replication of the model first articulated in Europe by those who saw a national literature as the refinement of indigenous folk expression. Locke and James Weldon Johnson applied this nineteenth-century model quite specifically to music, seeing in the spirituals the material that—in the hands of gifted black composers—would escape "the lapsing conditions and fragile vehicle of folk art and come firmly into the context of formal music" (Locke, "Negro" 199). The Fisk Jubilee Singers, performing concert settings composed by R. Nathaniel Dett and others, represent the first movement of Locke's envisioned symphony.

Folklorist Arthur Huff Fauset applied the same principle to literature. Writing in Locke's *The New Negro* (1925), Fauset decried the derogatory misrepresentations of authentic African folklore in its American survivals, called for a more professional ethnographic study of it, and predicted that "Negro writers themselves will shortly, no doubt[,] be developing [the folktales and oral traditions of the South] as arduously as [Joel] Chandler Harris, and we hope as successfully, or even more so" (243-44).

While Locke foresaw a great classical music born of the folk forms shaped by slavery, James Weldon Johnson surveyed Broadway's stages and declared a victory for Negro genius, citing the rhythmic impulse of African American music as "the genesis and foundation of our national popular medium for musical expression" (*American Negro Spirituals* 31). Johnson's political interpretation of this development was not hidden. In the preface to his 1926 collection of Negro spirituals, he noted that "America would not be precisely the America it is except for the silent power the Negro has exerted upon it, both positive and negative" (19). Johnson also asserted that authentic folk art posed a serious challenge for any academically trained artist who aspired to transcend, or even match, its distinctive qualities of honesty and emotionally overwhelming beauty.

That the type of reclamation effort Arthur Huff Fauset prescribed for African American folktales should also be required for the blues—a form that only emerged in the first decade of the century—should not surprise those who consider the carefully built and well-maintained mechanism of racism that was running at full throttle before World War II.

Texas A & M College professor Will H. Thomas's *Some Current Folk-Songs of the Negro* was the very first publication of the Texas Folklore Society. While this essay provides evidence that the blues was a widespread and authentic form in Texas in 1912—two years before W. C. Handy published "The St. Louis Blues" and launched its commercial development—the paper also offers disturbing documentation of white academics sitting around enjoying their own genteel version of "darkie" jokes. Sympathetic song collectors were also somewhat tainted by the general paternalism of the region and era. Folklorist John A. Lomax, one of the earliest commentators on the blues, characterized them as "Negro songs of self-pity" in an article published in *The Nation* in 1917. Even when employed by a liberal, such terminology supported the negative social construction of the African American image that James Weldon Johnson succinctly summarized as the view that black people were, at best, "wards" of American society.

Benjamin A. Botkin, writing in 1927, accepted the Texas folklorists' idea that self-pity was "a trait of the Negro, bred in him by centuries of oppression" (231); but Botkin was perceptive enough to understand that out of this "sense of self-pity develops an inevitable conviction of social injustice and an indictment of the existing order" (233). Botkin and Sterling Brown would become allies. They were the same age and shared similar interests in folklore, the experiments of the New Poetry movement, and a high regard for proletarian self-expression as encouraged by intellectuals connected with *The New Masses* and similar journals (Hutchinson 271-73); thus Botkin's annual anthology *Folk-Say: A Regional Miscellany* provided a venue for Brown's essays and the blues-influenced poems collected in **Southern Road** (1932).[2]

"The blues," wrote Brown in *Negro Poetry and Drama* (1937), "tell a great deal about folk-life. The genteel turn away from them in distaste, but blues persist with their terse and tonic shrewdness about human nature" (27). It is also true that the blues differ from the spirituals because the secular form highlights vicarious and ventriloquial qualities. "Ain't nobody here can go there for you, / You got to go there by yourself" is, as Brown puts it, the "sour truth" of the ancient spiritual **"Lonesome Valley"** (**Collected Poems** 98-99). The message of any blues, of course, is just the opposite. The blues singer bids his listener to learn from his or her example before, as Roosevelt Sykes put it, you "make a mistake in life." The poems Brown originally published as a sort of suite titled **"Lonesome Valley"** in Botkin's 1931 *Folk-Say* seem designed to explore this aspect of blues songs.[3]

Brown's three-part **"The New St. Louis Blues"** is deeply and pugnaciously political. In the first poem, even the natural disasters that are so often the topic of blues songs are politicized. After a tornado brings destruction and a flood of refugees, Brown sings:

> Newcomers dodge de mansions, and knocked on de
> po' folks' do',
> Dodged most uh de mansions, and knocked down de
> po' folks' do,
> Never knew us po' folks so popular befo'.
>
> ("**Lonesome Valley**" 119)

When he turns his attention to the way things go in the man-made world, the picture is bleaker still:

> Woman done quit me, my boy lies fast in jail,
> Woman done quit me, pardner lies fast in jail,
> Kin bum tobacco but I cain't bum de jack fo' bail.
>
> Church don't help me, 'cause I ain't got no Sunday
> clothes,
> Church don't help me, got no show-off Sunday
> clothes,
> Preachers and deacons, don't look to get no help from
> those.
>
> Dice are loaded an' de deck's all marked to hell,
> Dice are loaded an' de deck's all marked to hell,
> Whoever runs dis gamble sholy runs it well.
>
> ("**Lonesome Valley**" 121)

Another poem, **"Convicts"**—not written in the blues stanza form—comments on the Southern penal system. Jim, serving ninety days on the chain gang, passes his own home each day as he shuttles between "handcuffs / And a digny cell, / Daytime on the highways, / Nights in hell" (115).[4]

In the poems grouped as **"Lonesome Valley,"** Brown is quite deliberately revising both the folklorists' and the Broadway song-pluggers' misinterpretations of the blues. In his prose writings on the blues from the late 1930s to the early 1950s, Brown would explicitly restate the principles that informed his blues poems. "As well as self-pity there is stoicism in the blues," Brown wrote in 1937. He also directed attention to the collector Lawrence Gellert's discovery of songs that contained searing evidence of "otherwise inarticulate resentment against injustice." The arch language used here is, of course, intended to mock the Southern (and, perhaps also, academic) etiquette of oppression. Brown characterizes the songs Gellert collected as ironic, coded, but defiant protest, representing not self-pity but "a very

adept self-portraiture" (*Negro Poetry and Drama* 27-29). The kinds of songs Gellert collected can be judged by the following verses, recorded in Southern Pines, North Carolina:

> Ah wants no ruckus, but ah ain' dat kin'
> What lets you all shoe-shine on mah behin'.
>
> ("Negro Songs" 233)

Gellert, a contributor to *The New Masses,* met Brown in Boston while traveling with Nancy Cunard in 1932. The three impressed each other greatly (Gellert, "Remembering" 142-43). For his part, Brown cites Gellert's work in almost every article on the blues he subsequently published.

The development of the blues simultaneously as a folk music, vulnerable to scholarly misinterpretation, and as an offering of the commercial music industry, on phonograph records and on the vaudeville stage, is intriguing. For those interested in the study of "pure forms" this dual development offered problems from the start. Nevertheless, unlike Alain Locke, Sterling Brown seemed unworried about the possible fading away of authentic folk expression or its commercial exploitation. What remained important to him was that "the vigor of the creative impulse has not been snapped, even in the slums" of big cities, as far from the source of Southern tradition as anyone might imagine ("Negro Folk Expression" 61). Brown also clearly articulated his understanding of what the living blues form represented, and what the true purpose of the "creative impulse" embodied in the blues really is. "Socially considered," Brown wrote in 1952,

> the blues tell a great deal about one segment of Negro life. It is inaccurate, however, to consider them completely revelatory of the Negro folk, or of the folk transplanted in the cities, or of the lower class in general. The blues represent the secular, the profane, where the spirituals and gospel songs represent the religious.
>
> ("The Blues" 291)

As he had pointed out in 1930,

> There are so many Blues that any preconception might be proved about Negro folk life, as well as its opposite. As documentary proof of dogma about the Negro peasant, then, the Blues are satisfactory and unsatisfactory. As documents about humanity they are invaluable.
>
> ("The Blues as Folk Poetry" 372)

What becomes apparent to anyone who dips into the considerable musicological and sociological literature about African American music published in recent years is that Sterling Brown's early efforts to properly complicate our interpretations have, indeed, achieved a great measure of success.

The same cannot be said of Brown's interest in building a literary edifice on the unique blues form. Though Langston Hughes created masterpieces with that form, and though W. H. Auden, Raymond Patterson, James Emanuel, and Sterling Plumpp have—like Brown himself—also created notable blues works, the attempt to elevate the blues stanza to literary rank has not been so successful as the campaign for the sonnet. It may be fair to consider, however, that the partisans of the sonnet began to promote it 300 years before Sterling Brown discovered the blues.

What Brown certainly did accomplish, however, was to identify the authentic poetic voice of black America, making it heard above the din of racist parody and well-intentioned, sympathetic misinterpretation. In 1953, during the height of the McCarthyist assault on creative expression, Brown saw fit to foreground the political power inherent in the blues songs composed by his friend Waring Cuney and by the popular Josh White. These songs "on poverty, hardship, poor housing and jim crow military service, come from conscious propagandists, not truly folk," Brown wrote. "They make use of the folk idiom in both text and music, however, and the folk listen and applaud. They know very well what Josh White is talking about" ("Negro Folk Expression" 60).[5] It is interesting—and a subtle index of Sterling A. Brown's character—to note that, while in **"Ma Rainey,"** written in 1930, he was content to quote an audience member's appreciation that "'she jes catch hold of us, somekindaway,'" in the 1950s—at a time when it mattered—he was brave enough to explain exactly *why*.

Notes

1. An intriguing discussion of how the New Negro movement attempted to re-site the idea of tradition is offered by Charles H. Rowell's view of the poet as a sort of *adept*: "In a word, when Brown taught and traveled in the South, he became an insider to the multifarious traditions and verbal art forms indigenous to black folk, and through his adaptations of their verbal art forms and spirit he, as poet, became an instrument for their myriad voices. Hence *Southern Road*" (134). How this approach to reclaiming tradition in the service of literary innovation also served Alain Locke's program for the arts as an instrument of race "redemption" via political and social progress is indicated by a comment from Langston Hughes and Arna Bontemps in their introduction to *The Book of Negro Folklore* (1959): "The blues provided a tap-root of tremendous vitality for season after season, vogue after vogue of popular music, and became an American idiom in a broad sense" (vii).

2. Typically placing important but accessible essays by scholars such as Henry Nash Smith in the company of poems by John Gould Fletcher and others, *Folk-Say* was more literary anthology than academic journal. An excellent discussion of Botkin's project is found in Hirsch 12-14.

3. Sterling Brown actually uses the blues stanza form in three ways in his own poems. The earliest approach is found in "Ma Rainey," first published in *Folk-Say* in 1930. Here, as in Langston Hughes's poem "The Weary Blues" (1927), the actual blues verses are set within a more elaborate structure of different free-verse stanzas. The 1931 edition of *Folk-Say* contains Brown's "Tin Roof Blues" and "New St. Louis Blues," both of which are entirely composed in the standard three-line blues stanza form. In 1932 Brown published "Long Track Blues" and "Rent Day Blues"—and here the blues stanzas are disguised as quatrains.

It is important to distinguish between the poems in which Brown uses the actual blues stanza form and those poems which appear to have a "blues feeling" or depict a socioeconomic milieu that might be typical or evocative of the blues. The poem "Southern Road," for example, is not a blues song but a work song—quite specifically of the type used to accompany or "choreograph" the rhythms of sledgehammer or pickaxe work. Similarly, the poem "Memphis Blues" is not a blues; it is an elaborate structure similar to "Ma Rainey" which provides Brown with a setting for an apocalyptically parodistic spiritual.

4. The system of local prison farms and the practice of leasing convict labor were major concerns to African Americans in the South in the early years of the century. As Lawrence Gellert noted regarding his travels in South Carolina and Georgia in the 1920s, "These roads are kept in repair by chain-gangs. Work on them, of course, is in proportion to the number of convicts available. Hence no crime goes long unpunished. Not if there can be found a stray Negro within a hundred-mile radius" (229). This system was in place as early as 1906, as Ray Stannard Baker reported in *Following the Color Line* (95-99). John L. Spivak's contribution to Nancy Cunard's *Negro: An Anthology* includes photographs of prisoners in Georgia being tortured by fastening in stocks or being stretched between posts, situations even more brutally repressive than those recorded by Baker a quarter-century earlier. "No pretext had been necessary to kidnap Africans and bring them to America as slaves. But pretexts would be necessary to kidnap Black Americans and reenslave

them," observes H. Bruce Franklin. The answer was, of course, that "the victims would have to be perceived as criminals" (102).

Many of the songs Lawrence Gellert collected were recorded on the prison sites. Gellert's articles appeared originally in *The New Masses*; the field recordings he made have been released by Rounder Records as *Negro Songs of Protest* (see Bastin 64-67).

5. Testifying before the House Committee on Un-American Activities, White explained his performing for Communist-organized benefits and rallies in the following statement: "Dozens of artists of all races and colors . . . have also given their names and talent and time under the innocent impression that they were on the side of charity and equality. Let me make it clear, if I can, that I am still on that side. The fact that Communists are exploiting grievances for their own purpose does not make those grievances any less real" (*Josh White Songbook* 33).

Works Cited

Baker, Houston A., Jr. *Modernism and the Harlem Renaissance.* Chicago: U of Chicago P, 1987.

Baker, Ray Stannard. *Following the Color Line: An Account of Negro Citizenship in the American Democracy.* 1908. Williamstown: Corner House, 1973.

Bastin, Bruce. *Red River Blues: The Blues Tradition in the Southeast.* Urbana: U of Illinois P, 1986.

Botkin, B. A. "Self-Portraiture and Social Criticism in Negro Folk-Song." 1927. *The Politics and Aesthetics of "New Negro" Literature.* Ed. Cary D. Wintz. New York: Garland, 1996. 230-34.

Brown, Sterling A. "The Approach of the Creative Artist." *Journal of American Folklore* 59 (Oct.-Dec. 1946): 506-07.

———. "The Blues." *Phylon* 13 (1952): 286-92.

———. "The Blues as Folk Poetry." *Folk-Say: A Regional Miscellany.* Ed. B. A. Botkin. Norman: U of Oklahoma P, 1930. 324-39. Rpt. in Hughes and Bontemps, *The Book of Negro Folklore* 371-86.

———. *Collected Poems.* Ed. Michael S. Harper. 1980. Chicago: Tri-Quarterly P, 1989.

———. "Lonesome Valley" [9 poems]. *Folk-Say: A Regional Miscellany.* Ed. B. A. Botkin. Norman: U of Oklahoma P, 1931. 113-23.

———. "Negro Folk Expression: Spirituals, Seculars, Ballads and Work Songs." *Phylon* 14 (1953): 45-61.

———. *Negro Poetry and Drama.* 1937. New York: Arno P, 1969.

———. "Our Literary Audience." *Opportunity* 8 (Feb. 1930): 42-46, 61.

———. "Weep Some More My Ladie." *Opportunity* 10 (Mar. 1932): 87.

———, Arthur P. Davis, and Ulysses Lee, eds. *The Negro Caravan.* 1941. Salem: Ayer, 1987.

Cunard, Nancy, ed. *Negro: An Anthology.* 1934. New York: Ungar, 1970.

Eliot, T. S. "Tradition and the Individual Talent." *The Sacred Wood: Essays on Poetry and Criticism.* 1920. New York: Barnes and Noble, 1960. 47-59.

Fauset, Arthur Huff. "American Negro Folk Literature." Locke, *New Negro* 238-44.

Franklin, H. Bruce. *Prison Literature in America: The Victim as Criminal and Artist.* New York: Oxford UP, 1989.

Gabbin, Joanne V. *Sterling A. Brown: Building the Black Aesthetic Tradition.* 1985. Charlottesville: UP of Virginia, 1994.

Gellert, Lawrence. "Negro Songs of Protest." Cunard 226-37.

———. "Remembering Nancy Cunard." *Nancy Cunard: Brave Poet, Indomitable Rebel, 1896-1965.* Ed. Hugh Ford. Philadelphia: Chilton, 1968. 141-44.

Goldberg, Isaac. *George Gershwin: A Study in American Music.* 1931. New York: Ungar, 1958.

Henderson, Stephen E. "The Heavy Blues of Sterling Brown: A Study of Craft and Tradition." *Black American Literature Forum* 14 (Spring 1980): 32-44.

Hirsch, Jerrold. "Folklore in the Making: B. A. Botkin." *Journal of American Folklore* 100 (Jan.-Mar. 1987): 3-38.

Hughes, Langston, and Arna Bontemps, eds. *The Book of Negro Folklore.* New York: Dodd, Mead, 1959.

Hurston, Zora Neale. "Characteristics of Negro Expression." 1934. *The Sanctified Church.* Berkeley: Turtle Island, 1981. 49-68.

Hutchinson, George. *The Harlem Renaissance in Black and White.* Cambridge: Harvard UP, 1995.

Johnson, James Weldon, and J. Rosamond Johnson. *The Book of American Negro Spirituals.* 1926. New York: Da Capo P, 1981.

Locke, Alain. "The Negro Spirituals." Locke, *New Negro* 199-210.

———, ed. *The New Negro.* 1925. New York: Atheneum, 1992.

Lomax, John A. "Self-Pity in Negro Folk-Songs." *Nation* 9 Aug. 1917: 141-45.

Rowell, Charles H. "Sterling A. Brown and the Afro-American Folk Tradition." *Studies in the Literary Imagination* 7 (Fall 1974): 131-52.

Spivak, John L. "Flashes from Georgia Chain Gangs." Cunard 124-30.

Thomas, Will H. *Some Current Folk-Songs of the Negro.* 1912. Austin: Texas Folklore Society, 1936.

White, Josh, with Robert Shelton and Walter Raim. *The Josh White Songbook.* Chicago: Quadrangle, 1963.

Charles H. Rowell (essay date 1997)

SOURCE: Rowell, Charles H. "Sterling A. Brown and the Afro-American Folk Tradition." In *Harlem Renaissance Re-examined: A Revised and Expanded Edition,* edited by Victor A. Kramer and Robert A. Russ, pp. 333-53. Troy, N.Y.: The Whitson Publishing Company, 1997.

[*In the following essay, Rowell explores how Brown's studies of African American folk traditions and culture impacted his poetic work.*]

One of the concerted efforts of the "New Negro" writers of the Twenties and Thirties was the attempt to reinterpret black life in America and thereby provide a more accurate, more objective, representation of black people than that popularized in the reactionary and sentimental literature of the preceding decades. Alain Locke, a major voice of the New Negro Movement, wrote in the mid-Twenties that "the Negro to-day wishes to be known for what he is, even in his faults and short comings, and scorns a craven and precarious survival at the price of seeming to be what he is not."[1] In their creative works, many New Negro writers subscribed to that position, for they knew that much of the earlier literature about the black experience in the United States was fraught with distorted images of ante- and post-bellum black Americans—their life and culture and their history and traditions. That is, much of the poetry, fiction and drama about black people was based on the sentimental, plantation and minstrel traditions, and, therefore, had little or nothing to do with the lives of black people in America. However numerous their failings might be, New Negro writers, with a high degree of achievement, tried to create a new stage upon which to play out the kaleidoscopic drama of black life in America.

The effort to reinterpret Afro-American life and character went in various directions. Following the "just-like-white-folks philosophy," some writers, for example, created works which emphasized the similarities between blacks and whites. Other writers, subscribing to the decadent white belief in the "exotic Negro," emphasized the so-called "primitivism" of black people. There were, of course, other writers whose aesthetic visions were broader than those of the aforementioned groups. This third group realized that to express the souls of black folk, the artist has to divest himself of preconceived and false notions about black people, and create an art whose foundation is the ethos from which black life, history, culture, and traditions all spring.

It is this third group of New Negro writers—Langston Hughes, Jean Toomer, Zora Neale Hurston, and Sterling Brown among them—who set out to reevaluate "African-American history and folk culture."[2] It is this group of writers who tried to do what James Weldon Johnson said he attempted to do in his later poetry: to rear a superstructure of conscious art upon "the American Negro's cultural background and his creative folk-art."[3] This group of young writers was indeed familiar with the pronouncements that James Weldon Johnson, Alain Locke, and others made on the importance of the Afro-American folk tradition to the development of the black artist.[4] In their efforts to build a self-conscious art upon folk art, these writers, just as their black predecessors (Paul Laurence Dunbar and Charles W. Chesnutt) had done in their more balanced works, brought to Afro-American literature a quality that became one of its main currents: the ethos of black folk. However, of the younger New Negro writers, it was Sterling A. Brown and Zora Neale Hurston, as Larry Neal points out, who made the systematic studies of certain aspects of the Afro-American folk tradition.[5] And much of what Hurston and Brown discovered from their studies found its way into their conscious art. While Langston Hughes concentrated on urban black folk in *The Weary Blues* (1926) and *Fine Clothes to the Jew* (1927), Hurston and Brown, like Jean Toomer in *Cane* (1923), probed deeply into the life and culture of Southern black folk. But, whereas some may argue that Hurston occasionally failed aesthetically in fiction, Brown succeeded in poetry.

Unlike Zora Neale Hurston (1903-1960), whose background was small-town South, Brown was born and reared in Washington, D.C., where his father was a minister of distinction and a professor of religion at Howard University. After he graduated from Washington's Dunbar High School, Brown received the B.A. and M.A. degrees in English literature from Williams College (Massachusetts) and Harvard University, respectively. Such a background was not, however, a liability to him for his preparation as folklorist, critic of Afro-American literature, and poet in the folk manner. Instead his background proved to be an asset, for his New England education and wide reading developed in him a critical sensibility, one which he long used in positive service to the black community. Early in his career as litterateur, he discovered that the representations of black peasants in most books were very different from the black peasants he had known and seen in

Washington. Realizing that the images of black people in existing literature were largely false, Brown set out to correct what he saw.

"What motivates a middle-class Black man and a Harvard graduate . . . to devote his life to portraying less well-to-do folks?" queries Genevieve Ekaete. She answers:

> Being Black is the key. . . . According to [Sterling Brown], he was indignant at the corrupted folk speech publicized by "white comic writers like Octavus Roy Cohen." From his experience, Brown says, he knew his people didn't talk that way. It wasn't enough for him to enjoin them to "Stop knowing it all!" He had to bring some semblance of balance by putting his people down on black and white to counter the proliferating distortions from other sources.[6]

Then, too, early in his teaching career Brown read the new realistic poetry in American life:—that of Frost, Sandburg, Masters, Lindsay and Robinson, for example. In their "democratic approach to the people," Brown saw much that reflected his own thoughts about ordinary people. Brown recalls: "when Carl Sandburg said 'yes' to the American people, I wanted to say 'yes' to my people."[7] Brown's "yes" was to give us carefully wrought poems portraying "common" black folk "in a manner constant with them."[8] His "yes" to black people was also to give us a series of critical works which attempted to counter "the proliferating distortions" of black folk life and character. As early as the Twenties, Brown began writing a series of critical studies and reviews on the portrayal of blacks in American literature. In 1929, he observed that

> From Kennedy's "Swallow Barn," about the first treatment of the plantation, down to Dixon's rabid Ku Klux Klan propaganda, the Negro has been shown largely as an animal. Kennedy, doing a piece of special pleading, showed the Negro as parasitical, excessively loyal, contented, irresponsible, and so forth. Dixon showed his Negro characters, not as faithful dogs, but as mad curs. His brutes are given to rapine, treachery, bestiality, and gluttony.[9]

Like other New Negro writers, Brown knew that such portrayals were neither accurate characterizations nor true expressions of the souls of black folk.

After study at Williams and Harvard, Brown prepared himself to counter distorting images of black people perpetuated in American literature. To do so, he read widely and critically into the literature by and about black people, and carefully studied Afro-American history and folk culture. Hence his *Negro Poetry and Drama, The Negro in American Fiction* (both in 1938), and several important periodical essays and reviews—sources which no serious student of American literature can ignore. But to counter the distorting images as poet,

Brown knew he had to go beyond books and his Washington experiences for material: he went directly to black people in the South. That is, as he taught and traveled in the South, he lived among and carefully observed those peasants who created black folk traditions—traditions which sustained them in their daily lives. Writing in 1934 about Brown as "folk poet," Alain Locke asserted that

> Sterling Brown has listened long and carefully to the folk in their intimate hours, when they are talking to themselves, not, so to speak, as in Dunbar, but actually as they do when the masks of protective mimicry fall. Not only has he dared to give quiet but bold expression to this private thought and speech, but he has dared to give the Negro peasant credit for thinking.[10]

In a word, when Brown taught and traveled in the South, he became an insider to the multifarious traditions and verbal art forms indigenous to black folk, and through his adaptations of their verbal art forms and spirit he, as poet, became an instrument for their myriad voices. Hence *Southern Road.*

When *Southern Road* appeared in 1932, reviewers, as James Weldon Johnson had observed in his introduction to the collection, were quick to recognize Brown's absorption of the spirit and the verbal art of black folk. Critics realized that Brown had tapped the black folk ethos which later Afro-American poets would draw from, that he had captured the essence of black folk life and culture, without the distortion and sentimentality of earlier American writers. In form and content, most of Brown's poems reflect some aspect of the life and oral traditions of black people. And it is through his folk-oriented poems that he makes his most significant contribution to the corpus of Afro-American poetry.[11]

In the Preface to the 1921 edition of his *Book of American Negro Poetry,* James Weldon Johnson made an influential comment about the direction the black poet in America should take. Inherent in Johnson's seminal statement are the principles embodied in Brown's major poetry. Johnson asserted that what the black American poet

> needs to do is something like what Synge did for the Irish; he needs to find a form that will express the racial spirit by symbols from within rather than by symbols from without, such as the mere mutilation of English spelling and pronunciation. He needs a form that is freer and larger than dialect, but which will still hold the racial flavor; a form expressing the imagery, the idioms, and peculiar turns of thought, and the distinctive humor and pathos, too, of the Negro, but which will also be capable of voicing the deepest and highest emotions and aspirations, and allow of the widest range of subjects and the widest scope of treatment.[12]

To give voice to the common black man in poetry, Brown drew heavily on forms that grew directly out of the black American experience; he made use of Afro-

American folksongs—their techniques, idiom and spirit. Brown knew that the ideas and art of the folksongs were expressive of the people who created them; that Afro-American "folk forms and cultural responses," to use the words of George E. Kent, "were themselves definitions of black life created by blacks on the bloody and pine-scented Southern soil and upon the blackboard jungle of urban streets, tenement buildings, store-front churches, and dim-lit bars."[13] What, then, could be more appropriate modes for poetic reinterpretations of black life in America than the worksong, the blues, the spiritual, and the ballad?

In **"Southern Road,"** the title poem of his first collection, Brown draws upon the forms and spirit of the worksong and the blues. To express the tragic voice of despondency of black chain gangs so often seen on Southern roads, Brown fuses adapted techniques of the worksong and the blues. But the aesthetic and ideational result is something more than the blues or the worksong.

Because the worksong as a distinctive form has all but passed away, it is important here to make a brief comment on its nature and function. At one time the worksong was sung by black laborers throughout the Americas and Africa. Like much black music, the worksong is functional; it was composed not for the entertainment of an audience but as an accompaniment to labor. As a functional form of music, the worksong was variously "used to pace work" and "supply a rhythm for work," to give directions, to "help pass the time," and "to offer a partial outlet for . . . tensions and frustrations and angers." Moreover, for convicts, worksongs changed "the nature of the work by putting the work into the worker's framework rather than the guards'."[14] On the worksong accompanying voluntary and involuntary labor, Brown wrote that

> . . . worksongs accompany work in unison. Roustabouts on the levees, steel-drivers, axemen in the woods, the shantymen on the old windjammers, lighten their labor by singing in rhythm with it. A gang driving spikes will sing, punctuating their lines with a grunt as the hammer falls. . . . [T]he verses are somewhat unconnected, the men singing what first comes to their minds, concerned chiefly with the functional rhythm.[15]

Brown's comments are descriptive of the type of worksong which accompanies communal labor and requires group rhythm—what Bruce Jackson calls "timed work," such as cross-cutting, logging, flatweeding, and steel-driving.[16] The grunt ("hunh") Brown mentions is a rhythmical or timing device in some worksongs. In others such as **"Here, Rattler, Here,"** a repeated ejaculatory phrase or line following the song leader's assertion serves the same function. Brown's comments on the worksong, especially his observations on its rhythm and the inconsecutiveness of its stanzas, are essential to our

understanding and appreciation of his adaptation of its communal form in **"Southern Road."** The artistic techniques of a worksong like "John Henry Hammer Song" not only bear his comments out but suggest the kind of worksong he drew on for conscious poetry.

A comparison of the first stanzas of **"Southern Road"** and "John Henry Hammer Song" will show how Brown incorporates the rhythm of the worksong in his poem:

Swing dat hammer	/hunh/
Steady, bo';	
Swing dat hammer	/hunh/
Steady, bo';	
Ain't no rush, bebby,	
Long ways to go.	

(**"Southern Road"**)

Dis is de Hammer	/hunh/
Killt John Henry	/hunh/
Twon't kill me, baby,	/hunh/
Twon't kill me	

("John Henry Hammer Song")[17]

Brown punctuates lines one and three with "hunh," the "grunt" he refers to as being uttered "as the hammer falls." Although the transcriber of "John Henry Hammer Song" did not represent the "grunts," the rhythm of the work which the song accompanied probably required that "hunh" be uttered after the song leader's assertions in lines one, two, and three. The "bebby" in Brown's poem and the "baby" in the hammer song serve the same function: they, like the grunt, aid in the rhythm; and they signal the closing of each stanza. Moreover, they suggest the presence of not so much an auditor but a fellow worker, as does the directional "Steady, bo'" in stanza one of Brown's poem. In **"Southern Road,"** Brown, it should be remembered, does not imitate the rhythm of the worksong. Rather, like Johnson in his use of the rhythm of the folk sermon in *God's Trombones*, Brown adapts the rhythm of the communal worksong.

In addition to adapting the rhythm of the communal worksong, Brown takes the worksong to a high level of conscious art. He transforms the worksong into a piece of coherent art by creating stanzas which are connected in content as well as rhythm. Like most worksongs, **"Southern Road"** is not narrative. Brown's poem does, however, recount a unified and coherent series of situations or conditions of a despondent but stoic convict. That panoramic series produces one effect: sympathy or sorrow for the tragic fate of the speaker who has been sentenced to life imprisonment for murder.

Concentrating on the convict's woes, the poem takes into account the problems of his family in the outside world as well as his own within the confines of the prison. He can do nothing about those problems, for he is powerless. The first stanza is about his own and his fellow convicts' immediate situation. Their work, which has no private goal, is interminable—hence they need not rush. In the following stanzas we discover the cause of his imprisonment, and the mental anguish brought on by it and the condition of his family. In a state of powerlessness, he is tormented psychologically as well as physically, for his daughter has become a street woman; his son, a wanderer; and his wife, a hospitalized mother of a coming child. Moreover, the convict-speaker thinks of his poor mother rocking her misery, and he recalls his father cursing him on his deathbed. The last three stanzas move back to the convict's immediate condition: he is chained ("double-shackled") to dehumanizing labor, with a white guard damning his soul. The final stanza brings his suffering full circle: he is doomed; he is on the chain gang for life—"po' los' boy / Evahmo'." His appears to be an insurmountable despondency, for his powerlessness and that of his lost family, and the social and economic curse of the larger society render him helpless. Unlike the ironic and rebellious speaker in "John Henry Hammer Song" and other worksongs, the speaker in Brown's **"Southern Road"** assumes a blues attitude. He of necessity resigns himself to his tragic fate.

"No poem more pathetically depicts the despair of the entire race than **'Southern Road,'**" writes Jean Wagner.

> Here the entire spirit of revolt is already snuffed out and transcended, since it is seen as useless, and there is a stoic acceptance of destiny. Confronting a hostile universe, the black man knows that he is dolefully alone and has no surviving connection with an outside world that might offer him help or a gleam of hope.[18]

"Southern Road" is a lyrical expression of powerlessness and despondency—one picture of "the tragedy of the southern Negro." It is, then, important to remember that the speaker of the poem is a convict, not a Black Everyman; that his despondency is that of his people, but that other poems in Brown's first collection and elsewhere are needed to round out his picture of the tragic condition of Southern black folk. It is important to remember, too, that in the world of Sterling Brown the black man's response to the inhumanities of his white oppressors is not always acceptance. His response, however futile it may prove to be, is sometimes like that of Joe in **"The Ballad of Joe Meek"** or that of Sam in **"Sam Smiley"**: revolt in the face of inevitable destruction.

To express the powerlessness and despair of his convict-speaker, Brown also assimilates the stanzaic pattern of the blues. Like the traditional blues stanza, each stanza of **"Southern Road"** is divided into two parts. Part one constitutes a statement, or presents a situation or problem. Part two gives a response, the speaker's (or more accurately, singer's) reaction to the problem or the effect of the problem upon him. Moreover, as in the blues, the statement of the problem or situation is repeated in **"Southern Road"** but without the occasional variation. The statement is followed by a concluding response once presented—e.g., "Ball and chain, bebby, / On my min'." A reordering of one of Brown's stanzas reveals how closely it approximates the traditional stanza of the blues:

> Chain gang nevah—hunh—
> Let me go;
> Chain gang nevah—hunh—
> Let me go;
> Po' los' boy, bebby,
> Evahmo'. . . .

Rather than emphasize the speaker's response to the problem as in "John Henry Hammer Song," Brown concentrates on the problem through repetition, thus intensifying the tragic situation of the speaker. In Brown's hands the worksong is transformed into a new blues form, a blues-worksong, permeated with all the resignation and toughness of traditional blues. In the direct and terse idiom characteristic of the Afro-American folksong, Brown, in **"Southern Road,"** captures at once a single and, ultimately, a communal cry of the desponding Southern black voice.

Brown draws more directly on the traditional form, the subjects, and the idiom of the blues in other poems. In some of those, however, he, as self-conscious artist, is less successful than in others in which he fuses various folk and literary techniques. In the former, he, as Alvin Aubert observes of Langston Hughes's direct use of the blues mode,[19] almost replicates those artistic techniques marking the distinctiveness of the blues form. The three poems which comprise **"New St. Louis Blues,"** for instance, adhere too closely to the blues form. In them, Brown uses the two-part three line stanza form of classic blues, each line marked by a caesura. But instead of the common *aab* rhyme scheme, Brown's stanzas are triplets. Aesthetically, these poems are like Hughes's "Morning After" and "Midwinter Blues." They lack what George Kent calls the resources of the blues singer: "the singing voice, instrumental music, facial expression and gesture"—all of which help the singer drive his lyrics "into our spirit."[20]

Brown's poems in the blues mode are more captivating than Hughes's. What interests us most about Brown's poems in **"New St. Louis Blues"** is the broadness and variety of his subjects and his handling of them. In Hughes's blues mode poems, the central subject is usually love relationships, rendered in the first person and through the associational technique of the blues. Less individualized, Brown's poems in **"New St. Louis Blues"** cover various subjects. In **"Market Street Woman,"** there is the troubled life of the prostitute, to whom life is "dirty in a hundred onery ways." Written in the first person, **"Low Down"** describes the down-

and-outness of a "bummin' cut plug," who tragically internalizes society's vision of him as a worthless being and who views life and that which follows as a loaded game of dice. **"Tornado Blues"** recounts the havoc wrought by a storm on a poor black community, which must suffer not only from the storm's destructiveness but from the economic exploitation of the white community also. In **"Tornado Blues"** and such poems as **"Children of the Mississippi," "Foreclosure"** and **"Cabaret,"** the Southern black man is a victim of natural disasters as well as racial injustice. These six poems clearly support Jean Wagner's thesis that Brown's poetry "depicts the Negro as the victim not only of the white man, but of all that surrounds him."[21]

Beyond the obvious blues form previously noted, the art of **"New St. Louis Blues"** is an achievement, for here Brown takes blues techniques to a literary level. In **"Tornado Blues"** he skillfully uses personification, a figure of speech frequently used in the blues. In some blues such as Leadbelly's "Good Morning Blues," Bessie Smith's "In House Blues" and Leroy Carr's "Midnight Hour Blues," the blues itself is personified. Brown's personification of the merciless tornado and its effects gives irony to the situation in **"Tornado Blues."** After the heartless wind completes its work and disappears, it leaves in its wake destruction, fear, death and sorrow. The speaker in the poem comments:

> Newcomers dodge de mansions, and knocked on de
>   po' folks' do',
> Dodged most of the mansions, and knocked down de
>   po' folks' do',
> Never know us po' folks so popular befo'—

It is ironic that these poor black people, rather than rich white people, would be visited, for they had little to offer their cruel guests. Brown's extended use of personification gives coherence to **"Tornado Blues"**—a coherence less directly achieved through the usual associational technique of traditional blues.

In **"Ma Rainey,"** Brown uses the blues in another way, or rather he uses self-conscious poetry to comment on what Larry Neal refers to as the ethos of the blues.[22] Although **"Ma Rainey"** is a celebration of a single blues singer, Brown's poem is ultimately a description of the general effect and function of all blues singers and their art. The idea of Brown's poem is not unlike some of the views set forth by Larry Neal, Albert Murray and Ralph Ellison on the blues and blues singers. The blues singer, writes Neal, acts "as ritual poet" and "reflects the horrible and beautiful realities of life." "The blues singer," Neal continues, "is not an alienated artist attempting to impose his view on the world of others. His ideas are the reflection of an unstated general point-of-view."[23] Murray sees the blues musician as "fulfilling the same fundamental existential requirement that determines the mission of the poet, the priest, and the medicine man. He is making an affirmative and hence exemplary and heroic response to that which André Malraux describes as *la condition humaine*."[24] For Ellison, Bessie Smith was a "priestess"; she was "a celebrant who affirmed the values of the group and man's ability to deal with chaos."[25] That Brown's Ma Rainey was not "an alienated artist" but a priestess-poet-medicinewoman of the people is voiced throughout the poem. First of all, "as ritual poet" Ma Rainey attracted throngs of people wherever she performed—e.g., in Missouri and

> Fo' miles on down,
> To New Orleans delta
> An' Mobile town. . . .

And when she performed, her first person songs, which expressed the collective experience of her people, moved her auditors, for she could "Git way inside" them: "She jes' catch hold of us somekindaway." Her performance was ritual; and her songs, medicine to "keep us strong." In other words, her effect, though secular, was not unlike that of the black folk preacher in his sermons: it gave her auditors fortitude to confront and endure "de hard luck / Roun'" their "do'" and "de lonesome road" they "mus' go. . . ." Her songs bore witness to their many troubles and, thereby, made meaning of the chaotic world they confronted perpetually. No wonder, then, when Ma Rainey sang "Backwater Blues"—that song of personal and collective suffering from natural disaster—

> '. . . de folks, dey natchally bowed dey heads an'
>   cried,
> Bowed dey heavy heads, shet dey moufs up tight an'
>   cried,
> An' Ma lef' de stage, an' followed some de folks
>   outside.'

Brown's skillful use of the blues mode in part four of **"Ma Rainey"** is similar to Hughes's in "The Weary Blues." In neither poem is there mere replication. Rather the blues mode is thematically functional in each poem. Brown uses the form to illustrate further the effect of Ma Rainey's blues artist on her auditors. He excerpts and alters lines (one line of the statement and the response) from three stanzas of Bessie Smith's popular "Backwater Blues,"[26] and follows them with a stanza (quoted above) in the blues form. That stanza, a triplet, describes the effect of Ma Rainey's ritualized performance—an effect which is at once cathartic and entertaining.

It is important to note that Brown's selection of "Backwater Blues" is very appropriate. Not only do the lines further the poem thematically; they, like the poems of **"New St. Louis Blues,"** indirectly make a comment on the subject of the blues: that its subject is not limited to love relations. Because several women blues singers had popularized the form with lyrics dealing with love, many people concluded that the blues "are a woman's longing cry for her 'man'. The subject matter," wrote Brown in 1937,

> is not so limited, however, and blues aplenty can be found bewailing tornadoes, high water, hard times in farming, or insisting upon the need for traveling, for leaving this cold-hearted town. As well as self pity there is stoicism in the blues.[27]

Moreover, Brown's selection of "Backwater Blues" gave an air of immediacy to the poem—i.e., his readers were no doubt familiar with Bessie Smith's song and the countless problems caused by floods in the Mississippi Valley, and other river and lowland areas, as recounted in Brown's **"Children of the Mississippi,"** **"Foreclosure"** and other poems. Therefore, while implying that the range of the subject of the blues is not limited, Brown, in part four of **"Ma Rainey,"** provided his early readers with an experience that was as immediate to them as the threat of air pollution is to us.

Brown's use of other forms of black folk music is similar to his fusion of the blues mode in **"Ma Rainey."** His fusion of folk music forms with self-conscious literary techniques is thematically functional and constant with the folk and folk life he portrays. In **"Strong Men,"** for example, there are quoted lines from various black folksongs. **"Strong Men,"** it should be noted, is about black people's strength to survive in the face of racism and economic exploitation; the poem is a celebration of the stoicism of black Americans. In other words, in spite of the white man's dehumanization of him from the Middle Passage through the twentieth century, the black man has endured; he has never been completely broken, as it were, for "The strong men keep a-comin' on." In fact, "Gittin' stronger. . . ." To develop the idea of black stoicism, Brown juxtaposes his catalogue of inhumanities against black people to passages from spirituals and secular songs. The songs Brown quotes bespeak the black man's hope, strength and endurance—his dogged will to survive—born out of the suffering, profitless labor, racial segregation, etc., described in the poem. For centuries these songs and others have served as a solace and a source of strength for black people. As Brown says in **"Children's Children,"** these songs, though unknown or laughed at by first generation Great Migrators, were the "sole comfort" of a suffering Black South people, who have known

> Long days beneath the torrid Dixie sun
> In miasma'd riceswamps;
> The chopping of dried grass, on the third go round
> In strangling cotton;
> Wintry nights in mud-daubed makeshift huts
> With these songs, sole comfort.

The old undefeated black woman in **"Virginia Portrait"** has her "Old folksongs chanted underneath the stars . . . ," along with her religion and her pleasant memories of times past to help her survive the many problems she faces. Through his use of black folk music in **"Strong Men,"** **"Children's Children,"** and **"Virginia Portrait,"** Brown comments on Black South strength and, indirectly, the function of music in black life and culture. As in **"Strong Men,"** Brown uses excerpts from the spiritual for thematic purposes in **"When de Saints Go Ma'ching Home."** The lines from the spiritual of the same title are expressive of the dream of the speaker-musician: on Judgment Day he hopes to meet his mother in Heaven and be counted among the saints. The lines from the spiritual also have a technical function; they serve as transitions from one roll call to the next of persons the musician envisions as likely and unlikely saints. Brown's incorporation of passages from black folksongs in his poetry is not unlike a technique T. S. Eliot, Melvin Tolson, Ezra Pound and Robert Hayden employed in their poetry. But Brown's poetry makes fewer demands on the reader.

The stark simplicity and directness of expression in the catalogue of inhumanities in **"Strong Men"** and, especially, **"Old Lem"** are akin to those in the following slave secular recorded by Frederick Douglass in *My Bondage and My Freedom* (1853):

> We raise de wheat,
> Dey gib us de corn;
> We bake de bread,
> Dey gib us de crust;
> We sif de meal,
> Dey gib us de huss;
> We peel de meat,
> Dey gib us the skin;
> And dat's the way
> Dey take us in;
> We skim de pot.
> Dey gib us de liquor,
> And say dat's good enough for nigger.[28]

A passage from **"Old Lem"** will show Brown's ability to capture that same simplicity and directness of expression through the voice of Old Lem:

> "They weigh the cotton
> They store the corn
>   We only good enough
>   To work the rows;
> They run the commissary
> They keep the books
>   We gotta be grateful
>   For being cheated;
> Whippersnapper clerks
> Call us out of our name
>   We got to say mister
>   To spindling boys
> They make our figgers
> Turn somersets

We buck in the middle
　　Say, 'Thankyuh, sah.'"[29]

The voice of Old Lem adapts the cadence of the slave
secular. Moreover, like the speaker in the slave secular,
Old Lem, without resorting to excessive figures of
speech or bombastic, emotional language, articulates
the powerlessness of his people and the many injustices
heaped upon them. No rhetorical tricks becloud his
revelation of facts. The clarity and power of the dialect
he speaks belie the false image of the black man in the
literature of the minstrel and plantation traditions, in
which he is represented as a verbose clown, misusing
and mutilating polysyllabic words. Using collected
folklore, folksongs, and the living speech of the peasant
blacks he met and befriended as indices to rural black
dialect, Brown, in **"Old Lem"** and many other poems,
attempted to counter the vicious propaganda about black
dialect disseminated in American literature. In a word
Brown took the dialect of the black peasant and shaped
it into consummate art.

Not all of Brown's folk characters speak with the
simplicity and directness found in **"Old Lem."** Like
other dialects, black folk speech has its variety, and the
form used at a given moment depends upon the occasion as well as the nature of the speaker and his
linguistic region. Hence the dialect of the speaker in
"Sister Lou" is constant with her Southern character
and her vision of Heaven, whereas some of the
vocabulary ("down the country," "dicties," "pennies on
de numbers") of the speaker's dialect in **"Tin Roof
Blues"** reflects his Northern urban experience. In **"Sister Lou,"** the female speaker's vision of Heaven, that
place where she and her auditor hope to be relieved of
the troubles of this world, is couched in an idiom that is
replete with homely images. Her images and metaphors
are reflective of her experience and her status in
Southern society. As in spirituals and gospel songs, her
God, Jesus, and the saints are seen in anthropomorphic
terms. Her Heaven is reflective of places of earthly
wealth—places which, from her angle of vision, suggest comfort. The passage from this world to the next
will be by train, and, during her auditor's stay in heaven,
she should visit "Wid frien' Jesus fo' a spell." God and
His saints have human attributes, and her relation to
them will be a human relation. Although the organization of this Heaven is reflective of what she knows on
earth, God, the Master of the Big House in Heaven,
will change her role. No longer will she be the servant;
she will become a lady with her own room

　　. . . wid windows
　　Opening on cherry trees an' plum trees
　　Bloomin' everlastin'

She will, moreover, have servants, but they will not
disturb her room or her rest. She, a lady in Heaven, will
be done with all the rushing imposed on black servants

in this world. In short, Brown's poetic idiom of the
folk, however secular, is constant with the folk vision
of Heaven—a reflection of all that the folk have seen as
positive and wanted in this world.

Again in **"Memphis Blues,"** Brown employs the
rhythm idiom of black folk church. In fact, he fuses the
rhythm and imagery of the black folk sermon with the
ejaculatory response of the blues and gospel, and the
rhythm of folk rhymes. Parts one and three of **"Memphis Blues"** employ the rhythm of black folk rhymes.
Although part one uses the rhythm of the folk rhyme,
underlining its Biblical and historical allusions is the
black folk preacher's vision of the threat of destruction.
The threat here is not so much "the fire next time" for
which the sinner is to prepare his soul, but the destruction of Memphis, Tennessee, by floods and tornadoes.
Ultimately the poem is a comment on the transitory
nature of all things man-made. In other words, just as
great cities of the past fell to decay, so will Memphis.
But, because this Memphis does not belong to the black
man, the various speakers are indifferent to its inevitable
destruction; if Memphis falls, "Nigger won't worry," or
if "Memphis come back / Ain' no skin / Off de nigger's
back." Rather than prepare for the destruction as the
auditors of an exhorting preacher would expect his
congregation to do, the speakers stoically accept it
without reprimand from the general speaker. Their indifference is summed up in part three, an excellent
employment of the rhythm of black folk rhymes:

　　Memphis go
　　By Flood or Flame;
　　Nigger won't worry
　　All de same—
　　Memphis go
　　Memphis come back,
　　Ain' no skin
　　Off de nigger's back.
　　All dese cities
　　Ashes, rust. . . .
　　De win' sing sperrichals
　　Through deir dus'.

The rhythm of that stanza is similar to that in the following rhyme entitled "Aunt Kate":

　　Ole Aunt Date, she died so late
　　She couldn't get in at the Heaven Gate.
　　The Angels met her with a great big club,
　　Knocked her right back in the washin' tub.[30]

And in "Precious Things":

　　Hold my rooster, hold my hen,
　　Pray don't touch my Grecian Bend.

　　Hold my bonnet, hold my shawl,
　　Pray don't touch my waterfall.

　　Hold my hands by the finger tips,
　　But pray don't touch my sweet little lips.[31]

Through the rhythm of folk rhymes, Brown intensifies the black man's indifference toward the destruction of Memphis, for folk rhymes are not only humorous but playful. The threat of the destruction of Memphis is dismissed lightly, for it is of less concern to the black man than it is to the white man, who claims the city as his own.

Presenting each speaker's reaction to the threat of destruction, part two of **"Memphis Blues"** fuses the voices of the black folk preacher, and the blues and gospel singers. Each stanza is divided into two parts: a call in the voice of the preacher and a response in the voices of musicians. Like the black folk preacher using repetitious, formulaic and rhetorical questions to exhort his congregation to prepare their souls for Judgment Day, the general speaker calls:

> Watcha gonna do when de tall flames roar,
> Tall flames roar, Mistah Lovin' Man?

And the Loving Man responds:

> Gonna love my brownskin better'n before—
> Gonna love my baby lak a do right man,
> Gonna love my brown baby, oh, my Lawd!

The first two lines, which initiate the last three lines of each stanza, convey the threat of destruction, presented in terms of the traditional fire-water-wind-flame imagery found in the folk sermon. The general speaker's identification or address to each speaker responding by his vocation or avocation recalls the descriptive appellation of the "sinner man" and "gambling man." The repeated, formulaic call ("What you gonna do when . . ."), Presented in a carefully measured rhythm, exemplifies one of the techniques used by the folk preacher to "move" his congregation. Ironically, the response of each speaker in the poem has nothing to do with the impending destruction; while Memphis is being destroyed, each speaker plans to do what he thinks is best for him. On the other hand, the sentiment and repetition of the response recall the blues, but its ejaculatory "oh, my Lawd" is from the tradition of the "shout," and spiritual and gospel singing, which runs throughout "New Steps." **"Memphis Blues,"** then, is not a blues poem in the sense that **"New St. Louis Blues," "Kentucky Blues," "Riverbank Blues,"** and **"Ma Rainey"** are. But underlining each speaker's indifference in **"Memphis Blues"** is the sensibility of the blues singer—his stoic ability to transcend his deprived condition.

The dialect of the black folk figures in Brown's poetry is constant with their character. Honed in black folk life, the dialect he employs has none of the "humor and pathos" of the contrived speech used by "black" characters in the literature of the plantation tradition. Neither is the dialect in his poetry a transcription of how blacks supposedly spoke. Although he retains some of the pronunciations common to black speech, Brown does not arbitrarily mutilate the spellings of words to suggest the unlettered character of his folk. At a time when many black poets were avoiding black dialect as a medium for poetry, Brown, wrote Johnson in his Introduction to *Southern Road,* "infused his poetry with genuine characteristic flavor by adopting as his medium the common, racy, living speech of the Negro in certain phases of real life." From that speech, Brown, with a good ear and a sensibility attuned to the folk, selects its varied rhythms, idioms, metaphors and images, and transforms them into conscious art.

Like Euro-American and other Afro-American poets of the twentieth century, Brown has also employed the traditions of the folk ballad in his poetry. Influencing more than fifteen poems in *Southern Road,* the ballad, along with the blues mode, is the most frequently used form in the collection. At times, he adopts the ballad form; at others, he combines the narrative techniques of the ballad with artistic techniques of other forms. **"Ma Rainey"** and **"Georgie Grimes,"** in which he combines the narrative technique and the stanzaic patterns of the ballad with the ethos of the blues, are excellent examples of the fusion of folk forms. **"Ma Rainey"** is, says Stephen Henderson, an "invented . . . blues-ballad, which, as a literary phenomenon, is as distinctive as Wordsworth's 'lyrical ballad.'"[32] In other poems, such as **"Frankie and Johnny," "The Ballad of Joe Meek,"** and the Slim Greer series, Brown relies, in the main, on the ballad tradition to interpret the experience of black people.

His poems in the ballad tradition are not confined to the subjects iterated in Gordon Hall Gerould's *The Ballad of Tradition* or those B. Malcolm Laws sees as the prevailing themes of the black folk ballad.[33] Brown's literary ballads, while sometimes adhering closely to the folk ballad form, cover numerous subjects from black folk life. Racial injustice, exploits of folk heroes, tragic love affairs, religion, suffering in poverty, freedom, the need for travel—all of these and many others constitute the subjects of Brown's ballads. His poems in the ballad form alone, more than his poems employing other forms of Afro-American music, give us a broad slice of black life in America.

"Frankie and Johnny" is an example of Brown's use of the subject of a traditional ballad. In this poem, he retains the subject of a love relationship, but he changes the narrative from that found in the traditional ballad, variously called **"Frankie and Johnny"** to comment on the cruelty, and the sexual racism and fear of the rural South. In the traditional ballad, both lovers are black, but in Brown's poem Frankie is changed to a

white girl, "A halfwit" who "Kept a crazy love of torment when she got bigger." Moreover, the source of
conflict in the traditional ballad is the unfaithfulness of
Frankie's lover, Johnny, whom she, with a thirst for
revenge, kills without remorse. The conflict in Brown's
poem, on the other hand, is racial and sexual. Sadistic
Frankie seduces Johnny, a black plowman, to make
love to her. To torment her racist father, a "red-faced
cracker, with a cracker's thirst," Frankie spoke to him
about her affair with the black plowman. When her "pa-
ppy" discovers the truth, the inevitable occurs: Johnny
is lynched. The lynching brings pleasure to the sadistic
Frankie: "And Frankie yowled hilariously when the
thing was done." In spite of Untermeyer's assertion that
"Frankie and Johnny" is "a ballad which any genuine
lover of folk-songs ought to let alone,"[34] we can argue
that Brown's transformation of the story of the
traditional ballad is an achievement which points toward
one of the major sources of racism—sexual fear.

There is in some of Brown's other ballads a balance
between the narrative action and the characters portrayed—i.e., neither the characters nor the action is
subordinate to each other. The character portrayal and
the action in **"The Ballad of Joe Meek"**[35] seem to exist
as an illustration of the idea embodied in the first two
stanzas of part one and part five. In those sections of
the poem, Brown, again using the stanzaic pattern of
the traditional ballad, exploits the proverbial truth, folk
wisdom, of folklore. The truth is this: the external attributes and overt actions of a human being are not
always an index to his thoughts or probable actions. So
was the case of meek Joe, who, as the narrative
progresses, assumes the role of "bad nigger," a black
folk hero represented in folklore by Railroad Bill and
Stagolee, and in real life by Jack Johnson and Mu-
hammed Ali. The motivation of Joe's "badness" is not
akin to that of Stagolee, whose ego is insulted when
Billy Lyons steps on his Stetson hat. Joe's change from
meekness to badness is motivated by the hot weather
(dog days) and police brutality:

> Strolling down Claiborne
>   In the wrong end of town
> Joe saw two policemen
>   Knock a po' gal down

> He didn't know her at all,
>   Never saw her befo'
> But that didn't make no difference,
>   To my old boy Joe.

In his revenge of the "po' gal" Joe takes on the qualities of the supernatural hero:

> Shot his way to the station house,
>   Rushed right in,
> Wasn't nothing but space
>   Where the cops had been.

> They called the reserves,
>   And the national guard,
> Joe was in a cell
>   Overlooking the yard.

> The machine guns sputtered,
>   Didn't faze Joe at all—
> But evvytime *he* fired
>   A cop would fall.

> The tear-gas make him laugh
>   When they let it fly,
> Laughing gas made him hang
>   His head an' cry.

> He threw the hand grenades back
>   With a outshoot drop,
> An' evvytime he threw
>   They was one less cop.

In the end, Joe, like Railroad Bill, is shot in cold blood.
But, as in the legend of Railroad Bill, the white law-
men, in their attempt to capture and subdue Joe, bring
out a force larger than the defying black man. From the
narrative of **"The Ballad of Joe Meek"** emerges a well
drawn portrait of the "bad man" as hero. Here the
motivation for "badness," often absent from the folk
ballad about the badman, is explicit. But providing
motivation and folk wisdom, Brown raises the folk hero
to the level of a living character rather than a type or
stereotype.

The tragic and comic are fused in **"The Ballad of Joe
Meek."** In part one of the poem, Joe is represented as a
meek creature, whose abnormal humility is foolish. The
narrator humorously tells us how Joe went beyond what
was required by the Bible:

> The good book say
>   "Turn the other cheek,"
> But that warn't no turning
>   To my boy Joe Meek.

> He turned up all parts,
>   And baigged you to spank,
> Pulled down his breeches,
>   And supplied the plank.

The incongruity of the early meek Joe, "Soft as pie," in
part one and the image of the powerful, defying Joe in
the rest of the poem produces a folk humor that is
achieved only in the Slim Greer series and **"Sporting
Beasley."**

In addition to providing entertaining action, Brown's
ballads paint pictures of numerous folk characters and
various aspects of black folk life. There are suffering
chain gang Jim in **"Convict,"** protesting Scotty in
"Scotty Has His Say," indigent Sam contrasted with
wealthy Samuel in **"Mister Samuel and Sam,"** badman Mojo Pete and Deacon Cole in **"Checkers,"** ruined

Lulu in **"Seeking Religion,"** wandering working-man Big Boy in **"The Odyssey of Big Boy,"** tragic Johnny in **"Johnny Thomas,"** and many others. The sources of these portraits are not figures in Afro-American folklore. These portraits are informed by the black folk life of the rural South and some of the folk Brown met and befriended.

The series of ballads devoted to the adventures of Slim Greer gives us a highly developed character against a panoramic background of black folk life. The comic ballads are essentially tall tales. In **"Slim Greer,"** the narrator relates Slim's tall tale of how he, who is "no lighter / Than a dark midnight," passes for white. Here he is the trickster or "con man,"[36] who is able, for a while, to deceive "a nice white woman" and her family. "Slim wore the deadpan mask and behind it perpetuated the joke on white society, but his inner nature came out when he played the blues."[37] Slim again assumes, in **"Slim Hears 'The Call,'"**[38] the role of trickster when he is down and out, when "Big holes is the onlies / Things in" his pockets. He plans to become a bishop in order to get his "cake down here" and his "pie in the sky," a trick he learned from his old buddy. The final stanza of the poem points an accusing finger at the clergy. Having stated his plans to follow the example of his trickster-buddy, Slim concludes:

> An' I says to all de Bishops,
>   What is hearin' my song—
> Ef de cap fits you, brother,
>   Put it on.

In **"Slim Greer in Hell,"**[39] **"Slim in Atlanta,"** and **"Slim Lands a Job?"** Brown's traveling epic hero finds himself in humorous situations—but situations which recall the forms of oppression and racism which black people encounter. In addition to the ballad tradition, it is the black tradition of storytelling and folk humor that informs these ballads. Implied in them is the black man's ability to see not only the tragic aspects of his life, but those comic elements also—even in the absurdity of white racism.

The poetry of Sterling A. Brown gives a kaleidoscopic picture of black folk character and life in America—a picture that is constant with the folk themselves. In the main, Brown's are a Black South folk, who, through song, dogged will, ironic laughter, wisdom, "strange legacies," and faith, confront and survive a hostile universe, in spite of the dehumanization they encounter perpetually. "Illiterate, and somehow very wise," Brown's black folk are strong men who "keep-a-comin' on / Gittin' stronger. . . ." Although he concentrates on the folk of the rural South, he gives us a brief picture of the black folk of the urban North in Part Three, **"Tin Roof Blues,"** of *Southern Road.* Like their Southern brothers, they, too, face a hostile universe, but, cut off

from their Black South ancestral roots, Brown's Northern black folk act out their illusions of joy and "arrival" in what they thought would be a Promised Land. In his varied portrayals of black folk, Brown makes no apology for them or their lifestyles. Neither does he present distorted pictures of them. To counter the propagandistic images proliferated in American literature, he, with the integrity of the true artist, represents black folk realistically through forms created by them and a spirit that emanates from their lives. In short, his poems eloquently fulfill James Weldon Johnson's request that the black American poet turn inward for an aesthetic that bespeaks the souls of black folk.

Notes

1. "The New Negro" in *The New Negro,* ed. Alain Locke (New York: Atheneum, 1969), p. 11.

2. Larry Neal, "Eatonville's Zora Neale Hurston: A Profile," *Black Review No. 2,* ed. Mel Watkins (New York: William Morrow, 1979), p. 15. Hereafter referred to as *Black Review No. 2.*

3. *Along This Way* (New York: Viking, 1937), p. 152.

4. For the importance of the folk tradition to the New Negro writer, see Chapter 2, "Folk Art and the Harlem Renaissance," of Bernard Bell's *The Folk Roots of Contemporary Afro-American Poetry* (Detroit: Broadside Press, 1974), pp. 20-31.

5. *Black Review No. 2,* p. 15.

6. "Sterling Brown: A Living Legend," *New Directions: The Howard University Magazine* 1 (Winter 1974): 8-9.

7. Ekaete, "Folk Art and the Harlem Renaissance," p. 9.

8. Ekaete, "Folk Art and the Harlem Renaissance," p. 8.

9. "Negro Literature—Is it True? Complete" in *The Durham Fact-Finding Conference* (1929), p. 27.

10. "Sterling Brown: The New Negro Folk Poet," *Negro Anthology,* ed. Nancy Cunard (London: Wishart, 1934), p. 113.

11. "Folk oriented poems" and poems "in the folk manner" refer to Brown's poems that are about the "folk" or those poems which use some of the technique of folk poetry. The poems in Part Four of *Southern Road* fall into neither of the above classes; the poems in that section are "subjective" or "confessional." After the publication of *Southern Road,* Brown wrote other poems, some of which were published in periodicals, and others were collected in various anthologies.

12. *The Book of American Negro Poetry,* ed. James Weldon Johnson (New York: Harcourt, 1959), pp. 41-42.

13. "Langston Hughes and Afro-American Folk and Cultural Tradition," *Langston Hughes, Black Genius: A Critical Evaluation,* ed. Therman B. O'Daniel (New York: William Morrow, 1971), p. 183.

14. Bruce Jackson, ed., *Wake Up Dead Man: Afro-American Worksongs from Texas Prisons* (Cambridge: Harvard Univ. Press, 1972), pp. 29-30.

15. "Contributions of the American Negro," *One America,* ed. F. J. Brown and J. S. Roucek (New York: Prentice-Hall, 1945), p. 593.

16. Jackson, *Wake Up Dead Man,* pp. 31-33.

17. *The Negro Caravan,* ed. Sterling A. Brown, Arthur P. Davis and Ulysses Lee (New York: Arno, 1970), p. 465. Hereafter referred to as *The Negro Caravan.* Sterling Brown quotes a version of stanza one of the song with "grunts" at the end of the first three lines in his article, "Negro Folk Expression: Spirituals, Seculars, Ballads, and Songs," *Phylon* 14 (1953): 57.

18. *Black Poets of the United States: From Paul Laurence Dunbar to Langston Hughes,* trans. Kenneth Douglas (Chicago: Univ. of Illinois Press, 1973), p. 490. Hereafter referred to as *Black Poets of the United States.*

19. "Black American Poetry, Its Language, and the Folk Tradition," *Black Academy Review* 2 (Spring-Summer 1971): 75.

20. *Self-Conscious Writers and the Black Tradition.* Taped NCTE Distinguished Lecture, Stock No. 77785 (Urbana, Ill.: National Council of Teachers of English).

21. *Black Poets of the United States,* p. 483.

22. Larry Neal, "The Ethos of the Blues," *The Black Scholar* 3 (Summer 1972): 42-48.

23. Neal, "The Ethos of the Blues," pp. 44, 46.

24. Albert Murray, *The Omni-Americans* (New York: Avon, 1971), p. 89.

25. Ralph Ellison, *Shadow and Act* (New York: Random House, 1964), p. 257.

26. Chris Albertson, *Bessie* (New York: Stein & Day, 1972), pp. 127, 131.

27. Sterling Brown, *Negro Poetry and Drama* (Washington, DC: Associates in Negro Folk Education, 1937), p. 27.

28. *My Bondage and My Freedom* (New York: Arno, 1969), pp. 252-53.

29. For the text of "Old Lem," see *The Negro Caravan,* pp. 387-88.

30. Langston Hughes and Arna Bontemps, ed., *The Book of Negro Folklore* (New York: Dodd, Mead, 1958), p. 342.

31. *The Book of Negro Folklore,* p. 334.

32. *Understanding the New Black Poetry* (New York: William Morrow, 1973), p. 51.

33. See Laws's chapter on the Afro-American ballad in his *Native American Balladry* (Philadelphia: The American Folklore Society, 1964).

34. "New Light from an Old Mine," *Opportunity* 10 (Aug. 1932): 250.

35. See the following for the text of "The Ballad of Joe Meek": Bernard W. Bell, ed., *Modern and Contemporary Afro-American Poetry* (Boston: Allyn & Bacon, 1972), pp. 31-35.

36. S. P. Fullinwider, *The Mind and Mood of Black America* (Homewood, Ill.: Dorsey, 1969), p. 215; Stephen A. Henderson, "A Strong Man Called Sterling Brown," *Black World* 29 (Sept. 1970): 9.

37. Fullinwider, *Mind and Mood of Black America,* p. 215.

38. For the text of "Slim Hears 'The Call,'" see Jean Wagner's *Les Poètes Nègres des Etats-Unis* (Paris: Librarie Istra, 1963), pp. 596-600.

39. See B. A. Botkin's *Folk-Say—The Land is Ours* (Norman: Univ. Of Oklahoma Press, 1932), pp. 246-49, for the text of "Slim Greer in Hell."

Edward Hirsch (essay date March-April 1999)

SOURCE: Hirsch, Edward. "Reverberations of a Work Song." *The American Poetry Review* 28, no. 2 (March-April 1999): 43-7.

[*In the following essay, Hirsch asserts that Brown "turned to folk forms like the blues, spirituals, and work songs to create an accurate, unsentimentalized, and dignified portrait of southern black life in the twentieth century."*]

In 1980 I was energized by the publication of Sterling Brown's ***Collected Poems,*** which brought together three important books of poems: ***Southern Road*** (1932), one of the key books of American and perhaps the key book of African American poetry in the 1930s; ***The Last Ride of Wild Bill*** (1975), a uniquely narrative book of eight idiomatic literary ballads rewritten in African American terms out of the central tall tale tradition of American literature; and *No Hiding Place,* a group of poems mainly completed in the late 1930s but which found no publisher ready to hand and consequently had to wait some forty years for publication, a fierce durable book that stands as a dramatic companion to *Southern Road,* re-exploring in a sensitive folk idiom the social nature of the southern black experience. Brown was not, as he has sometimes been treated, a minor satellite of the Harlem Renaissance, but a poet of comparable stature to, say, Claude McKay and Countee Cullen, engaged in a different but parallel poetic revolution. As a young writer influenced by the poetical and social concept of the New Negro, energized by the sharp articulate writings of Alain Locke and W. E. Dubois, Brown turned his verbal gifts not to the urban life of his contemporaries but to the previously unmined world of southern blacks. As Langston Hughes experimented with jazz rhythms to render Harlem night life (at first in *Fine Clothes to the Jew,* 1927, and later, with greater success, in *Montage of a Dream Deferred,* 1951), so Brown turned to folk forms like the blues, spirituals, and work songs to create an accurate, unsentimentalized, and dignified portrait of southern black life in the twentieth century. In the deceptively simple forms of his chosen folk idiom Sterling Brown's poems successfully brought an unknown African American world into the realm of recorded history.

The operant formal influence on Brown's work was his radical reliance on both secular (blues, ballads, work songs) and sacred (spirituals) African American musical traditions. It was virtually unprecedented for Brown— who after all was from Washington, D.C., and educated at Williams College and Harvard University—to turn his considerable intellectual resources on rural folk forms. But then, as Sterling Stuckey has said, Brown always had a sense of the connecting timbre, "a feel for reciprocity between past and present." That same feeling was evidenced in his historical delineations and primary sourcebooks for black culture, *The Negro in American Fiction* (1937), *Negro Poetry and Drama* (1937), and *Negro Caravan* (1941), and in his fifty year teaching career at Howard University.

In *Southern Road* Brown was both resurrecting and affirming the essential dignity of folk forms (and, consequently, of black slave and farm experience conveyed through them) and implicitly redefining a recognizably American aesthetic of the local. (I think of William Carlos Williams's idea of putting into his poems "the speech of Polish mothers.") Even more radically, Brown's poems were first written in dialect at a time when dialect was associated not with a vigorous living speech but with the mawkish sentimentality and optimism of the plantation and blackface minstrel traditions.

In his introduction to the first edition of *Southern Road* James Weldon Johnson praised Brown for "adopting as his medium the common, racy, living speech of the Negro in certain phases of *real* life," thus reversing his earlier opinion that dialect was "an instrument with but two complete stops, humor and pathos" (*God's Trombones,* 1927). Johnson's polemical objections were to parodic traditions which, as he said, "had but slight relation, often no relation at all, to *actual* Negro life." (Think of the excesses of Tin Pan Alley or the pseudo-folk idiom of a poet like Vachel Lindsay.) What he discovered in Brown's poetry was both the denial and the dismantling of the exaggerated sentimentality of previous dialect tradition. *Southern Road* in effect rewrote and reformulated the nature of the black vernacular as it had been presented in American literature. By turning to an oral folk as opposed to a written literary tradition, Brown's poetry called the written tradition into question and instead privileged the external immediacy of black life.

As he later put it:

> I love Negro speech and I think it is rich and wonderful. It is not *dis* and *dat* and a split verb. But it is "Been down so long that down don't worry me," or it is what the spirituals had in one of the finest couplets in American literature: "I don't know what my mother wants to stay here for. / This old world ain't been no friend to her."

By using his poetry as an instrument to redefine the character of black speech and song Brown was also redefining the character of rural southern blacks, replacing geniality with fierce stoicism, ironic humor, and deep tragedy.

Now here is the title poem of *Southern Road*:

"Southern Road"

Swing dat hammer—hunh—
Steady, bo';
Swing dat hammer—hunh—
Steady bo';
Ain't no rush, bebby,
Long ways to go.

Burner tore his—hunh—
Black heart away;
Burner tore his—hunh—
Black heart away;
Got me life, bebby,
An' a day.

Gal's on Fifth Street—hunh—
Son done gone;
Gal's on Fifth Street—hunh—
Son done gone;
Wife's in de ward, bebby,
Babe's not bo'n.

My ole man died—hunh—
Cussin' me;
My ole man died—hunh—
Cussin' me;
Ole lady rocks, bebby,
Huh misery.

Doubleshackled—hunh—
Guard behin';
Doubleshackled—hunh—
Guard behin';
Ball an' chain, bebby,
On my min'.

White man tells me—hunh—
Damn yo' soul;
White man tells me—hunh—
Damn yo' soul;
Got no need, bebby,
To be tole.

Chain gang nevah—hunh—
Let me go;
Chain gang nevah—hunh—
Let me go;
Po' los' boy, bebby,
Evahmo'.

I first came across this fictive prison song in a section called "Poetry in the Folk Manner" in Langston Hughes and Arna Bontemps's *Book of Negro Folklore* (1958). The poem was called **"Dark of the Moon,"** which is the wry title of a *different* poem in **Southern Road.** ("Plant a fence post / On de dark un de moon," an old saying has it, "Yuh plant it fo' nothin', / Yuh plant it fo' rottin'.") Brown also contributed essays on the spirituals and on the blues as folk poetry to this anthology, which also contained a relevant section of work songs, like this one:

"Take This Hammer"

Take this hammer—huh!
And carry it to the captain—huh!
You tell him I'm gone—huh!
You tell him I'm gone—huh!

If he asks you—huh!
Was I runnin'—huh!
You tell him I was flyin'—huh!
You tell him I was flyin'—huh!

If he asks you—huh!
Was I laughin'—huh!
You tell him I was cryin'—huh!
You tell him I was cryin'—huh!

The work song is a utilitarian form whose main function is to synchronize the efforts of workers who must move together as in, say, a chain gang. A leader provides a strong rhythmic cue with two or three bars which are then answered by the ejaculatory word or words of moving workers. The rhythmic interaction and continual interplay create a call and response pattern, and make music a participant activity. The words tend to be an improvisatory mode of "signifying" (or as Henry Louis Gates, Jr. designates it "Signifyin(g)"), which Roger Abrahams calls "a technique of indirect argument or persuasion," "a language of implication." The singer creates a mask of address to the so-called "captain," the white boss, and at the same time satirizes and undercuts that very voice, thus building morale by subversively talking back to power.

John and Alan Lomax's *Folk Song U.S.A.* (1947) gives a classic description of a work song going at full swing:

> The hot southern sun shines down on the brown and glossy muscles of the work gang. The picks make whirling rainbow arcs around the shoulders of the singers. As the picks dig into the rock, the men give a deep, guttural grunt; their pent-up strength flows through the pick handle and they relax their bodies and prepare for the next blow.
>
> The song leader now begins—pick handle twirling in his palms, the pickhead flashing in the sun:
>
> *Take this hammo—Huh!*
>
> The men grunt as the picks bite in together. They join the leader on his line, trailing in, one in harmony, one talking the words, another grunting them out between clenched teeth, another throwing out a high falsetto cry above the rest. On the final syllable, the picks are descending and again they bite a chip out of the rock and again there is a grunting exhalation of breath:
>
> *Carry it to my Captain—Huh!*
>
> The picks whirl up together in the sunlight and down again, they ring on the earth together, with maybe one or two bounding a couple of times in a sort of syncopation. When the leader comes to the third—
>
> *Carry it to my Captain*
>
> he holds onto the word "captain" as long as he can, looks around at the boss and grins; his buddies chuckle and relax for a moment, knowing he is giving them a little rest; then, "wham" the steel bites at the rock and the whole gang roars out the final line, so that the hill gives back the sound.

The way the gang responds to the leader here—one voice slipping in harmonically, another talking words, a third grunting them, a fourth lifting a falsetto cry over the rest—is a polyrhythmic variation on the West African call and response pattern. The song puts a tremendous claim on experience. Some folklorists have persuasively argued that the work song actually challenges the nature of work itself by changing the framework of the workers. The singer supplies the beat and relieves the tedium, transposing the space, creating a different relationship to time. In *Black Culture and Black Consciousness,* the historian Lawrence Levine argues "Secular work songs resembled the spirituals in that their endless rhythmic and verbal repetitions could transport the singers beyond time, make them oblivious to their immediate surroundings and create a state of what Wilfred Mellers has referred to as 'ritualistic hypnosis.' The chant then becomes, again in Mellers's words, 'a positive rhythmic ecstasy rather than a negative numbing of pain.'" I am tempted to suggest that the singer of the work song is doing in the most literal way the essential work of the poet in society who more abstractly but just as genuinely works to ease and transfigure human suffering, who interpenetrates the secular and the sacred, the sacred and the secular, and who transfigures our relationship to historical time. The form creates a space of release for the reader who also has a charge and creative part to play, who also drifts off through the foremind of reverie, trailing in, talking back the words. The experience stops time, it is time-stopping. The poem becomes a medium of transcendence.

The lyric **"Southern Road"** resonates with a rich background context, a southern way of life, which it evokes in its very rhythms, its call and response pattern. The rhythm, like the vernacular language, calls up a whole painful history of chain gangs. But because it is a written and not an oral poem per se, it removes the work song from its immediate social and historical context. The work song loses its primary function (no one ever thought the poem **"Southern Road"** was going to be sung in the fields) and thus becomes non-utilitarian, a different kind of animal that behaves in an analogous but different way. Brown compensates by asking the poem to do a different kind of symbolic work. He inscribes the values of the work song. He creates a particular speaker with a particular history and textualizes the feeling of an individual testifying to a participating community. He models the relationship between the singer and the community. And he gives the poem a narrative or storytelling value. It has a lyric bluesy element.

In fact, if you change the lineation and drop the choral response you have a slightly foreshortened but otherwise classic three-line blues stanza:

> White man tells me damn yo' soul;
> White man tells me damn yo' soul;
> Got no need, bebby, to be tole.

The work song almost certainly contributed to the statement and response pattern of the blues which retain elements of the field holler. Like the classical four-line ballad stanza the blues form is a good vehicle for telling a story of any length, but it stages a different kind of drama through its repetitions. The blues have always retained a flexible style and structure, but have tended toward a twelve-bar tercet with an AAB pattern. The first line establishes the premise and the scene, the second repeats (sometimes with slight variations) and

hammers it in, the third line punches, develops, or turns it. Each line is an intact entity, each stanza a unit unto itself. Here's a traditional blues verse:

> I'm going to the river, take my rockin' chair,
> Goin' to the river, take my rockin' chair,
> If the blues overcome me, I'll rock on away from
>   here.

Brown also imitates the blues form undisguised and to great effect in his three-part sequence **"New St. Louis Blues."** Here's the first stanza of part two, **"Tornado Blues,"** which shows how he works the imagery and the form:

> Black wind come a-speedin' down de river from de
>   Kansas plains,
> Black wind come a-speedin' down de river from de
>   Kansas plains,
> Black wind come a-roarin' like a flock of giant
>   aeroplanes—

The blues are more highly personalized than the work song since the call and response pattern remains but the singer in essence answers and responds to himself or herself. In *Blues People* Amiri Baraka (Leroi Jones) persuasively argues that the form resonates with a powerful individual ethos that would have been alien to African society and thus shows a high degree of American acculturation. Thus the blues becomes a more characteristically American form of verbal art.

It's the voice of an individual testifying to the collective that I hear in **"Southern Road."** We know, for example, the speaker has got a "gal" on Fifth Street, a son who disappeared for good, a wife having a baby, a father who died putting a curse on him. He's not just a victim of white people alone, he participates in his own fate. Brown once said that he modeled the speaker on the character of Big Boy Davis, a traveling guitar player who is also the speaker in **"Odyssey of Big Boy,"** a poem which begins with a singer's call for community with a race's folk heroes:

> Lemme be wid Casey Jones,
>   Lemme be wid Stagolee,
> Lemme be wid such like men
>   When Death takes hol' on me,
>   When Death takes hol' on me.

Brown reported that he first heard from Davis about John Henry, about Stagolee, about "The Ballad of the Bollweevil." The same guitar player stands at the center of **"When de Saints Go Ma'ching Home,"** a poem in which the great spiritual becomes the vehicle for the singer to create his own "chant of saints." (The phrase gave Michael Harper and Robert Stepto the title for their gathering of African-American literature, art, and scholarship.) Rereading the three poems about Big Boy Davis I was reminded of something that William Williams said about Robert Hayden: "His speakers confront their history as active participants in its making and not as distant onlookers bemoaning their isolation."

Brown also captures the fierce undercurrent of pain in the blues. As he put it, "Irony, stoicism, and bitterness are deeply but not lingeringly expressed." There's a tragic undertow to: "Chain gang nevah—hunh— / Let me go; / Po' los' boy, bebby, / Evahmo' . . ." The three dots at the end of this poem tell everything. They are heartstopping. This suffering feels like it is going to go on and on endlessly.

One of Sterling Brown's main poetic tasks was to show "the extraordinary in ordinary lives." Early on he was influenced both in his idiom and in his themes by the American common man mythology, descending from Whitman to Edwin Arlington Robinson and Robert Frost. I think, for example, of Whitman's poem "A Song for Occupations" ("In the labor of engines and trades and the labor of fields I find the developments, / And find the eternal meanings"), of how he vows to put "the family kiss" on the cotton field drudge and the cleaner of privies, of how he remembers "The heave'e'yo of stevedores unloading ships by the wharves, / The refrain of the anchor lifters." Here is a passage from section 12 of "Song of Myself" where he closely follows the rhythmic movement of blacksmiths:

> Blacksmiths with grimed and hairy chests environ the anvil,
> Each has his main-sledge, they are all out, there is a great heat in the fire.
>
> From the cinder-strew'd threshold I follow their movements.
> The lithe sheer of their waists plays even with their massive arms,
> Overhand the hammers swing, overhand so slow, overhand so sure,
> They do not hasten, each man hits in his place.

It seems to me that the work song generates or opens up naturally in the direction of a poetry that becomes *about* working, and here one thinks how Brown's notion of "the extraordinary in ordinary lives" has reverberated through the work of such contemporary poets as Michael Harper Sherley A. Williams, and Yusef Komunyakaa, of Garrett Hongo and Philip Levine, who has written the best postwar book of poems on the subject, *What Work Is.* These poets share a fierce commitment to the lost and failed, to the poor, the marginal, the refused. They take up Whitman's chant, "Vivas to those who have failed!" Reading through two recent anthologies of poetry about work, *A Song of Occupations* and *Working Classics,* I started to feel that one of the main tasks of the poet in the late twentieth century who would write about the subject of work is to affirm a community of workers who no longer share a com-

mon transfiguring music. The poems mostly fail because they rely on a chopped up prose that doesn't do any of the figural or rhythmic work of poetry itself.

"Southern Road" is an American poem that participates in a deeply rooted tradition we do well to remember. The work song has been found wherever there are Africans in the New World. It was probably first sung in the United States when people who were enslaved were landed and forced to work. The subsequent black work song—the song of woodcutters and fishermen, of rail and prison road gangs—summons up the group labor songs of the West Indies and West Africa. As the anthropologist Melville Herskovitz explained:

> This tradition, carried over into the New World, is manifest in the tree-felling parties of the Suriname Bush Negroes, the *combites* of the Haitian peasant, and in various forms of group labor in agriculture, fishing, house-raising, and the like encountered in Jamaica, Trinidad, the French West Indies, and elsewhere.

The African-American work song traces back to Africa where music was always associated with dancing and with working.

So, too, the earliest indications of lyric activity, the Egyptian tomb inscriptions (ca. 2600 B.C.) also include work songs of shepherds, fishers, and chairmen. I'm reminded of Robert Graves's theory that the rhythm of Anglo-Saxon poetry was based on the slow pull and push of the oar:

> Then I of myself / Will make this known
> That awhile I was held / the Heodenings' scop,
> To my duke most dear / And Deor was my name.

According to Graves, the function of the Nordic *scop* (an old English name for a harpist and poet-singer who commanded full mastery of the complex oral-formulaic materials of old Germanic prosody) was twofold: the poet's first task was as a "shaper" of charms to protect the King and thus insure prosperity for the kingdom, but, secondarily, to persuade "a ship's crew to pull rhythmically and uncomplainingly on their oars against the rough waves of the North Sea by singing them ballads in time to the beat." The oldest meaning of the word "beat" is "to strike repeatedly," and thus it retains vestiges in poetry of that sense of repeated physical action.

Whereas Nordic verse-craft was linked to the movement of the oar, the Irish tradition developed a technique of craftsmanship based on the hammer and anvil. "When two hammers answer each other five times on the anvil—*ti-tum, ti-tum, ti-tum, ti-tum, ti-tum,*" Graves suggests, "there you have Chaucer's familiar hendeca-syllabic line:

> A knight there was, and that a worthy man
> That fro the tyme that he first began
> To ryden out, he loved chivalrie.

By contrast, Greek verse is connected to the ecstatic beat of dancers moving around a sacred altar. It has been plausibly suggested, as W. H. Auden has pointed out, that Greek verse, which has a quantitative meter, has its origins in ritual or play, but that English verse, which has a qualitative meter, has its origins in the physical action of work. Both were embodied.

The word "ballad" derives from the Old French "ballade," a dancing song. It would have had special resonance for Graves in his description of the Nordic scop because he believed, as he put it in a short critical survey of the English ballad (1927), "When the word 'ballad' was adopted by English singers, though the association with dancing did not survive, there remained latent in it the sense of *rhythmic group action* whether in work or in play." It seems likely that the medieval ballad originated in religious ritual, conjoining narrative and dancing, performed by a choral leader and a group of participants who both sang and danced. The leader would have sung the main body of the tale and the chorus would have followed with the refrain. Thus it has a strong parallel with the secular work song.

The traditional British ballad may be defined as a short narrative song (a poem that tells a story) preserved and transmitted orally, and Graves was correct that it retains vestiges of archaic modes of preliterature, of ritual participation. He was incorrect in his idea that the ballad was collectively as opposed to individually composed, though, as Northrop Frye has noted, the ballad is "so close to the poem of community as to have led some scholars to believe that its origin was in communal composition." The individual singer of the traditional ballad—of "Sir Patrick Spens" or "The Twa Corbies" or "Lord Randall"—stands in for the community, serving as the deputy of a public voice.

In traditional societies there were two main types of oral narrative poetry—epic and ballad—and both have oral formulaic elements. They are models of the fluid text, of fixity and flux, tradition and innovation. The epic is nonstanzaic (or stichic) and thus creates a strong sense of linear development, whereas the ballad, a much shorter form, is stanzaic and thus balances lyric and narrative elements. It slows down the narration. In his ground-breaking book *The Singer of Tales,* Albert Lord, following the lead of Milman Parry, demonstrated the connection between *The Iliad* and *The Odyssey* and the living epic tradition of Yugoslavia. The epic singer brings together a powerful memory and a strong improvisatory technique, using formulaic phrases, lines and half-lines, propulsive rhythms, stock descriptions, recurrent scenes and incidents to build an epic tale in song and verse. The singer of tales could also apply those same skills to work songs and funeral chants. So, too, the ballad singer could use formulaic elements to pace the narrative action, to expand and condense the story line, to emphasize recurrent lyric elements even as the song is being recomposed.

Dialogue is the main vehicle of action for the folk ballad which has been built up and scoured down by oral transmission to a masterpiece of rapid elliptical narration. There is very little description or analysis of the thoughts or feelings of the characters in the traditional ballad (as there is, say, in prose fiction). The audience supplies the background scene and information, the underlying motivation. The listeners actively collaborate in the making of meaning which only emerges in performance. Indeed, both the epic and the ballad give us strong cases of an emergent *poesis*.

I suspect that isolated writers have always understood the power of this interactive and emergent relationship. The writer would maintain his or her freedom through writing (Northrop Frye defines the lyric as the form of literature in which the writer turns his back on the audience), but would nonetheless tap into this participatory and communal model. Certainly this helps to explain the widespread popularity and recurrence of the written literary ballad for a couple of centuries—from Robert Burns and Sir Walter Scott to W. B. Yeats, W. H. Auden, and Graves himself, from Blake, Wordsworth, and Coleridge to Swinburne, Tennyson, and both Rossettis, from William Morris and Oscar Wilde to Thomas Hardy, Walter de la Mare, A. E. Housman, and Rudyard Kipling, Louis MacNiece and Edwin Muir, Sterling Brown and Robert Hayden. The writer would transcend isolation, seeking thus to stand-in as the expression of a primordial collective will. The ballad writer also tends to be in quest of an archaic way of knowing, and thus the very work, the rhythmic action, of the ballad becomes a way of attaining what Daniel Hoffman calls "barbarous knowledge." I recall how much Whitman loved Sir Walter Scott's collection of old ballads, *The Border Minstrelsy,* precisely because it seemed to take him back to the primitive roots of all poetry and thus offered a bardic model for his own "barbaric yawp." "Stop this day and night and you shall possess the origin of all poems," he wrote in "Song of Myself," where he tried to conjure up the earthly and divine origins of archaic poetry on behalf of a forward-looking democratic art. "Our heart is in the future," Pablo Neruda declared in a Whitmanesque line, "and our pleasure is ancient."

Poetry came of age with the chant and the dance. As the linguist Edward Sapir put it, "Poetry everywhere is inseparable in its origins from the singing voice and the measure of the dance." The origins of poetry are highly speculative. The earliest poetry recedes into the vast mist of centuries of oral tradition before writing inscribed and thus transfixed texts. We do know that throughout the world, throughout history, oral expression can and has existed without writing, but that writing has never existed without orality (Walter Ong). There is a strong continuity between oral and written verbal art forms. Writing is textuality. It immobilizes texts in visual space and thereby allows us to linger and internalize them, to scan them backward and forward, to reread and study them. It creates a space for introspection. It vastly enlarges the potentiality of language. But it is fundamental to remember in thinking about poetry that all over the world oral peoples have considered words to have magical potency, to be sounded and power-driven. The interaction—the interdependency—between the singer and the group provides one strong model of participation in literary exchange. Writing removes us from such face to face communication, but it also models it secondarily. It separates us but it also calls us deeply to each other. The written ballad, the written blues, the written work song—all these forms model a particular kind of participatory relationship between the poet and the community. These are all active forms with narrative and lyrical values. They are poems with stories and refrains. They would use these oral elements to empower the relationship between writer and reader. Perhaps we should speak more often of the *work* of poetry, the work that poetry does in rhythmically restructuring time. In the work song we have one of the fountainheads of that restructuring, and thus of poetry itself.

Elizabeth Davey (essay date summer 1999)

SOURCE: Davey, Elizabeth. "The Souths of Sterling A. Brown." *Southern Cultures* 5, no. 2 (summer 1999): 20-45.

[*In the following essay, Davey applauds Brown's attempts to present a fuller portrait of the African American experience in the South.*]

It is evident that Negro folk culture is breaking up. Where Negro met only with Negro in the black belt the old beliefs strengthened. But when mud traps give way to gravel roads, and black tops and even concrete highways with buses and jalopies and trucks lumbering over them, the world comes closer. The churches and the schools, such as they are, struggle against some of the results of isolation, and the radio plays a part. Even in the backwoods, aerials are mounted on shanties that seem ready to collapse from the extra weight on the roof, or from a good burst of static against the walls. The phonograph is common, the television set is by no means unknown, and down at the four corners store, a juke-box gives out the latest jive. Rural folk closer to towns and cities may on Saturday jaunts even see an occasional movie, where a rootin'-tootin' Western gangster film introduces them to the advancements of civilization. Newspapers, especially the Negro press,

give the people a sense of belonging to a larger world, and the tales of the returning veterans, true Marco Polos, also prod the inert into curiosity. Brer Rabbit and Old Jack no longer are enough. Increasingly in the churches the spirituals lose favor to singing out of the books or from broadsides, and city-born blues and jive take over the jook-joints.[1]

"'Folk' has no meaning without 'modern,'" historian Robin D. G. Kelley reminds us. In this description by Sterling A. Brown in 1953 of the technological transformation of southern black communities, the expansion of the modern brings the folk into sharp relief. The extension of electricity, roads, and the mass media into America's rural areas in the 1920s and 1930s inspired tremendous interest in the communities that lay on the edge of these transformations. The term "folk" suggests that these communities are outside the modern, the urban, and the industrial and values them as both threatened and unchanging in rapidly changing times. But in the essay "Negro Folk Expression," Brown chose the phrase "breaking up" to describe an African American folk culture that was both changing and dispersing. Migration had brought this folk creativity to the cities.

American literature and music were showing its influence. "Just as Huckleberry Finn and Tom Sawyer were fascinated by the immense lore of their friend Jim," Brown wrote, "American authors have been drawn to Negro folk life and character."[2]

During the late 1920s and early 1930s, ethnographic writings found wide audiences outside the discipline of anthropology. Publishers produced a small boom of folklore collections, many published by white authors on rural black folklore. Two University of North Carolina professors collected and published *The Negro and His Songs: A Study of Typical Negro Songs in the South* in 1925, and Carl Sandburg published *American Songbag* in 1927. In critical discussions of black poetry in the early 1930s, an embrace of folk poetry subsumed the previous decade's discussion and rejection of dialect verse, a change that can be explained in part by the emergence of "the folk" as a popular subject of American writing. Over the next decade, interest in the rural poor and working-class people would produce collections of folklore such as B. A. Botkin's series *Folk-Say* and Zora Neale Hurston's *Mules and Men,* as well as proletarian novels, poems, narratives, and stories that drew from folk idioms. This interest in the folk in American writing would culminate in the work of the New Deal Federal Writers' Project (FWP), which published a number of compilations of folklore, oral histories, and regional guides. By the mid-1930s, a discourse of the folk had considerable currency among black and white writers of various ideological persuasions.[3]

An exact contemporary of Langston Hughes, Sterling A. Brown was one of the most admired younger poets of the Harlem Renaissance. The books he published in the 1930s and 1940s—*Southern Road, The Negro in American Fiction, Negro Poetry and Drama,* and *The Negro Caravan*—established his reputation as a poet, literary critic, and anthologist attentive to African American folk traditions. He taught at Howard University for four decades, and his book reviews for *Opportunity,* the magazine of the National Urban League, brought him an audience outside literary circles. While he is best known for poems that tapped African American folk language and stories, his creative and critical work that struggles first with representations of the folk and then with representations of the South deserves more attention. In the 1920s and 1930s, Brown viewed popular interest in the folk—a folk most frequently imagined as southern black communities—as a critical moment in the representation of African Americans and the South. This interest could bring rich descriptions of these communities into discussions of American literature, politics, and music, or it could rearticulate simple stereotypes.

Brown was an astute and sardonic critic of the extreme simplifications and stereotypes of African Americans in white American writing. He began his keystone essay "Negro Character as Seen by White Authors," published in the *Journal of Negro Education* in 1933, with a mocking endorsement of the words of Roark Bradford, a popular white author who published folktales and fiction: "There are three types of Negroes, says Roark Bradford, in his sprightly manner: 'the nigger,' the 'colored person,' and 'the Negro'—upper case N. In his foreword to *Ol' Man Adam an' His Chillun,* the source from which Marc Connelly drew the *Green Pastures* and a book causing the author to be considered, in some circles, a valid interpreter of *the* Negro, Bradford defines *the* Negro's character and potentialities." Actually, Brown explained in the essay, the works of white American authors showed seven types of Negroes rather than three, and he proceeded to define them: the Contented Slave, the Wretched Freeman, the Comic Negro, the Brute Negro, the Tragic Mulatto, the Local Color Negro, and the Exotic Primitive. The essay demonstrates Brown's attention to southern authors and his impatience with any claim to represent "*the* Negro." His insistent italicized "the" reminded that "*the* Negro" was as false a figure as the "Contented Slave." "That mythical non-entity '*the* Negro,'" Brown chided in another review. No single individual, community, study, or creative work could represent the diversity of black Americans. "But if one wishes to learn of *the* Negro" he wrote, "it would be best to study *the* Negro himself; a study that might result in the discovery that *the* Negro is more difficult to find than the countless human beings called Negroes." "The sincere, sensitive artist," he concluded, "will be wary of confining a race's entire character to a half-dozen narrow grooves." American literature on African Americans was like a record that continuously skipped back to the same few grooves; the multiple notes, voices, words, and instruments of black culture had yet to be heard.[4]

Brown extended this critique in the manuscript of his second book of poems, *No Hiding Place.* The poems in a section titled "Harlem Stopover" all take place in Harlem and focus on the production of images of blackness for white audiences. **"Real Mammy Song,"** which bears the dedication "(*With proudful apologies to Irving Berlin et. al.*)" and **"The New Congo"**—"(*With no apologies to Vachel Lindsay*)"—contest images of blackness created by white artists in popular music and poetry. (Lindsay's racist poem "The Congo" was enormously popular in his public readings.) Beyond satirizing stereotypes, these poems argue that the repertoire of images of blacks that whites will accept is extremely limited, and they explore some of the "narrow grooves" functioning in American society in the 1930s. **"The Law for George,"** which instructs the black urban service worker, offers one rule: In the uniform of work, the uniform of service, the black man is allowed in the presence of the white woman; but without the uniform his image is uncontrolled, dangerous, and in danger:

"Redcap"

Carry her bags for her
Listen to her kiddin'
Laugh with her
But don't never offer
To help her with no bundles
When you ain't got
Yo' red cap on.
See?

"Houseman"
. . . . .
Don't never put on
No collar and no tie
Don't never hand her no flower
Without those overhalls on.
See?[5]

The evening bill of a Harlem cabaret in **"Roberta Lee"** expands the critique of the limited representations of blacks recognized and accepted by whites to include Harlem as a site for the production of such images. Roberta Lee, a "Lee of Leesburg," takes in a show "in this hell-hole of the North, / A Harlem cabaret / logical outcome of Appomattox." Her own femininity threatened by her companion's interest in the chorus dancers, she watches the show with disgust and hatred until the act changes:

Then he appeared.
Ape-like in body, with his long arms dangling,
Nearly to his feet resembling flatboats,

Upon his head a crazy hat, his face
A black mask, except for large white circles
About his eyes, and thickly painted lips.
He danced.[6]

"Oh isn't that lovely," Roberta gushes. "That's the kind of nigger I know." The clown exits the stage to great applause, and Roberta longs to "bring him back." Again and again in these "Harlem Stopover" poems, Brown suggests that white audiences will accept only a limited and familiar repertoire of representations: the mammy, the clown, the servant in uniform.

Brown's sometimes occasional, sometimes monthly book reviews for *Opportunity* combed through contemporary writing on the South with the same wit and attention to representation. Many of the book reviews Brown published in the 1920s and 1930s chronicled the popular literature that floated between fiction and folklore, exemplified by Roark Bradford's books. Brown reviewed five of these, including *John Henry,* a rewriting that relocated the folk hero from the railroad to the cotton fields and roustabouts' dock, and *Kingdom Coming,* a novel set in Civil War New Orleans that concludes as a slave mistakes a Yankee firing squad for a freedom ceremony. In his early assessments, Brown distinguished writers like Bradford, whose folklore and fiction continued traditions of local color and dialect literature, from writers whose use of local idiom and folk belief created original and complicated characters. Bradford's popularity and claims to insight into black culture outraged Brown, who conceded Bradford's skills as a local-color humorist in the tradition of Twain but vehemently contested claims that Bradford's tales recorded African American folk thought and experience. He frequently contrasted the claims on Bradford's book jackets—"Here is real American folklore . . . instinct with the genuine religious spirit of the Negro"—with Bradford's characters: preachers who scrambled biblical stories, slaves who did not understand or want freedom, a God who resembled a plantation owner.[7] Bradford's "folklore" was a new presentation of old stereotypes.

Brown initially placed Julia Peterkin, on the other hand, among a group of writers whose use of folklore produced human, tragic, and nuanced African American rural characters. He enthusiastically rifled his review of her 1927 novel *Black April* "The New Secession," for he saw in her work a break from past characterizations of African Americans:

> The Negroes in the writer's work are like none others we have had. Unlike Sherwood Anderson's, they are more than symbols, have further concerns than ejaculating deep-belied laughter; unlike the Harlemites of Van Vechten these are primitive, far from *Nigger Heaven,* being of the earth earthy; unlike Walter White's, they have no problem with the "Nordics" tangling their days.

They are more akin perhaps to Toomer's Karma and Karintha. If we leave literature and go to buncombe they differ from Dixon's in that they don't imitate Klansmen; and from Cohen's in that they are not jack-in-the-boxes.

As Peterkin published novels and essays in the 1930s, Brown's enthusiasm waned. Even though she knew a great deal about the black communities near her plantation in South Carolina, Brown argued, she chose to depict "the startling, the bizarre, the primitive, the *different*" in her novel *Bright Skin.* The novel tended towards local color—fiction that did not develop characters beyond their distinctive dialect and folk beliefs.[8]

Brown's focus expanded from representation of character to region in his 1934 review of *Roll, Jordan, Roll,* a book of text by Peterkin and photographs by Doris Ulmann. Peterkin's South lacked bitter memories of slavery, lacked racial violence, and was silent to the causes of poverty. Brown found her presentation geographically unspecific, generalizing the language and beliefs of her local area, a low-country plantation in South Carolina, to all rural southern black communities. In describing these communities as outside the "machine-age," Peterkin placed them back on the plantation. "Certainly 'this land,' wherever it is," Brown wrote, "is not representative of the South."[9] The title of the review, "Arcadia, South Carolina," encapsulates Brown's critique. "Arcadia" was his shorthand for nostalgic representations of a plantation life distinguished by the childlike and grateful devotion of slave to master. It was a literary representation developed, in his account, from the novels written to defend slavery from abolitionist attacks. Even with knowledge of the local language and customs of South Carolina Gullahs, Brown suggested, Peterkin repeats a literary representation rather than renders a full account of the lives of people within a particular community. *Roll, Jordan, Roll* was one of the early documentary books; the claims to realism made by the combination of texts and photographs made Peterkin's generalizations and elisions more dangerous.

Brown viewed southern literature in the 1930s as the battleground for representation of African American lives. The emerging interest in the folk increased literary interest in rural black communities, but it also created new opportunities for writers to repeat nostalgic and romantic views of an Old South. Folklore could easily serve representations of African Americans and the South that were severed from history and geography. Brown's reviews of 1930s southern literature trace a drama of competing representations of the South and southern history through the decade, a drama in which popular folklore and folkloric fiction are increasingly challenged by studies in history, politics, and economics, and by narrative works that introduce poor whites and the sharecropper into views of the South. Through his reviews of the work of writers such as Bradford and Peterkin, Brown's readers could follow the struggle between, as read his headlines, "Mississippi—Old Style" and "Mississippi, Alabama—New Style."[10]

During the 1930s the southern black communities of Brown's poetry became more geographically specific and defined more by historical events, by violence, and by exploitative economies than by a separation from modernity. A note describing Brown's poetry in his 1937 pamphlet *Negro Poetry and Drama* describes his first collection of poems, *Southern Road,* as "chiefly an attempt at folk portraiture of southern characters." It then goes on to describe his current project: "His second volume, to be called *No Hiding Place,* re-explores the southern scene with more emphasis on social themes." In a 1974 interview, Brown explained the organization of *Southern Road* as biographical and geographical, following the path of his early years teaching at Virginia Seminary College, Lincoln University in Missouri, and Fisk University in Nashville. But these places are unspecified; instead, the sections are structured by folk forms. The first section, "Road so Rocky," includes poems inspired by folk ballads and aphorisms, secular songs and spirituals; the second section, "On Restless River," draws from the forms and feeling of the blues. These two sections, comprising the bulk of the collection, create regions of the spirituals, regions of the blues. The result is a South a little out of time, a little off the map.[11]

The poems of Brown's second collection, *No Hiding Place,* have specific historical and geographical contexts. Rather than protectors of folk forms and folk knowledge, the old people in *No Hiding Place* are often historians of lost events. The opening lines of **"An Old Woman Remembers"** invite the expectation that she will sing or tell a tale:

> Her eyes were gentle, her voice was for soft singing
> In the stiff-backed pew, or on the porch when evening
> Comes slowly over Atlanta. But she remembered.

But instead of reciting a song or tale, she describes a race riot in Atlanta—whites beating up black men and women, looting businesses—that finally ended when "our folks got sick and tired / Of being chased and beaten and shot down" and went home, took out their shotguns, and sat ready on their porches. **"Remembering Nat Turner"** describes the older generation as historians of resistance rather than tellers of folk tales. As the narrator and his companion retrace the trail of Nat Turner's rebellion, they ask people about him:

> When we got to Cross Keys, they could tell us little
> of him,
> The Negroes had only the faintest recollections:

> "I ain't been here so long, I come from up roun' New-
> some;
> Yassah, a town a few miles up de road,
> The old folks who coulda told you is all dead an'
> gone.
> I heard something, sometime; I doan jis remember
> what.[12]

The poems in *No Hiding Place* carefully map the distinctive historical, cultural, and linguistic resources of black communities: the South breaks into the Cotton South, Louisiana, Atlanta, and Washington, D.C.; vernacular breaks into multiple regional dialects. And more than *Southern Road, No Hiding Place* represents the economic exploitation, relentless racial violence, and resistance that were part of these communities. Brown's review of Hurston's *Mules and Men,* on the other hand, describes the book as a rich collection of stories but argues that it erased the economic and social conditions of these communities: "Her characters are naive, quaint, complaisant, bad enough to kill each other in jooks, but meek otherwise, socially unconscious. Their life is made to appear easy going and carefree. This, to the reviewer, makes *Mules and Men* singularly *incomplete.* These people live in a land shadowed by squalor, poverty, disease, violence, enforced ignorance, and exploitation. Even if brow beaten, they do know a smoldering resentment. Many folk stories and songs from the South contain this resentment."[13] Brown's praise for Hurston's 1937 novel *Their Eyes Were Watching God* suggests that he did not hold fiction to the same standard of representation. His own poems in *No Hiding Place,* however, attempt a new literary construction of the "folk," one oriented against systems of oppression in the South rather than against the cultural changes wrought by urbanization.

RE-EXPLORING THE SOUTHERN SCENE

In 1932, the year *Southern Road* was published, Langston Hughes published two pamphlets of poems: *The Dream Keeper* and *Scottsboro Limited,* four poems and a verse play written in response to the 1931 convictions of nine young black men charged with raping two white women on a train passing through Scottsboro, Alabama. In a review of the year's writing by and about black America, Alain Locke, editor of the landmark Harlem Renaissance anthology *The New Negro,* reacted to the changing economic, political, and literary contexts in which black writing was produced and discussed. He singled out *Southern Road* as "the outstanding literary event of the year" and praised the poems for furthering the use of "Negro folk portraiture" begun by Langston Hughes and Jean Toomer. But following this praise of Brown's book, Locke criticized a shift in Hughes's poetry to a poetic influenced by the emerging proletarian writing:

> Meanwhile, as the folk-school tradition deepens, Lang-
> ston Hughes, formerly its chief exponent, turns more

and more in the direction of social protest and propaganda. . . . But the poet of *Scottsboro, Ltd.* is a militant and indignant proletarian reformer, proclaiming:

> "The voice of the red world
> Is our voice, too.
> The voice of the red world is you!
> With all of the workers
> Black or white,
> We'll go forward
> Out of the night."

Locke's distinction between a "folk-school tradition" exemplified by *Southern Road* and proletarian writing works largely to discredit Hughes's politically engaged verse. But it was a deceptively simple distinction in a time when folklore and proletarian writing shared an interest in the rural poor and the working class.[14]

Through the 1930s, Brown gave numerous public readings and published poems about sharecropping, labor organizing, and racial violence in magazines with black readerships (*Opportunity, Crisis, New Challenge*) and left and liberal periodicals and anthologies that published proletarian poetry and fiction (*New Masses, Partisan Review, The New Republic, The Nation, Get Organized*). Throughout the decade he had a substantial multiracial audience. Several of the biographical notes that accompanied his publications in the 1930s promise the imminent publication of *No Hiding Place.* The book was widely anticipated by black writers and intellectuals. "You forgot to send me the manuscript of the new book," wrote Walter White, head of the NAACP, in a letter to Brown in 1939. "I want to try my voice on reading one or two of the poems to some friends." Alain Locke, in the editorial forward to Brown's 1937 booklet *Negro Poetry and Drama,* boasted that Brown had received a Guggenheim fellowship and would use it to complete his second collection of poems. It is in that same book that the introductory note to Brown's work—probably written by Brown himself—previews the collection: "His second volume, to be called 'No Hiding Place,' re-explores the Southern scene with more emphasis on social themes."[15]

Most likely because of these "social themes," Brown's publisher, Harcourt Brace, rejected the manuscript, as did several other major publishers. Donald B. Elder of Doubleday, Doran and Company advised Brown to publish the poems with a novel in a package contract. "Until then—in view of the discouraging sales of poetry—I haven't enough of a selling point to put them across, despite the fact that everyone likes the poems," he explained in a letter. A more frank exchange over Brown's poetry between Eda Lou Walton and the publisher of her anthology *This Generation* suggests that the Doubleday editor's reassurance was perhaps insincere. With an eye towards sales in the South, the editor at Scott Foresman demanded that Walton drop several of Brown's poems from the anthology: "Unfortunately we have pretty definite evidence," he wrote, "that most of the selections from Brown would be pure dynamite throughout the Southern area."[16] Ultimately published in 1980 under the title "No Hiding Place" in *The Collected Poems of Sterling A. Brown,* the poems could have been explosive if published in the 1930s because they shared with the proletarian literature of the time an attention to the South's poverty, economic exploitation, and the possibilities of multiracial working-class solidarity. Brown's poems support labor organizing in the South but show interfacial organizing to be much more complex and dangerous than proletarian literature's images of solidarity between black and white workers.

The few critics who have written on Brown's relation to the proletarian literature of the decade emphasize his treatment of multiracial solidarity and focus on **"Sharecroppers,"** a poem that describes the beating and murder of a black man who is a member of a multiracial sharecroppers' union. First published by *New Masses* in November 1936, the poem was reprinted in the 1939 literary pamphlet *Get Organized: Stories and Poems about Trade Union People.* Notes in the Sterling A. Brown papers suggest that Brown sometimes read the poem to close his public readings. The anonymous hero of **"Sharecroppers"** is questioned by his landlord and the sheriff about the location of a union meeting and its participants; he is then whipped, dragged away from his home into the woods, clubbed, shot in the side, and left to die. The poem's closing lines, which shift from poetic diction to a quoted vernacular, state his refusal to relinquish a vision of taking control of the land, a vision of black and white coexisting and growing "side by side":

> Then to the dark woods and the moon
> He gave up one secret before he died:
> "We gonna clean out dis brushwood round here soon,
> Plant de white-oak and de black-oak side by side."

One critic finds many of the conventions of proletarian poetry at work in the poem, writing that "the defiance, the brutality, and the prophecy of black and white solidarity were the stock content of poems published in the *New Masses* and other left wing periodicals of the 1930s." Another critic sees in this same poem a warning that the promise of working-class solidarity is yet another false front in "the white's conspiracy." But read with attention to organizing efforts and to the repertoire of poetic techniques Brown developed to depict race relations, the poem offers a cautionary enthusiasm for multiracial organizing. The poems of *No Hiding Place* detail economic and social conditions that demand an organized response but question the enthusiastic images of solidarity that had been produced by proletarian writers and artists.[17]

To the poem's 1930s audiences, the murder of the anonymous sharecropper would have recalled publicized incidents of violent repression of sharecropper organizing, but it would have also reminded them of some of successful interracial organizing. In the early and mid-thirties, attempts to organize sharecroppers in the South were brutally repressed by landowners and local law enforcement. In its emphasis on the violence directed against black sharecroppers who attempted to unionize, the poem may refer to the July 1931 "Camp Hill Incident" in Tallapoosa County, Alabama, where police, investigating rumors of a meeting of a black sharecroppers' union (organized by the Communist Party), provoked a shootout with a sharecropper walking toward the meeting place. The sharecropper, Ralph Grey, was wounded and left for dead; the sharecroppers at the meeting had time to flee. The chief of police then formed a posse that grew to over five hundred men, and at the end of four days, Grey had been killed and over sixty black men arrested.

By suggesting the particular potential of a sharecroppers' union to bring together black and white in the South, Brown invoked the successes of the Southern Tenant Farmers' Union (STFU), a sharecroppers' union initiated by Socialist Party organizers in Tyronza, Arkansas, in 1934. The STFU targeted the agricultural policies of Roosevelt's New Deal as well as local landowners; in articulating their agenda in the national arena, the union brought national attention to the displacement and exploitation of sharecroppers. A majority of the STFU locals were segregated, and the leadership remained white through the union's existence. But the STFU was vocally and aggressively interfacial in its policies and platforms, and in two years it grew to a membership of thirty-one thousand in seven southern states. Yet the STFU was the target of unrelenting antiunion violence: members were evicted from plantations, meeting places were burned, threats were made against organizers. The union continued to grow. Five thousand workers in Arkansas, Missouri, Tennessee, Mississippi, and Alabama participated in the September 1935 cotton-picking strike, which won some wage increases and accelerated the momentum of the union's organizing. When "Sharecroppers" was published in *New Masses* in 1936, the STFU was nationally known, mounting a growing interfacial challenge to southern tenancy.[18]

Poems published with **"Sharecroppers"** in the section of *No Hiding Place* rifled "The Cotton South" use various poetic techniques to describe the economics of sharecropping. The relentless parallel structures of **"Master and Man"** and **"Old Lem"** outline relationships between the landowner's profits and the tenant's labor and poverty:

> The yellow ears are crammed in Mr. Cromartie's bin
> The wheat is tight sacked in Mr. Cromartie's barn.

> The timothy is stuffed in Mr. Cromartie's loft.
> The ploughs are lined up in Mr. Cromartie's shed.
> The cotton has gone to Mr. Cromartie's factory.
> The money is in Mr. Cromartie's bank.

The passive voice conceals the labor—and laborer—that earned and secured this prosperity. The second stanza continues the repetition, but shifts to images of waste and absence; within the pattern Mr. Cromartie's repositories of wealth are replaced by Uncle Ned's labor:

> Blackened sticks line the furrows that Uncle Ned laid.
> Bits of fluff are in the corners where Uncle Ned ginned.

Through the poem Mr. Cromartie is named as possessing things; Uncle Ned only has his work.

> The harvest is over: Uncle Ned's harvesting,
> Mr. Cromartie's harvest. Time now for rest.

Brown's account of this economy and its enforcement pays substantial attention to the shared economic oppression of black and white workers. The three words that close **"Sharecroppers"**—"side by side"—are repeated in two other poems in *No Hiding Place*, **"Colloquy"** and **"Side by Side,"** the collection's longest poem. In **"Side by Side,"** the title phrase, spoken once by a black worker, once by a white worker, and once by a narrator addressing them both, represents both the commonalities and the separation of the two workers. This poem insists on the similarities between the lives of "John Cracker" and "Joe Nigg" by using the same language, slightly transposed, to describe their neighborhoods, their food, their women, their dreams, their music, their churches:

> Your unpainted, ramshackly churches stand
> Side by side, Lord, side by side.
> In one John hears of hell for sinners,
> Of heaven for the hard-worked, meek, long-suffering;
> In the other Joe hears of heaven bright heaven
> For the meek, long-suffering, hard-worked,
> And of hell for sinners.

Though the recognition of the fact that they live "side by side" is a potential power, the poem reminds us that it is living "side by side" that enables their exploitation:

> Let the white workers strike, will break it with niggers
> Then let the niggers if they dare.
> They know how to keep you separate, separate,
> Poor white trash and nigger trash, side by side.

The narrator's direct address to both John Cracker and Joe Nigg at the poem's close suggests that Joe Nigg knows the message already and that John Cracker may never hear it:

> Listen, John:
> But you will probably never listen,

Your ears have been deafened by the roar so long,
You have told yourself there is nothing Joe can say
But "Yessuh" and "Nawsuh," and "Be right there,
  Mister John"
You have never gotten around to it, John,
Either to listening or thinking.

Brown again marked the narrow limits of the white imagination, for John Cracker is unable to imagine his black counterpart speaking any words beyond expressions of subservience. But the poem closes as Joe attempts to speak through the "roar" that has deafened John Cracker:

But Joe has said it, in moments when fear
Did not catch his tongue and throttle his breath:
"Mr. John, Mr. John
We cain't never make it dis way at all."
Listen, John Cracker,
Joe Nigg, I've an earful for yo.

An imperative "Listen" often commenced poems written for performance at political events in the 1930s, probably to gain attention and quiet an audience. Brown's audience included white labor and organizers, and the poem attempts to begin conversations between white and black workers.[19]

Brown used the image of "side by side" to remind white workers of the common struggles they shared with black workers and also to remind them of the disproportionate costs black workers would be made to pay for solidarity. In the early 1930s, Communist and white left literary critics favored works by black writers that affirmed and celebrated solidarity between black and white workers. Images of solidarity such as the interfacial handshake appeared frequently in poems, plays, magazine illustrations, articles, and letters. Langston Hughes, for example, often closed his poems and plays with a handclasp between a white worker and a black worker. Hughes's "Open Letter to the South," a poem addressed by a black southern worker to his white counterpart, closes with the lines, "White worker, / Here is my hand. / Today, / We're Man to Man." In *No Hiding Place* multiracial organizing is a far more complex and dangerous act than represented by the image of a black and a white hand clasping. Brown responds to that image directly in a stanza from **"Colloquy,"** a conversation between Mist' Charlie, a white worker, and Sam, a black worker:

"Shake hands, Sam. We'll be buddies now.
An' do our scrappin' side by side from this."
"Well, here's my hand. I never gave it before,
Scared I might draw back a wrist.

For now, let's return to **"Sharecroppers"** and the questions asked by critics writing on Brown's relation to proletarian poetry: does this poem affirm or reject the possibility of interracial working-class solidarity? How do we read the vision of the poem's closing lines: "We gonna clean out dis brushwood round here soon, / Plant de white-oak and de black-oak side by side"?[20] The poem affirms the message of interfacial solidarity figured in the sharecropper's dying vision by placing it in a closing couplet and shifting to a quoted vernacular, a language consistently valued in Brown's poems. The poem's allusion to a particular historical moment—the organizing campaign of the STFU—in which some reforms had been won through multiracial organizing, also suggests that Brown believed that interracial working-class solidarity was a necessary step towards economic justice in the South. But rather than use the handshakes and marches of proletarian literature to figure solidarity, Brown created an image of productive work—clearing, planting, making the land more useful. The image gestures towards the contributions of both black and white labor to the making of the southern landscape and economy, and anticipates the productivity of their solidarity. The narrative thoroughly measures the cost: an escalation of violence against the black worker. By publishing these poems in left periodicals and anthologies, Brown demanded the same complexity of representation in proletarian writing that he demanded in folklore.

A NEGRO LOOKS AT THE SOUTH

When Brown was appointed editor on Negro affairs for the Federal Writers' Project (FWP) in 1936, he brought this same attention to representation into a federal agency charged with recording and representing American regional life. Brown coordinated the collection of ex-slave narratives, directed an inventory of historical manuscripts relating to black Americans, and initiated several major studies of African American history and culture. But much of his time was consumed by the task of reviewing copy produced by State Writers' Project (SWP) offices for the *American Guides*—a series of book-length state guidebooks. Each of these American Guides was both a travel book that provided the visitor with maps, transportation information, and suggested "tours," and an inventory of local geology, history, culture, and economies. In a 1939 memo to the Works Progress Administration's publicity office, Brown wrote that the office on Negro affairs "was set up with the express purpose of helping to present the race adequately and without bias." Not surprisingly, Brown encountered many of the same "grooves" and omissions, which he fought with efforts to hire more black writers and to include essays on black life in the state guides. Brown drafted lists of questions white writers should ask about a black community and reviewed all copy produced by the project. His correspondence shows his diplomatic attempts to negotiate revisions of copy with white editors. In June 1937 Brown protested the erasure of black communities from the *Guides* in a memo to Henry Alsberg, director of the FWP. "This New South (or New Midwest or New North)," Brown wrote "from which the Negro is an exile, not self-imposed in this case, is hardly recognizable. . . . But if our publications are to be true guides to American life, the Negro cannot be so completely relegated to the background."[21]

In this context of continually revising representations of American regions, Brown began to compose his own narrative accounts of the South. A biographical note published in 1943 described the forthcoming project *A Negro Looks at the South* as "a book nearing completion in which Sterling Brown interprets southern people and scenes." A year later, a note in the Washington, D.C., magazine *The Record Changer* announced the book's imminent publication and urged his readers to ask for it in their local bookstore the following spring. The fate of the book *A Negro Looks at the South* is even less clear than that of the unpublished book of poems. A manuscript exists in scattered fragments in the Sterling A. Brown papers in the Moorland-Spingarn Research Center, and Brown published narrative sketches, most likely pieces of the project, in *Phylon, Survey Graphic, The Record Changer,* and *South Today.* The essay "Count Us In," which draws upon Brown's wartime travels to argue against segregation, also seems part of this project.[22]

If published, *A Negro Looks at the South* would have joined the books of documentary writing and photographs that often centered an account of Depression America around the South. Documentary writing shared with the decade's folk and proletarian literature an interest in presenting the poor, the "submerged" people of the Depression. In the early 1930s, left and radical journalists, photographers, and editors had developed narrative and representational strategies that attempted to record and present the economic and social impacts of the Depression as riveting and undeniable fact. They relied on techniques such as direct quotation of documents, direct quotation of informants, and a firsthand reportage that, as William Stott has described it, "tries to convey the texture of actuality as well as the facts."[23] By the end of the decade, through the work of the FWP and the Farm Security Administration (FSA), documentary became the aesthetic of the New Deal. The most well known of these documentary productions are the images compiled by photographers working for the FSA, which offered evidence of the need for FSA projects and later documented their results. A number of other folklorists and proletarian writers worked for the FWP, including B. A. Botkin, Zora Neale Hurston, and Jack Conroy. Brown took at least two extended tours through the South—probably one trip in 1937, another in the early 1940s, joining the ranks of the writers and photographers who toured the South during the 1930s and produced books such as *You Have Seen Their*

Faces (Erskine Caldwell), *American Exodus* (Dorothea Lange), *Land of the Free* (Archibald MacLeish), and *12 Million Black Voices* (Richard Wright), as well as the FWP's *American Guides.*

In his notes for the preface of his book, Brown challenged representations Of "the South" just as he had Bradford's claim of representing "the Negro" a decade earlier:

> Preface: Not given as "The South." Realize there are many Souths, some of which I could not enter. Certain Carcassones I have not seen. Disadvantage: color, education, border city, middle class. Places I could not reach: peonage farms, turpentine camps, Okefenokee swamp, prison camps, etc. Lynching. Time & money prevented seeing much of Florida, Texas, Arkansas. Yet Fla—Yankeeized state—Texas—nearly a nation in itself—Also levels of life: St Cecelia's aristocrats—on the outside of all that—Cotton factors, sheriffs—poor whites—Yet not too many disclaimers. Itinerary: all of the southern states east of the Mississippi. Alexandria to Alexandria, La.—Not chamber of Commerce South—not "So You're Seeing South"—tours, etc. Charleston, Miami—etc.—Twenty years of teaching in the South or travelling there—Have read enough of literature on South to realize that there are countless Souths: People I have seen and talked with, sometimes fleetingly, more often at length. Scenes I have witnessed. Note on dialect: wuz, ah, etc—tried instead to get idiom and cadence.[24]

Brown might have imagined a book that remained immersed in distinctive local scenes. Each of his published sketches describes an hour, afternoon, or evening spent in a particular place—a visit to a family that lives with cotton growing to their porch, an attempt to visit the home of Joel Chandler Harris, a pay dance in an auditorium in Atlanta. The outlines in Brown's notes suggest that the book would be arranged thematically, with chapters, formed from ten to twelve sketches, on topics such as education, agriculture, remembrance and history, segregation, music, and whites.

The book's structure emphasized multiplicity and difference, refusing to reduce any issue or topic to one place, example, or spokesperson, and served to illuminate differences between southern black communities. A chapter provisionally tided "Farm" would include visits to Gee's Bend, Alabama—an isolated black community talked up for its African cultural retentions—a family laboring for a cotton planter, a tenant farmer organizer, and a Creole landowner. Sketches about music described a search for first-wave jazz greats in New Orleans, a description of a jitterbug dance, a low-cotton family singing hymns, and competitions between quartets that sang with style and harmonies Brown had never before heard. Brown's chapters are alert to individual artistry and to difference. There are moments when he does not understand the dialect or even the language of his hosts. Of a visit with the aunt of a

Creole friend, Brown wrote, "With the two of them talking away in French, Gus less sure, Aunt Véronique fluent and precise and musical, with the lamplight glinting on the highly colored crucifix and Catholic emblems on the white clay walls, it was easy to imagine that I was in a farm home in France rather than in the American South."[25]

Brown often used the word "folklore" as a derisive label for accounts of southern locales and people given in other documentary narratives, including stories told in the FWP state guides. In these sketches he described visiting a local landmark with his local hosts and repeating to them the "folklore of the *Louisiana Guide*." In other sketches Brown used "folktale" to designate stories overheard or retold that were almost exclusively about contemporary "white folks." One "folktale of sharecropping" describes a landlord and son whittling down the annual payment they owe their best sharecropper. A section of the book published in the magazine *Survey Graphic* labels a series of stories of interfacial encounters between soldiers and civilians in the South with the heading "folktales": a southern white restaurant owner who refuses to provide box lunches to a train transporting black soldiers; a black woman's quip to a white soldier who refuses to share a bus seat; the story of a white community that spread a lavish picnic for a black aviator who had lost his squadron. In these sketches Brown redirected the appeal of the term "folktale" and its claims to authenticity towards stories of contemporary race relations.

For Brown, documentary writing, with its use of reportage and quotation, was a genre that could accommodate various forms of testimony against segregation in the South, and various forms of testimony to individual and organized acts of protest. Brown planned to begin the book with a chapter titled "Jim Crow Journal," revising the cross-country travel narrative into a firsthand account of negotiating systems of segregation. Brown documented protest by southern blacks that had been concealed but was growing in the late 1930s and early 1940s into stronger demands. "The protest I heard in my travels," Brown reported in his essay "Count Us In," "ranged from the quietly spoken aside, through twisted humor and sarcasm, to stridency." There are numerous stories of individuals who refused to give up a seat on the bus, individuals who challenged restrictions on voting within their communities. A sketch titled "One Language, One People" describes acts of protest against the segregation enforced at the meeting of the National Council of Teachers of English when it was held in Atlanta. Brown intended to include a section titled "Odyssey of an Organizer," a digest of the autobiography of Clinton Clark, a Louisiana sharecropper organizer who typed his life story on the back of union newsletters and mailed pages to Brown with requests for paper, typewriter ribbons, and old clothes.

Brown's retelling of Clark's story quotes heavily from Clark's manuscript but highlights the extent of organizing Clark accomplished without the knowledge of local whites. (When Clark was arrested and jailed after organizing a public meeting, local whites lined-up to view the previously unseen organizer through a peephole in the prison wall.) By assembling these various stories of individual and organized protest, Brown sought to form a South unseen in other documentary narratives.

In the later 1930s and early 1940s, the reformist use of documentary shifted even further toward patriotic causes. We see this most visibly in the transfer of the FSA photographers to the Domestic Operations Branch (DOB) of the Office of War Information in 1942. Instead of documenting the work of the FSA, they photographed the domestic war effort, including the internment of Japanese Americans. But in Brown's writing the onset of the war sharpened his documentation of domestic protest. The anecdotes and conversations he gathered on his trip during a "six month's stay in the deep South of wartime" repeatedly record the racial discrimination and segregation in the wartime rhetorics of "Unity" and "Victory." For example, Brown cited a sign printed under a large red "V" on a bus in Charleston: "Avoid friction. Be patriotic. White passengers will be seated from front to rear; colored passengers from rear to front." In articles published in 1942 and 1944 Brown recorded numerous examples of southern blacks responding with their own appropriations of wartime rhetoric. In an anecdote Brown credited to a white liberal, a black soldier is asked to move from a seat on a bus. "I'm fixing to go off and fight for democracy," he tells the bus driver. "I may as well start right now." In these anecdotes Brown forcefully used writing practices that had been developed to present evidence of economic deprivation instead to present evidence of discrimination, segregation, and increasing resistance. Brown described a wartime South where the lines of segregation increasingly were challenged, both by the influx of northern soldiers—black and white—and by southern blacks armed with the war's rhetorics of democracy. His work presciently argued that southern blacks would lead the struggle against racial oppression in the United States, and the individual acts of protest he described anticipate some of the tactics of the Civil Rights movement of the next decade.

Brown published these wartime anecdotes in "Count Us In," an essay published in the 1944 collection *What the Negro Wants*. The critic attentive to literary representation is present in the opening anecdote of a visiting foreign student who is shocked by a white writer's assertion that Georgia is 100 percent Anglo-Saxon. But as Brown argued against segregation and exclusion from the full rights of citizenship, he caught himself speaking for "*the* Negro":

However segregation may be rationalized, it is essentially the denial of belonging. I believe that Negroes want segregation abolished. I realize that here, as so often elsewhere, it is presumptuous to talk of what *the* Negro wants. I understand that Negroes differ in their viewpoints toward segregation: the half-hand on a back country farm, the lost people on Arkansas plantations, the stevedore on Savannah docks, the coal miner in Birmingham, the cook-waitress-nurse in Charleston, the man-on-the-street in Waco, Los Angeles, New York, Boston, the government workers, the newspaper editors, the professional men, the spokesmen for pressure groups—all see segregation from different angles. An illiterate couple on Red River may differ greatly in attitude from their children on River Rouge. On the part of many there has been a long accommodation to segregation; but I believe that satisfaction with it has always been short.[26]

In this passage Brown struggled to reconcile two decade-long projects: an insistence that American writing include nuanced attention to multiple African American lives and an attention to a shared experience of exclusion, exploitation, and violence. His strong stand against segregation may have prevented Brown from publishing *A Negro Looks at the South,* especially as World War II preempted other political and aesthetic projects. Perhaps his stand against segregation also prevented him from finishing the book. *A Negro Looks at the South* may have ended for Brown when his insistence on the multiplicity of black experience gave way to unanimous protest.

Brown had begun the decade listening to the "narrow grooves" with which the white imagination had represented African Americans. He welcomed the folk, proletarian, and documentary writings that directed literary attention to southern black communities and presumed to record details of rural, working-class, and dispossessed lives. As Brown pressed for more specific accounts of these communities, the violence directed against them, and their growing demands for equality, his attention to representation widened to the South itself. Although his contemporaries delighted in his *Opportunity* reviews and public readings, the censorship of book publishers, who rejected **No Hiding Place** and perhaps rejected or discouraged *A Negro Looks at the South,* has hidden these Souths from subsequent generations of readers. His poems and travel narratives provide vivid, sometimes biting, sometimes adoring, descriptions of work, talk, play, history, music, politics, violence, and loss in black communities from Washington, D.C., to Opelousas, Louisiana. The Souths of Sterling A. Brown grew more multivalent and restive through the 1930s and early 1940s, and with wit and panache, he challenged his contemporaries with his interpretations of these many different southern communities.

Notes

1. Sterling A. Brown, "Negro Folk Expression: Spirituals, Seculars, Ballads, and Work Songs," *Phylon* 14 (Winter 1953): 60. This essay, along with a number of others discussed here, has been usefully reprinted in *A Son's Return: Selected Essays of Sterling A. Brown,* ed. Mark A. Sanders (Northeastern University Press, 1996).

2. Robin D. G. Kelley, "Notes on Deconstructing 'the Folk,'" *American Historical Review* 97 (1992): 1402; Brown, "Negro Folk Expression," 61.

3. On the rise of ethnography, see George Marcus and Michael Fischer, *Anthropology as Cultural Critique: An Experimental Moment in the Human Sciences* (University of Chicago Press, 1986), 19, 119,129.

4. Sterling A. Brown, "Negro Character as Seen by White Authors," *Journal of Negro Education* 11 (April 1933): 179; Sterling A. Brown, "From the Southwest," review of *Tone the Bell Easy,* ed. J. Frank Dobie, and *Negrito,* by J. Mason Brewer, *Opportunity* (October 1933): 313; Brown, "Negro Character," 179-80, 203. Emphasis in the original.

5. Sterling A. Brown, *The Collected Poems of Sterling A. Brown* 1980; rprt. TriQuarterly Press, 1989) 172-73.

6. Brown, *Collected Poems,* 170.

7. Sterling A. Brown, "You Call That Religion," review of *Ol' King David an' the Philistine Boys,* by Roark Bradford, *Opportunity* (January 1931): 21. The ellipsis is Brown's.

8. Sterling A. Brown, "The New Secession—A Review," review of *Black April,* by Julia Peterkin, *Opportunity* (May 1927): 148; Sterling A. Brown, "Local Color or Interpretation," review of *Bright Skin,* by Julia Peterkin, *Opportunity* (July 1932): 223. Emphasis in the original.

9. Sterling A. Brown, "Arcadia, South Carolina," review of *Roll, Jordan, Roll,* by Julia Peterkin and Doris Ulmann, *Opportunity* (February 1934): 60.

10. Robert G. O'Meally's vital bibliographic work has guided me back to these reviews and to Brown's many other writings published in periodicals. His annotated bibliography of Brown's writings is published in both *The Collected Poems of Sterling A. Brown* and *A Son's Return: Selected Essays of Sterling A. Brown.*

11. Sterling A. Brown, *Negro Poetry and Drama* (1937; rprt. *The Negro in American Fiction and Negro Poetry and Drama,* Arno Press and *The*

New York Times, 1969), 77; Charles Rowell, "'Let Me Be With Ole Jazzbo': An Interview with Sterling A. Brown," *Callaloo* 14 (1991): 811.

12. Brown, *Collected Poems,* 188, 209.

13. Sterling Brown, "Old Time Tales," review of *Mules and Men,* by Zora Neale Hurston, *New Masses,* 25 February 1936, 25.

14. Alain Locke, "Black Truth and Black Beauty" *Opportunity* (January 1933): 14, 17.

15. The many invitations in his correspondence (held by the Moorland-Spingarn Research Center at Howard University) suggest that Brown read to a great variety of public groups. A biographical note can be found in "Contributors," *New Challenge* 2. 2 (1937): 93-94; Walter White to Sterling Brown, 26 May 1939, Sterling A. Brown Papers, Moorland-Spingarn Research Center, Howard University, Washington, D.C.; Brown, *Negro Poetry and Drama,* 77.

16. Donald B. Elder to Brown, 11 March 1939, Sterling A. Brown Papers, Moorland-Spingarn Research Center, Howard University, Washington, D.C.; see ed. George Anderson and Eda L. Walton, *This Generation* (1939; rprt. Scott, Foresman, 1949) 645-46.

17. Brown, *Collected Poems,* 182; James O. Young, *Black Writers of the Thirties* (Louisiana State University Press, 1973) 186; Jean Wagner, *Black Poets of the United States,* trans. Kenneth Douglas (University of Illinois Press, 1973), 483.

18. Dan T. Carter, *Scottsboro: A Tragedy of the American South* (1969; rprt. Louisiana State University Press, 1979), 123-27; Jerold S. Auerbach, "Southern Tenant Farmers: Socialist Critics of the New Deal," *Labor History* 7 (Winter 1966): 13, 17; Leah Wise and Sue Thrasher, "The Southern Tenant Farmers' Union," *Working Lives: The Southern Exposure History of Labor in the South,* ed. Marc S. Miller (Pantheon Books, 1980), 137.

19. Brown, *Collected Poems* 183, 219, 220, 222, 182. "Master and Man" was first published in *The New Republic,* 18 November 1936, 66.

20. Langston Hughes, *The Collected Poems of Langston Hughes,* ed. Arnold Rampersad and David Roessel (Knopf, 1994) 160-61; Brown, *Collected Poems,* 214. "Colloquy" was first published in Anderson and Walton, *This Generation.*

21. Sterling Brown's office to Mr. Dutton Ferguson, 8 February 1939, "Reports and Miscellaneous Records Pertaining to Negro Studies," FWP, RG 69, National Archives; Joanne Gabbin provides a useful summary of Brown's work in the FWP in her book *Sterling A. Brown: Building the Black Aesthetic Tradition* (Greenwood Press, 1985); Brown to Alsberg, 8 June 1937, "Reports and Miscellaneous Records Pertaining to Negro Studies," FWP, RG 69, National Archives.

22. Sterling A. Brown, "Words on a Bus," *South Today* (Spring 1943): 27; "Lemme Take This Chorus," *The Record Changer* (December 1944): 50.

23. William Stott, *Documentary Expression and Thirties America* (1973; rprt. University of Chicago Press, 1986), 144.

24. Sterling A. Brown, handwritten notes, Box 69, Sterling A. Brown Papers.

25. Sterling A. Brown, handwritten manuscript, Sterling A. Brown Papers.

26. Sterling A. Brown, "Count Us In," in *What the Negro Wants,* ed. Rayford Logan (University of North Carolina Press, 1944) 315, 318, 482, 336-37.

Joanne V. Gabbin (essay date 1999)

SOURCE: Gabbin, Joanne V. "The Poetry of Sterling A. Brown: A Study in Form and Meaning." In *African American Literary Criticism, 1773 to 2000,* edited by Hazel Arnett Ervin, pp. 247-58. New York: Twayne Publishers, 1999.

[In the following essay, Gabbin assesses the influence of blues, spirituals, and work songs on Brown's poetry.]

With the same literary perspective used in recreating folk subjects and themes, [Sterling] Brown adopted the language and form of Black folklore. In his poetry the language of Black folk—the dialect, the idioms, the imagery, the style—retains its richness and verve. Likewise, the spirituals, blues, ballads, work songs, tall tales, and aphorisms achieve another level of expressiveness as they are absorbed and integrated. Not once doubting the efficacy of folk speech to express all that the people were, Brown brought the use of dialect in poetry to new respectable heights, despite a debate over its value as a literary medium.

In 1922 James Weldon Johnson, writing in the preface of *The Book of American Negro Poetry,* recognized that Black writers were breaking away from the use of conventionalized Negro dialect. The long association of this kind of dialect with the conventionalized treatment of Black character had convinced Johnson and other writers like Countee Cullen that the poet could not "adequately or artistically" treat a broad spectrum of

Black life using this medium. Though Johnson generally applauded the tendency to discard dialect, he feared that Black poets, in an attempt to disassociate themselves from the spurious, often demeaning, traditions of dialect poetry, would lose the "quaint and musical folk speech as a medium of expression." Johnson's indictment, then, was not against dialect, as such, "but against the mold of convention in which Negro dialect in the United States had been set." In his now classic call for originality and authenticity in racial poetry, he anticipated a form of expression that would not limit the poet's emotional and intellectual response to Black American life.

> What the colored poet in the United States needs to do is something like what Synge did for the Irish; he needs to find a form that will express the racial spirit by symbols from within rather than by symbols from without, such as the mere mutilation of English spelling and pronunciation. He needs a form that is freer and larger than dialect, but which will still hold the racial flavor; a form expressing the imagery, the idioms, the peculiar turns of thought, and the distinctive humor and pathos, too, of the Negro, but which will also be capable of voicing the deepest and highest emotions and aspirations, and allow the widest range of subjects and the widest scope of treatment.

Ten years later Brown, with the publication of *Southern Road,* comes as close to achieving Johnson's ideal of original racial poetry as any Black American poet had before. Appropriately, Johnson had the distinction of introducing Brown's poems to the American reading public.

> Mr. Brown's work is not only fine, it is also unique. He began writing just after the Negro poets had generally discarded conventionalized dialect with its minstrel traditions to Negro life (traditions that had but slight relation, often no relation at all, to actual Negro life) with its artificial and false sentiment, its exaggerated geniality and optimism. He infused his poetry with genuine characteristic flavor by adopting as his medium the common, racy, living speech of the Negro in certain phases of real life.

In Brown, Johnson recognized a poet who mined the "unfailing sources" of Black poetry to enrich his own poems. He saw Brown exploring with uncompromising honesty the range of characteristically folk responses—the stoicism in **"Memphis Blues,"** the tragic despair in **"Southern Road,"** the ironical humor of the Slim Greer series, the alienation of **"Revelations,"** and the impulse to keep moving in such poems as **"Odyssey of Big Boy"** and **"Long Gone"**—which rang true to Johnson as they would have to the folk themselves.

Brown's exploration of the range of their responses led him to the sacred songs, the spirituals. "As the best expression of the slaves' deepest thoughts and yearnings," the spirituals are emotional, imaginative, and visionary. They reflect, often in rhythms as striking as the melodies are beautiful, the religious nature of Black folk. Their expression of emotions that move to tears and joy, their imaginative interpretation of life and scripture, their fascination with Biblical characters, their preoccupation with sin, evil, and the devil, their personal relationship with "King Jesus" and God, and their visionary treatment of heaven, hell and judgment day are all revealed in these songs.

Many of the essential qualities, themes, and idioms of the spirituals, Brown succeeds in transferring to his own poetry. In **"New Steps,"** an infrequently quoted poem in *Southern Road,* Brown imaginatively handles the themes of saints and sinners competing for the soul of a young man. Here the battle of good and evil is worked out in a rather homely fashion. Sister Annie, overjoyed with the fine "new steps a-climbing to de little Church do'," remains strong in the faith that the church will save her son from ruin. Encouraged that the church is now fine enough to attract her wayward son, she "struts herself down to the sinful Foot." To her disappointment, she sees that the sinners are busy sprucing up the dens of iniquity, "puttin' green paint" on "poolroom den" and "sportin' new lace next the dirty panes." Brown uses a language whose cadence and tone are reminiscent of the spiritual "By an' By," in which the unknown bard sings, "O, by an' by / I'm gwinter lay down my heavy load." He shows Sister Annie continuing the battle against sin in a gesture of one-upmanship though the weight of her armor seems onerous.

> Up de new steps that meeting' night
> Sister Annie drug a heavy an' a weary load.
> New steps a-climbin'—
> O my Lawd
> Lace curtains snow white
> Snow white curtains
> O my Lawd
> Upstairs, downstairs,
> New steps
> O my Lawd. . . .

Though the poet does not reveal who finally wins out, his message is clear and parallels thematically that of the traditional religious song, "Workin' on the Building."

> If I wus a sinner man, I tell you what I'd do,
> I'd lay down all my sinful ways an' work on the building too.
> I'm workin' on the building fer my Lord,
>   Fer my Lord, fer my Lord,
> I'm workin' on the building fer my Lord
>   I'm working on the building, too.

Continuing to work on the building, Sister Annie is a symbol of religious faith and spiritual fortitude.

"New Steps" mirrors the form of spiritual songs and projects the Christian concepts of faith, love, humility, and salvation. Many of the songs retell in capsulized, often dramatic, form significant events and stories recorded in the Old and New Testaments. Some, however, make no direct allusion to Biblical scenes but are inspired by local events, sermons, or the desire for religious social comment. In **"New Steps,"** Brown adopts the dramatic form of many spirituals to spotlight Sister Annie's attempt to bring her boy to salvation. The characters in the story are allegorized (Brother Luck, Miss Joy, Victory). They add to the symbolic richness of the poem in which every element of the setting—"new steps," "the dingy house," "the big white letters," "snow white curtains"—is charged with a metaphorical meaning like that evoked by the chariot, the wheel, and gospel shoes, standard images in the spirituals.

The language in the poem is characterized by economy of statement, and vivid, fresh images: "An the dingy house . . . / Runnin' over wid jazz an' scarlet noise." Brown also punctuates the poem with interjections—"Oh my Lawd"—a typical feature of Black music, and he occasionally, "worries the line" as he has his narrator interject bits of wisdom.

> Good times, seems like, ain't fuh las'—
> Nebber de real good times, dey ain't—

Finally Brown uses an effective incremental style in the chorus to evoke the most powerful image of the poem.

> O my Lawd
> Upstairs, downstairs
> New steps
> O my Lawd. . . .

The themes, the qualities, and the idiom characteristic of the spiritual receive their fullest exploration in another poem appearing in *Southern Road,* **"When De Saints Go Ma'ching Home."** Using two carefully selected similes and incorporating into his poem a line from the spiritual, he suggests the quiet dignity and solemnity of Big Boy Davis as he tunes up his guitar to play his "mother's favorite."

> Carefully as an old maid over needlework;
> Oh, as some black deacon, over his Bible, lovingly,
> He'd tune up specially for this. There'd be
> No chatter now, no patting of the feet.
> After a few slow chords, knelling and sweet—
> Oh when de saints go ma'chin' home,
> Oh when de sayaints goa ma'chin' home . . .
> He would forget
> The quieted bunch, his dimming cigarette
> Stuck into a splintered edge of the guitar;
> Sorrow deep hidden in his voice, a far
> And soft light in his strange brown eyes;
> Alone with his masterchords, his memories. . . .

As Big Boy sang the saints' triumph song, he would see "a gorgeous procession" of the faithful, those who had held out to the end, marching to the "Beulah Land."

There would be Old Deacon Zachary and Sis Joe. Elder Peter Johnson, "steamin' up de grade / Lak Wes' bound No. 9," and "little brown skinned chillen / Wid deir skinny legs a-dancin' would join the heavenly band." However, white folk, as goes his dream, would "have to stay outside." In keeping with God's promise to take care of his own, those who had shunted him would not be kept behind. Heaven is a place reserved for the righteous, and his folk shall occupy the best place. There would be "another mansion fo' white saints." Ironically, his vision of heaven takes on the pattern of earthly existence; segregation will be preserved.

According to Big Boy's dream, God's judgment was not color blind; it would fall as evenly on the Black folk as the white. Big Boy's buddies—Sportin' Legs and Lucky Sam, Smitty, Hambone, and Hardrock George—would go the way of "guzzlin', cuttin' shines" and bootleggers. Even Sophie, his strappin' brown, could not fit in with the saints of God. One, though, was assured a place. He sees his mother's "wrinkled face, / Her brown eyes, quick to tears—to joy."

> Mammy
> With deep religion defeating the grief
> Life piled so closely about her
> Ise so glad trouble doan last alway,
> And her dogged belief
> That some fine day
> She'd go a-ma'chin'
> When de saints go ma'chin' home.

Part of the effectiveness of the poem lies in Brown's skillful mixture of idiom and his evocation of religious imagery and lyrics in the spiritual. In profiling the saints in the heavenly band, Brown uses folk dialect to clothe the humble and simple faith they brought to their religion. Interspersed with the more formal language, these passages stand in bold relief.

"When De Saints Go Ma'ching Home" is one of the best examples of Brown's effective use of structure. Using the music of this spiritual as his dominant poetic referent, Brown has Big Boy's rendition of this favorite spiritual come alive with the fervor, ecstasy, and drama of Black religious music. Brown uses several of the techniques identified by Stephen Henderson in his important book *Understanding the New Black Poetry.* Brown makes a clear allusion to the song title and adopts it as the title of his poem. The title has the power to evoke the image of a bodacious New Orleans band parading from the cemetery amid the rejoicing of those who are very much alive, or Louis "Satchmo" Armstrong irreligiously belting out the "chant of saints," in one hand his handkerchief which has become a cliche and in the other hand his trumpet which will never be one. Brown forces the reader to incorporate into the structure of the poem his memory of specific passages from the spiritual. Here Big Boy sings the song with solemn, slow chords from his guitar. Brown takes care to write in the inflection and the syncopation.

> Oh when de saints go ma'chin' home
> Oh when de sayaints goa ma'chin' home. . . .

Above all, **"When De Saints Go Ma'ching Home"** is performance. Brown presents in six dramatic scenes the singer's remarkable vision. Attributing to his singer the skill of the visionary minister who, touched by the Holy Fire, recreates heaven's alabaster gates, the streets of gold, and the manna on celestial tables to coax his reluctant sheep to the fold, the poet imaginatively reenacts the singer's performance. Each section relates a different aspect of the singer's vision, as though the vision were a series of stills that could be viewed separately or run together to produce the moving picture. Kimberly W. Benston, in a brilliant exegesis of the poem, writes that it is "the mode of seeing the hero's songs, the perspectivizing of performance, which constitutes the inner concern" of the poem. In each section the "envisaged saints exist as possibilities not memories, which none is actually present but everyone, under the hero's watchful 'gaze' is immanently represented."

As performance, the poem speaks to the separation between singer and audience, between the self and the community. Benston sees the disjunction between the singer and the audience producing the "deep tension" in the poem and representing its "true subject." This "disjunction" is readily apparent in the structures of the poem. Benston writes, "The poem is framed by acute recognition of this discontinuity: 'He'd play after the bawdy songs and blues . . . he'd go where we / Never could flow'—divorce figured in the distinctions between 'he' and 'we' (self and community) and between the hero and poet (voice/dialect and text/formal diction)." Ultimately, by separating himself from his audience, the singer is capable of a higher vision that has the power to convince his hearers of their own possibility of revision, renewal and re-creation.

In Brown's **"Sister Lou,"** one of the most remarkable monologues in American literature, the speaker—much like the Indian-looking woman Brown met in Coolwell, Virginia—compresses her higher vision of heaven in images as familiar as hearthside implements. Sister Lou at the bedside of an ailing friend bolsters her courage with the familiar images of old dear friends that she will meet "When de man / Calls out de las' train."

Sister Lou has the train, the dominant symbol of escape and separation in folk parlance, serve as the heavenly chariot to take her friend "home." As with the folk, in the imagination of Sister Lou "the scenes of everyday life form continuous allegories" with the material found in the Bible. The woman, when she gets home, would show "Marfa" how to make "greengrape jellies" and bake "a passel of Golden Biscuits" for poor Lazarus, "scald some meal for li'l box plunkin' David and tell the Hebrew children her stories."

> Give a good talking' to
> To yo' favorite 'postle Peter,
> An' rub the po'head
> Of mixed-up Judas,
> An' joke awhile wid Jonah.

Matching the pantheon of Biblical heroes given in the spirituals, Brown establishes what he believes to be the intimate relationship that exists between Black folk and the heavenly host. Among them, they would be accepted. In heaven, there would be no back doors. "No mo' dataway / Not evah no mo!" There would be pearly gates and their own room, "Openin' on cherry trees an' plum trees / Bloomin' everlastin'." The saints would be compensated for enduring hardship and suffering pain. The folk had faith that their "belief in God enabled them to cling on to life, though poor, miserable, and dying, looking to God and expecting Him, through miraculous and spectacular means, to deliver them from their plight."

Sometimes, however, their faith is shaken. In the poem, **"Children of the Mississippi,"** the victims of the Mississippi flood recall the story of Noah but wonder why they did not receive the sign.

> De Lord tole Norah
> Dat de flood was due,
> Norah listened to de Lord
> An' got his stock on board,
> Wish dat de Lord
> Had tole us too.

In another poem, **"Crossing,"** Brown fuses the doubting of escaping slaves with the spiritual doubting of Christians. As in the spirituals, the freedom from sin gets all mixed up with physical freedom from oppression.

> We do not know
> If any have reached that Canaan
> We have received no word.
> Behind us the belling pack
> Beyond them the hunters
> Before us the dismal swamp.
> We do not know. . . .

It is appropriate that Brown couches their doubts in the poignant language of the sacred songs, for each journey involves uncertainty. Incorporating lines from several traditional songs, Brown effects, as Stephen Henderson suggested in *Understanding the New Black Poetry,* "a particularized response" resulting from the subjective feeling stirred by the reference. Henderson calls this technique the use of "subjective correlative," in contrast to the objective correlative that gained currency in the New Criticism. The following lines illustrates the technique:

> We know only
> That there lies not Canaan
> That this is no River Jordan.
>
> Still are we motherless children
> Still are we dragging travelers
> Alone, and a long ways from home.
>
> Still with the hard earth for our folding bed
> Still with our head pillowed upon a rock
>
> And still
> With one more river,
> Oh, one wide river to cross.

These lines evoke several spirituals. Dominating the poem is an allusion to the spiritual, "Wasn't Dat a Wide River."

> Oh, Jordan's River is deep and wide
> One mo' river to cross
> I don't know how to get on de other side
> One mo' river to cross.

The "ancient dusky rivers," that Hughes made symbols of the continuity of this people's racial spirit, for Brown become symbols of obstacles that must be bridged. Those who "leapt / From swamp land / Into marshes," those who "grow footsore / and muscle weary" inherit the hardships of their ancestors and stand in need of the encouragement and solace provided by the spirituals. Intrinsic to Brown's language are references to the spiritual lyrics: "Sometime I feel like a motherless child . . . A long ways from home" and "Let us cheer the weary traveler, along the heavenly way." However, his language is formal; departing from the dialect of the sacred song, it reflects a new period of struggle. The "crossing" is not to be considered entirely other-wordly—"This is not Jordan River / There lies not Canaan"—but the crossing represents also the immediate and real crossing over to freedom. . . .

Sterling Brown and his contemporary, Langston Hughes, more than any other New Negro writers, explored the oral tradition and experimented with its forms in the belief that Black folk were creating valuable, original art. They put great stock in the virtuosity of folk expression; they prized its innovation, its freshness of style, and its inclusive quality as artistic exemplars. Of all the forms, the blues received the greatest exploration in their poetry. According to Stephen Henderson, Hughes and Brown "expand and amplify the form without losing its distinctive blues flavor. Poems like Hughes' 'The Weary Blues' and 'Montage of a Dream Deferred' and Brown's **'Memphis Blues'** suggest something of their range, even in their respective first volumes of poetry."

Brown's absorption and intensification of the blues form and feeling vary from poem to poem. In **"Long Track Blues,"** Brown, handling the twin blues themes of loving and leaving, departs from the three-line stanza typical of the classic blues but uses the two-line form, the sentiments, the language, and verbal conventions of the standard blues. As folk artists had done before, he makes the railroad "the favored symbol of escape." He renders with fidelity the melancholy of a man who has lost his "lovin' babe."

> Heard a train callin'
> Blowin' long ways down the track;
> Ain't no train due here,
> Baby, what can bring you back?

The familiar ingredients are all here: the distant whistle of the train, the howling dog, the beckoning signal lights, the brakeman's lantern, all of which combine to express the man's lament. A comparison of the stanza from a folk blues and one from Brown's poem shows his close study of the form.

> I went down to de depot, I looked
> upon de board,
> Couldn't see no train, couldn't hear no
> whistle blow.
>
> Went down to the yards
> To see the signal lights come on;
> Looked down the track
> Where my lovin' babe done gone.

An analysis of these two stanzas shows that Brown approximates the cadence of the blues line with four stresses. He also uses an idiom that captures the sound and sense of railroad lore. However, in this poem the poet runs the risk of being, as George Kent suggests, "too reliant upon a folk form that has, itself, the alliance of the singing voice, instrumental music, facial expression and gesture, to drive itself into our spirit." Yet, to articulate the deeply personal feeling of departure and loss, Brown utilizes symbolism, among other literary conventions, to increase the power of the blues poem, stripped of the oral resources of the blues song. An example is the following stanza:

> Red light in my block,
> Green light down the line;
> Lawdy, let yo' green light
> Shine down on that babe o' mine.

The red light and green light that usually function to keep the rail traffic unsnarled, here have symbolic significance. The red light is a symbol for hard times, bad luck and danger; the green light is a symbol of good times, success, and safety. And on another level the green light represents the presence of spiritual grace and protection. Out there, somewhere down the line is grief, ugly grief,—not to be denied. Hauntingly, the poem suggests the poignancy that comes with preparing to face grief and loss and death.

In another poem, **"Rent Day Blues,"** Brown, using extended dialogue, tells the story of a couple facing rent day without any money. As the man wonders where they will get the rent, his woman turns up with the money from a mysterious source. Though the man is briefly troubled, he finally resolves to let their good fortune stand. In **"Rent Day Blues,"** Brown clearly presents one of the major themes of the blues—poverty and economic uncertainty—within the context of the blues' preoccupation with the love relationship. Here, Brown breaks with the blues tradition by having his blues poem "proceed in a narrative fashion." According to blues critic Charles Keil, the blues lyric rarely proceeds in this fashion but "is designed primarily to illustrate a particular theme or create a general mood." Using dialogue as a narrative technique, Brown is able to add a dramatic dimension and bits of characterization not typical of the blues lyric. For example, in the following stanzas the willingness of the woman to get the rent money any way she can and the man's suspicions and cynicism come through clearly.

> My baby says, "Honey,
> Dontcha worry 'bout the rent,
> Looky here, daddy,
> At de money what de good Lord sent."

> Says to my baby,
> "Baby, I been all aroun';
> Never knowed de good Lord
> To send no greenbacks down."

Brown is also experimenting with the rhythm of the blues poem. For example, he infuses a jazz-style offbeat rhythm in the poem. The established pattern appears to be iambic trimeter. However, in the first stanza cited above, the last line breaks from this basic pattern with a syncopated pentameter line. In a solidly aesthetic gesture, Brown is taking on the risk and challenge of the literary rather than the oral poet. . . .

In **"Ma Rainey,"** one of the finest poems in *Southern Road*, Brown skillfully brings together the ballad and blues forms and, demonstrating his inventive genius, creates the blues-ballad. On one level, the poem gives a glimpse of the folk heroine, Ma Rainey. Gertrude "Ma"

Rainey, on the vaudeville circuit at the age of fourteen, "heard the blues while trouping up and down her native south land, and started singing them herself to audiences that were spellbound as her deep, husky voice gave them back their songs." In many ways the mother of the blues, she took a youngster named Bessie Smith in her care and lovingly taught her the blues, and the child grew strong in timbre, cadence, and resonance, like her "Ma." Befitting the title Madam "Ma" Rainey, she made her entrance on innumerable stages with a sequined gown hugging her short, stocky frame, an elaborate gold necklace, tasseled earrings, and a brilliant gold-tooth grin crowning it all. Her professionalism was hard won in the Black minstrel shows, medicine shows, traveling road shows, and vaudeville shows where she trained her raspy voice to complement the new instrumental blues stylings.

But even more than being a portrait of the venerated blues singer, the poem serves as an emotional portrait of the people who flocked to hear "Ma do her stuff."

> An' some jokers keeps deir laughs a-going' in de crowded aisles,
> An' some folks sits dere waitin' wid deir aches an' miseries, . . .

Brown celebrates Ma Rainey's charisma that is more than flashy jewelry and sequined gown. He celebrates her skill in the art of improvisation, which Albert Murray says "will enable contemporary man to be at home with his sometimes tolerable but never quite certain condition of not being at home in the world and will also dispose him to regard his obstacles and frustrations as well as his achievements in terms of adventures and romance." Like Larry Neal and Ralph Ellison, Brown also celebrates the power of the blues singer "to reflect the horrible and beautiful realities of life" and to affirm "the value of the group and man's ability to deal with chaos."

In **"Ma Rainey,"** Brown has the blues mode function thematically and structurally to heighten the effect of the poem. In the poem he also uses a technique that is a common practice among several poets. Henderson describes the practice as "forcing the reader to incorporate into the structure of the poem his memory of a specific song or passage of a song, or even of a specific delivery technique." Throughout Brown's poetry there are several examples of this technique. **"When De Saints Go Ma'ching Home," "Strong Men,"** and **"Revelations"** are among the most notable examples. In the final section of the poem, Brown incorporates Bessie Smith's popular "Backwater Blues." The song, by suggesting the hardships and suffering of the victims of the Mississippi Valley floods, illustrates the dire problems faced by these people and gives, as Charles H. Rowell suggests, an "air of immediacy to the poem."

Brown has also fused the blues form with the ballad to invent the "blues-ballad," which Henderson hails as "a literary phenomenon . . . as distinctive as Wordsworth's lyrical ballad." As structurally effective as it is innovative, the blues-ballad combines the narrative framework of the ballad and the ethos of the blues. The ingenuity of his invention can be best appreciated when one sees how the two traditions come together in a blues-ballad like **"Ma Rainey."**

Ballads telling of the exploits of Black folk heroes, similar to sixteen-bar or eight-bar ballads of Anglo-Saxon origin, began to appear in America during the second half of the nineteenth century. With the abolition of slavery, Black folk, facing the prospect of freedom, were inspired to compose songs dedicated to the virtues and deeds of their heroes. These ballads bear their names: "John Hardy," "John Henry," "Casey Jones," "Railroad Bill," "Stagolee," and "Frankie and Johnny," among others. Aware of English, Irish, Scottish, and French ballad styles, Black balladeers adopted the classic ballad form which tells a story in a series of stanzas, usually in a progressive, chronologically developed narrative with or without a refrain.

At the close of the century, blues developed as a form out of the hollers of the solitary farmers who worked the rows of Southern fields. Often they sang their hollers, repeating the lines until new lines came to mind that completed the thought and expressed the emotion.

With the introduction of the guitar, capable of producing the moaning, whining, flattened sounds of the human voice, blues took shape. Though the early blues had the eight-bar or sixteen-bar stanzaic structure like the ballads, with the experimentation with the "blues notes" and the African pentatonic scale, the "twelve-bar blues" evolved. The most common but by no means the only structure consisted of three lines of four bars each.

Within this structure, the blues singer improvises his music, and in the act of creation he draws from a stock of favorite verses and familiar rhythmic patterns, and combines them with new lines extemporized out of his melancholy experience. He sings of love and infidelity, poverty and economic uncertainty, lonely travel and dislocation, drinking and drugs, and disasters and death. Unlike the balladeer who extols the virtues of a distant hero, the blues singer is the central character in this song. Therefore, the blues singers themselves become heroes to their hearers. Brownie McGhee, Blind Willie McTell, Huddie "Leadbelly" Ledbetter, Blind Lemon Jefferson, Gertrude "Ma" Rainey, Bessie Smith, Clara Smith, Mamie Smith, Ida Cox—the names are legion—look on their personal calamities and are not destroyed.

Clearly in this cultural tradition, Brown, with a conscious artistry, combines the intensely personal music of the blues singer with the heroic tales and epic scope of the balladeer. The genius of this invention is apparent in **"Ma Rainey."** Brown takes the explicit, chronological, and narrative elements of the ballad to tell how the people flock in to hear "Ma Rainey do her stuff." And though the ballad form functions well to spotlight this magnificent woman with the "gold-toofed smiles," it cannot accommodate the intimacy, the immediacy, and the emotional intensity that Brown intends for the poem. He needs the blues ethos to suggest the massive concentration of emotion present among the folk in Ma's audience—the work-weary soul, the laughing to keep from crying, the unspeakable sorrow, the needful catharsis. . . .

FURTHER READING

Biography

Pinckney, Darryl. "The Last New Negro." *New York Review of Books* 36, no. 4 (16 March 1989): 14-16.
    Overview of Brown's life and career.

Criticism

Benson, Kimberly W. "Sterling Brown's After-Song." *Callaloo* 5, nos. 1-2 (February-May 1982): 33-42.
    Contends that "When De Saints Go Ma'ching Home" "both explicates and stages the model of authentic expression which constitutes the touchstone of Brown's subtle poetics."

Collins, Michael. "Risk, Envy and Fear in Sterling Brown's Georgics." *Callaloo* 21, no. 4 (fall 1998): 950-67.
    Compares Brown's poetry to Virgil's *Georgics* and investigates the roles of risk and fear in Brown's verse.

Henderson, Stephen E. "The Heavy Blues of Sterling Brown: A Study of Craft and Tradition." *Black American Literature Forum* 14, no. 1 (spring 1980): 32-44.
    Discusses the influence of the blues tradition on Brown's poetry.

O'Meally, Robert G. "'Game to the Heart': Sterling Brown and the Badman." *Callaloo* 5, nos. 1-2 (February-May 1982): 43-54.
    Examines the image of the black badman in Brown's poetry.

Skinner, Beverly. "Sterling Brown's Poetic Ethnography: A Black and Blues Ontology." *Callaloo* 21, no. 4 (fall 1998): 998-1011.

> Explores the impact of Brown's field research, literary criticism, and social commentary on his verse.

Smethurst, James Edward. "'The Strong Men Gittin' Stronger': Sterling Brown and the Representation and Re-creation of the Southern Folk Voice." In *The New Red Negro: The Literary Left and African-American Poetry 1930-1946,* pp. 60-92. New York: Oxford University Press, 1999.

> Places Brown's poetics within the political and cultural events of the 1930s and 1940s and contrasts his work with that of Langston Hughes.

Additional coverage of Brown's life and career is contained in the following sources published by the Gale Group: *African American Writers,* **Eds. 1, 2;** *Black Literature Criticism,* **Ed. 1;** *Black Writers,* **Eds. 1, 3;** *Contemporary Authors,* **Vols. 85-88;** *Contemporary Authors New Revision Series,* **Vol. 26;** *Contemporary Authors—Obituary,* **Vol. 127;** *Contemporary Literary Criticism,* **Vols. 1, 23, 59;** *Dictionary of Literary Biography,* **Vols. 48, 51, 63;** *DISCovering Authors 3.0; DISCovering Authors Modules:Multicultural Authors* **and** *Poets; Harlem Renaissance: A Gale Critical Companion,* **Vol. 2;** *Literature Resource Center; Major 20ᵗʰ-Century Writers,* **Eds. 1, 2;** *Reference Guide to American Literature,* **Ed. 4; and** *World Poets.*

Barbara Guest
1920-

American poet, dramatist, novelist, essayist, and biographer.

The following entry provides information on Guest's life and works from 1997 through 2002.

INTRODUCTION

Guest was one of the core members of an informal group of writers called the New York School of poets in the late 1950s and 1960s. Their approach to poetry was influenced by the visual arts, especially surrealism and abstract expressionism. Although Guest eventually moved away from these early influences, critics continue to describe her work as "painterly" for its visual variety, linguistic texture, and use of language to evoke images and illusions of light and space.

BIOGRAPHICAL INFORMATION

Guest was born Barbara Ann Pinson in Wilmington, North Carolina, on September 6, 1920. She grew up in southern California, graduated from the University of California at Berkeley, and moved to New York City as a young adult. In 1952 a poem she had submitted to *Partisan Review* caught the attention of Frank O'Hara, one of the original poets in the group that would become known as the New York School. She soon became an integral member of the group, which also included John Ashbery, Kenneth Koch, and James Schuyler. Guest's poetry appeared in various literary journals, and she worked for a time as the poetry editor of *Partisan Review*. Her first collection of poetry, *The Location of Things* (1960), marked the beginning of a prolific career as a poet and essayist. However, in the late 1960s and 1970s, Guest's visibility as a poet was eclipsed by other women poets, including Denise Levertov and Adrienne Rich, whose work was more overtly political or feminist. As a result, Guest was all but forgotten by critics and scholars as a founding member of the New York group. She continued to work steadily, nonetheless, publishing volumes of original poetry regularly throughout the 1980s and 1990s. In 1998 she was awarded the Robert Frost Medal of the Poetry Society of America. Since the late 1990s, her earlier work has enjoyed renewed critical attention and additional volumes of new poetry and essays have appeared,

including *Rocks on a Platter: Notes on Literature* (1999), *Miniatures and Other Poems* (2002), and *Forces of Imagination: Writing on Writing* (2002).

MAJOR WORKS

Guest's early works, including *The Location of Things*, were strongly influenced by the efforts of the New York group of poets to use language to capture the tactile properties of modern art, abstract paintings, and other visual imagery. The work was vivid, fresh, and unlike previous trends in American poetry. Guest's personal knowledge of painting and painters, drawn in part from her work as a reviewer for *ArtNews* in the early 1950s, has been successfully employed in her literary collaborations with visual artists over the course of her career. Works such as *I Ching: Poems and Lithographs* (1969; with Sheila Isham) and *Symbiosis* (2000; with Laurie Reid) have been called creative innovations that transcend their visual and linguistic components, becoming more than poetry illustrated by art, or art enhanced by poetry. Many individual poems Guest has published over the course of more than four decades, including "The Poetess" (1973), and "The Farewell Stairway" (1989) were written for or about specific works of art.

A frequent traveler, Guest also infused her poetry with images garnered during international and domestic journeys. The diction and rhyme of Guest's poetry in *The Blue Stairs* (1968) evokes sensory richness and the influences of visits to such places as Siberia, Vladivostock, Yokohama, Morocco, Granada, and the Sierra Nevada. Standing in contrast to the wide-ranging experience of travel as an overt theme of this collection is Guest's strong sense of being centered in a place to which one returns gratefully, having left for the journey with mixed emotions.

Between 1973 and 1989 Guest published three major collections of poetry: *Moscow Mansions* (1973), *The Countess from Minneapolis* (1976), and *Fair Realism* (1989), along with smaller works, some of which were done in collaboration with visual artists. Among these are *The Türler Losses* (1979), *Biography* (1980), and *Quilts* (1980). In 1984 she also published the well-received biography of Hilda Doolittle, *Herself Defined: The Poet H. D. and Her World.*

In the 1990s Guest's work began to incorporate more of what she terms "space, sparseness, and openness." Her 1993 collection *Defensive Rapture* contains poems that have been described as oblique and elusive, traversing the spectrum of themes that appear throughout earlier works, including travel, nature, art, perception, and love. Following the death of her husband in 1990, Guest returned to Berkeley, California, and volumes of poetry began to appear more regularly. In 1995 came *Stripped Tales* and *Selected Poems*; in 1996, *Quill, Solitary AP-PARITION. The Confetti Trees: Motion Picture Stories,* a series of prose poems, was published in 1998. Since the turn of the twenty-first century, new works have appeared, including a collection of essays, *Forces of Imagination: Writing on Writing,* and a volume of verse, *Miniatures and Other Poems.*

CRITICAL RECEPTION

Having played a central role in the birth and development of Modernist poetry in the early 1950s, Guest was not long thereafter excluded from the living legacy of that time by critics, anthology editors, and commentators who preferred to canonize the New York School of poets as yet one more coterie of young men dedicated to leaving their mark on the American literary scene. The slight was only temporary, however. Renewed reader and critical interest in Guest's entire oeuvre at the turn of the twenty-first century, while she is still actively writing, has led to a reconsideration of her significant influence on the direction of poetry at the midpoint of the twentieth-century and beyond. Catherine Kasper characterizes Guest's poetry, throughout the evolution of her career, as "radically individual, and less easily summarized" than the works of her early peers, suggesting that Guest's exclusion from the roster of literary artists of the New York School is due to aesthetic preference as well as gender discrimination. In a similar way, Robert Kaufman describes Guest as "a supreme poet's poet," noting that throughout her career she has been "perhaps the most genuinely experimental, aesthetically fearless and uncompromising artist" of the original core group of New York School writers. Sara Lundquist likewise commends Guest's unique voice and "blithely individualistic" approach to writing and participating in the literary life of American poetry, asserting that she has remained "true to her own lights" and confident in her life's work regardless of critical attention, or the lack thereof. Lundquist writes, "Her poetry is still doing what it wants to do, and is ahead of what has been written about it."

PRINCIPAL WORKS

Poetry

The Location of Things 1960
Poems: The Location of Things, Archaics, The Open Skies 1962
The Blue Stairs 1968
I Ching: Poems and Lithographs (with Sheila Isham) 1969
Moscow Mansions 1973
The Countess from Minneapolis 1976
The Türler Losses 1979
Biography 1980
Quilts 1980
Fair Realism 1989
Defensive Rapture 1993
Selected Poems 1995
Quill, Solitary, APPARITION 1996
The Confetti Trees: Motion Picture Stories 1998
If So, Tell Me: Short Poems 1999
Rocks on a Platter: Notes on Literature 1999
Symbiosis (with Laurie Reid) 2000
Miniatures and Other Poems 2002

Other Major Works

The Ladies Choice (play) 1953
The Office (play) 1961
Port (play) 1965

Seeking Air (novel) 1978
Herself Defined: The Poet H. D. and Her World
    (biography) 1984
Forces of Imagination: Writing on Writing (essays) 2003

CRITICISM

Sara Lundquist (essay date summer 1997)

SOURCE: Lundquist, Sara. "Reverence and Resistance: Barbara Guest, Ekphrasis, and the Female Gaze." *Contemporary Literature* 38, no. 2 (summer 1997): 260-86.

[*In the following essay, Lundquist discusses gender perspective in Guest's ekphrastic poems—that is, poetry inspired by or written about specific works of art.*]

Composer John Gruen, in his reminiscence of the New York arts scene during the 1950s and 1960s, employs both photographs and text to show how ardent artistic endeavor merged in those days with fervent socializing. He chronicles the doings of a group of people whose admiration of each other's as-yet-unrecognized work coincided with delight in each other's conversation and company. Studio photographs of artists at work are mixed with photographs of parties in bars and on beaches; pictures of elegant gallery openings are mixed with comical posings and blurred informal snapshots of leisure and levity. A typical photograph full of people is accompanied by a half-page list of names—of poets, painters, sculptors, scriptwriters, musicians, everyone who was anyone or hoped to be. One photograph, tagged "Another patio group shot—another party" (from 1961), particularly compels interest because of the elusive presence there, among the crowd, of "poet Barbara Guest" (154). Barbara Guest sits far to the left in the photograph, on its very margin, her face turned from the camera and hidden by her hair, one of the few people who does not look aggressively or self-consciously out of the photograph toward its contemporary and future viewers. Her attention is entirely inward toward the company, and she thus deflects the attention of the viewer; she is *difficult to see,* mysteriously not there at the same time that she is ostensibly there.

Trying to see Barbara Guest in this photograph is similar to trying to "see" Barbara Guest in any of the many venues in which contemporary poets come to the attention of readers. She is provocatively *there,* by name in literary histories, by reputation in the written reminiscences of others, and as a primary source for writers of literary biographies. She was present as an influential art critic who wrote essays for *Partisan Review* and

helped edit *Art News* during the 1950s. Her biography of H. D. is generally acknowledged to be an important contribution to the reappraisal of the poet, "whose work, especially the long myth-laden poems of her later years, offers a uniquely female twist on modernism," in the words of one reviewer of Guest's book (Pollitt 7). But as a poet, Guest has remained strangely elusive, her volumes of poetry often difficult to obtain, reviews of her work infrequent, and academic critical studies sparse. Her name, in literary histories and anthologies, is almost invariably linked with those of Frank O'Hara, John Ashbery, Kenneth Koch, and James Schuyler as a member of the New York school of poets. Yet her poetry has not yet garnered the attention paid to the other four, certainly not the intense interest directed toward Ashbery and O'Hara from academic critics.

This disregard registers as particularly curious since Guest seems to fit so securely among these poets, engaged like them in beginnings, celebrations, *le merveilleux,* like them "saturate[d] . . . in language, the spoken, ordinary language, partly colloquial, partly slangy . . . wish[ing] to heighten the surface of a poem by intense, sophisticated interest in individual words" (Myers 24). And, like theirs, her poetry derives significant inspiration from painting. In books from *The Location of Things* in 1960 to *Defensive Rapture* in 1993, Guest has written poems about, for, and to paintings by artists as varied as Pinturicchio, Delacroix, Miró, Gris, Matisse, Kandinsky, Giacomo Balla, Robert Motherwell, Warren Brandt, Grace Hartigan, Mary Abbott, and Helen Frankenthaler. These poems can match Ashbery's and O'Hara's famous ekphrastic poems for sophistication, power, and subtlety.[1] But as Ashbery and O'Hara (and to a lesser extent Schuyler and Koch) have, over the years, entered the literary mainstream—favored by anthologists, reviewed in the literary and general presses, studied by literary scholars, critics, and theorists, and, as Geoff Ward puts it, "airlifted to the slippery slopes of the university syllabus" (9)—Guest's work remains marginal, or perhaps "out front." She is still likely to publish single poems in avant-garde publications like *Sulfur, Blue Mesa, Hambone, O.blek,* and *Temblor.* Her poem **"On the Verge of the Path"** must surely comment ruefully on the way her playful companions "Frank" and "John" of the 1950s have become "the shelves of O'Hara and Ashbery" (*Moscow Mansions* 68), strangely transformed, from her point of view, into "name" poets.

Of the two anthologies that responded to the new popularity of avant-garde poetry in New York—Ron Padgett and David Shapiro's *An Anthology of New York Poets* (1970) and John Myers's *The Poets of the New York School* (1969)—one (Myers's) includes more than twenty pages of Guest's poetry, beginning with a large, startlingly vivid photograph of the poet and interspersing reproductions of paintings by Robert Goodnough.

The other (Padgett and Shapiro's), although it includes three times as many poets (twenty-seven as opposed to Myers's nine), leaves out Barbara Guest.[2] Again a curious impression of absence/presence is created by considering the anthologies together: in one, Guest is securely in place and valued, and from the other she is carelessly or carefully excluded. Investigation into her reception and reputation yields a double sense of her both being there and not being there, creating a suspicion that, as Rachel Blau DuPlessis has suggested, "gender marginalization and invisibility have been an issue," and that Guest's career has suffered from the "strained and unexamined relationship to their female participants" often characteristic of groups dedicated to innovative poetries, which manifests itself in a "cavalier attitude toward women" ("Flavor" 23).

When Guest's poetry does come under critical discussion, it is likely to be described in such a way as to reinforce three persistent, true, but ultimately simplistic assumptions about her work: first, that it is difficult to the point of obduracy; second, that it is refined and cool, rather than passionate, personal, or emotionally urgent; and third, that it invariably avoids the political in favor of the aesthetic, preferring the sensualities of surface, texture, and wordplay over narrative, social commentary, and political naming.[3] "She seems serenely confident in her calling," writes Anthony Manousos, unbeset by "the political ardors of Denise Levertov and Adrienne Rich or with the confessional intensity of Sylvia Plath and Anne Sexton" (299, 296). While admiring her "assurance, taste, and intelligence" (Manousos 299), critics have noted the poetry's stylistic inaccessibility and have characterized her subject matter and tone as elite, perhaps elitist, working to refine rather than popularize American poetry. "She is . . . the most elegant of the New York poets," writes Robert F. Kiernan. "There is an inveterate chill to her poetry—a cosmopolitan refinement that supersedes anything truly personal" (144). Reviewing ***Moscow Mansions*** (1973), Alicia Ostriker claims: "the values are essentially and purely esthetic—line, texture, color, tone—rather than, say, moral, intellectual, or emotional"; "[The poems] are a little like conversations in refined places among refined persons. They are, like Alice's biscuits, very dry" (qtd. in Manousos 298, 296).[4] In an era when the poetry of women and feminist poetic theories richly sustain each other, Guest appears less than ardently feminist, difficult to place on a literary map whose coordinates are gender-based. This perhaps accounts for her exclusion from both editions of Florence Howe's influential anthology of twentieth-century poetry by women, *No More Masks!,* and for the troubling omission of any discussion of Guest's work from *Stealing the Language,* Ostriker's panoramic examination of American women's poetry. Unlike other women poets

slighted by the literary mainstream, Guest has not yet, with the notable exception of DuPlessis, been embraced or promoted by feminist readers.[5]

The issues of difficulty and the personal urgency and feminist vision of Guest's poems can be reevaluated by looking at her numerous ekphrastic poems, that is, her poems about paintings. In this kind of second-order discourse one finds the inner life, the erotic life, the conflicts and confusions, and the intellectual exigencies of Guest's poetic personality lying half-concealed and half-revealed. There one is also disabused of the notion that her poetry engages only in the driest and coolest of refined, cultural "high talk." Her stylistic choices also come to seem less dauntingly difficult if they are read as precise and passionate expressions of feeling, thought, vision, and commitment experienced in the presence of a particularly compelling painting. Guest herself becomes more visible when one acknowledges that the act of seeing is crucial to her art, and much can be learned by assessing the nature and quality of her gaze.

Ekphrasis is the literary term for poetry that is "verbal representation of visual representation," in James A. W. Heffernan's succinct definition (3). Inquiry into the complex relations between word and image has been pursued most recently by W. J. T. Mitchell in *Picture Theory* (1994), by Heffernan in his book on the history and poetics of ekphrasis, *Museum of Words* (1993), by Murray Krieger in *Ekphrasis* (1992), and by Wendy Steiner in *Pictures of Romance* (1988). Thanks to this work on ekphrasis, it is possible to recognize and analyze the lively and conflicted emotional, intellectual, and linguistic activity that lies subsumed under the words "inspired by." A vocabulary now exists to investigate the arena of conflict or seduction that a poet enters when she or he re-presents in words what has already been presented in images.

Guest's ekphrastic poems perform and illumine questions central to the genre of ekphrasis, which are usefully phrased by Mitchell this way: "what motivates the desire to construct an entire text as an evocation, incorporation, or substitute for a visual object or experience? Why do texts seem compelled to reach out to their semiotic 'others,' the objects of visual representation?" (109). The poetry also invites its readers to speculate on the fact of choice: why this painting, and why now? What does it reveal about the poet's temperament, her character, her situation in time and place? What does it reveal about her sense of self as artist, her aesthetic, political, and moral position vis-à-vis her chosen painter? Because Guest's work offers the rare perspective of a woman in the position of viewer, respondent, "envoicer," and maker of the poetic meaning, it offers to complicate and inform theories of gendered art criticism which analyze the male gaze. To look at a painting via a poem by Barbara Guest is to enter the arena of the "female gaze" and also compels us to consider in what respects Guest is indeed a feminist.

In Guest's work we encounter an embarrassment of riches in the ekphrastic genre.[6] Her work charts an entire lifetime of engagement with painting and sculpture, resulting in some of our century's most complex and beautiful ekphrastic poems, poems that help define what viewing art means in our time. The poems explore how (indeed *if*) aesthetic perception of the visual can be translated into the signification of words, and what is problematic or enabling about the attempt to do so. Guest's imagination engages both representational and abstract art, evoking the postmodern situation of having the entire history of art to "walk through" and choose from. A comprehensive list of her ekphrastic poems would require much space, but notable examples include **"Piazzas"** (for Mary Abbott Clyde), **"Heroic Stages"** (for Grace Hartigan), **"All Elegies Are Black and White"** (to Robert Motherwell), **"Roses"** (about Gertrude Stein and Juan Gris), **"The Rose Marble Table"** (about Matisse), **"The View from Kandinsky's Window," "Dora Maar," "Wild Gardens Overlooked by Night Lights," "The Screen of Distance," "The Nude,"** and **"The Surface as Object."** "Painting is the poems' cosmology," Barbara Einzig writes, "and the world is read as a painting" (9).

Two particular poems about paintings, because they are distinctly different, can serve as examples and illustrations and give a sense of the range of Guest's capabilities. The first is titled **"The Poetess,"** from the collection *Moscow Mansions* (1973). The poem, short, compressed, and pointed, describes a lyrical, abstract gouache and oil painting of shifting shapes and colors by the Spanish modernist painter Joan Miró titled *La Poétesse.* The second poem, **"The Farewell Stairway,"** from *Fair Realism* (1989), is long, repetitious, and meandering, lavishly spread over six pages of *Selected Poems.* It responds to a rigorously realist painting of three women descending a staircase, completed in 1909 by the Italian futurist Giacomo Balla. Both poems invite analysis of their gender configurations and contexts, since both are about paintings of women and present a female poet in colloquy, as it were, with a male painter. The paintings enhance access to the poems and vice versa, and both are revealing of the poetic personality of Guest herself. Similarly, the poems, though resplendently aesthetic, are not merely so; when contextualized, they reveal Guest's strong, judicious, clear understanding of cultural and social issues central to women.

"The Poetess," with its epigraph "after Miró," claims outright its ekphrastic nature, its entanglement with an Other. The painting *La Poétesse* is one in a series of

twenty-three collectively titled *Constellations,* completed by Miró during World War II, smuggled out of occupied France, and first displayed at the Pierre Matisse Gallery in New York in 1945.[7] When, in April 1994, Brown University held a conference to celebrate Guest's work, the announcement of the event reprinted **"The Poetess"** alongside a reproduction of *La Poétesse.* Such a singling out of this poem enhances its status as a "signature" poem, which bears distinctive marks of identity, individuality, personality. It can, in fact, be read as a subtle and powerful autobiographical poem, as if the reader were looking over the shoulder of Guest as she looked in a mirror, seeing her see herself. When an interviewer asked Guest, "Did you go in for confessional poetry?" she answered simply, "I think all poetry is confessional" ("Barbara Guest" 23). This response expresses, I believe, Guest's awareness that all artistic representation functions as autobiographical projection, necessarily telling a story of self. In ekphrastic poetry (by definition a representation of a representation), the central story of self becomes complicated and enriched by the simultaneous centrality of an Other. Two visions consort and conflict with each other, seduce and serve, bewilder and explain each other. In poems such as these, Guest is creating a risky, open-ended portrait of self-as-artist, a portrait that is always strangely and necessarily relational.

The title, **"The Poetess,"** invites reading of the poem for understanding of how Guest defines herself as a poet, and specifically as a woman poet. The title also begs the question of why a woman poet would so closely align herself with the troublesomely gendered word "poetess." The tradition of American women's poetry has been haunted by the specter of the poetess; most women poets took pains to dissociate themselves from her devalued status. In a refrainlike phrase, DuPlessis repeatedly expresses the fears and longing of H. D. about her career amid male modernist poets: "It was the struggle not to be reduced, not to become 'poetess.'" Women poets live and work, she writes, with inscribed "drives to self-abnegation . . . [that] could easily help to create poetesses from the raw material that would have made poets" (*Pink Guitar* 27, 28). Just a decade before Guest's poem was published, Robert Lowell, intending to extend high praise to Sylvia Plath's achievement in *Ariel,* declared her "certainly not another 'poetess'" (vii), while a generation earlier, a male critic, seeking to undermine the powerful poet and critic Amy Lowell, employed the humorous but immensely hurtful epithet "Hippo-poetess" (Gould 231-33).

It is strange and significant that a "signature" poem should also be an ekphrastic poem, one that owes its existence to another, one generated and interpolated by another. The poem has its eye trained not inward but outward, at a painter's brush marks, and yet those marks look to Guest like a mirror. The poet, it seems, has adopted Miró's *La Poétesse* as an amenable portrait of a woman poet, and an altogether truer and more satisfactory representation of her own self-as-poet than the stereotype of the "wailing" or "scribbling" poetess that has haunted literary criticism and the popular imagination. As the only woman poet of the first-generation New York poets, Guest may have seen in Miró's painting a visual validation of the inventive, humorous, fluid, elusive, urbane, whimsical, postsurrealist work she and they were doing and rejoiced to find it labeled feminine.

Neither painting nor poem, of course, is in any way a conventional portrait. The painting is essentially abstract: against a luminous brown-grey background geometrical and calligraphic shapes splay out over the painting's surface. Although J. H. Matthews complained that "however much good will we muster, we cannot be sure we discern a poet of either sex" (95), and although distinction between the figure and her surroundings is purposely minimized, a humanoid shape can be discerned and once seen is difficult to unsee. The poetess's body, with upraised "arms" reaching into the top corners, is drawn with a single continuous line, a section of which runs roughly parallel to the bottom margin of the painting. The contours of the body suggest a flowing and capacious robe as the poetess's apparel. Her head, in profile looking right just above the center, is marvelously odd but entirely Miróesque. Her eye, with its dilated pupil, startling white section, and eyelashes, is shaped like a stylized baby bird. Her nose or forehead is greatly elongated, even phallic shaped, and sports two extra sets of breasts. Her mouth is opened to reveal three sharp teeth. What is "inside" the poetess is very similar to what is "outside" her defining line: the same intense black, white, brown, and green, with primary yellow, red, and blue, the same linear tracery, curlicues, arabesques, asterisks, hourglass shapes, crescents, circles, barbells, triangles. Whenever line cuts through shape, it causes a color change. Inside the poetess's body, triangular shapes seem to represent breasts, and she displays the "awesome red and black vagina" that William Rubin has pointed out in another of the *Constellations* paintings (82). There are two of Miró's ubiquitous, mysterious "escape ladders." There are other "personages" and scattered minor characters in the form of childlike stick figures, biomorphic shapes, and floating eyes. The whole gives an impression of rhythm, humor, and delirious play among elements that are nonetheless delicately related and balanced.

La Poétesse, like the other *Constellations,* is imbued with spatial mystery and with sexuality that is "warm, abandoned, clean-cut, beautiful, and above all intense," in Robert Motherwell's description (117). About the period in which the paintings were made, Miró wrote:

> We had to leave Varengeville in haste. In this region which had remained calm the Germans opened up piti-less bombardments. With the Allied armies completely defeated and continuous bombardments we took the train from Paris. Pilar [Miró's wife, Pilar Juncosa de Miró] took Dolores, who was then a little girl, by the hand and I carried with me under my arm the portfolio containing those *Constellations* that were finished and the remainder of the sheets which were to serve for the completed series. . . .

> At this time . . . I was very depressed. I believed in an inevitable victory for Nazism, and that all that we love and that gives us our reason for living was sunk forever in the abyss. I believed that in this defeat there was no further hope for us, and had the idea of expressing this mood and this anguish by drawing signs and forms . . . which would go up and caress the stars, fleeing from the stink and decay of a world built by Hitler and his friends.

> (qtd. in Penrose 100-102)

Given the bleak and brutal context of world war in which these paintings were made, they seem to reflect Miró's wishful and stubborn need to assert human loveliness, sensuality, tenderness, humor, and benevolence in the order of things: in short, they posit what might be called a "feminized" cosmology. Miró, by titling *La Poétesse* as he did, made this painting stand out among the others and no doubt contributed to Guest's attraction to it.[8] The title suggests that the "mute ekphrastic object awaiting the . . . poetic voice already has a voice of its own" (as Mitchell puts it in another context [173]); indeed that it, *she,* "speaks" for the whole of the endangered world. In the cosmos of *Constellations,* the poet figure is a *poetess,* a circumstance in which Guest positively revels. She wrote in a letter about the poem: "Miró, being ignorant of the pejorative attitude toward the word Poetess, I believe, in his genuine educative ignorance chose the word as the correct word for a woman who was a poet. I took him at his word, and fearlessly had my own hyjinks with the painting." In other words, the poem does not partake of a recurrent motif among ekphrastic poems, what Mitchell calls "ekphrastic anxiety"—fear that the powerful image will silence and paralyze the poet who would approach it (170-76). To Guest, writing forty years after the fact, *La Poétesse* seems to have conferred instead a sense of entitlement and permission, an access to speech.

Here then is Guest's **"The Poetess"** (after Miró):

> A dollop is dolloping
> her a scoop is pursuing
> flee vain ignots   Ho
> coriander darks   thimble blues
> red okays adorn her
> buzz green circles in flight
> or submergence?   Giddy
> mishaps of blackness make
> stinging clouds what!
> a fraught climate

what natural c/o abnormal
loquaciousness   the
Poetess riddled
her asterisk
genial!   as space

(Selected Poems 78)

Compact and concrete, elegant and capricious, joyously "frontal" in its persistent present tense, this poem exuberantly describes Miró's painting. Guest emulates the painting's sensual surface, its oscillating rhythms. She sees both the poetess and her consequence, the difference she makes in occupying her field, the ripples she sends out, the stir and sensation she causes.

The poem leaps from the page like what Charles Olson would call a "high energy construct," in which words and phrases are shifting and indeterminate—in their parts of speech, in their syntactical relationships, in their symbolic depth and import. This effect is heightened by a lack of punctuation to order the affiliation of word with word, phrase with phrase. What punctuation there is—one question mark and two exclamation points—contributes to an aura of suggestion rather than assertion, possibility rather than certainty, excited discovery rather than orderliness or deliberation. Radical enjambment agitates both line and sentence. The "dollop" and the "scoop" probably refer to the two creatures in Miró's painting that flank the poetess's head. The dollop (to the left) is a pear-shaped, heavily jowled and mustached fellow, with staring red eyes; the scoop (on the right) is white and snakelike, with a black snout and ears and a blue pointed tail. In the first lines of the poem, the inert dollop undergoes a swift transformation from noun to verb and then, due to a deft enjambment, from intransitive verb to transitive. Even so lumpish a character in such a lively setting cannot merely be but must do, and do to. As the dollop dollops the poetess, the scoop courts her, chases her, attempts to capture her, perhaps in the recess of his scoop-like body. Yet these minor characters are collectively referred to by a neologism of charming and dismissive brevity—"ignots," which connotes, along with the adjective "vain," their ignorance, perhaps their ignominy, and their diminutive size in a field so clearly commanded by the poetess herself.

There are words of percussive interjection: "Ho" expresses surprise and joy and discovery. The word "dark" becomes plural, and "darks" are curiously characterized as "coriander"—to suggest, perhaps, the freshness, greenness, flavor of darkness in the painting. "Thimble," usually a noun, serves as an adjective describing blue, or perhaps blue is a verb, something the thimble does. "Okays" take on the concreteness of red-colored adornments. Are the buzzing "green circles in flight / or submergence"? Is "what!" meant to express strong excitement and elicit agreement? Or is it a

breathless inability to say what "mishaps of blackness" do to "stinging clouds" in this "fraught climate"? Is "as space," the final phrase of the poem, part of a metaphor that describes how genial the poetess's asterisk is, or does it begin a new, unseen sentence drifting off onto the white page, into space itself?

"Riddle" is what this poetess does, the compact poetic mode of surprise and enigma that, like Emily Dickinson, she has chosen. But she is also "riddled," shot through with the whole objective world, her boundaries, as in the painting, astonishingly permeable. One riddling phrase—"natural c/o abnormal"—forms a verbal labyrinth in its own right, a conundrum of skewed paradox describing the "loquaciousness" of the poetess. DuPlessis hears in this short phrase an entire mocking debate on the issue of women's speech ("Flavor" 23). By jamming two words into an adjectival phrase describing loquacity, Guest seems to question how fluency and readiness of speech in women can be "natural" and "abnormal" at the same time. On the other hand, the admiring tone of the phrase in which these words appear seems to strip both words of their pejorative sting. "Natural" speech, if by this we understand speech that is spontaneous and free from artificiality, affectation, or inhibition, is carried into poetry in the care of ("c/o") "abnormal / loquaciousness." Here we can read "abnormal" as the necessary deviation of poetic language from standard language, a deviation that revitalizes perception, emotion, thought, and standard language itself.

Pervasive variability is described in the poem as "a fraught climate." This "fraughtness" is a quality of both poem and painting, in the sense that they are both highly charged, full to their own edges, volatile, mercurial, sexual. The poetess lives and breathes this climate; she also creates it as an emanation of her natural, abnormal will toward speech. Poem and painting deny the notion of static essence in a celebration of motion, change, multiplicity, all that is dynamic; both imply a denial of the passivity, weakness, piety, sentimentality, and humorlessness traditionally understood to be inherent in the term "poetess." "Poetess," argues Svetlana Boym, will come to serve as a useful critical term only if it can be "rewritten and reinvented to resist all cultural insults and condescendingly precautionary quotation marks" (240). Guest recognized that Miró's abstract rendering of a woman poet is presented as just the kind of (very rare) poetess "without quotation marks" that Boym would like to see—a poet whose feminine suffix does not read as "a sign of cultural inferiority" (192). Miró's poetess generates and inhabits fraught space that is, by consequence, also "genial" space, conducive to life, growth, and comfort, and even (reviving an obsolete meaning of the word) "relating to or marked by genius." Like Miró, working inside and against the stresses of his wartime context, Guest can and does transform the critical context represented by the word "poetess" by an act of lyric and ekphrastic translation.

The second poem, **"The Farewell Stairway,"** also declares epigraphically its ekphrastic status: "After Balla." The poem responds to the futurist Giacomo Balla's painting of 1909 that is titled *Salutando* (*Saying Goodbye*) or *Gli Addii Scala* (*The Stairway of Farewells*). The painting depicts, from an uncustomary angle of vision, three women descending a staircase. So precisely and geometrically rendered are Balla's lines and angles, so naturalistic are his scaling and foreshortening that his painting, when reduced in size and reproduced in black and white, is often mistaken for a photograph. Guest's poem about this painting is divided into eleven sections, as if it contrived to be eleven successive looks at the painting, each with its own shape, its own lyric agenda, its own management of the page's white space. Guest presumes to name the figures in the painting, and to attribute to them emotions and thoughts not explicit there. Also, she "adds" to the painting what cannot be seen in it—usually fragments of outdoor imagery, strangely portentous and evasively allusive, but also bits of autobiographical reference. All of this creates a degree of dissonance between painter and poet that is absent from **"The Poetess."** Here there is a sense that Guest wishes to enter into an imaginative dialectic with Balla, rather than posit him as precursor to be admired and emulated. The poem evinces an intriguing mixture of reverence and resistance, displaying admiration for the painting but pointedly foregrounding and emphasizing all the ways in which *Salutando* does not correspond to the futurists' political and artistic agenda.

Here, the fact of choice is of immense significance, since Guest has chosen to respond to a painting executed by an ardent proponent of futurism *before he became a futurist,* before his period of greatest notoriety. She chose a painting from 1909, rather than one of those paintings from the next decade which, by and large, erase the human figure in favor of abstract depictions of light, movement, color. This puts Guest in the position of examining a "lost" moment in the history of modern art. She claims in the poem "I saw it futurally" and that the women in the painting are "futurally extended." I want to make much of the substitution of the word "futural" (coined as far as I can determine by Guest herself) for "futurist" or "futurism." The poem seems to wonder about and mourn the loss of female figures and female sensibility from Balla's artistic world, and the transformation of an artist capable of thinking and creating futurally into one who began to think and create and act futuristically instead. The suffix *-al* is amenable in its neutrality to Guest's appreciation of *Salutando*: it makes a noun adjectival in order to convey the unvexed meaning "of, related to, or characterized by." The suffix *-ist* (especially in the case of "futurist") denotes advocacy of a specified doctrine,

theory, or system of principles. Guest's admiration of and identification with *this* painting (expressed in a future beyond futurism) suggests a subtle reproof of futurist thought and propaganda.

The Italian futurists were "a tightly knit, ardently committed amalgam" (C. Taylor 1) whose aim was to express the energetic, dynamic, and violent quality of contemporary life, which they accomplished partly through a series of revolutionary manifestoes written between 1909 and 1933. They intended to blast through what they saw as current complaisance and compromise with a combination of "arrogance, bombast, and buffoonery" (C. Taylor 3). Futurism began with what Marjorie Perloff calls a period of "utopian buoyancy . . . a short-lived but remarkable rapprochement between avant-garde aesthetic, radical politics, and popular culture" (*Futurist Moment* xvii), but it later became known for its innate machismo, its glorification of war, its virulent disparagement of the female temperament, and after 1917 its much contested relationship with Fascism in Italy. Guest's poem responds most appreciatively to the features of Balla's painting that owe nothing to these negative components of futurist ideology.

First, Guest sees Balla celebrating an ordinary moment in present time, which is serene and domestic rather than aggressive or feverish, a moment remarkable for its non-revolutionary aspect.[9] This choice would seem to contravene the intent of the futurists to "create eternal, omnipresent speed" and to "exalt aggressive action, a feverish insomnia, the racer's stride, the mortal leap, the punch and the slap" (Marinetti 22, 21). Secondly, she points at the subject of his painting, three women carefully and respectfully depicted, which does not seem to evince the "scorn for woman" (whom futurists considered to be fatally passive, weak, and incapable of the hygienic violence of war) so pointedly called for in the manifestoes of futurism (Marinetti 22). And thirdly, she shows how the painting can be convincingly and successfully read in terms of mythology, despite the futurists' rejection of the "smelly gangrene" of mythological and historical subjects, their determination to "[s]weep the whole field of art clean of all themes and subjects which have been used in the past" (Boccioni et al. 26), and their declaration that "Mythology and the Mystic Ideal are defeated at last" (Marinetti 20). What Balla the modernist had to disparage and throw away, Guest the postmodernist can resuscitate and interpolate into Balla's painting itself.[10]

A description of the painting: the viewer's perspective is that of one who stands on the top landing of a spiral staircase, looking downward. Five turnings of the staircase are visible, each concentrically smaller, receding deep into the picture's space, each becoming less defined than the one before, until the limit of the visible is reached. The steps and the balusters fan out, precisely spaced, outlined by the curved brown line of the railing. The light is from above, suggesting a skylight. Color darkens from whites and grays to browns and purples as the stairway descends. The sensation is of a vortex, a drawing of the eye downward, inward, toward that blank, unseeable center of the staircase, which in the painting is off-center to the right and bisected by the bottom frame. The upper, outward region of the painting, where the staircase is wide and white, suggests openness, airiness, release; the inner, downward region suggests tightening, darkening, inexorable pull.

On the first turning of the staircase, three women are caught in the act of descending, their feet directed forward and downward, but all three have turned their heads and upper bodies backward and upward in gestures of farewell. They form a triangle. One wears a long purplish dress and a white hat; her right hand is on the inner railing. She seems to smile. Beside her stands a woman dressed all in black, her left hand resting on the outer rail, her right hand lifted in a wave. Of the three, she is the least distinct, her facial features most blurred, her figure most in shadow. The third woman, two steps above the other two, also raises her right (gloved?) hand. She wears pink; her dress floats. She wears a white hat; one has the impression that she is the youngest of the group. The three women express in their bodies' language a fleeting moment in going of staying. It is this looking backward, and Balla's care in depicting it, that feels unlike a futurist's stance. Also, the scene is domestic, social, even bourgeois: three well-dressed ladies, having made a visit, now descend the stairway to depart into the city and into the rest of the day. The techniques of photography rather than those of futurism provide visual drama here—not futurist whorls, force lines, vibrating intervals, and chaotic excitement, but photography's flattening of the image, the aerial view, the cropping rather than centering of the subject, the snapshot's ability to catch its subject in a normally unobserved daily activity.

Yet for all its ordinariness, its technical precision and photographic realism, the painting resonates with something mysterious and enigmatic, prompting, I think, Guest's impulse toward re-mythologizing it. When she speaks of, to, and for this painting, Guest names the women as Greek goddesses, as if stylish Roman matrons in the midst of their daily activities were unconsciously enacting ritual—their movements, when stilled, speak ancestrally, mythically, iconically. No commentary on this painting that I have seen makes this startling, inspired connection. To come "after Balla" is to re-mythologize, personally and vitally, what Balla has carefully, pointedly stripped of mythologies grown, for him and his generation of young men, conventional and stale. (Or perhaps she catches him in a moment of inadvertent, soon-to-be-disparaged mythologizing.) Guest "voices" Balla's silent painting in terms of the

mythical tale of Demeter, Persephone, and Hecate, revealing in the process her full-blown, personal involvement with the classic myth of periodic descent, female sexuality, relationships among women, and the position of human beings in relation to time and the future.

Guest's poem, however, evinces none of the feverish rush toward the future that characterizes futurism. Perhaps in admiring imitation Guest has built a poem that declines poetry's and mythology's access to the available "future" of its protagonists. Instead, the poem holds its futural promise firmly in check, obsessively retelling, rephrasing, and correcting its opening line— "The women without hesitancy began to descend" (**Fair Realism** 48)—in each of the ten other sections of the poem. Never do the women finish their descent, or even progress beyond the point of beginning it. A single moment in time, a single setting in space (the time and space that Balla captures with his snapshot-like picture) are revisited and retold in suggestive fragmentary descriptions and floating metaphors rather than in passages of forward-moving event. This lack of plot-driven narrative has, in fact, been Guest's practice in making use of mythological stories since she published the poems called "Archaics" in 1962. There likewise she does not attempt to narrate entire myths but instead captures Greek and Roman mythological personages in resonant moments of present time, as if the outcomes of their famous stories were yet unknown. Atalanta, famed for her swiftness in running, is pictured pacing in strenuous restlessness, heedless of the future, while the reader knows she will eventually be overtaken in a race by her future husband. The separate arbitrary and lazy doings of Hero and Leander are recounted in the hours before their fateful meeting. The poems set up a dialectic between the reader's prior knowledge of the stories' outcome and the richness of the present moments they portray.[11] In the present lyric moment of **"The Farewell Stairway,"** the reader must acknowledge the characters' situatedness in time, their wonderful ignorance of the future, and also must experience intimations that their story might have proceeded and ended otherwise. In this way the poem profoundly comments on and even "performs" the meaning of futurity, since it remains stuck in a perpetual present.

Because Guest, following Balla, refuses to "see" the future of the myth she has introduced, stop-frames her retelling of the Persephone myth at the moment of descent, depicts the women descending together, declares that they descend "without hesitancy," and declines to characterize the dark center ("Hades at the bottom" [48]), she seems to prefer one version of this famous myth to the other.

One account of the story is that Persephone and her mother, Demeter (Guest calls her by her Roman name, Ceres), were picking flowers together in a valley when

Persephone was abducted by Hades, who forced her to descend into the underworld and become his wife. Hecate heard Persephone cry out, but did not (or could not) prevent the abduction. Demeter grieved so at the loss of her daughter that she neglected her duties as goddess of the earth, causing the earth's vegetation to shrivel and die. Persephone was later allowed to return to her mother for two-thirds of the year. Hecate, after assisting in the search for Persephone, lighted her way back to earth.

The story has been important to feminist readers, who focus on Hades' abduction and rape of Persephone, interpreting it as "an encoding of patriarchal violence" (in Elizabeth T. Hayes's words), a representation of traumatic loss and grief, a resonant story of forced separation from matriarchal sources of identity and love, a paradigm of marriage as primitive abduction severely limiting the freedom of women, and an allegory of feminine power usurped by a dominant male, then partially restored, but in a derivative and damaged form (Hayes 9).

In another (older) version of the myth (which has also been important to feminists), there is no abduction; instead Persephone goes seriously but willingly to a Hades portrayed not as a man, or a male god, but as unpredictable mystery, the unknown, the dark, the future. She descends in fear and attraction to Hades, which is both vibrant with sexuality and redolent of death. In this version, the journey that Persephone takes through shadowy realms of uncertainty is read as a journey into the future and into maturity, leading ultimately to gains in wisdom and selfhood, rather than to irrevocable damage and loss of integrity.

"The Farewell Stairway" reveals Guest as more attracted to this second reading of the Persephone myth than to the first, as her opening line declares: "The women without hesitancy began to descend." The agency in this movement downward belongs entirely to the women; all suggestion of outside coercion is erased. At this determining moment all three women are together, serving as guides, companions, and models for each other. Guest renders the women in Balla's painting with deft and simple phrases of ekphrastic description in which they reveal their ancient personalities. Ceres/ Demeter, of the three the one understood as representing the aspect of woman in full maturity, the goddess of agriculture, appears "harried" and "bragg[ing] of cultivated grain" (48). She has pressing responsibilities; she is possessed of important accomplishments appropriate to middle age. She appears in the Balla painting as the woman dressed in purple. Hecate appears there as the woman dressed in black, the most indistinct of the three, the most shadowy, and in Guest as "the gray-wrapped woman. / in lumpy dark," who "managed me" (48, 51). Hecate's role is that of the dread and

wise crone; she stands for the old age aspect of woman, "funerary priestess and death mother . . . owner of the sacred lore," as Barbara Walker describes her, claiming her "our best guide in this long, dark, labyrinthine spiritual journey" (14). She haunts the fringes, as the goddess of the threshold and the crossroad; she "represents the seriousness and precariousness of all transitions" (Downing 234). That leaves the pink dress woman as Persephone; of the maiden-mother-crone triad, she alone remains unnamed in the poem, but significantly, it is she who merges from time to time with the narrative "I."[12] The "I" seems to be by turns the poet who looks at the picture and a character in the picture, both viewer and viewed.

In the poem, the women seem to oscillate back and forth between their mythological, portentous aspect and their contemporary ordinariness. The second line— "leaving flowers"—on the one hand evokes an image of the modern Roman women, having brought flowers and left them as a gift. On the other hand, read into the myth, it recalls the valley of flowers that Persephone "left" to begin her descent into Hades. Throughout the poem, mythological imagery and everyday imagery (borrowed from Balla, or making reference to the poet's own life) hold each other in balance, almost in an embrace. Sections referring to "tiny Arachne" and "gnarled Charon" (the boatman who carries the souls of the dead to Hades), "birds dropping south out of the wind," and the Greek town of Nauplia alternate with "common" scenes more linkable to the painting, where the women's clothes are described as "modish," the "*scala*," or stairway, is described as being "polished" and situated in the neighborhood of the "*stazione*." But either way, the poem holds the future in abeyance, refusing to foreknow it, refusing to fill in the darkness at the bottom of Balla's stairway, and, most significantly, refusing to name abduction, rape, violation of will, and severing of ties between women as the inevitable nature of "Hades." Instead, Guest sees Persephone, the "I" of the poem, in one section laughing and in another tearful, but always poised at a moment of choice, "pull," and desire as she steps into the future. This is accomplished daily, moment by moment, in the most unremarkable ways, Guest implies, trusting Balla the painter more than Balla of the manifestoes. Yet, she suggests, such moments are also crossed with immense significance, which can and should be understood in mythological terms. Suddenly speaking intimately to the reader who is outside both poem and painting, Guest invites her to imagine the future as vortex, inexorably "pulling" and yet, paradoxically, somehow also allowing "free movement":

> you who are outside. over there.
> can't feel the pull. it makes you wonder—

the oscillation. the whirling. urgent.
indicating air revolving in a circuit—

without interruption. free movement
in *cielo puro*—

(52)

Much art criticism and most discussions of ekphrastic poetry have assumed that the viewer of the art will be male, engendering an entire literature describing the desires and the appropriations of the "male gaze." Some theorists have even characterized the act of looking as itself characteristically male, intent on penetration and control, and granting authority to the viewer. Mitchell, among others, has discussed the tendency of poems in the ekphrastic tradition to treat the image as a "female other." The genre, he writes, "tends to describe an object of visual pleasure and fascination from a masculine perspective, often to an audience understood to be masculine as well" (168). Surely Linda Nochlin, in this passage, assumes that both the makers and the consumers of art have been and will be masculine:

> representations of women in art are founded upon and serve to reproduce indisputably accepted assumptions held by society in general, artists in particular, and some artists more than others, about men's power over, superiority to, difference from, and necessary control of women, assumptions which are manifested in the visual structures as well as the thematic choices of the pictures in question.

(13)

Besides working to understand the pervasive and powerful "male gaze," feminist critics document those many painful moments in art and literature when the female viewer or reader fails to find her image, or finds it distorted, disturbed and disturbing. Mary Ann Caws, for instance, has analyzed the difficulties that female viewers encounter when viewing fragmented, entrapped, doll-like, dominated, or violated images of women in surrealistic art; she would caution viewers always to ask, "Whose is the pleasure, where is it taken, and from whom?" (117).[13]

But Caws begins to move in another direction when she encourages female viewers, critics, and writers to find and chronicle their responses to positive images of women as well: "Instead of yielding our minds up with our modeled and remodeled bodies, we must give our . . . opinions as to which [images] deserve anger and which celebration" (133). To do so "turns us from consumer and consumed to creator and life-giver" (134). One area in which it is possible to find abundant, complex, surprising, and often beautiful and challenging chronicles of women's responses to art is in contemporary women's ekphrastic poetry, of which Guest has been a consistently vital and thoughtful practitioner.

Indeed, examination of the ways women poets go about seeing and responding to gender content in painting complicates and enriches ekphrastic theory itself, particularly the assertion that the relationship of poetry to painting is always of necessity intensely *paragonal* (to employ the word that James Heffernan likes to use), the assertion that ekphrasis invariably enacts a "struggle for mastery between word and image" (6). Cynthia Messenger, for instance, comes to another conclusion about Elizabeth Bishop's ekphrastic poems: that Bishop's ekphrasis is *not* the kind described by Grant F. Scott as a "cunning attempt to transform and master the image by inscribing it" (302). Instead, she writes, Bishop's poetry is "rather an admission of the impossibility of achieving the same" (109). Perhaps to do this, Bishop must, like Guest, seek out paintings that enable rather than paralyze their (often female) subjects, and therefore enable and give pleasure to their female viewers.

Guest's poems also seem singularly free of that fear of being silenced which provokes verbal acts that strive to dominate or erase the initiating image. Guest does not seem to posit the relationship of poem to painting as one of conflict and competition, but as one of division of labor and dialogue, one of both reverence and resistance, in which she, as viewer and maker of meaning, is equal to the painter as maker of meaning. To the claim of theorists that ekphrastic poetry speaks about, to, and for paintings, Guest's poems add an alternative: they speak *with* the paintings and, through them, *with* the painters; they speak relationally rather than paragonally. This ongoing poetic and critical project, never less than difficult, is always, intensely, both personal and political. Guest, responding to a friend's paintings, wrote in sympathetic infinitives that might also describe her own ekphrastic desires and accomplishments: "To find the picture, the animus, both physical and metaphysical; to be directed and to direct; to clarify and intensify; to be absorbed and to be free; to allow thought to enter passion as silence interrupts movement, these are the urgencies of a Goodnough painting" ("Robert Goodnough" 23). These are also the subtle and powerful urgencies of a Barbara Guest poem about painting.

Notes

1. James A. W. Heffernan calls Ashbery's "Self-Portrait in a Convex Mirror" "the most resoundingly ekphrastic poem ever written and certainly one of the longest" (170-71). For discussions of Ashbery and O'Hara in this regard, see also Altieri; Diggory; Miller; Moramarco; Perloff, *O'Hara*; and Wolf.

2. Twenty-two years later, David Shapiro wrote apologetically about this lapse: "It was a youthful indiscretion that Ron Padgett and I were not able to include her in our motley [anthology]: a misjudgment we have apologized for over the years, and an indication of the lopsided dogmatism of youth" (39).

3. It is true that, from her earliest collection of poems in 1960, Guest has exploited, for her own ends, much of the poetic experimentation that has contributed to difficult poetry of our century: the spareness and juxtapositional ambiguity of imagism, the allusive freedom of verbal collage, the arbitrary fictiveness and metonymic oddity of dada and surrealism, the broken "cubist" writing reminiscent of Gertrude Stein. Early and late, she has been a practitioner of "disjunctive" poetics, which has often manifested itself in severe paratactical fragmentation. In this, and because of the associative and improvisatory quality of her work, she has been admired and imitated recently by the language poets.

4. By no means have all Guest's readers been puzzled or faint in their praise. Some substantial appreciative reviews of her more recent poetry have provided useful avenues of approach. See DuPlessis, "Flavor"; Einzig; Shapiro; and Welish. See also Guest's 1992 interview with Mark Hillringhouse.

5. DuPlessis's "'All My Vast / Journeying Sensibility': Barbara Guest's Recent Work" discusses two important poems about paintings in which gender content is paramount: "Dora Maar" and "The Nude" (*Fair Realism* 22-25 and 57-64). At the National Poetry Foundation's 1996 conference on American poetry in the 1950s, the session on Guest featured a paper by Linda Kinnahan about women and experimental poetics, one by Lynn Keller titled "Barbara Guest's Feminine Mystique," and my "'The Imagination's at Its Turning': Barbara Guest's Ekphrastic Poems from the 1950s."

6. In addition to writing ekphrastic poetry, Guest has produced collaborative works with visual artists June Felter, Sheila Isham, Richard Tuttle, Warren Brandt, and Anne Dunn.

7. Guest's poem is not the first ekphrastic response to *La Poétesse*. André Breton's *Constellations*, published in 1959, is a series of surrealist prose poems inspired by Miró's *Constellations*. Part of the poem Breton wrote for *La Poétesse* reads (in translation from the French): "The games of love are going on under the peristyle with detonations of fire-arms. From the coppices where the bewitching song is brewing, the belladonna's nipple is breaking through in lightning flashes and undulating" (qtd. in Matthews 96).

8. Guest described Miró's act of titling this painting in "The Cradle of Culture": "He took a piece of crayon from his pocket / he began to draw stars, starfish, pebbles / a woman: 'The Poetess' you saw him write / above the triangles, circles, jingles of color" (*Fair Realism* 76).

9. Susan Barnes Robinson argues that ordinariness may have been precisely the point—that "ever-objective Balla" intended to counter "symbolist excesses," particularly in the form of Edward Burne-Jones's painting of 1880 *The Golden Stairs*. "Three ordinary Roman matrons descending the staircase of a Roman palazzo" represent, Robinson suggests, a realist alternative to Burne-Jones's "improbable architecture and visionary subject matter" (70).

10. The more usual reading of this painting is that it "anticipates some important desiderata of Futurism," explores "the dynamic potential of lines and shapes," and "is an imaginative analogue to the abstract oscillation patterns which Etienne-Jules Marey derived from his chronophotographic images of moving objects" (Guggenheim Museum 48).

11. Barbara Einzig describes Guest's method of handling mythology this way: "personages that are ancient and classical . . . cross over into the text, but they usually swim back, shy of a classical story, appearing instead as shards of their original narratives, clues, fragments of the mythologies of another time" (7).

12. In not naming Persephone, Guest follows precedent. C. Kerényi reports that during the ancient Elysian mystery rites dedicated to these goddesses, Persephone was never named but referred to as the "ineffable maiden," too sacred to be spoken of among the initiated (26).

13. See Mulvey and Rose as well as Caws and Nochlin for discussions of women as subjects and viewers of painting, photography, and film.

Works Cited

Altieri, Charles. "John Ashbery and the Challenge of Postmodernism in the Visual Arts." *Critical Inquiry* 14 (1988): 805-30.

Boccioni, Umberto, et al. "Manifesto of the Futurist Painters, 1910." Trans. Robert Brain. *Futurist Manifestos.* Ed. Umbro Apollonio. New York: Viking, 1973. 24-27.

Boym, Svetlana. *Death in Quotation Marks: Cultural Myths of the Modern Poet.* Cambridge, MA: Harvard UP, 1991.

Caws, Mary Ann. *The Art of Interference: Stressed Readings in Verbal and Visual Texts.* Princeton, NJ: Princeton UP, 1989.

Diggory, Terence. "Questions of Identity in *Oranges* by Frank O'Hara and Grace Hartigan." *Art Journal* 52 (1993): 41-50.

Downing, Christine. "Hekate, Rhea, and Baubo: Perspectives on Menopause." *The Long Journey Home: Re-Visioning the Myth of Demeter and Persephone for Our Time.* Ed. Christine Downing. Boston: Shambhala, 1994. 233-42.

DuPlessis, Rachel Blau. "'All My Vast/Journeying Sensibility': Barbara Guest's Recent Work." *Sulfur* 39 (1996): 39-48.

———. "The Flavor of Eyes: *Selected Poems* by Barbara Guest." *Women's Review of Books* 13 (1995): 23-24.

———. *The Pink Guitar: Writing as Feminist Practice.* New York: Routledge, 1990.

Einzig, Barbara. "The Surface as Object: Barbara Guest's *Selected Poems.*" *American Poetry Review* Jan.-Feb. 1996: 7-10.

Gould, Jean. *Amy: The World of Amy Lowell and the Imagist Movement.* New York: Dodd, 1975.

Gruen, John. *The Party's Over Now: Reminiscences of the Fifties.* New York: Viking, 1967.

Guest, Barbara. "Barbara Guest: An Interview by Mark Hillringhouse." *American Poetry Review* July-Aug. 1992: 23-30.

———. *Defensive Rapture.* Los Angeles: Sun & Moon, 1993.

———. *Fair Realism.* Los Angeles: Sun & Moon, 1989.

———. Letter to the author. 30 May 1996.

———. *Moscow Mansions.* New York: Viking, 1973.

———. *Poems: The Location of Things, Archaics, The Open Skies.* New York: Doubleday, 1962.

———. "Robert Goodnough." *School of New York: Some Younger Artists*: New York: Grove, 1959. 18-23.

———. *Selected Poems.* Los Angeles: Sun & Moon, 1995.

Guggenheim Museum. *Futurism: A Modern Focus.* Preface by Thomas A. Messer. New York: Guggenheim Foundation, 1973.

Hayes, Elizabeth T. *Images of Persephone: Feminist Readings in Western Literature.* Gainesville: UP of Florida, 1994.

Heffernan, James A. W. *Museum of Words: The Poetics of Ekphrasis from Homer to Ashbery.* Chicago: U of Chicago P, 1993.

Kerényi, C. *Eleusis: Archetypal Image of Mother and Daughter.* Trans. Ralph Manheim. New York: Schocken, 1977.

Kiernan, Robert F. *American Writing since 1945: A Critical Survey.* New York: Ungar, 1983.

Krieger, Murray. *Ekphrasis: The Illusion of the Natural Sign.* Baltimore, MD: Johns Hopkins UP, 1992.

Lanchner, Carolyn. *Joan Miró.* New York: Museum of Modern Art, 1993.

Lowell, Robert. Foreword. *Ariel.* By Sylvia Plath. New York: Harper, 1965. vii-ix.

Manousos, Anthony. "Barbara Guest." *Dictionary of Literary Biography: American Poets since World War II.* Ed. Donald J. Greiner. Vol. 5. Detroit, MI: Gale, 1980. 295-300.

Marinetti, F. T. "The Founding and Manifesto of Futurism 1909." Trans. R. W. Flint. *Futurist Manifestos.* Ed. Umbro Apollonio. New York: Viking, 1973. 19-24.

Matthews, J. H. "André Breton and Joan Miró: *Constellations.*" *Languages of Surrealism.* Columbia: U of Missouri P, 1986. 79-101.

Messenger, Cynthia. "'But How Do You Write a Chagall?': Ekphrasis and the Brazilian Poetry of P. K. Page and Elizabeth Bishop." *Canadian Literature* 142-43 (1994): 102-17.

Miller, Stephen Paul. "'Self-Portrait in a Convex Mirror,' the Watergate Affair, and Johns's Crosshatch Paintings: Surveillance and Reality-Testing in the Mid-Seventies." *Boundary 2* 20.2 (1993): 84-115.

Mitchell, W. J. T. *Picture Theory: Essays on Verbal and Visual Representation.* Chicago: U of Chicago P, 1994.

Moramarco, Fred. "John Ashbery and Frank O'Hara: The Painterly Poets." *Journal of Modern Literature* 5 (1976): 436-62.

Motherwell, Robert. "The Significance of Miró." *The Collected Writings of Robert Motherwell.* Ed. Stephanie Terenzio. New York: Oxford UP, 1992. 114-21.

Mulvey, Laura. *Visual and Other Pleasures.* Bloomington: Indiana UP, 1989.

Myers, John Bernard. Introduction. *The Poets of the New York School.* Philadelphia: Pennsylvania UP, 1969. 7-29.

Nochlin, Linda. "Women, Art, and Power." *Visual Theory: Painting and Interpretation.* Ed. Norman Bryson, Michael Ann Holly, and Keith Moxey. New York: Harper, 1991. 12-46.

Padgett, Ron, and David Shapiro, eds. *An Anthology of New York Poets.* New York: Random, 1970.

Penrose, Roland. *Miró.* New York: Abrams, 1969.

Perloff, Marjorie. *Frank O'Hara: Poet among Painters.* New York: Braziller, 1977.

———. *The Futurist Moment: Avant-Garde, Avant Guerre, and the Language of Rupture.* Chicago: U of Chicago P, 1986.

Pollitt, Katha. "She Was Neither Dryad nor Victim." Rev. of *Herself Defined: The Poet H. D. and Her World,* by Barbara Guest. *New York Times Book Review* 11 Mar. 1984: 7-8.

Robinson, Susan Barnes. *Giacomo Balla: Divisionism and Futurism 1871-1912.* Ann Arbor, MI: UMI Research, 1981.

Rose, Jacqueline. *Sexuality in the Field of Vision.* London: Verso, 1986.

Rubin, William. *Miró in the Collection of the Museum of Modern Art.* New York: Museum of Modern Art, 1973.

Scott, Grant F. "The Rhetoric of Dilation: Ekphrasis and Ideology." *Word & Image* 7 (1991): 301-10.

Shapiro, David. "A Salon of 1990: Maximalist Manifesto." Rev. of *Fair Realism,* by Barbara Guest. *American Poetry Review* Jan.-Feb. 1991: 37-47.

Steiner, Wendy. *Pictures of Romance: Form against Context in Painting and Literature.* Chicago: U of Chicago P, 1988.

Taylor, Christiana J. *Futurism: Politics, Painting, and Performance.* Ann Arbor, MI: UMI Research, 1979.

Taylor, Joshua C. *Futurism.* New York: Museum of Modern Art, 1961.

Walker, Barbara G. *The Crone: Woman of Age, Wisdom, and Power.* San Francisco: Harper, 1985.

Ward, Geoff. *Statutes of Liberty: The New York School of Poets.* New York: St. Martin's, 1993.

Welish, Marjorie. Rev. of *Fair Realism,* by Barbara Guest. *Sulfur* 26 (1990): 213-15.

Wolf, Leslie. "The Brushstroke's Integrity: The Poetry of John Ashbery and the Art of Painting." *Beyond Amazement: New Essays on John Ashbery.* Ed. David Lehman. Ithaca, NY: Cornell UP, 1980. 224-54.

Robert Kaufman (essay date July-August 2000)

SOURCE: Kaufman, Robert. "A Future for Modernism: Barbara Guest's Recent Poetry." *The American Poetry Review* 29, no. 4 (July-August 2000): 11-16.

[*In the following essay, Kaufman examines how Guest's poetry "dramatizes this critical process of discovering reality by means of lyric negation" and he predicts that the poet's reception among readers and critics will continue to grow.*]

Remember Borges' great figure Pierre Menard? The difficult *Symboliste* poet was discovered to have written—not to have copied, parodied, or pastiched, but actually to have imagined and written, word for word and line by line—nothing less than the *Quixote* of Miguel de Cervantes. Now consider a Borgesian tale that, in complex fidelity to our own moment, goes Borges one better, establishing itself not only as true fiction but as true fact:

For decades, a brilliant poet is excluded from American poetry's higher honors and publicity loops, excluded as well from a surprising number of alternative anthologies. But in a perverse and too-common form of recognition, she *is* regularly identified in the critical literature: she's *the woman* in one of American poetry's initiatory moments of post-Modernism, that of the first generation of New York School poets. Yet she is known also, by a sizeable readership, as a supreme poet's poet, as the New York School's perhaps most genuinely experimental, aesthetically fearless and uncompromising artist. And then on April 23, 1999, Barbara Guest—amidst an extraordinarily prolific output of luminous work during her eighth decade—is awarded the Poetry Society of America's Robert Frost Medal. The honor officially places her in the select company of such previous Frost-Medal recipients as Wallace Stevens, Marianne Moore, and John Ashbery (Guest's New York School colleague).[1]

At which point, the literary world, belatedly turning its attention to the *oeuvre* of this pioneer in a post-Modern experimentalism that can at last be accepted and codified, discovers in shock or chagrin that she's been a card-carrying, militant Modernist all along! Moreover, careful reading of the later work reveals an increasingly relentless investigation of the Modernist versus post-Modernist question itself, and the concomitant emergence of a powerful, apparently unexpected claim made in Guest's writing. The claim? That post-Modernism, far from having superseded Modernism, has actually prevented the latter from coming fully into being.

If this rehearsal of Guest's career appears structurally as a Borgesian reshuffling of historical sequence, its implicit form and content sound the overarching aesthetic and political themes of another great Modernist voice, that of the Frankfurt School philosopher and critic Theodor Adorno. There are many paths into the experimental modernity of Guest's poetry. But rumors about the comeback of both experimental Modernism and Adornian aesthetics make it especially interesting to approach Guest's work (and her plottings of a future for Modernism) via her poetry's intense engagement with Adorno. Indeed, it's worth backing up to note one of literary history's wonderful accidents, the sort of accident or contingency that art by its nature turns into necessity (at least, that's what art does until post-Modernism). It so happens that two of what Guest deems her most important early poems first appeared in a 1960 issue of the journal *Noonday*. The second of these two lyric poems, **"Lights of my Eyes,"** begins

Lights of my eyes
      my only
they're turning it off
      while we're asleep on this shore

and the poem later concludes,

   . . . I'll go on singing 'adieu'

By whatever quirk of fate and *Noonday* editorial decision, on the very page following Guest's poems appears
the first English translation of Adorno's "Looking Back
on Surrealism"; the brief essay was one of Adorno's attempts to reroute the theoretical efforts of his friend and
colleague Walter Benjamin, whose 1929 essay on Surrealism in many ways is the point of departure for Adorno's later undertaking.[2] There has long been heated
debate about the effectiveness, in his own lifetime, of
Benjamin's Marxian advocacy of those Surrealist and
allied artistic experiments that had highlighted what
Benjamin called "mechanical reproduction": the attempt
to jettison traditional notions about the "aura" created
through an individual artist's imaginative labor, and
likewise to abolish the contiguous concept of "aesthetic
autonomy."[3] Whatever the merits of the positions
expressed in that debate, the strong consensus is that
the real life of Benjamin's mechanical-reproduction
theory has occurred during its posthumous celebration
in post-Modernism. So *Adorno*'s Surrealism essay is
particularly relevant here, as would be his "On Lyric
Poetry and Society" (1957) and his final work, *Aesthetic
Theory* (1970).[4] These texts are motivated by a desire
(articulated largely within the Marxian vocabulary
Adorno shares with Benjamin) not to relinquish what
Adorno deems the "critical" nature of Modernism, by
Adorno's refusal to ratify the theory and practice of
"anti-aesthetic" mechanical reproduction.[5]

One could not do better, when seeking an exemplary
site for Guest's and Adorno's meeting on the terrain of
late Modernism, than those 1960, back-to-back pages of
Noonday. Guest's two early lyrics are already characterized by the sustained grace, radiance, and imaginative
reach for which she will become known. The poems
exhibit deep, multiple, elegant and musical intuitions of
experimental, in-process structure, where intense yet
deft acts of intellection are informed by melody, where
song quickens thought.

   We are living at an embarkation port
      where the gulls
      and the soft-shoed buoys
      make Atlantic soundings

   This air of ours is photographing fish

   and the rice and the white antelope pelts
   are asleep in the dark orchid hold
   where old women have sent their black lids to be
     parched

and young bronze boys are tying knots in their limbs
while spume and the salt
      send thick-painted pictures to
      the hatchway

                (from **"In Dock"**)

Guest fills the atmosphere, the air of her embarkation
port, with song (with "an air," as was once said) whose
Atlantic soundings make buoys and boys float into one
another. That melodic atmosphere in turn yields—
almost surreally, one wants to say—visual conceptualization, as the air "photographs" fish, carries spume and
salt as "pictures." And just as Guest's two lyrics finally
transport their readers to the next page of *Noonday*—
transport them, that is, to a rigorous theorization of
critical aesthetic subjectivity by someone named
Adorno—so will the very theorizations in Adorno's essay come to depend on Adorno's historical valuation of
a complex of song and intellectual construction, a
complex that Adorno will elsewhere identify as *lyric,* a
term that for him means the modern lyric traditions
whose trajectory runs from Romanticism through the
twentieth century.

Of course, a view that comes to one of its great
apotheoses in post-Modernist art and theory—a view
Adorno always seeks to refute—is that a critical poetics
should react against the Romantic and Modernist legacy
of auratic lyric subjectivity and the latter's allegedly
"aestheticizing" propagation of poetic false consciousness. A critical poetics, the apparently Benjaminian and
post-Modernist argument goes, should be anti-lyric,
anti-aesthetic, and committed to methods associated
with technologically oriented reproduction, all in order
to effect radical defamiliarization and the renewal of sociopolitical commitment. But, playing careful variations
on Benjamin's themes, Adorno holds throughout his
work that—at least since Baudelaire—the critical force
of poetry depends precisely on its ability to make lyric
itself critical. This is quite distinct from abolishing or
getting beyond auratic lyric subjectivity and modern
aesthetic autonomy. Preserving Benjamin's insights
about how Baudelaire brilliantly makes lyric vocation
confront the destruction of its own historical preconditions—the kind of temporal-reflective *experience* no
longer possible, Baudelaire's poems seem to declare, in
a radically commodified, high speed, high capitalist
modernity—Adorno nonetheless effectively defends a
lyric whose exponentially raised *via-negativa* aura
survives Benjamin's intermittent proclamations of
aura's death. Hence Adorno maintains (with Baudelaire,
Rimbaud, and Celan as pathfinders) that the refusal of
lyric aura *tout court* is for poetry the refusal of critique.[6]

It's not as if the 1960 accident of *Noonday* publication
and pagination somehow imprinted Adornian aesthetics
into the DNA of all Guest's subsequent poetry. That
poetry now makes up quite a body of work, from

Guest's early *The Location of Things* all the way to her 1995 *Selected Poems* and, most astonishingly, the five volumes she's written since publication of her *Selected*.[7] Across these years Guest certainly hasn't channeled Adorno, hasn't read his *Aesthetic Theory*—or any other philosophy, for that matter—as blueprint for poetry. (Though, truth be told, she has been known to paint onto canvas, as something of an *ars poetica,* Adorno's severe yet complicatedly lyric aphorism that "with Schönberg, affability ceases.") For all her decades of reading in philosophy and critical theory, Guest's genuine affinity with Adorno, and her on-going commitment to Modernism, prove themselves precisely because she doesn't *apply* theory to poetry. Rather—and I'll perversely take my formulation here, about experimental artistic constructivism, from Adorno's *Aesthetic Theory*—Guest enacts a

> subjective paradox of art: to produce what is blind, expression, by way of reflection, that is, through form; not to rationalize the blind but to produce it aesthetically, "To make things of which we do not know what they are."[8]

I'll turn shortly to the way Guest dramatizes this critical process of discovering reality by means of lyric negation (the dynamic whereby in poetry, to quote the title of a Guest poem, **"An Emphasis Falls on Reality"**). But I want first to note the related Adornian concern, explicitly articulated in Guest's prose, about the preservation and expansion of a critical lyric Modernism. This is an aesthetic with commitments far afield from parody, pastiche, and either nose-thumbing or solemnizing registrations of techno-mechanical reproducibility, the culture of copy and simulacrum. Guest's concern is present when, in **"Poetry the True Fiction,"** she makes a constellation that stretches from Cowper and Coleridge to Mallarmé and Stevens, linking them all to the way that Willem de Kooning locates, in Renaissance drawing, a proto-modern sense of "plastic," "movable" form—a notion crucial to much of Guest's thinking about poetry's palpable and musical structures.[9] The concern appears in a review of the poet and critic Susan Gevirtz's study of Dorothy Richardson, where Guest writes suggestively, in classic Enlightenment aesthetic vocabulary, of "enlargement of the scope of field" and the need to relate a dynamic "empathy" to "an extending modernity."[10] And it appears in Guest's powerful if unfashionable revivification of Romantic-Modernist poetic irony; not as a too-knowing cynicism, but as something qualitatively different—something fundamental to poetic experiment—is how Guest conceives the "bittersweet laughter" that "brings us closer to irony, the mole of poetry."[11] All of which, Guest has indicated on several occasions, are encapsulated for her in Norma Cole's "The Poetics of Vertigo"; delivered as the 1998 George Oppen Memorial Lecture, "The Poetics of Vertigo" had thought through Oppen's exploration of poetry's ways of *knowing* (and thought

through the path, Guest has emphasized, that led a poet as politically committed as Oppen to adumbrate an "asocial radicality claimed by and for poetry").[12]

Still, Guest's poetry always flows back in, even or especially back into the issues raised in the prose. So it's appropriate to quote as well from her remarkable poem **"Leaving Modernity"** in the award-winning volume *Quill, Solitary, APPARITION* (1996), a poem whose resonances seem to replay as undersong Adorno's repeated incantations of Rimbaud's *il faut être absolument moderne,* watchword for a sense of Modernism not as style or canonized authority but as continued experiment, as critical-exploratory approach to the given. In **"Leaving Modernity"** the poet makes us encounter musically "the idea of *departure* (simmered between brackets)," which she presents as the poem's difficult question. We confront too a "leaving (without ending)"; the poem enables us virtually to hear how

> "a disorder between space and form"
>
> interrupts Modernity
>
> with an aptitude unties
>
> the dissolving string
>
> * * *
>
> and thought of your vanishment, *Modernity*
> on the roadway

The poet and critic Marjorie Welish, an especially acute commentator on Guest's work, has rightly emphasized that Guest's recent poetry threads a terrifically distilled musicality and a disjunctive spatialization through each other, at once preserving and unsettling the lyricism.[13] One might add that Guest accomplishes this in a manner whose consonance with Benjamin's description of the Baudelairean lyric counter-tradition (and its constant, ever-increasing wager with/against aura) is readily evident. Since Baudelaire, that is, the poet can choose from two modes of resignation: the poet can blithely sing away, as if capitalist modernity had never happened, had not profoundly affected the experiential preconditions for intellectual and emotional processing of lyric and its contents; or, in awareness of how drastically modernity *has* altered the conditions for aesthetic experience, the poet—not wishing to participate in false comforts and illusory consolations—can just throw in the towel on song-based poetics. A third, admittedly paradoxical and ever-tentative alternative is the one Benjamin and Adorno try to chart in Baudelaire and the tradition of formal experiment associated with him. Here the poet begins with something like an attempt to sing, but does so haltingly, fragmentarily, or with confessions of paralytic bad faith, and so forth; yet the poet also or thereby seeks to reconjure beauty while simultaneously representing the unprecedented complexity—in all too many cases, the out-and-out horror—of really existing society. The poet begins with an attempt to sing song's apparent impossibility.

Guest's poetic is experimentally modern and Modernist in this Benjaminian-Adornian sense. Guest simultaneously invokes and takes leave of lyric, calls forth and questions modernity, places opulence of sound and suggestion of depth alongside ruthlessly stripped down narrative gesture. The technique more than recalls Adorno's notion that Schönberg's great achievement, in *Moses und Aron,* was first to have radically compressed and then interwoven monumental construction and extreme polyphony; indeed, Guest virtually courts melodic decomposition as her means toward reinventing poetry's version of "through-composed," architectonically conceived musicality. But the pre-condition for these particular modes of experiment—and this is Adorno's point about the Baudelairean tradition in poetry, not to mention Schönberg—is the necessarily difficult, almost constitutively negative reanimation of aura, the spectral presence-ing of aesthetic autonomy.

This would go a long way toward explaining the place in Guest's work of a lyric music rarely heard (or so frequently misheard) today, along with at least two of its interconnected forms of difficulty: that of hearing lyric at all in our culture; and of hearing a specifically difficult lyric whose seeming abstractness or hyper-distillation may appear wilfully recondite. The first sentence of Benjamin's "On Some Motifs in Baudelaire" echoes still: "Baudelaire envisaged readers to whom the reading of lyric poetry would present difficulties."[14] Adorno later begins unpacking the multiple meanings of such *difficulty* in Baudelaire (and in Benjamin) when he states that, with and after Baudelaire, "lyric poetry became a game in which one goes for broke." The modern experimental lyric poet risks audience incomprehension not out of a rebellious desire for obscurity but actually because he or she seeks to bring to light, through poetic form and with as much precision as possible, aspects of a modern social complexity whose reality can hardly correspond to socially available, already established, status-quo conceptions of present society. Nor will an older, ready-to-hand lyric language's formulae and concepts necessarily prove adequate for describing, understanding, and engaging those facets of the social. Moreover, the dynamic nature of the basic equation means that—with some possible exceptions that would, at a minimum, probably depend on the confluence of a culturally shared sense of social crisis (or at least of imminent and important transformation) coupled with a relatively large readership for "advanced" poetry—Baudelairean poets after Baudelaire will court ever greater risk, as the social and aesthetic problems that the poets engage in relation

to lyric aura seem necessarily to increase in complexity, making formal failure and/or audience refusal exponentially more likely.[15]

The ambitions, then, of Guest's poetry comprehend levels and combinations of difficulty that have at times, perhaps inevitably, caused it to be side-stepped or misunderstood in all the ways Benjamin and Adorno posit, and then some. Misreadings have ranged widely, and have often been based on interpretive options decidedly ironized or tweaked by the poems themselves. For example, Guest's evident interests in painting and the visual has led to hasty pronouncements that she is—with all the traditionally gendered connotations the term implicitly carries in modern poetics—merely a pictorialist. Meanwhile, awareness that lyric music matters tremendously to Guest has led to assumptions that she is a straightforward (if especially demure or muted, again because female) singer, in the line of Baudelairean-formal-experiment-and-its-aftermath-never-occurred. Finally, recognition of the emphatic disjunctions and dissonances in her work, and confusion about the ways that Guest has occasionally used the term *lyric* to signify the non-problematic strain that makes a wide detour around Baudelaire et al., have led to judgments that Guest must be some species of language poet.[16] Guest is none of these, but the relative familiarity of these options within poetics today makes them all too readily available as explanations of her work. This has meant that for various readers, Guest's poetry has beckoned with intriguing mystery, only to remain mostly mysterious. Put differently, the work—judged, for example, in terms of the language poetry or mainstream lyric which it is not—does not behave according to any current canons.

What probably makes the work appear to some as mysterious or frustratingly unrecognizable is the incomprehensibility today—the sheer foreignness—of the very notion of experimental vocation at the heart of Benjamin's and Adorno's readings of modern poetry (no small irony, given that the Frankfurt School authors are so often cited to lend ballast to championings of post-Modernist experimentalism). That is, Guest's lyric may seem inscrutable or unassimilable because it undertakes nothing less than to reimagine the ur-problem that modern lyric experiment poses for itself, a problem that, to be sure, harkens back to a task lyric poetry broaches long before modernity: how to build a solid artistic structure out of something as delicate and ephemeral as subjective song?

To this the Baudelairean poet must add the maddening fact of lyric aura's specifically modern "impossibility." That impossibility may be traced, in the Benjaminian-Adornian view, not only from the subjective perspective of the one who would voice or hear the song, but also from the direction of objectivity, of structural analysis of a capitalist modernity characterized by an all-pervasive structure that nevertheless, given the impressively fluid and everchanging character of capital itself, proves notoriously difficult to delineate and objectify. An earlier poetics had approached analogous if simpler conundrums by relying on achieved form as the principle of dynamic synthesis of subjective utterance and objective ground. The modern twist, visible in Baudelaire and accelerating thereafter, is the sense that the very categories of subject and object seem disconcertingly to have been erased well before they can be elegantly transmuted, via *poesis,* into each other.

Renderings of the social, formal, or musical look—thankfully—different among different poets within experimental traditions. Guest has gravitated toward what in Benjamin's and (especially) Adorno's eyes is the most ambitious task within lyric experiment: that of realizing poetic form anew in an architectonically-conceived structure, built, as it were, from hard to grasp musical materials. (Shared dedication to that confluence of powerful structure and lyric play is also, of course, one of the great bonds between New York School painters and poets.) In poem after poem, Guest constructs the edifice by musical phrase; the result is usually an architecture at once monumental and ghostly, seemingly held in place by the vibration of phrase-blocks one against another.[17] The sense of musical phrase testifies to an uncanny blending not only of poetic history's ways with melody, meter, and breath, but equally with those of musical performance, one ear pitched toward the classical, the other toward jazz (and with decided partiality in each toward the human voice and its string or reed kin). The architectural ambition, the sense of musical phrase as constructive unit, of music as metaphor that also metaphorizes into something provisionally concrete enough to build with, is perhaps nowhere so pronounced as in **"An Emphasis Falls on Reality"** (from *Fair Realism,* 1989). This poem's radical understanding of the nature and conceptualization of reality begins with its title, which posits apprehension of the real as a process of understanding that occurs through the imagining, making, and/or naming of figures that, in their "emphasis" on aspects of reality, fall like grace notes upon the latter. The act of apprehension—ultimately, the act of poetry—becomes part of its object, reality:

> Cloud fields change into furniture
> furniture metamorphizes into fields
> an emphasis falls on reality.
>
> "It snowed toward morning," a barcarole
> the words stretched severely
>
> silhouettes they arrived in trenchant cut
> the face of lilies. . . .

If the cloud (continually forming, disintegrating, reconstituting itself), metaphorically seen as field, turns into furniture and back into field and then both literally *and* metaphorically falls onto reality (earth) as snow, the whole transmission—"stretched severely"—turns into a musical form, a barcarole. Music moves like the air and its elements, moves through or rises and falls in time, and the barcarole (taking its name from the gondolier, who takes his name from the boat itself) is both literal and metaphorical instantiation of such movement. The gondolier's song, the barcarole, moves—like all music—in time, but also on the boat and water from which it is originally sung. That song moves historically into a form that is not only sung but also played instrumentally without words (the *barcarolles* of Chopin, Mendelssohn, Fauré), yet still in imitation of boat and water movement. In Guest's poem, the whole process signifies the mutually constitutive identity of metaphor, music, and movement. The complex of terms designates the activity of *emphasizing*: of figuratively understanding, making, imaginatively comprehending, *moving* reality and thereby becoming it. Musical cadence gently though swingingly sounds the desire for reality; with rhythmic grace and assonance expressive of that desiring subjectivity, it marks its difference from its object by recognizing musical metaphor's difference from, and effect on, the reality it seeks to know:

> I was envious of fair realism.
>
> I desired sunrise to revise itself
> as apparition, majestic in evocativeness,
> two fountains traced nearby on a lawn. . . .

Whether the *i*'s that call to one another are sunrise or its revision, apparition of actual sunrise or apparition caused by metaphorical sunrise, a shadow is cast on earth: on a lawn. As the poem hums its way through the literalization of figures and the metaphorization of reality—as poetry and reality shadow and inflect one another, yielding a notion, in a fair realism both fine and just, of poetry as a form *of* reality—the architectural, along with modernity itself, make their joint appearance:

> A column chosen from distance
> mounts into the sky while the font
> is classical,
>
> they will destroy the disturbed font
> as it enters modernity and is rare. . . .
>
> The necessary idealizing of you reality
> is part of the search, the journey
> where two figures embrace
>
> This house was drawn for them
> it looks like a real house
> perhaps they will move in today

The column that rises skyward from earth, and the classical, destroyed-as-it-enters-modernity font lead quickly to figures that may be actual people or just *figures*; they stand for both, and so for figuration as a process that would logically end in real embodiment. Figures of either kind are housed or "move into" structures that begin as "drawn" images, plans, blueprints: images that can be physically realized as actual houses. For Guest, critical lyric ideally aspires to the condition of works of art that are first made as figures, then made real enough for human beings to enter them; these ultimately would be weight-bearing structures, works of architecture. Yet the poem wants to build with foundations, girders, and beams composed of music, to maintain its structuring tensions through fluid sound and syntax: a barcarole built directly from—by severely stretching—the original *barca,* an architecture designed for flotation, movement, and song. The imagination's need to puzzle or stretch itself severely to project the creation or comprehension of such lyric architectonics appears as the price of an artistic-aesthetic ambition to apprehend, move on and into, reality. Or rather, in the wake of such necessarily idealized architectural-musical conceptualization ("The necessary idealizing of you reality / is part of the search"), reality is approached, made emphatic—fallen upon—through what looks like its photo-negation, as the poem's figures finally move

> into ephemeral dusk and
> move out of that into night
> selective night with trees,
>
> The darkened copies of all trees.

Grasping this poem's openly invoked architectonics—architecturalism in constantly decomposing and recomposing song-movement—allows us to perceive the same ambition in Guest's more recent, dramatically pared-down work, like the **"Leaving Modernity"** excerpt from *Quill, Solitary, APPARITION* quoted above. Call it experimental, barely or powerfully lyrical, Adornian; in any case, it helps to know that *Quill, Solitary, AP-PARITION*—if it makes sense to say this about a work that so courts the minimal—maximally references Baudelaire, from explicit naming and quotation to subtle allusion. Guest raises the stakes, so that musical architectonics investigates its conditions of possibility, internally explores its micro-units and simultaneously pushes outward; this poetic dares to enact *"'disorder between space and form'"* and then with virtuosic *"'aptitude unties / the dissolving string.'"* Even amid the volume's relentless compression, the coupling of a still achingly graceful literariness and a stark, spatially disorienting juxtaposition of poetic line recognizably extends the techniques of classical Modernism, while the poem's charged putting into relation of audible beauty and geometric abstraction further reminds us that we are in the realm of high aesthetic.

So it becomes necessary to ask: What makes Adorno in theory and Guest in poetry emphasize, against politically inflected critiques of elitist-aestheticist, canonical-

Modernist false consciousness, this frankly aesthetic, seemingly transcendental phenomenon of lyric? How does an aesthetic commitment to lyric *give us,* as Adorno frequently puts it, the social; how does it provide a genuinely critical purchase on the modern? The answer involves Adorno's teasing out—from Immanuel Kant's aesthetic treatise *Critique of Judgment* (the Third Critique) and Kant's Critical Philosophy as a whole, and from a kindred Romantic-Modernist poetics—of a constructivist theory of aesthetic experience and human agency. This effort allows Adorno to uncover and begin working out a crucial distinction between *aesthetic* and aesthetic*ization*. At issue will be the non- or quasi-conceptual character of aesthetic thought-experience.

The idea is that although the aesthetic may look like conceptual, objective, useful thought, the resemblance is only formal. Aesthetic thought-experience in some way precedes objective, use-oriented thought; in that sense, art or the aesthetic is formal because, rather than being determined by, it provides *the form for* conceptual, objective thought or cognition. But aesthetic thought-experience itself remains free (relative to more properly conceptual thought) from pre-existent concepts or cognitive rules. The aesthetic—with ephemeral lyric traditionally at its apex—actually serves as mold or frame for the construction of conceptual thought in general. The aesthetic serves also as the formal engine for new, experimental (because previously non-existent) concepts: new concepts that may bring obscured aspects of substantive social reality to light. Consequently, the aesthetic can provide a prerequisite of critical thought by affording formal means for the development of new (not even necessarily utopian) concepts. Lyric experiment thus helps construct the intellectual-emotional apparatus for accessing, and to that extent helps make available the social material of, the new. In short, far from effecting a false-consciousness escape from society and politics, this constructivist theory and practice sees that experiment in lyric—lyric *as* experiment—helps make new areas of the modern fitfully available *to* perception in the first place.[18]

One last point of aesthetic theory and poetic history before returning to Guest's work. There's a fascinating issue that literary critics and historians concerned with nineteenth- and twentieth-century poetry, and with Frankfurt School theory, have largely missed, perhaps because the issue is so subtly woven into scattered textual moments, its presence discernible largely in gesture and implication. Adorno's interest in Modernist constructivism, and in the relationship of critical human agency to processes of aesthetic and social construction more generally, of course traces itself back from his favorite twentieth-century exemplars: Celan, Beckett, Schönberg. But the tracing works back not just to later nineteenth-century lyric poetry and the well known case of Baudelaire; it goes back further, most specifically and surprisingly to a particular dynamic in the poetry of John Keats. The dynamic involves a constitutive tension between that famously ephemeral *negative capability* and Keats's equally celebrated *monumental constructivism*; the tension locates itself most memorably in Keats's lyric, but highly built and densely wrought, odes. Though it is possible to cull this history from the panoply of Adorno's writings, the connections are by no means obvious, a fact evidenced by the paucity of secondary literature on the subject.[19]

I recount this literary and aesthetic history because of a remarkable poem in Guest's *Rocks on a Platter: Notes on Literature* (1999); the near-identity of the book's subtitle with Adorno's *Notes to Literature* scarcely seems haphazard. The poem in question originally appeared in the journal *Avec* in 1995, under the title **"Others,"** though in *Rocks on a Platter,* the poem bears no title other than its first line,

    Intimacy of tone

—by which it is identified in the Table of Contents. The poem quickly reveals itself to be concerned not only with tone, but with form and form-construction as well; and that will be only the beginning:

        Intimacy of tone

   and form

     beyond the tangible itinerary

        mirror trap

   at 30 degrees

Guest's poem is notable for many reasons, not least for the ways it unearths and vivifies—as only an artwork can—the very poetic and aesthetic histories that inform Adorno's theory of Modernist constructivism. Guest discovers and makes visible buried touchstones of the theory, apprehends its foundations in the interanimating tension between Keatsian negative capability and monumental construction. Her poem accomplishes this sheerly by giving itself over to its own imaginative acts of investigatory *poesis,* pursued via Guest's formidable erudition and ability to sympathize with her materials, and animated by her ceaseless examination of the literary-historical constituents of her own experiments in musical architectonic. It would no doubt have delighted Adorno that the first powerful understanding of the Keatsian elements in his aesthetic theory emerges from a work of poetic art rather than criticism, and from a work struggling to reimagine Modernist legacies at that. For it turns out that among Guest's earliest impulses for the poem originally called **"Others"** was her transformative meditation on two ideas or problems.

The first involved Adorno's ruminations on the degree to which mimesis (artistic representation) is not a copying or transcription of the given, but instead, a dialectical or disseminative process involving what Adorno calls "the non-conceptual affinity of a subjective creation with its object and positive other."

A second found-speculation spurred and informed Guest's thinking, in this poem, about art's relationship to otherness, about otherness in and as art. This second idea grew from her rethinking of the "camelion-poet" hypothesized in Keats's letter on the "poetical character," a companion text to Keats's earlier "negative capability" letter. In the letter on the poetical character, Keats asserts that the poetical character "is not itself—it has no self—it is every thing and nothing—It has no character." And Keats consequently is led to insist that

> A Poet is the most unpoetical of any thing in existence; because he has no Identity—he is continually in for— and filling some other Body . . .

> . . . When I am in a room with People if I ever am free from speculating on creations of my own brain, then not myself goes home to myself: but the identity of every one in the room begins to press upon me that, I am in a very little time annihilated.[20]

Out of these and other sources and experiences taken into Guest's imagination comes the final version of the poem, with its acute Keats-Adorno fusion, its making of plastic fictions from materials that put monumental construction into conversation with an ephemeral, melodic sense of negation or negative capability. Guest makes audible and concrete a paradoxically social solitariness, a sympathetic projection or filiation in and through poetry. This is a poetic filled always with song, in which things sound one another to discover their present, or yet-to-be-learned, affinities:

   snow footprints adieu

   cold tears splashed acre is intimacy,

        and many chimed things,

     future's conduit.

Keats's alone-in-the-crowded-room experience of self, together with the marmoreality or monumentality of construction by which poetic making enables such subjectivity, is likewise evoked (in almost microscopic, Webernesque units),

   In a room

     "not alone"

 enters

    midday

appears

massive.

* * *

Cannot dream except in "two's" or be alone,
    is hollowed out.

Meanwhile this speculative, imaginative subjectivity
transgresses the rules of utility and socially predetermined options; the emergent, alternative mode
speaks in a language of politics, sensuous particularity,
and artistic metamorphosis. Cadence and diction
conspire to make minimalism feel inextricable from
lightness of touch, exclamatory impulse, and, above all,
effortless swing:

dissident morning!
with no ulterior purpose

image exchanged for a feather
le poisson on the watered page.

It bears noticing what distillation and condensation
mean to Guest, how her work on the text becomes part
of the poem's own understanding of its subject. One of
the earlier drafts of this poem (from which Guest had
read publically in November 1994) included the full
passages that I quoted above from Adorno and Keats.
Guest had initially placed those passages within the
body of the poem's text, into its twelfth, final page.
Then, just weeks prior to the poem's first publication in
1995 (as **"Others,"** in *Avec*), Guest rethought the inclusion of the Adorno comment, which in the earlier draft
had read,

mimesis: the non-conceptual affinity of a subjective
creation with its object and positive other

(Adorno)

Guest transformed that passage, and the longer quotation from Keats (about the poet having no identity or
self and so always "filling some other Body"), into the
following, finally revised, concluding page of the poem;

Bar of silence crossed the mouth
decorates it.

She watched skirts sweep the floor,
from that day of her sixteenth year
her skirt brushes the floor. What she
    is after

"trailing skirt," blossom
in mimetic hair

fills some other Body.

There's alchemy here. Poetic brooding over a philosophical formulation (a formulation about artistic
representation itself) passes into the poem's braided

suggestions of an irreducible mixture between lived and
literary history. We hear, envision, and feel mimesis,
"non-conceptual affinity with the objective" other. How?
As a skirt sweeping the floor, as a teenage girl imitating
or assimilating that movement; as linked weight-and-
rhythm traces (in the poem's images and sounds) that
blossom in "mimetic" hair whose movement, in turn,
echoes the original sweep of skirts (as does our reading
experience).

The marvel is that Guest's realization of "non-
conceptual affinity" has traveled in two different directions, establishing affinity with two distinct others, two
discrete conceptual or historical objects. One object is
the evanescent, elliptical yet lived human experience
evoked by literal and then metaphoric movement-traces
of skirt and hair. The second object is, of course, Adorno's and Keats's theoretical conceptualization of how
art, in its very non-conceptuality, allows us to imagine
and construct affinity with conceptual or empirical
objects, and with other subjects. In this second case,
rather than metaphorize an already existing object (hair
and skirt metaphorizing not only one another, but also
the objective experience of an incident in a personal
history, wherein movement and perception were
experienced as one), Guest's art now embodies—literal-
izes—an abstract concept (the poem as a whole concret-
izing something that began not as a phenomenological
experience but as a theoretical-conceptual insight; and,
the specific abstract *concept* to which Guest's poem
lends concrete particularity wonderfully happens to have
posited art's *quasi*-conceptual, particularizing character).
As with metaphor generally, these two directions in
which non-conceptual affinity travels keep turning back
into each other, aided here by the gliding of lines that
on the page—at least at first glance—look like they
might read in staccato clip rather than the luxurious
flow that the combination of punctuation, enjambment,
and breath invites. And in an ultimate working-through
of the haunting logic whereby art and conceptual-
objective knowledge shadow and provisionally disap-
pear into their opposite numbers, the poem's original,
abstract, conceptual-sounding title, **"Others,"** finally
disappears from—disappears into—the text. The poem
henceforth will be known (as it appears in *Rocks on a
Platter: Notes on Literature*) not by a name, but merely
by a part of its own body, by its first line: **"Intimacy of
tone."**

The poem's difficult structure and stringent lyricism
help underscore its Modernism. Still, even without
knowledge of Guest's linkages to Adorno, questions
would arise about this Modernism's presumably
nostalgic melancholia or pessimism, and about the use;
the political efficacy, of such poetry and theory. We
have to do here with an aesthetics admittedly susceptible
to accusations of—in a word—formalism. The latter
was, you'll recall, one of the repeated charges hurled

(usually preceded by the modifier *bourgeois*) against both high Modernism and Adornian aesthetics as post-Modernism took center stage in art and theory. But post-Modernist culture and critique, by presuming that Modernist aesthetic formalism turns material, socio-political history into art's forgotten other, often miss the central point. For aesthetic form, as in Guest's poem, can be precisely the attempt to imagine or engage, however imperfectly and provisionally, otherness. From that perspective, modern lyric aura or transcendence simply signifies the imagining of positions and experiences beyond those already known to the subject—which is why Benjamin and Adorno so emphasize lyric's historical relation to critical thought and emancipatory possibility.

It would take another essay to explore the intriguing reception Guest's recent poetry has had in circles that, though seeing their poetics within experimental traditions, are known for far more explicit rhetorics of sociopolitical commitment than that which is legible on the surface, at any rate, of Guest's work. (Interestingly, this reception has included not only the U.S. and Western Europe but also Latin America, particularly among poets and critics whose literary and political work has involved attempts to remake and repoliticize public space, and whose previous work had involved the question of Argentina's, Chile's, and Brazil's "disappeared.")[21] It is tempting to say that such reception merely involves close and deep reading of Guest's sense of poetic form and vocation, that the reading locates itself in the hidden layers of places like the first epigraph—it is from Hölderlin—in **Rocks on a Platter**: "To live is to defend a form." And whatever its future parameters, Guest's broader reception will one day profitably be read together with the perceptive commentaries on her work that have started to appear during the last few years.[22]

There are few bankable guarantees these days in poetry, aesthetics, or politics. But Guest's relentlessly investigatory, authentically experimental, pitch-perfect work—which always has been, and always will be, recent—may yet point to a future for Modernism.

Notes

For their responses to earlier versions of this essay, I am indebted to Charles Altieri, Adam Casdin, Joshua Clover, Norma Cole, Terence Diggory, Geoffrey Galt Harpham, Robert Hass, Brenda Hillman, Robert Hullot-Kentor, Michael Kelly, Laura Moriarty, Michael Palmer, and Marjorie Welish.

1. For thoughtful, interestingly heterodox analyses of Ashbery's and Guest's recent work—paying generous tribute to both poets' decades of achievement—see the poet and critic Garrett Caples' two reviews, "Ashbery Returns to Reinvention" [reviewing *Girls on the Run], San Francisco Chronicle Book Review,* April 4, 1999, p. 2, and "Masterful Variety from Poet Barbara Guest" [reviewing *Rocks on a Platter: Notes on Literature, The Confetti Trees,* and *If So, Tell Me], San Francisco Chronicle Book Review,* January 9, 2000, p. 12.

2. See *Noonday* 3 (1960), pp. 13-20; see also "Surrealism: The Last Snapshot of the European Intelligentsia" in Walter Benjamin, *Reflections: Essays, Aphorisms, Autobiographical Writings,* ed. and with an Introduction by Peter Demetz, trans. Edmund Jephcott (New York: Schocken, 1986), pp. 177-192. Adorno's "Looking Back on Surrealism" (first published in German in 1956) can now be found in Adorno, *Notes to Literature,* ed. Rolf Tiedemann, trans. Shierry Weber Nicholsen (New York: Columbia University Press, 1991) Vol. I, pp. 86-90.

3. See, e.g., "The Work of Art in the Age of Mechanical Reproduction" in Benjamin, *Illuminations,* ed. and with an Introduction by Hannah Arendt, trans. Harry Zohn (New York: Schocken, 1969), pp. 217-251.

4. "On Lyric Poetry and Society" in *Notes to Literature,* Vol. I, pp. 37-54; *Aesthetic Theory,* ed., translated, and with a translator's Introduction by Robert Hullot-Kentor (Minneapolis: University of Minnesota Press, 1997).

5. Within the field of what had once been broadly identified as experimental modern art, Peter Bürger has very usefully distinguished an "Avant-Gardist" desire to deconstruct or abolish aesthetic aura and autonomy from a "Modernist" commitment to art's provisional distance from reality and society. Thus in Bürger's particular terminology, Avant-Garde and Modernist are no longer synonymous, though both these tendencies within modern art are still seen to understand their projects as experimental. And, as Bürger and others have noted, progressive/ Left artists and critics have been found on either side of this divide. Arguments for art-into-life (and/or for art's self-assimilation to advanced techniques of mechanical/technological reproduction), and counter-arguments for the value of aesthetic distance, have both been made in pursuit of a critical art that would contribute to emancipatory agendas. Numerous artists and critics have observed that post-Modernist culture—as the very term implies—has been far more often associated with Avant-Gardist reproductionism than with Modernist aesthetic aura or distance. See Peter Bürger, *Theory of the Avant-Garde,* trans. Michael Shaw (Minneapolis: University of Minnesota Press, 1984).

6. See, e.g., "On Lyric Poetry and Society" and *Aesthetic Theory*; see too Benjamin, "On Some Motifs in Baudelaire," *Illuminations* pp. 155-200.

7. Like much contemporary experimental poetry, a good deal of Guest's work has been published by smaller presses whose books may prove hard to find. I should therefore add that all or most of the texts mentioned in this essay are available through the (non-profit) Small Press Distribution, the leading such distributor in the United States, at 1341 Seventh Street, Berkeley, CA 94710, (510)524-1668 or (800)869-7553, fax (510)524-0852, order-sspdbooks.org, http://www.spdbooks.org. Where it appears that SPD may not carry the text in question, I have tried to list the appropriate alternative resource.

8. *Aesthetic Theory*, p. 114.

9. Guest, "Poetry the True Fiction," in *Exact Change Yearbook* No. 1, ed. Peter Gizzi (1995), pp. 97-102 [Exact Change, P.O. Box 1917, Boston, MA 02205; distributed by: Distributed Art Publishers, (800) 338-BOOK].

10. Guest, review of Susan Gevirtz's *Narrative's Journey: The Fiction and Film Writing of Dorothy Richardson* (Peter Lang Publishers, 1996), in *Sulfur* 40 (Spring 1997), pp. 186-188.

11. Guest, "A Reason for Poetics," *Ironwood* 24 (1984), pp. 153-155.

12. Cole's "The Poetics of Vertigo," which Guest originally heard delivered to The Poetry Center and American Poetry Archives at San Francisco State University, has since been published in the *Denver Quarterly* 34: 4 (Winter 2000), pp. 71-99; the passage about the "asocial radicality claimed by and for poetry" appears on p. 86.

13. Marjorie Welish, "The Lyric Lately (a work-in-progress)," *Jacket* #10 http://www.jacket.zip.com.au/jacket10/welish-on-guest.html.

14. "On Some Motifs in Baudelaire," p. 155.

15. See Adorno, "On Lyric Poetry and Society," pp. 43-46. [Adorno's "On Lyric Poetry and Society," in accord with his work in general, often uses the terms *totality* and/or *objectivity* to signify society, or rather, to designate the genuinely social, objective reality that dominant forces in society do not and/or cannot articulate about the society they dominate.]

16. Far from rejecting or condemning lyric, Guest has tried to suggest that her impulse toward it is so powerful that, if her musicality is to figure in the tradition of critical lyric and not simply overwhelm it, lyric impulse must be initially resisted: that is, it must be kept in tense relationship to what would seem the non or minimally lyric (i.e., kept in something like charged suspension, as an intensely stretched undersong, an apparently mute but in fact barely beneath the surface verbal music). For an excellent discussion see Welish, "The Lyric Lately (a work-in-progress)." See also Terence Diggory's insightful contrast between Guest's work and language-identified poetics, "Barbara Guest and the Mother of Beauty," presented at the Barnard College conference "Where Lyric Tradition Meets Language Poetry: Innovation in Contemporary American Poetry by Women," April 1999; the essay will be published in a special issue—focussed on Guest and edited by Catherine Kasper—of *Women's Studies: An Interdisciplinary Journal.*

17. See Welish's discussion in "The Lyric Lately (a work-in-progress)" of Guest's composition processes.

18. For sustained discussion of these points see Kaufman, "Red Kant, or The Persistence of the Third *Critique* in Adorno and Jameson," *Critical Inquiry* 26:4 (Summer 2000).

19. For extended treatment of the topic see Kaufman, "Negatively Capable Dialectics: Keats, Vendler, Adorno, and the Theory of the Avant-Garde," *Critical Inquiry* 27:2 (Winter 2001). For discussion of a somewhat parallel dialogue between late twentieth-century and Romantic experimentalism see Kaufman, "Everybody Hates Kant: Blakean Formalism and the Symmetries of Laura Moriarty," *Modern Language Quarterly* 61:1 (March 2000).

20. Keats's letter to Richard Woodhouse on the poetical character is dated October 27, 1818; the negative-capability letter, written to George and Tom Keats, is dated December 21-27, 1817. The texts are included in most editions of, or anthology excerpts from, Keats's *Letters*.

21. I am grateful to Francine Masiello for directing my attention to the scope of this Latin American reception.

22. See, e.g., Kathleen Fraser, "Barbara Guest: The location of her (A memoir)" and "'One Hundred and Three Chapters of Little Times': Collapsed and transfigured moments in the cubist fiction of Barbara Guest" in Fraser's *Translating the Unspeakable: Poetry and the Innovative Necessity* (Tuscaloosa and London: University of Alabama Press, 2000), pp. 124-130, 161-173; Marjorie Welish, "The Lyric Lately (a work-in-progress)" [cited in n.13 above] and Welish's review of *Fair Real-*

ism in *Sulfur* 26 (Spring 1990), pp. 213-215; Susan Gevirtz, "Belief's Afterimage," *Jacket* #10 http://www.jacket.zip.com.au/jacket10/guest-by-gevirtz.html; Rachel Blau DuPlessis, "The Flavor of Eyes: *Selected Poems* by Barbara Guest," *Women's Review of Books* 13 (1995), pp. 23-24, and "'All My Vast/Journeying Sensibility': Barbara Guest's Recent Work," *Sulfur* 39 (1996), pp. 39-48; Barbara Einzig. "The Surface as Object: Barbara Guest's *Selected Poems, American Poetry Review* (Jan/Feb 1996), pp. 7-10; Brenda Hillman, "The Artful Dare: Barbara Guest's *Selected Poems*," *Talisman* 16 (Fall 1996), pp. 207-220; Sara Lundquist, "Reverence and Resistance: Barbara Guest, Ekphrasis, and the Female Gaze," *Contemporary Literature* 38:2 (1997), pp. 260-286; and Norma Cole, untitled poem with dedication "for Barbara Guest" in Cole, *The Vulgar Tongue* (San Francisco: a+bend press, 2000), p. 3 [a+bend press is distributed through jilith@aol.com].

Catherine Kasper (essay date fall 2001)

SOURCE: Kasper, Catherine. Review of *Rocks on a Platter: Notes on Literature. Chicago Review* 47, no. 3 (fall 2001): 145-48.

[*In the following essay, Kasper offers a review of* Rocks on a Platter: Notes on Literature.]

Rocks on a Platter contains some of Barbara Guest's most obscure and compelling lines since ***Defensive Rapture*** (1993). It has been interpreted by other reviewers as one long poem that examines the "implacable poet" as subject and vector in the process of creative production. While that may be the case, these poems are also literally "notes" on literature, as its subtitle suggests. The book can be seen as Guest's own jottings in response to her inspiring and eclectic research, with texts dissected and arranged to become poetic objects resonating as in a still-life painting.

Guest was one of the central members of the New York School, though David Lehman (in *The Last Avant-Garde*) omits her in favor of an unnecessarily reductive, masculine view of the group. It could be argued that Guest's work, and perhaps Guest herself, is more radically individual, and less easily summarized. Canonical practices have typically excluded such writers in favor of more homogenous categorization. While this tendency has long been under critical scrutiny, the practice of dropping particularly influential, but often more clairvoyant poets from critical schema persists (see, for instance Alan Kaufman's omission of Edward Dorn and his connections to Black Mountain and the Beats from *The Outlaw Bible of American Poetry*). But what critics

fail to recognize or like to forget is how different kinds of poets still speak to each other, still have friendships and discussions that are crucial to artistic germination whether or not they share the same aesthetics. The best poetry demonstrates this kind of complex engagement with different kinds of poetry and with a greater, interdisciplinary community. Most recently, Guest's work has been noted as one of the foundational influences for what could be considered a feminist "wing" of post-L=A=N=G=U=A=G=E poets such as Kathleen Fraser, Brenda Hillman, Mei-mei Berssenbrugge, Lisa Jarnot, Juliana Spahr, and Jena Osman.

Intrinsic to the New York School's poetics was a fundamental cross-fertilization with the visual arts. Painters such as Motherwell, Freilicher, and Rivers were just a few of those whose work and ideas coalesced with those of the poets. Frank O'Hara worked at MOMA and Ashbery worked as an art critic, as did Guest. Her own work often achieves a kind of poetic equivalent to Abstract Expressionism, forcing the literary critic to work with the vocabulary of the art critic: abstraction replaces representation, patina replaces simple imagery, chiaroscuro, diction. Her poetry reveals a primacy of page as "canvas" that draws from modernist sources, yet achieves a texture which is distinctly postmodern in its absence of a central, controlling ego.

That Guest is the artist of the collage on the cover of ***Rocks on a Platter*** confirms that her close relationship to the visual arts and to artists is one of the fertile resources of her work. The collage is composed of several subtle, textured surfaces in nearly indistinguishable tones of gray, black, white, and beige. The collage, like the poetry, appears to be composed of shadows, of water and sand as much as of paper. Placement here is as imbued with meaning as the weighty rocks. This cover evokes "natural" sculpture: nature "placed" on a created surface.

Rocks on a Platter is concerned with nature and the natural world, from the "flotsam of the world of appearances" to its "wet earth." One vision which emerges from these "Notes" is that of the natural world as element and object, as force and "life," animate and inanimate. Land is both ship's destiny or conquest and the very limits of language, "ground" is earth and page:

>   Ship
>   shoal   rocks
>
> to approach this land raving!
>
> Rocks, platter, words, words . . .
> X'   mammoth teeth.
>
>   (3)

The book begins with the aqueous beginnings of earth, with "Dreams set by / typography" like a ship in an immense sea. Ideas find themselves in trees and typography, on shore and ship. These "ideas" evolve into an impetus for prose, which yields an archetypal fairytale about children, a wolf, a king, and "baked apples." "Mobility" is "interseamed with print" in a voyage through printed texts: from "secular" mythologies, to references to Keats's "Urn" and other literary milestones, to the final, illusive or heavenly "Dolphin God," who "swims" on the page as a soon-extinct natural wonder, provoking a quotation from Hölderlin: "In ancient times / Heavenly Beings made sense of themselves and how / they have made off with the strength of the Gods."

We travel by way of "Childe Harold"—Browning's poem written amidst nineteenth century re-definitions of "nature"—moving from Darwin to Freud to Nietzsche. Quotations from Hegel, Adorno, and Hölderlin are interspersed with references to Williams, Eliot, and H. D., and quotations from Dr. Samuel Johnson: "To invest abstract ideas with form, and animate them with activity has always been the right of poetry." This poetic collage tries to get at the "reality" that is not an "empirical inner and outer world" but a "truer reality." This is something much of Guest's poetry confronts: those things that cannot be said, or those things that are suggested by gaps and silences, in the given air between the arrangement of "rocks." In this way, her art often creates "sacred places" where those emotions or intuitive bits of knowledge that are most difficult to express can be evoked. It is the place where human creation (platter) and earthly creation (rock) meet, where they work, often paradoxically, to become a third, entirely other thing that is neither artificial nor natural. In the following lines a kind of gardening becomes "story," an activity invested with plant-like "fragrance" which grows from both soil and words into its own life:

> She digs with her fingernails into the earth while
> speaking and
>
> weeping. Her face is also
> introduced into the story:
> a fragrant narration.
>
> (5)

Guest recognizes a nature which is no longer the "capital N" powerful nature but instead one which has become moveable as an object. It is a natural world with a late twentieth century lingering guilt: we believe we are capable of arranging it to our liking, to such an extent, perhaps, that we must try in a kind of quiet, desperate invocation to summon the return of some "Dolphin God." Beyond early American desires to "control" nature or tame it, beyond the atomic age recognition of our ability to obliterate it and ourselves, this is a kind of prophesy of a new age:

> An episode with new palm trees.
> Words in magnetic order

> Words in natural order.
>
> Vulnerable Dolphin skin
> and magnetic skin.
>
> (48)

This "magnetic" order of nature asks for an intuitive world, a "charged" set of relationships which imbues the world with a life both "vulnerable" and "magnetic." The natural "order" refers to that of language as well. In Guest's poetry, the "field" of poetry is "charged," which is one of the clearest keys, perhaps, to understanding Guestian poetics which emerge from Olson's "breath." Word placement substitutes "place" (Olson's Gloucester) as words themselves hold their own histories. And how better to "conduct" this charge than to flood the field with water—"the watered page,"—water whose immeasurable depths give the illusion of surface? "Entry into waterfield," she writes, "is the wax waterfield, / and savaging." ***Rocks on a Platter*** begins and ends in water, is at once a statement of poetics, a collage of literary and philosophical influences and responses, and an enigmatic key to Guest's oeuvre.

Sara Lundquist (essay date 2001)

SOURCE: Lundquist, Sara. "The Fifth Point of a Star: Barbara Guest and The New York 'School' of Poets." *Women's Studies: An Interdisciplinary Journal* 30 (2001): 11-41.

[*In the following essay, Lundquist examines Guest's literary reputation and places her among the five writers who were the originators of the New York School of poets in the 1950s and 1960s.*]

James Schuyler wrote in 1971 (with exasperated humor) to his friend and fellow poet, Barbara Guest, about what he believed was a general but mistaken belief that only Kenneth Koch, John Ashbery, and Frank O'Hara constituted the originators and core group of New York poets. "They do not realize that the Founders of the NY school [. . .] are not a trefoil, but a star, a five-pointed star, at the very least" (Guest papers). The star emblem allows for the happier inclusion, from his point of view, of himself and Guest in the group of poetic innovators known collectively for their celebrations of the energies of New York City, their passion for painting, especially abstract expressionism, their high-spirited wit and fondness for comedy, their experiments in surrealism and fantasy, their irony, their refusal of linguistic and social decorum, and for their poetic "method" of paying attention. From among the original five friends and obscure avant-gardians, Ashbery and O'Hara broke out to become the best-known, the ones accorded national attention, premier publishing venues, and academic canonization. Over the years, Koch and Schuyler (despite the latter's worry in this regard) have also won their fair share of attention and fame. Guest, as David Lehman offhandedly comments in his recent history of the New York school poets, has remained unsung, "the odd woman out" in critical appraisals of the group (244). Lehman's book, published by Doubleday in 1998, is described on its jacket as "a landmark work of cultural history." Yet, although it includes a detailed and appreciative chapter on each of the four other New York poets, it bafflingly extends to century's end one sort of official disregard to Guest. This despite a keen and pleasured, albeit belated, second embracing of Guest's particular contribution to American poetry during the last ten years or so by readers, fellow poets, and critics. Of Lehman's missed opportunity, one contributor to an email list-serve grumbled: "Would it have killed him to include a chapter on Barbara Guest?"

It may not have killed him, but it would have upset the theme and the form of Lehman's book to do so, for he makes much of the New York school as "the last avant-garde," a kind of guy gang, a band of rivals, who shared a "fraternal sympathy" with each other. He names a number of life and career circumstances experienced in common by at least three of the four men. David Yezzi's review of the book succinctly summarizes Lehman's characterization of their complex groupings, with O'Hara always serving as the common denominator: "All (save Schuyler) overlapped at Harvard, all (save Koch) were homosexual, all (save Ashbery) did military service, all (save Koch) reviewed art and all (save Ashbery, who soon moved to Paris) lived in New York during their formative years as poets." The neatness of this formulation, for one thing, would have been twisted by the fact of Guest's real presence, her complicating alignments and disalignments.

Lehman justifiably claims that his four "deviated boldly from the prevailing idea of masculinity in the 1950s and early '60s," given that three of them were homosexual, and that all proclaimed and performed an unapologetic aestheticism (13). Surely, a consideration of a woman poet's contribution to this critique of masculinity could only have added to the truth and complexity of the argument. For one thing, the very fact that the four of them did not consider her gender in judging her poetry or in counting her an intimate friend itself serves as a critique of the literary preserves and privileges of masculinity. But in choosing to concentrate at all, Lehman writes, "I must stint other admirable writers in their circle." He claims that the four poets "secretly" believed in their exclusive foursome, citing as proof of this secret belief a 1959 letter from Schuyler to Ashbery about contributions to *Locus Solus*, the literary magazine then in the planning stage (12), which was to become so crucial in finding and distributing experimental poetry during the early '60s.

Lehman writes: "When I lecture on the New York School, I am sometimes asked why relatively few women were involved in the movement. I reply that this is not true of its later manifestations." He cites as examples the poets Anne Waldman, Bernadette Mayer, Maureen Owen, and Alice Notley (12-13). But for Lehman to deflect the question to the second generation is surely to further erase the one woman who *was* there, and who no doubt, as least as much as her male friends, contributed to latter-day possibilities for poetry and for women in New York. Kathleen Fraser (for one) but she credits Barbara Guest's writing (in combination with that of Adrienne Rich) with her "awakening" to a new poetics whose source was in the as-yet-unexplored perspectives of modernist women writers. She found in Guest's work superior permissions and liberations based in "tenacious insistence on the primacy of reinventing language structures in order to catch one's own at-oddness with the presumed superiority of the central mainstream vision" (31). Fraser also wrote:

> I would like to note, particularly, Guest's generosity toward younger women aspiring to the vocation of poetry. It was the exception in the Sixties, when the word *mentor* more than often implied token male sponsorship based on dubious power relations. Her friendship was offered in dignity, assumed reciprocity of value and complementarity of interests [. . .]. Guest continues to provide a model for those of us engaged in finding full parity for women in the reading/writing community, beyond token representation.
>
> (127)

Other poets have declared their debt of gratitude to Guest's work and example: Susan Howe, Mei-mei Berssenbrugge, Rosmarie Waldrop, Rena Rossenwasser, Charles North, Charles Bernstein, Molly McQuade, Rachel Blau DuPlessis, Brenda Hillman, Marjorie Welish, Susan Gevirtz, Harry Mathews, Ann Lauterbach, Barbara Einzig, to mention a few. She is known, writes Robert Kaufman, "as a supreme poet's poet, known even as the New York School's most genuinely experimental, aesthetically fearless and uncompromising artist" (11). And as Paul Hoover points out, "she has had a greater following among younger poets than any New York school member other than John Ashbery.

Probably the publication in 1995 of **Selected Poems** marked a turning point and sparked a desire to reassess Guest's achievement. Her work has been very well represented in recent anthologies: Douglas Messerli's *From the Other Side of the Century* (1994), Paul Hoover's *Postmodern American Poetry* (1994) and the latest (4th) edition of the "canon-defining" *Norton Anthology of Poetry,* 1996. The Poetry Society of America awarded her on April 23, 1999 the prestigious Frost Medal, previously received by Wallace Stevens and Marianne Moore. The same month she appeared as an honored guest at a crucial conference about experimental poetry at Barnard College in New York. Important critical work includes, of course, this issue of *Women's Studies: An Interdisciplinary Journal* and *The Scene of My Selves: New Work on New York Poets* edited by Terence Diggory and Stephen Paul Miller, which contains four essays on Guest. Internet magazines of poetry and poetics have been very keen to obtain work by and about Guest.

One must look back, however, to re-establish Guest's centrality to the group of friends who found themselves fashioned during the postwar era into a "school" and to narrate her relationships with the four men who were the other "points of the star." During the 1950s and '60s Barbara Guest contributed, more centrally than has usually been acknowledged, to the group's sense of identity, as it shifted and changed and evolved and came to be seen as a literary and historical event. To paint it as an entirely male phenomenon, albeit one that investigated and parodied oppressive socially-constructed notions of masculinity, is to distort the truth. She was there. She gave poetry readings; she published; she had her plays produced; she wrote gallery reviews for *Art News* and collaborated with painters (notably Grace Hartigan, Helen Frankenthaler, and Mary Abbott); she served briefly as the poetry editor of *Partisan Review*; she partied and joked and visited and traveled, corresponded, fought and made up with the other four poets; they admired her work, she admired theirs. They wrote letters and poems to and about her, and she wrote letters and poems to and about them. She was one of what Lehman calls the "band of rivals," for whom "competitiveness provided an incentive to excel" (85). John Bernard Myers at the Tibor de Nagy Art Gallery followed the crucial publishing of O'Hara's *A City Winter* in 1952, Koch's *Poems* and Ashbery's *Turandot* in 1953 with ***The Location of Things,*** Barbara Guest's first book in 1960 (and then with Schuyler's *May 24th or So,* 1966). Her name was then and is now included in literary histories of the period. Her work was printed in important mid-century and subsequent anthologies of American poetry. This cannot be mere tokenism, but the tip of an iceberg under which lies a complicated real story and a substantial body of work that only requires attention to shine.

Four poems by Barbara Guest appeared in Donald Allen's *The New American Poetry* (1960), an anthology that is widely credited for identifying poets with the energy and confidence capable of disturbing the becalmed waters of mid-century academic verse. Myers included more than twenty pages of Guest's work in *The Poets of the New York School* (1969), with the result that the *New York Times* reviewer wrote: "to my mind, the presence of Barbara Guest in the Myers book almost balances the weight of the other poets" (Lask). In the introduction, Myers described her work and its affinity with the others': their debt to Breton's surreal-

ism, their excitability, their attention to brilliant surfaces. Myers thought constantly about his coterie of poets and how they might be described and promoted. "Honey, send me a good poem about a page long," he wrote to Guest in 1961.

> I have been asked by a California mag called *Nomad* to edit a NY School presentation of about 20 pages with a tiny forward. My line is as follows [. . .] the new work is marked by a clear understanding of the word as *different* from the thing it stands for, an absence of simile, and a new rhetoric based on daily events [. . .]. The tone is never merely personal. The humor can be either *noir* or *blanche*—and sometimes both. The new poetry is urban, colloquial, but never corny. It is not "poetic." Send me a poem [. . .]. I'm having Berkson, Koch, O'Hara, Schuyler, Ashbery, and Elmslie. OK?
>
> (Guest papers)

Ron Padgett and David Shapiro's *An Anthology of New York Poets* of the following year on the other hand, was something of a shock and a sobering lesson to Kathleen Fraser, just beginning to make her own way among the poets in New York:

> When the second generation of the New York School emerged full of ego and ambition, a major anthology came out. Barbara Guest, a major figure in the painting and poetry scene throughout the Fifties and Sixties, publishing her poems and art criticism in many New York magazines and reading on various New York School programs—by then, author of three poem collections and one monograph on the painter Robert Goodnough—was left out of the anthology. Meanwhile, twenty-six men were included—some of them brilliant poets [. . .], others merely adequate camp followers. [. . .] Guest's erasure was my first in-person encounter with this common historic practice.
>
> (29-30)

"No matter how it is parsed, this is a shocking erasure," writes DuPlessis, one that checked the desire of readers and writers to know Guest as fully as they might otherwise have. A combination of a "cavalier attitude" evinced by avant-grade artists toward the women among them, and a distrust of language-centered poetries among the more essentialist feminist groups, according to DuPlessis, contributed to Guest's comparative lack of visibility after that first most intense decade or so ("Gendered Marvelous" 190, "Flavor" 23).

Yet, the poets of her own generation knew intimately what kind of role she played during that particular moment in literary history and how she contributed to their maverick and instigatory poetics. The letters preserved in the Guest archive at the Beinecke library attest to her valued entanglement in the by-now-famous web of vital friendship that the poets and painters wove. In demonstration, it is worth quoting directly from some of these teasing, funny, intimate, and affectionate letters.

In a characteristic letter, John Ashbery wrote to Guest from Paris:

> It was nice of you to say all those things about my poetry. I have been wondering increasingly if I haven't been barking up the wrong Trees [no doubt a reference to Ashbery's first book *Some Trees*, published in 1956]. [. . .] To have you say they mean something to you means very much to me—I don't know how else to phrase it! You know how very much I love yours which are quite different. I was just rereading "Candles [?]" which impressed me with its subtle false perspectives, shiftings of emphasis just where you don't expect it; a screen suddenly turns out to be a passageway and vice versa. The sum of all this is to set up quite a few currents of air which are very refreshing to breathe. Which is so rare in poetry now—being able to breathe I mean. I love the spaces between the things in your poems. [. . .] It will be lovely to see you in France which I hope will come to pass, especially in the south of it where the air is so wonderful it makes breathing a pleasure, as in your poems, rather than a duty. (There is some very nice smell in the air around Aix which seemingly can't be traced to anything that grows there). Give my love to Trumbull and any of my friends you see, especially Jane Hazan, and please hie thee hither at the first opportunity.

>   (Guest papers)

After Guest's **The Location of Things** was issued by Tibor de Nagy, Ashbery wrote:

> Dear Barbara, Here we are in drear-nighted November and I still haven't written to tell you that I think your book is the greatest thing since Hesiod. I have been meaning to many times but every time I start I feel like you when you walk down the Avenue de Messine. Anyway I've told so many returning travellers about it that I'm sure some word must have leaked back to you. **'All Gray-Haired My Sisters'** made me shed salt tears on Majorca. Harry Mathews loves them too, and he is going to print up a separate little folder of your work in the magazine and send you some for gift giving. One interesting thing about your work is that you employ the pronoun "I" a great deal, though you never seem to be talking about yourself. That is what poetry ought to do (the two together I mean).

>   (Guest papers)

Two postcards in 1961 from Ashbery: "John M. told me you're having a *hard*-backed book published and I'm wild with joy. Would you like to send some more poems for *Locus Solus*? I'm doing #3 which will be all poetry and very far out, I hope. Paris hath need of thee—I often think of you and of the restaurant on St. Germain where we had lunch and where I still go"; and: "the poems [. . .] are beautiful—rather like coming upon a city built in some completely new architectural style. Love to everybody except that mysterious unnamed unnamable person. John."

Frank O'Hara sent a typescript in 1956 of what has become one of his best-known poems, "A Step Away From Them," along with a typically lighthearted note:

"I thought you might like to see this little thing, which now that I type it over again [. . .] seems very flat. Do you think it would be better if I just wrote it all backwards? Da.DA" (Guest papers). And in 1959:

> Dear Barbara, How is the most beautiful poet of the English (and probably any other) speaking world today? I've been thinking of how lovely you looked, like a mirage, the other day and what an unexpected joy it was to see you [. . .]. I am so glad I got to sit next to you and Kenneth. [. . .] And I still don't see why we could't have been sitting upstairs at the bar underneath the Lippold, all jangling and quivering like a field of mushrooms at the approach of John Cage, or wading in one of the front fountains as is, so often, our wont. Now if I can only keep a firm hold on "Piazzas" [Guest's poem] in my memory I may get through all right. I am going to ask Grace [Hartigan] to let me copy it, if I may, and if she will really consent to let it out of her hands for a day which is doubtful. [. . .] Now I am also going to enclose a couple of poems and hope this will make you do likewise when you write me (and soon?). Best to Trumbull and the children, Love, Frank.

>   (Guest papers)

His notes and letters were full of jokes about publishing, which show how he understood their fortunes to be joined: "I am so delighted that *Partisan* is going to take 'Ode to Joy'—will you have something in the same issue? I hope so, it will bring us luck to follow our chain of appearances, *Folder, The Blue Angel*, and ultimately *The Sands*, leading us at last, but unerringly, to the National Book Award and the Academy Award Dinner, you in white fox and me in a TV blue evening shirt and moccasins." And: "I forgot to tell you just now that Kenneth just sold a poem to POETRY—and him so obscure [. . .]. I can't *believe* they understand. Maybe they are branching out, so why don't you send something. I think I'll send my James Dean poems to *The American Scholar* and let them worry about them, anything to get them out of the house—or maybe *Sewanee Review* would be interested." At the end, a hand written "Pfui!" (Guest papers).

James Schuyler sent Guest a poem he had dedicated to her, scribbling in the margins: "Dear Barbara, Is not this tattered cobweb worthy of Herrick? I like to think so! love, J." And he actively solicited her work:

> John Ashbery and Harry Mathews (do you know him?) have decided to conjure a new little magazine out of air and paper, and I'm to edit it. Its policy of course, will be class, which of course means (I hope) you. [. . .] [S]o far as I'm able to control things, it won't be printed on lumpy paper and bound in that rather ugh stuff they dug up for Frank's "Meditations." It's to be called *Locus Solus*, in honor of the great Roussel, and I've already wormed "Easter" out of Frank [. . .] and from Kenneth "Bertha" and a poem in the style of Roussel that sounds exactly like Kenneth. It's mostly a description of someone pasting a postage stamp on a

letter and, as John A. would say, is intensely moving. I hope you'll send me something—a group would be nice, recent or not recent, as you please, or both. As you know I'm a devotee of your poetry, and I thought the last two I saw in *Noonday* were superb. If Proust had recreated Anna de Naailles as a first rate poet, I think her work would have resembled yours. I hate asking for manuscripts when no money is going to change hands, but I think *Locus Solus* will be handsome; it won't be camp; and since money isn't involved I see no reason for including anything that isn't grand. I hope to hear and receive. My best to T. Love, Jimmy.

(Guest papers)

About the beginnings of this fervent artistic and social life in New York City, Frank O'Hara wrote years later: "we were all in our early twenties. John Ashbery, Barbara Guest, Kenneth Koch and I, being poets, divided our time between the literary bar, the San Remo, and the artists' bar, the Cedar Tavern. In the San Remo, we argued and gossiped: in the Cedar we often wrote poems while listening to the painters argue and gossip. [. . .] [F]or most of us non-Academic and indeed non-literary poets [. . .] the painters were the only generous audience for our poetry, and most of us read first publicly in art galleries or at The Club" (qtd. in Perloff 58-59). Guest herself wrote this to her relatives in 1952:

Last Wednesday my poems were read at the Art Club which is the center, socially and ideally for most of the painters here. I think I told you that a short time before I and two others read our poems at a gathering at Latouche's, the song-writer's penthouse. A very nice evening, lots of rich, young, talented, beautiful people and loads of food and drinks, and I quite the queen of it all. It's funny how a little fame spreads so rapidly, ever since the publication in *Partisan Review*. Well *PR* is *the* review, but I had no idea I'd be taken up and be introduced everywhere as Barbara G., 'the poet.' But New York is so small, so intimate, you keep crossing and recrossing the same circles and everyone knows everyone else, so that once you crash the fringes you are to a degree in.

(Guest papers)

She was in, of course, because her work corresponded aesthetically and thematically with that of this group of high-spirited, inventive, urbane, anti-academic, and painterly New York poets, and because she had her own provocative voice among them. Like them she eschewed the kind of overly earnest, melodramatic, conscience-ridden, serious poetry of the day with its formal imperatives, and its ponderous tones. She wrote sometimes like O'Hara with bristling and sensual appreciation of art and everyday life, sometimes like Ashbery, with a meandering personal surrealism, like Koch, but with subtler comedy like Schuyler, in alert, casual, tender descriptions of the natural and social worlds. She had her own sense of the mystery of things, the way people and objects occupy space, of gorgeous surfaces, and suggestive depths. Myers wrote: "The very rhythm of her lines implies a quicker breathing. [. . .] We are confronted with a newly found world that fills her and the reader with astonishment, with wonder" (25). Indeed all five of the poets were buoyant with intelligence, youth, and talent, all five impatient to write their own kind of poetry, to express their wonder at being alive and in New York City, all five ready to have their day. They wrote poetry with a startling sense of immediacy which was closely connected to the historical moment of its creation. Of course, to all of them, with their anti-programmatic good sense, the inflated concept of a New York "school" was something of a joke and a lark, sometimes indeed an embarrassment, a nuisance, and a limitation. However, if "New York School" must exist as a critical, literary, or historical category (and Lehman's book decisively promotes it as all of these), then discussions of it must include Guest as a defining and foundational "member."

Guest's early poems can be read in such a way as to show how clearly they qualify as a writing that expresses the group sensibility of the New York School. It is only in describing her work, explicating it, shining critical attention on it, that one can begin to repair the odd lack of detailed published discussion of its author's achievement. Indeed it remains to say what her individual achievement *was,* how it partakes of, departs, from, and transcends that very group ethos and aesthetic in which it is grounded. What is her particular subject and style? Is there anything particularly feminine or feminist about Guest's work? What did it mean to be a woman poet of the first generation of the New York School?

"Safe Flights" appeared in Guest's first book of poems in 1960, was included in Myers's inaugural New York school anthology in 1969, and was chosen by Guest for her *Selected Poems* of 1995. It was written during the time of the five friends' greatest geographical proximity and their most intimate cohesion as like-minded practitioners of experimental poetry. Like so much of their work, **"Safe Flights"** declines traditional verse form in favor of a more unusual organizing principle, in this case the anaphoric repetition of the phrase "to no longer" in two sentences of 13 lines each. It also avoids the lyrical pronoun "I," of which these poets were so wary and used so strangely, in favor of the second person "you" (that charming colloquial version of the pronoun "one," meaning "anyone of everybody, anyone whatever"). "You" lightens and brightens the poem with a certain tonic irony, lifting it out of the intense and agonizing self-focus of confessional poetry. The poem is a prime example of what Guest called "concealed autobiography," with its necessary and "deliberate ambiguity of the reigning person" ("Shifting Persona" 85), also a salient characteristic of Ashbery's poetry.

The subject of the poem is typically elusive, like an abstract painting by Pollock or Motherwell or Hartigan.

What *is* that a painting *of*? What is **"Safe Flights"** *about*? is a question difficult to answer in traditional terms. Like many of Guest's poems, it parries, at best, with mimesis. Indeed, Guest declares, the "poet whose sole urgency is his subject matter neglects the immensity of the depth to be rendered by Art" ("Mysteriously" 13). Other urgencies lie in the mysterious depths of spirit, timbre and tone, the play of language, range of reference, labyrinthine turns:

> To no longer like the taste of whisky
> A goldfinch in the breeze,
> To no longer wish winter to have explanations
> This is saying also no to you who are
> To lace your shoes in the snow
> With no need to remember,
> To no longer pull the two blankets
> Over your shoulders, to no longer feel the cold,
> To no longer pretend in the flower
> There is a secret, or in the earth a tomb,
> And no longer water on stone hurting the ear,
> Making those five noises of thunder
> And you tremble no longer.
> To no longer travel over mountains,
> Over small farms
> No longer the weather changing and the atmosphere
> Causing delicate breaks where the nerves confuse,
> To no longer have your name shouted
> And your birthmark again described,
> To no longer fear where the rapids break
> A miniature rock under your canoe,
> To no longer repeat the mirror is water,
> The house is a burden to the weak cyclone,
> You are under a tent where promises perform
> And the ring you grasp as an aerialist
> Glides, no longer.

>   (*Selected Poems* 17)

This subtle poem defies quick interpretation, despite its vivid materiality based in natural imagery. One might say that in the same way an abstract expressionist painting is about paint and the ways in which it meets and adheres to canvas, this poem is about words and the way they behave in lines and sentences. It draws attention to how very many emotively powerful verbs can follow the phrase "to no longer": *like, wish, need to remember, pull, feel, pretend, tremble, travel, fear.* What wistfulness and yearning inheres in these varied infinitives linked with a negated adverb of continuing action: *no longer.* In its tonal complexity, the poem renders its emotional state directly through sound and repetitive syntax rather than through meaning as meaning is usually understood. The New York School poets are known for just this particular sensitivity to the medium, to the look and feel and effect of word assemblage. Subject matter, rhetoric, argument, overt ideology have mattered less to them than new perception, approaches to the mysterious links between language and feeling. Writing about Kenneth Koch, Myers claims "the color and timbre of individual words, as well as clusters of words, *is* what poetry is [. . .]. The impact derives

from the surfaces: fat sounds, tinny sounds, smooth phrases, jagged phrases, silences, spaces, definite metre, no metre, occasional rhymes or half-rhymes, or even snatches of prose" (23-4). Guest wrote also of the "flesh of a poem. Even as a painting has flesh. The vibrancy of its skin." **"Safe Flights"** is a poem on just such vibrant emotional high-alert. Biographical details pertaining to the life of Barbara Guest, the person, are not revealed, but emotional experience is fully and candidly exposed, without self-pity or narcissism. She practices what George Butterick and Robert J. Bertholf have called, in relation to O'Hara's personal poems, a "detailed realism of feelings" (216). The poem evinces that quality Guest has named as one crucial to the art she admires: "a glowing impersonal empathy" ("Under the Shadow" 17).

Like so many of the poems in *The Location of Things,* this poem examines and performs the emotional dislocations and costs of change, a theme Guest made her own. "Am I to understand change, whether remarkable or hidden?" she wonderingly and plaintively asks in the first poem of that first book. The self of **"Safe Flights"** is in a state of flux, imagining another kind of self who no longer does, thinks, sees, feels the things she now does, both wanting and fearfully rejecting that new and as yet undefined self. The poem catalogues and then imagines away all things its "you" is accustomed to, from liking "the taste of whisky," to "feel[ing] the cold," to "hav[ing] your name shouted / And your birthmark again described." This last presents such an apt synecdoche of the intimate tedium of family life—surely each of the various scenarios makes a similarly succinct representation of past and ongoing sensual, imaginative, and "real" experience. These are things that have been true, and for some time, and often, and are now imagined as if true "no longer." Which of these particulars of "no longer," keenly imagined as elements of self, will be missed and yearned after? Which might be gratefully put down? Under the repeated "no longer" lie two potent and contradictory "if's": both the sense of "If these changes were to come to pass, I would no longer be myself, and thus be utterly lost," and the sense of "If only I could be free of these internal and external circumstances that have always so defined me." The repetition of the phrase "to no longer" is incantatory, employing its magic both for self-protection and self-projection. The very verb tense of the poem expresses a sense that the moment, any moment, is a flux, a turning point, a rich emotional conundrum, simultaneously a becoming and a lapsing. The word that names this tense is "infinitive," which, it can be noted, derives from the same Latin root as the words "unlimited," and "indefinite."

James E. B. Breslin has written of the New York poets, that they are "skeptical of rest, finality, or the comforts of a fixed position," that they love "plurality and movement, and of all their generation they are the most engaged with process, ongoingness, temporality" (1098). O'Hara wrote in 1959: "It may be that poetry makes life's nebulous events tangible to me and restores their detail; or conversely, that poetry brings forth the intangible quality of incidents which are all too concrete and circumstantial. Or each on specific occasions, or both all the time" ("Statement" 420). **"Safe Flights"** is only one of Guest's many poems that exhibit these selfsame skepticisms and passions, similar tangible intangibilities, and sensitivity to the prescient, the possible, the about-to-be. She is not anchored, but floating, exquisitely suspended in the "stranger ocean" of that most frequently anthologized, deliciously wry love poem from the early '60s, **"Parachutes, My Love, Could Carry Us Higher."**

Guest must have sensed opportunity and space in this aesthetic milieu for poetry of remarkable expressiveness, unhampered by societal expectations of the feminine, or by prejudices in literary circles about women's capacities as artists. Though seldom overtly gendered, and often strikingly different from them in tone, Guest's early poems about change can be read as of a piece with other women's poetry of the 1950s and 1960s that prepares to countenance and promote personal and cultural shifts of some magnitude. Guest believed she lived at a time when "the imagination [was] at its turning," when one could feel "the alphabet turning over," as she wrote in a poem dedicated to Mary Abbott, a time of risk, opportunity, and immense change, requiring a kind of unbridled and passionate language. She, like her male counterpart, James Schuyler, "freely espouses" in language charged with sensuality and celebration. She wrote poems even the most unfriendly critics could not read as the frail or lugubrious or static odes to love once thought to be the ruinous realm into which poetry by women was likely to fall.[1] If her persona is a lover, she is also "a heroine, an aerialist, an acrobat, a parachutist, a deep-sea diver, a pioneer, an adventuress, [. . .] and a restless traveler" (Lundquist 162). In a poem of progress and movement [comparable to O'Hara's "Poem (Khrushchev is coming on the right day!)"] called "On the Way to Dumbarton Oaks," excitement explodes in a series of exclamations, responsive to the entire passing scene of a winter trip to Washington, D.C.:

> The air! The colonial air! the walls, the brick,
> this November thunder! The clouds atlanticking,
> Canadianning, Alaska snowclouds,
> tunnel and sleigh, urban and mountain routes!
>
> (*Selected Poems* 15)

Everywhere feelings of flux and huge openness, proper nouns turning verbal, walls and bricks transfigured by their proximity to cloud and air and thunder. Everywhere the stimulation of modes of moving about,—"tunnel

and sleigh, urban and mountain routes." To travel in the "ordinary" eastern United States is to experience, via the very air, the huge Atlantic, all of Canada, far-away Alaska. This is a form of ecstasy; as in O'Hara's poem "the light seems to be eternal / and joy seems to be inexorable / I am foolish enough always to find it in wind" (*Collected Poems* 340).

"Fresh air," and indeed an element of foolishness were what poetry so desperately needed, Kenneth Koch declaimed in his comic poetic rant so titled.[2] Ashbery (per his letter, quoted above) was wise to inhale a great burst of it from Guest's poetry, cognizant or not that an extra dimension of her aerated poetry was no doubt glad escape from dark forms of domesticity, the suffocation of "delicate prisons." That selfsame freedom, fresh air, and determined light-heartedness so good for poetry, if taken seriously by its practitioners, could also contribute to the liberation of women from prevailing modes of social rigidity. In fact, "Air" is a constant motif from the beginning to the present in Guest's work. Sixteen poems in *Poems: The Location of Things* (1962) contain the word "air"; her novel of 1978 is titled *Seeking Air*; her most recent collaboration (*Symbiosis* 2000) contains one of Guest's suggestively weightless, iridescent references to air (happily consonant with Laurie Reid's transparent paintings): "A suggestion in mid air / dropped on the hid body no never binding nothing / attached / no weight no thing to litter; / free as unusual" (14). Yet, to Guest, air is remarkably variable in its texture, sometimes almost palpable, certainly always painterly: "air braided of wind," "wild wooden air," "cracked as the air," "the now doubling air," "mirroring air," "air enriched by plants," "air in the arch is black," "thick air circling snow," "that immigrant air," "that avid air of chance hanging," "held in mortar air," "bronze liquid air," "idleways into air" to choose but a few examples. In the early 1950s, air was the poets' element of choice, their currency, their shared medium. Two of O'Hara's poems about Guest, "With Barbara at Larré's (1955)" and "With Barbara Guest in Paris (1955)," are lunch poems, "personisms," in-crowd poems, "burning conversation" poems, famous landmark poems, friendship poems, poems of easy allusion, poems which posit future greatness—all markers of the New York aesthetic, O'Hara-style. It is also worth nothing both are poems ending in references to air:

> "This is quite an aerial table,
> isn't it?" To such a tryst we cannot come
> so frequently, guarding the effervescent from
> the air, the air from all the burning conversations.
>
> (*Collected Poems* 228)

> Care for the lap of Mallarmé
> and the place where heroes fell down
> is right in our Pushkinesque enclosure
> as greatness sleeps outside

          smiles and bears
          the purple city air

          (Collected Poems 310)

Guest's "air" poem, "On the Way to Dunbarton Oaks," turns global, as if travel could capture the world and history, and as if it allowed the self access to all its own creative potential and peculiarity. Lynn Keller writes that "the speaker discovers the virtually inexhaustible resources of her own sensibility"; her traveling experience becomes "a source of plenitude, fertility, and erotic connection" (222). She is a poet, an artist, a singer of stanzas. In a series of inspired repetitions, body and stanza and Chinese tree are similarly described and quantified, echoing each other's beauty of shape and style. The traveler does not bother to deny or hide the wonderfully strange fact that one of her "three precise-nesses" just happens to be a tail, no less exquisite than head or body. This must be, in part, a funny and exuberant claiming of one's own (female) intellect and body, one's right to precise and particular sexual and artistic individuality:

     Chinese tree
     your black branches and your three yellow leaves
     with you I traffick. My three
     yellow notes, my three yellow stanzas,
     my three precisenesses
     of head and body and tail joined
     carrying my scroll, my tree drawing

     this winter day I'm
     a compleat travel agency with my Australian
     aborigine sights, my moccasin feet padding
     into museums where I'll betray all my vast
     journeying sensibility in a tear dropped before
     "The Treasure of Petersburg"

Museums bring the world to our shores, enabling a sophisticated kind of travel through time as well as place, in which one experiences many cultures and many levels of history almost simultaneously. Archaic spellings (a fond stylistic trait of the New York School poets) of the words "traffick," and "compleat" are perhaps included as elegant linguistic traces of such a history. Guest, of course, shows herself throughout her career to be as sensitive to what can be seen in museums as to what is found in nature. Ekphrastic poetry is a genre in which all the New York School painters excelled, with their passionately personal responses to visual art. In this poem, Guest's affinity to painting and her propensity for travel merge—the moment of destination is anticipated as a moment when the traveler, marked by physical evidence of her farflung voyages, feels a transport of pathos and aesthetic pleasure before a painting, which itself transports her from Washington, D.C. to St. Petersburg. The poem ends as ecstatically as it began:

          and gorgeous this forever
     I've a raft of you left over

          like so many gold flowers and so many white
          and the stems! the stems I have left!

Never one to eschew the exclamation point when she felt it called for, Guest proves herself to be, along with her fellow New York Poets, one of our postmodern poets of joy, of irreverence (even stems enjoy her celebratory interest!), of things in extravagant quantity—"*so many* gold flowers and *so many* white," absolute "*rafts*" of gorgeous "*forever*" (my hardly necessary added emphasis). Here, revealed in heightened perception and immoderate speech, is Guest's version of Breton's surrealistic "le mérveilleux" (noted as a feature of her poetry in general by Myers 25).

"In New York," wrote James Schuyler, "the art world is a painter's world: writers and musicians are in the boat, but they don't steer. [. . .] New York poets [. . .] are affected most by the floods of paint in which we all scramble" (*Selected Art Writings* 1). (Among that "we" he naturally includes Guest along with himself, John Ashbery, and Frank O'Hara). Herein lies another gap to be filled up in a scenario presented by Lehman: "These poets aligned themselves with modern painters in their crises, their conflicts, and their sense of artistic aspiration and romantic possibility. A pretty good idea of the aesthetics of the New York School could be gleaned from such work as Koch's 'The Artist,' Ashbery's 'The Painter,' and 'Self-Portrait in a Convex Mirror,' and O'Hara's 'Memorial Day, 1950' and 'Why I Am Not a Painter.'" To this, for information and delight, could be added Guest's **"Piazzas"** (dedicated to Mary Abbott), **"Heroic Stages"** (dedicated to Grace Hartigan), **"All Elegies are Black and White"** (about Robert Motherwell's paintings), **"Sand"** (sections of which Mary Abbott wrote into a "poem-painting" collaboration) and **"In the Middle of the Easel"** to mention poems only from Guest's first hard-bound book.[3] *Poems* (1962) also contains **"The Hero Leaves His Ship"** as well as an entire series of poems called **"Archaics"** meant to accompany lithographs by Grace Hartigan, in which she and the painter tempt each other to the heroism of lives dedicated to work and art, to the labor and the thrill of getting it right, to risky experimentalism. The poems which acknowledge and engage the work of women painter's have a special power and poignance in this regard: it is heartening to think of the example and support they must have provided for each other in their aspirations for careers in the arts.[4]

Like Schuyler, O'Hara, and Ashbery, Guest wrote art criticism as well as poetry. Like theirs, her articulation of the painters' procedures, gestures, and abstentions was an investigation of what could be usefully borrowed for poetry. She wrote of the poets' longing for painting, which would serves them as

     an associative art within whose eye the poet might
     gaze for reassurance and for a glowing impersonal

empathy. [. . .] Painters are the revolutionaries to whom writers turn in their desire to break from the solemnity of the judicious rules of their craft. This need to go on a rampage was felt by poets during the explosive era of Abstract Expressionism. [. . .] The physical extravagance of paint, of enormous canvases can cause a nurturing envy in the poet that prods his greatest possession, the imagination, into an expansion of its borders. As an art critic, who happened to be a poet, I was exposed to the temperament of the explosion of Abstract Expressionism, and my personal relationships with its painters certainly influenced the way I saw both nature and image.

                                                            (**"Under"** 16)

Guest wrote a substantial article about Helen Frankenthaler for *Arts Magazine* in 1975 in which the parallel is clear between her own artistic goals and procedures, and those of Frankenthaler's abstract expressionism. Discussing Frankenthaler's progress (from "Mountains and Sea" and "Eden" of the 1950s to "Circe" and "The Sound of the Bassoon" from the early 1970s), Guest observes: "The joy of life is ripe," and "One does not observe quiet thoughts here [. . .] [but] action, sophistication, the attitude of a city graduate" (58). Guest agrees with Frankenthaler's critics that "her intelligence is dominant in her painting," but she wants also to make a case for "the sensuous appliqué of the paint," "sensitive use of the unconscious," the influence of surrealism, "her manner of flaunting space" (59). She emphasizes the painter's boldness, wit, sophistication, and surety. Any of Guest's poems of the same period radiate alertness and maturity, disciplined wildness and surprise, gestural abandon with her medium, all qualities to which she was so attuned in Frankenthaler's work. The poems in *The Blue Stairs* (1968) can serve as examples of the way Guest offers poetry as "non-representational" as Frankenthaler's painting. Poems and paintings are equally bold in presentation, restless and colorful, rife with emotion, formally vivid and unsettling. In Frankenthaler's cover illustration, a great wash of blue billows from the left, until it meets mid-page a single thick blue crayon line, which bends to the pressure, but also stands, pliant and erect, against that mass of blue. In this section from **"Fan Poems,"** Guest uses the resources of her own medium: tender apostrophe, sentences disarrayed by line breaks, imagistic fragments, the intimacy of the pronouns "we," "us" and "our," metapoetic references to form and inspiration, sibilant use of alliteration, heightened diction, depth and reach of emotion straining against stanza form, disquietingly unconventional use of metaphor. No less than Frankenthaler, Guest's "methods consist of a series of surprises sprung on us through color and gesture" (59):

Windows, Melissa, they contain what is best
of us, the glass your arm has arranged
into crystal by spinning eye, by alarms
taken when the rain has chosen a form

unlike the universe, similar to ups and downs
which vary or change as cowslips
in the meadow we cross have a natural tint,
the panes reflect our hesitations and delight

Repeatedly striking, i.e., to strike the imagination
another blow, neither heat nor cold,
but the power in the wing, the chill
smothering feather outlined narrowly
by vertebrae extended for an instant;
it makes one shudder, the quick umbrella
unfurled near the tearful statue.

                                                    (*Selected Poems* 31-32)

One can find in Guest's early poems a good number which, like much women's poetry of the time, investigate mythology from a gendered perspective as well as with characteristic New York School brio and beauty. **"All Grey-haired My Sisters"** addresses itself widely and very tenderly to ancestresses and "adventuresses." The speaker wonders about the wanderings of ancient women, and imagines their long lost lives with sensual immediacy. The poem borrows some of the typical language of the Homeric epics, while sweetening and brightening it. In making herself the songstress of the unnamed and unsung, the speaker fills in some of the felt reality of female adventures, which have never been portrayed as epic and yet were still the stuff of life, and could be made the stuff of poetry:

All grey-haired my sisters
what is it in the more enduring
clime of Spring that waits?
[. . .]

                Sombre
mysteries the garden illumines
a shape of honey hive
the vigorous drones lighting
up your face as fortunes pour
from your cold pockets into the heat
and glaze, fortresses
for those memories brisk
in the now doubling air,

Adventuresses
guided by the form and scent
of tree and flower blossoming
the willow once frail now image
cut of stone so to endure,

My darlings
you walked into the wars
with wreaths of pine cones, you lay
by the sea and your sweet dresses
were torn by waves as over each receded-
and pebbles were lifted at your feet
in the foam,

[. . .]
In the broad strange light,
a region of silences, The delphic
clouded tree knows its decline,
If you were to forget animosities, girls,
and in the pagan grass slide heedlessly

blossoms would return such songs
as I've sung of you, the youthful ashes
fling upward settling fragrant
brightness on your dusky marquetry [. . .]

(*Poems* 15-16)

Italicized stanzas of impassioned apostrophe express the speaker's intense identification with the women yet preserve wonder at the elusive and unknowable otherness and remoteness of them. Notably, the poem imagines for them little complaint or female anger at wrongs and injustices, a by-now familiar staple of modern lyric poems reclaiming the voices of historical women. Instead there is an acknowledgment of their usually unacknowledged adventure: some travel to war and to sea, but others travel into beauty and sensuality, into "sombre / mysteries the garden illumines," into "the broad strange light, / a region of silences," into "this afternoon's seraphicness." The poem implies that spiritual, meditative, philosophical, and erotic knowledge can be garnered as much from domesticity and intricate communality as from war, travel, and politics. Guest doesn't portray her "sisters" as women dwarfed by privative circumstances, or as teachers primarily of endurance or rebellion, but as possessors of secret, voluptuous, hallowed knowledge that must be imagined to be accessed, since it is lost to literature: "such songs / as I've sung of you, the youthful ashes / fling upward settling fragrant / brightness on your dusky marquetry." Thus does Guest, from her own corner, fulfill another New York School predilection: the necessity of paying attention. She takes it for granted that attention to the experiences of women will reward, and that it will renew vitality, intensity and precision to poetic language.

What did it mean to be a woman poet of the first generation New York School? In a sense it was very lonely, Guest confessed in a taped interview with Charles Bernstein. She had to wait a generation for poetic fellowship with women, "younger women with whom I could identify, as they could identify with me."

But also, initially, for Guest, it seems to have been a time of coincidence between the kind of poetry she wished to write and the kind of poetry admired by her friends and being written by them. "I believe the male poets of my generation were the ones with whom I identified, because we were involved in the same attitude toward poetry." Certainly the climate in which she wrote these poems was fraught with fewer debilitating gender assumptions than the ones that surrounded their contemporaries in the Beat and Black Mountain poetry movements, each with its version of artistic macho swagger and male verbal privilege. The first New York poets believed in relationship rather than competition and their social and artistic interactions were marked by friendships and collaborations between men and women. If we add the painters' names to the mixed artistic milieu they moved in, women emerge as absolutely central and quite numerous: Helen Frankenthaler, Grace Hartigan, the much-beloved Jane Freilicher, Nell Blaine, Lee Krasner, Joan Mitchell, Alice Neel, Elaine de Kooning. Amid 1950s and early '60s high anxiety about gender roles, these poets, as Lehman notes, loved the flamboyance of gay life; they embraced aestheticism; they saw the benefit to a mid-century poetry grown staid and humorless of camp, of sensuousness, of enthusiasm, of silliness, of love. One might go so far as to say there was something "feminine" about their ethos and poetics. Their poetry was humorous, fluid, elusive, learned, urbane, whimsical, and emotionally rich. In each other's company, despite the famous stuffiness and conformity of the post-war era, they found how much fun it was, and how productive, to be what they were, and to write with an assumption of freedom, an assumption that was then rather politically and socially incorrect if not altogether suspect. In this atmosphere, Guest could write poetry relieved of the necessity of an overtly feminist agenda, unburdened by self-consciousness, anger, fear of misunderstanding. This makes Guest's early poetry a very valuable, very rare phenomenon. She did not masculinize or degender it; neither was she compelled to limit it to the traditional "feminine" subjects or tonal range. She did not have to, since she was writing for an initial audience whose sensibilities matched hers in active and exciting ways. The New York poets, Guest by no means least among them, disturbed the binary clustering of emotions and attitudes attached to male and female to the benefit of them all, in what amounted to an access to and an outburst of freedom.

But as Charles Bernstein claims in his hilarious, poignantly titled poem about the absurdity of poets claiming school, group, and factional loyalty to each other, "Solidarity Is The Name We Give To What We Cannot Hold" (33). By 1978, after all, Fraser was writing to Guest about an upcoming reading at St. Mark's: "Lord knows what I can possibly say to those 17th generation New York School poets" (Guest papers). Attenuated indeed that lineage must have become, and what "solidarity" it expressed rather wishful or willed. But there is no doubt that the five poets whose affections and enthusiasms first led to the so-called school began careers within it that were rich and sustainable. Guest urged me in an email message to note that it was life and time (and no doubt O'Hara's early death) that led to changes in their relationships: not discord, disagreement, or any falling-off of talent or output. "N.B.," she writes, "various conditions altered relations among the New York Poets: Ashbery's stay in Paris, where his poetic developed in the direction of the French poets of the magazine *Tel Quel*; Schuyler's illnesses; Koch was traveling; and the direction of my poetry you have seen in *Moscow Mansions*. We retained the same concept of poetry." And in this statement from another email message, it is clear that the restless paradox of invention (newness, change, surprise) as a commonly held artistic "method," is one Guest still espouses: "The forces of that era are cemented in our poetry. The inventive attitudes, the attitude of invention as *ars poetica*."

That group name meant to be a joking homage to the painters they admired was bound to feel like a constricting label used by others, seeming to hold them to an earnest brand of solidarity that ill-expressed the very poetic license they had forged. They themselves did not try to hold what cannot be held, especially not by converting their fluid friendships, their electric compatibility, their ardor for amusing themselves ("another highly suspect activity"—Ashbery, "Introduction" viii) into a solid school of thought with codifiable principles. "You just go on your nerve," wrote the boyish, sophisticated, and nervy O'Hara in his mock manifesto (*Standing Still* 110). Thomas Lask reported Ashbery's paradoxical observation that "if the school did in fact have a program, it was only the absence of one. Poetry should be everything it wants to be" (29). In this "absence of a program," Guest again proves herself integral to the program, so to speak. She has remained a poet true to her own lights, blithely individualistic, non-polemical, elusive of definition, too restless and rich in her gifts to ever cover the same territory twice. Witness the astonishing range of her recent experimentation—from "stripped tales," to cinematic prose poetry, to poetic flirtations with aesthetic theory, to apparitional allusion, to odd latter-day imagism, to Schoenbergian stringencies, to a new collaboration with the young painter, Laurie Reid.

The five New York School poets sometimes expressed a half-serious ambition to silence their critics—to write a poem so immediate, so quick to the heart, so elusive to logic, so fresh in its idiom, so close to music or painting, so funny, so unparaphraseable, so contingent on the circumstances of its reading—that critical vocabulary would be disarmed. They wished to write a poetry that would "resist the intelligence almost successfully," to put one of Wallace Stevens' *Adagia* to work.[5] Barbara Guest, among the New York poets, most successfully (almost) resists the intelligence of her readers, to put rather oddly what is nevertheless true. (It goes without saying that the intelligence is mightily provoked and stimulated by the encounter). This is one way to understand the relative silence from critics, when compared to the veritable cottage industries that have grown up around Ashbery and O'Hara. It is hard for a critic to portray herself in print as one whose intelligence is actively resisted; she might not after all, be able to render that saving "almost" convincingly enough. Guest is formidable in this regard, an exhilarating test of all one's reading skills and expectations. Ashbery, Schuyler, Koch, and O'Hara have garnered

sufficient critical narrative so that we think we know them. But Guest remains unnarrated, and unappropriated to the use of criticism and literary history. Her poetry is still doing what it wants to do, and is ahead of what has been written about it, out in uncharted territory, "leading us further into an unprotected, ambitious future."[6] Her work, therefore, I stress again, must be understood as a last vital irritant, THE New York School poetry, which in its restless elusiveness staves off canonization, respectability, predictability, complacency—all those dullnesses that poets in their youth thumb their noses at. In this regard, surely Guest is the last of the last avant-garde. She, in her turbulent implacability, may well be for American poetry, "future's conduit," to use her own apt phrase, one who in the last year of the millennium published these lines as if to ready herself and poetry itself for yet another strange, beautiful "new idiom," another foray into the as-yet-unsaid:

> Without shyness or formality:
>
> "a gesture of *allowing oneself time*"
>
> Remember how starry it arrives the hope of another
>   idiom, beheld
>   that blush of inexactitude, and the furor, it
>   will return to you, flotsam blocked out.

*(**Rocks on a Platter** 37)*

Notes

1. She was, however, sometimes read as cool and detached, or refined and elitist, a charge that the poems themselves, with their variety of tone, and wide-ranging themes, do not support.

2. From Section 5 of "Fresh Air" by Kenneth Koch (1955):

   > Sun out! Perhaps there is a reason for the lack of poetry
   > In these ill-contented souls, perhaps they need air!
   >
   > Blue air, fresh air, come in, I welcome you, you are an
   > art student,
   > Take off your cap and gown and sit down on the chair.
   > Together we shall paint the poets—but no, air! Perhaps
   > you should go to them, quickly,
   >
   > Give them a little inspiration, they need it, perhaps
   > they are out of breath,
   > Give them a little inhuman company before they freeze
   > the English language to death! (And rust their typewriters a little, be sea air! Be noxious! Kill them, if you
   > must, but stop their poetry! . . .).

   (On the Great Atlantic Rainway 74)

3. Growing beyond the New York School, Guest has remained an ekphrastic poet, and a poet who turned to painting for inspiration and analogous techniques and emotions. Major poems in this

mode are "The Poetess" (Miró), "Roses" (Juan Gris), "The Rose Marble Table" (Matisse), "The View from Kandinsky's Window," "The Farewell Stairway" (Balla), "Fair Realism," "Dora Maar," "Wild Gardens Overlooked by Night Lights," "The Screen of Distance," "The Nude," and "The Surface As Object." She was and still is an avid collaborator with visual artists, many of whom have been women, besides the already mentioned Grace Hartigan and Mary Abbott, June Felter, Anne Dunn, and Laurie Reid as well as Richard Tuttle and Warren Brandt.

4. See Lundquist, "Another Poet Among Painters."

5. Guest is an admirer of Stevens's poetry and his poetics. This particular statement from the *Adagia* is one that Charles North has also found useful in describing his reader's relationship with Guest's poetry.

6. This is Guest's phrase describing Leatrice Rose who did the cover painting for *Fair Realism,* 1989 (13).

Works Cited

Allen, Donald, ed. *The New American Poetry, 1945-1960.* Berkeley: U of California P, 1999, c1960.

Ashbery, John. Letters to Barbara Guest, undated, 21 November 1960. Postcards to Barbara Guest, 1962. Guest Papers.

———. Introduction to *The Collected Poems of Frank O'Hara.* Ed. Donald Alleen. Berkeley: U of California P, 1995. vii-xi.

Bernstein, Charles. *My Way: Speeches and Poems.* Chicago: U of Chicago P, 1999.

Breslin, James E. B. "Poetry, 1945 to the Present." *Columbia Literary History of the United States.* Ed. Emory Elliot, et al. New York: Columbia UP, 1988. 1079-1100.

Butterick, George F. and Robert J. Bertholf. "Frank O'Hara." *Dictionary of Literary Biography* Volume 193; *American Poets Since World War II,* Sixth Series. Ed. Joseph Conte. Detroit, Gale, 1998. 213-233.

DuPlessis, Rachel Blau. "The Flavor of Eyes: *Selected Poems* by Barbara Guest." *Women's Review of Books* 13(1) October 1995. 23-4.

———. "The Gendered Marvelous: Barbara Guest, Surrealism, and Feminist Reception." *The Scene of My Selves: New Work on New York School Poets.* Eds. Terence Diggory and Stephen Paul Miller, Orono, ME: National Poetry Foundation, 2000. 189-214.

Einzig, Barbara. "The Surface as Object: Barbara Guest's *Selected Poems.*" *American Poetry Review* 25(1) January/February 1996. 7-10.

Fraser, Kathleen. Letter to Barbara Guest, 7 April 1978. (Guest papers).

———. *Translating the Unspeakable: Poetry and the Innovative Necessity.* Tuscaloosa: U of Alabama P, 2000.

Guest, Barbara. *The Blue Stairs.* New York: Corinth, 1968.

———. Email messages to Sara Lundquist, 2 June 2000.

———. *Fair Realism.* Los Angeles: Sun & Moon P, 1989.

———. Letter to Mr. and Mrs. John Pelzel, May 24, 1952. (Guest papers).

———. "Helen Frankenthaler: The Moment & The Distance." *Arts Magazine* 49 (April 1975): 58-9.

———. Interview. With Charles Bernstein. Audio Tape. LINEbreak Series. Buffalo, NY: Granolithic Productions, 1996.

———. Interview. With Mark Hillringhouse. *American Poetry Review* July/August 1992: 23-30.

———. "Leatrice Rose." *Arts Magazine* 59 (Summer 1985): 13.

———. *Moscow Mansions.* New York: Viking, 1973.

———. "Mysteriously Defining the Mysterious: Byzantine Proposals of Poetry." *HOW(ever)* 3(3) October 1986. 12-13.

———. *Poems: The Location of Things. Archaics, The Open Skies.* New York: Doubleday, 1962.

———. *The Location of Things.* New York: Tibor de Nagy, 1960.

———. Papers. Beinecke Rare Book and Manuscript Library. Yale University, New Haven, Conn.

Guest, Barbara. "Robert Goodnough." *School of New York: Some Younger Artists.* Ed. B. H. Friedman. New York: Grove, 1959. 18-23.

———. *Seeking Air.* Black Sparrow P, 1978.

———. *Selected Poems.* Los Angeles: Sun & Moon P, 1995

———. "Shifting persona." *Poetics Journal* 9# (June 1991): 85-8.

———. *Symbiosis.* (with Laurie Reid). Berkeley: Kelsey St. P, 2000.

———. "Under the Shadow of Surrealism." *PEN Newsletter* #62, no date. 16-17.

Hoover, Paul. "The Plot Against the Giant . . . : Review of *The Last Avant-Garde* by David Lehman. Jacket #6. (January 1999).

Kaufman, Robert. "The Future of Modernism: Barbara Guest's Recent Poetry." *American Poetry Review.* July/August 2000: 11-16.

Keller, Lynn. "Becoming 'a Compleat Travel Agency': Barbara Guest's Negotiations with the 'Fifties Feminine Mystique.'" *The Scene of My Selves: New Work on New York School Poets.* Eds. Terence Diggory and Stephen Paul Miller, Orono, ME: National Poetry Foundation, 2000. 215-228.

Koch, Kenneth. *On the Great Atlantic Rainway: Selected Poems 1950-1988.* New York: Knopf, 1994.

Lask, Thomas. "Lines from Gotham." *New York Times* June 6, 1970, 29.

Lehman, David. *The Last Avant-Grade: The Making of the New York School of Poets.* New York: Doubleday, 1998.

Lundquist, Sara. "Another Poet Among Painters: Barbara Guest, Grace Hartigan, Mary Abbott." *The Scence of My Selves: New Work on New York School Poets.* Eds. Terence Diggory and Stephen Paul Miller, Orono, ME: National Poetry Foundation, 2000. 245-264.

——. "Barbara Guest." *Dictionary of Literary Biography: American Poets Since World War* II Ed. Joseph Conte. Volume 193. Detroit: Bruccoli Clark Layman, 1998. 159-170.

Myers, John Bernard. Introduction to *The Poets of the New York School.* Philadelphia: Pennsylvania UP, 1969. 7-29.

——. Letter to Barbara Guest. October 18, 1961. Guest papers.

North, Charles. "10 Essays for Barbara Guest." *No Other Way: Selected Prose.* Brooklyn, NY: Hanging Loose Press, 1998. 152-156.

O'Hara, Frank. *Collected Poems.* ed. Donald Allen. Berkeley: U of California P, 1995.

——. Letters to Barbara Guest. 7 November 1955, 4 October 1956, 9 March 1958, 19 October 1959. Guest Papers.

——. *Standing Still and Walking In New York.* San Francisco: Grey Fox P, 1983.

——. Statement on Poetics. *The New American Poetry, 1945-1960.* Donald Allen, ed. Berkeley: U of California P, 1999, c1960. 419-20.

Padgett, Ron, and David Shapiro, eds. *An Anthology of New York Poets.* New York: Random House, 1970.

Perloff, Marjorie. *Frank O'Hara: Poet Among Painters.* Chicago: U of Chicago P, 1998.

Schuyler, James. *Selected Art Writings.* Ed. Simon Pettet. Santa Rosa: Black Sparrow P, 1998.

——. Letters to Barbara Guest. 18 February 1959, 16 May 1971, 7 October 1977. Guest papers.

Yezzi, David, "Last One Off the Barricade Turn Out the Lights." review of *The Last Avant-Garde* by David Lehman. *New York Times Books Review.* January 3, 1999.

Arielle Greenberg (essay date 2001)

SOURCE: Greenberg, Arielle. "A Sublime Sort of Exercise: Levity and the Poetry of Barbara Guest." *Women's Studies: An Interdisciplinary Journal* 30 (2001): 111-21.

[*In the following essay, Greenberg traces the evolution of humor and wit in Guest's poetry from 1960 through 1980.*]

Much of the recent critical work on Barbara Guest has focused on the importance of *painterly* light in her poems. I would like to discuss the importance of a *different* kind of light—light in the sense of levity, humor. I would ask that we read Guest as a poet possessed of great wit, and as a poet employing feminist strategies. I argue that these two characteristics can be seen as intrinsically linked.

This essay charts a trajectory in Guest's work from 1960 through 1980—from *Poems* (1962), *The Blue Stairs* (1968), *The Countess from Minneapolis* (1976), to *The Türler Losses* (1979)—and argues that her use of wit over those two decades parallels a change in her aesthetic: from work influenced by poetic tradition to a more liberated voice. I also argue that the use of levity is a feminist strategy; it serves as an undoing of the dominant order in both poetics and the culture at large. I argue that, ironically, levity *grounds* Guest's reader in poems which are often fragmented and spare, and that while a sense of humor is certainly present in the work of the New York School poets, Guest's work resonates more with that of contemporary avant-garde women writers who use the subversive power of wit to locate themselves within a female community.

As evidenced by this issue of *Women's Studies: An Interdisciplinary Journal* and other attentions paid to her in recent years, Guest has finally begun, in her fifth decade of publishing poetry, to receive real critical attention. But the ways in which she is read still encompass a very limited set of frameworks. As Sara Lundquist notes, discussion of Guest's poetry centers around

> three persistent, *true,* but ultimately simplistic assumptions about her work: first, that it is difficult to the point of obduracy; second, that it is refined and cool, rather than passionate, personal or emotionally urgent;

and third, that it [. . .] avoids the political in favor of the aesthetic, preferring the sensualites of surface, texture and wordplay over narrative, social commentary, and political naming.

(263)

I want to argue that Guest actually has that most forgiving and welcoming kind of warmth, the kind manifested in a sense of humor, and that this carries a political power. How can wit in women's writing be considered political or feminist? First, we can understand the very nature of women writing as feminist. From an ideological standpoint, the act of a woman writing is itself a subversive and resistant act, because language is power, and power is male-dominated. If women claim and use that power, we are working in opposition to structural oppressions.

Second, humor disrupts the order of things, celebrating chaos and confusion; it relies on otherness to exist. This is compounded when instigated by a woman. As Regina Barreca notes, "the woman writer's use of comedy is dislocating, anarchic and [. . .] unconventional," because language itself is imagined to be equivalent to the authority of the masculine perspective (*New Perspectives* 6). Barreca states, "Women's humor is about our reclamation of certain forms of control over our own lives. Humor allows us to gain perspective by ridiculing the implicit insanities of a patriarchial culture" (*Untamed* 12). A woman with a sense of humor is proving her intelligence, indicating her confidence, taking action.

By characterizing Guest's humor as *levity* I mean to indicate a breezy use of irony that doesn't betray femininity. The lack of closure often noted in Guest's work is an extension of this breeziness. As Guest uses it, levity allows a person to make light of herself while still retaining her dignity. It also signifies a certain confidence; to quote Lundquist again, "Guest's poems seem singularly free of that fear of being silenced" (283). As I will show, Guest's use of levity is tied to her sense of womanhood, and its development can be tracked along a path from control—of self, of line, of syntax—to liberation—of objects, of identity, and of language.

Guest's first major book, **Poems,** finds the poet drawing from a number of poetic movements. There is a lyrical, Romantic aesthetic at work, with metaphoric references to personified seasons, and an epigraph from Verlaine. There is also the influence of the narrative confessional present, with a strong use of the first-person voice. I see little in this book which is deeply resonant with the poems of O'Hara or Koch: the voice rarely gets chatty or witty, and feels rather restrained. The connection with the New York School, if one needs to be made, would probably hinge on Ashbery's more elusive and elegant writing.

What is evident here is a sense of being controlled and a desire for freedom, and many of the poems in this first collection refer to specifically gendered issues. **"All Grey-haired My Sisters"** is a case in point. The poem is addressed from a devoted speaker to a group of mythic women using classical Western roles—sisters, relatives, adventuresses, darlings, ancestresses, mermaids, girls; each term cements the speaker's community with these figures. The women are in concert with nature ("guided by the form and scent / of tree and flower blossoming") and have endured hardships throughout history ("*you walked into the wars*") (15). These hardships may have also included marriage, as indicated in the lines "*as daisies drop at your wrists / which flight are you making? / down the lime aisles*" (16).

This poem also contains lines which I would like to posit as one of Guest's first gendered jokes. In this section, an unidentified second-person emerges—"From your journals"—and then a moment of dialogue is quoted from an unknown "he" and "she" (16):

> He said: "In nymphic barque"
> She replied: "A Porcupine."
> And later,
> "Reason selects our otherness."

(16)

As I read this, a man is describing a woman in terms of nature and of a feminized creature of sweetness and innocence, the nymph. The response from a woman is a pointed, sharp animal.

A plea for liberty is present in the poem **"The First of May,"** in which the speaker begins: "My eye cannot turn toward you / Night / because it has Day watching" (73). Throughout the poem, the speaker yearns for autonomy and freedom:

> I would like to go for a walk
> in the dark
> without moonbeams
>
> down that path of mushrooms
> in my nightdress
> without shoes.

(73)

Her desire is manifested in a desire for sexual pleasure and rebellion: "I would like to steal . . . ," "I would like to go to a hotel / with you" (73). Day, the controller, blinds the speaker, and yet the speaker is reluctant to leave Day's power, because if she does disobey and "give you up Day forever," she will be forced to join "the guerrillas" who will "roast my bird / and eat it" (74). Thus freedom is seen as bringing treacherous consequences.

Published six years after **Poems, The Blue Stairs** opens with a daring declaration: "There is no fear / in taking the first step" (3). These first lines anticipate the liberation of language, line and spirit, the "quiet authority of [. . .] one," in Wendy Mulford's words, that runs throughout Guest's second collection. *The Blue Stairs* establishes the aesthetic now typically associated with Guest. Fragmentation occurs more often and in greater extremes: the average line in the book is five words long. The lines begin to move away from the left margin, with indentations bringing lines halfway across the page. The page looks airy; each idea is given its own room to breathe.

And although the first-person speaker does make appearances here, the first poem in the book, significantly, has hardly any "I" voice at all. In its place is a voice of declarative authority which seems to be calling for courage, ambition and dignity—a climb up a flight of metaphorical stairs: "In fact the top / can be reached / without disaster" (3). In my reading, this is a gendered quest. The speaker knows her own mind and her goal: "Its purpose / is to take you upward" (5). Once she has finished her journey to the pinnacle, she does not want to relinquish her position: "And having reached the summit / would like to stay there / even if the stairs are withdrawn" (6).

In other poems in *The Blue Stairs,* we can see a chatty, light-hearted humor which seems more related to the New York School mode than any of the poems in the previous collection. In **"Turkey Villas"** the voice becomes whimsical and intimate:

> Or
> to make a shorter story
> and relate in truth
> to my life
> as if it were San Francisco
> 1937
>
> (7)

The speaker later takes on a self-effacing tone, laughing at herself for being so personal. "Now to be a proper historian / of my dreams," she describes

> . . . a ship seen from
> A Hotel Hilton balcony
> Think of that
> Balcon Hilton!
>
> (8)

And then, as if sensing her own foray into O'Hara-ish exuberance, she pulls back the reigns: "Enough of this dizziness / let us apply the oars." (8)

But the speaker cannot help herself:

> I am spinning with ideas
> to the top of the Mosque
> I am an ice cream cone
> Muezzin
>
> (8)

A critique of gender roles is here, too; in the midst of a list of wishful thinking—"I shall go on collecting pottery / yet it shall be blue"—the speaker laughs "I shall be medieval and slim / at once!," a reference to her own body, and a joke on what is expected of it (9). Revealing this insecurity only adds to the humanity of this poem, and towards its end, the speaker is once again self-effacing: "My dreams / are stupidly turbulent," she claims, and yet as readers, we do not quite believe her (10). Her dreams have proven to be delightful in their wildness.

In the poem **"The Return of the Muses"** the speaker refers specifically to the problems and particulars of the female body. When the Muses leave the speaker, she is forced to alter herself:

> And I went on a diet
> I stopped eating regularly,
> I changed my ways several times
>
> "strict discipline, continuous devotion,
> receptiveness"
>
> were mine.
>
> (19)

In these lines, the speaker refers to dieting as a kind of religious ritual which she happily abandons when the Muses return: "Here you are back again. Welcome. / Farewell, 'strict, continuous, repetitive—'" (19).

The Blue Stairs concludes with one of Guest's most noted poems, **"A Handbook of Surfing."** The tone here is more serious than in previous poems—in an interview, Guest stated, "That poem is really an anti-Vietnam poem"—but the use of language is lively, and foreshadows the kind of fragmentation used in her more recent work (Hillringhouse 26). Lines are often broken in unexpected places; there is a lack of punctuation which makes phrases feel rushed together. This kind of bold usage and heightened language are interspersed with a pseudo-handbook tone, which is then deconstructed by the speaker so that a passage which reads "we would / like to tell here about paddling, standing and turning" receives the response (39),

> Everyone knows how to turn or turn about
> or make a reverse these are daily decisions both
> politic and poetic and they have historic sequences
> in the surf they are known as Changing Directions
>
> (39-40)

The Blue Stairs marks a rather dramatic change in direction for Guest, one that is followed through in the book-length poem, *The Countess from Minneapolis.* In it, a woman of European royalty is displaced in the American Midwest, where she observes the culture through the "unreasonable lenses" of an outsider (12).

The book alternates between lyric, fragmented poems and prose pieces that tend to be more down-to-earth—and humorous.

These prose pieces employ playful strategies: syntactic misuse, lists, parodies of formality, and surrealist juxtapositions. There is something subversive about the voice in these poems, in part because they are prose poems: they do not follow the "rules" of poetic form.

Laughing at the pretensions of European and aristocratic culture is a refrain throughout the prose poems in **Countess.** Minneapolis itself is not ridiculed for its perceived shortcomings; the contempt of The Countess is reserved for the cosmopolitan pretension she herself uses to describe her surroundings. Poem fourteen begins in the voice of Signor Reboneri, a visiting lecturer: "The refinement of what's special takes place between the meat and the bun. N'est-ce-pas?" (14). The professor proceeds to compare the Midwestern locals in a bar to Viking "'sauvages,'" but he "like[s] what he saw," a room full of "hefty maidens" and "god-like men" (14). In the end, the joke is on the Signor, who falls into a beer-induced reverie about the "hairy arms" of "these tribes" (14).

Surrealism is found in this text through the juxtaposition of everyday objects out of place. This is the case in poem twenty-five, which begins by pointing out "The further exoticism of reading a British novel while visiting Duluth," and in poem eleven (25):

> There was such an anachronism lurking
> in the snakelike room that Pedersen frequently mistook
> the potatoes in his soup for boulders and searched
> beneath them for hidden reptiles
>
> (11)

Most strikingly surrealist (and lovely, and funny) is the list of "ACTIVITIES" which make up poem thirty-seven:

> Grain Belt Beer, He Who Gets Slapped, Vikings vs
>   Dolphins,
> ice skating, fishing, Japanese food, meat, square
> dancing, collage, Rimbaud, New York Painting,
>   Showboats,
> Baskin-Robbins ice cream, La Strada, Basement
>   Studios
>
> (37)

This list points to the strangeness of cultural landscape; it mixes high and low culture in a manner reminiscent of the New York School (which itself is referenced here). In fact, despite the Countess's ancestry, her tone is often extremely casual and New Yorky, as in the letter she composes when an unnamed friend suggests, "'What you need is a sophisticated cat'" (24). The

Countess writes a "note to self": "Contact nearest available feline breeding—kennel—was it kennel—was it shed? Whatever. The sooner the better" (24).

Elsewhere Guest delights in the surfaces of language in a light-hearted way, as in the list of names the Countess reels off in poem fifteen, "AT THE GUTHRIE THEATER": ". . . Helm Wulfings and his assistants: Hnaef Hocings, Wald Woings, Wod Thurings, Seaferth Seggs . . ." and so on (15). These lists mock the social order and meaning, which can be read as a feminist strategy, a disruption (by the Countess) of the power structure.

In the last book Guest published in the '70s, a slim volume entitled **The Türler Losses,** the speaker, who one is safe to assume is Barbara Guest, has lost several expensive Türler watches, and the poems recount the losses. The *poems* feel likewise scattered. While they are too abstract and complex to utilize the kind of levity present in **Countess,** some places find Guest offering a warm welcome to the reader inside a difficult text, as in this section:

> I like innocuous rhythms, don't you?
> Loss isn't so important.
> When nothing lies there wearing its ring
>
> (3)

In this way, Guest takes herself lightly, and urges us to do the same, joking even about the importance of her watches and her carelessness in losing the costly objects: "After the second Türler loss / a lessening perhaps of fastidiousness / the Timex phase" (6).

I'd argue that by focusing on such a personal theme—the loss of a piece of jewelry—for a sustained experimental work, Guest is again using a feminist strategy: elevating the "woman's sphere" to the place of high art. Of course, the book is also about metaphoric losses, about space and time, but it often reads, between sections of dense imagery and assonant sound-play, more like an ethereal diary than anything else:

> Whisked to hotel. Sleepy hotel morning. Enjoyment
>   of eider-
> down. Waiter wheels in lunch. Step outside onto
>   balcony.
> Clouds. Descend to gardens. Pool where there is wave-
>   making
> machine, much discomfiture
>
> (11)

Certainly, this kind of reportage voice seems to be making fun of the very nature of such a personal book: a female voice masquerading as male news anchor. The use of the diary form feels womanly, as she herself remarks in a later section: "Safely home she duly recorded this event in her DIARY, JOURNAL, LETTERS, and the Sunday shopping lists later discovered nestling in the shrubbery outside her workroom" (14). When Guest uses the academic, scientific—i.e., masculine—mode of the footnote with no corresponding notation in the text, she is clearly making fun of it:

> SEE: INDEX, CROSS-FILING, UNIVERSITY, CORRESPONDENCE, ac-Va Yu, post, previous, subsequent, intervening, chronological, summary, additional material, endeavors, travel, quarrels, divorces, demises. N.B. All private papers withheld.
>
> (14)

In *The Türler Losses,* the voice is uniquely Guest's, representative of her commitment to the blend of the everyday and the spiritual, the philosophical and the capricious, a commitment which is evident in the poetry which has come since.

I want to close by quoting Guest herself, who once remarked "poetry should have more tension [. . .] I think it is coming into contemporary poetry more and I admire that" (qtd. in Hillringhouse 28). It is out of admiration for Guest that I put forward the reading I've outlined here, which I'm hoping will serve to complicate notions of her aesthetic—to heighten the tension, even. But I'm not asking that we read Guest only in this light. Rather, I see this essay as part of an exciting new effort—evidenced by this issue of *Women's Studies,* the recent panel on her work at the National Poetry Conference on North American poetry in the 1960s, and other events and publications—to place Guest in a new context, one which appreciates the fresh air she has breathed into language.

Works Cited

Barreca, Regina, ed. *New Perspectives on Women and Comedy.* Philadelphia: Gordon and Breach, 1992.

———, ed. *Untamed and Unabashed.* Detroit, Wayne State UP, 1994.

Guest, Barbara. *The Blue Stairs.* New York: Corinth Books, 1968.

———. *The Countess from Minneapolis.* Providence: Burning Deck, 1976.

———. *Poems: The Location of Things, Archaics, The Open Skies.* New York: Doubleday & Company, Inc., 1962.

———. *The Türler Losses.* Montréal: Mansfield Book Mart Ltd., 1979.

Hillringhouse, Mark. "Barbara Guest: An Interview by Mark Hillringhouse." *The American Poetry Review* July/August 1992: 23-30.

Lundquist, Sara. "The Midwestern New York Poet: Barbara Guest's 'The Countess From Minneapolis.'" *Jacket* #10: online, October 1999. Available: www.jacket.zip.com.au/jacket10/mulford-on-guest.html.

———. "Reverance and Resistance: Barbara Guest, Ekphrasis, and the Female Gaze." *Contemporary Literature* 38.2 (1997): 260-286.

Mulford, Wendy. "The Architecture of Dream: Barbara Guest's 'The Blue Stairs,' Corinth, 1968." *Jacket* #10: online, October 1999. Available: www.jacket.zip.com.au/jacket10/mulford-on-guest.html.

Garrett Caples (essay date 2001)

SOURCE: Caples, Garrett. "The Barbara Guest Experience." *Women's Studies: An Interdisciplinary Journal* 30 (2001): 123-29.

[*In the following essay, Caples discusses how Guest's later poetry incorporates the theme of "wandering."*]

> going to your desk in the meadow
> finding a token in the drawer . . .
>
> —Barbara Guest, **"Knight of the Swan,"** *Selected Poems*

"Poetry," Barbara Guest insists, "is an experience,"[1] and I quote these lines from "Knight of the Swan" (1973) freely out-of-context, for they strike me as very like the experience of reading her work. There's much imagery of wandering, then finding things, but the quest is never hurried, and the things you find are less things in themselves than proxies for them, tokens (but of what?). In *Rocks on a Platter* (1999), the image is an "Amulet cast from the pocket" (11), an object valued not so much for what it is as for what it conjures. But I'm less interested in the continuity of such imagery over a quarter century in and of itself than in its relationship to the structural development of Guest's poetry over that same period. **"Knight of the Swan,"** thematically her wandering poem *par excellence,* has the air of a New York School (NYS) romp on *The Faerie Queene,* epic giving way to absurdity, but also simultaneously to some of the most beautifully erotic love poetry ever produced by that school of shameless love poets. It is infused with a good deal of what is by now identified as "typical" NYS sleight-of-hand—rapid discontinuities and shifts in pronouns, sudden attention to "gingerale" giving way to a Donne-like sense of cosmos—the poem consists largely of the long rambling verse paragraphs characteristic of the group's earlier output. However, in more recent work such as *Rocks on a Platter* and *Symbiosis* (2000), a collaborative book with painter Laurie Reid, Guest has more literally incorporated this previously thematic wandering into the very structure of her poetry.[2] The poems have grown more sparse, discursive rambling giving way to more fragmentary clusters of lines, surrounded by space on the page. But these clusters, while isolated, are by no means sparse. They remain complex, even vivid objects, something like the tokens and amulets we still find depicted in them.

This "vividness," however, is not, or not merely, a matter of depiction. It has as much to do with the compelling symmetry of "token"—a lone *k* flanked by vowels, then bracketed by consonants—with the flagrant Frenchness of "amulet" against the Anglo-Saxon texture of our tongue. When Guest is occasionally (and imprecisely) identified as a "pictorialist," it is not, I assume, because she hangs out with painters or that her images are more "visualizable" than those of other poets. What such accounts are driving at is that she approaches the materials of her art much as we imagine a painter approaching her apparently more technical materials (pigments, texture of painting surface, and so on)—*as* material, real objects themselves, subject to physical manipulation. But words, not objects, are the poet's objects, though only language in general could be termed her material. That is to say, words are the discrete units the poet manipulates as distinct from their referents, the actual objects in the world. Perhaps it would be better to say that some of her objects are invisible, most obviously sound and sense, but also more abstract structural principles like syntax. Or perhaps some of her materials aren't objects at all. In any case, a material orientation is fundamental to Guest's sense of poetic experience, one that is chiefly linguistic rather than conceptual or representational, less involved with meaning and more with the forms meanings can take. Her manipulation of the physical properties of words themselves, ortho- and typographical as well as aural, generates her work.

In suggesting that "Poetry is an experience," Guest was responding to a question concerning the relation between **Rocks on a Platter** and **Symbiosis**: were they not both meditations of a kind, the first subheaded **Notes on Literature,** the second thematizing the very process of artistic collaboration? No, she replied, they are not meditations; neither work is a poem-of-ideas. "Poetry," she said, "is not thought, it's an experience," citing for evidence the line "O valley. O wine." from the following passage of **Symbiosis**:

> Plume of impatience the petal,
> a clue to ensnare the undrawn,
>
> O valley. O wine.

                                                                                    (15)

It was clear she referred to the primarily sensual appeal of this passage, which overwhelms considerations of sense or discursive thought. Isolated on their own page, marked as a self-contained unit through capitalization and punctuation though in truth only sentence fragments, the lines stand in no obvious relationship to those on surrounding pages. There's no context available in which to establish reference, save for the symbiotic one of relating them to the abstract grey-green strips Reid overlays Guest's poem with. Yet the lines still compel through sheer structural bravado. A

crucial relation seems to obtain between "Plume of impatience the petal" and "a clue to ensnare the undrawn" even in the absence of verbs or logical connectives. In fact their relation is aural; though an avant-gardist, Guest's facility with meter rivals that of any retrograde neo-formalist in the Richard Wilbur or Geoffrey Hill vein. Without undue obviousness her juxtaposition of these two lines creates a sort of aural chiasmus through opposite patterns of stress. The two dactyls plus a trochee of "Plume of impatience the petal," give way to a corresponding iamb with two anapests in "a clue to ensnare the undrawn," resembling something like the effect of crescendo followed by diminuendo, or the alternating intonations of question and answer. The security of their sounded arrangement momentarily forestalls potential objections (*What is the undrawn and how can a clue ensnare it? What is a plume of impatience, and how can a petal be this?* etc.). The accompanying apostrophes ("O valley. O wine.") communicate their rhythm and exultation of mood, but again, in the absence of a referential context, we are only left to imagine possible contexts in which objects of such different scale could be addressed from the same vantage point. In this respect her poetry may be termed "experimental," because, while their formal arrangements do to a large extent determine the course of our reading, they cannot fully calculate in advance a given reader's experience of previously unencountered combinations that result from her privileging the physicality of words over meanings.

The nature of Guest's experiment is, I think, what distinguishes her interest in experience from the seemingly similar process-orientation of language poetry. A language poet will, for example, write "a book-length prose poem [. . .] according to the Fibonacci number sequence"—whereby "the number of sentences in each paragraph equals the number of sentences in the previous two paragraphs" (Hoover 489)—and be righteously unconcerned over whether or not tedium comprises much of a reader's experience. The experiment of this poetry is largely the experience of composition, but Guest's work is less narcissistic, acknowledging the necessarily divided nature of poetic experience. In other words, she is as concerned with the intensity of the reader's experience of the composition as with her own of composing it. To this end, her poems tend to maximize the potential associative possibilities of a given unit of words by setting multiple organizational patterns against each other, syntax versus lineation, semantics versus sound. **Symbiosis** continues:

> This is the point where the strophes meet,
>   one line interweaves with another,
>
>   room of liberal fountains,
>   a different speech and metabolism,

                                                                                    (16)

Here the poem seems to straightforwardly address the situation of composition. In the absence of clear antecedent for "This"—the valley? the wine?—we might assume it refers to "this point in the poem," a familiar postmodernist gesture against closure sanctioned by language poetry, were it not for "strophe" itself, Greek as an *oktopous,* on an otherwise plain bed of English. The familiar begins to fracture. Like all the more technical terms of rhetoric and poetics, "strophe" already has a faint reek of arcana, and spurred on by the ostentatious Greekness of "symbiosis," we may be tempted to investigate. The dictionary offers a clue; "strophe" once signified both "a turn in dancing made by an ancient Greek chorus" and "lines recited during this." Thus one word is used to lend conceptual unity to a combination of two fundamentally different acts, recalling the title's implications. When Guest writes "one line interweaves with another," it seems less self-conscious scrutiny of the pattern of her own lines and more comment on their intersection with Reid's. The spacing of Guest's lines in fact encourages a certain disunity among them, as if each were also a freestanding unit all its own. Indeed, the syntax opens up, as the next two lines float free of clear grammatical connection, into dialogue with Reid's own abstractly connected visuals. The next page reads "near an ancient site of accord / and priority," the page break seemingly sewing the syntax shut. But the isolation of these lines, on a page shared only by Reid's art, encourages their separation from the sentence. Perhaps there's a suggestion of landscape in the juxtaposition of "site" with the horizontal orientation of the visuals. But the "ancient site of accord / and priority" also recalls the earlier divided sense of "strophe," the implied simultaneity of two arts, separate identities submerged into a union. Rather than lines simply titling a picture, the page instead alludes to a genre mentioned later in *Symbiosis,* the **"Poem-Painting"** (23), in which painter and writer literally compose on the same surface. Over the next two pages, a single sentence broken into two isolated passages reinforces such appearances:

> In no climate whatsoever
> noise traveling up the tower
>
> (18)

> bronze green in the tournament,
> each player hit a wood ball.
>
> (19)

Even as punctuation and capitalization insist on continuity, the repeated pattern of page- and line-breaks continues to maintain the feel of discreet poem-paintings. Meter again asserts its organizational prerogatives. The repeated stress pattern of "whatsoever" in "up the tower" mark them as a couplet, while the double stressed "bronze green" and "wood ball" audibly seal

off as a unit the lines they bracket. But then another more vertical pattern connects the two pages, if we notice that the word "tower" is scrambled throughout "whatsoever," and its French translation, "tour," is peeking out of "tournament." An orthographical maneuver transforms into an etymological one, proposing an alternative continuity to reunite the sundered whole.

It is to these competing patterns of organization that I refer when I claim Guest has incorporated wandering into the structure of recent poems. They encourage a good deal of pausing for reconsideration, turning back for another or closer look at various clusters of lines. To move forward is often at the same time to go back, as subsequent passages revise a reader's experience of previous ones. Unlike the *fait accompli* of process-oriented language poems, Guest's work offers the reader a generous share in poetic experience. The unstable and yet constitutive relationship of language to the world, much referred to by language poets, is implied in the delicate surrealism of her imagery. Yet she doesn't interpret such insight as necessitating the prohibition of certain forms, unlike the language poets, who, for example, have disavowed the use of line, metaphor, orality, and so forth as organizational units for contemporary poetry. As we have seen, even punctuation and capitalization—so unfashionable in poetry today—can be employed, not as a constraint on interpretation, but as one more pattern by which we can organize our experience of her work. Guest rules out nothing in advance, aware that forms are in themselves neutral, empty, even if every particular employment of one is a nexus in a web of contingent social relations too vast to even begin to enumerate in terms of literary criticism alone. Rather than deny her readers, she puts all of language at our disposal. It's a romantic gesture made through intensely aware avant-garde strategies. And why not, for the nature of poetic experience is dual.

Notes

1. Telephone Interview. 7/25/00.

2. This is not to suggest by any means that there is one line of stylistic development in Guest's work—or in the NY School, for that matter—as she is well-known to work in different modes simultaneously. Indeed this formed the primary subject of my review of the three books she published concurrently in 1999 ("Masterful Variety From Poet Barbara Guest," *San Francisco Chronicle Book Review* [January 9, 2000], 12).

Works Cited

Guest, Barbara. *Rocks on a Platter: Notes on Literature.* Hanover and London: Wesleyan, 1999.

———. *Selected Poems.* Los Angeles: Sun & Moon, 1995.

Guest, Barbara and Laurie Reid. *Symbiosis.* Berkeley: Kelsey St, 2000.

Hoover, Paul, ed. *Postmodern American Poetry.* NY and London: Norton, 1994.

Linda A. Kinnahan (essay date 2001)

SOURCE: Kinnahan, Linda A. "Reading Barbara Guest: The View from the Nineties." In *The Scene of My Selves: New Work on New York School Poets,* Terence Diggory and Stephen Paul Miller, pp. 229-43. Orono, Maine: The National Poetry Foundation, 2001.

[*In the following essay, Kinnahan offers an overview of recent critical assessment of the poetic work of Barbara Guest.*]

> Miss Guest abolishes relationship, and consequently abolishes value. . . . Where Miss Guest abolishes relationship, Miss Plath asserts it as central.
>
> -William Dickey ("Responsibilities" 758, 764)

> While O'Hara's energetic celebration of the whole of life, in its dailiness, was a great permission giver, it was Guest's linguistic mysteries that lingered, composed and collaged from the precise fragments of her painterly witness and her skeptical wariness of language's confinement and oversimplification.
>
> -Kathleen Fraser ("Tradition" 24)

> . . . we don't know her.
>
> -Rachel Blau DuPlessis ("Flavor of Eyes" 23)

The remarkable retrieval of linguistically experimental women writing in this century has led to rediscoveries of such poorly remembered figures as Mina Loy and Lola Ridge, to renewed considerations of Laura Riding, Marianne Moore, H. D., and to revised notions of such "personalities" as Gertrude Stein and Amy Lowell. The labors of feminist critics, particularly those working in the field of modernism—Carolyn Burke, Marianne DeKoven, Rachel Blau DuPlessis, Susan Stanford Friedman, to name just a handful—have enriched our literary histories while challenging their very parameters and defining narratives. Likewise, contemporary women practicing innovative poetries, especially those writing from the 1960s and 1970s to the present, have sought to "reconstruct that preexisting tradition of modernist women" and to conduct a "'dig' for a female tradition of language inventiveness" (Fraser, "Tradition" 26). The work of Barbara Guest, who began writing in the 1950s and continues until the present day, generationally bridges modernist and contemporary poets but suffers from decades of neglect that leads a poet/critic like Rachel Blau DuPlessis to bemoan "we don't know her" ("Flavor of Eyes" 23) despite an extraordinary career as a poet, novelist, essayist, biographer, and art critic.[1]

Although little in the way of academic literary criticism exists to help us know her, beyond her label as the only woman poet of the New York School of writers and artists, her work is currently being resituated by women poets who are interested in her formal innovations and particularly in a "feminist understanding of poetic innovation" exhibited in her work ("Flavor of Eyes" 23). Recent reviews by Rachel Blau DuPlessis and Barbara Einzig of Guest's 1995 *Selected Poems* describe a poetics radical both in form and in politics, a "new perspective on what linguistically-foregrounded poetry is about, suggesting that concentration upon the 'word-as-such' may offer a way of expressing within poetry the tension and violence of our time" (Einzig 7). Locating Guest's work within a line of women experimentalists in this century whose work with language has probed constructions of gender and culture but has been customarily marginalized for that very focus, DuPlessis sees in Guest "a test case of the crossings and vectors in contemporary poetry: the feminist understanding of poetic innovation; the approaches to proto-feminist analysis made by women innovators; the cavalier attitude to women artists sometimes evident in artistic groups" ("Flavor of Eyes" 23). These "crossings and vectors" emerge from and within an interactive history of literary discourses and cultural ideologies contextualizing Guest's initial reception, her subsequent marginalization, and the hopeful signs of a current reevaluation. In this essay, I am particularly interested in the gendered ideologies attending the cultural moments of Guest's earliest work and her recovery by women poets of the nineties. In part, this essay looks to the reception of Guest's work as a way of suggesting broader relationship between literary stature, formal innovation, and constructions of gender.

Prior to the recent reviews of DuPlessis and Einzig, the poet Kathleen Fraser had taken issue with the "benign critical neglect of Guest's work" and had devoted attention to Guest in essays and editorial efforts.[2] The founder of the journal *HOW(ever),* a forum for experimental poetry by women that was published from the mideighties until the early nineties, Fraser positions Guest within what she terms a "tradition of marginality," a tradition revealing the cultural, historical, and gendered dimensions of women's experimental writing. Mapping some of these dimensions in a 1988 essay, "The Tradition of Marginality," Fraser tellingly describes her own experience in the 1960s of a dual marginality: developing an increasingly linguistically-foregrounded poetry hybridizing both feminist politics and avant-garde practice, Fraser found herself nonetheless excluded from emerging mainstream feminist poetries (and their "call for the immediately accessible language of personal experience") and from male-dominated avant-garde poetries (24). This marginality typifies for Fraser the status of the woman experimentalist in twentieth-century American poetry and is furthered by the "historic practice" of the erasure of women from narratives of literary history and the mechanisms that support them—critical attention, anthology selections, editorial networks, etc.

The case of Barbara Guest provided Fraser's first "in-person encounter with this common historic practice" while, simultaneously, for the young woman poet in the early sixties, Guest offered Fraser her first model of the woman poet embracing "linguistic mysteries" and a questioning of the notion of self ("Tradition" 24). A "major figure in the poetry and painting scene through the fifties and sixties" and "the only woman poet in the first generation of the New York School," Guest was nonetheless excluded from the first major anthology representing the different generations of the school (with the work of twenty-six men and one woman), *An Anthology of New York Poets,* edited by David Shapiro and Ron Padgett and published in 1970.[3] Recounting the "shocking erasure" enacted by this exclusion from a "defining anthology," DuPlessis also notes that Guest's work suffered similar erasure from a defining anthology of women's feminist poetry, *No More Masks!* (edited by Florence Howe and Ellen Bass in 1973 and revised by Howe in 1993), which also omitted this copiously published poet, "probably because none of her work was felt to be readable, then or now, by feminist thematics."[4] The question of readability, of course, begs the question of who is reading and from what position. Excluded from the reading communities shaping and shaped by such anthologists as Shapiro and Padgett or Howe, Guest's work and its reception suggest the necessary revisions of aesthetic expectations and of reading practices that must be undertaken as part of an interactive poetic-critical project to establish the validity of women exploring the cultural work of language and the territory of gender's relation to formal innovation.

Such a project necessarily looks to dominant forms of literary, poetic, and critical discourse and attempts to trace both their impact and their ideological foundations. In this respect, Guest serves as an ideal "test case" of the gendered intersections of aesthetic and critical values, particularly as these take shape in a decade encouraging cultural containment and homogenous norms, the fifties. In a two-fold manner, I want to linger upon the moment of the late fifties and early sixties in America as a way of suggesting these gendered intersections: first, through a 1962 review essay of Guest's work, and secondly, through Kathleen Fraser's autobiographical comments on the New York poetry scene at this time.

With most of the decade of the fifties still ahead, Barbara Guest moved in her early twenties from California to New York City, where she began working as an editor for *Art News.* By 1955, having published a poem in the *Partisan Review* that caught the eye of a

group of writers and painters, she met John Myers, Frank O'Hara, and Jane Freilicher, beginning her involvement with the literary and visual artists who came to be called the New York School, including also John Ashbery, Kenneth Koch, and James Schuyler. When Delmore Schwartz left the *Partisan Review,* Guest was invited to fill the post as poetry editor, where she encouraged the publication of O'Hara and others. As the fifties drew to a close, Guest, at that point the only female poet associated with the New York School, gathered together her first book of poems, *The Location of Things,* published as the decade ended (1960). Guest followed with *Poems: The Location of Things, Archaics, the Open Skies* (1962), which was promptly reviewed by William Dickey in the (magisterially male) *Kenyon Review.*

In this review, Dickey denigrates Guest's poetry as incoherent, irresponsible, and capricious, complaints clustering around his perception of an uncertainty of voice and self within the work. His criteria for evaluating "good" poetry demonstrate the unease or "discomfort with women who do not assert the self in writing, who instead write in part to bring into question the very notion of the self" that Carolyn Burke (cited in Fraser, "Line" 165) claims to be common among critical responses to women experimentalists—even if, as in this case, they are not identified as such. In his review, commenting on six new books of poetry, Dickey includes two women, "Miss Guest" and "Miss Plath" amidst four men: John W. Clark, Christopher Middleton, John Hollander, and Frederic Will (none of them a "Mr."). On the whole, he is disappointed, experiencing "tedium" and "irritation" at the

> failure of some of these poets to show a sense of responsibility to the reader. They expect the reader to work devotedly for them to solve conundrums, to supply transitions, to make, out of a haphazard assortment of building materials, a habitable dwelling. The poets will not trouble to be intelligent or exact. They will be satisfied with fragments of thoughts, melanges of images, comparisons which have no basis in similitude, phrases whose sonority disguises a lack of meaning.
>
> ("Responsibilities" 756)

A surpassing, if unwitting, description of language-oriented poetries, Dickey's commentary disdains the inaccessibility of the poet who refuses the transparency of language, who offers the reader a collaborative role, or who obscures the poetic voice as primary vehicle of authenticity and expression. Plath in particular stands in opposition to Guest. Miss Guest "is herself . . . *that self . . . curiously without coherence,*" and Dickey finds in her poetry a disunity that "abolishes relationship" and refuses "a sense of intelligible structure" or "meaningful sequence" (758; italics added). Miss Plath, in the pre-*Ariel* and formally polished *Colossus,* contrasts with the verbal arbitrariness of Guest, for in

Plath's poetry, "Nothing is arbitrary. The words are there because they can be used, and for purposes of revelation, not concealment. Finally, each passage establishes a *consistent, personal tone of voice,* which contributes to the individuality and unity of the poem" (762; italics added). In gentlemanly fashion, Dickey implicitly allows that women—so carefully marked off by the modest, girlish "Miss"—can write poetry, but only rarely can they escape the irrational and incoherent female self to transcend to the perfect unity and control of revelation.

It is against the continuing power of this kind of critical discourse that Kathleen Fraser more recently has questioned the articulation of the subject or self in women's poetry:

> if the subject is yet to be brought into focus, what learned prohibitions have women poets worked against to uncover and catch partial knowledge, fragmentary perception that disappears almost as fast as it arrives? What if the subject, itself, is resistance, vulnerability, seeming lack of will, the conditioned self-denial that creates uncertainty, unsteadiness in the world? How can the line [or form in general] be made to reflect these states?

> ("Line" 165)

In large part, language-oriented poets like Fraser have been teaching us in the 1980s and 1990s how to read back into this critical moment of 1962, a moment bearing the weight of sexist ideologies dominating the postwar fifties, of which Fraser, as a young poet entering the field, became acutely aware. On a fundamental level, Dickey's strategy of counterpointing Guest with Plath reveals a larger pattern, one that would repeatedly position Guest outside of the mainstream of women's poetry in the 1960s and 1970s; the Plath/Guest opposition manifests a general critical division between the expressive (those advocating the accessible voice of female experience) and the experimental (those concerned with the coded play of language) that has presently become standard in literary criticism. However, for the literary establishment of the late fifties and early sixties, the division boiled down to good and bad, unified and fragmentary, coherent and irrational, serious poet and "Miss."

During this moment prior to the Women's Liberation movement, Kathleen Fraser encountered Barbara Guest and her poetry in New York, but only after experiencing some significantly gender-informed poetic practices and assumptions that set up particular models of female poetry we find echoing through Dickey's review. A recent college graduate (having, incidentally, studied no women poets or authors at Occidental College), Fraser arrived in New York in the early 1960s to work as a journalist and ended up joining poetry workshops with Stanley Kunitz and Robert Lowell. With Kunitz, Fraser

read the poems of Elizabeth Bishop—presented as good because genderless—and then, by 1962, began hearing through these men of Sylvia Plath:

> In 1962 we read her poems; by 1963, she was dead. Plath was my first female role model in poetry. The male poets and editors were in love with her. Lowell read her poems at his reading. Not only did she have the superb craft and ear, but there was something seductive for the male literary world in her 'madness' and her tragic end.

> ("Tradition" 23)

Yearning for a "female role model, for a teacher who could show how one might attempt to be in the world as a woman poet, without choosing nervous breakdown, total isolation, or suicide as a solution," Fraser registered for a workshop by a woman poet unknown to her, Daisy Aldan ("Tradition" 23). Illness prevented Aldan's appearance, and she was replaced by Kenneth Koch, who taught Fraser many "healthy" things (a skepticism about sentimentality or high seriousness, an embrace of playfulness in language) but, she remembers, "I watched uneasily as he divided us into male poets and female sex objects who wrote poetry" ("Tradition" 23). Presumably, Fraser faced the prospect of becoming a "Miss Fraser," although Koch did introduce the young poet to Barbara Guest.

Risking oversimplification, I want to emphasize a primary and obvious division between the regard accorded male and female poets in these narratives of critical and poetic attitudes; but further, to suggest that a gendered set of aesthetic values exemplified by Dickey or Lowell or Koch becomes mirrored in the categorizations created by female poets themselves in the sixties and seventies, even as they discard a poetics of male-identification through strategies of emphatic feminization of self-expression (Plath, Sexton) and/or assertion of a feminist politics (Rich, Levertov). The establishment's valuing of voice (initially perceived as genderless) in the late-1950s perceptions of poets like Plath, Rich, or Levertov is carried over into the feminist privileging of a female voice of authenticity in the 1960s celebration and growth of women's poetry. My point is not to diminish this feminist accomplishment but to note parallels between Dickey's dismissal of Guest, Fraser's feelings of marginality, and, some twenty-five years later, a continuing stress upon identifying Guest's work against the "political ardors of Denise Levertov and Adrienne Rich or . . . the confessional intensity of Sylvia Plath and Anne Sexton," with whom she would have "no truck," the *Dictionary of Literary Biography* tells us (Manousos 296). As Fraser's memoir-essay testifies, the experiencing of this division was (and remains) acute as poets of female experience demanded a language of reportage and transparency and voice, and thus remained skeptical of women—like Guest or Fraser—whose work investigated the assumptions of language's access to truth and experience. This oppositional division, taken up and experienced by women poets, seems sustained by an unfortunate resistance to examining its contradictory connections to male-derived discourses already set up, in the late fifties and early sixties. Protected by this resistance, expectations about women's poetry, particularly with respect to the role of voice and self, often went unchallenged.

In what seems a deliberate blurring of these oppositional categories (useful as they can be), Guest's response to a 1992 interview question—"Did you go for confessional poetry?"—is telling: "I think all poetry is confessional" (Interview with Hillringhouse, 23). While this assertion validates a basis in the autobiographical that her carefully crafted poems often obscure, on another level, it speaks to a concept of self and experience that opens beyond the conventional assumptions of unity, authenticity, and voice that circumscribe Dickey's review and, by extension, a whole tradition of reading the lyric. Guest's poetics exhibits a concern with structures of female subjectivity that Fraser describes as the formal project of many contemporary women poets interested in language operations:

> the frame of the page, the measure of the line, has provided . . . the difficult pleasure of reinventing the givens of poetry, imagining in visual, structural terms core states of female social and psychological experience not yet adequately tracked: hesitancy, silencing or speechlessness, continuous disruption of time, 'illogical' resistance, simultaneous perception, social marginality.

("Line" 153)

What Dickey might read as incoherent or arbitrary, Fraser instructs us to think of as structural responses to female socialization and psychology that, within the "givens of poetry" or the norms of discourse, will seem deviant. In Guest's 1962 *Poems,* Dickey's displeasure might well have been provoked by **"Belgravia"** (Guest *SP* [*Selected Poems*] 13-14), which situates itself within conventions of love poetry while demonstrating the gendered constructions shaping voice, subjectivity, and language in these naturalized (i.e. masculine) rules of reading. The poem commits numerous sins for a reader like Dickey: an enfolded and veiled use of image ("fragment of thoughts, melanges of images"); an anticipation of expectations of the love lyric that are not carried through (a lack of "meaningful sequence" or "intelligible structure"); a speaking "I" that seems deferred and buried ("curiously without coherence"); a discursiveness characterized by limpid, passive, and open-ended structures (a refusal to be "intelligent or exact"); a generality and musicality of diction ("phrases whose sonority disguises a lack of meaning"); a movement toward variability and ambiguity rather than

revelation ("a failure . . . to show a sense of responsibility" and a "haphazard assortment of building materials"). Indeed, the poem conveys a peculiar sense of absence or disembodiment in its representational choices of image, diction and syntactical configurations—all of which dwell upon a "man" who, nonetheless, remains elusive, unspecified, yet omnipresent; and a female speaker, whose subjectivity is located in relationship to the construction of masculinity enacted by the poem's formal and linguistic moves.

The poem opens with an obvious gesture toward the love lyric—the first line and continuing refrain is "I am in love with a man"—while simultaneously reconsidering the genre in the first stanza's refusal of specificity, offering a generic man who is never personalized or directly addressed. The poem displaces the love relationship with a relationship between this man and his house while suspending any direct comment upon the "I" and the man:

> I am in love with a man
> Who is more fond of his own house
> Than many interiors which are, of course, less unique,
> But more constructed to the usual sensibility,
> Yet unlike those rooms in which he lives
> Cannot be filled with crystal objects.
>
> There are embroidered chairs
> Made in Berlin to look like cane, very round
> And light which do not break, but bend
> Ever so slightly, and rock at twilight as the cradle
> Rocks itself if given a slight push and a small
> Tune can be heard when several of the branches creak.

As the poem's seven stanzas develop, the metaphor of the house clearly tells us much about this man; the arrangement of the house suggests a controlling subjectivity that is privileged, composed, reflective, distant, analytical, and orderly. An elaborate conceit develops in the poem, but the poem's deliberately discursive arrangement of the female "I" extends the conceit into the arena of linguistic constructions of gender norms. Rather than the "authentic I," the speaking voice signifies a construction socialized to exist in support of masculinity and of a particular set of ideologies privileging masculine rationality, speech and power. Simultaneously, however, the poem's formal operations void the masculine subject, or, more precisely, reveal the naturalized masculine subject as a carefully constructed "self" that depends upon a singularity and unity of perspective, a regulated viewpoint of gender within our culture.

These first two stanzas establish a pattern of the lyric "I's" deferral and non-emergence. A characteristic syntactical doubling in the opening lines sets this pattern in motion, playing with our expectations of lineal development in the love poem: "I am in love with a man / who is more fond of his own house." This "more-than" structure, following as it does a statement of love, initially suggests that the "I" or "me" will be the object of comparison, and, hence, the source of the love lyric's distress. After all, who would want to be in love with a man who loves his house more than his wife or lover? Instead, the "I" is displaced with the generalized word choice, "interiors," so that we are encouraged to think literally of other houses while also retaining the trace of the expected "me." Furthermore, passive constructions bury the agency of the "I" while also seeming to disembody the "man": objects in the poem are put into action but the syntax consistently refuses to identify the actor. Thus, rooms are "filled with crystal objects," "There are embroidered chairs," "the cradle / Rocks itself if given a slight push," and "a small / Tune can be heard"—and yet the agent doing the action is carefully omitted by the grammatical structures.

In gendered terms, as the poem continues, this elimination of grammatical agency has dual effects. Certain actions coded as feminine (as in rocking the cradle), when presented in passive terms, increase the passivity of the speaking "I" as if demonstrating the way female subjectivity is continually deflected through the discursive structures of our culture (women are nurturing, etc.) in a way that negates female agency. At the same time, the passive structures deemphasize the masculine body to demonstrate the hierarchical privileging of (masculine) mind over (female) body. The next stanzas in the poem pointedly reference physical activities only to relegate them to serving the superior workings of the "thinking" man:

> Many rooms are in his house
> And they can all be used for exercise.
> There are mileposts cut into the marble,
> A block, ten blocks, a mile
> For the one who walks here always thinking,
> Who finds a meaning at the end of a mile
> And wishes to entomb his discoveries.

A singularly non-muscular diction and controlled calmness mark this retreat of the body into the mind, a deadening process that makes use of the body only to find and "entomb" "meaning." The body is never present (except in the generalized "one who walks") in these linguistic structures of passivity that disembody the masculine subject while recording the material effects of his subjectivity as it leaves evidence of its arranging and measuring mastery upon the environment: "There are embroidered chairs"; "There are mileposts cut into the marble"; and the rooms "can all be used for exercise." The sense of the "man" who transcends body but nonetheless leaves the marks of his agency chillingly defines the role of the speaking "I" in the next stanzas:

> I am in love with a man
> Who knows himself better than my youth,

> My experience or my ability
> Trained now to reflect his face
> As rims reflect their glasses,
> Or as mirrors, filigreed as several European
> Capitals have regarded their past
> Of which he is the living representative,
> Who alone is nervous with history.

> I am in love with a man
> In this open house of windows,
> Locks and balconies,
> This man who reflects and considers
> The brokenhearted bears who tumble in the leaves.

The female "I" is arranged within this masculine structure as carefully as the chairs or crystal objects, serving to reflect back to the man his masculine identity. Within this structure, the feminine role of "mirror" keeps the masculine subject from being "alone with history," allowing him to transcend the historical and social through a fixing of gender subjectivities. In this house of locks and windows, the man "reflects and considers" the activity on the lawn rather than engaging with the "brokenhearted bears" (his children?), removing himself through mental contemplation from the messiness of materiality associated, in this image of the bears, with the feminine role of maternity. Thus, the feminine saves him from history by mirroring a contained and unified masculinity, a universalized vision of a civilized, rational self and past ("filigreed as several European / Capitals have regarded their past"); at the same time, the feminine embodies history—the maternal body, the one who bodies forth generations, the body denied the ability to reflect and consider so that men may do so. As a "living representative" of a western narrative of history and self, "filigreed" as though needing a shiny veneer, the man is "nervous with history" or with the threat that the veneer might be stripped or peeled away to reveal the "representation" as representation. To reduce the naturalized image of the unified and privileged masculine self to a fiction constructed through history is to leave the "one who walks" necessarily "nervous with history" if facing it "alone." The feminized mirror, the "other," supports the place of man in history.

The poem's attention to ideological foundations of masculinity takes on additional resonance when considered within the context of the fifties and early sixties in America, a time of rigid attempts to homogenize and define gender identity in ways that supported the privileged status of men. Guest's poem, like Simone de Beauvoir's *The Second Sex* (1949, trans. 1953) or Betty Friedan's *The Feminine Mystique* (1963), responds in part to the post-war retreat into domesticity, privacy, and tradition that relegated women (at least in the ideal) to subservient positions, both in the home and in the public sphere. The dominance of gender norms encouraged in the fifties depended, of course, upon a denial of the performative and the constructed quality of gender, encouraged by a regulated view of masculinity or femininity as natural rather than historically circumscribed, as universal rather than culturally scripted. The poem's final stanzas, set in a garden outside the house, emphasize the careful arrangement of perspective shaping apprehensions of both self and other, signalling the careful construction of subjectivity within the gendered space of the conventional love poem and the culture it inhabits:

> In the garden which thus has escaped all intruders
> There when benches are placed
> Side by side, watching separate entrances,
> As one might plan an audience
> That cannot refrain from turning ever so little
> In other directions and witnessing
> The completion of itself as seen from all sides,
>
> I am in love with him
> Who only among the invited hastens my speech.

Subordinate clauses defer, for an entire stanza, the grammatical subject and verb of the main clause—the "I am" of the final "I am in love." This accumulative syntax, pushing the "I" further from our view while also enclosing it with a verbal density, incrementally builds an image of enclosure and performance, wherein the garden is set up in such a way as to ensure the "audience" has the proper perspective and to discourage the audience from turning their gaze upon themselves—from "turning ever so little / In other directions and witnessing / The completion of itself as seen from all sides." It is within this structure, within this directed gaze, that the "I" loves, a love progressively deromanticized by the poem's emphasis upon the constructions of gender scripting this performance. The final lines enact a linguistic doubleness in their grammatical ambiguity: does the "him" hasten her speech "only among the invited," suggesting that he permits her to speak in front of the audience he has chosen and is directing; or is he himself among "the invited," a circumstance hastening her to speak of the conditions of masculinity, a speaking that suggests an assertion of her agency (being the one to invite) and voice (her choice to speak) that emerges from such exposure of the structures relegating her to object status? A palimpsestic layering of textual meaning, what Barbara Einzig calls a "syntactic mobility," offers us both readings at once, allowing them to interact and resonate through the poem's various constructions and deconstructions of gendered subjectivity (Einzig 8).

Kathleen Fraser has likened "overlaying" of details and thoughts in Guest's work to "bits of fine-colored tissue used in collage," and quotes Honor Johnson's delineation of Guest's "techniques of abstraction and methods of composition that might be applied to words and their reinvented relations inside the poem" ("Line" 162). Similarly evoking a painting analogy, Marianne DeK-

oven describes the "palette" of Fraser's own writing as made of a "nonreferential combination of precision and generality. . . . [P]articular expressions of emotion . . . [are] combined with both rigorous refusal, in the abstract diction, of specifying context or narrative coherence . . . and also diction which establishes very precise, very specific actions or objects" (14). That Fraser has learned from Guest something about "the mysteries of language" takes on an historical significance within post-war avant-garde practice, for both women, in generational sequence and overlap, have conducted careers "in relation" to specific "reading communities" (various avant-gardes, feminist, New Critical, confessional, etc.) and to the "socio-poetic forces they represent," as DuPlessis describes the history of Guest's reception ("Flavor of Eyes" 23). That poets like DuPlessis, Fraser, and Einzig continue or extend Guest's "increasing focus on the surface of language," as Einzig puts it (7), suggests to us the necessary and practical project of a feminist innovative poetics that involves developing communities of women poets to resist the isolation and erasure of the "token woman" in avant-garde circles; establishing networks of publication and commentary; and identifying predecessors like Guest or the early modernists. Their innovative work validates, contextualizes, and instructs the poetics of linguistically-oriented women poets, confirming a relationship between feminism, feminine subjectivity, and poetic innovation.

Notes

1. Guest's *Selected Poems* (1995) is preceded by numerous books of poetry, a biography of H. D. (*Herself Defined*), a novel (*Seeking Air*), a variety of collaborative works with artists, and art criticism (primarily for *Art News*).

2. As editor of *HOW(ever)*, Fraser published Guest's work. Additionally, she discusses Guest in two essays on the topic of women experimental writers, "The Tradition of Marginality" and "Line." On *Seeking Air*, Guest's novel, see Fraser, "One Hundred and Three Chapters."

3. Fraser notes that, despite having been published by the time of the anthology in at least four books and many New York School magazines, Guest's work was unfavorably judged by the men putting together the collection: "Bill Berkson, who advised Shapiro and Padgett, explained to me later: 'We didn't think her work was that interesting'" ("Tradition" 24).

4. "Flavor of Eyes" 23. DuPlessis notes that Guest was included in Donald Allen's *New American Poetry* (1960) and its revision, *The Postmoderns* (1982), indicating a degree of recognition within a post-1945 American avant garde.

Barbara Guest (essay date September-October 2002)

SOURCE: Guest, Barbara. "Three Essays." *The American Poetry Review* 31, no. 5 (September-October 2002): 13-15.

[*In the following essay, including three pieces that appear in Guest's 2003 publication,* Forces of Imagination: Writing on Writing, *the poet considers the aim of poetry, the role of imagination, and the many aspects of art at large.*]

WOUNDED JOY

The most important act of a poem is to reach further than the page, so that we are aware of another aspect of the art. This will introduce us to its spiritual essence. This essence has no limits. What we are setting out to do is to *delimit* the work of art, so that it appears to have *no beginning and no end, so that it overruns the boundaries of the poem on the page.* All of the arts share this need for delimiting.

Coleridge said that a poem must be both *obscure and clear.* This is what we search for in our poem, this beautiful balance between the *hidden and the open.*

What is this poem that appears to be opening within our hands? Mallarmé says that Poetry is the intensely musical and emotional state of the Soul.

Do you ever notice as you write that no matter what there is on the written page something appears to be in *back of everything that is said, a little ghost.* I judge that this ghost is there to remind us there is always more, an elsewhere, a hiddenness, a secondary form of speech, an eye blink. Not on the print before us. And yet the secret is that this secondary form of writing is what backs up the primary one, it is the *obscure essence that lies within the poem that is not necessary to put into language, but that the poem must hint at, must say "this is not all I can tell you. There is something more I do not say." Leave this little echo to haunt the poem, do not give it form, but let it assume its own ghost-like shape.* It has the shape of your own soul as you write.

John Donne wrote this very modern paragraph describing the state of his mind troubling his prayers, but he might as well be describing, and probably is, the state of his mind as he approaches a poem:

> A memory of yesterday's pleasures, a fear of tomorrow's dangers, a straw under my knee, a noise in mine ear, a light in mine eye, and anything a nothing, a fancy a chimera in my braine troubles me.

He can also be saying that these things trouble him as he reaches for his pen to make a poem. The presence of a hidden anxiety about a poem might be a necessary prodding to go intensely into the poem. A poem should tremble a little. Again remember, "Poetry is nothing but the intensely musical and emotional state of the Soul."

Baudelaire tells us that a poem should have within it "a dose of the bizarre." This can be a wakeup call within the poem, to say the poet is nodding, has become too mundane, too involved with a daily recounting. I love this phrase. I suppose it is the basis of Surrealism, but in Surrealism *everything is bizarre.* I prefer this little dosage. When one is nodding or recapitulating events of daily life and we become mundane, then this little *"dose of the bizarre," like holding a minnow in your hands, or a feather of a riotous color, not too much, or the bizarre will overwhelm the poem and to have nothing but a bizarre account can be very boring.*

To sail off on a ship of delight, a brief, necessary voyage, within the poem to encourage pleasure, to escape the mundane, the chain of struggle. If and when necessary, this pleasure will sparkle at the hour of a poem's struggle to endure, the poem's midnight.

René de Gourmont suggested that the past must constantly be re-invented. As you take issue with the poetry of the past, remember that it has its usages, its declarations and affirmation, because it has existed so long. Think of the past as the modern poem runs along beside you. As the past darkens the window.

In the youth of my poetry I was fortunate to be surrounded by painters in the Art movement of Abstract Expressionism and I learned from them.

First I noticed these painters appeared to have a lot more joy than did the poets. They were more playful! Their ideas were exploding on the canvas and they had a sense of freedom the poets were only beginning to learn from them. This was perhaps a heritage of Surrealism, but the fact that they were a MOVEMENT and were accepted even by the commercial world, which meant money, lent them this freedom. Not only were they enjoying themselves, but they were a MOVEMENT. And a profitable one. The entire city of New York liked their art. More importantly the air around them was hesitating as it turned into *the moment.* The idea of a moment with its special apparatus is a good thing for poetry, also.

No subject is introduced, the painting is spontaneous. The subject is found as you explore the canvas. And that is a useful idea. I remember when a painter visited and I had a little poem in the typewriter and he looked at it, the little unwritten poem, but with its title already secured. The painter said "never give a poem a title, let the poem find its subject."

Remember Picasso said, "you may give a painting a title, but it always turns out to be something else." Frank O'Hara's poem, "Sardines," plays with this idea.

Another thing these painters borrowed from Surrealism, was the use of "accident." I know that I have accidentally typed a wrong word and thought, "well that's a better word, anyway."

Behind these sentences is the idea of no pre-planning. I can always tell when I am reading a pre-planned poem; there is no freshness in it. No mysterious element of change, as when the poem lies quivering on its page, its contents wounded, yet the poet is joyful.

An admonishment not to be fearful of tarnishing your wings. To rest in the glow of great poets; they always have something to tell you. To welcome the substance that glitters and rubs off.

I cannot end a discussion of poetics without stressing the power of the Imagination. To lean on it! To trust it! Imagination is the single most important element in poetry. When I examine a poem, it is not for its form or style. There are plenty of "successful" poems. One must look for the vibrating imagination hid under those stones of form or style. How empty is all their dazzle without imagination.

Coleridge wrote that in his youth he was *"trembling with imaginative power." Imagination is the absent flower of Mallarmé, a turbulent presence to be evoked.*

THE FORCE OF IMAGINATION

The forces of the imagination from which strength is drawn have a disruptive and capricious power. If the imagination is indulged too freely, it may run wild and destroy or be destructive to the artist. "The frenzied addiction to art," wrote Baudelaire, is a canker that devours.

If not used imagination may shrivel up. Even in old age Goethe wrote that he feared the wild tricks of a lively imagination. "What is the good," he said, "of shaping the intellect, securing the supremacy of reason? Imagination lies in wait."

Plato also suspected imagination. He thought man could be transformed by the imagination and suggested laws that would prohibit the miming of extravagant evil characters. He advised changing from dramatic to narrative language if writing became too overwrought. It is fear of what begins as fiction ending as reality.

Plato said, "If any poet were to come to us and show his art we should kneel down before him as a rare and holy and delightful being, but we should not permit him to stay. We should anoint him with myrrh and set a garland of wool upon his head and send him away to another city."

These words express fear of the possibility of a destructive risk that lurks in poetry. Baudelaire continually reminds us that the magic of art is inseparable from its risks. And this risk is also a necessary component of poetry as it performs its balancing act between reality and the imaginative force at work within the poem. The poet enters the poem with a hood over the poet's eyes. The poet has arrived from a distance from a real world. The poet is a conjurer balancing on the barre of risk like a dancer, or acrobat. Have you ever wondered why the painter is prone to painting acrobats, and not only in the famous painting of Picasso? It is because in all the arts the practitioner, the poet, the artist, even the musician with a new set of rules maintains a balancing act between reality or rules, and the imagination. And there is where the risk lies, in that balancing act, so filled with fervor and terror as the little word is placed on its spool of light.

Hegel's language is radical. He believes that art exists in absolute freedom, and is allowed to attach itself freely, he says, to any form it chooses that will help it "exercise the imagination." We can view the poem as existing for a time in pure space, exercising imagination, no matter how mundane the exercise may appear, how untidy the bag of words it carries with it. The poem is enjoying a spatial freedom before it settles into images and rhythm and order of its new habitat on the page.

In this state of suspension the art that is created is infinitely susceptible to new shapes because no shape can be regarded as final. No form is safe when the poet is in a state of perpetual self-transformation, or where, as Hegel suggests, the artist is in a condition of "infinite plasticity." This position of "subjectivity" or "openness" the poem desires to obtain, free to be molded by forces that shall condition the imagination of the poet.

In the sixteenth century Ariosto complains that Chivalry is being destroyed by the introduction of firearms. This is what Orlando Furioso is about, and I borrowed the title in my own mock epic, ***Rocks on a Platter***. In Orlando Furioso we are given a setting of pure fantasy and fantasy is written all over the poem. The reader can have no doubt of its unreality.

It is the innovation of Ariosto we admire, an alarming innovation and bespeaks the power of innovation when we are told the poem may have aided in the destruction of the codes of chivalry.

The idea of "infinite plasticity" is a noble one. It causes the poet to breathe more freely. One thinks of Prometheus Unbound. And it is the blood of "boundlessness" that enters the poem.

When I was a young poet I was immensely influenced, as you know, by painters with whom I circulated. Their ideas of painting took up my young life. I envied their freedom. I began to use some of their methods. Often titles arrived after the poem was finished, as O'Hara illustrates so humorously in his poem, *Sardines.*

The idea belonged to Picasso, who said about subject matter: "You have to have an idea of what you are going to do, but it should be a vague idea. It's always something else in the end." This idea of Picasso's also, for some reason, lends an idea of space to the poem.

Painters also gave me a sense of being unconfined to a page. I became experimental without using that word. I wrote **"Parachutes, My Love Could Carry Us Higher"** without considering whether my parachutes went up or down.

The Hollywood songwriter wrote, "Imagination is funny, it makes the whole world sunny."

André Breton said, "to imagine is to see."

SHIFTING PERSONA

I

The windows are normally independent of one another, although you may pass back and forth from one view to the other. This absurd interdependence is like a lark at break of day. The altitude is assumed by the upper window. The lark song. The other window is the lark.

The person inside a literary creation can be both viewer and insider. The window is open and the bird flies in. It closes and a drama between the bird and its environment begins.

When the person who is you is the viewer, you believe an extraordinary strength exists in that position. You are outside the arena of dispute or creativity or blasphemy, dwelling in a private space where emotive speculation is stronger than fact or action each of which passes before you in an attempt at dissimulation which you are free to dispute. This is called the orchid position, because of the extravagant attention the viewer demands.

Sometimes it is the flap of a tent held back, or a cushion pushed next to a door or a turban lifted over one eye, even a mountain top is offered where the person who is outside the scene can take up an observation post and gaze closely down into the valley.

Without the person outside there would be no life inside. The scene relies on that exterior person to explain the plangent obsessions with which Art is adorned.

Yet inside the window is the person who is you, who are now looking out, shifted from the observer to the inside person and this shows in your work. When you are the inside person you can be both heavy and delicate, depending upon your mood; you have a sense of responsibility totally different from the you outside. You occupy the lotus position.

You are depending upon yourself to a degree that can cause extreme unease, but this is acute to all species of creativity. You find you cannot always depend upon yourself as absorbedly as when you assumed the orchid position, because you are more vulnerable, dependent upon the psychic phenomena that occupy your meditation. The lotus position is one of exaggerated self-dependency, in which the eye goes inward so frequently that rest stops are required, something like paragraphic encasings.

These rest stops can be seen in the shifts that take place between the persona of the creator and the persona of the observer. In a well-developed persona the shifts take place before our eyes without revealing themselves, as if gauze had been spun especially for the purpose and a curtain falls slyly between the persona of the person and the persona that is now accepted. We travel back to the mountain-top and the valley with the shifting of spatial contacts.

II

The ability to project both windows is a sign of originality and is rare. In writing concealed within a limited physical environment, as in the work of Jane Austen, the threat of claustrophobia hangs over the whole body of the novels. In order to relieve this environmental tension, the writer with her strokes of genius elevates the characters above a physical dimension, so that although their persons appear to inhabit a closed drawing-room they are actually removed from the interior to the exterior as they move beyond their limited space through the projection of the author.

They are persons who are capable in their minds, even in an obtuse mind, of looking outside themselves into another place, of shifting their persons. They are relieved of ordained claustrophobia, as is the reader, who might be stuck in that drawing-room, who is lifted by the author's inked quill, her euphemism for time, to project beyond singularity.

She has even trained us to watch for the apparitions of ourselves moving alongside the characters. This is on a grand scale, her knowledge of sequence in time caught in a limited physical dimension. The person of the author travels from afar.

III

There is a book about Picasso that records him during his labors while attempting to create his version of Las Meninas of Velázquez. What emerges from this devastating account is his conflict with the person of Velázquez as Picasso attempted to stabilize his own persona. Picasso consistently refused to consider his position as revisionist.

Picasso went into the Velázquez painting very far. Yet his enormous struggle which involved his wife and friends took place far less within the realm of Art than in the psychological struggle of an artist to survive the atmosphere of an originating persona. We are also aware of Picasso's need to endow Velázquez with the Picasso persona.

The painting of Velázquez is even more complicated as several persons compete for the dominating person within Las Meninas.

> Picasso said it was a very peculiar affair.
>
> Velázquez had painted the King and Queen in the mirror as if they were outside the canvas—which is the fact—but as if it was they who were painting the canvas, since he, Velázquez, was inside it with Las Meninas.
>
> And we said it was an even more peculiar affair for Picasso to paint in that position, while Picasso painted the mirror in which he might have added himself to the King and Queen, who in fact must be on the same side as Velázquez opposite Las Meninas, etc. etc.[1]

Finally out of the hundreds of studies Picasso made of this painting, one in particular succeeds. It is called "The Studio" and there are no persons inside that space.

One of the lessons to be learned from this shortened account of Picasso and Las Meninas is that the deliberate ambiguity of the reigning person produces the Velázquez painting's magnificent climaxes, and prevents revision of the work of the originating person. Las Meninas has added to the mystery of the person in Art.

IV

In *The Uses of Literature,* Italo Calvino writes (I quote from him because he has so rapidly summed up the stunning performance of Flaubert):

> Gustave Flaubert the author of the complete works of Gustave Flaubert projects outside himself the Gustave Flaubert who is the author of Madame Bovary, who in turn projects from himself the character of a middle-class married woman in Rouen, Emma Bovary, who projects from herself that Emma Bovary whom she dreams of being. . . . It was Flaubert himself who gave us the precise clue to this with his famous phrase, "Mme. Bovary, c'est moi."

V

The person with the omnipotence of a cloud hovers over a poem pointing to the direction which it should take.

The poem's concealed autobiography. A memoir of itself which is released as it becomes a presence existing in time.

When the poem is on its feet, to leave it alone to express its own person. The relief from the intensity of the poem's presence as it heats up.

An astonishment throughout the poem at the vibrations of its ego. "I" becomes the bystander and the poem is propelled by the force of the "person" stripped bare.

Richard Wollheim writes: "The artist is essentially a spectator of his work."

VI

A landscape appears before us, solitary in its incidents of meadow broken by low running water, the sky dour, the earth in twists moving like the water into continuous dark drainage. This landscape appears solitary and yet there in the short grass is the hidden person placed there by the writer who desired a human instrument to bear witness to this attempt to construct with a fictional or real landscape a syllabus of art.

The person is given a place of habitation within the construction and endowed with a knowledge not only of the force of nature, but the aesthetic purpose behind the writer's decision to create this scene.

This witness, positioned inside the work of art, conveys to us the secret intent of the writer so that following the instructions now transmitted we may work our way through to the pitch of the art before us, the center where the writing rocks back and forth before taking its plunge into space.

The person is our conduit. Hidden arms are stretched pointing to the variations, the hollows, the deliberate judgments of time within the work of art.

The person has a voice. It echoes the tone of the writer and it is this echoing voice that assembles what we call the "tone" of poetry or prose.

It is the gathering together of varying instructions by the concealed person that presents us with what we may call a "reliable" landscape.

Note

1. Helen Parmelin, *Picasso Plain* (New York: St. Martin's Press, 1963). See also Richard Wollheim, *Painting as an Art,* The A. W. Mellon Lectures in the Fine Arts, Bollingen Series (Princeton, N.J.: Princeton University Press, 1984), pp. xxxv-33.

This essay appeared in *Poetics Journal,* ed. Lyn Hejinian, Barrett Watten, 1990.

FURTHER READING

Criticism

Diggory, Terence. "Barbara Guest and the Mother of Beauty." *Women's Studies: An Interdisciplinary Journal* 30 (2001): 75-94.

Examines Guest's role as a central figure among contemporary American poets.

DuPlessis, Rachel Blau. "The Gendered Marvelous: Barbara Guest, Surrealism and Feminist Reception." In *The Scene of My Selves: New Work on New York School Poets,* Terence Diggory and Stephen Paul Miller, pp. 189-213. Orono, Maine: The National Poetry Foundation, 2001.

Considers feminist criticism of Guest's poetics through an examination of works including "The Poetess," "The Farewell Stairway," "The Nude," and "Dora Maar."

Hillringhouse, Mark. "Barbara Guest: An Interview by Mark Hillringhouse." *The American Poetry Review* 21, no. 4 (July-August 1992): 23-30.

Guest discusses her poetry and the cultural aesthetics that inspire her.

Keller, Lynn. "Becoming "A Compleat Travel Agency": Barbara Guest's Negotiations with the Fifties Feminine Mystique." In *The Scene of My Selves: New Work on New York School Poets,* Terence Diggory and Stephen Paul Miller, pp. 215-27. Orono, Maine: The National Poetry Foundation, 2001.

Considers the influence of American cultural standards for women in the 1950s on the voices and themes of Guest's poetry.

William Morris
1834-1896

English poet, novelist, essayist, short story writer, and translator.

The following entry provides information on Morris's life and career from 1858 through 2000.

INTRODUCTION

Morris was a member of the Pre-Raphaelite circle of artists and poets that included Charles Algernon Swinburne, Edward Burne-Jones, Canon Dixon, and Dante Gabriel Rossetti, their inspirational leader. Nineteenth-century English life, radically altered by the rise of industrial capitalism, was intolerable to Morris and his circle. In their rejection of this way of life, the Pre-Raphaelites looked to an era whose values were deeper than profit and production—the age of medievalism with its tradition of romance and craftsmanship. The love of things medieval is apparent in all Morris's works: his architecture, painting, graphics, and furniture design, as well as his literary efforts.

BIOGRAPHICAL INFORMATION

Morris was born on March 24, 1834 in Walthamstow, Essex, England. He entered Exeter College, Oxford, with the intention of joining the ministry. However, after meeting Burne-Jones and reading the works of John Ruskin, he became interested in the Gothic revival in art and architecture. He began writing romances and poetry and turned his attention to architecture, taking a position with an architectural firm upon his graduation. After meeting Rossetti, however, he abandoned his architectural career for painting. Later, he formed his own design company and pioneered the modern movement toward functional simplicity in furniture and design. Morris's devotion to aesthetics and opposition to machine-aided industry contributed to his interest in socialism. In the 1880s he was an active member of the Democratic Federation and then the Socialist League, editor of the Socialist organ *Commonweal,* and a tireless lecturer on the relationship of art to society and industry. In 1890, he founded the Kelmscott Press, which published books similar to the illuminated manuscripts of the Middle Ages. Morris's research into typography and medieval printing techniques spurred a revival of the art of fine book production in England.

He was offered the post of poet laureate in 1892, but he refused the invitation and spent his last years writing prose romances. He died on October 3, 1896.

MAJOR WORKS

Morris's poetry is marked by several distinct influences. *The Defence of Guenevere* (1858) echoes Thomas Malory's *Le Morte D'Arthur* in its adaptation of medieval material, and borrows many of its images from the paintings of Rossetti. The romantic poetry of the volume revives the splendor of the Middle Ages as well as the haunting qualities of Gothic fantasy. Though at the time of publication reviewers took little notice of the work, several later critics regretted that Morris never returned to the style of the collection with its dramatic narratives and dream poems. Morris's next work, *The Life and Death of Jason* (1867), is a departure from his earlier style. In *Jason* as well as in his following work, *The Earthly Paradise* (1868-70), Morris clearly follows his avowed master, Geoffrey Chaucer. With *Jason*, Morris was hailed for restoring an art of narrative nearly forgotten since Chaucer's time. In retelling the Greek legend of Jason and his quest for the golden fleece, Morris regarded the heroic age from a medieval viewpoint. Critics liken his scenes of crowds, processions, and battles to tapestries that portray the romance of the human race.

The theme that Morris first treated in *Jason*—the desire to escape death and celebrate beauty and life—was elaborated in *The Earthly Paradise*. Critics hailed this work for its execution and masterly poetic design, in which the months of a year provide the framework for the retelling of two tales, one from Greek mythology and one from Norse and medieval sources. *The Earthly Paradise* signaled a change in Morris's style. Influenced by his visit to Iceland in 1869 and by his experience translating *Völsunga Saga*, Morris turned from Chaucer to the Norse eddas, and from the narrative to the epic form. His grand epic venture is *Sigurd the Volsung* (1876), a "magnificent chant" which recounts the story of Sigurd. While some reviewers found the work inordinately long and marred with verbal archaisms, to many it was Morris's most important contribution.

CRITICAL RECEPTION

Morris's narrative and epic poetry no longer command the attention they attracted in the late nineteenth and early twentieth centuries. Moreover, his poetic works have always drawn mixed reviews. Some commentators feel his works lack action and feeling, and are no more than lovely pictures conveyed in tedious, sterile verse. To others Morris was a master storyteller with a supreme gift of invention, who recreated the worlds of garden, court, and battlefield in a clear, expressive style. He was devoted to the belief that to find meaning one must create beauty and he sought to convey his artistic ideals in all of his work. He is viewed as an important figure in the Pre-Raphaelite movement and a prolific contributor in several genres, including political writing, fantasy, short fiction, furniture design, architecture, and book printing. Several critical studies have investigated his noteworthy role in nineteenth-century literature, politics, and art.

PRINCIPAL WORKS

Poetry

The Defence of Guenevere, and Other Poems 1858
The Life and Death of Jason 1867
The Earthly Paradise. 3 vols. 1868-70

Love Is Enough; or, The Freeing of Pharamond 1873
The Story of Sigurd the Volsung, and the Fall of the Niblungs (poetry and short stories) 1876
Chants for Socialists 1884
The Pilgrims of Hope 1886
Poems by the Way 1891
The Collected Works of William Morris. 24 vols. (poetry and prose) 1910-15
William Morris: Artist, Writer, Socialist. 2 vols. (poetry and prose) 1936

Other Major Works

A Dream of John Ball, and A King's Lesson (short stories) 1888
A Tale of the House of the Wolfings and All the Kindreds of the Mark (short stories) 1889
News from Nowhere (novel) 1890
The Story of the Glittering Plain (novel) 1891
The Wood beyond the World (novel) 1894
The Well at the World's End (novel) 1896
The Sundering Flood (novel) 1897
The Water of the Wondrous Isles (novel) 1897
The Letters of William Morris to His Family and Friends (letters) 1950
The Unpublished Lectures of William Morris (lectures) 1969

CRITICISM

Richard Garnett (essay date 1858)

SOURCE: Garnett, Richard. Review of *The Defence of Guenevere*, by William Morris. In *William Morris: The Critical Heritage*, edited by Peter Faulkner, pp. 32-7. London: Routledge & Kegan Ltd., 1973.

[*In the following review, which was originally published in March 1858, Garnett investigates the poetic influences on Morris's* The Defence of Guenevere.]

It might not be easy to find a more striking example of the indestructibility of anything truly beautiful, than the literary resurrection of King Arthur and his Knights, after so many centuries' entombment in the Avalon of forgetfulness. The Israfel of this revival was Mr. Tennyson, the first peal of whose awakening trumpet sounded some twenty-six years ago in his marvellous 'Lady of Shalott,' followed by utterances of no inferior beauty, some made public for our delight, others, it is whispered, as yet withheld from us. But the movement thus inaugurated has taken a direction which Mr. Tennyson cannot have anticipated. We are not alluding to Sir E.

Bulwer's elegant but affected and artificial 'King Arthur,' nor to Mr. Arnold's lovely 'Tristram and Iseult.' These are remarkable poems, but not startling phenomena. But the pre-Raphaelite poets and painters have made the Arthurian cyclus their own, by a treatment no less strange and original than that which has already thrown such novel light on the conceptions of Shakespeare and the scenery of Palestine. Not long since our columns contained a notice of certain fresco illustrations of Arthurian romance attempted at Oxford by painters of this school, who, being for the most part utterly unknown to fame, may be supposed to have been invented on purpose. One of these gentlemen has now enabled us to form some opinion of his qualifications for his task by the publication of the book before us; and we do not hesitate to pronounce, that if he do but wield the brush to half as much purpose as the pen, his must be pictures well worth a long pilgrimage to see.

In advocating the claims of an unknown poet to public attention, it is before all things necessary to establish his originality—a very easy matter in the present instance. It might almost have seemed impossible for any one to write about Arthur without some trace of Tennysonian influences, yet, for Mr. Morris, the Laureate might never have existed at all. Every one knows Tennyson's 'Sir Galahad'—Mr. Morris's exquisite poem on the same subject is unfortunately much too long for quotation, but our meaning will be sufficiently illustrated by a few of the initiatory stanzas:

> It is the longest night in all the year,
>   Near on the day when the Lord Christ was born;
> Six hours ago I came and sat down here,
>   And ponder'd sadly, wearied and forlorn.
>
> The winter wind that pass'd the chapel-door,
>   Sang out a moody tune, that went right well
> With mine own thoughts: I look'd down on the floor,
>   Between my feet, until I heard a bell
>
> Sound a long way off through the forest deep,
>   And toll on steadily; a drowsiness
> Came on me, so that I fell half asleep,
>   As I sat there not moving: less and less
>
> I saw the melted snow that hung in beads
>   Upon my steel-shoes, less and less I saw
> Between the tiles the bunches of small weeds:
>   Heartless and stupid, with no touch of awe
>
> Upon me, half-shut eyes upon the ground,
>   I thought; O! Galahad, the days go by,
> Stop and cast up now that which you have found,
>   So sorely you have wrought and painfully.

The difference between the two poets obviously is that Tennyson writes of mediæval things like a modern, and Mr. Morris like a contemporary. Tennyson's 'Sir Galahad' is Tennyson himself in an enthusiastic and devotional mood; Mr. Morris's is the actual champion,

just as he lived and moved and had his being some twelve hundred years ago. Tennyson is the orator who makes a speech for another; Mr. Morris the reporter who writes down what another man says. Whatever mediævalists may assert, poetry flourishes far more in the nineteenth century than it ever did in the seventh; accordingly the Laureate is as superior in brilliance of phrase, finish of style, and magic of versification, as he is inferior in dramatic propriety and *couleur locale.* We might continue this parallel for ever, but shall bring the matter to a head by observing that Mr. Morris's poems bear exactly the same relation to Tennyson's as Rossetti's illustrations of the Laureate to the latter's own conceptions. We observed in noticing these designs that they illustrated anything in the world rather than Tennyson, and have certainly seen no reason to change our opinion. The more we view them, the more penetrated we become with their wonderful beauty (always excepting that remarkable angel in the Robinson Crusoe cap), but also the more impressed with their utter incompatibility with their text. Tennyson is the modern *par excellence,* the man of his age; Rossetti and Morris are the men of the middle age; and while this at once places them in a position of inferiority as regards Tennyson, it increases their interest towards ourselves, as giving us what it would be vain to expect from any one else. Who but Mr. Rossetti or his double could have written anything like this?—

> For these vile things that hem me in,
> These Pagan beasts who live in sin,
> The sickly flowers pale and wan,
> The grim blue-bearded castellan,
> The stanchions half worn-out with rust,
> Whereto their banner vile they trust—
> Why, all these things I hold them just
> Like dragons in a missal-book,
> Wherein, whenever we may look,
> We see no horror, yea, delight
> We have, the colours are so bright;
> Likewise we note the specks of white,
> And the great plates of burnish'd gold.
>
> Just so this Pagan castle old,
> And everything I can see there,
> Sick-pining in the marshland air,
> I note; I will go over now,
> Like one who paints with knitted brow,
> The flowers and all things one by one,
> From the snail on the wall to the setting sun.
>
> Four great walls, and a little one
> That leads down to the barbican,
> Which walls with many spears they man,
> When news comes to the castellan
> Of Launcelot being in the land.
>
> And as I sit here, close at hand
> Four spikes of sad sick sunflowers stand,
> The castellan with a long wand
> Cuts down their leaves as he goes by,
> Ponderingly, with screw'd up eye,

And fingers twisted in his beard—
Nay, was it a knight's shout I heard?

Other pieces are yet more characteristic; for example, **'Golden Wings,'** which seems to conduct us through a long gallery of Mr. Rossetti's works, with all their richness of colouring, depth of pathos, poetical but eccentric conception, and loving elaboration of every minute detail. After all, those who have read the beautiful poems, contributed by the painter to the defunct *Oxford and Cambridge Magazine,* will probably think this dissertation and Mr. Morris's dedication equally superfluous.

Another influence, however, has done something towards making Mr. Morris what he is. In spite of his having taken every precaution that human foresight can suggest to render himself unintelligible, it is impossible that so fine a poet and deep a thinker as Mr. Browning should remain without influence on a generation so accessible as our own to the fascination of genius. Accordingly his influence widens day by day, and he already counts several disciples of unusual talent, from Mr. Owen Meredith downwards. These, however, are too undisguisedly imitators to earn a higher praise than that of considerable adroitness. In Mr. Morris's volume we for the first time trace the influence of Browning on a writer of real original genius, and the result is very curious. **'Sir Peter Harpdon's End'** shows that Mr. Morris possesses considerable dramatic power, and is so far satisfactory, otherwise it appears to us ultra-Browningian, unpleasant and obscure. **'The Judgment of God'** reads exactly like Browning's dramatic lyrics, but is, we think, better than any but the very best of them. By far the best of these pieces, however, is **'The Haystack in the Floods,'** where Mr. Morris's native romance and pathos unite with his model's passion and intensity to form a whole unsurpassed, we will venture to say, by any man save Tennyson, since the golden age of British poetry expired with Byron at Missolonghi. We regret that it is too long to quote here.

To describe any one as Rossetti *plus* Browning, is as much as to say that he is not a little affected and obscure. This, perhaps, is Mr. Morris's misfortune; his carelessness and inattention to finish is his fault, and a serious one. It has ruined the first two poems in his volume, which should have been the finest. A little trouble will, perhaps, make **'Queen Guenevere's Defence'** what it ought to be, but **'King Arthur's Tomb'** will never be fit for anything but the fire. We can only suppose Mr. Morris's frequent indifferent grammar, atrocious rhymes, and lines unscannable on any imaginable metrical system, to be the consequence of an entirely erroneous notion of poetry. Let him be assured that poetry is just as much an art as painting, and that the selfsame principle which forbids his drawing a lady with three feet ought to keep him from pen-

ning an iambic verse with six. All arts are but modifications of the one archetypal beauty, and the laws of any one, *mutatis mutandis,* bind all the rest.

No fleck, happily, mars the pure beauty of **'Sir Galahad'** and **'The Chapel in Lyoness,'** pieces in which the rough chivalry of the middle ages appears as it were transfigured, and shining with a saintly halo of inexpressible loveliness. Of **'Sir Peter Harpdon'** we have already spoken. **'Rapunzel,'** the next poem, will be a fearful stumbling-block to prosy people, and we must own that it is, if possible, too romantically ethereal in its wild, weird beauty. Like Shelley, Mr. Morris is often guilty of what we may call luminous indistinctness. We are delighted with his poetry, but cannot very well tell what it is all about; 'we see a light, but no man.' This is particularly the case with those very remarkable pieces, **'Golden Wings,' 'The Blue Closet,' 'Spell-bound,'** and **'The Wind,'** in which it is true that something exciting happens, but, as the courier in *Little Dorrit* has it, there is no why. We return to **'Rapunzel,'** to borrow two passages of perfect beauty:—

[quotes **'A Duel'** and **'Guendolen'**]

The minor poems may be distributed into three classes, the Arthurian, the Froissartian, and the purely imaginative. Though bewildered with a perfect *embarras de richesses,* we are fain to content ourselves with a single example of each:—

[quotes **'Riding Together'**, **'The Eve of Crecy'** and **'Summer Dawn'**]

The barbarous rhyme, *dawn* and *corn,* is but a sample of that carelessness of which the author must get the better if he is ever to rank as a master of his art. Still his volume is of itself a sufficient proof that it is not necessary to be a master in order to delight and astonish. Mr. Morris is an exquisite and original genius, a poet whom poets will love.

Walter Pater (essay date 1868)

SOURCE: Pater, Walter. "Poems by William Morris." In *Pre-Raphaelitism: A Collection of Critical Essays,* edited by James Sambook, pp. 105-17. Chicago: The University of Chicago Press, 1974.

[*In the following essay, originally published in* The Westminster Review *in 1868, Pater gives a reading of Morris's oeuvre with an emphasis on the mixture of Hellenic, medieval, and modern influences in the poet's works.*]

This poetry is neither a mere reproduction of Greek or mediaeval life or poetry, nor a disguised reflex of modern sentiment. The atmosphere on which its effect depends belongs to no actual form of life or simple form of poetry. Greek poetry, mediaeval or modern poetry, projects above the realities of its time a world in which the forms of things are transfigured. Of that world this new poetry takes possession, and sublimates beyond it another still fainter and more spectral, which is literally an artificial or "earthly paradise." It is a finer ideal, extracted from what in relation to any actual world is already an ideal. Like some strange second flowering after date, it renews on a more delicate type the poetry of a past age, but must not be confounded with it. The secret of the enjoyment of it is that inversion of homesickness known to some, that incurable thirst for the sense of escape, which no actual form of life satisfies, no poetry even, if it be merely simple and spontaneous. It is this which in these poems defines the temperament or personality of the workman.

The writings of the romantic school mark a transition not so much from the pagan to the mediaeval ideal, as from a lower to a higher degree of passion in literature. The end of the eighteenth century, swept by vast disturbing currents, experienced an excitement of spirit of which one note was a reaction against an outworn classicalism severed not more from nature than from the genuine motives of ancient art; and a return to true Hellenism was as much a part of this reaction as the sudden pre-occupation with things mediaeval. The mediaeval tendency is in Goethe's *Goetz von Berlichingen,* the Hellenic in his *Iphigenie.* At first this mediaevalism was superficial. Adventure, romance in the poorest sense, grotesque individualism—that is one element in mediaeval poetry, and with it alone Scott and Goethe dealt. Beyond them were the two other elements of the mediaeval spirit; its mystic religion at its apex in Dante and Saint Louis, and its mystic passion, passing here and there into the great romantic loves of rebellious flesh, of Lancelot and Abelard. That stricter, imaginative mediaevalism which recreates the mind of the middle age, so that the form, the presentment grows outward from within, came later with Victor Hugo in France, with Heine in Germany.

The *Defence of Guenevere: and Other Poems,* published ten years ago, are a refinement upon this later, profounder mediaevalism. The poem which gives its name to the volume is a thing tormented and awry with passion, like the body of Guenevere defending herself from the charge of adultery, and the accent falls in strange, unwonted places with the effect of a great cry. These Arthurian legends, pre-Christian in their origin, yield all their sweetness only in a Christian atmosphere. What is characteristic in them is the strange suggestion of a deliberate choice between Christ and a rival lover. That religion shades into sensuous love, and sensuous love into religion, has been often seen; it is the experience of Rousseau as well as of the Christian mystics. The Christianity of the middle age made way among a people whose loss was in the life of the senses only by the possession of an idol, the beautiful idol of the Latin hymn-writers, who for one moral or spiritual sentiment have a hundred sensuous images. Only by the inflaming influence of such idols can any religion compete with the presence of the fleshly lover. And so in these imaginative loves, in their highest expression the Provençal poetry, it is a rival religion with a new rival cultus that we see. Coloured through and through with Christian sentiment, they are rebels against it. The rejection of one idolatry for the other is never lost sight of. The jealousy of that other lover, for whom these words and images and strange ways of sentiment were first devised, is the secret here of a triumphant colour and heat. It is the mood of the cloister taking a new direction, and winning so a later space of life it never anticipated. Who knows whether, when the simple belief in them has faded away, the most cherished sacred writings may not for the first time exercise their highest influence as the most delicate amorous poetry in the world?

Hereon, as before in the cloister, so now in the chateau, the reign of reverie set in. The idolatry of the cloister knew that mood thoroughly, and had sounded all its stops. For in that idolatry the idol was absent or veiled, not limited to one supreme plastic form like Zeus at Olympia or Athena in the Acropolis, but distracted, as in a fever dream, into a thousand symbols and reflections. Quite in the way of one who handles the older sorceries, the Church has a thousand charms to make the absent near. Like the woman in the idyll of Theocritus—ελκε τυ τηνον εμον ποτι δωμα τον ανδρα,[1] is the cry of all her bizarre rites. Into this kingdom of reverie, and with it into a paradise of ambitious refinements, the earthly love enters, and becomes a prolonged somnambulism. Of religion it learns the art of directing towards an imaginary object sentiments whose natural direction is towards objects of sense. Hence a love defined by the absence of the beloved, choosing to be without hope, protesting against all lower uses of love, barren, extravagant, antinomian. It is the love which is incompatible with marriage, for the chevalier who never comes, of the serf for the chatelaine, the rose for the nightingale, of Rudel for the Lady of Tripoli.[2] Another element of extravagance came in with the feudal spirit: Provençal love is full of the very forms of vassalage. To be the servant of love, to have offended, to taste the subtle luxury of chastisement, of reconciliation—the religious spirit, too, knows that, and meets just there, as in Rousseau, the delicacies of the earthly love. Here, under this strange complex of conditions, as in some medicated air, exotic flowers of sentiment expand, among people of a remote and unaccustomed beauty, somnambulistic, frail, androgynous, the light almost shining through them, as the flame of a little taper shows through the Host. Such loves were too fragile and adventurous to last more than for a moment.

That whole religion of the middle age was but a beautiful disease of disorder of the senses; and a religion which is a disorder of the senses must always be subject to illusions. Reverie, illusion, delirium; they are the three stages of a fatal descent both in the religion and the loves of the middle age. Nowhere has the impression of this delirium been conveyed as by Victor Hugo in *Notre Dame de Paris*. The strangest creations of sleep seem here, by some appalling licence, to cross the limit of the dawn. The English poet too has learned the secret. He has diffused through **"King Arthur's Tomb"** the maddening white glare of the sun, and tyranny of the moon, not tender and far-off, but close down—the sorcerer's moon, large and feverish. The colouring is intricate and delirious, as of "scarlet lilies." The influence of summer is like a poison in one's blood, with a sudden bewildered sickening of life and all things. In **"Galahad: a Mystery,"** the frost of Christmas night on the chapel stones acts as a strong narcotic; a sudden shrill ringing pierces through the numbness; a voice proclaims that the Grail has gone forth through the great forest. It is in the **"Blue Closet"** that this delirium reaches its height with a singular beauty, reserved perhaps for the enjoyment of the few:

> How long ago was it, how long ago,
> He came to this tower with hands full of snow?
> "Kneel down, O love Louise, kneel down," he said,
> And sprinkled the dusty snow over my head.
> He watch'd the snow melting, it ran through my hair,
> Ran over my shoulders, white shoulders, and bare.
> "I cannot weep for thee, poor love Louise,
> For my tears are all hidden deep under the seas.
> In a gold and blue casket she keeps all my tears;
> But my eyes are no longer blue, as in old years;
> For they grow grey with time, grow small and dry—
> I am so feeble now, would I might die."
> Will he come back again, or is he dead?
> O! is he sleeping, my scarf round his head?
> Or did they strangle him as he lay there,
> With the long scarlet scarf I used to wear?
> Only I pray thee, Lord, let him come here!
> Both his soul and his body to me are most dear.
> Dear Lord, that loves me, I wait to receive
> Either body or spirit this wild Christmas-eve.

A passion of which the outlets are sealed, begets a tension of nerve, in which the sensible world comes to one with a reinforced brilliance and relief—all redness is turned into blood, all water into tears. Hence a wild, convulsed sensuousness in the poetry of the middle age, in which the things of nature begin to play a strange delirious part. Of the things of nature the mediaeval mind had a deep sense; but its sense of them was not objective, no real escape to the world without one. The aspects and motions of nature only reinforced its prevailing mood, and were in conspiracy with one's own brain against one. A single sentiment invaded the world; everything was infused with a motive drawn from the soul. The amorous poetry of Provence, making the starling and the swallow its messengers, illustrates the whole attitude of nature in this electric atmosphere, bent as by miracle or magic to the service of human passion.

The most popular and gracious form of Provençal poetry was the *nocturn,* sung by the lover at night at the door or under the window of his mistress. These songs were of different kinds, according to the hour at which they were intended to be sung. Some were to be sung at midnight—songs inviting to sleep, the *serena,* or *serenade;* others at break of day—waking songs, the *aube,* or *aubade.*[3] This waking-song is put sometimes into the mouth of a comrade of the lover, who plays sentinel during the night, to watch for and announce the dawn; sometimes into the mouth of one of the lovers, who are about to separate. A modification of it is familiar to us all in *Romeo and Juliet,* where the lovers debate whether the song they hear is of the nightingale or the lark; the aubade, with the two other great forms of love-poetry then floating in the world, the sonnet and the epithalamium, being here refined, heightened, and inwoven into the structure of the play. Those, in whom what Rousseau calls *les frayeurs nocturnes* are constitutional, know what splendour they give to the things of the morning; and how there comes something of relief from physical pain with the first white film in the sky. The middle age knew those terrors in all their forms; and these songs of the morning win hence a strange tenderness and effect. The crown of the English poet's book is one of these songs of the dawn:

> Pray but one prayer for me 'twixt thy closed lips,
>   Think but one thought of me up in the stars.
> The summer-night waneth, the morning light slips,
>   Faint and grey 'twixt the leaves of the aspen,
>   betwixt the cloud-bars,
> That are patiently waiting there for the dawn:
>   Patient and colourless, though Heaven's gold
> Waits to float through them along with the sun.
> Far out in the meadows, above the young corn,
>   The heavy elms wait, and restless and cold
> The uneasy wind rises; the roses are dun;
> Through the long twilight they pray for the dawn,
> Round the lone house in the midst of the corn.
>   Speak but one word to me over the corn,
>   Over the tender, bow'd locks of the corn.

It is the very soul of the bridegroom which goes forth to the bride; inanimate things are longing with him; all the sweetness of the imaginative loves of the middle age, with a superadded spirituality of touch all its own, is in that!

The **Defence of Guenevere** was published in 1858; the **Life and Death of Jason** in 1867; and the change of manner wrought in the interval is entire, it is almost a revolt. Here there is no delirium or illusion, no experiences of mere soul while the body and the bodily senses sleep or wake with convulsed intensity at the prompting of imaginative love; but rather the great primary passions under broad daylight as of the pagan Veronese. This simplification interests us not merely for the sake of an individual poet—full of charm as he is—but chiefly because it explains through him a transition which, under many forms, is one law of the life of the human spirit, and of which what we call the Renaissance is only a supreme instance. Just so the monk in his cloister, through the "open vision," open only to the spirit, divined, aspired to and at last apprehended a better daylight, but earthly, open only to the senses. Complex and subtle interests, which the mind spins for itself may occupy art and poetry or our own spirits for a time; but sooner or later they come back with a sharp rebound to the simple elementary passions—anger, desire, regret, pity and fear—and what corresponds to them in the sensuous world—bare, abstract fire, water, air, tears, sleep, silence—and what De Quincey has called the "glory of motion."[4]

This reaction from dreamlight to daylight gives, as always happens, a strange power in dealing with morning and the things of the morning. Think of this most lovely waking with the rain on one's face—(Iris comes to Argus as he sleeps; a rainbow, when he wakes, is to be the pledge she has been present:)

> Then he, awaking in the morning cold,
> A sprinkle of fine rain felt on his face,
> And leaping to his feet, in that wild place,
> Looked round and saw the morning sunlight throw
> Across the world the many-coloured bow,
> And trembling knew that the high gods, indeed,
> Had sent the messenger unto their need.
>
> [XI, 194-200]

Not less is this Hellenist of the middle age master of dreams, of sleep and the desire of sleep—sleep in which no one walks, restorer of childhood to men—dreams, not like Galahad's or Guenevere's, but full of happy, childish wonder as in the earlier world. It is a world in which the centaur and the ram with the fleece of gold are conceivable. The song sung always claims to be sung for the first time. There are hints at a language common to birds and beasts and men. Everywhere there is an impression of surprise, as of people first waking from the golden age, at fire, snow, wine, the touch of water as one swims, the salt taste of the sea. And this simplicity at first hand is a strange contrast to the sought-out simplicity of Wordsworth. Desire here is towards the body of nature for its own sake, not because a soul is divined through it.

And yet it is one of the charming anachronisms of a poet, who, while he handles an ancient subject, never becomes an antiquarian, but vitalizes his subject by keeping it always close to himself, that betweenwhiles we have a sense of English scenery as from an eye well practised under Wordsworth's influence, in the song of the brown river-bird among the willows, the casement half opened on summer-nights, the

> Noise of bells, such as in moonlit lanes
> Rings from the grey team on the market night.

Nowhere but in England is there such a nation of birds, the fern-owl, the water-hen, the thrush in a hundred sweet variations, the ger-falcon, the kestrel, the starling, the pea-fowl; birds heard from the field by the townsman down in the streets at dawn; doves everywhere, pink-footed, grey-winged, flitting about the temple, troubled by the temple incense, trapped in the snow. The sea-touches are not less sharp and firm, surest of effect in places where river and sea, salt and fresh waves, conflict.

All this is in that wonderful fourteenth book, the book of the Syrens. The power of an artist will sometimes remain inactive over us, the spirit of his work, however much one sees of it, be veiled, till on a sudden we are *found* by one revealing example of it which makes all he did precious. It is so with this fourteenth book of **Jason.** There is a tranquil level of perfection in the poem, by which in certain moods, or for certain minds, the charm of it might escape. For such the book of the Syrens is a revealing example of the poet's work. The book opens with a glimpse of white bodies, crowned and girt with gold, moving far-off on the sand of a little bay. It comes to men nearing home, yet so longing for rest that they might well lie down before they reach it. So the wise Medea prompts Orpheus to plead with the Argonauts against the Syrens,

> Sweetly they sung, and still the answer came
> Piercing and clear from him, as bursts the flame
> From out the furnace in the moonless night;
> Yet, as their words are no more known aright
> Through lapse of many ages, and no man
> Can any more across the waters wan,
> Behold those singing women of the sea,
> Once more I pray you all to pardon me,
> If with my feeble voice and harsh I sing
> From what dim memories may chance to cling
> About men's hearts, of lovely things once sung
> Beside the sea, while yet the world was young.
>
> [XIV, 113-24]

Then literally like an echo from the Greek world, heard across so great a distance only as through some miraculous calm, subdued in colour and cadence, the ghosts of passionate song, come those matchless lyrics.

In handling a subject of Greek legend, anything in the way of an actual revival must always be impossible. Such vain antiquarianism is a waste of the poet's power. The composite experience of all the ages is part of each one of us; to deduct from that experience, to obliterate any part of it, to come face to face with the people of a past age, as if the middle age, the Renaissance, the eighteenth century had not been, is as impossible as to become a little child, or enter again into the womb and be born. But though it is not possible to repress a single phase of that humanity, which, because we live and move and have our being in the life of humanity, makes us what we are; it is possible to isolate such a phase, to throw it into relief, to be divided against ourselves in zeal for it, as we may hark back to some choice space of our own individual life. We cannot conceive the age; we can conceive the element it has contributed to our culture; we can treat the subjects of the age bringing that into relief. Such an attitude towards Greece, aspiring to but never actually reaching its way of conceiving life, is what is possible for art.

The modern poet or artist who treats in this way a classical story comes very near, if not to the Hellensim of Homer, yet to that of the middle age, the Hellenism of Chaucer. No writer on the Renaissance has hitherto cared much for this exquisite early light of it. Afterwards the Renaissance takes its side, becomes exaggerated and facile. But the choice life of the human spirit is always under mixed lights, and in mixed situations; when it is not too sure of itself, is still expectant, girt up to leap forward to the promise. Such a situation there was in that earliest return from the overwrought spiritualities of the middle age to the earlier, more ancient life of the senses; and for us the most attractive form of classical story is the monk's conception of it, when he escapes from the sombre legend of his cloister to that true light. The fruits of this mood, which, divining more than it understands, infuses into the figures of the Christian legend some subtle reminiscence of older gods, or into the story of Cupid and Psyche that passionate stress of spirit which the world owes to Christianity, have still to be gathered up when the time comes.

And so, before we leave *Jason,* a word must be said about its mediaevalisms, delicate inconsistencies which, coming in a Greek poem, bring into this white dawn thoughts of the delirious night just over and make one's sense of relief deeper. The opening of the fourth book describes the embarkation of the Argonauts; as in a dream the scene shifts and we go down from Iolchos to the sea through a pageant of the fourteenth century in some French or Italian town. The gilded vanes on the spires, the bells ringing in the towers, the trellis of roses at the window, the close planted with apple-trees, the grotesque undercroft with its close-set pillars, change by a single touch the air of these Greek cities and we are at Glastonbury by the tomb of Arthur. The nymph in furred raiment who seduces Hylas is conceived frankly in the spirit of Teutonic romance; her song is of a garden enclosed, such as that with which the glass-stainer of the middle ages surrounds the mystic bride of the song of songs. Medea herself has a hundred

touches of the mediaeval sorceress, the sorceress of the Streckelberg or the Blocksberg; her mystic changes are Christabel's. Here again is an incident straight out of the middle age,

> But, when all hushed and still the palace grew,
> She put her gold robes off, and on her drew
> A dusky gown, and with a wallet small
> And cutting wood-knife girt herself withal,
> And from her dainty chamber softly passed
> Through stairs and corridors, until at last
> She came down to a gilded watergate,
> Which with a golden key she opened straight,
> And swiftly stept into a little boat,
> And, pushing off from shore, began to float
> Adown the stream, and with her tender hands
> And half-bared arms, the wonder of all lands,
> Rowed strongly through the starlit gusty night.
>
> [VII, 117-29]

It is precisely this effect, this grace of Hellenism relieved against the sorrow of the middle age, which forms the chief motive of *The Earthly Paradise,* with an exquisite dexterity the two threads of sentiment are here interwoven and contrasted. A band of adventurers sets out from Norway, most northerly of northern lands, where the plague is raging, and the host-bell is continually ringing as they carry the sacrament to the sick. Even in Mr. Morris's earliest poems snatches of the sweet French tongue had always come with something of Hellenic blitheness and grace. And now it is below the very coast of France, through the fleet of Edward III., among the painted sails of the middle age, that we pass to a reserved fragment of Greece, which by some Θεια τυχη [wondrous chance] lingers on in the Western Sea into the middle age. There the stories of *The Earthly Paradise* are told, Greek story and romantic alternating; and for the crew of the "Rose Garland" coming across the sins of the earlier world with the sign of the cross and drinking Rhine wine in Greece, the two worlds of sentiment are confronted.

We have become so used to austerity and concentration in some noble types of modern poetry, that it is easy to mislike the lengthiness of this new poem. Yet here mere mass is itself the first condition of an art which deals with broad atmospheric effects. The water is not less medicinal, not less gifted with virtues, because a few drops of it are without effect; it is water to bathe and swim in. The songs, **"The Apology to the Reader,"** the month-interludes, especially those of April and May, which are worthy of Shakespeare, detach themselves by their concentrated sweetness from the rest of the book. Partly because in perfect story-telling like this the manner rises and falls with the story itself, **"Atalanta's Race,"** **"The Man born to be King,"** **"The Story of Cupid and Psyche,"** and in **"The Doom of King Acrisius,"** the episode of Danae and the shower of gold, have in a pre-eminent degree what is characteristic of the whole book, the loveliness of things newly washed with fresh water; and this clarity and chasteness, mere qualities here of an exquisite art, remind one that the effectual preserver of all purity is perfect taste.

One characteristic of the pagan spirit these new poems have which is on their surface—the continual suggestion, pensive or passionate, of the shortness of life; this is contrasted with the bloom of the world and gives new seduction to it; the sense of death and the desire of beauty; the desire of beauty quickened by the sense of death. "*Arriéré!*" you say, "here in a tangible form we have the defect of all poetry like this. The modern world is in possession of truths; what but a passing smile can it have for a kind of poetry which, assuming artistic beauty of form to be an end in itself, passes by those truths and the living interests which are connected with them, to spend a thousand cares in telling once more these pagan fables as if it had but to choose between a more and a less beautiful shadow?" It is a strange transition from the earthly paradise to the sad-coloured world of abstract philosophy. But let us accept the challenge; let us see what modern philosophy, when it is sincere, really does say about human life and the truth we can attain in it, and the relation of this to the desire of beauty.

To regard all things and principles of things as inconstant modes or fashions has more and more become the tendency of modern thought. Let us begin with that which is without,—our physical life. Fix upon it in one of its more exquisite intervals—the moment, for instance, of delicious recoil from the flood of water in summer heat. What is the whole physical life in that moment but a combination of natural elements to which science gives their names? But those elements, phosphorus and lime, and delicate fibres, are present not in the human body alone; we detect them in places most remote from it. Our physical life is a perpetual motion of them—the passage of the blood, the wasting and repairing of the lenses of the eye, the modification of the tissues of the brain by every ray of light and sound—processes which science reduces to simpler and more elementary forces. Like the elements of which we are composed, the action of these forces extends beyond us; it rusts iron and ripens corn. Far out on every side of us these elements are broadcast, driven by many forces; and birth and gesture and death and the springing of violets from the grave are but a few out of ten thousand resulting combinations. That clear, perpetual outline of face and limb is but an image of ours under which we group them—a design in a web the actual threads of which pass out beyond it. This at least of flame-like our life has, that it is but the concurrence renewed from moment to moment of forces parting sooner or later on their ways.

Or if we begin with the inward world of thought and feeling, the whirlpool is still more rapid, the flame more eager and devouring. There it is no longer the gradual darkening of the eye and fading of colour from the wall, the movement of the shore side, where the water flows down indeed, though in apparent rest, but the race of the midstream, a drift of momentary acts of sight and passion and thought. At first sight experience seems to bury us under a flood of external objects, pressing upon us with a sharp, importunate reality, calling us out of ourselves in a thousand forms of action. But when reflection begins to act upon those objects they are dissipated under its influence, the cohesive force is suspended like a trick of magic, each object is loosed into a group of impressions, colour, odour, texture, in the mind of the observer. And if we continue to dwell on this world, not of objects in the solidity with which language invests them, but of impressions unstable, flickering, inconsistent, which burn, and are extinguished with our consciousness of them, it contracts still further, the whole scope of observation is dwarfed to the narrow chamber of the individual mind. Experience, already reduced to a swarm of impressions, is ringed round for each one of us by that thick wall of personality through which no real voice has ever pierced on its way to us, or from us to that, which we can only conjecture to be without. Every one of those impressions is the impression of an individual in his isolation, each mind keeping as a solitary prisoner its own dream of a world.

Analysis goes a step further still, and tells us that those impressions of the individual to which, for each one of us, experience dwindles down, are in perpetual flight; that each of them is limited by time, and that as time is infinitely divisible, each of them is infinitely divisible also, all that is actual in it being a single moment, gone while we try to apprehend it, of which it may ever be more truly said that it has ceased to be than that it is. To such a tremulous wisp constantly reforming itself on the stream, to a single sharp impression, with a sense in it, a relic more or less fleeting, of such moments gone by, what is real in our life fines itself down. It is with the movement, the passage and dissolution of impressions, images, sensations, that analysis leaves off, that continual vanishing away, that strange perpetual weaving and unweaving of ourselves.

Such thoughts seem desolate at first; at times all the bitterness of life seems concentrated in them. They bring the image of one washed out beyond the bar in a sea at ebb, losing even his personality, as the elements of which he is composed pass into new combinations. Struggling, as he must, to save himself, it is himself that he loses at every moment.

"Philosophiren," says Novalis, "ist dephlegmatisiren, vivificiren."[5] The service of philosophy, and of religion and culture as well, to the human spirit, is to startle it into a sharp and eager observation. Every moment some form grows perfect in hand or face; some tone on the hills or sea is choicer than the rest; some mood of passion or insight or intellectual excitement is irresistibly real and attractive for us for that moment only. Not the fruit of experience but experience itself is the end. A counted number of pulses only is given to us of a variegated, dramatic life. How may we see in them all that is to be seen in them by the finest senses? How can we pass most swiftly from point to point, and be present always at the focus where the greatest number of vital forces unite in their purest energy?

To burn always with this hard gem-like flame, to maintain this ecstasy, is success in life. Failure is to form habits; for habit is relative to a stereotyped world; meantime it is only the roughness of the eye that makes any two things, persons, situations—seem alike. While all melts under our feet, we may well catch at any exquisite passion, or any contribution to knowledge that seems by a lifted horizon to set the spirit free for a moment, or any stirring of the senses, strange dyes, strange flowers and curious odours, or work of the artist's hands, or the face of one's friend. Not to discriminate every moment some passionate attitude in those about us and in the brilliance of their gifts some tragic dividing of forces on their ways, is on this short day of frost and sun to sleep before evening. With this sense of the splendour of our experience and of its awful brevity, gathering all we are into one desperate effort to see and touch, we shall hardly have time to make theories about the things we see and touch. What we have to do is to be for ever curiously testing opinion and courting new impressions, never acquiescing in a facile orthodoxy of Comte or of Hegel or of our own. Theories, religious or philosophical ideas, as points of view, instruments of criticism, may help us to gather up what might otherwise pass unregarded by us. "La philosophie," says Victor Hugo, "c'est le microscope de la pensée." The theory or idea or system which requires of us the sacrifice of any part of this experience, in consideration of some interest into which we cannot enter, or some abstract morality we have not identified with ourselves, or what is only conventional, has no real claim upon us.

One of the most beautiful places in the writings of Rousseau is that in the sixth book of the *Confessions,* where he describes the awakening in him of the literary sense. An undefinable taint of death had always clung about him, and now in early manhood he believed himself stricken by mortal disease. He asked himself how he might make as much as possible of the interval that remained; and he was not biassed by anything in his previous life when he decided that it must be by intellectual excitement, which he found in the clear, fresh writings of Voltaire. Well, we are all *condamnés,* as Hugo somewhere says: we have an interval and then we cease to be. Some spend this interval in listlessness, some in high passions, the wisest in art and song. For

our one chance is in expanding that interval, in getting as many pulsations as possible into the given time. High passions give one this quickened sense of life, ecstasy and sorrow of love, political or religious enthusiasm, or the "enthusiasm of humanity." Only, be sure it is passion, that it does yield you this fruit of a quickened, multiplied consciousness. Of this wisdom, the poetic passion, the desire of beauty, the love of art for art's sake, has most; for art comes to you professing frankly to give nothing but the highest quality to your moments as they pass, and simply for those moments' sake.

Notes

1. [My magic wheel, draw to my house the man I love. (Idyll II, 17-63, refrain.)]

2. [Geoffroi Rudel, Prince de Blaye, a Provençal poet of the twelfth century, was the author of a famous song celebrating distant love and thought to refer to the Countess of Tripoli; cf. Robert Browning, "Rudel to the Lady of Tripoli," in *Bells and Pomegranates,* III (1842).]

3. [Claude-Charles] Fauriel's "Historie de la poésie provençal" [Paris, 1846], Tome 2, ch. xviii.

4. [*The English Mail-Coach.*]

5. [Philosophizing is dephlegmatizing, vivifying. "Lolologische Fragmente 15," *Schriften,* ed. R. Samuel (1960), 2: 526. The original reads "Philosophistisiren."]

W. J. Courthope (essay date 1872)

SOURCE: Courthope, W. J. "An English View of the Limitations of Morris's Poetry." In *William Morris: The Critical Heritage,* edited by Peter Faulkner, pp. 182-88. London: Routledge & Kegan Ltd., 1973.

[*In the following essay, which initially appeared in the* Quarterly Review *in 1872, Courthope delineates the major flaws in Morris's* Earthly Paradise.]

Without in any way affecting the character of a mystic, Mr. Morris withdraws himself, perhaps, even farther than Mr. Rossetti from all sympathy with the life and interests of his time:—

> Of Heaven and Hell I have no power to sing,
> I cannot ease the burden of your fears,
> Or make quick-coming death a little thing.
> Or bring again the pleasures of past years,
> Nor for my words shall ye forget your tears,
> Or hope again for aught that I can say,
> The idle singer of an empty day.

[quotes next two stanzas]

Such is Mr. Morris's apology for taking us back to a kind of mediæval legend for the scheme of his *Earthly Paradise.* 'Certain gentlemen and mariners of Norway having considered all that they had heard of the "Earthly Paradise" set sail to find it, and, after many troubles, and the lapse of many years, came old men to some western land of which they had never before heard: there they died when they had dwelt there certain years much honoured of the strange people.' The narrative of their wanderings is told with much grace and pathos. A proposal by a priest of the strange people that feasts should be instituted, for the wanderers to hear some of the tales of their Greek ancestors, connects the stories of the poem with the introduction. Mr. Morris ascribes his inspiration to Chaucer, but we think that the design of **The Earthly Paradise** bears much more resemblance to the *Decameron* than to *The Canterbury Tales.* The characters are far more like the colourless ladies and gentlemen who left Florence during the plague, and serve so conveniently as narrators and audience of the Tales in the *Decameron,* than Chaucer's vivacious company of pilgrims. At the end of each of Boccaccio's stories, his ladies 'praise the tale,' or 'laugh very pleasantly', or 'feel their cheeks suffused with blushes'. In like manner Mr. Morris's wanderers 'watch the shades of the dead hopes pass by,' sit 'silent, soft-hearted, and compassionate,' or are 'wrapped up in soft self pity.' We are never interested in their actions, as in the quarrel between the Frere and the Sompnoure; indeed it is clear that the racy incidents of real life would be out of place among his legendary shadows. The symmetrical division of the Tales by periods of time is after the manner of the *Decameron*; but the institution of monthly feasts for the mere purpose of telling stories is a somewhat clumsy contrivance for connecting the tales with the introduction, and for giving the poet an excuse for a graceful prelude to every month of the year. In spite, however, of small blemishes, there is a beauty and completeness in the design of the **Earthly Paradise,** which gives it a fine distinction among the crowd of chaotic fragments that darken modern literature.

Of the manner in which Mr. Morris has executed his task we cannot speak with unmixed praise. In the first place it is clear that he has expended his whole skill upon investing his poems with an antique air. The closeness with which he reproduces the effect of the old romance style in his loosely constructed verse is often surprising as a poetical *tour de force.* A passage in the **'Lovers of Gudrun,'** where Guest the seer watches the sons of Olaf bathing, strikes us as particularly noticeable, but there are many parts of his tales, and especially the openings, where the ancient simplicity has been imitated with great fidelity. In his description of nature, also, the out-of-door freshness and *naïveté* of the romances has been very happily caught.

His command of the ancient style has, however, been acquired at the cost of other qualities far more essential to real success in narrative. In delineation of character, vivacity of incident, and energy of versification, Mr. Morris shows himself either negligent or incapable. His poetical method may be contrasted not unfairly with that of Ariosto. Like the great poet, he professedly appears 'in raiment clad of stories oft besung.' Ariosto's style, however, is extremely idiomatic, and generally ironical. Yet, though no revivalist, and while looking on the marvels of Turpin's Chronicle with the eye of a humourist, he had a poet's appreciation of all that was noble in the idea of chivalry. Mr. Morris, on the other hand, while trying above all things to tell his stories in the language of romance, often misses the romantic spirit; indeed, so far is he from feeling it, that he is for ever breathing into his Neo-Gothic verse the expression of that decrepit love-longing, which is the peculiar product of modern poetry. There is nothing heroic about his heroes. They perform great deeds, it is true, because the old stories so represent them; but the only adventures in which Mr. Morris shows any interest are their love affairs. Thus when Perseus falls in with Andromeda, several pages are taken up with a recital of all that they felt and said, but when the sea-monster appears, he is despatched in as many lines. Perseus is armed with the Gorgon's head, a weapon of such tremendous power, that he ought to have felt it should be used only on great occasions; yet he employs it on the least provocation, and against the most ignoble foes, merely, as it appears, that Mr. Morris may have the pleasure of conducting him back as quickly as possible to the embraces of Andromeda. Ruggiero, in the *Orlando Furioso,* has a similar enchanted shield, but he keeps it carefully under cover, and when on one occasion he gains the victory, by the accidental removal of the case, he flings the shield into a well. Even the lovers in Mr. Morris's stories do not command our respect. In the **'Lovers of Gudrun,'** perhaps the best story of the collection, our sympathy is claimed for Kiartan, who is deprived of his mistress by the treachery of his friend. In the old story we should probably feel compassion for such a man, for, though the knights of romance are by no means immaculate, their infidelities are generally lightly passed over in the *naïve* simplicity of the narrative. But how can we waste our sympathy on Mr. Morris's soft-hearted lover, who loiters in Norway, scarcely sending a meagre message to Gudrun, while he amuses himself with the king's sister Ingibiorg, who

> More than well
> Began to love him, and he let her love,
> Saying withal that nought at all might move
> His heart from Gudrun; and for very sooth
> He might have held that word; and yet for ruth
> *And a soft pleasure that he might not name*
> All unrebuked he let her soft eyes claim
> Kindness from his.

More tiresome still is Acontius. This youth having fallen in love with a lady whom he has just seen 'through half-shut eyes,' learns to his horror that she is to be sacrificed to Diana. Yet though he afterwards sees her twice, he has never the heart to speak to her, much less to effect her escape. It is characteristic of Mr. Morris, that after a thousand lines filled with languishing and lamentation, without one act of courage or ingenuity on his part, this most detestable of lovers, through the intervention of Venus, is rewarded by the hand of the beautiful Cydippe.

The heroines of the tales, on the other hand, are as forward as the heroes are languid. We have no objection to their falling in love at first sight—though the occasional appearance of some shrewish Katharine would certainly be a relief—but it appears to us that their unconcealed complaisance would have disenchanted any lovers more particular than Mr. Morris's. Even Aslaug, fostered in the rudest retirement, on the appearance of a ship off her coast, speculates whether 'the great lord' to whom it belongs will fall in love with her. Mr. Morris, in fact, seems to think that shame and reserve are qualities incompatible with simplicity. Yet he might remember that Homer's Nausicaa, on approaching her father's town with Ulysses in her waggon, bids him leave her, lest she should provoke comment by appearing in the company of a stranger.

Again, the author has the very slenderest appreciation of the value of incident. This is not the fault of his originals. Both the Greek and the Norse legends have their full complement of the marvellous, but for the marvellous Mr. Morris cares nothing. We confess that we approached these stories with delighted expectation. The reappearance of the dragon in poetry, and in the face of a sceptical age, is an event which all readers of poetry should welcome. We recalled the spirit-stirring combat between Ruggiero and the Ork, and the magnificent description of the dragon in the first book of the *Faery Queen*. But Mr. Morris cannot 'see' a dragon, much less can his dragons fight. When the Chimæra appears, the messenger who reports it to King Jobates confesses to having been so frightened as to be unable to say what it was like. When Mr. Morris himself has to describe the sea-beast killed by Perseus, this is all he has to say of him:—

> He beholding Jove's son drawing near
> A huge black fold against him did uprear,
> Maned with a hairy tuft, as some old tree
> Hung round with moss *in lands where vapours be!*

It excites neither surprise nor admiration that this most feeble and incapable monster should succumb beneath one whisk of the hero's magic sword.

Lastly, the natural languor of Mr. Morris's style makes his verse at once diffuse and tedious. An incurable habit of gossiping causes him to loiter in his narratives, when he should be swift and stirring. If one of his heroes, say the man born to be a King, sets out on a journey of life and death, we are told all that he thought about, whether the apples that he saw were ripe, and how many old women he passed, going to market. If a princess has occasion to look out of a window, Mr. Morris peeps to see what sort of a carpet she is standing on; and when he has married a pair of lovers in the middle of a story, he pauses to breathe a tearful blessing after them, telling them to make the most of their time, as they will probably some day grow tired of each other's company and at any rate they will have to die.

This tendency to diffuseness is encouraged by the metre of the poems. The heroic couplet, properly so called with all its proved capacities, is set aside in favour of the elementary style of Chaucer, who, if he were now alive, would be the first to own that the noble metre which he invented had received its last development from later hands. But Mr. Morris is far more diffuse than Chaucer himself. The latter, though he does not observe the couplet, rarely makes a break in the middle of a line, so that his rhymes are clearly marked. Mr. Morris, on the other hand, writes by sentences, and, as his chief aim is to give each sentence an archaic turn, his verse resembles old prose with incidental rhymes. In this way his rhymes become useless not only as points of rhetoric, but as points of limitation. We select a passage at random to illustrate our meaning.

> So Bodli nothing loth went every day
> When so they would to make the lovers gay,
> When so they would to get him gone, that these
> Even with such yearning looks their souls might please
> As must be spoken, but sound folly still
> To aught but twain, because no tongue hath skill
> To tell their meaning. Kinder, Kiartan deemed,
> Grew Bodli day by day, and ever seemed
> Well nigh as happy as the happy twain,
> And unto Bodli life seemed nought but gain,
> And fair the days were.

The octosyllabic metre, with its inherent facility, does not become vigorous in the hands of Mr. Morris, nor can we approve of his revival of the seven-line stanza, after its long supersession by the Spenserian stanza. It is in this measure, however, we think, that Mr. Morris writes best; indeed, when obliged to consider the ways and means of metre, he shows that he can be concise and forcible enough. The following stanza describes the feelings of Atalanta at her first interview with Milanion before the race:—

> What mean these longings, vague, without a name,
> And this vain pity never felt before,
> This sudden languor, this contempt of fame,
> This tender sorrow for the time past o'er,
> These doubts that grow each minute more and more?
> Why does she tremble as the time draws near,
> And weak defeat and woeful victory fear?

In the graceful epilogue to *The Earthly Paradise,* Mr. Morris sends forth his book to find the spirit of Chaucer, who, he says, will understand and sympathize with his attempt

> to lay
> The ghosts that crowd about life's empty day.

We confess we do not think that Chaucer, however gratified he might be with Mr. Morris's preference and real appreciation, would at all sanction his method of laying ghosts. Of all poets Chaucer shows the most vigorous enjoyment of the activity and incident of life, from which his fastidious scholar so delicately withdraws himself. With his quick perception of character and his genial humour, we believe that the father of our poetry would never have found the present a mere 'empty day.' Such a phrase might characterize the society that existed at Rome under the latter empire, where all the springs of political and social life were dried. But a nation like England, whose historical fame is still recent, and whose liberties are not extinct, does not subside at once into such a state of torpor as the expression indicates. It is true that the picturesqueness of life that marked the period of Chaucer, has almost entirely disappeared; it is true also that other arts like those of journalism and novel-writing have done much to supersede poetry in the representation of national manners; yet after all deductions, enough remains of passion in politics, and individuality in character to give opportunities to the poet who knows how to seize them. That the opportunities have not been seized argues, we think, less the emptiness of the day, than the incapacity of the poets.

Edmund Clarence Stedman (essay date 1887)

SOURCE: Stedman, Edmund Clarence. "Latter-Day Singers: Robert Buchanan, Dante Gabriel Rossetti, William Morris." In *Victorian Poets,* pp. 366-78. Boston: Houghton Mifflin Co., 1887.

[*In the following excerpt, Stedman provides an overview of Morris's poetic oeuvre.*]

It is but natural, then, that we should find in William Morris a poet who may be described, to use the phrase of Hawthorne, as an Artist of the Beautiful. He delights in the manifestation of objective beauty. Byron felt himself one with Nature. Morris is absorbed in the loveliness of his romantic work, and as an artist seems to find enchantment and content.

In this serenity of mood he possesses that which has been denied to greater poets. True, he sings of himself,

> Dreamer of dreams, born out of my due time,
> Why should I strive to set the crooked straight?

but what time could be to him more fortunate? Amid the problems of our day, and the uncertainty as to what kind of art is to result from its confused elements, there is at least repose in the enjoyment of absolute beauty. There is safety in an art without a purpose other than to refresh and charm. People who labor in "six counties overhung with smoke" are willing enough to forget them. Morris's proffer of the means to this end could not have been more timely. Keats had juster cause for dissatisfaction: he could not know how eagerly men would turn to his work when the grandiloquent period, in which he found himself so valueless, should have worn itself away. Besides, he never fairly attained his ideal. To him the pursuit of Beauty, rather than the possession, was a passion and an appetite. He followed after, and depicted her, but was not at rest in her presence. Had Keats lived,—had he lived to gain the feeling of Morris, to pass from aspiration to attainment, and had his delicious poems been succeeded by others, comparing with **"Isabella"** and **"The Eve of St. Agnes,"** as *The Earthly Paradise* compares with **"The Defence of Guenevere,"** then indeed the world would have listened to a singer

> Such as it had
> In the ages glad,
> Long ago!

Morris appears to have been devoted from youth to the service of the beautiful. He has followed more than one branch of art, and enjoys, besides his fame as a poet, a practical reputation as an original and graceful designer in decorative work of many kinds. The present era, like the Venetian, and others in which taste has sprung from the luxury of wealth, seems to breed a class of handicraftsmen who are adepts in various departments of creative art. Rossetti, Morris, Linton, Scott, Woolner, Hamerton, among others, follow the arts of song or of design at will. Doubtless the poet Morris, while making his unique drawings for stained glass, wall-paper, or decorative tile-work, finds a pleasure as keen as that of the artist Morris in the construction of his metrical romances. There is balm and recreation to any writer in some tasteful pursuit which may serve as a foil to that which is the main labor and highest purpose of his life.

As for his poetry, it is of a sort which must be delightful to construct: wholly removed from self, breeding neither anguish nor disquiet, but full of soft music and a familiar olden charm. So easeful to read, it cannot be unrestful to compose, and to the maker must be its own reward. He keeps within his self-allotted region; if it be that of a lotos-eater's dream, he is willing to be deluded, and no longing for the real makes him "half sick of shadows." In this respect he is a wise, sweet, and very fortunate bard.

Some years ago, judging of Morris by *The Defence of Guenevere, and Other Poems,* the only volume which he then had printed, I wrote of him: "Never a slovenly writer, he gives us pieces that repay close reading, but also compel it, for they smack of the closet and studio rather than of the world of men and women, or that of the woods and fields. He, too, sings the deeds of Arthur and Lancelot." Let me now say that there is no purer or fresher landscape, more clearly visible both to the author and the reader, than is to be found everywhere in the course of Morris's later volumes. Not only are his descriptions of every aspect of Nature perfect, but he enters fully into the effect produced by her changes upon our lives and feelings. He sings of June,

> And that desire that rippling water gives
> To youthful hearts to wander anywhere;

of the drowsy August languor,

> When men were happy, they could scarce tell why,
> Although they felt the rich year slipping by.

A thousand similar examples may be selected from his poems. But his first work was quite in sympathy with that of Rossetti: an effort to disconnect poetry from modern thought and purpose, through a return not so much to nature as to models taken from the age of ballad-romance. It was saturated with the Pre-Chaucerian spirit. In mediæval tone, color, and somewhat rigid drawing, it corresponded to the missal-work style of the Pre-Raphaelites in art. The manner was too studied to permit of swift movement or broad scope; the language somewhat ancient and obscure. There is much that is fine, however, in the plumed and heroic ballad, **"Riding Together,"** and **"The Haystack in the Flood"** is a powerful conception, wrought out with historic truth of detail and grim dramatic effect.

These thirty poems, fitly inscribed to Rossetti, made up a work whose value somewhat depended upon its promise for the future. The true Pre-Raphaelite is willing to bury his own name in order to serve his art; to spend a life, if need be, in laying the ground-wall upon which his successors can build a new temple that shall replace the time-worn structure he has helped to tear away. But, to a man of genius, the higher service often is given later in his own career.

Morris's second volume showed that he had left the shadows of ballad minstrelsy, and entered the pleasant sunlight of Chaucer. After seven years of silence *The Life and Death of Jason* was a surprise, and was welcomed as the sustained performance of a true poet. It is a narrative poem, of epic proportions, all story and action, composed in the rhymed pentameter, strongly and sweetly carried from the first book to the last of seventeen. In this production, as in all the works of Morris,—in some respects the most notable raconteur since the time of his avowed master, Geoffrey Chau-

cer,—the statement is newly illustrated, that imaginative poets do not invent their own legends, but are wise in taking them from those historic treasuries of fact and fiction, the outlines of which await only a master-hand to invest them with living beauty. The invention of *Jason,* for instance, does not consist in the story of the Golden Fleece, but in new effects of combination, and in the melody and vigor of the means by which these old adventurous Greeks again are made to voyage, sing, love, fight, and die before us. Its author has a close knowledge of antiquities. Here and there his method is borrowed from Homer,—as in the gathering of the chiefs, which occupies the third book. Octosyllabic songs are interspersed, such as that of Orpheus,

> O bitter sea, tumultuous sea,
> Full many an ill is wrought by thee!

after which,

> Then shouted all the heroes, and they drove
> The good ship forth, so that the birds above,
> With long white wings, scarce flew so fast as they.

These three lines convey an idea of the general diction; nor can any be selected from the ten thousand which compose the work that do not show how well our Saxon English is adapted for the transmission of the Homeric spirit. The poem is fresh and stirring, and the style befits the theme, though not free from harshness and careless rhymes; moreover, it must be confessed that the reader often grows weary of the prolonged tale. This is an Odyssean epic, but written with continuity of effort; not growing of itself with the growth of a nation, nor builded at long intervals like the "Idyls of the King." The poet lacks variety. His voice is in a single key, and, although it be a natural one that does not tire the ear, we are content as we close the volume, and heave a sigh of satisfied appetite rather than of regret that the entertainment has reached an end.

In his learned taste for whatever is curious and rare Morris has made researches among the Sagas of Norse literature, especially those of Iceland. The admirable translations which he made, in company with E. Magnusson, from the Icelandic Grettis and Volsunga Sagas, show how thoroughly every class of work is fashioned by his hands, and illustrate the wealth of the resources from which he obtained the conception of his latest poem.[1] *The Story of Grettir the Strong,* and *The Story of the Volsungs and Niblungs,* appeared in 1869; but in 1868, five years after the completion of *Jason,* the public had been delighted with the early installments of a charming production, which, whatever he may accomplish hereafter, fairly exhibits his powers in their most sustained and varied form.

The plan of *The Earthly Paradise* was conceived in a day that should be marked with a white stone, since for this poet to undertake it was to complete it. The effort was so sure to adjust itself to his genius (which is epic rather than dramatic), that the only question was one of time, and that is now a question of the past. In this important work Morris reaches the height of his success as a relator. His poems always have been stories. Even the shortest ballads in his first book are upon themes from the old chronicles. *The Earthly Paradise* has the universe of fiction for a field, and reclothes the choicest and most famous legends of Asia and Europe with the delicate fabric of its verse. Greek and Oriental lore, the tales of the Gesta Romanorum, the romance of the Nibelungen-Lied, and even the myths of the Eddas, contribute to this thesaurus of narrative song. All these tales are familiar: many of a type from which John Fiske or Müller would prove their long descent, tracing them far as the "most eastern East"; but never before did they appear in more attractive shape, or fall so musically from a poet's honeyed mouth. Their fascination is beyond question. We listen to the narrator, as Arabs before the desert fire hang upon the lips of one who recites some legend of the good Haroun. Here is a successor to Boccaccio and to Chaucer. The verse, indeed, is exclusively Chaucerian, of which three styles are used, the heroic, sestina, and octosyllabic. Chance quotations show with what felicity and perfect ease the modern poet renews the cadences of his master. Take one from **"Atalanta's Race"**:

> Through thick Arcadian woods a hunter went,
> Following the beasts up, on a fresh spring day;
> But since his horn-tipped bow, but seldom bent,
> Now at the noontide naught had happed to slay,
> Within a vale he called his hounds away,
> Hearkening the echoes of his lone voice cling
> About the cliffs, and through the beech-trees ring.

Another from **"The Man Born to be King"**:

> So long he rode he drew anigh
> A mill upon the river's brim,
> That seemed a goodly place to him,
> For o'er the oily, smooth millhead
> There hung the apples growing red,
> And many an ancient apple-tree
> Within the orchard could he see,
> While the smooth millwalls, white and black,
> Shook to the great wheel's measured clack,
> And grumble of the gear within;
> While o'er the roof that dulled that din
> The doves sat crooning half the day,
> And round the half-cut stack of hay
> The sparrows fluttered twittering.

And this, from **"The Story of Cupid and Psyche"**:

> From place to place Love followed her that day
> And ever fairer to his eyes she grew,
> So that at last when from her bower she flew,
> *And underneath his feet the moonlit sea*
> *Went shepherding his waves disorderly,*
> He swore that of all gods and men, no one
> Should hold her in his arms but he alone.

The couplet which I have italicized has an imaginative quality not frequent in Morris's verse, for the excellence of this poet lies rather in his clear vision and exquisite directness of speech. Examples, otherwise neither better nor worse than the foregoing, may be taken from any one of the sixteen hundred pages of his great work. I can give but the briefest statement of its method and range.

In each of these metrical forms the verse is smooth and transparent,—the choice result of the author's Chaucerian studies, with what addition of beauty and suggestiveness his genius can bestow. His language is so pure that there absolutely is no resisting medium to obscure the interest of a tale. We feel that he enjoys his story as we do, yet the technical excellence, seen at once by a writer, scarcely is thought of by the lay reader, to whom poetry is in the main addressed. Morris easily grasps the feeling of each successive literature from which his stories are derived. He is at will a pagan, a Christian, or a worshipper of Odin and Thor; and especially has caught the spirit of those generations which, scarcely emerged from classicism in the South, and bordered by heathendom on the North, peopled their unhallowed places with beings drawn from either source. Christ reigned, yet the old gods had not wholly faded out, but acted, whether fair or devilish, as subjects and allies of Satan. All this is magically conveyed in such poems as **"The Ring Given to Venus"** and **"The Lady of the Land."** The former may be consulted (and any other will do almost as well) for evidence of the advantage possessed by Morris through his knowledge of mediæval costumes, armor, dances, festivals, and all the curious paraphernalia of days gone by. So well equipped a virtuoso, and so facile a rhythmist, was warranted in undertaking to write *The Earthly Paradise,* broad as it is in scope, and extended to the enormous length of forty thousand lines. The result shows that he set himself a perfectly feasible task.

In this work he avoids the prolonged strain of *Jason,* by making, with few exceptions, each story of a length that can be read at a sitting. His harmonic turn is shown in the arrangement of them all under the signs of the zodiac. We have one classical and one mediæval legend for each month of the year. I take it that the framework of the whole, the romance of voyagers in search of an earthly Paradise, is familiar to the reader. While Morris claims Chaucer, as Dante claimed Virgil, for his master, this only relates to the purpose and form of his poetry, for the freshness and sweetness are his own. He has gone to Chaucer, but also to nature,—to the earth whence sprang that well of English undefiled. His descriptive preludes, that serenely paint each phase of the revolving year, and the scenic touches throughout his stories, are truthful and picturesque. He uses but few and often-repeated adjectives; like the early rhapsodists, once having chosen an epithet for a certain thing, he clings to it, never introducing, for novelty's sake, another that is poorer than the best.

Morris fairly escapes from our turmoil and materialism by this flight to the refuge of amusement and simple art. A correlative moral runs through all of his poetry; one which, it must be owned, savors of pagan fatalism. The thought conveyed is that nothing should concern men but to enjoy what hollow good the gods award us, and this in the present, before the days come when we shall say we have no pleasure in them,—before death come, which closes all. He not only chooses to be a dreamer of dreams, and will not "strive to set the crooked straight," but tells us,

> Yes, ye are made immortal on the day
> Ye cease the dusty grains of time to weigh;

and in every poem has some passage like this:

> Fear little, then, I counsel you,
> What any son of man can do;
> Because a log of wood will last
> While many a life of man goes past,
> And all is over in slight space.

His hoary voyagers have toiled and wandered, as they find, in vain:

> Lo,
> A long life gone, and nothing more they know,
> Why they should live to have desire and foil,
> And toil, that, overcome, brings yet more toil,
> Than that day of their vanished youth, when first
> They saw Death clear, and deemed all life accurst
> By that cold, overshadowing threat,—the End.

They have nothing left but to beguile the remnant of their hours with story and repose, until the grave shall be reached, in which there is neither device, nor knowledge, nor wisdom. The poet's constant injunction is to seize the day, to strive not for greater or new things, since all will soon be over, and who knoweth what is beyond? In his epilogue to the entire work he faithfully epitomizes its spirit:

> Death have we hated, knowing not what it meant;
> Life have we loved, through green leaf and through
>   sere,
> Though still the less we knew of its intent:
> The Earth and Heaven through countless year on year,
> Slow changing, were to us but curtains fair,
> Hung round about a little room, where play
> Weeping and laughter of man's empty day.

This tinge of fatalism has a saddening effect upon Morris's verse, and thus far lessens its charm. A shadow falls across the feast. One of his critics has well said that "A poet, in this age of the world, who would be immortal, must write as if he himself believed in im-

mortality." His personages, moreover, are phantasmal, and really seem as if they issued from the ivory gate. Again, while his latest work is a marvel of prolonged strength and industry, its length gives it somewhat of an encyclopedic character. The last volume was not received so eagerly as the first. I would not quote against the author that saying of Callimachus, "a great book is a great evil"; nevertheless we feel that he has a too facile power,—a story once given him,—of putting it into rippling verse as rapidly as another man can write it in prose. Still, *The Earthly Paradise* is a library of itself, and in yielding to its spell we experience anew the delights which the "Arabian Nights" afforded to our childhood. What more tempting than to loll in such an "orchard-close" as the poet is wont to paint for us, and—with clover blooming everywhere, and the robins singing about their nests—to think it a portion of that fairy-land **"East of the Sun and West of the Moon"**; or to read the fay-legends of **"The Watching of the Falcon"** and **"Ogier the Dane,"** or that history of **"The Lovers of Gudrun,"** which possibly is the finest, as it is the most extended, of all our author's romantic poems? What more potent spell to banish care and pain? And let there be some one near to sing:

> In the white-flowered hawthorn brake,
> Love, be merry for my sake;
> Twine the blossoms in my hair,
> Kiss me where I am most fair,—
> Kiss me, love! for who knoweth
> What thing cometh after death?

We have seen that the poetry of William Morris is thoroughly sweet and wholesome, fair with the beauty of green fields and summer skies, and pervaded by a restful charm. Yet it is but the choicest fashion of romantic narrative-verse. The poet's imagination is clear, but never lofty; he never will rouse the soul to elevated thoughts and deeds. His low, continuous music reminds us of those Moorish melodies whose delicacy and pathos come from the gentle hearts of an expiring race, and seem the murmurous echo of strains that had an epic glory in the far-away past. Readers who look for passion, faith, and high imaginings, will find his measures cloying in the end. Rossetti's work has been confined to Pre-Chaucerian minstrelsy, and to the spiritualism of the early Italian school. Morris advances to a revival of the narrative art of Chaucer. The next effort, to complete the cyclic movement, should renew the fire and lyric outburst of the dramatic poets. Let us estimate the promise of what already has been essayed in that direction;—but to do this we must listen to the voice of the youngest and most impassioned of the group that stand with feet planted upon the outer circuit of the Victorian choir, and with faces looking eagerly toward the future.

Note

1. He now is said to be engaged upon a lineal and literal translation of Virgil,—a work which he can hardly fail to execute speedily and well.

W. J. Dawson (essay date 1906)

SOURCE: Dawson, W. J. "William Morris." In *The Makers of English Poetry*, pp. 368-79. New York: Fleming H. Revell Co., 1906.

[*In the following essay, Dawson credits Morris, along with Dante Gabriel Rossetti and Algernon Charles Swinburne, with the revival of Romanticism in English poetry and analyzes Morris's development as a poet.*]

William Morris is the third great name connected with the revival of Romanticism in modern poetry. His *Defence of Guinevere,* published in 1858, and dedicated to Rossetti, is marked by that same return to the mediæval spirit which so strikingly distinguished Rossetti, and which bore partial fruit in the early poems of Swinburne. The chief thing to be noticed about all three poets is that their poetry disdains modern thought and purpose, and deliberately seeks its inspiration in other times, and more ancient sources of emotion. Rossetti alone remained absolutely true to the mediæval spirit: his last poems had as distinctly as his first the impress and mould of mediæval Romanticism. Swinburne, as we have seen, did his best work under the shadows of Greek Classicism, and has besides grown more modern in spirit as he has grown older, handling purely modern themes, as in his *Songs before Sunrise,* with all his early vehemence and metrical skill. With William Morris the fascination of present-day life is a thing of very recent growth, and it can scarcely be said that it has done anything to help his poetry. As a poet he has three distinct periods. First comes the period when, in common with Rossetti, the fascination of ballad-romance was strong upon him, and its fruit is the thirty poems contained in his earliest volume. When he next appealed to the public he had cast off the glamour of mediævalism, and had become an epic poet. This is the period of *Jason* and the *Earthly Paradise.* The last period, if such it may be called, is marked by an awakening to the actual conditions of modern life, and is signalized by a series of *Chants for Socialists,* which are remarkable rather for political passion than poetic power. It may be well for us briefly to glance at these three periods.

William Morris's first volume, the *Defence of Guinevere,* is a remarkable book. It is not only significant for its revival of mediæval feeling, but also for its artistic feeling, its sense of colour, its touches of frank yet inoffensive sensuousness, its simplicity and directness of poetic effect. As a matter of fact, the question whether Morris should devote his life to art or literature for a long time hung in the balance, and it is only natural that his poetry should be remarkable for richness of colour and objective effect. The *Defence of Guinevere* is a fragment, but its very abruptness and incompleteness are effective. Its involution of thought, its curious touches of indirect introspection, its vivid glow of colour, its half-grotesque yet powerful imagery, are essentially mediæval. Such lines as the following at once recall the very method of Rossetti, and bear in themselves the marks of their relationship to the *Blessed Damozel:*

> Listen: suppose your time were come to die,
> And you were quite alone and very weak:
> Yea, laid a-dying, while very mightily
>
> The wind was ruffling up the narrow streak
> Of river through your broad lands running well:
> Suppose a hush should come, then some one speak:
>
> "One of those cloths is heaven, and one is hell,
> Now choose one cloth forever, which they be
> I will not tell you, you must somehow tell
>
> "Of your own strength and mightiness: here, see!"
> Yea, yea, my lord, and you to ope your eyes,
> At foot of your familiar bed to see
>
> A great God's angel standing, with such dyes
> Not known on earth, on his great wings, and hands,
> Held out two ways, light from the inner skies
>
> Showing him well, and making his commands
> Seem to be God's commands; moreover, too,
> Holding within his hands the cloths on wands:
>
> And one of these strange choosing-cloths was blue
> Wavy and long, and one cut short and red;
> No man could tell the better of the two.
>
> After a shivering half-hour you said
> "God help! heaven's colour, the blue;" and he said,
>   "Hell."
> Perhaps you then would roll upon your bed,
>
> And cry to all good men who loved you well,
> "Ah Christ! if only I had known, known, known."

It is characteristic of mediæval imagination to dwell in the borderland of spiritual mystery, and to utter itself with perfect unrestraint, much as a child speaks of such things, with a fearlessness which is unconscious of wrong, and a quaintness which gives a touch of sublimity to what in other lips would sound simply grotesque. It is precisely this frank and fascinating quaintness which William Morris has admirably reproduced in this remarkable poem. His description of the angel is the description of a mediæval artist, who notices first the celestial dyes upon hands and wings, and the colour of the choosing-cloths, and afterwards ponders the spiritual mystery of his presence. The chief quality in both Morris's and Rossetti's poetry is its sensitive appreciation of colour; each has carried to its furthest point the art of painting in words.

There are other poems in this slight volume which are equally remarkable with the *Defence of Guinevere.* The "Haystack in the Floods" is one of the most realistic poems in modern literature. All the troubled terror of the Middle Ages, the fierce passions and hasty vengeances, the barbaric strength and virility of love, the popular ignorance and cruelty, are brought home to us with an intense vividness in this brief poem. Every line of the poem is simple and direct, and it is by a score or so of natural touches of description that the whole scene is put before us. It is a piece of grim tragedy, painted, rather than told, with realistic fidelity and force. The landscape is as clear to us as the figures of the actors; we see the whole episode in its tragic misery and rudeness when we read the opening lines—

> Along the dripping, leafless woods
> The stirrup touching either shoe,
> She rode astride as troopers do,
> With kirtle kilted to her knee,
> To which the mud splashed wretchedly;
> And the wet dripped from every tree
> Upon her head and heavy hair,
> And on her eyelids broad and fair;
> The tears and rain ran down her face.

It is so Jehane rides on into the deepening shadows of fate. Her lover

> Seemed to watch the rain: yea, too,
> His lips were firm; he tried once more
> To touch her lips; she reached out, sore
> And vain desire so tortured them,
> The poor gray lips.

But the vision she sees through the dripping forest glades is

> The court at Paris: those six men,
> The gratings of the Chatelet;
> The swift Seine on some rainy day
> Like this, and people standing by,
> And laughing, while my weak hands try
> To recollect how strong men swim.

One would have supposed that poetry so original and powerful as this would have been sure of recognition. The book, however, fell dead from the press. Little of it is even now known save the spirited ballad, "Riding Together." It was not until twenty-five years later that the significance of this first volume of Morris's was realized. By that time he had reached his second period;

he had outgrown much of his early mediævalism, or rather he had "worked out for himself a distinct and individual phrase of the mediæval movement."

Eight years after his first volume William Morris published the *Life and Death of Jason,* and this was followed in 1868 by the first installment of the *Earthly Paradise.* Of the first poem it is enough to say that it is a noble epic, full of sustained narrative power, but too long, and occasionally too deficient in interest, to obtain the highest honours of the epic. It marks, however, his emancipation from the spell of mediæval minstrelsy. He had now entered a larger world, where pleasant sunlight had taken the place of tragic shadows of terror, and where his genius moved freely with a sense of conscious power. It was evident also that his mind had developed new and unsuspected qualities. The old simplicity and directness are here, the old keen sense of colour is still predominant; but there is something new—a gift of larger utterance, a power of word-painting, inimitably fresh and truthful, a sort of childlike joy in dreams, and a corresponding power of setting them forth, which interests and fascinates us. And there is the same sort of childlike delight in Nature. He sees her with a fresh eye, and tells us what he sees in the simplest phrases. We rarely meet an epithet which surprises us by the keenness of its observation, or the intensity of its vision, but we never meet a description of Nature that is not truthful and sincere. We are never startled into delight, but we are always soothed and refreshed. "The art of William Morris," said Mary Howitt, "is Nature itself, rough at times, but quaint, fresh, and dewy beyond anything I ever saw or felt in language."

The scenery Morris loves to paint, and which he paints best, is familiar scenery; the dewy meads, the orchards with their snowy bloom, the white mill with its cozy quiet, the flower-gardens where the bee sucks, and where the soft wet winds murmur in the leaves of "immemorial elms." The charm of such pictures is in their unintentional art, the entire absence of any effort to be fine. The breaking day has been described a thousand times, and often the most laboured descriptions have been most admired; yet there is still delight to be found in so simple a sketch as this:

> So passed the night; the moon arose and grew,
> From off the sea a little west wind blew,
> Rustling the garden leaves like sudden rain,
> And ere the moon had 'gun to fall again
> The wind grew cold, a change was in the sky,
> And in deep silence did the dawn draw nigh.

How clearly is the colourist seen also in this companion picture:

> The sun is setting in the west, the sky
> Is clear and hard, and no clouds come anigh
> The golden orb, but further off they lie,

Steel-gray and black, with edges red as blood,
And underneath them is the weltering flood
Of some huge sea, whose tumbling hills, as they
Turn restless sides about, are black, or gray,
Or green, or glittering with the golden flame:
The wind has fallen now, but still the same
The mighty army moves, as if to drown
This lone bare rock, whose sheer scarped sides of
 brown
Cast off the weight of waves in clouds of spray.

Sometimes there is a flash of imaginative intensity, as in the lines:

And underneath his feet the moonlit sea
Went shepherding his waves disorderly;

but such touches are rare. William Morris has the infrequent gift of using commonplace phrases in a way that is not commonplace. Tennyson would scarcely deign to use so well-worn a phrase as "the golden orb"; he would probably have invented some felicitous double adjective which would strike us as much by its ingenuity as its truth. Morris is never troubled by any such scruples. He uses the handiest phrases, and somehow he makes us feel that they are after all the truest. He is always pictorial, and his pictures are painted with so great a breadth that the absence of any delicate filigree work of ingenious phrase-making is not remarked. Perhaps this also is part of his charm. While almost every other poet of our day aims at the invention of new phrases which shall allure us by their originality, Morris is simply intent upon telling us his story; and the very absence of pretension in his style fills us with a new delight, and strikes us as a new species of genius.

The aim and scope of the *Earthly Paradise* Morris has himself set forth in his **"Apology"** and **"L'Envoi."**

Of heaven and hell I have no power to sing;
 I cannot ease the burden of your fears,
Or make quick-coming death a little thing,
 Or bring again the pleasure of past years;
 Nor for my words shall ye forget your tears,
Or hope again for aught that I can say—
The idle singer of an empty day.

Dreamer of dreams, born out of my due time,
 Why should I strive to set the crooked straight?
Let it suffice me that my murmuring rhyme
 Beats with light wing against the ivory gate,
 Telling a tale not too importunate
To those who in the sleepy region stay,
Lulled by the singer of an empty day.

In **"L'Envoi"** he boldly claims Geoffrey Chaucer as his master, and sounds the same note of gentle pessimism as regards the fortunes of his own day. From a moral point of view this pessimism is the most striking thing about the *Earthly Paradise.* He turns to dreamland, and bids us travel with him into the realms of faery, because he cannot unravel the mystery of human life, and believes that any attempt to do so can only end in bewilderment and despair. When he ventures upon any counsel it is simply the old pagan counsel of *carpe diem.* The thought of death is always with him, and the true wisdom of life is to gather the roses while we may. Death, the great spoliator, will soon be upon us, and the days will come all too soon when we have no pleasure in them.

In the white-flowered hawthorn brake,
Love, be merry for my sake:
Twine the blossoms in my hair,
Kiss me where I am most fair—
Kiss me, love! for who knoweth
What thing cometh after death?

This is the note which sounds throughout the *Earthly Paradise.* Ogier the Dane, at the bidding of the fairy, renounces life just when its consummation is at hand, and puts aside the crown of Charlemaine, saying:

Lie there, O crown of Charlemaine,
Worn by a mighty man and worn in vain.
Because he died, and all the things he did
Were changed before his face by earth was hid.

Ambition, the fierce race for wealth, the battle even for what seem to be great causes and sufficing ideals, are all in vain, and end in disillusionment and sorrow. It is better still to dream. In dreams everything is beautiful; in actual life the sordid and the vulgar intrude at every turn. It is better still to dream, because dreams never disappoint us. There, at least, we can forget the shadow of death and wander in the meads of a perpetual spring; and, so far as dreams bring the jaded mind refreshment and release, it is wise to dream. The imaginative faculty needs exercise as well as the practical, and no full or fair life can be lived where it is stunted or ignored. And we are only too ready to hail a singer who bids us

Forget six counties overhung with smoke,
Forget the snorting steam and piston-stroke,
Forget the spreading of the hideous town;
Think rather of the pack-horse on the down,
And dream of London—small, and white, and clean—
The clear Thames bordered by its gardens green.

But, after all, he is not the highest poet who only bids us dream. The highest poet is he who, knowing life and death, bids us not ignore the one nor fear the other, but prepares us equally for both by the inspiration of his courage and the serenity of his faith. This William Morris does not do in his greatest poems, and has not sought to do. He knows the limitations of his nature, and confesses his inability to sing the songs which humanity has ever counted the noblest. He has left to others the battles of faith and philosophy. He has sought only to be the singer of an empty day, the dreamer of dreams, in whose bright spells weary men may rest awhile, and those who are vexed by life's disasters may find a brief refreshment and repose. Nor is this a slight aim nor a contemptible achievement. It is something to have amid the fierce strain of modern life one poet who does not excite, but soothe us; who does not make us think, but bids us enjoy; who lures us back again into the simplicities of childhood, and who, in all his writings, has not written a page that a child might not read, and has written many with so lucid an art that a child might enjoy and comprehend them.

Of the third period of William Morris it is only necessary to add a sentence or two. The dreamer of the *Earthly Paradise* at last wakes from his dream, and casts away his spells, and breaks his magic wand. He discovers that the nineteenth century is not an empty day, nor is it a time when any man who has helpful hands may dare to be idle or unserviceable. The social problem, which is the great and real problem of our time, powerfully affected Morris's mature life. With his socialistic harangues at street corners, his "wrestles with policemen, or wrangles with obtuse magistrates about freedom of speech," we have nothing to do here. Here we have only to deal with his work in literature, and with the exception of a few spirited verses such as these:

> Then a man shall work and bethink him, and rejoice
>   in the deeds of his hand,
> Nor yet come home in the even, too faint and weary
>   to stand,
> For that which the worker winneth shall then be his
>   indeed,
> Nor shall half be reaped for nothing by him that sowed
>   no seed.
> Then all *mine* and *thine* shall be *ours*, and no more
>   shall any man crave
> For riches that serve for nothing but to fetter a friend
>   for a slave,

the socialistic propaganda has gained nothing by his poetic art. Perhaps it was too late in life for Morris to catch the true lyric fire of the revolutionary poet. It is, however, profoundly interesting to remark how the huge shadow of this social problem has been gradually projected over the entire field of literature, politics, and philosophy.

It is by his earlier work in mediæval romance, and his *Earthly Paradise* that Morris will be remembered. Concerning the latter it is but uttering a commonplace to say that no writer since Chaucer has displayed so masterly a power of continuous narrative, or has rested his fame so completely upon the arts of simplicity and lucidity. In this he occupies a unique place among modern poets. He has imitators, but he has no real competitor. He has drunk deep of the well of English undefiled, and has again taught the old lesson of the potency of plain and idiomatic Saxon as an unrivalled

vehicle of poetic utterance. If he has added nothing new to the wealth of metrical expression he has enriched modern literature by the recoining of ancient forms of speech, and by the recurrence to the free simplicity of our older poetry. If he falls far behind Rossetti in the art of beautiful expression, and behind Swinburne in vehemence and lyric fire, he is the superior of both in the more enduring qualities of strength and breadth of style, and has a nobler inventiveness and a wholesomer view of life. To be the modern Chaucer is a far greater thing than to be an English Baudelaire or Villon, simply because Chaucer was an infinitely greater man than either, and carried in his sweet and sunny nature the secret seed of a more enduring immortality. This William Morris is—the nearest approach to Chaucer which the nineteenth century can produce, or that any intervening period has produced. This is much to say, but it is not too much to say of the author of the *Life and Death of Jason* and the *Earthly Paradise.* Separated as they are by a vast stretch of time, different as they are by so much as five centuries of civilization can constitute of difference, still they are alike in spirit; and Chaucer is indeed the master of William Morris's art, and he the most faithful and successful of his disciples.

G. K. Chesterton (essay date 1906)

SOURCE: Chesterton, G. K. "William Morris and His School." In *Varied Types,* pp. 15-26. New York: Dodd, Mead, and Company, 1906.

[*In the following essay, Chesterton views Morris as a prime representative of the Victorian era and outlines the limitations of his verse.*]

It is proper enough that the unveiling of the bust of William Morris should approximate to a public festival, for while there have been many men of genius in the Victorian era more despotic than he, there have been none so representative. He represents not only that rapacious hunger for beauty which has now for the first time become a serious problem in the healthy life of humanity, but he represents also that honourable instinct for finding beauty in common necessities of workmanship which gives it a stronger and more bony structure. The time has passed when William Morris was conceived to be irrelevant to be described as a designer of wall-papers. If Morris had been a hatter instead of a decorator, we should have become gradually and painfully conscious of an improvement in our hats. If he had been a tailor, we should have suddenly found our frockcoats trailing on the ground with the grandeur of mediæval raiment. If he had been a shoemaker, we should have found, with no little consternation, our shoes gradually approximating to the antique sandal. As a hairdresser, he would have invented some massing of the hair worthy to be the crown of Venus; as an iron-monger, his nails would have had some noble pattern, fit to be the nails of the Cross.

The limitations of William Morris, whatever they were, were not the limitations of common decoration. It is true that all his work, even his literary work, was in some sense decorative, had in some degree the qualities of a splendid wall-paper. His characters, his stories, his religious and political views, had, in the most emphatic sense, length and breadth without thickness. He seemed really to believe that men could enjoy a perfectly flat felicity. He made no account of the unexplored and explosive possibilities of human nature, of the unnameable terrors, and the yet more unnameable hopes. So long as a man was graceful in every circumstance, so long as he had the inspiring consciousness that the chestnut colour of his hair was relieved against the blue forest a mile behind, he would be serenely happy. So he would be, no doubt, if he were really fitted for a decorative existence; if he were a piece of exquisitely coloured cardboard.

But although Morris took little account of the terrible solidity of human nature—took little account, so to speak, of human figures in the round, it is altogether unfair to represent him as a mere æsthete. He perceived a great public necessity and fulfilled it heroically. The difficulty with which he grappled was one so immense that we shall have to be separated from it by many centuries before we can really judge of it. It was the problem of the elaborate and deliberate ugliness of the most self-conscious of centuries. Morris at least saw the absurdity of the thing. He felt it was monstrous that the modern man, who was pre-eminently capable of realising the strangest and most contradictory beauties, who could feel at once the fiery aureole of the ascetic and the colossal calm of the Hellenic god, should himself, by a farcical bathos, be buried in a black coat, and hidden under a chimney-pot hat. He could not see why the harmless man who desired to be an artist in raiment should be condemned to be, at best, a black and white artist. It is indeed difficult to account for the clinging curse of ugliness which blights everything brought forth by the most prosperous of centuries. In all created nature there is not, perhaps, anything so completely ugly as a pillar-box. Its shape is the most unmeaning of shapes, its height and thickness just neutralising each other; its colour is the most repulsive of colours—a fat and soulless red, a red without a touch of blood or fire, like the scarlet of dead men's sins. Yet there is no reason whatever why such hideousness should possess an object full of civic dignity, the treasure-house of a thousand secrets, the fortress of a thousand souls. If the old Greeks had had such an institution, we may be sure that it would have been surmounted by the severe, but graceful, figure of the god of letter-writing. If the mediæval Christians had possessed it, it would have

had a niche filled with the golden aureole of St. Rowland of the Postage Stamps. As it is, there it stands at all our street-corners, disguising one of the most beautiful of ideas under one of the most preposterous of forms. It is useless to deny that the miracles of science have not been such an incentive to art and imagination as were the miracles of religion. If men in the twelfth century had been told that the lightning had been driven for leagues underground, and had dragged at its destroying tail loads of laughing human beings, and if they had then been told that the people alluded to this pulverising portent chirpily as "The Twopenny Tube," they would have called down the fire of Heaven on us as a race of half-witted atheists. Probably they would have been quite right.

This clear and fine perception of what may be called the anæsthetic element in the Victorian era was, undoubtedly, the work of a great reformer: it requires a fine effort of the imagination to see an evil that surrounds us on every side. The manner in which Morris carried out his crusade may, considering the circumstances, be called triumphant. Our carpets began to bloom under our feet like the meadows in spring, and our hitherto prosaic stools and sofas seemed growing legs and arms at their own wild will. An element of freedom and rugged dignity came in with plain and strong ornaments of copper and iron. So delicate and universal has been the revolution in domestic art that almost every family in England has had its taste cunningly and treacherously improved, and if we look back at the early Victorian drawing-rooms it is only to realise the strange but essential truth that art, or human decoration, has, nine times out of ten in history, made things uglier than they were before, from the "coiffure" of a Papuan savage to the wall-paper of a British merchant in 1830.

But great and beneficent as was the æsthetic revolution of Morris, there was a very definite limit to it. It did not lie only in the fact that his revolution was in truth a reaction, though this was a partial explanation of his partial failure. When he was denouncing the dresses of modern ladies, "upholstered like armchairs instead of being draped like women," as he forcibly expressed it, he would hold up for practical imitation the costumes and handicrafts of the Middle Ages. Further than this retrogressive and imitative movement he never seemed to go. Now, the men of the time of Chaucer had many evil qualities, but there was at least one exhibition of moral weakness they did not give. They would have laughed at the idea of dressing themselves in the manner of the bowmen at the battle of Senlac, or painting themselves an æsthetic blue, after the custom of the ancient Britons. They would not have called that a movement at all. Whatever was beautiful in their dress or manners sprang honestly and naturally out of the life they led and preferred to lead. And it may surely be maintained that any real advance in the beauty of modern dress must spring honestly and naturally out of the life we lead and prefer to lead. We are not altogether without hints and hopes of such a change, in the growing orthodoxy of rough and athletic costumes. But if this cannot be, it will be no substitute or satisfaction to turn life into an interminable historical fancy-dress ball.

But the limitation of Morris's work lay deeper than this. We may best suggest it by a method after his own heart. Of all the various works he performed, none, perhaps, was so splendidly and solidly valuable as his great protest for the fables and superstitions of mankind. He has the supreme credit of showing that the fairy tales contain the deepest truth of the earth, the real record of men's feeling for things. Trifling details may be inaccurate, Jack may not have climbed up so tall a beanstalk, or killed so tall a giant; but it is not such things that make a story false; it is a far different class of things that makes every modern book of history as false as the father of lies; ingenuity, self-consciousness, hypocritical impartiality. It appears to us that of all the fairy-tales none contains so vital a moral truth as the old story, existing in many forms, of Beauty and the Beast. There is written, with all the authority of a human scripture, the eternal and essential truth that until we love a thing in all its ugliness we cannot make it beautiful. This was the weak point in William Morris as a reformer: that he sought to reform modern life, and that he hated modern life instead of loving it. Modern London is indeed a beast, big enough and black enough to be the beast in Apocalypse, blazing with a million eyes, and roaring with a million voices. But unless the poet can love this fabulous monster as he is, can feel with some generous excitement his massive and mysterious *joie-de-vivre,* the vast scale of his iron anatomy and the beating of his thunderous heart, he cannot and will not change the beast into the fairy prince. Morris's disadvantage was that he was not honestly a child of the nineteenth century: he could not understand its fascination, and consequently he could not really develop it. An abiding testimony to his tremendous personal influence in the æsthetic world is the vitality and recurrence of the Arts and Crafts Exhibitions, which are steeped in his personality like a chapel in that of a saint. If we look round at the exhibits in one of these æsthetic shows, we shall be struck by the large mass of modern objects that the decorative school leaves untouched. There is a noble instinct for giving the right touch of beauty to common and necessary things, but the things that are so touched are the ancient things, the things that always to some extent commended themselves to the lover of beauty. There are beautiful gates, beautiful fountains, beautiful cups, beautiful chairs, beautiful reading-desks. But there are no modern things made beautiful. There are no beautiful lamp-posts, beautiful letter-boxes, beautiful engines, beautiful bicycles. The spirit of William Morris has not seized hold of the century and made its humblest necessities beautiful. And this was because, with all his healthiness and energy, he had not the supreme courage to face the ugliness of things; Beauty shrank from the Beast and the fairy-tale had a different ending.

But herein, indeed, lay Morris's deepest claim to the name of a great reformer: that he left his work incomplete. There is, perhaps, no better proof that a man is a mere meteor, merely barren and brilliant, than that his work is done perfectly. A man like Morris draws attention to needs he cannot supply. In after-years we may have perhaps a newer and more daring Arts and Crafts Exhibition. In it we shall not decorate the armour of the twelfth century, but the machinery of the twentieth. A lamp-post shall be wrought nobly in twisted iron, fit to hold the sanctity of fire. A pillar-box shall be carved with figures emblematical of the secrets of comradeship and the silence and honour of the State. Railway signals, of all earthly things the most poetical, the coloured stars of life and death, shall be lamps of green and crimson worthy of their terrible and faithful service. But if ever this gradual and genuine movement of our time towards beauty—not backwards, but forwards—does truly come about, Morris will be the first prophet of it. Poet of the childhood of nations, craftsman in the new honesties of art, prophet of a merrier and wiser life, his full-blooded enthusiasm will be remembered when human life has once more assumed flamboyant colours and proved that this painful greenish grey of the æsthetic twilight in which we now live is, in spite of all the pessimists, not of the greyness of death, but the greyness of dawn.

A. Clutton-Brock (essay date 1914)

SOURCE: Clutton-Brock, A. "Morris as a Romantic Poet." In *William Morris: His Work and Influence,* pp. 79-96. New York: Henry Holt and Company, 1914.

[*In the following essay, Clutton-Brock discusses Morris as a Romantic poet, contending that of "all the Romantic poets Morris, in his early poetry was the most romantic; for he was more consciously discontented with the circumstances of his own time than any of them."*]

The word Romantic, as applied to a certain movement in art, has been used vaguely and in different senses. We know better who the Romantic poets are than why we call them Romantic. But if we examine their works, and especially those which any one would choose as being peculiarly romantic, we shall find that they have this in common—namely, that they interest us through their unlikeness, rather than through their likeness, to our own experience. In poems like Keats's "Eve of St.

Agnes" and "La Belle Dame sans Merci," or like Col-eridge's "Christabel" and "The Ancient Mariner," there is a continual insistence upon the strangeness of the circumstances. It is not merely that the story belongs to the past; most stories told by poets do. But Homer and Chaucer do not incessantly remind us that their stories belong to the past, whereas Keats and Coleridge do. Homer and Chaucer tell a story because they think it a good one; but Coleridge in "Christabel" and Keats in the "Eve of St. Agnes" have very little story to tell. The aim of these poems is to carry us into a strange world and its strangeness is more important than what hap-pens in it. Wordsworth, again, in his poems about peas-ants, though he does not carry us into the past, does carry us into a world different from our own, and he is always insisting upon the difference. Indeed, many of his incidents are chosen to illustrate the difference between his peasants and the people for whom he writes. In fact, the Romantic movement expressed a general dissatisfaction with the circumstances and sur-roundings of the life of the Romantic poets. It was not merely an attempt to enrich the subject-matter of poetry or to deliver it from the prosaic methods of the eighteenth century. It was rather a revolt against the whole urban civilization of that century; and the Romantic poets ranged the past because they were sick of the present. Some of them were liberal in their politics, others were conservative; but Scott, the most conservative of them all, did not like the urban civiliza-tion of his time well enough to write about it. He, too, not only found his stories in the past, but enjoyed it because it was unlike the present; and whenever he draws a character well from life it is a countryman sharply distinguished from the run of educated and well-to-do townspeople of the day. Shakespeare took Hamlet from a primitive Danish story and turned him into a gentleman of his own time. A Romantic poet would have made him even more primitive than he was in the original story; for he would have chosen that story as a way of escape from the present, and would have peopled it with strange, not with familiar, characters.

Now of all the Romantic poets Morris, in his early poetry was the most romantic; for he was more consciously discontented with the circumstances of his own time than any of them. At the very beginning of the Romantic movement the Middle Ages had been discovered; that is to say, they had become interesting instead of being merely dull and barbarous. Horace Walpole built himself what he took to be a Gothic villa at Strawberry Hill, and wrote what he thought was a mediæval romance in the "Castle of Otranto." At first this interest in the Middle Ages was merely a new fashion, like the earlier fashion which produced Pastoral poetry, and it had results just as absurd. But it was a fashion that lasted, and people went on being interested in the Middle Ages without quite knowing why. To Keats and Coleridge they were full of a strange

inexplicable beauty, well expressed in these lines from "Christabel"—

> The moon shines dim in the open air,
> And not a moonbeam enters here.
> But they without its light can see
> The chamber carved so curiously,
> Carved with figures strange and sweet,
> All made out of the carver's brain,
> For a lady's chamber meet:
> The lamp with twofold silver chain
> Is fastened to an angel's feet.

Then came Ruskin, who explained the causes and condi-tions of this beauty and why it could not be imitated now; and for Morris, who had learnt from Ruskin, and who studied the Middle Ages with the passion of an artist and of a man of science, their beauty was no longer fantastic or inexplicable. For him their art was as normal and rational as classical art seemed to the masters of the High Renaissance in Italy. It was the art of his own people and his own country, which had been for a time ousted by a foreign art, just as the southern art of Italy was for a time ousted by the Gothic.

But still it was not the art which he saw being produced about him. The tradition of it had been lost and would have to be recovered; and that could not be done by mere imitation. Meanwhile, however, he felt himself, as he said in the Introduction to *The Earthly Paradise,* to be born out of his due time. This feeling was not the result of a vague dislike of reality, but of a very clear liking for a reality different from that in which he found himself. And in his first volume of poems we see him trying to throw himself back into that reality, and describing it as if it were something he remembered from his own childhood. The detail of poems such as **"The Defence of Guenevere"** or **"King Arthur's Tomb"** is not the vague detail of earlier poets. It is all precise, and described as if the poet were telling of what he had seen with his own eyes. But he insists continually on it because he wishes, not only to tell a story or express a passion, but also to describe a world different from that in which he lives. He is not entirely occupied with strange circumstance; for Guenevere and Lancelot and all the people of the "Morte d'Arthur" were real people to him; but they were more real than the people he met in the street just because he thought of them as living in this world of his desires. So he could not bring them to life without also bringing that world to life; and **"The Defence of Guenevere"** and **"King Arthur's Tomb"** are troubled and confused with this twofold task. Morris has too much to say in them; he is like a child trying to tell a story and at the same time to express its own delighted interest in every detail of the story; and he becomes both breathless and rambling in the effort. He is full of strange news about wonderful people in a wonderful world of his own discovery; and he tells it all as news, making no distinction of emphasis between one fact and another. Tennyson writes of the Court of King Arthur as if it were an old tale worth exploiting by a modern civilized poet. For him it is a story of no time or place; but for Morris it is a story of a time better than his own, not, of course, the real legendary time of King Arthur, but the Middle Ages still familiar to Mallory. And whereas Tennyson's treatment of circumstance is like the vague treatment of some idealist eighteenth-century painter, Morris reminds us of Mantegna in his mixture of living passion and detail drawn from the past. For Mantegna looked back to the Roman past just as Morris looked back to the past of the Middle Ages, and he too expressed his desire for another state of being in his art with a passion that freed his detail from pedantry.[1]

The Defence of Guenevere contains one or two of Morris's earliest poems, such as the beautiful **"Summer Dawn,"** in which he seems to dream without energy. In the later and mediæval poems he is still dreaming, but with an energy too fierce for a pure dreamer such as he still took himself to be. And it is this dreaming energy which makes those poems unlike other romantic poetry. The romantic game had been played in verse often enough, but here it is played in deadly earnest. Morris does not make use of the Middle Ages for artistic purposes; he writes about them as a poet writes of love when he is in love himself. In poems like **"The Haystack in the Floods"** we can see that he has taken his method from Browning. He tells a great deal of his story by means of allusion, and by the same means manages to introduce detail without labour or digression. But whereas Browning used this method to express his curiosity about many past ages, Morris used it to express his passion for one. He writes not like a curious traveller through all the past, but like one who has travelled to find what he wants and has found it. No one, perhaps, could see at the time that there was more than dreaming in those poems, but we can see now that they were written by a man who would try to make his dreams come true.

In *The Defence of Guenevere* volume there is one poem, **"Sir Peter Harpdon's End,"** in blank verse and dramatic in form. After the publication of that volume Morris started to write a series of **"Scenes from the Fall of Troy,"** also dramatic and in blank verse. He never finished them, partly because at the time he was too busy with the firm and partly because his mind was being drawn more and more to narrative. It was contrary to his practical nature to write drama that was not completely a play and that was not meant to be acted. He showed in these experiments that he had more dramatic power than most modern poets, both in his invention and in the style of his blank verse, which is poetry yet sounds like natural speech; but he never developed this dramatic power for want of a theatre and actors. The tale of Troy, like the tale of King Arthur,

was to him a story of the Middle Ages, but one which the Middle Ages had got from a past already far remote. He saw it, whereas most modern writers only think of it; but he saw it faint in an infinite distance and through a transforming mist. He always felt the sadness "of old unhappy far-off things and battles long ago"; but this sadness is heavier in the Troy scenes than in any other work of his. The people all seem like ghosts, acting their past faintly over again with a fore-knowledge of its futile end. It is as if he had evoked them and then soon dismissed them out of pity; but in these fragments, there is a real evocation and, however pale the ghosts may be, we believe at least that they are ghosts.

After this Morris wrote little verse for six or seven years, and when he began again in London he made no more experiments. Then he set to work upon narrative poetry, knowing exactly what he meant to do and well able to do it. He was lucky in that he had a great natural talent for a kind of poetry that has not often been written well in England. Since the *Canterbury Tales* most of our narrative poems that have been poetical have not told a story well; and most of those which have told a story well have been either prosaic or poetic only by artifice. Morris told his stories naturally in verse because he could conceive them as poems; and at this time he was content to be a poetic teller of old stories. Chaucer was his master in this art and from him he seems to have learnt, without practice on his own account, all that can be learnt of it; and in particular how to make the poetry issue naturally out of the story instead of using the story as a pretext for irrelevant poetry. And, like Chaucer in the *Canterbury Tales,* Morris in his *Earthly Paradise* devises circumstances that provide a plausible reason for storytelling. But, whereas Chaucer's pilgrims tell stories fitted to their own individual characters, the narrators of *The Earthly Paradise* tell each a story of his own race or country. Since, then, his stories were half Greek and half from other sources, he had to contrive a setting in which Greeks surviving from the ancient world meet with men of the Middle Ages and of many different countries. Hence the Prologue, a fine story in itself, in which, in the time of Edward III, a crew of sailors set out to find the Earthly Paradise, and after many adventures and disappointments come to an island where there are Greeks still keeping their old way of life unknown to the rest of mankind. Thus this great exchange of tales is made possible.

But Morris, for all his love of a story, could not tell one as Chaucer could. Chaucer often thought he was relating history and, like a good historian, put all his knowledge of living men into it. Morris knew that he was simply telling stories; and in *The Earthly Paradise* he tells most of them as if he knew they were mere stories and as if he were passing them on as best he could. He set himself a task and performed it at a great pace. But no man who ever lived could tell all these diverse stories so as to express his own experience through them. Morris when he wrote *The Earthly Paradise* had still the romantic conception of poetry, namely, that it should interest by its unlikeness rather than by its likeness to our experience. Therefore he lays his stress upon the wonderful events in his tales and upon their strangeness of circumstance rather than upon those passions and characters that are constant to men. It is events and circumstances that we remember rather than people. The poetry of *The Earthly Paradise* has been rather foolishly compared to the design of his wall-papers and chintzes; but it is true that Morris often gives as faint an image of reality in a story as in a pattern, and that he relies on the story, as on the pattern, to justify the faintness. No modern English poet had written a long poem of any kind so easy to read. Begin one of the tales of *The Earthly Paradise* and you find that it draws you along with its own current. Begin Swinburne's "Tristram," and you find that after each splendid lyrical passage you have to set yourself to the story with an effort. All the best of it is digression; but there are no digressions in **"The Man born to be King,"** and, as it is all poetry, this is high praise. But I, for one, can never feel quite satisfied with *The Earthly Paradise,* and I even feel that its popularity has injured Morris's fame. A great deal of it is merely pleasure-giving poetry, and if he had written nothing else he would indeed have been the idle singer of an empty day. Perhaps, being at this time a little bewildered by life and the state of the world, seeing that things were wrong and not having got any clear determination to right them, he set himself a task and tried to satisfy his enormous energy with that. He liked to think of poetry as a craft; and he had mastered the craft of story-telling so that it was almost too easy to him, and so that he could practise it without giving the whole of his mind to it. Indeed, one feels a kind of absence of mind in many of these stories, as if the writer knew them so well that he could think of something else while he was telling them; and for that reason he often seems to be telling us something to amuse us rather than because he must tell it.

He had meant *The Life and Death of Jason* to be part of *The Earthly Paradise*; but as he wrote it, it grew too large to take its place there. It is a poem of pure romance, told for its wonder and very well told; until near the end when Medea, from having been only a wonderful enchantress, becomes a mother, and has to subdue the tenderness common to all mothers before she can slay her children. Then Morris surprises us with a power like Chaucer's of expressing passion in the simplest words. There is the same power in **"The Lovers of Gudrun,"** which comes at the end of the third part of *The Earthly Paradise.* Two years before it was published Morris had begun to learn Icelandic, and he soon read through most of the sagas. He enjoyed all good stories; but these were to him among the stories of the world what Gothic was among all the different kinds of architecture; and he put the whole force of his mind into **"The Lovers of Gudrun,"** telling it not merely for its strangeness, but because he loved the men and women in it. But of this change in his poetry [Clutton-Brock speaks in a later chapter not reproduced here]. Two years after *The Earthly Paradise* was finished he made another dramatic experiment. **"Love is Enough"** is more remote from reality than any of his poems. Mr. Mackail has given a lucid account of its peculiar form with its receding planes of action, five in all; the aim of which is, starting from a representation of the outer world and particular persons, to reach in the furthest plane an expression, almost in pure music, of that passion which possesses the chief character of the play. For success in such a design, a very sharp contrast would be needed between the nearer and the more distant planes; and the contrast in the poem is not sharp. The rustics in the nearest plane are as faint as any persons in *The Earthly Paradise* and all the other characters are shadows; so that the lyrics of the furthest plane seem nearer to us than anything else in the poem. **"Love is Enough"** seems a shadowy romance; but it is really a religious play, a confession of faith made almost unconsciously. The love of which the lyrics tell is not the love of one human being for another, though that may be a preparation for it. It is rather a state of mind which, to those who know it, is better than happiness, indeed the best that man can attain to in this life.

But Morris can express it better than I can explain it—

> Ye know not how void is your hope and your living:
>   Depart with your helping lest yet ye undo me.
>   Ye know not that at nightfall she draweth near to me,
> There is soft speech between us and words of forgiving,
>   Till in dead of the midnight her kisses thrill through me.
>   Pass by me, and hearken, and waken me not.

The language of that is recognized at once by any one who has an ear for it. It is the language of religious ecstasy, expressing a desire so strong that it can use the terms of earthly love, and so sweet to those who feel it that it has in it also the delight of earthly love. Morris, like all great men of his kind, was unworldly, not so much from contempt of the world, certainly not from contempt of the earth, as because there was something desired by his soul compared with which things of the world seemed to him of little account. As a rule he acted upon this desire more than he thought about it. He was not by nature speculative, and shared the scepticism of his time about all supernatural things. He set himself so many tasks that he was more concerned with performing them than with asking himself why he did so. But sometimes that high passion, which was the motive force of his life, expressed itself suddenly in his poetry so that it seems to tell a secret of which he was hardly aware himself, a secret only to be understood by those who know it already. In ordinary speech Morris, though very frank, told no secrets about himself; and all his friends knew that there was a part of him which he shared with no one. Here he reveals it in his art, telling all the world that there is a source outside him from which he gets his strength and purpose; and then he turns proudly on the world as if he had told it too much—

> Wherewith will ye buy it, ye rich who behold me?
>   Draw out from your coffers your rest and your laughter,
>   And the fair gilded hope of the dawn coming after.
>
> Nay, this I sell not—though ye bought me and sold me—
>   For your house stored with such things from threshold to rafter,
>   Pass by me. I hearken, and think of you not.

When he wrote this he was still, like an eremite, half afraid of the world, and withdrawing from it to listen to the whispers of his familiar. But these very whispers were to send him into the world again so that he might labour to change what he hated.

"Love is Enough" is half a failure as a romantic poem because Morris could no longer soothe his disgust of reality by writing of strange things. The romantic part of it persists from mere habit and has become as faint as a fading memory. Indeed, the music of the lyrics makes us forget it altogether, and they break through it as if the poet himself had forgotten it. In them we hear no longer the idle singer of an empty day but one whose music is making itself out of his own experience.

Note

1. See Mr. Borenson's interesting essay on Mantegna.

Karl Litzenberg (essay date May 1936)

SOURCE: Litzenberg, Karl. "Allusions to the Elder *Edda* in the 'Non-Norse' Poems of William Morse." *Scandinavian Studies and Notes* 14, no. 2 (May 1936): 17-24.

[*In the following essay, Litzenberg traces Morris's allusions to Eddic matters in his pre-1869 verse.*]

I

Although William Morris is noted for the Norse adaptations he made in such poems as **"The Lovers of Gudrun"** and *Sigurd the Volsung,* in composing which he drew directly upon the *Laxdœla* and *Völsunga Sagas,* his "non-Norse" poems do not contain any large body of Norse allusions. It is a rather curious fact, however, that the poet actually employed more allusions to the *Edda* in poems written before he studied the Old Icelandic language and literature than he did after he and Eiríkr Magnússon composed their joint translations. In 1869, after a short period of study with Magnússon, Morris began to publish his long series of Scandinavian works. But before 1869, Morris had published a few poems in which he alluded to certain Eddic matters. While such allusions are by no means vast in number, they are especially significant, for they help to explain what Morris knew about Scandinavian myth before he commenced his collaboration with Magnússon.

The first Eddic allusion occurs in **"The Wanderers,"** the framework poem of *The Earthly Paradise.* Encountering certain cannibals, the speaker says:

> For with our grief such fearful foes we grew
> That Odin's gods had scarcely scared men more
> As fearless through the naked press we bore.[1]

The gods of Odin's Asgard, except for Thor, whose aspect is generally fearsome, and Loki, whose mischief-making is a by-word, are generally represented as kindly in their treatment of men. But Morris apparently knew as early as 1865-68 (when **"The Wanderers"** was probably composed) that the inhabitants of Asgard were not always gentle creatures. These gods were the eternal enemies of the giants; they often fought viciously among themselves, and were even known to play tricks upon unsuspecting men when they visited Midgard. Morris apparently appreciated the fact that, given the same circumstances, Odin's gods would have been just as fierce as the Norwegian Mariners about whom Rolf speaks in **"The Wanderers."** That Odin and his lesser gods were not capable of the sublimity of the Christian God of Love, Morris seemed fully to understand. The wrath of the Norse gods, as for example in the *Lokasenna* and the *Thrymskvitha,* was terrific when once aroused.[2]

A second allusion in **"The Wanderers"** is more subtle in implication. For a considerable time after Christianity was introduced into the Scandinavian peninsula, the practice of the people was to rely both upon the God of their missionaries, and upon the old Odinic worship which their ancestors had followed. The wanderers in Morris's poem had accepted the Christian faith; moreover, they had a priest in their party; but they had not forgotten the heathen tales of long ago.[3]

> Though we worshipped God,
> And heard mass duly, still of Swithiod
> The Greater, Odin, and his house of gold
> The noble stories ceased not to be told.[4]

"Swithiod the Greater," or Sweden the Great (*Svíþjóð hin mikla*), also called Godhome,[5] was the home of the gods (in certain sagas); but the term found no general use in legitimate Eddic material. Magnússon ventures the opinion that it was synonymous with Valhalla.[6] Morris probably got it from the *Ynglinga Saga* in English translation, or from some English epitome of Eddic and saga stories such as those made by Dasent and Thorpe. The names *Svíþjóð* and *Goðheimar* occur frequently in the *Ynglinga Saga*.

If it is true that *Svíþjóð* and Valhalla are synonymous, then the phrases, "Swithiod the Greater" and "Odin's house of gold," in the Morris poem, are redundant; for *Glaðsheimr* (Odin's house of gold) was the fifth home of the gods ("In my Father's house there are many mansions") and contains within it Valhalla. Says Odin, disguised as Grimnir:

> The fifth is Glathsheim, and gold-bright there
> Stands Valhall stretching wide;[7]

Following the lines from **"The Wanderers"** concerning Swithiod, the speaker continues to note the contrast between the old and new in times and religion:

> A little and unworthy land[8] it seemed,
> And all the more of Asgard's days I dreamed,
> And worthier seemed the ancient faith of praise.[9]

In closing this phase of the discussion, we should note that Morris's respect for the "ancient faith of praise" and the worthy aspiration toward Valhalla—matters with which he was obviously acquainted before he could read the Old Norse language—are not the least of the many things which the Old Norse literature taught him. There may be "more than meets the eye" in the poet's statement: "In religion I am a pagan."

II

To only three other Norse gods—Heimdall, Baldur, and Thor—does Morris allude in his non-Norse poems. The reference to Heimdall in the incomplete **"In Arthur's House"** testifies to Morris's early recognition of the importance of *ragna rök*:

> E'en as the sun arising wan
> In the black sky when Heimdall's horn
> Screams out and the last day is born,
> This blade to the eyes of men shall be
> On that dread day I shall not see—[10]

The old carle who is speaking to Arthur's entourage refers to *rogna rök*, the last battle of the gods with their ancient enemies, the giants, by telling of the harbinger which shall herald the battle: the sound of Heimdall's horn. Heimdall, the "white god," dwells in *Himinbjörg*, close to *Bifröst*, the Bridge of the *æsir*. He is the watchman of the gods, and when the giants come raging over *Bifröst*, he will blow "Yeller-Horn" (*Gjallarhorn*) to warn the gods.[11] Then the gods will arise and take counsel: Yggdrasil will tremble, and the æsir will attack

their invaders. There will be much slaughter and mutual-killing in duels; the world will be burned, and the gods and champions of mankind will be dead.[12] Then the "dread day" which Morris's old carle says he will not see, will have come. Since **"In Arthur's House"** was doubtless written as early as 1865, we have in this reference to Heimdall's horn ample proof that Morris recognized the significance of the Norse day of judgment at least five years before he composed his first great Norse poem, and at least three years before he began his comprehensive study of Scandinavian literature.

Baldur's chief characteristics—his beauty and brightness—were apparent to Morris of course. In order to describe another man whose aspect he wished to appear shining also, Morris employed a Baldur simile by way of illustration. The elder woman in *Anthony* pictures a youth for the maiden to whom she speaks:

> Southland may,
> Almost would he have moved thy solemn heart;
> Baldur come back to life[13] again he seemed
> A sun to light the dim hall's glimmering dusk—[14]

This information concerning Baldur is given many times in both *Eddas*; Morris may have recalled a passage from Snorri, paraphrased by one of the English adaptors, which reads (in a modern translation): "'The second son of Odin is Baldr, and good things are to be said of him . . . he is so fair of feature, and so bright, that light shines from him.'"[15]

Possibly the most elusive of all references to the gods in Morris's non-Norse poems is one which makes mention of Thor. In **"Ogier the Dane,"** the twelfth tale of **The Earthly Paradise,** Ogier scolds the multitude in the following manner:

> S[ain]t Mary! do such men as ye
> Fight with the wasters from across the sea?
> Then certes, are ye lost, however good
> Your hearts may be; not such were those who stood
> Beside the Hammer-bearer years agone.[16]

Although we cannot be sure of the particular incident to which Morris refers, the following explanation seems logical to the present writer: The "Hammer-bearer" is of course Thor (*Hlorriði, Vingþórr*: "Thor the Hurler"), and "those who stood" are probably the other gods. The allusion seems to contrast the inadequacy of Ogier's warriors in battle with the strength of the æsir. They "stood beside the Hammer-bearer" while Loki wrangled and accused the Ásynjur of infidelity, and the accumulated rage of "they who stood" when they heard Loki vilify Sif, Thor's wife, drove Loki out of Asgard. He then hid in Franang's Waterfall, and was fished out by the gods in the form of a salmon. This concludes a long series of misdeeds perpetrated by Loki, and henceforth he lies bound with the guts of his son, Vali,[17] waiting, as Snorri says, "Till the weird of the Gods."[18]

While these three references to the gods Heimdall, Baldur, and Thor, seem casual enough, they indicate, when their full implication is laid bare, that he who used them knew rather a great deal about the Norse stories from which they came.

III

After the completion of the translations of the *Gunnlaugs Saga* and the *Grettis Saga,* made in collaboration with Eiríkr Magnússon and published in 1869, Morris turned his attention to the heroic lays of the *Elder Edda* and the *Völsunga Saga* from both of which he acquired that vast body of legendary material concerning the Volsungs and Niblungs which he later used in **Sigurd the Volsung.** Although Magnússon states elsewhere that Morris was familiar with the *Eddas* from the Thorpe and Dasent versions before he had studied the originals, he leads one to suppose in his Preface to the last volume of the *Saga Library,*[19] that Morris's first real understanding of the Volsung stories came to him while Morris was working over the translations which he and the Icelander made together in 1870. Certainly the two allusions to the Volsung legends which occur in Morris's poems written previous to 1870 do not disprove Magnússon's theory. But they do indicate that Morris was at least slightly acquainted with the general ideas of the Volsung-Niblung stories. Both of these references mention the Hoard of the Niblungs. The "link" following **"The Writing on the Image"** in **The Earthly Paradise,** Part II, contains these lines:

> They praised the tale, and for a while they talked
> Of other tales of treasure-seekers balked,
> And shame and loss for men insatiate stored
> Nitocris' tomb, the Niblungs fatal hoard,[20]

The other Niblung allusion speaks of the Hoard figuratively as a kenning for gold:

> [On the Sword, Tyrfing]
> "The ruddy kin of Niblung's [sic] curse
> O'er the tresses of a sea-wife's hair
> Was wrapped about the handle fair";[21]

The "ruddy kin" is easily explicable, but the "sea-wife's hair" is not so readily interpreted. Ægir, the Norse Sea-god, had a wife, Ran, who was *the* sea-wife in most Eddic stories concerning the deities of the waters. Her "hair" may pertain to the net in which she caught those ship-wrecked within her domain, or it may refer to gold itself.[22] The vague allusion to "sea-wife's hair" probably was intended by Morris to represent simply one of the attributes of Tyrfing, or perhaps to signify the fetter which bound Tyrfing to its scabbard so that its unwary possessor might not pull it out and thereby kill himself, for Tyrfing always took a life when it was bared. The passage is mysterious enough to lend to the sword that glamour of the supernatural which was so definitely a feature of the charmed weapons of the Norsemen. But it actually does not tell us any more about the Hoard of the Niblungs than the mere fact that it existed.[23]

IV

The Norse allusions in the non-Norse poems of William Morris are of no small importance to the study of his relations with the Old Norse literature. We have seen that before he studied Old Icelandic with Magnússon, he had a fairly broad and general knowledge of Scandinavian mythology. We have likewise observed that he undoubtedly knew much more of the gods than he did of the Volsung heroes. English versions of the *Eddas* as paraphrased and translated by Dasent and Thorpe probably contributed to Morris the substance of his Norse allusions; and it may even be that some of them came from the incidental mythological references in Laing's English version of the *Heimskringla.* We should not overlook the importance of the allusions in these poems of **The Earthly Paradise** period, written mostly between 1865 and 1868, no matter how inconsequential they may appear at first view. The fact that Morris had *some* understanding of Norse matters before he worked with Magnússon allows us more easily to comprehend the phenomenal speed with which the English poet and the Icelandic philologist worked. Within a few months after the commencement of their collaboration, their first English version of a saga—that of *Gunnlaug the Wormtongue*—appeared; others followed in more than rapid succession.

Miscellaneous Norse allusions ceased to appear in Morris's poems after 1870, for after Morris had once plunged into the lays and sagas written in the Old Icelandic tongue, nothing other than the direct adaptation of *whole stories* could satisfy the artistic urge which now possessed the English "*Frún-smiðr* of the Northern Olympus." Morris's desire to recreate in his own language the Norse stories of another age brought forth those magnificent poems of a later date: **"The Lovers of Gudrun"** and **Sigurd the Volsung.** Yet we cannot say that such a line as

'And all the more of Asgard's days I dreamed'

does not have its private and exemplary significance in the genesis of that aesthetic which produced the noble hexameters of **Sigurd.**

Notes

1. *The Collected Works of William Morris,* With Introductions by his Daughter, May Morris (London and New York, 1910-1915), III, 48.

2. See also *Gylfaginning,* ch. 51, and *Völuspá,* stanzas 43-66.

3. For a modern treatment of the same paradoxical dual worship, see Sigrid Undset's *Kristin Lavrans-datter.*

4. *Collected Works*, III, 6.

5. See *Ynglinga Saga* (*Saga Library*, London, 1891-1905, III, 25-26), where Swegdir searches for Godhome so that he may find Odin.

6. See *Saga Library*, VI, "Godhome," Index II, p. 252.

7. *Grimnismál*, stanza 8, Bellows' translation (*The Poetic Edda*, translated by Henry Adams Bellows, New York, 1923). Cf. also *Gylfagynning*, Chapter XIV, wherein Gladsheim (*Glaðsheimr*) is the *first* house. "It was their [the gods'] first work to make that court in which their twelve seats stand, and another, the high-seat which the Allfather himself has. That house is the best-made of any on earth, and the greatest; without and within, it is all like one piece of gold; men call it Gladsheim." (*The Prose Edda*, translated by Arthur Gilchrist Brodeur, New York, 1929.)

8. That is, the land in which he, the speaker, lived.

9. *Collected Works*, III, 6.

10. *Collected Works*, XXIV, 323.

11. *Gylfaginning*, chapter XXVII.

12. See Snorri's *Edda*, chapters LI, LII, LIII.

13. "Baldur come back to life": cf. "Ah! when thy Balder comes back," in Morris's *Iceland First Seen, Collected Works*, IX, 126; and also "And Baldr comes back" [*mun baldr koma*], *Völuspá*, stanza 62. The coming of *ragna rök* and the return of Baldur were two important events which Morris later incorporated into his social philosophy. The present author has discussed these matters in a previous article: "The Social Philosophy of William Morris and the Doom of the Gods," *Michigan Essays and Studies in English and Comparative Literature*, X (Ann Arbor, 1933), 183-203. It is exceedingly interesting to observe that one of the first things Morris knew about Norse myth was the destruction on the dread day of *ragna rök*, for he made considerable use of this idea in his later works.

14. *Collected Works*, XXIV, 335. This poem belongs in the 1865-68 period also.

15. *Gylfaginning*, chapter XXII, Brodeur's translation, p. 36.

16. *Collected Works*, IV, 235-236. While it is appropriate that Ogier the Dane should himself make a Scandinavian allusion, the poem, *Ogier the Dane*, can scarcely be considered a Norse poem. It is even less characteristically Scandinavian than Morris's "Aslaug," or his "Swanhild," both of which were written before he could read Norse. The real Norse poems are "Gudrun" and "Sigurd."

17. Loki's expulsion for his abuse of the gods is found in the *Elder Edda, Lokasenna*, stanzas 60-65. Cf. also *Thrymskvitha* for Thor's wrath and the passive nature of his companions, stanzas 30-33.

18. In Snorri's version, however, Loki is punished by the gods for his part in Baldur's death. See *Gylfaginning*, chapter L.

19. *Saga Library*, VI, Preface, pp. xv-xvi.

20. *Collected Works*, IV, 85.

21. *In Arthur's House*, in *Collected Works*, XXIV, 320.

22. "Ran's light" was a kenning for gold, since Ægir used gold instead of torches to illuminate his palace. See Snorri's *Edda, Skáldskaparmál*, chapter XXXIII.

23. In contrast to these vague Volsung allusions, cf. the lines:

> My Sigurd's sword, my Brynhild's fiery bed,
> The tale of years of Gudrun's drearihead,

from *Love is Enough*, composed *after* Morris had delved into the *Völsunga Saga* in the original. "Sigurd's sword" was Gram, which Regin made from the shards of Sigmund's broken brand. "Brynhild's fiery bed" symbolizes the well-known Volsung episode: Sigurd, in the person of Gunnar, rode through the flames that surrounded Brynhild, on his horse, Grani; and slept with her three nights in the guise of Gunnar, placing Gram between them. Gudrun's later knowledge of this, the subsequent murder of Sigurd by Gunnar and the brothers, and the ensuing life of tragedy made up those events which are "The tale of years of Gudrun's drearihead." The two lines quoted above from *Love is Enough* show that when he wrote that poem Morris was well informed concerning the Volsung tradition.

Lawrence Perrine (essay date April 1960)

SOURCE: Perrine, Lawrence. "Morris's Guenevere: An Interpretation." *Philological Quarterly* 39, no. 2 (April 1960): 234-41.

[*In the following essay, Perrine provides an interpretation of Queen Guenevere's character in "The Defence of Guenevere" and finds her guilty of adultery in the poem.*]

"The Defence of Guenevere" is a poem that has been widely admired without being fully understood. An initial difficulty lies in its central situation. The Queen is pleading her innocence of an accusation made by

Gauwaine. Whether she is innocent or guilty, however, and, indeed, what exactly the accusation has been—though it includes the charge of adultery—are not stated. Critics of Morris have either disagreed, admitted their perplexity, or dodged the issue altogether. A few of their comments follow:

> Though wedded to Arthur, [Guenevere] has loved Launcelot, but not sinned with him. This she confesses, at the same time denying the baser charge.[1]

> Were it not for **"King Arthur's Tomb,"** which follows, and which may be taken as a sequel to **"The Defence of Guenevere,"** the Queen's guilt would not be indubitable. . . . With Guenevere talking like this [boasting of her beauty], and with Morris leaving it uncertain whether he intended her to be guilty of adultery or not, you cannot help thinking that a dash of clear 18th-century reason would have made his poetry . . . a stronger thing than it is.[2]

> Morris does not settle clearly whether Guenevere is innocent or not. Instead he leaves us with the memory of the suffering Queen.[3]

> [Morris's] "romanticism" seems to have clouded his power of judging fairly. The argument is exceedingly weak. The reader is left uncertain of the Queen's guilt.[4]

> What Guinevere meant by saying that Gawain lied is never cleared up.[5]

> ["**The Defence of Guenevere"**] is a defence of the virtue of King Arthur's queen, a lady whose fair fame, like Helen's, it was reserved for our politeness to vindicate.[6]

Since the essence of the poem lies in the characterization of the Queen, the question of her technical guilt or innocence is an exceedingly important one. The answer to the question, however, is only one clue to the interpretation of her character. In this paper I shall, first, establish the fact of Guenevere's guilt; second, provide an interpretation of her character; and, third, comment briefly on Morris's attitude toward her.

I

There can be no doubt—nor has there ever been—that the source of the poem is the *Morte Darthur.* **"The Defence"** was written within a year or two of Morris's purchase of a copy of Malory in 1855 and probably within a year of his having heard Rossetti describe the *Morte Darthur* and the Bible as the two greatest books in the world. It was written during a period when Morris and his friends talked constantly of Malory and Morris did three murals for Rossetti's ill-fated project of decorating the new Union Society building at Oxford with a series of ten scenes from Malory.[7] The details of the poem conform, with two minor exceptions, to the story as told by Malory. And these variations—the substitution of Gauwaine for Mordred as Guenevere's accuser, and the substitution of Agravaine for Gaheris

as the slayer of Gaheris's and Gauwaine's mother—are not explainable by any other source. They are the kind of mistakes a man might make who was writing from a vivid impression of his reading, and whose philosophy of the best way to retell an old romance was, as Morris told his daughter, to "read it through, then shut the book and write it out again as a new story for yourself."[8]

Not only does Morris's poem stem from Malory as a source; it requires a knowledge of Malory for its comprehension. Such an allusion as that to the death of Gauwaine's mother ("Remember in what grave your mother sleeps," etc., lines 153-157) is unintelligible without familiarity with the *Morte Darthur*; for the reader who has that familiarity, it calls up the whole dramatic story of the enmity of Gauwaine and his brethren for Lamorak and of the various amours of Gauwaine's mother Margause, whom her own son Gaheris finally slew when he took her in bed with Lamorak. Guenevere's implication in reminding Gauwaine of this affair is simply "Remember that your own mother was guilty of the same crime of which you are accusing me." The episode of Mellyagraunce's accusation and of his fight with Launcelot is similarly not understandable without knowledge of the Malory source; yet Morris devotes nineteen stanzas—one fifth of his poem—to this episode. One fact stands out from these considerations, and its recognition is essential to correct interpretation of the poem. **"The Defence of Guenevere"** *is written by a reader of Malory for readers of Malory.* Morris has chosen to explore one moment from the *Morte Darthur* in all its dramatic implications and to make it vivid, exciting, and alive. In the *Morte Darthur* Guenevere had been given no "defence." The "defence" is Morris's invention; the rest is dependent on Malory. It is for this reason that Morris has not stated the guilt or innocence of the Queen. He assumes that the story told by Malory will be as vivid in his reader's mind as it is in his own.

The episode in Malory which occasions Morris's poem is the third of three occasions on which Launcelot saves Guenevere from being burned at the stake. The first of these episodes (Book XVIII, chs. 3-8) is not mentioned by Morris. The second (Book XIX, chs. 1-9) is the episode referred to in the Mellyagraunce stanzas. On this occasion Guenevere, in the castle of Mellyagraunce, had slept the night in the same chamber with the wounded knights of her escort, that she might tend them if needed. During the night Launcelot climbed to her window, they had a long talk, and then "both wished to come to each other." Launcelot broke the iron bars, cutting his hand, and "went unto bed with the queen, and he took no force of his hurt hand, but took his pleasaunce and his liking until it was in the dawning of the day." When Mellyagraunce found blood on the Queen's bed, he accused her of having lain with one of her wounded knights. In the trial by combat which followed, with the fire prepared for Guenevere, Launcelot fought Mellyagraunce with his left side exposed and his left hand tied behind him, and slew him.

The third episode (Book XX, chs. 1-8) is the famous one which provides the basis for Morris's poem. Mordred and Agravaine, suspecting that Launcelot lay "daily and nightly with the queen" and plotting to take the pair together, sent word to Guenevere that Arthur would not return from a hunting trip that night. Then Mordred and Agravaine with twelve other knights secreted themselves in the castle until night, and when Guenevere and Launcelot were together, came crying outside their door. Launcelot, unarmed except for his sword, opened the door and killed all but Mordred, who fled. Then Launcelot took farewell of the Queen, promising to rescue her on the morrow should Arthur condemn her to death, as indeed Arthur did. In the morning, therefore, Guenevere was led forth from Carlisle, stripped to her smock, and shriven by her ghostly father. One of Launcelot's spies informed Launcelot and his men, who were hidden in the woods near Carlisle, and "then was there but spurring and plucking up of horses, and right so they came to the fire," and slew many knights, and rescued Guenevere. Though it is not stated definitely whether Launcelot and Guenevere were abed on this occasion, their guilt on previous occasions has been made amply clear.

The evidence for Guenevere's guilt, in Morris's poem, is thus practically conclusive. She is guilty in Malory. Morris has written his poem so that it requires knowledge of Malory for its complete comprehension. Had Morris intended a different conception, he would surely have taken pains to avoid misinterpretation. Had he intended the Queen to be innocent, he would not have included the tell-tale incident of Mellyagraunce and the blood on Guenevere's bed. And he would not have portrayed, in his sequel poem, **"King Arthur's Tomb,"** a repentant Guenevere lamenting her sin.

II

"The Defence of Guenevere" is something more, however, than the cold-blooded denial by a guilty woman of her guilt. It is the desperate battle of a proud queen and passionate woman for life and for everything which makes life dear to her. And it is given dignity by her genuine feeling that she has been done, and is being done, a great injustice.

Guenevere is moved in her defence primarily by three emotions—anger, fear, and love. Her anger is over her very real sense of a just grievance—of having been bought in marriage "by Arthur's great name and his little love" and of being denied her love for Launcelot. Her fear is for her life, which she clings to with all the force of a person who is still young, beautiful, and intensely physically alive. Her love is for Launcelot and is what makes life a priceless possession to her and the prospect of losing it terrible. Her defence is a mixture of passionate sincerity, sheer bluff, and bold lies, prompted by desperation, and receives its force from all of these. She knows that Launcelot is coming to rescue her and that she will be safe if she can stave off the lighting of the faggots until then. She is striving, in her defence, to justify her conduct; to dazzle, threaten, or cajole her judges into releasing her; and to stall for time until Launcelot's arrival.

In the parable of the choosing-cloths Guenevere's defence is genuine and sincere. Here she is making a plea for a larger moral frame of reference than that which obtains in Camelot. She is suggesting that Camelot's law and God's law are not necessarily the same, that in the eyes of God she may be innocent. Her choice has been between fidelity to a marriage without love or to love without marriage. She has chosen love, and her judges have declared her wrong. Obviously, however, Guenevere does not believe that she is wrong. Love, for her, has a law of its own. Love is that which she had deemed would ever move round her "glorifying all things"; and now that she has experienced it, it has not disappointed her. How can one do wrong in following love? She has not been breaking law, she implies, but following law—only it has been the law of love rather than that of Camelot. She says, in effect, "I am not guilty. I know a higher law than you are aware of. Better true love without marriage than marriage without love."

Guenevere boasts of her feeling for Launcelot. In her recounting the growth of her love, she obviously takes glory in it. Her fighting it off for a year and a half, she would imply, attests both to the genuineness of her own motives and to the reality of the love. She denies, however, that she has been guilty of adultery, and the vehemence of her denial is such that it almost seems to carry some color of truth:

> Nevertheless you, O Sir Gauwaine, lie,
> Whatever may have happened through these years,
> God knows I speak truth, saying that you lie.

Not improbably Gauwaine, in accordance with his hot nature, has stated his accusation in broader terms than a mere flat charge of adultery. He has called her, perhaps, a harlot, a strumpet, or a traitor. If such is the case, though Guenevere is consciously and deliberately lying in denying the technical charge against her, she is passionately in earnest in repudiating the broader imputation. She is legally guilty, though she denies it, but she believes firmly that morally she is innocent.

The rest of Guenevere's defence is mostly bluff and virtuosity. She uses every trick and weapon at her command in order to get mercy from her judges. She tries to draw forth their pity—

> Gauwaine be friends now, speak me lovingly.
> Do I not see how God's dear pity creeps
> All through your frame, and trembles in your mouth?
> Remember in what grave your mother sleeps. . . .

She tries to frighten them with the judgment of God upon them for a false decision—

> Yet Mellyagraunce was shent,
> For Mellyagraunce had fought against the Lord;
> Therefore, my lords, take heed lest you be blent
> With all this wickedness.

She tries to sway them by her beauty—

> See my breast rise,
> Like waves of purple sea, as here I stand;
> And how my arms are moved in wonderful wise,
> . . . how in my hand
> The shadow lies like wine within a cup
> Of marvelously colour'd gold.

Guenevere is proud of her beauty and uses it as a strong man would use his strong right arm. She "dares" her judges to condemn to the fire anything as beautiful as she. She plays deliberately upon the reluctance of human nature to believe that anything beautiful can be corrupt:

> Will you dare,
> When you have looked a little on my brow,
> To say this thing is vile?

She is not, however, a coolly designing schemer. She is a woman who has been faithful to one great love, and whose lies arise from the heat of her passion, danger, and desperation.

The task of establishing her innocence—since she is not innocent—is, of course, an impossible one. Nevertheless, Guenevere attacks it boldly:

> Let God's justice work! Gauwaine, I say,
> See me hew down your proofs.

The proofs that Gauwaine has advanced are two: (1) that on the occasion when Guenevere slept in one room with her wounded knights, Mellyagraunce found blood on her sheets; (2) that, more recently, Launcelot has been found in her chamber. Guenevere's "hewing down" of these proofs consists (1) in asserting that a queen does not need to offer proofs—that it would have been undignified in her, on the first occasion, to stoop to answer Mellyagraunce's unseemly accusations; and (2) in suggesting that Launcelot, on the recent occasion, could have come to her chamber and spent the night in it for entirely innocent reasons. Needless to say, both arguments are sophistical. Guenevere then urges further that her very tears are proof of her innocence:

> Being such a lady could I weep these tears
> If this were true? A great queen such as I

> Having sinn'd this way, straight her conscience sears;
> And afterwards she liveth hatefully,
> Slaying and poisoning, certes never weeps.

This argument, of course, is no better than the first two. The lowest harlot is capable of real tears, and any actress can simulate them.

At least two of the critics previously cited have held the weakness of Guenevere's logic to be a weakness in the poem. Nothing could be further from the truth. Morris's whole characterization of Guenevere is that of a person whose motivating force is passion, not principle or reason. As a woman of passion, and one, moreover, who is legally guilty, Guenevere defends herself, not logically, but boldly, and altogether as such a person might, under the circumstances.

And after all, what first impresses the reader about Guenevere's defence is not its weakness but its strength—even its magnificence. The initial reaction is one, not of moral indignation, but of admiration. Be she ever so guilty, one cannot help feeling, as Morris has written in a discarded introduction, that her plea has been spoken by "brave lips and beautiful."[9] Moreover, her defence has "worked." Whether it persuades any of her judges of her *moral* innocence, each reader must determine by his own reaction—since he is ultimately the judge himself, but it does stave off the lighting of the fire until Launcelot can come to the rescue; and the reader of Malory will remember that Guenevere outlives her accusers and dies a holy woman. But her defence accomplishes even more than that. It has persuaded some scholars of her *technical* innocence.

III

One further misunderstanding about the poem needs clearing up. The poem has been referred to by some critics as being *Morris's* defence of Guenevere. The implication is that when Guenevere pleads for her moral innocence, in the parable of the choosing-cloths, Morris is pleading for her. The temptation, of course, is to contrast Morris's exculpation of her behavior with Tennyson's later Victorian condemnation of it. This contrast, however, is unjustified. The true contrast is between the importance of the didactic element in Tennyson and the complete absence of it in Morris. Morris's poetry as a whole is notable for its absence of philosophical ideas, and one looks in vain for moral judgments in *The Defence of Guenevere* volume. Morris, at the time of its composition, was strongly under the influence of Browning. When asked, before its publication, in whose style the title poem was written, he answered, "More like Browning than anyone else, I suppose."[10] What influenced Morris, in Browning's poetry, was not its philosophy, but its dramatic character. Browning took persons good, bad, and indifferent, and let them speak for themselves and attempt to justify themselves. In *The Defence of Guenevere* volume Morris follows suit. Nearly all of the poems are dramatic. The speakers are so many medieval knights and ladies, not Morris himself. Though most of them are good, some are bad. In **"The Judgment of God"** and **"Golden Wings"** the speakers are murderers, but in neither does Morris express any moral judgment. And there is no more reason for supposing that Morris is justifying these characters than there is to believe that Browning is defending the Duke of Ferrara or the Bishop of St. Praxed's.

The only moral sympathies that Morris expresses in **"The Defence of Guenevere"** are admiration for Guenevere's beauty and bravery—

> Still she stood right up, and never shrunk
> But spoke on bravely, glorious lady fair!

Courage and physical beauty command admiration always in Morris's poetry. But Morris no more necessarily condones Guenevere's conduct than Milton does Satan's when he describes the archfiend as a "great Commander" and as possessing "dauntless courage." The poem is not Morris's defence of Guenevere, but Guenevere's defence of herself. Morris has merely taken one of Malory's characters in a moment of stress and brought her intensely alive. His task has been not to excuse or to blame, but to vivify.

Notes

1. James Ormerod, *The Poetry of William Morris* (Derby, 1938), p. 4.

2. Howard Maynadier, *The Arthur of the English Poets* (Boston, 1907), pp. 359-360.

3. B. Ifor Evans, *William Morris & his Poetry* (London, 1925), p. 28.

4. Margaret J. C. Reid, *The Arthurian Legend* (Edinburgh, [1938]), p. 98.

5. August J. App, *Lancelot in English Literature* (Washington, 1929), pp. 177-178.

6. *Saturday Review of Politics, Literature, Science, and Art,* VI (November 20, 1858), 506-507.

7. See J. W. Mackail, *The Life of William Morris,* 2 vols. (London, 1899).

8. *The Collected Works of William Morris, With introductions by his daughter May Morris* (London, 1910), XVII, xxxix.

9. *Collected Works,* I, xx.

10. Mackail, I, 131-132.

Robert L. Stallman (essay date autumn 1969)

SOURCE: Stallman, Robert L. "'Rapunzel' Unravelled." *Victorian Poetry* 7, no. 3 (autumn 1969): 221-32.

[*In the following essay, Stallman perceives Morris's "Rapunzel" as an archetypal Victorian treatment of the mythic quest and a "rite of passage" tale.*]

Morris' youthful little drama challenges modern readers of poetry quite as much as it did his Victorian peers. They met the challenge by ignoring the poem, but it hardly seems admirable of us to dismiss it as "bewitching" or as having an inexplicable "dark weirdness" about it.[1] If the poem is effective, there must be some rationale to its effect on us as readers, perhaps an effect that can be illuminated rather than explained away. Certainly, as we read the poem, we have the uncomfortable feeling of walking over thin ice that hides a vast world beneath its surface glitter. This is somewhat the same feeling we have on reading the original tale in *Grimm's Fairy Tales,* but Morris' treatment seems more intense and dramatic.

In Grimm's tale the Prince overhears the Witch's magic words and climbs the tower secretly to spend time with Rapunzel. The witch catches him and casts him into the thorns below which blind him. He wanders about until by supernatural aid he recovers his sight, kills the Witch and wins Rapunzel for his love. Morris creates from this original a series of dramatic tableaux, a drama of moods not actions. Examining the four scene changes in the poem, we find that in each a shift in perception rather than action precipitates the change and so advances the plot. Perhaps the answer to the effectiveness of **"Rapunzel"** may be found by examining this dramatic structure and the psychological and mythical bases on which it rests.

The opening scene is dramatic and represents by the arrangement of the speeches the three characters, the Prince, the Witch, and the Maiden standing, let us say, left, center, and right on a stage. Each speech group consists of a stanza, quatrains for the Prince and Maiden, two short lines for the Witch, each speech being separated in the same order: Prince, Witch, Maiden; Prince, Witch, Maiden, suggesting the position of the Witch between the two lovers. In addition, each speaker breaks into the syntax of the one before, so that it appears they are all speaking simultaneously. The scene thus gains something of the effect of three separate soliloquies proceeding at once.

The Prince reminisces about his reasons for taking up the quest; the Maiden bewails her sad plight; and the Witch repeats the ritual, "Rapunzel, Rapunzel, / Let down your hair!" While this scene serves to supply background, a skeleton story of sorts, and suggests the separation of the lovers, it also gives characteristic images and speech modes for each of the characters. The Prince moves in a dream of action:

> I put my armor on,
> 　Thinking on what they said:
> "Thou are a king's own son,
> 　'Tis fit that thou should'st wed."
>
> 　　　　　　　　　　　　　　(ll. 21-24)
>
> . . . . .
>
> I rode throughout the town,
> 　Men did not bow the head,
> Though I was the king's own son;
> 　"He rides to dream," they said.
>
> 　　　　　　　　　　　　　　(ll. 31-34)

The Maiden's speeches are characteristically sorrowful for the imprisonment she endures and are excessively concerned with her golden hair.

> Is it not true that every day
> She climbeth up the same strange way,
> Her scarlet cloak spread broad and gay,
> 　　Over my golden hair?
>
> 　　　　　　　　　　　　　　(ll. 7-10)
>
> . . . . .
>
> See, on the marble parapet
> The faint red stains with tears are wet;
> The long years pass, no help comes yet
> 　　To free my golden hair.
>
> 　　　　　　　　　　　　　　(ll. 37-40)

The Witch's speeches, on the other hand, have the repetitious effect of an evil rite:

> Rapunzel, Rapunzel,
> Let down your hair!
>
> 　　　　　　　　　　　　　　(ll. 25-26)
>
> . . . . .
>
> Rapunzel, Rapunzel,
> Wind up your hair!
>
> 　　　　　　　　　　　　　　(ll. 35-36)

While the two young people seem nearer to being realistic characters, the Witch represents some timeless evil quality that hangs about their lives and separates them like a paralyzing mist. Her speeches are chants, repetitions of the refrain which dazzles the lovers and challenges them at the same time. Even in her defeat, the Witch seems powerful because she has no really human qualities, but only the steadfastness of evil itself which we know will endure though it be cast into hell.

The first scene, then, is this triple soliloquy. The second scene, told in retrospect, shows the Prince blind and wandering, Rapunzel praying in her tower, the Witch secure in her evil. Scene three, seemingly without transition, shows the Prince and Maiden united, the banner of the Witch being tossed down, and their descent from the tower into the real world of grass and flowers. The fourth and fifth scenes may be united as one, since they both concern the successful aftermath of the adventure with both Prince and Maiden assuming their proper names and the Witch vanquished. In none of these scenes is there the violent action we might expect. The fall of the Prince from the tower into the thorns, the fight with the Witch, the Prince's triumph: none of this is shown. The first two scenes are told in dreamy retrospect, the last three in present time, breaking the poem evenly into a dream-like bondage in the first half, and a realistic (with real names) victory and freedom in the last half. The effect so gained is not so much that of a real knight defeating a realistic power of evil, as of Everyman caught in a magic mist from which he seems powerless to escape; then, by some supernatural insight or sudden awakening, finding his love and victory. As in Browning's "Childe Roland" it seems to be a problem of perception rather than battle, and when the victory occurs, it is a simple emergence of the sun where before there was fog. The timelessness of the first half of the poem, especially of the Prince's speeches in scene two, where he mixes past and present in his blindness, makes victory impossible. The Prince is snared in time, and although he can hear the Witch and hear Rapunzel's song, and each morning whets his sword as if to do battle, still the golden mist blinds him and he cannot act. Then when the change comes, suddenly it is all over. There has been no real battle at all, it seems.

The story of Rapunzel is, of course, the tale of a quest, a pattern that in this case is also a "rite of passage."[2] But this time the knight's quest seems impeded by dreams and blindness, and more importantly, by the poet's lack of emphasis on the heart of the quest, the battle. If this knight is to pass his "rite," and bring back to his land the "glorious lady fair" that is his reward, he cannot in this case do actual battle with the Witch. He must undergo a change of perception, a much more difficult task than fighting visible and tangible dragons. In a later story written for inclusion in *The Earthly Paradise,* Morris again used this sort of moral rite of passage. In **"The Lady of the Land,"** his wanderer found the lovely lady of gold who warned him that not swords but moral courage would win her reward. The adventurer, secretly fearing for his life, girt his sword on for a battle that was purely a test of faith. And with this faulty preparation, he failed his rite and was cast into darkness forever. In **"Rapunzel,"** then, the secret of success for the hero is to achieve the proper state of mind. Battle is not the answer in this moral cause. For this reason there is no violent action in the poem, and for this reason too, the drama exhibits unusual scene shifts, depending on association of ideas and changes of mood rather than on physical action.

The shift from scene one to scene two illustrates Morris' manner of advancing the plot by association, as in a dream, rather than by dramatic action.

[Scene one]

RAPUNZEL:

> And yet—but I am growing old,
> For want of love my heart is cold;
> Years pass, the while I loose and fold
> The fathoms of my hair.

[Scene two]

THE PRINCE (IN THE MORNING):

> I have heard tales of men, who in the night
> Saw paths of stars let down to earth from
> heaven,
> Who followed them until they reached the light
> Wherein they dwell, whose sins are all forgiven.

(ll. 47-54)

The shift is accomplished by reference to the golden ladder of Rapunzel's hair, the paradoxical symbol of love that contains possibilities for both evil and good.

Such associative shifts help to create an atmosphere of dream appropriate to the rite of passage in the first half of the poem. We find that the Prince has had the unheroic boyhood usual to future heroes, that he was

> "patient of the scoff
> That met [him] always there from day to day,
> From any knave or coward of them all."

(ll. 66-68)

And he has ridden out to look for love, feeling himself about to be born anew:

> Not born as yet, but going to be born,
> No naked baby as I was at first,
> But an arméd knight, whom fire, hate and scorn
> Could turn from nothing.

(ll. 95-98)

He knows that his quest is irreversible, like any rite of passage, and that he must not hesitate or turn back:

> But who went backward when they saw the gate
> Of diamond, nor dared to enter in;
> All their life long they were content to wait,
> Purging them patiently of every sin.

(ll. 55-58)

Then, at the moment of his victory, the Prince finds himself helpless. And his plight is not relieved by his knightly prowess, for the frightening power of the Witch has blinded him:

> And every morning do I whet my sword,
> Yet Rapunzel still weeps within the tower,
> And still God ties me down to the green sward,
> Because I cannot see the gold stair floating lower.

(ll. 152-155)

The sight he remembers as paralyzing him in his progress was that of the Witch's abusing Rapunzel's hair, swinging on its plaits like devil's bats. The tower in which Rapunzel is immured is a distinctly feminine counterpart of the usual Freudian tower with "No belfry for the swinging of great bells . . . amber and rose walls . . . flower-carven marble" and in all "a dwelling for a queen."

Rapunzel's hair is, of course, symbolic in both the fairy tale and in Morris' retelling of it of the woman's sexual maturity. The accompanying menses are represented by the Witch's "scarlet cloak spread broad and gay, / Over my golden hair." In such a mixture of sexual symbolism and romantically conceived myth as we have here, the hair represents both the romantic conception of love, which was probably what Morris had in mind, and the mystery of woman, which is capable of being both heaven and hell. The golden hair may be the delight and law of marriage, or the perversion and non-law of promiscuity (as in **"The Defence of Guenevere"**).[3] Since the Witch's abuse centers on Rapunzel's hair, we presume it refers to some sexual perversion, possibly the simple fact of enforced virginity, which is a perversion, as well as the prevention of romantic love in its "proper" form. In Grimm's tale, it is the sad result of the mother's lust for the forbidden rampion root that leads to the daughter's imprisonment. In either case the symbolism smacks of sexual perversion or prevention. The poem is highly charged with sexual symbols, readily recognizable in our own post-Freudian day, but acting only in a subliminal manner for the Victorians. The whole point here, however, is that there is more to be gained from the poem than a simple job of symbol-picking will accomplish.

In the first two scenes of the poem, in addition to the picture of the Prince as the typical hero undergoing the rite of passage and the creation of a dream mood, there are images which seem to place the tower of Rapunzel in some inaccessible location beneath the sea. The hair is often said to "float," and the word "fathoms" is used several times: "Fathoms below my hair grows wet / With the dew," and "while I loose and fold / The fathoms of my hair." The Prince uses the same word once, then speaks of Rapunzel "Bearing within her arms waves of her yellow hair." And before his eyes "a film of gold / Floated, as now it floats," and again he cannot act "Because [he] cannot see the gold stair floating lower." In Rapunzel's song at the end of the second scene, there is explicit reference to her situation as beneath the sea: she "can see no more / The crayfish on the leaden floor, / That mock with feeler and grim claw" (ll. 197-199). And, of course, throughout the first half of the poem, the creation of a dream-like atmosphere adds to the unearthly setting. The whole reminds one of the old Danish fairy tale called "The Wizard's Daughter," in which the daughter is trapped in a glass castle under the sea, from which the young man must rescue her by outwitting her father the Wizard.[4] The symbolism of release from the bondage of childhood to the freedom of adult love is nearly the same, although the details are different.

At any rate, the image of the depths of the sea is appropriate to this particular quest since the sea has, for as long as our myths can remember, been associated with the undifferentiated life of childhood before the breaking away of the ego (by means of the rites of passage) into individual life and being. The poem would then be an enactment of the rite that takes the young man from the undifferentiated life of the child, scoffed at and mocked, through the difficult trial of attaining adult perception (surmounting the blindness, of which more in a moment), and attaining love and individuality, represented by the individual names given the Prince and the Maiden in the second half of the poem.

The trial which the Prince must undergo is explained partially in the first half of the poem, partially in the second. Blindness which Morris describes as only temporary, a sort of golden haze before the eyes, inhibits the Prince from his goal. Now we recognize, of course, Freud's interpretation of blindness as infantile castration fear, coupled with what Jung (or in this case Neumann) calls "loss of the conscious realization of the ego."[5] These two interpretations have similar results, namely the loss of power or confidence in oneself through a faulty perception, or more accurately, fear (usually thought of as fear of the parent). The fact that the blindness is a golden mist suggests his trouble might also be a faulty (lustful) perception of love, i.e., the sexual mystery, noted as inherent in the golden hair, which fills his sight to the exclusion of all else. He is blind to complete love. But the Prince is also inhibited from his goal by the usual fear which accompanies the passage from child to adult, the fear of the "Witch" or the parent, which holds the child in thrall. The sudden resolution of this thralldom is one of the startling shifts arising from Morris' dramatic method.

In terms of the dramatic method which was mentioned earlier, the shift from scene two to scene three, or symbolically the successful passing of the rite, is accomplished by the Maiden's invocation of Christ and Mary. But if we are aware of the sexual drama also going on here, we are not surprised to find that the maiden has added a few lines of her own to the ritual prayer. In this addition, she invokes the phallic power that will free her from the parental prison:

> Yet besides I have made this
> By myself: *Give me a kiss*
> *Dear God, dwelling up in heaven!*
> Also: *Send me a true knight*
> *Lord-Christ, with a steel sword, bright,*
> *Broad and trenchant; yea, and seven*
> *Spans from hilt to point, O Lord!*
> *And let the handle of his sword*
> *Be gold on silver, Lord in heaven!*
> *Such a sword as I see gleam*
> *Sometimes, when they let me dream.*
>
> (ll. 165-175)

Although Morris himself would never have dreamed (or perhaps it would be correct to say would *only* have dreamed) of such a meaning, it is the phallic power of the young knight that finally brings freedom and individuality to the young lovers, severing them from the bondage of the parent. It is clear also that this phallic power is a moral force that must be properly perceived before it can be used.

The rite of passage is psychologically sound in terms of our own understanding, read in this way as the freeing of the individual from the undifferentiated sea of the parental power, as well as the awakening, sexual and otherwise, of the sort of true love Morris approved of. It is this invocation to God and the phallic power that shifts the mood of the poem suddenly from dream-like stasis in the first two scenes to the real victory and real world of the second half of the poem. The shift is dramatically correct in terms of Morris' method of association also, for the last lines of scene two lead by association directly into scene three.

> I behold a face,
> Which sometime, if God give me grace,
> May kiss me in this very place.
>
> [Scene three]

RAPUNZEL:

> (*Evening in the tower*)
> It grows half way between the dark and light;
> Love, we have been six hours here alone.
>
> (ll. 204-208)

The maiden has been dreaming of just such an event, and suddenly as if in dream-like fulfillment of her wishes, she and the Prince are together. Not only is such a wish fulfillment appropriate to the dream, but it fits the moral scheme of the poem, for the proper conjunction of moods has been reached in both characters. The scene changes; the rite is accomplished; a new perception has occurred.

As the Prince and the maiden speak together, apparently undisturbed any further by the Witch, a battle is spoken of which at first sight seems irrelevant to the poem as a whole. The Prince asks the maiden, "Now tell me, did you ever see a death, / Or ever see a man take mortal harm?" (ll. 213-214). Rapunzel thereupon tells of having seen two knights destroy each other below the tower once in an apparently causeless battle. The description of the knights is done in Morris' usual, accurate medieval vein, and the incident might be taken as simply added to the old fairy tale to give color and action. The Prince, upon hearing of the battle, remarks,

> Ah, they were brothers then,
> And often rode together, doubtless where
> The swords were thickest, and were loyal men,
> Until they fell in these same evil dreams.
>
> (ll. 244-247)

This is left to hang cryptically for some lines, while the lovers prepare to depart from the tower. The Prince tells the maiden how he came to find her, lured on by the dream of her golden hair. He says then that if he had not come to find her,

> O child I should have slain my brother, too,
>   My brother, Love, lain moaning in the grass,
> Had I not ridden out to look for you,
>   When I had watch'd the gilded courtiers pass
> From the golden hall.
>
> (ll. 271-275)

It is this speech which justifies the inclusion of the battle scene and also indicates the moral nature of the Prince's quest as opposed to the quest involving physical prowess. The "evil dreams" are exemplified in the first half of the poem in the Prince's blindness and in the story of the brothers battling each other. It is evidently an evil dream to imagine the maiden can be won by such battles, or to seek the results of a moral quest with force of arms. The brothers remind us of the many other avatars of this situation: Tennyson's Balin and Balan (from Malory, Book II), and the tale repeated in the *Idylls* ("Lancelot and Elaine") of the brother kings who slew each other; these in turn possibly springing from the Celtic myth of Belinus and Bran, or Balyn and Bran, counterparts of this Prince Sebald who might have killed his brother if he had not been steadfast in the moral quest for love.[6]

The brother battle here is similar also to such tales of the "doppelganger" as Poe's "William Wilson" and Dostoievsky's *The Double,* which show a man divided against himself to his ultimate self-destruction when his energies are not directed outward toward the finding of his own individuality. Certainly Morris was familiar with the idea of the alter-ego or soul-double from De La Motte Fouque's tale, "Undine," in which Undine and Bertalda are "two faces opening from a single stem," even though one was a human child and one a fairy changeling.[7] Otto Rank mentions this double image as the basic spiritual principle of the "gradual freeing of the individual from dependence," and seeking rebirth as a whole individual that will unite his conflict-

ing self-images instead of causing them to war against each other.[8] In general, Rank goes too far afield in connecting art and the artist, but in this case he seems to have hit on a basic truth that Morris perhaps perceived intuitively: man wars against himself unless he succeeds in completing the rite of passage from undifferentiated union with the parent to successfully differentiated adult. He in effect destroys himself with the conflicting impulses of the urge toward freedom versus the urge toward regression into the parental power.[9] There is also something of a sexual parallel here comparable to the perversion indicated by the Witch's misuse of Rapunzel's hair. The self-battle is a perversion of the natural energies that should be directed outward. In this sense too, the battle is quite appropriate to the poem.

It is immediately after the telling of this battle that the final symbol of the Witch's power falls. Rapunzel notes the sense "Of fluttering victory," and a few lines later the Prince, now Prince Sebald, plucks the crimson banner of the Witch and tosses it down to the green grass below. In terms of the obvious color symbolism in the poem, the red (evil, perverted, static) banner lies "below, / Above it in the wind let grasses laugh." The green (youthful, growing) grass conquers the red much as the two lovers emerge from their dream tower into a real world in scene four.

The shift from scene three to scene four is again accomplished by an associative leap that changes the mood and results in a change in perception. As the lovers leave the tower victorious, they symbolically leave the dream world in which the rite has taken place. It is fitting, therefore, that they emerge into a real outdoor world and possess real, worldly names.

[end of scene three]

>   But it is strange your name
> Is not the same the minstrel sung of yore;
>   You called it Rapunzel, 'tis not the name.
>   See love, the stems shine through the open door.

[scene four]
  (*Morning in the woods*)

RAPUNZEL:

> O Love! me and my unknown name you have well
>   won;
>   The witch's name was Rapunzel; eh! not so
>   sweet?
> No!—but is this real grass, love, that I tread upon?
> What call they these blue flowers that lean across
>   my feet?
>
> (ll. 275-282)

Not very surprisingly, her name is Guendolen, the same as the lass in the song that had inspired the Prince originally. The change of identity not only makes the song fit into the tale as the supernatural help requisite to the successful rite of passage, it confirms the maiden's reality in this real world. Even the alliteration of "golden Guendolen" as opposed to red Rapunzel, assists the change of mood that must occur in scenes four and five. The fact that the Witch's name was Rapunzel and that Guendolen was called only by her name makes the equation with parental power complete.[10] And the name suggests the fleshly sins symbolized in the fairy tale by the rampion root, while the change indicates the maiden's purification from these sins. This connection also accounts for the ambiguity concerning the golden hair: that it seems yet to contain the potential for both good and evil, indicated in scene five when Guendolen sings:

> I was unhappy once in dreams,
> And even now a harsh voice seems
>   To hang about my hair.

(ll. 336-338)

The golden hair is both talisman of love and possibility of evil, for the flesh is both the salvation and the ever-present danger of damnation if misused. The Witch is incredulous, screaming (in capitals) the final stanza of the poem.

> WOE! THAT ANY MAN COULD DARE
> TO CLIMB UP THE YELLOW STAIR,
> GLORIOUS GUENDOLEN'S GOLDEN HAIR.

(ll. 339-341)

This last stanza, occupying as it does the final word in the poem, contains the essence of the quest for differentiated consciousness. It seems incredible that any man would dare to leave the safety of his parents' power for the quest, so dangerous and so uncertain. But this danger and ultimate uncertainty makes the victory all the more conclusive once the rite of passage is completed.

So, what we have here is the naive Victorian enactment of a primitive rite of passage from undifferentiated consciousness to adulthood, complete with new names and love. The fact that Sebald and Guendolen become king and queen reinforces the victory and gives them the parental status and power once possessed by their progenitors. Morris utilizes the fairy tale as a vehicle to recount the usual mythic form of the quest, and in so doing, gives a drama of moods and symbols which creates an opposite of dream-like stasis and frustration in the first half of the poem, and a release from bondage into the freedom of reality in the last half. Constructed in this dramatic way, a rite of passage or archetype of regeneration is transformed into an insightful psychological drama describing a youth's quest for manhood. The absence of action and the tale of the brother-battle underline and enforce the fact that his victory must be a moral one.

Such archetypal situations are common to poetry, of course, but in this case it seems the craftsman Morris has given us an exquisite example of the concentration and power possible in the retelling of even the oldest tales. In his own mind, Morris was probably placing the emphasis on the burgeoning love relationship, skirting around the battles as of secondary importance. Certainly the dramatic character of the poem is arrived at partially by its separation into tableaux which seem to arise like dreams from the ultimately happy state of the lovers. In the first half of the poem it is as if the lovers were remembering, or dreaming of the past, perhaps omitting the pain and struggle as our memories wipe out physical pain. **"Rapunzel"** owes its success to a combination in its form of the successful rite of passage and a dramatic framework using one of Morris' favorite moods, the dream reverie.

Notes

1. Alfred Noyes, *William Morris* (London, 1908), p. 29; and B. Ifor Evans, *William Morris and his Poetry* (London, 1925), p. 48 respectively. More recently than this, we seem to have ignored the poem altogether.

2. The classic work on this subject is Arnold Van Gennep, *The Rites of Passage,* trans. Mokika B. Vizedom and Gabrielle L. Caffer (Chicago, 1960), originally published in 1908.

3. Erich Fromm, *The Forgotten Language* (New York, 1957), p. 240, gives a simple example of this sort of symbolism in the story of "Little Red Cap."

4. This tale can be found in *Danish Fairy Tales,* trans. J. Grant Cramer (Boston, 1912), p. 89. It is of course cognate with many other legends of like import.

5. Erich Neumann, *The Origins and History of Consciousness,* trans. R. F. C. Hull (New York, 1954), p. 311.

6. John Rhys, *Studies in Arthurian Legend* (Oxford, 1891), pp. 119-120, 285. Rhys traces Balyn to the Celtic divinity of the sun, called Apollo Belenus or Belinus in Latin. His brother-enemy was said to have a black face, and kept mostly concealed for purposes of destruction and death. Rhys makes the equation common to his time of Balyn with the sun and his opponent with darkness, so that the story of the struggle is a variant of the sun myth. At times the myth of the brothers doing battle does indeed fit this sort of light-dark structure. But the "sun-myth" theory does not plumb the depths of the myth's symbolic import.

7. De La Motte Fouque, *Undine and Other Tales,* trans. F. E. Burnett (New York, n. d. [circa 1905]), p. 57. Morris later considered a poem on Balin and Balan after completing *The Earthly Paradise.*

8. *Art and Artist,* trans. Francis Atkinson (New York, 1932), p. xxiii.

9. The image of the doppelganger was doubtless a topic of conversation among the Pre-Raphaelites since Rossetti painted a picture depicting a young couple meeting themselves in a garden as a prelude to their death. The painting itself was not completed until 1860, but designs were made for such a picture as early as 1851, and H. C. Marilliar (*Dante Gabriel Rossetti* [London, 1904], pp. 27-28) notes that the subject was one that fascinated Rossetti from boyhood.

10. As an interesting sidelight on this equation of witch with mother, I have had personal experience with a child of eight who related to me a dream, about which she said excitedly, "And then my mother turned into a witch and chased me over the bridge." The dream was incomprehensible to the child who professed to love her mother although she resented her heavy handed educational regimen. Jung notes this phenomenon also in *Contributions to Analytical Psychology,* trans. H. G. and Cary F. Baynes (New York, 1928), pp. 122-124.

Frederick Kirchhoff (essay date winter 1977)

SOURCE: Kirchhoff, Frederick. "*Love is Enough*: A Crisis in William Morris's Poetic Development." *Victorian Poetry* 15, no. 4 (winter 1977): 297-306.

[*In the following essay, Kirchhoff views* Love is Not Enough *to be a transitional work in Morris's poetic development.*]

The notion of William Morris' career as a gradual flowering into inevitable Marxism and the very different notion of Morris as a "happy craftsman" have equally obscured the actual shape of his literary development.[1] Granted, fully understanding Morris entails fully understanding his work in all three fields. But at this—still relatively innocent—stage in the criticism of his poetry, what is needed is not another brave attempt to synthesize his achievement as a whole, but a painstaking examination of his poetry *as* poetry and of his poetic development as a strictly literary phenomenon. It is not just oversimplification but plain misunderstanding to argue that art led Morris to socialism. His art and his socialism were alternative solutions to the same problem of bridging the gap between the actual world and that vision of an intense yet familiar happiness so characteristic of his work. Morris' particular version of this age-old problem has encouraged critics to draw parallels between him and Keats.[2] And, whatever the limitations of the comparison, it does sug-

gest that, like Keats's, Morris' literary development should be seen as a process of experiment and self-correction. His *Earthly Paradise* (1868-70) is a series of variations on the theme of Keats's "Ode on a Grecian Urn"; his political activism, a logical consequence of the questions Keats asked himself in *The Fall of Hyperion.* In the first, Morris' attempt to use art as a means of arresting the flux of time faces him—ultimately—with a melancholy awareness of the limitations of art. In the second, his recognition of the claims of society does not obliterate the poet's sense of a private vision. While it is true that Morris neither renounced art nor turned his back on the Party, it is also true that he came in time to face the inadequacy of both the aesthetic and the political solutions to the problem of being human. Thus, the high tragedy of *Sigurd the Volsung* (1877) reevaluates the aesthetic of his 1860's poetry, and the psychological realism of the last romances corrects the psychological naiveté of *News from Nowhere* (1890).

This movement of experiment and self-adjustment suggests that the pattern of Morris' literary career is a dialectic, in which the prose romances stand as a final synthesis of his commitments to art and to the cause of "fellowship," with his acceptance of the potentially tragic limitations of both. If this paradigm is valid, then the early 1870's and the early 1890's, when (respectively) the aesthetic and the political solutions confront their antitheses, are the two crucial periods in Morris' development. This essay is concerned with the earlier and more purely literary of these two periods—specifically, with the most clearly "transitional" of Morris' longer poems.

Love is Enough, which Morris began shortly after his return from Iceland in the fall of 1871, marks a crisis in his development as a poet. Its narrative subject—Pharamond's all-for-love desertion of his kingdom and search for the dream-maiden Azalais—could be straight out of *The Earthly Paradise.* But Morris' complex, at times self-contradictory, treatment of this subject expresses a new phase in his thinking. The protagonists of the twenty-four tales within the Wanderers' frame-story either succeed or fail in their quests for happiness; Pharamond both succeeds *and* fails. Significantly, the polarities of the earlier poem are reversed: the Wanderers' quest leads them from plague-stricken Norway to a succession of false paradises in the warm South; Pharamond's takes him from an unspecified middle latitude to a northern country geologically akin to Iceland. While the later poem expresses itself in a mood and literary style far removed from the boisterous realism of the *Icelandic Journals* (1871, 1873), it is nevertheless very much a response to Morris' formative confrontation with the North. What Iceland taught Morris was an essentially tragic view of human experience. As rendered in his *Journals,* the Icelandic landscape becomes the symbolic expression of both a material order ultimately indifferent to human fate, the recognition of which frees man once and for all from the protean vestiges of natural religion, and the Icelanders themselves, the living representatives of a greatness that does not lie in evading the potential tragedy of life but in looking at it squarely and accepting the consequences. Thus, without necessarily denigrating the quest for an Earthly Paradise, Iceland offered Morris the image of a higher nobility than the Wanderers' refined disillusionment.

Love is Enough embodies the poet's struggle to revise an earlier aesthetic—not by rejecting the materials of his earlier poetry, but by attempting to recast them to new significance. The poem attempts to fuse a quest for the ideal with an affirmation of the earthly and to combine a dramatic reliance on poetic justice (through which happy endings are not only possible but likely) with a ruthless philosophical materialism. As in the case of the Romantic quest-narratives with which it has most in common, *Alastor* and *Endymion,* the result is a poem uniquely difficult to evaluate. E. P. Thompson, who sees *Love is Enough* as a regression in Morris' development as a socialist, dismisses it as "the lowest ebb of Morris's creative life."[3] May Morris, on the other hand, seems to have liked it best of her father's poetry. "No glimpse of the inner life of Morris," she argues, "was ever vouchsafed even to his closest friends— *secretum meum mihi.* It was a subject on which he never spoke except in *Love is Enough.*"[4] Seizing on her hints, later critics have tended to see the poem as an expression of Morris' disillusionment with his marriage.[5] But May's interpretation is not the daughter's oblique acknowledgment of her father's unhappy love-life. Instead, she is referring to what she considers his "belief in the life of the spirit" and "the mysteries that lie beyond the life of man" (I, 442). As this paper will argue, her reading is far from satisfactory.

Thompson, even in damning the poem, takes us closer to the grounds for its significance:

> "Love" is not presented in the poem as a human relationship, but as a languorous yearning, a saturation of the senses, a weakening of the will, in short, as the attraction of the unconscious. Indeed, towards the end of the narrative the longing for death and the yearning for "Love" become almost indistinguishable. . . . The superficial subject may be "Love," but the underlying theme is the desire for unconsciousness and death.
>
> (p. 153)

Thompson fails to recognize that this confrontation with "the desire for unconsciousness and death" is not an evasion of the lessons of Iceland, but a necessary stage in Morris' response to the North. Pharamond's melancholia corresponds to the sickness of heart Morris records again and again in the *Icelandic Journals*—his "nausea" in facing up to the implications of the barren, "awful" landscape: "a piece of turf under your feet, and

the sky overhead, that's all; whatever solace your life is to have here must come out of yourself or these old stories, not over hopeful themselves."[6] *Love is Enough* brings the unspecified death wish of *The Earthly Paradise* into the open. Thus Morris is able at once to reevaluate the earlier poem and to advance to a higher level of self-knowledge. Although it does not follow that *Love is Enough* is a more successful poem than the best narratives of *The Earthly Paradise* or even *The Life and Death of Jason* (1867), neither is it in any pejorative sense a "regression." Pharamond is the hero of a romance who is almost but not quite the hero of a tragedy. His indecision reflects Morris' own inability to sort out just what he must discard from the past from what he wishes to continue holding onto with all his might. The narrative of his quest is Morris' effort at weighing the alternatives.

Moreover, even to speak, as Thompson does, of "Love" in the singular ignores the multiple meanings of the term the poem offers us. To begin with, Love is both a state of Pharamond's consciousness and an independent character in the poem. The central event in *Love is Enough* is a masque celebrating the nuptials of an unnamed Emperor and Empress; they, the Mayor, who acts as a master of ceremonies, and the peasant couple Giles and Joan, who have come to see the whole affair, offer three concentric frames of commentary—noble, bourgeois, and rustic—on the story "Of Pharamond the Freed." The masque itself contains three elements: (1) a sequence of lyric poems designated "The Music"; (2) six scenes narrating in sequence Pharamond's discontent with his kingship, his decision to search for the maiden who has been revealed to him in a group of related dreams or dream-visions, the final stages in his quest, his meeting with Azalais, and his presumably temporary return to his former kingdom; and (3) the figure of "Love," who acts both as an external interpreter of the action and as a controlling force within the action.

The allegorical Love appears seven times. He speaks the prologue to each scene of the masque and the epilogue to the completed drama. Thus he mediates between the two elements of the poem—the masque and its audience—and, by extension, between the reader and the masque. (Morris is making the point that it is Love which connects the elements of the poem and is therefore responsible for its unity as a work of art and—by extension—that it is the common experience of Love which constitutes the reader's relationship to the poem as a whole.) But Love is also an actor in the masque: immediately prior to the appearance of Azalais, Love, who has previously stood before the curtain for his speeches, literally steps into the action and holds a dialogue with Pharamond. This confrontation, not Pharamond's union with Azalais, is the turning point in his quest. The physical setting is that of his former dreams. Now Love awakens him to the "real" scene.

Significantly, Pharamond's confrontation with the power behind his own sexuality takes place in a landscape influenced by Morris' first Icelandic expedition. The poem seems to be arguing that this awakening is possible because Pharamond's quest for love has become that very quest for oblivion that Thompson dismisses as a "desire for unconsciousness and death." Certainly Pharamond himself does not regard this apparent dead end as a defeat—"Cruel wert thou, O Love, yet have thou and I conquered" (IX, 49). In regarding the defeat of the Imagination as a spiritual victory, Pharamond reveals his kinship with the protagonist of *Alastor.* He has given up power and human ties to follow a vision that has finally led him into an empty and alien landscape. Nevertheless, like Shelley's Poet, he refuses to renounce his vision. What was for the Wanderers of **The Earthly Paradise** a willful persistence in unfounded hope is sharpened into an issue of moral self-determination.

But unlike the Poet of *Alastor,* Pharamond is rewarded for his persistence with the fulfillment of his vision. Keats achieved a similar victory for Endymion by melting the ideal Cynthia and the earthly Indian Maid into one and the same figure. Morris' strategy, on the other hand, hinges on Pharamond's recognition of the essential dualism of his own desire: it is not the imagination alone nor the sexual drive alone but "thou and I" together who have "conquered." The teasing problem in *Alastor* is the ambiguous identity of Eros. Is it an expression of the protagonist's Imaginative passion for "all of wonderful, or wise, or beautiful, which the poet, the philosopher, or the lover could depicture"? Or is it only one more manifestation of Nature, working in this instance through the Poet's own repressed sexuality? Morris eliminates this ambiguity by restating it as an essential and unavoidable dualism. As a consequence, Pharamond is not trapped into asking the unanswerable questions—and hence into the dubious self-consciousness—of Shelley's quester Poet. He need not puzzle over the meaning of Love; he need simply accept it as inevitable. Insofar as his quest for Azalais is in part a function of the "natural" erotic, his drive towards "freed" life is also and equally a drive towards participation in the cycle of reproduction and death. Pharamond's response to this fact may be profound melancholy, but at least it is intellectually consistent. And it is precisely his acceptance of the ambivalence of his own desire that distinguishes him from the heroes of **The Earthly Paradise.**

This—or something close to it—seems to have been Morris' intention in the poem. The strategy is bold, but it is not entirely successful, both because it tends to reduce the stature of the lover-hero by emphasizing his passivity and responsiveness, and because the presence of the allegorical figure "Love" raises more difficulties than it solves. Insofar as Morris' allegory is a mode of psychological analysis, it enables him to clarify the terms of Pharamond's self-confrontation. But Love is bigger than Pharamond's individual sexuality. Moreover, Love's double role as participant in and commentator on the action suggests that Pharamond is the victim of duplicity. The Love who determines his quest and ultimately intervenes to unite him with Azalais is also a figure detached from his fate, using the story of Pharamond as an exemplum of his own power. And to the extent that Pharamond is such an example, the heroism of his individual quest is diminished.

But these are not the only problems. What, after all, is the connection between Pharamond's confrontation with Love and his subsequent meeting with Azalais? Pharamond recognizes that his quest for ideal love is based on biological necessity, and as a consequence "Biological Necessity" (in capital letters) rewards him with the girl of his dreams. "Love," insofar as he effects the dénouement of Pharamond's quest, implies a providential order in the universe in some sense responsible for the affairs of mankind. Since this notion is at odds with Morris' philosophical materialism, Morris must find a means of using the allegorical figure while at the same time disavowing its implications.

Accordingly, Love offers himself in many guises. He appears—sequentially—"crowned as a king," "clad as an image-maker," "clad as a maker of Pictured Cloths," "with a cup of bitter drink and his hands bloody," "clad as a pilgrim," and finally "holding a crown and palm-branch." These transformations parallel the stages in Pharamond's quest, but whether they reflect any sympathy between Love and his victim, Morris is careful to keep uncertain. Thus, when the bloody-handed Love protests "how the tears well up / From my grieved heart my blinded eyes to grieve" (IX, 48), the gesture may be merely emblematic. Moreover, when Love appears "holding a crown and palm-branch" to speak the epilogue to Pharamond's story, he calls into question even the significance of these triumphal symbols themselves:

> —Reward of what?—Life springing fresh again.—
> Life of delight?—I say it not—Of pain?
> It may be—Pain eternal?—Who may tell?
> Yet pain of Heaven, beloved, and not of Hell.
> —What sign, what sign, ye cry, that so it is?
> The sign of Earth, its sorrow and its bliss,
> Waxing and waning, steadfastness and change;
> Too full of life that I should think it strange
> Though death hang over it; too sure to die
> But I must deem its resurrection nigh.

> (IX, 77)

It is the cyclic nature of earth itself which guarantees the coming round of delight after pain—and, as surely, of pain after delight. But it is far from clear just how this interpretation harmonizes with Love's argument that it is Pharamond's total obedience that brings about his union with Azalais. Instead of affirming his particular justice to the individual Pharamond, Love merely offers the reader a barrage of general promises. He speaks of "the many mansions of my house" where his followers may expect "A wedding-garment, and a glorious seat / Within my household." And he looks forward to their fighting beneath his banner "when the hosts are met / On Armageddon's plain" (IX, 78-79). Morris is not Christianizing his poem. He is merely following a medieval precedent in secularizing the imagery of the New Testament. But even if Morris does not mean for us to take them seriously, Love's pseudo-apocalyptics are an evasion of his responsibility for the present state of things.

Nor is this the only evasion by Morris' allegorical figure. "Clad as a maker of Pictured Cloths," Love carefully distinguishes his "true" dreams from mere illusions:

—Those tales of empty striving, and lost days
Folk tell of sometimes—never lit my fire
Such ruin as this; but Pride and Vain-desire,
My counterfeits and foes, have done the deed.

(IX, 38)

Similarly, what the poet takes for Love—and wrestles with, Jacob-fashion—turns out to be "a Shadow of the Night" (IX, 47). These distinctions may be meant to clarify the nature of "real" Love, but they succeed only in reminding the reader of just how easy it is to be misled. Thus, while the poem is structured as what appears to be a cause-and-effect sequence of vision, trial, and reward, Morris offers no surer explanation for Pharamond's union with Azalais than the proposition that liberated ("freed") Eros must needs participate in the earthly cycles of pleasure and pain. (Hence, May Morris' view that *Love is Enough* affirms her father's "belief in the life of the spirit" ignores the genuinely problematic nature of the poem.)

By evading full responsibility for his treatment of Pharamond, Love is able to act like a representative of providence while questioning the notion of an order in Nature particularly favorable to individual heroes. Aside from its intellectual shortcomings, this strategy has the further disadvantage—as previously suggested—of reducing the stature of the hero. Morris attempts to correct this reduction by his curious treatment of the final scene of the masque, in which Pharamond returns to his kingdom. Philip Henderson draws a parallel with Morris' private life. Pharamond, he tells us, finds his dream mistress "only to lose her again at once. He has become, in effect, another idle singer of an empty day, returning to his kingdom at last to find his throne usurped and his people disaffected—much as Morris had returned from Iceland to find Rossetti in his place."[7] True, the two

returns are parallel—and the analogy suggests that Pharamond, like Morris, will return to the North. But Henderson's verb "lose" is misleading. Pharamond leaves Azalais intentionally—not just to get back his kingdom, but for motives more complex. "Something hard to understand," Love tells us, "Dulls the crowned work to which I set my hand" (IX, 64).

Pharamond justifies his return as a "gift" to his foster-father Master Oliver, the companion of his quest for Azalais. But Love recognizes the hunger of Pharamond's Imagination at work: "our one desire / Fulfilled at last, what next shall feed the fire?" (IX, 64). He goes on to summarize a collection of possible motives:

Well, Pharamond fulfilled of love must turn
Unto the folk that still he deemed would yearn
To see his face, and hear his voice once more;
And he was mindful of the days passed o'er,
And fain had linked them to these days of love;
And he perchance was fain the world to move
While love looked on; and he perchance was fain
Some pleasure of the strife of old to gain.

(IX, 65)

The notion of a link or connection is important. Pharamond is attempting not to go back to the past, but to forge a bond between the past and present—between public and private desire, the material world of kingship and the imaginative world of Love. This connection is an element in the archetypal quest. The hero returns to his society in order to integrate with it whatever power he has gained in the world outside his society.[8] Moreover, the gesture is not merely a sign of his duty to his society. It is also an integration of the hero's own past—conceived both as his own earlier experience and as his participation in the collective spirit of his society—with his achieved present. Further, Pharamond's return, interpreted as an active gesture towards integration, enables Morris to present his hero as the master of his own fate. For once, Love is not the guiding force behind his behavior.

Significantly, however, this gesture of independence is a practical—if not a spiritual—failure. Pharamond is able to assert his individuality only by deserting the woman he loves. Moreover, instead of the desired integration, he returns to discover that he is no longer capable of participating in the political and military life of his kingdom. A reversal has taken place. The dream world of Azalais and her northern valley has become the norm for reality, against which the usurper Theobald's retinue is at best a "pageant," at worst "shadows" (IX, 73). King Theobald and Honorius, the Councillor who is the power behind his throne, are offered as alternatives to Pharamond's newfound life of "freed" Eros. Both he rejects: Theobald, because the most powerful king is limited by the mundane nature of his power—"wert thou the crown of all rulers, / No field shouldst thou ripen, free no frost-bound river" (IX, 73); Honorius, the more efficient ruler, for the dehumanization implicit in all political dealings—

> —Thou lovest not mercy, yet shalt thou be merciful;
> Thou joy'st not in justice, yet shall thy doom be;
> No deep hell thou dreadest, nor dream'st of high heaven;
> No gleam of love leads thee; no gift men may give thee;
> For no kiss, for no comfort the lone way thou wearest,
> A blind will without life, lest thou faint ere the end come.
>
> (IX, 74)

Pharamond's first decision to leave his kingdom in search of his dream maiden may be judged wanton egoism or a weak-spirited capitulation to his own hitherto repressed sexuality. His second decision to leave is a reasoned moral choice. He has achieved the end of his quest and has been transformed by it past the recognition of his former self. The masque ends with Pharamond contemplating his return to Azalais.

To call Pharamond "another idle singer of an empty day" is simply to pay careless attention to the action of the poem. Nevertheless, the final scene of the narrative cannot be described as a triumphant vindication of Eros. Morris deliberately refrains from reuniting the lovers. "Love were enough," murmurs Pharamond, "if thy lips were not lacking." The last glimpse of the hero is of a man cut off from both political power and erotic consummation. Whether or not he returns to Azalais, Pharamond's failure to integrate the two elements of his personality is potentially tragic. The "love" that is "enough" is seen in the closing lines of the masque as a form of compensation for a higher but impossible synthesis. Unlike the Wanderers, Pharamond achieves the goal of his quest. But his very success eliminates the need for a mediating aesthetic—like the story-telling of *The Earthly Paradise.* What had seemed the Wanderers' substitute for ultimate achievement turns out to be the very means of saving them from the alienation of Pharamond.

This alienation is not merely the product of Pharamond's final indecisiveness. It is also a function of the elaborate distancing inherent in the structure of the poem. Not only are we the readers placed at several removes from the events of the masque; the onlookers themselves are never allowed to forget that Pharamond and Azalais are characters in a play "Wrought long ago for some dead poet's glory" (IX, 12). Instead of empathizing with the dramatis personae, both the Emperor and Empress and Giles and Joan experience impulses to identify with the actors who play the parts of Pharamond and Azalais. Moreover, both the Emperor and Empress and Giles and Joan appear capable of an adjustment to life denied to Pharamond. The imperial

couple are, after all, both rulers *and* lovers. The peasants' pastoral felicity is undisturbed by the memory of past sacrifices.

On the other hand, both alternative states have limitations. The very conventionality of the peasants, who speak in the language and metrics of Marlowe's "Passionate Shepherd,"[9] suggests that their low-key happiness has all the liabilities implicit in its literary genre. And the royal stereotype of the Emperor and Empress, while allowing them a voice of passionate intensity, is equally limiting. Thus, while they may reward the actor and actress with rich gifts, they cannot step out of the formal boundaries of the ruler-subject relationship. (Giles and Joan, on the other hand, can invite the actors home for a few days of pastoral merry-making.) Jessie Kocmanová points out that "the surroundings of the fulfilled love of Pharamond and Azalais are not those of the great king, but transfer us to the simple world of Giles and Joan, the peasants."[10] This is true. But, significantly, Morris' revisions of the poem eliminated much of the material emphasizing the "peasant" element of Pharamond's betrothal. And, more to the point, the poem does not end with his return to Azalais, but with the hero unable to integrate with and therefore alienated from both worlds.

Pharamond, because he attempts to be at once Emperor and peasant—to take on the responsibilities of a just king without sacrificing his "freed" Eros—is a larger figure than any of the onlookers of the drama. The Wanderers, whose story-telling softens the acuteness of a similar dilemma, are not tragic figures. Pharamond, who faces it, very nearly is. And for this reason *Love is Enough* anticipates Morris' strongest expression of tragic fate, in *Sigurd the Volsung.* But neither Pharamond's alienation nor Sigurd's doom is a final statement of the poet's vision. It is precisely because *Love is Enough* makes explicit and therefore untenable the death wish of his earlier poetry that it points the way to the profounder writing of his final decades. From Pharamond it is an easy transition to the narrator of *News from Nowhere,* also in search of erotic fulfillment in a pastoral world integrated with the political life that makes it possible. The heroes of the last prose romances undertake versions of the same quest,[11] and Pharamond's alienation—his "desire for unconsciousness and death"—is a stage in the development of these later figures. It is a stage which must be rejected, but it is a stage without which the final integration of the hero with his society and the integration of the hero's social world with the natural world defining both its province and boundaries are not possible.

The stage is crucial. No wonder Morris, who prided himself on the effortlessness of his verse-making, had trouble completing *Love is Enough.* And May Morris' account of "the curious detached sort of way" he later spoke of the poem comes as no surprise: "Talking of early English poetry with a friend one day, he said: 'You know, I wrote an alliterative poem myself once on a time'—almost as though it had been written by someone else, written on another planet" (IX, xxxi). "A fantastic little book," Morris himself called it in a letter to Andreas Scheu.[12] This is not the distance of disavowal. May Morris may have been wrong in her interpretation, but not in her sense that **Love is Enough** takes us closest to the pain and heroic self-awareness of her father's most crucial years.

Notes

1. I wish to thank the National Endowment for the Humanities for making possible the Summer Seminar in connection with which this essay was completed, and U. C. Knoepflmacher, director of the Seminar, for his criticism and encouragement.

2. For example: Maud Bodkin, *Archetypal Patterns in Poetry* (Oxford Univ. Press, 1934), p. 120; George Ford, *Keats and the Victorians* (1944; rpt. London, 1962), p. 162; Elizabeth Strode, "The Crisis of *The Earthly Paradise*: Morris and Keats," *VP* [*Victorian Poetry*], 13, Nos. 3 & 4 (1975), 71-81.

3. *William Morris: Romantic to Revolutionary* (1955; rev. & rpt. New York, 1977), p. 152.

4. *William Morris: Artist, Writer, Socialist* (Oxford, 1936), I, 441.

5. This, for example, is Thompson's view.

6. *The Collected Works of William Morris,* ed. May Morris (1910-15; rpt. New York, 1966), VIII, 108; hereafter cited in the text.

7. *William Morris: His Life, Work and Friends* (New York, 1967), p. 128.

8. This pattern is clearly expressed in romances like Morris' *Roots of the Mountains* and *The Well at the World's End;* it is implicit in the didactics of his utopian dream vision in *News from Nowhere.*

9. Thompson calls them "sentimentalized," but they are better described as deliberately conventional.

10. *The Poetic Maturing of William Morris* (New York, 1970), p. 129.

11. Indeed, this quest is their central concern, and the pattern of two women representing successive stages of the hero's erotic development suggests just why Pharamond may find it difficult to go back to Azalais.

12. *The Letters of William Morris to his Family and Friends,* ed. Philip Henderson (New York, 1950), p. 186.

Margaret A. Lourie (essay date fall 1977)

SOURCE: Lourie, Margaret A. "The Embodiment of Dreams: William Morris' 'Blue Closet' Group." *Victorian Poetry* 15, no. 3 (fall 1977): 193-206.

[*In the following essay, Lourie examines the seven Morris poems that make up the "The Blue Closet" group, maintaining that by studying these poems "we will perhaps have learned something essential about the Pre-Raphaelite contribution to English poetry."*]

Pre-Raphaelite poetry, that influential resurgence of Romanticism in mid-nineteenth-century England, has been accurately perceived from the beginning to be such stuff as dreams are made on. When in 1858 William Morris published the first Pre-Raphaelite volume under the title **The Defence of Guenevere, and Other Poems,** it was greeted by the reviewer for the *Athenaeum* with a damaging comparison to Tennyson: "That strange dream ['The Lady of Shalott'], which, however beautiful, quaint, and touching it be, quivers on the furthest verge of Dream-land to which sane Fancy can penetrate, has been 'the point of departure' for Mr. Morris" (April 3, 1858, p. 427). This insistence upon Pre-Raphaelite dreaminess has been frequently reiterated in the twentieth century. William Gaunt retitled his popular account of this important movement *The Pre-Raphaelite Dream* (London, 1943). In 1950 John Heath-Stubbs confidently characterized the Pre-Raphaelite literary achievement as dream-poetry.[1] And a few years later W. W. Robson ascribed to the Pre-Raphaelites "the static, dreamy atmosphere, which has not the transitory vividness of real dreams, but rather the insubstantiality of a waking dream or reverie."[2] Perhaps the latest entrant into this particular field of Pre-Raphaelite commentary is David Larkin's collection of Pre-Raphaelite paintings with the predictable title *The English Dreamers* (New York, 1975).

If critics of the Pre-Raphaelites seem to have concentrated much of their attention on the quality of reverie, at least they derive their authority from the Pre-Raphaelites themselves. Rossetti, for instance, described Burne-Jones as "one of the nicest young fellows in—*Dreamland.* For there most of the writers in that miraculous piece of literature [*The Oxford and Cambridge Magazine,* published by Morris and his undergraduate friends during 1856] seem to be."[3] With similar insight, Morris confessed, "My work is the embodiment of dreams in one form or another."[4]

The problem for modern critics, then, is not to dissociate dreams from the Pre-Raphaelites, who rather fancied themselves residents of dreamland anyway, but to determine what it has typically meant for critics to call these poets dreamers. Victorian critics like the reviewer of Morris' **Guenevere** volume for the *Athenaeum* simply espoused an entirely different aesthetic from the one on which Pre-Raphaelite poetry was predicated. For them, the proper function of poetry was to teach its readers how to live humanely in an increasingly ugly and impersonal world, or, like Tennyson's *In Memoriam,* to illuminate the darkness which was gathering around philosophical and religious issues. Poetry therefore needed to be more or less forthright, realistic, logical, active. What it emphatically did not need, as Arnold observed when he withdrew *Empedocles on Etna* from the 1853 collection of his poems, was either introspection or inaction. Not surprisingly, critics of Arnold's persuasion often disparaged poets of the dream. For these critics, dreams meant mist, distance, stasis, fuzzy thinking, and an irresponsible refusal to confront daily life. It is small wonder that the Pre-Raphaelites were not enthusiastically received by the Victorian literary establishment.

It is, however, a matter for somewhat greater wonder that post-Freudian critics have largely failed to abandon the Victorian attitude toward dreams when they discuss the Pre-Raphaelites. No longer hampered by sanctions against introspection or inaction in literature, twentieth-century critics have become increasingly sensitive to the delicate operations of the human mind as they are mirrored in literature. But this sensitivity has scarcely begun to be extended to the Pre-Raphaelites; and we have yet to apply our knowledge of dreams as windows on the pre-rational life of the unconscious to a serious reading of Pre-Raphaelite poetry.

Curiously, it was a Victorian critic, Walter Pater, who pointed the way for such a reading in his essay "Aesthetic Poetry." Pater saw that in Morris' *Guenevere* poems, as in Victor Hugo's *Notre Dame de Paris,* "the strangest creations of sleep seem here, by some appalling licence, to cross the limit of the dawn." Furthermore, in the Morris poems, "a passion of which the outlets are sealed, begets a tension of nerve, in which the sensible world comes to one with a reinforced brilliancy and relief." And that sensible world does not exist objectively but is "bent as by miracle or magic to the service of human passion."[5] In short, Pater understood that these are poems of the mind turned in upon itself. He also understood that Morris' poem **"The Blue Closet"** epitomizes these excursions into dreamland. Following Pater's lead, we would do well to reexamine **"The Blue Closet"** and, I would add, the six other *Guenevere* poems which most resemble it: **"The Sailing of the Sword," "Spell-bound," "The Wind," "The Tune of Seven Towers," "Golden Wings,"** and **"Near Avalon."** If we can discover how the poems in the **"Blue Closet"** group operate, we will perhaps have learned something essential about the Pre-Raphaelite contribution to English poetry.

Insofar as **"The Blue Closet"** yields to plot summary, it seems to be a poem about Lady Alice, Lady Louise,

and their two attendants, who have all been imprisoned in an isolated and untended tower. Once every year on Christmas eve they are permitted to vent their captive spirits by entering a Blue Closet and singing of the long-ago visit of Louise's knight, Arthur, who "sprinkled the dusty snow over [her] head" (l. 40)[6] in token of his return. This year, in answer to their choral prayer for his second coming, a red lily shoots through the floor as a sign that Arthur at last dwells in *"the land of the dead"* (l. 62) and can now come back for the ladies. In the last section, Arthur comes among them, and together everyone leaves the Blue Closet, crossing a bridge into "the happy golden land" (l. 72). Throughout the poem a refrain reiterates that a *"great bell overhead / Booms in the wind a knell for the dead,"* suggesting that all these characters bear only the most tenuous connection to life. And by the end of the poem they are certainly both dead and happy.

The eerie emotional effect of such a plot line is immediately obvious. But **"The Blue Closet"** does not so readily present itself for intellectual analysis. As the reviewer for the *Saturday Review* (November 20, 1858, p. 507) remarked of the entire volume, "You cannot quite make out what it means, or whether it means anything taken altogether." Yet, as we shall see, it is largely the refusal of this poem to mean anything or to lend itself to rational interpretation that provides its special power; for in **"The Blue Closet"** Morris transcends the normal processes of waking thought and cuts off the usual orientation of the mind toward the phenomenal world. As a result, he can journey down into the pre-logical and primarily image-making reaches of the psyche. The many critics who accuse Morris of escapism are quite right; he does wish to escape from the world of external reality. But what they too often fail to see is that he escapes *to* a more universal internal reality. Let us understand how he engineers this escape.

Morris' very choice of plot materials for **"The Blue Closet"** undermines the rational faculty in at least two ways. First, he bases his story line on the pre-rational superstitions encoded in the folklore which he gleaned from E. H. Wehnert's 1853 translation of Grimm's *Marchen* and Benjamin Thorpe's 1851 collection of *Northern Mythology.* These are the racial hopes and fears which precede reasoning but which have nevertheless retained their primordial appeal through centuries of Western civilization. Second, Morris synthesizes these fears and superstitions into an entirely new narrative and thereby subverts the desire of the intellect to draw parallels with an original. A glance at some folklore analogues will illustrate both these points at once. Grimm has several tales of women locked up in towers—either young women, like Rapunzel, locked away from the world, or older women imprisoned for displeasing their husbands. But none of these tales matches **"The Blue Closet"** in any other particular. For

Cecil Lang, the tone and color scheme of this poem recall Perrault's "Barbe Bleue," but even fewer details from that story match this one.[7] Or again, if lines like "Between the wash of the tumbling seas" (l. 2) and "the sea-salt oozes through / The chinks of the tiles of the Closet Blue" (ll. 32-33) imply an underwater setting for this poem, then several superstitions in Thorpe's *Northern Mythology* come to mind. Thorpe reveals that the depths of the water were equated in Germanic tradition with the nether world (I, 288), and Morris seems to make the same association between an underwater existence and a life outside the world. In one of Thorpe's stories, "The Bell-Pond," "it is related that every year at Christmas, from the hour of twelve till one, a bell is heard tolling from [the depth of the pond]" (III, 118). Specters in Thorpe also hold their masses between twelve and one. In other places in Thorpe, water sprites lure young girls away to their underwater abodes (I, 248) just as Arthur has been mysteriously lured by the woman who has hidden his tears "deep under the seas"; white lilies spring from the graves of the unjustly executed (I, 290n) just as a red one here betokens the return of the dead Arthur; and the ghosts of the drowned, often graphically described (III, 10), appear to loved ones just as the ghastly Arthur, although not necessarily drowned, appears to Louise.

Shifting from fairytale to Biblical analogues yields the same emotional resonance but no more intellectual clarity. Arthur may recall Christ, a possibility reinforced by Tennyson's association of King Arthur with Christ in his "Morte d'Arthur." And it is true that the remembered visit in the snow suggests baptism, that the Christmas eve setting suggests the imminence of Christ, that the ladies pray for Arthur's return as centuries of Christians have for the return of Christ, that Arthur finally chaperones the ladies Christ-like to their salvation. But, as with the other analogues, some aspects of the poem confound a Christian reading. What can the withholding of Arthur's tears by an unnamed maiden of the sea have to do with Christian suffering? And it is something of a sacrilege to place more emphasis on body than on spirit by portraying a Christ figure in such gruesome posthumous detail as this:

> What matter that his cheeks were pale,
>   His kind kiss'd lips all grey?
>
>   . . . . .
>
> What if his hair that brush'd her cheek
>   Was stiff with frozen rime?
> His eyes were grown quite blue again,
>   As in the happy time.
>
> (ll. 63-64, 67-70)

Why the stress on his physical ailments—the weariness and feebleness in his first visit, the blindness in his second? And what sort of Christian paradise is "the happy golden land"? Altogether, the poem simply does not yield very gracefully to a spiritual interpretation. It is too crammed with concrete physical detail for that. Apparently, these fairytale and Biblical analogues to "**The Blue Closet**" do not function like the sources of Morris' Arthurian and Froissartian poems; they can neither be pinpointed clearly nor used to help understand the meaning of the poem. Rather, they work by nuance and indirection, not appealing to the analytic faculties but increasing the universality of the poem and enriching its emotional texture. Source studies of the six other poems in the "**Blue Closet**" group would produce similar results.

If a source study of "**The Blue Closet**" proves intellectually frustrating, Morris compounds the difficulty by his treatment of causality in this poem. One thing human rationality seeks persistently to know is how event leads to event and what motivates people to act as they do. Yet Morris omits the causal dimension from "**The Blue Closet**." We cannot tell who locked these ladies up or why. We never know what delays Arthur's return. Nor can we answer the question posed in the refrain, "*Was he asleep, or was he dead?*" (l. 15). We have no idea why Arthur's tears have been locked away or who the subaqueous "she" is who keeps them in a "gold and blue casket" (l. 45). Finally, we do not know why Arthur chooses this year to return in answer to the annual prayer. Morris' other fantasy poems work this way too. The woman in "**The Wind**" dies from no apparent cause and for no apparent reason. It is impossible to see why the knight in "**Spell-bound**" has been tied up with silken chains or why Oliver in "**The Tune of Seven Towers**" would be willing to ride toward his death. The reviewer for the *Literary Gazette* (March, 1858, p. 227) summarized this tendency of the "**Blue Closet**" group: "It is true that something exciting happens, but, as the courier in 'Little Dorrit' has it, there is no why." It is quite possibly this absence of causality that makes these poems slightly frightening, since they are beyond our intellectual control. But it is equally important to recall, as Freud points out in *The Interpretation of Dreams*, that all causal connections decay into a mere sequence of images in dreams. Perhaps Morris has penetrated the thinking apparatus to a more primitive and more universal place in the psyche. It is not enough simply to call this dream-poetry. We must realize that it actually operates the way dreams do.

Another way Morris undoes thought is to present a pre-rational means of dealing with the world. If one important function of rationality is to cope effectively with the data of experience—Freud's "reality principle"—then the spectral characters of "**The Blue Closet**" do not possess it. They simply allow themselves to be acted upon. The ladies are far from contriving to escape from the tower, and Arthur is helpless even to regain his own tears. In fact, for a redeemer, Arthur is not only unusually passive but pathetically weary, aged, and pale: his eyes "grow grey with time, grow small and dry" (l. 47), and he admits, "I am so feeble now, would I might die" (l. 48). He may be *strong in the land of the dead*" (l. 62) but not strong enough to arrive at the tower under his own steam. Even his final act of redemption loses its potential strength when he must be led from the tower blind. Similarly, the ladies of the poem participate in a ritual conjuring of their savior, one that ultimately succeeds through no realistic effort on their part. Incapable of manipulating the external world to achieve their ends, these characters get what they want through magic and wish-fulfillment. They are dominated not by the "reality principle" but by the "pleasure principle," which governs the unconscious life and dreams.

Morris' prevailing technique in **"The Blue Closet,"** then, is to undercut the human intellect, that faculty which both operates by the rules of logic and devises practical solutions to problems encountered in the phenomenal world. When rationality has been thus stripped away, the faculty that remains is visual perception. For Freud, the ability to see concretely characterizes the most primitive mental process. Predictably, it is also the chief characteristic of dreams, which consist of visual sequences without clear logical connection. It should come as no surprise that Morris fixes in **"The Blue Closet"** on visual detail. In this and Morris' other poems of dreamland, visual certitude replaces thought.

In **"The Blue Closet"** the clarity of visual detail is especially pronounced because the poem was written as a companion piece to Rossetti's watercolor of the same title, which Morris commissioned in 1856. In all probability Morris meant the poem to accompany the picture, creating an integrated unit, just as Rossetti wrote poems to accompany pictures like *The Girlhood of Mary Virgin*. Rossetti seems to confirm this hypothesis in a letter to a friend: "To one of my water-colours, called *The Blue Closet,* [Morris] has written a stunning poem" (*Letters*, I, 312). This hypothesis would also explain why, considered together, painting and poem seem to complement each other with respect to visual detail. Where Rossetti supplies the most detail, Morris supplies the least, perhaps merely to avoid redundancy. Whenever Morris does repeat a detail from Rossetti, he nearly always accepts the Rossetti version without alteration. In the painting, the two queens lay their "long hands on the keys" (l. 4). The ladies in waiting, garbed appropriately in "purple and green" (l. 17), are indeed "ready to sing" (l. 3). Gold strings, blue tiles, patch of earth, lily red, and bells are all there, even though Morris substitutes a "*great bell overhead*" (l. 6) for Rossetti's string of little bells. Morris even picks up Rossetti's subtler touches, like the seasonal suggestion of the holly bough which falls across the top of the instrument in the painting. Finally, each of Rossetti's ladies, her eyes

disengaged from any worldly object, wears a dreamy, introspective expression, which Morris perfectly captures in his narrative of the inner life.

But where he ventures off Rossetti's canvas, Morris bears sole responsibility for grounding his fantasy in concrete detail. So it is at these points, notably the descriptions of Arthur's first and second comings, that Morris' use of detail is most elaborate. Thus, the baptism of snow is presented in tangible detail: the snow has a "dusty" texture, runs through Louise's hair, descends over her bare white shoulders. The hiding away of Arthur's tears, which would otherwise seem an incredible and incomprehensible event, is anchored to the perceptual world by the "gold and blue casket." Most strikingly, the dead Arthur who returns for his friends is not permitted the usual disembodiment of death but is represented in almost ghoulish detail with pale cheeks, gray lips, rime-encrusted hair, and blind blue eyes. Nearly every aspect of Morris' eerie narrative can, it seems, be visualized, especially by the reader who can supplement the poem with Rossetti's painting.

These details, so concretely portrayed in both poem and painting, are nonetheless not the sights of this world. In the careful balance and special purity of his color, Rossetti has no wish to represent nature but instead seems to paint the figures of dream, even of hallucination, so vivid and insistent are his hues. In the same way, Morris' Arthur is clearly a character limned not from life but from a nightmare vision of death. Although our eyes are focused in **"The Blue Closet"** as our intellects cannot be, they are not fixed on the external world but turned inward as in dreams and visions. Once again, Morris instinctively represents what Freud would call "primary process," the kind of mental activity that produces simple image sequences without logical connection. It is the process deepest in our minds and comprehensible only because it dominates our dreams.

Morris, then, intuitively grasped much of what Freud later outlined as the "dreamwork." In his poems of dreamland he suppressed reason and exalted the perception of the inward-looking eye. **"The Blue Closet"** would scarcely compel attention if it only shared its irreality and mystery with dreams. Instead it seems to operate on the same informing principles as dreams do.

What is more, the dream state of absolute withdrawal into the self retains a profound and primitive attraction for us, since it suggests the cessation of all conflict—Morris' "happy golden land." But at the same time such a withdrawal also entails the end of all bodily activity. Put another way, to dream forever is to be forever asleep, and Morris knew this perfectly well. That is why the action of **"The Blue Closet"** centers on the progressive dissolution of physical existence or, in Yeats's lovely phrase, "the autumn of the body."

From the start, the corporal existence of these personages seems tentative. In the first place, all of them are somehow physically immobilized. The ladies are incarcerated in a neglected tower. Arthur's tears are also locked away. And he has been mysteriously prevented for what seems an eternity from returning to the tower. A similar paralysis afflicts the characters in Morris' other poems of dreamland. The speaker in **"Spell-bound"** has been bound in silken chains by a wizard. The armorer in **"The Wind,"** succumbing to sleep, complains that "something keeps me still" (l. 28). Jehane in **"Golden Wings"** is an unwilling captive of the idyllic Ladies' Gard. In **"Rapunzel,"** of course, the heroine is also imprisoned in a tower while her lover feels that "still God ties me down to the green sward" (l. 154). The effect of this pervasive bodily inaction is to heighten the ambience of interiority. When all bodily movement is cut off, the mind is forced out of the world and back upon itself. It is the beginning of the body's death in deference to the dream.

Indeed, the ladies of **"The Blue Closet"** seem from the outset to inhabit a kind of middle kingdom between life and death. In their untended tower they are locked away from the living world. The seemingly underwater location of the tower recalls those folk traditions which equate the watery depths with the nether world. The burden tolls a constant death knell. And recurring images of snow, blue, and rime reinforce the sense that the damozels are already dead to ordinary life and wait in a wearying and almost timeless limbo for Arthur's return. Before that return Arthur himself has, if possible, a still more curious mode of existence. Even the ladies do not know whether to consider him asleep or dead. What are we to make of a knight whose "tears are all hidden deep under the seas" (l. 44) and whose very eyes change from blue to gray with age and infirmity? Although not perhaps literally dead at this point in the poem, Arthur betrays no abundance of vitality. He, too, seems trapped in a sort of passive limbo, neither very much alive nor truly dead. Not only is bodily movement denied in this poem, but life itself seems all but extinguished.

Morris further explores this half-life in other poems from the **"Blue Closet"** group. The knight in **"Spell-bound"** has been chained "Above the golden-waving plains, / Where never reaper cometh near" (ll. 75-76) in a land apparently beyond time and mortal activity. Yoland in **"The Tune of Seven Towers"** sings of "the desolate battlements all arow" (l. 3), revealing that

> No one walks there now;
>   Except in the white moonlight
> The white ghosts walk in a row;
>   If one could see it, an awful sight.
>
> (ll. 7-10)

Although less sinister than these settings, Ladies' Gard in **"Golden Wings"** is a timeless paradise outside of real life, for "no drop of blood, / Drawn from men's bodies by sword-blows, / Came ever there, or any tear" (ll. 36-38). And the knights and ladies of **"Near Avalon"** occupy, as the title suggests, a space somewhere between life and death. Already well out of the life of Victorian England, all these characters want to dream themselves out of any life at all, even a medieval one. This necessary connection between the dream and death is strengthened by the aging armorer's dream of death in **"The Wind."**

Suspended halfway between life and death, the restless women of **"The Blue Closet"** pray for the finality of death. Oddly, however, their impulse toward oblivion is framed as an invocation to a long-awaited lover. Jehane in **"Golden Wings"** also identifies love-longing with the death wish, expecting death to restore her lover. And Yoland of **"The Tune of Seven Towers"** lovingly sends her knight Oliver toward those desolate towers of death, as if only his death could redeem her happiness. For when all emotion is turned inward, love can never be outwardly consummated but becomes an intense and involuted passion which only death can assuage and which therefore takes death as its object. Thus, all these ladies of the dream are attracted to death as a kind of substitute lover, trusting to it their singular and ultimate fulfillment.

For the ladies of **"The Blue Closet"** the annual song of love and death is finally answered. Arthur at last returns to usher them out of limbo into that "happy golden land" beyond all earthly existence. And the blindness of their savior in the last stanza hints at what the ladies must sacrifice to gain that land across the bridge. From the first they have been turned inward to a place behind thought and all coping with the world. Now in this ultimate transmigration they must forego even that rudimentary faculty of perceiving images. Perhaps what continues to haunt us most about this poem is how cheerfully Morris was willing to purchase at the expense of life this last and deepest stretch of the interior.

As the quintessential example of Pre-Raphaelite dream-poetry, **"The Blue Closet"** has sufficient intrinsic interest to merit close attention. But comprehending this poem also allows us to isolate a strain in Victorian Romanticism which perhaps began with early Tennyson poems like "Mariana," "The Lotos-Eaters," and "The Lady of Shalott" and certainly culminated, as I shall briefly suggest, in the early work of William Butler Yeats. It is a strain which rejects Arnold's "powerful application of ideas to life" in favor of a movement downward out of life and into primeval levels of consciousness. It is a strain which ran from Tennyson through Morris and other Pre-Raphaelites to Walter Pater and, from there, to Yeats's friends in the Rhymers'

Club, whose movement out of life was all too often literal. Finally and most importantly, it came to Yeats himself. As this long genealogy implies, much of the Yeatsian version of this life-defying interiority bore the stamp of other and perhaps more central influences than Morris. Still, as he frequently acknowledged, Yeats felt a particular attachment for Morris, who had shown him dream-poetry at its purest.

Yeats announced in the *Autobiography* (New York, 1953, p. 70) that as a young man he had been "in all things pre-Raphaelite," and prominent among those "things pre-Raphaelite" were dreams. For much of Yeats's poetic inspiration came to him in waking dreams or trances. Of "The Cap and Bells," he remarks, "I dreamed this story exactly as I have written it."[8] Indeed, Yeats claimed that the symbolic value of the images in *The Wind Among the Reeds* (1899) was revealed to him most often in sleep. And the word "dream" wove through all his early poetry, a recurrent symbol of the ideal or interior world.

Dominated, like the young Morris, by the dream, Yeats also discovered in dreams many of the virtues Morris had instinctively located there. In 1893 Yeats wrote in *The Celtic Twilight* (London, p. 95): "I love better than any theory the sound of the Gate of Ivory, turning upon its hinges." But where Morris easily and naturally avoided theory, Yeats spent the whole decade of the nineties trying to purify his poetry of ideas or what he sometimes called "rhetoric." He saw "that Swinburne in one way, Browning in another, and Tennyson in a third, had filled their work with what I called 'impurities,' curiosities about politics, about science, about history, about religion; and that we must create once more the pure work" (*Autobiography,* p. 102). For Yeats the "pure work" would be "wrought about a mood,"[9] one of those pre-rational and almost ineffable emotional states common to all generations of mankind. Like the dream, it would get back to the essential inner life, not theorize about the ever-changing objective world. As Morris had before him, Yeats refused to compose the Victorian poetry of social responsibility and maintained that people would "more and more reject the opinion that poetry is a 'criticism of life,' and be more and more convinced that it is a revelation of a hidden life."[10]

Yeats agreed with Morris that one way back to that hidden life, one which cut through the political, moral, and intellectual tangles of any given age, lay through myth and legend. For Yeats, as for Morris, legends preserved those timeless human hopes and fears which precede rational thought and remain constant while conscious thinking changes. Morris in **"The Blue Closet"** relied on the folk traditions of northern Europe to provide this universality, whereas Yeats, committed to revitalizing his native Ireland, chose Irish legend. But both were using these traditional materials to the same end: to excise whatever was ephemeral and external from their poetry and mirror through legend the oldest and most enduring truths of the human heart.

Yeats not only wrote criticism in which he advocated the poetic exploration of the pre-intellectual dreamscape; he actually set out as one of these poetic explorers himself. "You write my sort of poetry," Morris remarked to Yeats after reading *The Wanderings of Oisin* in 1889 (*Autobiography,* p. 89), and it was truer then than it ever would be again. For in this long first poem Yeats derives both mood and method from poems like **"The Blue Closet."** In this early poem Yeats, like Morris, casts his retreat from the external world as a trip to fairyland. His hero passes "three centuries . . . / Of dalliance with a demon thing" (I. 3-4) on various enchanted islands, one of them apparently under water and all sharing with the deserted tower of **"The Blue Closet"** an absence of mortal time or change. On Yeats's Isle of Forgetfulness this enchantment is literally equated with continual dreaming. And, like the ladies of **"The Blue Closet,"** Oisin chafes under the yoke of his seemingly interminable sentence to this fairyland.

As for method, both poets rely on concrete visual detail, just as actual dreams do, to permit access to areas of consciousness otherwise remote from daily life. Hence, Yeats's enchanted islands are landscaped like Morris' many earthly paradises. The Isle of Dancing in particular has the same carven boats, swans, and stoats that surround the enchanted island in Morris' **"Golden Wings."** Further, Yeats uses color to specify the otherworldly creatures of his dream islands in *Oisin*:

> Their brows were white as fragrant milk,
> Their cloaks made out of yellow silk,
> And trimmed with many a crimson feather.
>
> (I. 204-206)

Such a description anchors the imaginary in the perceptible just as the insubstantial damozels of **"The Blue Closet"** are substantiated by color: "Two damozels wearing purple and green" (l. 17). The effect in both Yeats and Morris is as if their dreams were painted on a Pre-Raphaelite canvas.

Yeats pursued the inner fire at the expense of the phenomenal world throughout the nineties until it finally burned itself out in the 1899 volume, *The Wind Among the Reeds*. In the opening poem of this volume the same Niamh who ten years before had seduced Oisin to those enchanted islands still beckons, *"Away, come away."* For *The Wind Among the Reeds,* like Morris' **"Blue Closet"** group, articulates the attractions of life outside the world, life in a fairyland of the mind's interior where only those deep-seated and primal "moods" persist. And, although Yeats's poetic methods had now diverged considerably from Morris', his fairyland in the 1899 volume still has more in common with Morris' than just getting behind intellect to human essentials. It, too, imposes upon its inhabitants an "autumn of the body." The immobility of Morris' enchanted creatures finds its parallel in "The Hosting of the Sidhe":

> *if any gaze on our rushing band.*
> *We come between him and the deed of his hand,*
> *We come between him and the hope of his heart.*
>
> (ll. 10-12)

And, as in Morris, this fairyland introversion admits of no mortal love and looks forward either to personal death or to an apocalypse as a time of amorous fulfillment. "He hears the Cry of the Sedge" is one among numerous examples:

> I wander by the edge
> Of this desolate lake
> Where wind cries in the sedge:
> *Until the axle break*
> *That keeps the stars in their round,*
> *And hands hurl in the deep*
> *The banners of East and West,*
> *And the girdle of light is unbound,*
> *Your breast will not lie by the breast*
> *Of your beloved in sleep.*

As in the **Guenevere** poems, in this volume all love is thwarted and celibate. And, like Morris, Yeats knew that for the dream to survive in all its passionate intensity, the body and perhaps the world must die.

Although Morris' withdrawal from the world predicts many aspects of Yeats's inwardness in the nineties, the two poets radically disagree in one respect. Morris, as we have seen, gladly purchased his dream at the cost of all external experience. This was, however, a sacrifice which for Yeats was as terrifying as it was attractive. In *The Wind among the Reeds* Yeats is almost as anxious for those "sweet everlasting voices" of fairyland to be still as he is to be lulled by them. For Yeats, more than Morris, could become homesick for life and the things of this world, for

> All things uncomely and broken, all things worn out
>   and old,
> The cry of a child by the roadway, the creak of a
>   lumbering cart,
> The heavy steps of the ploughman, splashing the
>   wintry mould.
>
> (**"The Lover Tells of the Rose in His Heart,"** ll. 1-3)

So great for Yeats was the cost of this total retreat to the interior that after the turn of the century he more and more insisted on yoking the body back to the soul.

In 1902 Yeats wrote an essay on Morris called "The Happiest of the Poets." This may seem a strange epithet for a poet who began his career with poems of

nightmare and death like **"The Blue Closet."** And it is true that the essay concentrates largely on the later Morris who celebrated natural abundance. Yet the epithet could apply to the poet of **"The Blue Closet"** as well. For to Yeats, Morris had that rare pleasure of finding total sustenance in the dream, a pleasure forever denied his own more complicated sensibility. Still, even as Yeats went on to the waking life and twentieth-century poetry, he never forgot the power of that inner vision which he partly learned from William Morris; it was what he brought to the birthing of modern poetry.

Notes

1. "Pre-Raphaelitism and the Aesthetic Withdrawal," *The Darkling Plain: A Study of the Later Fortunes of Romanticism in English Poetry from George Darley to W. B. Yeats* (London, 1950), p. 157.

2. "Pre-Raphaelite Poetry," *From Dickens to Hardy: The Pelican Guide to English Literature,* VI, ed. Boris Ford (London, 1958), p. 364.

3. *Letters of D. G. Rossetti,* ed O. Doughty and J. R. Wahl (Oxford Univ. Press, 1965), I, 293.

4. *The Letters of William Morris to His Family and Friends,* ed. Philip Henderson (London, 1950), p. 17.

5. *Selected Works,* ed. Richard Aldington (New York, 1948), p. 79.

6. William Morris, *The Defence of Guenevere, and Other Poems* (London, 1858). All subsequent references to poems in the "Blue Closet" group are to this edition.

7. *The Pre-Raphaelites and Their Circle,* ed. Cecil Y. Lang (Boston, 1968), p. 511.

8. *The Variorum Edition of the Poems of W. B. Yeats,* ed. Peter Allt and Russell K. Alspach (New York, 1957), p. 808. All references to poems by Yeats are to this edition.

9. "The Moods," *Essays and Introductions* (New York, 1961), p. 195.

10. W. B. Yeats, John Eglinton, AE, and W. Larminie, *Literary Ideals in Ireland* (London, 1899), p. 36.

Charlotte H. Oberg (essay date 1978)

SOURCE: Oberg, Charlotte H. "The Apology and Prologue as Overture." In *A Pagan Prophet: William Morris,* pp. 25-38. Charlottesville: University of Virginia Press, 1978.

[*In the following essay, Oberg argues that the "Apology" and the Prologue to* The Earthly Paradise *function to foreshadow and amplify Morris's central poetic themes.*]

The Earthly Paradise begins with **"An Apology"** in which the narrator, introducing himself as "the idle singer of an empty day," foreshadows the substance of his theme, at once evoking and disclaiming the epic tradition of Virgil, Dante, and Milton:

> Of Heaven or Hell I have no power to sing,
> I cannot ease the burden of your fears,
> Or make quick-coming death a little thing,
> Or bring again the pleasure of past years,
> Nor for my words shall ye forget your tears,
> Or hope again for aught that I can say,
> The idle singer of an empty day.
>
> [III, 1]

What is frankly spelled out in this stanza is demonstrated through the length of *The Earthly Paradise.* Morris will postulate no afterlife—we will read nothing of heaven or hell in the usual sense of these concepts. Those few characters who attain paradisaical bliss within these twenty-four tales will do so on earth, without dying. Translation from the flesh into a spiritual body is not among the hopes of Morris's wanderers, even though they set sail from a Christianized Europe. In fact, one of Morris's recurrent preoccupations in the northern tales is with that most characteristic and familiar of nineteenth-century themes, the passing of paganism, the world "grown grey" from the breath of the "pale Galilean."[1] The contrast between paganism and Christianity is emphasized in the Prologue, as the wanderers' spokesman, Rolf, tells of his attraction to the religion of his ancestors, and forms the subject matter of an important part of the story **"The Lovers of Gudrun,"** in which the Christianization of Iceland results in part from the conversion of the hero Kiartan. In **"The Land East of the Sun,"** John, when questioned by his mother about the heaven promised by the "new faith," replies:

> "Nought know I, mother, of the dead,
> More than thou dost—let be—we live
> This day at least, great joy to give
> Each unto other. . . ."
>
> [V, 67]

The here and now, not the afterlife promised by Christianity, is Morris's concern not only in *The Earthly Paradise* but throughout his work.

The Apology continues with the first of many references to the heroic pagan substitute for immortality, the cult of fame, which in many literary contexts is referred to metaphorically in terms of the Blessed Isles, or the earthly paradise of heroes in Greek mythology (Valhalla of Germanic mythology is similarly attained only by great warriors):

> So let me sing of names rememberèd,
> Because they, living not, can ne'er be dead,

> Or long time take their memory quite away
> From us poor singers of an empty day.
>
> [III, 1]

In the next stanza the singer disclaims a social message:

> Dreamer of dreams, born out of my due time,
> Why should I strive to set the crooked straight?
> Let it suffice me that my murmuring rhyme
> Beats with light wing against the ivory gate,
> Telling a tale not too importunate.
> To those who in the sleepy region stay,
> Lulled by the singer of an empty day.
>
> [III, 1]

Rather, the proclaimed mission of the singer is to

> strive to build a shadowy isle of bliss
> Midmost the beating of the steely sea,
> Where tossed about all hearts of men must be. . . .
>
> [III, 2]

Like the "wizard to a northern king," the singer will cause the drear December wind to be unheard as he creates illusions of spring, summer, and autumn. Thus the present age is likened to winter in the passage of world ages, and the golden spring and summer of the past can be recaptured only through the magic of illusion, or art. The "shadowy isle of bliss" to be created by the singer in his song is the only earthly paradise possible in this December of the world—impossible to be realized even in the autumnal Middle Ages of the wanderers.

In this manner, then, the major themes of *The Earthly Paradise* are foreshadowed, somewhat in the fashion of musical themes in an overture. Because the golden past is dead, because man's life is short and full of trouble, because there is no hope beyond the grave—in short, because there is no paradise, earthly or unearthly—the singer can only beguile us into forgetfulness and into dreams of the dead golden past, the springtime of the world when heroic deeds were still possible, when the crooked could still be set straight. Such is the overt message of the idle singer of the Apology.

Morris amplifies his theme in the Prologue, which opens with a nightmarish vision of the London of his day: ". . . six counties overhung with smoke, . . . the snorting steam and piston stroke, . . . the spreading of the hideous town" (III, 3). He evokes this hellish vision only to dismiss it in favor of Chaucer's city, "small and white and clean," its green gardens bordering a clear Thames. But though idyllic, the London of Chaucer is far from Edenic—it is to serve only as an emblem of the fourteenth century, the time of the wanderers. Morris, despite his disclaimers in the voice of the idle singer as to didactic social intentions, seems to be a *laudator temporis acti* more extreme than Carlyle in *Past and*

Present, for Morris's superior model is not the medieval system (despite his famous "medievalism"), but the primitive and pagan heroic culture that preceded the Christian Middle Ages. The wanderers are to leave their medieval homes to search for a more remote and unattainable golden past, to be realized in the earthly paradise of their destination, a paradise not to be understood in terms of the Christian church's teachings about immortality.

The "nameless city" to which the narrator directs attention is the home of descendants of Greek wanderers of a more distant time. In this city of "marble palaces" and "pillared council-house," "Thronged with much people clad in ancient guise," the culture of the inhabitants' Ionian forebears is preserved. So, in the twilight of their own culture, the northern wanderers succeed only in finding a vestige of a culture already dead. It is the pattern of the Prologue that the search for unending life inevitably results in an encounter with a memento mori. Rolf's history, as told to the elders of the city, illustrates the deterioration of northern culture. Although born a Christian in Byzantium, he had learned in youth the stories of Norse mythology and, on visiting his ancestral home, had been struck by the contrast between the harsh realities of northern life and his childhood dreams of Asgard:

> But when I reached one dying autumn-tide
> My uncle's dwelling near the forest side,
> And saw the land so scanty and so bare,
> And all the hard things men contend with there,
> A little and unworthy land it seemed,
> And all the more of Asgard's days I dreamed,
> And worthier seemed the ancient faith of praise.

[III, 6]

The "autumn-tide" of his visit metaphorically underscores the state of decay of northern culture in the fourteenth century as contrasted with its heroic legendary springtime. The balance Morris sets up between the vestigial Greek culture of the nameless host city and the attenuated northern, or Germanic, culture represented by the various wanderers is a telling comment upon the nature of civilization in general and Western Europe in particular, regardless of the singer's earlier denials of social comment. Elsewhere Morris would compare "the Great Story of the North," as he termed the *Volsunga Saga* (thus showing the intensity of his heart's affection), to the "Tale of Troy" in its significance for posterity (VII, 286); the juxtaposition of these two cultures, Germanic and Greek, is integral to Morris's primitivist major theme in *The Earthly Paradise*: the alternation between stories of Greek and northern legend represents in symbolic fashion his idea of the parallelism of these two cultures. Oswald Spengler, many years later, in synthesizing the anthropology and mythology of the Cambridge School and others, formulated his "contemporary and spiritual epochs" which he charted for

Indian, Classical, Arabian, and Western civilizations in periods designated "Spring" through "Winter."[2] He was widely regarded as a prophet in his own day but is now, except in one important sense, a prophet without honor. But the truth of poetry is not the truth of history nor the truth of science; what remains valid in Spengler's lucubration is the truth of poetry, and this truth is almost precisely (or is in every way analogous) to Morris's "truth" in these tales. Morris believed himself to be living near the final collapse of the civilization of the north, that is, of Western Europe, a demise that would repeat that of the already dead Greek civilization. The widespread Aryan fever of the nineteenth century had its effect on Morris, whose enthusiasm for Icelandic subjects led him to abandon wife, children, home, and friends for months on end, but he was always able to view the civilization of the north with a certain amount of objectivity, an objectivity that places Morris in the vanguard of nineteenth-century thinkers on mythology and anthropology.

Rolf's dreams of Asgard were mingled with the ancient legends of the earthly paradise, "gardens ever blossoming / Across the western sea where none grew old" (III, 7), told him by the Breton squire Nicholas. Now, Rolf's longing for the golden past is identified with the quest for the earthly paradise, the vestigial golden age of man's infancy. These two concepts of immortality—the golden days of Asgard and the Blessed Isles of legend—are supplemented by a third concept, the alchemist's search for the elixir of immortality, or fountain of youth, carried on by Laurence, the Swabian priest. The fountain of youth is frequently associated with the terrestrial paradises of legend and literature, and Sabine Baring-Gould, the clergyman turned novelist and mythographer, makes much of it in a fine collection that was widely known in its day.[3] Laurence is fascinated with stories of vanished earthly heroes who live yet and will return:

> Tales of the Kaiser Redbeard could he tell
> Who neither went to Heaven nor yet to Hell,
> When from that fight upon the Asian plain
> He vanished, but still lives to come again
> Men know not how or when; but I listening
> Unto this tale thought it a certain thing
> That in some hidden vale of Swithiod
> Across the golden pavement still he trod.

[III, 8]

The motif of the returning hero, to be stressed in **"Ogier the Dane,"** which is based upon the legends clustering around Charlemagne and his knights, suggests other parallels in legend and myth. The expected return of King Arthur is an obvious analogue; a more spectacular one is the prophesied Second Coming of Jesus Christ, an event that is to coincide with the world cataclysm ushering in the millennium, that is, the new heaven and the new earth of Revelation, when death will be overcome and eternity will conquer time. (The Judeo-Christian idea is that time will come to an end, whereas the classical pagan conception is that the apocalypse is followed by a new paradisaical period.)[4] The reference to the tales of heroes told by Laurence, then, is the first hint of the relationship between the hero and the renewal of society and the rebirth of the world itself into a new cycle of ages. This relationship is to form a basic pattern within the tales of *The Earthly Paradise,* as well as in Morris's other writings.

It is on a "bright September afternoon" (III,8), the autumn weather corresponding to the autumnal lengthening shadows of their fourteenth-century civilization, that these three, Rolf, Nicholas, and Laurence, decide to leave their pestilence-ridden home in search of the earthly paradise (recalling the dusk into which the aged Ulysses and his mariners sail in Tennyson's poem). Nicholas, making the suggestion, invites his friends to

> go with me to-night,
> Setting your faces to undreamed delight,
> Turning your backs unto this troublous hell. . . .
>
> [III, 9]

This is the only hell to be found in the pages of *The Earthly Paradise*—the hard life of mortals in the world of reality. In **"The Watching of the Falcon"** Morris suggests that only the gift of death keeps this world from becoming a hell (IV, 161-62). The implication is, then, that eternal life per se is not enough—the world must be changed, or renewed.

Continuing his history, Rolf tells of the encounter with the English king Edward III. Although he is not identified by name, there is, in the first discarded version of the Prologue, a note calling for an illustration of "Edward on his galley at Sluse" (XXIV, 95). Edward, victorious against the French in the naval battle off Sluis, was later forced to vitiate his triumph by making a truce. Thus the aging king, surrounded by the trappings of heroic martial feats, is emblematic of the crepuscular civilization of which he is the epitome—a society in which heroic virtues have limited power. Morris presents Edward as the prototype of the noble leader who governs his people wisely and honorably but is approaching the twilight of his life and reign (though the historical Edward was at the time of Sluis actually only a little more than halfway through his reign):

> Broad-browed he was, hook-nosed, with wide grey
>   eyes
> No longer eager for the coming prize,
> But keen and steadfast; many an ageing line,
> Half hidden by his sweeping beard and fine,
> Ploughed his thin cheeks, his hair was more than grey,
> And like to one he seemed whose better day
> Is over to himself, though foolish fame
> Shouts louder year by year his empty name.
>
> [III, 16]

Nevertheless, the principle of heroic leadership that Edward III represents is still valid—we shall see that one of Morris's major concerns in *The Earthly Paradise* is the necessity for such leadership and its inherent problems—and dreams of heroic death are awakened in Rolf by the stirring challenge of the king to follow him:

> Ah, with such an one
> Could I from town to town of France have run
> To end my life upon some glorious day
> Where stand the banners brighter than the May
> Above the deeds of men, as certainly
> This king himself has full oft wished to die.
>
> [III, 15]

Either to follow or to oppose such a king would be glorious:

> Nor had it been an evil lot to stand
> On the worse side, with people of the land
> 'Gainst such a man, when even this might fall,
> That it might be my luck some day to call
> My battle-cry o'er his low-lying head,
> And I be evermore rememberèd.
>
> [III, 15]

Nicholas, fearing Rolf's acceptance of the king's invitation to follow him, explains their mission and elicits a rueful response from the king:

> "For you the world is wide—but not for me,
> Who once had dreams of one great victory
> Wherein that world lay vanquished by my throne,
> And now, the victor in so many an one,
> Find that in Asia Alexander died
> And will not live again; . . .
>
>   . . . . .
>   "Farewell, it yet may hap that I a king
> Shall be remembered but by this one thing,
> That on the morn before ye crossed the sea
> Ye gave and took in common talk with me."
>
> [III, 20-21]

Thus all the pagan concepts of immortality are introduced in the Prologue: Asgard, the earthly paradise or Blessed Isles, the elixir of life, the cult of fame. But the wanderers will be granted only visions of death, and that soon.

Upon finding land, which we may assume is somewhere in Central America, the wanderers are delirious with joy, thinking that they have "reached the gates of Paradise / And endless bliss" (III, 28). (The equating of the Americas with the earthly paradise has historical authority, as may be inferred from our earlier quotation from Christopher Columbus.[5] The plausible historicity of the events of the Prologue is an important point, and we shall return to it later.) Following a pathway up a hill, they find a monstrous burial place of kings:

And there a rude shrine stood, of unhewn stones
Both walls and roof, with a great heap of bones
Piled up outside it. . . .

[III, 32]

Inside the shrine is a golden idol, and hanging on the walls are the corpses of dead kings. On the mountain's summit is yet another grisly tableau, the meaning of which is not completely explained until much later: clad like his predecessors within the shrine, a dying king lies on the rocky ground surrounded by embalmed corpses "Set up like players at a yule-tide feast" (III, 33), depicting various stations of life. These dread reminders of death-in-life, ironically juxtaposed with the wanderers' meeting with Edward III, illustrate the futility of human striving in a world where even kings must die.

Forcibly wrenched into awareness that this cannot be the land of immortality, the wanderers are nonetheless favorably impressed with the inhabitants of this forest community:

And sure of all the folk I ever saw
These were the gentlest: if they had a law
We knew not then, but still they seemed to be
Like the gold people of antiquity.

[III, 37]

These noble savages live in a vestigial Bronze Age culture:

But nought of iron did they seem to know,
For all their cutting tools were edged with flint,
Or with soft copper, that soon turned and bent. . . .

[III, 37]

These handsome people, "comely and well knit," clad in their cotton or woven garments with ornaments of beaten gold, represent an earlier and more primitive, hence more admirable, level of culture. Ironically, when asked about the whereabouts of the "good land," these aborigines point eastward, and, told that the wanderers had come from the east, they kneel down to worship their more "civilized" visitors. Conversely, the wanderers are infused with new hope by finding the simpler bronze culture, as if, so much of the past being found still alive, the age of gold might yet exist:

But we, though somewhat troubled at this thing,
Failed not to hope, because it seemed to us
That this so simple folk and virtuous,
So happy midst their dreary forest bowers,
Showed at the least a better land than ours,
And some yet better thing far onward lay.

[III, 37]

But though their quest will take them further into barbarity and bestiality—the heart of darkness—the wanderers will never gain the paradisaical past they seek. From this point Rolf is haunted by dreams as well as by actual experiences of death and decay: at the next landing site Rolf is wakened from a dream of love and death by an attack of wild men (III, 40-41). The dream is prophetic: Kirstin, the beloved of Nicholas, is killed in the fighting.

Several fruitless encounters with the wild people are followed by another landing, and the experience of the wanderers at this place recalls the earlier visit with the Bronze Age forest folk. These naked brown people are even more primitive, "most untaught and wild, / Nigh void of arts, but harmless, good and mild" (III, 44). When they are questioned as to the location of the earthly paradise, they tell of the land beyond the mountains:

Beyond them lay a fair abode of bliss
Where dwelt men like the Gods, and clad as we,
Who doubtless lived on through eternity
Unless the very world should come to nought;
But never had they had the impious thought
To scale those mountains; since most surely, none
Of men they knew could follow up the sun,
The fearful sun, and live; but as for us
They said, who were so wise and glorious
It might not be so.

[III, 45]

This passage underscores one of the central ironies of the Prologue: the Promethean aspects of the northern civilization represented by Rolf and the other wanderers have been turned to regressive aims, their quest essentially denying the validity of the civilization this Prometheanism has produced, while the simpler, acquiescent cultures with which the wanderers come in contact consistently regard their visitors as godlike because of their superior technology. Rolf's speech rousing his companions to conquer the mountains illustrates the basic paradox of their quest to find a land where quests will be unnecessary:

"Did ye then deem the way would not be rough
Unto the lovely land ye so desire?
        . . . . .
    "Lo now, if but the half will come with me,
The summit of those mountains will I see,
Or else die first; . . .
            . . . . .
            . . . alone, O friends, will I
Seek for my life, for no man can die twice,
And death or life may give me Paradise!"

[III, 46-47]

The chastening of the Promethean spirit that is implicit in the story of the wanderers recurs often in the verse tales: the legend of the rebellious fire-bringer, associated since its earliest version in Hesiod with the end of the golden age, implies faith in progress, a concept inimical to primitivism.[6]

By this time some of the wanderers have already learned their lesson—"yet are we grown too wise / Upon this earth to seek for Paradise" (III, 47-48)—and they choose to remain behind. Their renunciation of the quest will be repeated by others and is shown to be justified by the outcome of the expedition to brave the mountains. Rolf and his diminished band of followers suffer greatly and, in the end, find only a land of cannibals. The series of cultures found by the wanderers illustrates a return to primitivism, but a primitivism unacceptable to the wanderers' preconceived ideals. This cultural retrogression is echoed in their own natures: in their quest for the happy land they become increasingly brutalized, mercilessly killing prisoners taken in skirmishes with the wild men: "So with the failing of our hoped delight / We grew to be like devils" (III, 49). Once again, death being found where life is sought, the wanderers are themselves participants in death.

Next, in a respite from their struggle, they dwell for a number of years as honored guests in a beautiful city inhabited by a people kin to the forest dwellers, also a Bronze Age culture:

> Their arms were edged with copper or with gold,
> Whereof they had great plenty, or with flint;
> No armour had they fit to bear the dint
> Of tools like ours, and little could avail
> Their archer craft; their boats knew nought of sail,
> And many a feat of building could we show,
> Which midst their splendour still they did not know.
>
> [III, 58]

The wanderers, with their superior military skill, deliver their hosts from the persecutions of a tyrant conqueror who periodically demands human tribute for sacrifice, a motif prefiguring a number of tales in *The Earthly Paradise*. Though tempted to remain amid their grateful hosts, Rolf and Nicholas are not yet resigned to the failure of their quest and so push on to the conclusion of their hopes:

> And we had lived and died as happy there
> As any men the labouring earth may bear,
> But for the poison of that wickedness
> That led us on God's edicts to redress.
>
> [III, 59]

A bitterly ironic episode ends this history. Dupes of a young man pretending to lead them to the land of immortality, the wanderers are kept as captive gods and treated to a final and most horrifying spectacle of death:

> Bound did we sit, each in his golden chair,
> Beholding many mummeries that they wrought
> About the altar; till at last they brought,
> Crowned with fair flowers, and clad in robes of gold,
> The folk that from the wood we won of old.
> Why make long words? before our very eyes
> Our friends they slew, a fitting sacrifice

> To us their new-gained Gods, who sought to find
> Within that land, a people just and kind
> That could not die, or take away the breath
> From living men.
>
> [III, 73]

While the city is under attack, the wanderers succeed in escaping. Though their erstwhile captors regard them as potential saviors, they are pleased to see the downfall of their worshipers as they desert the city and, for the last time, take to the sea. This episode is the most cynical comment upon the nature of religion in all *The Earthly Paradise*; its impact is reinforced in the verse tales by repeated rescues from religious sacrifice and the generally capricious nature of the gods depicted by Morris.

The story of the wanderers is the characteristic epic voyage in reverse. Odysseus returns to Ithaca and Penelope after a great war still accomplishing great deeds, killing the usurpers and reestablishing his own sovereignty; Aeneas similarly carves a heroic path to his new home, slaughtering with godlike mercilessness the enemies of the divinely ordained Rome. But these wanderers desert their homes, rejecting heroism and the immortality of fame in hope of earthly immortality in a land where striving ceases. Their quest is psychologically regressive: their wish to find paradise, or the golden age of man, is, on the psychological level, an attempt to return to a state of infancy, or sensual gratification without attendant anxiety or care. By contrast, Tolstoy's Ivan Ilyitch achieves salvation by regression to a state of infancy, but the authorial outlook is Christian, not pagan: Tolstoy's protagonist must, through his illness, become as a little child before he can be saved from the mindless triviality of his bourgeois existence. But the wanderers, like Tennyson's mariners tempted in the land of the lotos-eaters, want "long rest or death, dark death, or dreamful ease." Except for those who stay behind with the brown-skinned people, the wanderers do not establish a new home, but find only a series of temporary havens, their final hosts being the elders of the nameless city. There, the wanderers have no thought of taking wives and founding families—another aspect of their mortality, for their flesh will not even have biological continuity with future beings. As in Tennyson's "Ulysses," where the same curious mixture of Victorian Prometheanism and regressive death wish results in a last quest for the "Happy Isles," the journey's end for the wanderers is in fact seen to be a voyage to the end of night.[7]

On the other hand, the wanderers represent a warrior culture, though a decrepit one, as constant references to their superior weapons and military prowess emphasize, and the turning away from deeds by these "children of a warrior race" (III, 74) implies that heroism is not possible in this fourteenth-century twilight of the northern race. Now they can only thrill to stories of deeds done long before the earth (and they themselves) grew old:

> many things like these
> They talked about, till they seemed young again,
> Remembering what a glory and a gain
> Their fathers deemed the death of kings to be.
>
> . . . . .
>
> The minstrels raised some high heroic strain
> That led men on to battle in old times;
> And midst the glory of its mingling rhymes,
> Their hard hearts softened, and strange thoughts arose
> Of some new end to all life's cruel foes.
>
> 　　　　　　　　　　　　　　　　　[III, 266]

The implication of the Prologue is that the wanderers should have been content to remain with the Bronze Age cultures with which they first came in contact. Retrogression to a heroic age, in which great deeds could be done by great men, before commercialism had sullied pagan virtues, is as far back as man can travel. Such a concept is in accord with the heroic subject matter of most of Morris's writings. The wanderers are now able to experience deeds of heroism only vicariously, through art, and the stories they tell, as they are remembered and retold, will constitute their only immortality. Their aged condition metaphorically represents the world grown old, while the young people with whom they are surrounded, and the young heroes and heroines of their stories, represent the young world of long ago. Their deeds are now the subject of tales told in an old world where deeds are no longer possible.

The age of the wanderers, now old and withered, is contrasted with youth in the links that separate the tales. For instance:

> And now the watery April sun lit up
> Upon the fair board golden ewer and cup,
> And over the bright silken tapestry
> The fresh young boughs were gladdening every eye,
> And round the board old faces you might see
> Amidst the blossoms and their greenery.
>
> 　　　　　　　　　　　　　　　　　[III, 170]

Or:

> Then round about the grave old men they drew,
> Both youths and maidens; and beneath their feet
> The grass seemed greener and the flowers more sweet
> Unto the elders, as they stood around.
>
> 　　　　　　　　　　　　　　　　　[IV, 126]

The descriptions of the pastoral activities of the young people of the nameless city give a sense of what the wanderers have lost through their fruitless quest:

> Neath the bright sky cool grew the weary earth,
> And many a bud in that fair hour had birth
> Upon the garden bushes; in the west
> The sky got ready for the great sun's rest,

> And all was fresh and lovely; none the less,
> Although those old men shared the happiness
> Of the bright eve, 'twas mixed with memories
> Of how they might in old times have been wise,
> Not casting by for very wilfulness
> What wealth might come their changing life to bless;
> Lulling their hearts to sleep, amid the cold
> Of bitter times, that so they might behold
> Some joy at last, e'en if it lingered long;
> That, wearing not their souls with grief and wrong,
> They still might watch the changing world go by,
> Content to live, content at last to die.
> 　　Alas! if they had reached content at last,
> It was perforce when all their strength was past;
> And after loss of many days once bright,
> With foolish hopes of unattained delight.
>
> 　　　　　　　　　　　　　　　　　[IV, 186]

By seeking the phantasmal earthly paradise, they have paradoxically lost the only happiness possible to man in a real world—a simple life in accord with nature's rhythms. This natural state, the only Edenic state possible, has been lost through Promethean disobedience, refusal to accept the limitations of mortality. The pattern of the wanderers' lives is the pattern of the Fall; the pattern of redemption is found in the verse tales that follow the Prologue.

Notes

1. Algernon Charles Swinburne, "Hymn to Proserpine," l. 35.

2. *The Decline of the West,* Vol. I, *Form and Actuality,* trans. Charles Francis Atkinson (1926; rpt. New York, 1947), following p. 428.

3. *Curious Myths of the Middle Ages* (1867; rpt. New Hyde Park, N. Y., 1967), pp. 250-65.

4. See Mircea Eliade, *The Myth of the Eternal Return,* trans. Willard R. Trask (New York, 1954), pp. 126-30, and M. H. Abrams, *Natural Supernaturalism: Tradition and Revolution in Romantic Literature* (New York, 1971), pp. 34-37.

5. On this point see Baudet, pp. 26 ff., Giamatti, p. 4, and Abrams, pp. 411-12.

6. See Lovejoy and Boas, pp. 196-99; Abrams, pp. 56-65, discusses the relationship of the idea of progress to Judeo-Christian millennial concepts.

7. "The Lotos-Eaters," l. 98, and "Ulysses," l. 63.

Thomas T. Barker (essay date November 1981)

SOURCE: Barker, Thomas T. "The Shadow on the Tapestry: Irony in William Morris' *The Earthly Paradise.*" *The Journal of Pre-Raphaelite Studies* 2, no. 1 (November 1981): 111-26.

[*In the following essay, Barker compares* The Earthly Paradise *to Alfred Tennyson's "The Lotos-Eaters" and Edmund Spenser's* The Faerie Queene *to show that Morris's poem is more ironic than escapist in nature.*]

A review of the critics' reception of *The Earthly Paradise* shows that they have identified it with the trend toward escapist art which flourished in the late nineteenth century. Oscar Maurer's study of the work's original reviewers confirms this. Critics did not question Morris' escapism because it seemed easily proven by a literal reading of such passages in the **"Apology"** as "Dreamer of dreams, born out of my time, / Why should I strive to set the crooked straight?"[1] Commentators after the turn of the century[2] agreed with the reviewers of Morris' time. Paul Elmer More, typical of these, writes that Morris' "aim was to waft the reader into a 'shadowy isle of bliss' which is . . . the world's refuge of romance." Early modern critics[3] have generally followed this line of criticism. F. L. Lucas based his critique on the assumption that poets are "poor masters of the art of living," and concluded that the realities of the Victorian age drove Morris to escape via an art that reflected "the happiness of a day-dream." Holbrook Jackson, more sympathetic in view of Morris' later political activity, suggested that the period of the poem's composition reflected Morris' "retreatist (not 'escapist') attitude towards affairs." The idea that social criticism was alive but dormant in Morris while *The Earthly Paradise* was being written recurs time and again. One finds it early in Mackail's *Studies of English Poets:* the opening lines of the poem were Morris' "last cry out of the darkness before he reached the light" of socialist fellowship. Few modern critics[4] make any such attempt to evade the blatant escapist statements in the work. Northrop Frye categorizes it as "cuddle fiction: the romance that is physically associated with comfortable beds or chairs around fireplaces and warm spots generally."

Many of the critics who see the poem as escapist focus on the **"Apology."** (Oscar Maurer describes the **"Apology"** as a "manifesto of 'escapism.'") The voice we hear at the opening of the poem is that of the poet in the guise of an "idle singer of an empty day":

> Of Heaven or Hell I have no power to sing,
> I cannot ease the burden of your fears,
> Or make quick-coming death a little thing,
> Or bring again the pleasure of past years,
> Nor for my words shall ye forget your tears,
> Or hope again for aught that I can say,
> The idle singer of an empty day.
>
>   But rather, when aweary of your mirth,
> From full hearts still unsatisfied ye sigh,
> And, feeling kindly unto all the earth,
> Grudge every minute as it passes by,
> Made the more mindful that the sweet days die—
> —Remember me a little then I pray,
> The idle singer of an empty day.
>
>   The heavy trouble, the bewildering care
> That weighs us down who live and earn our bread,
> These idle verses have no power to bear;
> So let me sing of names remembered,
> Because they, living not, can ne'er be dead,

> Or long time take their memory quite away
> From us poor singers of an empty day.
>
>   Dreamer of dreams, born out of my due time,
> Why should I strive to set the crooked straight?
> Let it suffice me that my murmuring rhyme
> Beats with light wing against the ivory gate,
> Telling a tale not too importunate
> To those who in the sleepy region stay,
> Lulled by the singer of an empty day.[5]

(v. 3, "Apology")

Here the poet declares his intention to sing not of the realities of spiritual and physical life, but merely of imaginary characters. Although I will show that there are other personae, this persona of the poet as a "dreamer of dreams" has most often been identified with Morris himself. Supporting this identification, Holbrook Jackson, in *Dreamers of Dreams,* quotes Morris as saying, "My work is the embodiment of dreams in one form or another."

Although the arguments for reading the poem as escapist are numerous, I hope to show that there is an ironic structural element. Since there are many similarities between the two poems, *The Earthly Paradise* invites comparison with Tennyson's "The Lotos-Eaters," a poem that strongly embodies the moral aesthetic of the nineteenth century. Indeed, Morris presents an even stronger argument against escapism than Tennyson does. Morris alienates the reader from the escapist elements of the poem by establishing reader identification with the main character of the "Prologue," Rolf—an identification which he reinforces throughout the work in order to impress upon the reader a painful yet powerful vision of the stasis and frustration resulting from the consciousness of mortality, or the triumph of time. Morris contrasts this vision with the vision of the stasis of art that we find in the poem, and develops the didactic theme of the dangers to the reader who naively identifies with escapist "dreams." (We find this theme of the deceptiveness of literature in other works, notably in Spenser's "Bower of blisse" episode in Book II of the *Faerie Queene.* Along with other similarities between these two works, I propose to show how Morris uses the Spenserian technique of blending art and nature to involve the reader in the poem. By comparing *The Earthly Paradise* to the *Faerie Queene* in this way we see that Morris' innovative use of reader-response irony places *The Earthly Paradise* in a new context, that of the great moral poems of English literature.)

The Earthly Paradise and "The Lotos-Eaters" have many features in common. Most obviously, they both appear to argue against the moral aesthetic. They present a rationale for neglecting the past, families, the world of strife—in short, all social concerns. Both visions are drawn in attractive colors and vivid details that suggest the stasis of the plastic arts rather than the motion and change of life. Yet though they attract, they deceive;

"Adam and Eve." An engraving by William Morris.

and in each poem we can find that escapism is qualified by its associations with death.

The argument for the neglect of social concerns in ***The Earthly Paradise*** is summed up in these two lines from the **"Apology"**:

> Dreamer of dreams, born out of my due time,
> Why should I strive to set the crooked straight?

They carry the same rhetorical effect as the mariners' choric song in "The Lotos-Eaters": "Why should we toil, the roof and crown of things?" "What pleasure can we have / To war with evil?"[6] Jessie Kocmanova suggests that Morris was later to find an answer to the question "Why should I strive to set the crooked straight?" by taking up direct political action.[7] But here it seems obvious that we are being presented with a purely rhetorical question, as a rationalization of idleness based, as in "The Lotos-Eaters," on fatalism. Behind the mask of comforting rhyme and non-commitment expressed in ***The Earthly Paradise*** lies a deep-seated and unstated submission to the forces of death that the reader is tacitly asked to condone. The reader accepts this fatalism willingly because of the at-

tractiveness of a visionary realm free from death. The poet promises to deal with "names remembered / Because they, living not, can ne'er be dead." He knows that the passage of time troubles his readers; he assumes that they "Grudge every minute as it passes by," and he offers them an escape.

The use of colorful details and word painting in each poem makes its vision even more alluring. For example, the following passage of word painting from **"The Land East of the Sun and West of the Moon"** in *The Earthly Paradise* enhances the feeling of calm and stasis:

> Calm was the sea 'twixt wall and wall
> Of the green bight; the surf did fall
> With little noise upon the sand,
> Where 'neath the moon the smooth curved strand
> Shone white 'twixt dark sea, rocks, and turf.
>
> (v. 4, p. 24)

Tennyson too shows a land where time appears conquered, "A land where all things always seem the same." His word painting conveys the feeling of stillness, as in this passage:

> . . . far off, three mountain-tops
> Three silent pinnacles of aged snow,
> Stood sunset-flushed; and, dewed with showery drops
> . . .
>
> (ll. 15-17)

Thus we have a sensation of stasis, rather than strife or action, in both poems. These suggestions of stasis are further reinforced in ***The Earthly Paradise*** by Morris' preference for extended similes over metaphors. Robert Wahl, exploring the decorative function of Morris' similes, tells us that "separate free-standing" ornaments such as "Then through her limbs a tremor did there flit / As through white water runs the summer wind" bring the movement of the verse "to a standstill."[8]

In the early part of the "Prologue" the poet emphasizes the emotional response which his images of beauty and grandeur are to evoke in the reader: "wonder" and amazement; but it is worth noting that emotion here is always attached to visual perception. For example, the emotions rendered in the following passage recur throughout the poem:

> Pondering on them the city grey-beards *gaze*
> *Through kindly eyes,* midst thoughts of other days,
> And pity for poor souls, and *vague regret*
> For all the things that might have happened yet.
>
> (v. 3, p. 4; [italics] added)

The poet here subtly manipulates the reader into an acceptance of the emotions felt by the characters in the poem. Tennyson also does this, but in a different way.

He presents us with a rhythmically soothing and beautiful picture of slumber and peace, aiming to create a feeling in the reader similar to that of a lotos-eater:

> Full-faced above the valley stood the moon;
> And, like a downward smoke, the slender stream
> Along the cliff to fall and pause and fall did seem.
>
> (ll. 7-9)

These lines effectively draw the reader's eye downwards with the poet's eye, teasing the reader out of thought and leading him to ignore, temporarily, the qualifications of escapism in the poem. It invites him to relax and enjoy the spectacle before him.

Such reader manipulation is more overt in the opening scenes of *The Earthly Paradise.* The beginning of the "Prologue" involves the reader as a character in the poem, and asks him to replace the cares of daily life with a vision of his own city, London, in a state of purity and innocence.

> Forget six counties overhung with smoke,
> Forget the snorting steam and piston stroke,
> Forget the spreading of the hideous town;
> Think rather of the pack-horse on the down,
> And dream of London, small and white, and clean,
> The clear Thames bordered by its gardens green . . .

The focus in the opening scenes of the "Prologue" is on the visual spectacle and, like television, it captivates and holds the viewer. The poet gives the reader instructions on how to view this spectacle. He says, for instance, that he will "set before your eyes" a picture of a distant city: "A pillared council house *may you behold,* / Within whose porch are images of gold" (v. 3, p. 4; [italics] added). After presenting the setting the narrator moves the reader around in it:

> *Pass now between them, push the brazen door,*
> *And standing on the polished marble floor*
> *Leave* all the noises of the square behind;
> Most calm that reverent chamber *shall ye find,*
> Silent at first, but for *the noise you made*
> *When on the brazen door your hand you laid*
> *To shut it after you . . .*
>
> (v. 3, p. 4; [italics] added)

Later he says, "*but now behold* / The city rulers on their thrones of gold . . ." and then, "*drop your eyes and see* / Soldiers and peasants standing reverently . . ." (v. 3., p. 4; [italics] added). This conveys the power of an imaginary transport in concrete terms. Thus, to an extent almost unprecedented in previous literature the reader is made an actual character in the action of the poem.

Although "The Lotos-Eaters" lacks this style of direct reader address, it uses some degree of subtle reader manipulation to suggest inertia and passivity. In the opening stanzas the perceiving eye is mentioned only twice: "They saw the gleaming river seaward flow" and "Through mountain clefts the dale / Was seen. . . ." However, the transition from the active to the passive voice in the verb suggests increasing inertia rather than movement to the reader.

One of the central ironies of *The Earthly Paradise* can be seen in Morris' use of reader manipulation. Rather than making a simple shift from the active to the passive voice, he first involves the reader as a character and then abandons him. Later in the poem, in the sections that deal with the elders, the reader is no longer overtly involved. Evidently, Morris' purpose was to alienate the reader from this vision of escape. He does this by not only inviting the reader to identify with the scene of purity and innocence, but by making him actually take part in it, and later refusing to acknowledge his presence. This major ironic turn is essential to the poem's structure and its didactic theme.

It can also be shown that Tennyson and Morris consciously distance themselves from the dominant escapist motifs of their poems by creating an ambiguity about the authorial voice. Tennyson's displacement into the mythic past and the mask of the semi-dramatic choric song in "The Lotos-Eaters" enables him to appear as a disinterested recorder. For Morris the problem is more complex, because most readers take the direct authorial address in the **"Apology"** at face value. However, not all critics rely on a literal interpretation. Kocmanova, for instance, suggests that the latent Marxism of the poem is lost if we identify Morris with the escapist attitude of the "idle singer of an empty day," and Fleissner found himself faced with a similar ambiguity about the author's philosophy. The problem is that in the **"Apology"** the narrator has two distinct voices. Fleissner subsumes them both under the one enigmatic figure of the "masked minstrel."[9] However, it seems to me that for the purposes of Morris' irony these two voices must remain distinct. The dominant voice is that of the "idle singer of an empty day," the dreamer who, in the **"Apology,"** offers the reader an entrancing vision of escape. To hear only this, however, would be to forfeit the larger, more real vision of the overall structure of the work. Morris hints at that larger perspective by providing an alternate poetic voice in the **"Apology:"**

> Folk say, a wizard to a northern king
> At Christmas-tide such wondrous things did show,
> That through one window men beheld the spring,
> And through another saw the summer glow,
> And through a third the fruited vines arow,
> While still, unheard, but in its wonted way,
> Piped the drear wind of that December day.
>
> (v. 3, "Apology")

On the surface this suggests a power over the force of time and natural change. The wizard, a parallel to Morris, can compress the natural cycle of the year into one moment, to captivate the king, with whom the reader identifies. Yet the scene also emphasizes the *"drear wind* of that December day" which pipes "unheard" around the king. This larger reality that surrounds both the king and reader shows that the wizard is master of illusion only and is powerless to control time and natural decay. I contend that Morris put this subtle ironic voice into his important prefatory poem in order to begin to unhinge the reader's expectations of a victory over time.

We have seen how both poems offer entrancing visions of escape. Tennyson, though, is reluctant to dispense fully with the moral aesthetic. This reluctance is reflected in the pejorative connotations of sleep in "The Lotos-Eaters." The states of sleep and slumber unite with death by alliteration in this line: "Give us rest or death, dark death or dreamful ease." Also, the lotos-eaters speak with "thin" voices, as "voices from the grave." In *The Earthly Paradise,* on the other hand, the pejorative connotations of stasis that equate it with death occur more frequently and with a stronger, more explicit meaning as to the ultimate end of escapism. Suggestions of death associated with the land of stasis and calm can be found throughout the work. The following scene demonstrates the way Morris relates the stasis of the wanderers to the natural decay that surrounds them:

> But though, indeed, the outworn dwindled band
> Had no tears left for that once longed-for land,
> The very wind must moan for their decay.
>
> (v. 4, p. 255)

The aged story tellers are most commonly pictured in the evening when "in the west / The sky got ready for the great sun's rest," (v. 4, p. 186) or in the night as they watch "the dark night hide the gloomy earth" (v. 4, p. 186). The aged elders' presence in the youthful scenes foreshadows inevitable change:

> Round the old men the white porch-pillars stood,
> Gold-stained, as with the sun, streaked as with blood,
> Blood of the earth, at least, and to and fro
> Before them did the high-girt maidens go,
> Eager, bright-eyed, and careless of to-morn;
> And young men with them, nowise made forlorn
> By love and autumn-tide.
>
> (v. 5, p. 122-3)

The flowery symbols of growth around the elders, in the following scene suggest the floral tribute of a funeral:

> And now the watery April sun lit up
> Upon the fair board golden ewer and cup,
> And over the bright silken tapestry
> The fresh young boughs were gladdening every eye,
> And round the board old faces you might see
> Amidst the blossoms and their greenery.
>
> (v. 3, p. 170)

Finally, in the "Epilogue" to the poem Morris emphasizes death as the end of all: "They saw Death clear, and deemed all life accurst / By that cold overshadowing threat,—the End" (v. 6, p. 327).

The calm, peaceful exterior of both poems is thus in reality a mute submission to time. The pejorative connotations of death in "The Lotos-Eaters" lie buried in the alliteration, yet their force pervades the poem. In *The Earthly Paradise* death is more clearly present. It stalks almost every page, suggesting that not only is this poem *not* escapist, but that, in this instance at least, Morris is more the prophet of the moral aesthetic than Tennyson.

Morris, then, alienates the reader from escapist elements in the poem by showing that escapism ultimately leads to death. Also alienating is the way the reader's expectations of overt dramatic involvement in the poem are thwarted. As shown in my discussion of the **"Apology"**, there is good reason to expect other occasions for reader involvement in the poem: Morris iterates his concern that the reader "read aright." In fact, he usually provides for a proto-reader, who reflects the reader's experience, such as the king in the **"Apology."** The primary proto-reader throughout the poem, however, is Rolf, the captain of the wanderers who make the quest for the fountains of youth. Hence Rolf's development as proto-reader provides an illustration of how and why the escapist reader becomes disillusioned in *The Earthly Paradise.*

Rolf, the narrator and main character of the "Prologue," clearly exhibits many of the same responses to literature and life that are expected of the reader. We are implicitly invited to identify with Rolf and the "little band / Who bear such arms as guard the English land." It all began back in Norway where he, in his youth and innocence, was led by a Breton Squire to a belief in a mythical earthly paradise. Basing their hopes on the Squire's tales, Rolf, the little band of wanderers, the Breton Squire, and a Swabian Priest named Lawrence set off from their plague-ridden homeland in search of the land of immortality. Rolf's initial reaction to the tales parallels the reader's initial response to the poem:

> Yet [the Squire] spoke of gardens ever blossoming
> Across the western sea where none grew old,
> E'en as the books at Micklegarth had told,
> And said moreover that an English knight
> Had had the Earthly Paradise in sight,
> And heard the songs of those that dwelt therein,
> But entered not, being hindered by his sin.
> Shortly, so much of this and that he said
> That in my heart the sharp barb entered,
> And like real life would empty stories seem
> And life from day to day an empty dream.
>
> (v. 3, p. 7)

Further proof of Rolf's function as the proto-reader is contained in the last two lines of this passage which, recalling the **"Apology,"** suggest a parallel between the Breton Squire, as story-teller, and Morris.

After entering wholeheartedly into the hopes of the tales and rejecting plague-ridden Norway, Rolf's and the reader's expectations of immortality suffer an encounter with death. In the first land that the wanderers reach in their search for the fabled Earthly Paradise they find, not the fountains of youth, but death. They climb a mountain

> . . . in good hope soon to see
> Some signs of man, which happened presently;
> For two thirds up the hill we reached a space
> Leveled by man's hand in the mountain's face,
> And there a rude shrine stood, of unhewn stones
> Both walls and roof, with a great heap of bones
> Piled up outside it . . . therein could we see,
>
> . . . . .
>
> Against the wall men's bodies brown and dry,
> Which gaudy rags of raiment wretchedly
> Did wrap about. . . .
>
> (v. 3, p. 32)

Instead of a land of ever-blossoming life they find the land of the dead. This emphasis on decay, which reinforces the foreshadowings of decay associated with the elders in the "Prologue," is repeated in the next scene where the wanderers discover an aging king surrounded by the corpses of his vassals and left to die:

> We saw a group of well-wrought images,
> Or so they seemed at first, who stood around
> An old hoar man laid on the rocky ground
> Who seemed to live as yet; now drawing near
> We saw indeed what things these figures were;
> Dead corpses, by some deft embalmer dried,
> And on this mountain after they had died
> Set up like players at a yule-tide feast. . . .
>
> (v. 3, p. 33)

The reader and the wanderers begin to doubt the possibility of escaping death. Going back down the mountain Rolf remarks,

> . . . but we went by
> The chapel of the gold god silently,
> For doubts had risen in our hearts at last
> If yet the bitterness of death were past.
>
> (v. 3, p. 34)

The objective point of view from which the wanderers and the reader view these images of death changes in the course of the narrative to a subjective identification with death. The wanderers soon find themselves trapped and even worshiped as priests of dying:

> They brought us to the dais scarce alive,
> And changed our tattered robes again, and there
> Bound did we sit, each in his golden chair,
> Beholding many mummeries that they wrought

> About the altar; till at last they brought,
> Crowned with fair flowers, and clad in robes of gold,
> The folk that from the wood we won of old.
> Why make long words? Before our very eyes
> Our friends they slew, a fitting sacrifice
> To us their new-gained gods, who sought to find
> Within that land, a people just and kind,
> That could not die, or take away the breath
> From living men.
>
> (v. 3, p. 73)

The wanderers and the reader are again forced to question their original desire to escape time, to find immortality. This is reflected in the disillusionment of the proto-reader, Rolf: "What thing but that same death / Had we left now to hope for?" (v. 3, p. 73).

We remember that the quest for the fountains of youth was based on the tales told by the Breton Squire. After the first failure of that quest, Rolf was again led to hope that all was not lost, only to find himself trapped as above. At first it appeared that he was hoodwinked by a young man who claimed to be immortal. However, the true cause, as Morris shows, lay in Rolf's too innocent acceptance of the literal truth of myths and legends. Just before the young stranger arrived Rolf had been poring over "long stories from the priests." The stranger promised to lead him to the fountains of youth in a distant land and Rolf responded,

> The trap I saw not, . . . to the notes of years
> I turned, long parchments blotted with my tears, . . .
> Yet in the end it seemed that what he said
> Tallied with that, heaped up so painfully.
>
> (v. 3, pp. 62-3)

He goes on, "Thus easily I fell into the snare;" but we see by Morris' insistent reference to his naive response to tales that the real trap which caused his disillusionment, and the reader's, was the snare of escapist literature.

To strengthen the irony of his poem Morris focuses the reader's attention on this important emotional state of mental constraint and despair. The effect of their being trapped is expressed in terms of time. They are shown "hemmed in" by "an eternity of woe," as "The time went past, the dreary days went by / In dull unvarying round of misery / Nor can I tell if it went fast or slow" (v. 3, p. 73). They are trapped, as we have seen, in a temple, and worshiped as gods; yet on another level they are trapped by the awareness of the triumph of time. The feeling of static, hopeless frustration expressed in the above lines is another of the central ironies of the poem. We remember that as a young man in Norway Rolf was "half maddened by the lazy lapse of time" while he anticipated his quest for the fountains of youth. After he, and the reader, experience the two shocking scenes of death on the mountainside, their attitudes towards time are expanded. Rolf's description of this transition uses first the images of the two gates of life, birth and death:

> Two gates unto the road of life there are,
> And to the happy youth both seem afar;
> Both seem afar: so far the past one seems;
> The gate of birth, made dim with many dreams,
> Bright with remembered hopes, beset with flowers;
> So far it seems he cannot count the hours
> That to this midway path have led him on
> Where every joy of life now seemeth won—
>
> (v. 3, p. 59-60)

But more than merely commenting on Rolf's life, these lines reflect the experiences of the reader. The mention of dreams recalls the voice of the poet as a "dreamer of dreams" who led the reader into the world of escapism at the opening of the poem. In the next lines we see that with the passage of time the "happy youth" becomes aware of his mortality and his blindness to it in his earlier days:

> So far, he thinks not of the other gate,
> Within whose shade the ghosts of dead hopes wait
> To call upon him as he draws anear,
> Despoiled, alone, and dull with many a fear;
> "Where is thy work? how little thou hast done;
> Where are thy friends, why art thou so alone?"
>
> (v. 3, p. 60)

The poetic experience in these lines reflects both Rolf's and the reader's growing awareness of death. The attitude towards dreams shifts from dreams as escape to dreams as limited perspective, which typifies the ironic viewpoint of the whole poem.

In the final passage of Rolf's reflection, experience is seen through the image of a journey up a hill:

> How shall he weigh his life? slow goes the time
> The while the fresh dew-sprinkled hill we climb,
> Thinking of what shall be the other side;
> Slow pass perchance the minutes we abide
> On the gained summit, blinking at the sun;
> But when the downward journey is begun
> No more our feet may loiter; past our ears
> Shrieks the harsh wind scarce noted midst our fears,
> And battling with the hostile things we meet
> Till, ere we know it, our weak shrinking feet
> Have brought us to the end, and all is done.[10]
>
> (v. 3, p. 60)

This larger vision is a product of the ironic voice. Its presence in the description of Rolf's perception of his imminent downward journey is indicated, as in the **"Apology,"** by the "harsh wind." In the **"Apology"** we saw that the "murmuring rhyme" of the "idle singer of an empty day" beat with a light wing against the "ivory gate" of escapism. I suggest that in the passage where Rolf expresses his fears of death and his sorrow for the past, we see the "harsh wind" of the ironic voice beating against the "twin gates" of birth and death, symbols of the larger reality in the poem.

Thus we can see that **The Earthly Paradise** presents the reader with two visions of stasis: the stasis of art, associated with the escapist world of the elders and voiced through the persona of the "idle singer of an empty day"; and that of the ironic voice of the poem, introduced with the persona of the poet as wizard and the "harsh wind"—the stasis of consciousness through the painful struggle of the proto-reader, Rolf, with time: the constraint of the desires either to move forward or backward in time, as in the passage where Rolf expresses his fears for the future and regret for the lost past. By revealing that the stasis of art is a mute submission to death and by refusing to fulfill the reader's expectations of dramatic involvement, Morris alienates the reader from the world of art. By showing the elders as "resting in a dream" and emphasizing that "All was a picture in those later days" he underscores the idea that not only is this vision fatalistic, it is unreal.

The positive identification through the proto-reader shows that Morris wanted to orient his audience towards the larger vision of the stasis of consciousness. There is considerable evidence that Morris regarded this vision as the more realistic one. For example, we saw that the "Prologue" began with a direct address to the reader and that later in the poem Morris omitted this device in the scenes with the elders. This omission functions to strengthen the ironic reversal of the reader's expectations of escape into the world of immortality. The only direct addresses to the reader in the body of the poem are not in the scenes of calm and escape, but in the lyric poems which accompany each month and which portray the stasis of consciousness. For example ([italics] added): "Are *thine* eyes weary? is *thy* heart too sick . . . ?" ("November") or, "O *thou* who clingest still to life and love . . ." ("December"). Morris reinforces the realism of this vision through dramatic shifts of time in the lyric poems from the world of art in the mythic past to the real world of contemporary England. "Across the gap made by our English hinds" ("August") announces the poet's presence in the real world of both author and reader. Thus **The Earthly Paradise** exists on two levels of time: the real present of Victorian England, and the mythic past of art where the elders rest "in a dream." The central irony of the poem lies in the coexistence of these two temporal perspectives.

Morris' blending of reality and art, truth and beauty, in **The Earthly Paradise** and his constant injunctions to the reader to "read aright," along with the many examples in the poem of not reading aright, as in Rolf's naive acceptance of the literal truth of tales, suggests therefore that the poem needs to be seen as part of the tradition of didactic literature: the tradition represented by Spenser's "Bower of Blisse" episode in Book II of *The Faerie Queene.*[11] As well as similarities of technique, there are shared motifs in both poems. Both, for example, use the motif of the trap, or net, to reflect the intertwining of illusion and reality. They both envision their hero on a journey; the Breton Squire guides Rolf on his quest, and the Palmer guides Guyon, Spenser's hero in Book II. Finally, both portray, although in different ways, "blisse . . . turned to balefulness" (stanza 83). In Morris this can be seen in Rolf's enshrinement as a god of death and the reader's ultimately frustrated attempts to avert his eyes from "the heavy trouble and bewildering care" (**"Apology"**) of real life.

The following stanza by Spenser shows the merging of art with nature to entice the reader through his weakness for pure pleasure:

> One would have thought, (so cunningly, the rude
>   And scornèd parts were mingled with the fine,)
> That nature had for wantonesse ensude
> Art, and that Art at nature did repine;
> So striving each th' other to undermine,
> Each did the others worke more beautifie;
> So diff'ring both in willes, agreed in fine:
> So all agreed through sweete diversitie,
> This Gardin to adorne with all varietie.
>
> (stanza 59)

Comparably, *The Earthly Paradise* entices the reader into a world of escape through a mingling of art and reality. The following passage shows Morris' application of the Spenserian technique:

> The dull day long had faded into night
> Ere all was done; taper and red fire-light
> Cast on the wall's fair painted images
> Shadows confused of some, amidst of these,
> The old men on the dais. . . .
>
> (v. 6, p. 278)

By surrounding the elders with images of art Morris makes escapism more attractive, yet by blending the shadows of the elders with the pictures on the wall he shows that escape is artificial.

Morris adopts the same technique when he represents the effect of the deceptiveness of art on the proto-reader, Rolf. As he and the wanderers approached the tomb on the mountain-side in their first encounter with death, Rolf at first remarked that he saw "a group of well-wrought images" (v. 3, p. 33), yet as they drew closer they discovered "what these figures were; / Dead corpses, by some deft embalmer dried" (v. 3, p. 33). Thus Morris shows the reader through Rolf that behind the illusory beauty of the images of art is the death which Rolf discovers when he looks closer. By thus reversing Rolf's expectations Morris ironically denies

escape through art while at the same time he emphasizes the pit-falls resulting from a naive acceptance of art's literal truth.

Spenser and Morris are also similar in their desire to show the reader the consequences of seeing only the superficial level of art. Spenser does this in a rather negative way by obliterating art itself and revealing to the reader the righteous indignation of Guyon and the Palmer. We see Art personified in the "Enchauntress" Acrasia who is finally netted by the Palmer for her sinful, tempting wiles. Pursuing a like aim, Morris shows that the tempting stasis of art is a realm of death. Although the elders are not netted as Acrasia is in *The Faerie Queene*, Morris nets the elders, in a sense, by weaving their shadows amidst the images on the tapestry.

I would like to suggest that in this poem Morris went one step further than Spenser through his recourse to reader involvement. In creating Rolf he showed how through a lack of discrimination and by seeing only the promise of escape—the literal level of the tales—a person may be trapped and finally debilitated by the stasis of consciousness. And through Rolf in his function as proto-reader Morris trapped the reader who at first saw only the escapist elements of *The Earthly Paradise,* leaving him also in his own stasis of consciousness, his painful awareness of the triumph of time.

Notes

1. Oscar Maurer, "William Morris and the Poetry of Escape," *Nineteenth Century Studies,* ed. Herbert Davis, (Ithaca: Cornell University Press, 1940), 246-7.

2. Andrew Lang, *Adventures Among Books,* (London: Longman's, Green, and Co., 1905), 101-2; Alfred Noyes, *William Morris,* (London: G. P. Putnam's Sons, 1910), 106; Henry James, *Ten Victorian Poets,* (Boston: Ball Pub. Co., 1908), 73.

3. F. L. Lucas, *Ten Victorian Poets,* (Cambridge: Cambridge University Press, 1948), 144; Holbrook Jackson, *Dreamers of Dreams,* (London: Faber and Faber, 1948), 139; J. W. Mackail, *Studies of English Poets,* (London: Longman's, Green and Co., 1926), 195.

4. Some recent criticism is beginning to argue against the escapist thesis. Charlotte H. Oberg, arguing in *A Pagan Prophet* (Charlottesville: University Press of Virginia, 1978) a "primivist" theme, points out some of the ironies in the wanderer's regressive quest for a deathless land; Blue Calhoun, in *The Pastoral Vision of William Morris: The Earthly Paradise,* (Athens: Univ. of Georgia Press, 1975) contrasts the Prologue with an earlier version

called "The Wanderers," finding it conventionally romantic and the Prologue more ironic and ambiguous. Two articles, *The Earthly Paradise: Lost,*" by Carole G. Silver, and "The Crisis of *The Earthly Paradise:* Morris and Keats," by Elizabeth Strode, both in *Victorian Poetry,* vol. 13, Nos. 3 and 4, also argue that the poem is anti-escapist.

5. All quotations from *The Earthly Paradise* are from William Morris, *The Collected Works of William Morris,* May Morris, ed., (London: Messrs. Longman's, Green and Co.), 24 volumes.

6. Quotations from "The Lotos-Eaters" are from *The Poetry of Tennyson,* edited by Christopher Ricks.

7. "The Poetic Maturing of William Morris: From 'The Earthly Paradise' to 'The Pilgrims of Hope,'" *BRNO Studies in English,* 5 (1964), 15-16.

8. "The Mood of Energy and the Mood of Idleness: A Note on 'The Earthly Paradise,'" *English Studies in Africa,* 2, No. 2 (March, 1959) 93.

9. R. F. Fleissner, "*Percute Hic*: Morris's Terrestrial Paradise," *Victorian Poetry,* 3, No. 3 (Summer, 1965), 171.

10. A similar poetic situation can be found in other poems of the period, most notably, Dante Gabriel Rossetti's sonnet "Hill Summit," from *The House of Life.*

11. Quotations from *The Faerie Queene* are from *Edmund Spenser's Poetry,* Hugh Maclean, ed., (New York: W. W. Norton and Co., 1968), Book II, Canto xii, 175-195.

Josephine Koster Tarvers (essay date spring 1987)

SOURCE: Tarvers, Josephine Koster. "'The Deep Still Land of Colours': Color Imagery in *The Defence of Guenevere and Other Poems.*" *Studies in Philology* 84, no. 2 (spring 1987): 180-93.

[*In the following essay, Tarvers contends that Morris utilizes vivid color imagery in* The Defence of Guenevere and Other Poems *to manipulate "readers' emotional responses to the character and situations in his poetry."*]

From the beginning of the Pre-Raphaelite movement, bright and vivid color was a striking feature of the pictures produced by members of the Brotherhood. For example, artists such as Dante Gabriel Rossetti and William Holman Hunt, by the use of a white wet-ground[1] for their paintings, went against the prevalent French technique, so deplored by Ruskin,[2] of toning colors with grey, and created instead brighter, more intense effects.[3] Meanwhile, unlike their paintings, the poetry of the Pre-Raphaelites, while laden with exotic, sensuous details, can be better described as "studies in light and shade" than "works in colour."[4] Individual Pre-Raphaelite poems contain vivid color imagery, but the use of color as a literary device is not characteristic of their work as a whole.

The most notable exception to this generalization is the early poetry of William Morris. Probably because of his famous remark about his art—"Well, if this is poetry, it is very easy to write"[5]—it has become traditional to pay little attention to his literary craftsmanship. Many critics have noticed in passing the vividness of Morris' imagery,[6] but only a few have grasped the complexity which Morris created in his "deep still land of colours."[7] A careful examination of *The Defence of Guenevere and Other Poems* (1858), in which Morris' use of color is most frequent and intricate, shows how carefully he employs color as a means of manipulating readers' emotional responses to the characters and situations in his poetry.

A perceptive artist like Morris is bound to have been aware of the importance of color, and his writings, early and late, reflect his attention to the subject. In an 1855 letter to Cormell Price, Morris expressed his disappointment with some reproductions of a Fra Angelico painting: "the loss of colour makes of course a most enormous difference, where the colour is so utterly lovely as in the original."[8] His observations of other medieval art forms also reflect this interest: of stained glass he wrote, "Whatever key of colour may be chosen, the colour should always be bright, clear, and emphatic," and of thirteenth-century English manuscripts, "Nothing can exceed . . . the loveliness of the colour found at this period in the best-executed books."[9]

There are several reasons why a young poet, living in the artistic community of Oxford in the mid 1850's, might become interested in color. First, Goethe's early and admittedly unsystematic speculations about color and Greek color terms had led, in England, to a lively philological debate over color terms in the *Iliad* and *Odyssey.* This culminated in William Gladstone's 1858 book, *Studies in Homer and the Homeric Age,* which asserted that Homer had been color-blind.[10] In addition, Goethe's work had sparked a great deal of interest in France, especially in the artistic community. Works such as Frédéric Portal's *Des Couleurs Symboliques dans l'antiquité, le moyen âge et les temps moderns* (1837), and, in 1854, an English translation of Chevreul's *de la Loi du Contraste Simultané* (1839) became available, to the great interest of the English art world on whose fringes Morris resided.

Second, Oxford was also home to an interest in color on another front—the liturgical. The rise of the Tractarian Movement, in which Morris was interested,[11] had fostered research into church ceremonial and symbolism, and in particular into liturgical vestments. As a result, a great deal of research was done on the origins of the colors of vestments, particularly red, gold, green, and white, tracing the use of these colors through medieval manuscript citations and illustrations back to their biblical and patristic sources.[12] Finally, the great Victorian vogue for matters medieval had affected Morris ever since he was a boy,[13] and Mackail tells us that the student Morris spent hours in the Bodleian Library while at Oxford poring over manuscripts, both insular and continental, and that he studied Middle English poetry closely.[14] Here Morris could see instances of traditional, religious-based color symbolism employed by consummate artists such as Dante and Chaucer to give depth and texture to their poetry.[15] An examination of the colors most frequently used by Morris in *The Defence* volume shows that, using them in an emblematic manner much like that of his favorite medieval authors, he employs their full range of connotation to elicit various emotional responses in his readers.

In *The Defence* volume, gold and red are the most frequently mentioned colors. The traditional interpretations of the color gold associate it with spiritual union and revelation, and this is the meaning given to it by Dante in *Paradiso* XVII [Beatrice's smile] and XXI-XXII [the golden ladder] and, in ironic fashion, by Chaucer in *The Hous of Fame* 529-30 [the golden eagle].[16] Frédéric Portal in 1837 wrote of gold: "Les langues divines et sacrées désignaient par l'or et le jaune l'union de l'âme à Dieu, et par oposition l'adultère spirituel. Dans la langue profane, cet emblème matérialisé représente l'amour légitime et l'adultère charnel qui rompt les liens du mariage."[17] In *The Defence,* Morris employs all of these possible meanings. Chiefly, gold represents an advanced spiritual state—if not redemption, then at least achieving a higher state of the soul. Thus, when the dying Ozana le Cure Hardy in **"The Chapel in Lyoness"** lies within a golden screen, he is not only within the physical sanctuary of a church, which as Morris knew in medieval times was customarily surrounded by some sort of carved screen or parclose, but also within the embrace of spiritual union. For Ozana, "the sunlight slips . . . And night comes on apace" (ll. 10-12),[18] and he sees "With inward eye . . . the sun / Fade off the pillars one by one," and his "heart faints when the day is done" (ll. 21-23) until Galahad revives him with the dew of a rose. Then he is again bathed in golden light, signifying his elevation to higher spiritual status through Galahad's agency.

In the physical world of the poems, Morris focuses chiefly on the corruption of the golden state. In **"King Arthur's Tomb,"** Launcelot recalls that he and Guenevere used to sit in the sunlight "among the flowers, till night" (l. 25) when their love was in its initial, most Platonic state; but once their relationship has been physically consummated, they fall from these spiritual heights. Their meetings move indoors "ere the sun grew high" into a "cool green room" (ll. 85-86) as their emotional stability lessens and their spiritual level sinks. (Morris was no doubt aware that yellow had, in medieval terms, associations with avarice and deceit; Chaucer's pardoner has hair "yellow as wex" [*General Prologue* 675] and Avarice in *Piers Plowman* wears a "tawny" tabard in the version of that poem available in Morris' day.)[19]

Guenevere reflects her fallen spiritual state in **"King Arthur's Tomb"** when she recalls that in church, where one would expect her to sense the presence of the divine, "Launcelot's red-golden hair would play, / Instead of sunlight, on the painted wall" (ll. 306-07). The visual image conjures up not only the memory of the beloved's appearance, but also the substitution of the earthly for the divine. We become aware of her fallen spiritual state by the suggested comparison of her to the painting of the repentant Mary Magdalen. Like Mary's, Guenevere's eyes are "dimmed . . . scorch'd and red at sight of hell," and there is "no gold light" on her hair (ll. 315-16). The queen's golden hair, once emblematic of her beauty (l. 137), is now veiled in colorless white; divinity is no longer seen in her.

Yet, although neither Guenevere nor Launcelot in their fallen states are able to perceive it, Morris ensures that we remain aware of the possibility of their return to the golden spiritual state. The characters see the world only in terms of dust and greyness, but we are told repeatedly in **"King Arthur's Tomb"** that the sun still shines on this world; it makes "the Glastonbury gilded towers shine" (l. 10) and night lets "the sun flame over all" (l. 105). To Guenevere Launcelot appears to be a "black-bended shield / Sinister-wise across the fair gold ground" (ll. 368-69), but Morris reminds us by the presence of the sun that in Malory's story, both Launcelot and Guenevere join religious communities and die in a state of grace.

In the Froissart poems, by contrast with the Arthurian ones, the color gold is almost entirely absent. This is consistent with the apparent absence of spiritual values and elevation there. Only in the conclusion of **"Concerning Geoffray Teste Noire"** does Morris give gold its usual emblematic spiritual meaning, when the gilded hair on the effigies of the long-dead lovers replaces their once-golden hair and armor. On the other hand, the so-called "fantasy" poems which constitute the rest of the volume are rich in gold imagery, mainly associated with something that inspires men to nobler action. Ladies with golden hair inspire the knightly heroes of **"The Gilliflower of Gold," "The Little Tower,"** and **"A Good Knight in Prison."** Gold symbolizes the motivating love of the hero in **"Two Red Roses Across The Moon"**; it is used ironically in **"The Eve of**

Crecy," where Margaret, who wears "Gold on her head, and gold on her feet, / And gold where the hems of her kirtle meet, / And a golden girdle," becomes the ideal for which the doomed and impecunious banneret will give his life (ll. 1-3).

In the two fantasy poems where gold appears most often, Morris plays the various meanings of gold against each other to elicit ambivalent responses from us. In "Rapunzel" the heroine's golden hair drives Sebald to free her from her tower and rejuvenate his kingdom, but we are not permitted to forget that it has also been fouled by witches' rites. The witch's final curse (ll. 339-41) indicates that Guendolen's golden beauty is more dangerous than it seems. In "Golden Wings," Jehane du Castel beau casts a spell by using gold wings and gold hair to make her lover come back and restore her to full participation in the romantic world of Ladies' Gard. When he does not come back, she kills herself in the golden light of dawn, hoping to be reunited with him in death; the perversion of the divine golden state causes the total destruction of this charmed world. In both poems, gold seems not only appropriate to but also fatal to those who want it, and in both poems the association of the color with witchcraft and sorcery suggests its devaluation as a symbol of spirituality.

Gold is the color which indicates the spiritual state; red indicates the state of the heart. This follows the traditional interpretations of the color red, which associate it not only with love, fervor, holy zeal, and youth, but also with blood and martyrdom. Portal writes: "Le feu du sacrifice . . . est le symbole du feu céleste qui repose dans le coeur. . . . Ainsi le troisième attribut divin ou le Saint-Esprit, l'amour de Dieu, et le culte ont le même symbole, le feu, qui se traduit dans la langue des couleurs par le rouge."[20] Morris could have found many references to these symbolic meanings in his reading: young Hugh of Lincoln in Chaucer's *Prioress's Tale* 610 is "of martirdom the ruby bright;" and the martyrs Valerian and Cecile in the *Second Nun's Tale* 20ff. are given crowns of roses. Similarly, *caritas,* the virtue of love, is described in *Purgatorio* XXIX 122-23 as "l'una tanto rossa / ch'a pena fora dentro al foco nota," and the river of love in *Paradiso* XXX 66 gives off drops "quasi rubin che oro circonscrive."

Red, significantly, is the color Morris mentions most often in the four Arthurian poems. He uses many of its various shades and hues: not only red, but crimson, blood, rust, roan, scarlet, blush, and flame, to name a few. The color red is not in and of itself an unfavorable emblem, or necessarily the opposite of gold's spirituality. It is the color of love and lovers, whether earthly love like Guenevere's and Launcelot's, or divine, like that of Galahad for the deity in "Sir Galahad: A Christmas Mystery." Red can be the color of the physical "cheek of flame" ("Defence of Guenevere," l.

9); it can color the red robe of Launcelot "strange in the twilight with many unnamed colours" ("King Arthur's Tomb," ll. 46-47); or it can clothe God "With raiment half blood-red" and his angels in "white, without a stain, / And scarlet wings" ("Sir Galahad," ll. 88, 139-40). Appropriately, the angelic blazon adorning Galahad's surcoat is "white, with a red cross" ("Sir Galahad," stage direction after l. 152). This evokes not only the Cross of *Paradiso* XIV 66 ("ché con tanto lucore e tanto robbi") but also Spenser's Redcross Knight, reminding us that love can be holy as well as profane.

The redeeming power of love is also suggested in the red imagery in "The Chapel in Lyoness." Ozana, dying of love, cannot bleed, but lies under a "samite cloth of white and red" with a red rose across his face (ll. 7, 15-16). He is trapped between the mortal and divine worlds, paralyzed by fear of the profane nature of his love, and not until Galahad breaks the spell by placing "a faint wild rose" on his lips can Ozana see the divine nature of his love and die. It may also be significant that in the poem's last line Galahad sees a vision of Ozana and his lady "against the jasper sea," because jasper, which in classical times had signified a green stone, was by Morris' time used to refer to a number of stones red-gold in color.[21] If the sea has indeed turned red-gold (as it might at sunset), then what Galahad sees may be Ozana and his lady in the perfect fusion of love and spiritual grace—the very state longed for by the characters in many of these poems.

Red need not, therefore, necessarily impute any fault or moral flaw to the person with whom it is associated. But levels of love vary, and Morris carefully employs the different shades of red in the poems to direct our responses. We have already noted how Launcelot's "red-golden hair" has prevented Guenevere from seeing the light, either figuratively or literally. Likewise his shield in "King Arthur's Tomb" turns to "flame" (l. 260) as he fights for Guenevere's favor and honor. Launcelot's love, symbolized as a "great snake of green / That twisted on the quartered white and red" in Morris' original version of "The Defence," becomes increasingly passionate and transmuted into hotter flame.[22] The silver lilies to which "lily-like" Guenevere has been compared are transformed into "scarlet lilies" after she and Launcelot become lovers ("King Arthur's Tomb," ll. 57, 79). Her snow-white bedsheets, as she recalls, became sprinkled with blood as a result of the pair's intemperance ("Defence," ll. 173-178). Mary Magdalene's eyes are red because of her sins of passion ("King Arthur's Tomb," l. 315). And the queen uses vivid color images to remind her accuser, Gauwaine, of how passionate acts (including his murder of a maiden and conspiracy to commit matricide) have stained his life: "my eyes / Wept all away to grey, may bring some sword, / To drown you in your blood" ("Defence," ll. 224-26). Clearly the colors mentioned by the queen, whom Jonathan F. S. Post calls a "surrogate artist,"[23] are designed by Morris to express her passions and emotions; her recollections of her abduction are that Mellyagraunce's blood curdled at the thought of a duel with Launcelot, and that this duel—provoked by the bloodstains on her sheets—ended in "a spout of blood on the hot land" (**"Defence,"** ll. 187, 214). In fact, when her emotions are strongly moved, Guenevere's usual response is to turn red (**"Defence,"** ll. 9, 179, 293; **"King Arthur's tomb,"** l. 220). It is worth noting too that in Morris' one surviving oil painting, *Queen Guenevere,* the queen's sleeves and tunic embroidery are scarlet, and her bed is hung with a rich red undercover and red-embroidered draperies. Clearly the color and the character were connected in Morris' perception of her, and he uses these hues to direct our response to her.

Of course, the most famous and problematic association of red with Guenevere in the poems is her parable of the red and blue cloths (**"Defence,"** ll. 16-41). Most critics make the assumption that because the blue is simply "Heaven's colour" (and therefore that the red is Hell's, a far from traditional association), Guenevere's choice of the blue cloth brings her divine condemnation for her hypocrisy. Others associate the blue cloth with Launcelot, and argue that she is condemned for her infidelity. One recent critic has contended that her choice of the blue cloth proves Guenevere's infidelity to Arthur and that her marriage is a hell.[24] But Morris' constant association of red with Guenevere in these poems suggests yet another interpretation.

Both Guenevere and Launcelot, as shown above, are strongly linked with the color red in Morris' poems. Thus, the affirmative suggestions that the blue cloth represents Launcelot or that Guenevere's choice represents a defiant act of rebellion against a hellish marriage seem contradicted by the actual evidence of the poetry. Instead, Guenevere seems to be condemned for not being true to herself. Her instincts and emotions lead her to ally herself with red time and time again. Yet at this moment, possibly the most crucial time of her life, she attempts to make a rational choice, picking the color she thinks she ought to choose ("God help! heaven's colour, the blue") instead of the one all her instincts and emotions must pull her toward. Red signifies not only her guilty passion, but also the death of her marriage—a martyr's color. She laments "If only I had known!" but finds that knowledge cannot replace love. She is condemned for trying logically to decide an event that is predicated on chance. We cannot know what fate would have befallen her if she had chosen the red cloth, for after all her love is morally tainted, but we do know, as sympathetic readers, caught up by the strength of her emotions, and conditioned by Morris to associate her with red, that the choice of blue is a mistake.

In the Froissart poems, the associations of red with love and passion are also clear. In **"Sir Peter Harpdon's End,"** the besieged knight envisions his reunion with his lady, who "changes from pale to red"; subsequently, after Sir Peter's betrayal and murder, it is the Lady Alice who finds her dream of reunion with her lover "among the poppies" transformed into a nightmare of mice "all about my feet / Red shod and tired" (ll. 91, 538, 541-42). In **"Concerning Geoffray Teste Noir"** John of Castel Neuf is struck by the clarity of the red wine (ll. 58-59) and the red lion on the banners (l. 54) as he muses on the passion of dead lovers while waiting to ambush his enemy. In **"The Haystack in the Floods,"** Godmar's red pennon and flushed face are emblematic of his passion for Jehane. In all three poems red is an ominous color, reflecting both the intensity and the destructive power of passion.

The fantasy poems share this ambiguous red imagery. In most of them, red signifies dangerous and perhaps polluting passion: the witch's red cloak in **"Rapunzel"**; the blood-spouting heart as a device on an opponent's shield in **"The Gilliflower of Gold"**; the bloodied lover's corpse in **"The Wind"**; Ellayne's golden girdle, held together only by red silk after her ravishment by the red-pennant-bearing Robert in **"Welland River"**; the "tatter'd scarlet banners" of **"Near Avalon."** The strangest of all these red images is that of the mysterious red lily in **"The Blue Closet,"** which appears when Arthur, possibly having been strangled with a scarlet scarf, returns from the otherworld to reclaim Queen Louise in a curious perversion of the Orpheus myth. There are favorable red images as well—the red hair of Mary in **"A Good Knight in Prison"**; the red roof and ripe apples of **"Golden Wings"**; the war cry in **"Two Red Roses Across The Moon"**—but these have neither the power nor the haunting evocativeness of their ominous counterparts.

In Morris' early romances, green has its traditional associations with growth, hope, trust, and life; but in *The Defence* volume, its function is largely ironic, associated with destroyed hope, broken faith, and betrayal, as Morris once more exploits the range of symbolic connotations associated with the color. Again, according to Portal: "Le vert, comme les autres couleurs, eut une signification néfaste; si elle était le symbole de la régénération de l'âme et de la sagesse, elle signifia, par opposition, la dégradation morale et la folie. . . . Dans la langue sacrée, le vert était le symbole de l'espérance dans l'immortalité; dans la langue populaire, le vert était la couleur de l'esperance dans ce monde."[25]

Here again, Morris manipulates a wide range of traditional meanings to control the reader's response to his poems. The "green hope" of Guenevere's love for Arthur is only a memory, as is her fidelity to him (**"Defence,"** l. 255). In the heat of her passion, she betrays her husband in a "cool green room" of his castle ("**King Arthur's Tomb**," l. 86); and the once-golden stars and moon (which, curiously, is described as a star the queen has shed along with her divine status) grow pale against the green sky. But green, Morris reminds us, can represent more than ironic fidelity, for the four virgin martyrs in "**Sir Galahad**" are dressed "in gowns of green and red" (stage directions following l. 152, a close echo of Dante's first vision of Beatrice in *Purgatorio* XXX 32-33, "sotto verde manto / vestita di color di fiamma viva"), reflecting both their hope that Galahad will achieve the Grail and ascend to their spiritual level, and their roles as his spiritual lady-loves. And the jasper sea at the end of "**The Chapel in Lyoness**" may represent the green and eternal spiritual hope of men for redemption as well as a fusion of earthly and divine love.

This fluctuation between straightforward and ironic use of green is also found throughout the Froissart and fantasy poems. Sebald in "**Rapunzel**" wears green; faithful Alicia in "**The Sailing of the Sword**" carries a holly branch; the damozels in "**The Blue Closet**" wear purple and green gowns; the friends in "**Riding Together**" pass along a "green-banked stream"—all symbolizing fidelity. In some cases Morris deliberately makes us see double meanings: the green grass in "**Rapunzel**" is the setting where lovers pledge undying love, but also where brother kills brother; in "**The Little Tower**" the doomed retainers wear green; the tomb for the slain lovers in "**Concerning Geoffray Teste Noire**" is "in a green nook pure"; and fair Ellayne in "**Welland River**" is both "pale and green"—not only because of her fidelity to Robert, but also because, pregnant outside of wedlock, she is suffering from morning sickness. In some cases the color seems to evoke almost entirely unfavorable responses: the green-surrounded, moss-covered castle of lovers in "**Golden Wings**" degenerates into a world of sour green apples and green weeds; and the weird green banners decorating the barge in "**Near Avalon**" bear Guenevere's portrait on the sails. These mixed images and the mixed associations they evoke seem to reinforce Morris' theme of the impossibility of fidelity in the mundane world.

White is the most problematic color in the poems, for it seems to have several meanings. Portal sums it up succinctly: "Le couleur blanche devait être le symbole de la verité absolue, de celui qui est; elle seule réfléchit tous les rayons lumineux; elle est l'unité . . . [des] mille nuances qui colorent la nature."[26] In Morris' poems, it represents not only traditional purity and innocence, both real and ironic, but also intensity; and while the degrees of these states vary, the interpretation does not. Everything in the poems that is white is starkly, vividly, and connotatively white. In some cases Morris gives the color its traditional association with the purity of faith, as Chaucer used it with "the White

Lamb Celestial" of the *Prioress' Tale* 581 and Dante for the Mystic Rose of *Paradiso* XXXI 1. For example, there is the purity of the deity and of the angels' clothing ("**Sir Galahad**," ll. 88, 139); and the purity of Galahad's white hand ("**King Arthur's Tomb**," l. 331). There is the purity of passion, such as Palomydes growing pale for love of Iseult ("**Sir Galahad**," l. 29) or Guenevere's growing "white with flame" for Launcelot ("**Defence**," l. 70). There is the natural purity of the world, reflected in the snow-covered roofs of winter ("**Defence**," ll. 66-67) and the snow outside the chapel door in "**Sir Galahad**." There is the supposed purity of "lily-like Guenevere" ("**King Arthur's tomb**," l. 57) and the intensity of Launcelot's recognition of their sin and her repudiation ("**King Arthur's Tomb**," l. 362). Finally there is the pure and intense terror which strikes both Mellyagraunce ("**Defence**," l. 186) and the guilty lovers ("**Defence**," ll. 226, 269, 276).

The other poems in the volume share this interpretation. We see it in Roger's vision of pale Ellen in "**The Judgment of God**," the pure beauty of the ladies in "**A Good Knight in Prison**" and "**In Praise of My Lady**," the frigidly pure ladies whom Lord Roland exchanges in "**The Sailing of the Sword**," and the moonlight and white ghosts of "**The Tune of Seven Towers**." It seems clear that Morris uses white as an intensifying color, to bring out more sharply or more strangely his other effects, as well as for its symbolic value.

Of the half-dozen or so other colors mentioned in *The Defence* volume, the most significant seems to be grey. Again Portal's remark is particularly appropriate to Morris' poetry: "Je trouve encore un vestige de la symbolique des couleurs dans le mot *gris* pris dans le sens d'une demi-ivresse; la raison et la sagesse étaient représentées par le blanc, comme les passions honteuses par le noir."[27] In the first two poems, "**The Defence**" and "**King Arthur's Tomb**," it is clearly a replacement color, appearing when all other colors are exhausted. Guenevere's eyes have been leached of all other color by her tears; thus the eyes she turns on Sir Gauwaine are "wept all away to grey." The roan charger which once brought Launcelot to Guenevere's rescue ("**Defence**," l. 294) is replaced in "**King Arthur's Tomb**" by a "lone grey horse . . . on the grey road" (ll. 99-101). For both lovers, the red images are no longer vital but memories. It seems for a while that, no longer ruled by either their reason or their passions, they have no emotions left. But in fact, previous feelings have been replaced by a new emotion—guilt. In Guenevere's case "the grey downs bare / Grew into lumps of sin" ("**King Arthur's Tomb**," ll. 139-40) as she realizes the enormity of her passion's consequences. Launcelot is so overwhelmed by events that he collapses on the grey stone of "a tomb / Not knowing it was Arthur's" ("**King Arthur's Tomb**," ll. 125-26). There is no longer heat, or the color which connotes it;

there are only the cold grey downs for Guenevere and the cold grey stones for Launcelot. These are the only objects they can still perceive. Grey here does not seem to have its symbolic connotation of repentance, although Lancelot as he sits on the tomb may echo the Angel of Penance on the steps of Purgatory (*Purgatorio* IX 115-16): "Cenere, o terra che secca si cavi, / d'un color fora col suo vestimento."

Grey in the other poems seems to signify a similar absence of spiritual or emotional sensibility. Arthur in **"The Blue Closet"** and Robert in **"The Haystack in the Floods"** are incapable of using their "grey lips" to kiss their lovers; Oliver's lady in **"The Tune of Seven Towers"** dispatches her doomed suitor to a grey castle which reminds her of a row of grey tombstones (l. 39); and there are frequent references to grey light, grey rain, and grey night—to a world devoid of life and beauty—in situations of futility, despair, and certain death. The color grey in Morris' poems is the negative antithesis of his other symbolizing shades; he uses it when aspiration, passion, fidelity, and purity are no longer possible.[28]

To assume that Morris' intention was to use colors as symbols systematically in these poems would be fallacious. Like the other Pre-Raphaelite poets, he was not as much concerned with painting symbolic pictures as with creating vivid, compelling images. But his use of conventional color imagery and its associated values to direct response to the poems, very probably influenced by his reading and the temper of his surroundings at the time the poems were written, seems too careful and consistent to be merely casual, notwithstanding his remarks about the composition of poetry. The visual quality of his early poems, which makes them stand out from the body of Pre-Raphaelite verse, was the product of a characteristically calculated effort of design. Like Keats' descriptions in "The Eve of Saint Agnes" and Tennyson's careful use of red and white flowers to add depth to the portraits in *Maud*, Morris' exploitation of the traditional range of color imagery adds texture and vitality to his poems, both in this volume and throughout his work. He strives for—and often achieves—what he called in an 1891 lecture one of the most important qualities of Pre-Raphaelite art: "definite, harmonious, conscious beauty."[29]

Notes

1. Timothy Hilton, *The PreRaphaelites* (1970; NY: Praeger, 1974), 56, has a clear discussion of Pre-Raphaelite technique; see also Richard D. Buck, "A Note on the Methods and Materials of the Pre-Raphaelite Painters," in *Paintings and Drawings of the Pre-Raphaelites and their Circle* (Cambridge, MA: Fogg Museum of Art, Harvard University, 1946).

2. John Ruskin, *Academy Notes, 1858,* in *The Works of John Ruskin,* ed. E. T. Cook and Alexander Wedderburn (London: George Allen, 1904), 14: 178. There is no good modern study of Victorian color psychology or color theory, although there are many studies of the technique of individual artists. Alice Edwards Pratt gives a useful statistical and lexical survey of color references in English literature from Chaucer to Keats in *The Use of Color in the Verse of the English Romantic Poets* (Chicago: University of Chicago Press, 1898), but much work remains to be done with color in the works of the Victorians and their predecessors from a critical point of view.

3. Any collection of color reproductions of Pre-Raphaelite paintings will illustrate this point. Perhaps the classic example of color functioning as an element of meaning is found in Rossetti's *Ecce Ancilla Domini* (1849-50), in which the whiteness of the painting is relieved only by the blue drape behind the Virgin and the embroidered red stole in front of her.

4. John Ruskin, *Pre-Raphaelitism,* in *Works,* 12, 366.

5. J. W. Mackail, *The Life of William Morris* (1899; rpt. London: Longmans, Green, 1911), I, 52.

6. See, for example, the essays by William E. Fredeman and Dennis R. Balch in the special Morris double number of *Victorian Poetry,* 13, iii-iv (1975): xix-xxx and 61-70; and Jonathan F. S. Post, "Guenevere's Critical Performance," *Victorian Poetry* 17 (1979): 317-327.

7. See, for example, passing mention of the subject in Margaret A. Lourie, "The Embodiment of Dreams: William Morris' 'Blue Closet' Group," *Victorian Poetry* 15 (1977): 193-206; Wendell Stacy Johnson, "Style in Ruskin and Ruskin on Style," *Victorian Newsletter* 59 (Spring 1981): 1-6, esp. n. 6; Carole Silver, *The Romance of William Morris* (Athens, OH: Ohio University Press, 1982), xii, 13, 18, 21, 25, 33, etc.; and Robert Keane, "Rossetti and Morris: 'This Ever-Diverse Pair,'" in Carole Silver, ed., *The Golden Chain* (NY: The William Morris Society, 1982), 115-48.

8. Norman Kelvin, ed., *The Collected Letters of William Morris,* I (Princeton: Princeton University Press, 1984), 14. Morris' letters to his business associates are full of references to color; cf. especially his letters to Thomas Wardle and Catherine Holiday about the colors of dyes and tapestry materials.

9. May Morris, ed., *William Morris: Artist, Writer, Socialist* (Oxford: Basil Blackwell, 1936), I, 359, 341.

10. William E. Gladstone, *Studies in Homer and the Homeric Age* (Oxford: Oxford University Press, 1858), III, 457 ff.

11. See Mackail, I, 38 ff. Raymond Chapman, *Faith and Revolt: Studies in the Literary Influence of the Oxford Movement* (London: Weidenfeld and Nicolson, 1970), presents (Chapter 9 passim.) a thorough account of Morris' involvement with Tractarianism and the Broad Church Movement.

12. Some forty years of liturgical controversy over color are summarized in E. C. G. F. Atchley, "On English Liturgical Colours," *Essays on Ceremonial, The Library of Liturgiology and Ecclesiology for English Readers,* 4 (1904), 89-176.

13. Mackail, I, Chapter 1 passim.

14. Mackail, I, 38-39, 61, 81.

15. Keane (op. cit.) would have us believe (e.g. p. 128) that the symbolism in *The Defence* volume is largely a product of Rossetti's influence. While this is a possibility, Morris was certainly exposed to color symbolism elsewhere and used it in works written before his association with Rossetti had begun.

16. Citations from Dante are to *The Divine Comedy* in 3 vols., edited by Charles S. Singleton, Bollingen Series XXX (Princeton: Princeton University Press, 1970, 1973, 1975); citations from Chaucer are to F. N. Robinson, ed., *The Works of Geoffrey Chaucer,* 2nd ed. (London: Oxford University Press, 1957). Hereafter references to Dante will be made by section, canto and line number in the text; references to Chaucer will be made by title and line number in the text.

17. Frédéric Portal, *Des Couleurs Symboliques dans l'Antiquité, le Moyen-Age et les Temps Modernes* (1837; Paris: Editions Niclaus, 1938), 56.

18. All citations from Morris' poetry will be taken from *The Defence of Guenevere and Other Poems,* ed. Margaret A. Lourie (NY: Garland, 1981) and will be cited by title and line number in the text.

19. The version of *Piers Plowman* available in Morris's time, edited by Thomas Wright and published in 1842, reads "tawny" for B V 195. Although this reading is supported by 9 manuscripts of the poem (George Kane and E. Talbot Donaldson, eds., *Piers Plowman: The B Version* [London: Athlone, 1975]), it is actually a scribal variant of the heraldic color "tenné," orange brown (cp. *OED* 'tenné, tenny,' a., sb.). Whether Morris' knowledge of heraldry at this time would have allowed him to distinguish between the terms is not certain. I am indebted to Professor Kane for pointing out this distinction.

20. Portal, 73.

21. *OED* s. v. *jasper,* sb. 1. b.

22. Printed as an Appendix in the Lourie edition, 257-58.

23. Post, 321.

24. Criticism of this episode is neatly summarized in the Balch article cited above, 61-62.

25. Portal, 132-33.

26. Portal, 23.

27. Portal, 178.

28. Silver, *Romance* (p. 66), notes the increased use of grey as a counterpoint to other color references in *The Earthly Paradise,* in most cases agreeing generally with the interpretation presented here.

29. "Address on the Collections of Paintings of the English Pre-Raphaelite School in the City of Birmingham Museum and Art Gallery, on Friday, October 24, 1891," in May, *Morris,* I, 302.

David Latham (essay date fall 1987)

SOURCE: Latham, David. "Paradise Lost: Morris's Rewriting of *The Earthly Paradise*." *The Journal of Pre-Raphaelite and Aesthetic Studies* 1, no. 1 (fall 1987): 67-75.

[*In the following essay, Latham analyzes Morris's omissions and revisions to* The Earthly Paradise *and establishes a chronology for the composition of the poem.*]

> We know that the faculty for speed in his writing allowed Morris to indulge to the full his practice of rewriting, casting aside beginnings that did not work out to his liking. Here is evidence of it in concrete form, in the mass of *Earthly Paradise* MS.—a collection so important, so unique as showing a poet at work at his craft that one can but hope that, unluckily scattered as it now is, it will find its way in time to the British Museum for the benefit of students.[1]

So hoped May Morris in 1936, but the manuscripts of the longest poem in English remain scattered around the world. Having tracked down this scattered mass, I wish here to focus on those sections which William Morris chose to omit from *The Earthly Paradise.* First, I attempt to establish the chronology of their composition according to watermarks, numbered notebooks, advertisements for forthcoming tales, and contemporary correspondence. Second, I discuss examples of revisions that demonstrate his careful craftsmanship. Third, I conclude that the poem is a demonstration of those aesthetic principles practised by Morris to define the purpose of art and its relations to society.

Between 1860 and 1870, William Morris considered at least twelve tales for *The Earthly Paradise* in addition to the twenty-four that he eventually published. Three important lists of the tales exist that help determine the chronology in which the tales were written and the order in which Morris intended to present them. The first list is one printed by May Morris from the notebooks numbered by her father:

1. The Prologue.
2. Prologue, continued.
   Cupid and Psyche.
3. Cupid and Psyche, concluded.
   The Lady of the Land.
   The Palace East of the Sun.
   The Story of Adrastus.
   The Doom of Acrisius.
4. The Doom of Acrisius, continued.
   The Proud King.
5. The Proud King, concluded.
   The Watching of the Falcon.
   The Hill of Venus.
6. Hill of Venus, concluded.
   Writing on the Image.
   The Story of Dorothea.
   The Deeds of Jason.[2]

All but the second and fifth notebooks have been lost or perhaps fragmented. The second notebook, containing much of the rejected Prologue, is in the British Library and is on paper watermarked with an 1859 date.[3] The fifth notebook, also in the British Library, is an account book on unwatermarked paper (Add. MS. 45306). May Morris correctly identifies its date as 1861: "The first draft of '**The Watching of the Falcon**' is written in a little kind of notebook of work for the Firm, which begins with the date January 1861. 'The Proud King' is also here" (*AWS* [*William Morris: Artist, Writer, Socialist*] 1: 392).

Two tales from this list were not included in *The Earthly Paradise*. They are "**The Story of Dorothea**" and "**The Deeds of Jason**." ("**The Story of Adrastus**" was renamed "**The Son of Croesus**" in *The Earthly Paradise*.) Of the two known copies of "**The Story of Dorothea**," one is an amanuensis's copy (in the British Library) of the other. This other is a draft which K. L. Goodwin describes as "a lightly corrected holograph in The Fitzwilliam Museum, Cambridge, obviously posterior to a lost draft."[4] This draft may be the copy from the sixth notebook or it may be a transcription of it. If the former, then it has been separated from "**The Deeds of Jason**" and the other tales in the notebook. The draft ends with the note: "Death of Sidero by." As Charles Fairfax Murray (who had owned this manuscript) notes: "On the last leaf the mention of 'The Death of Sidero' shows that this story was followed in the Ms. book by '**The Deed** [sic] **of Jason**.'"[5] This note suggests indeed that the Fitzwilliam draft was removed from the sixth notebook.

But the draft for "**Dorothea**" could not have been written before the date on the paper, "Joyson 1864." While such watermark dates can only determine the earliest date for which a manuscript was composed, those on Morris's manuscripts may be more useful. In virtually all of his holographs for which the date of composition is known, the date of the watermark is within one year of the composition date. "**The Man Who Never Laughed Again**," a tale written after "**Dorothea**," is written on paper watermarked "W Stradling 1863" (BL Add. MS. 45303); therefore, it was probably written in 1863 or 1864. An exception to this pattern is *The Sundering Flood*, which Morris was writing in 1896 but which is on paper watermarked "Cansell 1890" and "Cansell 1891" (45326). While it cannot be denied that other exceptions may be among the unverifiable manuscripts, it is unlikely that the sixth notebook would be composed in 1864 or later, at least three years after the date recorded in the fifth notebook: "Jan: 1861." More likely, the 1864 watermarked draft of "**Dorothea**" is a transcription of an earlier draft in the sixth notebook. "**The Deeds of Jason**," which ended the sixth notebook, is the tale that grew so disproportionately longer than the other tales that Morris published it separately as *The Life and Death of Jason* (1867).

During the three-year period between the publication of *The Life and Death of Jason* and the final volume of *The Earthly Paradise*, Morris included in his announcements of forthcoming contents of *The Earthly Paradise* nine tales that he never published. The first list of tales was announced in 1867 at the end of *Jason*, while the second list was announced in 1868 at the end of the first volume of *The Earthly Paradise*. The 1867 list reveals little about the intended order for the tales, since it curiously cites the twelve Classical tales first, followed by the twelve Gothic tales. I have numbered the tales which were never included in the poem:

Prologue. The Wanderers; or the Search for Eternal Youth.
1. The Story of Theseus.
   The Son of Croesus.
   The Story of Cupid and Psyche.
2. The King's Treasure-House.
3. The Story of Orpheus and Eurydice.
   The Story of Pygmalion.
   Atalanta's Race.
   The Doom of King Acrisius.
   The Story of Rhodope.
4. The Dolphins and the Lovers.
5. The Fortunes of Gyges.
   The Story of Bellerophon.
   The Watching of the Falcon.
   The Lady of the Land.
   The Hill of Venus.
6. The Seven Sleepers.
   The Man who never Laughed again.
   The Palace East of the Sun.
7. The Queen of the North.
8. The Story of Dorothea.

The Writing on the Image.
The Proud King.
The Ring given to Venus.
The Man Born to be King.
Epilogue.

The 1868 list does suggest the order Morris was considering for the tales since it alternates the twelve remaining tales in pairs, each Classical tale followed by a Gothic one. A ninth tale that never was published is added to the list:

The Story of Theseus.
The Hill of Venus.
The Story of Orpheus and Eurydice.
The Story of Dorothea.
The Fortunes of Gyges.
The Palace East of the Sun.
The Dolphins & the Lovers.
The Man who never Laughed again.
The Story of Rodope.
9. Amys and Amillion.
The Story of Bellerophon.
The Ring given to Venus.
The Epilogue to the Earthly Paradise.

May Morris quotes Edmund Gosse remembering Morris reading "in his full, slightly monotonous voice a long story of Amis and Amyllion (I think those were the names) which has never, to my knowledge, appeared in print" (*CW* [*Collected Works*] 3: xiii). If Gosse was not thinking of Morris's prose translation of "The Friendship of Amis and Amile" published in his *Old French Romances*,[6] then this tale along with three of the following five listed by May have been lost: "For one reason or another quite a number of [these titles] were discarded, though five of them were written. These are **'The King's Treasure-House,' 'The Story of Orpheus,' 'The Dolphins and the Lovers,' 'The Fortunes of Gyges,' 'The Story of Dorothea'"** (*CW* 3: xiii). While May Morris had only Gosse's word that "Amis and Amyllion" was ever written, we have only May's and Mackail's that **"The King's Treasure-House," "The Dolphins and the Lovers,"** and **"The Fortunes of Gyges"** were.[7] She speculates that the draft and fair copy of the fragment **"In Arthur's House"** may be the tale first entitled **"The Queen of the North"**: "The fragment beginning 'In Arthur's house whileome was I,' though the subject suggests the earlier conceived Arthurian poems, is of a rather later period, and may be one of the projected stories for *The Earthly Paradise*. I please myself by imagining that it is the beginning of that tale on the list which is called **'The Queen of the North,'** but this we shall never know" (*CW* 24: xxxi). The draft of the poem is written on paper watermarked "E. Towgood 1872" (45308). Thus, the poem was not written until at least two years after the publication of the final volume of *The Earthly Paradise*.

Two additional tales that were written for *The Earthly Paradise* are **"The Wooing of Swanhild"** and **"The Story of Aristomenes."** Neither was completed, but the manuscripts for both are in the British Library (45308). This brings the total number of titles considered for the longest poem in the English language to thirty-six. Of the twelve that were not included in the poem, four are known to have existing manuscripts: **"The Story of Dorothea," "The Story of Orpheus and Eurydice," "The Wooing of Swanhild,"** and **"The Story of Aristomenes."** To these four tales should be added the original Prologue whose title, May Morris says, was emended from **"The Fools' Paradise,"** to **"The Wanderers,"** and finally to **"The Terrestrial Paradise"** (*CW* 3: xiii).

May Morris identified four versions of the rejected Prologue, all of which are now lost. One is a complete draft in quatrains entitled The Fool's Paradise /The Wanderers/. Then she mentions "a few verses of two other beginnings in the same measure." The fourth version is the beginning of a fair copy: "In the ten pages of the fair copy the title is **'The Terrestrial Paradise.'"**[8] When she edited the rejected Prologue for the last volume of the *Collected Works,* she chose the complete draft for her copy-text, which includes Morris's marginal notes to Burne-Jones: "An added charm to the manuscript itself moreover are the little side-notes every here and there of the drawings he wanted Burne-Jones to make for the story" (*CW* 24: xxix). In her introduction to the Prologue she includes quotations from the ten pages of the fair copy of **"The Terrestrial Paradise"** that reveal variants with the text of the rejected **"Wanderers."** These variants occur in the Argument, in the designated speakers (The People of the City and the People of the Ship), and in the punctuation.

May Morris curiously neglects to mention a fifth manuscript of the rejected Prologue, the one included in the first and second notebooks of her list. The only manuscript known now to be extant appears to be this second notebook, beginning more than a third of the way into the poem and ending with stanzas from **"Cupid and Psyche."**[9] But this manuscript has no "side-notes" for illustrations and has many variants from the complete draft that May edited. Her complete draft is listed in a bookseller's catalogue issued in 1929 by Maggs Bros.[10] The draft is described as "The Original Manuscript of the First Prologue entirely in the Autograph of the Poet, and written on 135 pp." Unfortunately, this manuscript remains lost. From the collection of Charles Fairfax Murray, it included Murray's note on the fly-leaf: "This MS., the first draft of the 'Prologue,' is referred to in Mackails [sic] Life of Wm. Morris, Vol. I., p. 188. It is entirely unpublished & was written two years earlier than the poem which replaced it." If Murray and Mackail are accurate, then this version of the Prologue was written in 1865, since "in the summer of 1867 he is reading the new Prologue to his friends by the side of one of the beautiful reaches of the river above Oxford" (*CW,* III, xv). But the earlier draft, the only one now known to be extant is watermarked "1859" and was probably written between 1860 and 1861, not long before he began the other four notebooks that occupied him in 1861.

The Prologue and **"The Story of Dorothea"** belong to the same early period of composition, the Prologue being written off and on from 1860 to 1865 and **"Dorothea"** from 1861 to 1864 or '65. K. L. Goodwin notes that Burne-Jones designed a cartoon for an embroidery of Saints Cecilia and Dorothea in 1861. The figure of Dorothea is modelled after Jane Morris and the ground is decorated with a pattern of flower trios similar to Morris's first wallpaper, "Daisy," designed in 1862 (Goodwin 92).

The other three tales—**"The Story of Orpheus and Eurydice," "The Wooing of Swanhild,"** and **"The Story of Aristomenes"**—belong together, but to a later period. Mackail mistakenly states that the Orpheus and Aristomenes tales "were written in 1866" (1: 182). **"The Story of Orpheus and Eurydice"** could not have been written before 1869. Its four drafts are written on a mixture of folios watermarked "E Towgood 1868" or "J. Allen & Sons Superfine 1869" (45307, 45308). As the 1869 watermark is on some of the six folios of a draft which he abandoned as a false beginning, no drafts of the poem in its present form were even considered before 1869. **"The Story of Aristomenes"** was written in the Spring and Summer of 1870. Most of its folios were watermarked "J. Allen & Sons Superfine 1870." The untitled first folio of the earliest draft in the British Library is dated by Morris in the top right corner: "Begun June 25th" (45308). The watermark proves it was written no earlier than June 25, 1870 and a letter dated 8 September 1870 from Dante Gabriel Rossetti to William Bell Scott proves that Morris had abandoned the poem by September:

> Morris wrote a long poem about Aristomenes and the Revolution of the Messenians against Sparta, but it got longer and longer till at last he couldn't get it into the EP at all & had to give it up. He had already made a mull after much work (or he thought it one) of the Orpheus story; & now in despair has written a rather short one about Hercules to fill the last empty classical gap. I haven't heard the Hercules yet. The Aristomenes was very fine especially in the fighting parts.[11]

The earliest surviving draft is on six folios from an oblong notebook which includes a draft of "A Prologue in Verse" for Morris's prose translation of *The Story of the Volsungs and Niblungs.*[12] As the prologue was written after mid-March when the translation was completed,[13] and the whole work was published in May 1870 (Mackail 1: 208), the Aristomenes fragments were probably written in early Spring.

The earliest surviving draft of **"The Wooing of Swanhild"** is on paper watermarked "E Towgood 1868,"

while the fair copy is on unwatermarked paper (45308). As the tale is "taken from the last chapters of the Volsunga Saga," it may have been composed in the Spring of 1870. But I believe the incomplete tale was written before the Volsunga translation for the following reason. Morris began studying and translating the Icelandic sagas with Eirikr Magnusson in the Autumn of 1868. By January 1869 the two men had published *The Saga of Gunnlaug Worm-Tongue* in the *Fortnightly Review.* By June the two had published *The Story of Grettir the Strong* (*AWS* 2: 633). Mackail states that Morris began **"The Lovers of Gudrun,"** the first Icelandic tale for *The Earthly Paradise,* in April after the Grettir Saga was completed and that he had finished **"Gudrun"** by June.[14] Another Icelandic tale, **"The Fostering of Aslaug,"** written on paper watermarked "J. Allen & Sons Superfine 1869," belongs to this same period. **"The Wooing of Swanhild"** appears to be the third tale from these Icelandic sagas featuring Gudrun and Sigurd. While the source for the completed **"Fostering of Aslaug"** is second-hand, through Thorpe's *Northern Mythology,* Morris went directly to the *Volsunga Saga* for the source of the unfinished **"Wooing of Swanhild."** But his dissatisfaction with his own version may have led him back to translating the Icelandic source to ingrain himself with the spirit of the original saga. If this supposition is correct, then **"The Wooing of Swanhild"** was composed towards the end of 1869. Morris would appear to have practised his translating from Autumn 1868 to Spring 1869, turned to composing three of his own versions for *The Earthly Paradise* through the remainder of 1869, and then returned to translating in 1870.

We can now attempt to establish the chronology of these five extant texts. While Rossetti's letter to Scott indicates that **"Orpheus"** was written before **"Aristomenes,"** there is no conclusive evidence to prove that **"Orpheus"** was written before **"Swanhild."** But the advertisements for forthcoming tales indicate that **"Orpheus"** was considered for *The Earthly Paradise* as early as 1867. Thus, the chronology follows this order, one which reverses the published poem's Classical/ Gothic pairings to Gothic/Classical pairings:

The First Prologue	1860-65
The Story of Dorothea	1861-65
The Story of Orpheus and Eurydice	1869-70
The Wooing of Swanhild	1869-70
The Story of Aristomenes	1870

May Morris identifies the manuscripts for *The Earthly Paradise* as "a collection so important, so unique as showing a poet at work at his craft" (*AWS* 1: 402). Entitled "William Morris as a Writer," her discussion remains the most important study of Morris's creative process.[15] After searching for the method of his revisions, she concludes that he followed no consistent system. To illustrate her conclusion, she draws on two of the earliest tales, both written in his "rough 'minstrel-lay' manner": **"The Proud King"** and **"The Watching of the Falcon."** Speaking of the first tale, she observes:

> The method of revision is simplicity itself; the idea is to retain the original rhymed endings, but to alter not only single words, but whole passages, whole verses. . . . Then we turn to **"The Watching of the Falcon,"** another of the earliest tales, and we naturally look for the same system of revision. Not a bit of it; the poet is in a different writing mood: for a larger part of the tale, the easy rhymed couplets which come next to **"The Proud King"** in the little notebook, . . . stand unaltered in the published version, revision mostly consisting of insertions of fresh matter, while one or two passages are cut out and written anew. So much for the "system."

> (*AWS* 1: 406)

Still, as May notes, some generalizations can be made as the manuscripts reveal "the poet forming his style. The young diction changes, he is careful that nothing that might strike readers as affectation, even in this romantic atmosphere, should remain." She regrets that Morris occasionally loses in his revisions for the finished work "a touch here and there of freshness— . . . the careless simplicity of the wandering singer." She quotes examples from **"The Story of Rhodope"**:

> *The goods she had been cheapening at her back*

is altered to

> *The wares she had just dealt for at her back.*

And again

> *By these glittering tamers of the sea*

becomes

> *And by these glittering folk oversea.*

> (*AWS* 1: 423)

In her discussion of the manuscripts for **"The Land East of the Sun and West of the Moon,"** she adds that "here and there the drafts show that in revision Morris has cut out a phrase that seemed to him too emphatically to lift the picture out of the far-off atmosphere to that of more recent days of romance—somewhat to our regret: though one must allow the artist to know his business" (*AWS* 1: 413).

The generalization that Morris's revisions show his impatience with youthful diction, obtrusive affectation, and jarring images that dispel the atmosphere of the distant dream-world is consistent with his shift away from the awkward cadence and vivid, grotesque imagery associated with his "rough minstrel-lay" *Defence of Guenevere* period toward the even cadence and muted imagery associated with *The Earthly Paradise.* But

when each example is examined in its context, the motive for the revision appears more complicated. Here is a sample revision from **"The Wooing of Swanhild"** that supports the above generalization, but shows as well that the artist fully knew his business:

> Then on a while silence oer all did die
>
> Yet for those twain no rest for heart or eye
>
> /Then in the gathering light oer all did lie
>
> Deep silence but no rest of heart or eye./
>
> (45308. ll. 1089-90)

In the first version "silence" is awkwardly personified as dying over the men, rendering them quiet but restless—as might well be expected of anyone over whom a shroud is drawn. In the revision, little is lost while much is gained. The revision turns the striking image into an equally striking paradox as the gathering light of dawn does not awaken hope but merely marks the loss of another day passed without love. The revision not only improves the rhythm but unifies the two lines by exploiting alliteration, assonance, consonance, and enjambment (*l*ight oer a*ll did lie*/*D*eep si*l*ence) to momentarily create the tension of a heroic couplet, until the thought spills over into the next two lines.

Another sample revision from **"The Wooing of Swanhild"** initially reveals a slight shift from the concrete to the abstract:

> Of the grey dove, that now in the black shade
> Of summer or
> Of moon blessed woods in the high aspen swayed
>
> Of the brown thrush hushed by the mysteries the dove,
>   that in the shade
> Of moon blessed woods now on the high tree swayed.
>
> (45308. ll. 999-1001)

The motivation for the shift from "the black shade" to "the mysteries," from "high aspen" to "high tree," is clouded by Morris's realization that he has forgotten a line in this stanza. Moreover, the revision shows that Morris is thinking already in abstract terms. The interchangeable grey and brown colours of interchangeable birds suggest grounds for Douglas Bush's complaint about *The Earthly Paradise:* "All eyes are grey, all hair is golden, all bosoms are hidden or half-bare, all legs are limbs, all feet are dainty."[16]

But a study of the total effect of the revision reveals that, again, the artist knew his business. The focus of the revision is not on the reduction of the concrete "black shade" to the abstract "mysteries," but on the intensification of the drama through sound and sense. The "grey dove that now in" becomes the "brown thrush hushed by," wherein the subject and verb are joined in an internal rhyme bracketed by the alliterative "brown" and "by." The visual focus changes from the dark shade to the awesome moonlight, an image which again (as in 1089-90) pictures the silencing effect of light entering upon a dark landscape.

Swinburne was the first to voice the common complaint against the immensely popular *Earthly Paradise.* In a letter to D. G. Rossetti (10 December 1869), Swinburne praised **"The Lovers of Gudrun"** as "excellently told . . . and of keen interest" and the monthly lyrics as "exquisite":

> but I find generally no change in the *trailing* style of work: his Muse is like Homer's Trojan women ελκεσίπεπλους—drags her robes as she walks; I really think a Muse (when she is neither resting nor flying) ought to tighten her girdle, tuck up her skirts, and step out. . . . Top's is spontaneous and slow; and especially my ear hungers for more force and variety of sound in the verse. It looks as if he purposely avoided all strenuous emotion or strength of music in thought and word.[17]

Rossetti responded to Swinburne's criticism with a defence of Morris (12 December 1869): "So excellent a poet must after all be allowed his own style in forms of poetry where deliberateness and delay are not absolutely inadmissable."[18]

The revisions in Morris's manuscripts reveal the subtleties of a mature artist at work. They reveal a shift away from the intense, emotional style of the lyric toward the more controlled pace of the narrative romance. Thus youthful diction, obtrusive affectation, awkward syntax, and jarring imagery are replaced by mature restraint, subtle sophistication, rhythmic pace, and dramatic paradox.

The common assumption that Morris paid little attention to punctuation is disproved by his revisions. Each subsequent draft for a tale shows an increase in care with punctuation, as he appears to ignore punctuation in his first drafts, is careless with it in his transcriptions, but is then careful to add or correct the punctuation for his fair copies. Thus in line 794 of **"The Story of Aristomenes"** (where he writes that "one voice sent out a mighty cry,—"), the punctuation evolves from "cry" in one draft to "cry;—" in the next, meaning that he had no punctuation in one draft, used a semicolon in the next draft, which he then crossed out in favor of a comma and a dash. In line 2211 of **"Aristomenes,"** he shows a rare concern for correcting the punctuation in an early draft: "Thereon in the cold moonlight,/—/ dashed/groaned/the heavy key" (45308). Here he deletes the comma after moonlight and inserts a dash.

For the most part, Morris's penmanship shows the care of an artist who wants to be understood. While he often signifies a dash with a dot in his hastily written drafts,

he places the dot in the middle of a line, as opposed to his periods which rest at the bottom. However, his upper and lower-case K's are virtually indistinguishable, making it difficult to determine whether he has capitalized the "k" in "king" or in "knight." He normally distinguishes upper and lower-case C's, S's, and W's by their size, but their size is sometimes inconsistent. The similarity of his n's and v's makes it difficult to distinguish such words as "loveliness" and "loneliness." The context does not always eliminate the confusion. Perhaps in no other poem as in Morris's elegiac *Earthly Paradise* are the root-words "love" and "lone" so often interchangeable.

A biographer might want to pursue these manuscripts to step further backwards to discover the personality behind the artist's craftsmanship and inspiration. One might note with interest where Morris pauses after a word or a line to draw or merely doodle. In a draft for **"The Wooing of Swanhild,"** Morris writes of the reaction of the wooing Randver to the King's warning: "And all the tumult of his *spirit sank*" (45308. 52). One might argue that Morris suddenly identifies with his character's spirit, as Morris pauses to underline the letters of "spirit sank" sixteen times. J. W. Mackail believes that *The Earthly Paradise* reveals much about its author:

> Shy and reserved in life, as to many matters that lay near his heart, he had all the instinct of the born man of letters for laying himself open in his books, and having no concealments from the widest circle of all. In the verses that frame the stories of *The Earthly Paradise* there is an autobiography so delicate and so outspoken that it must be left to speak for itself.
>
> (1: 210)

To regard the poem's concern with the loss of love and fear of death as Morris's personal obsession is to oversimplify the scope of *The Earthly Paradise.* Morris is writing about the fragmentation of nineteenth-century society and identity, of unity and paradise, self-expression and tradition. The poem presents a logical progression from the decaying world of Camelot (in *The Defence of Guenevere and Other Poems*) to the dying world of Troy about to be levelled after a decade of seige (in *Scenes from the Fall of Troy*). The imminent collapse of the dying Troy anticipates the dead society of Morris's London, those six dehumanized counties of smoke and assembly lines:

> Forget six counties overhung with smoke,
> Forget the snorting steam and piston stroke,
> Forget the spreading of the hideous town.
>
> (*CW* 3: 3)

The subject of all three works is the loss of paradise. Only the third poem concerns its rediscovery. The gathering of Nordic sailors and Greek settlers results in a mutual exchange of tales from Classical and Gothic mythology that provides a framework for Morris to explore the relation between personal vision and cultural tradition. The tales reveal the difference between a culture that has maintained its heritage and one that has lost it. The Greek settlers tell of accomplished quests while the discontented Nordic wanderers tell of failed quests. In the nuptial month of June, for example, the Greek tells of the consummation of an unselfish love in his tale of **"The Love of Alcestis,"** while the wanderer tells of the failure and death of a mariner in the quest for the love of a damsel in **"The Lady of the Land."** The contrast serves to demonstrate that an earthly paradise must be based on the renewal of traditions through the songs and stories developed from cultural roots. The Greek settlers represent a society in touch with its ancient culture despite its isolation in order to demonstrate that paradise is not a geographical location but a state of mind.

The way to reach that state of mind is to replace the Victorian ideal (based on technological progress toward leisure) with a Gothic ideal (based on the craftsman's unified sensibility). The Gothic ideal rejects the "division of labour" for that which demonstrates the "growth and unity of mankind."[19] The wanderers finally reject personal immortality for the higher realm of the Gothic spirit which "depended not on individual genius but on the collective genius or tradition."[20] It can be achieved through the universality of art, which depends upon the original expression of traditional sources:

> Every real poet can do something which no other poet can do. . . . This is what is meant by the much abused word "originality" which by no means signifies that the idea expressed is the sole property of the author . . . but that the author has been able to express it in his own way, and become the voice through which the poetry of mankind speaks so far.[21]

Notes

1. May Morris, *William Morris. Artist, Writer, Socialist* (Oxford: Blackwells, 1936) 1: 402. Hereafter cited in the text as *AWS*.

2. May Morris, ed., *The Collected Works of William Morris* (London: Longmans, 1910) 3: xv. Hereafter cited in the text as *CW*.

3. British Library, Add. MS. 45305.

4. K. L. Goodwin, "An Unpublished Tale from *The Earthly Paradise*," *Victorian Poetry* 13 (Fall-Winter 1975): 95.

5. Fitzwilliam Museum, Cambridge University, 25F, inside flyleaf.

6. *Old French Romances,* trans. William Morris (London: George Allen, 1896) 29-61.

7. J. W. Mackail states that a number of the tales "were destroyed by their author. Of 'The Fortunes of Gyges' only two pages have been preserved by some accident." *The Life of William Morris* (London: Longmans, 1899) 1: 208.

8. *CW* 3: xiii. In addition, the manuscript for the revised Prologue published in *The Earthly Paradise* is in the British Library, Add. MS. 37499.

9. See note 3. May mentions this manuscript in a footnote to her introduction in volume 4: "Search in a family treasure-chest brings to light also an oblong clasped notebook containing most of the First Prologue and a considerable portion of 'Cupid and Psyche' (*CW* 4: ix.) She then describes its contents in her *AWS* 1: 400-401, but wrongly adds that it was "composed two years before the published Prologue."

10. *English Verse & Dramatic Poetry. From Chaucer to the Present Day,* no. 517 (London: Maggs Bros., 1929) 373.

11. Troxell Collection, Princeton University Library, Princeton, New Jersey, Trox n. 14.

12. Humanities Research Center, University of Texas, ms. file (Morris, W), Works B.

13. Mackail quotes a letter to Janey dated 14 March 1870: "I have been hard at work . . . but have not done much except the translations, as they are rather pressing now, and I want to get all my Volsung work done this week." (Mackail, *Life* 1: 209). "A Prologue in Verse" is appended to the manuscript. (Oxford University, Bodl. MS. Eng. misc. d. 268).

14. Mackail states that Morris began the tale after the Grettir Saga was *published* in April, but he should have said that Morris began the tale after he had finished *translating* the saga (Mackail 1: 201).

15. For a later study, see my article "A Matter of Craftsmanship: Morris's Method of Composition," *The Journal of the William Morris Society* 6 (Summer 1985): 2-11. What are alleged to be Morris's first drafts, I argue, are really transcriptions from scrap paper.

16. Douglas Bush, *Mythology and the Romantic Tradition in English Poetry* (Cambridge, Mass.: Harvard UP, 1937) 320.

17. Cecil Lang, ed., *The Swinburne Letters* (New Haven: Yale UP, 1959) 2: 68.

18. Oswald Doughty and John Robert Wahl, eds., *Letters of Dante Gabriel Rossetti* (Oxford: Oxford UP, 1965) 2: 773.

19. Morris, "The Gothic Revival," in *Unpublished Lectures of William Morris,* ed. Eugene Le Mire (Detroit: Wayne State, 1969) 82. John Ruskin

recognized that the term "division of labour" was a misnomer: "It is not, truly speaking, the labour that is divided, but the men: Divided into mere segments of men—broken into small fragments and crumbs of life" (*The Works of Ruskin,* ed. Cook and Wedderburn (London: George Allen, 1904) 10: 196.

20. "The Gothic Revival" 67. Thus, the term "Gothic" is used for folk tales from Medieval, Eastern or Northern sources.

21. Quoted from Morris's letters by Jessie Kocmanova, "The Aesthetic Opinions of William Morris," *Comparative Literature Studies* 4 (1967): 422.

Isolde Karen Herbert (essay date summer 1991)

SOURCE: Herbert, Isolde Karen. "'A Strange Diagonal': Ideology and Enclosure in the Framing Sections of *The Princess* and *The Earthly Paradise.*" *Victorian Poetry* 29, no. 2 (summer 1991): 145-59.

[*In the following essay, Herbert contrasts the function of the frame structures of Alfred Tennyson's* The Princess *and Morris's* The Earthly Paradise.]

After reading the first volume of *The Earthly Paradise,* Browning complimented Morris on the poem's "continuous key and recurring forms,—the New masked in the Old and perpetually looking out of the eyeholes of its disguise."[1] Recurrence and disguise in the form of framing strategies shape Tennyson's *The Princess* and Morris' *The Earthly Paradise* into narratives in which similar structural designs create antithetical effects. Tennyson's enigmatic hint that "there is scarcely anything in the story which is not prophetically glanced at in the prologue"[2] and May Morris' recollection that the Prologue to *The Earthly Paradise* gave Morris "more trouble than all the rest of the work" suggest that the frame sections in these poems have more than usual significance.[3] Tennyson's extensive revisions and additions to his framing sequences in the third and fifth editions and Morris' rewriting of his entire Prologue indicate again each poet's determination to create a frame which precisely expresses his purpose.

Most readings of the two poems are arguments for unity. While I agree that the frames contribute structural and thematic coherence to the tales, I argue, conversely, for the autonomy of the "framing fictions," to use Judith M. Davidoff's term, as statements of poetic methodology.[4] As self-reflexive comments on poetic composition, the embedding narratives obliquely relate the perceptual acts of linguistic and social "framing." In the Prologue and Conclusion to *The Princess,* Tennyson evokes disturbing ideas that he is willing to confront only in the context of the protective distancing devices of the dramatic narrative and the persona. Morris, however, uses the frame to reduce the distance between the reader and the poem in order to confront the audience with its own misconceptions of society and of art. As a means to express, yet control, revolutionary social ideas, Tennyson's frame is an enclosure that, contrary to the overt subject of the work, constrains social and linguistic freedom within its monophonic voice. Possibly, this voice is the "rowdy, or bullying, element" in *The Princess* that Morris finds offensive;[5] if so, this characteristic of Tennyson's poem may well have influenced Morris' construction of *The Earthly Paradise* frame as a form in which polyphonic voices depict and advance the liberation of language and society.[6] Whereas Tennyson's contemporary frame functions as a barrier controlled by a single, regulative consciousness, the frame of *The Earthly Paradise* provides a perceptual entrance to a Brechtian chorus of interchangeable tellers and listeners.

William E. Buckler argues that the contemporary relevance of the poet and poetry, rather than the equality of the sexes, is the subject of *The Princess.*[7] As Buckler suggests, the poem explores the relevance of the poetic imagination to perceptual renewal; although I agree that the work is self-reflexive, I interpret the focus of this self-consciousness to be the tension both in poetry and in society between conservation and renewal. Accordingly, although the poet figure in the Prologue invokes progressive linguistic and social forces, he resists the disorder implicit in these forces. The narrator contradicts his egalitarian voice when he responds, structurally and thematically, to threats to his autonomy by assuming an autocratic voice. Because he controls the point of view, the narrator constructs the frame (and the work as a whole) according to his selective principles of exclusion and modulation. In the context of W. David Shaw's study of the framing consciousness and John Keble's "reserve," *The Princess*' Prologue and Conclusion reveal the narrator's fear of losing the "sovereignty of the framing mind" when his response to his subject, rather than the subject itself, begins to predominate.[8] This anxiety underlies the concern of the frame with voice and with the modes of generic renewal; moreover, because the poetic consciousness vacillates between the equally untenable options of the acceptance or rejection of democratic polyphony, Keble's reticence occurs as the "unsaid" which is central to the frame: the impropriety of any desire to relinquish poetic, social, or political control. Because this ideological "gap," a form of Pierre Macherey's textual "silence," contradicts the thesis and design of the poem,[9] the narrator uses layering techniques to attempt to conceal and order the chaos implied by the popular voice. This heroic compulsion to create and confront the forces of insurrection silently and unobtrusively while remaining within the protected enclosure of the dominant poetic voice generates the hermeneutic and structural tension, or the "strange diagonal" (Conclusion, l. 27), of the poet figure's framing configurations.[10] Tennyson, writes Thomas Carlyle, is "carrying a bit of Chaos about him, in short, which he is manufacturing into Cosmos";[11] *The Princess* dramatizes the irresolvable conflicts of this process as the censoring consciousness of the poet structures the frame of *The Princess* into a triple enclosure of dramatic design, imagery, and incident.

Tennyson's Prologue begins with a description of Sir Walter Vivian's annual opening of the grounds of his estate to the public. Although the entertainment on this day is egalitarian (demonstrations by the Mechanics' Institute of "popular" aspects of scientific advances and inventions) the retreat of the gentry to the Abbey ruins maintains the hierarchical distinctions between past and present, aristocrat and plebeian, and art and life. To complement these social and aesthetic barriers, the poet-narrator's selective imagination records a "medley" of images of linguistic and social restraint. The opening verse stanza introduces the issue of "mock" equality: the chronological limit of diurnal time ("until the set of sun" [Prologue, l. 2]) and the inset spatial frame of the "lawns" (Prologue, l. 2) control popular access to the aristocratic world. Diction subverts the democratic intent of the occasion: "flocked," "borough," and "patron" (Prologue, ll. 3, 5, 6) suggest obedience, corruption (in the sense of the "rotten" borough), and patriarchal charity. "We were seven" (Prologue, l. 9) echoes Wordsworth's "We are Seven" and emphasizes the inferred perceptual limitations of the populace; in addition, the narrator's omission of the "thousand" (Prologue, l. 57) in his count of seven indicates that he, like the child in Wordsworth's poem, reasons according to a perceptual bias which modulates objective reality.

These indications of spatial separation and perceptual exclusion recur throughout the Prologue. Sir Walter collects symbols of the ruin of marginalized cultures, geological epochs, and undeveloped geographical resources. This appropriation of universal time and space is a reductive process which domesticates images of the "Other" by trivializing them into commodities: "toys in lava" (Prologue, l. 18) and "the cursed Malayan crease" (Prologue, 21) are metonyms for the colonial control of natural and cultural forces. As inset framing images, the "ivory sphere in sphere" (Prologue, l. 20) and the Vivians' coat of arms hung between "monstrous horns of elk and deer" (Prologue, l. 23) replicate in miniature the Empire's global power. This encyclopedic collection identifies the house as an imperialist's version of a "palace of art."

The demonstrations of the Mechanics' Institute represent the local "frame" of the ongoing appropriation of man and nature. Each experiment creates a reciprocal

disturbance of the elements as nature resists its diminution into "sport" (Prologue, l. 79). As a palliative, this reduction of the size and strength of natural forces reassures the people of the progress of civilization and, at the same time, diverts their attention from the actuality of the French rebellion where real "cannon" (Prologue, l. 66) forcefully suppress a popular uprising. The narrator's reluctance to admit even this controlled form of social disorder into his consciousness, or, by extension, into his narrative, moves him to construct a verbal restraint, or frame, around his vision of potential chaos: the framing phrase "strange was the sight" (Prologue, ll. 54, 89) encloses the popular scene within the connotations of aberrant social behavior. At the level of statement, equality is sanctioned; at the level of suggestion, it is censored.

The picnic on the grass as "trim as any garden lawn" (Prologue, l. 95) encircled by the Abbey ruins extends the domestication of nature and of the past to the story-telling location. The view of previously described images of control (the park, the house, and the crowd) is framed by the Gothic arches which, because they seclude and distance the patrician from the popular sensibility, function as an architectural complement to the narrator's verbal frame mentioned above. Paradoxically, the carnivalized image of genealogical superiority (the scarf-draped statue of Sir Ralph) and the ruins of feudal hierarchy (the Abbey walls) protect the aristocratic sensibility. Hence, in order to retain their privilege, representatives of the "great Sirs" (Conclusion, l. 102), an expression indicative of the narrator's point of view, retreat into a microcosmic facsimile of the estate's controlled area. As a gesture of toleration and appeasement, the people are allowed restricted access into the regulative frames of the estate—and of the poem—where they function as the hegemony's literal and emblematic "view" of a tolerable democracy.

Michael André Bernstein's interpretation of carnival as a licensed and therefore, permissible freedom within hegemonic jurisdiction applies to the dramatic frame of *The Princess*.[12] Because the narrator is apprehensive of any democratic tendencies, he interprets both the popular activities and the generically bizarre tale in the terms of the incongruities of carnival. Also relevant here is Pugin's condemnation of the arbitrary conjunction of styles, notably the Greek and the Gothic (the ornamental style of Vivian-place), as a "*carnival* of architecture."[13] These social, linguistic, and architectural anomalies anticipate the breakdown of the Princess' order when "Love in the sacred halls / Held carnival at will" (7.69-70). Inversions of the social and natural hierarchies temporarily transform Vivian-place into a sanctioned parody of the market-place. Sir Walter's collection, like the scientific experiments and the oral tale, reflects the heterogeneity and arbitrary juxtapositions of carnival.

Spatially, the inward movement from the park and the house to the ruin parallels the increasing seclusion of the narrative voice within the privileged space of the origin of the poem. As I note above, Sir Ralph's statue may be read as the sign of a degenerate tradition; however, Lilia's decoration of the statue also transforms the "sward" (Prologue, l. 95) into the linguistic center of the poem. From this standpoint, the scarf is a symbol of the poetic imagination's perspective on the past and its traditions; whether this creative act veils, distorts, or transforms past and present realities depends upon the perceiving consciousness. These multiple connotations of the image of the broken statue reflect the tension between the narrator's allegiance to traditional poetics and politics and his desire to confront the disorder of radical change. When Walter asks the poet, "'What, if you drest it [the tale] up poetically?'" (Conclusion, l. 6), he asks for a literary analogue to Lilia's modulation of the significance of the statue: Sir Ralph's artistic legacy (the sculpture of the statue and the narrative of the chronicle), is susceptible to revision by either libertarian or traditionalist aesthetics. Although both Lilia and the poet "frame" or modulate an existent work of art, their approaches are quite different. Lilia is the rebellious voice of the poem; she resents her brother's condescension and interrupts the story-telling at the beginning of Part V to protest against the generic direction of the tale. In the Conclusion, when Lilia tears the grass, she symbolically disturbs the "trim" (Prologue, l. 95) order of the imaginative center of the poem, thereby resisting the control of the poet's reactionary voice. The narrator's admission that Lilia's silence pleases him (Conclusion, l. 29) indicates the momentary triumph of his dominant consciousness.

The contrast between Aunt Elizabeth's propagandist "text" of "universal culture" (Prologue, ll. 108, 109) and the students' "unworthier" (Prologue, l. 110) tales of their mutinous escapades at Cambridge, together with the narrator's initial relegation of feminine heroism to the historical romance of the chronicle, are conservative interpretations of potentially rebellious material that anticipate the work's concluding affirmation of the status quo. Throughout the Prologue, figures of imprisonment and constraint increase the effect of the linguistic, topographical, and architectural enclosures: the "gate" and "walls" (Prologue, ll. 33, 34) in the chronicle, the "spikes," "bars," and "cloisters" (Prologue, ll. 111, 112, 181) at Cambridge, the image of the cage, and, the epitome of confinement, the tomb in the Abbey ruins, reflect the narrator's divided awareness of the proximity of convention to "sinecure" and of innovation to "game" (Prologue, ll. 180, 191).

The "tale from mouth to mouth" (Prologue, l. 189) suggests a democratic narrative form, and yet the censorial device of the frame represses any advance toward polyphony. Terry Eagleton, however, exaggerates when he concludes that "the poem displays no *dialectic* of discourses whatsoever";[14] the narrator's persistent construction of framing devices in order to suppress dialectics suggests that his fear of the emergence of seditious voices becomes the subject of the poem. When the poet asserts, "The words are mostly mine" (Conclusion, l. 3), he reveals the dominance of his framing consciousness. Because the "words" of the Prologue and the Conclusion, like those of the tale itself, are the narrator's, the reader questions whether the poet's bias distorts the descriptions and events selected for the frame. Hence, the poet's material appropriation of the original text—"(I kept the book and had my finger in it)" (Prologue, l. 53)—foreshadows his subsequent admission of his artistic control of the derivative poem. This comprehensive framing act foregrounds the subjectivity of the framing consciousness and, by implication, points to the ethical responsibility of the poet who refashions inherited genres.

The poet's intent to "bind the scattered scheme of seven / Together in one sheaf" (Conclusion, ll. 8-9) indicates his determination to subdue polyphony and his compulsion to create the symmetry of closure.[15] Chiasmus, the "scheme" (this word is repeated to accentuate the conscious artistry suggested both by chiasmus and by generic adaptation [Conclusion, ll. 2, 8]) of the poet's "strange diagonal" (Conclusion, l. 27), provides a verbal, thematic, and graphic model of the containment of rebellious tendencies: like the tale, revolutions are "'Too comic for the solemn things they are, / Too solemn for the comic touches in them'" (Conclusion, ll. 67-68). Mary Ann Caws's description of chiasmus as a semantic form of the frame that frequently indicates a moment of insight suggests that Tennyson uses this device to enclose the "absence" crucial to the poem: the irreconcilable tension between feelings of attraction and repulsion toward forces which threaten stability and order.[16]

In the Conclusion, dialogue elaborates on this division within the narrative consciousness: while the autocratic and Tory voice asserts its traditional authority to be "'firm against the crowd'" (Conclusion, l. 57), the democratic voice, now weaker, is unable to refute these hegemonic claims. Instead, when the narrator asserts that the "'genial day'" (Conclusion, l. 75) has increased his faith, he implies that this faith refers to the disciplinary power of the establishment to repress or to construct an ideological "framework" (Conclusion, l. 22) around the freedom of unlicensed carnival. Another control, reveals the narrator, is the "'hand that guides'" (Conclusion, l. 79); again, the poet's recourse to the consolation of the divine plan evokes the concept of an ordered hierarchy. Moreover, the poet's consistently patriarchal tone reflects his conservative approach to religion and society. Throughout the Prologue and the Conclusion, the selection of imagery, diction, and metaphor exposes the narrator's belief that his role is that of the vatic poet, or Christ figure: the people, or the "multitude" (Prologue, l. 57) "flock[ed]" (Prologue, l. 3) to the "pasture" (Prologue, l. 55); his "sevenfold story" (Prologue, l. 198) parodies the Biblical creation, and, as he admits, he is Logos or the origin of "words" (Conclusion, l. 3). Similarly, after his ascent to Vivian-place, the poet assumes a prophetic stance. The view of pastoral, geographic, and political boundaries elicits the student's appreciation of the "narrow seas" (Conclusion, l. 70) which protect England from the "mock heroics" (Conclusion, l. 64) of the French uprising. Although the narrator's response to this patriotism begins with a criticism of England's "social wrong" (Conclusion, l. 73), his prophecy of progress implies that this "wrong" is the revolutionary impulse. Pertinently, Tennyson notes that these lines were "written just after the disturbances in France, February 1848, when Louis Philippe was compelled to abdicate" (Ricks, p. 294).

By praising Sir Walter excessively, the narrator attempts to overcome the doubts generated by his reflections on political instability. This apostrophe describes the landowner in the terms of his accumulated assets and, therefore, functions as a closural frame to complement the collection of artifacts in the Prologue. Repetition of "closed" in reference to the tale and the gates and in the circular syntax of "such as closed / Welcome, farewell, and welcome" (Conclusion, ll. 94-95) accentuates the poet's determination to structure his narrative according to his conception of an ordered and traditional poetic form. However, when darkness conceals the frames, or the symbols of linguistic and social power, the narrator transcends the finite concerns of poetic and social control during a moment of vision when he intuits a truth that is beyond language:

> we sat
> But *spoke not,* rapt in *nameless* reverie,
> *Perchance* upon the future man: the walls
> Blackened about us, bats wheeled, and owls whooped.
>
> (Conclusion, ll. 107-110; my italics)

Shakespeare's words fill the silence left by this loss of language. Thus, quotations from the chronicler and from Shakespeare frame the tale with inherited, or borrowed, language, and indicate the narrator's awareness of the insufficiency of his poetical consciousness to compose convincing accounts either of heroic resistance or of visionary consolation.

Whether Lilia's removal of her scarf from the statue symbolizes her renunciation of the revolutionary forces of carnival and poetry, or the triumph of these forces over the "ruins" of the narrator's dominant voice, remains uncertain. Before her silence, Lilia demands of her aunt, "'You—tell us what we are'" (Conclusion, l. 34). Lilia's request is futile because her aunt is a traditionalist (Prologue, ll. 107-109) who relegates poetic control to the equally conservative narrator ("As you will; / Heroic if you will, or what you will" [Prologue, ll. 214-215]). Moreover, the shout of the crowd disturbs nature and prevents a reply to Lilia's question because, despite the narrator's accumulation of framing images of control, he can neither repress nor ignore the populism which unsettles his dominant, or framing, voice.

Whereas Tennyson designs boundary images and structures as means of perceptual enclosure, Morris' framing pattern in **The Earthly Paradise** represents and encourages perceptual liberation. In sequence, the Apology, the Prologue's explanation of the circumstances and events of the quest journey, and the reflective lyrics inserted between each pair of tales present Morris' frame(s) as a chorus of voices. Tennyson's substitution of a "summer's" for a "winter's tale" (Prologue, l. 204) reflects the exclusive configurations in *The Princess*; in contrast, the "wizard" (3:2) in Morris' Apology creates an inclusive vision of all seasons within the windowed room of the poem.[17] As "the soul's perceptual opening," the window, like **The Earthly Paradise,** is an ordering frame around a picture of the homogeneity of romance and realism.[18] When the Wanderers meet King Edward they learn that because his historical role excludes romance from the "narrow space / Betwixt the four walls of a fighting place" (3:20), he seeks perceptual release in the pastoral songs of the saga. Similarly, the reader, confined within the contemporary frame of cultural and social degeneration, and the human frame of birth and death, obtains a temporary liberation of perception within the imaginative layers of Morris' poem. The wizard, King Edward, and the narrator of the November lyric who presents nature as an alternative to life's "four walls, hung with pain and dreams" (5:206) extend the motif of the imaginative release from enclosure to each of the three narrative levels of **The Earthly Paradise.**[19]

In **The Earthly Paradise,** polyphony, or the tale-telling process, generates cosmic, communal, and personal harmony through memory and reflection. The multiple frames of the dramatic mode offer access, rather than obstruction, to the central truth of the work—"nameless" for Morris (3:3) as for Tennyson (*The Princess,* Conclusion, l. 108). The story-telling situation itself is the unrecognized goal of the quest.[20] "Bliss" (3:2) or immortality is the evaluative recreation of individual and communal existence by the linguistic cycles, or frames, of listening, telling, reading, and writing. The way to understand reality is to see it through the perceptual change induced by romance. Accordingly, the Prologue allows the reader to share the "reality" of the Wanderers' journey; subsequently, the reader and the Wanderers together participate in the romance of the tales as a gloss on the quest experience. In the internal frames where the narrative returns to the story-telling location at the conclusion of each tale, the responses of the listeners guide the reader toward a viable interpretation of romance. The material purpose of the Wanderers' tales as payment for the Elder's hospitality accentuates the verisimilitude of these reminders of the setting of the work.

Beyond the outer frame of the Prologue, the Apology initiates the thesis of chronological, spatial, and perceptual movement across predetermined cognitive limits. This progression contrasts with the fixity implied in *The Princess* by the criterion of a tale which is "made to suit with Time and place" (Prologue, l. 224). Moreover, **The Earthly Paradise** begins with a formal movement across generic boundaries: the Apology argues for a realistic, yet lyrical, approach to romance narrative. Art, the narrator advises, cannot banish mortality, yet, with the appropriate perception, both the poet and his audience may endure mortality with equanimity. Like Morris, the tellers do not "*strive* to set the crooked straight" (3:1; italics added). Instead, their tales create a renewed perception by indirection and repetition; consequently, when the tellers "*strive* to build a shadowy isle of bliss / Midmost the beating of the steely sea" (3:2; emphasis added) obliquely, they transform the consciousness within the framing periphery of the actual. "Bliss," this raised consciousness, and "beating" suggest the union of the head and heart or, alternatively, Morris' moods of idleness and energy. Thus, in a correct reading of Morris' poetic narrative, these dialectics ensure that "the ivory gate" (3:1) remains a passage, and not a barrier, to the interpretation of illusion and actuality. The framework of **The Earthly Paradise** presents concentric circles of the lyric, or private voice, and the narrative, or public voice, as an exemplary configuration of democratic polyphony in which frame and picture repeat each other in a form of complementary repetition.

Unlike Tennyson's poet figure, Morris' narrator disavows the effectiveness of the "words" (3:1) of the individual, or autocratic, poetic voice and asserts that polyphony, or the plurality of singers through time, maintains the transformative power of the "singers" (3:1) and their songs. As a prescriptive introduction to the function of the poet and his art, the Apology directs the reader toward appropriate interpretative methods and reveals the narrator's intent to transfer the autonomy of his private, lyrical voice to the collective voice of the poets of the oral tradition who "living not, can ne'er be dead" (3:1); thus, he is as anxious to relinquish his control as the poet in *The Princess* is to retain his.

The thematic frame of the sea provides access both to the quest and to the poem. Because the concept of a definitive earthly paradise contradicts Morris' belief in the dialectics of the natural cycles, the process of the tales conducts the reader and the listeners through, not to, an earthly paradise. In a similar manner, the layers of the frame function as levels of a lyrical and dramatic spiral which raises consciousness. Reassertion of the negative, the narrator's advice to "forget" (3:3) the "hideous town" (3:3), effaces, and yet recreates, memories of the present that for the duration of the narrative, should be set aside. Although Rolf's desire for escape is an erroneous premise for his quest, he, too, leaves behind a "dreary" (3:11) town; in the November framing lyric, the reference to "smoke-tinged mist-wreaths" (5:206) completes the thematic cycle of the degradation of civilization through the various framing levels. Love, death and rebirth, and the "tale" itself are among other motifs Morris uses to foreground the homogeneity of the multiple narrative voices. Accordingly, the narrator's reference to his "hollow puppets" (3:3) does not suggest that his "rhymes" (3:3) are superficial but that wisdom is hidden within narrative frames and voices: although the narrator's lyrical expressions appear to be subjective reflections, they enclose a dramatic recreation of the insights of the Classical and European oral heritages. This revelation of wisdom through the juxtaposition of cultures contrasts with the incongruity of carnival suggested by the Gothic and Greek architecture in *The Princess*.

The "nameless city in a distant sea" (3:3) relocates and pluralizes the Apology's lyrical image of the island as consciousness within the inset frame of the narrative of the Prologue. Consciousness and imagination become dramatized functions rather than, as they are in the Apology, metaphoric: details of touch, sound, and sight contribute to the materiality of the linguistic center of the work. The reader accompanies the narrator through a series of borders leading to the *locus amoenus*: the sea, the island, the city walls, the market-place, and, finally, the council house door. Although these borders initially appear as exclusive as the perimeters in Tennyson's Prologue (especially in the command to close the door), the reader's participation in the movement through the framing layers indicates the accessibility of narrative as a means of perceptual renewal. Moreover, as an extension of the market square, the council house encloses both reflective silence, or idleness, and communal activity, or energy: rulers, soldiers, peasants, and the narrator with his reader/listener form the innermost structural and thematic enclosure of the poem. Whereas this center invites egalitarian discourse from the representatives of an active community, in *The Princess* the Abbey walls exclude the community and its popular (or, in the narrator's opinion, "pithy" [Conclusion, l. 94]) language.

With the introduction of the dramatic mode in Morris' Prologue, the authorial voice recedes behind the multiple consciousnesses of the personae; simultaneously, the narrator replaces his "map" of the city's imagined reality with the "real" topography of episodic fiction. Rolf's account of the Wanderers' journey focuses on the misreadings of language that initiate their quest.[21] His recollection of his naïve understanding of saga and myth includes the most precise statement of the implied thesis of the work: "And like real life would empty stories seem, / And life from day to day an empty dream" (3:7). As in *The Princess,* schematic parallelism accentuates this syntactic framing of the central "silence" of the poem. The recreation of the quest in the language of myth teaches Rolf and the reader that, if interpreted correctly and viewed as complementary, yet distinct, aspects of experience, neither life nor myth need be "empty." Differentiated repetition, structured as framing phrases which contrast "fact" with "fiction," traces the development of Rolf's awareness of the relevance of illusion to life. Initially, Rolf does not distinguish between "false and true" (3:12); although Nicholas recognizes that in myth "truth perchance touched lies" (3:13), his use of words to deceive the crew indicates the power of language to corrupt when the framing consciousness excludes morality. Before the first tale, the narrator recapitulates the Prologue's dramatization of the Apology's directive to "read aright" (3:2): the Elders and the Wanderers discuss the concerns of the community and, in times of "idleness," recite poets' tales which are "Not true nor false, but sweet to think upon" (3:83). Thus, the concern with the reader's/listener's appropriate response to language and narrative associates the lyrical frame, the quest, and the story-telling location with the cycle of tales.

Whereas the Apology distances the reader from his/her preconceptions about the authority of the individual voice of the lyric poet, the first verse paragraphs of the Prologue create a psychological distance between contemporary and mythological place and time. During the recreation of the "realistic" past of the quest, the reader's point of view becomes that of the representatives of the community who also experience the journey in retrospect; thus, the reader joins the inner frame of the circle of listeners. Like the Wanderers, the reader moves toward integration with the community. In the linking sections between the tales, the reader has the opportunity to contrast his/her response to each tale with that of the community of fictive listeners. In yet another formal margin, the private voice in the lyrics, removed from the tale-telling situation because of the absence of collective response, engages the reader's private sympathy and critical assessment. Thus, Morris fashions the thematic and structural frames into dialectical patterns which develop the antitheses of individual and community, private and public, and illusion and reality into comprehensive strategies for perceptual renewal.

E. P. Thompson's criticism of the frame of *The Earthly Paradise* as a "static" structure which is "the pretext, not the occasion for the stories"[22] fails to consider how the interlacement of framing and framed voices guides the reader toward a new perception of romance narrative. The transformation of the rigid conceptual barrier between truth and falsehood into the dialectic of actuality and romance organizes the layers of *The Earthly Paradise* as a polyphony of the voices of universal experience. In a *mise en abîme* effect, the frames allow the reader to observe others who also observe and participate in this polyphony: the young acquire wisdom and the old, by reliving their hopes and fears in articulated memories, learn to read the meaning of their quest and of narrative itself: "My old self grows unto myself grown old" (3:26). Narrative distance, or the linguistic "framing" of experience, shows Rolf that, ironically, the "slow decay" (3:72) of the false paradise in the Prologue is the criterion of the earthly paradise he seeks. Repetition of enclosure images (the walls, marketplace, temple, "brazen gate" (3:69), and dais) emphasizes the contrast between the city of "unending life" (3:72) and the Elders' city, where the experience of narrative as a social activity develops into Morris' dialectical ideal of individual perceptual clarity within an harmonious community. Thus, models of illusory and attainable, or authentic, earthly paradises frame the Prologue; moreover, these models repeat and frame Rolf's discovery of the mundane reality of kingship, another experience which tempers illusion with reality.

The flexible movement of the story-telling center among seasons and times of day and between urban and pastoral settings reflects the universal applicability and democratic function of narrative. The tales, as oral or written versions of existent myths or as original contributions to the cultural heritage, enrich the popular mythology. At the end of the Prologue, the Elders predict this cultural renewal: as story-tellers, the Wanderers are a "living chronicle" (3:80) and their tales, recorded by scribes, will bring enjoyment and instruction to present and future generations. The Elder's analogy of the tales as royal children who receive "the people's blessing on their birth" (3:80) attests to the veracity of the inherited discourse and communal function of the mythical tradition.

In the Epilogue, the narrator reassumes his obliquely instructive and lyrical voice as he emphasizes that a desire to challenge death, while an inevitable part of life, must be accompanied with the understanding that this heroic gesture is foredoomed. In a reference to the self-destructive tendency of the escapist search for the ideal, repetition frames a verbal paradox analogous to the thematic paradox of the poem as a whole: "They thought that every good thing would be won, / If they might win a refuge from it" (6:327). Thematic repetition (the allusions to the "flowery land" [6:328], to the true and false paradises, and to the organic cycle of tale-telling) again relates the lyrical to the narrative frames and reminds us that our renewed perception enables us to fashion the form and content of the poetic layers into a unified chorus of voices.

The Envoi addresses the book as a material object. The book encloses, or frames, a message which endures through historical time. Metaphorically, Morris expresses his concern that, as the language of the individual poet, the frame-work of *The Earthly Paradise* may prove inadequate to its task of the transmission of myth: the "limbs and heart" or unity of the work (6:330) may not merit inclusion in the community's legacy of egalitarian narrative. Nevertheless, the metaphorical "journey" (6:330) through space and time unites the book, as another "quester," with Chaucer's vernacular canon. Because the completion of the work ends the poet's active participation in the tradition of popular narrative, he speaks in his individual, rather than collective, voice. Thus, the poet's role returns to that of the Apology: the solitary speaker whose autonomous, and therefore less effectual, voice alienates him from the collective voices, whether oral or written, of inherited myth and legend. This alienation threatens to restrict his function to that of an "idle singer of an empty day" (6:330, 331, 332, 333).

Diction, image, structure, and point of view link the poet's individual and lyrical quest for method and for love to the cooperative search of the narrative voices for communal integration. The imagery of the "flower" and "seed" (6:333) frames *The Earthly Paradise* with the affirmation of the power of the "tale" to rejuvenate the perception of those made "weary" (6:333) by modern "life's empty day" (6:333). Jessie Kocmanová suggests that Morris' sense of design prevents him from allowing the frame to gain precedence over the "picture."[23] However, the embedding sections are not subordinate to the narratives they present; instead, Morris constructs the frame as a holistic and organic network which activates the dialectics between form and content and makes the framing consciousness a part of the vision it encloses.

The contrast between Morris' organic image of the book and Tennyson's allusion to the cooperative tales as "Seven-headed monsters" (Prologue, l. 200) reflects each poet's response to the tension generated by the social implications of the methodology proposed in their Prologues. For Morris, this tension results from

his desire to suppress his authoritarian voice and, by complex layering techniques, to induce the perceptual change needed to remove the earthly paradise from its traditional associations with retreat and escapism. Thus, Morris relocates the ideal within, not beyond, the social function of art wherein narrative records, interprets, and enhances experience. In *The Princess,* the conflict between the narrator's desire to appear democratic and his inclination to retain his authoritarian voice creates tension. In both frames, the poets express dissatisfaction with the results of their search for an appropriate framing voice to articulate the "nameless" (*The Princess,* Conclusion, l. 108; Morris, 3:3) contradiction between individual and social expression. The "silence" in Morris' poetic layers is the identification of the earthly paradise with the act of communal story-telling; the unspoken thesis in the Prologue and Conclusion to *The Princess* is the poet's fear of his egalitarian impulses. Morris encapsulates this fear in his caricature of Tennyson in *The Tables Turned*: "I don't want to understand Socialism," explains the fictive Tennyson, "it doesn't belong to my time."[24] Tennyson's framing of collective perception as the licensed enclosure of the aberrancies of carnival and Morris' layered vision of the communal consciousness as the operative basis of society are, to use Paul Ricoeur's terms, expressions of the "reproductive," or ideological, and the "productive," or utopian, imagination respectively.[25]

Notes

1. *William Morris: Artist, Writer, Socialist,* intro. May Morris (New York, 1966), 1:641-642.

2. Hallam Tennyson, *Alfred Lord Tennyson: A Memoir* (London, 1898), 1:251.

3. *The Collected Works of William Morris,* ed. May Morris (New York, 1966), 3:xiii.

4. Judith M. Davidoff, *Beginning Well: Framing Fictions in Late Middle English Poetry* (London, 1988), p. 17.

5. J. W. Mackail, *The Life of William Morris* (London, 1901), 1:45.

6. Mikhail Bakhtin, *Rabelais and His World,* trans. Hélène Iswolsky (Bloomington, 1984) and *Problems of Dostoevsky's Poetics,* ed. and trans. Caryl Emerson (Minneapolis, 1984). I use the terms "carnival" and "polyphony" in the Bakhtinian sense.

7. William E. Buckler, *The Victorian Imagination: Essays in Aesthetic Exploration* (New York, 1980), pp. 132-163. See also Herbert F. Tucker's argument for the dialectic between the lyric mode of discontent and the idyllic mode of containment in *Tennyson and the Doom of Romanticism* (Cambridge, Massachusetts, 1988), pp. 346-376.

8. W. David Shaw, *The Lucid Veil: Poetic Truth in the Victorian Age* (Madison, 1987), p. 48.

9. Pierre Macherey, *A Theory of Literary Production,* trans. Geoffrey Wall (London, 1978), pp. 82-89.

10. Quotations from *The Princess* are identified by section and line number and are from Christopher Ricks's edition, vol. 2 (Berkeley, 1987).

11. *The Correspondence of Thomas Carlyle and Ralph Waldo Emerson 1834-1872,* ed. Charles Eliot Norton (London, 1883), 2:66.

12. Michael André Bernstein, "When the Carnival Turns Bitter: Preliminary Reflections Upon the Abject Hero," in *Bakhtin: Essays and Dialogues on His Work,* ed. Gary Saul Morson (Chicago, 1986), pp. 99-121.

13. A. Welby Pugin, *An Apology for the Revival of Christian Architecture* (London, 1843), p. 2.

14. Terry Eagleton, "Tennyson: Politics and Sexuality in *The Princess* and *In Memoriam,*" in *1848: The Sociology of Literature: Proceedings of the Essex Conference on the Sociology of Literature, July 1977* (University of Essex, 1978), pp. 102-103.

15. See also James Harrison, "The Role of Anachronism in *The Princess,*" *ESC* [*English Studies in Canada*] 1 (1975): 304-316. In his study, Harrison suggests that none of the points of view can be attributed to Tennyson, who uses the multiple personae "to absolve him[self] of clear authorial responsibility" (p. 313).

16. Mary Ann Caws, *Reading Frames in Modern Fiction* (Princeton, 1985), p. 167.

17. Quotations from *The Earthly Paradise* are identified by volume and page number in the May Morris *Collected Works* edition.

18. Gerhard Joseph, "Victorian Frames: The Windows and Mirrors of Browning, Arnold, and Tennyson," *VP* [*Victorian Poetry*] 16 (1978): 72.

19. See also Florence S. Boos, "The Evolution of 'The Wanderers' Prologue,'" *PLL* [*Papers on Language and Literature: A Journal for Scholars and Critics of Language and Literature*] 20 (1984): 397-417 and her study of the reciprocity between the framing levels and the tales they enclose: "The Argument of *The Earthly Paradise,*" *VP* 23 (1985): 75-92.

20. Frederick Kirchhoff, "The Aesthetic Discipline of *The Earthly Paradise,*" *VP* 18 (1980): 229-240. Kirchhoff suggests that the opening lines of the work indicate Morris' rejection of "Wordsworthian dominance" (p. 236).

21. See Thomas T. Barker's "The Shadow on the Tapestry: Irony in William Morris' *The Earthly Paradise,*" *JPRS* [*The Journal of Pre-Raphaelite Studies*] 2 (1981): 111-126 for an interpretation of Morris' use of reader-response as irony.

22. E. P. Thompson, *William Morris: Romantic to Revolutionary* (New York, 1977), p. 114.

23. Jessie Kocmanová, *The Poetic Maturing of William Morris: From "The Earthly Paradise" to "The Pilgrims of Hope"* (Praha, 1964), p. 22.

24. William Morris, "The Tables Turned: Or Nupkins Awakened," in *William Morris: Artist, Writer, Socialist* (New York, 1966), 2:549.

25. Paul Ricoeur, *Lectures on Ideology and Utopia,* ed. George H. Taylor (New York, 1986), pp. 265-266, 309-310.

I am grateful for the financial assistance of the Social Sciences and Humanities Research Council of Canada during the preparation of this article.

Virginia S. Hale and Catherine Barnes Stevenson (essay date summer 1992)

SOURCE: Hale, Virginia S., and Catherine Barnes Stevenson. "Morris' Medieval Queen: A Paradox Resolved." *Victorian Poetry* 30, no. 2 (summer 1992): 171-78.

[*In the following essay, Hale and Stevenson determine Queen Guenevere's guilt in "Defence of Guenevere," contending that "Morris created a fully sexual woman who makes no apology for her adulterous love but rather celebrates herself and her status as loyal queen."*]

William Morris' **"Defence of Guenevere"** has perplexed a number of scholars because of a seeming dichotomy between the Queen's apparent denial of the accusation of adultery—"you, O Sir Gauwaine, lie" (l. 46)—and her vivid evocation of her adulterous love for Launcelot (to which she devotes a full eighty lines of the poem).[1] Focusing on this perceived contradiction, some critics characterize Guenevere as inconsistent and her defense as paradoxical. Carole Silver, for example, argues that "the poem's title is ironic. Guenevere intends a speech of self-vindication, but her words and actions persuade the reader of her adultery."[2] Margaret Lourie finds Guenevere inconsistent and emotional in her defense of herself against the charge of adultery.[3] Blue Calhoun identifies "conflicting styles" in Guenevere's self-vindication: an "assertion of innocence that is unconscious and self-revealing" and expressed in a "highly conscious manipulative" rhetoric.[4] Dennis Balch discusses opposing desires at odds in her monologue: "Guenevere's desire to save herself from burning coexists with the contradictory desire to insist on punishment and thereby make some amends for her sin against Arthur."[5]

These seeming contradictions and inconsistencies are resolved, at least in part, by a thorough knowledge of the medieval background of the poem and of the actual text of Malory read by Morris (an 1817 edition by Robert Southey). In light of these, it is clear that Guenevere, as presented by Malory and as reimagined by Morris, is not, as previous commentators have assumed, defending herself against the charge of adultery. Furthermore, when seen in the medieval context of the code of courtly love and the law of kynde, Guenevere emerges as a highly conscious, sophisticated woman of the medieval court who would not have assumed that her love for Launcelot required any defense. In fact, far from "defending" or vindicating herself against the charge of adultery, Morris' Guenevere audaciously celebrates herself as a woman and a lover.

In an early and still important article, Laurence Perrine asserts that "**'The Defence of Guenevere'** is written by a reader of Malory for readers of Malory. . . . Morris has not stated the guilt or innocence of the Queen. He assumes that the story told by Malory will be as vivid in his reader's mind as it is in his own" (p. 236). The story told by Malory describes the Queen's condemnation as follows:

> Soo thenne there was made grete ordynaunce in this hete, that the quene must be judged to the deth. And the lawe was suche in tho dayes that what someuer they were, of what estate or degree, yf they were fonde gylty of treason, there shold be none other remedy bu dethe . . . and ryght soo was it ordeyned for quene guenever, by cause sir Mordred was escaped sore wounded, and the dehte of thyrtten knyghtes of the round table. These preues and experyences caused kyng Arthur to commaunde the quene to the fyre.[6]

Guenevere is to be burned for treason, for an offense against the kingdom. The narrator here makes clear that the deaths of Arthur's knights and of Mordred are the cause of her being sentenced "to the fire." In the 1352 statute that defined treason, behaviors like imagining the king's death, raping the king's wife or unmarried daughter, making war against the king, aiding the enemies of the king, and counterfeiting are identified as treasonous.[7] Neither in this statute nor in Malory's description of Guenevere's condemnation does the Queen's sexual conduct seem to be in the foreground. Morris was steeped not only in Malory's text but in Chaucer, in medieval chronicles, romances, and poems.[8] As a result he was able to portray a Queen Guenevere who, accused of treason, mounts a rhetorically sophisticated defense,[9] in which she contemptuously dismisses that charge, while at the same time offering a celebration of her love in the medieval tradition of the "defence d'amor." She thereby asserts her reality as a queenly and fully sexual woman.

In the course of her defense Guenevere alludes several times to incidents which in Malory's text involve trea-

son.[10] For example, she directly addresses Gauwaine twice with accusations of lying:

> "Nevertheless you, O Sir Gauwaine, lie,
> Whatever happened on through all those years
> God knows I speak truth, saying that you lie.
>
> "Being such a lady could I weep these tears
> If this were true? A great queen such as I
> Having sinn'd this way, straight her conscience sears;
>
> "And afterwards she liveth hatefully,
> Slaying and poisoning, certes never weeps.
>
> (ll. 142-149)

Surely, in referring to a queen who has "sinn'd this way," Guenevere is alluding to the crime of treason not adultery. Specifically, this passage seems to call to mind the occasion in Malory in which the Queen prepared a banquet for Sir Gauwaine and included "for him all manner of fruit, for Sir Gauwaine was a passing hot knight of nature" (p. 129). At that banquet Sir Pinel le Savage tried to poison Gauwaine, but by mistake Sir Patrise ate the poisoned apple. On that occasion Guenevere was accused of treason (p. 321) and threatened with burning only to be eventually vindicated by Launcelot's defeat of the dead man's cousin. In that instance Sir Bors argued that "the queen is not guilty . . . [but] howsomever the game goeth, there was treason among us" (p. 325). In Morris' poem, the Queen attempts to prove her innocence of the charge of treason by reminding Gauwaine of her earlier vindication on that same charge. By subtly hinting at a parallel between the circumstances surrounding these two accusations, Guenevere suggests that among her accusers now are men who are themselves treacherous conspirators. In the *Morte D'Arthur* this is in fact the case.

Instead of joining her enemies as he does in Morris' poem, Gauwaine in the *Morte* encourages Arthur to see Guenevere's assignation with Launcelot's in the context of the courtly relationship between a lady and her champion: "Though it were so that Sir Lancelot were fonde in the quenes chamber, yet it myghte be soo that he came thyder for none euylle, for ye knowe my lord said Syr Gawayne that the Quene is moche beholden unto Syr Lancelot" (Book 20, Chap. 7). Reading **"The Defence"** through the lenses of the *Morte*, it seems unlikely that Gauwaine would be accusing the Queen of adultery since he was the one who affirmed the legitimacy of her relationship with Launcelot within the courtly code. (In fact, he only turned on Lancelot and Guenevere because of Launcelot's seemingly unchivalrous act of slaying Gauwaine's unarmed brothers.) Guenevere in Morris' poem incorporates the very arguments that Malory attributes to Gauwaine. She repeatedly alludes to her status as Queen, a position which commanded the absolute loyalty of all knights of the round table:

"Is there a good knight then would stand aloof,
When a queen says with gentle queenly sound:
'O true as steel, come now and talk with me.'"

(ll. 243-245)

Later in the poem Guenevere advances her defense through a long discussion of her abduction by Sir Mellygraunce. After kidnapping her and wounding her knights, Mellygraunce discourteously enters her bedchamber and accuses the Queen of sleeping with one of her knights when he finds blood on the bedcovers. Specifically in the *Morte* he charges her with "hyghe treason" (p. 376). In point of fact, it is Mellygraunce, that "setter of traps," that unworthy and unchivalrous knight, who is the real traitor in Guenevere's eyes and in Malory's text: "And whanne the Kynge and the Quene and all the lordes knew of the treason of Sir Mellygraunce, they were all ashamed on his behalf" (p. 279). Again, Guenevere cleverly alludes to a situation in which she was accused of treason by those who themselves were acting against the best interests of the state.

In defending herself against the charges of doing ill to the kingdom, Guenevere, like the great rhetorician she is, begins by acknowledging the power and authority of the court:

God wot I ought to say, I have done ill,
And pray you all forgiveness heartily!
Because you must be right, such great lords—still.

(ll. 13-15)

That single syllable—"still"—alerts us that she intends to separate the political issues from the personal: she will make a case against the "lie" that she is a traitorous Queen while simultaneously making a case for herself as a "true" woman and lover in light of two bodies of law appropriate to a medieval woman of courtly stature: the law of kynde and the law of courtly love.[11]

The law of kynde, with which Morris was undoubtedly familiar through Chaucer's more than forty appeals to it, underlies Guenevere's initial justification of herself. Recalling her vision of her own life before she was "bought" by her husband, Guenevere reflects:

Must I give up for ever then, I thought,

"That which I deemed would ever round me move
Glorifying all things; for a little word,
Scarce ever meant at all, must I now prove

"Stone-cold for ever? Pray you does the Lord
Will that all folks should be quite happy and good?

(ll. 84-89)

Her question poses the issue of human law and human nature. Broadly construed, the natural law is derived from the essence of the creature. It implies that not only

are human beings free and equal, but that they are obliged to answer to the order of the universe by rationally following their natural inclinations. In the medieval period, Christian theologians appealed to Paul's Letter to the Romans (2.14-15), which said: "When the Gentiles who have not the law do by nature what the law requires, they are a law to themselves, even though they do not have the law. They show that what the law requires is written on their hearts." Malory allows the Fair Maid of Astolat to use natural law to justify her love for Lancelot. Having been urged by a priest to abandon thoughts of Lancelot, she replies: "Why should I leue suche thoughtes, am I not an erthely woman, and alle the whyle the brethe is in mu body I may complayne me, for my byleue is I doo none offence though I loue an erthely man" (p. 351). Similarly, Guenevere argues that since the essence of her nature is the warmth of human affection, which "glorifies all things" in the world, a God of love and mercy who wishes humans to be "happy and good" would wish her to love. If this were not so, she suggests, she would be free to "cut the cord" that binds her to God and to this life.

Not only does Guenevere conceptualize her emotional and sexual life in terms of the progress of the seasons,[12] she imagines herself as part of the natural world of her garden—transparent to its light, enraptured by it, empowered by its energy. She is the spirit of May and the spirit of Summer and thus the spirit of love. When Launcelot enters her walled garden and they share their first kiss, Guenevere simply obeys natural law. In opposition to the "lie" that the men of the court tell about her, Guenevere asserts the veracity of her passion:

this is true, the kiss
Wherewith we kissed in meeting that spring day,
I scarce dare talk of the remember'd bliss,

"When both our mouths went wandering in one way,
And aching sorely, met among the leaves;
Our hands being left behind strained far away.

(ll. 133-138)

In chapter 25 of Book 18 of the *Morte,* Malory exhorts the lovers to remember May as Guenevere did "that whil she lyued she was a tru lover, and therfore she had a god ende."

Southey's introduction and notes in his edition of Malory would certainly have encouraged Morris to see Guenevere as a "true lover," not as an adulteress. Southey twice directly addresses the issue of the sexual "morality" of the Arthurian romances. First, he refutes Addison's negative description of female chastity in romance by claiming that "Amadis was the first romance in which the female character was made respectable; and even there, although the author designed to make the women as admirable as the heroes of his tale, he thought the virtue of chastity might be dispensed with, provided they were constant in their love" (p. xxix). Later Southey corrects Roger Ascham's descriptions of the Arthurian tales as compendia of "open manslaghter and bolde bawdrie." "I believe," he writes in his notes, "that books of chivalry, instead of increasing the corruption of the age, tended very greatly to raise the standard of morals. It is to the story of Lancelot and Guenevere that we owe one of the finest passages in Dante" (p. 490). Indeed, Carole Silver concludes that Southey's attitude toward adultery enabled the Pre-Raphaelites to select "those sources which would extenuate Arthurian women" and to "reinterpret the figures they derived from the Morte D'Arthur . . . [so that] constancy and passion in chivalric love replace marital fidelity as a test of virtue"(p. 251).[13]

Guenevere's virtue is grounded in the knowledge that she has been true to the kingdom (in the sense of wishing no harm to come to it or to the king) and true to her passional self. She urges her accusers not to join the ranks of those like Mellygraunce who "fought against the Lord" (both Arthur and the divine order) and were "shent." Put simply, Guenevere argues that her beautiful face means a beautiful soul:

> Therefore, my lords, take heed lest you be blent
>
> "With all this wickedness; say no rash word
> Against me, being so beautiful; my eyes,
> Wept all away to grey, may bring some sword
>
> "To drown you in your blood; see my breast rise,
> Like waves of purple sea, as here I stand;
> And how my arms are moved in wonderful wise
>
> . . . . .
>
> . . . will you dare
> When you have looked a little on my brow,
>
> "To say this thing is vile? or will you care
> For any plausible lies of cunning woof,
> When you can see my face with no lie there
>
> For ever? am I not gracious proof?
>
> (ll. 222-241)

In medieval times, physiognomy, "the art of discovering the characteristic qualities of the mind or temper of a man by observation of his form and the movement of his face or body, or both,"[14] existed as a bona fide branch of medical science, like astrology—to which it is closely allied—and alchemy. Every educated man or woman in the later Middle Ages would have believed it possible "to judge with a certain degree of accuracy and with approximate infallibility the inner character of a man from the study of his form and features" (Curry, p. 57). In a medieval framework her argument from beauty makes sense.

As a medieval woman, Guenevere's sense of the rightness of her love and of her truth to her sexual self would have existed in the context of the code of courtly love. And it is in this frame of reference that she can most fully be understood. The very first rule of courtly love, according to Andreas Capellanus, is that "Marriage is no real excuse for not loving."[15] This rule is elaborated in a decision rendered in one of the courts of love by the Countess of Champagne: "We declare and hold as firmly established that love cannot exert its powers between two people who are married. . . . A precept of love tells us that no woman, even if she is married, can be crowned with the reward of the King of Love unless she is seen to be enlisted in the service of Love outside the bonds of wedlock" (pp. 106-107). This is the context for Guenevere's contemptuous reference to her marriage as being "bought by Arthur's great name and his little love" (ll. 82-83), and her allusion to her marriage vow as "a little word / Scarce ever meant at all" (ll. 86-87). In light of this one can understand her warm praise for her champion Launcelot who defended her against Mellygraunce, that gross violator of courtly norms:

> my knight cried and said:
> 'Slayer of unarm'd men . . .
>
> "'Setter of traps, I pray you guard your head,
> By God I am so glad to fight with you,
> Stripper of ladies.
>
> (ll. 188-192)

She continues:

> as I saw my knight
> "Along the lists look to my stake and pen
> With such a joyous smile, it made me sigh
> From agony beneath my waist chain.
>
> (ll. 204-207)

Launcelot was his lady's true champion, a courtly lover who lived up to Capellanus' injunction that "every man is bound in time of need to come to the aid of his beloved" (p. 151). In a courtly context, the love of Guenevere and Launcelot would draw plaudits.

In the Victorian era when women's sexuality generated enormous cultural uneasiness and marital fidelity was sanctified, Morris created a fully sexual woman who makes no apology for her adulterous love but rather celebrates herself and her status as loyal Queen. There is no inconsistency in Guenevere's self-presentation because Morris, like a true champion of his lady, was able to enter into the medieval frame of mind fully enough to allow his Queen never to doubt—or to need to defend—her sexuality or her adulterous love.

Notes

1. *The Pre-Raphaelites and Their Circle,* ed. Cecil Y. Lang (Boston, 1968), pp. 161-170.

2. Carole E. Silver, *The Romance of William Morris* (Athens, Ohio, 1982), p. 24.

3. Margaret A. Lourie, *William Morris: The Defence of Guenevere and Other Poems* (New York, 1981), p. 14.

4. Blue Calhoun, *The Pastoral Vision of William Morris: The Earthly Paradise* (Athens, Georgia, 1975), p. 46.

5. Dennis R. Balch, "Guenevere's Fidelity to Arthur in 'The Defence of Guenevere' and 'King Arthur's Tomb,'" *VP* [*Victorian Poetry*] 13, nos. 3-4 (1975): 65. A sizeable body of criticism about this poem is devoted to two interlocked questions: the nature and the extent of Guenevere's guilt and the verbal strategies that she employs in order to win over her audiences—her auditors within the imagined context of the poem and her readers. See also the following: Laurence Perrine, "Morris's Guenevere: An Interpretation," *PQ* [*Philological Quarterly*] 39 (1960): 196-200; Meredith B. Raymond, "The Arthurian Group in *The Defence of Guenevere and Other Poems*," *VP* 4 (1966): 213-218; Carole G. Silver, "'The Defence of Guenevere': A Further Interpretation," *SEL* [*Studies in English Literature, 1500-1900*] 9 (1969): 695-702; Angela Carson, "Morris' Guenevere: A Further Note," *PQ* 42 (1963): 131-134; and John Hollow, "William Morris and the Judgment of God," *PMLA* [*Publications of the Modern Language Association of America*] 86 (1971): 446-451.

6. Thomas Malory, *The Byrth, Lyf, and Actes of King Arthur,* ed. Robert Southey, 2 vols. (London, 1817), p. 400.

7. Alan Harding, *A Social History of English Law* (Baltimore, 1966), p. 79.

8. Jack Lindsay, *William Morris: His Life and Work* (London, 1975), p. 53; J. W. Mackail, *The Life of William Morris* (London, 1897), 1:39.

9. Jonathan F. S. Post, "Guenevere's Critical Performance," *VP* 17 (1979): 318, pays tribute to the Queen's "majesty" as a verbal artist gifted with enormous "rhetorical energy." On the other hand, Ellen Sternberg, "Verbal and Visual Seduction in 'The Defence of Guenevere,'" *JPRS* [*The Journal of Pre-Raphaelite Studies*] 6, no. 2 (1986), finds Guenevere's pleas "specious" and her arguments "capricious or disingenuous, . . . [or] forensically hollow" (p. 47). She sees Guenevere as an artist who "triumphs" not through reasoned argument but through beauty and passion (p. 51).

10. Malory's interest in treason may have been more than idle. His checkered career includes a number of fines and imprisonments for crimes ranging from cattle rustling to rape, but he is recorded as pleading guilty only to non-payment of a debt. The crime for which he spent the last years of his life in jail has been variously described, and the precise term "treason" has not been used, but most scholars regard it as a political matter. One strong piece of evidence to support that view is the fact that Malory was twice specifically excluded from general pardons issued by Edward IV. It is possible that he was released when Henry VI was restored to the throne in 1470, but his burial at the Gray Friars near Newgate suggests he may have died in prison.

11. J. M. S. Tompkins, *William Morris: An Approach to the Poetry* (London, 1988), p. 55, aptly observes that Guenevere "is a figure imagined by a young mid-nineteenth century poet, in close accordance with the fifteenth-century text, fit to move in its scenes and to be and do what Malory describes. Her beliefs and assumptions are within the mediaeval frame."

12. For discussions of the seasonal patterns employed in this poem, see Robert Stallman, "The Lovers' Progress: An Investigation of William Morris' 'The Defence of Guenevere' and 'King Arthur's Tomb,'" *SEL* 15 (1975): 657-670; Audrey Shaw Bledsoe, "The Seasons of Camelot: William Morris' Arthurian Poems," *South Atlantic Bulletin* 42 (1977): 114-122; and Calhoun, pp. 42-44.

13. We are indebted here to Carole Silver's excellent work on Morris, particularly to her article "Victorian Spellbinders: Arthurian Women and the Pre-Raphaelite Circle," *The Passing of Arthur: New Essays in the Arthurian Tradition,* ed. Christopher Baswell and William Sharpe (New York, 1988), pp. 249-259, in which she points out the influence of Southey's notes on Morris' interpretation of Guenevere.

14. Walter Clyde Curry, *Chaucer and the Medieval Sciences* (New York, 1960), p. 56.

15. Andreas Capellanus, *The Art of Courtly Love* (New York, 1941), p. 92.

Norman Talbot (essay date spring 1997)

SOURCE: Talbot, Norman. "The 'Pomona' Lyric and Female Power." *Victorian Poetry* 35, no. 1 (spring 1997): 71-81.

[*In the following essay, Talbot offers a feminist perspective on "Pomona" and maintains that Morris was aware and concerned with feminist and ecological issues.*]

1

Admirers of William Morris were (until relatively recently) inclined to assume that his later poetry dispenses with the erotic complexities of the *Defence of Guinevere* volume and the menacing mortal implications of most of the *Earthly Paradise* narratives.[1] Critics who had not read most of the ten prose romances of his last decade were especially prone to believe that his later poetry consisted simply of "affirmations," such as that brave London Lads will rise and Kelmscott four-posters tranquillize. Undoubtedly, affirmation is there, but as a hard-earned fictive triumph, not a cosy guarantee. Many recent readings of the later work, including those of Frederick Kirchhoff and Carole Silver,[2] are undoubtedly more alert; however, the tapestry lyrics have not been studied at length, and the present essay seeks both to remedy this and to connect one of their crucial motifs with elements in the major romances.

The lyric **"Pomona"**[3] indicates something of the resilience and integrity of Morris' later imagination. Although, like its companion **"Flora,"** the poem was written for inclusion in an eponymous tapestry,[4] unlike the tapestries the poems do not form a diptych: Morris, rightly, printed **"Flora"** second, though naturalism would dictate that flowers come before fruit.

"Pomona"

I am the ancient Apple-Queen,
As once I was so am I now.
For evermore a hope unseen,
Betwixt the blossom and the bough.

Ah, where's the river's hidden Gold!
And where the windy grave of Troy?
Yet come I as I came of old,
From out the heart of summer's joy.

"Pomona" is certainly less dark, in the two senses of intellectually obscure and imagistically gloomy, than, say, **"The Blue Closet"** or **"The Ring Given to Venus."**[5] The palette and voice of the lyric belong, after all, to a goddess, and goddesses (even those deconstructed from classical mythology and constructed into the phenomena of the seasons) must comprehend something of their own mystery. If **"The Blue Closet"** had been sung by the sea-witch instead of the incarcerated ladies, the human tragedy would not have been averted, but it would have been both more highly sexed and more explicable. Had **"The Ring Given to Venus"** been focalized by Venus rather than being reliant on mortal understanding, we would have had a different perspective on whether the hard-to-get young human male were more to be despised, pitied, or admired; we would have put on some of the goddess' knowledge with her power.

The apparent simplicity of **"Pomona"** should not mislead us. The speaker's "exquisite promise of renewal"[6] is, from mortal viewpoints, complicated. She is ancient and timelessly recurrent, certainly, but that takes only two lines to affirm. Though she is always the same,

may not human beings be very different from those who, two thousand years ago, consciously believed in vegetation goddesses? After all, the poem and its companion were written to accompany quite sophisticated figures designed not for worship but as decorative aesthetic objects. Relations between mortals and immortal dispensers of apples have never been reassuring: the fruit of the tree of the knowledge of good and evil in the Garden of Eden was, traditionally, an apple.[7]

Structurally, the joyous pride of the goddess affirming her integrity and eternal recurrence begins and ends—that is, it frames—an affirmation of mystery (ll. 3 and 4) and two rhetorical questions (ll. 5 and 6). This envelope design, where major assertions form a strong, clear border to much more problematic material, would not surprise a tapestry weaver as much as it does a lyric poet.[8] Of course, the frame is part of the poem's voice, not a frame for the voice.[9]

In lines three and four Pomona offers a more elusive mystery than that of Edenic disobedience. The point at which flower becomes fruit, intercourse becomes fertility, is invisible in space, undetectable in time. Geneticists cannot explain away the mystery; they merely re-express it. Blake, Morris' great predecessor in radical vision, evokes it superbly:

Every Time less than a pulsation of the artery
Is equal in its period & value to Six Thousand years,
For in this Period the Poet's Work is Done, & all the great
Events of Time start forth & are conceived in such a Period,
Within a Moment, a Pulsation of the Artery.[10]

No mortal science or art can locate, temporally or spatially, Pomona's work and essence: she bloweth where she listeth. But we can hear the assertion as either consoling or challenging, even taunting.

The two questions that follow explain this, but their explanation changes the poem's balance so that the final assertion carries a different weight from the beginning. Each is unerringly selected to pull down masculine vanity by evoking a heroic tale that males think of as ancient, and as about males. Like the paired tales in *The Earthly Paradise,* one comes from Morris' beloved Northern story-hoard, the other from the classics.[11] In fact they evoke, in one line each, the most massive and revered epics of those traditions.

Males often assume that maleness is "what makes the world go round," what makes time human and measurable, what makes history. They traditionally treasure stories that seem to embody and justify masculine, heroic qualities such as active aggression, competitive daring, acquisitive pride, and decisive leadership. To be "male," males are taught, is to do, while the "female" role is simply to be. Natural recurrence such as Pomona proclaims and identifies with is marginalized into negatives such as inaction, denial of development, passivity, effeminacy. The womb gives birth to the hero and justifies his quest, and he may impregnate a few wombs himself (indeed he must, to pass on his sterling qualities and well-earned kingdom and treasure to a dynasty of male heirs), but good stories aren't "love-stories." Love, fertility, and nurture are mere stasis at best, and can actually discourage the hero.

In such male-transmitted stories, action seems to be male-engendered. Energy is celebrated as the pursuit of change, whether to epic triumph or to tragedy. The "Gold" of line five evokes the story-group of the *Volsungasaga* and *Nibelungenlied.* "Troy," in line six, necessarily evokes the *Iliad,* but also, because the question is about Troy's grave, the two travel-epics that begin with its fall, the *Odyssey* and the *Aeneid.* Morris translated three of these five, and also wrote his own **Sigurd the Volsung.**

The northern story-group is divided on the causes of the tragedy. The *Volsungasaga* hinges on male conflict, at the divine level, over Andvari's hoard, hidden in a river. From it the ring Andvari's-Loom enters the mortal world of violence and deception.[12] Its use as a love-token between Brynhild and Sigurd proves that it was he, in Gunnar's shape, who won her. Though Sigurd did not intend to deceive her, she and Gudrun, the focalizations who give their names to the last two of the four books of **Sigurd the Volsung,** are deeply wronged. All three female heroes, Signy, Brynhild, and Gudrun, are wed to male falsehood and murder.

The *Nibelungenlied* focuses on Kriemhild and Hagen almost throughout, but Siegfried uses his invisibility to lend Gunther an unmerited status, deceiving and defeating the mighty Brunhild. When this invisible brother-in-law "masters" her and, perhaps impulsively, steals her gold ring and girdle, she is deflowered and robbed of her previous virgin strength. It is psychologically most apt that she should resent and revile her husband's supposed liegeman and precipitate his murder. The tragedy hinges on the vicious taunting and flyting of the two queens, but this is provoked by their husbands' deceptions. Later, the treasure earned by Siegfried's mighty deeds is stolen from Kriemhild by Hagen and her brothers and sunk in the Rhine near Locheim, but none of the treacherous Burgundians lives to reveal its hiding-place. It ends as "the river's hidden Gold."[13]

The Trojan conflict is over treasure in female form. In the *Iliad* Helen's role as actant (however intriguing such more complex images as her weaving may be) is strictly to be a prize for the victor, like Cryseis and Briseis in the "wrath of Achilles" contention that begins the epic. Helen is only the cause of the war in a passive way: she is the wife won by a king, then seduced from his possession by a prince, then treasured (held in protective custody) by his father, the super-paterfamilias King Priam, while male armies fight over her. Superficially, only male prowess is privileged, but in another reading, male values are interrogated, by the fates and responses of Andromache and Hecuba, for example.

But this obvious set of narrative ironies does not account for the ambiguous register of Pomona's questions. Whether readers construct her as primarily mocking and challenging or more consolatory and compassionate, she is speaking from a position of knowledge and power, an eternal female and generative power. All heroes fall; even swords of untarnished fame soon rust to impotence. The male contribution to the "hope unseen" is minimal and anonymous: some pollen may be needed, but it scarcely matters whose.

Curses like the one on Andvari's-Loom and the plottings of apparently subordinate "wise" women are what bring Norse heroes low. As for the male ego, once the candidates enter their more permanent state of death the Valkyries, as choosers of the slain, are the only judges of who, if anyone, counts as heroic. The "grave" of Troy is dug because Helen has no choice about falling in love with Paris: the rivalry of three goddesses, and specifically Paris' bribery by Aphrodite, causes that. Again, these three are rivals because another goddess, malevolently jealous, has given a golden apple to start their strife. The helplessness of the mortal bait-and-reward females during the action of the *Iliad* contrasts with the power of Thetis and Hera on Olympus, who find even Zeus remarkably pliant. Athene is the major figure in the *Odyssey,* no matter what other divinities the hero offends, and Venus is the will behind every step Aeneas takes, even the blood-smeared climactic step over Turnus' body.

Performers and readers must choose the tone they need for Pomona's last proclamation. "Yet" can be concessive: "in spite of the triviality of male self-aggrandising story," or "though you power-males don't deserve it," or "the state of the world may seem to deny it, but," or even "though you humans sometimes realize your striving is irrelevant." It can be iterative, meaning "still," which may also be given an ominous tilt: "so far" or "as yet." This last sense has a hortatory aspect: we must not take our apples for granted.

As the voice of Pomona is autumnal, a richer meaning still is available, adding subtlety to the affirmative reading. A whole story can be folded into a question, but it can also be unfolded again. These stories, and our awareness of their past-ness, are aspects of the harvest. Where the gold and the grave are is not only a matter for archaeologists: all the "male" energy expended on acquiring gold, on burying a city, has been conserved in story, laid in store to be fuel for our communal winter. At least as artist, the male can be nurturing and fertile. Like the apples, his tales harmonize sweetness and astringency, pleasurable nourishment, and thoughtful memory. Story harvests and redeems history.

2

Poems by the Way is a dismissive title. May Morris glossed it as identifying poems written "as a distraction in the midst of more important productions" (*CW, [Collected Works]* 9:xxxiv). Today we are less likely to accept clear divisions between important work and trivia, crucial work and distraction (or to take the author's word for anything much). It is especially unwise to take Morris' dismissive comments for truths; he was addicted to deprecation of his own work, and of poetry in general. He was also accustomed to working in large poetic units, which neither were nor could have been all "poetry" in the honorific sense.

We have abundant evidence, too, that he used various arts as "distraction" from each other, moving restlessly between them to avoid being left without any occupation or bored by the one he was in. It is typical that he should contribute good verse to a tapestry.[14] No competent critic will fall into Gardner's error of quoting May Morris' categorization of the group of poems **"Pomona"** belongs to, "verses written for pictures, tapestries and embroidery" (p. xxxvii), as if it were a derogatory literary judgment (he even adds dismissive words like "slightness" and "inconsequential").[15]

Far from Morris sharing the post-Eliotian sentimentality that a poem designed to be woven into a tapestry must necessarily be trivial compared to a poem printed in a book of poems, he would have argued the opposite to be the case: no one need ever open a particular book at a particular page unless that page were enjoyable in itself. However, a tapestry or carving, if a thing of beauty worth looking at in its own right, must add a special, complex pleasure and a social availability to poems presented in that mode.

"Flora" (9:193), the voice of Spring and Summer flowering, is physically parallel to **"Pomona."** **"Flora"** cannot ever be as fruitful of story as Autumn, and her emphasis is on her role as servant: "I am the handmaid of the earth." This echo of Mary's self-description, "the handmaid of the Lord," foreshadows the pregnancy that replaces the blossoms in the Goddess' Pomona-aspect. But "the Lord" is a very male sky-god, while Flora serves the mother-goddess Earth,[16] who bears the children of the year herself rather than commissioning a virgin to do so.

Flora claims no centrality to her own story. Her verbs are "broider" and "deck"; her attention touches on "gown," "garland," and "hem," that they should be "fair" and "glorious," so that she stimulates "mirth" and "renown." When the Mother gives birth, as she does abundantly, Flora becomes, briefly, a charming nurse-maid. To amuse the children she tosses her only gift, her petals, into the sun and wind which gave them. This openhanded self-forgetfulness contrasts with the cowardice, or the assertiveness, of lesser lives. If not a Cleopatra, she is at least a Charmian.

Another complex celebration of Spring from *Poems by the Way,* **"Spring's Bedfellow"** (9:132), describes a scene of mutual seduction. Sadder and wiser from a winter of self-misled male egoism, one form of love-sickness, young Sorrow lies asleep; Spring, tender as Flora and fruitful of stories as Pomona, leans over him, singing of heroic "days of old," "life and deeds." In response Sorrow sings of love, and the exchange makes him bolder and she sweeter till "they sang the same." Then they can make love and beget "an earthly bliss."

Like the pan-seasonal magic of the famous **"Apology"** for *The Earthly Paradise,* the season-poetry of *Poems by the Way* relates to the role of the artist amid the flux of time. Now, however, the narrator-wizard's male vanity, that delights in making Nature do as she is told, has been pulled down. The four quatrains on the seasons, printed near **"Pomona"** and **"Flora"** and also written for visual art-work, have a similar pattern of acceptance to theirs, perhaps even more emphatic in the alternative **"Winter"** text May Morris quotes in the Introduction (p. xxxvii). Their androgynous responsiveness and their delight in their contrary truths oppose the "male" capitalist ego-obsession that Morris stigmatizes in **"Mine and Thine"** (p. 200), from the same collection:

> Two words about the world we see
> And nought but Mine & Thine they be.
> . . . . .
> No manslayer then the whole world o'er
> When Mine & Thine are known no more.
> . . . . .
> But now so rageth greediness
> That each desireth nothing less
> Than all the world, and all his own;
> And all for him and him alone.
>
> (ll. 1-20)

The poem is supposed to come from a medieval Flemish original, but man-slaying, mercantile greed, and generalized lusts for dominance still typify "male" rather than "female" thinking.

My implication that Morris, who was never associated with women's suffrage, anticipates major concerns of feminist theology,[17] may surprise some readers. Far less surprising is his kinship, as a pioneer environmental conservationist, with those twentieth-century socio-ecological critics who accuse a male-centered "Culture" of attempting to equate the female with a victimized and debauched "Nature" provided specifically for male (that is, active human) exploration, subjugation, and industrial and agricultural exploitation.[18]

Women's suffrage is a non-issue for Morris (as it was for George Eliot, for example), because he saw the vote as a trivializing placebo to the real social diseases of his time. The work of the late Linda Richardson establishes his consistent alertness to the major issues that engaged the Victorian versions of radical feminist movements.[19] Though he endured males-only school years and ambiguous male University life, Morris always lived in, and worked best in, female-dominated households like that of his childhood. His many remarkable female allies included (to name but two late examples) Louise Michel, fiery hero of the barricades of the Paris Commune and influence on *The Pilgrims of Hope,* and Annie Besant, whose collaboration with him in radical endeavors included financial backing for the first modern strike, that of the Match-Girls.

Morris had a clearer awareness of the ecological and gender ironies of the culture he so generously opposed than any of its writers that I have read. In *News from Nowhere* it is a woman (and the lover and mother Clara rather than the chrono-visionary Ellen) who indicts Victorian and pre-Victorian science and technology as a literally un-natural neurotic male drive towards "mastery" born of economic slavery:

> "Was not their mistake once more bred of the life of slavery that they had been living?—a life which was always looking upon everything, except mankind, animate and inanimate—'nature,' as people used to call it—as one thing, and mankind as another? It was natural to people thinking this way, that they should try to make 'nature' their slave, since they thought 'nature' was something outside them."[20]

Urban critics are sometimes tempted to equate celebration of the seasons with sentimentality, but this is as illogical as assuming that the celebration of love is itself sentimental. The motif of female power both offers a subject generative and generous enough for any lyric, and implies complexity and danger: mother-goddesses can have other priorities than the reassurance of mortal males. The two ancient tales evoked in **"Pomona"** do not insist on their more dismaying implications, but juxtaposition with Morris' larger late works will justify a reading that problematizes the "charm" of the tapestries.

3

In the great romances of Morris' last decade[21] time, change, and inevitable personal death condition all action and characterization, not only of female and male mortals but even of demi-goddesses, including Pomona-principles almost above mortality. Some of these are rulers or exploiters, but being female is no better excuse for power-hunger than being male.

The powerful and beautiful Wood-Sun in *The House of the Wolfings* is a renegade Valkyrie, whose attempt to preserve the life of Thiodolf, her mortal lover, almost destroys his people—the focus of his name, the story, and its title. Their daughter, the tribal shaman Hall-Sun, not only accepts heroic death but weaves it into the communal epic of the tribe's continuity. Pomona, the sum of these two sun-women, presides over the end of male deeds.

In *The Wood Beyond the World,* Walter is preserved by the Maid, a recognizable Flora, who replaces the self-indulgent Lady, Pomona as Fatal Woman. The Maid asserts that she did not strike the actual blow that fells the Lady, but she does not prove it: Walter has to choose to believe her. He does so, and accepts his passive share of the guilt in the death. In their escape back into the world, the Maid employs her maiden Flora-power in replacing the dead Pomona-Lady, but later, marrying Walter and becoming a mortal queen, she casts aside any but mortal authority.

The Well at the World's End also presents the replacement of one Pomona by a girl, initially an innocent Flora. In this case, though, the Lady of Abundance (who, however bad she has been for others, is certainly good to Ralph) is not destroyed by Ursula. She is cut down by her own jealous husband, for reasons she well understands: for centuries her possession of the Well's power had divided and scattered peoples rather than unified them, and used up her male warrior lovers rather than fulfilled them. It has also effectively ended. Sorry to leave Ralph's embraces, she directly bequeaths him to Ursula, both before her death, by an emblematic gift to her successor, and after it, by a strange instructive appearance in his dreams.[22]

The most eloquent alignment of ironies about Pomona-power is in *The Water of the Wondrous Isles.* The fate of the self-styled Queen of the Isles, a travestied Pomona, is sealed when Birdalone, as Flora, comes to her magic island. Birdalone later sends knights to that island (on the male quest of liberating the captive maidens there) and one of them, forced to the Queen's bed as object of her lust, discovers her supply of a mortality-defying drug. Meanwhile Birdalone, having used this unheroic masculine quest to free her three maiden friends into the chaos and truth of unmagicked life, makes passionate supplication to the Earth-powers—she does not want Pomona attributes but the love of Arthur, one of the knights. The answer to her prayer is vivid and violent, and makes her, de facto, a destroyer of masculine standards of right conduct. This has an inevitable and bloody cost, and a strange mixture of pathos and black comedy attends her attempts to make reparation—from respectable female needlework to dressing as an imitation knight. The generosity that harmonizes her story comes not from an orchard-goddess but Habundia, a wild-crab Pomona, spirit of that dark ecological lucidity, the woodland miscalled Evilshaw.

In all the romances, women as well as men are subject to the story's logic. There is no naive stacking of the cards against males. On the other hand, women are shown to respond more readily to the Pomona-principle that stimulates, ripens, and harvests the story and the passions of its mortal role-players. Males often find themselves helpless; this drives mad the heroic Arthur and the formidable Baron of Sunway, and tests all the others sharply, sometimes fatally. **"Pomona"** is the voice of a goddess that mortal males can hear variously, but should try to respond to with delight—mixed with an awe that is wholly salutary.

Notes

1. Geoffrey Grigson's glib dismissal in his Faber selection, *A Choice of William Morris's Verse* (London: 1969), is only slightly extreme for his generation: "What has so often been called his tapestry verse . . . hardly bears reprinting." He duly fails to reprint "Pomona," and much else of value.

2. For example, Frederick Kirchhoff, *"Love is Enough*: A Crisis in William Morris' Poetic Development," *VP* [*Victorian Poetry*] 15 (1977): 297-306, and Carole Silver, *The Romance of William Morris* (Athens: Ohio Univ. Press, 1982), pp. 86-93 and 98-100, both read Morris' most complex later poem, *Love is Enough,* in terms of a fierce warfare between ironic negation and passionate longing, even though the one regards the work as a powerful evocation of psychological agony, and the other as far from successful. Kirchhoff's Twayne biography of Morris (Boston, 1979) and his study of the relationship of poetry to emotional biography in *William Morris: the Construction of a Male Self 1856-72* (Athens: Ohio Univ. Press, 1990) are the fullest of his many important contributions to Morris studies. Silver's book is especially valuable on the later works.

3. 9:193; hereafter cited as *CW* [*Collected Works*]. Page numbers follow parenthetically in the text when other poems or phrases of the introduction are quoted from volume 9

4. The very restrained figures are by Edward Burne-Jones.

5. "The Blue Closet," *CW,* 1:111-113, is from *The Defence of Guenevere;* "The Ring Given to Venus," *CW,* 6:136-174, is a January tale from *The Earthly Paradise.* They are specified here simply as successful early narratives hinging on a mortal male's meeting with the goddess.

6. The phrase is from Brian Spittles' review of Peter Faulkner, ed., *William Morris: Selected Poems,* in *JWMS* 10, no. 1 (1992): 39.

7. For whatever reason, Dante Gabriel Rossetti never finished his nightmare vision of the apple-giver as Fatal Woman, "The Orchard-Pit," which he forecast to Janey Morris in 1869 "will be I hope the best thing I have done" (*Dante Gabriel Rossetti and Jane Morris: The Correspondence,* ed. John Bryson [Oxford: Clarendon Press, 1976], p. 30). W. M. Rossetti's edition of his brother's *Works* (London 1911) reprints it, pp. 239-240, along with its extended short story version, pp. 607-609. We can be sure Morris saw the poem's draft; at any rate "Pomona" is a superb antidote to its misogyny, yet implies quite as much awe.

8. However, song-writers like Burns often use a framing chorus that is far more striking and memorable than any of the verses, and offers a "timeless" perspective on their consecutive events. Burns also uses an annular design, ending a song by repeating its first lines; "Ae Fond Kiss," for example, seems anti-climactic without its music.

9. Consistently with his habitual denigration of Burne-Jones' figures, Paul Thompson (*The Work of William Morris* [New York: Viking Press, 1972], p. 200) claims that the "Pomona" and "Flora" tapestries are only successful "because the background dominates." If this were true, would this material still be "background"? The poems, as dramatic monologues, can only imply background; typically, and fortunately, Thompson does not mention either poem!

10. William Blake, *Milton,* First Book, Plate 28, line 62, to Plate 29, line 3, in *William Blake's Writings,* ed. G. E. Bentley, Jr., 2 vols. (Oxford: Clarendon Press, 1978), 1:379-380.

11. Carole Silver has taken to task both my early study, "Women and Goddesses in the Romances of William Morris" (*Southern Review* [Adelaide] 3, no. 4 [1969]: 339-357) and Charlotte Oberg's *A Pagan Prophet* (Charlottesville: Univ. Press of Virginia, 1978), because we "seem unaware that Morris, supporting the ideas of Jacob and Wilhelm Grimm, depicts all female deities as varied, but essentially interchangeable, aspects of one primal goddess" (*The Romance of William Morris,* p. 213, n. 21). I must admit that such interchangeability, however unproductive and question-begging in narrative terms, and especially when applied to the developing relationship of mortal and divine femaleness, undoubtedly privileges the alignment of superficially contrasting cultural set-pieces. Compare the radical feminist approach to mythology and legend of such collections as Merlin

Stone's *Ancient Mirrors of Womanhood* (Boston: Beacon Press, 1991), first published 1979 by New Sibylline Books.

12. In *Sigurd the Volsung* (*CW,* vol. 12), the accursed ring is called "Andvari's Ring of Gain." When Sigurd chooses it before any other treasure in Fafnir's hoard, the savage autumnal ironies of this choice, perhaps hinted in "the Ransom's utmost grain," are made overt in "first of all the harvest" (p. 118).

13. Similarly, in Richard Wagner's libretto to the first opera in his *Ring das Nibelungen* sequence, *Das Rheingold,* the Rhinemaidens properly resent the male theft and treachery that deprives them of their treasured gold, and curse it.

14. Apropos of "Pomona," Peter Faulkner, in *Against the Age: An Introduction to William Morris* (Boston: Allen and Unwin, 1980), p. 124, emphasizes Morris' readiness to employ poetry as merely one among the crafts and arts, "not a key to higher truths." Even if the lyric does not secrete metaphysical profundity, its implications seem as rich as those of most eight-line poems.

15. Delbert R. Gardner, *An Idle Singer and His Audience* (The Hague: Mouton, 1975), pp. 90-91. May Morris was merely, and usefully, pointing out that some of these had previously been printed in their exhibition catalogues.

16. The earlier "earth" becomes "Earth" in line five.

17. See, for example, the pioneering work of Mary Daly, *The Church and the Second Sex* (New York: Harper & Row, 1968) and especially *Beyond God the Father* (Boston: Beacon Press, 1973). A particularly valuable perspective on Flora-Pomona ironies, with rich implications for the perilous topic of the virgin birth is Clarissa W. Atkinson, Constance H. Buchanan, and Margaret R. Miles, *Immaculate and Powerful: the Female in Sacred Image and Social Reality* (Boston: Beacon Press, 1985). See also Ann Loades, ed., *Feminist Theology* (London: SPCK Press, 1990). This comparison does not of course imply that Morris was a Christian, or generally sympathetic to any of the Churches of his day.

18. See, for example, Carolyn Merchant, *The Death of Nature* (San Francisco: Harper & Row, 1980) and Susan Griffin, *Pornography and Silence: Culture's Revenge against Nature* (London: Women's Press, 1981).

19. Her Oxford D.Phil. dissertation, "William Morris and Women: Experience and Representation," though unfortunately unpublished (due to her untimely death in 1990), can be consulted in the William Morris Society library, Kelmscott House, Hammersmith, London. The society has also printed in *The Journal of the William Morris Society* two short articles she derived from the dissertation, "Louise Michel and William Morris" (8, no. 2 [1989]: 26-29) and her feminist interrogation of "William Morris's Childhood and Schooling" (9, no. 1 [1990]: 15-19).

20. *News From Nowhere, CW,* 16:179.

21. *The House of the Wolfings* and *The Story of the Glittering Plain* share volume 14, *The Roots of the Mountains* is 15, *The Wood Beyond the World* and *Child Christopher* share 17 with translations of some minor French romances, *The Well at the World's End* fills 18 and 19, *The Water of the Wondrous Isles* is 20, and *The Sundering Flood* is 21. Though all are relevant, only the most emphatic Pomona-figures are overtly referred to here.

22. Her apparition "gets wrong" Ursula's name, using the deliberate mistake "Dorothea," which means "gift of the Goddess."

Florence S. Boos (essay date February 2000)

SOURCE: Boos, Florence S. "'The Banners of the Spring to Be': The Dialectical Pattern of Morris's Later Poetry." *English Studies* 81, no. 1 (February 2000): 14-40.

[*In the following essay, Boos provides an "inclusive and eclectic view" of Morris's poetic development.*]

William Morris's contemporaries viewed him primarily as the author of ***The Earthly Paradise,*** and to a lesser extent of ***The Life and Death of Jason*** and a few later works. Most later critics sharply reversed this judgment, in favor of ***The Defence of Guenevere,*** which they interpreted as a youthful proto-modernist text of implosive intensity.[1] This profile persists, for example, in Fiona MacCarthy's comprehensive biography, *William Morris: A Life for Our Time.* MacCarthy makes some sustained efforts to evaluate the poems on their own aesthetic terms, but reimposes the usual canon in her summary assessment: 'I would not press the claims of Morris's own favourite ***Sigurd the Volsung***; it is too large, too chant-like. Volsungs are out of fashion . . . But there is much to reward the modern reader in Morris's early poems, ***The Defence of Guenevere,*** short, spare, edgy narratives of violence and loss. And most of all his 1890s novels repay reading [:] *The Wood Beyond the World;The Water of the Wondrous Isles; The Well at the World's End . . .*'[2]

Ironically, perhaps, ***The Earthly Paradise***'s length, epic conventions, and narrative architectonic alienate many readers, but so also do the relative brevity, randomness, and apparent disparity of Morris's later work. In this essay I hope to offer a more inclusive and eclectic view of Morris's poetic development, and suggest that other parts of his poetic *oeuvre* remain valuable for the variety of their plots and aesthetic effects; for the novelty of their experimental efforts to blend poetry and prose; and for their embodiments of complex and philosophically sophisticated beliefs about language, history, and the fundamental sources of emotion.

Morris's substantial poetic output after the publication of *The Earthly Paradise* included the four volumes of *Love Is Enough, Sigurd the Volsung, Poems by the Way,* and *The Pilgrims of Hope,* a number of uncollected poems, and many lovely paeans interspersed through the prose romances. Only measured against the scale of Morris's other literary achievements—translations from French, Greek, Latin, and Icelandic, writings for *Commonweal* and essays on art and socialism, and historical, political and quasi-Scandinavian prose romances—might his later poems seem in any sense 'slight'.

I will trace the evolution of Morris's later poetry in this essay, and note how its many interrelations developed as he grew older, reevaluated his sense of audience, and recast poetic approaches originally devised for the final sections of *The Earthly Paradise.* Morris had already revised extensively the manner of his earlier poems, of course; the later medieval tales of *The Earthly Paradise* differed substantially from *Jason,* and both from the tone of *The Defence.*

Less closely observed has been the degree to which Morris's subsequent poems—*Love Is Enough, Sigurd the Volsung, The Pilgrims of Hope, Poems By the Way,* and all the shorter lyrics—are metrically and historically diverse. Morris's aims were consistent, but he had an experimental bent. Study of the experimental aspects of Morris's later poetry can help us understand his purposes, for they evolved alongside his political convictions, and merged into the mighty torrent of his prose. I will argue that these later works embodied a deeply-held idiosyncratic view of the purpose of poetry, or at least of his poetry: to blend poetic techniques with the language of narrative to attain 'popular' and folk-lore-derived ends.

Similar ideals had animated German and English romantic poets, of course, but Morris emulated neither their techniques nor their sources. Each new attempt was for him an experiment—some quite brilliant—and dissatisfaction with one led him to try another. Parts of *Love Is Enough* and *Sigurd,* in particular, are as good as anything he ever wrote. Generations have responded to **'For the Bed at Kelmscott'** and **'The Message of the March Wind',** but he also wrote small inset gems of historical interpretation into his longer translations.

All these works—'occasional', lyrical or realistic—embed allegories of loss, and the longer ones employ complexly iterated patterns of doubling and opposition. These dualities also reflected dialectical oppositions in Morris's own sensibility, for the author of the cloudless lyric **'Hymn to Venus'** also wrote the extended and gruesome scene in *Sigurd* in which Gunnar and his kin ravage themselves and each other both verbally and physically—one of the most repellently powerful set-pieces of its kind in English poetry.

As Morris composed *The Earthly Paradise,* his style gained in narrative complexity, emotional resonance, and prosodic skill. He chose stories of an increasingly fantastic, mythical and intricately ironic cast, and shaped the plots of the stories to reflect recurrent passions, obsessions, and ideals. His evolving preoccupations and radical changes in poetic style recognized the fragility of human relations and achievements. They also celebrated the origins of popular literature in anonymous storytelling, and the recurrent roles of transmitter, speaker, and audience as authentic sources of this literature's unwritten history.

Certain significant aspects of this *Earthly Paradise* style persisted throughout Morris's later writing. Among these were his tendencies to

(a) project a *direct lyric voice,* often in the guise of a poet or 'singer'—most conspicuously in the **'Apology'** and the lyrics of the months;

(b) *refract* or *relativize* this voice, often in imbricated series of narrative frames—a muted version of this appears in the **'Apology'**-poet's ironic self-characterization as the 'idle singer of an empty day', and this 'singer' later intervenes in **'The Doom of King Acrisius', 'The Writing on the Image',** and other tales;

(c) deploy certain forms of explicit *moral and metaphysical allegory*—most conspicuously, perhaps, in **'Ogier the Dane'** and in **'Bellerophon in Lycia';**

(d) make extensive *mythopoetic use of folk and saga material*—more generically in **'The Fostering of Aslaug',** and more concretely and 'realistically' in **'The Lovers of Gudrun'.**

Refracted variants of the 'singer's' direct voice reappear, for example, in *Love Is Enough, The Pilgrims of Hope, Poems by the Way* and the hymnodic **'Chants for Socialists',** and inset counterparts linger in the lyrics of the prose romances, often cast as communal 'songs'. Temporal and narrative shifts of perspective are present in *Love Is Enough* and *The Pilgrims of Hope.* Explicit allegory, finally, is central to *Love Is Enough,* and myth-entwined counterparts of moral allegory permeate the saga-derived conflicts between revenge and remorse which rule *Sigurd the Volsung.*

Love Is Enough: Aesthetic Displacement
and Autobiography

Morris kept an extensive journal during his visit to Iceland in 1871, and the experiences there in 1871 and 1873 inflected his poetic sensibility in lasting ways. For *Jason* and *The Earthly Paradise,* he had drawn on wide knowledge of classical and medieval sources, but his stay in *Ultima Thule* gave him a chance to think about *his own plot*—to reevaluate what he admired, and reconsider ways to resolve the *aporiai* of his life. The conclusions he reached directed the future course of his poetic as well as his political career.

Certain aspects of Morris's style-shift emerged in *Love Is Enough,* a radically personal verse 'masque' which he set down in several heavily reworked drafts over a three month period in 1872 and published in 1873. Arranged in a miniature fractal series of narrative iterations, the poem meditates on the displacement of love into hope, and makes open-ended appeals for universality and audience-participation. Indeed, Morris's later poetry and prose romances can be viewed as a series of attempts to resolve a dialectical conflict between the reconciliatory ethos of *Love Is Enough* and its 'negation' in the bitterly tragic *Sigurd the Volsung.* In the end, the resilient spirit of 'Love' determined the fluidity and pace of his final imaginative writings.

The basic tenet of *Love Is Enough* is that fulfillment and deferral are in some sense concurrent, that life preserves and celebrates hope amid loss, and that absence and displacement paradoxically preserve hope. *Love Is Enough* grants its hero Pharamond renewed energy after many dislocations and reversals, but refracts his own perspective in a series of larger prismatic frames.

Formally, *Love Is Enough* describes the progress of a medieval poetic masque, performed by a troupe of players for an Emperor and Empress, a bourgeois Mayor, and a mixed audience of onlookers that includes the peasant lovers Giles and Joan. The players enact the story of King Pharamond, a benevolent ruler who abdicates his rule to search for a woman in a distant land. Accompanied by his servant and companion Oliver, Pharamond sails to a country of stark, quasi-Icelandic beauty, falls asleep in despair, and is awakened by Azalais, the object of his search, who has been drawn to him in turn. The two tell their life-histories, embrace, and sing a joint hymn in praise of love as an eternal narrative—past, passing, and to come.

Oliver's failing health and Pharamond's worries about his kingdom prompt them to return home, where they learn that a certain Theobald has gained the people's sympathies. Pharamond believes he would have been a better and more generous monarch, but accedes to Theobald's claim, and sets forth again to return to look for Azalais. He has not yet found her when the inner story ends, and calls to her in its final tableau, 'Yea, Love were enough if thy lips were not lacking'.

Allegorical personifications of Music and Love now step onto the stage, praise this tale of apparent uncertainty and deferral, and exhort the play's onlookers (and us) to:

> Fear not; no vessel to dishonour born
> Is in my house . . .
>   this life great stories made;
> All cast aside for love, and then and then
> Love filched away; the world an adder-den,
> And all folk foes; and one, the one desire—
> —How shall we name it?—grown a poisoned fire,
> God once, God still, but God of wrong and shame
> A lying God, a curse without a name.
> So turneth love to hate, the wise world saith.
> —Folly—I say 'twixt love and hate lies death,
> They shall not mingle: neither died this love,
> But through a dreadful world all changed must move
> . . .

The heterosexual couples in the play's audience then make its art 'real' by meeting and socializing with the *players,* but such attempts to assimilate signified and signifier have inherent limitations, as Joan tells Giles:

> Too wide and dim, love, lies the sea,
> That we should look on face to face
> This Pharamond and Azalais.
> Those only from the dead come back
> Who left behind them what they lack.

The onlookers retire, and pray that Love will engender in them the origins of more such tales:

> —O Love, go with us as we go,
> And from the might of thy fair hand
> Cast wide about the blooming land
> The seed of such-like tales as this!

The allegorical personifications of Love have many disguises, all male: a King, an 'image-maker', 'a maker of Pictured Cloths', a 'Pilgrim', and a priest-like figure 'with a cup of bitter drink'. Love and his ally 'The Music' provide a choral accompaniment for the biblically-cadenced masque and wedding-feast. The latter takes place beneath tapestries of sorrow and reconciliation in a kind of secular church, decorated with artistic images of the celebrants.

In his discussion of the ideology of *Love Is Enough* in *Victorian Poets and Romantic Poems,* Anthony Harrison claims that Morris opposed its 'wholly optimistic amatory ideology' (154) to D. G. Rossetti's fatalism, and identifies 'Endymion' as the poem's principal Romantic 'precursor'.[3] This seems too simple, for Morris's 'wholly optimistic . . . ideology' *also* foresees that natural cycles inevitably bring new 'sign[s] of Earth, its sorrow and its bliss':

—Reward of what?—Life springing fresh again.—
Life of delight?—I say it not—Of pain?
It may be—Pain eternal?—Who may tell?
Yet pain of Heaven, beloved, and not of Hell.
—What sign, what sign, ye cry, that so it is?
The sign of Earth, its sorrow and its bliss,
Waxing and waning, steadfastness and change;
Too full of life that I should think it strange
Though death hang over it; too sure to die
But I must deem its resurrection nigh.

Love Is Enough also evolved into a more and more emblematic allegory as Morris discarded 'realistic' details from successive drafts. The poem has distant archival origins, as May Morris records—in the *Mabinogion*'s tale of Maxen Wledig, 'Emperor of Rome'. Wledig dreams of and journeys to a fair isle, and courts there a maiden who sits in a chair of ruddy gold. Offered gifts of her choice, she requests the Island of Britain for her father, and three of its castles for herself. Wledig and his wife live together for seven years, and he then returns to Rome to manage various wars.[4] No traces of symbolism or moral allegory grace this plot, and Morris infused everything of worth in the poem from his own experience—the hero's vision, travels to a remote land, and awareness of the tensions between inner exile and external responsibility.

May Morris also observed that earlier drafts gave Azalais a different, markedly more 'northern' name (Bertha, or 'bright one'); made Love a speaking character in the inner masque; included many more details of Bertha's village life; and added Pharamond's efforts to win her disguised as a smith in her father's house.[5] Some of these atmospheric details recall Morris's early prose tale **'Gertha's Lovers'.** These comparisons also suggest that Morris began with the prototype of an unused *Earthly Paradise* tale, like **'The Wooing of Swanhild',** and later abandoned its plot details to express deeper preoccupations.

Morris's fractal iterations of art within art and stories within stories can usually be (re)interpreted as generic appeals for universality and audience participation, and so it is here. We, his readers, are to construe and apply the allegories of Love's Music to ourselves, and to our own lives. Nineteenth-century readers also understood the uses of such daedal self-referentiality, and contemporary reviewers of *Love Is Enough* make essentially the same point. Morris could often count on a practical critical eye for formal metric patterns and ear for aural cadence to convey this hermeneutic. For Victorian readers the poem's verbal polyrhythms reinforced its sense of delicate mystery. G. A. Simcox wrote in the December 1872 *Academy* that:

> It is hard to pronounce upon a single trial whether the revival of alliterative rhythm will be a permanent addition to our poetical resources. We are inclined to think that Mr. Morris himself has gained more of the

eloquence of passion, and this without any sacrifice of delicacy . . . [on Azalais's speech to the sleeping Pharamond] Perhaps the anapaestic movement is here as elsewhere too unbroken . . . But we feel it is ungracious to criticize music at once so rich and so simple.

> . . . it is impossible to speak too highly of the rich rapturous melody of the songs, which are all in long anapaestic stanzas with double rhymes . . .[6]

Sidney Colvin added his praise in the January 1873 *Fortnightly Review*:

> Reading yourself into [the poem], you find much loveliness and a singular originality. There is the originality of using a metrical system of anapaests without rhyme, and with an irregular alliterative tendency, roughly resembling the common form of early English verse [which] is certainly proved capable of effects of great metrical charm and dignity . . . Some strokes of the lyric interludes, some passages, like that where Azalais comes upon Pharamond in his sleep, are of an almost perfect poetry.[7]

Also interesting is the topographical specificity of the inner masque. Morris found geography and landscape never-failing sources of pleasure, and the masque's carefully delineated Icelandic-like landscapes are individuated in remarkable ways. We don't *know* what the lovers looked like, or where they lived, and we aren't *supposed* to know. But we *see* Pharamond's approach to the coast of Iceland in surreal detail:

> And I woke and looked forth, and the dark sea, long
> changeless,
> Was now at last barred by a dim wall that swallowed
> The red shapeless moon, and the whole sea was roll-
> ing,
> Unresting, unvaried, as grey as the void is,
> Toward that wall 'gainst the heavens as though rest
> were behind it.
> Still onward we fared and the moon was forgotten,
> And colder the sea grew, and grey, green-besprinked,
> And the sky seemed to breach it; and lo at the last
> Many islands of mountains, and a city amongst them.
> White clouds of the dawn, not moving yet waning,
> Wreathed the high peaks about; and the sea beat for
> ever
> 'Gainst the green sloping hills and the black rocks and
> beachless.

Other descriptions of enclosed valleys, rock, and mist clearly reflected Morris's Icelandic experiences, and added poignance and personal resonance to the other autobiographical elements in the poem.

Love Is Enough also introduced a relatively new variety of female protagonist. Most of Morris's heroines had either been passively loving, or active but neurotic and/or capricious. One welcome exception is the energetically loving Philonoë ('lover of thought') in **'Bellerophon in Lycia',** the final classical tale of *The Earthly Paradise.* Like Azalais, Philonoë is beautiful, forthright, demonstrative, and affectionate—an Ellen-like expression of unfragile natural goodness, neither static nor entrapped. Azalais too is never at rest, but travels toward Pharamond as he in turn seeks her. Almost no other early Morrisean heroine is so distinguished by her capacity for active sympathy and shared experience.

Consider, for example, Azalais's good-Samaritan-like encounter with Pharamond, as he lies asleep at the side of the road:

> —Ah! what lieth there by the side of the highway?
> Is it death stains the sunlight, or sorrow or sickness?
> [going up to Pharamond]
> . . . I will wait till he wakens and gaze on his beauty,
> Lest I never again in the world should behold him.
> —Maybe I may help him; he is sick and needs tend-
>   ing,
> He is poor, and shall scorn not our simpleness surely
>   . . .
> Then . . .
> I shall be part of thy rest for a little.
> And then—who shall say—wilt thou tell me thy story,
> And what thou hast loved, and for what thou hast
>   striven?
> —Thou shalt see me, and my love and my pity, as
>   thou speakest,
> And it may be thy pity shall mingle with mine.

Most *Earthly Paradise* heroines are beautiful, of course, many are passionate or intelligent, and some are even loving, but this heroine's interior poise and quick mental life are relatively new. The poem's plot grimly permits the lovers only a few actual moments together, but even *imagined* informality and shared experiences between men and women were rare in Morris's writings to this point.

Azalais also turns out to be unproblematically faithful. She does not cease to love Pharamond, and she embodies the qualities I have described throughout the interior play. This sweet-tempered, clear-minded spirit of ardent affection and symbol of freedom from erotic anxiety does reappear several times in Morris's later writings. A few of Azalais's specific traits—her vaguely Scandinavian ambience, her idealism, her general firmness—have counterparts in the more ambivalent character of Brynhild, and straightforwardness and mental quickness reappear in the heroine of the *Pilgrims of Hope* and several women in the prose romances. Here, above all, her keen generosity confirms the poem's message of loyal alliance and disinterested love.

Morris's design for *Love Is Enough* effectively refracted or displaced the poem's essentially autobiographical preoccupations, and several aspects of 'refraction' are discernible in the poem's imbricated frames.[8] Obvious referents in Morris's life can be found for the narrator's multiple roles, Pharamond's three

years of emotional turmoil and distaste for usurpers, the onlookers' fears before their own marriages, Love's insistence that (true) love can never 'turn [. . .] to hate', and his desire to inhabit a house filled with storied tapestries. Other allusions to Morris's personal experiences include Pharamond's intense (near-epileptic?) dream-visions, the mediating presence of his male comrades and associates, the protagonist's two journeys to a remote island, and the resonance he finds between the island's stark Northern landscapes and his deepest personal emotions.

Love Is Enough, in short, allegorizes Morris's increasing search for fulfillment, resignation, and peace as he approached middle age: his understanding of the inherent incompleteness of life and its aspirations and endeavors; his need to balance friendship and love, privacy and marriage, work and rest; and his growing awareness that change and loss rekindle life, and that 'love'—redefined as a search for moments of affection and illumination—can dignify these cycles and elevate them to myth. Morris/Pharamond's 'individual solution' freed him from the need to cast blame or judgment on others, and enabled him to accept his own finitude and fallibility. Humans must cope incessantly with absence and pain, but some are granted the good fortune to decorate the rafters of Love's house, and comforted by the unexpected recurrences of affection and generosity. I have argued in my book that such an ethic of unillusioned stoic acceptance is already discernible in several *Earthly Paradise* plots, and this ethic animated, in fact, all of Morris's later work, from *Love Is Enough* to the end of his life.[9] Assured of his ability to think 'bigly and kindly', Morris and some of his protagonists began to shift their energies to more active endeavors and wider social concerns.

SIGURD THE VOLSUNG: HISTORY'S PATTERN OF MYTH AND HOPE

In 1870, Morris and his collaborator and eventual fellow traveler Eiríkur Magnússon published their translation of the *Volsungasaga,* and in 1877, four years after *Love Is Enough,* Morris brought out *Sigurd the Volsung,* a four-book epic poem based loosely on the *Volsungasaga.* Morris's extended 'nordic' poem of twilit struggle is utterly remote in plot from the delicate allegory of renunciation of *Love Is Enough,* but even here he managed to project some of the patterns mentioned above into an originary tale of brutal conflict between two aristocratic houses of medieval Northern Europe. In *Sigurd,* Morris tried to write a sophisticated 'popular' epic, which would draw on the Icelandic historical and legendary materials he had learned. As he had already done in 'The Lovers of Gudrun', *The Earthly Paradise*'s dramatic reworking of the *Laxdaela Saga,* Morris rearranged legendary materials in rather drastic ways. He expanded and interpreted hundreds of incidents in *Sigurd* to express his personal preoccupations with love and endurance, and transmuted the original epic's carnage and macabre disruptions into a poetic tragedy of fulfilled prophecy and fate.

Morris chose the grim tale of the Volsungs with a good deal of thought, and it held personal as well as cultural significance for him. His co-published prose rendering of the *Volsunga Saga* is still considered a model of Victorian translation, and in its preface, Morris expressed hope that the saga's beauty and power would endure:

> For this is the Great Story of the North, which should be to all our race what the Tale of Troy was to the Greeks—to all our race first, and afterwards, when the change of the world has made our race nothing more than a name of what has been—a story too—then should it be to those that come after us no less than the Tale of Troy has been to us.

Morris also inserted an introspective prefatory poem, which makes its parallel claim in different terms:

> Naught vague, naught base our tale, that seems to say,—
>   'Be wide-eyed, kind; curse not the hand that smites,
> Curse not the kindness of a past good day,
>   Or hope of love; cast by all earth's delights,
>   For very love: through weary days and nights,
> Abide thou, striving howsoe'er in vain,
> The inmost love of one more heart to gain!'
>
> So draw ye round and hearken, English Folk,
>   Unto the best tale pity ever wrought!
> Of how from dark to dark bright Sigurd broke,
>   Of Brynhild's glorious soul with love distraught,
>   Of Gudrun's weary wandering unto naught,
> Of utter love defeated utterly,
> Of grief too strong to give Love time to die!

Morris expressed his admiration for the saga even more directly in a letter to the American critic and translator Charles Eliot Norton: 'I daresay you have read abstracts of the story, but however fine it seemed to you thus, it would give you little idea of the depth and intensity of the complete work . . . the scene of the last interview between Sigurd and the despairing and terrible Brynhild touches me more than anything I have ever met with in literature; there is nothing wanting in it, nothing forgotten, nothing repeated, nothing overstrained; all tenderness is shown without the use of a tender word, all misery and despair without a word of raving, complete beauty without an ornament'.[10]

In what follows, I will note some features of the poem's scene-patterning, and emphasize a few plot-elements which I believe have been neglected by earlier critics. These include: proto-feminist roles of women as active agents in the poem's tragic sequence of events, and the presence of certain female wisdom-figures; motifs of

prophesy, foresight, and cyclical unraveling, which permit deeply flawed characters to reform and express incongruously noble social ideals; and 'All-father's' (Odin's) role as heroic mentor, reminiscent of Homeric divinities and certain facilitating male guardians in *Love Is Enough*, and of the quasi-angelic Steelhead in Morris's *The Sundering Flood*. Finally, I will also remark on the poem's prosody and contemporary critical responses, and consider the role of rhythms, brocaded patterns, and sense of fate in the poem's final complex tonalities.

The four 'books' of *Sigurd the Volsung* tell relatively self-contained stories, but their interrelations of scene, plot, and motif reverberate with ironic, iconic, and prophetic significance. As the reader traces through the work's many superposed and retrospective debates between female protagonists, scenes of courtship and mating, pledges of 'brotherhood' undermined by male ambition and Grimhild's evil and narrow-minded counsel, allusions to the originary tree 'Branstock' ('Fire-trunk') and the rings of Andvari ('Vigilance'), these contrapuntal echoes accumulate, and gradually heighten a sense of oppressive subjectivity and implacable fate.

Consider, for example, several scenes of the interrelations between thwarted and/or vaguely transgressive sexuality. In one, Sigurd kneels beside the recumbent Brynhild. In another, Sigurd and Brynhild lie transfixed beside each other like figures on a medieval frieze or tomb. And in a third, Sigurd comes to Brynhild's bed in the shape of his 'blood brother' Gunnar. Each of these unions is interdicted in some way—by a sword, a distortion, a disguise, or death itself, on Sigurd's funeral pyre. When Sigurd first enters the ring of fire and finds Brynhild asleep in her coat of armor, he uses 'Wrath' (his mighty Branstock sword) to free and—symbolically—to enter her.

> . . . the sharp Wrath biteth and rendeth, and before it fall the rings,
> And, lo, the gleam of the linen, and the light of golden things:
> Then he driveth the blue steel onward, and through the skirt, and out,
> Till nought but the rippling linen is wrapping her about;
> Then he deems her breath comes quicker and her breast begins to heave,
> So he turns about the War-Flame and rends down either sleeve . . .

(II, **'How Sigurd awoke Brynhild upon Hindfell'**)

Parallel descriptions attend Sigurd's later visit to Lymdale, when the two exchange antiphonal vows, foresee their ultimate destinies, and fatalistically embrace. All these pledges, vows, and embraces are ironically recapitulated when Sigurd later enters the fiery ring in the guise of Gunnar, to exchange another 'pledge' with her on Gunnar's behalf:

> There they went in one bed together; but the foster-
>   brother laid
> 'Twixt him and the body of Brynhild his bright blue
>   battle-blade,
> And she looked and heeded it nothing; but, e'en as
>   the dead folk lie,
> With folded hands she lay there, and let the night go
>   by;
> And as still lay that Image of Gunnar as the dead of
>   life forlorn,
> And hand on hand he folded as he waited for the
>   morn.
> So oft in the moonlit minster your father may ye see
> By the side of the ancient mothers await the day to
>   be.
> Thus they lay as brother by sister—and e'en such had
>   they been to behold,
> Had he borne the Volsung's semblance and the shape
>   she knew of old.

(III: **'Sigurd rideth with the Niblungs, and wooeth Brynhild for King Gunnar'**)

This frieze-frame of recumbent stasis also persists in other scenes. In one, Brynhild sleeps beside Gunnar, and 'the Lie is laid between them, as the sword lay while agone' (III, **'Of the Contention betwixt the Queens'**). In another, Gudrun sleeps at Sigurd's side before his murder by Guttorm's sword. In a third, Brynhild lies abed and relates a bitter dream: 'Dead-cold was thy bed, O Gunnar, and thy land was parched with dearth' (III, 'Of the passing away of Brynhild'). In the final such scene, Brynhild orders her laying-out on Sigurd's funeral pyre:

> There lay me adown by Sigurd and my head beside
>   his head:
> But ere ye leave us sleeping, draw his Wrath from out
>   the sheath,
> And lay that Light of the Branstock, and the blade
>   that frighted death
> Betwixt my side and Sigurd's, as it lay that while
>   agone,
> When once in one bed together we twain were laid
>   alone . . .

(*Ibid.*)

Similar associations also accrete around much simpler dramatic images—ring, cup, bed, sword, tree, and sun, as well as fire.

Generative Women, and Generational 'Grief and Wrack'

As in Morris's other poems, *Sigurd*'s women characters also assume much more active roles than in his sources. The epic plot ostensibly celebrates male heroism in a warrior-dominated society, but the poem's most important women determine much of its action, and all but Grimhild—a stereotypical meddling mother-in-

law—are admirable and/or courageous in their culture's terms. Morris's rhetorical legerdemain of prophetic visions, frozen tableaux, patterned reversals *et alia,* permitted him to portray these women as innocent as well as complicitous, providentially wise as well as vengeful, and active initiators in many cases of the events they witness and record.

They are also prophetic, or at least chastened by what they behold. When Brynhild in *Sigurd* learns that Sigurd has connived in Gunnar's deception, she predicts the downfall of the Volsungs, and her prophesy prompts Gunnar to conspire in Sigurd's assassination. Brynhild's powerful rhetoric thus leads indirectly to Sigurd's death, but her pronouncements can be interpreted as simple acts of the sort of clairvoyance central to her character. Gudrun, in her turn, is clearly motivated by insecurity about her husband's affections when she tells Brynhild of the origins of the ring, but she is devastated by her husband's murder, and lives to preserve as well as avenge Sigurd's memory.

Sigurd's aunt, Signy, daughter of the original King Volsung, provides in Book I another roughly parallel exemplar of vengeful courage and doomed clairvoyance. King Volsung, her father, triggers the bloody events of the poem's entire plot when he arranges Signy's marriage to Siggeir the Goth, for reasons of cupidity:

> But the King's heart laughed within him and the
>   King's sons deemed it good;
> For they dreamed how they fared with the Goths o'er
>   ocean and acre and wood;
> Till all the north was theirs, and the utmost southern
>   lands.

Like most of the tale's women, Signy has prophetic gifts. Volsung asks her whether she is willing to submit to this marriage, and she grimly consents, but foretells dire consequences for herself and others:

> A fire lit up her face, and her voice was e'en as a cry:
> 'I will sleep in a great king's bed, I will bear the lords
>   of the earth,
> And the wrack and the grief of my youth-days shall
>   be held for nothing
>   worth.

A faint hint of Morris's later socialist critique of marriage appears in Signy's apparent self-sacrifice for her father's gain. Pathetic in her terrible foreknowledge, she goes unillusioned to her marital doom. In the destructive field of her world's social forces, Signy's complicity in this marriage she loathes is a mark of forced solidarity, but her subsequent liberation of her brother Sigmund, Sigurd's father, helps ensure that this branch of the Volsung line will continue to exist.

Signy and Sigmund later survive Siggeir's treacherous assault on his in-laws, and she resolutely commits herself to revenge their deaths. She disguises herself and visits Sigmund in his cave hideout, where they conceive a son, Sinfiotli. When Sigmund and his adult son later attack Siggeir in his dwelling, Signy prompts Sinfiotli to kill two of Siggeir's children, his half-siblings, but when Sigurd and Sinfiotli set fire to the king's house, she immolates herself in the flames.

Sinfiotli is later poisoned by Borghild, Sigmund's new queen, but Sigmund remarries in old age before he dies in a final battle. His prophetically gifted wife, Hiordis, survives to bear Sigurd, their son, whom she carries away to safety in the neighboring land of the friendly Helper and his son Elf, where Regin ('Gods') nurtures and trains Sigurd, as Sigmund had done with Sinfiotli. The bloody collaboration of Sigmund's skill with Signy's and Hiordis's foresight and ironwilled loyalty thus bring the dynasty through the first book.

Another striking woman appears very briefly in Book III, in an addition by Morris which briefly highlights the victimization of women and children by war. As Gudrun is mourning Sigurd's murder, a 'war-chattel' interrupts with a grimmer tale:

> Then spake a Queen of Welshland, and Herborg hight was she:
> 'O frozen heart of sorrow, the Norns dealt worse with me:
> Of old, in the days departed, were my brave ones under shield,
> Seven sons, and the eighth, my husband, and they fell in the Southland field:
> Yet lived my father and mother, yet lived my brethren four,
> And I bided their returning by the sea-washed bitter shore:
> But the winds and death played with them, o'er the wide sea swept the wave,
> The billows beat on the bulwarks and took what the battle gave . . .'

Gudrun ignores this 'chattel's' eloquent lament, and with it a possible moment of genuinely prophetic insight and solidarity. The Welshland Queen's account, a medieval 'ubi sunt' lament in female voice, recalls the 'Lay of Gormley' as well as the plight of Hecuba in Euripides's Troy cycle, and her sorrow overshadows—in some perspectives, at least—the collective griefs of Gudrun, Brynhild, Gunnar, and the rest of the self-lacerating Volsung/Niblung line.

Sigurd the Volsung's most conspicuously impressive heroine, in any case, remains Brynhild, who is clearly a woman of quick intelligence and resolute will. Brynhild's utterances in the original *Volsunga Saga* are full of flat, sententious Polonian bits, such as the following:

> Let not thy mind be overmuch crossed by unwise men at thronged meetings of folk; for oft these speak worse than they wot of; lest thou be called a dastard, and art minded to think that thou art even as is said; slay such an one on another day, and so reward his ugly talk.[11]

Morris's Brynhild, by contrast, speaks in resonant biblical periods. When she first meets Sigurd she interprets the Gods' motives, and enjoins Sigurd to constancy of purpose in eloquent, Ecclesiastes-like cadences:

> 'Be wise, and cherish thine hope in the freshness of the days,
> And scatter its seed from thine hand in the field of the people's praise;
> Then fair shall it fall in the furrow, and some the earth shall speed,
> And the sons of men shall marvel at the blossom of the deed:
> But some the earth shall speed not; nay rather, the wind of the heaven
> Shall waft it away from thy longing—and a gift to the Gods hast thou given,
> And a tree for the roof and the wall in the house of the hope that shall be,
> Though it seemeth our very sorrow, and the grief of thee and me . . .
> 'I have spoken the words, beloved, to thy matchless glory and worth;
> But thy heart to my heart hath been speaking, though my tongue hath set it forth:
> For I am she that loveth, and I know what thou wouldst teach
> From the heart of thine unlearned wisdom, and I need must speak thy speech.'

This iconically vatic Brynhild is Sigurd's 'speech-friend' indeed. She is more articulate than any of Morris's poetic heroines, with the possible exception of Guenevere, and more fluently eloquent and loving than any other female character in Morris's work before the advent of Birdalone and Elfhild, in the last prose romances. Sigurd learns his destiny well, and falters only when he is drugged by the devious Grimhild. At their original meeting, the newly-plighted lovers even projected a 'day of better things', in language that recalls Christ's view of kingdoms of the earth, or Aurora and Romney's vision of the New Jerusalem at the end of *Aurora Leigh*:

> And they saw their crowned children and the kindred of the kings,
> And deeds in the world arising and the day of better things.

The poem provides *sources* for all this vatic wisdom, in the first appearance of yet another motif to which Morris recurs in the late prose romances. Male protagonists are helped by their Allfather, Odin, but Brynhild learns her lore from a female figure—'Wisdom' herself:

> 'I saw the body of Wisdom and of shifting guise was she wrought,
> And I stretched out my hands to hold her, and a mote of the dust they caught;
> And I prayed her to come for my teaching, and she came in the midnight dream—
> And I woke and might not remember, nor betwixt her tangle deem:

> She spake, and how might I hearken; I heard, and
> how might I know;
> I knew, and how might I fashion, or her hidden glory
> show?
> All things I have told thee of Wisdom are but fleeting
> images
> Of her hosts that abide in the Heavens, and her light
> that Allfather sees . . .

Morris later fashioned brief versions of such tutelage for other, comparably mythic heroines—Birdalone, for example, in *Water of the Wondrous Isles,* who learns nature's lore from the benign witch Habundia.

Another, less visionary woman is central to Morris's version of the plot: the bitterly wronged and vengeful Gudrun, whose marriage to Sigurd precipitates much woe. Aware that a bond exists between Sigurd and Brynhild, Gudrun boasts idly to Brynhild that she has spent the night with 'the best of men' (Sigurd), which goads the momentarily petty Brynhild to retort that Sigurd is 'the serving-man of Gunnar . . . King of the King-folk who rode the Wavering Fire'. Gudrun then shows Brynhild the ring of Andvari that Brynhild had herself given Sigurd, and he in turn to her.

Gudrun is later devastated by Sigurd's murder, ordered by Gunnar, and she flees the royal homestead to live for seven years among the peasantry, an echo, perhaps, of Nebuchadnezzar's seven years in the fields. In the poem's final book, Gunnar sends again for Gudrun and asks her to marry his oppressive royal neighbor Atli. She consents, but incites Atli to murder her brothers in revenge for Sigurd's death. Shamed by the aftermath of all this vengeful carnage, she then torches Atli's palace, stabs her terrified husband in his bedchamber with the sword of the Branstock, and leaps to her death:

> —Begin, O day of Atli! O ancient sun, arise,
> With the light that I loved aforetime, with the light
> that blessed mine eyes,
> When I woke and looked on Sigurd, and he rose on
> the world and shone!' . . .
> She hath spread out her arms as she spake it, and
> away from the earth she leapt
> And cut off her tide of returning; for the sea-waves
> over her swept,
> And their will is her will henceforward; and who
> knoweth the deeps of the sea,
> And the wealth of the bed of Gudrun, and the days
> that yet shall be?

The more wholeheartedly evil Sthenoboea in **'Bellerophon in Argos'**, a late *Earthly Paradise* tale, also leapt to her death from a cliff. Here, Gudrun's courageous and spectacular leap 'away from the earth' finally ends the noble Volsung line, and brings the cycle to its close.

BLOOD-DRENCHED ANTIHEROES AND NUMINOUS VISIONS

The poem's many prophecies and intermittent expressions of introspective remorse and atonement interdict final judgments in complicated ways, and one such example of narrative redemption occurs earlier in Book IV. Gunnar, Sigurd's 'blood-brother', and contractor of his murder, struggles heroically to organize the Niblung's doomed resistance to Atli's treacherous attack (itself an analogue of Siggeir's murders in Book I), in one of the grimmer battle scenes in modern English poetry. He and a few survivors are then overwhelmed, and withstand imprisonment in a snake pit, where he refuses under torture to divulge to Atli the secret location of Andvari's gold, 'the ransom of Odin'.

In the final scenes of his life, Gunnar even becomes a skald, and chants several truly beautiful songs as he fights and withstands torture. Like Orpheus and the Gunnar of the *Njálssaga,* the Niblung Gunnar sings most poignantly, as it were, from beyond the grave. His social conscience awakened, he even chants the merits of the 'brother' he has killed:

> The praise of the world he was, the hope of the biders
> in wrong,
> The help of the lowly people, the hammer of the
> strong:
> Ah, oft in the world henceforward, shall the tale be
> told of the deed,
> And I, e'en I, will tell it in the day of the Niblungs'
> Need:
> For I sat night-long in my armour, and when light was
> wide o'er the land,
> I slaughtered Sigurd my brother, and looked on the
> work of mine hand . . .

This sudden *afflatus* of physical heroism and prophetic powers adds unexpected power and eloquence to the poem's final book. Gudrun witnesses all this, and her horror at it is one of the reasons for her final murder of Atli and despairing suicide.

Gunnar's redemptive fervor and remarkable end help create, in effect, a kind of collective protagonist for the poem, drawn from all of the Volsungs and Niblungs, more specifically from the original incestual unit of Signy, Sigmund, and Sinfiotli, and their tragically mismated descendants—Brynhild, Sigurd, Gudrun, and Gunnar. All but Sigurd and Brynhild are complicit in the poem's many crimes, and all have epiphanies of courage and self-knowledge.

One recurring quasi-religious motif of the cycle, mentioned earlier, is Odin's advent at moments of stress. The appearances of 'All-father' in many guises are too numerous to trace, but each beneficiary sees him in a different form. Old-Testamental echoes abound, but these 'sendings' sometimes bring a simple sense of renewed purpose, and sometimes comfort. After Sigurd has fallen prey to Grunhild's spell, for example, he struggles to regain clarity and falls into a visionary trance:

But frail and alone he fareth, and as one in the sphere-
    stream's draft,
By the starless empty places that lie beyond the life:
Then at last is he stayed in his drifting, and he saith,
    It is blind and dark;
Yet he seeth the earth at his feet, and there cometh a
    change and a spark . . .
A man in the raiment of Gods, nor fashioned worser
    than they:
Full sad he gazeth on Sigurd from the great wide eyes
    and grey;
And the Helm that aweth the people is set on the
    golden hair,
And the Mail of Gold enwraps him, and the Wrath in
    his hand is bare.

(III, **'Sigurd rideth with the Niblungs, and wooeth
Brynhild for King Gunnar'**)

Sigurd's manifold effects are also heightened by its intricate variations in meter and stanza-form, which follow the narrative with the fidelity of a skillful movie-soundtrack. Morris uses one such quasi-musical device, for example—antiphonally-rhymed interlocution, in which two speakers declaim in rhymed alternation—to present lovers' vows and marital conversations, to report events, and to create a stylized form for hostile confrontations. Consider, for example, Atli's exchange with Gunnar before he throws him and Hogni into the pit of adders:

'Yet words of mine shalt thou hearken,' said Atli, 'or
    ever thou die.'
'So crieth the fool,' said Gunnar, 'on the God that his
    folly hath slain.'
'Yet meeter were thy silence;' said Atli, 'for thy folk
    make ready to sing.'
'O Gunnar, I long for the Gold with the heart and the
    will of a king.'
'This were good to tell,' said Gunnar, 'to the Gods
    that fashioned the earth!'
'Make me glad with the Gold,' said Atli, 'live on in
    honour and worth!'
With a dreadful voice cried Gunnar: 'O fool, hast thou
    heard it told
Who won the Treasure aforetime and the ruddy rings
    of the Gold?

A LOST ART

Exquisitely sensitive to such metrical nuances, classically-trained Victorian reviewers praised *Sigurd in excelsis.* May Morris cites George Saintsbury's long analysis of the poem's varied seven-beat line,[12] and a reviewer for the *Saturday Review* affirmed that: 'We regard this **Story of Sigurd** as his greatest and most successful effort; of all poetical qualities—strength, subtlety, vividness, mystery, melody, variety—there is hardly one that it does not exhibit in a very high degree . . . (January 1877). North American reviews were equally favorable:

After all, quotation . . . is vain, as every worthy reader
will acknowledge when he turns the last page of the
poem, and feels for a moment as if the whole earth

were made void by its ending . . . [Morris] has now, as it seems to us, fixed forever the most appropriate form of rhymed verse for an English epic.

(*Atlantic Monthly,* April 1877)

[His] is the most satisfying English measure ever yet adopted for the telling of a long story in verse . . . It is noble, yet changeful; supple and sustained. There is a kind of wistful sweetness, both in its hurrying anapests and its lingering iambics, which makes them cling to the memory; while the frequent use of alliteration marks its kinship with the primeval forms of Scandinavian story. Whatever its immediate reception may be, William Morris's *Sigurd* is certain eventually to take its place among the few great epics of the English tongue.

(*Literary World,* February 1877)

[Mr. Morris] has produced a work whose grandeur and beauty will make it for all time to come monumental in the annals of English literature.[13]

(*International Review,* September 1877)

Peter Faulkner is surely correct to suggest that critical indifference did *not* move Morris to abandon the writing of long poems.[14] After one allows for cliques, fashions and evanescent hyperbole, these remain remarkable reviews. They are also just appreciations, I believe, of the poem's depth and passion.

The polar tensions of the 'dialectical conflicts' between loss, renunciation, and the attainment of ultimate meaning are more apparent in *Sigurd* than in other works—in the unrepentant vengefulness of many of its major characters, for example, and the horrific, near-masochistic descriptions of the cycle's extended final battle-scenes, unique in Victorian poetic representation of war. Critics have justly noted that *Sigurd*'s protagonists sporadically express certain social ideals, but their agonistic lives of unceasing dynastic conflict, in my view, provide few plausible realizations of them. What the poem's antiphonal patterns do furnish are intricate motives of prophecy, foresight, and cyclical unraveling, which permit deeply flawed characters to 'reform' before their death, and express incongruously noble ideals. Viewed in this light, *Sigurd*'s dramatic embrace of opposites in suspension yields a work of prosodic brilliance, structural originality, and emotional intensity and narrative depth.

THE SOCIAL TURN: 'HOW THE CHANGE CAME'

One may wonder why Morris ceased to write such strikingly polarized poetic works (I have in mind the stark contrast between **Love Is Enough** and *Sigurd*) at the height of his technical powers. He continued to be moved by a contrapuntal sense of 'tragic' and 'romantic' approaches to a common subject matter, and might well have found other poetically and historically appropriate subjects for these polarities, and consolidated his reputation as a poet of epic scope into the twentieth century.

One possible answer is that Morris, in the end—like Pharamond, his hero in *Love Is Enough*—set aside one 'love' for another. Wider sympathies and a mature social conscience led him to attempt new subjects and literary media—poetic prose, for example; novellas-in-poetry; and lyric-within-narrative, a genre he virtually made his own. His growing radicalism and socialist commitments also impelled him to seek ways to appeal to audiences broader and less formally educated than the readers of the *Fortnightly Review* or the *Athenaeum*.

Many years later, May Morris recalled her father's wry remark that 'A man shouldn't write poetry after fifty'.[15] Morris was fifty in 1884, the year he left the Social Democratic Federation to co-found the Socialist League. He continued to write poetry all the same, with a social and communal focus, and in more accessible forms, but he sought to write for a literate 'popular' audience, and talk to it about certain recurrent human needs—for social justice ('fellowship'), and for a new aesthetic, one that might express the harmonies of a better social order, and encourage forms of affection wider than individual and familial 'love'.

Pilgrims of Hope: Love's Bloody Cup and the Religion of Socialism

The Pilgrims of Hope, which appeared serially from April to June, 1885, was the first poem Morris published in *Commonweal* after he became its editor in January of that year. He considered it too rough for republication in book form, but included its opening lyric (**'The Message of the March Wind'**) and fourth section (**'Mother and Son'**) in the 1891 volume *Poems by the Way.* The hero's lifelong commitment to the cause of socialism and acceptance of his late wife's preference for another man reflect personal and political aspects of wider egalitarian values Morris wanted to realize and diffuse, and I have elsewhere argued that linkage of these autobiographical concerns made *Pilgrims* a proto-feminist work—indeed, the *only* male-authored nineteenth century poem which set forth programmatic 'socialist-feminist' tenets about a woman's right to sexual autonomy.[16] I will not elaborate these points here, or discuss the poem's depictions of contemporary socialism or the fall of the Paris Commune, but will focus instead on the poem's qualities as an experimental verse-novel, its disrupted time-sequence, and its lyrical interludes of visionary emotion. Interesting resonances also emerged in Morris's factually commonplace but politically unorthodox plot, in which a male hero survives his wife's early death to raise alone their infant child.

The poem's six-beat line is more balladic than *Sigurd*'s seven-beat anapaests, but it permitted rapid immediacy, colloquial informality, and credible evocations of the poem's social ambiance. Consider the following sample, in which Morris's narrator attends a gathering at which soldiers are sent off to an imperial war. Born and bred in a rural village, the hero Richard sadly describes a crowd of lost proletarian onlookers who '. . . *never never never / shall be slaves*':

> And earth was foul with its squalor—that stream of every day,
> The hurrying feet of labour, the faces worn and grey
> . . .
> . . . these are the sons of the free,
> Who shall bear our name triumphant o'er every land and sea.

(III, 'Sending to the War')

In *Love Is Enough,* Pharamond witnesses a Eucharist-like tableau, in which the figure of Love offers a blood-filled cup. Here, Morris refits popular Christian iconography to serve the cause of socialism: 'I was born once long ago: I am born again tonight' (V, **'New Birth'**).

Richard begins the poem as a twenty-five-year-old joiner-carpenter, the son of an unmarried village woman whom Richard's father deserted before he was born. A small inheritance comes to him unexpectedly at his father's death, and this enables Richard and his wife to rent a small cottage outside London. He and his wife share radical views, and his employer fires him shortly after his father's lawyers have swindled him out of his money. Lower middle-class Victorian readers wisely feared such reversals, and all could identify with the humiliations that attended them:

> I take up fear with my chisel, fear lies 'twixt me and my plane,
> And I wake in the merry morning to a new unwonted pain.

('The New Proletarian')

The poem's sections incorporate two interesting shifts of voice. In sections two, three, five, and six, Richard describes his youth, marriage, political radicalization, and unemployment. In section four, the anonymous wife sets forth her view of life in a wryly intelligent, soft-spoken monologue to her uncomprehending infant son, and she describes in section seven Richard's arrest and imprisonment for political agitation. In section eight, **'The Half of Life Gone',** the narrative suddenly flashes forward. Richard now grieves for his dead wife, and seems to see her working in a field, then admits to himself that

> She is gone. She was and she is not; there is no such thing on the earth
> But e'en as a picture painted; and for me there is void and dearth
> That I cannot name or measure.

Richard recalls the intervening events in sections nine through thirteen. After Richard's release from prison, a young middle-class socialist named Arthur has befriended them and visited their house. The three friends decide to leave the couple's son in the care of friends—contrary to Victorian expectations—and join the Communards. Shortly before they leave for France, Richard learns that Arthur and his wife have fallen in love. The three young idealists leave together all the same, and they know when they find their way to the Commune that they have made the right decision:

> . . . at last I knew indeed that our word of the com-
> ing day,
> That so oft in grief and in sorrow I had preached, and
> scarcely knew
> If it was but despair of the present or the hope of the
> day that was due—
> I say that I saw it now, real, solid, and at hand.

(XI, 'The Glimpse of the Coming Day')

Later Richard, his now-estranged wife ('A sister amidst of the strangers—and, alas! a sister to me'), and Arthur have become street-fighters as the siege tightens. In one engagement, Richard's wife turns to see Arthur die, and is killed herself as she runs toward him across the path of an exploding artillery shell. Richard, who has run after her, is severely wounded by the same shell, but lives to remember that:

> she never touched the man
> Alive and she also alive; but thereafter as they lay
> Both dead on one litter together, then folk who knew
> not us,
> But were moved by seeing the twain so fair and so
> piteous,
> Took them for husband and wife who were fated there
> to die,
> Or, it may be lover and lover indeed—but what know
> I?

(XIII, 'The Story's Ending')

In the final section, the now solitary and recovered 'pilgrim of hope' has managed to return to England, where he finds work, raises his son, and clings resolutely to '. . . the love of the past and the love of the day to be'.

Richard's valedictory in section thirteen is very brief for a work filled with reflective flashbacks, descriptions of nature, and evocations of socialist ideals, and the poem would have benefited from more counterparts of the wife's lovely dramatic monologues in four and seven, in which she gives her own view of Richard and Arthur, or describes her experiences in the Commune. There is something deeply beautiful, nonetheless, about the abrupt dissolve from the wife's monologue in section seven, to the husband's sorrowing elegy in section eight. *Women* often survived the deaths of *male* lovers in Morris's literary writings, but Morris never again closed a tale in this way.[17]

The poem's disjunctions and discontinuities remain interesting, however, for they show in rough-cast the emergence of a verse-novel style that Morris might well have refined and developed had he not turned in the last decades of his life to prose. Problems of time-ellipsis are not peculiar to Morris, of course—they are conspicuously present in other first-person-narrated verse-novels, such as *Aurora Leigh,* in which the poet must balance narrative immediacy, absence of plausible foreknowledge, and the importance of retrospective self-knowledge. *Pilgrims* maintains this balance, and some of its *hiatūs*—like the abrupt dissolve mentioned above—actually heighten the poem's effect, as do skillfully-managed cinematic flashforwards and flashbacks. Richard's experiences—of familial disruption and social upheaval—are themselves fragmentary and disjointed, and the meditative hand-held camera of Morris's poetry reflects them well.

Though she cannot compete with the iconic figures of Signy, Brynhild, and Gudrun, *Pilgrims'* unnamed 'wife' is a brave woman of strong character, and *Pilgrims* is a good-faith first effort to explore in a contemporary context controversial questions of female sexual autonomy and participation in war. **'Mother and Son'** has suffered unjust neglect in comparison with better-known, 'canonical' monologues of the period—Browning's 'Pompilia', for example. Morris's working-class heroine also has some strong socialist-feminist lines—among them the following, spoken to her son in section 4:

> Prudence begets her thousands: 'Good is a housekeep-
> er's life,
> So shall I sell my body that I may be matron and
> wife.'
> 'And I shall endure foul wedlock and bear the children
> of need.'

Whatever his deficiencies as a feminist, Morris did understand completely that 'the personal is political'. *Pilgrims of Hope* is the *only* long English poem of the period which presented political ideals and conflicts from any sort of socialist or communist perspective, and this surely has something to do with its neglect. This near-unique document in the social history of nineteenth-century poetry blended and recombined basic motifs from *Love Is Enough* and *Sigurd the Volsung* in a vastly different, near-contemporary setting, and its tone of mingled celebration and empathetic regret lingered in its two immediate prose successors, *A Dream of John Ball* and *The House of the Wolfings*. The poem's colloquial flexibility, satiric precision, and utopian insight reappeared in *News from Nowhere* and *The Roots of the Mountains,* and some of *Pilgrims'* lyrical passages—like other shorter poems Morris wrote for *Commonweal* and the Socialist League—anticipated the hymnlike vision of a transmuted world found in poetic interludes of the last prose romances.

Late Poems and 'Chants', and Hymns of the Folk

Six years later, in 1891, Morris published *Poems By the Way,* whose modestly casual title reflected the fact that he had first drafted a number of its poems around 1870 or shortly thereafter. Several of these recast Scandinavian accounts of ill-fated love in artful stanzaic and metrical variations.[18] **'The Wooing of Hallbiorn'**, for example, which Morris glossed as 'A Story from the Land-Settling Book of Iceland, Chapter XXX', skillfully darkens each taunting repetition of one of its refrains, first sung at the wedding feast of Hallbiorn and Hallgerd by Snaebiorn, Hallgerd's once and future lover. Among the volume's other poems is **'The King of Denmark's Sons'**, a tale of fratricide and paternal grief in rhymed couplets, patterned loosely after Rossetti's 'The White Ship'. **'The Son's Sorrow: From the Icelandic'** is another refrain-poem, remarkable in this case for the naturalistic plausibility of the death it mourns—that of the speaker's wife, who has died bearing her third son. **'The God of the Poor'** and **'The Burghers' Battle'** celebrate medieval conflicts against evil rulers. Some of the volume's poems—among them **'The Hall and the Wood'**, **'The Folk Mote By the River'**, and **'Goldilocks and Goldilocks'**, the latter written by Morris especially for the volume in 1891—reflected his more anthropological, 'folk'-centered priorities in meliorative stories of rewarded love.[19] He also intoned several poems—**'Hope Dieth: Love Liveth'**, **'Error and Loss'**, **'Meeting in Winter'**, **'Love Fulfilled'**, **'Thunder in the Garden'**, **'Love's Reward'**, **'Love's Gleaning Tide'**, **'Pain and Time Strive Not'**, and **'The Half of Life Gone'**—in the unmediated personal voice of *The Earthly Paradise*'s lyric singer, but he had already inscribed most of these in his physically lovely manuscript *Book of Verse* in 1870.

Three of the volume's better-known poems emerged from Morris's visits to Iceland in 1871 and 1873: **'To the Muse of the North'**, **'Iceland First Seen'**, and **'Gunnar's Howe Above the House at Lithend'**. The last of these records the speaker's profound response at the grave of the murdered *Njálssaga* warrior, who was heard in the saga singing at night in his grave:

> O young is the world yet meseemeth and the hope of
>   it flourishing green,
> When the words of a man unremembered so bridge all
>   the days that have been,
> As we look round about on the land that these nine
>   hundred years he hath seen.

This aspect of the legend clearly influenced Morris's elevation of another Gunnar's defiant last songs in *Sigurd the Volsung.*

I have seen Gunnar's grave. The 'howe' (*haugr*) is a barely-discernible grass-swept elevation on a gentle slope above a green, treeless, receding plain, and Morris effectively recorded a moment of his own spiritual autobiography in his meditation over its solitary, windswept *Útsýn*. His deepest preoccupations with 'men unremembered' resonated in its lines.

The speaker's relief and happiness spring from his recognition that nine hundred years have not (yet) entirely effaced Gunnar's gallantry in the face of death. Retrieval of such tenuous memories from the abyss of oblivion seems to him a kind of psychological resurrection: if he helps preserve it, the 'bridge' of days still stands, and something in himself may stand as well. Morris closed the poem with a tribute to the enduring qualities of the long Icelandic summer twilight, in which 'day and night toileth the summer lest deedless his time pass away'.

Morris's *Chants for Socialists* and **'A Death Song for Alfred Linnell'** adapted hymnodic forms to new circumstances. Socialists set Morris's *Chants* to familiar tunes, and sang them at their meetings, which competed for some of their audiences with the Salvation Army and the uncertain harmonies of the local pub. Morris remarked in his 1887 'Socialist Diary' that he found it difficult to convey socialist doctrine to semi-literate audiences, but he expressed in his songs the movement's basic verities: that workers have a right to the fruits of their labor, and should act in solidarity to secure that right for all the dispossessed. Morris's hymns remained staples in socialist and labor circles for many decades, as generations of labor-songbooks show.[20]

All these motifs resonated in **'A Death Song of Alfred Linnell'**, written for the funeral of an innocent bystander killed by the police in Trafalgar Square in 1886:

> We asked them for a life of toilsome earning,
> They bade us bide their leisure for our bread;
> We craved to speak to them our woeful learning:
> We come back speechless, bearing back our dead.
> *Not one, not one, nor thousands must they slay,*
> *But one and all if they would dusk the day . . .*
>
> Here lies the sign that we shall break our prison;
> Amidst the storm he won a prisoner's rest;
> But in the cloudy dawn the sun arisen
> Brings us our day of work to win the best.
> *Not one, not one, nor thousands must they slay,*
> *But one and all if they would dusk the day.*

Morris hardly belonged in the extensive company of Victorian hymn writers, but he did in effect write successful hymns for the 'religion of humanity' of a different, secular church.

Most critics have also neglected the eighty-odd pages of poems Morris interspersed in his prose romances, especially in the 'German' romances, *The House of the*

Wolfings and *The Roots of the Mountains,* which he wrote for *Commonweal* in 1888 and 1889. Almost all moments of high emotion in *The House of the Wolfings*—prophecies, histories, avowals of love and commemorations of the dead—provided occasion for such interspersed lyrics, and they heightened and varied the tales' prose narration in sometimes surprising ways.

Wolfings, in part, is a gentler successor to **Sigurd,** especially in its fatalistic acceptance of 'good' heroic death, and its careful attention to the implications of many marginal skirmishes with an evil enemy might even allegorize aspects of concurrent Socialist League struggles. The poetic speeches of the prophetess Hall-Sun; the resolute action of the selfless chieftain Thiodolf; and the ardor of the half-divine Wood-Sun, who lies to Thiodolf about the efficacy of the hauberk she gives him, in the hope that this will save his life—all these characters' interactions form a stately antiphony to the tale's archaic prose and simple plot. The analogy between the Roman enemies of the Goths and imperialist English exploiters of sweated labor may have been clearer to Morris than it was to his contemporaries, but *Wolfings* provided especially striking instances of the framing of poetry in an accessible prose narrative, and interspersal of choral and expressive verse into otherwise terse accounts of locally significant quasi-historical events. In several of the interpolated poems Morris experimented boldly with medieval Scandinavian meters, and these unexpected rhythms bring to the narrative a sense of surprise, exoticism, and heightened authenticity.

In *The Roots of the Mountains,* the poetic interludes were briefer, and their more formal, generic and iconically abstract meters served to celebrate social aspects of Wolfing life, memorialize past conflicts, and honor the Wolfing dead. An antiphonal poem sung by Bow-may and Gold-mane, for example, as they prepare to join the Wolfings' defensive campaign against raiders from Silverdale, became a poetic celebration of a male-female partnership in battle. Paradoxically this provided a gracious interlude in the tale, for in Morris's writings, men and women often share love, but seldom labor; and women's love typically requires that their male partners risk loneliness and death. Here, the (unromantically attached) warriors sing:

> *She singeth:*
> Bare are my feet for the rough waste's wending,
>> Wild is the wind, and my kirtle's thin;
> Faint shall I be ere the long way's ending
>> Drops down to the Dale and the grief therein.
> *He singeth:*
> . . . Come, for how from thee shall I sunder?
>> Come, that a tale may arise in the land;
> Come, that the night may be held for a wonder,
>> When the Wolf was led by a maiden's hand!
> *She singeth:*

> Now will I fare as ye are faring,
>> And wend no way but the way ye wend;
> And bear but the burdens ye are bearing,
>> And end the day as ye shall end . . .
>> *They sing together:*
> Over the moss through the wind and the weather,
>> Through the morn and the even and the death
> of the day,
> Wend we man and maid together,
>> For out of the waste is born the fray.

After the tale's final battle, the Wolfings return home to bury their dead, and consecrate their Mote-House with song:

> We are the men of joy belated;
>> We are the wanderers over the waste;
> We are but they that sat and waited,
>> Watching the empty winds make haste.
>
> Long, long we sat and knew not others,
>> Save alien folk and the foes of the road;
> Till late and at last we met our brothers,
>> And needs must we to the old abode . . .
>
> Over the waste we came together:
>> There was the tangle athwart the way;
> There was the wind-storm and the weather;
>> The red rain darkened down the day.
>
> For here once more is the Wolf abiding,
>> Nor ever more from the Dale shall wend,
> And never again his head be hiding,
>> Till all days be dark and the world have end.

Morris also intended the tale's retrospectively utopian lyrics to express the values of a quasi-democratic 'tribal' society at peace with itself, and these poems' antiphonal patterns suggest deep natural recurrences that underlie human desires. They resonate with assurance, and are unique achievements of their kind.

In summary, Morris's poetry continued to evolve after *The Earthly Paradise,* as he recast traditional legends and meters, balanced tales of ill-fated love with celebrations of natural cycles of rebirth, and found new ways to blend the rhythms of poetry and natural speech. His quasi-populist efforts to seek less 'elite' and more varied audiences and explore new styles and modes of expression expressed his personal belief in utopian communism and the efficacy of 'hope,' but they also anticipated and paralleled some of the generic and thematic innovations of the *fin de siècle.*

Conclusion: Was Morris a 'Fin-de-Siècle' Poet?

The originality and experimental qualities of Morris's poetry might have been better appreciated had he accomplished less in other areas of his life. As we approach the end of the twentieth century, we typically evaluate the literature of the previous 'end of century' in terms of something notoriously ill-defined called 'modernity'. How should one compare Morris's later poetry with that of his 'decadent' near-contemporaries, among them Oscar Wilde, Aubrey Beardsley, Thomas Hardy, Ernest Dowson, Olive Schreiner, Sarah Grand, or Vernon Lee?

To what extent, for example, was this vigorously romantic late-Victorian dissident also a proto-aesthetic poet? It seems to me that the elegantly muted visual patterns Morris designed in the 80s and 90s were as proto-'modernist' as the delicately colorful ones he crafted in the late 60s and 70s were 'Victorian'. Both types of patterns were excellent of their kind. And so, I believe, were the different modes of poetry Morris cultivated during his career.

Morris's poetry—early, middle, and late—anticipated one theme that became central in various ways to *fin de siècle* writers—the blocking or interdiction of love. Poets and other writers in the 90s often argued explicitly or implicitly that gratified love (hetero- or homosexual) is not only *unattainable,* but in some cases even *unimaginable.* Examples abound: Wilde's 'Ballad of Reading Gaol', Mary Coleridge's 'The Other Side of the Mirror', Rosamond Marriott Watson's 'The Witch', Hardy's 'Satires of Circumstance', Arthur Symons's 'The Loom of Dreams', and Lionel Johnson's poignant 'The Dark Angel'. In his preoccupation with doomed or postponed love—displacement and sublimation, if you will—Morris also seemed to anticipate certain forms of Freudian *Unbehagen in der Kultur* (the original title of *Civilization and Its Discontents*) that one commonly associates with the age that followed him.

Even Morris's historicism and fondness for archaic medievalism in the 1880s and 90s had 'modern' aspects, for his later research methods were self-consciously anthropological and receptive to the original sources he knew—as deeply grounded in them as his early work had been in the romantic renditions of Walter Scott, Charles Kingsley, and medieval compendia in the 1850s and 60s. Josephine Guy has remarked in *The British Avant Garde in the Nineteenth Century* that British writers who wished to subvert authority typically sought to find radical antecedents in reconstructions of the historical past, whereas their continental analogues tended to reject such antecedents.[21] If Guy is right (and I believe she is), it becomes thoroughly understandable why the late Victorian poet who most fervently embraced radically revolutionary ideals experimented with so many traditional aesthetic forms.

Likewise the quasi-biblical imagery and overtones of Morris's secular-humanist 'religion of humanity' is surprisingly consistent with a *fin de siècle* affinity for iconic, ritualistic, or spiritualist turns, found in such late-century and turn-of-the-century poets as Alice Meynell, Michael Field, or Francis Thompson, and even W. B. Yeats. The emblematic, strongly patterned, and self-referential aspects of Morris's poems are equally 'aesthetic', and his social concerns allied him with several contemporary and subsequent writers of 'new woman' fiction.

It is not coincidental, therefore, that his writings—especially *News from Nowhere* and his essays on the decorative arts—were admired by contemporary feminists such as Charlotte Perkins Gilman and Emma Lazarus, and by feminist-utopian writers of subsequent generations. Many writers have commented by now on the 'tree-hugging' qualities of Morris's belief in a communion between the natural world and its inhabitants, and Morris's political ideals and their ecological urgency seem much clearer now than they did to Morris's own socialist descendants half a century ago.

Morris's attempts to recreate/invent a 'tongue of the folk', by contrast, found few immediate emulators. The rise of critical interest in the poetic prose of his romances suggests that Morris's later work blended the boundaries of poetic and fictional, historicist and utopian modes of writing in unexpected ways. His eclectic work contributed both to efforts to create a 'vernacular revival', and to the complex mixtures of sensational and quotidian elements in the work of modernist writers such as Lewis Grassic Gibbon, Charlotte Mew, James Joyce, and their successors.

Despite his apparent 'simplicity', then, Morris had as much in common with later disillusioned poetic dissectors of the heart such as Wilde or Mary Coleridge or T. S. Eliot as he did with Browning and Tennyson. His most distinctive attribute, however, was his ability to reconcile this unillusioned 'level gaze' with an organic view of the possibilities of earthly renewal—a complex synthesis which mediated to his poetic successors one of the strongest legacies of his century's romantic sensibility.

Many significant aspects of Morris's poetry and beliefs were independent of the trends that flowed around him, however—as he would have wished. Modern appeals to alienation, 'silence and cunning', for example, were utterly foreign to Morris's firm belief in the social nature of identity. His temperamental holism and awareness of the interrelatedness of human lives—indeed, of all life—prompted him to hope for a literature that would benefit an entire people. This ambitious aspiration remains one of the broadest visions ever indited of fully social literature, in an even broader kingdom of aesthetic ends.

No writer could accomplish more than a modest part of such a task, of course, or even suggest what forms its realization might take. But this was hardly to Morris's discredit. He was exactly right when he wrote to Bruce Glasier, without false modesty, that 'my life ha[s] been passed in being defeated; as surely every man's life must be who finds himself forced into a position of being a little ahead of the average in his aspirations'.[22]

As for the emerging political ideals which underlay much of his later poetry from **Love Is Enough** through **The Pilgrims of Hope,** these surfaced first in the realms of allegory—in his many apostrophic appeals to 'love', 'courage', and 'hope'. Morris once wrote to his wife that he thought 'imaginative people . . . want to live to see the play played out fairly—they have hopes that they are not conscious of'. The mingled effortlessness and strenuously urgent qualities of Morris's poetry similarly expressed the healing power of such 'hope'— eternally recurrent, yet eternally deferred.

In the end, Morris's sense of such 'allegorical' ideals was neither Victorian nor *fin de siècle*—not of its own time, or perhaps of any other. It expressed his deeply personal desire to resolve into words new forms of political and artistic 'hope'—an infinite task, for the object(s) of hope can never be fully represented, at least in any language we may hope to speak. But the resonance of Morris's poetry with the practical and visual arts, and its attention to the need for such hope, will continue to evoke surprise and recognition from the readers who follow us, and inspire creative interpretations in the generations to come.

Notes

1. Recent North American critics—Florence Boos, Blue Calhoun, Frederick Kirchhoff, Charlotte Oberg, Carole Silver, Jeffrey Skoblow—have shown more interest in *The Earthly Paradise.* A volume on *Sigurd the Volsung, After Summer Seed: Reconsiderations of William Morris's Sigurd the Volsung,* edited by John Hollow, was published by the William Morris Society in 1978. The 1996 Morris special issue of *Victorian Poetry* includes articles on *The Earthly Paradise, Sigurd the Volsung,* and *Poems By the Way.*

2. London, 1995, ix.

3. Harrison, *Victorian Poets and Romantic Poems: Intertextuality and Ideology,* Charlottesville, 1990. He argues that 'The poem deliberately presents itself, in fact, as doubly dream-bound; a self-conscious retreat into the idealities of love within the idealities of art' (170). *Love Is Enough* does make emblematic use of Keatsian 'colored images', but its allegorical structure also recalls Shelley's *Prometheus Unbound,* whose hero is surrounded by refracting and mirroring spirits who declaim messages of fortitude, hymnlike closure, and meditations on first and last things.

4. *Artist, Writer, Socialist* (Oxford, 1938) I: 444-45.

5. May Morris, *Collected Works* (London, 1910-1915), 266. In May's words, Morris's aim was to 'curtail [. . .] and discard [. . .] incidents that might strike a note of commonplace, however pretty in themselves, until at last the charming but rather discursive piece of narrative is remoulded into drama close-knit and passionate'.

6. Peter Faulkner, ed., *William Morris: The Critical Heritage* (London, 1973), 207-208.

7. Faulkner, 209-210.

8. See Florence Boos, '*Love Is Enough* as Secular Theodicy', *Papers on Language and Literature* 24. 4 (1988): 53-80.

9. Florence Boos, *The Design of William Morris' The Earthly Paradise,* Lewiston, New York, 1991.

10. *Artist, Writer, Socialist* I: 472. Other critics have commented on his softening of the cruelty of the saga's prose source, and traced the poem's carefully patterned structures of pervasive images and recurrent motifs—seasonal and weather images, for example, the presence of light and the sun, and the setting of fires. They have also interpreted Andvari's gold ring as an emblem of the corrosive effects of wealth, emphasized Sigurd's reformist vision of just rule, and alluded to the quasi-'revolutionary' aspects of Ragnarök, the 'twilight of the gods'. *Sigurd*'s protagonists sporadically express certain social ideals, but I am not convinced that these aspects of the poem's economic subtext are borne out in other elements of its plot, or that an agonistic life of unceasing conflict best represents the ideal of a just ruler.

For some of these lines of argument, see *After Summer Seed: Reconsiderations of William Morris's Sigurd the Volsung,* edited by John Hollow, Pennsylvania: William Morris Society, 1978. A recent discussion of the poem's ethos and style appears in Herbert Tucker, 'All for the Tale: The Epic Macropoetics of *Sigurd the Volsung*', *Victorian Poetry* 34:3 (1996): 373-94.

11. Intro. Robert Gutman, 1962, 155.

12. May Morris, *William Morris: Artist, Writer, Socialist* I, 476-77.

13. Peter Faulkner, *William Morris: The Critical Heritage,* 267.

14. Faulkner, 14-16.

15. *Artist, Writer, Socialist,* I, 496.

16. Florence Boos, 'Narrative Design in *The Pilgrims of Hope*', *Socialism and the Literary Artistry of William Morris,* eds. Florence Boos and Carole

Silver, Columbia, Missouri, 1990, 147-66. See also Anne Janowitz, 'The Pilgrims of Hope: William Morris and the dialectic of romanticism', *Cultural Politics at the Fin de Siècle,* ed. Sally Ledger and Scott McCracken (Cambridge, 1995) and Nicholas Salmon, 'The Serialisation of *The Pilgrims of Hope*', *William Morris Society Journal* 12. 2 (1997), 14-25.

17. Some of the poem's narrative discontinuities probably reflected the exigencies of its serial composition and appearance. This was Morris's sole effort to bring out a poem in shorter units: even the four volume *Earthly Paradise* appeared in several-hundred page bound 'parts'. Had Morris ever chosen to revise the poem, he might well have enlarged and reordered its final sections, and perhaps added a socialist lyric to supplement the opening 'Message of the March Wind'.

18. Among these are 'The Wooing of Hallbiorn', 'The Raven and the King's Daughter', 'The Lay of Christine', 'Hildebrand and Hellelil', and 'Hafbur and Signy'.

19. See Peter Faulkner, 'The Male as Lover, Fool, and Hero: "Goldilocks" and the Late Prose Romances,' *Victorian Poetry* 34. 3 (1996): 413-24 and Ken Goodwin, 'The Summation of a Poetic Career: *Poems By the Way*', *Victorian Poetry* 34. 3 (1996): 397-410.

20. Chris Waters, 'Morris's 'Chants' and the Problems of Socialist Culture', in *Socialism and the Literary Artistry of William Morris,* 127-146; Florence and William Boos, 'Orwell's Morris and Old Major's Dream', *English Studies* 71. 4 (1990): 361-71.

21. Brighton, 1990.

22. Kelvin, ed., Vol. 2, 1885-88, 684, letter of August 15th, 1887.

A. A. Markley (essay date March 2000)

SOURCE: Markley, A. A. "'Love for the Sake of Love': William Morris's Debt to Robert Browning in 'Riding Together.'" *English Language Notes* 37, no. 3 (March 2000): 47-55.

[*In the following essay, Markley determines the influence of Robert Browning on Morris's "Riding Together."*]

Published in 1856 in the *Oxford and Cambridge Magazine,* and later in the 1858 collection, *The Defence of Guenevere and Other Poems,* William Morris's poem **"Riding Together,"** like other poems among Morris's

early works, is an impressive formal experiment in fusing the dramatic monologue and the old English ballad. In this sense, Morris was clearly working in the tradition of the Romantics, and was obviously highly influenced by such works as *Lyrical Ballads* and particularly Keats's "La Belle Dame Sans Merci."[1] More importantly, however, **"Riding Together"** illustrates the extent to which Morris was influenced by Robert Browning in his experimentation with the form of the dramatic monologue. Browning's influence on this aspect of Morris's poetry has been well documented, but a close look at his unusually strong influence on this particular poem provides valuable evidence concerning the composition date of Morris's poem.[2] Moreover, of particular interest in terms of Browning's influence on Morris is the manner in which Morris appropriates images and language from Browning's poems celebrating heterosexual love, particularly "The Last Ride Together," in a poem that foregrounds love and companionship between male comrades.

In her edition of *The Defence of Guenevere and Other Poems,* Margaret Lourie suggests that **"Riding Together,"** originally titled **"The Captive,"** could have been written as early as 1853 because of its inclusion in manuscript form with other manuscripts dated that year.[3] The poem's similarities to Browning's "The Last Ride Together," however, demand a reconsideration of its dating after Morris's exposure to Browning's poem, published in *Men and Women* in 1855. It is probable that Morris at least renamed **"Riding Together"** after the publication of *Men and Women.* An understanding of **"Riding Together"** therefore requires a close look at Browning's work, and particularly at Browning's "The Last Ride Together," because of Morris's reference to this particular piece in his praise of Browning's poetry.

In his essay on Robert Browning's *Men and Women,* written in 1856 for the *Oxford and Cambridge Magazine,* William Morris discusses a number of the poems published in Browning's volume of the previous year, and he praises Browning's "love-poems" for their splendid evocations of a deep sense of what Morris defines as "love for love's sake." Morris writes,

> And in these love-poems of Robert Browning there is one thing that struck me particularly; that is their intense, unmixed love; love for the sake of love, and if that is not obtained, disappointment comes, falling-off, misery. I suppose the same kind of thing is to be found in all very earnest love-poetry, but I think more in him than in almost anybody else. "Any Wife to Any Husband," "The Last Ride Together:" read them, and I think you will see what I mean. I cannot say it clearly, it cannot be said so but in verse; love for love's sake, the only true love, I must say. Pray Christ some of us attain to it before we die![4]

"Any Wife to Any Husband" is a monologue in which a woman expresses the intensity of her love for her husband, her frustration that death will separate them, and her anxiety that her husband will love another. "The Last Ride Together" also focuses on frustrated love; in this poem the speaker, whom Morris described as "disappointed in his best hopes of love" persuades his lover to accompany him on "one more last ride with me" (line 11).[5] Morris described the "calm, hopeless eyes" with which the speaker views his situation—he faces the failure of his love without a struggle. Morris continued, "then over him comes a strange feeling; he does not know, it is all so blissful, so calm: 'She has not spoke so long;' suppose it be that it was Heaven now at this moment!" (344).

In the second stanza of the poem, Browning's speaker gains his wish for one last ride, and says that "one day more am I deified," beginning the theme of the eternalizing of the "good minute" that will dominate the poem. The speaker acknowledges his interest in living for the moment in his assertion in line 22 that "Who knows but the world may end tonight?" In a prelude to the realization of his idealized "good minute," the speaker describes in stanza three his lady's lying a moment on his breast as a physical realization of heaven—indicated by the drawing of "Cloud, sunset, moonrise, star-shine too" down to the earth. In the conflation of celestial imagery here with lying on the lover's breast, the reader is reminded of Keats's sonnet, "Bright Star, Would I Were Steadfast As Thou Art," in which the speaker wishes he were as steadfast as the star he addresses, so as to live forever "Pillow'd upon my fair love's ripening breast" (10).[6] The description of the eternalized moment in stanza three is an erotic one; indeed one might read the situation of the last ride together as a euphemism for a final sexual encounter.

The speaker describes the beginning of the last ride as a spiritual experience, allowing his soul to smooth itself out and flutter in the wind (34-36). He perceives his spirit as flying above other regions and cities, and from this vantage point he can speculate on the futility of human labors. As the poem progresses, the speaker again idealizes the perfection of both the conception and the carrying out of this eternalized moment with his lover, and again he does so in erotic terms with, "What will but felt the fleshly screen? / We ride and I see her bosom heave" (59-60). These lines recall the "Pleasure Thermometer" passage in the first book of Keats's "Endymion," in which the speaker describes the sensual experiences of life as providing one with the state of a "floating spirit's" (796), and in which the degrees of sensual experience lead up to the ultimate opportunity of losing one's self in physical love. The full importance of the influence of "Endymion" on Browning is seen in the lines at the end of Keats's passage in which Keats describes earthly love as having the power to make "Men's being mortal, immortal" (844).

In the final two stanzas of "The Last Ride Together," Browning's speaker explains his contentment with his achievement of the "good minute." Had fate decreed a full realization of his bliss with his lover, then Heaven would hold no promise of a happier life beyond. The speaker goes on to consider whether or not the good moment actually is heaven—the fixed, frozen moment in which one realizes life's best: "The instant made eternity—" (108).

In "The Last Ride Together," Browning uses repetition in order to emphasize the importance of the actual moment of the ride to the speaker. Browning uses a form of the verb "to ride" in the last line of all but two of the ten stanzas of the poem, and three times in the last line of the final stanza. Like Browning, Morris uses repetition to the hilt in **"Riding Together,"** repeating various forms of the verb "to ride," or similar verbs such as "gallop'd" and "dash'd" in nearly every stanza. Moreover, Morris uses the word "together" as the last word in the first line of every stanza in the poem except for stanza three, where it is the last word in the third line of the quatrain. In addition, Morris rhymes "together" with the word "weather" in all thirteen stanzas. The repetition of "together" creates a thematic refrain in which the reader constantly and consistently is reminded of the main theme of the poem—togetherness; and the repetition of "weather" creates a visual refrain out of the most active symbolic image in the poem—the condition of the weather. These refrains heighten one's sense of the poem as a ballad, as does the speaker's disinterested tone of calmness and control, qualities which Morris admired in the speaker in Browning's "The Last Ride Together."

Morris's **"Riding Together"** has a striking number of similarities to Browning's poem. The poet's use of repetition, particularly of the word "together," and the fact that he changed the title of the piece from **"The Captive"** to **"Riding Together"**—a change that reflects an emphasis on the speaker's relationship with his companion rather than merely on the speaker himself as narrator—suggests that he intended for the reader to recall Browning's poem. But despite the many similarities between the two poems, Morris's poem is not a monologue about heterosexual romantic love. **"Riding Together"** is a poem which recounts an incident from the Crusades, most likely borrowed from Jean de Joinville's account of the Battle with the Saracens at Mansura in 1250, from his *Life of Saint Louis*.[7] While the poem's focus is on the speaker's romantic associations of a "last ride," the ride that he recalls is one shared by comrades-at-arms.

In composing this poem focusing on male camaraderie in the Crusades, Morris reconfigures the eroticism of Browning's dramatic portrayal of heterosexual "love for the sake of love." His incorporation of Browning's technique of repetition of word and image allows him to emphasize the companionship and love between the two comrades, and thus to amplify the emotional content of the poem. Readers familiar with the plight of the dejected narrator in "The Last Ride Together" would bring a host of preconceptions concerning that lover and his feelings for his beloved to Morris's obviously allusive **"Riding Together"**; preconceptions that would have amplified greatly their perception of the speaker's grief in Morris's poem. In appropriating expressions of heterosexual love to amplify love between male friends, surely Morris was following Tennyson's lead; in his elegy *In Memoriam* (1850), Tennyson had woven together an array of examples of love in a variety of human relationships in order to emphasize the depth of his speaker's love for his lost friend.

The setting of **"Riding Together"** in Medieval history and in a military situation may in part account for the contemporary acceptability of its homoerotic overtones. After all, Victorian readers of poetry would have been well acquainted with the tradition of male love in the ancient epics—Achilles's love for Patroclus in Homer's *Iliad,* for example, and Virgil's account of the lovers Nisus and Euryalus in the *Aeneid,* Book IX. Lord Byron had drawn on this tradition in two pieces on military themes in his *Hours of Idleness* (1807). "The Episode of Nisus and Euryalus" is a paraphrase of Virgil, in which the warrior Nisus dies in battle after avenging his beloved companion Euryalus. Similarly, "The Death of Calmar and Orla: An Imitation of MacPherson's Ossian," is a prose passage heavily based on the Nisus and Euryalus story in its focus on two men's unflagging loyalty to each other, and on their deaths together in battle, including the same death scene detail of one companion's dying in the embrace of his dead lover. Of Calmar Byron wrote, "No maid was the sigh of his soul: his thoughts were given to friendship,—to dark-haired Orla, destroyer of heroes! Equal were their swords in battle."[8]

Critics have discussed the importance of male companionship and love amongst comrades in Medieval romance, a genre of particular relevance here, given its importance as an influence on *The Defence of Guenevere* collection. Susan Crane, for example, has explored the complex analogy between love and combat in Medieval romance in her work on gender and romance in Chaucer's *Canterbury Tales.* Crane discusses the degree to which heterosexual relations are patterned after male-male relations in this tradition. She explains that in many cases in which men are presented as learning to negotiate the social requirement to establish a heterosexual bond, they do so by maintaining strong homosocial bonds, "by redoubling and extending masculine relations through courtship."[9] Thus, drawing on the manner in which male relationships have often been depicted in literary tradition, Morris's speaker concentrates his narrative on the strong emotional bond that he shares with his primary companion at arms.

"Riding Together" divides thematically into two sections of six stanzas each, with one stanza between the two sections (stanza seven) serving as a turning point in the action. The first section sets up the situation of a band of knights riding in a campaign, although their quest is not made clear until the latter half of the poem. The opening stanzas emphasize how far the knights have journeyed from home by reiterating the condition of the hot, clear weather of the East, and their isolation: "Yet we met neither friend nor foe" (6),[10] emphasizing the gradually developing theme of togetherness between the companions. In the third stanza the poet introduces an unusual description of "clear-cut" trees "with shadows very black" (10). The trees' shadows visually foreshadow the speaker's situation at the poem's conclusion.

In stanza six the knights gallop into the wind with banners streaming, an image that recalls the flowing stream of stanza four, as well as Keats's "floating spirits," and Browning's description of the speaker's happiness in lines 34-36 of "The Last Ride Together": "My soul / Smoothed itself out, a long-cramped scroll / Freshening and fluttering in the wind." The following stanza provides a turning point in the action of **"Riding Together."** Here the knights' spears symbolically sink down as they see a thick army of pagans approaching. The mention of "pagans" indicates that this campaign is indeed a crusade, as the mention of "our Lady's Feast" and of the rood earlier may have led one to imagine. In lines 25-26 we are told at last how many knights are riding together with the mention of "threescore spears." Up to this point it has been impossible to determine whether or not the speaker is with one companion only, or among a larger band. By saving this detail until the midpoint of the poem, Morris has effectively emphasized the importance of the companion to the speaker.

In lines 27-28, Morris's speaker for the first time describes his particular companion specifically: "His eager face in the clear fresh weather, / Shone out that last time by my side." The moment is frozen in the speaker's mind—the last time that he saw his friend's face alive, much like the eternalized "good minute" in Browning's poems. Here the reader may also recall Browning's "Childe Roland to the Dark Tower Came," also from the *Men and Women* collection, in which the speaker flashes back to thoughts of former companions in firming his present resolve to persevere. Browning's speaker describes an indelible image of one of his companions as follows:

> I fancied Cuthbert's reddening face
> Beneath its garniture of curly gold,
> Dear fellow, till I almost felt him fold
> An arm in mine to fix me to the place,
> That way he used.

(91-95)

The second thematic division of **"Riding Together"** begins with stanza eight as the knights meet the pagans on a bridge, which rocks "to the crash of the meeting spears" (29-30). Nature, which has played such an active role in the poem's imagery thus far, now reflects the emotion of the impending situation in an effective use of objective correlative: "Down rain'd the buds of the dear spring weather, / The elm-tree flowers fell like tears" (31-32).

In stanza nine the knights and the pagans "roll'd and writhed together" in a physical confrontation which is almost sexual, following naturally the dashing, rocking, and crashing images of the preceding stanza. In lines 34-36, the speaker witnesses his companion's demise, and he describes his almost Achillean rage that follows as a kind of madness, although in relating the incident he does not break out of the controlled, calm tone that has characterized the poem thus far. The speaker throws up his arms as he sees his companion fall "in the lovely weather"—an ironic reminder of the beauty of their natural surroundings—and in stanza ten he slays his companion's slayer and describes his victim as having "thoughts of death"—again in the lovely weather (39), and "gapingly mazed at my madden'd face" (40).

In the penultimate stanza the speaker's hands are bound together by his captors—another ironic detail, since it uses the poem's main image of togetherness to represent captivity rather than companionship. In line 46 the corpse of the speaker's companion is bound, nodding by his side. For a third time the speaker indicates that his friend is "by my side" (see also lines 28 and 35). Again they ride together, though the companion is now dead, giving a poignant double reference to the poem's title.

Line 49 poignantly emphasizes the fact that the two companions are permanently separated: "We ride no more, no more together." Here the speaker for the first time switches from the past tense to the present. The speaker tells us that "my prison bars are thick and strong" (50), visually recalling the earlier imagery of the trees and spears, and he says that "I take no heed of any weather, / The sweet Saints grant that I live not long" (51-52). It is appropriate not only that there is no reference to the actual condition of the weather here, but also that the speaker explains that he no longer takes notice of the weather, his life, in effect, being over—a fact which he mentions with resignation. The resignation of the speaker, and the switch of verb tenses in this last stanza may remind the reader of Tennyson's "Mariana," published in the 1830 volume of *Poems, Chiefly Lyrical,* in which Mariana alters her consistent refrain of "He cometh not," to "He will not come" in the final stanza (82).[11]

Morris recognizes in "The Last Ride Together" Browning's perfect evocation of the power of the emotion of love, love for the sake of love, to whatever degree it may have been frustrated, and he draws on Browning's creation of a character capable of appreciating a "good minute" for its own sake, and even capable of seeing the eternal in that minute. Inspired by Browning's strong evocation of heterosexual love, Morris extends the conventional boundaries of gender roles in order to allow his speaker to express an honest feeling of "intense, unmixed love" for his lost friend. His success with this technique allows him to achieve in his poem a much greater degree of emotional resonance and a much more profound sense of pathos.[12]

Notes

1. According to Ronald Gorell Barnes Gorell in *John Keats: the Principle of Beauty* (London: Sylvan P, 1948), Morris said when correcting the proofs for the Kelmscott Keats that "La Belle Dame Sans Merci" was "the germ from which all the poetry of [his] group had sprung" (cited in J. M. S. Tompkins, *William Morris, the Poetry* [London: Cecil Woolf, 1988] 45). E. P. Thompson called Morris in his *Defence* poems "the true inheritor of the mantle of Keats" (*William Morris: Romantic to Revolutionary* [London: Lawrence and Wishart, 1955, 1961]).

2. For Browning's influence on Morris's poetry, see Robert Stallman, "The Lover's Progress: An Investigation of William Morris's 'The Defence of Guenevere' and 'King Arthur's Tomb,'" *Studies in English Literature* 15 (1975): 657-70; Frederic Kirchhoff, "William Morris's 'Childe Roland': The Deformed Not Quite Transformed," *Pre-Raphaelite Review* 1 (1977): 95; J. M. S. Tompkins, *William Morris, the Poetry,* 58; and Amanda Hodgson, "Riding Together: William Morris and Robert Browning," *Journal of the William Morris Society* 9 (1992): 3-7.

3. William Morris, *The Defence of Guenevere and Other Poems,* Margaret Lourie, ed. (New York: Garland, 1981) 249.

4. William Morris, *The Collected Works of William Morris.* May Morris, ed. (London: Longmans Green, 1910) 340.

5. Quotations from Robert Browning's poetry are taken from *The Complete Works of Robert Browning.* Roma A. King, Jr., et al., eds. (Athens: U Ohio P, 1969-1981).

6. Quotations from Keats's poetry are taken from *The Poems of John Keats,* Jack Stillinger, ed. (Cambridge: Harvard UP, 1978, 1982).

7. Lourie, ed., *The Defence of Guenevere and Other Poems,* 249-50.

8. Quotations from Byron's poetry are taken from *Lord Byron: The Complete Poetical Works,* Jerome J. McGann, ed. 7 Vols. (Oxford: Oxford UP, 1980).

9. Susan Crane, *Gender and Romance in Chaucer's Canterbury Tales* (Princeton: Princeton UP, 1994) 54.

10. Quotations from Morris's "Riding Together" are taken from Margaret Lourie's edition of *The Defence of Guenevere and Other Poems.*

11. Tennyson's poetry is quoted from *The Poems of Tennyson,* Christopher Ricks, ed. 3 vols. (Essex: Longman, 1987).

12. I am most grateful to Allan Life, Mary Edmonds, Vincent Lankewish, and my student Kea Anderson for their assistance with this research.

Catherine Stevenson and Virginia Hale (essay date fall 2000)

SOURCE: Stevenson, Catherine, and Virginia Hale. "Medieval Drama and Courtly Romance in William Morris' 'Sir Galahad, A Christmas Mystery.'" *Victorian Poetry* 38, no. 3 (fall 2000): 383-91.

[*In the following essay, Stevenson and Hale view "Sir Galahad: A Christmas Mystery" as a hybrid of the conventions of medieval religious drama, courtly romance, and medieval mystery play.*]

Writing of William Morris' use of medieval sources, David Staines observes that the four poems in ***The Defence of Guenevere*** volume based on Malory—**"The Defence of Guenevere," "King Arthur's Tomb," "Sir Galahad, A Christmas Mystery,"** and **"A Chapel in Lyoness"**—give evidence of a "decreasing fidelity" to the original materials. Of **"Sir Galahad, A Christmas Mystery"** he asserts: "Instead of taking a particular moment in Malory and reshaping it in his own manner, as he did in the Guenevere poem, Morris now creates his own particular incident out of the many similar incidents in Malory."[1] What is strikingly absent from Staines's account is an acknowledgment of the other medieval materials that shaped **"Sir Galahad,"** those referenced in the poem's very title—mystery or cycle plays.[2] For while the characters and some of the events in the poem derive "loosely" from Malory's romance (p. 448), the structure, the content, the emotional tenor, and the spiritual vision of the poem owe a great debt to medieval mystery plays. **"Sir Galahad, A Christmas Mystery"** is a particularly striking hybrid of the conventions and motifs of both courtly romance and medieval religious drama. While commentary on the poem has concentrated on its affinities with romance, a strong argument can be made for its derivation from another medieval mode of artistic creation. In fact, **"Sir Galahad"** and the poems that immediately precede and follow it in the ***Defence of Guenevere*** volume comprise a sort of nascent mystery cycle based on episodes in Malory.[3] By fusing romance and drama in this poem, Morris is able to create a psychologically intriguing Galahad and to express the paradoxical nature of this figure who is simultaneously of this world and too perfect for it, a spiritual visionary and a knight errant.

Morris' early familiarity with the Middle Ages and interest in romance are, of course, well documented.[4] As Carole Silver observes: "The many facets of romance . . . satisfied Morris's political, social, and artistic cravings" (p. xvi). Morris' poem about Galahad incorporates several of the characteristics of what W. R. J. Barron calls the "romance mode": first, a hero who is "superior to other men in *degree* . . . in personal qualities and to his environment by virtue of his superlative, even supernatural, abilities"; second, a series of independent episodes dealing with conventional motifs ("mysterious challenge, . . . lonely journey through hostile territory, . . . single combat against overwhelming odds or a monstrous opponent") that are loosely held together by the quest structure—the quest being always "to some extent symbolic." Finally, romance is characterized by the vision of a social ideal "inspired by a vision of what might be rather than by objective fact."[5]

"Superlative" is a word aptly suited to describe Galahad's strength, virtue, and status in Malory; he is, after all, the knight for whom the Siege Perilous is reserved—the one fated to find the Grail. In the opening section of Morris' poem, however, this super-human being is not apparent. Instead, the speaker is an all-too-human knight who, with melted snow hanging in beads on his steel-shoes, comes to shelter on the longest night in the year.[6] Galahad's previous trials—the episodes of testing and trial so central to the romance quest—are only indirectly referenced: he has wrought "sorely" and "painfully" having been many nights alone with his horse, "dismal and unfriended." Past hardships are not named specifically, but the knight's isolation and the loneliness are made palpable. The opening monologue—evocative, as we shall later see, of the medieval complaint—captures a deeply human, suffering Galahad that we do not see in either Malory or Tennyson. Revelation of character and creation of mood take precedence over the narrative of romantic adventure.

The episodic nature of romance is part of the substructure of Morris' **"Sir Galahad"**; the journeys and the extraordinary tests of strength frame the lonely moment in the chapel on which the poem focuses. Galahad will remain alone in this chapel for only a brief space, and then impelled by the imperative of the quest, will move on to further adventures continuing in the romance mode. In many medieval romances the love of the lady is the motivating factor impelling knights to face great dangers and perform feats of daring. In **"Sir Galahad,"** ironically, the quest precludes earthly fulfillment, and Galahad's opening monologue expresses his anguish at the absence of a lady in his life. Galahad reflects enviously on Palomydes' and Lancelot's romantic relationships: Palomydes is the courtly lover whose chivalry serves a lady without necessarily gaining the reward of her favor; Lancelot, in contrast, is the lover who has tangible possession of his beloved. Galahad imagines the sensuality of Guenevere's "round, / Warm and lithe" arms as they wrap around his father. As Galahad plunges into self-pity, he envisions himself being found dead in the snow, at which people would say "This Galahad / If he had lived had been a right good knight, / Ah! poor chaste body!" Here he fixes on a central contradiction of medieval romance: chastity is a highly prized virtue but, in the Arthurian world, so is the love of ladies. Unlike Tennyson's perfectly pure youth, Morris' Galahad is a knight fighting an internal battle between the ideal and the human. This emotional and spiritual conflict rather than the battle against external enemies is the central dramatic focus of Morris' poem.

A final characteristic of the romance form is its projection of a social ideal "inspired by a vision of what might be" (Barron, p. 4). Arthur's court at Camelot offered just such a social ideal; yet Galahad left that world to seek a demanding spiritual ideal. Galahad (like his creator) tries in the dramatic episode represented by the poem to reconcile his longing for earthly rewards and delights with the more austere spiritual goal to which he has been called. The poem dramatically enacts his conflict and its resolution through a transfiguring experience which enables the final completion of the quest.

The debt of **"Sir Galahad"** to romance then is obvious; less apparent but equally important is its adaptation of the conventions of the medieval mystery play, a literary form which Morris had a number of opportunities to encounter during his Oxford years, 1853-55.[7] Morris' use of the term "mystery" reveals not only a familiarity with the available scholarly material on medieval drama but also an understanding of the distinction between "mystery" and "miracle" plays. He and his friend Burne-Jones as undergraduates "devoured anything of any kind written about the Middle Ages."[8] The distinction between the two major forms of medieval drama appears to have been introduced in the eighteenth century to differentiate formally between religious plays based on Biblical stories and factual narratives (the mystery) and those based on legends of the saints (the miracle). By the nineteenth century, mystery plays came to be associated with the guilds that performed them, each of which had its own craft or "mystery."[9] Morris'

own "Christmas Mystery" would have been an appropriate tribute to the patron saint of the brotherhood or "Order" he and Burne-Jones planned to establish.[10]

Meredith Raymond argues that **"Sir Galahad"** and the **"Chapel in Lyoness"** should be seen as companion poems that examine "spiritual love and heavenly grace" as opposed to the other two Arthurian poems which examine "human corruption, earthly love, frailty, and sin" (pp. 214-215). We would argue instead that **"Sir Galahad"** and the poems that immediately precede and follow it in the *Defence of Guenevere* volume (written 1856-57) constitute a miniature cycle of mystery plays which echo and complement each other while tracing out a seasonal/liturgical year. **"King Arthur's Tomb"** (written October 1857) takes place on a summer afternoon, and concludes with the penitent, prone Lancelot awakening to the sound of a mysterious but clearly symbolic bell. **"Sir Galahad"** (written in the winter of 1856) unfolds in Christmastide and uses the physical environment to reify Galahad's chilly isolation. The bell and the swooning hero from the preceding poem are also echoed in **"Sir Galahad"**: Lancelot falls upon the ground in a swoon of longing for Guenevere, rising to the sound of a bell; Galahad, who has been languishing for lack of the very human love which destroyed his father, falls in dread before the divine voice whose presence is presaged by a bell (l. 89). **"The Chapel in Lyoness"** (written in September 1876) also subtitled "a mystery," completes the liturgical cycle by covering the period from Christmas to Whit-Sunday. In it a knight lies dying in winter in a kind of bizarre realization of Galahad's nightmare vision of his own fate (ll. 49-50); ironically, he is "saved" by Galahad's kiss as Galahad earlier was "saved" by the intervention of the divine presence. Raymond argues that Galahad progresses from being a "somewhat self-centered" figure in the poem that bears his name to a savior capable of imparting grace in **"The Chapel in Lyoness"** (p. 218). This transformation is effected through the ritualized drama at the center of **"Sir Galahad: A Christmas Mystery."**

The earliest mystery plays were designed around the liturgy of a season and were performed at Easter and Christmas. Eventually the cycles of plays became associated with the feast of Corpus Christi. This feast was not idly chosen. The transubstantiation of the Mass, the changing of bread and wine into the corpus of Christ, was the central fact of Christian life and the center of the drama of the Mass. Like the medieval mystery cycle, Morris' **"Sir Galahad"** accords a central place to the mystery of the Eucharist. In stanza 20 Galahad is summoned by a bell beside the door of the chapel:

> "And I leapt up when something pass'd me by.
>
> Shrill ringing going with it, still half blind
> I stagger'd after, a great sense of awe
> At every step gathering on my mind."[11]

This scene evokes, without actually depicting, the procession of bell-ringer and priest carrying the consecrated host. It is immediately followed by a visionary scene in which the sacramental Eucharist becomes the living body of Christ "sitting on the altar as on a throne, / Whose face no man could say he did not know." The vision consoles Galahad: "Good Knight of God . . . I come to make you glad."

The vast number of cycle plays begin with a monologue or a dialogue which sets both the subject and the tone of the play. *Abraham and Isaac,* for example, offers a monologue on the plight of the patriarch in the face of God's command; several of the shepherd plays begin with speeches lamenting the poverty, misery, and general harshness of the life of everyday human beings; two Noah plays feature complaints by God about the distressful condition of his creation. These openings are often followed by the vision or dream of an angel who addresses the complaints and directs the figures to action which will restore their hope or fulfill their role in God's plan. Once that action is initiated, the pattern brings in other characters whose interaction with the main figure dramatizes the biblical story and often casts it in the terms of a contemporary dilemma. Thus, Noah's family becomes a model of a typical family replete with obedient and recalcitrant offspring and a shrewish wife.

Like these dramas, Morris' **"Sir Galahad"** opens with a complaint. The "wearied and forlorn" protagonist ponders his lonely, celibate state, questioning the choices he has made. Galahad's opening plaint resembles the lament of another celibate man, St. Joseph, in the "Pageant of the Shearmen and Taylors":

> A weylle-awey Joseoff as thow ar olde
> Lyke a fole now may I stand and truse
> But in feyth Mare thu art in syn
> Soo moche ase I have cheryischyd the chyd the, dame,
> and all thi kyn
> Be hynd my bak to serve me thus
> All olde men insampull take be me
> How I am begylid here may you see
> To wed soo yong a chyld.
> Now fare well Mare leyve the here alone
> Worthe the, dam, and thy workis ycheone
> For I woll noo more be gylid be for frynd nor foe
> Now of this ded I am so dull
> And of my lyf I am so full no further ma I goo.

(Sharp, p. 87; Middle English spelling has been regularized for clarity)

The "Pageant of the Weavers" also from the Coventry Corpus Christi plays, presents another lamentation by Joseph that is very close in spirit to Galahad's:

> I wandur abowt myself alone,
> Turtulis or dovis can I none see.

> Now, Kyng of hevin, thow amend my mone:
> For I trow I seke nott where thei be!
> My myght, my strenth ys worne fro me:
> For age I am waxun almost blynd.
> Those fowlys thei are full far fro me
> And verrie yvill for me to fynde.
>
> I loke fast and nevre the nere;
> My wynd for feynt ys allmost gone.
> Lord, *benedissete!* Whatt make I here
> Among these heggis myself alone?
>
> For-were I ma no lengur stond;
> These buskis thei teyre me on evere syde.
> Here woll I sytt upon this londe,
> Oure Lordis wyll for to abyde.[12]

(Middle English spelling regularized for clarity)

When Joseph has reached his lowest point, he is interrupted by an angelic voice offering comfort through revelation of the divine mystery. Then the sacred drama unfolds and the cast broadens to include shepherds, singing angels, wise men, and, of course, Herod. The York play of *Joseph's Troubles About Mary,* the Christmas plays in the pageant of the Shearmen and Taylors, and the Pageant of the Weavers all follow this same pattern.

Similarly, Morris' Galahad, feeling utterly unloved, opens his monologue by mentally revisiting the romantic entanglements available to his fellow knights but forbidden to him. These self-punishing musings are interrupted by the arrival of a consolatory divine voice: "Rise up and look and listen Galahad . . . I come to make you glad" (ll. 94-96). The formal complexity of this poem is illustrated by the fact that here, in an act of dramatic ventriloquism, Galahad recreates in his narrative the voice of the divine speaker. Lionel Stevenson characterizes the poem as an "interior monologue" which later shifts to "dramatic action" (p. 141). But, in fact, as in many medieval cycle plays, the "interior monologue" is actually a kind of performance for an unspecified audience; the knight becomes a dramatic impersonator (stanzas 12, 14, and 25-35) who evokes the voices of others: Palomides, Father Launcelot, "they" of the courtly world, and finally Christ.

Although the first two thirds of the poem are enriched monologue, in the middle of line 153 the poem shifts into the present tense ("the bell comes near") and blossoms into a full-scale drama, complete with stage directions, angels, four saintly ladies, and three characters from the *Morte D'Arthur.* This bold shift to pure drama signals not only a narrative transition but also a psychological and spiritual transformation of the character. The blend of romance and cycle drama enables Morris to create a Galahad who, unlike Tennyson's hero, is emotionally complex, conflicted, and palpably human. The shift to the pure dramatic mode serves as a caesura in the poem signaling a transition in the character of Galahad from a figure out of romance to a spiritual, iconographic hero. Galahad is to be a knight of a higher order. The encounter with the divine has transformed him in ways that are symbolized, not directly narrated.

The stage direction "Enter" (between lines) introduces four saintly women, all virgin martyrs,[13] who begin a ritual enactment bridging the sacred and the courtly worlds of the poem. This rite combines the traditional arming of the warrior for battle with the ritual vesting of a priest for mass[14] and draws upon the tradition in the Arthurian stories wherein an armed knight was a *Miles Christi*. Recalling St. Paul's Epistle to the Ephesians, Chapter 6, the Christian knight was counselled to "be strengthened in the Lord, in the might of his power. Put you on the armor of God, so that you may be able to stand against the deceits of the devil." The chivalric ideal, however modified and tarnished by practice and human imperfection, was the imitation of Christ, the effort to realize in the individual and in society the perfection to which human nature aided by grace could aspire.

The dramatic action figures forth the transformation in Galahad which reaffirms the intersection of the Christian and courtly ideals. Galahad, having partaken of a salutary vision, has to reenter the human world to complete the quest that was interrupted for the duration of this long night.

With the entrance of the courtly company, the poem finds its dénouement in a retreat from the dramatically enacted spiritual vision and sacred ritual. Bors's final speech reintroduces the human world of pain, struggle, and partial vision in which good knights can see "the light" only briefly and at a distance, while great warriors like Gawain and Lionel come back from the Quest "merely shamed" or like Lancelot have not yet returned. Others like poor Dinadan, the level-headed, witty companion of Sir Tristram, have met a shocking fate: "in a little wood / . . . found all hack'd and dead." "In vain" (Morris repeats the phrase twice for emphasis), they "struggle for the vision fair."

Unlike the knights described in the poem's final three stanzas, Galahad will not quest in vain. In fact, in stanzas 22 through 34, he has already achieved on the emotional and psychological levels the realization of the Christian mystery which the others are still vainly seeking. The solitary knight, filled with despair, has

been embraced by consolatory grace dramatically embodied. The poem concludes with Galahad poised to reenter the world of romance. As the child of Lancelot as well as of the Christ who addresses him as "son" (stanzas 29 and 32), he departs for further adventures before achieving the foregone conclusion—the physical realization of the Grail quest.

In **"Sir Galahad, A Christmas Mystery"** Morris has created an imaginary episode that conflates, in a most original way, medieval religious drama and courtly romance. Galahad speaks like a Joseph from the cycle plays, a vulnerable man complaining about his fate. He is consoled by the vision of a compassionate Christ who speaks about the human trials of Lancelot and Palomides, while also exhorting Galahad to keep his eyes on heavenly rewards. As in the medieval mysteries, human trials and concerns are voiced, at the same time as heavenly, consolatory, miraculous responses are given. Galahad as dramatic protagonist experiences a metamorphic ritual. In Morris' hands, then, the Christian mystery play served as a flexible literary form within which to explore the psychological and spiritual life of a character, taken for a transcendent moment out of the kinetic world of romance.

Notes

1. David Staines, "Morris' Treatment of His Medieval Sources," *SP* [*Studies in Philology*] 70 (1973): 448; hereinafter cited in parentheses in the text.

2. In his 1972 study *The Pre-Raphaelite Poets* (Chapel Hill: Univ. of North Carolina Press, 1972), Lionel Stevenson observes that William Morris' "The Chapel in Lyoness," "Rapunzel," and "The Blue Closet" can all be described as "mysteries" because "they follow the form of medieval folk drama . . . in being a series of set speeches in lyric rhythms" (p. 147). Unaccountably, Stevenson leaves out of his list "Sir Galahad" subtitled "A Christmas Mystery." Margaret A. Lourie, *The Defence of Guenevere and Other Poems* (New York: Garland, 1981), cites Stevenson and comments (inaccurately, it turns out) that "Lionel Stevenson points out that the medieval mystery play or folk drama determined the form of this poem" (p. 195).

3. Curtis Dahl, "Morris's 'The Chapel in Lyoness'": An Interpretation," *SP* 60 (1954): 482-491, and Meredith Raymond, "The Arthurian Group in 'The Defence of Guenevere and Other Poems,'" *VP* [*Victorian Poetry*] 4 (1966): 213-218, speak of the four poems based on Malory as "spiritual drama" but do not draw the specific parallel to medieval liturgical drama.

4. Frederick Kirchhoff, *William Morris: The Construction of a Male Self 1856-1872* (Athens: Ohio Univ. Press, 1990); Carole Silver, *The Romance of William Morris* (Athens: Ohio Univ. Press, 1982); and David G. Riede, "Morris, Modernism, and Romance," *ELH* 7 (1984): 85-105.

5. W. R. J. Barron, *English Medieval Romance* (London: Longman, 1987), pp. 2, 4-5.

6. This opening parallels "Sir Gawain and the Green Knight," the manuscript of which was acquired by the British Museuem in 1802. As in "Gawain," external nature sets a mood akin to despair on the part of the questing knight.

7. He and Burne-Jones might have seen a mystery play in performance, although existing records in Oxford do not list any college or University performances during those years. Printed versions of plays were available to him, however, from at least two sources, both of which are owned by the Bodleian Library, where we know that he and Burne-Jones read Chaucer and studied the illuminated manuscripts. See Jack Lindsay, *William Morris: His Life and Work* (London: Constable, 1975), p. 53. In 1825 Thomas Sharp had published a detailed and beautifully illustrated study of medieval dramatic practice at Coventry entitled *A Dissertation on the Pageants or Dramatic Mysteries Anciently Performed at Coventry by Trading Companies of that City.* In addition to precise information about the material circumstances of medieval drama gleaned from a study of the records of the guilds that produced the plays, Sharp also printed the complete text of the "Pageant of the Shearmen and Taylors Company." In addition, William Marriott's *A Collection of English Miracle-Plays or Mysteries* (1838) made available ten dramas from the Chester, Coventry, and Towneley series, including two of the Ludus Coventriae ("Joseph's Jealousy" and the "Trial of Mary and Joseph") which he wrongly attributes to the Coventry cycle.

8. Georgiana Burne-Jones, *Memorials of Edward Burne-Jones* (London: Macmillan, 1904), 1:104.

9. Vincent Hopper and Gerald Leahy, *Medieval Mysteries, Moralities and Interludes* (New York: Barron's, 1962), p. 9.

10. J. W. Mackail, *The Life of William Morris* (London, 1899), 1:63, and Philip Henderson, *William Morris, His Life, Work and Friends* (New York: McGraw Hill, 1967).

11. William Morris, *The Collected Works of William Morris,* Vol. 1 (1910; repr. New York: Russell and Russell, 1969); hereinafter cited in parentheses in the text.

12. *Two Coventry Corpus Christi Plays,* ed. Harden Craig, Early English Text Society Extra Series, 87, 2nd ed. (London: Oxford Univ. Press, 1957), p. 49.

13. At least two of the saints—Mary of Antioch and Katherine of Alexandria—were identified as those whose voices spoke to Joan of Arc.

14. The arming of the warrior has a tradition going back to classical and folk-epics. In the medieval romances with which Morris was probably familiar, there are any number of arming passages: Beves of Hampton, Guy of Warwick, and Sir Gawain and the Green Knight are three popular British romances that he would probably have known. Squires, of course, do most of the arming, but Josian, the lady of Sir Beves, participates in his preparation and in Chrétien de Troyes's "Erec and Enid," the heroine herself arms her warrior knight.

FURTHER READING

Biographies

McGann, Jerome. "'A Thing to Mind': The Materialist Aesthetic of William Morris." *Huntington Library Quarterly* 55, no. 1 (winter 1992): 55-74.

Details Morris's involvement with books and printing.

Stansky, Peter. *William Morris.* Oxford: Oxford University Press, 1983, 96 p.

Biographical and critical study.

Criticism

Boos, Florence S. "Ten Journeys to the Venusberg: Morris' Drafts for 'The Hill of Venus.'" *Victorian Poetry* 39, no. 4 (winter 2001): 597-615.

Traces the various drafts of "The Hill of Venus."

Calhoun, Blue. *The Pastoral Vision of William Morris: The Earthly Paradise.* Athens: University of Georgia Press, 1975, 263 p.

Explores the pastoral vision of *The Earthly Paradise.*

Holzman, Michael. "Propaganda, Passion, and Literary Art in William Morris's *The Pilgrims of Hope*." *Texas Studies in Literature and Language* 24, no. 4 (winter 1982): 372-93.

Offers readings of *The Pilgrim of Hope* as propa-

-ganda, Pre-Raphaelite love poetry, and a formal literary exercise.

Oberg, Charlotte H. *William Morris: A Pagan Prophet.* Charlottesville: University Press of Virginia, 1978, 189 p.

Examines aspects of Morris's literary oeuvre.

Additional coverage of Morris's life and career is contained in the following sources published by the Gale Group: *British Writers,* **Vol. 5;** *Concise Dictionary of British Literary Biography,* **Vol. 1832-1890;** *Dictionary of Literary Biography,* **Vols. 18, 35, 57, 156, 178, 184;** *Literature Resource Center;* *Nineteenth-Century Literature Criticism,* **Vol. 4;** *Reference Guide to English Literature,* **Ed. 2;** *St. James Guide to Fantasy Writers;* *St. James Guide to Science Fiction Writers,* **Ed. 4; and** *Supernatural Fiction Writers.*

How to Use This Index

The main references

> **Calvino, Italo**
> 1923-1985 .... **CLC 5, 8, 11, 22, 33, 39, 73; SSC 3, 48**

list all author entries in the following Gale Literary Criticism series:

AAL = Asian American Literature
BG = The Beat Generation: A Gale Critical Companion
BLC = Black Literature Criticism
BLCS = Black Literature Criticism Supplement
CLC = Contemporary Literary Criticism
CLR = Children's Literature Review
CMLC = Classical and Medieval Literature Criticism
DC = Drama Criticism
HLC = Hispanic Literature Criticism
HLCS = Hispanic Literature Criticism Supplement
HR = Harlem Renaissance: A Gale Critical Companion
LC = Literature Criticism from 1400 to 1800
NCLC = Nineteenth-Century Literature Criticism
NNAL = Native North American Literature
PC = Poetry Criticism
SSC = Short Story Criticism
TCLC = Twentieth-Century Literary Criticism
WLC = World Literature Criticism, 1500 to the Present
WLCS = World Literature Criticism Supplement

The cross-references

> See also CA 85-88, 116; CANR 23, 61;
> DAM NOV; DLB 196; EW 13; MTCW 1, 2;
> RGSF 2; RGWL 2; SFW 4; SSFS 12

list all author entries in the following Gale biographical and literary sources:

AAYA = Authors & Artists for Young Adults
AFAW = African American Writers
AFW = African Writers
AITN = Authors in the News
AMW = American Writers
AMWR = American Writers Retrospective Supplement
AMWS = American Writers Supplement
ANW = American Nature Writers
AW = Ancient Writers
BEST = Bestsellers
BPFB = Beacham's Encyclopedia of Popular Fiction: Biography and Resources
BRW = British Writers
BRWS = British Writers Supplement
BW = Black Writers
BYA = Beacham's Guide to Literature for Young Adults
CA = Contemporary Authors
CAAS = Contemporary Authors Autobiography Series
CABS = Contemporary Authors Bibliographical Series
CAD = Contemporary American Dramatists
CANR = Contemporary Authors New Revision Series
CAP = Contemporary Authors Permanent Series
CBD = Contemporary British Dramatists
CCA = Contemporary Canadian Authors
CD = Contemporary Dramatists
CDALB = Concise Dictionary of American Literary Biography
CDALBS = Concise Dictionary of American Literary Biography Supplement
CDBLB = Concise Dictionary of British Literary Biography

CMW = *St. James Guide to Crime & Mystery Writers*
CN = *Contemporary Novelists*
CP = *Contemporary Poets*
CPW = *Contemporary Popular Writers*
CSW = *Contemporary Southern Writers*
CWD = *Contemporary Women Dramatists*
CWP = *Contemporary Women Poets*
CWRI = *St. James Guide to Children's Writers*
CWW = *Contemporary World Writers*
DA = *DISCovering Authors*
DA3 = *DISCovering Authors 3.0*
DAB = *DISCovering Authors: British Edition*
DAC = *DISCovering Authors: Canadian Edition*
DAM = *DISCovering Authors: Modules*
   DRAM: *Dramatists Module;* **MST:** *Most-studied Authors Module;*
   MULT: *Multicultural Authors Module;* **NOV:** *Novelists Module;*
   POET: *Poets Module;* **POP:** *Popular Fiction and Genre Authors Module*
DFS = *Drama for Students*
DLB = *Dictionary of Literary Biography*
DLBD = *Dictionary of Literary Biography Documentary Series*
DLBY = *Dictionary of Literary Biography Yearbook*
DNFS = *Literature of Developing Nations for Students*
EFS = *Epics for Students*
EXPN = *Exploring Novels*
EXPP = *Exploring Poetry*
EXPS = *Exploring Short Stories*
EW = *European Writers*
FANT = *St. James Guide to Fantasy Writers*
FW = *Feminist Writers*
GFL = *Guide to French Literature,* Beginnings to 1789, 1798 to the Present
GLL = *Gay and Lesbian Literature*
HGG = *St. James Guide to Horror, Ghost & Gothic Writers*
HW = *Hispanic Writers*
IDFW = *International Dictionary of Films and Filmmakers: Writers and Production Artists*
IDTP = *International Dictionary of Theatre: Playwrights*
LAIT = *Literature and Its Times*
LAW = *Latin American Writers*
JRDA = *Junior DISCovering Authors*
MAICYA = *Major Authors and Illustrators for Children and Young Adults*
MAICYAS = *Major Authors and Illustrators for Children and Young Adults Supplement*
MAWW = *Modern American Women Writers*
MJW = *Modern Japanese Writers*
MTCW = *Major 20th-Century Writers*
NCFS = *Nonfiction Classics for Students*
NFS = *Novels for Students*
PAB = *Poets: American and British*
PFS = *Poetry for Students*
RGAL = *Reference Guide to American Literature*
RGEL = *Reference Guide to English Literature*
RGSF = *Reference Guide to Short Fiction*
RGWL = *Reference Guide to World Literature*
RHW = *Twentieth-Century Romance and Historical Writers*
SAAS = *Something about the Author Autobiography Series*
SATA = *Something about the Author*
SFW = *St. James Guide to Science Fiction Writers*
SSFS = *Short Stories for Students*
TCWW = *Twentieth-Century Western Writers*
WLIT = *World Literature and Its Times*
WP = *World Poets*
YABC = *Yesterday's Authors of Books for Children*
YAW = *St. James Guide to Young Adult Writers*

Literary Criticism Series
Cumulative Author Index

Andrews, Cicily Fairfield
See West, Rebecca

Andrews, Elton V.
See Pohl, Frederik

Andreyev, Leonid (Nikolaevich)
1871-1919 .... **TCLC 3**
See Andreev, Leonid
See also CA 104; 185

Andric, Ivo 1892-1975 .... **CLC 8; SSC 36;**
TCLC 135
See also CA 81-84; 57-60; CANR 43, 60;
CDWLB 4; DLB 147; EW 11; EWL 3;
MTCW 1; RGSF 2; RGWL 2, 3

Androvar
See Prado (Calvo), Pedro

Angelique, Pierre
See Bataille, Georges

Angell, Roger 1920- .... **CLC 26**
See also CA 57-60; CANR 13, 44, 70; DLB
171, 185

Angelou, Maya 1928- ... **BLC 1; CLC 12, 35,**
64, 77, 155; PC 32; WLCS
See also AAYA 7, 20; AMWS 4; BPFB 1;
BW 2, 3; BYA 2; CA 65-68; CANR 19,
42, 65, 111; CDALBS; CLR 53; CP 7;
CPW; CSW; CWP; DA; DA3; DAB;
DAC; DAM MST, MULT, POET, POP;
DLB 38; EWL 3; EXPN; EXPP; LAIT 4;
MAICYA 2; MAICYAS 1; MAWW;
MTCW 1, 2; NCFS 2; NFS 2; PFS 2, 3;
RGAL 4; SATA 49, 136; WYA; YAW

Angouleme, Marguerite d'
See de Navarre, Marguerite

Anna Comnena 1083-1153 .... **CMLC 25**

Annensky, Innokentii Fedorovich
See Annensky, Innokenty (Fyodorovich)
See also DLB 295

Annensky, Innokenty (Fyodorovich)
1856-1909 .... **TCLC 14**
See also CA 110; 155; EWL 3

Annunzio, Gabriele d'
See D'Annunzio, Gabriele

Anodos
See Coleridge, Mary E(lizabeth)

Anon, Charles Robert
See Pessoa, Fernando (Antonio Nogueira)

Anouilh, Jean (Marie Lucien Pierre)
1910-1987 . **CLC 1, 3, 8, 13, 40, 50; DC**
8, 21
See also CA 17-20R; 123; CANR 32; DAM
DRAM; DFS 9, 10; EW 13; EWL 3; GFL
1789 to the Present; MTCW 1, 2; RGWL
2, 3; TWA

Anthony, Florence
See Ai

Anthony, John
See Ciardi, John (Anthony)

Anthony, Peter
See Shaffer, Anthony (Joshua); Shaffer,
Peter (Levin)

Anthony, Piers 1934- .... **CLC 35**
See also AAYA 11, 48; BYA 7; CA 200;
CAAE 200; CANR 28, 56, 73, 102; CPW;
DAM POP; DLB 8; FANT; MAICYA 2;
MAICYAS 1; MTCW 1, 2; SAAS 22;
SATA 84, 129; SATA-Essay 129; SFW 4;
SUFW 1, 2; YAW

Anthony, Susan B(rownell)
1820-1906 .... **TCLC 84**
See also CA 211; FW

Antiphon c. 480B.C.-c. 411B.C. .... **CMLC 55**

Antoine, Marc
See Proust, (Valentin-Louis-George-Eugene)
Marcel

Antoninus, Brother
See Everson, William (Oliver)

Antonioni, Michelangelo 1912- .... **CLC 20,**
144
See also CA 73-76; CANR 45, 77

Antschel, Paul 1920-1970
See Celan, Paul
See also CA 85-88; CANR 33, 61; MTCW
1

Anwar, Chairil 1922-1949 .... **TCLC 22**
See Chairil Anwar
See also CA 121; 219; RGWL 3

Anzaldua, Gloria (Evanjelina)
1942- .... **HLCS 1**
See also CA 175; CSW; CWP; DLB 122;
FW; LLW 1; RGAL 4

Apess, William 1798-1839(?) .... **NCLC 73;**
NNAL
See also DAM MULT; DLB 175, 243

Apollinaire, Guillaume 1880-1918 .... **PC 7;**
TCLC 3, 8, 51
See Kostrowitzki, Wilhelm Apollinaris de
See also CA 152; DAM POET; DLB 258;
EW 9; EWL 3; GFL 1789 to the Present;
MTCW 1; RGWL 2, 3; TWA; WP

Apollonius of Rhodes
See Apollonius Rhodius
See also AW 1; RGWL 2, 3

Apollonius Rhodius c. 300B.C.-c.
220B.C. .... **CMLC 28**
See Apollonius of Rhodes
See also DLB 176

Appelfeld, Aharon 1932- ... **CLC 23, 47; SSC**
42
See also CA 112; 133; CANR 86; CWW 2;
EWL 3; RGSF 2

Apple, Max (Isaac) 1941- .... **CLC 9, 33; SSC**
50
See also CA 81-84; CANR 19, 54; DLB
130

Appleman, Philip (Dean) 1926- .... **CLC 51**
See also CA 13-16R; CAAS 18; CANR 6,
29, 56

Appleton, Lawrence
See Lovecraft, H(oward) P(hillips)

Apteryx
See Eliot, T(homas) S(tearns)

Apuleius, (Lucius Madaurensis)
125(?)-175(?) .... **CMLC 1**
See also AW 2; CDWLB 1; DLB 211;
RGWL 2, 3; SUFW

Aquin, Hubert 1929-1977 .... **CLC 15**
See also CA 105; DLB 53; EWL 3

Aquinas, Thomas 1224(?)-1274 ..... **CMLC 33**
See also DLB 115; EW 1; TWA

Aragon, Louis 1897-1982 .... **CLC 3, 22;**
TCLC 123
See also CA 69-72; 108; CANR 28, 71;
DAM NOV, POET; DLB 72, 258; EW 11;
EWL 3; GFL 1789 to the Present; GLL 2;
LMFS 2; MTCW 1, 2; RGWL 2, 3

Arany, Janos 1817-1882 .... **NCLC 34**

Aranyos, Kakay 1847-1910
See Mikszath, Kalman

Aratus of Soli c. 315B.C.-c.
240B.C. .... **CMLC 64**
See also DLB 176

Arbuthnot, John 1667-1735 .... **LC 1**
See also DLB 101

Archer, Herbert Winslow
See Mencken, H(enry) L(ouis)

Archer, Jeffrey (Howard) 1940- .... **CLC 28**
See also AAYA 16; BEST 89:3; BPFB 1;
CA 77-80; CANR 22, 52, 95; CPW; DA3;
DAM POP; INT CANR-22

Archer, Jules 1915- .... **CLC 12**
See also CA 9-12R; CANR 6, 69; SAAS 5;
SATA 4, 85

Archer, Lee
See Ellison, Harlan (Jay)

Archilochus c. 7th cent. B.C.- .... **CMLC 44**
See also DLB 176

Arden, John 1930- .... **CLC 6, 13, 15**
See also BRWS 2; CA 13-16R; CAAS 4;
CANR 31, 65, 67, 124; CBD; CD 5;
DAM DRAM; DFS 9; DLB 13, 245;
EWL 3; MTCW 1

Arenas, Reinaldo 1943-1990 .. **CLC 41; HLC**
1
See also CA 124; 128; 133; CANR 73, 106;
DAM MULT; DLB 145; EWL 3; GLL 2;
HW 1; LAW; LAWS 1; MTCW 1; RGSF
2; RGWL 3; WLIT 1

Arendt, Hannah 1906-1975 .... **CLC 66, 98**
See also CA 17-20R; 61-64; CANR 26, 60;
DLB 242; MTCW 1, 2

Aretino, Pietro 1492-1556 .... **LC 12**
See also RGWL 2, 3

Arghezi, Tudor .... **CLC 80**
See Theodorescu, Ion N.
See also CA 167; CDWLB 4; DLB 220;
EWL 3

Arguedas, Jose Maria 1911-1969 .... **CLC 10,**
18; HLCS 1; TCLC 147
See also CA 89-92; CANR 73; DLB 113;
EWL 3; HW 1; LAW; RGWL 2, 3; WLIT
1

Argueta, Manlio 1936- .... **CLC 31**
See also CA 131; CANR 73; CWW 2; DLB
145; EWL 3; HW 1; RGWL 3

Arias, Ron(ald Francis) 1941- .... **HLC 1**
See also CA 131; CANR 81; DAM MULT;
DLB 82; HW 1, 2; MTCW 2

Ariosto, Ludovico 1474-1533 ... **LC 6, 87; PC**
42
See also EW 2; RGWL 2, 3

Aristides
See Epstein, Joseph

Aristophanes 450B.C.-385B.C. .... **CMLC 4,**
51; DC 2; WLCS
See also AW 1; CDWLB 1; DA; DA3;
DAB; DAC; DAM DRAM, MST; DFS
10; DLB 176; LMFS 1; RGWL 2, 3; TWA

Aristotle 384B.C.-322B.C. .... **CMLC 31;**
WLCS
See also AW 1; CDWLB 1; DA; DA3;
DAB; DAC; DAM MST; DLB 176;
RGWL 2, 3; TWA

Arlt, Roberto (Godofredo Christophersen)
1900-1942 .... **HLC 1; TCLC 29**
See also CA 123; 131; CANR 67; DAM
MULT; EWL 3; HW 1, 2; LAW

Armah, Ayi Kwei 1939- . **BLC 1; CLC 5, 33,**
136
See also AFW; BW 1; CA 61-64; CANR
21, 64; CDWLB 3; CN 7; DAM MULT,
POET; DLB 117; EWL 3; MTCW 1;
WLIT 2

Armatrading, Joan 1950- .... **CLC 17**
See also CA 114; 186

Armitage, Frank
See Carpenter, John (Howard)

Armstrong, Jeannette (C.) 1948- .... **NNAL**
See also CA 149; CCA 1; CN 7; DAC;
SATA 102

Arnette, Robert
See Silverberg, Robert

Arnim, Achim von (Ludwig Joachim von
Arnim) 1781-1831 ..... **NCLC 5; SSC 29**
See also DLB 90

Arnim, Bettina von 1785-1859 ...... **NCLC 38,**
123
See also DLB 90; RGWL 2, 3

Arnold, Matthew 1822-1888 ..... **NCLC 6, 29,**
89, 126; PC 5; WLC
See also BRW 5; CDBLB 1832-1890; DA;
DAB; DAC; DAM MST, POET; DLB 32,
57; EXPP; PAB; PFS 2; TEA; WP

Arnold, Thomas 1795-1842 .... **NCLC 18**
See also DLB 55

Barker, Clive 1952- .... **CLC 52; SSC 53**
See also AAYA 10; BEST 90:3; BPFB 1;
CA 121; 129; CANR 71, 111; CPW; DA3;
DAM POP; DLB 261; HGG; INT CA-
129; MTCW 1, 2; SUFW 2

Barker, George Granville
1913-1991 .... **CLC 8, 48**
See also CA 9-12R; 135; CANR 7, 38;
DAM POET; DLB 20; EWL 3; MTCW 1

Barker, Harley Granville
See Granville-Barker, Harley
See also DLB 10

Barker, Howard 1946- .... **CLC 37**
See also CA 102; CBD; CD 5; DLB 13,
233

Barker, Jane 1652-1732 .... **LC 42, 82**
See also DLB 39, 131

Barker, Pat(ricia) 1943- ...... **CLC 32, 94, 146**
See also BRWS 4; CA 117; 122; CANR 50,
101; CN 7; DLB 271; INT CA-122

Barlach, Ernst (Heinrich)
1870-1938 .... **TCLC 84**
See also CA 178; DLB 56, 118; EWL 3

Barlow, Joel 1754-1812 .... **NCLC 23**
See also AMWS 2; DLB 37; RGAL 4

Barnard, Mary (Ethel) 1909- .... **CLC 48**
See also CA 21-22; CAP 2

Barnes, Djuna 1892-1982 .... **CLC 3, 4, 8, 11,
29, 127; SSC 3**
See Steptoe, Lydia
See also AMWS 3; CA 9-12R; 107; CAD;
CANR 16, 55; CWD; DLB 4, 9, 45; EWL
3; GLL 1; MTCW 1, 2; RGAL 4; TUS

Barnes, Jim 1933- .... **NNAL**
See also CA 108; 175; CAAE 175; CAAS
28; DLB 175

Barnes, Julian (Patrick) 1946- . **CLC 42, 141**
See also BRWS 4; CA 102; CANR 19, 54,
115; CN 7; DAB; DLB 194; DLBY 1993;
EWL 3; MTCW 1

Barnes, Peter 1931- .... **CLC 5, 56**
See also CA 65-68; CAAS 12; CANR 33,
34, 64, 113; CBD; CD 5; DFS 6; DLB
13, 233; MTCW 1

Barnes, William 1801-1886 .... **NCLC 75**
See also DLB 32

Baroja (y Nessi), Pío 1872-1956 .... **HLC 1;
TCLC 8**
See also CA 104; EW 9

Baron, David
See Pinter, Harold

Baron Corvo
See Rolfe, Frederick (William Serafino
Austin Lewis Mary)

Barondess, Sue K(aufman)
1926-1977 .... **CLC 8**
See Kaufman, Sue
See also CA 1-4R; 69-72; CANR 1

Baron de Teive
See Pessoa, Fernando (Antonio Nogueira)

Baroness Von S.
See Zangwill, Israel

Barres, (Auguste-)Maurice
1862-1923 .... **TCLC 47**
See also CA 164; DLB 123; GFL 1789 to
the Present

Barreto, Afonso Henrique de Lima
See Lima Barreto, Afonso Henrique de

Barrett, Andrea 1954- .... **CLC 150**
See also CA 156; CANR 92

Barrett, Michele .... **CLC 65**

Barrett, (Roger) Syd 1946- .... **CLC 35**

Barrett, William (Christopher)
1913-1992 .... **CLC 27**
See also CA 13-16R; 139; CANR 11, 67;
INT CANR-11

Barrie, J(ames) M(atthew)
1860-1937 .... **TCLC 2**
See also BRWS 3; BYA 4, 5; CA 104; 136;
CANR 77; CDBLB 1890-1914; CLR 16;
CWRI 5; DA3; DAB; DAM DRAM; DFS
7; DLB 10, 141, 156; EWL 3; FANT;
MAICYA 1, 2; MTCW 1; SATA 100;
SUFW; WCH; WLIT 4; YABC 1

Barrington, Michael
See Moorcock, Michael (John)

Barrol, Grady
See Bograd, Larry

Barry, Mike
See Malzberg, Barry N(athaniel)

Barry, Philip 1896-1949 .... **TCLC 11**
See also CA 109; 199; DFS 9; DLB 7, 228;
RGAL 4

Bart, Andre Schwarz
See Schwarz-Bart, Andre

Barth, John (Simmons) 1930- ... **CLC 1, 2, 3,
5, 7, 9, 10, 14, 27, 51, 89; SSC 10**
See also AITN 1, 2; AMW; BPFB 1; CA
1-4R; CABS 1; CANR 5, 23, 49, 64, 113;
CN 7; DAM NOV; DLB 2, 227; EWL 3;
FANT; MTCW 1; RGAL 4; RGSF 2;
RHW; SSFS 6; TUS

Barthelme, Donald 1931-1989 ... **CLC 1, 2, 3,
5, 6, 8, 13, 23, 46, 59, 115; SSC 2, 55**
See also AMWS 4; BPFB 1; CA 21-24R;
129; CANR 20, 58; DA3; DAM NOV;
DLB 2, 234; DLBY 1980, 1989; EWL 3;
FANT; LMFS 2; MTCW 1, 2; RGAL 4;
RGSF 2; SATA 7; SATA-Obit 62; SSFS
17

Barthelme, Frederick 1943- ...... **CLC 36, 117**
See also AMWS 11; CA 114; 122; CANR
77; CN 7; CSW; DLB 244; DLBY 1985;
EWL 3; INT CA-122

Barthes, Roland (Gerard)
1915-1980 .... **CLC 24, 83; TCLC 135**
See also CA 130; 97-100; CANR 66; DLB
296; EW 13; EWL 3; GFL 1789 to the
Present; MTCW 1, 2; TWA

Barzun, Jacques (Martin) 1907- ..... **CLC 51,
145**
See also CA 61-64; CANR 22, 95

Bashevis, Isaac
See Singer, Isaac Bashevis

Bashkirtseff, Marie 1859-1884 .... **NCLC 27**

Basho, Matsuo
See Matsuo Basho
See also PFS 18; RGWL 2, 3; WP

Basil of Caesaria c. 330-379 .... **CMLC 35**

Basket, Raney
See Edgerton, Clyde (Carlyle)

Bass, Kingsley B., Jr.
See Bullins, Ed

Bass, Rick 1958- .... **CLC 79, 143; SSC 60**
See also ANW; CA 126; CANR 53, 93;
CSW; DLB 212, 275

Bassani, Giorgio 1916-2000 .... **CLC 9**
See also CA 65-68; 190; CANR 33; CWW
2; DLB 128, 177; EWL 3; MTCW 1;
RGWL 2, 3

Bastian, Ann .... **CLC 70**

Bastos, Augusto (Antonio) Roa
See Roa Bastos, Augusto (Antonio)

Bataille, Georges 1897-1962 .... **CLC 29**
See also CA 101; 89-92; EWL 3

Bates, H(erbert) E(rnest)
1905-1974 .... **CLC 46; SSC 10**
See also CA 93-96; 45-48; CANR 34; DA3;
DAB; DAM POP; DLB 162, 191; EWL
3; EXPS; MTCW 1, 2; RGSF 2; SSFS 7

Bauchart
See Camus, Albert

Baudelaire, Charles 1821-1867 . **NCLC 6, 29,
55; PC 1; SSC 18; WLC**
See also DA; DA3; DAB; DAC; DAM
MST, POET; DLB 217; EW 7; GFL 1789
to the Present; LMFS 2; RGWL 2, 3;
TWA

Baudouin, Marcel
See Peguy, Charles (Pierre)

Baudouin, Pierre
See Peguy, Charles (Pierre)

Baudrillard, Jean 1929- .... **CLC 60**
See also DLB 296

Baum, L(yman) Frank 1856-1919 .. **TCLC 7,
132**
See also AAYA 46; BYA 16; CA 108; 133;
CLR 15; CWRI 5; DLB 22; FANT; JRDA;
MAICYA 1, 2; MTCW 1, 2; NFS 13;
RGAL 4; SATA 18, 100; WCH

Baum, Louis F.
See Baum, L(yman) Frank

Baumbach, Jonathan 1933- .... **CLC 6, 23**
See also CA 13-16R; CAAS 5; CANR 12,
66; CN 7; DLBY 1980; INT CANR-12;
MTCW 1

Bausch, Richard (Carl) 1945- .... **CLC 51**
See also AMWS 7; CA 101; CAAS 14;
CANR 43, 61, 87; CSW; DLB 130

Baxter, Charles (Morley) 1947- . **CLC 45, 78**
See also CA 57-60; CANR 40, 64, 104;
CPW; DAM POP; DLB 130; MTCW 2

Baxter, George Owen
See Faust, Frederick (Schiller)

Baxter, James K(eir) 1926-1972 .... **CLC 14**
See also CA 77-80; EWL 3

Baxter, John
See Hunt, E(verette) Howard, (Jr.)

Bayer, Sylvia
See Glassco, John

Baynton, Barbara 1857-1929 .... **TCLC 57**
See also DLB 230; RGSF 2

Beagle, Peter S(oyer) 1939- .... **CLC 7, 104**
See also AAYA 47; BPFB 1; BYA 9, 10,
16; CA 9-12R; CANR 4, 51, 73, 110;
DA3; DLBY 1980; FANT; INT CANR-4;
MTCW 1; SATA 60, 130; SUFW 1, 2;
YAW

Bean, Normal
See Burroughs, Edgar Rice

Beard, Charles A(ustin)
1874-1948 .... **TCLC 15**
See also CA 115; 189; DLB 17; SATA 18

Beardsley, Aubrey 1872-1898 .... **NCLC 6**

Beattie, Ann 1947- ..... **CLC 8, 13, 18, 40, 63,
146; SSC 11**
See also AMWS 5; BEST 90:2; BPFB 1;
CA 81-84; CANR 53, 73; CN 7; CPW;
DA3; DAM NOV, POP; DLB 218, 278;
DLBY 1982; EWL 3; MTCW 1, 2; RGAL
4; RGSF 2; SSFS 9; TUS

Beattie, James 1735-1803 .... **NCLC 25**
See also DLB 109

Beauchamp, Kathleen Mansfield 1888-1923
See Mansfield, Katherine
See also CA 104; 134; DA; DA3; DAC;
DAM MST; MTCW 2; TEA

Beaumarchais, Pierre-Augustin Caron de
1732-1799 .... **DC 4; LC 61**
See also DAM DRAM; DFS 14, 16; EW 4;
GFL Beginnings to 1789; RGWL 2, 3

Beaumont, Francis 1584(?)-1616 .. **DC 6; LC
33**
See also BRW 2; CDBLB Before 1660;
DLB 58; TEA

**Beauvoir, Simone (Lucie Ernestine Marie
Bertrand) de** 1908-1986 .... **CLC 1, 2, 4,
8, 14, 31, 44, 50, 71, 124; SSC 35;
WLC**
See also BPFB 1; CA 9-12R; 118; CANR
28, 61; DA; DA3; DAB; DAC; DAM

Bennett, Elizabeth
See Mitchell, Margaret (Munnerlyn)
Bennett, George Harold 1930-
See Bennett, Hal
See also BW 1; CA 97-100; CANR 87
Bennett, Gwendolyn B. 1902-1981 .... **HR 2**
See also BW 1; CA 125; DLB 51; WP
Bennett, Hal .... **CLC 5**
See Bennett, George Harold
See also DLB 33
Bennett, Jay 1912- .... **CLC 35**
See also AAYA 10; CA 69-72; CANR 11,
42, 79; JRDA; SAAS 4; SATA 41, 87;
SATA-Brief 27; WYA; YAW
Bennett, Louise (Simone) 1919- .... **BLC 1;
CLC 28**
See also BW 2, 3; CA 151; CDWLB 3; CP
7; DAM MULT; DLB 117; EWL 3
Benson, A. C. 1862-1925 .... **TCLC 123**
See also DLB 98
Benson, E(dward) F(rederic)
1867-1940 .... **TCLC 27**
See also CA 114; 157; DLB 135, 153;
HGG; SUFW 1
Benson, Jackson J. 1930- .... **CLC 34**
See also CA 25-28R; DLB 111
Benson, Sally 1900-1972 .... **CLC 17**
See also CA 19-20; 37-40R; CAP 1; SATA
1, 35; SATA-Obit 27
Benson, Stella 1892-1933 .... **TCLC 17**
See also CA 117; 154, 155; DLB 36, 162;
FANT; TEA
Bentham, Jeremy 1748-1832 .... **NCLC 38**
See also DLB 107, 158, 252
Bentley, E(dmund) C(lerihew)
1875-1956 .... **TCLC 12**
See also CA 108; DLB 70; MSW
Bentley, Eric (Russell) 1916- .... **CLC 24**
See also CA 5-8R; CAD; CANR 6, 67;
CBD; CD 5; INT CANR-6
ben Uzair, Salem
See Horne, Richard Henry Hengist
Beranger, Pierre Jean de
1780-1857 .... **NCLC 34**
Berdyaev, Nicolas
See Berdyaev, Nikolai (Aleksandrovich)
Berdyaev, Nikolai (Aleksandrovich)
1874-1948 .... **TCLC 67**
See also CA 120; 157
Berdyayev, Nikolai (Aleksandrovich)
See Berdyaev, Nikolai (Aleksandrovich)
Berendt, John (Lawrence) 1939- ...... **CLC 86**
See also CA 146; CANR 75, 93; DA3;
MTCW 1
Beresford, J(ohn) D(avys)
1873-1947 .... **TCLC 81**
See also CA 112; 155; DLB 162, 178, 197;
SFW 4; SUFW 1
Bergelson, David (Rafailovich)
1884-1952 .... **TCLC 81**
See Bergelson, Dovid
See also CA 220
Bergelson, Dovid
See Bergelson, David (Rafailovich)
See also EWL 3
Berger, Colonel
See Malraux, (Georges-)Andre
Berger, John (Peter) 1926- .... **CLC 2, 19**
See also BRWS 4; CA 81-84; CANR 51,
78, 117; CN 7; DLB 14, 207
Berger, Melvin H. 1927- .... **CLC 12**
See also CA 5-8R; CANR 4; CLR 32;
SAAS 2; SATA 5, 88; SATA-Essay 124
Berger, Thomas (Louis) 1924- .. **CLC 3, 5, 8,
11, 18, 38**
See also BPFB 1; CA 1-4R; CANR 5, 28,
51; CN 7; DAM NOV; DLB 2; DLBY
1980; EWL 3; FANT; INT CANR-28;
MTCW 1, 2; RHW; TCWW 2

Bergman, (Ernst) Ingmar 1918- ...... **CLC 16,
72**
See also CA 81-84; CANR 33, 70; DLB
257; MTCW 2
Bergson, Henri(-Louis) 1859-1941 . **TCLC 32**
See also CA 164; EW 8; EWL 3; GFL 1789
to the Present
Bergstein, Eleanor 1938- .... **CLC 4**
See also CA 53-56; CANR 5
Berkeley, George 1685-1753 .... **LC 65**
See also DLB 31, 101, 252
Berkoff, Steven 1937- .... **CLC 56**
See also CA 104; CANR 72; CBD; CD 5
Berlin, Isaiah 1909-1997 .... **TCLC 105**
See also CA 85-88; 162
Bermant, Chaim (Icyk) 1929-1998 ... **CLC 40**
See also CA 57-60; CANR 6, 31, 57, 105;
CN 7
Bern, Victoria
See Fisher, M(ary) F(rances) K(ennedy)
Bernanos, (Paul Louis) Georges
1888-1948 .... **TCLC 3**
See also CA 104; 130; CANR 94; DLB 72;
EWL 3; GFL 1789 to the Present; RGWL
2, 3
Bernard, April 1956- .... **CLC 59**
See also CA 131
Berne, Victoria
See Fisher, M(ary) F(rances) K(ennedy)
Bernhard, Thomas 1931-1989 ..... **CLC 3, 32,
61; DC 14**
See also CA 85-88; 127; CANR 32, 57; CD-
WLB 2; DLB 85, 124; EWL 3; MTCW 1;
RGWL 2, 3
Bernhardt, Sarah (Henriette Rosine)
1844-1923 .... **TCLC 75**
See also CA 157
Bernstein, Charles 1950- .... **CLC 142,**
See also CA 129; CAAS 24; CANR 90; CP
7; DLB 169
Berriault, Gina 1926-1999 .... **CLC 54, 109;
SSC 30**
See also CA 116; 129; 185; CANR 66; DLB
130; SSFS 7,11
Berrigan, Daniel 1921- .... **CLC 4**
See also CA 33-36R, 187; CAAE 187;
CAAS 1; CANR 11, 43, 78; CP 7; DLB 5
Berrigan, Edmund Joseph Michael, Jr.
1934-1983
See Berrigan, Ted
See also CA 61-64; 110; CANR 14, 102
Berrigan, Ted .... **CLC 37**
See Berrigan, Edmund Joseph Michael, Jr.
See also DLB 5, 169; WP
Berry, Charles Edward Anderson 1931-
See Berry, Chuck
See also CA 115
Berry, Chuck .... **CLC 17**
See Berry, Charles Edward Anderson
Berry, Jonas
See Ashbery, John (Lawrence)
See also GLL 1
Berry, Wendell (Erdman) 1934- ... **CLC 4, 6,
8, 27, 46; PC 28**
See also AITN 1; AMWS 10; ANW; CA
73-76; CANR 50, 73, 101; CP 7; CSW;
DAM POET; DLB 5, 6, 234, 275; MTCW
1
Berryman, John 1914-1972 ... **CLC 1, 2, 3, 4,
6, 8, 10, 13, 25, 62**
See also AMW; CA 13-16; 33-36R; CABS
2; CANR 35; CAP 1; CDALB 1941-1968;
DAM POET; DLB 48; EWL 3; MTCW 1,
2; PAB; RGAL 4; WP
Bertolucci, Bernardo 1940- ...... **CLC 16, 157**
See also CA 106; CANR 125

Berton, Pierre (Francis Demarigny)
1920- .... **CLC 104**
See also CA 1-4R; CANR 2, 56; CPW;
DLB 68; SATA 99
Bertrand, Aloysius 1807-1841 .... **NCLC 31**
See Bertrand, Louis oAloysiusc
Bertrand, Louis oAloysiusc
See Bertrand, Aloysius
See also DLB 217
Bertran de Born c. 1140-1215 .... **CMLC 5**
Besant, Annie (Wood) 1847-1933 ..... **TCLC 9**
See also CA 105; 185
Bessie, Alvah 1904-1985 .... **CLC 23**
See also CA 5-8R; 116; CANR 2, 80; DLB
26
Bestuzhev, Aleksandr Aleksandrovich
1797-1837 .... **NCLC 131**
See also DLB 198
Bethlen, T. D.
See Silverberg, Robert
Beti, Mongo .... **BLC 1; CLC 27**
See Biyidi, Alexandre
See also AFW; CANR 79; DAM MULT;
EWL 3; WLIT 2
Betjeman, John 1906-1984 ...... **CLC 2, 6, 10,
34, 43**
See also BRW 7; CA 9-12R; 112; CANR
33, 56; CDBLB 1945-1960; DA3; DAB;
DAM MST, POET; DLB 20; DLBY 1984;
EWL 3; MTCW 1, 2
Bettelheim, Bruno 1903-1990 .... **CLC 79;
TCLC 143**
See also CA 81-84; 131; CANR 23, 61;
DA3; MTCW 1, 2
Betti, Ugo 1892-1953 .... **TCLC 5**
See also CA 104; 155; EWL 3; RGWL 2, 3
Betts, Doris (Waugh) 1932- ..... **CLC 3, 6, 28;
SSC 45**
See also CA 13-16R; CANR 9, 66, 77; CN
7; CSW; DLB 218; DLBY 1982; INT
CANR-9; RGAL 4
Bevan, Alistair
See Roberts, Keith (John Kingston)
Bey, Pilaff
See Douglas, (George) Norman
Bialik, Chaim Nachman
1873-1934 .... **TCLC 25**
See also CA 170; EWL 3
Bickerstaff, Isaac
See Swift, Jonathan
Bidart, Frank 1939- .... **CLC 33**
See also CA 140; CANR 106; CP 7
Bienek, Horst 1930- .... **CLC 7, 11**
See also CA 73-76; DLB 75
Bierce, Ambrose (Gwinett)
1842-1914(?) .... **SSC 9; TCLC 1, 7, 44;
WLC**
See also AAYA 55; AMW; BYA 11; CA
104; 139; CANR 78; CDALB 1865-1917;
DA; DA3; DAC; DAM MST; DLB 11,
12, 23, 71, 74, 186; EWL 3; EXPS; HGG;
LAIT 2; RGAL 4; RGSF 2; SSFS 9;
SUFW 1
Biggers, Earl Derr 1884-1933 .... **TCLC 65**
See also CA 108; 153
Billiken, Bud
See Motley, Willard (Francis)
Billings, Josh
See Shaw, Henry Wheeler
Billington, (Lady) Rachel (Mary)
1942- .... **CLC 43**
See also AITN 2; CA 33-36R; CANR 44;
CN 7
Binchy, Maeve 1940- .... **CLC 153**
See also BEST 90:1; BPFB 1; CA 127; 134;
CANR 50, 96; CN 7; CPW; DA3; DAM
POP; INT CA-134; MTCW 1; RHW
Binyon, T(imothy) J(ohn) 1936- .... **CLC 34**
See also CA 111; CANR 28

MST, NOV, POP; DLB 2, 8; EXPN; EXPS; HGG; LAIT 3, 5; LATS 1; LMFS 2; MTCW 1, 2; NFS 1; RGAL 4; RGSF 2; SATA 11, 64, 123; SCFW 2; SFW 4; SSFS 1; SUFW 1, 2; TUS; YAW

Braddon, Mary Elizabeth
1837-1915 .... **TCLC 111**
See also BRWS 8; CA 108; 179; CMW 4; DLB 18, 70, 156; HGG

Bradfield, Scott (Michael) 1955- .... **SSC 65**
See also CA 147; CANR 90; HGG; SUFW 2

Bradford, Gamaliel 1863-1932 .... **TCLC 36**
See also CA 160; DLB 17

Bradford, William 1590-1657 .... **LC 64**
See also DLB 24, 30; RGAL 4

Bradley, David (Henry), Jr. 1950- .... **BLC 1; CLC 23, 118**
See also BW 1, 3; CA 104; CANR 26, 81; CN 7; DAM MULT; DLB 33

Bradley, John Ed(mund, Jr.) 1958- . **CLC 55**
See also CA 139; CANR 99; CN 7; CSW

Bradley, Marion Zimmer
1930-1999 .... **CLC 30**
See Chapman, Lee; Dexter, John; Gardner, Miriam; Ives, Morgan; Rivers, Elfrida
See also AAYA 40; BPFB 1; CA 57-60; 185; CAAS 10; CANR 7, 31, 51, 75, 107; CPW; DA3; DAM POP; DLB 8; FANT; FW; MTCW 1, 2; SATA 90, 139; SATA-Obit 116; SFW 4; SUFW 2; YAW

Bradshaw, John 1933- .... **CLC 70**
See also CA 138; CANR 61

Bradstreet, Anne 1612(?)-1672 ...... **LC 4, 30; PC 10**
See also AMWS 1; CDALB 1640-1865; DA; DA3; DAC; DAM MST, POET; DLB 24; EXPP; FW; PFS 6; RGAL 4; TUS; WP

Brady, Joan 1939- .... **CLC 86**
See also CA 141

Bragg, Melvyn 1939- .... **CLC 10**
See also BEST 89:3; CA 57-60; CANR 10, 48, 89; CN 7; DLB 14, 271; RHW

Brahe, Tycho 1546-1601 .... **LC 45**

Braine, John (Gerard) 1922-1986 . **CLC 1, 3, 41**
See also CA 1-4R; 120; CANR 1, 33; CD-BLB 1945-1960; DLB 15; DLBY 1986; EWL 3; MTCW 1

Braithwaite, William Stanley (Beaumont)
1878-1962 .... **BLC 1; HR 2; PC 52**
See also BW 1; CA 125; DAM MULT; DLB 50, 54

Bramah, Ernest 1868-1942 .... **TCLC 72**
See also CA 156; CMW 4; DLB 70; FANT

Brammer, William 1930(?)-1978 ...... **CLC 31**
See also CA 77-80

Brancati, Vitaliano 1907-1954 .... **TCLC 12**
See also CA 109; DLB 264; EWL 3

Brancato, Robin F(idler) 1936- .... **CLC 35**
See also AAYA 9; BYA 6; CA 69-72; CANR 11, 45; CLR 32; JRDA; MAICYA 2; MAICYAS 1; SAAS 9; SATA 97; WYA; YAW

Brand, Max
See Faust, Frederick (Schiller)
See also BPFB 1; TCWW 2

Brand, Millen 1906-1980 .... **CLC 7**
See also CA 21-24R; 97-100; CANR 72

Branden, Barbara .... **CLC 44**
See also CA 148

Brandes, Georg (Morris Cohen)
1842-1927 .... **TCLC 10**
See also CA 105; 189

Brandys, Kazimierz 1916-2000 .... **CLC 62**
See also EWL 3

Branley, Franklyn M(ansfield)
1915-2002 .... **CLC 21**
See also CA 33-36R; 207; CANR 14, 39; CLR 13; MAICYA 1, 2; SAAS 16; SATA 4, 68, 136

Brant, Beth (E.) 1941- .... **NNAL**
See also CA 144; FW

Brathwaite, Edward Kamau
1930- .... **BLCS; CLC 11**
See also BW 2, 3; CA 25-28R; CANR 11, 26, 47, 107; CDWLB 3; CP 7; DAM POET; DLB 125; EWL 3

Brathwaite, Kamau
See Brathwaite, Edward Kamau

Brautigan, Richard (Gary)
1935-1984 .... **CLC 1, 3, 5, 9, 12, 34, 42; TCLC 133**
See also BPFB 1; CA 53-56; 113; CANR 34; DA3; DAM NOV; DLB 2, 5, 206; DLBY 1980, 1984; FANT; MTCW 1; RGAL 4; SATA 56

Brave Bird, Mary .... **NNAL**
See Crow Dog, Mary (Ellen)

Braverman, Kate 1950- .... **CLC 67**
See also CA 89-92

Brecht, (Eugen) Bertolt (Friedrich)
1898-1956 ..... **DC 3; TCLC 1, 6, 13, 35; WLC**
See also CA 104; 133; CANR 62; CDWLB 2; DA; DA3; DAB; DAC; DAM DRAM, MST; DFS 4, 5, 9; DLB 56, 124; EW 11; EWL 3; IDTP; MTCW 1, 2; RGWL 2, 3; TWA

Brecht, Eugen Berthold Friedrich
See Brecht, (Eugen) Bertolt (Friedrich)

Bremer, Fredrika 1801-1865 .... **NCLC 11**
See also DLB 254

Brennan, Christopher John
1870-1932 .... **TCLC 17**
See also CA 117; 188; DLB 230; EWL 3

Brennan, Maeve 1917-1993 ... **CLC 5; TCLC 124**
See also CA 81-84; CANR 72, 100

Brent, Linda
See Jacobs, Harriet A(nn)

Brentano, Clemens (Maria)
1778-1842 .... **NCLC 1**
See also DLB 90; RGWL 2, 3

Brent of Bin Bin
See Franklin, (Stella Maria Sarah) Miles (Lampe)

Brenton, Howard 1942- .... **CLC 31**
See also CA 69-72; CANR 33, 67; CBD; CD 5; DLB 13; MTCW 1

Breslin, James 1930-
See Breslin, Jimmy
See also CA 73-76; CANR 31, 75; DAM NOV; MTCW 1, 2

Breslin, Jimmy .... **CLC 4, 43**
See Breslin, James
See also AITN 1; DLB 185; MTCW 2

Bresson, Robert 1901(?)-1999 .... **CLC 16**
See also CA 110; 187; CANR 49

Breton, Andre 1896-1966 .. **CLC 2, 9, 15, 54; PC 15**
See also CA 19-20; 25-28R; CANR 40, 60; CAP 2; DLB 65, 258; EW 11; EWL 3; GFL 1789 to the Present; LMFS 2; MTCW 1, 2; RGWL 2, 3; TWA; WP

Breytenbach, Breyten 1939(?)- .. **CLC 23, 37, 126**
See also CA 113; 129; CANR 61, 122; CWW 2; DAM POET; DLB 225; EWL 3

Bridgers, Sue Ellen 1942- .... **CLC 26**
See also AAYA 8, 49; BYA 7, 8; CA 65-68; CANR 11, 36; CLR 18; DLB 52; JRDA; MAICYA 1, 2; SAAS 1; SATA 22, 90; SATA-Essay 109; WYA; YAW

Bridges, Robert (Seymour)
1844-1930 .... **PC 28; TCLC 1**
See also BRW 6; CA 104; 152; CDBLB 1890-1914; DAM POET; DLB 19, 98

Bridie, James .... **TCLC 3**
See Mavor, Osborne Henry
See also DLB 10; EWL 3

Brin, David 1950- .... **CLC 34**
See also AAYA 21; CA 102; CANR 24, 70, 125, 127; INT CANR-24; SATA 65; SCFW 2; SFW 4

Brink, Andre (Philippus) 1935- . **CLC 18, 36, 106**
See also AFW; BRWS 6; CA 104; CANR 39, 62, 109; CN 7; DLB 225; EWL 3; INT CA-103; LATS 1; MTCW 1, 2; WLIT 2

Brinsmead, H. F(ay)
See Brinsmead, H(esba) F(ay)

Brinsmead, H. F.
See Brinsmead, H(esba) F(ay)

Brinsmead, H(esba) F(ay) 1922- ...... **CLC 21**
See also CA 21-24R; CANR 10; CLR 47; CWRI 5; MAICYA 1, 2; SAAS 5; SATA 18, 78

Brittain, Vera (Mary) 1893(?)-1970 . **CLC 23**
See also CA 13-16; 25-28R; CANR 58; CAP 1; DLB 191; FW; MTCW 1, 2

Broch, Hermann 1886-1951 .... **TCLC 20**
See also CA 117; 211; CDWLB 2; DLB 85, 124; EW 10; EWL 3; RGWL 2, 3

Brock, Rose
See Hansen, Joseph
See also GLL 1

Brod, Max 1884-1968 .... **TCLC 115**
See also CA 5-8R; 25-28R; CANR 7; DLB 81; EWL 3

Brodkey, Harold (Roy) 1930-1996 .. **CLC 56; TCLC 123**
See also CA 111; 151; CANR 71; CN 7; DLB 130

Brodskii, Iosif
See Brodsky, Joseph

Brodsky, Iosif Alexandrovich 1940-1996
See Brodsky, Joseph
See also AITN 1; CA 41-44R; 151; CANR 37, 106; DA3; DAM POET; MTCW 1, 2; RGWL 2, 3

Brodsky, Joseph . **CLC 4, 6, 13, 36, 100; PC 9**
See Brodsky, Iosif Alexandrovich
See also AMWS 8; CWW 2; DLB 285; EWL 3; MTCW 1

Brodsky, Michael (Mark) 1948- .... **CLC 19**
See also CA 102; CANR 18, 41, 58; DLB 244

Brodzki, Bella ed. .... **CLC 65**

Brome, Richard 1590(?)-1652 .... **LC 61**
See also DLB 58

Bromell, Henry 1947- .... **CLC 5**
See also CA 53-56; CANR 9, 115, 116

Bromfield, Louis (Brucker)
1896-1956 .... **TCLC 11**
See also CA 107; 155; DLB 4, 9, 86; RGAL 4; RHW

Broner, E(sther) M(asserman)
1930- .... **CLC 19**
See also CA 17-20R; CANR 8, 25, 72; CN 7; DLB 28

Bronk, William (M.) 1918-1999 .... **CLC 10**
See also CA 89-92; 177; CANR 23; CP 7; DLB 165

Bronstein, Lev Davidovich
See Trotsky, Leon

Bronte, Anne 1820-1849 ..... **NCLC 4, 71, 102**
See also BRW 5; BRWR 1; DA3; DLB 21, 199; TEA

Byron, Robert 1905-1941 .... **TCLC 67**
    See also CA 160; DLB 195
C. 3. 3.
    See Wilde, Oscar (Fingal O'Flahertie Wills)
Caballero, Fernan 1796-1877 .... **NCLC 10**
Cabell, Branch
    See Cabell, James Branch
Cabell, James Branch 1879-1958 .... **TCLC 6**
    See also CA 105; 152; DLB 9, 78; FANT;
    MTCW 1; RGAL 4; SUFW 1
Cabeza de Vaca, Alvar Nunez
    1490-1557(?) .... **LC 61**
Cable, George Washington
    1844-1925 .... **SSC 4; TCLC 4**
    See also CA 104; 155; DLB 12, 74; DLBD
    13; RGAL 4; TUS
Cabral de Melo Neto, Joao
    1920-1999 .... **CLC 76**
    See Melo Neto, Joao Cabral de
    See also CA 151; DAM MULT; LAW;
    LAWS 1
Cabrera Infante, G(uillermo) 1929- . **CLC 5,**
    25, 45, 120; HLC 1; SSC 39
    See also CA 85-88; CANR 29, 65, 110; CD-
    WLB 3; DA3; DAM MULT; DLB 113;
    EWL 3; HW 1, 2; LAW; LAWS 1; MTCW
    1, 2; RGSF 2; WLIT 1
Cade, Toni
    See Bambara, Toni Cade
Cadmus and Harmonia
    See Buchan, John
Caedmon fl. 658-680 .... **CMLC 7**
    See also DLB 146
Caeiro, Alberto
    See Pessoa, Fernando (Antonio Nogueira)
Caesar, Julius .... **CMLC 47**
    See Julius Caesar
    See also AW 1; RGWL 2, 3
Cage, John (Milton, Jr.) 1912-1992 . **CLC 41**
    See also CA 13-16R; 169; CANR 9, 78;
    DLB 193; INT CANR-9
Cahan, Abraham 1860-1951 .... **TCLC 71**
    See also CA 108; 154; DLB 9, 25, 28;
    RGAL 4
Cain, G.
    See Cabrera Infante, G(uillermo)
Cain, Guillermo
    See Cabrera Infante, G(uillermo)
Cain, James M(allahan) 1892-1977 .. **CLC 3,**
    11, 28
    See also AITN 1; BPFB 1; CA 17-20R; 73-
    76; CANR 8, 34, 61; CMW 4; DLB 226;
    EWL 3; MSW; MTCW 1; RGAL 4
Caine, Hall 1853-1931 .... **TCLC 97**
    See also RHW
Caine, Mark
    See Raphael, Frederic (Michael)
Calasso, Roberto 1941- .... **CLC 81**
    See also CA 143; CANR 89
Calderon de la Barca, Pedro
    1600-1681 .... **DC 3; HLCS 1; LC 23**
    See also EW 2; RGWL 2, 3; TWA
Caldwell, Erskine (Preston)
    1903-1987 .... **CLC 1, 8, 14, 50, 60; SSC**
    19; TCLC 117
    See also AITN 1; AMW; BPFB 1; CA 1-4R;
    121; CAAS 1; CANR 2, 33; DA3; DAM
    NOV; DLB 9, 86; EWL 3; MTCW 1, 2;
    RGAL 4; RGSF 2; TUS
Caldwell, (Janet Miriam) Taylor (Holland)
    1900-1985 .... **CLC 2, 28, 39**
    See also BPFB 1; CA 5-8R; 116; CANR 5;
    DA3; DAM NOV, POP; DLBD 17; RHW
Calhoun, John Caldwell
    1782-1850 .... **NCLC 15**
    See also DLB 3, 248

Calisher, Hortense 1911- ..... **CLC 2, 4, 8, 38,**
    134; SSC 15
    See also CA 1-4R; CANR 1, 22, 117; CN
    7; DA3; DAM NOV; DLB 2, 218; INT
    CANR-22; MTCW 1, 2; RGAL 4; RGSF
    2
Callaghan, Morley Edward
    1903-1990 ..... **CLC 3, 14, 41, 65; TCLC**
    145
    See also CA 9-12R; 132; CANR 33, 73;
    DAC; DAM MST; DLB 68; EWL 3;
    MTCW 1, 2; RGEL 2; RGSF 2
Callimachus c. 305B.C.-c.
    240B.C. .... **CMLC 18**
    See also AW 1; DLB 176; RGWL 2, 3
Calvin, Jean
    See Calvin, John
    See also GFL Beginnings to 1789
Calvin, John 1509-1564 .... **LC 37**
    See Calvin, Jean
Calvino, Italo 1923-1985 .... **CLC 5, 8, 11, 22,**
    33, 39, 73; SSC 3, 48
    See also CA 85-88; 116; CANR 23, 61;
    DAM NOV; DLB 196; EW 13; EWL 3;
    MTCW 1, 2; RGSF 2; RGWL 2, 3; SFW
    4; SSFS 12
Camara Laye
    See Laye, Camara
    See also EWL 3
Camden, William 1551-1623 .... **LC 77**
    See also DLB 172
Cameron, Carey 1952- .... **CLC 59**
    See also CA 135
Cameron, Peter 1959- .... **CLC 44**
    See also AMWS 12; CA 125; CANR 50,
    117; DLB 234; GLL 2
Camoens, Luis Vaz de 1524(?)-1580
    See Camoes, Luis de
    See also EW 2
Camoes, Luis de 1524(?)-1580 . **HLCS 1; LC**
    62; PC 31
    See Camoens, Luis Vaz de
    See also DLB 287; RGWL 2, 3
Campana, Dino 1885-1932 .... **TCLC 20**
    See also CA 117; DLB 114; EWL 3
Campanella, Tommaso 1568-1639 .... **LC 32**
    See also RGWL 2, 3
Campbell, John W(ood, Jr.)
    1910-1971 .... **CLC 32**
    See also CA 21-22; 29-32R; CANR 34;
    CAP 2; DLB 8; MTCW 1; SCFW; SFW 4
Campbell, Joseph 1904-1987 .... **CLC 69;**
    TCLC 140
    See also AAYA 3; BEST 89:2; CA 1-4R;
    124; CANR 3, 28, 61, 107; DA3; MTCW
    1, 2
Campbell, Maria 1940- .... **CLC 85; NNAL**
    See also CA 102; CANR 54; CCA 1; DAC
Campbell, (John) Ramsey 1946- ..... **CLC 42;**
    SSC 19
    See also AAYA 51; CA 57-60; CANR 7,
    102; DLB 261; HGG; INT CANR-7;
    SUFW 1, 2
Campbell, (Ignatius) Roy (Dunnachie)
    1901-1957 .... **TCLC 5**
    See also AFW; CA 104; 155; DLB 20, 225;
    EWL 3; MTCW 2; RGEL 2
Campbell, Thomas 1777-1844 .... **NCLC 19**
    See also DLB 93, 144; RGEL 2
Campbell, Wilfred .... **TCLC 9**
    See Campbell, William
Campbell, William 1858(?)-1918
    See Campbell, Wilfred
    See also CA 106; DLB 92
Campion, Jane 1954- .... **CLC 95**
    See also AAYA 33; CA 138; CANR 87
Campion, Thomas 1567-1620 .... **LC 78**
    See also CDBLB Before 1660; DAM POET;
    DLB 58, 172; RGEL 2

Camus, Albert 1913-1960 ...... **CLC 1, 2, 4, 9,**
    11, 14, 32, 63, 69, 124; DC 2; SSC 9;
    WLC
    See also AAYA 36; AFW; BPFB 1; CA 89-
    92; DA; DA3; DAB; DAC; DAM DRAM,
    MST, NOV; DLB 72; EW 13; EWL 3;
    EXPN; EXPS; GFL 1789 to the Present;
    LATS 1; LMFS 2; MTCW 1, 2; NFS 6,
    16; RGSF 2; RGWL 2, 3; SSFS 4; TWA
Canby, Vincent 1924-2000 .... **CLC 13**
    See also CA 81-84; 191
Cancale
    See Desnos, Robert
Canetti, Elias 1905-1994 .. **CLC 3, 14, 25, 75,**
    86
    See also CA 21-24R; 146; CANR 23, 61,
    79; CDWLB 2; CWW 2; DA3; DLB 85,
    124; EW 12; EWL 3; MTCW 1, 2; RGWL
    2, 3; TWA
Canfield, Dorothea F.
    See Fisher, Dorothy (Frances) Canfield
Canfield, Dorothea Frances
    See Fisher, Dorothy (Frances) Canfield
Canfield, Dorothy
    See Fisher, Dorothy (Frances) Canfield
Canin, Ethan 1960- .... **CLC 55; SSC 70**
    See also CA 131; 135
Cankar, Ivan 1876-1918 .... **TCLC 105**
    See also CDWLB 4; DLB 147; EWL 3
Cannon, Curt
    See Hunter, Evan
Cao, Lan 1961- .... **CLC 109**
    See also CA 165
Cape, Judith
    See Page, P(atricia) K(athleen)
    See also CCA 1
Capek, Karel 1890-1938 .... **DC 1; SSC 36;**
    TCLC 6, 37; WLC
    See also CA 104; 140; CDWLB 4; DA;
    DA3; DAB; DAC; DAM DRAM, MST,
    NOV; DFS 7, 11; DLB 215; EW 10; EWL
    3; MTCW 1; RGSF 2; RGWL 2, 3; SCFW
    2; SFW 4
Capote, Truman 1924-1984 . **CLC 1, 3, 8, 13,**
    19, 34, 38, 58; SSC 2, 47; WLC
    See also AMWS 3; BPFB 1; CA 5-8R; 113;
    CANR 18, 62; CDALB 1941-1968; CPW;
    DA; DA3; DAB; DAC; DAM MST, NOV,
    POP; DLB 2, 185, 227; DLBY 1980,
    1984; EWL 3; EXPS; GLL 1; LAIT 3;
    MTCW 1, 2; NCFS 2; RGAL 4; RGSF 2;
    SATA 91; SSFS 2; TUS
Capra, Frank 1897-1991 .... **CLC 16**
    See also AAYA 52; CA 61-64; 135
Caputo, Philip 1941- .... **CLC 32**
    See also CA 73-76; CANR 40; YAW
Caragiale, Ion Luca 1852-1912 ...... **TCLC 76**
    See also CA 157
Card, Orson Scott 1951- .... **CLC 44, 47, 50**
    See also AAYA 11, 42; BPFB 1; BYA 5, 8;
    CA 102; CANR 27, 47, 73, 102, 106;
    CPW; DA3; DAM POP; FANT; INT
    CANR-27; MTCW 1, 2; NFS 5; SATA
    83, 127; SCFW 2; SFW 4; SUFW 2; YAW
Cardenal, Ernesto 1925- .... **CLC 31, 161;**
    HLC 1; PC 22
    See also CA 49-52; CANR 2, 32, 66; CWW
    2; DAM MULT, POET; DLB 290; EWL
    3; HW 1, 2; LAWS 1; MTCW 1, 2;
    RGWL 2, 3
Cardozo, Benjamin N(athan)
    1870-1938 .... **TCLC 65**
    See also CA 117; 164
Carducci, Giosue (Alessandro Giuseppe)
    1835-1907 .... **PC 46; TCLC 32**
    See also CA 163; EW 7; RGWL 2, 3
Carew, Thomas 1595(?)-1640 . **LC 13; PC 29**
    See also BRW 2; DLB 126; PAB; RGEL 2

Caute, (John) David 1936- .... **CLC 29**
See also CA 1-4R; CAAS 4; CANR 1, 33, 64, 120; CBD; CD 5; CN 7; DAM NOV; DLB 14, 231

Cavafy, C(onstantine) P(eter) .... **PC 36; TCLC 2, 7**
See Kavafis, Konstantinos Petrou
See also CA 148; DA3; DAM POET; EW 8; EWL 3; MTCW 1; RGWL 2, 3; WP

Cavalcanti, Guido c. 1250-c. 1300 .... **CMLC 54**

Cavallo, Evelyn
See Spark, Muriel (Sarah)

Cavanna, Betty .... **CLC 12**
See Harrison, Elizabeth (Allen) Cavanna
See also JRDA; MAICYA 1; SAAS 4; SATA 1, 30

Cavendish, Margaret Lucas 1623-1673 .... **LC 30**
See also DLB 131, 252, 281; RGEL 2

Caxton, William 1421(?)-1491(?) .... **LC 17**
See also DLB 170

Cayer, D. M.
See Duffy, Maureen

Cayrol, Jean 1911- .... **CLC 11**
See also CA 89-92; DLB 83; EWL 3

Cela, Camilo Jose 1916-2002 .... **CLC 4, 13, 59, 122; HLC 1**
See also BEST 90:2; CA 21-24R; 206; CAAS 10; CANR 21, 32, 76; DAM MULT; DLBY 1989; EW 13; EWL 3; HW 1; MTCW 1, 2; RGSF 2; RGWL 2, 3

Celan, Paul .... **CLC 10, 19, 53, 82; PC 10**
See Antschel, Paul
See also CDWLB 2; DLB 69; EWL 3; RGWL 2, 3

Celine, Louis-Ferdinand .. **CLC 1, 3, 4, 7, 9, 15, 47, 124**
See Destouches, Louis-Ferdinand
See also DLB 72; EW 11; EWL 3; GFL 1789 to the Present; RGWL 2, 3

Cellini, Benvenuto 1500-1571 .... **LC 7**

Cendrars, Blaise .... **CLC 18, 106**
See Sauser-Hall, Frederic
See also DLB 258; EWL 3; GFL 1789 to the Present; RGWL 2, 3; WP

Centlivre, Susanna 1669(?)-1723 .... **LC 65**
See also DLB 84; RGEL 2

Cernuda (y Bidon), Luis 1902-1963 . **CLC 54**
See also CA 131; 89-92; DAM POET; DLB 134; EWL 3; GLL 1; HW 1; RGWL 2, 3

Cervantes, Lorna Dee 1954- ..... **HLCS 1; PC 35**
See also CA 131; CANR 80; CWP; DLB 82; EXPP; HW 1; LLW 1

Cervantes (Saavedra), Miguel de 1547-1616 ... **HLCS; LC 6, 23, 93; SSC 12; WLC**
See also BYA 1, 14; DA; DAB; DAC; DAM MST, NOV; EW 2; LAIT 1; LATS 1; LMFS 1; NFS 8; RGSF 2; RGWL 2, 3; TWA

Cesaire, Aime (Fernand) 1913- .... **BLC 1; CLC 19, 32, 112; DC 22; PC 25**
See also BW 2, 3; CA 65-68; CANR 24, 43, 81; DA3; DAM MULT, POET; EWL 3; GFL 1789 to the Present; MTCW 1, 2; WP

Chabon, Michael 1963- ... **CLC 55, 149; SSC 59**
See also AAYA 45; AMWS 11; CA 139; CANR 57, 96, 127; DLB 278; SATA 145

Chabrol, Claude 1930- .... **CLC 16**
See also CA 110

Chairil Anwar
See Anwar, Chairil
See also EWL 3

Challans, Mary 1905-1983
See Renault, Mary
See also CA 81-84; 111; CANR 74; DA3; MTCW 2; SATA 23; SATA-Obit 36; TEA

Challis, George
See Faust, Frederick (Schiller)
See also TCWW 2

Chambers, Aidan 1934- .... **CLC 35**
See also AAYA 27; CA 25-28R; CANR 12, 31, 58, 116; JRDA; MAICYA 1, 2; SAAS 12; SATA 1, 69, 108; WYA; YAW

Chambers, James 1948-
See Cliff, Jimmy
See also CA 124

Chambers, Jessie
See Lawrence, D(avid) H(erbert Richards)
See also GLL 1

Chambers, Robert W(illiam) 1865-1933 .... **TCLC 41**
See also CA 165; DLB 202; HGG; SATA 107; SUFW 1

Chambers, (David) Whittaker 1901-1961 .... **TCLC 129**
See also CA 89-92

Chamisso, Adelbert von 1781-1838 .... **NCLC 82**
See also DLB 90; RGWL 2, 3; SUFW 1

Chance, James T.
See Carpenter, John (Howard)

Chance, John T.
See Carpenter, John (Howard)

Chandler, Raymond (Thornton) 1888-1959 .... **SSC 23; TCLC 1, 7**
See also AAYA 25; AMWC 2; AMWS 4; BPFB 1; CA 104; 129; CANR 60, 107; CDALB 1929-1941; CMW 4; DA3; DLB 226, 253; DLBD 6; EWL 3; MSW; MTCW 1, 2; NFS 17; RGAL 4; TUS

Chang, Diana 1934- .... **AAL**
See also CWP; EXPP

Chang, Eileen 1921-1995 .... **AAL; SSC 28**
See Chang Ai-Ling
See also CA 166; CWW 2

Chang, Jung 1952- .... **CLC 71**
See also CA 142

Chang Ai-Ling
See Chang, Eileen
See also EWL 3

Channing, William Ellery 1780-1842 .... **NCLC 17**
See also DLB 1, 59, 235; RGAL 4

Chao, Patricia 1955- .... **CLC 119**
See also CA 163

Chaplin, Charles Spencer 1889-1977 .... **CLC 16**
See Chaplin, Charlie
See also CA 81-84; 73-76

Chaplin, Charlie
See Chaplin, Charles Spencer
See also DLB 44

Chapman, George 1559(?)-1634 . **DC 19; LC 22**
See also BRW 1; DAM DRAM; DLB 62, 121; LMFS 1; RGEL 2

Chapman, Graham 1941-1989 .... **CLC 21**
See Monty Python
See also CA 116; 129; CANR 35, 95

Chapman, John Jay 1862-1933 .... **TCLC 7**
See also CA 104; 191

Chapman, Lee
See Bradley, Marion Zimmer
See also GLL 1

Chapman, Walker
See Silverberg, Robert

Chappell, Fred (Davis) 1936- .... **CLC 40, 78, 162**
See also CA 5-8R, 198; CAAE 198; CAAS 4; CANR 8, 33, 67, 110; CN 7; CP 7; CSW; DLB 6, 105; HGG

Char, Rene(-Emile) 1907-1988 .... **CLC 9, 11, 14, 55**
See also CA 13-16R; 124; CANR 32; DAM POET; DLB 258; EWL 3; GFL 1789 to the Present; MTCW 1, 2; RGWL 2, 3

Charby, Jay
See Ellison, Harlan (Jay)

Chardin, Pierre Teilhard de
See Teilhard de Chardin, (Marie Joseph) Pierre

Chariton fl. 1st cent. (?)- .... **CMLC 49**

Charlemagne 742-814 .... **CMLC 37**

Charles I 1600-1649 .... **LC 13**

Charriere, Isabelle de 1740-1805 .. **NCLC 66**

Chartier, Alain c. 1392-1430 .... **LC 94**
See also DLB 208

Chartier, Emile-Auguste
See Alain

Charyn, Jerome 1937- .... **CLC 5, 8, 18**
See also CA 5-8R; CAAS 1; CANR 7, 61, 101; CMW 4; CN 7; DLBY 1983; MTCW 1

Chase, Adam
See Marlowe, Stephen

Chase, Mary (Coyle) 1907-1981 .... **DC 1**
See also CA 77-80; 105; CAD; CWD; DFS 11; DLB 228; SATA 17; SATA-Obit 29

Chase, Mary Ellen 1887-1973 .... **CLC 2; TCLC 124**
See also CA 13-16; 41-44R; CAP 1; SATA 10

Chase, Nicholas
See Hyde, Anthony
See also CCA 1

Chateaubriand, Francois Rene de 1768-1848 .... **NCLC 3, 134**
See also DLB 119; EW 5; GFL 1789 to the Present; RGWL 2, 3; TWA

Chatterje, Sarat Chandra 1876-1936(?)
See Chatterji, Saratchandra
See also CA 109

Chatterji, Bankim Chandra 1838-1894 .... **NCLC 19**

Chatterji, Saratchandra .... **TCLC 13**
See Chatterje, Sarat Chandra
See also CA 186; EWL 3

Chatterton, Thomas 1752-1770 .... **LC 3, 54**
See also DAM POET; DLB 109; RGEL 2

Chatwin, (Charles) Bruce 1940-1989 .... **CLC 28, 57, 59**
See also AAYA 4; BEST 90:1; BRWS 4; CA 85-88; 127; CPW; DAM POP; DLB 194, 204; EWL 3

Chaucer, Daniel
See Ford, Ford Madox
See also RHW

Chaucer, Geoffrey 1340(?)-1400 .. **LC 17, 56; PC 19; WLCS**
See also BRW 1; BRWC 1; BRWR 2; CD-BLB Before 1660; DA; DA3; DAB; DAC; DAM MST, POET; DLB 146; LAIT 1; PAB; PFS 14; RGEL 2; TEA; WLIT 3; WP

Chavez, Denise (Elia) 1948- .... **HLC 1**
See also CA 131; CANR 56, 81; DAM MULT; DLB 122; FW; HW 1, 2; LLW 1; MTCW 2

Chaviaras, Strates 1935-
See Haviaras, Stratis
See also CA 105

Chayefsky, Paddy .... **CLC 23**
See Chayefsky, Sidney
See also CAD; DLB 7, 44; DLBY 1981; RGAL 4

Chayefsky, Sidney 1923-1981
See Chayefsky, Paddy
See also CA 9-12R; 104; CANR 18; DAM DRAM

Clark, J. P.
See Clark Bekederemo, J(ohnson) P(epper)
See also CDWLB 3; DLB 117

Clark, John Pepper
See Clark Bekederemo, J(ohnson) P(epper)
See also AFW; CD 5; CP 7; RGEL 2

Clark, Kenneth (Mackenzie)
1903-1983 .... **TCLC 147**
See also CA 93-96; 109; CANR 36; MTCW 1, 2

Clark, M. R.
See Clark, Mavis Thorpe

Clark, Mavis Thorpe 1909-1999 ...... **CLC 12**
See also CA 57-60; CANR 8, 37, 107; CLR 30; CWRI 5; MAICYA 1, 2; SAAS 5; SATA 8, 74

Clark, Walter Van Tilburg
1909-1971 .... **CLC 28**
See also CA 9-12R; 33-36R; CANR 63, 113; DLB 9, 206; LAIT 2; RGAL 4; SATA 8

Clark Bekederemo, J(ohnson) P(epper)
1935- .... **BLC 1; CLC 38; DC 5**
See Clark, J. P.; Clark, John Pepper
See also BW 1; CA 65-68; CANR 16, 72; DAM DRAM, MULT; DFS 13; EWL 3; MTCW 1

Clarke, Arthur C(harles) 1917- .... **CLC 1, 4, 13, 18, 35, 136; SSC 3**
See also AAYA 4, 33; BPFB 1; BYA 13; CA 1-4R; CANR 2, 28, 55, 74; CN 7; CPW; DA3; DAM POP; DLB 261; JRDA; LAIT 5; MAICYA 1, 2; MTCW 1, 2; SATA 13, 70, 115; SCFW; SFW 4; SSFS 4, 18; YAW

Clarke, Austin 1896-1974 .... **CLC 6, 9**
See also CA 29-32; 49-52; CAP 2; DAM POET; DLB 10, 20; EWL 3; RGEL 2

Clarke, Austin C(hesterfield) 1934- .. **BLC 1; CLC 8, 53; SSC 45**
See also BW 1; CA 25-28R; CAAS 16; CANR 14, 32, 68; CN 7; DAC; DAM MULT; DLB 53, 125; DNFS 2; RGSF 2

Clarke, Gillian 1937- .... **CLC 61**
See also CA 106; CP 7; CWP; DLB 40

Clarke, Marcus (Andrew Hislop)
1846-1881 .... **NCLC 19**
See also DLB 230; RGEL 2; RGSF 2

Clarke, Shirley 1925-1997 .... **CLC 16**
See also CA 189

Clash, The
See Headon, (Nicky) Topper; Jones, Mick; Simonon, Paul; Strummer, Joe

Claudel, Paul (Louis Charles Marie)
1868-1955 .... **TCLC 2, 10**
See also CA 104; 165; DLB 192, 258; EW 8; EWL 3; GFL 1789 to the Present; RGWL 2, 3; TWA

Claudian 370(?)-404(?) .... **CMLC 46**
See also RGWL 2, 3

Claudius, Matthias 1740-1815 .... **NCLC 75**
See also DLB 97

Clavell, James (duMaresq)
1925-1994 .... **CLC 6, 25, 87**
See also BPFB 1; CA 25-28R; 146; CANR 26, 48; CPW; DA3; DAM NOV, POP; MTCW 1, 2; NFS 10; RHW

Clayman, Gregory .... **CLC 65**

Cleaver, (Leroy) Eldridge
1935-1998 .... **BLC 1; CLC 30, 119**
See also BW 1, 3; CA 21-24R; 167; CANR 16, 75; DA3; DAM MULT; MTCW 2; YAW

Cleese, John (Marwood) 1939- .... **CLC 21**
See Monty Python
See also CA 112; 116; CANR 35; MTCW 1

Cleishbotham, Jebediah
See Scott, Sir Walter

Cleland, John 1710-1789 .... **LC 2, 48**
See also DLB 39; RGEL 2

Clemens, Samuel Langhorne 1835-1910
See Twain, Mark
See also CA 104; 135; CDALB 1865-1917; DA; DA3; DAB; DAC; DAM MST, NOV; DLB 12, 23, 64, 74, 186, 189; JRDA; LMFS 1; MAICYA 1, 2; NCFS 4; SATA 100; SSFS 16; YABC 2

Clement of Alexandria
150(?)-215(?) .... **CMLC 41**

Cleophil
See Congreve, William

Clerihew, E.
See Bentley, E(dmund) C(lerihew)

Clerk, N. W.
See Lewis, C(live) S(taples)

Cliff, Jimmy .... **CLC 21**
See Chambers, James
See also CA 193

Cliff, Michelle 1946- .... **BLCS; CLC 120**
See also BW 2; CA 116; CANR 39, 72; CD-WLB 3; DLB 157; FW; GLL 2

Clifford, Lady Anne 1590-1676 .... **LC 76**
See also DLB 151

Clifton, (Thelma) Lucille 1936- .... **BLC 1; CLC 19, 66, 162; PC 17**
See also AFAW 2; BW 2, 3; CA 49-52; CANR 2, 24, 42, 76, 97; CLR 5; CP 7; CSW; CWP; CWRI 5; DA3; DAM MULT, POET; DLB 5, 41; EXPP; MAICYA 1, 2; MTCW 1, 2; PFS 1, 14; SATA 20, 69, 128; WP

Clinton, Dirk
See Silverberg, Robert

Clough, Arthur Hugh 1819-1861 ... **NCLC 27**
See also BRW 5; DLB 32; RGEL 2

Clutha, Janet Paterson Frame 1924-2004
See Frame, Janet
See also CA 1-4R; CANR 2, 36, 76; MTCW 1, 2; SATA 119

Clyne, Terence
See Blatty, William Peter

Cobalt, Martin
See Mayne, William (James Carter)

Cobb, Irvin S(hrewsbury)
1876-1944 .... **TCLC 77**
See also CA 175; DLB 11, 25, 86

Cobbett, William 1763-1835 .... **NCLC 49**
See also DLB 43, 107, 158; RGEL 2

Coburn, D(onald) L(ee) 1938- .... **CLC 10**
See also CA 89-92

Cocteau, Jean (Maurice Eugene Clement)
1889-1963 ...... **CLC 1, 8, 15, 16, 43; DC 17; TCLC 119; WLC**
See also CA 25-28; CANR 40; CAP 2; DA; DA3; DAB; DAC; DAM DRAM, MST, NOV; DLB 65, 258; EW 10; EWL 3; GFL 1789 to the Present; MTCW 1, 2; RGWL 2, 3; TWA

Codrescu, Andrei 1946- .... **CLC 46, 121**
See also CA 33-36R; CAAS 19; CANR 13, 34, 53, 76, 125; DA3; DAM POET; MTCW 2

Coe, Max
See Bourne, Randolph S(illiman)

Coe, Tucker
See Westlake, Donald E(dwin)

Coen, Ethan 1958- .... **CLC 108**
See also CA 126; CANR 85

Coen, Joel 1955- .... **CLC 108**
See also CA 126; CANR 119

The Coen Brothers
See Coen, Ethan; Coen, Joel

Coetzee, J(ohn) M(axwell) 1940- ..... **CLC 23, 33, 66, 117, 161, 162**
See also AAYA 37; AFW; BRWS 6; CA 77-80; CANR 41, 54, 74, 114; CN 7; DA3; DAM NOV; DLB 225; EWL 3; LMFS 2; MTCW 1, 2; WLIT 2; WWE 1

Coffey, Brian
See Koontz, Dean R(ay)

Coffin, Robert P(eter) Tristram
1892-1955 .... **TCLC 95**
See also CA 123; 169; DLB 45

Cohan, George M(ichael)
1878-1942 .... **TCLC 60**
See also CA 157; DLB 249; RGAL 4

Cohen, Arthur A(llen) 1928-1986 ...... **CLC 7, 31**
See also CA 1-4R; 120; CANR 1, 17, 42; DLB 28

Cohen, Leonard (Norman) 1934- ...... **CLC 3, 38**
See also CA 21-24R; CANR 14, 69; CN 7; CP 7; DAC; DAM MST; DLB 53; EWL 3; MTCW 1

Cohen, Matt(hew) 1942-1999 .... **CLC 19**
See also CA 61-64; 187; CAAS 18; CANR 40; CN 7; DAC; DLB 53

Cohen-Solal, Annie 19(?)- .... **CLC 50**

Colegate, Isabel 1931- .... **CLC 36**
See also CA 17-20R; CANR 8, 22, 74; CN 7; DLB 14, 231; INT CANR-22; MTCW 1

Coleman, Emmett
See Reed, Ishmael

Coleridge, Hartley 1796-1849 .... **NCLC 90**
See also DLB 96

Coleridge, M. E.
See Coleridge, Mary E(lizabeth)

Coleridge, Mary E(lizabeth)
1861-1907 .... **TCLC 73**
See also CA 116; 166; DLB 19, 98

Coleridge, Samuel Taylor
1772-1834 .... **NCLC 9, 54, 99, 111; PC 11, 39; WLC**
See also BRW 4; BRWR 2; BYA 4; CD-BLB 1789-1832; DA; DA3; DAB; DAC; DAM MST, POET; DLB 93, 107; EXPP; LATS 1; LMFS 1; PAB; PFS 4, 5; RGEL 2; TEA; WLIT 3; WP

Coleridge, Sara 1802-1852 .... **NCLC 31**
See also DLB 199

Coles, Don 1928- .... **CLC 46**
See also CA 115; CANR 38; CP 7

Coles, Robert (Martin) 1929- .... **CLC 108**
See also CA 45-48; CANR 3, 32, 66, 70; INT CANR-32; SATA 23

Colette, (Sidonie-Gabrielle)
1873-1954 .... **SSC 10; TCLC 1, 5, 16**
See Willy, Colette
See also CA 104; 131; DA3; DAM NOV; DLB 65; EW 9; EWL 3; GFL 1789 to the Present; MTCW 1, 2; RGWL 2, 3; TWA

Collett, (Jacobine) Camilla (Wergeland)
1813-1895 .... **NCLC 22**

Collier, Christopher 1930- .... **CLC 30**
See also AAYA 13; BYA 2; CA 33-36R; CANR 13, 33, 102; JRDA; MAICYA 1, 2; SATA 16, 70; WYA; YAW 1

Collier, James Lincoln 1928- .... **CLC 30**
See also AAYA 13; BYA 2; CA 9-12R; CANR 4, 33, 60, 102; CLR 3; DAM POP; JRDA; MAICYA 1, 2; SAAS 21; SATA 8, 70; WYA; YAW 1

Collier, Jeremy 1650-1726 .... **LC 6**

Collier, John 1901-1980 . **SSC 19; TCLC 127**
See also CA 65-68; 97-100; CANR 10; DLB 77, 255; FANT; SUFW 1

Collier, Mary 1690-1762 .... **LC 86**
See also DLB 95

Corso, (Nunzio) Gregory 1930-2001 . **CLC 1, 11; PC 33**
See also AMWS 12; BG 2; CA 5-8R; 193; CANR 41, 76; CP 7; DA3; DLB 5, 16, 237; LMFS 2; MTCW 1, 2; WP

Cortazar, Julio 1914-1984 ... **CLC 2, 3, 5, 10, 13, 15, 33, 34, 92; HLC 1; SSC 7**
See also BPFB 1; CA 21-24R; CANR 12, 32, 81; CDWLB 3; DA3; DAM MULT, NOV; DLB 113; EWL 3; EXPS; HW 1, 2; LAW; MTCW 1, 2; RGSF 2; RGWL 2, 3; SSFS 3; TWA; WLIT 1

Cortes, Hernan 1485-1547 .... **LC 31**

Corvinus, Jakob
See Raabe, Wilhelm (Karl)

Corwin, Cecil
See Kornbluth, C(yril) M.

Cosic, Dobrica 1921- .... **CLC 14**
See also CA 122; 138; CDWLB 4; CWW 2; DLB 181; EWL 3

Costain, Thomas B(ertram) 1885-1965 .... **CLC 30**
See also BYA 3; CA 5-8R; 25-28R; DLB 9; RHW

Costantini, Humberto 1924(?)-1987 . **CLC 49**
See also CA 131; 122; EWL 3; HW 1

Costello, Elvis 1954- .... **CLC 21**
See also CA 204

Costenoble, Philostene
See Ghelderode, Michel de

Cotes, Cecil V.
See Duncan, Sara Jeannette

Cotter, Joseph Seamon Sr. 1861-1949 .... **BLC 1; TCLC 28**
See also BW 1; CA 124; DAM MULT; DLB 50

Couch, Arthur Thomas Quiller
See Quiller-Couch, Sir Arthur (Thomas)

Coulton, James
See Hansen, Joseph

Couperus, Louis (Marie Anne) 1863-1923 .... **TCLC 15**
See also CA 115; EWL 3; RGWL 2, 3

Coupland, Douglas 1961- .... **CLC 85, 133**
See also AAYA 34; CA 142; CANR 57, 90; CCA 1; CPW; DAC; DAM POP

Court, Wesli
See Turco, Lewis (Putnam)

Courtenay, Bryce 1933- .... **CLC 59**
See also CA 138; CPW

Courtney, Robert
See Ellison, Harlan (Jay)

Cousteau, Jacques-Yves 1910-1997 .. **CLC 30**
See also CA 65-68; 159; CANR 15, 67; MTCW 1; SATA 38, 98

Coventry, Francis 1725-1754 .... **LC 46**

Coverdale, Miles c. 1487-1569 .... **LC 77**
See also DLB 167

Cowan, Peter (Walkinshaw) 1914- .... **SSC 28**
See also CA 21-24R; CANR 9, 25, 50, 83; CN 7; DLB 260; RGSF 2

Coward, Noel (Peirce) 1899-1973 . **CLC 1, 9, 29, 51**
See also AITN 1; BRWS 2; CA 17-18; 41-44R; CANR 35; CAP 2; CDBLB 1914-1945; DA3; DAM DRAM; DFS 3, 6; DLB 10, 245; EWL 3; IDFW 3, 4; MTCW 1, 2; RGEL 2; TEA

Cowley, Abraham 1618-1667 .... **LC 43**
See also BRW 2; DLB 131, 151; PAB; RGEL 2

Cowley, Malcolm 1898-1989 .... **CLC 39**
See also AMWS 2; CA 5-8R; 128; CANR 3, 55; DLB 4, 48; DLBY 1981, 1989; EWL 3; MTCW 1, 2

Cowper, William 1731-1800 ..... **NCLC 8, 94; PC 40**
See also BRW 3; DA3; DAM POET; DLB 104, 109; RGEL 2

Cox, William Trevor 1928-
See Trevor, William
See also CA 9-12R; CANR 4, 37, 55, 76, 102; DAM NOV; INT CANR-37; MTCW 1, 2; TEA

Coyne, P. J.
See Masters, Hilary

Cozzens, James Gould 1903-1978 . **CLC 1, 4, 11, 92**
See also AMW; BPFB 1; CA 9-12R; 81-84; CANR 19; CDALB 1941-1968; DLB 9; DLBD 2; DLBY 1984, 1997; EWL 3; MTCW 1, 2; RGAL 4

Crabbe, George 1754-1832 .... **NCLC 26, 121**
See also BRW 3; DLB 93; RGEL 2

Crace, Jim 1946- .... **CLC 157; SSC 61**
See also CA 128; 135; CANR 55, 70, 123; CN 7; DLB 231; INT CA-135

Craddock, Charles Egbert
See Murfree, Mary Noailles

Craig, A. A.
See Anderson, Poul (William)

Craik, Mrs.
See Craik, Dinah Maria (Mulock)
See also RGEL 2

Craik, Dinah Maria (Mulock) 1826-1887 .... **NCLC 38**
See Craik, Mrs.; Mulock, Dinah Maria
See also DLB 35, 163; MAICYA 1, 2; SATA 34

Cram, Ralph Adams 1863-1942 ..... **TCLC 45**
See also CA 160

Cranch, Christopher Pearse 1813-1892 .... **NCLC 115**
See also DLB 1, 42, 243

Crane, (Harold) Hart 1899-1932 .... **PC 3; TCLC 2, 5, 80; WLC**
See also AMW; AMWR 2; CA 104; 127; CDALB 1917-1929; DA; DA3; DAB; DAC; DAM MST, POET; DLB 4, 48; EWL 3; MTCW 1, 2; RGAL 4; TUS

Crane, R(onald) S(almon) 1886-1967 .... **CLC 27**
See also CA 85-88; DLB 63

Crane, Stephen (Townley) 1871-1900 ...... **SSC 7, 56, 70; TCLC 11, 17, 32; WLC**
See also AAYA 21; AMW; AMWC 1; BPFB 1; BYA 3; CA 109; 140; CANR 84; CDALB 1865-1917; DA; DA3; DAB; DAC; DAM MST, NOV, POET; DLB 12, 54, 78; EXPN; EXPS; LAIT 2; LMFS 2; NFS 4; PFS 9; RGAL 4; RGSF 2; SSFS 4; TUS; WYA; YABC 2

Cranmer, Thomas 1489-1556 .... **LC 95**
See also DLB 132, 213

Cranshaw, Stanley
See Fisher, Dorothy (Frances) Canfield

Crase, Douglas 1944- .... **CLC 58**
See also CA 106

Crashaw, Richard 1612(?)-1649 .... **LC 24**
See also BRW 2; DLB 126; PAB; RGEL 2

Cratinus c. 519B.C.-c. 422B.C. ..... **CMLC 54**
See also LMFS 1

Craven, Margaret 1901-1980 .... **CLC 17**
See also BYA 2; CA 103; CCA 1; DAC; LAIT 5

Crawford, F(rancis) Marion 1854-1909 .... **TCLC 10**
See also CA 107; 168; DLB 71; HGG; RGAL 4; SUFW 1

Crawford, Isabella Valancy 1850-1887 .... **NCLC 12, 127**
See also DLB 92; RGEL 2

Crayon, Geoffrey
See Irving, Washington

Creasey, John 1908-1973 .... **CLC 11**
See Marric, J. J.
See also CA 5-8R; 41-44R; CANR 8, 59; CMW 4; DLB 77; MTCW 1

Crebillon, Claude Prosper Jolyot de (fils) 1707-1777 .... **LC 1, 28**
See also GFL Beginnings to 1789

Credo
See Creasey, John

Credo, Alvaro J. de
See Prado (Calvo), Pedro

Creeley, Robert (White) 1926- .. **CLC 1, 2, 4, 8, 11, 15, 36, 78**
See also AMWS 4; CA 1-4R; CAAS 10; CANR 23, 43, 89; CP 7; DA3; DAM POET; DLB 5, 16, 169; DLBD 17; EWL 3; MTCW 1, 2; RGAL 4; WP

Crevecoeur, Hector St. John de
See Crevecoeur, Michel Guillaume Jean de
See also ANW

Crevecoeur, Michel Guillaume Jean de 1735-1813 .... **NCLC 105**
See Crevecoeur, Hector St. John de
See also AMWS 1; DLB 37

Crevel, Rene 1900-1935 .... **TCLC 112**
See also GLL 2

Crews, Harry (Eugene) 1935- ..... **CLC 6, 23, 49**
See also AITN 1; AMWS 11; BPFB 1; CA 25-28R; CANR 20, 57; CN 7; CSW; DA3; DLB 6, 143, 185; MTCW 1, 2; RGAL 4

Crichton, (John) Michael 1942- .... **CLC 2, 6, 54, 90**
See also AAYA 10, 49; AITN 2; BPFB 1; CA 25-28R; CANR 13, 40, 54, 76, 127; CMW 4; CN 7; CPW; DA3; DAM NOV, POP; DLB 292; DLBY 1981; INT CANR-13; JRDA; MTCW 1, 2; SATA 9, 88; SFW 4; YAW

Crispin, Edmund .... **CLC 22**
See Montgomery, (Robert) Bruce
See also DLB 87; MSW

Cristofer, Michael 1945(?)- .... **CLC 28**
See also CA 110; 152; CAD; CD 5; DAM DRAM; DFS 15; DLB 7

Criton
See Alain

Croce, Benedetto 1866-1952 .... **TCLC 37**
See also CA 120; 155; EW 8; EWL 3

Crockett, David 1786-1836 .... **NCLC 8**
See also DLB 3, 11, 183, 248

Crockett, Davy
See Crockett, David

Crofts, Freeman Wills 1879-1957 .. **TCLC 55**
See also CA 115; 195; CMW 4; DLB 77; MSW

Croker, John Wilson 1780-1857 .... **NCLC 10**
See also DLB 110

Crommelynck, Fernand 1885-1970 .. **CLC 75**
See also CA 189; 89-92; EWL 3

Cromwell, Oliver 1599-1658 .... **LC 43**

Cronenberg, David 1943- .... **CLC 143**
See also CA 138; CCA 1

Cronin, A(rchibald) J(oseph) 1896-1981 .... **CLC 32**
See also BPFB 1; CA 1-4R; 102; CANR 5; DLB 191; SATA 47; SATA-Obit 25

Cross, Amanda
See Heilbrun, Carolyn G(old)
See also BPFB 1; CMW; CPW; MSW

Crothers, Rachel 1878-1958 .... **TCLC 19**
See also CA 113; 194; CAD; CWD; DLB 7, 266; RGAL 4

Croves, Hal
See Traven, B.

Crow Dog, Mary (Ellen) (?)- .... **CLC 93**
See Brave Bird, Mary
See also CA 154

Crowfield, Christopher
   See Stowe, Harriet (Elizabeth) Beecher
Crowley, Aleister .... **TCLC 7**
   See Crowley, Edward Alexander
   See also GLL 1
Crowley, Edward Alexander 1875-1947
   See Crowley, Aleister
   See also CA 104; HGG
Crowley, John 1942- .... **CLC 57**
   See also BPFB 1; CA 61-64; CANR 43, 98;
   DLBY 1982; FANT; SATA 65, 140; SFW
   4; SUFW 2
Crud
   See Crumb, R(obert)
Crumarums
   See Crumb, R(obert)
Crumb, R(obert) 1943- .... **CLC 17**
   See also CA 106; CANR 107
Crumbum
   See Crumb, R(obert)
Crumski
   See Crumb, R(obert)
Crum the Bum
   See Crumb, R(obert)
Crunk
   See Crumb, R(obert)
Crustt
   See Crumb, R(obert)
Crutchfield, Les
   See Trumbo, Dalton
Cruz, Victor Hernandez 1949- ... **HLC 1; PC
   37**
   See also BW 2; CA 65-68; CAAS 17;
   CANR 14, 32, 74; CP 7; DAM MULT,
   POET; DLB 41; DNFS 1; EXPP; HW 1,
   2; LLW 1; MTCW 1; PFS 16; WP
Cryer, Gretchen (Kiger) 1935- .... **CLC 21**
   See also CA 114; 123
Csath, Geza 1887-1919 .... **TCLC 13**
   See also CA 111
Cudlip, David R(ockwell) 1933- .... **CLC 34**
   See also CA 177
Cullen, Countee 1903-1946 .... **BLC 1; HR 2;
   PC 20; TCLC 4, 37; WLCS**
   See also AFAW 2; AMWS 4; BW 1; CA
   108; 124; CDALB 1917-1929; DA; DA3;
   DAC; DAM MST, MULT, POET; DLB 4,
   48, 51; EWL 3; EXPP; LMFS 2; MTCW
   1, 2; PFS 3; RGAL 4; SATA 18; WP
Culleton, Beatrice 1949- .... **NNAL**
   See also CA 120; CANR 83; DAC
Cum, R.
   See Crumb, R(obert)
Cummings, Bruce F(rederick) 1889-1919
   See Barbellion, W. N. P.
   See also CA 123
Cummings, E(dward) E(stlin)
   1894-1962 .. **CLC 1, 3, 8, 12, 15, 68; PC
   5; TCLC 137; WLC**
   See also AAYA 41; AMW; CA 73-76;
   CANR 31; CDALB 1929-1941; DA;
   DA3; DAB; DAC; DAM MST, POET;
   DLB 4, 48; EWL 3; EXPP; MTCW 1, 2;
   PAB; PFS 1, 3, 12, 13; RGAL 4; TUS;
   WP
Cunha, Euclides (Rodrigues Pimenta) da
   1866-1909 .... **TCLC 24**
   See also CA 123; 219; LAW; WLIT 1
Cunningham, E. V.
   See Fast, Howard (Melvin)
Cunningham, J(ames) V(incent)
   1911-1985 .... **CLC 3, 31**
   See also CA 1-4R; 115; CANR 1, 72; DLB
   5
Cunningham, Julia (Woolfolk)
   1916- .... **CLC 12**
   See also CA 9-12R; CANR 4, 19, 36; CWRI
   5; JRDA; MAICYA 1, 2; SAAS 2; SATA
   1, 26, 132

Cunningham, Michael 1952- .... **CLC 34**
   See also CA 136; CANR 96; DLB 292;
   GLL 2
Cunninghame Graham, R. B.
   See Cunninghame Graham, Robert
   (Gallnigad) Bontine
Cunninghame Graham, Robert (Gallnigad)
   Bontine 1852-1936 .... **TCLC 19**
   See Graham, R(obert) B(ontine) Cunning-
   hame
   See also CA 119; 184
Curnow, (Thomas) Allen (Monro)
   1911-2001 .... **PC 48**
   See also CA 69-72; 202; CANR 48, 99; CP
   7; EWL 3; RGEL 2
Currie, Ellen 19(?)- .... **CLC 44**
Curtin, Philip
   See Lowndes, Marie Adelaide (Belloc)
Curtin, Phillip
   See Lowndes, Marie Adelaide (Belloc)
Curtis, Price
   See Ellison, Harlan (Jay)
Cusanus, Nicolaus 1401-1464 .... **LC 80**
   See Nicholas of Cusa
Cutrate, Joe
   See Spiegelman, Art
Cynewulf c. 770- .... **CMLC 23**
   See also DLB 146; RGEL 2
Cyrano de Bergerac, Savinien de
   1619-1655 .... **LC 65**
   See also DLB 268; GFL Beginnings to
   1789; RGWL 2, 3
Cyril of Alexandria c. 375-c. 430 . **CMLC 59**
Czaczkes, Shmuel Yosef Halevi
   See Agnon, S(hmuel) Y(osef Halevi)
Dabrowska, Maria (Szumska)
   1889-1965 .... **CLC 15**
   See also CA 106; CDWLB 4; DLB 215;
   EWL 3
Dabydeen, David 1955- .... **CLC 34**
   See also BW 1; CA 125; CANR 56, 92; CN
   7; CP 7
Dacey, Philip 1939- .... **CLC 51**
   See also CA 37-40R; CAAS 17; CANR 14,
   32, 64; CP 7; DLB 105
Dagerman, Stig (Halvard)
   1923-1954 .... **TCLC 17**
   See also CA 117; 155; DLB 259; EWL 3
D'Aguiar, Fred 1960- .... **CLC 145**
   See also CA 148; CANR 83, 101; CP 7;
   DLB 157; EWL 3
Dahl, Roald 1916-1990 .... **CLC 1, 6, 18, 79**
   See also AAYA 15; BPFB 1; BRWS 4; BYA
   5; CA 1-4R; 133; CANR 6, 32, 37, 62;
   CLR 1, 7, 41; CPW; DA3; DAB; DAC;
   DAM MST, NOV, POP; DLB 139, 255;
   HGG; JRDA; MAICYA 1, 2; MTCW 1,
   2; RGSF 2; SATA 1, 26, 73; SATA-Obit
   65; SSFS 4; TEA; YAW
Dahlberg, Edward 1900-1977 .. **CLC 1, 7, 14**
   See also CA 9-12R; 69-72; CANR 31, 62;
   DLB 48; MTCW 1; RGAL 4
Daitch, Susan 1954- .... **CLC 103**
   See also CA 161
Dale, Colin .... **TCLC 18**
   See Lawrence, T(homas) E(dward)
Dale, George E.
   See Asimov, Isaac
Dalton, Roque 1935-1975(?) ..... **HLCS 1; PC
   36**
   See also CA 176; DLB 283; HW 2
Daly, Elizabeth 1878-1967 .... **CLC 52**
   See also CA 23-24; 25-28R; CANR 60;
   CAP 2; CMW 4
Daly, Mary 1928- .... **CLC 173**
   See also CA 25-28R; CANR 30, 62; FW;
   GLL 1; MTCW 1

Daly, Maureen 1921- .... **CLC 17**
   See also AAYA 5; BYA 6; CANR 37, 83,
   108; CLR 96; JRDA; MAICYA 1, 2;
   SAAS 1; SATA 2, 129; WYA; YAW
Damas, Leon-Gontran 1912-1978 .... **CLC 84**
   See also BW 1; CA 125; 73-76; EWL 3
Dana, Richard Henry Sr.
   1787-1879 .... **NCLC 53**
Daniel, Samuel 1562(?)-1619 .... **LC 24**
   See also DLB 62; RGEL 2
Daniels, Brett
   See Adler, Renata
Dannay, Frederic 1905-1982 .... **CLC 11**
   See Queen, Ellery
   See also CA 1-4R; 107; CANR 1, 39; CMW
   4; DAM POP; DLB 137; MTCW 1
D'Annunzio, Gabriele 1863-1938 ... **TCLC 6,
   40**
   See also CA 104; 155; EW 8; EWL 3;
   RGWL 2, 3; TWA
Danois, N. le
   See Gourmont, Remy(-Marie-Charles) de
Dante 1265-1321 .... **CMLC 3, 18, 39; PC 21;
   WLCS**
   See also DA; DA3; DAB; DAC; DAM
   MST, POET; EFS 1; EW 1; LAIT 1;
   RGWL 2, 3; TWA; WP
d'Antibes, Germain
   See Simenon, Georges (Jacques Christian)
Danticat, Edwidge 1969- .... **CLC 94, 139**
   See also AAYA 29; CA 152, 192; CAAE
   192; CANR 73; DNFS 1; EXPS; LATS 1;
   MTCW 1; SSFS 1; YAW
Danvers, Dennis 1947- .... **CLC 70**
Danziger, Paula 1944- .... **CLC 21**
   See also AAYA 4, 36; BYA 6, 7, 14; CA
   112; 115; CANR 37; CLR 20; JRDA;
   MAICYA 1, 2; SATA 36, 63, 102; SATA-
   Brief 30; WYA; YAW
Da Ponte, Lorenzo 1749-1838 .... **NCLC 50**
Dario, Ruben 1867-1916 .... **HLC 1; PC 15;
   TCLC 4**
   See also CA 131; CANR 81; DAM MULT;
   DLB 290; EWL 3; HW 1, 2; LAW;
   MTCW 1, 2; RGWL 2, 3
Darley, George 1795-1846 .... **NCLC 2**
   See also DLB 96; RGEL 2
Darrow, Clarence (Seward)
   1857-1938 .... **TCLC 81**
   See also CA 164
Darwin, Charles 1809-1882 .... **NCLC 57**
   See also BRWS 7; DLB 57, 166; LATS 1;
   RGEL 2; TEA; WLIT 4
Darwin, Erasmus 1731-1802 .... **NCLC 106**
   See also DLB 93; RGEL 2
Daryush, Elizabeth 1887-1977 ...... **CLC 6, 19**
   See also CA 49-52; CANR 3, 81; DLB 20
Das, Kamala 1934- .... **PC 43**
   See also CA 101; CANR 27, 59; CP 7;
   CWP
Dasgupta, Surendranath
   1887-1952 .... **TCLC 81**
   See also CA 157
Dashwood, Edmee Elizabeth Monica de la
   Pasture 1890-1943
   See Delafield, E. M.
   See also CA 119; 154
da Silva, Antonio Jose
   1705-1739 .... **NCLC 114**
Daudet, (Louis Marie) Alphonse
   1840-1897 .... **NCLC 1**
   See also DLB 123; GFL 1789 to the Present;
   RGSF 2
d'Aulnoy, Marie-Catherine c.
   1650-1705 .... **LC 100**
Daumal, Rene 1908-1944 .... **TCLC 14**
   See also CA 114; EWL 3
Davenant, William 1606-1668 .... **LC 13**
   See also DLB 58, 126; RGEL 2

Davenport, Guy (Mattison, Jr.)
1927- .... **CLC 6, 14, 38; SSC 16**
See also CA 33-36R; CANR 23, 73; CN 7;
CSW; DLB 130

David, Robert
See Nezval, Vitezslav

Davidson, Avram (James) 1923-1993
See Queen, Ellery
See also CA 101; 171; CANR 26; DLB 8;
FANT; SFW 4; SUFW 1, 2

Davidson, Donald (Grady)
1893-1968 .... **CLC 2, 13, 19**
See also CA 5-8R; 25-28R; CANR 4, 84;
DLB 45

Davidson, Hugh
See Hamilton, Edmond

Davidson, John 1857-1909 .... **TCLC 24**
See also CA 118; 217; DLB 19; RGEL 2

Davidson, Sara 1943- .... **CLC 9**
See also CA 81-84; CANR 44, 68; DLB
185

Davie, Donald (Alfred) 1922-1995 .... **CLC 5,
8, 10, 31; PC 29**
See also BRWS 6; CA 1-4R; 149; CAAS 3;
CANR 1, 44; CP 7; DLB 27; MTCW 1;
RGEL 2

Davie, Elspeth 1919-1995 .... **SSC 52**
See also CA 120; 126; 150; DLB 139

Davies, Ray(mond Douglas) 1944- ... **CLC 21**
See also CA 116; 146; CANR 92

Davies, Rhys 1901-1978 .... **CLC 23**
See also CA 9-12R; 81-84; CANR 4; DLB
139, 191

Davies, (William) Robertson
1913-1995 .... **CLC 2, 7, 13, 25, 42, 75,
91; WLC**
See Marchbanks, Samuel
See also BEST 89:2; BPFB 1; CA 33-36R;
150; CANR 17, 42, 103; CN 7; CPW;
DA; DA3; DAB; DAC; DAM MST, NOV,
POP; DLB 68; EWL 3; HGG; INT CANR-
17; MTCW 1, 2; RGEL 2; TWA

Davies, Sir John 1569-1626 .... **LC 85**
See also DLB 172

Davies, Walter C.
See Kornbluth, C(yril) M.

Davies, William Henry 1871-1940 ... **TCLC 5**
See also CA 104; 179; DLB 19, 174; EWL
3; RGEL 2

Da Vinci, Leonardo 1452-1519 ..... **LC 12, 57,
60**
See also AAYA 40

Davis, Angela (Yvonne) 1944- .... **CLC 77**
See also BW 2, 3; CA 57-60; CANR 10,
81; CSW; DA3; DAM MULT; FW

Davis, B. Lynch
See Bioy Casares, Adolfo; Borges, Jorge
Luis

Davis, Frank Marshall 1905-1987 ...... **BLC 1**
See also BW 2, 3; CA 125; 123; CANR 42,
80; DAM MULT; DLB 51

Davis, Gordon
See Hunt, E(verette) Howard, (Jr.)

Davis, H(arold) L(enoir) 1896-1960 . **CLC 49**
See also ANW; CA 178; 89-92; DLB 9,
206; SATA 114

Davis, Rebecca (Blaine) Harding
1831-1910 .... **SSC 38; TCLC 6**
See also CA 104; 179; DLB 74, 239; FW;
NFS 14; RGAL 4; TUS

Davis, Richard Harding
1864-1916 .... **TCLC 24**
See also CA 114; 179; DLB 12, 23, 78, 79,
189; DLBD 13; RGAL 4

Davison, Frank Dalby 1893-1970 ..... **CLC 15**
See also CA 217; 116; DLB 260

Davison, Lawrence H.
See Lawrence, D(avid) H(erbert Richards)

Davison, Peter (Hubert) 1928- .... **CLC 28**
See also CA 9-12R; CAAS 4; CANR 3, 43,
84; CP 7; DLB 5

Davys, Mary 1674-1732 .... **LC 1, 46**
See also DLB 39

Dawson, (Guy) Fielding (Lewis)
1930-2002 .... **CLC 6**
See also CA 85-88; 202; CANR 108; DLB
130; DLBY 2002

Dawson, Peter
See Faust, Frederick (Schiller)
See also TCWW 2, 2

Day, Clarence (Shepard, Jr.)
1874-1935 .... **TCLC 25**
See also CA 108; 199; DLB 11

Day, John 1574(?)-1640(?) .... **LC 70**
See also DLB 62, 170; RGEL 2

Day, Thomas 1748-1789 .... **LC 1**
See also DLB 39; YABC 1

Day Lewis, C(ecil) 1904-1972 . **CLC 1, 6, 10;
PC 11**
See Blake, Nicholas
See also BRWS 3; CA 13-16; 33-36R;
CANR 34; CAP 1; CWRI 5; DAM POET;
DLB 15, 20; EWL 3; MTCW 1, 2; RGEL
2

Dazai Osamu .... **SSC 41; TCLC 11**
See Tsushima, Shuji
See also CA 164; DLB 182; EWL 3; MJW;
RGSF 2; RGWL 2, 3; TWA

de Andrade, Carlos Drummond
See Drummond de Andrade, Carlos

de Andrade, Mario 1892-1945
See Andrade, Mario de
See also CA 178; HW 2

Deane, Norman
See Creasey, John

Deane, Seamus (Francis) 1940- ...... **CLC 122**
See also CA 118; CANR 42

**de Beauvoir, Simone (Lucie Ernestine Marie
Bertrand)**
See Beauvoir, Simone (Lucie Ernestine
Marie Bertrand) de

de Beer, P.
See Bosman, Herman Charles

de Brissac, Malcolm
See Dickinson, Peter (Malcolm)

de Campos, Alvaro
See Pessoa, Fernando (Antonio Nogueira)

de Chardin, Pierre Teilhard
See Teilhard de Chardin, (Marie Joseph)
Pierre

Dee, John 1527-1608 .... **LC 20**
See also DLB 136, 213

Deer, Sandra 1940- .... **CLC 45**
See also CA 186

De Ferrari, Gabriella 1941- .... **CLC 65**
See also CA 146

de Filippo, Eduardo 1900-1984 ... **TCLC 127**
See also CA 132; 114; EWL 3; MTCW 1;
RGWL 2, 3

Defoe, Daniel 1660(?)-1731 .. **LC 1, 42; WLC**
See also AAYA 27; BRW 3; BRWR 1; BYA
4; CDBLB 1660-1789; CLR 61; DA;
DA3; DAB; DAC; DAM MST, NOV;
DLB 39, 95, 101; JRDA; LAIT 1; LMFS
1; MAICYA 1, 2; NFS 9, 13; RGEL 2;
SATA 22; TEA; WCH; WLIT 3

de Gourmont, Remy(-Marie-Charles)
See Gourmont, Remy(-Marie-Charles) de

de Gournay, Marie le Jars
1566-1645 .... **LC 98**
See also FW

de Hartog, Jan 1914-2002 .... **CLC 19**
See also CA 1-4R; 210; CANR 1; DFS 12

de Hostos, E. M.
See Hostos (y Bonilla), Eugenio Maria de

de Hostos, Eugenio M.
See Hostos (y Bonilla), Eugenio Maria de

Deighton, Len .... **CLC 4, 7, 22, 46**
See Deighton, Leonard Cyril
See also AAYA 6; BEST 89:2; BPFB 1; CD-
BLB 1960 to Present; CMW 4; CN 7;
CPW; DLB 87

Deighton, Leonard Cyril 1929-
See Deighton, Len
See also CA 9-12R; CANR 19, 33, 68;
DA3; DAM NOV, POP; MTCW 1, 2

Dekker, Thomas 1572(?)-1632 ..... **DC 12; LC
22**
See also CDBLB Before 1660; DAM
DRAM; DLB 62, 172; LMFS 1; RGEL 2

de Laclos, Pierre Ambroise Franois
See Laclos, Pierre Ambroise Francois

Delacroix, (Ferdinand-Victor-)Eugene
1798-1863 .... **NCLC 133**
See also EW 5

Delafield, E. M. .... **TCLC 61**
See Dashwood, Edmee Elizabeth Monica
de la Pasture
See also DLB 34; RHW

de la Mare, Walter (John)
1873-1956 . **SSC 14; TCLC 4, 53; WLC**
See also CA 163; CDBLB 1914-1945; CLR
23; CWRI 5; DA3; DAB; DAC; DAM
MST, POET; DLB 19, 153, 162, 255, 284;
EWL 3; EXPP; HGG; MAICYA 1, 2;
MTCW 1; RGEL 2; RGSF 2; SATA 16;
SUFW 1; TEA; WCH

de Lamartine, Alphonse (Marie Louis Prat)
See Lamartine, Alphonse (Marie Louis Prat)
de

Delaney, Franey
See O'Hara, John (Henry)

Delaney, Shelagh 1939- .... **CLC 29**
See also CA 17-20R; CANR 30, 67; CBD;
CD 5; CDBLB 1960 to Present; CWD;
DAM DRAM; DFS 7; DLB 13; MTCW 1

Delany, Martin Robison
1812-1885 .... **NCLC 93**
See also DLB 50; RGAL 4

Delany, Mary (Granville Pendarves)
1700-1788 .... **LC 12**

Delany, Samuel R(ay), Jr. 1942- .... **BLC 1;
CLC 8, 14, 38, 141**
See also AAYA 24; AFAW 2; BPFB 1; BW
2, 3; CA 81-84; CANR 27, 43, 115, 116;
CN 7; DAM MULT; DLB 8, 33; FANT;
MTCW 1, 2; RGAL 4; SATA 92; SCFW;
SFW 4; SUFW 2

De la Ramee, Marie Louise (Ouida)
1839-1908
See Ouida
See also CA 204; SATA 20

de la Roche, Mazo 1879-1961 .... **CLC 14**
See also CA 85-88; CANR 30; DLB 68;
RGEL 2; RHW; SATA 64

De La Salle, Innocent
See Hartmann, Sadakichi

de Laureamont, Comte
See Lautreamont

Delbanco, Nicholas (Franklin)
1942- .... **CLC 6, 13, 167**
See also CA 17-20R, 189; CAAE 189;
CAAS 2; CANR 29, 55, 116; DLB 6, 234

del Castillo, Michel 1933- .... **CLC 38**
See also CA 109; CANR 77

Deledda, Grazia (Cosima)
1875(?)-1936 .... **TCLC 23**
See also CA 123; 205; DLB 264; EWL 3;
RGWL 2, 3

Deleuze, Gilles 1925-1995 .... **TCLC 116**
See also DLB 296

Delgado, Abelardo (Lalo) B(arrientos)
1930- .... **HLC 1**
See also CA 131; CAAS 15; CANR 90;
DAM MST, MULT; DLB 82; HW 1, 2

Dickson, Carter
See Carr, John Dickson
Diderot, Denis 1713-1784 .... **LC 26**
See also EW 4; GFL Beginnings to 1789;
LMFS 1; RGWL 2, 3
Didion, Joan 1934- . **CLC 1, 3, 8, 14, 32, 129**
See also AITN 1; AMWS 4; CA 5-8R;
CANR 14, 52, 76, 125; CDALB 1968-
1988; CN 7; DA3; DAM NOV; DLB 2,
173, 185; DLBY 1981, 1986; EWL 3;
MAWW; MTCW 1, 2; NFS 3; RGAL 4;
TCWW 2; TUS
Dietrich, Robert
See Hunt, E(verette) Howard, (Jr.)
Difusa, Pati
See Almodovar, Pedro
Dillard, Annie 1945- .... **CLC 9, 60, 115**
See also AAYA 6, 43; AMWS 6; ANW; CA
49-52; CANR 3, 43, 62, 90, 125; DA3;
DAM NOV; DLB 275, 278; DLBY 1980;
LAIT 4, 5; MTCW 1, 2; NCFS 1; RGAL
4; SATA 10, 140; TUS
Dillard, R(ichard) H(enry) W(ilde)
1937- .... **CLC 5**
See also CA 21-24R; CAAS 7; CANR 10;
CP 7; CSW; DLB 5, 244
Dillon, Eilis 1920-1994 .... **CLC 17**
See also CA 9-12R; 182; 147; CAAE 182;
CAAS 3; CANR 4, 38, 78; CLR 26; MAI-
CYA 1, 2; MAICYAS 1; SATA 2, 74;
SATA-Essay 105; SATA-Obit 83; YAW
Dimont, Penelope
See Mortimer, Penelope (Ruth)
Dinesen, Isak .... **CLC 10, 29, 95; SSC 7**
See Blixen, Karen (Christentze Dinesen)
See also EW 10; EWL 3; EXPS; FW; HGG;
LAIT 3; MTCW 1; NCFS 2; NFS 9;
RGSF 2; RGWL 2, 3; SSFS 3, 6, 13;
WLIT 2
Ding Ling .... **CLC 68**
See Chiang, Pin-chin
See also RGWL 3
Diphusa, Patty
See Almodovar, Pedro
Disch, Thomas M(ichael) 1940- ... **CLC 7, 36**
See Disch, Tom
See also AAYA 17; BPFB 1; CA 21-24R;
CAAS 4; CANR 17, 36, 54, 89; CLR 18;
CP 7; DA3; DLB 8; HGG; MAICYA 1, 2;
MTCW 1, 2; SAAS 15; SATA 92; SCFW;
SFW 4; SUFW 2
Disch, Tom
See Disch, Thomas M(ichael)
See also DLB 282
d'Isly, Georges
See Simenon, Georges (Jacques Christian)
Disraeli, Benjamin 1804-1881 ... **NCLC 2, 39,
79**
See also BRW 4; DLB 21, 55; RGEL 2
Ditcum, Steve
See Crumb, R(obert)
Dixon, Paige
See Corcoran, Barbara (Asenath)
Dixon, Stephen 1936- .... **CLC 52; SSC 16**
See also AMWS 12; CA 89-92; CANR 17,
40, 54, 91; CN 7; DLB 130
Djebar, Assia 1936- .... **CLC 182**
See also CA 188; EWL 3; RGWL 3; WLIT
2
Doak, Annie
See Dillard, Annie
Dobell, Sydney Thompson
1824-1874 .... **NCLC 43**
See also DLB 32; RGEL 2
Doblin, Alfred .... **TCLC 13**
See Doeblin, Alfred
See also CDWLB 2; EWL 3; RGWL 2, 3

Dobroliubov, Nikolai Aleksandrovich
See Dobrolyubov, Nikolai Alexandrovich
See also DLB 277
Dobrolyubov, Nikolai Alexandrovich
1836-1861 .... **NCLC 5**
See Dobroliubov, Nikolai Aleksandrovich
Dobson, Austin 1840-1921 .... **TCLC 79**
See also DLB 35, 144
Dobyns, Stephen 1941- .... **CLC 37**
See also AMWS 13; CA 45-48; CANR 2,
18, 99; CMW 4; CP 7
Doctorow, E(dgar) L(aurence)
1931- .... **CLC 6, 11, 15, 18, 37, 44, 65,
113**
See also AAYA 22; AITN 2; AMWS 4;
BEST 89:3; BPFB 1; CA 45-48; CANR
2, 33, 51, 76, 97; CDALB 1968-1988; CN
7; CPW; DA3; DAM NOV, POP; DLB 2,
28, 173; DLBY 1980; EWL 3; LAIT 3;
MTCW 1, 2; NFS 6; RGAL 4; RHW;
TUS
Dodgson, Charles L(utwidge) 1832-1898
See Carroll, Lewis
See also CLR 2; DA; DA3; DAB; DAC;
DAM MST, NOV, POET; MAICYA 1, 2;
SATA 100; YABC 2
Dodsley, Robert 1703-1764 .... **LC 97**
See also DLB 95; RGEL 2
Dodson, Owen (Vincent) 1914-1983 .. **BLC 1;
CLC 79**
See also BW 1; CA 65-68; 110; CANR 24;
DAM MULT; DLB 76
Doeblin, Alfred 1878-1957 .... **TCLC 13**
See Doblin, Alfred
See also CA 110; 141; DLB 66
Doerr, Harriet 1910-2002 .... **CLC 34**
See also CA 117; 122; 213; CANR 47; INT
CA-122; LATS 1
Domecq, H(onorio Bustos)
See Bioy Casares, Adolfo
Domecq, H(onorio) Bustos
See Bioy Casares, Adolfo; Borges, Jorge
Luis
Domini, Rey
See Lorde, Audre (Geraldine)
See also GLL 1
Dominique
See Proust, (Valentin-Louis-George-Eugene)
Marcel
Don, A
See Stephen, Sir Leslie
Donaldson, Stephen R(eeder)
1947- .... **CLC 46, 138**
See also AAYA 36; BPFB 1; CA 89-92;
CANR 13, 55, 99; CPW; DAM POP;
FANT; INT CANR-13; SATA 121; SFW
4; SUFW 1, 2
Donleavy, J(ames) P(atrick) 1926- .... **CLC 1,
4, 6, 10, 45**
See also AITN 2; BPFB 1; CA 9-12R;
CANR 24, 49, 62, 80, 124; CBD; CD 5;
CN 7; DLB 6, 173; INT CANR-24;
MTCW 1, 2; RGAL 4
Donnadieu, Marguerite
See Duras, Marguerite
See also CWW 2
Donne, John 1572-1631 ... **LC 10, 24, 91; PC
1, 43; WLC**
See also BRW 1; BRWC 1; BRWR 2; CD-
BLB Before 1660; DA; DAB; DAC;
DAM MST, POET; DLB 121, 151; EXPP;
PAB; PFS 2, 11; RGEL 2; TEA; WLIT 3;
WP
Donnell, David 1939(?)- .... **CLC 34**
See also CA 197
Donoghue, P. S.
See Hunt, E(verette) Howard, (Jr.)

Donoso (Yanez), Jose 1924-1996 ... **CLC 4, 8,
11, 32, 99; HLC 1; SSC 34; TCLC 133**
See also CA 81-84; 155; CANR 32, 73; CD-
WLB 3; DAM MULT; DLB 113; EWL 3;
HW 1, 2; LAW; LAWS 1; MTCW 1, 2;
RGSF 2; WLIT 1
Donovan, John 1928-1992 .... **CLC 35**
See also AAYA 20; CA 97-100; 137; CLR
3; MAICYA 1, 2; SATA 72; SATA-Brief
29; YAW
Don Roberto
See Cunninghame Graham, Robert
(Gallnigad) Bontine
Doolittle, Hilda 1886-1961 . **CLC 3, 8, 14, 31,
34, 73; PC 5; WLC**
See H. D.
See also AMWS 1; CA 97-100; CANR 35;
DA; DAC; DAM MST, POET; DLB 4,
45; EWL 3; FW; GLL 1; LMFS 2;
MAWW; MTCW 1, 2; PFS 6; RGAL 4
Doppo, Kunikida .... **TCLC 99**
See Kunikida Doppo
Dorfman, Ariel 1942- .... **CLC 48, 77; HLC 1**
See also CA 124; 130; CANR 67, 70; CWW
2; DAM MULT; DFS 4; EWL 3; HW 1,
2; INT CA-130; WLIT 1
Dorn, Edward (Merton)
1929-1999 .... **CLC 10, 18**
See also CA 93-96; 187; CANR 42, 79; CP
7; DLB 5; INT CA-93-96; WP
Dor-Ner, Zvi .... **CLC 70**
Dorris, Michael (Anthony)
1945-1997 .... **CLC 109; NNAL**
See also AAYA 20; BEST 90:1; BYA 12;
CA 102; 157; CANR 19, 46, 75; CLR 58;
DA3; DAM MULT, NOV; DLB 175;
LAIT 5; MTCW 2; NFS 3; RGAL 4;
SATA 75; SATA-Obit 94; TCWW 2; YAW
Dorris, Michael A.
See Dorris, Michael (Anthony)
Dorsan, Luc
See Simenon, Georges (Jacques Christian)
Dorsange, Jean
See Simenon, Georges (Jacques Christian)
Dorset
See Sackville, Thomas
Dos Passos, John (Roderigo)
1896-1970 ... **CLC 1, 4, 8, 11, 15, 25, 34,
82; WLC**
See also AMW; BPFB 1; CA 1-4R; 29-32R;
CANR 3; CDALB 1929-1941; DA; DA3;
DAB; DAC; DAM MST, NOV; DLB 4,
9; DLBD 1, 15, 274; DLBY 1996; EWL
3; MTCW 1, 2; NFS 14; RGAL 4; TUS
Dossage, Jean
See Simenon, Georges (Jacques Christian)
Dostoevsky, Fedor Mikhailovich
1821-1881 .. **NCLC 2, 7, 21, 33, 43, 119;
SSC 2, 33, 44; WLC**
See Dostoevsky, Fyodor
See also AAYA 40; DA; DA3; DAB; DAC;
DAM MST, NOV; EW 7; EXPN; NFS 3,
8; RGSF 2; RGWL 2, 3; SSFS 8; TWA
Dostoevsky, Fyodor
See Dostoevsky, Fedor Mikhailovich
See also DLB 238; LATS 1; LMFS 1, 2
Doty, M. R.
See Doty, Mark (Alan)
Doty, Mark
See Doty, Mark (Alan)
Doty, Mark (Alan) 1953(?)- .... **CLC 176; PC
53**
See also AMWS 11; CA 161, 183; CAAE
183; CANR 110
Doty, Mark A.
See Doty, Mark (Alan)
Doughty, Charles M(ontagu)
1843-1926 .... **TCLC 27**
See also CA 115; 178; DLB 19, 57, 174

Douglas, Ellen .... **CLC 73**
See Haxton, Josephine Ayres; Williamson, Ellen Douglas
See also CN 7; CSW; DLB 292

Douglas, Gavin 1475(?)-1522 .... **LC 20**
See also DLB 132; RGEL 2

Douglas, George
See Brown, George Douglas
See also RGEL 2

Douglas, Keith (Castellain)
1920-1944 .... **TCLC 40**
See also BRW 7; CA 160; DLB 27; EWL 3; PAB; RGEL 2

Douglas, Leonard
See Bradbury, Ray (Douglas)

Douglas, Michael
See Crichton, (John) Michael

Douglas, (George) Norman
1868-1952 .... **TCLC 68**
See also BRW 6; CA 119; 157; DLB 34, 195; RGEL 2

Douglas, William
See Brown, George Douglas

Douglass, Frederick 1817(?)-1895 ..... **BLC 1; NCLC 7, 55; WLC**
See also AAYA 48; AFAW 1, 2; AMWC 1; AMWS 3; CDALB 1640-1865; DA; DA3; DAC; DAM MST, MULT; DLB 1, 43, 50, 79, 243; FW; LAIT 2; NCFS 2; RGAL 4; SATA 29

Dourado, (Waldomiro Freitas) Autran
1926- .... **CLC 23, 60**
See also CA 25-28R; 179; CANR 34, 81; DLB 145; HW 2

Dourado, Waldomiro Autran
See Dourado, (Waldomiro Freitas) Autran
See also CA 179

Dove, Rita (Frances) 1952- . **BLCS; CLC 50, 81; PC 6**
See also AAYA 46; AMWS 4; BW 2; CA 109; CAAS 19; CANR 27, 42, 68, 76, 97; CDALBS; CP 7; CSW; CWP; DA3; DAM MULT, POET; DLB 120; EWL 3; EXPP; MTCW 1; PFS 1, 15; RGAL 4

Doveglion
See Villa, Jose Garcia

Dowell, Coleman 1925-1985 .... **CLC 60**
See also CA 25-28R; 117; CANR 10; DLB 130; GLL 2

Dowson, Ernest (Christopher)
1867-1900 .... **TCLC 4**
See also CA 105; 150; DLB 19, 135; RGEL 2

Doyle, A. Conan
See Doyle, Sir Arthur Conan

Doyle, Sir Arthur Conan
1859-1930 .... **SSC 12; TCLC 7; WLC**
See Conan Doyle, Arthur
See also AAYA 14; BRWS 2; CA 104; 122; CDBLB 1890-1914; CMW 4; DA; DA3; DAB; DAC; DAM MST, NOV; DLB 18, 70, 156, 178; EXPS; HGG; LAIT 2; MSW; MTCW 1, 2; RGEL 2; RGSF 2; RHW; SATA 24; SCFW 2; SFW 4; SSFS 2; TEA; WCH; WLIT 4; WYA; YAW

Doyle, Conan
See Doyle, Sir Arthur Conan

Doyle, John
See Graves, Robert (von Ranke)

Doyle, Roddy 1958(?)- .... **CLC 81, 178**
See also AAYA 14; BRWS 5; CA 143; CANR 73; CN 7; DA3; DLB 194

Doyle, Sir A. Conan
See Doyle, Sir Arthur Conan

Dr. A
See Asimov, Isaac; Silverstein, Alvin; Silverstein, Virginia B(arbara Opshelor)

Drabble, Margaret 1939- ...... **CLC 2, 3, 5, 8, 10, 22, 53, 129**
See also BRWS 4; CA 13-16R; CANR 18, 35, 63, 112; CDBLB 1960 to Present; CN 7; CPW; DA3; DAB; DAC; DAM MST, NOV, POP; DLB 14, 155, 231; EWL 3; FW; MTCW 1, 2; RGEL 2; SATA 48; TEA

Drakulic, Slavenka 1949- .... **CLC 173**
See also CA 144; CANR 92

Drakulic-Ilic, Slavenka
See Drakulic, Slavenka

Drapier, M. B.
See Swift, Jonathan

Drayham, James
See Mencken, H(enry) L(ouis)

Drayton, Michael 1563-1631 .... **LC 8**
See also DAM POET; DLB 121; RGEL 2

Dreadstone, Carl
See Campbell, (John) Ramsey

Dreiser, Theodore (Herman Albert)
1871-1945 .... **SSC 30; TCLC 10, 18, 35, 83; WLC**
See also AMW; AMWC 2; AMWR 2; BYA 15, 16; CA 106; 132; CDALB 1865-1917; DA; DA3; DAC; DAM MST, NOV; DLB 9, 12, 102, 137; DLBD 1; EWL 3; LAIT 2; LMFS 2; MTCW 1, 2; NFS 8, 17; RGAL 4; TUS

Drexler, Rosalyn 1926- .... **CLC 2, 6**
See also CA 81-84; CAD; CANR 68, 124; CD 5; CWD

Dreyer, Carl Theodor 1889-1968 ...... **CLC 16**
See also CA 116

Drieu la Rochelle, Pierre(-Eugene)
1893-1945 .... **TCLC 21**
See also CA 117; DLB 72; EWL 3; GFL 1789 to the Present

Drinkwater, John 1882-1937 .... **TCLC 57**
See also CA 109; 149; DLB 10, 19, 149; RGEL 2

Drop Shot
See Cable, George Washington

Droste-Hulshoff, Annette Freiin von
1797-1848 .... **NCLC 3, 133**
See also CDWLB 2; DLB 133; RGSF 2; RGWL 2, 3

Drummond, Walter
See Silverberg, Robert

Drummond, William Henry
1854-1907 .... **TCLC 25**
See also CA 160; DLB 92

Drummond de Andrade, Carlos
1902-1987 .... **CLC 18; TCLC 139**
See Andrade, Carlos Drummond de
See also CA 132; 123; LAW

Drummond of Hawthornden, William
1585-1649 .... **LC 83**
See also DLB 121, 213; RGEL 2

Drury, Allen (Stuart) 1918-1998 .... **CLC 37**
See also CA 57-60; 170; CANR 18, 52; CN 7; INT CANR-18

Dryden, John 1631-1700 ..... **DC 3; LC 3, 21; PC 25; WLC**
See also BRW 2; CDBLB 1660-1789; DA; DAB; DAC; DAM DRAM, MST, POET; DLB 80, 101, 131; EXPP; IDTP; LMFS 1; RGEL 2; TEA; WLIT 3

du Bellay, Joachim 1524-1560 .... **LC 92**
See also GFL Beginnings to 1789; RGWL 2, 3

Duberman, Martin (Bauml) 1930- ..... **CLC 8**
See also CA 1-4R; CAD; CANR 2, 63; CD 5

Dubie, Norman (Evans) 1945- .... **CLC 36**
See also CA 69-72; CANR 12, 115; CP 7; DLB 120; PFS 12

Du Bois, W(illiam) E(dward) B(urghardt)
1868-1963 ..... **BLC 1; CLC 1, 2, 13, 64, 96; HR 2; WLC**
See also AAYA 40; AFAW 1, 2; AMWC 1; AMWS 2; BW 1, 3; CA 85-88; CANR 34, 82; CDALB 1865-1917; DA; DA3; DAC; DAM MST, MULT, NOV; DLB 47, 50, 91, 246, 284; EWL 3; EXPP; LAIT 2; LMFS 2; MTCW 1, 2; NCFS 1; PFS 13; RGAL 4; SATA 42

Dubus, Andre 1936-1999 ..... **CLC 13, 36, 97; SSC 15**
See also AMWS 7; CA 21-24R; 177; CANR 17; CN 7; CSW; DLB 130; INT CANR-17; RGAL 4; SSFS 10

Duca Minimo
See D'Annunzio, Gabriele

Ducharme, Rejean 1941- .... **CLC 74**
See also CA 165; DLB 60

du Chatelet, Emilie 1706-1749 .... **LC 96**

Duchen, Claire .... **CLC 65**

Duclos, Charles Pinot- 1704-1772 .... **LC 1**
See also GFL Beginnings to 1789

Dudek, Louis 1918-2001 .... **CLC 11, 19**
See also CA 45-48; 215; CAAS 14; CANR 1; CP 7; DLB 88

Duerrenmatt, Friedrich 1921-1990 ... **CLC 1, 4, 8, 11, 15, 43, 102**
See Durrenmatt, Friedrich
See also CA 17-20R; CANR 33; CMW 4; DAM DRAM; DLB 69, 124; MTCW 1, 2

Duffy, Bruce 1953(?)- .... **CLC 50**
See also CA 172

Duffy, Maureen 1933- .... **CLC 37**
See also CA 25-28R; CANR 33, 68; CBD; CN 7; CP 7; CWD; CWP; DFS 15; DLB 14; FW; MTCW 1

Du Fu
See Tu Fu
See also RGWL 2, 3

Dugan, Alan 1923-2003 .... **CLC 2, 6**
See also CA 81-84; 220; CANR 119; CP 7; DLB 5; PFS 10

du Gard, Roger Martin
See Martin du Gard, Roger

Duhamel, Georges 1884-1966 .... **CLC 8**
See also CA 81-84; 25-28R; CANR 35; DLB 65; EWL 3; GFL 1789 to the Present; MTCW 1

Dujardin, Edouard (Emile Louis)
1861-1949 .... **TCLC 13**
See also CA 109; DLB 123

Duke, Raoul
See Thompson, Hunter S(tockton)

Dulles, John Foster 1888-1959 .... **TCLC 72**
See also CA 115; 149

Dumas, Alexandre (pere)
1802-1870 .... **NCLC 11, 71; WLC**
See also AAYA 22; BYA 3; DA; DA3; DAB; DAC; DAM MST, NOV; DLB 119, 192; EW 6; GFL 1789 to the Present; LAIT 1, 2; NFS 14; RGWL 2, 3; SATA 18; TWA; WCH

Dumas, Alexandre (fils) 1824-1895 ...... **DC 1; NCLC 9**
See also DLB 192; GFL 1789 to the Present; RGWL 2, 3

Dumas, Claudine
See Malzberg, Barry N(athaniel)

Dumas, Henry L. 1934-1968 .... **CLC 6, 62**
See also BW 1; CA 85-88; DLB 41; RGAL 4

du Maurier, Daphne 1907-1989 .. **CLC 6, 11, 59; SSC 18**
See also AAYA 37; BPFB 1; BRWS 3; CA 5-8R; 128; CANR 6, 55; CMW 4; CPW; DA3; DAB; DAC; DAM MST, POP;

DLB 191; HGG; LAIT 3; MSW; MTCW
1, 2; NFS 12; RGEL 2; RGSF 2; RHW;
SATA 27; SATA-Obit 60; SSFS 14, 16;
TEA

Du Maurier, George 1834-1896 ..... **NCLC 86**
See also DLB 153, 178; RGEL 2

Dunbar, Paul Laurence 1872-1906 ... **BLC 1;
PC 5; SSC 8; TCLC 2, 12; WLC**
See also AFAW 1, 2; AMWS 2; BW 1, 3;
CA 104; 124; CANR 79; CDALB 1865-
1917; DA; DA3; DAC; DAM MST,
MULT, POET; DLB 50, 54, 78; EXPP;
RGAL 4; SATA 34

Dunbar, William 1460(?)-1520(?) .... **LC 20**
See also BRWS 8; DLB 132, 146; RGEL 2

Dunbar-Nelson, Alice .... **HR 2**
See Nelson, Alice Ruth Moore Dunbar

Duncan, Dora Angela
See Duncan, Isadora

Duncan, Isadora 1877(?)-1927 .... **TCLC 68**
See also CA 118; 149

Duncan, Lois 1934- .... **CLC 26**
See also AAYA 4, 34; BYA 6, 8; CA 1-4R;
CANR 2, 23, 36, 111; CLR 29; JRDA;
MAICYA 1, 2; MAICYAS 1; SAAS 2;
SATA 1, 36, 75, 133, 141; SATA-Essay
141; WYA; YAW

Duncan, Robert (Edward)
1919-1988 .... **CLC 1, 2, 4, 7, 15, 41, 55;
PC 2**
See also BG 2; CA 9-12R; 124; CANR 28,
62; DAM POET; DLB 5, 16, 193; EWL
3; MTCW 1, 2; PFS 13; RGAL 4; WP

Duncan, Sara Jeannette
1861-1922 .... **TCLC 60**
See also CA 157; DLB 92

Dunlap, William 1766-1839 .... **NCLC 2**
See also DLB 30, 37, 59; RGAL 4

Dunn, Douglas (Eaglesham) 1942- .... **CLC 6,
40**
See also CA 45-48; CANR 2, 33, 126; CP
7; DLB 40; MTCW 1

Dunn, Katherine (Karen) 1945- .... **CLC 71**
See also CA 33-36R; CANR 72; HGG;
MTCW 1

Dunn, Stephen (Elliott) 1939- .... **CLC 36**
See also AMWS 11; CA 33-36R; CANR
12, 48, 53, 105; CP 7; DLB 105

Dunne, Finley Peter 1867-1936 ...... **TCLC 28**
See also CA 108; 178; DLB 11, 23; RGAL
4

Dunne, John Gregory 1932-2003 ..... **CLC 28**
See also CA 25-28R; CANR 14, 50; CN 7;
DLBY 1980

Dunsany, Lord .... **TCLC 2, 59**
See Dunsany, Edward John Moreton Drax
Plunkett
See also DLB 77, 153, 156, 255; FANT;
IDTP; RGEL 2; SFW 4; SUFW 1

**Dunsany, Edward John Moreton Drax
Plunkett** 1878-1957
See Dunsany, Lord
See also CA 104; 148; DLB 10; MTCW 1

Duns Scotus, John 1266(?)-1308 ... **CMLC 59**
See also DLB 115

du Perry, Jean
See Simenon, Georges (Jacques Christian)

Durang, Christopher (Ferdinand)
1949- .... **CLC 27, 38**
See also CA 105; CAD; CANR 50, 76; CD
5; MTCW 1

Duras, Marguerite 1914-1996 . **CLC 3, 6, 11,
20, 34, 40, 68, 100; SSC 40**
See Donnadieu, Marguerite
See also BPFB 1; CA 25-28R; 151; CANR
50; CWW 2; DLB 83; EWL 3; GFL 1789
to the Present; IDFW 4; MTCW 1, 2;
RGWL 2, 3; TWA

Durban, (Rosa) Pam 1947- .... **CLC 39**
See also CA 123; CANR 98; CSW

Durcan, Paul 1944- .... **CLC 43, 70**
See also CA 134; CANR 123; CP 7; DAM
POET; EWL 3

Durfey, Thomas 1653-1723 .... **LC 94**
See also DLB 80; RGEL 2

Durkheim, Emile 1858-1917 .... **TCLC 55**

Durrell, Lawrence (George)
1912-1990 ..... **CLC 1, 4, 6, 8, 13, 27, 41**
See also BPFB 1; BRWS 1; CA 9-12R; 132;
CANR 40, 77; CDBLB 1945-1960; DAM
NOV; DLB 15, 27, 204; DLBY 1990;
EWL 3; MTCW 1, 2; RGEL 2; SFW 4;
TEA

Durrenmatt, Friedrich
See Duerrenmatt, Friedrich
See also CDWLB 2; EW 13; EWL 3;
RGWL 2, 3

Dutt, Michael Madhusudan
1824-1873 .... **NCLC 118**

Dutt, Toru 1856-1877 .... **NCLC 29**
See also DLB 240

Dwight, Timothy 1752-1817 .... **NCLC 13**
See also DLB 37; RGAL 4

Dworkin, Andrea 1946- .... **CLC 43, 123**
See also CA 77-80; CAAS 21; CANR 16,
39, 76, 96; FW; GLL 1; INT CANR-16;
MTCW 1, 2

Dwyer, Deanna
See Koontz, Dean R(ay)

Dwyer, K. R.
See Koontz, Dean R(ay)

Dybek, Stuart 1942- .... **CLC 114; SSC 55**
See also CA 97-100; CANR 39; DLB 130

Dye, Richard
See De Voto, Bernard (Augustine)

Dyer, Geoff 1958- .... **CLC 149**
See also CA 125; CANR 88

Dyer, George 1755-1841 .... **NCLC 129**
See also DLB 93

Dylan, Bob 1941- .... **CLC 3, 4, 6, 12, 77; PC
37**
See also CA 41-44R; CANR 108; CP 7;
DLB 16

Dyson, John 1943- .... **CLC 70**
See also CA 144

Dzyubin, Eduard Georgievich 1895-1934
See Bagritsky, Eduard
See also CA 170

E. V. L.
See Lucas, E(dward) V(errall)

Eagleton, Terence (Francis) 1943- .. **CLC 63,
132**
See also CA 57-60; CANR 7, 23, 68, 115;
DLB 242; LMFS 2; MTCW 1, 2

Eagleton, Terry
See Eagleton, Terence (Francis)

Early, Jack
See Scoppettone, Sandra
See also GLL 1

East, Michael
See West, Morris L(anglo)

Eastaway, Edward
See Thomas, (Philip) Edward

Eastlake, William (Derry)
1917-1997 .... **CLC 8**
See also CA 5-8R; 158; CAAS 1; CANR 5,
63; CN 7; DLB 6, 206; INT CANR-5;
TCWW 2

Eastman, Charles A(lexander)
1858-1939 .... **NNAL; TCLC 55**
See also CA 179; CANR 91; DAM MULT;
DLB 175; YABC 1

Eaton, Edith Maude 1865-1914 .... **AAL**
See Far, Sui Sin
See also CA 154; DLB 221; FW

Eaton, (Lillie) Winnifred 1875-1954 .... **AAL**
See also CA 217; DLB 221; RGAL 4

Eberhart, Richard (Ghormley)
1904- .... **CLC 3, 11, 19, 56**
See also AMW; CA 1-4R; CANR 2, 125;
CDALB 1941-1968; CP 7; DAM POET;
DLB 48; MTCW 1; RGAL 4

Eberstadt, Fernanda 1960- .... **CLC 39**
See also CA 136; CANR 69

**Echegaray (y Eizaguirre), Jose (Maria
Waldo)** 1832-1916 .... **HLCS 1; TCLC 4**
See also CA 104; CANR 32; EWL 3; HW
1; MTCW 1

Echeverria, (Jose) Esteban (Antonino)
1805-1851 .... **NCLC 18**
See also LAW

Echo
See Proust, (Valentin-Louis-George-Eugene)
Marcel

Eckert, Allan W. 1931- .... **CLC 17**
See also AAYA 18; BYA 2; CA 13-16R;
CANR 14, 45; INT CANR-14; MAICYA
2; MAICYAS 1; SAAS 21; SATA 29, 91;
SATA-Brief 27

Eckhart, Meister 1260(?)-1327(?) ... **CMLC 9**
See also DLB 115; LMFS 1

Eckmar, F. R.
See de Hartog, Jan

Eco, Umberto 1932- .... **CLC 28, 60, 142**
See also BEST 90:1; BPFB 1; CA 77-80;
CANR 12, 33, 55, 110; CPW; CWW 2;
DA3; DAM NOV, POP; DLB 196, 242;
EWL 3; MSW; MTCW 1, 2; RGWL 3

Eddison, E(ric) R(ucker)
1882-1945 .... **TCLC 15**
See also CA 109; 156; DLB 255; FANT;
SFW 4; SUFW 1

Eddy, Mary (Ann Morse) Baker
1821-1910 .... **TCLC 71**
See also CA 113; 174

Edel, (Joseph) Leon 1907-1997 .. **CLC 29, 34**
See also CA 1-4R; 161; CANR 1, 22, 112;
DLB 103; INT CANR-22

Eden, Emily 1797-1869 .... **NCLC 10**

Edgar, David 1948- .... **CLC 42**
See also CA 57-60; CANR 12, 61, 112;
CBD; CD 5; DAM DRAM; DFS 15; DLB
13, 233; MTCW 1

Edgerton, Clyde (Carlyle) 1944- ...... **CLC 39**
See also AAYA 17; CA 118; 134; CANR
64, 125; CSW; DLB 278; INT CA-134;
YAW

Edgeworth, Maria 1768-1849 .... **NCLC 1, 51**
See also BRWS 3; DLB 116, 159, 163; FW;
RGEL 2; SATA 21; TEA; WLIT 3

Edmonds, Paul
See Kuttner, Henry

Edmonds, Walter D(umaux)
1903-1998 .... **CLC 35**
See also BYA 2; CA 5-8R; CANR 2; CWRI
5; DLB 9; LAIT 1; MAICYA 1, 2; RHW;
SAAS 4; SATA 1, 27; SATA-Obit 99

Edmondson, Wallace
See Ellison, Harlan (Jay)

Edson, Russell 1935- .... **CLC 13**
See also CA 33-36R; CANR 115; DLB 244;
WP

Edwards, Bronwen Elizabeth
See Rose, Wendy

Edwards, G(erald) B(asil)
1899-1976 .... **CLC 25**
See also CA 201; 110

Edwards, Gus 1939- .... **CLC 43**
See also CA 108; INT CA-108

Edwards, Jonathan 1703-1758 .... **LC 7, 54**
See also AMW; DA; DAC; DAM MST;
DLB 24, 270; RGAL 4; TUS

Edwards, Sarah Pierpont 1710-1758 .. **LC 87**
See also DLB 200

Efron, Marina Ivanovna Tsvetaeva
See Tsvetaeva (Efron), Marina (Ivanovna)

Endo Shusaku
    See Endo, Shusaku
    See also DLB 182; EWL 3
Engel, Marian 1933-1985 .... **CLC 36; TCLC 137**
    See also CA 25-28R; CANR 12; DLB 53;
    FW; INT CANR-12
Engelhardt, Frederick
    See Hubbard, L(afayette) Ron(ald)
Engels, Friedrich 1820-1895 .. **NCLC 85, 114**
    See also DLB 129; LATS 1
Enright, D(ennis) J(oseph)
    1920-2002 .... **CLC 4, 8, 31**
    See also CA 1-4R; 211; CANR 1, 42, 83;
    CP 7; DLB 27; EWL 3; SATA 25; SATA-
    Obit 140
Enzensberger, Hans Magnus
    1929- .... **CLC 43; PC 28**
    See also CA 116; 119; CANR 103; EWL 3
Ephron, Nora 1941- .... **CLC 17, 31**
    See also AAYA 35; AITN 2; CA 65-68;
    CANR 12, 39, 83
Epicurus 341B.C.-270B.C. .... **CMLC 21**
    See also DLB 176
Epsilon
    See Betjeman, John
Epstein, Daniel Mark 1948- .... **CLC 7**
    See also CA 49-52; CANR 2, 53, 90
Epstein, Jacob 1956- .... **CLC 19**
    See also CA 114
Epstein, Jean 1897-1953 .... **TCLC 92**
Epstein, Joseph 1937- .... **CLC 39**
    See also CA 112; 119; CANR 50, 65, 117
Epstein, Leslie 1938- .... **CLC 27**
    See also AMWS 12; CA 73-76, 215; CAAE
    215; CAAS 12; CANR 23, 69
Equiano, Olaudah 1745(?)-1797 . **BLC 2; LC 16**
    See also AFAW 1, 2; CDWLB 3; DAM
    MULT; DLB 37, 50; WLIT 2
Erasmus, Desiderius 1469(?)-1536 ..... **LC 16, 93**
    See also DLB 136; EW 2; LMFS 1; RGWL
    2, 3; TWA
Erdman, Paul E(mil) 1932- .... **CLC 25**
    See also AITN 1; CA 61-64; CANR 13, 43,
    84
Erdrich, Louise 1954- .... **CLC 39, 54, 120, 176; NNAL; PC 52**
    See also AAYA 10, 47; AMWS 4; BEST
    89:1; BPFB 1; CA 114; CANR 41, 62,
    118; CDALBS; CN 7; CP 7; CPW; CWP;
    DA3; DAM MULT, NOV, POP; DLB 152,
    175, 206; EWL 3; EXPP; LAIT 5; LATS
    1; MTCW 1; NFS 5; PFS 14; RGAL 4;
    SATA 94, 141; SSFS 14; TCWW 2
Erenburg, Ilya (Grigoryevich)
    See Ehrenburg, Ilya (Grigoryevich)
Erickson, Stephen Michael 1950-
    See Erickson, Steve
    See also CA 129; SFW 4
Erickson, Steve .... **CLC 64**
    See Erickson, Stephen Michael
    See also CANR 60, 68; SUFW 2
Erickson, Walter
    See Fast, Howard (Melvin)
Ericson, Walter
    See Fast, Howard (Melvin)
Eriksson, Buntel
    See Bergman, (Ernst) Ingmar
Eriugena, John Scottus c.
    810-877 .... **CMLC 65**
    See also DLB 115
Ernaux, Annie 1940- .... **CLC 88, 184**
    See also CA 147; CANR 93; NCFS 3, 5
Erskine, John 1879-1951 .... **TCLC 84**
    See also CA 112; 159; DLB 9, 102; FANT

Eschenbach, Wolfram von
    See Wolfram von Eschenbach
    See also RGWL 3
Eseki, Bruno
    See Mphahlele, Ezekiel
Esenin, Sergei (Alexandrovich)
    1895-1925 .... **TCLC 4**
    See Yesenin, Sergey
    See also CA 104; RGWL 2, 3
Eshleman, Clayton 1935- .... **CLC 7**
    See also CA 33-36R, 212; CAAE 212;
    CAAS 6; CANR 93; CP 7; DLB 5
Espriella, Don Manuel Alvarez
    See Southey, Robert
Espriu, Salvador 1913-1985 .... **CLC 9**
    See also CA 154; 115; DLB 134; EWL 3
Espronceda, Jose de 1808-1842 ..... **NCLC 39**
Esquivel, Laura 1951(?)- ... **CLC 141; HLCS 1**
    See also AAYA 29; CA 143; CANR 68, 113;
    DA3; DAM NOV; LAIT 3; LMFS 2; MTCW
    1; NFS 5; WLIT 1
Esse, James
    See Stephens, James
Esterbrook, Tom
    See Hubbard, L(afayette) Ron(ald)
Estleman, Loren D. 1952- .... **CLC 48**
    See also AAYA 27; CA 85-88; CANR 27,
    74; CMW 4; CPW; DA3; DAM NOV,
    POP; DLB 226; INT CANR-27; MTCW
    1, 2
Etherege, Sir George 1636-1692 .... **LC 78**
    See also BRW 2; DAM DRAM; DLB 80;
    PAB; RGEL 2
Euclid 306B.C.-283B.C. .... **CMLC 25**
Eugenides, Jeffrey 1960(?)- .... **CLC 81**
    See also AAYA 51; CA 144; CANR 120
Euripides c. 484B.C.-406B.C. .... **CMLC 23, 51; DC 4; WLCS**
    See also AW 1; CDWLB 1; DA; DA3;
    DAB; DAC; DAM DRAM, MST; DFS 1,
    4, 6; DLB 176; LAIT 1; LMFS 1; RGWL
    2, 3
Evan, Evin
    See Faust, Frederick (Schiller)
Evans, Caradoc 1878-1945 ... **SSC 43; TCLC 85**
    See also DLB 162
Evans, Evan
    See Faust, Frederick (Schiller)
    See also TCWW 2
Evans, Marian
    See Eliot, George
Evans, Mary Ann
    See Eliot, George
Evarts, Esther
    See Benson, Sally
Everett, Percival
    See Everett, Percival L.
    See also CSW
Everett, Percival L. 1956- .... **CLC 57**
    See Everett, Percival
    See also BW 2; CA 129; CANR 94
Everson, R(onald) G(ilmour)
    1903-1992 .... **CLC 27**
    See also CA 17-20R; DLB 88
Everson, William (Oliver)
    1912-1994 .... **CLC 1, 5, 14**
    See also BG 2; CA 9-12R; 145; CANR 20;
    DLB 5, 16, 212; MTCW 1
Evtushenko, Evgenii Aleksandrovich
    See Yevtushenko, Yevgeny (Alexandrovich)
    See also RGWL 2, 3
Ewart, Gavin (Buchanan)
    1916-1995 .... **CLC 13, 46**
    See also BRWS 7; CA 89-92; 150; CANR
    17, 46; CP 7; DLB 40; MTCW 1
Ewers, Hanns Heinz 1871-1943 ..... **TCLC 12**
    See also CA 109; 149

Ewing, Frederick R.
    See Sturgeon, Theodore (Hamilton)
Exley, Frederick (Earl) 1929-1992 .... **CLC 6, 11**
    See also AITN 2; BPFB 1; CA 81-84; 138;
    CANR 117; DLB 143; DLBY 1981
Eynhardt, Guillermo
    See Quiroga, Horacio (Sylvestre)
Ezekiel, Nissim 1924-2004 .... **CLC 61**
    See also CA 61-64; CP 7; EWL 3
Ezekiel, Tish O'Dowd 1943- .... **CLC 34**
    See also CA 129
Fadeev, Aleksandr Aleksandrovich
    See Bulgya, Alexander Alexandrovich
    See also DLB 272
Fadeev, Alexandr Alexandrovich
    See Bulgya, Alexander Alexandrovich
    See also EWL 3
Fadeyev, A.
    See Bulgya, Alexander Alexandrovich
Fadeyev, Alexander .... **TCLC 53**
    See Bulgya, Alexander Alexandrovich
Fagen, Donald 1948- .... **CLC 26**
Fainzilberg, Ilya Arnoldovich 1897-1937
    See Ilf, Ilya
    See also CA 120; 165
Fair, Ronald L. 1932- .... **CLC 18**
    See also BW 1; CA 69-72; CANR 25; DLB
    33
Fairbairn, Roger
    See Carr, John Dickson
Fairbairns, Zoe (Ann) 1948- .... **CLC 32**
    See also CA 103; CANR 21, 85; CN 7
Fairfield, Flora
    See Alcott, Louisa May
Fairman, Paul W. 1916-1977
    See Queen, Ellery
    See also CA 114; SFW 4
Falco, Gian
    See Papini, Giovanni
Falconer, James
    See Kirkup, James
Falconer, Kenneth
    See Kornbluth, C(yril) M.
Falkland, Samuel
    See Heijermans, Herman
Fallaci, Oriana 1930- .... **CLC 11, 110**
    See also CA 77-80; CANR 15, 58; FW;
    MTCW 1
Faludi, Susan 1959- .... **CLC 140**
    See also CA 138; CANR 126; FW; MTCW
    1; NCFS 3
Faludy, George 1913- .... **CLC 42**
    See also CA 21-24R
Faludy, Gyoergy
    See Faludy, George
Fanon, Frantz 1925-1961 .... **BLC 2; CLC 74**
    See also BW 1; CA 116; 89-92; DAM
    MULT; DLB 296; LMFS 2; WLIT 2
Fanshawe, Ann 1625-1680 .... **LC 11**
Fante, John (Thomas) 1911-1983 .... **CLC 60; SSC 65**
    See also AMWS 11; CA 69-72; 109; CANR
    23, 104; DLB 130; DLBY 1983
Far, Sui Sin .... **SSC 62**
    See Eaton, Edith Maude
    See also SSFS 4
Farah, Nuruddin 1945- ...... **BLC 2; CLC 53, 137**
    See also AFW; BW 2, 3; CA 106; CANR
    81; CDWLB 3; CN 7; DAM MULT; DLB
    125; EWL 3; WLIT 2
Fargue, Leon-Paul 1876(?)-1947 .... **TCLC 11**
    See also CA 109; CANR 107; DLB 258;
    EWL 3
Farigoule, Louis
    See Romains, Jules

Firbank, Louis 1942-
See Reed, Lou
See also CA 117
Firbank, (Arthur Annesley) Ronald
1886-1926 .... **TCLC 1**
See also BRWS 2; CA 104; 177; DLB 36;
EWL 3; RGEL 2
Fish, Stanley
See Fish, Stanley Eugene
Fish, Stanley E.
See Fish, Stanley Eugene
Fish, Stanley Eugene 1938- .... **CLC 142**
See also CA 112; 132; CANR 90; DLB 67
Fisher, Dorothy (Frances) Canfield
1879-1958 .... **TCLC 87**
See also CA 114; 136; CANR 80; CLR 71,;
CWRI 5; DLB 9, 102, 284; MAICYA 1,
2; YABC 1
Fisher, M(ary) F(rances) K(ennedy)
1908-1992 .... **CLC 76, 87**
See also CA 77-80; 138; CANR 44; MTCW
1
Fisher, Roy 1930- .... **CLC 25**
See also CA 81-84; CAAS 10; CANR 16;
CP 7; DLB 40
Fisher, Rudolph 1897-1934 .... **BLC 2; HR 2;**
SSC 25; TCLC 11
See also BW 1, 3; CA 107; 124; CANR 80;
DAM MULT; DLB 51, 102
Fisher, Vardis (Alvero) 1895-1968 .... **CLC 7;**
TCLC 140
See also CA 5-8R; 25-28R; CANR 68; DLB
9, 206; RGAL 4; TCWW 2
Fiske, Tarleton
See Bloch, Robert (Albert)
Fitch, Clarke
See Sinclair, Upton (Beall)
Fitch, John IV
See Cormier, Robert (Edmund)
Fitzgerald, Captain Hugh
See Baum, L(yman) Frank
FitzGerald, Edward 1809-1883 .... **NCLC 9**
See also BRW 4; DLB 32; RGEL 2
Fitzgerald, F(rancis) Scott (Key)
1896-1940 ... **SSC 6, 31; TCLC 1, 6, 14,**
28, 55; WLC
See also AAYA 24; AITN 1; AMW; AMWC
2; AMWR 1; BPFB 1; CA 110; 123;
CDALB 1917-1929; DA; DA3; DAB;
DAC; DAM MST, NOV; DLB 4, 9, 86,
219; DLBD 1, 15, 16, 273; DLBY 1981;
1996; EWL 3; EXPN; EXPS; LAIT 3;
MTCW 1, 2; NFS 2; RGAL 4; RGSF 2;
SSFS 4, 15; TUS
Fitzgerald, Penelope 1916-2000 . **CLC 19, 51,**
61, 143
See also BRWS 5; CA 85-88; 190; CAAS
10; CANR 56, 86; CN 7; DLB 14, 194;
EWL 3; MTCW 2
Fitzgerald, Robert (Stuart)
1910-1985 .... **CLC 39**
See also CA 1-4R; 114; CANR 1; DLBY
1980
FitzGerald, Robert D(avid)
1902-1987 .... **CLC 19**
See also CA 17-20R; DLB 260; RGEL 2
Fitzgerald, Zelda (Sayre)
1900-1948 .... **TCLC 52**
See also AMWS 9; CA 117; 126; DLBY
1984
Flanagan, Thomas (James Bonner)
1923-2002 .... **CLC 25, 52**
See also CA 108; 206; CANR 55; CN 7;
DLBY 1980; INT CA-108; MTCW 1;
RHW

Flaubert, Gustave 1821-1880 .... **NCLC 2, 10,**
19, 62, 66, 135; SSC 11, 60; WLC
See also DA; DA3; DAB; DAC; DAM
MST, NOV; DLB 119; EW 7; EXPS; GFL
1789 to the Present; LAIT 2; LMFS 1;
NFS 14; RGSF 2; RGWL 2, 3; SSFS 6;
TWA
Flavius Josephus
See Josephus, Flavius
Flecker, Herman Elroy
See Flecker, (Herman) James Elroy
Flecker, (Herman) James Elroy
1884-1915 .... **TCLC 43**
See also CA 109; 150; DLB 10, 19; RGEL
2
Fleming, Ian (Lancaster) 1908-1964 . **CLC 3,**
30
See also AAYA 26; BPFB 1; CA 5-8R;
CANR 59; CDBLB 1945-1960; CMW 4;
CPW; DA3; DAM POP; DLB 87, 201;
MSW; MTCW 1, 2; RGEL 2; SATA 9;
TEA; YAW
Fleming, Thomas (James) 1927- ...... **CLC 37**
See also CA 5-8R; CANR 10, 102; INT
CANR-10; SATA 8
Fletcher, John 1579-1625 .... **DC 6; LC 33**
See also BRW 2; CDBLB Before 1660;
DLB 58; RGEL 2; TEA
Fletcher, John Gould 1886-1950 .... **TCLC 35**
See also CA 107; 167; DLB 4, 45; LMFS
2; RGAL 4
Fleur, Paul
See Pohl, Frederik
Flooglebuckle, Al
See Spiegelman, Art
Flora, Fletcher 1914-1969
See Queen, Ellery
See also CA 1-4R; CANR 3, 85
Flying Officer X
See Bates, H(erbert) E(rnest)
Fo, Dario 1926- .... **CLC 32, 109; DC 10**
See also CA 116; 128; CANR 68, 114;
CWW 2; DA3; DAM DRAM; DLBY
1997; EWL 3; MTCW 1, 2
Fogarty, Jonathan Titulescu Esq.
See Farrell, James T(homas)
Follett, Ken(neth Martin) 1949- .... **CLC 18**
See also AAYA 6, 50; BEST 89:4; BPFB 1;
CA 81-84; CANR 13, 33, 54, 102; CMW
4; CPW; DA3; DAM NOV, POP; DLB
87; DLBY 1981; INT CANR-33; MTCW
1
Fontane, Theodor 1819-1898 .... **NCLC 26**
See also CDWLB 2; DLB 129; EW 6;
RGWL 2, 3; TWA
Fontenot, Chester .... **CLC 65**
Fonvizin, Denis Ivanovich
1744(?)-1792 .... **LC 81**
See also DLB 150; RGWL 2, 3
Foote, Horton 1916- .... **CLC 51, 91**
See also CA 73-76; CAD; CANR 34, 51,
110; CD 5; CSW; DA3; DAM DRAM;
DLB 26, 266; EWL 3; INT CANR-34
Foote, Mary Hallock 1847-1938 .. **TCLC 108**
See also DLB 186, 188, 202, 221
Foote, Shelby 1916- .... **CLC 75**
See also AAYA 40; CA 5-8R; CANR 3, 45,
74; CN 7; CPW; CSW; DA3; DAM NOV,
POP; DLB 2, 17; MTCW 2; RHW
Forbes, Cosmo
See Lewton, Val
Forbes, Esther 1891-1967 .... **CLC 12**
See also AAYA 17; BYA 2; CA 13-14; 25-
28R; CAP 1; CLR 27; DLB 22; JRDA;
MAICYA 1, 2; RHW; SATA 2, 100; YAW

Forche, Carolyn (Louise) 1950- .... **CLC 25,**
83, 86; PC 10
See also CA 109; 117; CANR 50, 74; CP 7;
CWP; DA3; DAM POET; DLB 5, 193;
INT CA-117; MTCW 1; PFS 18; RGAL 4
Ford, Elbur
See Hibbert, Eleanor Alice Burford
Ford, Ford Madox 1873-1939 ... **TCLC 1, 15,**
39, 57
See Chaucer, Daniel
See also BRW 6; CA 104; 132; CANR 74;
CDBLB 1914-1945; DA3; DAM NOV;
DLB 34, 98, 162; EWL 3; MTCW 1, 2;
RGEL 2; TEA
Ford, Henry 1863-1947 .... **TCLC 73**
See also CA 115; 148
Ford, Jack
See Ford, John
Ford, John 1586-1639 .... **DC 8; LC 68**
See also BRW 2; CDBLB Before 1660;
DA3; DAM DRAM; DFS 7; DLB 58;
IDTP; RGEL 2
Ford, John 1895-1973 .... **CLC 16**
See also CA 187; 45-48
Ford, Richard 1944- .... **CLC 46, 99**
See also AMWS 5; CA 69-72; CANR 11,
47, 86; CN 7; CSW; DLB 227; EWL 3;
MTCW 1; RGAL 4; RGSF 2
Ford, Webster
See Masters, Edgar Lee
Foreman, Richard 1937- .... **CLC 50**
See also CA 65-68; CAD; CANR 32, 63;
CD 5
Forester, C(ecil) S(cott) 1899-1966 ... **CLC 35**
See also CA 73-76; 25-28R; CANR 83;
DLB 191; RGEL 2; RHW; SATA 13
Forez
See Mauriac, Francois (Charles)
Forman, James
See Forman, James D(ouglas)
Forman, James D(ouglas) 1932- .... **CLC 21**
See also AAYA 17; CA 9-12R; CANR 4,
19, 42; JRDA; MAICYA 1, 2; SATA 8,
70; YAW
Forman, Milos 1932- .... **CLC 164**
See also CA 109
Fornes, Maria Irene 1930- .... **CLC 39, 61,**
187; DC 10; HLCS 1
See also CA 25-28R; CAD; CANR 28, 81;
CD 5; CWD; DLB 7; HW 1, 2; INT
CANR-28; LLW 1; MTCW 1; RGAL 4
Forrest, Leon (Richard)
1937-1997 .... **BLCS; CLC 4**
See also AFAW 2; BW 2; CA 89-92; 162;
CAAS 7; CANR 25, 52, 87; CN 7; DLB
33
Forster, E(dward) M(organ)
1879-1970 ...... **CLC 1, 2, 3, 4, 9, 10, 13,**
15, 22, 45, 77; SSC 27; TCLC 125;
WLC
See also AAYA 2, 37; BRW 6; BRWR 2;
BYA 12; CA 13-14; 25-28R; CANR 45;
CAP 1; CDBLB 1914-1945; DA; DA3;
DAB; DAC; DAM MST, NOV; DLB 34,
98, 162, 178, 195; DLBD 10; EWL 3;
EXPN; LAIT 3; LMFS 1; MTCW 1, 2;
NCFS 1; NFS 3, 10, 11; RGEL 2; RGSF
2; SATA 57; SUFW 1; TEA; WLIT 4
Forster, John 1812-1876 .... **NCLC 11**
See also DLB 144, 184
Forster, Margaret 1938- .... **CLC 149**
See also CA 133; CANR 62, 115; CN 7;
DLB 155, 271
Forsyth, Frederick 1938- .... **CLC 2, 5, 36**
See also BEST 89:4; CA 85-88; CANR 38,
62, 115; CMW 4; CN 7; CPW; DAM
NOV, POP; DLB 87; MTCW 1, 2

Forten, Charlotte L. 1837-1914 .... **BLC 2; TCLC 16**
See Grimke, Charlotte L(ottie) Forten
See also DLB 50, 239

Fortinbras
See Grieg, (Johan) Nordahl (Brun)

Foscolo, Ugo 1778-1827 .... **NCLC 8, 97**
See also EW 5

Fosse, Bob .... **CLC 20**
See Fosse, Robert Louis

Fosse, Robert Louis 1927-1987
See Fosse, Bob
See also CA 110; 123

Foster, Hannah Webster
1758-1840 .... **NCLC 99**
See also DLB 37, 200; RGAL 4

Foster, Stephen Collins
1826-1864 .... **NCLC 26**
See also RGAL 4

Foucault, Michel 1926-1984 . **CLC 31, 34, 69**
See also CA 105; 113; CANR 34; DLB 242;
EW 13; EWL 3; GFL 1789 to the Present;
GLL 1; LMFS 2; MTCW 1, 2; TWA

**Fouque, Friedrich (Heinrich Karl) de la
Motte** 1777-1843 .... **NCLC 2**
See also DLB 90; RGWL 2, 3; SUFW 1

Fourier, Charles 1772-1837 .... **NCLC 51**

Fournier, Henri-Alban 1886-1914
See Alain-Fournier
See also CA 104; 179

Fournier, Pierre 1916- .... **CLC 11**
See Gascar, Pierre
See also CA 89-92; CANR 16, 40

Fowles, John (Robert) 1926- . **CLC 1, 2, 3, 4,
6, 9, 10, 15, 33, 87; SSC 33**
See also BPFB 1; BRWS 1; CA 5-8R;
CANR 25, 71, 103; CDBLB 1960 to
Present; CN 7; DA3; DAB; DAC; DAM
MST; DLB 14, 139, 207; EWL 3; HGG;
MTCW 1, 2; RGEL 2; RHW; SATA 22;
TEA; WLIT 4

Fox, Paula 1923- .... **CLC 2, 8, 121**
See also AAYA 3, 37; BYA 3, 8; CA 73-76;
CANR 20, 36, 62, 105; CLR 1, 44, 96;
DLB 52; JRDA; MAICYA 1, 2; MTCW
1; NFS 12; SATA 17, 60, 120; WYA;
YAW

Fox, William Price (Jr.) 1926- .... **CLC 22**
See also CA 17-20R; CAAS 19; CANR 11;
CSW; DLB 2; DLBY 1981

Foxe, John 1517(?)-1587 .... **LC 14**
See also DLB 132

Frame, Janet .. **CLC 2, 3, 6, 22, 66, 96; SSC
29**
See Clutha, Janet Paterson Frame
See also CN 7; CWP; EWL 3; RGEL 2;
RGSF 2; TWA

France, Anatole .... **TCLC 9**
See Thibault, Jacques Anatole Francois
See also DLB 123; EWL 3; GFL 1789 to
the Present; MTCW 1; RGWL 2, 3;
SUFW 1

Francis, Claude .... **CLC 50**
See also CA 192

Francis, Dick 1920- .... **CLC 2, 22, 42, 102**
See also AAYA 5, 21; BEST 89:3; BPFB 1;
CA 5-8R; CANR 9, 42, 68, 100; CDBLB
1960 to Present; CMW 4; CN 7; DA3;
DAM POP; DLB 87; INT CANR-9;
MSW; MTCW 1, 2

Francis, Robert (Churchill)
1901-1987 .... **CLC 15; PC 34**
See also AMWS 9; CA 1-4R; 123; CANR
1; EXPP; PFS 12

Francis, Lord Jeffrey
See Jeffrey, Francis
See also DLB 107

Frank, Anne(lies Marie)
1929-1945 .... **TCLC 17; WLC**
See also AAYA 12; BYA 1; CA 113; 133;
CANR 68; DA; DA3; DAB; DAC; DAM
MST; LAIT 4; MAICYA 2; MAICYAS 1;
MTCW 1, 2; NCFS 2; SATA 87; SATA-
Brief 42; WYA; YAW

Frank, Bruno 1887-1945 .... **TCLC 81**
See also CA 189; DLB 118; EWL 3

Frank, Elizabeth 1945- .... **CLC 39**
See also CA 121; 126; CANR 78; INT CA-
126

Frankl, Viktor E(mil) 1905-1997 ...... **CLC 93**
See also CA 65-68; 161

Franklin, Benjamin
See Hasek, Jaroslav (Matej Frantisek)

Franklin, Benjamin 1706-1790 .... **LC 25;
WLCS**
See also AMW; CDALB 1640-1865; DA;
DA3; DAB; DAC; DAM MST; DLB 24,
43, 73, 183; LAIT 1; RGAL 4; TUS

**Franklin, (Stella Maria Sarah) Miles
(Lampe)** 1879-1954 .... **TCLC 7**
See also CA 104; 164; DLB 230; FW;
MTCW 2; RGEL 2; TWA

Fraser, Antonia (Pakenham) 1932- . **CLC 32,
107**
See also CA 85-88; CANR 44, 65, 119;
CMW; DLB 276; MTCW 1, 2; SATA-
Brief 32

Fraser, George MacDonald 1925- ...... **CLC 7**
See also AAYA 48; CA 45-48, 180; CAAE
180; CANR 2, 48, 74; MTCW 1; RHW

Fraser, Sylvia 1935- .... **CLC 64**
See also CA 45-48; CANR 1, 16, 60; CCA
1

Frayn, Michael 1933- . **CLC 3, 7, 31, 47, 176**
See also BRWC 2; BRWS 7; CA 5-8R;
CANR 30, 69, 114; CBD; CD 5; CN 7;
DAM DRAM, NOV; DLB 13, 14, 194,
245; FANT; MTCW 1, 2; SFW 4

Fraze, Candida (Merrill) 1945- .... **CLC 50**
See also CA 126

Frazer, Andrew
See Marlowe, Stephen

Frazer, J(ames) G(eorge)
1854-1941 .... **TCLC 32**
See also BRWS 3; CA 118; NCFS 5

Frazer, Robert Caine
See Creasey, John

Frazer, Sir James George
See Frazer, J(ames) G(eorge)

Frazier, Charles 1950- .... **CLC 109**
See also AAYA 34; CA 161; CANR 126;
CSW; DLB 292

Frazier, Ian 1951- .... **CLC 46**
See also CA 130; CANR 54, 93

Frederic, Harold 1856-1898 .... **NCLC 10**
See also AMW; DLB 12, 23; DLBD 13;
RGAL 4

Frederick, John
See Faust, Frederick (Schiller)
See also TCWW 2

Frederick the Great 1712-1786 .... **LC 14**

Fredro, Aleksander 1793-1876 .... **NCLC 8**

Freeling, Nicolas 1927-2003 .... **CLC 38**
See also CA 49-52; 218; CAAS 12; CANR
1, 17, 50, 84; CMW 4; CN 7; DLB 87

Freeman, Douglas Southall
1886-1953 .... **TCLC 11**
See also CA 109; 195; DLB 17; DLBD 17

Freeman, Judith 1946- .... **CLC 55**
See also CA 148; CANR 120; DLB 256

Freeman, Mary E(leanor) Wilkins
1852-1930 .... **SSC 1, 47; TCLC 9**
See also CA 106; 177; DLB 12, 78, 221;
EXPS; FW; HGG; MAWW; RGAL 4;
RGSF 2; SSFS 4, 8; SUFW 1; TUS

Freeman, R(ichard) Austin
1862-1943 .... **TCLC 21**
See also CA 113; CANR 84; CMW 4; DLB
70

French, Albert 1943- .... **CLC 86**
See also BW 3; CA 167

French, Antonia
See Kureishi, Hanif

French, Marilyn 1929- .. **CLC 10, 18, 60, 177**
See also BPFB 1; CA 69-72; CANR 3, 31;
CN 7; CPW; DAM DRAM, NOV, POP;
FW; INT CANR-31; MTCW 1, 2

French, Paul
See Asimov, Isaac

Freneau, Philip Morin 1752-1832 .. **NCLC 1,
111**
See also AMWS 2; DLB 37, 43; RGAL 4

Freud, Sigmund 1856-1939 .... **TCLC 52**
See also CA 115; 133; CANR 69; DLB 296;
EW 8; EWL 3; LATS 1; MTCW 1, 2;
NCFS 3; TWA

Freytag, Gustav 1816-1895 .... **NCLC 109**
See also DLB 129

Friedan, Betty (Naomi) 1921- .... **CLC 74**
See also CA 65-68; CANR 18, 45, 74; DLB
246; FW; MTCW 1, 2; NCFS 5

Friedlander, Saul 1932- .... **CLC 90**
See also CA 117; 130; CANR 72

Friedman, B(ernard) H(arper)
1926- .... **CLC 7**
See also CA 1-4R; CANR 3, 48

Friedman, Bruce Jay 1930- ...... **CLC 3, 5, 56**
See also CA 9-12R; CAD; CANR 25, 52,
101; CD 5; CN 7; DLB 2, 28, 244; INT
CANR-25; SSFS 18

Friel, Brian 1929- .... **CLC 5, 42, 59, 115; DC
8**
See also BRWS 5; CA 21-24R; CANR 33,
69; CBD; CD 5; DFS 11; DLB 13; EWL
3; MTCW 1; RGEL 2; TEA

Friis-Baastad, Babbis Ellinor
1921-1970 .... **CLC 12**
See also CA 17-20R; 134; SATA 7

Frisch, Max (Rudolf) 1911-1991 ... **CLC 3, 9,
14, 18, 32, 44; TCLC 121**
See also CA 85-88; 134; CANR 32, 74; CD-
WLB 2; DAM DRAM, NOV; DLB 69,
124; EW 13; EWL 3; MTCW 1, 2; RGWL
2, 3

Fromentin, Eugene (Samuel Auguste)
1820-1876 .... **NCLC 10, 125**
See also DLB 123; GFL 1789 to the Present

Frost, Frederick
See Faust, Frederick (Schiller)
See also TCWW 2

Frost, Robert (Lee) 1874-1963 .. **CLC 1, 3, 4,
9, 10, 13, 15, 26, 34, 44; PC 1, 39;
WLC**
See also AAYA 21; AMW; AMWR 1; CA
89-92; CANR 33; CDALB 1917-1929;
CLR 67; DA; DA3; DAB; DAC; DAM
MST, POET; DLB 54, 284; DLBD 7;
EWL 3; EXPP; MTCW 1, 2; PAB; PFS 1,
2, 3, 4, 5, 6, 7, 10, 13; RGAL 4; SATA
14; TUS; WP; WYA

Froude, James Anthony
1818-1894 .... **NCLC 43**
See also DLB 18, 57, 144

Froy, Herald
See Waterhouse, Keith (Spencer)

Fry, Christopher 1907- .... **CLC 2, 10, 14**
See also BRWS 3; CA 17-20R; CAAS 23;
CANR 9, 30, 74; CBD; CD 5; CP 7; DAM
DRAM; DLB 13; EWL 3; MTCW 1, 2;
RGEL 2; SATA 66; TEA

Granzotto, Giovanni Battista
1914-1985 .... **CLC 70**
See also CA 166

Grass, Guenter (Wilhelm) 1927- ... **CLC 1, 2, 4, 6, 11, 15, 22, 32, 49, 88; WLC**
See also BPFB 2; CA 13-16R; CANR 20, 75, 93; CDWLB 2; DA; DA3; DAB; DAC; DAM MST, NOV; DLB 75, 124; EW 13; EWL 3; MTCW 1, 2; RGWL 2, 3; TWA

Gratton, Thomas
See Hulme, T(homas) E(rnest)

Grau, Shirley Ann 1929- .... **CLC 4, 9, 146; SSC 15**
See also CA 89-92; CANR 22, 69; CN 7; CSW; DLB 2, 218; INT CA-89-92, CANR-22; MTCW 1

Gravel, Fern
See Hall, James Norman

Graver, Elizabeth 1964- .... **CLC 70**
See also CA 135; CANR 71

Graves, Richard Perceval
1895-1985 .... **CLC 44**
See also CA 65-68; CANR 9, 26, 51

Graves, Robert (von Ranke)
1895-1985 .. **CLC 1, 2, 6, 11, 39, 44, 45; PC 6**
See also BPFB 2; BRW 7; BYA 4; CA 5-8R; 117; CANR 5, 36; CDBLB 1914-1945; DA3; DAB; DAC; DAM MST, POET; DLB 20, 100, 191; DLBD 18; DLBY 1985; EWL 3; LATS 1; MTCW 1, 2; NCFS 2; RGEL 2; RHW; SATA 45; TEA

Graves, Valerie
See Bradley, Marion Zimmer

Gray, Alasdair (James) 1934- .... **CLC 41**
See also BRWS 9; CA 126; CANR 47, 69, 106; CN 7; DLB 194, 261; HGG; INT CA-126; MTCW 1, 2; RGSF 2; SUFW 2

Gray, Amlin 1946- .... **CLC 29**
See also CA 138

Gray, Francine du Plessix 1930- ..... **CLC 22, 153**
See also BEST 90:3; CA 61-64; CAAS 2; CANR 11, 33, 75, 81; DAM NOV; INT CANR-11; MTCW 1, 2

Gray, John (Henry) 1866-1934 ...... **TCLC 19**
See also CA 119; 162; RGEL 2

Gray, Simon (James Holliday)
1936- .... **CLC 9, 14, 36**
See also AITN 1; CA 21-24R; CAAS 3; CANR 32, 69; CD 5; DLB 13; EWL 3; MTCW 1; RGEL 2

Gray, Spalding 1941-2004 .... **CLC 49, 112; DC 7**
See also CA 128; CAD; CANR 74; CD 5; CPW; DAM POP; MTCW 2

Gray, Thomas 1716-1771 .... **LC 4, 40; PC 2; WLC**
See also BRW 3; CDBLB 1660-1789; DA; DA3; DAB; DAC; DAM MST; DLB 109; EXPP; PAB; PFS 9; RGEL 2; TEA; WP

Grayson, David
See Baker, Ray Stannard

Grayson, Richard (A.) 1951- .... **CLC 38**
See also CA 85-88, 210; CAAE 210; CANR 14, 31, 57; DLB 234

Greeley, Andrew M(oran) 1928- ...... **CLC 28**
See also BPFB 2; CA 5-8R; CAAS 7; CANR 7, 43, 69, 104; CMW 4; CPW; DA3; DAM POP; MTCW 1, 2

Green, Anna Katharine
1846-1935 .... **TCLC 63**
See also CA 112; 159; CMW 4; DLB 202, 221; MSW

Green, Brian
See Card, Orson Scott

Green, Hannah
See Greenberg, Joanne (Goldenberg)

Green, Hannah 1927(?)-1996 .... **CLC 3**
See also CA 73-76; CANR 59, 93; NFS 10

Green, Henry .... **CLC 2, 13, 97**
See Yorke, Henry Vincent
See also BRWS 2; CA 175; DLB 15; EWL 3; RGEL 2

Green, Julian (Hartridge) 1900-1998
See Green, Julien
See also CA 21-24R; 169; CANR 33, 87; DLB 4, 72; MTCW 1

Green, Julien .... **CLC 3, 11, 77**
See Green, Julian (Hartridge)
See also EWL 3; GFL 1789 to the Present; MTCW 2

Green, Paul (Eliot) 1894-1981 .... **CLC 25**
See also AITN 1; CA 5-8R; 103; CANR 3; DAM DRAM; DLB 7, 9, 249; DLBY 1981; RGAL 4

Greenaway, Peter 1942- .... **CLC 159**
See also CA 127

Greenberg, Ivan 1908-1973
See Rahv, Philip
See also CA 85-88

Greenberg, Joanne (Goldenberg)
1932- .... **CLC 7, 30**
See also AAYA 12; CA 5-8R; CANR 14, 32, 69; CN 7; SATA 25; YAW

Greenberg, Richard 1959(?)- .... **CLC 57**
See also CA 138; CAD; CD 5

Greenblatt, Stephen J(ay) 1943- ...... **CLC 70**
See also CA 49-52; CANR 115

Greene, Bette 1934- .... **CLC 30**
See also AAYA 7; BYA 3; CA 53-56; CANR 4; CLR 2; CWRI 5; JRDA; LAIT 4; MAICYA 1, 2; NFS 10; SAAS 16; SATA 8, 102; WYA; YAW

Greene, Gael .... **CLC 8**
See also CA 13-16R; CANR 10

Greene, Graham (Henry)
1904-1991 .... **CLC 1, 3, 6, 9, 14, 18, 27, 37, 70, 72, 125; SSC 29; WLC**
See also AITN 2; BPFB 2; BRWR 2; BRWS 1; BYA 3; CA 13-16R; 133; CANR 35, 61; CBD; CDBLB 1945-1960; CMW 4; DA; DA3; DAB; DAC; DAM MST, NOV; DLB 13, 15, 77, 100, 162, 201, 204; DLBY 1991; EWL 3; MSW; MTCW 1, 2; NFS 16; RGEL 2; SATA 20; SSFS 14; TEA; WLIT 4

Greene, Robert 1558-1592 .... **LC 41**
See also BRWS 8; DLB 62, 167; IDTP; RGEL 2; TEA

Greer, Germaine 1939- .... **CLC 131**
See also AITN 1; CA 81-84; CANR 33, 70, 115; FW; MTCW 1, 2

Greer, Richard
See Silverberg, Robert

Gregor, Arthur 1923- .... **CLC 9**
See also CA 25-28R; CAAS 10; CANR 11; CP 7; SATA 36

Gregor, Lee
See Pohl, Frederik

Gregory, Lady Isabella Augusta (Persse)
1852-1932 .... **TCLC 1**
See also BRW 6; CA 104; 184; DLB 10; IDTP; RGEL 2

Gregory, J. Dennis
See Williams, John A(lfred)

Grekova, I. .... **CLC 59**

Grendon, Stephen
See Derleth, August (William)

Grenville, Kate 1950- .... **CLC 61**
See also CA 118; CANR 53, 93

Grenville, Pelham
See Wodehouse, P(elham) G(renville)

Greve, Felix Paul (Berthold Friedrich)
1879-1948
See Grove, Frederick Philip
See also CA 104; 141; 175; CANR 79; DAC; DAM MST

Greville, Fulke 1554-1628 .... **LC 79**
See also DLB 62, 172; RGEL 2

Grey, Lady Jane 1537-1554 .... **LC 93**
See also DLB 132

Grey, Zane 1872-1939 .... **TCLC 6**
See also BPFB 2; CA 104; 132; DA3; DAM POP; DLB 9, 212; MTCW 1, 2; RGAL 4; TCWW 2; TUS

Griboedov, Aleksandr Sergeevich
1795(?)-1829 .... **NCLC 129**
See also DLB 205; RGWL 2, 3

Grieg, (Johan) Nordahl (Brun)
1902-1943 .... **TCLC 10**
See also CA 107; 189; EWL 3

Grieve, C(hristopher) M(urray)
1892-1978 .... **CLC 11, 19**
See MacDiarmid, Hugh; Pteleon
See also CA 5-8R; 85-88; CANR 33, 107; DAM POET; MTCW 1; RGEL 2

Griffin, Gerald 1803-1840 .... **NCLC 7**
See also DLB 159; RGEL 2

Griffin, John Howard 1920-1980 ..... **CLC 68**
See also AITN 1; CA 1-4R; 101; CANR 2

Griffin, Peter 1942- .... **CLC 39**
See also CA 136

Griffith, D(avid Lewelyn) W(ark)
1875(?)-1948 .... **TCLC 68**
See also CA 119; 150; CANR 80

Griffith, Lawrence
See Griffith, D(avid Lewelyn) W(ark)

Griffiths, Trevor 1935- .... **CLC 13, 52**
See also CA 97-100; CANR 45; CBD; CD 5; DLB 13, 245

Griggs, Sutton (Elbert)
1872-1930 .... **TCLC 77**
See also CA 123; 186; DLB 50

Grigson, Geoffrey (Edward Harvey)
1905-1985 .... **CLC 7, 39**
See also CA 25-28R; 118; CANR 20, 33; DLB 27; MTCW 1, 2

Grile, Dod
See Bierce, Ambrose (Gwinett)

Grillparzer, Franz 1791-1872 .... **DC 14; NCLC 1, 102; SSC 37**
See also CDWLB 2; DLB 133; EW 5; RGWL 2, 3; TWA

Grimble, Reverend Charles James
See Eliot, T(homas) S(tearns)

Grimke, Angelina (Emily) Weld
1880-1958 .... **HR 2**
See Weld, Angelina (Emily) Grimke
See also BW 1; CA 124; DAM POET; DLB 50, 54

Grimke, Charlotte L(ottie) Forten
1837(?)-1914
See Forten, Charlotte L.
See also BW 1; CA 117; 124; DAM MULT, POET

Grimm, Jacob Ludwig Karl
1785-1863 .... **NCLC 3, 77; SSC 36**
See also DLB 90; MAICYA 1, 2; RGSF 2; RGWL 2, 3; SATA 22; WCH

Grimm, Wilhelm Karl 1786-1859 .. **NCLC 3, 77; SSC 36**
See also CDWLB 2; DLB 90; MAICYA 1, 2; RGSF 2; RGWL 2, 3; SATA 22; WCH

Grimmelshausen, Hans Jakob Christoffel von
See Grimmelshausen, Johann Jakob Christoffel von
See also RGWL 2, 3

Haig-Brown, Roderick (Langmere)
1908-1976 .... **CLC 21**
See also CA 5-8R; 69-72; CANR 4, 38, 83;
CLR 31; CWRI 5; DLB 88; MAICYA 1,
2; SATA 12

Haight, Rip
See Carpenter, John (Howard)

Hailey, Arthur 1920- .... **CLC 5**
See also AITN 2; BEST 90:3; BPFB 2; CA
1-4R; CANR 2, 36, 75; CCA 1; CN 7;
CPW; DAM NOV, POP; DLB 88; DLBY
1982; MTCW 1, 2

Hailey, Elizabeth Forsythe 1938- ..... **CLC 40**
See also CA 93-96, 188; CAAE 188; CAAS
1; CANR 15, 48; INT CANR-15

Haines, John (Meade) 1924- .... **CLC 58**
See also AMWS 12; CA 17-20R; CANR
13, 34; CSW; DLB 5, 212

Hakluyt, Richard 1552-1616 .... **LC 31**
See also DLB 136; RGEL 2

Haldeman, Joe (William) 1943- .... **CLC 61**
See Graham, Robert
See also AAYA 38; CA 53-56, 179; CAAE
179; CAAS 25; CANR 6, 70, 72; DLB 8;
INT CANR-6; SCFW 2; SFW 4

Hale, Janet Campbell 1947- .... **NNAL**
See also CA 49-52; CANR 45, 75; DAM
MULT; DLB 175; MTCW 2

Hale, Sarah Josepha (Buell)
1788-1879 .... **NCLC 75**
See also DLB 1, 42, 73, 243

Halevy, Elie 1870-1937 .... **TCLC 104**

Haley, Alex(ander Murray Palmer)
1921-1992 .... **BLC 2; CLC 8, 12, 76;
TCLC 147**
See also AAYA 26; BPFB 2; BW 2, 3; CA
77-80; 136; CANR 61; CDALBS; CPW;
CSW; DA; DA3; DAB; DAC; DAM MST,
MULT, POP; DLB 38; LAIT 5; MTCW
1, 2; NFS 9

Haliburton, Thomas Chandler
1796-1865 .... **NCLC 15**
See also DLB 11, 99; RGEL 2; RGSF 2

Hall, Donald (Andrew, Jr.) 1928- ...... **CLC 1,
13, 37, 59, 151**
See also CA 5-8R; CAAS 7; CANR 2, 44,
64, 106; CP 7; DAM POET; DLB 5;
MTCW 1; RGAL 4; SATA 23, 97

Hall, Frederic Sauser
See Sauser-Hall, Frederic

Hall, James
See Kuttner, Henry

Hall, James Norman 1887-1951 ..... **TCLC 23**
See also CA 123; 173; LAIT 1; RHW 1;
SATA 21

Hall, Joseph 1574-1656 .... **LC 91**
See also DLB 121, 151; RGEL 2

Hall, (Marguerite) Radclyffe
1880-1943 .... **TCLC 12**
See also BRWS 6; CA 110; 150; CANR 83;
DLB 191; MTCW 2; RGEL 2; RHW

Hall, Rodney 1935- .... **CLC 51**
See also CA 109; CANR 69; CN 7; CP 7;
DLB 289

Hallam, Arthur Henry
1811-1833 .... **NCLC 110**
See also DLB 32

Halldor Kiljan Gudjonsson 1902-1998
See Halldor Laxness
See also CA 103; 164; CWW 2

Halldor Laxness .... **CLC 25**
See Halldor Kiljan Gudjonsson
See also DLB 293; EW 12; EWL 3; RGWL
2, 3

Halleck, Fitz-Greene 1790-1867 .... **NCLC 47**
See also DLB 3, 250; RGAL 4

Halliday, Michael
See Creasey, John

Halpern, Daniel 1945- .... **CLC 14**
See also CA 33-36R; CANR 93; CP 7

Hamburger, Michael (Peter Leopold)
1924- .... **CLC 5, 14**
See also CA 5-8R, 196; CAAE 196; CAAS
4; CANR 2, 47; CP 7; DLB 27

Hamill, Pete 1935- .... **CLC 10**
See also CA 25-28R; CANR 18, 71, 127

Hamilton, Alexander
1755(?)-1804 .... **NCLC 49**
See also DLB 37

Hamilton, Clive
See Lewis, C(live) S(taples)

Hamilton, Edmond 1904-1977 .... **CLC 1**
See also CA 1-4R; CANR 3, 84; DLB 8;
SATA 118; SFW 4

Hamilton, Eugene (Jacob) Lee
See Lee-Hamilton, Eugene (Jacob)

Hamilton, Franklin
See Silverberg, Robert

Hamilton, Gail
See Corcoran, Barbara (Asenath)

Hamilton, Jane 1957- .... **CLC 179**
See also CA 147; CANR 85

Hamilton, Mollie
See Kaye, M(ary) M(argaret)

Hamilton, (Anthony Walter) Patrick
1904-1962 .... **CLC 51**
See also CA 176; 113; DLB 10, 191

Hamilton, Virginia (Esther)
1936-2002 .... **CLC 26**
See also AAYA 2, 21; BW 2, 3; BYA 1, 2,
8; CA 25-28R; 206; CANR 20, 37, 73,
126; CLR 1, 11, 40; DAM MULT; DLB
33, 52; DLBY 01; INT CANR-20; JRDA;
LAIT 5; MAICYA 1, 2; MAICYAS 1;
MTCW 1, 2; SATA 4, 56, 79, 123; SATA-
Obit 132; WYA; YAW

Hammett, (Samuel) Dashiell
1894-1961 .... **CLC 3, 5, 10, 19, 47; SSC
17**
See also AITN 1; AMWS 4; BPFB 2; CA
81-84; CANR 42; CDALB 1929-1941;
CMW 4; DA3; DLB 226; DLBD 6; DLBY
1996; EWL 3; LAIT 3; MSW; MTCW 1,
2; RGAL 4; RGSF 2; TUS

Hammon, Jupiter 1720(?)-1800(?) .... **BLC 2;
NCLC 5; PC 16**
See also DAM MULT, POET; DLB 31, 50

Hammond, Keith
See Kuttner, Henry

Hamner, Earl (Henry), Jr. 1923- .... **CLC 12**
See also AITN 2; CA 73-76; DLB 6

Hampton, Christopher (James)
1946- .... **CLC 4**
See also CA 25-28R; CD 5; DLB 13;
MTCW 1

Hamsun, Knut .... **TCLC 2, 14, 49**
See Pedersen, Knut
See also EW 8; EWL 3; RGWL 2, 3

Handke, Peter 1942- .... **CLC 5, 8, 10, 15, 38,
134; DC 17**
See also CA 77-80; CANR 33, 75, 104;
CWW 2; DAM DRAM, NOV; DLB 85,
124; EWL 3; MTCW 1, 2; TWA

Handy, W(illiam) C(hristopher)
1873-1958 .... **TCLC 97**
See also BW 3; CA 121; 167

Hanley, James 1901-1985 ..... **CLC 3, 5, 8, 13**
See also CA 73-76; 117; CANR 36; CBD;
DLB 191; EWL 3; MTCW 1; RGEL 2

Hannah, Barry 1942- .... **CLC 23, 38, 90**
See also BPFB 2; CA 108; 110; CANR 43,
68, 113; CN 7; CSW; DLB 6, 234; INT
CA-110; MTCW 1; RGSF 2

Hannon, Ezra
See Hunter, Evan

Hansberry, Lorraine (Vivian)
1930-1965 ... **BLC 2; CLC 17, 62; DC 2**
See also AAYA 25; AFAW 1, 2; AMWS 4;
BW 1, 3; CA 109; 25-28R; CABS 3;
CAD; CANR 58; CDALB 1941-1968;
CWD; DA; DA3; DAB; DAC; DAM
DRAM, MST, MULT; DFS 2; DLB 7, 38;
EWL 3; FW; LAIT 4; MTCW 1, 2; RGAL
4; TUS

Hansen, Joseph 1923- .... **CLC 38**
See Brock, Rose; Colton, James
See also BPFB 2; CA 29-32R; CAAS 17;
CANR 16, 44, 66, 125; CMW 4; DLB
226; GLL 1; INT CANR-16

Hansen, Martin A(lfred)
1909-1955 .... **TCLC 32**
See also CA 167; DLB 214; EWL 3

Hansen and Philipson eds. .... **CLC 65**

Hanson, Kenneth O(stlin) 1922- .... **CLC 13**
See also CA 53-56; CANR 7

Hardwick, Elizabeth (Bruce) 1916- . **CLC 13**
See also AMWS 3; CA 5-8R; CANR 3, 32,
70, 100; CN 7; CSW; DA3; DAM NOV;
DLB 6; MAWW; MTCW 1, 2

Hardy, Thomas 1840-1928 .... **PC 8; SSC 2,
60; TCLC 4, 10, 18, 32, 48, 53, 72, 143;
WLC**
See also BRW 6; BRWC 1, 2; BRWR 1;
CA 104; 123; CDBLB 1890-1914; DA;
DA3; DAB; DAC; DAM MST, NOV,
POET; DLB 18, 19, 135, 284; EWL 3;
EXPN; EXPP; LAIT 2; MTCW 1, 2; NFS
3, 11, 15; PFS 3, 4, 18; RGEL 2; RGSF
2; TEA; WLIT 4

Hare, David 1947- .... **CLC 29, 58, 136**
See also BRWS 4; CA 97-100; CANR 39,
91; CBD; CD 5; DFS 4, 7, 16; DLB 13;
MTCW 1; TEA

Harewood, John
See Van Druten, John (William)

Harford, Henry
See Hudson, W(illiam) H(enry)

Hargrave, Leonie
See Disch, Thomas M(ichael)

**Hariri, Al- al-Qasim ibn 'Ali Abu
Muhammad al-Basri**
See al-Hariri, al-Qasim ibn 'Ali Abu Mu-
hammad al-Basri

Harjo, Joy 1951- ..... **CLC 83; NNAL; PC 27**
See also AMWS 12; CA 114; CANR 35,
67, 91; CP 7; CWP; DAM MULT; DLB
120, 175; EWL 3; MTCW 2; PFS 15;
RGAL 4

Harlan, Louis R(udolph) 1922- .... **CLC 34**
See also CA 21-24R; CANR 25, 55, 80

Harling, Robert 1951(?)- .... **CLC 53**
See also CA 147

Harmon, William (Ruth) 1938- .... **CLC 38**
See also CA 33-36R; CANR 14, 32, 35;
SATA 65

Harper, F. E. W.
See Harper, Frances Ellen Watkins

Harper, Frances E. W.
See Harper, Frances Ellen Watkins

Harper, Frances E. Watkins
See Harper, Frances Ellen Watkins

Harper, Frances Ellen
See Harper, Frances Ellen Watkins

Harper, Frances Ellen Watkins
1825-1911 .... **BLC 2; PC 21; TCLC 14**
See also AFAW 1, 2; BW 1, 3; CA 111; 125;
CANR 79; DAM MULT, POET; DLB 50,
221; MAWW; RGAL 4

Harper, Michael S(teven) 1938- ... **CLC 7, 22**
See also AFAW 2; BW 1; CA 33-36R;
CANR 24, 108; CP 7; DLB 41; RGAL 4

Harper, Mrs. F. E. W.
See Harper, Frances Ellen Watkins

Harpur, Charles 1813-1868 .... **NCLC 114**
See also DLB 230; RGEL 2

Harris, Christie
See Harris, Christie (Lucy) Irwin

Harris, Christie (Lucy) Irwin
1907-2002 .... **CLC 12**
See also CA 5-8R; CANR 6, 83; CLR 47;
DLB 88; JRDA; MAICYA 1, 2; SAAS 10;
SATA 6, 74; SATA-Essay 116

Harris, Frank 1856-1931 .... **TCLC 24**
See also CA 109; 150; CANR 80; DLB 156,
197; RGEL 2

Harris, George Washington
1814-1869 .... **NCLC 23**
See also DLB 3, 11, 248; RGAL 4

Harris, Joel Chandler 1848-1908 ..... **SSC 19;**
TCLC 2
See also CA 104; 137; CANR 80; CLR 49;
DLB 11, 23, 42, 78, 91; LAIT 2; MAI-
CYA 1, 2; RGSF 2; SATA 100; WCH;
YABC 1

Harris, John (Wyndham Parkes Lucas)
Beynon 1903-1969
See Wyndham, John
See also CA 102; 89-92; CANR 84; SATA
118; SFW 4

Harris, MacDonald .... **CLC 9**
See Heiney, Donald (William)

Harris, Mark 1922- .... **CLC 19**
See also CA 5-8R; CAAS 3; CANR 2, 55,
83; CN 7; DLB 2; DLBY 1980

Harris, Norman .... **CLC 65**

Harris, (Theodore) Wilson 1921- .... **CLC 25,**
159
See also BRWS 5; BW 2, 3; CA 65-68;
CAAS 16; CANR 11, 27, 69, 114; CD-
WLB 3; CN 7; CP 7; DLB 117; EWL 3;
MTCW 1; RGEL 2

Harrison, Barbara Grizzuti
1934-2002 .... **CLC 144**
See also CA 77-80; 205; CANR 15, 48; INT
CANR-15

Harrison, Elizabeth (Allen) Cavanna
1909-2001
See Cavanna, Betty
See also CA 9-12R; 200; CANR 6, 27, 85,
104, 121; MAICYA 2; SATA 142; YAW

Harrison, Harry (Max) 1925- .... **CLC 42**
See also CA 1-4R; CANR 5, 21, 84; DLB
8; SATA 4; SCFW 2; SFW 4

Harrison, James (Thomas) 1937- ...... **CLC 6,**
14, 33, 66, 143; SSC 19
See Harrison, Jim
See also CA 13-16R; CANR 8, 51, 79; CN
7; CP 7; DLBY 1982; INT CANR-8

Harrison, Jim
See Harrison, James (Thomas)
See also AMWS 8; RGAL 4; TCWW 2;
TUS

Harrison, Kathryn 1961- .... **CLC 70, 151**
See also CA 144; CANR 68, 122

Harrison, Tony 1937- .... **CLC 43, 129**
See also BRWS 5; CA 65-68; CANR 44,
98; CBD; CD 5; CP 7; DLB 40, 245;
MTCW 1; RGEL 2

Harriss, Will(ard Irvin) 1922- .... **CLC 34**
See also CA 111

Hart, Ellis
See Ellison, Harlan (Jay)

Hart, Josephine 1942(?)- .... **CLC 70**
See also CA 138; CANR 70; CPW; DAM
POP

Hart, Moss 1904-1961 .... **CLC 66**
See also CA 109; 89-92; CANR 84; DAM
DRAM; DFS 1; DLB 7, 266; RGAL 4

Harte, (Francis) Bret(t)
1836(?)-1902 ... **SSC 8, 59; TCLC 1, 25;**
WLC
See also AMWS 2; CA 104; 140; CANR
80; CDALB 1865-1917; DA; DA3; DAC;
DAM MST; DLB 12, 64, 74, 79, 186;
EXPS; LAIT 2; RGAL 4; RGSF 2; SATA
26; SSFS 3; TUS

Hartley, L(eslie) P(oles) 1895-1972 ... **CLC 2,**
22
See also BRWS 7; CA 45-48; 37-40R;
CANR 33; DLB 15, 139; EWL 3; HGG;
MTCW 1, 2; RGEL 2; RGSF 2; SUFW 1

Hartman, Geoffrey H. 1929- .... **CLC 27**
See also CA 117; 125; CANR 79; DLB 67

Hartmann, Sadakichi 1869-1944 ... **TCLC 73**
See also CA 157; DLB 54

Hartmann von Aue c. 1170-c.
1210 .... **CMLC 15**
See also CDWLB 2; DLB 138; RGWL 2, 3

Hartog, Jan de
See de Hartog, Jan

Haruf, Kent 1943- .... **CLC 34**
See also AAYA 44; CA 149; CANR 91

Harvey, Caroline
See Trollope, Joanna

Harvey, Gabriel 1550(?)-1631 .... **LC 88**
See also DLB 167, 213, 281

Harwood, Ronald 1934- .... **CLC 32**
See also CA 1-4R; CANR 4, 55; CBD; CD
5; DAM DRAM, MST; DLB 13

Hasegawa Tatsunosuke
See Futabatei, Shimei

Hasek, Jaroslav (Matej Frantisek)
1883-1923 .... **SSC 69; TCLC 4**
See also CA 104; 129; CDWLB 4; DLB
215; EW 9; EWL 3; MTCW 1, 2; RGSF
2; RGWL 2, 3

Hass, Robert 1941- ... **CLC 18, 39, 99; PC 16**
See also AMWS 6; CA 111; CANR 30, 50,
71; CP 7; DLB 105, 206; EWL 3; RGAL
4; SATA 94

Hastings, Hudson
See Kuttner, Henry

Hastings, Selina .... **CLC 44**

Hathorne, John 1641-1717 .... **LC 38**

Hatteras, Amelia
See Mencken, H(enry) L(ouis)

Hatteras, Owen .... **TCLC 18**
See Mencken, H(enry) L(ouis); Nathan,
George Jean

Hauptmann, Gerhart (Johann Robert)
1862-1946 .... **SSC 37; TCLC 4**
See also CA 104; 153; CDWLB 2; DAM
DRAM; DLB 66, 118; EW 8; EWL 3;
RGSF 2; RGWL 2, 3; TWA

Havel, Vaclav 1936- ..... **CLC 25, 58, 65, 123;**
DC 6
See also CA 104; CANR 36, 63, 124; CD-
WLB 4; CWW 2; DA3; DAM DRAM;
DFS 10; DLB 232; EWL 3; LMFS 2;
MTCW 1, 2; RGWL 3

Haviaras, Stratis .... **CLC 33**
See Chaviaras, Strates

Hawes, Stephen 1475(?)-1529(?) .... **LC 17**
See also DLB 132; RGEL 2

Hawkes, John (Clendennin Burne, Jr.)
1925-1998 .. **CLC 1, 2, 3, 4, 7, 9, 14, 15,**
27, 49
See also BPFB 2; CA 1-4R; 167; CANR 2,
47, 64; CN 7; DLB 2, 7, 227; DLBY
1980, 1998; EWL 3; MTCW 1, 2; RGAL
4

Hawking, S. W.
See Hawking, Stephen W(illiam)

Hawking, Stephen W(illiam) 1942- . **CLC 63,**
105
See also AAYA 13; BEST 89:1; CA 126;
129; CANR 48, 115; CPW; DA3; MTCW
2

Hawkins, Anthony Hope
See Hope, Anthony

Hawthorne, Julian 1846-1934 .... **TCLC 25**
See also CA 165; HGG

Hawthorne, Nathaniel 1804-1864 ... **NCLC 2,**
10, 17, 23, 39, 79, 95; SSC 3, 29, 39;
WLC
See also AAYA 18; AMW; AMWC 1;
AMWR 1; BPFB 2; BYA 3; CDALB
1640-1865; DA; DA3; DAB; DAC; DAM
MST, NOV; DLB 1, 74, 183, 223, 269;
EXPN; EXPS; HGG; LAIT 1; NFS 1;
RGAL 4; RGSF 2; SSFS 1, 7, 11, 15;
SUFW 1; TUS; WCH; YABC 2

Haxton, Josephine Ayres 1921-
See Douglas, Ellen
See also CA 115; CANR 41, 83

Hayaseca y Eizaguirre, Jorge
See Echegaray (y Eizaguirre), Jose (Maria
Waldo)

Hayashi, Fumiko 1904-1951 .... **TCLC 27**
See Hayashi Fumiko
See also CA 161

Hayashi Fumiko
See Hayashi, Fumiko
See also DLB 180; EWL 3

Haycraft, Anna (Margaret) 1932-
See Ellis, Alice Thomas
See also CA 122; CANR 85, 90; MTCW 2

Hayden, Robert E(arl) 1913-1980 ..... **BLC 2;**
CLC 5, 9, 14, 37; PC 6
See also AFAW 1, 2; AMWS 2; BW 1, 3;
CA 69-72; 97-100; CABS 2; CANR 24,
75, 82; CDALB 1941-1968; DA; DAC;
DAM MST, MULT, POET; DLB 5, 76;
EWL 3; EXPP; MTCW 1, 2; PFS 1;
RGAL 4; SATA 19; SATA-Obit 26; WP

Hayek, F(riedrich) A(ugust von)
1899-1992 .... **TCLC 109**
See also CA 93-96; 137; CANR 20; MTCW
1, 2

Hayford, J(oseph) E(phraim) Casely
See Casely-Hayford, J(oseph) E(phraim)

Hayman, Ronald 1932- .... **CLC 44**
See also CA 25-28R; CANR 18, 50, 88; CD
5; DLB 155

Hayne, Paul Hamilton 1830-1886 . **NCLC 94**
See also DLB 3, 64, 79, 248; RGAL 4

Hays, Mary 1760-1843 .... **NCLC 114**
See also DLB 142, 158; RGEL 2

Haywood, Eliza (Fowler)
1693(?)-1756 .... **LC 1, 44**
See also DLB 39; RGEL 2

Hazlitt, William 1778-1830 ...... **NCLC 29, 82**
See also BRW 4; DLB 110, 158; RGEL 2;
TEA

Hazzard, Shirley 1931- .... **CLC 18**
See also CA 9-12R; CANR 4, 70, 127; CN
7; DLB 289; DLBY 1982; MTCW 1

Head, Bessie 1937-1986 ...... **BLC 2; CLC 25,**
67; SSC 52
See also AFW; BW 2, 3; CA 29-32R; 119;
CANR 25, 82; CDWLB 3; DA3; DAM
MULT; DLB 117, 225; EWL 3; EXPS;
FW; MTCW 1, 2; RGSF 2; SSFS 5, 13;
WLIT 2; WWE 1

Headon, (Nicky) Topper 1956(?)- ..... **CLC 30**

Heaney, Seamus (Justin) 1939- ..... **CLC 5, 7,**
14, 25, 37, 74, 91, 171; PC 18; WLCS
See also BRWR 1; BRWS 2; CA 85-88;
CANR 25, 48, 75, 91; CDBLB 1960 to
Present; CP 7; DA3; DAB; DAM POET;
DLB 40; DLBY 1995; EWL 3; EXPP;
MTCW 1, 2; PAB; PFS 2, 5, 8, 17; RGEL
2; TEA; WLIT 4

Hoffman, Daniel (Gerard) 1923- . **CLC 6, 13, 23**
See also CA 1-4R; CANR 4; CP 7; DLB 5

Hoffman, Eva 1945- .... **CLC 182**
See also CA 132

Hoffman, Stanley 1944- .... **CLC 5**
See also CA 77-80

Hoffman, William 1925- .... **CLC 141**
See also CA 21-24R; CANR 9, 103; CSW; DLB 234

Hoffman, William M(oses) 1939- ..... **CLC 40**
See Hoffman, William M.
See also CA 57-60; CANR 11, 71

Hoffmann, E(rnst) T(heodor) A(madeus)
1776-1822 .... **NCLC 2; SSC 13**
See also CDWLB 2; DLB 90; EW 5; RGSF 2; RGWL 2, 3; SATA 27; SUFW 1; WCH

Hofmann, Gert 1931- .... **CLC 54**
See also CA 128; EWL 3

Hofmannsthal, Hugo von 1874-1929 ... **DC 4; TCLC 11**
See also CA 106; 153; CDWLB 2; DAM DRAM; DFS 17; DLB 81, 118; EW 9; EWL 3; RGWL 2, 3

Hogan, Linda 1947- ..... **CLC 73; NNAL; PC 35**
See also AMWS 4; ANW; BYA 12; CA 120; CANR 45, 73; CWP; DAM MULT; DLB 175; SATA 132; TCWW 2

Hogarth, Charles
See Creasey, John

Hogarth, Emmett
See Polonsky, Abraham (Lincoln)

Hogg, James 1770-1835 .... **NCLC 4, 109**
See also DLB 93, 116, 159; HGG; RGEL 2; SUFW 1

Holbach, Paul Henri Thiry Baron
1723-1789 .... **LC 14**

Holberg, Ludvig 1684-1754 .... **LC 6**
See also RGWL 2, 3

Holcroft, Thomas 1745-1809 .... **NCLC 85**
See also DLB 39, 89, 158; RGEL 2

Holden, Ursula 1921- .... **CLC 18**
See also CA 101; CAAS 8; CANR 22

Holderlin, (Johann Christian) Friedrich
1770-1843 .... **NCLC 16; PC 4**
See also CDWLB 2; DLB 90; EW 5; RGWL 2, 3

Holdstock, Robert
See Holdstock, Robert P.

Holdstock, Robert P. 1948- .... **CLC 39**
See also CA 131; CANR 81; DLB 261; FANT; HGG; SFW 4; SUFW 2

Holinshed, Raphael fl. 1580- .... **LC 69**
See also DLB 167; RGEL 2

Holland, Isabelle (Christian)
1920-2002 .... **CLC 21**
See also AAYA 11; CA 21-24R; 205; CAAE 181; CANR 10, 25, 47; CLR 57; CWRI 5; JRDA; LAIT 4; MAICYA 1, 2; SATA 8, 70; SATA-Essay 103; SATA-Obit 132; WYA

Holland, Marcus
See Caldwell, (Janet Miriam) Taylor (Holland)

Hollander, John 1929- .... **CLC 2, 5, 8, 14**
See also CA 1-4R; CANR 1, 52; CP 7; DLB 5; SATA 13

Hollander, Paul
See Silverberg, Robert

Holleran, Andrew 1943(?)- .... **CLC 38**
See Garber, Eric
See also CA 144; GLL 1

Holley, Marietta 1836(?)-1926 .... **TCLC 99**
See also CA 118; DLB 11

Hollinghurst, Alan 1954- .... **CLC 55, 91**
See also CA 114; CN 7; DLB 207; GLL 1

Hollis, Jim
See Summers, Hollis (Spurgeon, Jr.)

Holly, Buddy 1936-1959 .... **TCLC 65**
See also CA 213

Holmes, Gordon
See Shiel, M(atthew) P(hipps)

Holmes, John
See Souster, (Holmes) Raymond

Holmes, John Clellon 1926-1988 ...... **CLC 56**
See also BG 2; CA 9-12R; 125; CANR 4; DLB 16, 237

Holmes, Oliver Wendell, Jr.
1841-1935 .... **TCLC 77**
See also CA 114; 186

Holmes, Oliver Wendell
1809-1894 .... **NCLC 14, 81**
See also AMWS 1; CDALB 1640-1865; DLB 1, 189, 235; EXPP; RGAL 4; SATA 34

Holmes, Raymond
See Souster, (Holmes) Raymond

Holt, Victoria
See Hibbert, Eleanor Alice Burford
See also BPFB 2

Holub, Miroslav 1923-1998 .... **CLC 4**
See also CA 21-24R; 169; CANR 10; CD-WLB 4; CWW 2; DLB 232; EWL 3; RGWL 3

Holz, Detlev
See Benjamin, Walter

Homer c. 8th cent. B.C.- .... **CMLC 1, 16, 61; PC 23; WLCS**
See also AW 1; CDWLB 1; DA; DA3; DAB; DAC; DAM MST, POET; DLB 176; EFS 1; LAIT 1; LMFS 1; RGWL 2, 3; TWA; WP

Hongo, Garrett Kaoru 1951- .... **PC 23**
See also CA 133; CAAS 22; CP 7; DLB 120; EWL 3; EXPP; RGAL 4

Honig, Edwin 1919- .... **CLC 33**
See also CA 5-8R; CAAS 8; CANR 4, 45; CP 7; DLB 5

Hood, Hugh (John Blagdon) 1928- . **CLC 15, 28; SSC 42**
See also CA 49-52; CAAS 17; CANR 1, 33, 87; CN 7; DLB 53; RGSF 2

Hood, Thomas 1799-1845 .... **NCLC 16**
See also BRW 4; DLB 96; RGEL 2

Hooker, (Peter) Jeremy 1941- .... **CLC 43**
See also CA 77-80; CANR 22; CP 7; DLB 40

Hooker, Richard 1554-1600 .... **LC 95**
See also BRW 1; DLB 132; RGEL 2

hooks, bell
See Watkins, Gloria Jean

Hope, A(lec) D(erwent) 1907-2000 .... **CLC 3, 51**
See also BRWS 7; CA 21-24R; 188; CANR 33, 74; DLB 289; EWL 3; MTCW 1, 2; PFS 8; RGEL 2

Hope, Anthony 1863-1933 .... **TCLC 83**
See also CA 157; DLB 153, 156; RGEL 2; RHW

Hope, Brian
See Creasey, John

Hope, Christopher (David Tully)
1944- .... **CLC 52**
See also AFW; CA 106; CANR 47, 101; CN 7; DLB 225; SATA 62

Hopkins, Gerard Manley
1844-1889 .... **NCLC 17; PC 15; WLC**
See also BRW 5; BRWR 2; CDBLB 1890-1914; DA; DA3; DAB; DAC; DAM MST, POET; DLB 35, 57; EXPP; PAB; RGEL 2; TEA; WP

Hopkins, John (Richard) 1931-1998 .. **CLC 4**
See also CA 85-88; 169; CBD; CD 5

Hopkins, Pauline Elizabeth
1859-1930 .... **BLC 2; TCLC 28**
See also AFAW 2; BW 2, 3; CA 141; CANR 82; DAM MULT; DLB 50

Hopkinson, Francis 1737-1791 .... **LC 25**
See also DLB 31; RGAL 4

Hopley-Woolrich, Cornell George 1903-1968
See Woolrich, Cornell
See also CA 13-14; CANR 58; CAP 1; CMW 4; DLB 226; MTCW 2

Horace 65B.C.-8B.C. .... **CMLC 39; PC 46**
See also AW 2; CDWLB 1; DLB 211; RGWL 2, 3

Horatio
See Proust, (Valentin-Louis-George-Eugene) Marcel

Horgan, Paul (George Vincent O'Shaughnessy) 1903-1995 .. **CLC 9, 53**
See also BPFB 2; CA 13-16R; 147; CANR 9, 35; DAM NOV; DLB 102, 212; DLBY 1985; INT CANR-9; MTCW 1, 2; SATA 13; SATA-Obit 84; TCWW 2

Horkheimer, Max 1895-1973 .... **TCLC 132**
See also CA 216; 41-44R; DLB 296

Horn, Peter
See Kuttner, Henry

Horne, Frank (Smith) 1899-1974 .... **HR 2**
See also BW 1; CA 125; 53-56; DLB 51; WP

Horne, Richard Henry Hengist
1802(?)-1884 .... **NCLC 127**
See also DLB 32; SATA 29

Hornem, Horace Esq.
See Byron, George Gordon (Noel)

Horney, Karen (Clementine Theodore Danielsen) 1885-1952 .... **TCLC 71**
See also CA 114; 165; DLB 246; FW

Hornung, E(rnest) W(illiam)
1866-1921 .... **TCLC 59**
See also CA 108; 160; CMW 4; DLB 70

Horovitz, Israel (Arthur) 1939- .... **CLC 56**
See also CA 33-36R; CAD; CANR 46, 59; CD 5; DAM DRAM; DLB 7

Horton, George Moses
1797(?)-1883(?) .... **NCLC 87**
See also DLB 50

Horvath, odon von 1901-1938
See von Horvath, Odon
See also EWL 3

Horvath, Oedoen von -1938
See von Horvath, Odon

Horwitz, Julius 1920-1986 .... **CLC 14**
See also CA 9-12R; 119; CANR 12

Hospital, Janette Turner 1942- .... **CLC 42, 145**
See also CA 108; CANR 48; CN 7; DLBY 2002; RGSF 2

Hostos, E. M. de
See Hostos (y Bonilla), Eugenio Maria de

Hostos, Eugenio M. de
See Hostos (y Bonilla), Eugenio Maria de

Hostos, Eugenio Maria
See Hostos (y Bonilla), Eugenio Maria de

Hostos (y Bonilla), Eugenio Maria de
1839-1903 .... **TCLC 24**
See also CA 123; 131; HW 1

Houdini
See Lovecraft, H(oward) P(hillips)

Houellebecq, Michel 1958- .... **CLC 179**
See also CA 185

Hougan, Carolyn 1943- .... **CLC 34**
See also CA 139

Household, Geoffrey (Edward West)
1900-1988 .... **CLC 11**
See also CA 77-80; 126; CANR 58; CMW 4; DLB 87; SATA 14; SATA-Obit 59

Housman, A(lfred) E(dward)
1859-1936 .... **PC 2, 43; TCLC 1, 10; WLCS**
See also BRW 6; CA 104; 125; DA; DA3; DAB; DAC; DAM MST, POET; DLB 19, 284; EWL 3; EXPP; MTCW 1, 2; PAB; PFS 4, 7; RGEL 2; TEA; WP

Author Index

DLB 36, 100, 162, 195, 255; EWL 3;
EXPN; LAIT 5; LMFS 2; MTCW 1, 2;
NFS 6; RGEL 2; SATA 63; SCFW 2;
SFW 4; TEA; YAW

Huxley, T(homas) H(enry)
1825-1895 .... **NCLC 67**
See also DLB 57; TEA

Huysmans, Joris-Karl 1848-1907 ... **TCLC 7,
69**
See also CA 104; 165; DLB 123; EW 7;
GFL 1789 to the Present; LMFS 2; RGWL
2, 3

Hwang, David Henry 1957- .. **CLC 55; DC 4**
See also CA 127; 132; CAD; CANR 76,
124; CD 5; DA3; DAM DRAM; DFS 11,
18; DLB 212, 228; INT CA-132; MTCW
2; RGAL 4

Hyde, Anthony 1946- .... **CLC 42**
See Chase, Nicholas
See also CA 136; CCA 1

Hyde, Margaret O(ldroyd) 1917- ..... **CLC 21**
See also CA 1-4R; CANR 1, 36; CLR 23;
JRDA; MAICYA 1, 2; SAAS 8; SATA 1,
42, 76, 139

Hynes, James 1956(?)- .... **CLC 65**
See also CA 164; CANR 105

Hypatia c. 370-415 .... **CMLC 35**

Ian, Janis 1951- .... **CLC 21**
See also CA 105; 187

Ibanez, Vicente Blasco
See Blasco Ibanez, Vicente

Ibarbourou, Juana de 1895-1979 ..... **HLCS 2**
See also DLB 290; HW 1; LAW

Ibarguengoitia, Jorge 1928-1983 ..... **CLC 37;
TCLC 148**
See also CA 124; 113; EWL 3; HW 1

Ibn Battuta, Abu Abdalla
1304-1368(?) .... **CMLC 57**
See also WLIT 2

Ibn Hazm 994-1064 .... **CMLC 64**

Ibsen, Henrik (Johan) 1828-1906 .... **DC 2;
TCLC 2, 8, 16, 37, 52; WLC**
See also AAYA 46; CA 104; 141; DA; DA3;
DAB; DAC; DAM DRAM, MST; DFS 1,
6, 8, 10, 11, 15, 16; EW 7; LAIT 2; LATS
1; RGWL 2, 3

Ibuse, Masuji 1898-1993 .... **CLC 22**
See Ibuse Masuji
See also CA 127; 141; MJW; RGWL 3

Ibuse Masuji
See Ibuse, Masuji
See also DLB 180; EWL 3

Ichikawa, Kon 1915- .... **CLC 20**
See also CA 121

Ichiyo, Higuchi 1872-1896 .... **NCLC 49**
See also MJW

Idle, Eric 1943- .... **CLC 21**
See Monty Python
See also CA 116; CANR 35, 91

Ignatow, David 1914-1997 .... **CLC 4, 7, 14,
40; PC 34**
See also CA 9-12R; 162; CAAS 3; CANR
31, 57, 96; CP 7; DLB 5; EWL 3

Ignotus
See Strachey, (Giles) Lytton

Ihimaera, Witi (Tame) 1944- .... **CLC 46**
See also CA 77-80; CN 7; RGSF 2

Ilf, Ilya .... **TCLC 21**
See Fainzilberg, Ilya Arnoldovich
See also EWL 3

Illyes, Gyula 1902-1983 .... **PC 16**
See also CA 114; 109; CDWLB 4; DLB
215; EWL 3; RGWL 2, 3

Imalayen, Fatima-Zohra
See Djebar, Assia

Immermann, Karl (Lebrecht)
1796-1840 .... **NCLC 4, 49**
See also DLB 133

Ince, Thomas H. 1882-1924 .... **TCLC 89**
See also IDFW 3, 4

Inchbald, Elizabeth 1753-1821 ...... **NCLC 62**
See also DLB 39, 89; RGEL 2

Inclan, Ramon (Maria) del Valle
See Valle-Inclan, Ramon (Maria) del

Infante, G(uillermo) Cabrera
See Cabrera Infante, G(uillermo)

Ingalls, Rachel (Holmes) 1940- .... **CLC 42**
See also CA 123; 127

Ingamells, Reginald Charles
See Ingamells, Rex

Ingamells, Rex 1913-1955 .... **TCLC 35**
See also CA 167; DLB 260

Inge, William (Motter) 1913-1973 ..... **CLC 1,
8, 19**
See also CA 9-12R; CDALB 1941-1968;
DA3; DAM DRAM; DFS 1, 3, 5, 8; DLB
7, 249; EWL 3; MTCW 1, 2; RGAL 4;
TUS

Ingelow, Jean 1820-1897 .... **NCLC 39, 107**
See also DLB 35, 163; FANT; SATA 33

Ingram, Willis J.
See Harris, Mark

Innaurato, Albert (F.) 1948(?)- ... **CLC 21, 60**
See also CA 115; 122; CAD; CANR 78;
CD 5; INT CA-122

Innes, Michael
See Stewart, J(ohn) I(nnes) M(ackintosh)
See also DLB 276; MSW

Innis, Harold Adams 1894-1952 .... **TCLC 77**
See also CA 181; DLB 88

Insluis, Alanus de
See Alain de Lille

Iola
See Wells-Barnett, Ida B(ell)

Ionesco, Eugene 1912-1994 ... **CLC 1, 4, 6, 9,
11, 15, 41, 86; DC 12; WLC**
See also CA 9-12R; 144; CANR 55; CWW
2; DA; DA3; DAB; DAC; DAM DRAM,
MST; DFS 4, 9; EW 13; EWL 3; GFL
1789 to the Present; LMFS 2; MTCW 1,
2; RGWL 2, 3; SATA 7; SATA-Obit 79;
TWA

Iqbal, Muhammad 1877-1938 .... **TCLC 28**
See also CA 215; EWL 3

Ireland, Patrick
See O'Doherty, Brian

Irenaeus St. 130- .... **CMLC 42**

Irigaray, Luce 1930- .... **CLC 164**
See also CA 154; CANR 121; FW

Iron, Ralph
See Schreiner, Olive (Emilie Albertina)

Irving, John (Winslow) 1942- ... **CLC 13, 23,
38, 112, 175**
See also AAYA 8; AMWS 6; BEST 89:3;
BPFB 2; CA 25-28R; CANR 28, 73, 112;
CN 7; CPW; DA3; DAM NOV, POP;
DLB 6, 278; DLBY 1982; EWL 3;
MTCW 1, 2; NFS 12, 14; RGAL 4; TUS

Irving, Washington 1783-1859 . **NCLC 2, 19,
95; SSC 2, 37; WLC**
See also AMW; CDALB 1640-1865; DA;
DA3; DAB; DAC; DAM MST; DLB 3,
11, 30, 59, 73, 74, 183, 186, 250, 254;
EXPS; LAIT 1; RGAL 4; RGSF 2; SSFS
1, 8, 16; SUFW 1; TUS; WCH; YABC 2

Irwin, P. K.
See Page, P(atricia) K(athleen)

Isaacs, Jorge Ricardo 1837-1895 ... **NCLC 70**
See also LAW

Isaacs, Susan 1943- .... **CLC 32**
See also BEST 89:1; BPFB 2; CA 89-92;
CANR 20, 41, 65, 112; CPW; DA3; DAM
POP; INT CANR-20; MTCW 1, 2

Isherwood, Christopher (William Bradshaw)
1904-1986 .... **CLC 1, 9, 11, 14, 44; SSC
56**
See also BRW 7; CA 13-16R; 117; CANR
35, 97; DA3; DAM DRAM, NOV; DLB
15, 195; DLBY 1986; EWL 3; IDTP;
MTCW 1, 2; RGAL 4; RGEL 2; TUS;
WLIT 4

Ishiguro, Kazuo 1954- .. **CLC 27, 56, 59, 110**
See also BEST 90:2; BPFB 2; BRWS 4;
CA 120; CANR 49, 95; CN 7; DA3;
DAM NOV; DLB 194; EWL 3; MTCW
1, 2; NFS 13; WLIT 4; WWE 1

Ishikawa, Hakuhin
See Ishikawa, Takuboku

Ishikawa, Takuboku 1886(?)-1912 ..... **PC 10;
TCLC 15**
See Ishikawa Takuboku
See also CA 113; 153; DAM POET

Iskander, Fazil (Abdulovich) 1929- .. **CLC 47**
See also CA 102; EWL 3

Isler, Alan (David) 1934- .... **CLC 91**
See also CA 156; CANR 105

Ivan IV 1530-1584 .... **LC 17**

Ivanov, Vyacheslav Ivanovich
1866-1949 .... **TCLC 33**
See also CA 122; EWL 3

Ivask, Ivar Vidrik 1927-1992 .... **CLC 14**
See also CA 37-40R; 139; CANR 24

Ives, Morgan
See Bradley, Marion Zimmer
See also GLL 1

Izumi Shikibu c. 973-c. 1034 .... **CMLC 33**

J. R. S.
See Gogarty, Oliver St. John

Jabran, Kahlil
See Gibran, Kahlil

Jabran, Khalil
See Gibran, Kahlil

Jackson, Daniel
See Wingrove, David (John)

Jackson, Helen Hunt 1830-1885 .... **NCLC 90**
See also DLB 42, 47, 186, 189; RGAL 4

Jackson, Jesse 1908-1983 .... **CLC 12**
See also BW 1; CA 25-28R; 109; CANR
27; CLR 28; CWRI 5; MAICYA 1, 2;
SATA 2, 29; SATA-Obit 48

Jackson, Laura (Riding) 1901-1991 .... **PC 44**
See Riding, Laura
See also CA 65-68; 135; CANR 28, 89;
DLB 48

Jackson, Sam
See Trumbo, Dalton

Jackson, Sara
See Wingrove, David (John)

Jackson, Shirley 1919-1965 . **CLC 11, 60, 87;
SSC 9, 39; WLC**
See also AAYA 9; AMWS 9; BPFB 2; CA
1-4R; 25-28R; CANR 4, 52; CDALB
1941-1968; DA; DA3; DAC; DAM MST;
DLB 6, 234; EXPS; HGG; LAIT 4;
MTCW 2; RGAL 4; RGSF 2; SATA 2;
SSFS 1; SUFW 1, 2

Jacob, (Cyprien-)Max 1876-1944 .... **TCLC 6**
See also CA 104; 193; DLB 258; EWL 3;
GFL 1789 to the Present; GLL 2; RGWL
2, 3

Jacobs, Harriet A(nn)
1813(?)-1897 .... **NCLC 67**
See also AFAW 1, 2; DLB 239; FW; LAIT
2; RGAL 4

Jacobs, Jim 1942- .... **CLC 12**
See also CA 97-100; INT CA-97-100

Jacobs, W(illiam) W(ymark)
1863-1943 .... **TCLC 22**
See also CA 121; 167; DLB 135; EXPS;
HGG; RGEL 2; RGSF 2; SSFS 2; SUFW
1

Jacobsen, Jens Peter 1847-1885 .... **NCLC 34**

Jacobsen, Josephine (Winder)
1908-2003 .... **CLC 48, 102**
See also CA 33-36R; 218; CAAS 18; CANR
23, 48; CCA 1; CP 7; DLB 244

Jacobson, Dan 1929- .... **CLC 4, 14**
See also AFW; CA 1-4R; CANR 2, 25, 66;
CN 7; DLB 14, 207, 225; EWL 3; MTCW
1; RGSF 2

Jacqueline
See Carpentier (y Valmont), Alejo

Jacques de Vitry c. 1160-1240 ...... **CMLC 63**
See also DLB 208

Jagger, Mick 1944- .... **CLC 17**

Jahiz, al- c. 780-c. 869 .... **CMLC 25**

Jakes, John (William) 1932- .... **CLC 29**
See also AAYA 32; BEST 89:4; BPFB 2;
CA 57-60, 214; CAAE 214; CANR 10,
43, 66, 111; CPW; CSW; DA3; DAM
NOV, POP; DLB 278; DLBY 1983;
FANT; INT CANR-10; MTCW 1, 2;
RHW; SATA 62; SFW 4; TCWW 2

James I 1394-1437 .... **LC 20**
See also RGEL 2

James, Andrew
See Kirkup, James

James, C(yril) L(ionel) R(obert)
1901-1989 .... **BLCS; CLC 33**
See also BW 2; CA 117; 125; 128; CANR
62; DLB 125; MTCW 1

James, Daniel (Lewis) 1911-1988
See Santiago, Danny
See also CA 174; 125

James, Dynely
See Mayne, William (James Carter)

James, Henry Sr. 1811-1882 .... **NCLC 53**

James, Henry 1843-1916 .... **SSC 8, 32, 47;**
TCLC 2, 11, 24, 40, 47, 64; WLC
See also AMW; AMWC 1; AMWR 1; BPFB
2; BRW 6; CA 104; 132; CDALB 1865-
1917; DA; DA3; DAB; DAC; DAM MST,
NOV; DLB 12, 71, 74, 189; DLBD 13;
EWL 3; EXPS; HGG; LAIT 2; MTCW 1,
2; NFS 12, 16; RGAL 4; RGEL 2; RGSF
2; SSFS 9; SUFW 1; TUS

James, M. R.
See James, Montague (Rhodes)
See also DLB 156, 201

James, Montague (Rhodes)
1862-1936 .... **SSC 16; TCLC 6**
See James, M. R.
See also CA 104; 203; HGG; RGEL 2;
RGSF 2; SUFW 1

James, P. D. .... **CLC 18, 46, 122**
See White, Phyllis Dorothy James
See also BEST 90:2; BPFB 2; BRWS 4;
CDBLB 1960 to Present; DLB 87, 276;
DLBD 17; MSW

James, Philip
See Moorcock, Michael (John)

James, Samuel
See Stephens, James

James, Seumas
See Stephens, James

James, Stephen
See Stephens, James

James, William 1842-1910 .... **TCLC 15, 32**
See also AMW; CA 109; 193; DLB 270,
284; NCFS 5; RGAL 4

Jameson, Anna 1794-1860 .... **NCLC 43**
See also DLB 99, 166

Jameson, Fredric (R.) 1934- .... **CLC 142**
See also CA 196; DLB 67; LMFS 2

Jami, Nur al-Din 'Abd al-Rahman
1414-1492 .... **LC 9**

Jammes, Francis 1868-1938 .... **TCLC 75**
See also CA 198; EWL 3; GFL 1789 to the
Present

Jandl, Ernst 1925-2000 .... **CLC 34**
See also CA 200; EWL 3

Janowitz, Tama 1957- .... **CLC 43, 145**
See also CA 106; CANR 52, 89; CN 7;
CPW; DAM POP; DLB 292

Japrisot, Sebastien 1931- .... **CLC 90**
See Rossi, Jean-Baptiste
See also CMW 4; NFS 18

Jarrell, Randall 1914-1965 .... **CLC 1, 2, 6, 9,**
13, 49; PC 41
See also AMW; BYA 5; CA 5-8R; 25-28R;
CABS 2; CANR 6, 34; CDALB 1941-
1968; CLR 6; CWRI 5; DAM POET;
DLB 48, 52; EWL 3; EXPP; MAICYA 1,
2; MTCW 1, 2; PAB; PFS 2; RGAL 4;
SATA 7

Jarry, Alfred 1873-1907 .... **SSC 20; TCLC 2,**
14, 147
See also CA 104; 153; DA3; DAM DRAM;
DFS 8; DLB 192, 258; EW 9; EWL 3;
GFL 1789 to the Present; RGWL 2, 3;
TWA

Jarvis, E. K.
See Ellison, Harlan (Jay)

Jawien, Andrzej
See John Paul II, Pope

Jaynes, Roderick
See Coen, Ethan

Jeake, Samuel, Jr.
See Aiken, Conrad (Potter)

Jean Paul 1763-1825 .... **NCLC 7**

Jefferies, (John) Richard
1848-1887 .... **NCLC 47**
See also DLB 98, 141; RGEL 2; SATA 16;
SFW 4

Jeffers, (John) Robinson 1887-1962 .. **CLC 2,**
3, 11, 15, 54; PC 17; WLC
See also AMWS 2; CA 85-88; CANR 35;
CDALB 1917-1929; DA; DAC; DAM
MST, POET; DLB 45, 212; EWL 3;
MTCW 1, 2; PAB; PFS 3, 4; RGAL 4

Jefferson, Janet
See Mencken, H(enry) L(ouis)

Jefferson, Thomas 1743-1826 . **NCLC 11, 103**
See also ANW; CDALB 1640-1865; DA3;
DLB 31, 183; LAIT 1; RGAL 4

Jeffrey, Francis 1773-1850 .... **NCLC 33**
See Francis, Lord Jeffrey

Jelakowitch, Ivan
See Heijermans, Herman

Jelinek, Elfriede 1946- .... **CLC 169**
See also CA 154; DLB 85; FW

Jellicoe, (Patricia) Ann 1927- .... **CLC 27**
See also CA 85-88; CBD; CD 5; CWD;
CWRI 5; DLB 13, 233; FW

Jelloun, Tahar ben 1944- .... **CLC 180**
See Ben Jelloun, Tahar
See also CA 162; CANR 100

Jemyma
See Holley, Marietta

Jen, Gish .... **AAL; CLC 70**
See Jen, Lillian
See also AMWC 2

Jen, Lillian 1956(?)-
See Jen, Gish
See also CA 135; CANR 89

Jenkins, (John) Robin 1912- .... **CLC 52**
See also CA 1-4R; CANR 1; CN 7; DLB
14, 271

Jennings, Elizabeth (Joan)
1926-2001 .... **CLC 5, 14, 131**
See also BRWS 5; CA 61-64; 200; CAAS
5; CANR 8, 39, 66, 127; CP 7; CWP;
DLB 27; EWL 3; MTCW 1; SATA 66

Jennings, Waylon 1937- .... **CLC 21**

Jensen, Johannes V(ilhelm)
1873-1950 .... **TCLC 41**
See also CA 170; DLB 214; EWL 3; RGWL
3

Jensen, Laura (Linnea) 1948- .... **CLC 37**
See also CA 103

Jerome, Saint 345-420 .... **CMLC 30**
See also RGWL 3

Jerome, Jerome K(lapka)
1859-1927 .... **TCLC 23**
See also CA 119; 177; DLB 10, 34, 135;
RGEL 2

Jerrold, Douglas William
1803-1857 .... **NCLC 2**
See also DLB 158, 159; RGEL 2

Jewett, (Theodora) Sarah Orne
1849-1909 .... **SSC 6, 44; TCLC 1, 22**
See also AMW; AMWC 2; AMWR 2; CA
108; 127; CANR 71; DLB 12, 74, 221;
EXPS; FW; MAWW; NFS 15; RGAL 4;
RGSF 2; SATA 15; SSFS 4

Jewsbury, Geraldine (Endsor)
1812-1880 .... **NCLC 22**
See also DLB 21

Jhabvala, Ruth Prawer 1927- . **CLC 4, 8, 29,**
94, 138
See also BRWS 5; CA 1-4R; CANR 2, 29,
51, 74, 91; CN 7; DAB; DAM NOV; DLB
139, 194; EWL 3; IDFW 3, 4; INT CANR-
29; MTCW 1, 2; RGSF 2; RGWL 2;
RHW; TEA

Jibran, Kahlil
See Gibran, Kahlil

Jibran, Khalil
See Gibran, Kahlil

Jiles, Paulette 1943- .... **CLC 13, 58**
See also CA 101; CANR 70, 124; CWP

Jimenez (Mantecon), Juan Ramon
1881-1958 .... **HLC 1; PC 7; TCLC 4**
See also CA 104; 131; CANR 74; DAM
MULT, POET; DLB 134; EW 9; EWL 3;
HW 1; MTCW 1, 2; RGWL 2, 3

Jimenez, Ramon
See Jimenez (Mantecon), Juan Ramon

Jimenez Mantecon, Juan
See Jimenez (Mantecon), Juan Ramon

Jin, Ha .... **CLC 109**
See Jin, Xuefei
See also CA 152; DLB 244, 292; SSFS 17

Jin, Xuefei 1956-
See Jin, Ha
See also CANR 91; SSFS 17

Joel, Billy .... **CLC 26**
See Joel, William Martin

Joel, William Martin 1949-
See Joel, Billy
See also CA 108

Johann Sigurjonsson 1880-1919 .... **TCLC 27**
See also CA 170; DLB 293; EWL 3

John, Saint 10(?)-100 .... **CMLC 27, 63**

John of Salisbury c. 1115-1180 ..... **CMLC 63**

John of the Cross, St. 1542-1591 .... **LC 18**
See also RGWL 2, 3

John Paul II, Pope 1920- .... **CLC 128**
See also CA 106; 133

Johnson, B(ryan) S(tanley William)
1933-1973 .... **CLC 6, 9**
See also CA 9-12R; 53-56; CANR 9; DLB
14, 40; EWL 3; RGEL 2

Johnson, Benjamin F., of Boone
See Riley, James Whitcomb

Johnson, Charles (Richard) 1948- .... **BLC 2;**
CLC 7, 51, 65, 163
See also AFAW 2; AMWS 6; BW 2, 3; CA
116; CAAS 18; CANR 42, 66, 82; CN 7;
DAM MULT; DLB 33, 278; MTCW 2;
RGAL 4; SSFS 16

Johnson, Charles S(purgeon)
1893-1956 .... **HR 3**
See also BW 1, 3; CA 125; CANR 82; DLB
51, 91

Johnson, Denis 1949- . **CLC 52, 160; SSC 56**
See also CA 117; 121; CANR 71, 99; CN 7; DLB 120

Johnson, Diane 1934- .... **CLC 5, 13, 48**
See also BPFB 2; CA 41-44R; CANR 17, 40, 62, 95; CN 7; DLBY 1980; INT CANR-17; MTCW 1

Johnson, E. Pauline 1861-1913 .... **NNAL**
See also CA 150; DAC; DAM MULT; DLB 92, 175

Johnson, Eyvind (Olof Verner)
1900-1976 .... **CLC 14**
See also CA 73-76; 69-72; CANR 34, 101; DLB 259; EW 12; EWL 3

Johnson, Fenton 1888-1958 .... **BLC 2**
See also BW 1; CA 118; 124; DAM MULT; DLB 45, 50

Johnson, Georgia Douglas (Camp)
1880-1966 .... **HR 3**
See also BW 1; CA 125; DLB 51, 249; WP

Johnson, Helene 1907-1995 .... **HR 3**
See also CA 181; DLB 51; WP

Johnson, J. R.
See James, C(yril) L(ionel) R(obert)

Johnson, James Weldon 1871-1938 .. **BLC 2; HR 3; PC 24; TCLC 3, 19**
See also AFAW 1, 2; BW 1, 3; CA 104; 125; CANR 82; CDALB 1917-1929; CLR 32; DA3; DAM MULT, POET; DLB 51; EWL 3; EXPP; LMFS 2; MTCW 1, 2; PFS 1; RGAL 4; SATA 31; TUS

Johnson, Joyce 1935- .... **CLC 58**
See also BG 3; CA 125; 129; CANR 102

Johnson, Judith (Emlyn) 1936- .... **CLC 7, 15**
See Sherwin, Judith Johnson
See also CA 25-28R; 153; CANR 34

Johnson, Lionel (Pigot)
1867-1902 .... **TCLC 19**
See also CA 117; 209; DLB 19; RGEL 2

Johnson, Marguerite Annie
See Angelou, Maya

Johnson, Mel
See Malzberg, Barry N(athaniel)

Johnson, Pamela Hansford
1912-1981 .... **CLC 1, 7, 27**
See also CA 1-4R; 104; CANR 2, 28; DLB 15; MTCW 1, 2; RGEL 2

Johnson, Paul (Bede) 1928- .... **CLC 147**
See also BEST 89:4; CA 17-20R; CANR 34, 62, 100

Johnson, Robert .... **CLC 70**

Johnson, Robert 1911(?)-1938 .... **TCLC 69**
See also BW 3; CA 174

Johnson, Samuel 1709-1784 .... **LC 15, 52; WLC**
See also BRW 3; BRWR 1; CDBLB 1660-1789; DA; DAB; DAC; DAM MST; DLB 39, 95, 104, 142, 213; LMFS 1; RGEL 2; TEA

Johnson, Uwe 1934-1984 .. **CLC 5, 10, 15, 40**
See also CA 1-4R; 112; CANR 1, 39; CD-WLB 2; DLB 75; EWL 3; MTCW 1; RGWL 2, 3

Johnston, Basil H. 1929- .... **NNAL**
See also CA 69-72; CANR 11, 28, 66; DAC; DAM MULT; DLB 60

Johnston, George (Benson) 1913- .... **CLC 51**
See also CA 1-4R; CANR 5, 20; CP 7; DLB 88

Johnston, Jennifer (Prudence)
1930- .... **CLC 7, 150**
See also CA 85-88; CANR 92; CN 7; DLB 14

Joinville, Jean de 1224(?)-1317 ..... **CMLC 38**

Jolley, (Monica) Elizabeth 1923- ..... **CLC 46; SSC 19**
See also CA 127; CAAS 13; CANR 59; CN 7; EWL 3; RGSF 2

Jones, Arthur Llewellyn 1863-1947
See Machen, Arthur
See also CA 104; 179; HGG

Jones, D(ouglas) G(ordon) 1929- ..... **CLC 10**
See also CA 29-32R; CANR 13, 90; CP 7; DLB 53

Jones, David (Michael) 1895-1974 .... **CLC 2, 4, 7, 13, 42**
See also BRW 6; BRWS 7; CA 9-12R; 53-56; CANR 28; CDBLB 1945-1960; DLB 20, 100; EWL 3; MTCW 1; PAB; RGEL 2

Jones, David Robert 1947-
See Bowie, David
See also CA 103; CANR 104

Jones, Diana Wynne 1934- .... **CLC 26**
See also AAYA 12; BYA 6, 7, 9, 11, 13, 16; CA 49-52; CANR 4, 26, 56, 120; CLR 23; DLB 161; FANT; JRDA; MAICYA 1, 2; SAAS 7; SATA 9, 70, 108; SFW 4; SUFW 2; YAW

Jones, Edward P. 1950- .... **CLC 76**
See also BW 2, 3; CA 142; CANR 79; CSW

Jones, Gayl 1949- ...... **BLC 2; CLC 6, 9, 131**
See also AFAW 1, 2; BW 2, 3; CA 77-80; CANR 27, 66, 122; CN 7; CSW; DA3; DAM MULT; DLB 33, 278; MTCW 1, 2; RGAL 4

Jones, James 1921-1977 ...... **CLC 1, 3, 10, 39**
See also AITN 1, 2; AMWS 11; BPFB 2; CA 1-4R; 69-72; CANR 6; DLB 2, 143; DLBD 17; DLBY 1998; EWL 3; MTCW 1; RGAL 4

Jones, John J.
See Lovecraft, H(oward) P(hillips)

Jones, LeRoi .... **CLC 1, 2, 3, 5, 10, 14**
See Baraka, Amiri
See also MTCW 2

Jones, Louis B. 1953- .... **CLC 65**
See also CA 141; CANR 73

Jones, Madison (Percy, Jr.) 1925- ...... **CLC 4**
See also CA 13-16R; CAAS 11; CANR 7, 54, 83; CN 7; CSW; DLB 152

Jones, Mervyn 1922- .... **CLC 10, 52**
See also CA 45-48; CAAS 5; CANR 1, 91; CN 7; MTCW 1

Jones, Mick 1956(?)- .... **CLC 30**

Jones, Nettie (Pearl) 1941- .... **CLC 34**
See also BW 2; CA 137; CAAS 20; CANR 88

Jones, Peter 1802-1856 .... **NNAL**

Jones, Preston 1936-1979 .... **CLC 10**
See also CA 73-76; 89-92; DLB 7

Jones, Robert F(rancis) 1934-2003 .... **CLC 7**
See also CA 49-52; CANR 2, 61, 118

Jones, Rod 1953- .... **CLC 50**
See also CA 128

Jones, Terence Graham Parry
1942- .... **CLC 21**
See Jones, Terry; Monty Python
See also CA 112; 116; CANR 35, 93; INT CA-116; SATA 127

Jones, Terry
See Jones, Terence Graham Parry
See also SATA 67; SATA-Brief 51

Jones, Thom (Douglas) 1945(?)- ..... **CLC 81; SSC 56**
See also CA 157; CANR 88; DLB 244

Jong, Erica 1942- .... **CLC 4, 6, 8, 18, 83**
See also AITN 1; AMWS 5; BEST 90:2; BPFB 2; CA 73-76; CANR 26, 52, 75; CN 7; CP 7; CPW; DA3; DAM NOV, POP; DLB 2, 5, 28, 152; FW; INT CANR-26; MTCW 1, 2

Jonson, Ben(jamin) 1572(?)-1637 . **DC 4; LC 6, 33; PC 17; WLC**
See also BRW 1; BRWC 1; BRWR 1; CD-BLB Before 1660; DA; DAB; DAC; DAM DRAM, MST, POET; DFS 4, 10; DLB 62, 121; LMFS 1; RGEL 2; TEA; WLIT 3

Jordan, June (Meyer)
1936-2002 .. **BLCS; CLC 5, 11, 23, 114; PC 38**
See also AAYA 2; AFAW 1, 2; BW 2, 3; CA 33-36R; 206; CANR 25, 70, 114; CLR 10; CP 7; CWP; DAM MULT, POET; DLB 38; GLL 2; LAIT 5; MAICYA 1, 2; MTCW 1; SATA 4, 136; YAW

Jordan, Neil (Patrick) 1950- .... **CLC 110**
See also CA 124; 130; CANR 54; CN 7; GLL 2; INT CA-130

Jordan, Pat(rick M.) 1941- .... **CLC 37**
See also CA 33-36R; CANR 121

Jorgensen, Ivar
See Ellison, Harlan (Jay)

Jorgenson, Ivar
See Silverberg, Robert

Joseph, George Ghevarughese .... **CLC 70**

Josephson, Mary
See O'Doherty, Brian

Josephus, Flavius c. 37-100 .... **CMLC 13**
See also AW 2; DLB 176

Josiah Allen's Wife
See Holley, Marietta

Josipovici, Gabriel (David) 1940- ...... **CLC 6, 43, 153**
See also CA 37-40R; CAAS 8; CANR 47, 84; CN 7; DLB 14

Joubert, Joseph 1754-1824 .... **NCLC 9**

Jouve, Pierre Jean 1887-1976 .... **CLC 47**
See also CA 65-68; DLB 258; EWL 3

Jovine, Francesco 1902-1950 .... **TCLC 79**
See also DLB 264; EWL 3

Joyce, James (Augustine Aloysius)
1882-1941 .... **DC 16; PC 22; SSC 3, 26, 44, 64; TCLC 3, 8, 16, 35, 52; WLC**
See also AAYA 42; BRW 7; BRWC 1; BRWR 1; BYA 11, 13; CA 104; 126; CD-BLB 1914-1945; DA; DA3; DAB; DAC; DAM MST, NOV, POET; DLB 10, 19, 36, 162, 247; EWL 3; EXPN; EXPS; LAIT 3; LMFS 1, 2; MTCW 1, 2; NFS 7; RGSF 2; SSFS 1; TEA; WLIT 4

Jozsef, Attila 1905-1937 .... **TCLC 22**
See also CA 116; CDWLB 4; DLB 215; EWL 3

Juana Ines de la Cruz, Sor
1651(?)-1695 ...... **HLCS 1; LC 5; PC 24**
See also FW; LAW; RGWL 2, 3; WLIT 1

Juana Inez de La Cruz, Sor
See Juana Ines de la Cruz, Sor

Judd, Cyril
See Kornbluth, C(yril) M.; Pohl, Frederik

Juenger, Ernst 1895-1998 .... **CLC 125**
See Junger, Ernst
See also CA 101; 167; CANR 21, 47, 106; DLB 56

Julian of Norwich 1342(?)-1416(?) . **LC 6, 52**
See also DLB 146; LMFS 1

Julius Caesar 100B.C.-44B.C.
See Caesar, Julius
See also CDWLB 1; DLB 211

Junger, Ernst
See Juenger, Ernst
See also CDWLB 2; EWL 3; RGWL 2, 3

Junger, Sebastian 1962- .... **CLC 109**
See also AAYA 28; CA 165

Juniper, Alex
See Hospital, Janette Turner

Junius
See Luxemburg, Rosa

Kemelman, Harry 1908-1996 .... **CLC 2**
  See also AITN 1; BPFB 2; CA 9-12R; 155;
  CANR 6, 71; CMW 4; DLB 28

Kempe, Margery 1373(?)-1440(?) ... **LC 6, 56**
  See also DLB 146; RGEL 2

Kempis, Thomas a 1380-1471 .... **LC 11**

Kendall, Henry 1839-1882 .... **NCLC 12**
  See also DLB 230

Keneally, Thomas (Michael) 1935- ... **CLC 5, 8, 10, 14, 19, 27, 43, 117**
  See also BRWS 4; CA 85-88; CANR 10,
  50, 74; CN 7; CPW; DA3; DAM NOV;
  DLB 289; EWL 3; MTCW 1, 2; NFS 17;
  RGEL 2; RHW

Kennedy, Adrienne (Lita) 1931- .... **BLC 2; CLC 66; DC 5**
  See also AFAW 2; BW 2, 3; CA 103; CAAS
  20; CABS 3; CANR 26, 53, 82; CD 5;
  DAM MULT; DFS 9; DLB 38; FW

Kennedy, John Pendleton
  1795-1870 .... **NCLC 2**
  See also DLB 3, 248, 254; RGAL 4

Kennedy, Joseph Charles 1929-
  See Kennedy, X. J.
  See also CA 1-4R, 201; CAAE 201; CANR
  4, 30, 40; CP 7; CWRI 5; MAICYA 2;
  MAICYAS 1; SATA 14, 86, 130; SATA-
  Essay 130

Kennedy, William 1928- ... **CLC 6, 28, 34, 53**
  See also AAYA 1; AMWS 7; BPFB 2; CA
  85-88; CANR 14, 31, 76; CN 7; DA3;
  DAM NOV; DLB 143; DLBY 1985; EWL
  3; INT CANR-31; MTCW 1, 2; SATA 57

Kennedy, X. J. .... **CLC 8, 42**
  See Kennedy, Joseph Charles
  See also CAAS 9; CLR 27; DLB 5; SAAS
  22

Kenny, Maurice (Francis) 1929- ..... **CLC 87; NNAL**
  See also CA 144; CAAS 22; DAM MULT;
  DLB 175

Kent, Kelvin
  See Kuttner, Henry

Kenton, Maxwell
  See Southern, Terry

Kenyon, Robert O.
  See Kuttner, Henry

Kepler, Johannes 1571-1630 .... **LC 45**

Ker, Jill
  See Conway, Jill K(er)

Kerkow, H. C.
  See Lewton, Val

Kerouac, Jack 1922-1969 ...... **CLC 1, 2, 3, 5, 14, 29, 61; TCLC 117; WLC**
  See Kerouac, Jean-Louis Lebris de
  See also AAYA 25; AMWC 1; AMWS 3;
  BG 3; BPFB 2; CDALB 1941-1968;
  CPW; DLB 2, 16, 237; DLBD 3; DLBY
  1995; EWL 3; GLL 1; LATS 1; LMFS 2;
  MTCW 2; NFS 8; RGAL 4; TUS; WP

Kerouac, Jean-Louis Lebris de 1922-1969
  See Kerouac, Jack
  See also AITN 1; CA 5-8R; 25-28R; CANR
  26, 54, 95; DA; DA3; DAB; DAC; DAM
  MST, NOV, POET, POP; MTCW 1, 2

Kerr, (Bridget) Jean (Collins)
  1923(?)-2003 .... **CLC 22**
  See also CA 5-8R; 212; CANR 7; INT
  CANR-7

Kerr, M. E. .... **CLC 12, 35**
  See Meaker, Marijane (Agnes)
  See also AAYA 2, 23; BYA 1, 7, 8; CLR
  29; SAAS 1; WYA

Kerr, Robert .... **CLC 55**

Kerrigan, (Thomas) Anthony 1918- .. **CLC 4, 6**
  See also CA 49-52; CAAS 11; CANR 4

Kerry, Lois
  See Duncan, Lois

Kesey, Ken (Elton) 1935-2001 ... **CLC 1, 3, 6, 11, 46, 64, 184; WLC**
  See also AAYA 25; BG 3; BPFB 2; CA
  1-4R; 204; CANR 22, 38, 66, 124;
  CDALB 1968-1988; CN 7; CPW; DA;
  DA3; DAB; DAC; DAM MST, NOV,
  POP; DLB 2, 16, 206; EWL 3; EXPN;
  LAIT 4; MTCW 1, 2; NFS 2; RGAL 4;
  SATA 66; SATA-Obit 131; TUS; YAW

Kesselring, Joseph (Otto)
  1902-1967 .... **CLC 45**
  See also CA 150; DAM DRAM, MST

Kessler, Jascha (Frederick) 1929- ...... **CLC 4**
  See also CA 17-20R; CANR 8, 48, 111

Kettelkamp, Larry (Dale) 1933- .... **CLC 12**
  See also CA 29-32R; CANR 16; SAAS 3;
  SATA 2

Key, Ellen (Karolina Sofia)
  1849-1926 .... **TCLC 65**
  See also DLB 259

Keyber, Conny
  See Fielding, Henry

Keyes, Daniel 1927- .... **CLC 80**
  See also AAYA 23; BYA 11; CA 17-20R,
  181; CAAE 181; CANR 10, 26, 54, 74;
  DA; DA3; DAC; DAM MST, NOV;
  EXPN; LAIT 4; MTCW 2; NFS 2; SATA
  37; SFW 4

Keynes, John Maynard
  1883-1946 .... **TCLC 64**
  See also CA 114; 162, 163; DLBD 10;
  MTCW 2

Khanshendel, Chiron
  See Rose, Wendy

Khayyam, Omar 1048-1131 ... **CMLC 11; PC 8**
  See Omar Khayyam
  See also DA3; DAM POET

Kherdian, David 1931- .... **CLC 6, 9**
  See also AAYA 42; CA 21-24R, 192; CAAE
  192; CAAS 2; CANR 39, 78; CLR 24;
  JRDA; LAIT 3; MAICYA 1, 2; SATA 16,
  74; SATA-Essay 125

Khlebnikov, Velimir .... **TCLC 20**
  See Khlebnikov, Viktor Vladimirovich
  See also DLB 295; EW 10; EWL 3; RGWL
  2, 3

Khlebnikov, Viktor Vladimirovich 1885-1922
  See Khlebnikov, Velimir
  See also CA 117; 217

Khodasevich, Vladislav (Felitsianovich)
  1886-1939 .... **TCLC 15**
  See also CA 115; EWL 3

Kielland, Alexander Lange
  1849-1906 .... **TCLC 5**
  See also CA 104

Kiely, Benedict 1919- ... **CLC 23, 43; SSC 58**
  See also CA 1-4R; CANR 2, 84; CN 7;
  DLB 15

Kienzle, William X(avier)
  1928-2001 .... **CLC 25**
  See also CA 93-96; 203; CAAS 1; CANR
  9, 31, 59, 111; CMW 4; DA3; DAM POP;
  INT CANR-31; MSW; MTCW 1, 2

Kierkegaard, Soren 1813-1855 ..... **NCLC 34, 78, 125**
  See also EW 6; LMFS 2; RGWL 3; TWA

Kieslowski, Krzysztof 1941-1996 .... **CLC 120**
  See also CA 147; 151

Killens, John Oliver 1916-1987 .... **CLC 10**
  See also BW 2; CA 77-80; 123; CAAS 2;
  CANR 26; DLB 33; EWL 3

Killigrew, Anne 1660-1685 .... **LC 4, 73**
  See also DLB 131

Killigrew, Thomas 1612-1683 .... **LC 57**
  See also DLB 58; RGEL 2

Kim
  See Simenon, Georges (Jacques Christian)

Kincaid, Jamaica 1949- ...... **BLC 2; CLC 43, 68, 137**
  See also AAYA 13; AFAW 2; AMWS 7;
  BRWS 7; BW 2, 3; CA 125; CANR 47,
  59, 95; CDALBS; CDWLB 3; CLR 63;
  CN 7; DA3; DAM MULT, NOV; DLB
  157, 227; DNFS 1; EWL 3; EXPS; FW;
  LATS 1; LMFS 2; MTCW 2; NCFS 1;
  NFS 3; SSFS 5, 7; TUS; WWE 1; YAW

King, Francis (Henry) 1923- .... **CLC 8, 53, 145**
  See also CA 1-4R; CANR 1, 33, 86; CN 7;
  DAM NOV; DLB 15, 139; MTCW 1

King, Kennedy
  See Brown, George Douglas

King, Martin Luther, Jr. 1929-1968 . **BLC 2; CLC 83; WLCS**
  See also BW 2, 3; CA 25-28; CANR 27,
  44; CAP 2; DA; DA3; DAB; DAC; DAM
  MST, MULT; LAIT 5; LATS 1; MTCW
  1, 2; SATA 14

King, Stephen (Edwin) 1947- .... **CLC 12, 26, 37, 61, 113; SSC 17, 55**
  See also AAYA 1, 17; AMWS 5; BEST
  90:1; BPFB 2; CA 61-64; CANR 1, 30,
  52, 76, 119; CPW; DA3; DAM NOV,
  POP; DLB 143; DLBY 1980; HGG;
  JRDA; LAIT 5; MTCW 1, 2; RGAL 4;
  SATA 9, 55; SUFW 1, 2; WYAS 1; YAW

King, Steve
  See King, Stephen (Edwin)

King, Thomas 1943- .... **CLC 89, 171; NNAL**
  See also CA 144; CANR 95; CCA 1; CN 7;
  DAC; DAM MULT; DLB 175; SATA 96

Kingman, Lee .... **CLC 17**
  See Natti, (Mary) Lee
  See also CWRI 5; SAAS 3; SATA 1, 67

Kingsley, Charles 1819-1875 .... **NCLC 35**
  See also CLR 77; DLB 21, 32, 163, 178,
  190; FANT; MAICYA 2; MAICYAS 1;
  RGEL 2; WCH; YABC 2

Kingsley, Henry 1830-1876 .... **NCLC 107**
  See also DLB 21, 230; RGEL 2

Kingsley, Sidney 1906-1995 .... **CLC 44**
  See also CA 85-88; 147; CAD; DFS 14;
  DLB 7; RGAL 4

Kingsolver, Barbara 1955- . **CLC 55, 81, 130**
  See also AAYA 15; AMWS 7; CA 129; 134;
  CANR 60, 96; CDALBS; CPW; CSW;
  DA3; DAM POP; DLB 206; INT CA-134;
  LAIT 5; MTCW 2; NFS 5, 10, 12; RGAL
  4

Kingston, Maxine (Ting Ting) Hong
  1940- .... **AAL; CLC 12, 19, 58, 121; WLCS**
  See also AAYA 8, 55; AMWS 5; BPFB 2;
  CA 69-72; CANR 13, 38, 74, 87;
  CDALBS; CN 7; DA3; DAM MULT,
  NOV; DLB 173, 212; DLBY 1980; EWL
  3; FW; INT CANR-13; LAIT 5; MAWW;
  MTCW 1, 2; NFS 6; RGAL 4; SATA 53;
  SSFS 3

Kinnell, Galway 1927- ..... **CLC 1, 2, 3, 5, 13, 29, 129; PC 26**
  See also AMWS 3; CA 9-12R; CANR 10,
  34, 66, 116; CP 7; DLB 5; DLBY 1987;
  EWL 3; INT CANR-34; MTCW 1, 2;
  PAB; PFS 9; RGAL 4; WP

Kinsella, Thomas 1928- .... **CLC 4, 19, 138**
  See also BRWS 5; CA 17-20R; CANR 15,
  122; CP 7; DLB 27; EWL 3; MTCW 1, 2;
  RGEL 2; TEA

Kinsella, W(illiam) P(atrick) 1935- . **CLC 27, 43, 166**
  See also AAYA 7; BPFB 2; CA 97-100;
  CAAS 7; CANR 21, 35, 66, 75; CN 7;
  CPW; DAC; DAM NOV, POP; FANT;
  INT CANR-21; LAIT 5; MTCW 1, 2;
  NFS 15; RGSF 2

Kinsey, Alfred C(harles)
 1894-1956 .... **TCLC 91**
 See also CA 115; 170; MTCW 2

Kipling, (Joseph) Rudyard 1865-1936 . **PC 3;**
 SSC 5, 54; TCLC 8, 17; WLC
 See also AAYA 32; BRW 6; BRWC 1, 2;
 BYA 4; CA 105; 120; CANR 33; CDBLB
 1890-1914; CLR 39, 65; CWRI 5; DA;
 DA3; DAB; DAC; DAM MST, POET;
 DLB 19, 34, 141, 156; EWL 3; EXPS;
 FANT; LAIT 3; LMFS 1; MAICYA 1, 2;
 MTCW 1, 2; RGEL 2; RGSF 2; SATA
 100; SFW 4; SSFS 8; SUFW 1; TEA;
 WCH; WLIT 4; YABC 2

Kirk, Russell (Amos) 1918-1994 .. **TCLC 119**
 See also AITN 1; CA 1-4R; 145; CAAS 9;
 CANR 1, 20, 60; HGG; INT CANR-20;
 MTCW 1, 2

Kirkland, Caroline M. 1801-1864 . **NCLC 85**
 See also DLB 3, 73, 74, 250, 254; DLBD
 13

Kirkup, James 1918- .... **CLC 1**
 See also CA 1-4R; CAAS 4; CANR 2; CP
 7; DLB 27; SATA 12

Kirkwood, James 1930(?)-1989 .... **CLC 9**
 See also AITN 2; CA 1-4R; 128; CANR 6,
 40; GLL 2

Kirsch, Sarah 1935- .... **CLC 176**
 See also CA 178; CWW 2; DLB 75; EWL
 3

Kirshner, Sidney
 See Kingsley, Sidney

Kis, Danilo 1935-1989 .... **CLC 57**
 See also CA 109; 118; 129; CANR 61; CD-
 WLB 4; DLB 181; EWL 3; MTCW 1;
 RGSF 2; RGWL 2, 3

Kissinger, Henry A(lfred) 1923- ..... **CLC 137**
 See also CA 1-4R; CANR 2, 33, 66, 109;
 MTCW 1

Kivi, Aleksis 1834-1872 .... **NCLC 30**

Kizer, Carolyn (Ashley) 1925- .. **CLC 15, 39,**
 80
 See also CA 65-68; CAAS 5; CANR 24,
 70; CP 7; CWP; DAM POET; DLB 5,
 169; EWL 3; MTCW 2; PFS 18

Klabund 1890-1928 .... **TCLC 44**
 See also CA 162; DLB 66

Klappert, Peter 1942- .... **CLC 57**
 See also CA 33-36R; CSW; DLB 5

Klein, A(braham) M(oses)
 1909-1972 .... **CLC 19**
 See also CA 101; 37-40R; DAB; DAC;
 DAM MST; DLB 68; EWL 3; RGEL 2

Klein, Joe
 See Klein, Joseph

Klein, Joseph 1946- .... **CLC 154**
 See also CA 85-88; CANR 55

Klein, Norma 1938-1989 .... **CLC 30**
 See also AAYA 2, 35; BPFB 2; BYA 6, 7,
 8; CA 41-44R; 128; CANR 15, 37; CLR
 2, 19; INT CANR-15; JRDA; MAICYA
 1, 2; SAAS 1; SATA 7, 57; WYA; YAW

Klein, T(heodore) E(ibon) D(onald)
 1947- .... **CLC 34**
 See also CA 119; CANR 44, 75; HGG

Kleist, Heinrich von 1777-1811 ...... **NCLC 2,**
 37; SSC 22
 See also CDWLB 2; DAM DRAM; DLB
 90; EW 5; RGSF 2; RGWL 2, 3

Klima, Ivan 1931- .... **CLC 56, 172**
 See also CA 25-28R; CANR 17, 50, 91;
 CDWLB 4; CWW 2; DAM NOV; DLB
 232; EWL 3; RGWL 3

Klimentev, Andrei Platonovich
 See Klimentov, Andrei Platonovich

Klimentov, Andrei Platonovich
 1899-1951 .... **SSC 42; TCLC 14**
 See Platonov, Andrei Platonovich; Platonov,
 Andrey Platonovich
 See also CA 108

Klinger, Friedrich Maximilian von
 1752-1831 .... **NCLC 1**
 See also DLB 94

Klingsor the Magician
 See Hartmann, Sadakichi

Klopstock, Friedrich Gottlieb
 1724-1803 .... **NCLC 11**
 See also DLB 97; EW 4; RGWL 2, 3

Kluge, Alexander 1932- .... **SSC 61**
 See also CA 81-84; DLB 75

Knapp, Caroline 1959-2002 .... **CLC 99**
 See also CA 154; 207

Knebel, Fletcher 1911-1993 .... **CLC 14**
 See also AITN 1; CA 1-4R; 140; CAAS 3;
 CANR 1, 36; SATA 36; SATA-Obit 75

Knickerbocker, Diedrich
 See Irving, Washington

Knight, Etheridge 1931-1991 ... **BLC 2; CLC**
 40; PC 14
 See also BW 1, 3; CA 21-24R; 133; CANR
 23, 82; DAM POET; DLB 41; MTCW 2;
 RGAL 4

Knight, Sarah Kemble 1666-1727 .... **LC 7**
 See also DLB 24, 200

Knister, Raymond 1899-1932 .... **TCLC 56**
 See also CA 186; DLB 68; RGEL 2

Knowles, John 1926-2001 ... **CLC 1, 4, 10, 26**
 See also AAYA 10; AMWS 12; BPFB 2;
 BYA 3; CA 17-20R; 203; CANR 40, 74,
 76; CDALB 1968-1988; CN 7; DA; DAC;
 DAM MST, NOV; DLB 6; EXPN; MTCW
 1, 2; NFS 2; RGAL 4; SATA 8, 89; SATA-
 Obit 134; YAW

Knox, Calvin M.
 See Silverberg, Robert

Knox, John c. 1505-1572 .... **LC 37**
 See also DLB 132

Knye, Cassandra
 See Disch, Thomas M(ichael)

Koch, C(hristopher) J(ohn) 1932- .... **CLC 42**
 See also CA 127; CANR 84; CN 7; DLB
 289

Koch, Christopher
 See Koch, C(hristopher) J(ohn)

Koch, Kenneth (Jay) 1925-2002 .... **CLC 5, 8,**
 44
 See also CA 1-4R; 207; CAD; CANR 6,
 36, 57, 97; CD 5; CP 7; DAM POET;
 DLB 5; INT CANR-36; MTCW 2; SATA
 65; WP

Kochanowski, Jan 1530-1584 .... **LC 10**
 See also RGWL 2, 3

Kock, Charles Paul de 1794-1871 . **NCLC 16**

Koda Rohan
 See Koda Shigeyuki

Koda Rohan
 See Koda Shigeyuki
 See also DLB 180

Koda Shigeyuki 1867-1947 .... **TCLC 22**
 See Koda Rohan
 See also CA 121; 183

Koestler, Arthur 1905-1983 ... **CLC 1, 3, 6, 8,**
 15, 33
 See also BRWS 1; CA 1-4R; 109; CANR 1,
 33; CDBLB 1945-1960; DLBY 1983;
 EWL 3; MTCW 1, 2; RGEL 2

Kogawa, Joy Nozomi 1935- ...... **CLC 78, 129**
 See also AAYA 47; CA 101; CANR 19, 62,
 126; CN 7; CWP; DAC; DAM MST,
 MULT; FW; MTCW 2; NFS 3; SATA 99

Kohout, Pavel 1928- .... **CLC 13**
 See also CA 45-48; CANR 3

Koizumi, Yakumo
 See Hearn, (Patricio) Lafcadio (Tessima
 Carlos)

Kolmar, Gertrud 1894-1943 .... **TCLC 40**
 See also CA 167; EWL 3

Komunyakaa, Yusef 1947- .. **BLCS; CLC 86,**
 94; PC 51
 See also AFAW 2; AMWS 13; CA 147;
 CANR 83; CP 7; CSW; DLB 120; EWL
 3; PFS 5; RGAL 4

Konrad, George
 See Konrad, Gyorgy
 See also CWW 2

Konrad, Gyorgy 1933- .... **CLC 4, 10, 73**
 See Konrad, George
 See also CA 85-88; CANR 97; CDWLB 4;
 CWW 2; DLB 232; EWL 3

Konwicki, Tadeusz 1926- .... **CLC 8, 28, 54,**
 117
 See also CA 101; CAAS 9; CANR 39, 59;
 CWW 2; DLB 232; EWL 3; IDFW 3;
 MTCW 1

Koontz, Dean R(ay) 1945- .... **CLC 78**
 See also AAYA 9, 31; BEST 89:3, 90:2; CA
 108; CANR 19, 36, 52, 95; CMW 4;
 CPW; DA3; DAM NOV, POP; DLB 292;
 HGG; MTCW 1; SATA 92; SFW 4;
 SUFW 2; YAW

Kopernik, Mikolaj
 See Copernicus, Nicolaus

Kopit, Arthur (Lee) 1937- ...... **CLC 1, 18, 33**
 See also AITN 1; CA 81-84; CABS 3; CD
 5; DAM DRAM; DFS 7, 14; DLB 7;
 MTCW 1; RGAL 4

Kopitar, Jernej (Bartholomaus)
 1780-1844 .... **NCLC 117**

Kops, Bernard 1926- .... **CLC 4**
 See also CA 5-8R; CANR 84; CBD; CN 7;
 CP 7; DLB 13

Kornbluth, C(yril) M. 1923-1958 .... **TCLC 8**
 See also CA 105; 160; DLB 8; SFW 4

Korolenko, V. G.
 See Korolenko, Vladimir Galaktionovich

Korolenko, Vladimir
 See Korolenko, Vladimir Galaktionovich

Korolenko, Vladimir G.
 See Korolenko, Vladimir Galaktionovich

Korolenko, Vladimir Galaktionovich
 1853-1921 .... **TCLC 22**
 See also CA 121; DLB 277

Korzybski, Alfred (Habdank Skarbek)
 1879-1950 .... **TCLC 61**
 See also CA 123; 160

Kosinski, Jerzy (Nikodem)
 1933-1991 .... **CLC 1, 2, 3, 6, 10, 15, 53,**
 70
 See also AMWS 7; BPFB 2; CA 17-20R;
 134; CANR 9, 46; DA3; DAM NOV;
 DLB 2; DLBY 1982; EWL 3; HGG;
 MTCW 1, 2; NFS 12; RGAL 4; TUS

Kostelanetz, Richard (Cory) 1940- .. **CLC 28**
 See also CA 13-16R; CAAS 8; CANR 38,
 77; CN 7; CP 7

Kostrowitzki, Wilhelm Apollinaris de
 1880-1918
 See Apollinaire, Guillaume
 See also CA 104

Kotlowitz, Robert 1924- .... **CLC 4**
 See also CA 33-36R; CANR 36

Kotzebue, August (Friedrich Ferdinand) von
 1761-1819 .... **NCLC 25**
 See also DLB 94

Kotzwinkle, William 1938- ..... **CLC 5, 14, 35**
 See also BPFB 2; CA 45-48; CANR 3, 44,
 84; CLR 6; DLB 173; FANT; MAICYA
 1, 2; SATA 24, 70, 146; SFW 4; SUFW 2;
 YAW

Kowna, Stancy
 See Szymborska, Wislawa

Kozol, Jonathan 1936- .... **CLC 17**
    See also AAYA 46; CA 61-64; CANR 16, 45, 96
Kozoll, Michael 1940(?)- .... **CLC 35**
Kramer, Kathryn 19(?)- .... **CLC 34**
Kramer, Larry 1935- .... **CLC 42; DC 8**
    See also CA 124; 126; CANR 60; DAM POP; DLB 249; GLL 1
Krasicki, Ignacy 1735-1801 .... **NCLC 8**
Krasinski, Zygmunt 1812-1859 .... **NCLC 4**
    See also RGWL 2, 3
Kraus, Karl 1874-1936 .... **TCLC 5**
    See also CA 104; 216; DLB 118; EWL 3
Kreve (Mickevicius), Vincas
    1882-1954 .... **TCLC 27**
    See also CA 170; DLB 220; EWL 3
Kristeva, Julia 1941- .... **CLC 77, 140**
    See also CA 154; CANR 99; DLB 242; EWL 3; FW; LMFS 2
Kristofferson, Kris 1936- .... **CLC 26**
    See also CA 104
Krizanc, John 1956- .... **CLC 57**
    See also CA 187
Krleza, Miroslav 1893-1981 .... **CLC 8, 114**
    See also CA 97-100; 105; CANR 50; CD-WLB 4; DLB 147; EW 11; RGWL 2, 3
Kroetsch, Robert 1927- .. **CLC 5, 23, 57, 132**
    See also CA 17-20R; CANR 8, 38; CCA 1; CN 7; CP 7; DAC; DAM POET; DLB 53; MTCW 1
Kroetz, Franz
    See Kroetz, Franz Xaver
Kroetz, Franz Xaver 1946- .... **CLC 41**
    See also CA 130; EWL 3
Kroker, Arthur (W.) 1945- .... **CLC 77**
    See also CA 161
Kropotkin, Peter (Aleksieevich)
    1842-1921 .... **TCLC 36**
    See Kropotkin, Petr Alekseevich
    See also CA 119; 219
Kropotkin, Petr Alekseevich
    See Kropotkin, Peter (Aleksieevich)
    See also DLB 277
Krotkov, Yuri 1917-1981 .... **CLC 19**
    See also CA 102
Krumb
    See Crumb, R(obert)
Krumgold, Joseph (Quincy)
    1908-1980 .... **CLC 12**
    See also BYA 1, 2; CA 9-12R; 101; CANR 7; MAICYA 1, 2; SATA 1, 48; SATA-Obit 23; YAW
Krumwitz
    See Crumb, R(obert)
Krutch, Joseph Wood 1893-1970 ..... **CLC 24**
    See also ANW; CA 1-4R; 25-28R; CANR 4; DLB 63, 206, 275
Krutzch, Gus
    See Eliot, T(homas) S(tearns)
Krylov, Ivan Andreevich
    1768(?)-1844 .... **NCLC 1**
    See also DLB 150
Kubin, Alfred (Leopold Isidor)
    1877-1959 .... **TCLC 23**
    See also CA 112; 149; CANR 104; DLB 81
Kubrick, Stanley 1928-1999 .... **CLC 16; TCLC 112**
    See also AAYA 30; CA 81-84; 177; CANR 33; DLB 26
Kumin, Maxine (Winokur) 1925- ..... **CLC 5, 13, 28, 164; PC 15**
    See also AITN 2; AMWS 4; ANW; CA 1-4R; CAAS 8; CANR 1, 21, 69, 115; CP 7; CWP; DA3; DAM POET; DLB 5; EWL 3; EXPP; MTCW 1, 2; PAB; PFS 18; SATA 12

Kundera, Milan 1929- . **CLC 4, 9, 19, 32, 68, 115, 135; SSC 24**
    See also AAYA 2; BPFB 2; CA 85-88; CANR 19, 52, 74; CDWLB 4; CWW 2; DA3; DAM NOV; DLB 232; EW 13; EWL 3; MTCW 1, 2; NFS 18; RGSF 2; RGWL 3; SSFS 10
Kunene, Mazisi (Raymond) 1930- ... **CLC 85**
    See also BW 1, 3; CA 125; CANR 81; CP 7; DLB 117
Kung, Hans .... **CLC 130**
    See Kung, Hans
Kung, Hans 1928-
    See Kung, Hans
    See also CA 53-56; CANR 66; MTCW 1, 2
Kunikida Doppo 1869(?)-1908
    See Doppo, Kunikida
    See also DLB 180; EWL 3
Kunitz, Stanley (Jasspon) 1905- .. **CLC 6, 11, 14, 148; PC 19**
    See also AMWS 3; CA 41-44R; CANR 26, 57, 98; CP 7; DA3; DLB 48; INT CANR-26; MTCW 1, 2; PFS 11; RGAL 4
Kunze, Reiner 1933- .... **CLC 10**
    See also CA 93-96; CWW 2; DLB 75; EWL 3
Kuprin, Aleksander Ivanovich
    1870-1938 .... **TCLC 5**
    See Kuprin, Aleksandr Ivanovich; Kuprin, Alexandr Ivanovich
    See also CA 104; 182
Kuprin, Aleksandr Ivanovich
    See Kuprin, Aleksander Ivanovich
    See also DLB 295
Kuprin, Alexandr Ivanovich
    See Kuprin, Aleksander Ivanovich
    See also EWL 3
Kureishi, Hanif 1954(?)- .... **CLC 64, 135**
    See also CA 139; CANR 113; CBD; CD 5; CN 7; DLB 194, 245; GLL 2; IDFW 4; WLIT 4; WWE 1
Kurosawa, Akira 1910-1998 ..... **CLC 16, 119**
    See also AAYA 11; CA 101; 170; CANR 46; DAM MULT
Kushner, Tony 1957(?)- .... **CLC 81; DC 10**
    See also AMWS 9; CA 144; CAD; CANR 74; CD 5; DA3; DAM DRAM; DFS 5; DLB 228; EWL 3; GLL 1; LAIT 5; MTCW 2; RGAL 4
Kuttner, Henry 1915-1958 .... **TCLC 10**
    See also CA 107; 157; DLB 8; FANT; SCFW 2; SFW 4
Kutty, Madhavi
    See Das, Kamala
Kuzma, Greg 1944- .... **CLC 7**
    See also CA 33-36R; CANR 70
Kuzmin, Mikhail (Alekseevich)
    1872(?)-1936 .... **TCLC 40**
    See also CA 170; DLB 295; EWL 3
Kyd, Thomas 1558-1594 .... **DC 3; LC 22**
    See also BRW 1; DAM DRAM; DLB 62; IDTP; LMFS 1; RGEL 2; TEA; WLIT 3
Kyprianos, Iossif
    See Samarakis, Antonis
L. S.
    See Stephen, Sir Leslie
Labrunie, Gerard
    See Nerval, Gerard de
La Bruyere, Jean de 1645-1696 .... **LC 17**
    See also DLB 268; EW 3; GFL Beginnings to 1789
Lacan, Jacques (Marie Emile)
    1901-1981 .... **CLC 75**
    See also CA 121; 104; DLB 296; EWL 3; TWA
Laclos, Pierre Ambroise Francois
    1741-1803 .... **NCLC 4, 87**
    See also EW 4; GFL Beginnings to 1789; RGWL 2, 3

Lacolere, Francois
    See Aragon, Louis
La Colere, Francois
    See Aragon, Louis
La Deshabilleuse
    See Simenon, Georges (Jacques Christian)
Lady Gregory
    See Gregory, Lady Isabella Augusta (Persse)
Lady of Quality, A
    See Bagnold, Enid
La Fayette, Marie-(Madelaine Pioche de la Vergne) 1634-1693 .... **LC 2**
    See Lafayette, Marie-Madeleine
    See also GFL Beginnings to 1789; RGWL 2, 3
Lafayette, Marie-Madeleine
    See La Fayette, Marie-(Madelaine Pioche de la Vergne)
    See also DLB 268
Lafayette, Rene
    See Hubbard, L(afayette) Ron(ald)
La Flesche, Francis 1857(?)-1932 ...... **NNAL**
    See also CA 144; CANR 83; DLB 175
La Fontaine, Jean de 1621-1695 .... **LC 50**
    See also DLB 268; EW 3; GFL Beginnings to 1789; MAICYA 1, 2; RGWL 2, 3; SATA 18
Laforgue, Jules 1860-1887 . **NCLC 5, 53; PC 14; SSC 20**
    See also DLB 217; EW 7; GFL 1789 to the Present; RGWL 2, 3
Layamon
    See Layamon
    See also DLB 146
Lagerkvist, Paer (Fabian)
    1891-1974 ..... **CLC 7, 10, 13, 54; TCLC 144**
    See Lagerkvist, Par
    See also CA 85-88; 49-52; DA3; DAM DRAM, NOV; MTCW 1, 2; TWA
Lagerkvist, Par .... **SSC 12**
    See Lagerkvist, Paer (Fabian)
    See also DLB 259; EW 10; EWL 3; MTCW 2; RGSF 2; RGWL 2, 3
Lagerloef, Selma (Ottiliana Lovisa)
    1858-1940 .... **TCLC 4, 36**
    See Lagerlof, Selma (Ottiliana Lovisa)
    See also CA 108; MTCW 2; SATA 15
Lagerlof, Selma (Ottiliana Lovisa)
    See Lagerloef, Selma (Ottiliana Lovisa)
    See also CLR 7; SATA 15
La Guma, (Justin) Alex(ander)
    1925-1985 . **BLCS; CLC 19; TCLC 140**
    See also AFW; BW 1, 3; CA 49-52; 118; CANR 25, 81; CDWLB 3; DAM NOV; DLB 117, 225; EWL 3; MTCW 1, 2; WLIT 2; WWE 1
Laidlaw, A. K.
    See Grieve, C(hristopher) M(urray)
Lainez, Manuel Mujica
    See Mujica Lainez, Manuel
    See also HW 1
Laing, R(onald) D(avid) 1927-1989 . **CLC 95**
    See also CA 107; 129; CANR 34; MTCW 1
Lamartine, Alphonse (Marie Louis Prat) de
    1790-1869 .... **NCLC 11; PC 16**
    See also DAM POET; DLB 217; GFL 1789 to the Present; RGWL 2, 3
Lamb, Charles 1775-1834 ..... **NCLC 10, 113; WLC**
    See also BRW 4; CDBLB 1789-1832; DA; DAB; DAC; DAM MST; DLB 93, 107, 163; RGEL 2; SATA 17; TEA
Lamb, Lady Caroline 1785-1828 ... **NCLC 38**
    See also DLB 116
Lamb, Mary Ann 1764-1847 .... **NCLC 125**
    See also DLB 163; SATA 17
Lame Deer 1903(?)-1976 .... **NNAL**
    See also CA 69-72

Lamming, George (William) 1927- ... **BLC 2; CLC 2, 4, 66, 144**
See also BW 2, 3; CA 85-88; CANR 26, 76; CDWLB 3; CN 7; DAM MULT; DLB 125; EWL 3; MTCW 1, 2; NFS 15; RGEL 2

L'Amour, Louis (Dearborn)
1908-1988 .... **CLC 25, 55**
See Burns, Tex; Mayo, Jim
See also AAYA 16; AITN 2; BEST 89:2; BPFB 2; CA 1-4R; 125; CANR 3, 25, 40; CPW; DA3; DAM NOV, POP; DLB 206; DLBY 1980; MTCW 1, 2; RGAL 4

Lampedusa, Giuseppe (Tomasi) di
.... **TCLC 13**
See Tomasi di Lampedusa, Giuseppe
See also CA 164; EW 11; MTCW 2; RGWL 2, 3

Lampman, Archibald 1861-1899 ... **NCLC 25**
See also DLB 92; RGEL 2; TWA

Lancaster, Bruce 1896-1963 .... **CLC 36**
See also CA 9-10; CANR 70; CAP 1; SATA 9

Lanchester, John 1962- .... **CLC 99**
See also CA 194; DLB 267

Landau, Mark Alexandrovich
See Aldanov, Mark (Alexandrovich)

Landau-Aldanov, Mark Alexandrovich
See Aldanov, Mark (Alexandrovich)

Landis, Jerry
See Simon, Paul (Frederick)

Landis, John 1950- .... **CLC 26**
See also CA 112; 122

Landolfi, Tommaso 1908-1979 .... **CLC 11, 49**
See also CA 127; 117; DLB 177; EWL 3

Landon, Letitia Elizabeth
1802-1838 .... **NCLC 15**
See also DLB 96

Landor, Walter Savage
1775-1864 .... **NCLC 14**
See also BRW 4; DLB 93, 107; RGEL 2

Landwirth, Heinz 1927-
See Lind, Jakov
See also CA 9-12R; CANR 7

Lane, Patrick 1939- .... **CLC 25**
See also CA 97-100; CANR 54; CP 7; DAM POET; DLB 53; INT CA-97-100

Lang, Andrew 1844-1912 .... **TCLC 16**
See also CA 114; 137; CANR 85; DLB 98, 141, 184; FANT; MAICYA 1, 2; RGEL 2; SATA 16; WCH

Lang, Fritz 1890-1976 .... **CLC 20, 103**
See also CA 77-80; 69-72; CANR 30

Lange, John
See Crichton, (John) Michael

Langer, Elinor 1939- .... **CLC 34**
See also CA 121

Langland, William 1332(?)-1400(?) ..... **LC 19**
See also BRW 1; DA; DAB; DAC; DAM MST, POET; DLB 146; RGEL 2; TEA; WLIT 3

Langstaff, Launcelot
See Irving, Washington

Lanier, Sidney 1842-1881 . **NCLC 6, 118; PC 50**
See also AMWS 1; DAM POET; DLB 64; DLBD 13; EXPP; MAICYA 1; PFS 14; RGAL 4; SATA 18

Lanyer, Aemilia 1569-1645 ...... **LC 10, 30, 83**
See also DLB 121

Lao-Tzu
See Lao Tzu

Lao Tzu c. 6th cent. B.C.-3rd cent.
B.C. .... **CMLC 7**

Lapine, James (Elliot) 1949- .... **CLC 39**
See also CA 123; 130; CANR 54; INT CA-130

Larbaud, Valery (Nicolas)
1881-1957 .... **TCLC 9**
See also CA 106; 152; EWL 3; GFL 1789 to the Present

Lardner, Ring
See Lardner, Ring(gold) W(ilmer)
See also BPFB 2; CDALB 1917-1929; DLB 11, 25, 86, 171; DLBD 16; RGAL 4; RGSF 2

Lardner, Ring W., Jr.
See Lardner, Ring(gold) W(ilmer)

Lardner, Ring(gold) W(ilmer)
1885-1933 .... **SSC 32; TCLC 2, 14**
See Lardner, Ring
See also AMW; CA 104; 131; MTCW 1, 2; TUS

Laredo, Betty
See Codrescu, Andrei

Larkin, Maia
See Wojciechowska, Maia (Teresa)

Larkin, Philip (Arthur) 1922-1985 ... **CLC 3, 5, 8, 9, 13, 18, 33, 39, 64; PC 21**
See also BRWS 1; CA 5-8R; 117; CANR 24, 62; CDBLB 1960 to Present; DA3; DAB; DAM MST, POET; DLB 27; EWL 3; MTCW 1, 2; PFS 3, 4, 12; RGEL 2

La Roche, Sophie von
1730-1807 .... **NCLC 121**
See also DLB 94

Larra (y Sanchez de Castro), Mariano Jose de 1809-1837 .... **NCLC 17, 130**

Larsen, Eric 1941- .... **CLC 55**
See also CA 132

Larsen, Nella 1893(?)-1963 .... **BLC 2; CLC 37; HR 3**
See also AFAW 1, 2; BW 1; CA 125; CANR 83; DAM MULT; DLB 51; FW; LATS 1; LMFS 2

Larson, Charles R(aymond) 1938- ... **CLC 31**
See also CA 53-56; CANR 4, 121

Larson, Jonathan 1961-1996 .... **CLC 99**
See also AAYA 28; CA 156

Las Casas, Bartolome de
1474-1566 .... **HLCS; LC 31**
See Casas, Bartolome de las
See also LAW

Lasch, Christopher 1932-1994 .... **CLC 102**
See also CA 73-76; 144; CANR 25, 118; DLB 246; MTCW 1, 2

Lasker-Schueler, Else 1869-1945 ... **TCLC 57**
See Lasker-Schuler, Else
See also CA 183; DLB 66, 124

Lasker-Schuler, Else
See Lasker-Schueler, Else
See also EWL 3

Laski, Harold J(oseph) 1893-1950 . **TCLC 79**
See also CA 188

Latham, Jean Lee 1902-1995 .... **CLC 12**
See also AITN 1; BYA 1; CA 5-8R; CANR 7, 84; CLR 50; MAICYA 1, 2; SATA 2, 68; YAW

Latham, Mavis
See Clark, Mavis Thorpe

Lathen, Emma .... **CLC 2**
See Hennissart, Martha; Latsis, Mary J(ane)
See also BPFB 2; CMW 4

Lathrop, Francis
See Leiber, Fritz (Reuter, Jr.)

Latsis, Mary J(ane) 1927(?)-1997
See Lathen, Emma
See also CA 85-88; 162; CMW 4

Lattany, Kristin
See Lattany, Kristin (Elaine Eggleston) Hunter

Lattany, Kristin (Elaine Eggleston) Hunter
1931- .... **CLC 35**
See also AITN 1; BW 1; BYA 3; CA 13-16R; CANR 13, 108; CLR 3; CN 7; DLB 33; INT CANR-13; MAICYA 1, 2; SAAS 10; SATA 12, 132; YAW

Lattimore, Richmond (Alexander)
1906-1984 .... **CLC 3**
See also CA 1-4R; 112; CANR 1

Laughlin, James 1914-1997 .... **CLC 49**
See also CA 21-24R; 162; CAAS 22; CANR 9, 47; CP 7; DLB 48; DLBY 1996, 1997

Laurence, (Jean) Margaret (Wemyss)
1926-1987 . **CLC 3, 6, 13, 50, 62; SSC 7**
See also BYA 13; CA 5-8R; 121; CANR 33; DAC; DAM MST; DLB 53; EWL 3; FW; MTCW 1, 2; NFS 11; RGEL 2; RGSF 2; SATA-Obit 50; TCWW 2

Laurent, Antoine 1952- .... **CLC 50**

Lauscher, Hermann
See Hesse, Hermann

Lautreamont 1846-1870 .. **NCLC 12; SSC 14**
See Lautreamont, Isidore Lucien Ducasse
See also GFL 1789 to the Present; RGWL 2, 3

Lautreamont, Isidore Lucien Ducasse
See Lautreamont
See also DLB 217

Laverty, Donald
See Blish, James (Benjamin)

Lavin, Mary 1912-1996 . **CLC 4, 18, 99; SSC 4, 67**
See also CA 9-12R; 151; CANR 33; CN 7; DLB 15; FW; MTCW 1; RGEL 2; RGSF 2

Lavond, Paul Dennis
See Kornbluth, C(yril) M.; Pohl, Frederik

Lawler, Ray
See Lawler, Raymond Evenor
See also DLB 289

Lawler, Raymond Evenor 1922- .... **CLC 58**
See Lawler, Ray
See also CA 103; CD 5; RGEL 2

Lawrence, D(avid) H(erbert Richards)
1885-1930 . **PC 54; SSC 4, 19; TCLC 2, 9, 16, 33, 48, 61, 93; WLC**
See Chambers, Jessie
See also BPFB 2; BRW 7; BRWR 2; CA 104; 121; CDBLB 1914-1945; DA; DAB; DAC; DAM MST, NOV, POET; DLB 10, 19, 36, 98, 162, 195; EWL 3; EXPP; EXPS; LAIT 2, 3; MTCW 1, 2; NFS 18; PFS 6; RGEL 2; RGSF 2; SSFS 2, 6; TEA; WLIT 4; WP

Lawrence, T(homas) E(dward)
1888-1935 .... **TCLC 18**
See Dale, Colin
See also BRWS 2; CA 115; 167; DLB 195

Lawrence of Arabia
See Lawrence, T(homas) E(dward)

Lawson, Henry (Archibald Hertzberg)
1867-1922 .... **SSC 18; TCLC 27**
See also CA 120; 181; DLB 230; RGEL 2; RGSF 2

Lawton, Dennis
See Faust, Frederick (Schiller)

Layamon fl. c. 1200- .... **CMLC 10**
See Layamon
See also RGEL 2

Laye, Camara 1928-1980 ..... **BLC 2; CLC 4, 38**
See Camara Laye
See also AFW; BW 1; CA 85-88; 97-100; CANR 25; DAM MULT; MTCW 1, 2; WLIT 2

Layton, Irving (Peter) 1912- .... **CLC 2, 15, 164**
See also CA 1-4R; CANR 2, 33, 43, 66; CP 7; DAC; DAM MST, POET; DLB 88; EWL 3; MTCW 1, 2; PFS 12; RGEL 2

Lazarus, Emma 1849-1887 ...... **NCLC 8, 109**

Lazarus, Felix
  See Cable, George Washington

Lazarus, Henry
  See Slavitt, David R(ytman)

Lea, Joan
  See Neufeld, John (Arthur)

Leacock, Stephen (Butler)
  1869-1944 .... **SSC 39; TCLC 2**
  See also CA 104; 141; CANR 80; DAC;
  DAM MST; DLB 92; EWL 3; MTCW 2;
  RGEL 2; RGSF 2

Lead, Jane Ward 1623-1704 .... **LC 72**
  See also DLB 131

Leapor, Mary 1722-1746 .... **LC 80**
  See also DLB 109

Lear, Edward 1812-1888 .... **NCLC 3**
  See also AAYA 48; BRW 5; CLR 1, 75;
  DLB 32, 163, 166; MAICYA 1, 2; RGEL
  2; SATA 18, 100; WCH; WP

Lear, Norman (Milton) 1922- .... **CLC 12**
  See also CA 73-76

Leautaud, Paul 1872-1956 .... **TCLC 83**
  See also CA 203; DLB 65; GFL 1789 to the
  Present

Leavis, F(rank) R(aymond)
  1895-1978 .... **CLC 24**
  See also BRW 7; CA 21-24R; 77-80; CANR
  44; DLB 242; EWL 3; MTCW 1, 2;
  RGEL 2

Leavitt, David 1961- .... **CLC 34**
  See also CA 116; 122; CANR 50, 62, 101;
  CPW; DA3; DAM POP; DLB 130; GLL
  1; INT CA-122; MTCW 2

Leblanc, Maurice (Marie Emile)
  1864-1941 .... **TCLC 49**
  See also CA 110; CMW 4

Lebowitz, Fran(ces Ann) 1951(?)- ... **CLC 11,
  36**
  See also CA 81-84; CANR 14, 60, 70; INT
  CANR-14; MTCW 1

Lebrecht, Peter
  See Tieck, (Johann) Ludwig

le Carre, John .... **CLC 3, 5, 9, 15, 28**
  See Cornwell, David (John Moore)
  See also AAYA 42; BEST 89:4; BPFB 2;
  BRWS 2; CDBLB 1960 to Present; CMW
  4; CN 7; CPW; DLB 87; EWL 3; MSW;
  MTCW 2; RGEL 2; TEA

Le Clezio, J(ean) M(arie) G(ustave)
  1940- .... **CLC 31, 155**
  See also CA 116; 128; DLB 83; EWL 3;
  GFL 1789 to the Present; RGSF 2

Leconte de Lisle, Charles-Marie-Rene
  1818-1894 .... **NCLC 29**
  See also DLB 217; EW 6; GFL 1789 to the
  Present

Le Coq, Monsieur
  See Simenon, Georges (Jacques Christian)

Leduc, Violette 1907-1972 .... **CLC 22**
  See also CA 13-14; 33-36R; CANR 69;
  CAP 1; EWL 3; GFL 1789 to the Present;
  GLL 1

Ledwidge, Francis 1887(?)-1917 .... **TCLC 23**
  See also CA 123; 203; DLB 20

Lee, Andrea 1953- .... **BLC 2; CLC 36**
  See also BW 1, 3; CA 125; CANR 82;
  DAM MULT

Lee, Andrew
  See Auchincloss, Louis (Stanton)

Lee, Chang-rae 1965- .... **CLC 91**
  See also CA 148; CANR 89; LATS 1

Lee, Don L. .... **CLC 2**
  See Madhubuti, Haki R.

Lee, George W(ashington)
  1894-1976 .... **BLC 2; CLC 52**
  See also BW 1; CA 125; CANR 83; DAM
  MULT; DLB 51

Lee, (Nelle) Harper 1926- .... **CLC 12, 60;
  WLC**
  See also AAYA 13; AMWS 8; BPFB 2;
  BYA 3; CA 13-16R; CANR 51; CDALB
  1941-1968; CSW; DA; DA3; DAB; DAC;
  DAM MST, NOV; DLB 6; EXPN; LAIT
  3; MTCW 1, 2; NFS 2; SATA 11; WYA;
  YAW

Lee, Helen Elaine 1959(?)- .... **CLC 86**
  See also CA 148

Lee, John .... **CLC 70**

Lee, Julian
  See Latham, Jean Lee

Lee, Larry
  See Lee, Lawrence

Lee, Laurie 1914-1997 .... **CLC 90**
  See also CA 77-80; 158; CANR 33, 73; CP
  7; CPW; DAB; DAM POP; DLB 27;
  MTCW 1; RGEL 2

Lee, Lawrence 1941-1990 .... **CLC 34**
  See also CA 131; CANR 43

Lee, Li-Young 1957- .... **CLC 164; PC 24**
  See also CA 153; CANR 118; CP 7; DLB
  165; LMFS 2; PFS 11, 15, 17

Lee, Manfred B(ennington)
  1905-1971 .... **CLC 11**
  See Queen, Ellery
  See also CA 1-4R; 29-32R; CANR 2; CMW
  4; DLB 137

Lee, Shelton Jackson 1957(?)- .. **BLCS; CLC
  105**
  See Lee, Spike
  See also BW 2, 3; CA 125; CANR 42;
  DAM MULT

Lee, Spike
  See Lee, Shelton Jackson
  See also AAYA 4, 29

Lee, Stan 1922- .... **CLC 17**
  See also AAYA 5, 49; CA 108; 111; INT
  CA-111

Lee, Tanith 1947- .... **CLC 46**
  See also AAYA 15; CA 37-40R; CANR 53,
  102; DLB 261; FANT; SATA 8, 88, 134;
  SFW 4; SUFW 1, 2; YAW

Lee, Vernon .... **SSC 33; TCLC 5**
  See Paget, Violet
  See also DLB 57, 153, 156, 174, 178; GLL
  1; SUFW 1

Lee, William
  See Burroughs, William S(eward)
  See also GLL 1

Lee, Willy
  See Burroughs, William S(eward)
  See also GLL 1

Lee-Hamilton, Eugene (Jacob)
  1845-1907 .... **TCLC 22**
  See also CA 117

Leet, Judith 1935- .... **CLC 11**
  See also CA 187

Le Fanu, Joseph Sheridan
  1814-1873 .... **NCLC 9, 58; SSC 14**
  See also CMW 4; DA3; DAM POP; DLB
  21, 70, 159, 178; HGG; RGEL 2; RGSF
  2; SUFW

Leffland, Ella 1931- .... **CLC 19**
  See also CA 29-32R; CANR 35, 78, 82;
  DLBY 1984; INT CANR-35; SATA 65

Leger, Alexis
  See Leger, (Marie-Rene Auguste) Alexis
  Saint-Leger

**Leger, (Marie-Rene Auguste) Alexis
  Saint-Leger** 1887-1975 .. **CLC 4, 11, 46;
  PC 23**
  See Perse, Saint-John; Saint-John Perse
  See also CA 13-16R; 61-64; CANR 43;
  DAM POET; MTCW 1

Leger, Saintleger
  See Leger, (Marie-Rene Auguste) Alexis
  Saint-Leger

Le Guin, Ursula K(roeber) 1929- ..... **CLC 8,
  13, 22, 45, 71, 136; SSC 12, 69**
  See also AAYA 9, 27; AITN 1; BPFB 2;
  BYA 5, 8, 11, 14; CA 21-24R; CANR 9,
  32, 52, 74; CDALB 1968-1988; CLR 3,
  28, 91; CN 7; CPW; DA3; DAB; DAC;
  DAM MST, POP; DLB 8, 52, 256, 275;
  EXPS; FANT; FW; INT CANR-32;
  JRDA; LAIT 5; MAICYA 1, 2; MTCW 1,
  2; NFS 6, 9; SATA 4, 52, 99; SCFW; SFW
  4; SSFS 2; SUFW 1, 2; WYA; YAW

Lehmann, Rosamond (Nina)
  1901-1990 .... **CLC 5**
  See also CA 77-80; 131; CANR 8, 73; DLB
  15; MTCW 2; RGEL 2; RHW

Leiber, Fritz (Reuter, Jr.)
  1910-1992 .... **CLC 25**
  See also BPFB 2; CA 45-48; 139; CANR 2,
  40, 86; DLB 8; FANT; HGG; MTCW 1,
  2; SATA 45; SATA-Obit 73; SCFW 2;
  SFW 4; SUFW 1, 2

Leibniz, Gottfried Wilhelm von
  1646-1716 .... **LC 35**
  See also DLB 168

Leimbach, Martha 1963-
  See Leimbach, Marti
  See also CA 130

Leimbach, Marti .... **CLC 65**
  See Leimbach, Martha

Leino, Eino .... **TCLC 24**
  See Lonnbohm, Armas Eino Leopold
  See also EWL 3

Leiris, Michel (Julien) 1901-1990 ..... **CLC 61**
  See also CA 119; 128; 132; EWL 3; GFL
  1789 to the Present

Leithauser, Brad 1953- .... **CLC 27**
  See also CA 107; CANR 27, 81; CP 7; DLB
  120, 282

le Jars de Gournay, Marie
  See de Gournay, Marie le Jars

Lelchuk, Alan 1938- .... **CLC 5**
  See also CA 45-48; CAAS 20; CANR 1,
  70; CN 7

Lem, Stanislaw 1921- ...... **CLC 8, 15, 40, 149**
  See also CA 105; CAAS 1; CANR 32;
  CWW 2; MTCW 1; SCFW 2; SFW 4

Lemann, Nancy (Elise) 1956- .... **CLC 39**
  See also CA 118; 136; CANR 121

Lemonnier, (Antoine Louis) Camille
  1844-1913 .... **TCLC 22**
  See also CA 121

Lenau, Nikolaus 1802-1850 .... **NCLC 16**

L'Engle, Madeleine (Camp Franklin)
  1918- .... **CLC 12**
  See also AAYA 28; AITN 2; BPFB 2; BYA
  2, 4, 5, 7; CA 1-4R; CANR 3, 21, 39, 66,
  107; CLR 1, 14, 57; CPW; CWRI 5; DA3;
  DAM POP; DLB 52; JRDA; MAICYA 1,
  2; MTCW 1, 2; SAAS 15; SATA 1, 27,
  75, 128; SFW 4; WYA; YAW

Lengyel, Jozsef 1896-1975 .... **CLC 7**
  See also CA 85-88; 57-60; CANR 71;
  RGSF 2

Lenin 1870-1924
  See Lenin, V. I.
  See also CA 121; 168

Lenin, V. I. .... **TCLC 67**
  See Lenin

Lennon, John (Ono) 1940-1980 .. **CLC 12, 35**
  See also CA 102; SATA 114

Lennox, Charlotte Ramsay
  1729(?)-1804 .... **NCLC 23, 134**
  See also DLB 39; RGEL 2

Lentricchia, Frank, (Jr.) 1940- .... **CLC 34**
  See also CA 25-28R; CANR 19, 106; DLB
  246

Lima Barreto, Afonso Henriques de
See Lima Barreto, Afonso Henrique de

Limonov, Edward 1944- .... **CLC 67**
See also CA 137

Lin, Frank
See Atherton, Gertrude (Franklin Horn)

Lincoln, Abraham 1809-1865 .... **NCLC 18**
See also LAIT 2

Lind, Jakov .... **CLC 1, 2, 4, 27, 82**
See Landwirth, Heinz
See also CAAS 4; EWL 3

Lindbergh, Anne (Spencer) Morrow
1906-2001 .... **CLC 82**
See also BPFB 2; CA 17-20R; 193; CANR
16, 73; DAM NOV; MTCW 1, 2; SATA
33; SATA-Obit 125; TUS

Lindsay, David 1878(?)-1945 .... **TCLC 15**
See also CA 113; 187; DLB 255; FANT;
SFW 4; SUFW 1

Lindsay, (Nicholas) Vachel
1879-1931 .... **PC 23; TCLC 17; WLC**
See also AMWS 1; CA 114; 135; CANR
79; CDALB 1865-1917; DA; DA3; DAC;
DAM MST, POET; DLB 54; EWL 3;
EXPP; RGAL 4; SATA 40; WP

Linke-Poot
See Doeblin, Alfred

Linney, Romulus 1930- .... **CLC 51**
See also CA 1-4R; CAD; CANR 40, 44,
79; CD 5; CSW; RGAL 4

Linton, Eliza Lynn 1822-1898 .... **NCLC 41**
See also DLB 18

Li Po 701-763 .... **CMLC 2; PC 29**
See also WP

Lipsius, Justus 1547-1606 .... **LC 16**

Lipsyte, Robert (Michael) 1938- ...... **CLC 21**
See also AAYA 7, 45; CA 17-20R; CANR
8, 57; CLR 23, 76; DA; DAC; DAM
MST, NOV; JRDA; LAIT 5; MAICYA 1,
2; SATA 5, 68, 113; WYA; YAW

Lish, Gordon (Jay) 1934- ... **CLC 45; SSC 18**
See also CA 113; 117; CANR 79; DLB 130;
INT CA-117

Lispector, Clarice 1925(?)-1977 .... **CLC 43;**
HLCS 2; SSC 34
See also CA 139; 116; CANR 71; CDWLB
3; DLB 113; DNFS 1; EWL 3; FW; HW
2; LAW; RGSF 2; RGWL 2, 3; WLIT 1

Littell, Robert 1935(?)- .... **CLC 42**
See also CA 109; 112; CANR 64, 115;
CMW 4

Little, Malcolm 1925-1965
See Malcolm X
See also BW 1, 3; CA 125; 111; CANR 82;
DA; DA3; DAB; DAC; DAM MST,
MULT; MTCW 1, 2

Littlewit, Humphrey Gent.
See Lovecraft, H(oward) P(hillips)

Litwos
See Sienkiewicz, Henryk (Adam Alexander
Pius)

Liu, E. 1857-1909 .... **TCLC 15**
See also CA 115; 190

Lively, Penelope (Margaret) 1933- .. **CLC 32,**
50
See also BPFB 2; CA 41-44R; CANR 29,
67, 79; CLR 7; CN 7; CWRI 5; DAM
NOV; DLB 14, 161, 207; FANT; JRDA;
MAICYA 1, 2; MTCW 1, 2; SATA 7, 60,
101; TEA

Livesay, Dorothy (Kathleen)
1909-1996 .... **CLC 4, 15, 79**
See also AITN 2; CA 25-28R; CAAS 8;
CANR 36, 67; DAC; DAM MST, POET;
DLB 68; FW; MTCW 1; RGEL 2; TWA

Livy c. 59B.C.-c. 12 .... **CMLC 11**
See also AW 2; CDWLB 1; DLB 211;
RGWL 2, 3

Lizardi, Jose Joaquin Fernandez de
1776-1827 .... **NCLC 30**
See also LAW

Llewellyn, Richard
See Llewellyn Lloyd, Richard Dafydd Viv-
ian
See also DLB 15

Llewellyn Lloyd, Richard Dafydd Vivian
1906-1983 .... **CLC 7, 80**
See Llewellyn, Richard
See also CA 53-56; 111; CANR 7, 71;
SATA 11; SATA-Obit 37

Llosa, (Jorge) Mario (Pedro) Vargas
See Vargas Llosa, (Jorge) Mario (Pedro)
See also RGWL 3

Llosa, Mario Vargas
See Vargas Llosa, (Jorge) Mario (Pedro)

Lloyd, Manda
See Mander, (Mary) Jane

Lloyd Webber, Andrew 1948-
See Webber, Andrew Lloyd
See also AAYA 1, 38; CA 116; 149; DAM
DRAM; SATA 56

Llull, Ramon c. 1235-c. 1316 .... **CMLC 12**

Lobb, Ebenezer
See Upward, Allen

Locke, Alain (Le Roy)
1886-1954 .... **BLCS; HR 3; TCLC 43**
See also BW 1, 3; CA 106; 124; CANR 79;
DLB 51; LMFS 2; RGAL 4

Locke, John 1632-1704 .... **LC 7, 35**
See also DLB 31, 101, 213, 252; RGEL 2;
WLIT 3

Locke-Elliott, Sumner
See Elliott, Sumner Locke

Lockhart, John Gibson 1794-1854 .. **NCLC 6**
See also DLB 110, 116, 144

Lockridge, Ross (Franklin), Jr.
1914-1948 .... **TCLC 111**
See also CA 108; 145; CANR 79; DLB 143;
DLBY 1980; RGAL 4; RHW

Lockwood, Robert
See Johnson, Robert

Lodge, David (John) 1935- .... **CLC 36, 141**
See also BEST 90:1; BRWS 4; CA 17-20R;
CANR 19, 53, 92; CN 7; CPW; DAM
POP; DLB 14, 194; EWL 3; INT CANR-
19; MTCW 1, 2

Lodge, Thomas 1558-1625 .... **LC 41**
See also DLB 172; RGEL 2

Loewinsohn, Ron(ald William)
1937- .... **CLC 52**
See also CA 25-28R; CANR 71

Logan, Jake
See Smith, Martin Cruz

Logan, John (Burton) 1923-1987 .... **CLC 5**
See also CA 77-80; 124; CANR 45; DLB 5

Lo Kuan-chung 1330(?)-1400(?) .... **LC 12**

Lombard, Nap
See Johnson, Pamela Hansford

London, Jack 1876-1916 .. **SSC 4, 49; TCLC**
9, 15, 39; WLC
See London, John Griffith
See also AAYA 13; AITN 2; AMW; BPFB
2; BYA 4, 13; CDALB 1865-1917; DLB
8, 12, 78, 212; EWL 3; EXPS; LAIT 3;
NFS 8; RGAL 4; RGSF 2; SATA 18; SFW
4; SSFS 7; TCWW 2; TUS; WYA; YAW

London, John Griffith 1876-1916
See London, Jack
See also CA 110; 119; CANR 73; DA; DA3;
DAB; DAC; DAM MST, NOV; JRDA;
MAICYA 1, 2; MTCW 1, 2

Long, Emmett
See Leonard, Elmore (John, Jr.)

Longbaugh, Harry
See Goldman, William (W.)

Longfellow, Henry Wadsworth
1807-1882 .... **NCLC 2, 45, 101, 103; PC**
30; WLCS
See also AMW; AMWR 2; CDALB 1640-
1865; DA; DA3; DAB; DAC; DAM MST,
POET; DLB 1, 59, 235; EXPP; PAB; PFS
2, 7, 17; RGAL 4; SATA 19; TUS; WP

Longinus c. 1st cent. - .... **CMLC 27**
See also AW 2; DLB 176

Longley, Michael 1939- .... **CLC 29**
See also BRWS 8; CA 102; CP 7; DLB 40

Longus fl. c. 2nd cent. - .... **CMLC 7**

Longway, A. Hugh
See Lang, Andrew

Lonnbohm, Armas Eino Leopold 1878-1926
See Leino, Eino
See also CA 123

Lonnrot, Elias 1802-1884 .... **NCLC 53**
See also EFS 1

Lonsdale, Roger ed. .... **CLC 65**

Lopate, Phillip 1943- .... **CLC 29**
See also CA 97-100; CANR 88; DLBY
1980; INT CA-97-100

Lopez, Barry (Holstun) 1945- .... **CLC 70**
See also AAYA 9; ANW; CA 65-68; CANR
7, 23, 47, 68, 92; DLB 256, 275; INT
CANR-7, -23; MTCW 1; RGAL 4; SATA
67

Lopez Portillo (y Pacheco), Jose
1920-2004 .... **CLC 46**
See also CA 129; HW 1

Lopez y Fuentes, Gregorio
1897(?)-1966 .... **CLC 32**
See also CA 131; EWL 3; HW 1

Lorca, Federico Garcia
See Garcia Lorca, Federico
See also DFS 4; EW 11; RGWL 2, 3; WP

Lord, Audre
See Lorde, Audre (Geraldine)
See also EWL 3

Lord, Bette Bao 1938- .... **AAL; CLC 23**
See also BEST 90:3; BPFB 2; CA 107;
CANR 41, 79; INT CA-107; SATA 58

Lord Auch
See Bataille, Georges

Lord Brooke
See Greville, Fulke

Lord Byron
See Byron, George Gordon (Noel)

Lorde, Audre (Geraldine)
1934-1992 .. **BLC 2; CLC 18, 71; PC 12**
See Domini, Rey; Lord, Audre
See also AFAW 1, 2; BW 1, 3; CA 25-28R;
142; CANR 16, 26, 46, 82; DA3; DAM
MULT, POET; DLB 41; FW; MTCW 1,
2; PFS 16; RGAL 4

Lord Houghton
See Milnes, Richard Monckton

Lord Jeffrey
See Jeffrey, Francis

Loreaux, Nichol .... **CLC 65**

Lorenzini, Carlo 1826-1890
See Collodi, Carlo
See also MAICYA 1, 2; SATA 29, 100

Lorenzo, Heberto Padilla
See Padilla (Lorenzo), Heberto

Loris
See Hofmannsthal, Hugo von

Loti, Pierre .... **TCLC 11**
See Viaud, (Louis Marie) Julien
See also DLB 123; GFL 1789 to the Present

Lou, Henri
See Andreas-Salome, Lou

Louie, David Wong 1954- .... **CLC 70**
See also CA 139; CANR 120

Louis, Adrian C. .... **NNAL**

Louis, Father M.
See Merton, Thomas (James)

Machado de Assis, Joaquim Maria
1839-1908 .... **BLC 2; HLCS 2; SSC 24;
TCLC 10**
See also CA 107; 153; CANR 91; LAW;
RGSF 2; RGWL 2, 3; TWA; WLIT 1

Machaut, Guillaume de c.
1300-1377 .... **CMLC 64**
See also DLB 208

Machen, Arthur .... **SSC 20; TCLC 4**
See Jones, Arthur Llewellyn
See also CA 179; DLB 156, 178; RGEL 2;
SUFW 1

Machiavelli, Niccolo 1469-1527 ... **DC 16; LC
8, 36; WLCS**
See also DA; DAB; DAC; DAM MST; EW
2; LAIT 1; LMFS 1; NFS 9; RGWL 2, 3;
TWA

MacInnes, Colin 1914-1976 .... **CLC 4, 23**
See also CA 69-72; 65-68; CANR 21; DLB
14; MTCW 1, 2; RGEL 2; RHW

MacInnes, Helen (Clark)
1907-1985 .... **CLC 27, 39**
See also BPFB 2; CA 1-4R; 117; CANR 1,
28, 58; CMW 4; CPW; DAM POP; DLB
87; MSW; MTCW 1, 2; SATA 22; SATA-
Obit 44

Mackay, Mary 1855-1924
See Corelli, Marie
See also CA 118; 177; FANT; RHW

Mackenzie, Compton (Edward Montague)
1883-1972 .... **CLC 18; TCLC 116**
See also CA 21-22; 37-40R; CAP 2; DLB
34, 100; RGEL 2

Mackenzie, Henry 1745-1831 .... **NCLC 41**
See also DLB 39; RGEL 2

Mackey, Nathaniel (Ernest) 1947- .... **PC 49**
See also CA 153; CANR 114; CP 7; DLB
169

MacKinnon, Catharine A. 1946- .... **CLC 181**
See also CA 128; 132; CANR 73; FW;
MTCW 2

Mackintosh, Elizabeth 1896(?)-1952
See Tey, Josephine
See also CA 110; CMW 4

MacLaren, James
See Grieve, C(hristopher) M(urray)

Mac Laverty, Bernard 1942- .... **CLC 31**
See also CA 116; 118; CANR 43, 88; CN
7; DLB 267; INT CA-118; RGSF 2

MacLean, Alistair (Stuart)
1922(?)-1987 .... **CLC 3, 13, 50, 63**
See also CA 57-60; 121; CANR 28, 61;
CMW 4; CPW; DAM POP; DLB 276;
MTCW 1; SATA 23; SATA-Obit 50;
TCWW 2

Maclean, Norman (Fitzroy)
1902-1990 .... **CLC 78; SSC 13**
See also CA 102; 132; CANR 49; CPW;
DAM POP; DLB 206; TCWW 2

MacLeish, Archibald 1892-1982 ... **CLC 3, 8,
14, 68; PC 47**
See also AMW; CA 9-12R; 106; CAD;
CANR 33, 63; CDALBS; DAM POET;
DFS 15; DLB 4, 7, 45; DLBY 1982; EWL
3; EXPP; MTCW 1, 2; PAB; PFS 5;
RGAL 4; TUS

MacLennan, (John) Hugh
1907-1990 .... **CLC 2, 14, 92**
See also CA 5-8R; 142; CANR 33; DAC;
DAM MST; DLB 68; EWL 3; MTCW 1,
2; RGEL 2; TWA

MacLeod, Alistair 1936- .... **CLC 56, 165**
See also CA 123; CCA 1; DAC; DAM
MST; DLB 60; MTCW 2; RGSF 2

Macleod, Fiona
See Sharp, William
See also RGEL 2; SUFW

MacNeice, (Frederick) Louis
1907-1963 .... **CLC 1, 4, 10, 53**
See also BRW 7; CA 85-88; CANR 61;
DAB; DAM POET; DLB 10, 20; EWL 3;
MTCW 1, 2; RGEL 2

MacNeill, Dand
See Fraser, George MacDonald

Macpherson, James 1736-1796 .... **LC 29**
See Ossian
See also BRWS 8; DLB 109; RGEL 2

Macpherson, (Jean) Jay 1931- .... **CLC 14**
See also CA 5-8R; CANR 90; CP 7; CWP;
DLB 53

Macrobius fl. 430- .... **CMLC 48**

MacShane, Frank 1927-1999 .... **CLC 39**
See also CA 9-12R; 186; CANR 3, 33; DLB
111

Macumber, Mari
See Sandoz, Mari(e Susette)

Madach, Imre 1823-1864 .... **NCLC 19**

Madden, (Jerry) David 1933- .... **CLC 5, 15**
See also CA 1-4R; CAAS 3; CANR 4, 45;
CN 7; CSW; DLB 6; MTCW 1

Maddern, Al(an)
See Ellison, Harlan (Jay)

Madhubuti, Haki R. 1942- ... **BLC 2; CLC 6,
73; PC 5**
See Lee, Don L.
See also BW 2, 3; CA 73-76; CANR 24,
51, 73; CP 7; CSW; DAM MULT, POET;
DLB 5, 41; DLBD 8; EWL 3; MTCW 2;
RGAL 4

Madison, James 1751-1836 .... **NCLC 126**
See also DLB 37

Maepenn, Hugh
See Kuttner, Henry

Maepenn, K. H.
See Kuttner, Henry

Maeterlinck, Maurice 1862-1949 ..... **TCLC 3**
See also CA 104; 136; CANR 80; DAM
DRAM; DLB 192; EW 8; EWL 3; GFL
1789 to the Present; LMFS 2; RGWL 2,
3; SATA 66; TWA

Maginn, William 1794-1842 .... **NCLC 8**
See also DLB 110, 159

Mahapatra, Jayanta 1928- .... **CLC 33**
See also CA 73-76; CAAS 9; CANR 15,
33, 66, 87; CP 7; DAM MULT

Mahfouz, Naguib (Abdel Aziz Al-Sabilgi)
1911(?)- .... **CLC 153; SSC 66**
See Mahfouz, Najib (Abdel Aziz al-Sabilgi)
See also AAYA 49; BEST 89:2; CA 128;
CANR 55, 101; CWW 2; DA3; DAM
NOV; MTCW 1, 2; RGWL 2, 3; SSFS 9

Mahfuz, Najib (Abdel Aziz al-Sabilgi)
.... **CLC 52, 55**
See Mahfouz, Naguib (Abdel Aziz Al-
Sabilgi)
See also AFW; DLBY 1988; EWL 3; RGSF
2; WLIT 2

Mahon, Derek 1941- .... **CLC 27**
See also BRWS 6; CA 113; 128; CANR 88;
CP 7; DLB 40; EWL 3

Maiakovskii, Vladimir
See Mayakovski, Vladimir (Vladimirovich)
See also IDTP; RGWL 2, 3

Mailer, Norman 1923- ... **CLC 1, 2, 3, 4, 5, 8,
11, 14, 28, 39, 74, 111**
See also AAYA 31; AITN 2; AMW; AMWC
2; AMWR 2; BPFB 2; CA 9-12R; CABS
1; CANR 28, 74, 77; CDALB 1968-1988;
CN 7; CPW; DA; DA3; DAB; DAC;
DAM MST, NOV, POP; DLB 2, 16, 28,
185, 278; DLBD 3; DLBY 1980, 1983;
EWL 3; MTCW 1, 2; NFS 10; RGAL 4;
TUS

Maillet, Antonine 1929- .... **CLC 54, 118**
See also CA 115; 120; CANR 46, 74, 77;
CCA 1; CWW 2; DAC; DLB 60; INT CA-
120; MTCW 2

Mais, Roger 1905-1955 .... **TCLC 8**
See also BW 1, 3; CA 105; 124; CANR 82;
CDWLB 3; DLB 125; EWL 3; MTCW 1;
RGEL 2

Maistre, Joseph 1753-1821 .... **NCLC 37**
See also GFL 1789 to the Present

Maitland, Frederic William
1850-1906 .... **TCLC 65**

Maitland, Sara (Louise) 1950- .... **CLC 49**
See also CA 69-72; CANR 13, 59; DLB
271; FW

Major, Clarence 1936- ... **BLC 2; CLC 3, 19,
48**
See also AFAW 2; BW 2, 3; CA 21-24R;
CAAS 6; CANR 13, 25, 53, 82; CN 7;
CP 7; CSW; DAM MULT; DLB 33; EWL
3; MSW

Major, Kevin (Gerald) 1949- .... **CLC 26**
See also AAYA 16; CA 97-100; CANR 21,
38, 112; CLR 11; DAC; DLB 60; INT
CANR-21; JRDA; MAICYA 1, 2; MAIC-
YAS 1; SATA 32, 82, 134; WYA; YAW

Maki, James
See Ozu, Yasujiro

Malabaila, Damiano
See Levi, Primo

Malamud, Bernard 1914-1986 .. **CLC 1, 2, 3,
5, 8, 9, 11, 18, 27, 44, 78, 85; SSC 15;
TCLC 129; WLC**
See also AAYA 16; AMWS 1; BPFB 2;
BYA 15; CA 5-8R; 118; CABS 1; CANR
28, 62, 114; CDALB 1941-1968; CPW;
DA; DA3; DAB; DAC; DAM MST, NOV,
POP; DLB 2, 28, 152; DLBY 1980, 1986;
EWL 3; EXPS; LAIT 4; LATS 1; MTCW
1, 2; NFS 4, 9; RGAL 4; RGSF 2; SSFS
8, 13, 16; TUS

Malan, Herman
See Bosman, Herman Charles; Bosman,
Herman Charles

Malaparte, Curzio 1898-1957 .... **TCLC 52**
See also DLB 264

Malcolm, Dan
See Silverberg, Robert

Malcolm X .... **BLC 2; CLC 82, 117; WLCS**
See Little, Malcolm
See also LAIT 5; NCFS 3

Malherbe, Francois de 1555-1628 .... **LC 5**
See also GFL Beginnings to 1789

Mallarme, Stephane 1842-1898 ...... **NCLC 4,
41; PC 4**
See also DAM POET; DLB 217; EW 7;
GFL 1789 to the Present; LMFS 2; RGWL
2, 3; TWA

Mallet-Joris, Francoise 1930- .... **CLC 11**
See also CA 65-68; CANR 17; DLB 83;
EWL 3; GFL 1789 to the Present

Malley, Ern
See McAuley, James Phillip

Mallon, Thomas 1951- .... **CLC 172**
See also CA 110; CANR 29, 57, 92

Mallowan, Agatha Christie
See Christie, Agatha (Mary Clarissa)

Maloff, Saul 1922- .... **CLC 5**
See also CA 33-36R

Malone, Louis
See MacNeice, (Frederick) Louis

Malone, Michael (Christopher)
1942- .... **CLC 43**
See also CA 77-80; CANR 14, 32, 57, 114

Malory, Sir Thomas 1410(?)-1471(?) . **LC 11,
88; WLCS**
See also BRW 1; BRWR 2; CDBLB Before
1660; DA; DAB; DAC; DAM MST; DLB
146; EFS 2; RGEL 2; SATA 59; SATA-
Brief 33; TEA; WLIT 3

Marsten, Richard
  See Hunter, Evan
Marston, John 1576-1634 .... **LC 33**
  See also BRW 2; DAM DRAM; DLB 58,
  172; RGEL 2
Martha, Henry
  See Harris, Mark
Marti, Jose
  See Marti (y Perez), Jose (Julian)
  See also DLB 290
Marti (y Perez), Jose (Julian)
  1853-1895 .... **HLC 2; NCLC 63**
  See Marti, Jose
  See also DAM MULT; HW 2; LAW; RGWL
  2, 3; WLIT 1
Martial c. 40-c. 104 .... **CMLC 35; PC 10**
  See also AW 2; CDWLB 1; DLB 211;
  RGWL 2, 3
Martin, Ken
  See Hubbard, L(afayette) Ron(ald)
Martin, Richard
  See Creasey, John
Martin, Steve 1945- .... **CLC 30**
  See also AAYA 53; CA 97-100; CANR 30,
  100; MTCW 1
Martin, Valerie 1948- .... **CLC 89**
  See also BEST 90:2; CA 85-88; CANR 49,
  89
Martin, Violet Florence 1862-1915 .. **SSC 56;**
  TCLC 51
Martin, Webber
  See Silverberg, Robert
Martindale, Patrick Victor
  See White, Patrick (Victor Martindale)
Martin du Gard, Roger
  1881-1958 .... **TCLC 24**
  See also CA 118; CANR 94; DLB 65; EWL
  3; GFL 1789 to the Present; RGWL 2, 3
Martineau, Harriet 1802-1876 ...... **NCLC 26,**
  137
  See also DLB 21, 55, 159, 163, 166, 190;
  FW; RGEL 2; YABC 2
Martines, Julia
  See O'Faolain, Julia
Martinez, Enrique Gonzalez
  See Gonzalez Martinez, Enrique
Martinez, Jacinto Benavente y
  See Benavente (y Martinez), Jacinto
Martinez de la Rosa, Francisco de Paula
  1787-1862 .... **NCLC 102**
  See also TWA
Martinez Ruiz, Jose 1873-1967
  See Azorin; Ruiz, Jose Martinez
  See also CA 93-96; HW 1
Martinez Sierra, Gregorio
  1881-1947 .... **TCLC 6**
  See also CA 115; EWL 3
Martinez Sierra, Maria (de la O'LeJarraga)
  1874-1974 .... **TCLC 6**
  See also CA 115; EWL 3
Martinsen, Martin
  See Follett, Ken(neth Martin)
Martinson, Harry (Edmund)
  1904-1978 .... **CLC 14**
  See also CA 77-80; CANR 34; DLB 259;
  EWL 3
Martyn, Edward 1859-1923 .... **TCLC 131**
  See also CA 179; DLB 10; RGEL 2
Marut, Ret
  See Traven, B.
Marut, Robert
  See Traven, B.
Marvell, Andrew 1621-1678 .... **LC 4, 43; PC**
  10; WLC
  See also BRW 2; BRWR 2; CDBLB 1660-
  1789; DA; DAB; DAC; DAM MST,
  POET; DLB 131; EXPP; PFS 5; RGEL 2;
  TEA; WP

Marx, Karl (Heinrich)
  1818-1883 .... **NCLC 17, 114**
  See also DLB 129; LATS 1; TWA
Masaoka, Shiki -1902 .... **TCLC 18**
  See Masaoka, Tsunenori
  See also RGWL 3
Masaoka, Tsunenori 1867-1902
  See Masaoka, Shiki
  See also CA 117; 191; TWA
Masefield, John (Edward)
  1878-1967 .... **CLC 11, 47**
  See also CA 19-20; 25-28R; CANR 33;
  CAP 2; CDBLB 1890-1914; DAM POET;
  DLB 10, 19, 153, 160; EWL 3; EXPP;
  FANT; MTCW 1, 2; PFS 5; RGEL 2;
  SATA 19
Maso, Carole 19(?)- .... **CLC 44**
  See also CA 170; GLL 2; RGAL 4
Mason, Bobbie Ann 1940- ... **CLC 28, 43, 82,**
  154; SSC 4
  See also AAYA 5, 42; AMWS 8; BPFB 2;
  CA 53-56; CANR 11, 31, 58, 83, 125;
  CDALBS; CN 7; CSW; DA3; DLB 173;
  DLBY 1987; EWL 3; EXPS; INT CANR-
  31; MTCW 1, 2; NFS 4; RGAL 4; RGSF
  2; SSFS 3,8; YAW
Mason, Ernst
  See Pohl, Frederik
Mason, Hunni B.
  See Sternheim, (William Adolf) Carl
Mason, Lee W.
  See Malzberg, Barry N(athaniel)
Mason, Nick 1945- .... **CLC 35**
Mason, Tally
  See Derleth, August (William)
Mass, Anna .... **CLC 59**
Mass, William
  See Gibson, William
Massinger, Philip 1583-1640 .... **LC 70**
  See also DLB 58; RGEL 2
Master Lao
  See Lao Tzu
Masters, Edgar Lee 1868-1950 ...... **PC 1, 36;**
  TCLC 2, 25; WLCS
  See also AMWS 1; CA 104; 133; CDALB
  1865-1917; DA; DAC; DAM MST,
  POET; DLB 54; EWL 3; EXPP; MTCW
  1, 2; RGAL 4; TUS; WP
Masters, Hilary 1928- .... **CLC 48**
  See also CA 25-28R, 217; CAAE 217;
  CANR 13, 47, 97; CN 7; DLB 244
Mastrosimone, William 19(?)- .... **CLC 36**
  See also CA 186; CAD; CD 5
Mathe, Albert
  See Camus, Albert
Mather, Cotton 1663-1728 .... **LC 38**
  See also AMWS 2; CDALB 1640-1865;
  DLB 24, 30, 140; RGAL 4; TUS
Mather, Increase 1639-1723 .... **LC 38**
  See also DLB 24
Matheson, Richard (Burton) 1926- .. **CLC 37**
  See also AAYA 31; CA 97-100; CANR 88,
  99; DLB 8, 44; HGG; INT CA-97-100;
  SCFW 2; SFW 4; SUFW 2
Mathews, Harry 1930- .... **CLC 6, 52**
  See also CA 21-24R; CAAS 6; CANR 18,
  40, 98; CN 7
Mathews, John Joseph 1894-1979 .. **CLC 84;**
  NNAL
  See also CA 19-20; 142; CANR 45; CAP 2;
  DAM MULT; DLB 175
Mathias, Roland (Glyn) 1915- .... **CLC 45**
  See also CA 97-100; CANR 19, 41; CP 7;
  DLB 27
Matsuo Basho 1644-1694 .... **LC 62; PC 3**
  See Basho, Matsuo
  See also DAM POET; PFS 2, 7
Mattheson, Rodney
  See Creasey, John

Matthews, (James) Brander
  1852-1929 .... **TCLC 95**
  See also DLB 71, 78; DLBD 13
Matthews, Greg 1949- .... **CLC 45**
  See also CA 135
Matthews, William (Procter III)
  1942-1997 .... **CLC 40**
  See also AMWS 9; CA 29-32R; 162; CAAS
  18; CANR 12, 57; CP 7; DLB 5
Matthias, John (Edward) 1941- .... **CLC 9**
  See also CA 33-36R; CANR 56; CP 7
Matthiessen, F(rancis) O(tto)
  1902-1950 .... **TCLC 100**
  See also CA 185; DLB 63
Matthiessen, Peter 1927- ... **CLC 5, 7, 11, 32,**
  64
  See also AAYA 6, 40; AMWS 5; ANW;
  BEST 90:4; BPFB 2; CA 9-12R; CANR
  21, 50, 73, 100; CN 7; DA3; DAM NOV;
  DLB 6, 173, 275; MTCW 1, 2; SATA 27
Maturin, Charles Robert
  1780(?)-1824 .... **NCLC 6**
  See also BRWS 8; DLB 178; HGG; LMFS
  1; RGEL 2; SUFW
Matute (Ausejo), Ana Maria 1925- .. **CLC 11**
  See also CA 89-92; EWL 3; MTCW 1;
  RGSF 2
Maugham, W. S.
  See Maugham, W(illiam) Somerset
Maugham, W(illiam) Somerset
  1874-1965 .. **CLC 1, 11, 15, 67, 93; SSC**
  8; WLC
  See also AAYA 55; BPFB 2; BRW 6; CA
  5-8R; 25-28R; CANR 40, 127; CDBLB
  1914-1945; CMW 4; DA; DA3; DAB;
  DAC; DAM DRAM, MST, NOV; DLB
  10, 36, 77, 100, 162, 195; EWL 3; LAIT
  3; MTCW 1, 2; RGEL 2; RGSF 2; SATA
  54; SSFS 17
Maugham, William Somerset
  See Maugham, W(illiam) Somerset
Maupassant, (Henri Rene Albert) Guy de
  1850-1893 . **NCLC 1, 42, 83; SSC 1, 64;**
  WLC
  See also BYA 14; DA; DA3; DAB; DAC;
  DAM MST; DLB 123; EW 7; EXPS; GFL
  1789 to the Present; LAIT 2; LMFS 1;
  RGSF 2; RGWL 2, 3; SSFS 4; SUFW;
  TWA
Maupin, Armistead (Jones, Jr.)
  1944- .... **CLC 95**
  See also CA 125; 130; CANR 58, 101;
  CPW; DA3; DAM POP; DLB 278; GLL
  1; INT CA-130; MTCW 2
Maurhut, Richard
  See Traven, B.
Mauriac, Claude 1914-1996 .... **CLC 9**
  See also CA 89-92; 152; CWW 2; DLB 83;
  EWL 3; GFL 1789 to the Present
Mauriac, Francois (Charles)
  1885-1970 .... **CLC 4, 9, 56; SSC 24**
  See also CA 25-28; CAP 2; DLB 65; EW
  10; EWL 3; GFL 1789 to the Present;
  MTCW 1, 2; RGWL 2, 3; TWA
Mavor, Osborne Henry 1888-1951
  See Bridie, James
  See also CA 104
Maxwell, William (Keepers, Jr.)
  1908-2000 .... **CLC 19**
  See also AMWS 8; CA 93-96; 189; CANR
  54, 95; CN 7; DLB 218, 278; DLBY
  1980; INT CA-93-96; SATA-Obit 128
May, Elaine 1932- .... **CLC 16**
  See also CA 124; 142; CAD; CWD; DLB
  44
Mayakovski, Vladimir (Vladimirovich)
  1893-1930 .... **TCLC 4, 18**
  See Maiakovskii, Vladimir; Mayakovsky,
  Vladimir
  See also CA 104; 158; EWL 3; MTCW 2;
  SFW 4; TWA

McNickle, (William) D'Arcy
1904-1977 .... **CLC 89; NNAL**
See also CA 9-12R; 85-88; CANR 5, 45;
DAM MULT; DLB 175, 212; RGAL 4;
SATA-Obit 22

McPhee, John (Angus) 1931- .... **CLC 36**
See also AMWS 3; ANW; BEST 90:1; CA
65-68; CANR 20, 46, 64, 69, 121; CPW;
DLB 185, 275; MTCW 1, 2; TUS

McPherson, James Alan 1943- . **BLCS; CLC
19, 77**
See also BW 1, 3; CA 25-28R; CAAS 17;
CANR 24, 74; CN 7; CSW; DLB 38, 244;
EWL 3; MTCW 1, 2; RGAL 4; RGSF 2

McPherson, William (Alexander)
1933- .... **CLC 34**
See also CA 69-72; CANR 28; INT
CANR-28

McTaggart, J. McT. Ellis
See McTaggart, John McTaggart Ellis

McTaggart, John McTaggart Ellis
1866-1925 .... **TCLC 105**
See also CA 120; DLB 262

Mead, George Herbert 1863-1931 . **TCLC 89**
See also CA 212; DLB 270

Mead, Margaret 1901-1978 .... **CLC 37**
See also AITN 1; CA 1-4R; 81-84; CANR
4; DA3; FW; MTCW 1, 2; SATA-Obit 20

Meaker, Marijane (Agnes) 1927-
See Kerr, M. E.
See also CA 107; CANR 37, 63; INT CA-
107; JRDA; MAICYA 1, 2; MAICYAS 1;
MTCW 1; SATA 20, 61, 99; SATA-Essay
111; YAW

Medoff, Mark (Howard) 1940- .... **CLC 6, 23**
See also AITN 1; CA 53-56; CAD; CANR
5; CD 5; DAM DRAM; DFS 4; DLB 7;
INT CANR-5

Medvedev, P. N.
See Bakhtin, Mikhail Mikhailovich

Meged, Aharon
See Megged, Aharon

Meged, Aron
See Megged, Aharon

Megged, Aharon 1920- .... **CLC 9**
See also CA 49-52; CAAS 13; CANR 1;
EWL 3

Mehta, Gita 1943- .... **CLC 179**
See also DNFS 2

Mehta, Ved (Parkash) 1934- .... **CLC 37**
See also CA 1-4R, 212; CAAE 212; CANR
2, 23, 69; MTCW 1

Melanchthon, Philipp 1497-1560 .... **LC 90**
See also DLB 179

Melanter
See Blackmore, R(ichard) D(oddridge)

Meleager c. 140B.C.-c. 70B.C. ...... **CMLC 53**

Melies, Georges 1861-1938 .... **TCLC 81**

Melikow, Loris
See Hofmannsthal, Hugo von

Melmoth, Sebastian
See Wilde, Oscar (Fingal O'Flahertie Wills)

Melo Neto, Joao Cabral de
See Cabral de Melo Neto, Joao
See also EWL 3

Meltzer, Milton 1915- .... **CLC 26**
See also AAYA 8, 45; BYA 2, 6; CA 13-
16R; CANR 38, 92, 107; CLR 13; DLB
61; JRDA; MAICYA 1, 2; SAAS 1; SATA
1, 50, 80, 128; SATA-Essay 124; WYA;
YAW

Melville, Herman 1819-1891 ..... **NCLC 3, 12,
29, 45, 49, 91, 93, 123; SSC 1, 17, 46;
WLC**
See also AAYA 25; AMW; AMWR 1;
CDALB 1640-1865; DA; DA3; DAB;
DAC; DAM MST, NOV; DLB 3, 74, 250,
254; EXPN; EXPS; LAIT 1, 2; NFS 7, 9;
RGAL 4; RGSF 2; SATA 59; SSFS 3;
TUS

Members, Mark
See Powell, Anthony (Dymoke)

Membreno, Alejandro .... **CLC 59**

Menander c. 342B.C.-c. 293B.C. .... **CMLC 9,
51; DC 3**
See also AW 1; CDWLB 1; DAM DRAM;
DLB 176; LMFS 1; RGWL 2, 3

Menchu, Rigoberta 1959- .. **CLC 160; HLCS
2**
See also CA 175; DNFS 1; WLIT 1

Mencken, H(enry) L(ouis)
1880-1956 .... **TCLC 13**
See also AMW; CA 105; 125; CDALB
1917-1929; DLB 11, 29, 63, 137, 222;
EWL 3; MTCW 1, 2; NCFS 4; RGAL 4;
TUS

Mendelsohn, Jane 1965- .... **CLC 99**
See also CA 154; CANR 94

Menton, Francisco de
See Chin, Frank (Chew, Jr.)

Mercer, David 1928-1980 .... **CLC 5**
See also CA 9-12R; 102; CANR 23; CBD;
DAM DRAM; DLB 13; MTCW 1; RGEL
2

Merchant, Paul
See Ellison, Harlan (Jay)

Meredith, George 1828-1909 ... **TCLC 17, 43**
See also CA 117; 153; CANR 80; CDBLB
1832-1890; DAM POET; DLB 18, 35, 57,
159; RGEL 2; TEA

Meredith, William (Morris) 1919- .... **CLC 4,
13, 22, 55; PC 28**
See also CA 9-12R; CAAS 14; CANR 6,
40; CP 7; DAM POET; DLB 5

Merezhkovsky, Dmitrii Sergeevich
See Merezhkovsky, Dmitry Sergeyevich
See also DLB 295

Merezhkovsky, Dmitry Sergeevich
See Merezhkovsky, Dmitry Sergeyevich
See also EWL 3

Merezhkovsky, Dmitry Sergeyevich
1865-1941 .... **TCLC 29**
See Merezhkovsky, Dmitrii Sergeevich;
Merezhkovsky, Dmitry Sergeevich
See also CA 169

Merimee, Prosper 1803-1870 ... **NCLC 6, 65;
SSC 7**
See also DLB 119, 192; EW 6; EXPS; GFL
1789 to the Present; RGSF 2; RGWL 2,
3; SSFS 8; SUFW

Merkin, Daphne 1954- .... **CLC 44**
See also CA 123

Merlin, Arthur
See Blish, James (Benjamin)

Mernissi, Fatima 1940- .... **CLC 171**
See also CA 152; FW

Merrill, James (Ingram) 1926-1995 .. **CLC 2,
3, 6, 8, 13, 18, 34, 91; PC 28**
See also AMWS 3; CA 13-16R; 147; CANR
10, 49, 63, 108; DA3; DAM POET; DLB
5, 165; DLBY 1985; EWL 3; INT CANR-
10; MTCW 1, 2; PAB; RGAL 4

Merriman, Alex
See Silverberg, Robert

Merriman, Brian 1747-1805 .... **NCLC 70**

Merritt, E. B.
See Waddington, Miriam

Merton, Thomas (James)
1915-1968 . **CLC 1, 3, 11, 34, 83; PC 10**
See also AMWS 8; CA 5-8R; 25-28R;
CANR 22, 53, 111; DA3; DLB 48; DLBY
1981; MTCW 1, 2

Merwin, W(illiam) S(tanley) 1927- ... **CLC 1,
2, 3, 5, 8, 13, 18, 45, 88; PC 45**
See also AMWS 3; CA 13-16R; CANR 15,
51, 112; CP 7; DA3; DAM POET; DLB
5, 169; EWL 3; INT CANR-15; MTCW
1, 2; PAB; PFS 5, 15; RGAL 4

Metcalf, John 1938- .... **CLC 37; SSC 43**
See also CA 113; CN 7; DLB 60; RGSF 2;
TWA

Metcalf, Suzanne
See Baum, L(yman) Frank

Mew, Charlotte (Mary) 1870-1928 .. **TCLC 8**
See also CA 105; 189; DLB 19, 135; RGEL
2

Mewshaw, Michael 1943- .... **CLC 9**
See also CA 53-56; CANR 7, 47; DLBY
1980

Meyer, Conrad Ferdinand
1825-1898 .... **NCLC 81**
See also DLB 129; EW; RGWL 2, 3

Meyer, Gustav 1868-1932
See Meyrink, Gustav
See also CA 117; 190

Meyer, June
See Jordan, June (Meyer)

Meyer, Lynn
See Slavitt, David R(ytman)

Meyers, Jeffrey 1939- .... **CLC 39**
See also CA 73-76, 186; CAAE 186; CANR
54, 102; DLB 111

**Meynell, Alice (Christina Gertrude
Thompson)** 1847-1922 .... **TCLC 6**
See also CA 104; 177; DLB 19, 98; RGEL
2

Meyrink, Gustav .... **TCLC 21**
See Meyer, Gustav
See also DLB 81; EWL 3

Michaels, Leonard 1933-2003 ..... **CLC 6, 25;
SSC 16**
See also CA 61-64; 216; CANR 21, 62, 119;
CN 7; DLB 130; MTCW 1

Michaux, Henri 1899-1984 .... **CLC 8, 19**
See also CA 85-88; 114; DLB 258; EWL 3;
GFL 1789 to the Present; RGWL 2, 3

Micheaux, Oscar (Devereaux)
1884-1951 .... **TCLC 76**
See also BW 3; CA 174; DLB 50; TCWW
2

Michelangelo 1475-1564 .... **LC 12**
See also AAYA 43

Michelet, Jules 1798-1874 .... **NCLC 31**
See also EW 5; GFL 1789 to the Present

Michels, Robert 1876-1936 .... **TCLC 88**
See also CA 212

Michener, James A(lbert)
1907(?)-1997 .. **CLC 1, 5, 11, 29, 60, 109**
See also AAYA 27; AITN 1; BEST 90:1;
BPFB 2; CA 5-8R; 161; CANR 21, 45,
68; CN 7; CPW; DA3; DAM NOV, POP;
DLB 6; MTCW 1, 2; RHW

Mickiewicz, Adam 1798-1855 . **NCLC 3, 101;
PC 38**
See also EW 5; RGWL 2, 3

Middleton, (John) Christopher
1926- .... **CLC 13**
See also CA 13-16R; CANR 29, 54, 117;
CP 7; DLB 40

Middleton, Richard (Barham)
1882-1911 .... **TCLC 56**
See also CA 187; DLB 156; HGG

Middleton, Stanley 1919- .... **CLC 7, 38**
See also CA 25-28R; CAAS 23; CANR 21,
46, 81; CN 7; DLB 14

Middleton, Thomas 1580-1627 ...... **DC 5; LC
33**
See also BRW 2; DAM DRAM, MST; DFS
18; DLB 58; RGEL 2

Migueis, Jose Rodrigues 1901-1980 . **CLC 10**
See also DLB 287

Mikszath, Kalman 1847-1910 .... **TCLC 31**
See also CA 170

Miles, Jack .... **CLC 100**
See also CA 200

Miles, John Russiano
See Miles, Jack

Miles, Josephine (Louise)
1911-1985 .... **CLC 1, 2, 14, 34, 39**
See also CA 1-4R; 116; CANR 2, 55; DAM POET; DLB 48

Militant
See Sandburg, Carl (August)

Mill, Harriet (Hardy) Taylor
1807-1858 .... **NCLC 102**
See also FW

Mill, John Stuart 1806-1873 .... **NCLC 11, 58**
See also CDBLB 1832-1890; DLB 55, 190, 262; FW 1; RGEL 2; TEA

Millar, Kenneth 1915-1983 .... **CLC 14**
See Macdonald, Ross
See also CA 9-12R; 110; CANR 16, 63, 107; CMW 4; CPW; DA3; DAM POP; DLB 2, 226; DLBD 6; DLBY 1983; MTCW 1, 2

Millay, E. Vincent
See Millay, Edna St. Vincent

Millay, Edna St. Vincent 1892-1950 .... **PC 6; TCLC 4, 49; WLCS**
See Boyd, Nancy
See also AMW; CA 104; 130; CDALB 1917-1929; DA; DA3; DAB; DAC; DAM MST, POET; DLB 45, 249; EWL 3; EXPP; MAWW; MTCW 1, 2; PAB; PFS 3, 17; RGAL 4; TUS; WP

Miller, Arthur 1915- ...... **CLC 1, 2, 6, 10, 15, 26, 47, 78, 179; DC 1; WLC**
See also AAYA 15; AITN 1; AMW; AMWC 1; CA 1-4R; CABS 3; CAD; CANR 2, 30, 54, 76; CD 5; CDALB 1941-1968; DA; DA3; DAB; DAC; DAM DRAM, MST; DFS 1, 3, 8; DLB 7, 266; EWL 3; LAIT 1, 4; LATS 1; MTCW 1, 2; RGAL 4; TUS; WYAS 1

Miller, Henry (Valentine)
1891-1980 .... **CLC 1, 2, 4, 9, 14, 43, 84; WLC**
See also AMW; BPFB 2; CA 9-12R; 97-100; CANR 33, 64; CDALB 1929-1941; DA; DA3; DAB; DAC; DAM MST, NOV; DLB 4, 9; DLBY 1980; EWL 3; MTCW 1, 2; RGAL 4; TUS

Miller, Jason 1939(?)-2001 .... **CLC 2**
See also AITN 1; CA 73-76; 197; CAD; DFS 12; DLB 7

Miller, Sue 1943- .... **CLC 44**
See also AMWS 12; BEST 90:3; CA 139; CANR 59, 91; DA3; DAM POP; DLB 143

Miller, Walter M(ichael, Jr.)
1923-1996 .... **CLC 4, 30**
See also BPFB 2; CA 85-88; CANR 108; DLB 8; SCFW; SFW 4

Millett, Kate 1934- .... **CLC 67**
See also AITN 1; CA 73-76; CANR 32, 53, 76, 110; DA3; DLB 246; FW; GLL 1; MTCW 1, 2

Millhauser, Steven (Lewis) 1943- .... **CLC 21, 54, 109; SSC 57**
See also CA 110; 111; CANR 63, 114; CN 7; DA3; DLB 2; FANT; INT CA-111; MTCW 2

Millin, Sarah Gertrude 1889-1968 ... **CLC 49**
See also CA 102; 93-96; DLB 225; EWL 3

Milne, A(lan) A(lexander)
1882-1956 .... **TCLC 6, 88**
See also BRWS 5; CA 104; 133; CLR 1, 26; CMW 4; CWRI 5; DA3; DAB; DAC; DAM MST; DLB 10, 77, 100, 160; FANT; MAICYA 1, 2; MTCW 1, 2; RGEL 2; SATA 100; WCH; YABC 1

Milner, Ron(ald) 1938- .... **BLC 3; CLC 56**
See also AITN 1; BW 1; CA 73-76; CAD; CANR 24, 81; CD 5; DAM MULT; DLB 38; MTCW 1

Milnes, Richard Monckton
1809-1885 .... **NCLC 61**
See also DLB 32, 184

Milosz, Czeslaw 1911- ...... **CLC 5, 11, 22, 31, 56, 82; PC 8; WLCS**
See also CA 81-84; CANR 23, 51, 91, 126; CDWLB 4; CWW 2; DA3; DAM MST, POET; DLB 215; EW 13; EWL 3; MTCW 1, 2; PFS 16; RGWL 2, 3

Milton, John 1608-1674 ..... **LC 9, 43, 92; PC 19, 29; WLC**
See also BRW 2; BRWR 2; CDBLB 1660-1789; DA; DA3; DAB; DAC; DAM MST, POET; DLB 131, 151, 281; EFS 1; EXPP; LAIT 1; PAB; PFS 3, 17; RGEL 2; TEA; WLIT 3; WP

Min, Anchee 1957- .... **CLC 86**
See also CA 146; CANR 94

Minehaha, Cornelius
See Wedekind, (Benjamin) Frank(lin)

Miner, Valerie 1947- .... **CLC 40**
See also CA 97-100; CANR 59; FW; GLL 2

Minimo, Duca
See D'Annunzio, Gabriele

Minot, Susan 1956- .... **CLC 44, 159**
See also AMWS 6; CA 134; CANR 118; CN 7

Minus, Ed 1938- .... **CLC 39**
See also CA 185

Mirabai 1498(?)-1550(?) .... **PC 48**

Miranda, Javier
See Bioy Casares, Adolfo
See also CWW 2

Mirbeau, Octave 1848-1917 .... **TCLC 55**
See also CA 216; DLB 123, 192; GFL 1789 to the Present

Mirikitani, Janice 1942- .... **AAL**
See also CA 211; RGAL 4

Miro (Ferrer), Gabriel (Francisco Victor)
1879-1930 .... **TCLC 5**
See also CA 104; 185; EWL 3

Misharin, Alexandr .... **CLC 59**

Mishima, Yukio ... **CLC 2, 4, 6, 9, 27; DC 1; SSC 4**
See Hiraoka, Kimitake
See also AAYA 50; BPFB 2; GLL 1; MJW; MTCW 2; RGSF 2; RGWL 2, 3; SSFS 5, 12

Mistral, Frederic 1830-1914 .... **TCLC 51**
See also CA 122; 213; GFL 1789 to the Present

Mistral, Gabriela
See Godoy Alcayaga, Lucila
See also DLB 283; DNFS 1; EWL 3; LAW; RGWL 2, 3; WP

Mistry, Rohinton 1952- .... **CLC 71**
See also CA 141; CANR 86, 114; CCA 1; CN 7; DAC; SSFS 6

Mitchell, Clyde
See Ellison, Harlan (Jay)

Mitchell, Emerson Blackhorse Barney
1945- .... **NNAL**
See also CA 45-48

Mitchell, James Leslie 1901-1935
See Gibbon, Lewis Grassic
See also CA 104; 188; DLB 15

Mitchell, Joni 1943- .... **CLC 12**
See also CA 112; CCA 1

Mitchell, Joseph (Quincy)
1908-1996 .... **CLC 98**
See also CA 77-80; 152; CANR 69; CN 7; CSW; DLB 185; DLBY 1996

Mitchell, Margaret (Munnerlyn)
1900-1949 .... **TCLC 11**
See also AAYA 23; BPFB 2; BYA 1; CA 109; 125; CANR 55, 94; CDALBS; DA3; DAM NOV, POP; DLB 9; LAIT 2; MTCW 1, 2; NFS 9; RGAL 4; RHW; TUS; WYAS 1; YAW

Mitchell, Peggy
See Mitchell, Margaret (Munnerlyn)

Mitchell, S(ilas) Weir 1829-1914 .... **TCLC 36**
See also CA 165; DLB 202; RGAL 4

Mitchell, W(illiam) O(rmond)
1914-1998 .... **CLC 25**
See also CA 77-80; 165; CANR 15, 43; CN 7; DAC; DAM MST; DLB 88

Mitchell, William (Lendrum)
1879-1936 .... **TCLC 81**
See also CA 213

Mitford, Mary Russell 1787-1855 ... **NCLC 4**
See also DLB 110; 116; RGEL 2

Mitford, Nancy 1904-1973 .... **CLC 44**
See also CA 9-12R; DLB 191; RGEL 2

Miyamoto, (Chujo) Yuriko
1899-1951 .... **TCLC 37**
See Miyamoto Yuriko
See also CA 170, 174

Miyamoto Yuriko
See Miyamoto, (Chujo) Yuriko
See also DLB 180

Miyazawa, Kenji 1896-1933 .... **TCLC 76**
See Miyazawa Kenji
See also CA 157; RGWL 3

Miyazawa Kenji
See Miyazawa, Kenji
See also EWL 3

Mizoguchi, Kenji 1898-1956 .... **TCLC 72**
See also CA 167

Mo, Timothy (Peter) 1950(?)- ... **CLC 46, 134**
See also CA 117; CN 7; DLB 194; MTCW 1; WLIT 4; WWE 1

Modarressi, Taghi (M.) 1931-1997 ... **CLC 44**
See also CA 121; 134; INT CA-134

Modiano, Patrick (Jean) 1945- .... **CLC 18**
See also CA 85-88; CANR 17, 40, 115; CWW 2; DLB 83; EWL 3

Mofolo, Thomas (Mokopu)
1875(?)-1948 .... **BLC 3; TCLC 22**
See also AFW; CA 121; 153; CANR 83; DAM MULT; DLB 225; EWL 3; MTCW 2; WLIT 2

Mohr, Nicholasa 1938- .... **CLC 12; HLC 2**
See also AAYA 8, 46; CA 49-52; CANR 1, 32, 64; CLR 22; DAM MULT; DLB 145; HW 1, 2; JRDA; LAIT 5; LLW 1; MAI-CYA 2; MAICYAS 1; RGAL 4; SAAS 8; SATA 8, 97; SATA-Essay 113; WYA; YAW

Moi, Toril 1953- .... **CLC 172**
See also CA 154; CANR 102; FW

Mojtabai, A(nn) G(race) 1938- ..... **CLC 5, 9, 15, 29**
See also CA 85-88; CANR 88

Moliere 1622-1673 ..... **DC 13; LC 10, 28, 64; WLC**
See also DA; DA3; DAB; DAC; DAM DRAM, MST; DFS 13, 18; DLB 268; EW 3; GFL Beginnings to 1789; LATS 1; RGWL 2, 3; TWA

Molin, Charles
See Mayne, William (James Carter)

Molnar, Ferenc 1878-1952 .... **TCLC 20**
See also CA 109; 153; CANR 83; CDWLB 4; DAM DRAM; DLB 215; EWL 3; RGWL 2, 3

Momaday, N(avarre) Scott 1934- ...... **CLC 2, 19, 85, 95, 160; NNAL; PC 25; WLCS**
See also AAYA 11; AMWS 4; ANW; BPFB 2; BYA 12; CA 25-28R; CANR 14, 34, 68; CDALBS; CN 7; CPW; DA; DA3; DAB; DAC; DAM MST, MULT, NOV, POP; DLB 143, 175, 256; EWL 3; EXPP; INT CANR-14; LAIT 4; LATS 1; MTCW 1, 2; NFS 10; PFS 2, 11; RGAL 4; SATA 48; SATA-Brief 30; WP; YAW

Monette, Paul 1945-1995 .... **CLC 82**
    See also AMWS 10; CA 139; 147; CN 7;
    GLL 1

Monroe, Harriet 1860-1936 .... **TCLC 12**
    See also CA 109; 204; DLB 54, 91

Monroe, Lyle
    See Heinlein, Robert A(nson)

Montagu, Elizabeth 1720-1800 .... **NCLC 7,
117**
    See also FW

Montagu, Mary (Pierrepont) Wortley
    1689-1762 .... **LC 9, 57; PC 16**
    See also DLB 95, 101; RGEL 2

Montagu, W. H.
    See Coleridge, Samuel Taylor

Montague, John (Patrick) 1929- ..... **CLC 13,
46**
    See also CA 9-12R; CANR 9, 69, 121; CP
    7; DLB 40; EWL 3; MTCW 1; PFS 12;
    RGEL 2

Montaigne, Michel (Eyquem) de
    1533-1592 .... **LC 8; WLC**
    See also DA; DAB; DAC; DAM MST; EW
    2; GFL Beginnings to 1789; LMFS 1;
    RGWL 2, 3; TWA

Montale, Eugenio 1896-1981 ... **CLC 7, 9, 18;
PC 13**
    See also CA 17-20R; 104; CANR 30; DLB
    114; EW 11; EWL 3; MTCW 1; RGWL
    2, 3; TWA

Montesquieu, Charles-Louis de Secondat
    1689-1755 .... **LC 7, 69**
    See also EW 3; GFL Beginnings to 1789;
    TWA

Montessori, Maria 1870-1952 ...... **TCLC 103**
    See also CA 115; 147

Montgomery, (Robert) Bruce 1921(?)-1978
    See Crispin, Edmund
    See also CA 179; 104; CMW 4

Montgomery, L(ucy) M(aud)
    1874-1942 .... **TCLC 51, 140**
    See also AAYA 12; BYA 1; CA 108; 137;
    CLR 8, 91; DA3; DAC; DAM MST; DLB
    92; DLBD 14; JRDA; MAICYA 1, 2;
    MTCW 2; RGEL 2; SATA 100; TWA;
    WCH; WYA; YABC 1

Montgomery, Marion H., Jr. 1925- .... **CLC 7**
    See also AITN 1; CA 1-4R; CANR 3, 48;
    CSW; DLB 6

Montgomery, Max
    See Davenport, Guy (Mattison, Jr.)

Montherlant, Henry (Milon) de
    1896-1972 .... **CLC 8, 19**
    See also CA 85-88; 37-40R; DAM DRAM;
    DLB 72; EW 11; EWL 3; GFL 1789 to
    the Present; MTCW 1

Monty Python
    See Chapman, Graham; Cleese, John
    (Marwood); Gilliam, Terry (Vance); Idle,
    Eric; Jones, Terence Graham Parry; Palin,
    Michael (Edward)
    See also AAYA 7

Moodie, Susanna (Strickland)
    1803-1885 .... **NCLC 14, 113**
    See also DLB 99

Moody, Hiram (F. III) 1961-
    See Moody, Rick
    See also CA 138; CANR 64, 112

Moody, Minerva
    See Alcott, Louisa May

Moody, Rick .... **CLC 147**
    See Moody, Hiram (F. III)

Moody, William Vaughan
    1869-1910 .... **TCLC 105**
    See also CA 110; 178; DLB 7, 54; RGAL 4

Mooney, Edward 1951-
    See Mooney, Ted
    See also CA 130

Mooney, Ted .... **CLC 25**
    See Mooney, Edward

Moorcock, Michael (John) 1939- ...... **CLC 5,
27, 58**
    See Bradbury, Edward P.
    See also AAYA 26; CA 45-48; CAAS 5;
    CANR 2, 17, 38, 64, 122; CN 7; DLB 14,
    231, 261; FANT; MTCW 1, 2; SATA 93;
    SCFW 2; SFW 4; SUFW 1, 2

Moore, Brian 1921-1999 ... **CLC 1, 3, 5, 7, 8,
19, 32, 90**
    See Bryan, Michael
    See also BRWS 9; CA 1-4R; 174; CANR 1,
    25, 42, 63; CCA 1; CN 7; DAB; DAC;
    DAM MST; DLB 251; EWL 3; FANT;
    MTCW 1, 2; RGEL 2

Moore, Edward
    See Muir, Edwin
    See also RGEL 2

Moore, G. E. 1873-1958 .... **TCLC 89**
    See also DLB 262

Moore, George Augustus
    1852-1933 .... **SSC 19; TCLC 7**
    See also BRW 6; CA 104; 177; DLB 10,
    18, 57, 135; EWL 3; RGEL 2; RGSF 2

Moore, Lorrie .... **CLC 39, 45, 68**
    See Moore, Marie Lorena
    See also AMWS 10; DLB 234

Moore, Marianne (Craig)
    1887-1972 .... **CLC 1, 2, 4, 8, 10, 13, 19,
47; PC 4, 49; WLCS**
    See also AMW; CA 1-4R; 33-36R; CANR
    3, 61; CDALB 1929-1941; DA; DA3;
    DAB; DAC; DAM MST, POET; DLB 45;
    DLBD 7; EWL 3; EXPP; MAWW;
    MTCW 1, 2; PAB; PFS 14, 17; RGAL 4;
    SATA 20; TUS; WP

Moore, Marie Lorena 1957- .... **CLC 165**
    See Moore, Lorrie
    See also CA 116; CANR 39, 83; CN 7; DLB
    234

Moore, Thomas 1779-1852 .... **NCLC 6, 110**
    See also DLB 96, 144; RGEL 2

Moorhouse, Frank 1938- .... **SSC 40**
    See also CA 118; CANR 92; CN 7; DLB
    289; RGSF 2

Mora, Pat(ricia) 1942- .... **HLC 2**
    See also AMWS 13; CA 129; CANR 57,
    81, 112; CLR 58; DAM MULT; DLB 209;
    HW 1, 2; LLW 1; MAICYA 2; SATA 92,
    134

Moraga, Cherrie 1952- ...... **CLC 126; DC 22**
    See also CA 131; CANR 66; DAM MULT;
    DLB 82, 249; FW; GLL 1; HW 1, 2; LLW
    1

Morand, Paul 1888-1976 .... **CLC 41; SSC 22**
    See also CA 184; 69-72; DLB 65; EWL 3

Morante, Elsa 1918-1985 .... **CLC 8, 47**
    See also CA 85-88; 117; CANR 35; DLB
    177; EWL 3; MTCW 1, 2; RGWL 2, 3

Moravia, Alberto .... **CLC 2, 7, 11, 27, 46;
SSC 26**
    See Pincherle, Alberto
    See also DLB 177; EW 12; EWL 3; MTCW
    2; RGSF 2; RGWL 2, 3

More, Hannah 1745-1833 .... **NCLC 27**
    See also DLB 107, 109, 116, 158; RGEL 2

More, Henry 1614-1687 .... **LC 9**
    See also DLB 126, 252

More, Sir Thomas 1478(?)-1535 .... **LC 10, 32**
    See also BRWC 1; BRWS 7; DLB 136, 281;
    LMFS 1; RGEL 2; TEA

Moreas, Jean .... **TCLC 18**
    See Papadiamantopoulos, Johannes
    See also GFL 1789 to the Present

Moreton, Andrew Esq.
    See Defoe, Daniel

Morgan, Berry 1919-2002 .... **CLC 6**
    See also CA 49-52; 208; DLB 6

Morgan, Claire
    See Highsmith, (Mary) Patricia
    See also GLL 1

Morgan, Edwin (George) 1920- .... **CLC 31**
    See also BRWS 9; CA 5-8R; CANR 3, 43,
    90; CP 7; DLB 27

Morgan, (George) Frederick
    1922-2004 .... **CLC 23**
    See also CA 17-20R; CANR 21; CP 7

Morgan, Harriet
    See Mencken, H(enry) L(ouis)

Morgan, Jane
    See Cooper, James Fenimore

Morgan, Janet 1945- .... **CLC 39**
    See also CA 65-68

Morgan, Lady 1776(?)-1859 .... **NCLC 29**
    See also DLB 116, 158; RGEL 2

Morgan, Robin (Evonne) 1941- .... **CLC 2**
    See also CA 69-72; CANR 29, 68; FW;
    GLL 2; MTCW 1; SATA 80

Morgan, Scott
    See Kuttner, Henry

Morgan, Seth 1949(?)-1990 .... **CLC 65**
    See also CA 185; 132

**Morgenstern, Christian (Otto Josef
Wolfgang)** 1871-1914 .... **TCLC 8**
    See also CA 105; 191; EWL 3

Morgenstern, S.
    See Goldman, William (W.)

Mori, Rintaro
    See Mori Ogai
    See also CA 110

Moricz, Zsigmond 1879-1942 .... **TCLC 33**
    See also CA 165; DLB 215; EWL 3

Morike, Eduard (Friedrich)
    1804-1875 .... **NCLC 10**
    See also DLB 133; RGWL 2, 3

Mori Ogai 1862-1922 .... **TCLC 14**
    See Ogai
    See also CA 164; DLB 180; EWL 3; RGWL
    3; TWA

Moritz, Karl Philipp 1756-1793 .... **LC 2**
    See also DLB 94

Morland, Peter Henry
    See Faust, Frederick (Schiller)

Morley, Christopher (Darlington)
    1890-1957 .... **TCLC 87**
    See also CA 112; DLB 9; RGAL 4

Morren, Theophil
    See Hofmannsthal, Hugo von

Morris, Bill 1952- .... **CLC 76**

Morris, Julian
    See West, Morris L(anglo)

Morris, Steveland Judkins 1950(?)-
    See Wonder, Stevie
    See also CA 111

Morris, William 1834-1896 . **NCLC 4; PC 55**
    See also BRW 5; CDBLB 1832-1890; DLB
    18, 35, 57, 156, 178, 184; FANT; RGEL
    2; SFW 4; SUFW

Morris, Wright 1910-1998 .. **CLC 1, 3, 7, 18,
37; TCLC 107**
    See also AMW; CA 9-12R; 167; CANR 21,
    81; CN 7; DLB 2, 206, 218; DLBY 1981;
    EWL 3; MTCW 1, 2; RGAL 4; TCWW 2

Morrison, Arthur 1863-1945 .... **SSC 40;
TCLC 72**
    See also CA 120; 157; CMW 4; DLB 70,
    135, 197; RGEL 2

Morrison, Chloe Anthony Wofford
    See Morrison, Toni

Morrison, James Douglas 1943-1971
    See Morrison, Jim
    See also CA 73-76; CANR 40

Morrison, Jim .... **CLC 17**
    See Morrison, James Douglas

Morrison, Toni 1931- ..... **BLC 3; CLC 4, 10, 22, 55, 81, 87, 173**
See also AAYA 1, 22; AFAW 1, 2; AMWC 1; AMWS 3; BPFB 2; BW 2, 3; CA 29-32R; CANR 27, 42, 67, 113, 124; CDALB 1968-1988; CN 7; CPW; DA; DA3; DAB; DAC; DAM MST, MULT, NOV, POP; DLB 6, 33, 143; DLBY 1981; EWL 3; EXPN; FW; LAIT 2, 4; LATS 1; LMFS 2; MAWW; MTCW 1, 2; NFS 1, 6, 8, 14; RGAL 4; RHW; SATA 57, 144; SSFS 5; TUS; YAW

Morrison, Van 1945- .... **CLC 21**
See also CA 116; 168

Morrissy, Mary 1957- .... **CLC 99**
See also CA 205; DLB 267

Mortimer, John (Clifford) 1923- ..... **CLC 28, 43**
See also CA 13-16R; CANR 21, 69, 109; CD 5; CDBLB 1960 to Present; CMW 4; CN 7; CPW; DA3; DAM DRAM, POP; DLB 13, 245, 271; INT CANR-21; MSW; MTCW 1, 2; RGEL 2

Mortimer, Penelope (Ruth) 1918-1999 .... **CLC 5**
See also CA 57-60; 187; CANR 45, 88; CN 7

Mortimer, Sir John
See Mortimer, John (Clifford)

Morton, Anthony
See Creasey, John

Morton, Thomas 1579(?)-1647(?) .... **LC 72**
See also DLB 24; RGEL 2

Mosca, Gaetano 1858-1941 .... **TCLC 75**

Moses, Daniel David 1952- .... **NNAL**
See also CA 186

Mosher, Howard Frank 1943- .... **CLC 62**
See also CA 139; CANR 65, 115

Mosley, Nicholas 1923- .... **CLC 43, 70**
See also CA 69-72; CANR 41, 60, 108; CN 7; DLB 14, 207

Mosley, Walter 1952- .... **BLCS; CLC 97, 184**
See also AAYA 17; AMWS 13; BPFB 2; BW 2; CA 142; CANR 57, 92; CMW 4; CPW; DA3; DAM MULT, POP; MSW; MTCW 2

Moss, Howard 1922-1987 . **CLC 7, 14, 45, 50**
See also CA 1-4R; 123; CANR 1, 44; DAM POET; DLB 5

Mossgiel, Rab
See Burns, Robert

Motion, Andrew (Peter) 1952- .... **CLC 47**
See also BRWS 7; CA 146; CANR 90; CP 7; DLB 40

Motley, Willard (Francis) 1909-1965 .... **CLC 18**
See also BW 1; CA 117; 106; CANR 88; DLB 76, 143

Motoori, Norinaga 1730-1801 .... **NCLC 45**

Mott, Michael (Charles Alston) 1930- .... **CLC 15, 34**
See also CA 5-8R; CAAS 7; CANR 7, 29

Mountain Wolf Woman 1884-1960 . **CLC 92; NNAL**
See also CA 144; CANR 90

Moure, Erin 1955- .... **CLC 88**
See also CA 113; CP 7; CWP; DLB 60

Mourning Dove 1885(?)-1936 .... **NNAL**
See also CA 144; CANR 90; DAM MULT; DLB 175, 221

Mowat, Farley (McGill) 1921- .... **CLC 26**
See also AAYA 1, 50; BYA 2; CA 1-4R; CANR 4, 24, 42, 68, 108; CLR 20; CPW; DAC; DAM MST; DLB 68; INT CANR-24; JRDA; MAICYA 1, 2; MTCW 1, 2; SATA 3, 55; YAW

Mowatt, Anna Cora 1819-1870 ..... **NCLC 74**
See also RGAL 4

Moyers, Bill 1934- .... **CLC 74**
See also AITN 2; CA 61-64; CANR 31, 52

Mphahlele, Es'kia
See Mphahlele, Ezekiel
See also AFW; CDWLB 3; DLB 125, 225; RGSF 2; SSFS 11

Mphahlele, Ezekiel 1919- ... **BLC 3; CLC 25, 133**
See Mphahlele, Es'kia
See also BW 2, 3; CA 81-84; CANR 26, 76; CN 7; DA3; DAM MULT; EWL 3; MTCW 2; SATA 119

Mqhayi, S(amuel) E(dward) K(rune Loliwe) 1875-1945 .... **BLC 3; TCLC 25**
See also CA 153; CANR 87; DAM MULT

Mrozek, Slawomir 1930- .... **CLC 3, 13**
See also CA 13-16R; CAAS 10; CANR 29; CDWLB 4; CWW 2; DLB 232; EWL 3; MTCW 1

Mrs. Belloc-Lowndes
See Lowndes, Marie Adelaide (Belloc)

Mrs. Fairstar
See Horne, Richard Henry Hengist

M'Taggart, John M'Taggart Ellis
See McTaggart, John McTaggart Ellis

Mtwa, Percy (?)- .... **CLC 47**

Mueller, Lisel 1924- .... **CLC 13, 51; PC 33**
See also CA 93-96; CP 7; DLB 105; PFS 9, 13

Muggeridge, Malcolm (Thomas) 1903-1990 .... **TCLC 120**
See also AITN 1; CA 101; CANR 33, 63; MTCW 1, 2

Muhammad 570-632 .... **WLCS**
See also DA; DAB; DAC; DAM MST

Muir, Edwin 1887-1959 . **PC 49; TCLC 2, 87**
See Moore, Edward
See also BRWS 6; CA 104; 193; DLB 20, 100, 191; EWL 3; RGEL 2

Muir, John 1838-1914 .... **TCLC 28**
See also AMWS 9; ANW; CA 165; DLB 186, 275

Mujica Lainez, Manuel 1910-1984 ... **CLC 31**
See Lainez, Manuel Mujica
See also CA 81-84; 112; CANR 32; EWL 3; HW 1

Mukherjee, Bharati 1940- ..... **AAL; CLC 53, 115; SSC 38**
See also AAYA 46; BEST 89:2; CA 107; CANR 45, 72; CN 7; DAM NOV; DLB 60, 218; DNFS 1, 2; EWL 3; FW; MTCW 1, 2; RGAL 4; RGSF 2; SSFS 7; TUS; WWE 1

Muldoon, Paul 1951- .... **CLC 32, 72, 166**
See also BRWS 4; CA 113; 129; CANR 52, 91; CP 7; DAM POET; DLB 40; INT CA-129; PFS 7

Mulisch, Harry 1927- .... **CLC 42**
See also CA 9-12R; CANR 6, 26, 56, 110; EWL 3

Mull, Martin 1943- .... **CLC 17**
See also CA 105

Muller, Wilhelm .... **NCLC 73**

Mulock, Dinah Maria
See Craik, Dinah Maria (Mulock)
See also RGEL 2

Munday, Anthony 1560-1633 .... **LC 87**
See also DLB 62, 172; RGEL 2

Munford, Robert 1737(?)-1783 .... **LC 5**
See also DLB 31

Mungo, Raymond 1946- .... **CLC 72**
See also CA 49-52; CANR 2

Munro, Alice 1931- .... **CLC 6, 10, 19, 50, 95; SSC 3; WLCS**
See also AITN 2; BPFB 2; CA 33-36R; CANR 33, 53, 75, 114; CCA 1; CN 7; DA3; DAC; DAM MST, NOV; DLB 53; EWL 3; MTCW 1, 2; RGEL 2; RGSF 2; SATA 29; SSFS 5, 13; WWE 1

Munro, H(ector) H(ugh) 1870-1916 .... **WLC**
See Saki
See also CA 104; 130; CANR 104; CDBLB 1890-1914; DA; DA3; DAB; DAC; DAM MST, NOV; DLB 34, 162; EXPS; MTCW 1, 2; RGEL 2; SSFS 15

Murakami, Haruki 1949- .... **CLC 150**
See Murakami Haruki
See also CA 165; CANR 102; MJW; RGWL 3; SFW 4

Murakami Haruki
See Murakami, Haruki
See also DLB 182; EWL 3

Murasaki, Lady
See Murasaki Shikibu

Murasaki Shikibu 978(?)-1026(?) ... **CMLC 1**
See also EFS 2; LATS 1; RGWL 2, 3

Murdoch, (Jean) Iris 1919-1999 ... **CLC 1, 2, 3, 4, 6, 8, 11, 15, 22, 31, 51**
See also BRWS 1; CA 13-16R; 179; CANR 8, 43, 68, 103; CDBLB 1960 to Present; CN 7; CWD; DA3; DAB; DAC; DAM MST, NOV; DLB 14, 194, 233; EWL 3; INT CANR-8; MTCW 1, 2; NFS 18; RGEL 2; TEA; WLIT 4

Murfree, Mary Noailles 1850-1922 .. **SSC 22; TCLC 135**
See also CA 122; 176; DLB 12, 74; RGAL 4

Murnau, Friedrich Wilhelm
See Plumpe, Friedrich Wilhelm

Murphy, Richard 1927- .... **CLC 41**
See also BRWS 5; CA 29-32R; CP 7; DLB 40; EWL 3

Murphy, Sylvia 1937- .... **CLC 34**
See also CA 121

Murphy, Thomas (Bernard) 1935- ... **CLC 51**
See also CA 101

Murray, Albert L. 1916- .... **CLC 73**
See also BW 2; CA 49-52; CANR 26, 52, 78; CSW; DLB 38

Murray, James Augustus Henry 1837-1915 .... **TCLC 117**

Murray, Judith Sargent 1751-1820 .... **NCLC 63**
See also DLB 37, 200

Murray, Les(lie Allan) 1938- .... **CLC 40**
See also BRWS 7; CA 21-24R; CANR 11, 27, 56, 103; CP 7; DAM POET; DLB 289; DLBY 2001; EWL 3; RGEL 2

Murry, J. Middleton
See Murry, John Middleton

Murry, John Middleton 1889-1957 .... **TCLC 16**
See also CA 118; 217; DLB 149

Musgrave, Susan 1951- .... **CLC 13, 54**
See also CA 69-72; CANR 45, 84; CCA 1; CP 7; CWP

Musil, Robert (Edler von) 1880-1942 .... **SSC 18; TCLC 12, 68**
See also CA 109; CANR 55, 84; CDWLB 2; DLB 81, 124; EW 9; EWL 3; MTCW 2; RGSF 2; RGWL 2, 3

Muske, Carol .... **CLC 90**
See Muske-Dukes, Carol (Anne)

Muske-Dukes, Carol (Anne) 1945-
See Muske, Carol
See also CA 65-68, 203; CAAE 203; CANR 32, 70; CWP

Musset, (Louis Charles) Alfred de 1810-1857 .... **NCLC 7**
See also DLB 192, 217; EW 6; GFL 1789 to the Present; RGWL 2, 3; TWA

Mussolini, Benito (Amilcare Andrea) 1883-1945 .... **TCLC 96**
See also CA 116

Mutanabbi, Al-
See al-Mutanabbi, Ahmad ibn al-Husayn Abu al-Tayyib al-Jufi al-Kindi

DLBD 12; DLBY 1980; EWL 3; EXPS;
LAIT 5; MAWW; MTCW 1, 2; NFS 3;
RGAL 4; RGSF 2; SSFS 2, 7, 10; TUS

O'Connor, Frank .... **CLC 23; SSC 5**
See O'Donovan, Michael Francis
See also DLB 162; EWL 3; RGSF 2; SSFS
5

O'Dell, Scott 1898-1989 .... **CLC 30**
See also AAYA 3, 44; BPFB 3; BYA 1, 2,
3, 5; CA 61-64; 129; CANR 12, 30, 112;
CLR 1, 16; DLB 52; JRDA; MAICYA 1,
2; SATA 12, 60, 134; WYA; YAW

Odets, Clifford 1906-1963 ..... **CLC 2, 28, 98;
DC 6**
See also AMWS 2; CA 85-88; CAD; CANR
62; DAM DRAM; DFS 3, 17; DLB 7, 26;
EWL 3; MTCW 1, 2; RGAL 4; TUS

O'Doherty, Brian 1928- .... **CLC 76**
See also CA 105; CANR 108

O'Donnell, K. M.
See Malzberg, Barry N(athaniel)

O'Donnell, Lawrence
See Kuttner, Henry

O'Donovan, Michael Francis
1903-1966 .... **CLC 14**
See O'Connor, Frank
See also CA 93-96; CANR 84

Oe, Kenzaburo 1935- .. **CLC 10, 36, 86, 187;
SSC 20**
See Oe Kenzaburo
See also CA 97-100; CANR 36, 50, 74, 126;
CWW 2; DA3; DAM NOV; DLB 182;
DLBY 1994; EWL 3; LATS 1; MJW;
MTCW 1, 2; RGSF 2; RGWL 2, 3

Oe Kenzaburo
See Oe, Kenzaburo
See also EWL 3

O'Faolain, Julia 1932- .... **CLC 6, 19, 47, 108**
See also CA 81-84; CAAS 2; CANR 12,
61; CN 7; DLB 14, 231; FW; MTCW 1;
RHW

O'Faolain, Sean 1900-1991 ...... **CLC 1, 7, 14,
32, 70; SSC 13; TCLC 143**
See also CA 61-64; 134; CANR 12, 66;
DLB 15, 162; MTCW 1, 2; RGEL 2;
RGSF 2

O'Flaherty, Liam 1896-1984 .... **CLC 5, 34;
SSC 6**
See also CA 101; 113; CANR 35; DLB 36,
162; DLBY 1984; MTCW 1, 2; RGEL 2;
RGSF 2; SSFS 5

Ogai
See Mori Ogai
See also MJW

Ogilvy, Gavin
See Barrie, J(ames) M(atthew)

O'Grady, Standish (James)
1846-1928 .... **TCLC 5**
See also CA 104; 157

O'Grady, Timothy 1951- .... **CLC 59**
See also CA 138

O'Hara, Frank 1926-1966 .... **CLC 2, 5, 13,
78; PC 45**
See also CA 9-12R; 25-28R; CANR 33;
DA3; DAM POET; DLB 5, 16, 193; EWL
3; MTCW 1, 2; PFS 8; 12; RGAL 4; WP

O'Hara, John (Henry) 1905-1970 . **CLC 1, 2,
3, 6, 11, 42; SSC 15**
See also AMW; BPFB 3; CA 5-8R; 25-28R;
CANR 31, 60; CDALB 1929-1941; DAM
NOV; DLB 9, 86; DLBD 2; EWL 3;
MTCW 1, 2; NFS 11; RGAL 4; RGSF 2

O Hehir, Diana 1922- .... **CLC 41**
See also CA 93-96

Ohiyesa
See Eastman, Charles A(lexander)

Okada, John 1923-1971 .... **AAL**
See also BYA 14; CA 212

Okigbo, Christopher (Ifenayichukwu)
1932-1967 .... **BLC 3; CLC 25, 84; PC 7**
See also AFW; BW 1, 3; CA 77-80; CANR
74; CDWLB 3; DAM MULT, POET; DLB
125; EWL 3; MTCW 1, 2; RGEL 2

Okri, Ben 1959- .... **CLC 87**
See also AFW; BRWS 5; BW 2, 3; CA 130;
138; CANR 65; CN 7; DLB 157, 231;
EWL 3; INT CA-138; MTCW 2; RGSF
2; WLIT 2; WWE 1

Olds, Sharon 1942- .. **CLC 32, 39, 85; PC 22**
See also AMWS 10; CA 101; CANR 18,
41, 66, 98; CP 7; CPW; CWP; DAM
POET; DLB 120; MTCW 2; PFS 17

Oldstyle, Jonathan
See Irving, Washington

Olesha, Iurii
See Olesha, Yuri (Karlovich)
See also RGWL 2

Olesha, Iurii Karlovich
See Olesha, Yuri (Karlovich)
See also DLB 272

Olesha, Yuri (Karlovich) 1899-1960 . **CLC 8;
SSC 69; TCLC 136**
See Olesha, Iurii; Olesha, Iurii Karlovich;
Olesha, Yury Karlovich
See also CA 85-88; EW 11; RGWL 3

Olesha, Yury Karlovich
See Olesha, Yuri (Karlovich)
See also EWL 3

Oliphant, Mrs.
See Oliphant, Margaret (Oliphant Wilson)
See also SUFW

Oliphant, Laurence 1829(?)-1888 .. **NCLC 47**
See also DLB 18, 166

Oliphant, Margaret (Oliphant Wilson)
1828-1897 .... **NCLC 11, 61; SSC 25**
See Oliphant, Mrs.
See also DLB 18, 159, 190; HGG; RGEL
2; RGSF 2

Oliver, Mary 1935- .... **CLC 19, 34, 98**
See also AMWS 7; CA 21-24R; CANR 9,
43, 84, 92; CP 7; CWP; DLB 5, 193;
EWL 3; PFS 15

Olivier, Laurence (Kerr) 1907-1989 . **CLC 20**
See also CA 111; 150; 129

Olsen, Tillie 1912- ... **CLC 4, 13, 114; SSC 11**
See also AAYA 51; AMWS 13; BYA 11;
CA 1-4R; CANR 1, 43, 74; CDALBS; CN
7; DA; DA3; DAB; DAC; DAM MST;
DLB 28, 206; DLBY 1980; EWL 3;
EXPS; FW; MTCW 1, 2; RGAL 4; RGSF
2; SSFS 1; TUS

Olson, Charles (John) 1910-1970 .. **CLC 1, 2,
5, 6, 9, 11, 29; PC 19**
See also AMWS 2; CA 13-16; 25-28R;
CABS 2; CANR 35, 61; CAP 1; DAM
POET; DLB 5, 16, 193; EWL 3; MTCW
1, 2; RGAL 4; WP

Olson, Toby 1937- .... **CLC 28**
See also CA 65-68; CANR 9, 31, 84; CP 7

Olyesha, Yuri
See Olesha, Yuri (Karlovich)

Olympiodorus of Thebes c. 375-c.
430 .... **CMLC 59**

Omar Khayyam
See Khayyam, Omar
See also RGWL 2, 3

Ondaatje, (Philip) Michael 1943- .... **CLC 14,
29, 51, 76, 180; PC 28**
See also CA 77-80; CANR 42, 74, 109; CN
7; CP 7; DA3; DAB; DAC; DAM MST;
DLB 60; EWL 3; LATS 1; LMFS 2;
MTCW 2; PFS 8; TWA; WWE 1

Oneal, Elizabeth 1934-
See Oneal, Zibby
See also CA 106; CANR 28, 84; MAICYA
1, 2; SATA 30, 82; YAW

Oneal, Zibby .... **CLC 30**
See Oneal, Elizabeth
See also AAYA 5, 41; BYA 13; CLR 13;
JRDA; WYA

O'Neill, Eugene (Gladstone)
1888-1953 ... **DC 20; TCLC 1, 6, 27, 49;
WLC**
See also AITN 1; AMW; AMWC 1; CA
110; 132; CAD; CDALB 1929-1941; DA;
DA3; DAB; DAC; DAM DRAM, MST;
DFS 2, 4, 5, 6, 9, 11, 12, 16; DLB 7; EWL
3; LAIT 3; LMFS 2; MTCW 1, 2; RGAL
4; TUS

Onetti, Juan Carlos 1909-1994 ... **CLC 7, 10;
HLCS 2; SSC 23; TCLC 131**
See also CA 85-88; 145; CANR 32, 63; CD-
WLB 3; DAM MULT, NOV; DLB 113;
EWL 3; HW 1, 2; LAW; MTCW 1, 2;
RGSF 2

O Nuallain, Brian 1911-1966
See O'Brien, Flann
See also CA 21-22; 25-28R; CAP 2; DLB
231; FANT; TEA

Ophuls, Max 1902-1957 .... **TCLC 79**
See also CA 113

Opie, Amelia 1769-1853 .... **NCLC 65**
See also DLB 116, 159; RGEL 2

Oppen, George 1908-1984 ..... **CLC 7, 13, 34;
PC 35; TCLC 107**
See also CA 13-16R; 113; CANR 8, 82;
DLB 5, 165

Oppenheim, E(dward) Phillips
1866-1946 .... **TCLC 45**
See also CA 111; 202; CMW 4; DLB 70

Opuls, Max
See Ophuls, Max

Origen c. 185-c. 254 .... **CMLC 19**

Orlovitz, Gil 1918-1973 .... **CLC 22**
See also CA 77-80; 45-48; DLB 2, 5

Orris
See Ingelow, Jean

Ortega y Gasset, Jose 1883-1955 ...... **HLC 2;
TCLC 9**
See also CA 106; 130; DAM MULT; EW 9;
EWL 3; HW 1, 2; MTCW 1, 2

Ortese, Anna Maria 1914-1998 .... **CLC 89**
See also DLB 177; EWL 3

Ortiz, Simon J(oseph) 1941- .... **CLC 45;
NNAL; PC 17**
See also AMWS 4; CA 134; CANR 69, 118;
CP 7; DAM MULT, POET; DLB 120,
175, 256; EXPP; PFS 4, 16; RGAL 4

Orton, Joe .... **CLC 4, 13, 43; DC 3**
See Orton, John Kingsley
See also BRWS 5; CBD; CDBLB 1960 to
Present; DFS 3, 6; DLB 13; GLL 1;
MTCW 2; RGEL 2; TEA; WLIT 4

Orton, John Kingsley 1933-1967
See Orton, Joe
See also CA 85-88; CANR 35, 66; DAM
DRAM; MTCW 1, 2

Orwell, George ...... **SSC 68; TCLC 2, 6, 15,
31, 51, 128, 129; WLC**
See Blair, Eric (Arthur)
See also BPFB 3; BRW 7; BYA 5; CDBLB
1945-1960; CLR 68; DAB; DLB 15, 98,
195, 255; EWL 3; EXPN; LAIT 4, 5;
LATS 1; NFS 3, 7; RGEL 2; SCFW 2;
SFW 4; SSFS 4; TEA; WLIT 4; YAW

Osborne, David
See Silverberg, Robert

Osborne, George
See Silverberg, Robert

Osborne, John (James) 1929-1994 .... **CLC 1,
2, 5, 11, 45; WLC**
See also BRWS 1; CA 13-16R; 147; CANR
21, 56; CDBLB 1945-1960; DA; DAB;
DAC; DAM DRAM, MST; DFS 4; DLB
13; EWL 3; MTCW 1, 2; RGEL 2

Parmenides c. 515B.C.-c.
450B.C. .... **CMLC 22**
See also DLB 176

Parnell, Thomas 1679-1718 .... **LC 3**
See also DLB 95; RGEL 2

Parr, Catherine c. 1513(?)-1548 .... **LC 86**
See also DLB 136

Parra, Nicanor 1914- ... **CLC 2, 102; HLC 2;**
PC 39
See also CA 85-88; CANR 32; CWW 2;
DAM MULT; DLB 283; EWL 3; HW 1;
LAW; MTCW 1

Parra Sanojo, Ana Teresa de la
1890-1936 .... **HLCS 2**
See de la Parra, (Ana) Teresa (Sonojo)
See also LAW

Parrish, Mary Frances
See Fisher, M(ary) F(rances) K(ennedy)

Parshchikov, Aleksei 1954- .... **CLC 59**
See Parshchikov, Aleksei Maksimovich

Parshchikov, Aleksei Maksimovich
See Parshchikov, Aleksei
See also DLB 285

Parson, Professor
See Coleridge, Samuel Taylor

Parson Lot
See Kingsley, Charles

Parton, Sara Payson Willis
1811-1872 .... **NCLC 86**
See also DLB 43, 74, 239

Partridge, Anthony
See Oppenheim, E(dward) Phillips

Pascal, Blaise 1623-1662 .... **LC 35**
See also DLB 268; EW 3; GFL Beginnings
to 1789; RGWL 2, 3; TWA

Pascoli, Giovanni 1855-1912 .... **TCLC 45**
See also CA 170; EW 7; EWL 3

Pasolini, Pier Paolo 1922-1975 .. **CLC 20, 37,**
106; PC 17
See also CA 93-96; 61-64; CANR 63; DLB
128, 177; EWL 3; MTCW 1; RGWL 2, 3

Pasquini
See Silone, Ignazio

Pastan, Linda (Olenik) 1932- .... **CLC 27**
See also CA 61-64; CANR 18, 40, 61, 113;
CP 7; CSW; CWP; DAM POET; DLB 5;
PFS 8

Pasternak, Boris (Leonidovich)
1890-1960 ...... **CLC 7, 10, 18, 63; PC 6;**
SSC 31; WLC
See also BPFB 3; CA 127; 116; DA; DA3;
DAB; DAC; DAM MST, NOV, POET;
EW 10; MTCW 1, 2; RGSF 2; RGWL 2,
3; TWA; WP

Patchen, Kenneth 1911-1972 .... **CLC 1, 2, 18**
See also BG 3; CA 1-4R; 33-36R; CANR
3, 35; DAM POET; DLB 16, 48; EWL 3;
MTCW 1; RGAL 4

Pater, Walter (Horatio) 1839-1894 . **NCLC 7,**
90
See also BRW 5; CDBLB 1832-1890; DLB
57, 156; RGEL 2; TEA

Paterson, A(ndrew) B(arton)
1864-1941 .... **TCLC 32**
See also CA 155; DLB 230; RGEL 2; SATA
97

Paterson, Banjo
See Paterson, A(ndrew) B(arton)

Paterson, Katherine (Womeldorf)
1932- .... **CLC 12, 30**
See also AAYA 1, 31; BYA 1, 2, 7; CA 21-
24R; CANR 28, 59, 111; CLR 7, 50;
CWRI 5; DLB 52; JRDA; LAIT 4; MAI-
CYA 1, 2; MAICYAS 1; MTCW 1; SATA
13, 53, 92, 133; WYA; YAW

Patmore, Coventry Kersey Dighton
1823-1896 .... **NCLC 9**
See also DLB 35, 98; RGEL 2; TEA

Paton, Alan (Stewart) 1903-1988 ...... **CLC 4,**
10, 25, 55, 106; WLC
See also AAYA 26; AFW; BPFB 3; BRWS
2; BYA 1; CA 13-16; 125; CANR 22;
CAP 1; DA; DA3; DAB; DAC; DAM
MST, NOV; DLB 225; DLBD 17; EWL
3; EXPN; LAIT 4; MTCW 1, 2; NFS 3,
12; RGEL 2; SATA 11; SATA-Obit 56;
TWA; WLIT 2; WWE 1

Paton Walsh, Gillian 1937- .... **CLC 35**
See Paton Walsh, Jill; Walsh, Jill Paton
See also AAYA 11; CANR 38, 83; CLR 2,
65; DLB 161; JRDA; MAICYA 1, 2;
SAAS 3; SATA 4, 72, 109; YAW

Paton Walsh, Jill
See Paton Walsh, Gillian
See also AAYA 47; BYA 1, 8

Patterson, (Horace) Orlando (Lloyd)
1940- .... **BLCS**
See also BW 1; CA 65-68; CANR 27, 84;
CN 7

Patton, George S(mith), Jr.
1885-1945 .... **TCLC 79**
See also CA 189

Paulding, James Kirke 1778-1860 ... **NCLC 2**
See also DLB 3, 59, 74, 250; RGAL 4

Paulin, Thomas Neilson 1949-
See Paulin, Tom
See also CA 123; 128; CANR 98; CP 7

Paulin, Tom .... **CLC 37, 177**
See Paulin, Thomas Neilson
See also DLB 40

Pausanias c. 1st cent. - .... **CMLC 36**

Paustovsky, Konstantin (Georgievich)
1892-1968 .... **CLC 40**
See also CA 93-96; 25-28R; DLB 272;
EWL 3

Pavese, Cesare 1908-1950 .... **PC 13; SSC 19;**
TCLC 3
See also CA 104; 169; DLB 128, 177; EW
12; EWL 3; RGSF 2; RGWL 2, 3; TWA

Pavic, Milorad 1929- .... **CLC 60**
See also CA 136; CDWLB 4; CWW 2; DLB
181; EWL 3; RGWL 3

Pavlov, Ivan Petrovich 1849-1936 . **TCLC 91**
See also CA 118; 180

Pavlova, Karolina Karlovna
1807-1893 .... **NCLC 138**
See also DLB 205

Payne, Alan
See Jakes, John (William)

Paz, Gil
See Lugones, Leopoldo

Paz, Octavio 1914-1998 . **CLC 3, 4, 6, 10, 19,**
51, 65, 119; HLC 2; PC 1, 48; WLC
See also AAYA 50; CA 73-76; 165; CANR
32, 65, 104; CWW 2; DA; DA3; DAB;
DAC; DAM MST, MULT, POET; DLB
290; DLBY 1990, 1998; DNFS 1; EWL
3; HW 1, 2; LAW; LAWS 1; MTCW 1, 2;
PFS 18; RGWL 2, 3; SSFS 13; TWA;
WLIT 1

p'Bitek, Okot 1931-1982 ..... **BLC 3; CLC 96**
See also AFW; BW 2, 3; CA 124; 107;
CANR 82; DAM MULT; DLB 125; EWL
3; MTCW 1, 2; RGEL 2; WLIT 2

Peacock, Molly 1947- .... **CLC 60**
See also CA 103; CAAS 21; CANR 52, 84;
CP 7; CWP; DLB 120, 282

Peacock, Thomas Love
1785-1866 .... **NCLC 22**
See also BRW 4; DLB 96, 116; RGEL 2;
RGSF 2

Peake, Mervyn 1911-1968 .... **CLC 7, 54**
See also CA 5-8R; 25-28R; CANR 3; DLB
15, 160, 255; FANT; MTCW 1; RGEL 2;
SATA 23; SFW 4

Pearce, Philippa
See Christie, Philippa
See also CA 5-8R; CANR 4, 109; CWRI 5;
FANT; MAICYA 2

Pearl, Eric
See Elman, Richard (Martin)

Pearson, T(homas) R(eid) 1956- .... **CLC 39**
See also CA 120; 130; CANR 97; CSW;
INT CA-130

Peck, Dale 1967- .... **CLC 81**
See also CA 146; CANR 72, 127; GLL 2

Peck, John (Frederick) 1941- .... **CLC 3**
See also CA 49-52; CANR 3, 100; CP 7

Peck, Richard (Wayne) 1934- .... **CLC 21**
See also AAYA 1, 24; BYA 1, 6, 8, 11; CA
85-88; CANR 19, 38; CLR 15; INT
CANR-19; JRDA; MAICYA 1, 2; SAAS
2; SATA 18, 55, 97; SATA-Essay 110;
WYA; YAW

Peck, Robert Newton 1928- .... **CLC 17**
See also AAYA 3, 43; BYA 1, 6; CA 81-84,
182; CANR 31, 63, 127; CLR
45; DA; DAC; DAM MST; JRDA; LAIT
3; MAICYA 1, 2; SAAS 1; SATA 21, 62,
111; SATA-Essay 108; WYA; YAW

Peckinpah, (David) Sam(uel)
1925-1984 .... **CLC 20**
See also CA 109; 114; CANR 82

Pedersen, Knut 1859-1952
See Hamsun, Knut
See also CA 104; 119; CANR 63; MTCW
1, 2

Peeslake, Gaffer
See Durrell, Lawrence (George)

Peguy, Charles (Pierre)
1873-1914 .... **TCLC 10**
See also CA 107; 193; DLB 258; EWL 3;
GFL 1789 to the Present

Peirce, Charles Sanders
1839-1914 .... **TCLC 81**
See also CA 194; DLB 270

Pellicer, Carlos 1900(?)-1977 .... **HLCS 2**
See also CA 153; 69-72; DLB 290; EWL 3;
HW 1

Pena, Ramon del Valle y
See Valle-Inclan, Ramon (Maria) del

Pendennis, Arthur Esquir
See Thackeray, William Makepeace

Penn, William 1644-1718 .... **LC 25**
See also DLB 24

PEPECE
See Prado (Calvo), Pedro

Pepys, Samuel 1633-1703 ... **LC 11, 58; WLC**
See also BRW 2; CDBLB 1660-1789; DA;
DA3; DAB; DAC; DAM MST; DLB 101,
213; NCFS 4; RGEL 2; TEA; WLIT 3

Percy, Thomas 1729-1811 .... **NCLC 95**
See also DLB 104

Percy, Walker 1916-1990 .... **CLC 2, 3, 6, 8,**
14, 18, 47, 65
See also AMWS 3; BPFB 3; CA 1-4R; 131;
CANR 1, 23, 64; CPW; CSW; DA3;
DAM NOV, POP; DLB 2; DLBY 1980,
1990; EWL 3; MTCW 1, 2; RGAL 4;
TUS

Percy, William Alexander
1885-1942 .... **TCLC 84**
See also CA 163; MTCW 2

Perec, Georges 1936-1982 .... **CLC 56, 116**
See also CA 141; DLB 83; EWL 3; GFL
1789 to the Present; RGWL 3

Pereda (y Sanchez de Porrua), Jose Maria
de 1833-1906 .... **TCLC 16**
See also CA 117

Pereda y Porrua, Jose Maria de
See Pereda (y Sanchez de Porrua), Jose
Maria de

Peregoy, George Weems
See Mencken, H(enry) L(ouis)

Perelman, S(idney) J(oseph)
1904-1979 .. **CLC 3, 5, 9, 15, 23, 44, 49; SSC 32**
See also AITN 1, 2; BPFB 3; CA 73-76; 89-92; CANR 18; DAM DRAM; DLB 11, 44; MTCW 1, 2; RGAL 4

Peret, Benjamin 1899-1959 .... **PC 33; TCLC 20**
See also CA 117; 186; GFL 1789 to the Present

Peretz, Isaac Leib 1851(?)-1915
See Peretz, Isaac Loeb
See also CA 201

Peretz, Isaac Loeb 1851(?)-1915 ...... **SSC 26; TCLC 16**
See Peretz, Isaac Leib
See also CA 109

Peretz, Yitzkhok Leibush
See Peretz, Isaac Loeb

Perez Galdos, Benito 1843-1920 ..... **HLCS 2; TCLC 27**
See Galdos, Benito Perez
See also CA 125; 153; EWL 3; HW 1; RGWL 2, 3

Peri Rossi, Cristina 1941- .. **CLC 156; HLCS 2**
See also CA 131; CANR 59, 81; DLB 145, 290; EWL 3; HW 1, 2

Perlata
See Peret, Benjamin

Perloff, Marjorie G(abrielle)
1931- .... **CLC 137**
See also CA 57-60; CANR 7, 22, 49, 104

Perrault, Charles 1628-1703 ... **DC 12; LC 2, 56**
See also BYA 4; CLR 79; DLB 268; GFL Beginnings to 1789; MAICYA 1, 2; RGWL 2, 3; SATA 25; WCH

Perry, Anne 1938- .... **CLC 126**
See also CA 101; CANR 22, 50, 84; CMW 4; CN 7; CPW; DLB 276

Perry, Brighton
See Sherwood, Robert E(mmet)

Perse, St.-John
See Leger, (Marie-Rene Auguste) Alexis Saint-Leger

Perse, Saint-John
See Leger, (Marie-Rene Auguste) Alexis Saint-Leger
See also DLB 258; RGWL 3

Perutz, Leo(pold) 1882-1957 .... **TCLC 60**
See also CA 147; DLB 81

Peseenz, Tulio F.
See Lopez y Fuentes, Gregorio

Pesetsky, Bette 1932- .... **CLC 28**
See also CA 133; DLB 130

Peshkov, Alexei Maximovich 1868-1936
See Gorky, Maxim
See also CA 105; 141; CANR 83; DA; DAC; DAM DRAM, MST, NOV; MTCW 2

Pessoa, Fernando (Antonio Nogueira)
1888-1935 ..... **HLC 2; PC 20; TCLC 27**
See also CA 125; 183; DAM MULT; DLB 287; EW 10; EWL 3; RGWL 2, 3; WP

Peterkin, Julia Mood 1880-1961 ...... **CLC 31**
See also CA 102; DLB 9

Peters, Joan K(aren) 1945- .... **CLC 39**
See also CA 158; CANR 109

Peters, Robert L(ouis) 1924- .... **CLC 7**
See also CA 13-16R; CAAS 8; CP 7; DLB 105

Petofi, Sandor 1823-1849 .... **NCLC 21**
See also RGWL 2, 3

Petrakis, Harry Mark 1923- .... **CLC 3**
See also CA 9-12R; CANR 4, 30, 85; CN 7

Petrarch 1304-1374 .... **CMLC 20; PC 8**
See also DA3; DAM POET; EW 2; LMFS 1; RGWL 2. 3

Petronius c. 20-66 .... **CMLC 34**
See also AW 2; CDWLB 1; DLB 211; RGWL 2, 3

Petrov, Evgeny .... **TCLC 21**
See Kataev, Evgeny Petrovich

Petry, Ann (Lane) 1908-1997 .. **CLC 1, 7, 18; TCLC 112**
See also AFAW 1, 2; BPFB 3; BW 1, 3; BYA 2; CA 5-8R; 157; CAAS 6; CANR 4, 46; CLR 12; CN 7; DLB 76; EWL 3; JRDA; LAIT 1; MAICYA 1, 2; MAICYAS 1; MTCW 1; RGAL 4; SATA 5; SATA-Obit 94; TUS

Petursson, Halligrimur 1614-1674 .... **LC 8**

Peychinovich
See Vazov, Ivan (Minchov)

Phaedrus c. 15B.C.-c. 50 .... **CMLC 25**
See also DLB 211

Phelps (Ward), Elizabeth Stuart
See Phelps, Elizabeth Stuart
See also FW

Phelps, Elizabeth Stuart
1844-1911 .... **TCLC 113**
See Phelps (Ward), Elizabeth Stuart
See also DLB 74

Philips, Katherine 1632-1664 . **LC 30; PC 40**
See also DLB 131; RGEL 2

Philipson, Morris H. 1926- .... **CLC 53**
See also CA 1-4R; CANR 4

Phillips, Caryl 1958- .... **BLCS; CLC 96**
See also BRWS 5; BW 2; CA 141; CANR 63, 104; CBD; CD 5; CN 7; DA3; DAM MULT; DLB 157; EWL 3; MTCW 2; WLIT 4; WWE 1

Phillips, David Graham
1867-1911 .... **TCLC 44**
See also CA 108; 176; DLB 9, 12; RGAL 4

Phillips, Jack
See Sandburg, Carl (August)

Phillips, Jayne Anne 1952- .... **CLC 15, 33, 139; SSC 16**
See also BPFB 3; CA 101; CANR 24, 50, 96; CN 7; CSW; DLBY 1980; INT CANR-24; MTCW 1, 2; RGAL 4; RGSF 2; SSFS 4

Phillips, Richard
See Dick, Philip K(indred)

Phillips, Robert (Schaeffer) 1938- .... **CLC 28**
See also CA 17-20R; CAAS 13; CANR 8; DLB 105

Phillips, Ward
See Lovecraft, H(oward) P(hillips)

Philostratus, Flavius c. 179-c.
244 .... **CMLC 62**

Piccolo, Lucio 1901-1969 .... **CLC 13**
See also CA 97-100; DLB 114; EWL 3

Pickthall, Marjorie L(owry) C(hristie)
1883-1922 .... **TCLC 21**
See also CA 107; DLB 92

Pico della Mirandola, Giovanni
1463-1494 .... **LC 15**
See also LMFS 1

Piercy, Marge 1936- .... **CLC 3, 6, 14, 18, 27, 62, 128; PC 29**
See also BPFB 3; CA 21-24R, 187; CAAE 187; CAAS 1; CANR 13, 43, 66, 111; CN 7; CP 7; CWP; DLB 120, 227; EXPP; FW; MTCW 1, 2; PFS 9; SFW 4

Piers, Robert
See Anthony, Piers

Pieyre de Mandiargues, Andre 1909-1991
See Mandiargues, Andre Pieyre de
See also CA 103; 136; CANR 22, 82; EWL 3; GFL 1789 to the Present

Pilnyak, Boris 1894-1938 . **SSC 48; TCLC 23**
See Vogau, Boris Andreyevich
See also EWL 3

Pinchback, Eugene
See Toomer, Jean

Pincherle, Alberto 1907-1990 ...... **CLC 11, 18**
See Moravia, Alberto
See also CA 25-28R; 132; CANR 33, 63; DAM NOV; MTCW 1

Pinckney, Darryl 1953- .... **CLC 76**
See also BW 2, 3; CA 143; CANR 79

Pindar 518(?)B.C.-438(?)B.C. .... **CMLC 12; PC 19**
See also AW 1; CDWLB 1; DLB 176; RGWL 2

Pineda, Cecile 1942- .... **CLC 39**
See also CA 118; DLB 209

Pinero, Arthur Wing 1855-1934 .... **TCLC 32**
See also CA 110; 153; DAM DRAM; DLB 10; RGEL 2

Pinero, Miguel (Antonio Gomez)
1946-1988 .... **CLC 4, 55**
See also CA 61-64; 125; CAD; CANR 29, 90; DLB 266; HW 1; LLW 1

Pinget, Robert 1919-1997 .... **CLC 7, 13, 37**
See also CA 85-88; 160; CWW 2; DLB 83; EWL 3; GFL 1789 to the Present

Pink Floyd
See Barrett, (Roger) Syd; Gilmour, David; Mason, Nick; Waters, Roger; Wright, Rick

Pinkney, Edward 1802-1828 .... **NCLC 31**
See also DLB 248

Pinkwater, Daniel
See Pinkwater, Daniel Manus

Pinkwater, Daniel Manus 1941- .... **CLC 35**
See also AAYA 1, 46; BYA 9; CA 29-32R; CANR 12, 38, 89; CLR 4; CSW; FANT; JRDA; MAICYA 1, 2; SAAS 3; SATA 8, 46, 76, 114; SFW 4; YAW

Pinkwater, Manus
See Pinkwater, Daniel Manus

Pinsky, Robert 1940- ...... **CLC 9, 19, 38, 94, 121; PC 27**
See also AMWS 6; CA 29-32R; CAAS 4; CANR 58, 97; CP 7; DA3; DAM POET; DLBY 1982, 1998; MTCW 2; PFS 18; RGAL 4

Pinta, Harold
See Pinter, Harold

Pinter, Harold 1930- .. **CLC 1, 3, 6, 9, 11, 15, 27, 58, 73; DC 15; WLC**
See also BRWR 1; BRWS 1; CA 5-8R; CANR 33, 65, 112; CBD; CD 5; CDBLB 1960 to Present; DA; DA3; DAB; DAC; DAM DRAM, MST; DFS 3, 5, 7, 14; DLB 13; EWL 3; IDFW 3, 4; LMFS 2; MTCW 1, 2; RGEL 2; TEA

Piozzi, Hester Lynch (Thrale)
1741-1821 .... **NCLC 57**
See also DLB 104, 142

Pirandello, Luigi 1867-1936 .. **DC 5; SSC 22; TCLC 4, 29; WLC**
See also CA 104; 153; CANR 103; DA; DA3; DAB; DAC; DAM DRAM, MST; DFS 4, 9; DLB 264; EW 8; EWL 3; MTCW 2; RGSF 2; RGWL 2, 3

Pirsig, Robert M(aynard) 1928- ... **CLC 4, 6, 73**
See also CA 53-56; CANR 42, 74; CPW 1; DA3; DAM POP; MTCW 1, 2; SATA 39

Pisarev, Dmitrii Ivanovich
See Pisarev, Dmitry Ivanovich
See also DLB 277

Pisarev, Dmitry Ivanovich
1840-1868 .... **NCLC 25**
See Pisarev, Dmitrii Ivanovich

Pix, Mary (Griffith) 1666-1709 .... **LC 8**
See also DLB 80

Pixerecourt, (Rene Charles) Guilbert de
1773-1844 .... **NCLC 39**
See also DLB 192; GFL 1789 to the Present

Powell, Anthony (Dymoke)
1905-2000 .... **CLC 1, 3, 7, 9, 10, 31**
See also BRW 7; CA 1-4R; 189; CANR 1,
32, 62, 107; CDBLB 1945-1960; CN 7;
DLB 15; EWL 3; MTCW 1, 2; RGEL 2;
TEA

Powell, Dawn 1896(?)-1965 .... **CLC 66**
See also CA 5-8R; CANR 121; DLBY 1997

Powell, Padgett 1952- .... **CLC 34**
See also CA 126; CANR 63, 101; CSW;
DLB 234; DLBY 01

Powell, (Oval) Talmage 1920-2000
See Queen, Ellery
See also CA 5-8R; CANR 2, 80

Power, Susan 1961- .... **CLC 91**
See also BYA 14; CA 160; NFS 11

Powers, J(ames) F(arl) 1917-1999 ..... **CLC 1,
4, 8, 57; SSC 4**
See also CA 1-4R; 181; CANR 2, 61; CN
7; DLB 130; MTCW 1; RGAL 4; RGSF
2

Powers, John J(ames) 1945-
See Powers, John R.
See also CA 69-72

Powers, John R. .... **CLC 66**
See Powers, John J(ames)

Powers, Richard (S.) 1957- .... **CLC 93**
See also AMWS 9; BPFB 3; CA 148;
CANR 80; CN 7

Pownall, David 1938- .... **CLC 10**
See also CA 89-92; 180; CAAS 18; CANR
49, 101; CBD; CD 5; CN 7; DLB 14

Powys, John Cowper 1872-1963 ... **CLC 7, 9,
15, 46, 125**
See also CA 85-88; CANR 106; DLB 15,
255; EWL 3; FANT; MTCW 1, 2; RGEL
2; SUFW

Powys, T(heodore) F(rancis)
1875-1953 .... **TCLC 9**
See also BRWS 8; CA 106; 189; DLB 36,
162; EWL 3; FANT; RGEL 2; SUFW

Prado (Calvo), Pedro 1886-1952 ... **TCLC 75**
See also CA 131; DLB 283; HW 1; LAW

Prager, Emily 1952- .... **CLC 56**
See also CA 204

Pratolini, Vasco 1913-1991 .... **TCLC 124**
See also CA 211; DLB 177; EWL 3; RGWL
2, 3

Pratt, E(dwin) J(ohn) 1883(?)-1964 . **CLC 19**
See also CA 141; 93-96; CANR 77; DAC;
DAM POET; DLB 92; EWL 3; RGEL 2;
TWA

Premchand .... **TCLC 21**
See Srivastava, Dhanpat Rai
See also EWL 3

Preseren, France 1800-1849 .... **NCLC 127**
See also CDWLB 4; DLB 147

Preussler, Otfried 1923- .... **CLC 17**
See also CA 77-80; SATA 24

Prevert, Jacques (Henri Marie)
1900-1977 .... **CLC 15**
See also CA 77-80; 69-72; CANR 29, 61;
DLB 258; EWL 3; GFL 1789 to the
Present; IDFW 3, 4; MTCW 1; RGWL 2,
3; SATA-Obit 30

Prevost, (Antoine Francois)
1697-1763 .... **LC 1**
See also EW 4; GFL Beginnings to 1789;
RGWL 2, 3

Price, (Edward) Reynolds 1933- ... **CLC 3, 6,
13, 43, 50, 63; SSC 22**
See also AMWS 6; CA 1-4R; CANR 1, 37,
57, 87; CN 7; CSW; DAM NOV; DLB 2,
218, 278; EWL 3; INT CANR-37; NFS
18

Price, Richard 1949- .... **CLC 6, 12**
See also CA 49-52; CANR 3; DLBY 1981

Prichard, Katharine Susannah
1883-1969 .... **CLC 46**
See also CA 11-12; CANR 33; CAP 1; DLB
260; MTCW 1; RGEL 2; RGSF 2; SATA
66

Priestley, J(ohn) B(oynton)
1894-1984 .... **CLC 2, 5, 9, 34**
See also BRW 7; CA 9-12R; 113; CANR
33; CDBLB 1914-1945; DA3; DAM
DRAM, NOV; DLB 10, 34, 77, 100, 139;
DLBY 1984; EWL 3; MTCW 1, 2; RGEL
2; SFW 4

Prince 1958- .... **CLC 35**
See also CA 213

Prince, F(rank) T(empleton)
1912-2003 .... **CLC 22**
See also CA 101; 219; CANR 43, 79; CP 7;
DLB 20

Prince Kropotkin
See Kropotkin, Peter (Alekseievich)

Prior, Matthew 1664-1721 .... **LC 4**
See also DLB 95; RGEL 2

Prishvin, Mikhail 1873-1954 .... **TCLC 75**
See Prishvin, Mikhail Mikhailovich

Prishvin, Mikhail Mikhailovich
See Prishvin, Mikhail
See also DLB 272; EWL 3

Pritchard, William H(arrison)
1932- .... **CLC 34**
See also CA 65-68; CANR 23, 95; DLB
111

Pritchett, V(ictor) S(awdon)
1900-1997 ... **CLC 5, 13, 15, 41; SSC 14**
See also BPFB 3; BRWS 3; CA 61-64; 157;
CANR 31, 63; CN 7; DA3; DAM NOV;
DLB 15, 139; EWL 3; MTCW 1, 2;
RGEL 2; RGSF 2; TEA

Private 19022
See Manning, Frederic

Probst, Mark 1925- .... **CLC 59**
See also CA 130

Prokosch, Frederic 1908-1989 ...... **CLC 4, 48**
See also CA 73-76; 128; CANR 82; DLB
48; MTCW 2

Propertius, Sextus c. 50B.C.-c.
16B.C. .... **CMLC 32**
See also AW 2; CDWLB 1; DLB 211;
RGWL 2, 3

Prophet, The
See Dreiser, Theodore (Herman Albert)

Prose, Francine 1947- .... **CLC 45**
See also CA 109; 112; CANR 46, 95; DLB
234; SATA 101

Proudhon
See Cunha, Euclides (Rodrigues Pimenta)
da

Proulx, Annie
See Proulx, E(dna) Annie

Proulx, E(dna) Annie 1935- ...... **CLC 81, 158**
See also AMWS 7; BPFB 3; CA 145;
CANR 65, 110; CN 7; CPW 1; DA3;
DAM POP; MTCW 2; SSFS 18

**Proust, (Valentin-Louis-George-Eugene)
Marcel** 1871-1922 .... **TCLC 7, 13, 33;
WLC**
See also BPFB 3; CA 104; 120; CANR 110;
DA; DA3; DAB; DAC; DAM MST, NOV;
DLB 65; EW 8; EWL 3; GFL 1789 to the
Present; MTCW 1, 2; RGWL 2, 3; TWA

Prowler, Harley
See Masters, Edgar Lee

Prus, Boleslaw 1845-1912 .... **TCLC 48**
See also RGWL 2, 3

Pryor, Richard (Franklin Lenox Thomas)
1940- .... **CLC 26**
See also CA 122; 152

Przybyszewski, Stanislaw
1868-1927 .... **TCLC 36**
See also CA 160; DLB 66; EWL 3

Pteleon
See Grieve, C(hristopher) M(urray)
See also DAM POET

Puckett, Lute
See Masters, Edgar Lee

Puig, Manuel 1932-1990 .... **CLC 3, 5, 10, 28,
65, 133; HLC 2**
See also BPFB 3; CA 45-48; CANR 2, 32,
63; CDWLB 3; DA3; DAM MULT; DLB
113; DNFS 1; EWL 3; GLL 1; HW 1, 2;
LAW; MTCW 1, 2; RGWL 2, 3; TWA;
WLIT 1

Pulitzer, Joseph 1847-1911 .... **TCLC 76**
See also CA 114; DLB 23

Purchas, Samuel 1577(?)-1626 .... **LC 70**
See also DLB 151

Purdy, A(lfred) W(ellington)
1918-2000 .... **CLC 3, 6, 14, 50**
See also CA 81-84; 189; CANR 17; CANR
42, 66; CP 7; DAC; DAM MST, POET;
DLB 88; PFS 5; RGEL 2

Purdy, James (Amos) 1923- .... **CLC 2, 4, 10,
28, 52**
See also AMWS 7; CA 33-36R; CAAS 1;
CANR 19, 51; CN 7; DLB 2, 218; EWL
3; INT CANR-19; MTCW 1; RGAL 4

Pure, Simon
See Swinnerton, Frank Arthur

Pushkin, Aleksandr Sergeevich
See Pushkin, Alexander (Sergeyevich)
See also DLB 205

Pushkin, Alexander (Sergeyevich)
1799-1837 .... **NCLC 3, 27, 83; PC 10;
SSC 27, 55; WLC**
See Pushkin, Aleksandr Sergeevich
See also DA; DA3; DAB; DAC; DAM
DRAM, MST, POET; EW 5; EXPS; RGSF
2; RGWL 2, 3; SATA 61; SSFS 9; TWA

P'u Sung-ling 1640-1715 .... **LC 49; SSC 31**

Putnam, Arthur Lee
See Alger, Horatio, Jr.

Puzo, Mario 1920-1999 .... **CLC 1, 2, 6, 36,
107**
See also BPFB 3; CA 65-68; 185; CANR 4,
42, 65, 99; CN 7; CPW; DA3; DAM
NOV, POP; DLB 6; MTCW 1, 2; NFS 16;
RGAL 4

Pygge, Edward
See Barnes, Julian (Patrick)

Pyle, Ernest Taylor 1900-1945
See Pyle, Ernie
See also CA 115; 160

Pyle, Ernie .... **TCLC 75**
See Pyle, Ernest Taylor
See also DLB 29; MTCW 2

Pyle, Howard 1853-1911 .... **TCLC 81**
See also BYA 2, 4; CA 109; 137; CLR 22;
DLB 42, 188; DLBD 13; LAIT 1; MAI-
CYA 1, 2; SATA 16, 100; WCH; YAW

Pym, Barbara (Mary Crampton)
1913-1980 .... **CLC 13, 19, 37, 111**
See also BPFB 3; BRWS 2; CA 13-14; 97-
100; CANR 13, 34; CAP 1; DLB 14, 207;
DLBY 1987; EWL 3; MTCW 1, 2; RGEL
2; TEA

Pynchon, Thomas (Ruggles, Jr.)
1937- ...... **CLC 2, 3, 6, 9, 11, 18, 33, 62,
72, 123; SSC 14; WLC**
See also AMWS 2; BEST 90:2; BPFB 3;
CA 17-20R; CANR 22, 46, 73; CN 7;
CPW 1; DA; DA3; DAB; DAC; DAM
MST, NOV, POP; DLB 2, 173; EWL 3;
MTCW 1, 2; RGAL 4; SFW 4; TUS

Pythagoras c. 582B.C.-c. 507B.C. . **CMLC 22**
See also DLB 176

Q
See Quiller-Couch, Sir Arthur (Thomas)

Qian, Chongzhu
See Ch'ien, Chung-shu

Qian Zhongshu
See Ch'ien, Chung-shu

Qroll
See Dagerman, Stig (Halvard)

Quarrington, Paul (Lewis) 1953- ..... **CLC 65**
See also CA 129; CANR 62, 95

Quasimodo, Salvatore 1901-1968 .... **CLC 10; PC 47**
See also CA 13-16; 25-28R; CAP 1; DLB 114; EW 12; EWL 3; MTCW 1; RGWL 2, 3

Quatermass, Martin
See Carpenter, John (Howard)

Quay, Stephen 1947- .... **CLC 95**
See also CA 189

Quay, Timothy 1947- .... **CLC 95**
See also CA 189

Queen, Ellery .... **CLC 3, 11**
See Dannay, Frederic; Davidson, Avram (James); Deming, Richard; Fairman, Paul W.; Flora, Fletcher; Hoch, Edward D(entinger); Kane, Henry; Lee, Manfred B(ennington); Marlowe, Stephen; Powell, (Oval) Talmage; Sheldon, Walter J(ames); Sturgeon, Theodore (Hamilton); Tracy, Don(ald Fiske); Vance, John Holbrook
See also BPFB 3; CMW 4; MSW; RGAL 4

Queen, Ellery, Jr.
See Dannay, Frederic; Lee, Manfred B(ennington)

Queneau, Raymond 1903-1976 ..... **CLC 2, 5, 10, 42**
See also CA 77-80; 69-72; CANR 32; DLB 72, 258; EW 12; EWL 3; GFL 1789 to the Present; MTCW 1, 2; RGWL 2, 3

Quevedo, Francisco de 1580-1645 .... **LC 23**

Quiller-Couch, Sir Arthur (Thomas) 1863-1944 .... **TCLC 53**
See also CA 118; 166; DLB 135, 153, 190; HGG; RGEL 2; SUFW 1

Quin, Ann (Marie) 1936-1973 .... **CLC 6**
See also CA 9-12R; 45-48; DLB 14, 231

Quincey, Thomas de
See De Quincey, Thomas

Quinn, Martin
See Smith, Martin Cruz

Quinn, Peter 1947- .... **CLC 91**
See also CA 197

Quinn, Simon
See Smith, Martin Cruz

Quintana, Leroy V. 1944- ...... **HLC 2; PC 36**
See also CA 131; CANR 65; DAM MULT; DLB 82; HW 1, 2

Quiroga, Horacio (Sylvestre) 1878-1937 .... **HLC 2; TCLC 20**
See also CA 117; 131; DAM MULT; EWL 3; HW 1; LAW; MTCW 1; RGSF 2; WLIT 1

Quoirez, Francoise 1935- .... **CLC 9**
See Sagan, Francoise
See also CA 49-52; CANR 6, 39, 73; CWW 2; MTCW 1, 2; TWA

Raabe, Wilhelm (Karl) 1831-1910 . **TCLC 45**
See also CA 167; DLB 129

Rabe, David (William) 1940- .. **CLC 4, 8, 33; DC 16**
See also CA 85-88; CABS 3; CAD; CANR 59; CD 5; DAM DRAM; DFS 3, 8, 13; DLB 7, 228; EWL 3

Rabelais, Francois 1494-1553 .... **LC 5, 60; WLC**
See also DA; DAB; DAC; DAM MST; EW 2; GFL Beginnings to 1789; LMFS 1; RGWL 2, 3; TWA

Rabinovitch, Sholem 1859-1916
See Aleichem, Sholom
See also CA 104

Rabinyan, Dorit 1972- .... **CLC 119**
See also CA 170

Rachilde
See Vallette, Marguerite Eymery; Vallette, Marguerite Eymery
See also EWL 3

Racine, Jean 1639-1699 .... **LC 28**
See also DA3; DAB; DAM MST; DLB 268; EW 3; GFL Beginnings to 1789; LMFS 1; RGWL 2, 3; TWA

Radcliffe, Ann (Ward) 1764-1823 ... **NCLC 6, 55, 106**
See also DLB 39, 178; HGG; LMFS 1; RGEL 2; SUFW; WLIT 3

Radclyffe-Hall, Marguerite
See Hall, (Marguerite) Radclyffe

Radiguet, Raymond 1903-1923 ...... **TCLC 29**
See also CA 162; DLB 65; EWL 3; GFL 1789 to the Present; RGWL 2, 3

Radnoti, Miklos 1909-1944 .... **TCLC 16**
See also CA 118; 212; CDWLB 4; DLB 215; EWL 3; RGWL 2, 3

Rado, James 1939- .... **CLC 17**
See also CA 105

Radvanyi, Netty 1900-1983
See Seghers, Anna
See also CA 85-88; 110; CANR 82

Rae, Ben
See Griffiths, Trevor

Raeburn, John (Hay) 1941- .... **CLC 34**
See also CA 57-60

Ragni, Gerome 1942-1991 .... **CLC 17**
See also CA 105; 134

Rahv, Philip .... **CLC 24**
See Greenberg, Ivan
See also DLB 137

Raimund, Ferdinand Jakob 1790-1836 .... **NCLC 69**
See also DLB 90

Raine, Craig (Anthony) 1944- .. **CLC 32, 103**
See also CA 108; CANR 29, 51, 103; CP 7; DLB 40; PFS 7

Raine, Kathleen (Jessie) 1908-2003 .. **CLC 7, 45**
See also CA 85-88; 218; CANR 46, 109; CP 7; DLB 20; EWL 3; MTCW 1; RGEL 2

Rainis, Janis 1865-1929 .... **TCLC 29**
See also CA 170; CDWLB 4; DLB 220; EWL 3

Rakosi, Carl .... **CLC 47**
See Rawley, Callman
See also CAAS 5; CP 7; DLB 193

Ralegh, Sir Walter
See Raleigh, Sir Walter
See also BRW 1; RGEL 2; WP

Raleigh, Richard
See Lovecraft, H(oward) P(hillips)

Raleigh, Sir Walter 1554(?)-1618 .... **LC 31, 39; PC 31**
See Ralegh, Sir Walter
See also CDBLB Before 1660; DLB 172; EXPP; PFS 14; TEA

Rallentando, H. P.
See Sayers, Dorothy L(eigh)

Ramal, Walter
See de la Mare, Walter (John)

Ramana Maharshi 1879-1950 .... **TCLC 84**

Ramoacn y Cajal, Santiago 1852-1934 .... **TCLC 93**

Ramon, Juan
See Jimenez (Mantecon), Juan Ramon

Ramos, Graciliano 1892-1953 .... **TCLC 32**
See also CA 167; EWL 3; HW 2; LAW; WLIT 1

Rampersad, Arnold 1941- .... **CLC 44**
See also BW 2, 3; CA 127; 133; CANR 81; DLB 111; INT CA-133

Rampling, Anne
See Rice, Anne
See also GLL 2

Ramsay, Allan 1686(?)-1758 .... **LC 29**
See also DLB 95; RGEL 2

Ramsay, Jay
See Campbell, (John) Ramsey

Ramuz, Charles-Ferdinand 1878-1947 .... **TCLC 33**
See also CA 165; EWL 3

Rand, Ayn 1905-1982 ...... **CLC 3, 30, 44, 79; WLC**
See also AAYA 10; AMWS 4; BPFB 3; BYA 12; CA 13-16R; 105; CANR 27, 73; CDALBS; CPW; DA; DA3; DAC; DAM MST, NOV, POP; DLB 227, 279; MTCW 1, 2; NFS 10, 16; RGAL 4; SFW 4; TUS; YAW

Randall, Dudley (Felker) 1914-2000 . **BLC 3; CLC 1, 135**
See also BW 1, 3; CA 25-28R; 189; CANR 23, 82; DAM MULT; DLB 41; PFS 5

Randall, Robert
See Silverberg, Robert

Ranger, Ken
See Creasey, John

Rank, Otto 1884-1939 .... **TCLC 115**

Ransom, John Crowe 1888-1974 .. **CLC 2, 4, 5, 11, 24**
See also AMW; CA 5-8R; 49-52; CANR 6, 34; CDALBS; DA3; DAM POET; DLB 45, 63; EWL 3; EXPP; MTCW 1, 2; RGAL 4; TUS

Rao, Raja 1909- .... **CLC 25, 56**
See also CA 73-76; CANR 51; CN 7; DAM NOV; EWL 3; MTCW 1, 2; RGEL 2; RGSF 2

Raphael, Frederic (Michael) 1931- ... **CLC 2, 14**
See also CA 1-4R; CANR 1, 86; CN 7; DLB 14

Ratcliffe, James P.
See Mencken, H(enry) L(ouis)

Rathbone, Julian 1935- .... **CLC 41**
See also CA 101; CANR 34, 73

Rattigan, Terence (Mervyn) 1911-1977 .... **CLC 7; DC 18**
See also BRWS 7; CA 85-88; 73-76; CBD; CDBLB 1945-1960; DAM DRAM; DFS 8; DLB 13; IDFW 3, 4; MTCW 1, 2; RGEL 2

Ratushinskaya, Irina 1954- .... **CLC 54**
See also CA 129; CANR 68; CWW 2

Raven, Simon (Arthur Noel) 1927-2001 .... **CLC 14**
See also CA 81-84; 197; CANR 86; CN 7; DLB 271

Ravenna, Michael
See Welty, Eudora (Alice)

Rawley, Callman 1903-
See Rakosi, Carl
See also CA 21-24R; CANR 12, 32, 91

Rawlings, Marjorie Kinnan 1896-1953 .... **TCLC 4**
See also AAYA 20; AMWS 10; ANW; BPFB 3; BYA 3; CA 104; 137; CANR 74; CLR 63; DLB 9, 22, 102; DLBD 17; JRDA; MAICYA 1, 2; MTCW 2; RGAL 4; SATA 100; WCH; YABC 1; YAW

Ray, Satyajit 1921-1992 .... **CLC 16, 76**
See also CA 114; 137; DAM MULT

Read, Herbert Edward 1893-1968 ..... **CLC 4**
See also BRW 6; CA 85-88; 25-28R; DLB 20, 149; EWL 3; PAB; RGEL 2

Read, Piers Paul 1941- .... **CLC 4, 10, 25**
See also CA 21-24R; CANR 38, 86; CN 7; DLB 14; SATA 21

Reade, Charles 1814-1884 .... **NCLC 2, 74**
See also DLB 21; RGEL 2

Reade, Hamish
See Gray, Simon (James Holliday)

Rulfo, Juan 1918-1986 .. **CLC 8, 80; HLC 2; SSC 25**
See also CA 85-88; 118; CANR 26; CD-WLB 3; DAM MULT; DLB 113; EWL 3; HW 1, 2; LAW; MTCW 1, 2; RGSF 2; RGWL 2, 3; WLIT 1

Rumi, Jalal al-Din 1207-1273 ...... **CMLC 20; PC 45**
See also RGWL 2, 3; WP

Runeberg, Johan 1804-1877 .... **NCLC 41**

Runyon, (Alfred) Damon
1884(?)-1946 .... **TCLC 10**
See also CA 107; 165; DLB 11, 86, 171; MTCW 2; RGAL 4

Rush, Norman 1933- .... **CLC 44**
See also CA 121; 126; INT CA-126

Rushdie, (Ahmed) Salman 1947- .... **CLC 23, 31, 55, 100; WLCS**
See also BEST 89:3; BPFB 3; BRWS 4; CA 108; 111; CANR 33, 56, 108; CN 7; CPW 1; DA3; DAB; DAC; DAM MST, NOV, POP; DLB 194; EWL 3; FANT; INT CA-111; LATS 1; LMFS 2; MTCW 1, 2; RGEL 2; RGSF 2; TEA; WLIT 4; WWE 1

Rushforth, Peter (Scott) 1945- .... **CLC 19**
See also CA 101

Ruskin, John 1819-1900 .... **TCLC 63**
See also BRW 5; BYA 5; CA 114; 129; CD-BLB 1832-1890; DLB 55, 163, 190; RGEL 2; SATA 24; TEA; WCH

Russ, Joanna 1937- .... **CLC 15**
See also BPFB 3; CA 5-28R; CANR 11, 31, 65; CN 7; DLB 8; FW; GLL 1; MTCW 1; SCFW 2; SFW 4

Russ, Richard Patrick
See O'Brian, Patrick

Russell, George William 1867-1935
See A.E.; Baker, Jean H.
See also BRWS 8; CA 104; 153; CDBLB 1890-1914; DAM POET; EWL 3; RGEL 2

Russell, Jeffrey Burton 1934- .... **CLC 70**
See also CA 25-28R; CANR 11, 28, 52

Russell, (Henry) Ken(neth Alfred)
1927- .... **CLC 16**
See also CA 105

Russell, William Martin 1947-
See Russell, Willy
See also CA 164; CANR 107

Russell, Willy .... **CLC 60**
See Russell, William Martin
See also CBD; CD 5; DLB 233

Russo, Richard 1949- .... **CLC 181**
See also AMWS 12; CA 127; 133; CANR 87, 114

Rutherford, Mark .... **TCLC 25**
See White, William Hale
See also DLB 18; RGEL 2

Ruyslinck, Ward .... **CLC 14**
See Belser, Reimond Karel Maria de

Ryan, Cornelius (John) 1920-1974 ..... **CLC 7**
See also CA 69-72; 53-56; CANR 38

Ryan, Michael 1946- .... **CLC 65**
See also CA 49-52; CANR 109; DLBY 1982

Ryan, Tim
See Dent, Lester

Rybakov, Anatoli (Naumovich)
1911-1998 .... **CLC 23, 53**
See also CA 126; 135; 172; SATA 79; SATA-Obit 108

Ryder, Jonathan
See Ludlum, Robert

Ryga, George 1932-1987 .... **CLC 14**
See also CA 101; 124; CANR 43, 90; CCA 1; DAC; DAM MST; DLB 60

S. H.
See Hartmann, Sadakichi

S. S.
See Sassoon, Siegfried (Lorraine)

Saba, Umberto 1883-1957 .... **TCLC 33**
See also CA 144; CANR 79; DLB 114; EWL 3; RGWL 2, 3

Sabatini, Rafael 1875-1950 .... **TCLC 47**
See also BPFB 3; CA 162; RHW

Sabato, Ernesto (R.) 1911- .... **CLC 10, 23; HLC 2**
See also CA 97-100; CANR 32, 65; CD-WLB 3; DAM MULT; DLB 145; EWL 3; HW 1, 2; LAW; MTCW 1, 2

Sa-Carneiro, Mario de 1890-1916 . **TCLC 83**
See also DLB 287; EWL 3

Sacastru, Martin
See Bioy Casares, Adolfo
See also CWW 2

Sacher-Masoch, Leopold von
1836(?)-1895 .... **NCLC 31**

Sachs, Hans 1494-1576 .... **LC 95**
See also CDWLB 2; DLB 179; RGWL 2, 3

Sachs, Marilyn (Stickle) 1927- .... **CLC 35**
See also AAYA 2; BYA 6; CA 17-20R; CANR 13, 47; CLR 2; JRDA; MAICYA 1, 2; SAAS 2; SATA 3, 68; SATA-Essay 110; WYA; YAW

Sachs, Nelly 1891-1970 .... **CLC 14, 98**
See also CA 17-18; 25-28R; CANR 87; CAP 2; EWL 3; MTCW 2; RGWL 2, 3

Sackler, Howard (Oliver)
1929-1982 .... **CLC 14**
See also CA 61-64; 108; CAD; CANR 30; DFS 15; DLB 7

Sacks, Oliver (Wolf) 1933- .... **CLC 67**
See also CA 53-56; CANR 28, 50, 76; CPW; DA3; INT CANR-28; MTCW 1, 2

Sackville, Thomas 1536-1608 .... **LC 98**
See also DAM DRAM; DLB 62, 132; RGEL 2

Sadakichi
See Hartmann, Sadakichi

Sade, Donatien Alphonse Francois
1740-1814 .... **NCLC 3, 47**
See also EW 4; GFL Beginnings to 1789; RGWL 2, 3

Sade, Marquis de
See Sade, Donatien Alphonse Francois

Sadoff, Ira 1945- .... **CLC 9**
See also CA 53-56; CANR 5, 21, 109; DLB 120

Saetone
See Camus, Albert

Safire, William 1929- .... **CLC 10**
See also CA 17-20R; CANR 31, 54, 91

Sagan, Carl (Edward) 1934-1996 .... **CLC 30, 112**
See also AAYA 2; CA 25-28R; 155; CANR 11, 36, 74; CPW; DA3; MTCW 1, 2; SATA 58; SATA-Obit 94

Sagan, Francoise .... **CLC 3, 6, 9, 17, 36**
See Quoirez, Francoise
See also CWW 2; DLB 83; EWL 3; GFL 1789 to the Present; MTCW 2

Sahgal, Nayantara (Pandit) 1927- .... **CLC 41**
See also CA 9-12R; CANR 11, 88; CN 7

Said, Edward W. 1935-2003 .... **CLC 123**
See also CA 21-24R; 220; CANR 45, 74, 107; DLB 67; MTCW 2

Saint, H(arry) F. 1941- .... **CLC 50**
See also CA 127

St. Aubin de Teran, Lisa 1953-
See Teran, Lisa St. Aubin de
See also CA 118; 126; CN 7; INT CA-126

Saint Birgitta of Sweden c.
1303-1373 .... **CMLC 24**

Sainte-Beuve, Charles Augustin
1804-1869 .... **NCLC 5**
See also DLB 217; EW 6; GFL 1789 to the Present

Saint-Exupery, Antoine (Jean Baptiste Marie Roger) de 1900-1944 .... **TCLC 2, 56; WLC**
See also BPFB 3; BYA 3; CA 108; 132; CLR 10; DA3; DAM NOV; DLB 72; EW 12; EWL 3; GFL 1789 to the Present; LAIT 3; MAICYA 1, 2; MTCW 1, 2; RGWL 2, 3; SATA 20; TWA

St. John, David
See Hunt, E(verette) Howard, (Jr.)

St. John, J. Hector
See Crevecoeur, Michel Guillaume Jean de

Saint-John Perse
See Leger, (Marie-Rene Auguste) Alexis Saint-Leger
See also EW 10; EWL 3; GFL 1789 to the Present; RGWL 2

Saintsbury, George (Edward Bateman)
1845-1933 .... **TCLC 31**
See also CA 160; DLB 57, 149

Sait Faik .... **TCLC 23**
See Abasiyanik, Sait Faik

Saki .... **SSC 12; TCLC 3**
See Munro, H(ector) H(ugh)
See also BRWS 6; BYA 11; LAIT 2; MTCW 2; RGEL 2; SSFS 1; SUFW

Sala, George Augustus 1828-1895 . **NCLC 46**

Saladin 1138-1193 .... **CMLC 38**

Salama, Hannu 1936- .... **CLC 18**
See also EWL 3

Salamanca, J(ack) R(ichard) 1922- .. **CLC 4, 15**
See also CA 25-28R; 193; CAAE 193

Salas, Floyd Francis 1931- .... **HLC 2**
See also CA 119; CAAS 27; CANR 44, 75, 93; DAM MULT; DLB 82; HW 1, 2; MTCW 2

Sale, J. Kirkpatrick
See Sale, Kirkpatrick

Sale, Kirkpatrick 1937- .... **CLC 68**
See also CA 13-16R; CANR 10

Salinas, Luis Omar 1937- ... **CLC 90; HLC 2**
See also AMWS 13; CA 131; CANR 81; DAM MULT; DLB 82; HW 1, 2

Salinas (y Serrano), Pedro
1891(?)-1951 .... **TCLC 17**
See also CA 117; DLB 134; EWL 3

Salinger, J(erome) D(avid) 1919- .. **CLC 1, 3, 8, 12, 55, 56, 138; SSC 2, 28, 65; WLC**
See also AAYA 2, 36; AMW; AMWC 1; BPFB 3; CA 5-8R; CANR 39; CDALB 1941-1968; CLR 18; CN 7; CPW 1; DA; DA3; DAB; DAC; DAM MST, NOV, POP; DLB 2, 102, 173; EWL 3; EXPN; LAIT 4; MAICYA 1, 2; MTCW 1, 2; NFS 1; RGAL 4; RGSF 2; SATA 67; SSFS 17; TUS; WYA; YAW

Salisbury, John
See Caute, (John) David

Salter, James 1925- .. **CLC 7, 52, 59; SSC 58**
See also AMWS 9; CA 73-76; CANR 107; DLB 130

Saltus, Edgar (Everton) 1855-1921 . **TCLC 8**
See also CA 105; DLB 202; RGAL 4

Saltykov, Mikhail Evgrafovich
1826-1889 .... **NCLC 16**
See also DLB 238:

Saltykov-Shchedrin, N.
See Saltykov, Mikhail Evgrafovich

Samarakis, Andonis
See Samarakis, Antonis
See also EWL 3

Samarakis, Antonis 1919- .... **CLC 5**
See Samarakis, Andonis
See also CA 25-28R; CAAS 16; CANR 36

Sanchez, Florencio 1875-1910 .... **TCLC 37**
See also CA 153; EWL 3; HW 1; LAW

Sanchez, Luis Rafael 1936- .... **CLC 23**
See also CA 128; DLB 145; EWL 3; HW 1;
WLIT 1

Sanchez, Sonia 1934- .... **BLC 3; CLC 5, 116;**
PC 9
See also BW 2, 3; CA 33-36R; CANR 24,
49, 74, 115; CLR 18; CP 7; CSW; CWP;
DA3; DAM MULT; DLB 41; DLBD 8;
EWL 3; MAICYA 1, 2; MTCW 1, 2;
SATA 22, 136; WP

Sancho, Ignatius 1729-1780 .... **LC 84**

Sand, George 1804-1876 ..... **NCLC 2, 42, 57;**
WLC
See also DA; DA3; DAB; DAC; DAM
MST, NOV; DLB 119, 192; EW 6; FW;
GFL 1789 to the Present; RGWL 2, 3;
TWA

Sandburg, Carl (August) 1878-1967 . **CLC 1,**
4, 10, 15, 35; PC 2, 41; WLC
See also AAYA 24; AMW; BYA 1, 3; CA
5-8R; 25-28R; CANR 35; CDALB 1865-
1917; CLR 67; DA; DA3; DAB; DAC;
DAM MST, POET; DLB 17, 54, 284;
EWL 3; EXPP; LAIT 2; MAICYA 1, 2;
MTCW 1, 2; PAB; PFS 3, 6, 12; RGAL
4; SATA 8; TUS; WCH; WP; WYA

Sandburg, Charles
See Sandburg, Carl (August)

Sandburg, Charles A.
See Sandburg, Carl (August)

Sanders, (James) Ed(ward) 1939- .... **CLC 53**
See Sanders, Edward
See also BG 3; CA 13-16R; CAAS 21;
CANR 13, 44, 78; CP 7; DAM POET;
DLB 16, 244

Sanders, Edward
See Sanders, (James) Ed(ward)
See also DLB 244

Sanders, Lawrence 1920-1998 .... **CLC 41**
See also BEST 89:4; BPFB 3; CA 81-84;
165; CANR 33, 62; CMW 4; CPW; DA3;
DAM POP; MTCW 1

Sanders, Noah
See Blount, Roy (Alton), Jr.

Sanders, Winston P.
See Anderson, Poul (William)

Sandoz, Mari(e Susette) 1900-1966 .. **CLC 28**
See also CA 1-4R; 25-28R; CANR 17, 64;
DLB 9, 212; LAIT 2; MTCW 1, 2; SATA
5; TCWW 2

Sandys, George 1578-1644 .... **LC 80**
See also DLB 24, 121

Saner, Reg(inald Anthony) 1931- .... **CLC 9**
See also CA 65-68; CP 7

Sankara 788-820 .... **CMLC 32**

Sannazaro, Jacopo 1456(?)-1530 .... **LC 8**
See also RGWL 2, 3

Sansom, William 1912-1976 . **CLC 2, 6; SSC**
21
See also CA 5-8R; 65-68; CANR 42; DAM
NOV; DLB 139; EWL 3; MTCW 1;
RGEL 2; RGSF 2

Santayana, George 1863-1952 .... **TCLC 40**
See also AMW; CA 115; 194; DLB 54, 71,
246, 270; DLBD 13; EWL 3; RGAL 4;
TUS

Santiago, Danny .... **CLC 33**
See James, Daniel (Lewis)
See also DLB 122

Santmyer, Helen Hooven
1895-1986 .... **CLC 33; TCLC 133**
See also CA 1-4R; 118; CANR 15, 33;
DLBY 1984; MTCW 1; RHW

Santoka, Taneda 1882-1940 .... **TCLC 72**

Santos, Bienvenido N(uqui)
1911-1996 .... **AAL; CLC 22**
See also CA 101; 151; CANR 19, 46; DAM
MULT; EWL; RGAL 4

Sapir, Edward 1884-1939 .... **TCLC 108**
See also CA 211; DLB 92

Sapper .... **TCLC 44**
See McNeile, Herman Cyril

Sapphire
See Sapphire, Brenda

Sapphire, Brenda 1950- .... **CLC 99**

Sappho fl. 6th cent. B.C.- ...... **CMLC 3; PC 5**
See also CDWLB 1; DA3; DAM POET;
DLB 176; RGWL 2, 3; WP

Saramago, Jose 1922- ..... **CLC 119; HLCS 1**
See also CA 153; CANR 96; DLB 287;
EWL 3; LATS 1

Sarduy, Severo 1937-1993 .... **CLC 6, 97;**
HLCS 2
See also CA 89-92; 142; CANR 58, 81;
CWW 2; DLB 113; EWL 3; HW 1, 2;
LAW

Sargeson, Frank 1903-1982 .... **CLC 31**
See also CA 25-28R; 106; CANR 38, 79;
EWL 3; GLL 2; RGEL 2; RGSF 2

Sarmiento, Domingo Faustino
1811-1888 .... **HLCS 2**
See also LAW; WLIT 1

Sarmiento, Felix Ruben Garcia
See Dario, Ruben

Saro-Wiwa, Ken(ule Beeson)
1941-1995 .... **CLC 114**
See also BW 2; CA 142; 150; CANR 60;
DLB 157

Saroyan, William 1908-1981 ... **CLC 1, 8, 10,**
29, 34, 56; SSC 21; TCLC 137; WLC
See also CA 5-8R; 103; CAD; CANR 30;
CDALBS; DA; DA3; DAB; DAC; DAM
DRAM, MST, NOV; DFS 17; DLB 7, 9,
86; DLBY 1981; EWL 3; LAIT 4; MTCW
1, 2; RGAL 4; RGSF 2; SATA 23; SATA-
Obit 24; SSFS 14; TUS

Sarraute, Nathalie 1900-1999 .... **CLC 1, 2, 4,**
8, 10, 31, 80; TCLC 145
See also BPFB 3; CA 9-12R; 187; CANR
23, 66; CWW 2; DLB 83; EW 12; EWL
3; GFL 1789 to the Present; MTCW 1, 2;
RGWL 2, 3

Sarton, (Eleanor) May 1912-1995 ..... **CLC 4,**
14, 49, 91; PC 39; TCLC 120
See also AMWS 8; CA 1-4R; 149; CANR
1, 34, 55, 116; CN 7; CP 7; DAM POET;
DLB 48; DLBY 1981; EWL 3; FW; INT
CANR-34; MTCW 1, 2; RGAL 4; SATA
36; SATA-Obit 86; TUS

Sartre, Jean-Paul 1905-1980 . **CLC 1, 4, 7, 9,**
13, 18, 24, 44, 50, 52; DC 3; SSC 32;
WLC
See also CA 9-12R; 97-100; CANR 21; DA;
DA3; DAB; DAC; DAM DRAM, MST,
NOV; DFS 5; DLB 72, 296; EW 12; EWL
3; GFL 1789 to the Present; LMFS 2;
MTCW 1, 2; RGSF 2; RGWL 2, 3; SSFS
9; TWA

Sassoon, Siegfried (Lorraine)
1886-1967 .... **CLC 36, 130; PC 12**
See also BRW 6; CA 104; 25-28R; CANR
36; DAB; DAM MST, NOV, POET; DLB
20, 191; DLBD 18; EWL 3; MTCW 1, 2;
PAB; RGEL 2; TEA

Satterfield, Charles
See Pohl, Frederik

Satyremont
See Peret, Benjamin

Saul, John (W. III) 1942- .... **CLC 46**
See also AAYA 10; BEST 90:4; CA 81-84;
CANR 16, 40, 81; CPW; DAM NOV,
POP; HGG; SATA 98

Saunders, Caleb
See Heinlein, Robert A(nson)

Saura (Atares), Carlos 1932-1998 .... **CLC 20**
See also CA 114; 131; CANR 79; HW 1

Sauser, Frederic Louis
See Sauser-Hall, Frederic

Sauser-Hall, Frederic 1887-1961 ...... **CLC 18**
See Cendrars, Blaise
See also CA 102; 93-96; CANR 36, 62;
MTCW 1

Saussure, Ferdinand de
1857-1913 .... **TCLC 49**
See also DLB 242

Savage, Catharine
See Brosman, Catharine Savage

Savage, Richard 1697(?)-1743 .... **LC 96**
See also DLB 95; RGEL 2

Savage, Thomas 1915-2003 .... **CLC 40**
See also CA 126; 132; 218; CAAS 15; CN
7; INT CA-132; SATA-Obit 147; TCWW
2

Savan, Glenn (?)- .... **CLC 50**

Sax, Robert
See Johnson, Robert

Saxo Grammaticus c. 1150-c.
1222 .... **CMLC 58**

Saxton, Robert
See Johnson, Robert

Sayers, Dorothy L(eigh)
1893-1957 .... **TCLC 2, 15**
See also BPFB 3; BRWS 3; CA 104; 119;
CANR 60; CDBLB 1914-1945; CMW 4;
DAM POP; DLB 10, 36, 77, 100; MSW;
MTCW 1, 2; RGEL 2; SSFS 12; TEA

Sayers, Valerie 1952- .... **CLC 50, 122**
See also CA 134; CANR 61; CSW

Sayles, John (Thomas) 1950- . **CLC 7, 10, 14**
See also CA 57-60; CANR 41, 84; DLB 44

Scammell, Michael 1935- .... **CLC 34**
See also CA 156

Scannell, Vernon 1922- .... **CLC 49**
See also CA 5-8R; CANR 8, 24, 57; CP 7;
CWRI 5; DLB 27; SATA 59

Scarlett, Susan
See Streatfeild, (Mary) Noel

Scarron 1847-1910
See Mikszath, Kalman

Schaeffer, Susan Fromberg 1941- ..... **CLC 6,**
11, 22
See also CA 49-52; CANR 18, 65; CN 7;
DLB 28; MTCW 1, 2; SATA 22

Schama, Simon (Michael) 1945- ..... **CLC 150**
See also BEST 89:4; CA 105; CANR 39,
91

Schary, Jill
See Robinson, Jill

Schell, Jonathan 1943- .... **CLC 35**
See also CA 73-76; CANR 12, 117

Schelling, Friedrich Wilhelm Joseph von
1775-1854 .... **NCLC 30**
See also DLB 90

Scherer, Jean-Marie Maurice 1920-
See Rohmer, Eric
See also CA 110

Schevill, James (Erwin) 1920- .... **CLC 7**
See also CA 5-8R; CAAS 12; CAD; CD 5

Schiller, Friedrich von 1759-1805 ...... **DC 12;**
NCLC 39, 69
See also CDWLB 2; DAM DRAM; DLB
94; EW 5; RGWL 2, 3; TWA

Schisgal, Murray (Joseph) 1926- .... **CLC 6**
See also CA 21-24R; CAD; CANR 48, 86;
CD 5

Schlee, Ann 1934- .... **CLC 35**
See also CA 101; CANR 29, 88; SATA 44;
SATA-Brief 36

Schlegel, August Wilhelm von
1767-1845 .... **NCLC 15**
See also DLB 94; RGWL 2, 3

Schlegel, Friedrich 1772-1829 .... **NCLC 45**
See also DLB 90; EW 5; RGWL 2, 3; TWA

Schlegel, Johann Elias (von)
    1719(?)-1749 .... **LC 5**
Schleiermacher, Friedrich
    1768-1834 .... **NCLC 107**
    See also DLB 90
Schlesinger, Arthur M(eier), Jr.
    1917- .... **CLC 84**
    See also AITN 1; CA 1-4R; CANR 1, 28,
    58, 105; DLB 17; INT CANR-28; MTCW
    1, 2; SATA 61
Schlink, Bernhard 1944- .... **CLC 174**
    See also CA 163; CANR 116
Schmidt, Arno (Otto) 1914-1979 ...... **CLC 56**
    See also CA 128; 109; DLB 69; EWL 3
Schmitz, Aron Hector 1861-1928
    See Svevo, Italo
    See also CA 104; 122; MTCW 1
Schnackenberg, Gjertrud (Cecelia)
    1953- .... **CLC 40; PC 45**
    See also CA 116; CANR 100; CP 7; CWP;
    DLB 120, 282; PFS 13
Schneider, Leonard Alfred 1925-1966
    See Bruce, Lenny
    See also CA 89-92
Schnitzler, Arthur 1862-1931 ..... **DC 17; SSC
    15, 61; TCLC 4**
    See also CA 104; CDWLB 2; DLB 81, 118;
    EW 8; EWL 3; RGSF 2; RGWL 2, 3
Schoenberg, Arnold Franz Walter
    1874-1951 .... **TCLC 75**
    See also CA 109; 188
Schonberg, Arnold
    See Schoenberg, Arnold Franz Walter
Schopenhauer, Arthur 1788-1860 .. **NCLC 51**
    See also DLB 90; EW 5
Schor, Sandra (M.) 1932(?)-1990 ..... **CLC 65**
    See also CA 132
Schorer, Mark 1908-1977 .... **CLC 9**
    See also CA 5-8R; 73-76; CANR 7; DLB
    103
Schrader, Paul (Joseph) 1946- .... **CLC 26**
    See also CA 37-40R; CANR 41; DLB 44
Schreber, Daniel 1842-1911 .... **TCLC 123**
Schreiner, Olive (Emilie Albertina)
    1855-1920 .... **TCLC 9**
    See also AFW; BRWS 2; CA 105; 154;
    DLB 18, 156, 190, 225; EWL 3; FW;
    RGEL 2; TWA; WLIT 2; WWE 1
Schulberg, Budd (Wilson) 1914- .. **CLC 7, 48**
    See also BPFB 3; CA 25-28R; CANR 19,
    87; CN 7; DLB 6, 26, 28; DLBY 1981,
    2001
Schulman, Arnold
    See Trumbo, Dalton
Schulz, Bruno 1892-1942 .. **SSC 13; TCLC 5,
    51**
    See also CA 115; 123; CANR 86; CDWLB
    4; DLB 215; EWL 3; MTCW 2; RGSF 2;
    RGWL 2, 3
Schulz, Charles M(onroe)
    1922-2000 .... **CLC 12**
    See also AAYA 39; CA 9-12R; 187; CANR
    6; INT CANR-6; SATA 10; SATA-Obit
    118
Schumacher, E(rnst) F(riedrich)
    1911-1977 .... **CLC 80**
    See also CA 81-84; 73-76; CANR 34, 85
Schuyler, George Samuel 1895-1977 .... **HR 3**
    See also BW 2; CA 81-84; 73-76; CANR
    42; DLB 29, 51
Schuyler, James Marcus 1923-1991 .. **CLC 5,
    23**
    See also CA 101; 134; DAM POET; DLB
    5, 169; EWL 3; INT CA-101; WP
Schwartz, Delmore (David)
    1913-1966 ... **CLC 2, 4, 10, 45, 87; PC 8**
    See also AMWS 2; CA 17-18; 25-28R;
    CANR 35; CAP 2; DLB 28, 48; EWL 3;
    MTCW 1, 2; PAB; RGAL 4; TUS

Schwartz, Ernst
    See Ozu, Yasujiro
Schwartz, John Burnham 1965- .... **CLC 59**
    See also CA 132; CANR 116
Schwartz, Lynne Sharon 1939- .... **CLC 31**
    See also CA 103; CANR 44, 89; DLB 218;
    MTCW 2
Schwartz, Muriel A.
    See Eliot, T(homas) S(tearns)
Schwarz-Bart, Andre 1928- .... **CLC 2, 4**
    See also CA 89-92; CANR 109
Schwarz-Bart, Simone 1938- . **BLCS; CLC 7**
    See also BW 2; CA 97-100; CANR 117;
    EWL 3
Schwerner, Armand 1927-1999 .... **PC 42**
    See also CA 9-12R; 179; CANR 50, 85; CP
    7; DLB 165
**Schwitters, Kurt (Hermann Edward Karl
    Julius)** 1887-1948 .... **TCLC 95**
    See also CA 158
Schwob, Marcel (Mayer Andre)
    1867-1905 .... **TCLC 20**
    See also CA 117; 168; DLB 123; GFL 1789
    to the Present
Sciascia, Leonardo 1921-1989 .. **CLC 8, 9, 41**
    See also CA 85-88; 130; CANR 35; DLB
    177; EWL 3; MTCW 1; RGWL 2, 3
Scoppettone, Sandra 1936- .... **CLC 26**
    See Early, Jack
    See also AAYA 11; BYA 8; CA 5-8R;
    CANR 41, 73; GLL 1; MAICYA 2; MAI-
    CYAS 1; SATA 9, 92; WYA; YAW
Scorsese, Martin 1942- .... **CLC 20, 89**
    See also AAYA 38; CA 110; 114; CANR
    46, 85
Scotland, Jay
    See Jakes, John (William)
Scott, Duncan Campbell
    1862-1947 .... **TCLC 6**
    See also CA 104; 153; DAC; DLB 92;
    RGEL 2
Scott, Evelyn 1893-1963 .... **CLC 43**
    See also CA 104; 112; CANR 64; DLB 9,
    48; RHW
Scott, F(rancis) R(eginald)
    1899-1985 .... **CLC 22**
    See also CA 101; 114; CANR 87; DLB 88;
    INT CA-101; RGEL 2
Scott, Frank
    See Scott, F(rancis) R(eginald)
Scott, Joan .... **CLC 65**
Scott, Joanna 1960- .... **CLC 50**
    See also CA 126; CANR 53, 92
Scott, Paul (Mark) 1920-1978 ...... **CLC 9, 60**
    See also BRWS 1; CA 81-84; 77-80; CANR
    33; DLB 14, 207; EWL 3; MTCW 1;
    RGEL 2; RHW; WWE 1
Scott, Ridley 1937- .... **CLC 183**
    See also AAYA 13, 43
Scott, Sarah 1723-1795 .... **LC 44**
    See also DLB 39
Scott, Sir Walter 1771-1832 .... **NCLC 15, 69,
    110; PC 13; SSC 32; WLC**
    See also AAYA 22; BRW 4; BYA 2; CD-
    BLB 1789-1832; DA; DAB; DAC; DAM
    MST, NOV, POET; DLB 93, 107, 116,
    144, 159; HGG; LAIT 1; RGEL 2; RGSF
    2; SSFS 10; SUFW 1; TEA; WLIT 3;
    YABC 2
Scribe, (Augustin) Eugene 1791-1861 . **DC 5;
    NCLC 16**
    See also DAM DRAM; DLB 192; GFL
    1789 to the Present; RGWL 2, 3
Scrum, R.
    See Crumb, R(obert)
Scudery, Georges de 1601-1667 .... **LC 75**
    See also GFL Beginnings to 1789
Scudery, Madeleine de 1607-1701 .. **LC 2, 58**
    See also DLB 268; GFL Beginnings to 1789

Scum
    See Crumb, R(obert)
Scumbag, Little Bobby
    See Crumb, R(obert)
Seabrook, John
    See Hubbard, L(afayette) Ron(ald)
Sealy, I(rwin) Allan 1951- .... **CLC 55**
    See also CA 136; CN 7
Search, Alexander
    See Pessoa, Fernando (Antonio Nogueira)
Sebastian, Lee
    See Silverberg, Robert
Sebastian Owl
    See Thompson, Hunter S(tockton)
Sebestyen, Igen
    See Sebestyen, Ouida
Sebestyen, Ouida 1924- .... **CLC 30**
    See also AAYA 8; BYA 7; CA 107; CANR
    40, 114; CLR 17; JRDA; MAICYA 1, 2;
    SAAS 10; SATA 39, 140; WYA; YAW
Secundus, H. Scriblerus
    See Fielding, Henry
Sedges, John
    See Buck, Pearl S(ydenstricker)
Sedgwick, Catharine Maria
    1789-1867 .... **NCLC 19, 98**
    See also DLB 1, 74, 183, 239, 243, 254;
    RGAL 4
Seelye, John (Douglas) 1931- .... **CLC 7**
    See also CA 97-100; CANR 70; INT CA-
    97-100; TCWW 2
Seferiades, Giorgos Stylianou 1900-1971
    See Seferis, George
    See also CA 5-8R; 33-36R; CANR 5, 36;
    MTCW 1
Seferis, George .... **CLC 5, 11**
    See Seferiades, Giorgos Stylianou
    See also EW 12; EWL 3; RGWL 2, 3
Segal, Erich (Wolf) 1937- .... **CLC 3, 10**
    See also BEST 89:1; BPFB 3; CA 25-28R;
    CANR 20, 36, 65, 113; CPW; DAM POP;
    DLBY 1986; INT CANR-20; MTCW 1
Seger, Bob 1945- .... **CLC 35**
Seghers, Anna .... **CLC 7**
    See Radvanyi, Netty
    See also CDWLB 2; DLB 69; EWL 3
Seidel, Frederick (Lewis) 1936- .... **CLC 18**
    See also CA 13-16R; CANR 8, 99; CP 7;
    DLBY 1984
Seifert, Jaroslav 1901-1986 . **CLC 34, 44, 93;
    PC 47**
    See also CA 127; CDWLB 4; DLB 215;
    EWL 3; MTCW 1, 2
Sei Shonagon c. 966-1017(?) .... **CMLC 6**
Sejour, Victor 1817-1874 .... **DC 10**
    See also DLB 50
Sejour Marcou et Ferrand, Juan Victor
    See Sejour, Victor
Selby, Hubert, Jr. 1928- .... **CLC 1, 2, 4, 8;
    SSC 20**
    See also CA 13-16R; CANR 33, 85; CN 7;
    DLB 2, 227
Selzer, Richard 1928- .... **CLC 74**
    See also CA 65-68; CANR 14, 106
Sembene, Ousmane
    See Ousmane, Sembene
    See also AFW; CWW 2; EWL 3; WLIT 2
Senancour, Etienne Pivert de
    1770-1846 .... **NCLC 16**
    See also DLB 119; GFL 1789 to the Present
Sender, Ramon (Jose) 1902-1982 ...... **CLC 8;
    HLC 2; TCLC 136**
    See also CA 5-8R; 105; CANR 8; DAM
    MULT; EWL 3; HW 1; MTCW 1; RGWL
    2, 3
Seneca, Lucius Annaeus c. 4B.C.-c.
    65 .... **CMLC 6; DC 5**
    See also AW 2; CDWLB 1; DAM DRAM;
    DLB 211; RGWL 2, 3; TWA

Snow, Frances Compton
See Adams, Henry (Brooks)

Snyder, Gary (Sherman) 1930- . **CLC 1, 2, 5, 9, 32, 120; PC 21**
See also AMWS 8; ANW; BG 3; CA 17-20R; CANR 30, 60, 125; CP 7; DA3; DAM POET; DLB 5, 16, 165, 212, 237, 275; EWL 3; MTCW 2; PFS 9; RGAL 4; WP

Snyder, Zilpha Keatley 1927- .... **CLC 17**
See also AAYA 15; BYA 1; CA 9-12R; CANR 38; CLR 31; JRDA; MAICYA 1, 2; SAAS 2; SATA 1, 28, 75, 110; SATA-Essay 112; YAW

Soares, Bernardo
See Pessoa, Fernando (Antonio Nogueira)

Sobh, A.
See Shamlu, Ahmad

Sobh, Alef
See Shamlu, Ahmad

Sobol, Joshua 1939- .... **CLC 60**
See Sobol, Yehoshua
See also CA 200; CWW 2

Sobol, Yehoshua 1939-
See Sobol, Joshua
See also CWW 2

Socrates 470B.C.-399B.C. .... **CMLC 27**

Soderberg, Hjalmar 1869-1941 ...... **TCLC 39**
See also DLB 259; EWL 3; RGSF 2

Soderbergh, Steven 1963- .... **CLC 154**
See also AAYA 43

Sodergran, Edith (Irene) 1892-1923
See Soedergran, Edith (Irene)
See also CA 202; DLB 259; EW 11; EWL 3; RGWL 2, 3

Soedergran, Edith (Irene)
1892-1923 .... **TCLC 31**
See Sodergran, Edith (Irene)

Softly, Edgar
See Lovecraft, H(oward) P(hillips)

Softly, Edward
See Lovecraft, H(oward) P(hillips)

Sokolov, Alexander V(sevolodovich) 1943-
See Sokolov, Sasha
See also CA 73-76

Sokolov, Raymond 1941- .... **CLC 7**
See also CA 85-88

Sokolov, Sasha .... **CLC 59**
See Sokolov, Alexander V(sevolodovich)
See also CWW 2; DLB 285; EWL 3; RGWL 2, 3

Sokolov, Sasha .... **CLC 59**

Solo, Jay
See Ellison, Harlan (Jay)

Sologub, Fyodor .... **TCLC 9**
See Teternikov, Fyodor Kuzmich
See also EWL 3

Solomons, Ikey Esquir
See Thackeray, William Makepeace

Solomos, Dionysios 1798-1857 .... **NCLC 15**

Solwoska, Mara
See French, Marilyn

Solzhenitsyn, Aleksandr I(sayevich)
1918- .. **CLC 1, 2, 4, 7, 9, 10, 18, 26, 34, 78, 134; SSC 32; WLC**
See Solzhenitsyn, Aleksandr Isaevich
See also AAYA 49; AITN 1; BPFB 3; CA 69-72; CANR 40, 65, 116; DA; DA3; DAB; DAC; DAM MST, NOV; EW 13; EXPS; LAIT 4; MTCW 1, 2; NFS 6; RGSF 2; RGWL 2, 3; SSFS 9; TWA

Solzhenitsyn, Aleksandr Isaevich
See Solzhenitsyn, Aleksandr I(sayevich)
See also EWL 3

Somers, Jane
See Lessing, Doris (May)

Somerville, Edith Oenone
1858-1949 .... **SSC 56; TCLC 51**
See also CA 196; DLB 135; RGEL 2; RGSF 2

Somerville & Ross
See Martin, Violet Florence; Somerville, Edith Oenone

Sommer, Scott 1951- .... **CLC 25**
See also CA 106

Sondheim, Stephen (Joshua) 1930- . **CLC 30, 39, 147; DC 22**
See also AAYA 11; CA 103; CANR 47, 67, 125; DAM DRAM; LAIT 4

Sone, Monica 1919- .... **AAL**

Song, Cathy 1955- .... **AAL; PC 21**
See also CA 154; CANR 118; CWP; DLB 169; EXPP; FW; PFS 5

Sontag, Susan 1933- .... **CLC 1, 2, 10, 13, 31, 105**
See also AMWS 3; CA 17-20R; CANR 25, 51, 74, 97; CN 7; CPW; DA3; DAM POP; DLB 2, 67; EWL 3; MAWW; MTCW 1, 2; RGAL 4; RHW; SSFS 10

Sophocles 496(?)B.C.-406(?)B.C. .... **CMLC 2, 47, 51; DC 1; WLCS**
See also AW 1; CDWLB 1; DA; DA3; DAB; DAC; DAM DRAM; MST; DFS 1, 4, 8; DLB 176; LAIT 1; LATS 1; LMFS 1; RGWL 2, 3; TWA

Sordello 1189-1269 .... **CMLC 15**

Sorel, Georges 1847-1922 .... **TCLC 91**
See also CA 118; 188

Sorel, Julia
See Drexler, Rosalyn

Sorokin, Vladimir .... **CLC 59**
See Sorokin, Vladimir Georgievich

Sorokin, Vladimir Georgievich
See Sorokin, Vladimir
See also DLB 285

Sorrentino, Gilbert 1929- .. **CLC 3, 7, 14, 22, 40**
See also CA 77-80; CANR 14, 33, 115; CN 7; CP 7; DLB 5, 173; DLBY 1980; INT CANR-14

Soseki
See Natsume, Soseki
See also MJW

Soto, Gary 1952- .. **CLC 32, 80; HLC 2; PC 28**
See also AAYA 10, 37; BYA 11; CA 119; 125; CANR 50, 74, 107; CLR 38; CP 7; DAM MULT; DLB 82; EWL 3; EXPP; HW 1, 2; INT CA-125; JRDA; LLW 1; MAICYA 2; MAICYAS 1; MTCW 2; PFS 7; RGAL 4; SATA 80, 120; WYA; YAW

Soupault, Philippe 1897-1990 .... **CLC 68**
See also CA 116; 147; 131; EWL 3; GFL 1789 to the Present; LMFS 2

Souster, (Holmes) Raymond 1921- .... **CLC 5, 14**
See also CA 13-16R; CAAS 14; CANR 13, 29, 53; CP 7; DA3; DAC; DAM POET; DLB 88; RGEL 2; SATA 63

Southern, Terry 1924(?)-1995 .... **CLC 7**
See also AMWS 11; BPFB 3; CA 1-4R; 150; CANR 1, 55, 107; CN 7; DLB 2; IDFW 3, 4

Southerne, Thomas 1660-1746 .... **LC 99**
See also DLB 80; RGEL 2

Southey, Robert 1774-1843 .... **NCLC 8, 97**
See also BRW 4; DLB 93, 107, 142; RGEL 2; SATA 54

Southworth, Emma Dorothy Eliza Nevitte
1819-1899 .... **NCLC 26**
See also DLB 239

Souza, Ernest
See Scott, Evelyn

Soyinka, Wole 1934- .. **BLC 3; CLC 3, 5, 14, 36, 44, 179; DC 2; WLC**
See also AFW; BW 2, 3; CA 13-16R; CANR 27, 39, 82; CD 5; CDWLB 3; CN 7; CP 7; DA; DA3; DAB; DAC; DAM DRAM, MST, MULT; DFS 10; DLB 125; EWL 3; MTCW 1, 2; RGEL 2; TWA; WLIT 2; WWE 1

Spackman, W(illiam) M(ode)
1905-1990 .... **CLC 46**
See also CA 81-84; 132

Spacks, Barry (Bernard) 1931- .... **CLC 14**
See also CA 154; CANR 33, 109; CP 7; DLB 105

Spanidou, Irini 1946- .... **CLC 44**
See also CA 185

Spark, Muriel (Sarah) 1918- ..... **CLC 2, 3, 5, 8, 13, 18, 40, 94; SSC 10**
See also BRWS 1; CA 5-8R; CANR 12, 36, 76, 89; CDBLB 1945-1960; CN 7; CP 7; DA3; DAB; DAC; DAM MST, NOV; DLB 15, 139; EWL 3; FW; INT CANR-12; LAIT 4; MTCW 1, 2; RGEL 2; TEA; WLIT 4; YAW

Spaulding, Douglas
See Bradbury, Ray (Douglas)

Spaulding, Leonard
See Bradbury, Ray (Douglas)

Speght, Rachel 1597-c. 1630 .... **LC 97**
See also DLB 126

Spelman, Elizabeth .... **CLC 65**

Spence, J. A. D.
See Eliot, T(homas) S(tearns)

Spencer, Anne 1882-1975 .... **HR 3**
See also BW 2; CA 161; DLB 51, 54

Spencer, Elizabeth 1921- .... **CLC 22; SSC 57**
See also CA 13-16R; CANR 32, 65, 87; CN 7; CSW; DLB 6, 218; EWL 3; MTCW 1; RGAL 4; SATA 14

Spencer, Leonard G.
See Silverberg, Robert

Spencer, Scott 1945- .... **CLC 30**
See also CA 113; CANR 51; DLBY 1986

Spender, Stephen (Harold)
1909-1995 .... **CLC 1, 2, 5, 10, 41, 91**
See also BRWS 2; CA 9-12R; 149; CANR 31, 54; CDBLB 1945-1960; CP 7; DA3; DAM POET; DLB 20; EWL 3; MTCW 1, 2; PAB; RGEL 2; TEA

Spengler, Oswald (Arnold Gottfried)
1880-1936 .... **TCLC 25**
See also CA 118; 189

Spenser, Edmund 1552(?)-1599 ..... **LC 5, 39; PC 8, 42; WLC**
See also BRW 1; CDBLB Before 1660; DA; DA3; DAB; DAC; DAM MST, POET; DLB 167; EFS 2; EXPP; PAB; RGEL 2; TEA; WLIT 3; WP

Spicer, Jack 1925-1965 .... **CLC 8, 18, 72**
See also BG 3; CA 85-88; DAM POET; DLB 5, 16, 193; GLL 1; WP

Spiegelman, Art 1948- .... **CLC 76, 178**
See also AAYA 10, 46; CA 125; CANR 41, 55, 74, 124; MTCW 2; SATA 109; YAW

Spielberg, Peter 1929- .... **CLC 6**
See also CA 5-8R; CANR 4, 48; DLBY 1981

Spielberg, Steven 1947- .... **CLC 20**
See also AAYA 8, 24; CA 77-80; CANR 32; SATA 32

Spillane, Frank Morrison 1918-
See Spillane, Mickey
See also CA 25-28R; CANR 28, 63, 125; DA3; MTCW 1, 2; SATA 66

Spillane, Mickey .... **CLC 3, 13**
See Spillane, Frank Morrison
See also BPFB 3; CMW 4; DLB 226; MSW; MTCW 2

Stifle, June
See Campbell, Maria
Stifter, Adalbert 1805-1868 .. **NCLC 41; SSC 28**
See also CDWLB 2; DLB 133; RGSF 2; RGWL 2, 3
Still, James 1906-2001 .... **CLC 49**
See also CA 65-68; 195; CAAS 17; CANR 10, 26; CSW; DLB 9; DLBY 01; SATA 29; SATA-Obit 127
Sting 1951-
See Sumner, Gordon Matthew
See also CA 167
Stirling, Arthur
See Sinclair, Upton (Beall)
Stitt, Milan 1941- .... **CLC 29**
See also CA 69-72
Stockton, Francis Richard 1834-1902
See Stockton, Frank R.
See also CA 108; 137; MAICYA 1, 2; SATA 44; SFW 4
Stockton, Frank R. .... **TCLC 47**
See Stockton, Francis Richard
See also BYA 4, 13; DLB 42, 74; DLBD 13; EXPS; SATA-Brief 32; SSFS 3; SUFW; WCH
Stoddard, Charles
See Kuttner, Henry
Stoker, Abraham 1847-1912
See Stoker, Bram
See also CA 105; 150; DA; DA3; DAC; DAM MST, NOV; HGG; SATA 29
Stoker, Bram . **SSC 62; TCLC 8, 144; WLC**
See Stoker, Abraham
See also AAYA 23; BPFB 3; BRWS 3; BYA 5; CDBLB 1890-1914; DAB; DLB 36, 70, 178; LATS 1; NFS 18; RGEL 2; SUFW; TEA; WLIT 4
Stolz, Mary (Slattery) 1920- .... **CLC 12**
See also AAYA 8; AITN 1; CA 5-8R; CANR 13, 41, 112; JRDA; MAICYA 1, 2; SAAS 3; SATA 10, 71, 133; YAW
Stone, Irving 1903-1989 .... **CLC 7**
See also AITN 1; BPFB 3; CA 1-4R; 129; CAAS 3; CANR 1, 23; CPW; DA3; DAM POP; INT CANR-23; MTCW 1, 2; RHW; SATA 3; SATA-Obit 64
Stone, Oliver (William) 1946- .... **CLC 73**
See also AAYA 15; CA 110; CANR 55, 125
Stone, Robert (Anthony) 1937- ... **CLC 5, 23, 42, 175**
See also AMWS 5; BPFB 3; CA 85-88; CANR 23, 66, 95; CN 7; DLB 152; EWL 3; INT CANR-23; MTCW 1
Stone, Ruth 1915- .... **PC 53**
See also CA 45-48; CANR 2, 91; CP 7; CSW; DLB 105
Stone, Zachary
See Follett, Ken(neth Martin)
Stoppard, Tom 1937- ... **CLC 1, 3, 4, 5, 8, 15, 29, 34, 63, 91; DC 6; WLC**
See also BRWC 1; BRWR 2; BRWS 1; CA 81-84; CANR 39, 67, 125; CBD; CD 5; CDBLB 1960 to Present; DA; DA3; DAB; DAC; DAM DRAM, MST; DFS 2, 5, 8, 11, 13, 16; DLB 13, 233; DLBY 1985; EWL 3; LATS 1; MTCW 1, 2; RGEL 2; TEA; WLIT 4
Storey, David (Malcolm) 1933- . **CLC 2, 4, 5, 8**
See also BRWS 1; CA 81-84; CANR 36; CBD; CD 5; CN 7; DAM DRAM; DLB 13, 14, 207, 245; EWL 3; MTCW 1; RGEL 2
Storm, Hyemeyohsts 1935- ... **CLC 3; NNAL**
See also CA 81-84; CANR 45; DAM MULT
Storm, (Hans) Theodor (Woldsen)
1817-1888 .... **NCLC 1; SSC 27**
See also CDWLB 2; DLB 129; EW; RGSF 2; RGWL 2, 3

Storni, Alfonsina 1892-1938 . **HLC 2; PC 33; TCLC 5**
See also CA 104; 131; DAM MULT; DLB 283; HW 1; LAW
Stoughton, William 1631-1701 .... **LC 38**
See also DLB 24
Stout, Rex (Todhunter) 1886-1975 ..... **CLC 3**
See also AITN 2; BPFB 3; CA 61-64; CANR 71; CMW 4; MSW; RGAL 4
Stow, (Julian) Randolph 1935- ... **CLC 23, 48**
See also CA 13-16R; CANR 33; CN 7; DLB 260; MTCW 1; RGEL 2
Stowe, Harriet (Elizabeth) Beecher
1811-1896 .... **NCLC 3, 50, 133; WLC**
See also AAYA 53; AMWS 1; CDALB 1865-1917; DA; DA3; DAB; DAC; DAM MST, NOV; DLB 1, 12, 42, 74, 189, 239, 243; EXPN; JRDA; LAIT 2; MAICYA 1, 2; NFS 6; RGAL 4; TUS; YABC 1
Strabo c. 64B.C.-c. 25 .... **CMLC 37**
See also DLB 176
Strachey, (Giles) Lytton
1880-1932 .... **TCLC 12**
See also BRWS 2; CA 110; 178; DLB 149; DLBD 10; EWL 3; MTCW 2; NCFS 4
Stramm, August 1874-1915 .... **PC 50**
See also CA 195; EWL 3
Strand, Mark 1934- .... **CLC 6, 18, 41, 71**
See also AMWS 4; CA 21-24R; CANR 40, 65, 100; CP 7; DAM POET; DLB 5; EWL 3; PAB; PFS 9, 18; RGAL 4; SATA 41
Stratton-Porter, Gene(va Grace) 1863-1924
See Porter, Gene(va Grace) Stratton
See also ANW; CA 137; CLR 87; DLB 221; DLBD 14; MAICYA 1, 2; SATA 15
Straub, Peter (Francis) 1943- ... **CLC 28, 107**
See also BEST 89:1; BPFB 3; CA 85-88; CANR 28, 65, 109; CPW; DAM POP; DLBY 1984; HGG; MTCW 1, 2; SUFW 2
Strauss, Botho 1944- .... **CLC 22**
See also CA 157; CWW 2; DLB 124
Strauss, Leo 1899-1973 .... **TCLC 141**
See also CA 101; 45-48; CANR 122
Streatfeild, (Mary) Noel
1897(?)-1986 .... **CLC 21**
See also CA 81-84; 120; CANR 31; CLR 17, 83; CWRI 5; DLB 160; MAICYA 1, 2; SATA 20; SATA-Obit 48
Stribling, T(homas) S(igismund)
1881-1965 .... **CLC 23**
See also CA 189; 107; CMW 4; DLB 9; RGAL 4
Strindberg, (Johan) August
1849-1912 ... **DC 18; TCLC 1, 8, 21, 47; WLC**
See also CA 104; 135; DA; DA3; DAB; DAC; DAM DRAM, MST; DFS 4, 9; DLB 259; EW 7; EWL 3; IDTP; LMFS 2; MTCW 2; RGWL 2, 3; TWA
Stringer, Arthur 1874-1950 .... **TCLC 37**
See also CA 161; DLB 92
Stringer, David
See Roberts, Keith (John Kingston)
Stroheim, Erich von 1885-1957 ..... **TCLC 71**
Strugatskii, Arkadii (Natanovich)
1925-1991 .... **CLC 27**
See also CA 106; 135; SFW 4
Strugatskii, Boris (Natanovich)
1933- .... **CLC 27**
See also CA 106; SFW 4
Strummer, Joe 1953(?)- .... **CLC 30**
Strunk, William, Jr. 1869-1946 ...... **TCLC 92**
See also CA 118; 164; NCFS 5
Stryk, Lucien 1924- .... **PC 27**
See also CA 13-16R; CANR 10, 28, 55, 110; CP 7
Stuart, Don A.
See Campbell, John W(ood, Jr.)

Stuart, Ian
See MacLean, Alistair (Stuart)
Stuart, Jesse (Hilton) 1906-1984 ... **CLC 1, 8, 11, 14, 34; SSC 31**
See also CA 5-8R; 112; CANR 31; DLB 9, 48, 102; DLBY 1984; SATA 2; SATA-Obit 36
Stubblefield, Sally
See Trumbo, Dalton
Sturgeon, Theodore (Hamilton)
1918-1985 .... **CLC 22, 39**
See Queen, Ellery
See also AAYA 51; BPFB 3; BYA 9, 10; CA 81-84; 116; CANR 32, 103; DLB 8; DLBY 1985; HGG; MTCW 1, 2; SCFW; SFW 4; SUFW
Sturges, Preston 1898-1959 .... **TCLC 48**
See also CA 114; 149; DLB 26
Styron, William 1925- .... **CLC 1, 3, 5, 11, 15, 60; SSC 25**
See also AMW; AMWC 2; BEST 90:4; BPFB 3; CA 5-8R; CANR 6, 33, 74, 126; CDALB 1968-1988; CN 7; CPW; CSW; DA3; DAM NOV, POP; DLB 2, 143; DLBY 1980; EWL 3; INT CANR-6; LAIT 2; MTCW 1, 2; NCFS 1; RGAL 4; RHW; TUS
Su, Chien 1884-1918
See Su Man-shu
See also CA 123
Suarez Lynch, B.
See Bioy Casares, Adolfo; Borges, Jorge Luis
Suassuna, Ariano Vilar 1927- .... **HLCS 1**
See also CA 178; HW 2; LAW
Suckert, Kurt Erich
See Malaparte, Curzio
Suckling, Sir John 1609-1642 . **LC 75; PC 30**
See also BRW 2; DAM POET; DLB 58, 126; EXPP; PAB; RGEL 2
Suckow, Ruth 1892-1960 .... **SSC 18**
See also CA 193; 113; DLB 9, 102; RGAL 4; TCWW 2
Sudermann, Hermann 1857-1928 .. **TCLC 15**
See also CA 107; 201; DLB 118
Sue, Eugene 1804-1857 .... **NCLC 1**
See also DLB 119
Sueskind, Patrick 1949- .... **CLC 44, 182**
See Suskind, Patrick
Suetonius c. 70-c. 130 .... **CMLC 60**
See also AW 2; DLB 211; RGWL 2, 3
Sukenick, Ronald 1932- .... **CLC 3, 4, 6, 48**
See also CA 25-28R; 209; CAAE 209; CAAS 8; CANR 32, 89; CN 7; DLB 173; DLBY 1981
Suknaski, Andrew 1942- .... **CLC 19**
See also CA 101; CP 7; DLB 53
Sullivan, Vernon
See Vian, Boris
Sully Prudhomme, Rene-Francois-Armand
1839-1907 .... **TCLC 31**
See also GFL 1789 to the Present
Su Man-shu .... **TCLC 24**
See Su, Chien
See also EWL 3
Summerforest, Ivy B.
See Kirkup, James
Summers, Andrew James 1942- .... **CLC 26**
Summers, Andy
See Summers, Andrew James
Summers, Hollis (Spurgeon, Jr.)
1916- .... **CLC 10**
See also CA 5-8R; CANR 3; DLB 6
Summers, (Alphonsus Joseph-Mary Augustus) Montague
1880-1948 .... **TCLC 16**
See also CA 118; 163
Sumner, Gordon Matthew .... **CLC 26**
See Police, The; Sting

441

Transtroemer, Tomas Gosta
See Transtromer, Tomas (Goesta)

Transtromer, Tomas
See Transtromer, Tomas (Goesta)

Transtromer, Tomas (Goesta)
1931- .... **CLC 52, 65**
See also CA 117; 129; CAAS 17; CANR 115; DAM POET; DLB 257; EWL 3

Transtromer, Tomas Gosta
See Transtromer, Tomas (Goesta)

Traven, B. 1882(?)-1969 .... **CLC 8, 11**
See also CA 19-20; 25-28R; CAP 2; DLB 9, 56; EWL 3; MTCW 1; RGAL 4

Trediakovsky, Vasilii Kirillovich
1703-1769 .... **LC 68**
See also DLB 150

Treitel, Jonathan 1959- .... **CLC 70**
See also CA 210; DLB 267

Trelawny, Edward John
1792-1881 .... **NCLC 85**
See also DLB 110, 116, 144

Tremain, Rose 1943- .... **CLC 42**
See also CA 97-100; CANR 44, 95; CN 7; DLB 14, 271; RGSF 2; RHW

Tremblay, Michel 1942- .... **CLC 29, 102**
See also CA 116; 128; CCA 1; CWW 2; DAC; DAM MST; DLB 60; EWL 3; GLL 1; MTCW 1, 2

Trevanian .... **CLC 29**
See Whitaker, Rod(ney)

Trevor, Glen
See Hilton, James

Trevor, William .. **CLC 7, 9, 14, 25, 71, 116; SSC 21, 58**
See Cox, William Trevor
See also BRWS 4; CBD; CD 5; CN 7; DLB 14, 139; EWL 3; LATS 1; MTCW 2; RGEL 2; RGSF 2; SSFS 10

Trifonov, Iurii (Valentinovich)
See Trifonov, Yuri (Valentinovich)
See also RGWL 2, 3

Trifonov, Yuri (Valentinovich)
1925-1981 .... **CLC 45**
See Trifonov, Iurii (Valentinovich); Trifonov, Yury Valentinovich
See also CA 126; 103; MTCW 1

Trifonov, Yury Valentinovich
See Trifonov, Yuri (Valentinovich)
See also EWL 3

Trilling, Diana (Rubin) 1905-1996 . **CLC 129**
See also CA 5-8R; 154; CANR 10, 46; INT CANR-10; MTCW 1, 2

Trilling, Lionel 1905-1975 .... **CLC 9, 11, 24**
See also AMWS 3; CA 9-12R; 61-64; CANR 10, 105; DLB 28, 63; EWL 3; INT CANR-10; MTCW 1, 2; RGAL 4; TUS

Trimball, W. H.
See Mencken, H(enry) L(ouis)

Tristan
See Gomez de la Serna, Ramon

Tristram
See Housman, A(lfred) E(dward)

Trogdon, William (Lewis) 1939-
See Heat-Moon, William Least
See also CA 115; 119; CANR 47, 89; CPW; INT CA-119

Trollope, Anthony 1815-1882 .... **NCLC 6, 33, 101; SSC 28; WLC**
See also BRW 5; CDBLB 1832-1890; DA; DA3; DAB; DAC; DAM MST, NOV; DLB 21, 57, 159; RGEL 2; RGSF 2; SATA 22

Trollope, Frances 1779-1863 .... **NCLC 30**
See also DLB 21, 166

Trollope, Joanna 1943- .... **CLC 186**
See also CA 101; CANR 58, 95; CPW; DLB 207; RHW

Trotsky, Leon 1879-1940 .... **TCLC 22**
See also CA 118; 167

Trotter (Cockburn), Catharine
1679-1749 .... **LC 8**
See also DLB 84, 252

Trotter, Wilfred 1872-1939 .... **TCLC 97**

Trout, Kilgore
See Farmer, Philip Jose

Trow, George W. S. 1943- .... **CLC 52**
See also CA 126; CANR 91

Troyat, Henri 1911- .... **CLC 23**
See also CA 45-48; CANR 2, 33, 67, 117; GFL 1789 to the Present; MTCW 1

Trudeau, G(arretson) B(eekman) 1948-
See Trudeau, Garry B.
See also CA 81-84; CANR 31; SATA 35

Trudeau, Garry B. .... **CLC 12**
See Trudeau, G(arretson) B(eekman)
See also AAYA 10; AITN 2

Truffaut, Francois 1932-1984 ... **CLC 20, 101**
See also CA 81-84; 113; CANR 34

Trumbo, Dalton 1905-1976 .... **CLC 19**
See also CA 21-24R; 69-72; CANR 10; DLB 26; IDFW 3, 4; YAW

Trumbull, John 1750-1831 .... **NCLC 30**
See also DLB 31; RGAL 4

Trundlett, Helen B.
See Eliot, T(homas) S(tearns)

Truth, Sojourner 1797(?)-1883 ...... **NCLC 94**
See also DLB 239; FW; LAIT 2

Tryon, Thomas 1926-1991 .... **CLC 3, 11**
See also AITN 1; BPFB 3; CA 29-32R; 135; CANR 32, 77; CPW; DA3; DAM POP; HGG; MTCW 1

Tryon, Tom
See Tryon, Thomas

Ts'ao Hsueh-ch'in 1715(?)-1763 .... **LC 1**

Tsushima, Shuji 1909-1948
See Dazai Osamu
See also CA 107

Tsvetaeva (Efron), Marina (Ivanovna)
1892-1941 .... **PC 14; TCLC 7, 35**
See also CA 104; 128; CANR 73; DLB 295; EW 11; MTCW 1, 2; RGWL 2, 3

Tuck, Lily 1938- .... **CLC 70**
See also CA 139; CANR 90

Tu Fu 712-770 .... **PC 9**
See Du Fu
See also DAM MULT; TWA; WP

Tunis, John R(oberts) 1889-1975 ..... **CLC 12**
See also BYA 1; CA 61-64; CANR 62; DLB 22, 171; JRDA; MAICYA 1, 2; SATA 37; SATA-Brief 30; YAW

Tuohy, Frank .... **CLC 37**
See Tuohy, John Francis
See also DLB 14, 139

Tuohy, John Francis 1925-
See Tuohy, Frank
See also CA 5-8R; 178; CANR 3, 47; CN 7

Turco, Lewis (Putnam) 1934- ..... **CLC 11, 63**
See also CA 13-16R; CAAS 22; CANR 24, 51; CP 7; DLBY 1984

Turgenev, Ivan (Sergeevich)
1818-1883 ..... **DC 7; NCLC 21, 37, 122; SSC 7, 57; WLC**
See also DA; DAB; DAC; DAM MST, NOV; DFS 6; DLB 238, 284; EW 6; LATS 1; NFS 16; RGSF 2; RGWL 2, 3; TWA

Turgot, Anne-Robert-Jacques
1727-1781 .... **LC 26**

Turner, Frederick 1943- .... **CLC 48**
See also CA 73-76; CAAS 10; CANR 12, 30, 56; DLB 40, 282

Turton, James
See Crace, Jim

Tutu, Desmond M(pilo) 1931- .. **BLC 3; CLC 80**
See also BW 1, 3; CA 125; CANR 67, 81; DAM MULT

Tutuola, Amos 1920-1997 ..... **BLC 3; CLC 5, 14, 29**
See also AFW; BW 2, 3; CA 9-12R; 159; CANR 27, 66; CDWLB 3; CN 7; DA3; DAM MULT; DLB 125; DNFS 2; EWL 3; MTCW 1, 2; RGEL 2; WLIT 2

Twain, Mark .. **SSC 34; TCLC 6, 12, 19, 36, 48, 59; WLC**
See Clemens, Samuel Langhorne
See also AAYA 20; AMW; AMWC 1; BPFB 3; BYA 2, 3, 11, 14; CLR 58, 60, 66; DLB 11; EXPN; EXPS; FANT; LAIT 2; NCFS 4; NFS 1, 6; RGAL 4; RGSF 2; SFW 4; SSFS 1, 7; SUFW; TUS; WCH; WYA; YAW

Tyler, Anne 1941- . **CLC 7, 11, 18, 28, 44, 59, 103**
See also AAYA 18; AMWS 4; BEST 89:1; BPFB 3; BYA 12; CA 9-12R; CANR 11, 33, 53, 109; CDALBS; CN 7; CPW; CSW; DAM NOV, POP; DLB 6, 143; DLBY 1982; EWL 3; EXPN; LATS 1; MAWW; MTCW 1, 2; NFS 2, 7, 10; RGAL 4; SATA 7, 90; SSFS 17; TUS; YAW

Tyler, Royall 1757-1826 .... **NCLC 3**
See also DLB 37; RGAL 4

Tynan, Katharine 1861-1931 .... **TCLC 3**
See also CA 104; 167; DLB 153, 240; FW

Tyutchev, Fyodor 1803-1873 .... **NCLC 34**

Tzara, Tristan 1896-1963 ..... **CLC 47; PC 27**
See also CA 153; 89-92; DAM POET; EWL 3; MTCW 2

Uchida, Yoshiko 1921-1992 .... **AAL**
See also AAYA 16; BYA 2, 3; CA 13-16R; 139; CANR 6, 22, 47, 61; CDALBS; CLR 6, 56; CWRI 5; JRDA; MAICYA 1, 2; MTCW 1, 2; SAAS 1; SATA 1, 53; SATA-Obit 72

Udall, Nicholas 1504-1556 .... **LC 84**
See also DLB 62; RGEL 2

Ueda Akinari 1734-1809 .... **NCLC 131**

Uhry, Alfred 1936- .... **CLC 55**
See also CA 127; 133; CANR 112; CD 5; CSW; DA3; DAM DRAM, POP; DFS 11, 15; INT CA-133

Ulf, Haerved
See Strindberg, (Johan) August

Ulf, Harved
See Strindberg, (Johan) August

Ulibarri, Sabine R(eyes)
1919-2003 .... **CLC 83; HLCS 2**
See also CA 131; 214; CANR 81; DAM MULT; DLB 82; HW 1, 2; RGSF 2

Unamuno (y Jugo), Miguel de
1864-1936 .. **HLC 2; SSC 11, 69; TCLC 2, 9, 148**
See also CA 104; 131; CANR 81; DAM MULT, NOV; DLB 108; EW 8; EWL 3; HW 1, 2; MTCW 1, 2; RGSF 2; RGWL 2, 3; TWA

Uncle Shelby
See Silverstein, Shel(don Allan)

Undercliffe, Errol
See Campbell, (John) Ramsey

Underwood, Miles
See Glassco, John

Undset, Sigrid 1882-1949 ..... **TCLC 3; WLC**
See also CA 104; 129; DA; DA3; DAB; DAC; DAM MST, NOV; EW 9; EWL 3; FW; MTCW 1, 2; RGWL 2, 3

Ungaretti, Giuseppe 1888-1970 ... **CLC 7, 11, 15**
See also CA 19-20; 25-28R; CAP 2; DLB 114; EW 10; EWL 3; RGWL 2, 3

Unger, Douglas 1952- .... **CLC 34**
See also CA 130; CANR 94

Verhaeren, Emile (Adolphe Gustave)
1855-1916 .... **TCLC 12**
See also CA 109; EWL 3; GFL 1789 to the
Present

Verlaine, Paul (Marie) 1844-1896 .. **NCLC 2,**
51; PC 2, 32
See also DAM POET; DLB 217; EW 7;
GFL 1789 to the Present; LMFS 2; RGWL
2, 3; TWA

Verne, Jules (Gabriel) 1828-1905 ... **TCLC 6,**
52
See also AAYA 16; BYA 4; CA 110; 131;
CLR 88; DA3; DLB 123; GFL 1789 to
the Present; JRDA; LAIT 2; LMFS 2;
MAICYA 1, 2; RGWL 2, 3; SATA 21;
SCFW; SFW 4; TWA; WCH

Verus, Marcus Annius
See Aurelius, Marcus

Very, Jones 1813-1880 .... **NCLC 9**
See also DLB 1, 243; RGAL 4

Vesaas, Tarjei 1897-1970 .... **CLC 48**
See also CA 190; 29-32R; EW 11; EWL 3;
RGWL 3

Vialis, Gaston
See Simenon, Georges (Jacques Christian)

Vian, Boris 1920-1959(?) .... **TCLC 9**
See also CA 106; 164; CANR 111; DLB
72; EWL 3; GFL 1789 to the Present;
MTCW 2; RGWL 2, 3

Viaud, (Louis Marie) Julien 1850-1923
See Loti, Pierre
See also CA 107

Vicar, Henry
See Felsen, Henry Gregor

Vicente, Gil 1465-c. 1536 .... **LC 99**
See also DLB 287; RGWL 2, 3

Vicker, Angus
See Felsen, Henry Gregor

Vidal, Gore 1925- ...... **CLC 2, 4, 6, 8, 10, 22,**
33, 72, 142
See Box, Edgar
See also AITN 1; AMWS 4; BEST 90:2;
BPFB 3; CA 5-8R; CAD; CANR 13, 45,
65, 100; CD 5; CDALBS; CN 7; CPW;
DA3; DAM NOV, POP; DFS 2; DLB 6,
152; EWL 3; INT CANR-13; MTCW 1,
2; RGAL 4; RHW; TUS

Viereck, Peter (Robert Edwin)
1916- .... **CLC 4; PC 27**
See also CA 1-4R; CANR 1, 47; CP 7; DLB
5; PFS 9, 14

Vigny, Alfred (Victor) de
1797-1863 .... **NCLC 7, 102; PC 26**
See also DAM POET; DLB 119, 192, 217;
EW 5; GFL 1789 to the Present; RGWL
2, 3

Vilakazi, Benedict Wallet
1906-1947 .... **TCLC 37**
See also CA 168

Villa, Jose Garcia 1914-1997
See Villa, Jose Garcia

Villa, Jose Garcia 1914-1997 .... **AAL; PC 22**
See also CA 25-28R; CANR 12, 118; EWL
3; EXPP

Villarreal, Jose Antonio 1924- .... **HLC 2**
See also CA 133; CANR 93; DAM MULT;
DLB 82; HW 1; LAIT 4; RGAL 4

Villaurrutia, Xavier 1903-1950 ...... **TCLC 80**
See also CA 192; EWL 3; HW 1; LAW

Villaverde, Cirilo 1812-1894 .... **NCLC 121**
See also LAW

Villehardouin, Geoffroi de
1150(?)-1218(?) .... **CMLC 38**

Villiers de l'Isle Adam, Jean Marie Mathias
Philippe Auguste 1838-1889 ... **NCLC 3;**
SSC 14
See also DLB 123, 192; GFL 1789 to the
Present; RGSF 2

Villon, Francois 1431-1463(?) . **LC 62; PC 13**
See also DLB 208; EW 2; RGWL 2, 3;
TWA

Vine, Barbara .... **CLC 50**
See Rendell, Ruth (Barbara)
See also BEST 90:4

Vinge, Joan (Carol) D(ennison)
1948- .... **CLC 30; SSC 24**
See also AAYA 32; BPFB 3; CA 93-96;
CANR 72; SATA 36, 113; SFW 4; YAW

Viola, Herman J(oseph) 1938- .... **CLC 70**
See also CA 61-64; CANR 8, 23, 48, 91;
SATA 126

Violis, G.
See Simenon, Georges (Jacques Christian)

Viramontes, Helena Maria 1954- .... **HLCS 2**
See also CA 159; DLB 122; HW 2; LLW 1

Virgil
See Vergil
See also CDWLB 1; DLB 211; LAIT 1;
RGWL 2, 3; WP

Visconti, Luchino 1906-1976 .... **CLC 16**
See also CA 81-84; 65-68; CANR 39

Vitry, Jacques de
See Jacques de Vitry

Vittorini, Elio 1908-1966 .... **CLC 6, 9, 14**
See also CA 133; 25-28R; DLB 264; EW
12; EWL 3; RGWL 2, 3

Vivekananda, Swami 1863-1902 .... **TCLC 88**

Vizenor, Gerald Robert 1934- .... **CLC 103;**
NNAL
See also CA 13-16R, 205; CAAE 205;
CAAS 22; CANR 5, 21, 44, 67; DAM
MULT; DLB 175, 227; MTCW 2; TCWW
2

Vizinczey, Stephen 1933- .... **CLC 40**
See also CA 128; CCA 1; INT CA-128

Vliet, R(ussell) G(ordon)
1929-1984 .... **CLC 22**
See also CA 37-40R; 112; CANR 18

Vogau, Boris Andreyevich 1894-1938
See Pilnyak, Boris
See also CA 123; 218

Vogel, Paula A(nne) 1951- ... **CLC 76; DC 19**
See also CA 108; CAD; CANR 119; CD 5;
CWD; DFS 14; RGAL 4

Voigt, Cynthia 1942- .... **CLC 30**
See also AAYA 3, 30; BYA 1, 3, 6, 7, 8;
CA 106; CANR 18, 37, 40, 94; CLR 13,
48; INT CANR-18; JRDA; LAIT 5; MAI-
CYA 1, 2; MAICYAS 1; SATA 48, 79,
116; SATA-Brief 33; WYA; YAW

Voigt, Ellen Bryant 1943- .... **CLC 54**
See also CA 69-72; CANR 11, 29, 55, 115;
CP 7; CSW; CWP; DLB 120

Voinovich, Vladimir (Nikolaevich)
1932- .... **CLC 10, 49, 147**
See also CA 81-84; CAAS 12; CANR 33,
67; MTCW 1

Vollmann, William T. 1959- .... **CLC 89**
See also CA 134; CANR 67, 116; CPW;
DA3; DAM NOV, POP; MTCW 2

Voloshinov, V. N.
See Bakhtin, Mikhail Mikhailovich

Voltaire 1694-1778 .... **LC 14, 79; SSC 12;**
WLC
See also BYA 13; DA; DA3; DAB; DAC;
DAM DRAM, MST; EW 4; GFL Begin-
nings to 1789; LATS 1; LMFS 1; NFS 7;
RGWL 2, 3; TWA

von Aschendrof, Baron Ignatz
See Ford, Ford Madox

von Chamisso, Adelbert
See Chamisso, Adelbert von

von Daeniken, Erich 1935- .... **CLC 30**
See also AITN 1; CA 37-40R; CANR 17,
44

von Daniken, Erich
See von Daeniken, Erich

von Hartmann, Eduard
1842-1906 .... **TCLC 96**

von Hayek, Friedrich August
See Hayek, F(riedrich) A(ugust von)

von Heidenstam, (Carl Gustaf) Verner
See Heidenstam, (Carl Gustaf) Verner von

von Heyse, Paul (Johann Ludwig)
See Heyse, Paul (Johann Ludwig von)

von Hofmannsthal, Hugo
See Hofmannsthal, Hugo von

von Horvath, Odon
See von Horvath, Odon

von Horvath, Odon
See von Horvath, Odon

von Horvath, Odon 1901-1938 .... **TCLC 45**
See von Horvath, Oedoen
See also CA 118; 194; DLB 85, 124; RGWL
2, 3

von Horvath, Oedoen
See von Horvath, Odon
See also CA 184

von Kleist, Heinrich
See Kleist, Heinrich von

von Liliencron, (Friedrich Adolf Axel)
Detlev
See Liliencron, (Friedrich Adolf Axel) De-
tlev von

Vonnegut, Kurt, Jr. 1922- . **CLC 1, 2, 3, 4, 5,**
8, 12, 22, 40, 60, 111; SSC 8; WLC
See also AAYA 6, 44; AITN 1; AMWS 2;
BEST 90:4; BPFB 3; BYA 3, 14; CA
1-4R; CANR 1, 25, 49, 75, 92; CDALB
1968-1988; CN 7; CPW 1; DA; DA3;
DAB; DAC; DAM MST, NOV, POP;
DLB 2, 8, 152; DLBD 3; DLBY 1980;
EWL 3; EXPN; EXPS; LAIT 4; LMFS 2;
MTCW 1, 2; NFS 3; RGAL 4; SCFW;
SFW 4; SSFS 5; TUS; YAW

Von Rachen, Kurt
See Hubbard, L(afayette) Ron(ald)

von Rezzori (d'Arezzo), Gregor
See Rezzori (d'Arezzo), Gregor von

von Sternberg, Josef
See Sternberg, Josef von

Vorster, Gordon 1924- .... **CLC 34**
See also CA 133

Vosce, Trudie
See Ozick, Cynthia

Voznesensky, Andrei (Andreievich)
1933- .... **CLC 1, 15, 57**
See Voznesensky, Andrey
See also CA 89-92; CANR 37; CWW 2;
DAM POET; MTCW 1

Voznesensky, Andrey
See Voznesensky, Andrei (Andreievich)
See also EWL 3

Wace, Robert c. 1100-c. 1175 .... **CMLC 55**
See also DLB 146

Waddington, Miriam 1917- .... **CLC 28**
See also CA 21-24R; CANR 12, 30; CCA
1; CP 7; DLB 68

Wagman, Fredrica 1937- .... **CLC 7**
See also CA 97-100; INT CA-97-100

Wagner, Linda W.
See Wagner-Martin, Linda (C.)

Wagner, Linda Welshimer
See Wagner-Martin, Linda (C.)

Wagner, Richard 1813-1883 ..... **NCLC 9, 119**
See also DLB 129; EW 6

Wagner-Martin, Linda (C.) 1936- .... **CLC 50**
See also CA 159

Wagoner, David (Russell) 1926- .... **CLC 3, 5,**
15; PC 33
See also AMWS 9; CA 1-4R; CAAS 3;
CANR 2, 71; CN 7; CP 7; DLB 5, 256;
SATA 14; TCWW 2

Wah, Fred(erick James) 1939- .... **CLC 44**
See also CA 107; 141; CP 7; DLB 60

Waters, Frank (Joseph) 1902-1995 .. **CLC 88**
See also CA 5-8R; 149; CAAS 13; CANR
3, 18, 63, 121; DLB 212; DLBY 1986;
RGAL 4; TCWW 2

Waters, Mary C. .... **CLC 70**

Waters, Roger 1944- .... **CLC 35**

Watkins, Frances Ellen
See Harper, Frances Ellen Watkins

Watkins, Gerrold
See Malzberg, Barry N(athaniel)

Watkins, Gloria Jean 1952(?)- .... **CLC 94**
See also BW 2; CA 143; CANR 87, 126;
DLB 246; MTCW 2; SATA 115

Watkins, Paul 1964- .... **CLC 55**
See also CA 132; CANR 62, 98

Watkins, Vernon Phillips
1906-1967 .... **CLC 43**
See also CA 9-10; 25-28R; CAP 1; DLB
20; EWL 3; RGEL 2

Watson, Irving S.
See Mencken, H(enry) L(ouis)

Watson, John H.
See Farmer, Philip Jose

Watson, Richard F.
See Silverberg, Robert

Watts, Ephraim
See Horne, Richard Henry Hengist

Watts, Isaac 1674-1748 .... **LC 98**
See also DLB 95; RGEL 2; SATA 52

Waugh, Auberon (Alexander)
1939-2001 .... **CLC 7**
See also CA 45-48; 192; CANR 6, 22, 92;
DLB 14, 194

Waugh, Evelyn (Arthur St. John)
1903-1966 .. **CLC 1, 3, 8, 13, 19, 27, 44,
107; SSC 41; WLC**
See also BPFB 3; BRW 7; CA 85-88; 25-
28R; CANR 22; CDBLB 1914-1945; DA;
DA3; DAB; DAC; DAM MST, NOV,
POP; DLB 15, 162, 195; EWL 3; MTCW
1, 2; NFS 13, 17; RGEL 2; RGSF 2; TEA;
WLIT 4

Waugh, Harriet 1944- .... **CLC 6**
See also CA 85-88; CANR 22

Ways, C. R.
See Blount, Roy (Alton), Jr.

Waystaff, Simon
See Swift, Jonathan

Webb, Beatrice (Martha Potter)
1858-1943 .... **TCLC 22**
See also CA 117; 162; DLB 190; FW

Webb, Charles (Richard) 1939- .... **CLC 7**
See also CA 25-28R; CANR 114

Webb, James H(enry), Jr. 1946- ...... **CLC 22**
See also CA 81-84

Webb, Mary Gladys (Meredith)
1881-1927 .... **TCLC 24**
See also CA 182; 123; DLB 34; FW

Webb, Mrs. Sidney
See Webb, Beatrice (Martha Potter)

Webb, Phyllis 1927- .... **CLC 18**
See also CA 104; CANR 23; CCA 1; CP 7;
CWP; DLB 53

Webb, Sidney (James) 1859-1947 .. **TCLC 22**
See also CA 117; 163; DLB 190

Webber, Andrew Lloyd .... **CLC 21**
See Lloyd Webber, Andrew
See also DFS 7

Weber, Lenora Mattingly
1895-1971 .... **CLC 12**
See also CA 19-20; 29-32R; CAP 1; SATA
2; SATA-Obit 26

Weber, Max 1864-1920 .... **TCLC 69**
See also CA 109; 189; DLB 296

Webster, John 1580(?)-1634(?) ...... **DC 2; LC
33, 84; WLC**
See also BRW 2; CDBLB Before 1660; DA;
DAB; DAC; DAM DRAM, MST; DFS
17; DLB 58; IDTP; RGEL 2; WLIT 3

Webster, Noah 1758-1843 .... **NCLC 30**
See also DLB 1, 37, 42, 43, 73, 243

Wedekind, (Benjamin) Frank(lin)
1864-1918 .... **TCLC 7**
See also CA 104; 153; CANR 121, 122;
CDWLB 2; DAM DRAM; DLB 118; EW
8; EWL 3; LMFS 2; RGWL 2, 3

Wehr, Demaris .... **CLC 65**

Weidman, Jerome 1913-1998 .... **CLC 7**
See also AITN 2; CA 1-4R; 171; CAD;
CANR 1; DLB 28

Weil, Simone (Adolphine)
1909-1943 .... **TCLC 23**
See also CA 117; 159; EW 12; EWL 3; FW;
GFL 1789 to the Present; MTCW 2

Weininger, Otto 1880-1903 .... **TCLC 84**

Weinstein, Nathan
See West, Nathanael

Weinstein, Nathan von Wallenstein
See West, Nathanael

Weir, Peter (Lindsay) 1944- .... **CLC 20**
See also CA 113; 123

Weiss, Peter (Ulrich) 1916-1982 .. **CLC 3, 15,
51**
See also CA 45-48; 106; CANR 3; DAM
DRAM; DFS 3; DLB 69, 124; EWL 3;
RGWL 2, 3

Weiss, Theodore (Russell)
1916-2003 .... **CLC 3, 8, 14**
See also CA 9-12R; 189; 216; CAAE 189;
CAAS 2; CANR 46, 94; CP 7; DLB 5

Welch, (Maurice) Denton
1915-1948 .... **TCLC 22**
See also BRWS 8, 9; CA 121; 148; RGEL
2

Welch, James (Phillip) 1940-2003 ..... **CLC 6,
14, 52; NNAL**
See also CA 85-88; 219; CANR 42, 66, 107;
CN 7; CP 7; CPW; DAM MULT, POP;
DLB 175, 256; LATS 1; RGAL 4; TCWW
2

Weldon, Fay 1931- . **CLC 6, 9, 11, 19, 36, 59,
122**
See also BRWS 4; CA 21-24R; CANR 16,
46, 63, 97; CDBLB 1960 to Present; CN
7; CPW; DAM POP; DLB 14, 194; EWL
3; FW; HGG; INT CANR-16; MTCW 1,
2; RGEL 2; RGSF 2

Wellek, Rene 1903-1995 .... **CLC 28**
See also CA 5-8R; 150; CAAS 7; CANR 8;
DLB 63; EWL 3; INT CANR-8

Weller, Michael 1942- .... **CLC 10, 53**
See also CA 85-88; CAD; CD 5

Weller, Paul 1958- .... **CLC 26**

Wellershoff, Dieter 1925- .... **CLC 46**
See also CA 89-92; CANR 16, 37

Welles, (George) Orson 1915-1985 .. **CLC 20,
80**
See also AAYA 40; CA 93-96; 117

Wellman, John McDowell 1945-
See Wellman, Mac
See also CA 166; CD 5

Wellman, Mac .... **CLC 65**
See Wellman, John McDowell; Wellman,
John McDowell
See also CAD; RGAL 4

Wellman, Manly Wade 1903-1986 ... **CLC 49**
See also CA 1-4R; 118; CANR 6, 16, 44;
FANT; SATA 6; SATA-Obit 47; SFW 4;
SUFW

Wells, Carolyn 1869(?)-1942 .... **TCLC 35**
See also CA 113; 185; CMW 4; DLB 11

Wells, H(erbert) G(eorge) 1866-1946 . **SSC 6,
70; TCLC 6, 12, 19, 133; WLC**
See also AAYA 18; BPFB 3; BRW 6; CA
110; 121; CDBLB 1914-1945; CLR 64;
DA; DA3; DAB; DAC; DAM MST, NOV,
DLB 34, 70, 156, 178; EWL 3; EXPS;
HGG; LAIT 3; LMFS 2; MTCW 1, 2;

NFS 17; RGEL 2; RGSF 2; SATA 20;
SCFW; SFW 4; SSFS 3; SUFW; TEA;
WCH; WLIT 4; YAW

Wells, Rosemary 1943- .... **CLC 12**
See also AAYA 13; BYA 7, 8; CA 85-88;
CANR 48, 120; CLR 16, 69; CWRI 5;
MAICYA 1, 2; SAAS 1; SATA 18, 69,
114; YAW

Wells-Barnett, Ida B(ell)
1862-1931 .... **TCLC 125**
See also CA 182; DLB 23, 221

Welsh, Irvine 1958- .... **CLC 144**
See also CA 173; DLB 271

Welty, Eudora (Alice) 1909-2001 .. **CLC 1, 2,
5, 14, 22, 33, 105; SSC 1, 27, 51; WLC**
See also AAYA 48; AMW; AMWR 1; BPFB
3; CA 9-12R; 199; CABS 1; CANR 32,
65; CDALB 1941-1968; CN 7; CSW; DA;
DA3; DAB; DAC; DAM MST, NOV,
DLB 2, 102, 143; DLBD 12; DLBY 1987,
2001; EWL 3; EXPS; HGG; LAIT 3;
MAWW; MTCW 1, 2; NFS 13, 15; RGAL
4; RGSF 2; RHW; SSFS 2, 10; TUS

Wen I-to 1899-1946 .... **TCLC 28**
See also EWL 3

Wentworth, Robert
See Hamilton, Edmond

Werfel, Franz (Viktor) 1890-1945 ... **TCLC 8**
See also CA 104; 161; DLB 81, 124; EWL
3; RGWL 2, 3

Wergeland, Henrik Arnold
1808-1845 .... **NCLC 5**

Wersba, Barbara 1932- .... **CLC 30**
See also AAYA 2, 30; BYA 6, 12, 13; CA
29-32R, 182; CAAE 182; CANR 16, 38;
CLR 3, 78; DLB 52; JRDA; MAICYA 1,
2; SAAS 2; SATA 1, 58; SATA-Essay 103;
WYA; YAW

Wertmueller, Lina 1928- .... **CLC 16**
See also CA 97-100; CANR 39, 78

Wescott, Glenway 1901-1987 .. **CLC 13; SSC
35**
See also CA 13-16R; 121; CANR 23, 70;
DLB 4, 9, 102; RGAL 4

Wesker, Arnold 1932- .... **CLC 3, 5, 42**
See also CA 1-4R; CAAS 7; CANR 1, 33;
CBD; CD 5; CDBLB 1960 to Present;
DAB; DAM DRAM; DLB 13; EWL 3;
MTCW 1; RGEL 2; TEA

Wesley, John 1703-1791 .... **LC 88**
See also DLB 104

Wesley, Richard (Errol) 1945- .... **CLC 7**
See also BW 1; CA 57-60; CAD; CANR
27; CD 5; DLB 38

Wessel, Johan Herman 1742-1785 .... **LC 7**

West, Anthony (Panther)
1914-1987 .... **CLC 50**
See also CA 45-48; 124; CANR 3, 19; DLB
15

West, C. P.
See Wodehouse, P(elham) G(renville)

West, Cornel (Ronald) 1953- .... **BLCS; CLC
134**
See also CA 144; CANR 91; DLB 246

West, Delno C(loyde), Jr. 1936- .... **CLC 70**
See also CA 57-60

West, Dorothy 1907-1998 .. **HR 3; TCLC 108**
See also BW 2; CA 143; 169; DLB 76

West, (Mary) Jessamyn 1902-1984 ... **CLC 7,
17**
See also CA 9-12R; 112; CANR 27; DLB
6; DLBY 1984; MTCW 1, 2; RGAL 4;
RHW; SATA-Obit 37; TCWW 2; TUS;
YAW

West, Morris
See West, Morris L(anglo)
See also DLB 289

Wilder, Thornton (Niven)
1897-1975 .. **CLC 1, 5, 6, 10, 15, 35, 82; DC 1; WLC**
See also AAYA 29; AITN 2; AMW; CA 13-16R; 61-64; CAD; CANR 40; CDALBS; DA; DA3; DAB; DAC; DAM DRAM, MST, NOV; DFS 1, 4, 16; DLB 4, 7, 9, 228; DLBY 1997; EWL 3; LAIT 3; MTCW 1, 2; RGAL 4; RHW; WYAS 1

Wilding, Michael 1942- ...... **CLC 73; SSC 50**
See also CA 104; CANR 24, 49, 106; CN 7; RGSF 2

Wiley, Richard 1944- .... **CLC 44**
See also CA 121; 129; CANR 71

Wilhelm, Kate .... **CLC 7**
See Wilhelm, Katie (Gertrude)
See also AAYA 20; BYA 16; CAAS 5; DLB 8; INT CANR-17; SCFW 2

Wilhelm, Katie (Gertrude) 1928-
See Wilhelm, Kate
See also CA 37-40R; CANR 17, 36, 60, 94; MTCW 1; SFW 4

Wilkins, Mary
See Freeman, Mary E(leanor) Wilkins

Willard, Nancy 1936- .... **CLC 7, 37**
See also BYA 5; CA 89-92; CANR 10, 39, 68, 107; CLR 5; CWP; CWRI 5; DLB 5, 52; FANT; MAICYA 1, 2; MTCW 1; SATA 37, 71, 127; SATA-Brief 30; SUFW 2

William of Malmesbury c. 1090B.C.-c. 1140B.C. .... **CMLC 57**

William of Ockham 1290-1349 ..... **CMLC 32**

Williams, Ben Ames 1889-1953 ..... **TCLC 89**
See also CA 183; DLB 102

Williams, C(harles) K(enneth)
1936- .... **CLC 33, 56, 148**
See also CA 37-40R; CAAS 26; CANR 57, 106; CP 7; DAM POET; DLB 5

Williams, Charles
See Collier, James Lincoln

Williams, Charles (Walter Stansby)
1886-1945 .... **TCLC 1, 11**
See also BRWS 9; CA 104; 163; DLB 100, 153, 255; FANT; RGEL 2; SUFW 1

Williams, Ella Gwendolen Rees
See Rhys, Jean

Williams, (George) Emlyn
1905-1987 .... **CLC 15**
See also CA 104; 123; CANR 36; DAM DRAM; DLB 10, 77; IDTP; MTCW 1

Williams, Hank 1923-1953 .... **TCLC 81**
See Williams, Hiram King

Williams, Helen Maria
1761-1827 .... **NCLC 135**
See also DLB 158

Williams, Hiram Hank
See Williams, Hank

Williams, Hiram King
See Williams, Hank
See also CA 188

Williams, Hugo (Mordaunt) 1942- ... **CLC 42**
See also CA 17-20R; CANR 45, 119; CP 7; DLB 40

Williams, J. Walker
See Wodehouse, P(elham) G(renville)

Williams, John A(lfred) 1925- . **BLC 3; CLC 5, 13**
See also AFAW 2; BW 2, 3; CA 53-56, 195; CAAE 195; CAAS 3; CANR 6, 26, 51, 118; CN 7; CSW; DAM MULT; DLB 2, 33; EWL 3; INT CANR-6; RGAL 4; SFW 4

Williams, Jonathan (Chamberlain)
1929- .... **CLC 13**
See also CA 9-12R; CAAS 12; CANR 8, 108; CP 7; DLB 5

Williams, Joy 1944- .... **CLC 31**
See also CA 41-44R; CANR 22, 48, 97

Williams, Norman 1952- .... **CLC 39**
See also CA 118

Williams, Sherley Anne 1944-1999 ... **BLC 3; CLC 89**
See also AFAW 2; BW 2, 3; CA 73-76; 185; CANR 25, 82; DAM MULT, POET; DLB 41; INT CANR-25; SATA 78; SATA-Obit 116

Williams, Shirley
See Williams, Sherley Anne

Williams, Tennessee 1911-1983 . **CLC 1, 2, 5, 7, 8, 11, 15, 19, 30, 39, 45, 71, 111; DC 4; WLC**
See also AAYA 31; AITN 1, 2; AMW; AMWC 1; CA 5-8R; 108; CABS 3; CAD; CANR 31; CDALB 1941-1968; DA; DA3; DAB; DAC; DAM DRAM, MST; DFS 17; DLB 7; DLBD 4; DLBY 1983; EWL 3; GLL 1; LAIT 4; LATS 1; MTCW 1, 2; RGAL 4; TUS

Williams, Thomas (Alonzo)
1926-1990 .... **CLC 14**
See also CA 1-4R; 132; CANR 2

Williams, William C.
See Williams, William Carlos

Williams, William Carlos
1883-1963 .... **CLC 1, 2, 5, 9, 13, 22, 42, 67; PC 7; SSC 31**
See also AAYA 46; AMW; AMWR 1; CA 89-92; CANR 34; CDALB 1917-1929; DA; DA3; DAB; DAC; DAM MST, POET; DLB 4, 16, 54, 86; EWL 3; EXPP; MTCW 1, 2; NCFS 4; PAB; PFS 1, 6, 11; RGAL 4; RGSF 2; TUS; WP

Williams, David (Keith) 1942- ..... **CLC 56**
See also CA 103; CANR 41; CD 5; DLB 289

Williamson, Ellen Douglas 1905-1984
See Douglas, Ellen
See also CA 17-20R; 114; CANR 39

Williamson, Jack .... **CLC 29**
See Williamson, John Stewart
See also CAAS 8; DLB 8; SCFW 2

Williamson, John Stewart 1908-
See Williamson, Jack
See also CA 17-20R; CANR 23, 70; SFW 4

Willie, Frederick
See Lovecraft, H(oward) P(hillips)

Willingham, Calder (Baynard, Jr.)
1922-1995 .... **CLC 5, 51**
See also CA 5-8R; 147; CANR 3; CSW; DLB 2, 44; IDFW 3, 4; MTCW 1

Willis, Charles
See Clarke, Arthur C(harles)

Willy
See Colette, (Sidonie-Gabrielle)

Willy, Colette
See Colette, (Sidonie-Gabrielle)
See also GLL 1

Wilmot, John 1647-1680 .... **LC 75**
See Rochester
See also BRW 2; DLB 131; PAB

Wilson, A(ndrew) N(orman) 1950- .. **CLC 33**
See also BRWS 6; CA 112; 122; CN 7; DLB 14, 155, 194; MTCW 2

Wilson, Angus (Frank Johnstone)
1913-1991 . **CLC 2, 3, 5, 25, 34; SSC 21**
See also BRWS 1; CA 5-8R; 134; CANR 21; DLB 15, 139, 155; EWL 3; MTCW 1, 2; RGEL 2; RGSF 2

Wilson, August 1945- ... **BLC 3; CLC 39, 50, 63, 118; DC 2; WLCS**
See also AAYA 16; AFAW 2; AMWS 8; BW 2, 3; CA 115; 122; CAD; CANR 42, 54, 76; CD 5; DA; DA3; DAB; DAC; DAM DRAM, MST, MULT; DFS 3, 7, 15, 17; DLB 228; EWL 3; LAIT 4; LATS 1; MTCW 1, 2; RGAL 4

Wilson, Brian 1942- .... **CLC 12**

Wilson, Colin 1931- .... **CLC 3, 14**
See also CA 1-4R; CAAS 5; CANR 1, 22, 33, 77; CMW 4; CN 7; DLB 14, 194; HGG; MTCW 1; SFW 4

Wilson, Dirk
See Pohl, Frederik

Wilson, Edmund 1895-1972 .. **CLC 1, 2, 3, 8, 24**
See also AMW; CA 1-4R; 37-40R; CANR 1, 46, 110; DLB 63; EWL 3; MTCW 1, 2; RGAL 4; TUS

Wilson, Ethel Davis (Bryant)
1888(?)-1980 .... **CLC 13**
See also CA 102; DAC; DAM POET; DLB 68; MTCW 1; RGEL 2

Wilson, Harriet
See Wilson, Harriet E. Adams
See also DLB 239

Wilson, Harriet E.
See Wilson, Harriet E. Adams
See also DLB 243

Wilson, Harriet E. Adams
1827(?)-1863(?) .... **BLC 3; NCLC 78**
See Wilson, Harriet; Wilson, Harriet E.
See also DAM MULT; DLB 50

Wilson, John 1785-1854 .... **NCLC 5**

Wilson, John (Anthony) Burgess 1917-1993
See Burgess, Anthony
See also CA 1-4R; 143; CANR 2, 46; DA3; DAC; DAM NOV; MTCW 1, 2; NFS 15; TEA

Wilson, Lanford 1937- ... **CLC 7, 14, 36; DC 19**
See also CA 17-20R; CABS 3; CAD; CANR 45, 96; CD 5; DAM DRAM; DFS 4, 9, 12, 16; DLB 7; EWL 3; TUS

Wilson, Robert M. 1941- .... **CLC 7, 9**
See also CA 49-52; CAD; CANR 2, 41; CD 5; MTCW 1

Wilson, Robert McLiam 1964- .... **CLC 59**
See also CA 132; DLB 267

Wilson, Sloan 1920-2003 .... **CLC 32**
See also CA 1-4R; 216; CANR 1, 44; CN 7

Wilson, Snoo 1948- .... **CLC 33**
See also CA 69-72; CBD; CD 5

Wilson, William S(mith) 1932- .... **CLC 49**
See also CA 81-84

Wilson, (Thomas) Woodrow
1856-1924 .... **TCLC 79**
See also CA 166; DLB 47

Wilson and Warnke eds. .... **CLC 65**

Winchilsea, Anne (Kingsmill) Finch
1661-1720
See Finch, Anne
See also RGEL 2

Windham, Basil
See Wodehouse, P(elham) G(renville)

Wingrove, David (John) 1954- .... **CLC 68**
See also CA 133; SFW 4

Winnemucca, Sarah 1844-1891 .... **NCLC 79; NNAL**
See also DAM MULT; DLB 175; RGAL 4

Winstanley, Gerrard 1609-1676 .... **LC 52**

Wintergreen, Jane
See Duncan, Sara Jeannette

Winters, Janet Lewis .... **CLC 41**
See Lewis, Janet
See also DLBY 1987

Winters, (Arthur) Yvor 1900-1968 .... **CLC 4, 8, 32**
See also AMWS 2; CA 11-12; 25-28R; CAP 1; DLB 48; EWL 3; MTCW 1; RGAL 4

Winterson, Jeanette 1959- .... **CLC 64, 158**
See also BRWS 4; CA 136; CANR 58, 116; CN 7; CPW; DA3; DAM POP; DLB 207, 261; FANT; FW; GLL 1; MTCW 2; RHW

Winthrop, John 1588-1649 .... **LC 31**
See also DLB 24, 30

PC Cumulative Nationality Index

Nationality Index

PC-55 Title Index

ISBN 0-7876-7453-2

9 780787 674533